LEGAL ETHICS IN THE PRACTICE OF LAW

FOURTH EDITION

LEGAL ETHICS IN THE PRACTICE OF LAW

Fourth Edition

Richard Zitrin
Lecturer in Law
University of California, Hastings College of the Law

Carol M. Langford
Adjunct Professor of Law
University of San Francisco School of Law

Liz Ryan Cole
Professor of Law
Vermont Law School

ISBN: 978-0-7698-5283-6
Looseleaf ISBN: 978-0-7698-5303-1
eBook ISBN: 978-0-3271-7755-5

Library of Congress Cataloging-in-Publication Data

Zitrin, Richard A., 1947- author.
    Legal ethics in the practice of law / Richard Zitrin, Lecturer in Law, University of California, Hastings College of the Law; Carol M. Langford, Adjunct Professor of Law, University of San Francisco School of Law; Liz Ryan Cole, Professor of Law, Vermont Law School. -- Fourth edition.
pages cm
    Includes index.
    ISBN 978-0-7698-5283-6
    1. Legal ethics--United States. I. Langford, Carol M. (Carol Mae), 1958- author. II. Cole, Liz Ryan, 1947- author. III. Title.
KF306.Z57   2013
174'.30973--dc23

2013037879

This publication is designed to provide authoritative information in regard to the subject matter covered. It is sold with the understanding that the publisher is not engaged in rendering legal, accounting, or other professional services. If legal advice or other expert assistance is required, the services of a competent professional should be sought.

LexisNexis and the Knowledge Burst logo are registered trademarks of Reed Elsevier Properties Inc., used under license. Matthew Bender and the Matthew Bender Flame Design are registered trademarks of Matthew Bender Properties Inc.

NOTE TO USERS
To ensure that you are using the latest materials available in this area, please be sure to periodically check the LexisNexis Law School web site for downloadable updates and supplements at www.lexisnexis.com/lawschool.

Editorial Offices
121 Chanlon Rd., New Providence, NJ 07974 (908) 464-6800
201 Mission St., San Francisco, CA 94105-1831 (415) 908-3200
www.lexisnexis.com

MATTHEW◆BENDER

(2013–Pub.3083)

DEDICATION

To Jesse, Gabriel, and Maya (RZ)

To Gregory . . . and to Nicholas (CML)

For Chuck and Griz — Who are always there (LRC)

ACKNOWLEDGMENTS

The creation of this fourth edition was made more challenging and interesting by all the sea changes in the world of legal ethics that have occurred since 2007. We could not have kept up with these changes without the help of many people, and we are indebted to each. Over the years we have had the help of many colleagues — academics and practitioners alike. Ethics professors Steve Berenson, Kathleen Clark, Steve Derian, Mary Jo Eyster, Monroe Freedman, Peter Joy, Drew Kershen, Rory Little, Judith Maute, Morris Ratner, Cindy Slane, and especially Bob Kuehn, now at Washington (St. Louis), have provided valuable comments over the years.

Practitioners who serve as adjunct professors have been no less helpful. Jim Schaller, who has taught for years at George Washington, and his colleague Ezio Borchini, provided us with a detailed list of errors from the third edition, many typographical and some substantive, which will make this new edition much cleaner. Richard Heafy of Oakland has provided us a stream of cases over the years, Rob Waring of San Francisco and Hon. Gary Miller of Indianapolis have provided video excerpts related to each of our problems, and Brian Faughnan gave us valuable information on state-by-state solutions to the perjury "trilemma." William M. Balin provided across-the-board input in many areas, while Victoria Zitrin, a non-practicing J.D., used her skill as a book editor to help her husband out of tight linguistic squeezes.

Law students have worked tirelessly to assist us on this edition. Vermont Law School students Ruth White and Tracy Ullom wrote a valuable paper that helped us significantly in revising our technology problem. Pauline Dachman, Phillip Foy, Ryan Gadapee, Jeffrey Guevin, Justin Kjolseth, Bob Liu, Eric Nickel, Ida Rose Nininger, Dan O'Connor, James Ostendorf, Christa Shute, Andrew Stone, Kami Todd, Jocelyn Walters-Hird, and Nicole Zub all assisted Prof. Cole at Vermont to research new material. Aishlin Hicks, R. Stone Lee, MD, and Amber Lu provided similar invaluable assistance to Prof. Zitrin at UC Hastings. Special heartfelt gratitude to recent Hastings grad Eugenée Heeter, who was responsible for coordinating all the permissions for this edition, which she did with grace, patience, and exceptional organization.

At the same time, we are reminded of those whose help was invaluable during our preparation of the first three editions. Claude Piller, researcher extraordinaire, gave both inspiration and perspiration to both the first and second editions, combing the archives and the Internet for the most interesting potential new readings. Jane Nydorf was our rock for these earlier editions, unsparingly giving us her tireless and ever-cheerful help. Bob D'Arcy read every word of the first two editions and provided consistent editorial wisdom. For the second edition, Waqar Hasib made certain that every reading was accounted for and properly cited.

We again thank others who helped us along the way, particularly the first time around: Elona Baum, the law firm of Carroll, Burdick & McDonough, Mark Hsen Wu Chu, Peter Cling, Joan Cortez, Nancy Castor, Ralph Francis, Diane Gamlowski, Ted Gest, Manoj Gorantla Govindaiah, Michael Hartmann, Terry Inghroff, Kimbery B. Janas, Steve Kassirer, Janet Loduca, Joe Levin, Peter McGaw, Margaret Moses, Laurie Robertson, Tracy Swann, Kenneth Wang, Maureen Kay Wurfel, Arthur Zitrin, Charlotte Zitrin, and Elizabeth Zitrin.

We would like to single out for thanks the following: our friends at LexisNexis, particularly our wonderful editors, Ally VonHockman for the second edition, and Pali Parekh for the last two; Lee Freudberg, who as director of law school publications for the Michie Company years ago was among the first to have the vision to see the value of a book such as this; former University of San Francisco dean Jay Folberg, who may have been the first to see the value of this volume; Shannon Lovely, who as Prof. Cole's administrative assistant guided us through hardcopy and on-line exchanges without which we could not have drafted the text of this book; and above all our friend and colleague, law professor Susan McGuigan, who assisted us fundamentally in researching much of this book and continues to work with us on future projects. Finally, we are forever grateful to the hundreds of students at the University of California's Hastings campus, the University of San Francisco, and Vermont Law School, who over the last 35 years have tested both our materials and our teaching methods, and who consistently challenge us and help to make us wiser teachers and better lawyers.

Richard Zitrin

Carol M. Langford

Liz Ryan Cole

October 2013

PREFACE TO FOURTH EDITION

For students and those teachers who have not previously read this book, the first part of our Introduction, which follows, serves to explain our practice-oriented, "real world," problem-driven approach. It also outlines both our approach to the discipline of legal ethics and the book's organizational structure. We suggest you begin there.

The purpose of this Preface is to give those with some working familiarity with our first three editions a brief overview of what has changed — in the world of legal ethics and in this volume.

In both instances, the changes have been substantial. Following the adoption of the ALI's Restatement (Third) of the Law Governing Lawyers and the wholesale revision to of the ABA's Model Rules of Professional Conduct in 2002 and 2003, widespread rule modification has slowed down. But rules revisions continue in several venues, most importantly: the ABA's Ethics 20/20 Commission, whose rules modifications on technology and international issues were largely adopted by the House of Delegates in 2012 and 2013; and a series of controversial changes in conflict of interest rules to allow broader "advance waivers" and more screening than previously permitted — changes by no means universally adopted by the states. Substantively, we have seen many changes in several areas of law and ethics. Most significantly, technology and ethics continues to evolve at a rapid pace. Some issues: What is a secure, confidential communication? Must we now encrypt information we transmit? What does it mean to "friend" someone as a lawyer, or reach out to people on LinkedIn? How does commercial free speech relate to lawyer blogs and other Internet presence?

In this Fourth Edition, we have tried to be responsive to these changes, while keeping intact the core of what seemed to work well in previous editions. Throughout, we have maintained our predisposition for accessible, readable materials that still satisfy necessary academic rigor.

Without exception, every Problem (for we continue to divide the book by Problems rather than Chapters) is changed from the last edition, and while several have mostly nips, tucks, and updates of citations, many more have undergone more substantial revision. We have excerpted several dozen new articles and cases that were published since our last edition, but we have maintained the last edition's structure and, we're glad to report, only modestly lengthened the text despite our desire to maintain a "full coverage" approach to this discipline.

Among the most important new material we have added are:

- A new half of a problem and several readings addressing the ethics of mass multi-plaintiff cases;
- An increased emphasis on wellness, including a recent detailed prescriptive article, our own key suggestions, and an article about developing trust between lawyer and client;
- Deeper discussions about mentoring, changes in the law school curriculum, and the adequacy of current law school training;
- Confidentiality and the emerging issue of whether law firms should be able to consult themselves about possible mistakes on their own clients' cases;

- Confidentiality and the wrongfully convicted;
- Further updated readings on technology and "the Cloud," including tweeting, "virtual" law offices, and seven recent ethics opinions on use of the Cloud;
- Detailed analysis of the state of the law on the ethical requirements of electronic discovery;
- Updated readings reflecting the evolution of conflicts of interest law, especially as it relates to disqualification, law firm imputation, waivers, and screening;
- Extensive revisions and expansion of material on multi-cultural and cross-cultural lawyering;
- An entire reworking and modernization of the problem on advertising and solicitation.

We hope you, both professors and students, find the changes useful and enjoyable. Anyone with questions or comments can reach us at zitrinr@uchastings.edu, langford@usfca.edu, and lcole@vermontlaw.edu. We look forward to hearing from you.

Richard Zitrin

Carol M. Langford

Liz Ryan Cole

October 2013

TABLE OF CONTENTS

TABLE OF CONTENTS

TABLE OF CONTENTS

TABLE OF CONTENTS

TABLE OF CONTENTS

TABLE OF CONTENTS

TABLE OF CONTENTS

TABLE OF CONTENTS

TABLE OF CONTENTS

TABLE OF CONTENTS

Chapter 5   WHO CONTROLS THE CASE? HOW SHOULD LAWYERS AND CLIENTS SHARE DECISIONMAKING? 361

TABLE OF CONTENTS

TABLE OF CONTENTS

TABLE OF CONTENTS

TABLE OF CONTENTS

TABLE OF CONTENTS

TABLE OF CONTENTS

TABLE OF CONTENTS

TABLE OF CONTENTS

TABLE OF CONTENTS

TABLE OF CONTENTS

TABLE OF CONTENTS

TABLE OF CONTENTS

TABLE OF CONTENTS

PART ONE

RULES AND REFLECTIONS

"There is a vague popular belief that lawyers are necessarily dishonest. . . . Let no young man choosing the law for a calling for a moment yield to the popular belief. Resolve to be honest at all events; and if in your own judgment you cannot be an honest lawyer, resolve to be honest without being a lawyer."

—Abraham Lincoln, 1850

INTRODUCTION

A. A PRACTICING LAWYER'S APPROACH TO ETHICS

Imagine yourself two or three years from now practicing law. You're an associate in a law firm, working hard for your clients, and trying to impress the partners that one day you should make partner yourself. But a problem comes up in a matter you are handling for one of the firm's largest clients. It seems that either you or your assistant miscalculated by a day the deadline to serve your opposition to a summary judgment motion by mail, and your opponent has refused to stipulate to electronic service. You've got the pleadings done, but you're a day late and the motions judge is a stickler with a reputation for not even considering pleadings that are not timely served. You're in a panic, thinking about losing your job and how you'd make your student loan payments, not to mention the payments on the sports sedan you treated yourself to when you passed the bar. You confide in a fellow associate who was a couple of years ahead of you at law school. She asks whether you're serving electronically and you tell her your opponent insisted on mail service. "Great," she tells you. "Here's what you can do. Just turn the postage meter back a day, backdate the date on your opposition, and mail it out this morning. Sometimes the postal service rejects backdated mail, but usually if you get it in the mail early enough, they don't. It'll probably get you off the hook, and no one will know the difference."

You walk away from the conversation feeling confused and upset. You know that turning back the postage meter is not the right thing to do, yet it seems so easy, and the ethics of the situation raised little concern with your more experienced friend, whose sense of "right" and "wrong" you have always admired. You feel enormous pressure, not just for yourself, but to protect your client's case. You know your law school ethics teacher would have cited you a rule — probably several — that your conduct would violate. You also recall how your supervising partner always talks about "whatever it takes to get the job done." You consider whether turning back the postage meter may be a situation of "no harm, no foul," since no one will be the wiser. You don't know how to resolve your dilemma, and you're not sure how fully your ethics course prepared you to deal with this situation.

Law schools teach students legal ethics in many different ways. Some professors focus on lecturing on the formal rules that govern "professional responsibility." They believe that a thorough knowledge of the black-letter "law of lawyering" provides the best curriculum.

Our focus is a little different. We ask this question: What is the role of a legal ethics text if not to prepare students for the "real world"? We do not underestimate the importance of the rules, codes, opinions, and decisional law that articulate the underlying basic precepts of legal ethics. But the goal of this volume is considerably broader than just teaching these precepts. It is to help you prepare for the ethical dilemmas you will certainly face as a practicing lawyer. We want to explore not just the traditional principles of legal ethics, but *how* these principles are used, how they interact, indeed how they conflict, in the real world practice of law. We also want to examine the relationship between these ethical principles and other important issues concerning the conduct of attorneys: legal malpractice and related torts; bar discipline; court sanctions; and contempt, among others.

No ethical precepts conflict more frequently or graphically than the two presented in our brief opening hypothetical — the competent, diligent, and vigorous advocacy of a client's interests versus the basic moral obligation to be truthful in one's words and deeds. And it would be naive for us to ignore one more element of the equation — the practical and economic consequences of doing things by the book when doing it that way could jeopardize your job. After all, if you do not get that summary judgment opposition heard, the consequences to the client, and to your future at your firm, could be dire.

The focus of this book will be on the problem areas, ethical dilemmas rather than bright line tests, conflicts among ethical principles rather than resolution, and recognition of these dilemmas, rather than concrete solutions. There is an excellent reason for this approach. While some ethical issues can be answered simply and concretely, many of the day-to-day issues confronting practicing lawyers are far more subtle. As we will see throughout this volume, these are issues on which reasonable minds — including those of thoughtful ethics experts — often differ. Experience has shown us that while most lawyers learn the rules of ethics well enough to pass a short-answer ethics bar exam, too many simply aren't able to recognize ethical dilemmas in their own practices until it's too late.

The lawyer who learns to recognize ethical problems early is halfway to a solution. If you are able to recognize the warning signs, consider the dilemma you face, and articulate the issues to yourself, finding a response to the situation becomes much easier. This will be the case whether you practice estate planning, criminal defense, civil litigation, transactional contract work, or public interest law.

Many of the most interesting ethical "grey areas" — the issues that create dilemmas and conflict over ethical principles — arise because of tension between black letter rules of legal ethics and society's sense of right and wrong. Some ethical principles, including those that justify why the clearly guilty criminal defendant should be vigorously represented, and why that defendant's confidences must be strictly protected, have their genesis in our Constitution. That document is a major source of the strong precepts of loyal and devoted advocacy for our clients, right or wrong, that have long been a fundamental part of our ethical rules. We will examine the tension between these rules and other important principles of our society: the obligation to tell the truth; the duty of fairness; the avoidance of racial, ethnic, and gender bias; the duty not to allow others to use our legal skills for their own illegal ends; the increasing significance of our multi-cultural society; and the obligation not to allow harm to come to others by virtue of our conduct, even if it means "blowing the whistle" on a client.

We will examine these issues in the context of the rules of legal ethics. In that analysis, however, we will not attempt to define morality any more than the rules of ethics could successfully legislate it. Rather, we hope that you will take your own sense of personal morality along with you as you analyze the principles of legal ethics that you learn here, in a way that helps you to develop a deeper understanding of yourself as an ethical lawyer.

You may wonder what we mean by the term "ethics" in the context of the practice of law. We believe that there is no one single answer to this complex question. Some commentators believe that legal ethics refers to "the law of lawyering," or the formal body of rules and opinions and cases that govern our behavior. Others agree with us that an understanding of legal ethics involves more — the consideration of both individual and group morality. A lawyer evaluating this moral component might ask questions like "How do I want to live my life as a practitioner?" and "What do I think the legal profession should be, and what is my role in that profession?" A *group moral component* has been defined by some as a law firm ethic, culture, or attitude. We hope that our own answer to the question of what "legal ethics" means will be more fully defined throughout the course of this book.

B.   A BRIEF WORD ABOUT THE ORGANIZATION OF THIS BOOK

This book adopts a problem-driven approach. The primary divisions in the syllabus are *problems*, not chapters. These problems are real world examples of the situations that face practicing lawyers every day; each one is based on actual experiences either we or lawyers of our acquaintance have had. We have tried to keep the problems simple, believing that a "blank canvas" without too much detail will allow for the broadest possible analysis. The problems deal with many important black letter principles of legal ethics, but we have also tried to infuse these problems with an element of reality. We recognize as practicing lawyers that often, lawyers will consider the practical as well as the ethical consequences of their behavior.

We follow each problem with a series of readings, most of which are directly relevant to the problem, but some of which concern other related issues. Many of the readings are excerpts from cases, law review articles, and formal ethics opinions. Many other readings are more colloquial — accounts from legal periodicals, newspaper accounts in the popular press, and a good deal of our own narrative discussion and analysis, which we often find is the most efficient way to express or stitch together important ideas. Certain readings provide more black letter law analysis, while others, including many sections that we have written, are important for making ethical principles more accessible and easier to grasp, digesting a series of points or issues, or providing a strong dose of reality. We consider both the excerpted readings and our narrative segments to be of primary importance.

When we teach with these materials, we prefer to have our students lead discussions on most of the problems. The analysis of each problem will be more complete and informative if it includes a review of the readings that follow and, importantly, a discussion of which ethical rules apply. We discuss the formation and organization of the most important codified rules later in this Introduction. These rules can be found in our own supplementary volume or other similar volumes from other publishers. Your professor will recommend how to find the ABA Model Rules as well as the rules that apply in your jurisdiction, and may recommend or require a "rules supplement" book. We want to point out, however, that this text contains *relatively few extensive discussions of the rules themselves.* This is intentional. We believe that when ethical problems arise in the real-world practice of law, lawyers themselves will have to research, discover, and then apply the relevant rules on each occasion.

Moreover, no discussion of a problem is complete if it stops with an analysis of the governing rules. Discussing the rules provides a framework and a foundation, a beginning but not the end result.

We suggest that as you read a problem and the readings that follow it, you consider the following questions: (1) What conduct described in the problem either does or might violate a formal ethical rule, and which rule(s)? (2) What conduct appears to violate some other obligation of a lawyer? (3) Might the conduct result in civil liability for the lawyer or law firm? (4) Is there tension or conflict between competing interests or rules of conduct, and if so, in what respect? (5) How do you feel a lawyer *should* be acting in these circumstances, and why? (6) If there is a tension or conflict between what you feel a lawyer *should* do in this situation and what the black letter rules seem to say a lawyer *must* do, what do *you* do? and (7) What practical considerations may be difficult to ignore in determining how a lawyer may behave in these circumstances? This is not a definitive list, but rather a checklist we recommend as a tool to develop a full, well-rounded approach to identifying and resolving ethical issues as they arise — in this book and in life.

The readings that follow each problem are organized into sections, and have been written or edited by us specifically for this book. In many sections, the text consists entirely of our own narrative. Where we have excerpted a case, article, or other "outside" reading, we have provided our own comments beforehand, and after most, we conclude with a *NOTES* section that reflects some of our own thoughts. Each outside reading is clearly demarcated with its author and title; in doing the editing, we have generally eliminated footnotes and citations without further reference.

We end the material on each problem with a summary of several supplemental readings, each of which we briefly describe. We often use the supplemental readings to point you to interesting discussions that are either less adaptable to brief excerpting, concern narrower or interesting but collateral issues, or develop concepts somewhat more challenging or complex. These readings are for those who are particularly interested in the subject matter raised and wish further resources. Since we prefer to teach these materials by using student discussion leaders for each problem, the students often use these supplemental readings as further source materials for their analysis.

C.   THE RULES AND STANDARDS OF OUR PROFESSION

The Early Days. Before the ABA established its Canons of Ethics in 1908, there were no uniform rules of professional conduct. The principal guidance to the legal profession came from common law edicts setting forth a lawyer's duties, such as to advocate zealously for one's client and to maintain a client's confidences. These early standards were statements of principle with little, if any, disciplinary enforcement. Early guidance also came from treatises such as Baltimore lawyer David Hoffman's 1836 volume, *A Course of Legal Study*, which included "Fifty Resolutions" that he believed reflected the values important to attorneys of his time. In 1854 came Judge George Sharswood's *A Compend of Lectures on the Aims and Duties of the*

Profession of Law, the publication of his lectures on the profession at the University of Pennsylvania.

The first ethical code originated in Alabama in 1887, based in part on Sharswood's precepts. In 1908, the ABA issued its first ethical principles, in the form of 32 Canons of Professional Ethics. But the ABA of 1908 was a far cry from the ABA today, exclusionary in membership and more interested in protecting those lawyers who represented large monied interests than the millions who formed the constituency for the populist politicians of the time. The stimulus for the ABA's Canons came not so much from a desire to control lawyer conduct as from a speech critical of the profession given at Harvard in 1905 by the country's number one populist, President Theodore Roosevelt. Henry St. George Tucker, a wealthy Virginia lawyer, was then president of the ABA. Tucker was a political opponent of Roosevelt, and took personally the President's criticism of corporate lawyers who made their living advising clients on ways to evade regulatory control. Tucker formed a committee to draft rules of conduct. Perhaps not surprisingly, the resulting Canons reflected more closely the concerns of wealthy "gentlemen" practitioners than they did the views of the President.

Of the original 32 Canons, some clearly set a moral tone while others provided more specific regulatory principles. In reality, the former may have been designed primarily to regulate what powerful Philadelphia lawyer Henry Drinker called "Russian Jew boys" and other riff-raff who had become lawyers from "up out of the gutter." Drinker personified the elitism of the bar of the early 20th century. He felt threatened by the idea that lawyers would lose professional status through creeping diversity, and so took matters into his own hands. As Chair of the ABA Committee on Professional Ethics for over a decade, he became a leading advocate of the Pennsylvania Preceptor Plan, a program designed to keep the bar clean by forbidding membership to lawyers from different ethnic backgrounds and lower social strata.

The early Canons addressed issues such as advertising and fee arrangements, not because these were seen as purely ethical concerns, but largely to control the conduct of sole practitioners and non-corporate lawyers who had to hustle for business, unlike Drinker and his colleagues, whose client base emanated from their social and Big Business connections. This helped to ensure that the balance of power in the profession would remain securely entrenched in the hands of those who held it throughout most of the 19th century.

The ABA Model Code. Over the first half of this century, the ABA Canons were expanded and improved on, finally increasing in number to 47. But not until 1964, when then ABA President and future Supreme Court Justice Lewis F. Powell formed a committee to develop a new set of standards, did the ABA begin to modernize its approach. The result of Powell's initiative was the passage of the Model Code of Professional Responsibility in 1969. The Model Code began its life successfully. Although membership in the ABA is entirely voluntary and the Code was only a model, within a few years most states had adopted the Code, in whole or in part, as their own rules of professional conduct. Unlike the Canons, the Code had a clear and detailed structure: Nine Canons, in effect chapters, each embodying a very broad general principle, and within each Canon, a series of Disciplinary Rules

(DRs) and Ethical Considerations (ECs). The Code's Preamble explains the function of the different elements of the Code:

> The Canons are statements of axiomatic norms, expressing in general terms the standards of professional conduct expected of lawyers in their relationships with the public, with the legal system, and with the legal profession. They embody the general concepts from which the Ethical Considerations and the Disciplinary Rules are derived.
>
> The Ethical Considerations are aspirational in character and represent the objectives toward which every member of the profession should strive.
>
> . . .
>
> The Disciplinary Rules, unlike the Ethical Considerations, are mandatory in character. The Disciplinary Rules state the minimum level of conduct below which no lawyer can fall without being subject to disciplinary action. . . .

The ABA Model Rules. Despite the success of the Code, some lawyers felt that the ABA had not progressed enough in articulating a modern set of standards. They argued for an approach along the lines adopted by the American Law Institute in forming its restatements of law, with black letter rules followed by annotated comments. Thus, in 1977, only eight years after passage of the Code, the ABA formed another rules commission, this time led by noted Kansas City Attorney Robert J. Kutak, with Yale Professor Geoffrey Hazard, Jr. acting as Reporter, or chief of staff to the Commission. Popularly known as the Kutak Commission, this group set out to develop standards that better reflected the modern practice of law. Unlike the committee that drafted the Code, much of the Kutak Commission's work occurred in the light of public scrutiny, and the Commission provided drafts of its rules for criticism and debate to the public as well as to lawyers.

The Kutak Commission published three drafts of its work in progress, in 1980 and 1981, and its 1982 submission to the ABA House of Delegates. True to its mission, the Commission recommended significant changes in certain traditional ethical precepts. Perhaps the most controversial was the idea that lawyers who see their clients doing harm to the public should have broad powers to abrogate attorney-client confidentiality where it is necessary for public protection. "Whistle-blowing" provisions were drafted into both the rule on confidentiality and the rule describing the obligations of corporate counsel. While supported by much of the public, these provisions were excoriated by the majority of lawyers, especially trial lawyers and corporate counsel. By the time the ABA House of Delegates passed the Model Rules of Professional Conduct in August 1983, these whistleblowing provisions had been removed. Indeed, one of the introductory paragraphs describing the scope of the Rules specifically warns against second-guessing lawyers who, because of confidentiality, decide *not* to disclose information.

The ABA Model Rules are divided into brief black letter rules and longer Comment sections. According to the introduction, the purpose of the Comments is to explain and interpret: "The Comments are intended as guides to interpretation, but the text of each Rule is authoritative." Tables were provided that cross-referenced the sections of the Rules with their Code counterparts. These tables proved necessary, because many states, having so recently adopted the Model Code, were reluctant to adopt so soon a new set of Rules based on a wholly different organizational scheme.

It took some time, but by 2010, only one state, California, still had not adopted the Model Rules. California had never adopted the Model Code, preferring instead to revise its own rules codification in 1989. However, after the "Ethics 2000" Commission (see the next paragraph), California formed a Commission to, at last, harmonize California's rules with those of the ABA. Nevertheless, by early 2013, the state Supreme Court still had yet to consider or even study the suggested rules revisions, and California's rules remained separate and distinct from the ABA's.

"Ethics 2000," and the New Edition of the Model Rules. In the late 1990s, the ABA undertook yet another revision of the rules. It began as a modest effort to modify the ABA Model Rules with a few nips and tucks, and to harmonize them with the American Law Institute's new Restatement of the Law Governing Lawyers. By 2000, it was clear that the ABA Ethics 2000 Commission, or "E2K," as it became known, had taken on a full-scale revision of the rules. Unlike the Kutak Commission, Ethics 2000 did not create a new rules structure but rather kept revisions within the same organizational structure as the existing Model Rules. Many rules changed little, while others were substantially modified. The commission conducted widespread public hearings and consulted an extensive advisory council in an effort to get as many divergent views as possible. The result was a complete revision of the ABA Model Rules, passed by the House of Delegates in 2002 and 2003.

A decade later, most states have taken what changes they wanted from this 2002–03 version and incorporated them into their own rules. The extent of this incorporation varies state by state. Because of this, we as teachers rely most on a "red-lined" version of the rules — such as in our own rules volume — that compares the earlier and later versions in legislative format.

ALI's Restatement, Third, of the Law Governing Lawyers. The American Law Institute, which had begun to create its Restatement of lawyering in 1986, continued to revise that document throughout the 1990s. As with most rules-making processes, the ALI had its own injection of politics. Criticizing the politicization of the Restatement, as exemplified by an incident in which insurance industry lawyers overtly lobbied for votes, one of the ALI's 3,000 members, Georgetown Professor Sherman L. Cohn, wrote in 1997 that if the ALI had ever been considered "an objective, disinterested body [of lawyers that] struggled for a restatement of the law based upon their own consciousness of what the law is, . . . it is clearly not true today."[1]

Nevertheless, the ALI navigated through its issues and approved the Restatement, Third, of the Law Governing Lawyers[2] before the Ethics 2000 version of the Model Rules was completed. While its purpose (unlike the ABA's) was not to create

---

[1] Sherman L. Cohn, *The Organization Client: Attorney-Client Privilege and the No-Contact Rule*, 10 GEO. J. LEGAL ETHICS 739, 789 (1997).

[2] There is no Restatement Second or First. The "Third" refers to the fact that the ALI is in its third edition of Restatements. This is the *first* ALI ethics codification, one of the indications of the increasing importance of ethics in the legal world in the last generation.

a work that would actually become the officially-approved ethical standard in any jurisdiction, the Restatement has become second in importance to the ABA Model Rules — an extensive and sophisticated work that has gradually garnered significant acceptance among both academics and courts.

The Ethics 20/20 Commission. In 2009, the ABA formed yet another commission to examine the ethics rules. The stated purpose of the Ethics 20/20 Commission was to evaluate the Model Rules in light of technological advances in the law and the development of global law practices. The Commission held hearings and presented its two sets of proposals to the House of Delegates in 2012 and 2013. These proposals, limited in scope to technological and global-law issues, were adopted by the ABA virtually in their entirety. Significantly, the 20/20 changes pervasively modified the definitions of various forms of communication and documentation to include all electronic and digital means.

Sources of Guidance Beyond the Rules. Neither the ABA's nor the individual states' rules of ethics stand alone. The ABA Standing Committee on Ethics and Professional Responsibility drafts opinions on ethical issues. So too do the ethics committees of most states and several local bars. These opinions supplement and explain the rules in their respective jurisdictions. In addition, there are other sources of ethical guidance provided by both the ABA and other organizations. In the 1970s, the ABA developed Standards Relating to the Administration of Criminal Justice for both prosecutors and defense lawyers. In 2010, the ABA formed a commission to implement a revision and update of these standards, which have not changed materially since their creation and have not been modified at all since 1993. The Standards do not have the same authority as the ABA Model Rules themselves, and that authority has materially diminished as the Standards became more outdated. However, these standards have been useful guidelines, relied on by state and federal courts in the past when evaluating the conduct of the criminal bar. Their revision would likely substantially increase their value, but the revision process has been slow: As of March 2013, the commission had not yet published even a proposed draft of revised standards.

Numerous voluntary associations of lawyers have also created their own ethical guidelines. In addition to the ALI, the Federal Bar Association, for example, an organization made up of lawyers practicing federal law, issued its Model Rules of Professional Conduct for Federal Lawyers in 1990. The American Trial Lawyers Foundation, concerned by provisions in the ABA's proposed Model Rules, published the American Lawyer's Code of Conduct (ALCC) in 1982, and has significantly revised that Code since. Other practice-specific organizations, such as the National District Attorneys Association, the National Association of Criminal Defense Lawyers, and the Association of Corporate Counsel, have developed their own ethics codes, have their own ethics committees, and write their own ethics opinions. Many other groups, from associations of labor lawyers, to patent attorneys, employment lawyers, mediators and arbitrators, and so on, do the same. These codes and opinions, though not binding in individual states, provide important guidance from thoughtful colleagues who are engaged in a similar practice. So too do the "ethics hotlines" that many practice-oriented groups have formed to help colleagues who find themselves in sticky ethical situations.

D. READINGS

1. The Way It Was

As we will do throughout the course of this book, we now present readings that we find relevant to our discussion above. Our first is an excerpt from historian Jerold S. Auerbach's fascinating 1976 book on the history of lawyers in America. We focus on the period before America's entry into the First World War, the time when the ABA's first Canons of Ethics were taking shape. There are many more interesting stories in this book, which is still in print and recommended to anyone interested in American legal history.

JEROLD S. AUERBACH, UNEQUAL JUSTICE: LAWYERS AND SOCIAL CHANGE IN MODERN AMERICA
(1976)[3]

The bar association movement was a characteristic feature of the decades surrounding 1900. . . . [T]he American Bar Association, organized in 1878, had [these stated] purposes: To promote the administration of justice, to advance jurisprudence, to uphold professional honor, and to encourage social intercourse among lawyers. But the ABA exuded the genial tone of a social club, set by its predominantly Southern members who came to Saratoga Springs each year to escape the summer heat. The "benefit of the waters," one member declared, rivaled in importance the professional business of the association. Simeon Baldwin, the moving spirit behind the association, labored to confine membership "to leading men or those of high promise. . . ." Local associations often were similarly exclusive. The Boston Bar Association seemed to exist solely for the benefit of State Street and Federal Street lawyers. The Chicago Bar Association, founded (in the words of one of its presidents) to bring "the better and the best elements of the profession together," charged high admission fees and annual dues to achieve its purpose. The strongest pillars of the Association of the Bar of the City of New York were Yale, Harvard, and Protestantism. . . .

Bar associations did venture timidly into the shallower waters of law reform, but they usually skirted the dangerous shoals of substantive change. In 1912 ABA president Stephen Gregory declared that professional associations were "the chief instrumentality of constructive legal reform." Rarely, however, did their concern extend to such problems as the provision of legal services. At best, they preoccupied themselves with the most technical, professional aspects of legal issues — for example, the ethical proprieties of contingent fees rather than the social and individual cost of lives broken in industrial accidents. The result was that law reform served as "a banner of rectitude waved in the public eye," a shield to deflect public criticism. . . .

During the second decade of the twentieth century the American Bar Association began to assert itself aggressively as a professional protective organization. Its purpose was twofold: To preserve its own exclusiveness (and the status that

---

[3] Copyright © 1976 by Oxford University Press, Inc. Reprinted by permission.

accompanied its preservation) and to exert professional leverage upon the political process. Two prewar episodes provided a test of its strength and scope: The admission of black lawyers and the nomination of Louis D. Brandeis to the Supreme Court.

In 1912 the executive committee of the American Bar Association unknowingly admitted three black lawyers to membership. Informed of its carelessness, it quickly passed a resolution rescinding the admission and — "since the settled practice of the Association has been to elect only white men as members" — referring the matter for determination by the entire association. Attorney General George W. Wickersham protested (one of the contested members, a Harvard law school graduate, was his assistant in the Department of Justice)— not from any commitment to racial equality but from disgust with procedural irregularities that violated association by-laws. He was assured by the association's secretary that the rescission resolution had been adopted only with "a sincere purpose to do what seemed . . . to be right and just. . . ." And he was sternly chastised for his "discourteous and dogmatic" criticism, a display of pique unbecoming an association member. But Moorfield Storey, a past president of the bar association and the first president of the National Association for the Advancement of Colored People, was incensed. "It is a monstrous thing," he complained, "that we should undertake to draw a color line in the Bar Association." Storey repudiated the notion that blacks were excluded by association policy, although he conceded that none had ever been admitted. The association was in a quandary. Claiming to be a national organization, it functioned as a restricted social club. The admission of blacks, in the words of its membership chairman, posed "a question of keeping pure the Anglo-Saxon race." A compromise resolution precluded future associational miscegenation. Prodded by Storey, members permitted the three duly elected black lawyers to remain but provided that all future applicants must identify themselves by race. The association thereby committed itself to lily-white membership for the next half-century. It had elevated racism above professionalism.

Professionalism converged with politics in the Brandeis donnybrook. The first of several dramatic twentieth-century Court nomination controversies, it brought into sharp focus the public implications of professional parochialism. More was at stake than a judicial seat, although a place on the Supreme Court was hardly inconsequential at a time when the judiciary was praised or blamed as the most reliable defender of vested property interests against public regulation. On the surface the division seemed clear. Brandeis' opponents, drawn largely from State Street law firms and from the American Bar Association, could plausibly see the Boston people's attorney as a threat to their restricted professional world. They spoke of the law as a bulwark of private property; Brandeis, who would not have disagreed, had often used it as an instrument of social change to make property owners more responsible to the public. They devoted their careers to counseling private interests; Brandeis committed much of his to public service . . . . They were Protestant; he was the first Jewish nominee to the Supreme Court.

These differences masked some striking similarities between Brandeis and his critics: His commitment to efficiency and order; his application of business values to the operation of his law firm; his admiration for the great New York firms; his fear of radical challenges to American institutions; and his insistence that only lawyers were competent to criticize and remedy defects in the administration of law and justice. But the differences were crucial. They determined that the challenge to Brandeis would cut across every major professional concern of the day: Ethnicity; the social functions of law; the role of lawyers; and standards of professional character, conduct, and ethics . . . . His confirmation fight was a symbolic crusade, pitting the newest defenders of the established professional order against the outsider who was especially dangerous because he shared so many of their attributes yet put them to such different use. It was precisely because Brandeis' credentials were so impeccable — a brilliant record at Harvard Law School and a lucrative corporate practice — that the opposition to his appointment was so revealing.

. . . .

Brandeis' opponents staked their claim on the ground of ethics and character. Moorfield Storey . . . testified to Brandeis' reputation as "an able lawyer, very energetic, ruthless in the attainment of his objects, not scrupulous in the methods he adopts, and not to be trusted." . . . Dipping his pen in vitriol, [former President and future Chief Justice] William Howard Taft dispatched letter after letter of calumny to friends and family, berating Brandeis for his ethics, politics, and religion.

By resting their public opposition on ethical and character defects, opponents of the nomination avoided a direct confrontation on the grounds of religion or reform. Storey, for example, vigorously denied that criticism of Brandeis was attributable to anti-Semitism or to politics. Lawyers, he insisted, objected to Brandeis solely "on the ground of his character." But "character" already had become a term of art in the legal profession, applied unerringly to those lawyers — and only to those — whose religion, national origin, or politics threatened the professional status quo. Certainly it is impossible to know (and unnecessary to establish) what distressed his opponents more: His Jewishness, his public service, his successful practice, his outspoken opposition to corporate arrogance, his social approach to legal problems, or his judgments upon the justness of a client's case. Success aside, these traits made Brandeis a professional outsider — reason enough to contest his nomination.

NOTES

Brandeis, of course, made it to the Court, albeit by the slimmest of margins. What about the attitude of the early bar associations, including the ABA? Does it surprise you? Remember the times in which this exclusionary, elitist conduct occurred: The Jim Crow segregated South, mass immigration in the North that threatened the established white Protestant order, and the exponential growth of trade unions and the workers' rights movement. Perhaps this history shows that lawyers are products of their times, and have as much difficulty as anyone else in rising above them. Think about the state of the legal profession today. Are the same circumstances true, with the only change the definition of "outsider" — perhaps "Muslim" or "defender of terrorists" instead of Jew or personal-injury lawyer? Or is it possible for legal institutions to have staked out a higher moral ground? And if institutions can't do this, can individual lawyers?

2. The Way It Is?

Professor William Henderson, an expert on law firm economics, has written an article that sketches out the rise and then the glory days of large corporate law firms, and suggests their possible fall unless they change the way they do business. About one-half of the million or more active attorneys in this country remain in solo or small firm practices. As for the other half, do you think that Henderson has it right?

William D. Henderson, *Three Generations of U.S. Lawyers: Generalists, Specialists, Project Managers*
70 MD L. REV. 373 (2011)[4]

The legal services industry is in the midst of a significant economic recession. In response to harsh economic conditions, the nation's corporate clients have tightened their legal budgets and altered their spending habits. As a result, large law firms, who in recent years hired roughly twenty-five percent of all law school graduates, have dramatically cut the sizes of their incoming associate classes. In turn, highly qualified law school graduates have expanded their job searches to markets and to employers that are normally reserved for the broad middle tier of law school graduates.[5]

Does (this) mark the beginning of a true sea change for traditional corporate law firms and, by extension, U.S. law schools? The answer to this question is yes. . . .

[This is] a relatively simple narrative in which successive generations of U.S. corporate lawyers have evolved from generalists, to specialists, to someday, in the not too distant future, project managers . . . . The U.S. legal profession is exiting a period of profound economic prosperity. This prosperity was set in motion by a handful of innovations in law firm structure and lawyer training that occurred several decades ago (that) gave American lawyers the tools and the platform to help create and grow a highly dynamic, regulated global economy. Unfortunately, those of us who have benefited . . . do not understand the history . . . [s]o we are the last to see the end of an era. The story fits the old adage, "nothing fails like success."

I. THE GENERALIST

In the United States circa 1900, the great industrialists and financiers were building empires. . . . Unfortunately, sophisticated business lawyers were in short supply. . . . The small number of elite institutions that provided systematic training in legal doctrine made no attempt to go beyond a generalist legal education. . . . When the need for more sophisticated business lawyers presented itself — because businesses were becoming larger, more complex, and more heavily regulated — law firms assumed this responsibility.

The major innovation of Paul Cravath (of the Cravath, Swaine & Moore firm) was

---

[4] Copyright © 2011 by Maryland Law Review. Reprinted by permission.

[5] [Editors' Note: We cannot let this comment pass without pointing out that many top students, even when "top" is measured by grades, prefer work outside the large law firm system/culture.]

to make [a] training system scaleable to fit the needs of sprawling industrial and financial clients. One important part of the Cravath system was an incentive structure that rewarded lawyers for working together as a team for the benefit of clients. A second key element was an advancement system that required lawyers to master the "art of delegation." A third feature was the emphasis on a structured program of training, which ensured that lawyers had someone coming up through the ranks to whom work could be delegated. . . . [V]irtually all major business law firms organized themselves along similar principles.

II. THE SPECIALIST

[In 1949,] the median salary of a lawyer working in private practice was $5,199, which was less than the $5,518 median salary paid to a lawyer employed by a government entity. In contrast, lawyers working in large law firms of nine or more partners enjoyed median incomes 400% higher. But their numbers were slight, as they comprised less than 1.5% of all lawyers working in private practice. These lawyers had become relatively wealthy because their workplace organization enabled them to become specialists. . . . Because clients were dependent on the expertise of their outside legal counsel, and because the size and scope of the legal issues continued to grow, clients were usually willing to pay for the training of junior lawyers.

. . . With the rise of the general counsel position in the 1970s, in-house lawyers assumed the position of trusted advisors to the company's owners or senior executives while outside law firms were called upon for their specialized skills and technical expertise.

. . . This vibrant market for specialized lawyers, however, also has consequences for junior career lawyers and recent law school graduates. . . . As the size of the corporate bar has expanded over the last several decades, the total volume of technically sophisticated lawyers (specialists) is at an all-time high. This reality strongly reduces the incentive of clients to subsidize the training of entry-level lawyers, particularly at inflated pay scales that are disconnected from the value provided to clients.

The end of the specialist era is the flipside of the same dynamic that gave rise to it in the first instance: The relative supply of sophisticated business lawyers has increased relative to demand, thanks to the growth of large law firms and the training they provided over a period of several decades (albeit at the clients' expense). Now, however, the amount of money spent on legal services by large corporate clients is vast. And, this purchasing power is disproportionately centralized among a few hundred general counsel.

The beginning of the project manager era — which I believe is now dawning — is marked by sophisticated corporate counsel looking for methods of workplace organization and process that will deliver higher quality legal inputs and outputs (a bundle of both services and products) for a predictable fee.

III. The Project Manager

. . . I grew up in Cleveland, Ohio during the 1970s and early 1980s, when the U.S. automotive industry peaked and then headed into decline. At the time, it would have been hard to imagine how quickly the industry would unravel. As a region, we believed that things would rebound or stabilize. We were wrong. . . .

I relate two concrete examples of how the traditional pyramidal law firm is being undercut by innovations — one by a client and another by a legal services firm — using innovative technology, project management, and process improvement. These examples reflect modes of problem solving that are completely foreign to the training and socialization of most successful corporate law firm lawyers — and that is why they are so disruptive to established hierarchies. . . .

[A]t Cisco Systems, Inc., a Fortune 100 technology company . . . the General Counsel . . . is expected to contain costs on par with any other department in the organization. One strategy the legal department has used to contain costs is to bring in-house legal work that is core to the company's competitive advantage (meaning, build rather than buy). As the legal department grew, the General Counsel and his staff wanted to capture the full learning of each matter so that each similar, subsequent matter could build upon it as a starting point. . . . The goal of the project was to better archive information, capture the full context of prior work, facilitate information sharing, develop internal expertise, save time, and obtain better legal outcomes.

Cisco's legal department promises to provide an answer to any legal question asked by any other corporate department . . . .

Novus Law, which was started less than five years ago, specializes in reviewing, managing, and analyzing documents for litigation, investigations, and transaction-based due diligence. . . . [T]he principals have M.B.A. degrees, not law degrees. Their work has been relied upon in complex civil, white-collar criminal, and major class actions and multidistrict litigation in federal courts. What is the value proposition for clients? Sixty percent lower cost than a traditional law firm and near perfect quality — far better than any large law firm with an army of top law school graduates.

Although a small portion of the cost savings comes from using less expensive lawyers in the United States and abroad, the efficiency and quality is entirely a function of world class project management and process engineering. . . . But Novus Law's real comparative advantage is a project management and process orientation that dramatically increases quality. . . . [A] one-touch, multifaceted approach to processing information can supply the client with a basis for an early resolution or dismissal, which can further reduce the cost of litigation.

The fact that Novus Law can measure and warrantee quality, and offer price certainty, endears it to large corporate clientele. . . . [Meanwhile,] traditional law firms . . . will reduce the number of entry-level hires . . . produc[ing] a general "graying" of the corporate bar and a large cohort of lawyers who will be less inclined to reinvent themselves. And this, unfortunately, reminds me of Cleveland.

I now see the same adversarial dynamics setting in between many large U.S.

corporations and their outside counsel [as occurred in the automobile industry between the Big Three auto-makers and union workers]. Rather than setting up long-term relationships in which information and the benefits of innovation will be shared between supplier and buyer, many general counsel are pressuring their law firms for discounted fees. Clients are also refusing to pay for first- or second-year associates. Law firms can attempt to prop up profitability by slashing entry-level hiring and by cutting costs on professional development along with other nonessential expenses. But in the long run, an organization — or, worst yet, an industry — cannot credibly compete on the basis of quality when it underinvests in its most important asset — legal talent.

. . . .

Thus, over the next several years, lawyers working for large corporate clients will increasingly layer the skills of project manager on top of their specialized legal knowledge. To the extent that lawyers resist this gravitational pull, they will lose their seat at the economic table.

NOTES

What do you think of Professor Henderson's predictions? As we look at the ethical issues to come in this volume, recall his extolling the virtues of Novus Law. Is this a law firm, or is it a bunch of MBAs practicing law, something that almost all jurisdictions still do not allow? And how does Novus, which works for all sides at all times, determine who its client is, or even whether it has a client.

E. SUPPLEMENTAL READINGS

1. Our supplemental readings will appear after each segment of this book — including at the end of each Problem and the subsequent Readings. For this Introduction, they are all websites with valuable information on legal ethics. We begin by referencing the website of the ABA's Center for Professional Responsibility, www.abanet.org/cpr/home.html. Other websites of particular value in researching and evaluating legal ethics issues include the following.

2. www.legalethics.com, a site maintained by cyberethics expert Peter Krakaur, that posts ethics information focused on Internet ethics and other cyberspace issues. There are also links to a wide variety of other information. Professor David Hricik, who worked with Krakaur for some time in maintaining this site, has his own home page at http://www.hricik.com/Welcome.html that features risk management and intellectual property issues as well as technology issues, and contains a straightforward series of links to ethics sources in each state.

3. Freivogel on Conflicts at www.freivogelonconflicts.com and now also available at simply *freivogel.com*, is quite an extraordinary site, chock full of summaries of a huge number of conflicts of interest cases, a similarly extensive and easy-to-navigate table of contents, and a "what's new" section that gives recent updates. Attorney William Freivogel, long involved in malpractice avoidance and insurance issues, maintains the site, which is designed as a "practical online guide to conflicts of interest for lawyers with sophisticated business and litigation practices." It's

straightforward enough for any researcher to understand, breaking conflicts of interest issues into about three dozen separate categories.

4. *legalethicsforum.com* is perhaps the most significant and popular ethics blog: A group of about 10 law school ethics professors from across the country lead a vigorous and dynamic discussion on a wide variety of current issues. Numerous threads are posted daily. One of its principal blogger/hosts, John Steele, who teaches ethics at various Northern California law schools, publishes an annual list of the year's most important ethics issues, which he also posts on this blog.

5. http://www.aprl.net/ is the home to the Association of Professional Responsibility Lawyers, an organization of ethics and malpractice "mavens" from across the country, and many lawyers from both sides of the disciplinary fence: prosecutors and "respondents' counsel." APRL takes *amicus* positions, publishes monographs, and has a website with an extensive amount of information, some of which, like the archives of its exceptionally active listserv, require membership.

6. Cornell University's Legal Information Institute operated its ethics site at www.law.cornell.edu/ethics. Sadly, this site, formerly maintained primarily by Cornell ethics Professor Roger Cramton, officially closed in March 2013 because of the difficulty in keeping current the vast repository of information. The material is largely still available, but a warning states that "some portions of the collection may already be severely out of date, so please be cautious in your use of this material."

Chapter 1

INITIAL REFLECTIONS ON ETHICS, MORALITY, AND JUSTICE IN AN ADVERSARY SYSTEM

A. READINGS

1. Some Initial Reflections, and Some Thoughts from Abe Lincoln

We are about to embark on a journey through the practice of law — one that quite naturally begins with the formation of a special relationship between lawyer and client. In our adversary system of justice, it is that special relationship that has long been given primacy in defining our behavior as lawyers. But before we begin our analysis and discussion of that relationship, we want to take note of what we believe to be the central ethical issue that drives modern American jurisprudential thinking. Consider this:

First, how do we balance two conflicting considerations: on one hand, our strong Anglo-American tradition of advocacy, where the client's needs are considered paramount and lawyers serve as the willing tools of their clients; and on the other, our obligations to the system of justice, and a society of laws in which we all work and live? Second, how do we reconcile our roles as ethical, professionally responsible attorneys, acting loyally and vigorously (some might say "zealously") on our clients' behalves, with our duties to society as a whole and with our own personal moral beliefs — our private selves, human beings each with our own strongly held beliefs?

Indeed, it is precisely this issue that is most often raised in disapproval by those outside the profession. There, the tenor of the inquiry may be more along the lines of, "How can you in good conscience act the way you do?" Or, more bluntly, "Why do lawyers seem so morally bankrupt? Why are they such jerks?" And we must ask *ourselves* these same questions, in order to ensure our own personal well-being and sense of self-worth. For, we suggest, we will not best serve our clients or society unless we remain true to ourselves.

We will return to these questions, and the tension between the goals of a client-oriented adversary system and a society-based system of morality, on more than one occasion in these pages. Like a diamond — or perhaps more apt, Rubik's cube — it is an issue that has many facets, and appears to look quite different depending on the perspective that we have at the time.

We begin with the perspective of perhaps the one American lawyer whose public image remains almost completely untarnished — Abraham Lincoln. In his succinct way, he reminds us of both our legal duties and the duties we owe ourselves.

Abraham Lincoln, *Notes for a Law Lecture*
(July 1, 1850)[1]

Discourage litigation. Persuade your neighbors to compromise whenever you can. Point out to them how the nominal winner is often the real loser — in fees, expenses and waste of time. As a peacemaker, the lawyer has a superior opportunity of being a good man. Never stir up litigation. A worse man can scarcely be found than one who does this.

. . . .

There is a vague popular belief that lawyers are necessarily dishonest. . . . [T]he impression is common, almost universal. Let no young man choosing the law for a calling for a moment yield to the popular belief. Resolve to be honest at all events; and if in your own judgment you cannot be an honest lawyer, resolve to be honest without being a lawyer. Choose some other occupation, rather than one in the choosing of which you do in advance, consent to be a knave.

2.   The Duty of Advocacy and Defending the Guilty

We begin by reaching back almost two centuries, to the beginnings of what has long been — and still is — the number one question lay people ask lawyers at cocktail parties: "How can you lawyers represent someone you know is guilty?" For an answer, we go back to England in 1840, to the story of Charles Phillips and his client Courvoisier, as described some 40 years ago by legal ethics scholar David Mellinkoff's wonderful 1973 monograph THE CONSCIENCE OF A LAWYER.

To set the stage, Courvoisier was accused of murdering Lord William Russell. Courvoisier had the good fortune to have Phillips, one of the leading barristers of his day, as his attorney. Professor Mellinkoff describes Phillips' vigorous defense of Courvoisier, who nevertheless was convicted and sentenced to death. During the course of the case, Courvoisier had confessed his guilt to his lawyer, putting Phillips in the unenviable position of having to decide whether to advocate on behalf of a guilty man. When he chose to do so, he gained little but disapprobation, as Professor Mellinkoff tells us in these excerpts. But Phillips's actions helped to cement, over time, the concepts of loyalty, confidentiality, and vigorous representation that are essential to our legal system.

---

[1] These "notes" have been quoted in many sources, including several books on legal quotations, among them 2000 FAMOUS LEGAL QUOTATIONS by M. Frances McNamara (1967) and THE OXFORD BOOK OF LEGAL QUOTATIONS (1993), and in collections of Lincoln's writings, including Volume 2 of THE COLLECTED WORKS OF ABRAHAM LINCOLN, edited by Roy P. Basler.

David Mellinkoff, The Conscience of a Lawyer
(1973)[2]

[I]n the same Monday morning newspapers carrying the story of Courvoisier's conviction and the first accounts of his confession of guilt, the word was out that before Charles Phillips spoke to the jury Courvoisier had confessed his guilt to his counsel. Of all the confessions of Courvoisier, this one was to have the most lasting effects, surviving Courvoisier's making peace with man and God, clouding the remaining years of Charles Phillips, following Phillips into the final estimate of his contemporaries, stirring controversy over the role of Courvoisier's counsel and counsel in general, and ultimately influencing the ethical canons of lawyers in England, America, and wherever the Anglo-American system of legal representation has taken hold.

. . . .

Some immediately struck out at the fundamental horror, as repellant to Victorian London as to many today: Phillips had been trying to persuade a jury to acquit a man he knew was guilty.

"One of the Profession" summed up the public's outrage in a letter to *The Times*:

> Sir, — After reading the eloquent and impassioned address of Mr. C. Phillips in defence of Courvoisier, a doubt suggested itself to my mind whether a profession in which a man employs his talent 'to screen the guilty, and to varnish crime', can be considered honorable.

> The culprit had avowed his guilt . . .

> I seek not to impeach Mr. Phillips' character, which, from report, I believe to be of a high order [but] I am simple enough to consider that he who defends the guilty, knowing him to be so, forgets alike honour and honesty, and is false to God and man!

> If my friend is to protect the butcher of my sleeping parent, though conscious of his guilt, Lord save me from my friends.

. . . .

A legal periodical *The Jurist* tackled the "grave and difficult question" raised by Courvoisier's case. It editorialized that the customary rule of the English bar requiring counsel to defend regardless of his opinion as to guilt or innocence is "inconsistent with the laws of morality, since it amounts to neither more nor less than that a man is bound to deceive, if it be for the interest of his client." To Lord Erskine's argument that "[i]f the advocate refuses to defend, he assumes the character of the judge; nay, he assumes it before the hour of judgment . . . .", *The Jurist* replied that in the unlikely event that no lawyer would take a man's case, he would have himself to thank for it that "the evidence . . . on his own shewing, was so strong as to afford irresistible inference of his guilt." "We contend," *The Jurist* bluntly concluded, "that if an accused person be really guilty, he has no moral right to any defence."

---

[2] Copyright © 1973 by the West Academic Publishing Corporation. Reprinted by permission.

The Bishop of London brought the moral issue (in "what had occurred on a late most melancholy and remarkable occasion") onto the floor of the House of Lords. He presented a petition from "the inhabitants of London" asking that the legislation of 1836 giving prisoner's counsel a right to address the jury be now reconsidered, as being "a principle of exceedingly questionable propriety." He found himself unable to reconcile some "passages of God's word . . . with the propriety of any man taking a reward to prove that to be otherwise which the accused himself had distinctly confessed."

In the Lords when the Bishop of London spoke was Charles Phillips' friend Lord Brougham, who two decades earlier in the same chamber had successfully defended Queen Caroline against a charge of adultery, and in doing so had pulled out the last stop in speaking of the zeal a lawyer must bring to his client's cause: " . . . If once a barrister is to be allowed to refuse a brief, and to say he will not defend a man because he is in the wrong, many will be found who will refuse to defend men, not on account of the case, but because they are weak men, under the pressure of unpopularity, against whom power has set its mark, because they are the victims of oppression, or are about to be made so. . . ."

The argument between the Bishop of London and Lord Brougham has been continued in a thousand forums since, and has not ended. It renewed not only the fundamental questioning of the morality of the profession of law, but even more basic questions of the purpose of the system of justice.

NOTES

As Mellinkoff notes, early American ethics pioneers David Hoffman and George Sharswood (see our Introduction) argued the same issue on this side of the Atlantic. Hoffman's *A Course of Legal Study* had objected to lawyers who "screen such foul offenders from merited penalties." Sharswood countered that even a guilty man "has a constitutional right to a trial according to law . . . . It is not to be termed screening the guilty from punishment, for the advocate to exert all his ability, learning, and ingenuity in such a defense, even if he should be perfectly assured in his own mind of the actual guilt of the prisoner." "Nothing," continued Sharswood, "seems plainer than the proposition, that a person accused of a crime is to be tried and convicted, if convicted at all, *upon evidence*, and *whether guilty or not guilty*, if the evidence is insufficient to convict him, he has a *legal right* to be acquitted."

3. Should Legal Ethics Ignore Social Morality?

Both Lord Brougham and Judge Sharswood rose to Charles Phillips' defense by arguing that Phillips did the ethical thing. But what does this conduct say about the *morality* of being a lawyer? Professor Mellinkoff himself asks this larger question. Do we as lawyers have the luxury of answering it? Should a lawyer consider the morality as well as the ethics of his or her conduct? Should morality ever be the deciding factor?

As Mellinkoff notes, the debate about defending the known guilty party has continued in "a thousand forums," as vibrant an issue today as it was in 1973 and, indeed, in 1840. Many cases in recent years — sensational cases from O.J. Simpson to Casey Anthony and others featured by Nancy Grace, or the representation of supposed "known" terrorists — have made it clear that this issue continues to resonate with the American public, and with lawyers and legal scholars as well. We will focus on it specifically in Problem 15.

Before we leave the topic, read this brief excerpt from an article now a quarter-century old but still having currency, as a journalist deftly compares lawyers to Machiavelli — unfavorably.

Richard Cohen, *A Rolling Ethic Gathers No Moss*
WASHINGTON POST MAGAZINE (May 1, 1988)[3]

I asked a lawyer, an eminent and well-respected one, what he would do if he discovered that the murder suspect he was defending was guilty. Without pausing, he gave his answer. He would make sure his client did not take the stand to testify. That would ensure that the defendant would not commit perjury. Other than that, the lawyer would give the murderer the best defense possible. It was, the lawyer said, the ethical thing to do.

Notice the use of the word "ethical." It's a powerful word, much in vogue nowadays if only because every profession has its code of ethics. But notice, too, how it obscures all sorts of moral questions. Take the case of the lawyer with a guilty client on his hands. He said, as most lawyers would, that it was not his obligation to determine guilt or innocence. That was the jury's job. It was his obligation to provide the best defense possible.

Yes, but the client is a killer and the lawyer knows it. A jury verdict of innocence would not change that fact. Nor would it change the fact that a murderer had gone free, possibly to murder again. If the killer did kill again, would the lawyer hold himself morally responsible? Not likely. Instead, he would say he did the ethically proper thing.

. . . .

Niccolo Machiavelli, the great Florentine thinker whose name the French came to use as a synonym for immorality, is the father of modern ethics. Writing in the late 15th and early 16th century from a Florence that was being buffeted by every regional war, that was a constant pawn in the struggles between the church, France and the Holy Roman Empire, Machiavelli yearned for a leader who could rescue his poor city-state. Such a man — a prince — would have to be both ruthless and cynically realistic. He would have to understand the base nature of man. It might be immoral to slaughter your enemies, as Cesare Borgia, a ruthless leader in Machiavelli's time, had done, but if in the long run such policies resulted in stability and peace, then ethically, according to Machiavelli, they were permissible. Morality would be considered but could be disregarded; ethics would replace it.

But at least Machiavelli — a poet, novelist, romantic and, ultimately, religious man — knew the meaning and importance of morality. He knew right from wrong.

---

[3] Copyright © 1988 by Washington Post Writers Group. Reprinted by permission.

The end might justify the means, but he recognized that the means nevertheless might be immoral. The concept of morality still had meaning. Not so with the contemporary professional. To him, everything comes down to ethics, usually an ethical code. If something is permitted, it's right — and how dare anyone question.

Probably in the long run it's best that lawyers defend anyone in need of a defense. Their ethical code makes sense. It has a utility. Ultimately, it serves society's interests. The same is probably true for journalists. (If you think I'm going to also pardon lobbyists, you're wrong.) But these ethical codes (sometimes merely oral traditions) are too often cited as if nothing more need be — or could be — said, as if they replaced individual morality or, if you will, character. For instance, Lloyd Cutler, a Washington lawyer of such eminence that there is no one more eminent, defended his role as a lobbyist for the makers of dangerous all-terrain vehicles by saying, "It's the duty of a lawyer to represent anyone for whom a responsible argument could be made." In other words, since it's ethical, how dare anyone question his morality.

NOTES

Is it as simple as Cohen states, that lawyers ignore the moral in choosing the ethical? Would some lawyers at least consider morality before deciding to do what their profession requires? Might some lawyers even argue that defending the guilty person is not only ethical, but also has a *moral* justification? For example, suppose a lawyer argued that while *truth* might not be served, *justice*, including forcing the state to meet its heavy burden of proof, would be. What is your reaction to this justification? Can you think of others?

4. "Moral Costs"

In the courtrooms and legislatures of 1990s America, a morality play was staged in the national political theater. The subject was the dangerous and addictive properties of tobacco smoke, and the efforts made by the tobacco industry both to adjust nicotine levels and to prevent public disclosure of the industry's own highly damaging scientific studies. Lawyers, of course, were central members of the cast. From the mid-1950s onward, tobacco company lawyers successfully hid behind the shield that all clients should be afforded zealous representation and complete confidentiality, even as these arguments sounded increasingly tenuous and hollow. Still, until 1992, tobacco lawyers had a perfect record of protecting the industry from outside scrutiny. The first chink in the armor was a series of disclosures made in a single New Jersey federal court case that was reversed on appeal.[4]

By 1998, however, with the settlement of lawsuits brought by states' attorneys general and the release by Congress of 39,000 formerly secret documents, it became clear that lawyers were directly involved in the tobacco industry's attempt to cover up what it knew about the dangers of its product. Some lawyers went even further: The Council on Tobacco Research (CTR), supposedly an organization for scientific study, turned out to be a repository of damaging information for which

---

[4] Haines v. Liggett Group, Inc., 140 F.R.D. 681 (D.N.J. 1992), *rev'd*, 975 F.2d 81 (3d Cir. 1992).

confidentiality was claimed, and maintained, because the CTR was largely run by *lawyers*, not scientists. In the years since the tobacco disclosures there have been other instances, from Enron to the creation of mortgage backed securities and the multiple malfeasances that precipitated the financial crisis of 2008. Today the American public and the governments in Washington and almost every state, seem to be insisting on more: a moral imperative to lawyer conduct.

Over 30 years ago, Gerald Postema wrote a particularly thoughtful and pioneering article about the interrelationship between a lawyer's ethical conduct and the moral imperative of that lawyer's actions. His ideas still have resonance today.

Gerald Postema, *Moral Responsibility in Professional Ethics*
55 N.Y.U. L. REV. 63 (1980)[5]

The requirements of professional ethics can sometimes move some distance from the concerns of private or ordinary morality, a phenomenon we might call *moral distance*. . . .

Morality seems to require not only that one be able to apply moral principles properly to one's own or another's conduct, but also that one be able to appreciate the moral costs of one's actions, perhaps even when those actions are unintentional. By "moral costs" I mean those features of one's action and its consequences . . . that, in the absence of specific justification, would provide substantial if not conclusive moral reasons against performing it.

. . . .

Since the lawyer often acts as an extension of the legal and moral personality of the client, the lawyer is under great temptation to refuse to accept responsibility for his professional actions and their consequences. Moreover, except when his beliefs coincide with those of his client, he lives with a recurring dilemma: He must engage in activities, make arguments, and present positions which he himself does not endorse or embrace. The lawyer's integrity is put into question by the mere exercise of the duties of his profession.

To preserve his integrity, the lawyer must carefully distance himself from his activities. Publicly, he may sharply distinguish statements or arguments he makes for the client and statements on which he stakes his professional honor. The danger in this strategy is that a curious two-stage distancing may result. First, the lawyer distances himself from the argument: It is not his argument, but that of his client. His job is to construct the arguments; the task of evaluating and believing them is left to others. Second, after detaching himself from the argument, he is increasingly tempted to identify with this stance of detachment. What first offers itself as a device for distancing oneself from personally unacceptable positions becomes a defining feature of one's professional self-concept. This, in turn, encourages an uncritical, uncommitted state of mind, or worse, a deep moral skepticism. When such detachment is defined as a professional ideal, as it is by the standard conception, the lawyer is even more apt to adopt these attitudes.

. . . .

Consider first the personal costs the lawyer must pay to act in this detached manner. . . . In a large portion of his daily experience, in which he is acting regularly in the moral arena, he is alienated from his own moral feelings and attitudes and indeed from his moral personality as a whole. Moreover, in light of the strong pressures for role identification, it is not unlikely that the explicit and conscious adoption of the minimal identification strategy involves a substantial element of self-deception.

The social costs of cutting off professional deliberation and action from their sources in ordinary moral experience are even more troubling. . . . [M]ost importantly, when professional action is estranged from ordinary moral experience, the lawyer's sensitivity to the moral costs in both ordinary and extraordinary situations tends to atrophy. The ideal of neutrality permits, indeed requires, that the lawyer regard his professional activities and their consequences from the point of view of the uninvolved spectator. One may abstractly regret that the injury is done, but this regret is analogous to the regret one feels as a spectator. . . . This has troubling consequences . . . . As Bernard Williams argued, "only those who are reluctant or disinclined to do the morally disagreeable when it is really necessary have much chance of not doing it when it is not necessary. . . ."

. . . .

Finally, the moral detachment of the lawyer adversely affects the quality of the lawyer-client relationship. Unable to draw from the responses and relations of ordinary experience, the lawyer is capable of relating to the client only as a client. He puts his moral faculties of reason, argument, and persuasion wholly at the service of the client, but simultaneously disengages his moral personality. He views himself not as a moral actor but as a legal technician. In addition, he is barred from recognizing the client's moral personality. . . .

The unavoidable social costs of the standard conception of professional legal behavior argue strongly for a radical rethinking of the lawyer's role. One alternative . . . is to recognize the unavoidable discontinuities in the moral landscape and to bridge them with a unified conception of moral personality. Each lawyer [would be] integrating his own sense of moral responsibility into the role itself. Such a conception must improve upon the current one by allowing a broader scope of engaged moral judgment in day-to-day professional activities while encouraging a keener sense of personal responsibility for the consequences of these activities.

NOTES

In the three decades since Professor Postema's piece, examination and discussion of the moral component of lawyering has increased substantially. Are Postema's assumptions — that lawyers create "moral distance," engage in self-deceptive detachment, and allow themselves to become mere "uninvolved spectators" to their clients' bad acts — still valid? Or has the profession grown a greater moral conscience since 1980?

One current commentator, Columbia law professor Katherine Franke, writing about the Occupy movement in late 2011, sees no improvement. Closely echoing Postema, she writes: "Too often, being a 'good lawyer' has meant . . . providing effective legal cover for otherwise borderline, or worse, practices." She argues "effective and ethical representation . . . does not relieve lawyers of responsibility for the harmful effects on others created by our clients' actions . . . ."[6]

Some observers suggest that newer lawyer regulations — such as the Sarbanes-Oxley Act, which can require attorneys in certain regulatory situations to candidly disclose the conduct of their clients, or changes to the ABA's rules to provide more whistleblowing exceptions to confidentiality (more on both later)— show that society is compelling lawyers to develop more public-protective and less client-centric thinking. But if a change in behavior is externally imposed, is it real change? Can morality be legislated? Franke, apparently, would say "no"; she sees many lawyers today who "regard all legal rules simply as the price of misconduct discounted by the probability of enforcement." If this unhappy view is correct, real change may have to be internal — through the way lawyers perceive themselves. Put another way, true moral lawyering may have to come "from within." Thus Franke urges law professors to inculcate "responsible moral judgment" in their students, and urges students to be, as Justice Brandeis put it 100 years ago, lawyers and "public citizens."

5.   Some Further Thoughts on Ethics and Morality

The first part of this book — Problems 1 through 14 — discusses the lawyer-client relationship, while the second part addresses the balance between client advocacy and a lawyer's other duties — to the legal system and, perhaps, to "justice." As you evaluate the problems you read, we think it's useful to keep Professor Postema in mind. His perspective about "moral costs" and lawyers' perceptions of their own actions recurs in different contexts throughout this volume. Consider also how the public feels about these issues. After all, the public criticism of lawyers has rested on the foundation that in "zealously" (arguably overzealously) representing their clients, lawyers fail society's greater good. But when a member of the public changes hats and becomes a client, that same individual may want, even insist on, that same narrowly focused, "zealous" representation.

Consider too how you view yourself as a prospective attorney. Is there a gulf between your vision of an ethical, professionally responsible lawyer and a moral citizen of the world, or do these two ideas merge in your mind? Should legal ethics be defined in terms of the four corners of legal representation, or as part of a larger canvas, in which the needs of society are considered? Finally, should "ethics" be determined by defining what the written rules permit a lawyer to "get away with" or by defining "the ethical lawyer" as one who meets a different standard based in part on moral responsibility?

We don't presume to tell anyone how to answer these questions; the issues they raise are far too personal. But permit us to throw in our "two cents" before we

---

[6] *Occupy Wall Street's Message for Lawyers*, THE NATIONAL L.J., at Nov. 21, 2011.

move on.

Practicing lawyers understand full well that clients retain us to meet *their* needs, not our own or those of society. Most of the time, clients couldn't care less what "society" or "the public" thinks is the proper way for us to act, or the ethical thing for us to do. Most clients are members of the public who expect *lawyers in the abstract* to be fair-minded and evenhanded, but want *their own* lawyer to do whatever it takes to win.

Some years ago, a student, while leading a class discussion on a problem that now appears in this book, said that to act in a particular way would be immoral and wrong, but it would be "ethical." When we asked what she meant, she said that the conduct was clearly wrong, even repugnant, but applying the rules of ethics, she could "get away with it." Should "ethical" be defined by what one may "get away with"? Or is a better definition one attorney commenting on another: "You know, there goes a really 'ethical' lawyer?" Many lawyers adopt the first conception: "Here's how we have to do it in order to stay out of trouble." Ethics opinions, as valuable as they are, foster this view by concentrating on conduct that can be sanctioned by suspension or disbarment, rather than on what is the "right" thing for an "ethical" lawyer to do, especially under the ABA Model Rules, which don't have "ethical considerations" to tell us what we *should* do.

When we asked our student what path she would take, the morally "right" course or the technically "ethical" one, she became confused. She looked at her personal morality as so distinct from what she had learned about the rules of ethics that she had never truly considered the two concepts together. As a result, she was unable to give us a practical answer to the question we find most important — "What would *you* do if this happens to *you*?"

As practicing lawyers *and* ethics teachers and advisors, we have some sympathy for Professor Postema's basic thesis; lawyers who separate their professional obligations from their personal morality will often find themselves in the same quandary that faced our student. Should lawyers then try to merge their legal and moral selves? The rules of ethics, after all, do appear to have a strong moral component. But thoughtful lawyers, practitioners, and ethicists alike disagree widely on whether their legal ethics and personal morality should be merged or even commingled.

One way to look at the body of work we call "legal ethics" is to integrate, even internalize, it along with one's own personal morality. It's as if one's sense of what is moral expands to absorb and include one's sense of what is "ethical." How then do you deal with the dilemmas faced every day in the practice of law? What do you do about revealing your knowledge of the body buried in the mine shaft (a question we'll examine in detail in Problem 4)? The desire to inform a distraught family is pitted against the duty and promise to the client to keep the information confidential. Are you stuck in the same place as our student, between what is moral and what is ethical? Perhaps these issues can be viewed as *moral dilemmas*, a term with which we are all familiar. Evaluating the situation as an integrated person, with professional ethics and personal morality absorbed into one integrated belief system, may not help to come up with the *right* answer, but it may make it easier to find *an* answer.

6. "Is There a Collective or Institutional Ethic Beyond the Ethics of the Individual?"

This is the question asked by investment banker Bowen "Buzz" McCoy in the next article. McCoy tells us about his own compelling experience in a situation literally involving life or death, and the lessons he learned about the development of individual and group ethics.

Bowen H. McCoy, *The Parable of the Sadhu*
HARVARD BUSINESS REVIEW (1983)[7]

Last year . . . I spent . . . three months in Nepal, walking 600 miles through 200 villages in the Himalayas . . . . On the trip my sole Western companion was an anthropologist who shed light on the cultural patterns of the villages we passed through.

During the Nepal hike, something occurred that had a powerful impact on my thinking about corporate ethics. Although some might argue that the experience has no relevance to business, it was a situation in which a basic ethical dilemma suddenly intruded into the lives of a group of individuals. How the group responded I think holds a lesson for all organizations no matter how defined.

The Sadhu

The Nepal experience was more rugged and adventuresome than I had anticipated. . . . My friend Stephen, the anthropologist, and I were halfway through the 60-day Himalayan part of the trip when we reached the high point, an 18,000-foot pass over a crest that we'd have to traverse to reach to the village of Muklinath, an ancient holy place for pilgrims.

Six years earlier I had suffered pulmonary edema, an acute form of altitude sickness, at 16,500 feet in the vicinity of Everest base camp, so we were understandably concerned about what would happen at 18,000 feet. Moreover, the Himalayas were having their wettest spring in 20 years; hip-deep powder and ice had already driven us off one ridge. If we failed to cross the pass, I feared that the last half of our "once in a lifetime" trip would be ruined.

The night before we would try the pass, we camped at a hut at 14,500 feet. In the photos taken at that camp, my face appears wan. The last village we'd passed through was a sturdy two-day walk below us, and I was tired.

During the late afternoon, four backpackers from New Zealand joined us, and we spent most of the night awake, anticipating the climb. Below we could see the fires of two other parties, which turned out to be two Swiss couples and a Japanese hiking club.

To get over the steep part of the climb before the sun melted the steps cut in the ice, we departed at 3:30 A.M. The New Zealanders left first, followed by Stephen and myself, our porters and Sherpas, and then the Swiss. The Japanese lingered in

---

their camp. The sky was clear, and we were confident that no spring storm would erupt that day to close the pass.

At 15,500 feet, it looked to me as if Stephen was shuffling and staggering a bit, which are symptoms of altitude sickness . . . . I felt strong, my adrenaline was flowing, but I was very concerned about my ultimate ability to get across. A couple of our porters were also suffering from the height, and Pasang, our Sherpa sirdar (leader) was worried.

Just after daybreak, while we rested at 15,500 feet, one of the New Zealanders, who had gone ahead, came staggering down toward us with a body slung across his shoulders. He dumped the almost naked, barefoot body of an Indian holy man — a sadhu — at my feet. He had found the pilgrim lying on the ice, shivering and suffering from hypothermia. I cradled the sadhu's head and laid him out on the rocks. The New Zealander was angry. He wanted to get across the pass before the bright sun melted the snow. He said, "Look, I've done what I can. You have porters and Sherpa guides. You care for him. We're going on!" He turned and went back up the mountain to join his friends.

I took a carotid pulse and found that the sadhu was still alive. We figured he had probably visited the holy shrines at Muklinath and was on his way home. It was fruitless to question why he had chosen this desperately high route instead of the safe, heavily traveled caravan route through the Kali Gandaki gorge. Or why he was almost naked and with no shoes, or how long he had been lying in the pass. The answers weren't going to solve our problem.

Stephen and the four Swiss began stripping off outer clothing and opening their packs. The sadhu was soon clothed from head to foot. He was not able to walk, but he was very much alive. I looked down the mountain and spotted below the Japanese climbers marching up with a horse.

Without a great deal of thought, I told Stephen and Pasang that I was concerned about withstanding the heights to come and wanted to get over the pass. I took off after several of our porters who had gone ahead.

On the steep part of the ascent where, if the ice steps had given way, I would have slid down about 3,000 feet, I felt vertigo. I stopped for a breather, allowing the Swiss to catch up with me. I inquired about the sadhu and Stephen. They said that the sadhu was fine and that Stephen was just behind. I set off again for the summit.

Stephen arrived at the summit an hour after I did. Still exhilarated by victory, I ran down the snow slope to congratulate him. He was suffering from altitude sickness, walking 15 steps, then stopping, walking 15 steps, then stopping. Pasang accompanied him all the way up. When I reached them, Stephen glared at me and said: "How do you feel about contributing to the death of a fellow man?"

I did not fully comprehend what he meant.

"Is the sadhu dead?" I inquired.

"No," replied Stephen, "but he surely will be!"

After I had gone, and the Swiss had departed not long after, Stephen had remained with the sadhu. When the Japanese had arrived, Stephen had asked to use their horse to transport the sadhu down to the hut. They had refused. He had then asked Pasang to have a group of our porters carry the sadhu. Pasang had resisted the idea, saying that the porters would have to exert all their energy to get themselves over the pass. He had thought they could not carry a man down 1,000 feet to the hut, reclimb the slope, and get across safely before the snow melted. Pasang had pressed Stephen not to delay any longer.

The Sherpas had carried the sadhu down to a rock in the sun at about 15,000 feet and had pointed out the hut another 500 feet below. The Japanese had given him food and drink. When they had last seen him he was listlessly throwing rocks at the Japanese party's dog, which had frightened him.

We do not know if the sadhu lived or died.

For many of the following days and evenings Stephen and I discussed and debated our behavior toward the sadhu. Stephen is a committed Quaker with deep moral vision. He said, "I feel that what happened with the sadhu is a good example of the breakdown between the individual ethic and the corporate ethic. No one person was willing to assume ultimate responsibility for the sadhu. Each was willing to do his bit just so long as it was not too inconvenient. When it got to be a bother, everyone just passed the buck to someone else and took off. . . ."

I defended the larger group, saying, "Look, we all cared. We all stopped and gave aid and comfort. Everyone did his bit. The New Zealander carried him down below the snow line. I took his pulse and suggested we treat him for hypothermia. You and the Swiss gave him clothing and got him warmed up. The Japanese gave him food and water. The Sherpas carried him down to the sun and pointed out the easy trail toward the hut. He was well enough to throw rocks at a dog. What more could we do?"

"You have just described the typical affluent Westerner's response to a problem. Throwing money — in this case food and sweaters — at it, but not solving the fundamentals!" Stephen retorted.

"What would satisfy you?" I said. "Here we are, a group of New Zealanders, Swiss, Americans, and Japanese who have never met before and who are at the apex of one of the most powerful experiences of our lives. Some years the pass is so bad no one gets over it. What right does an almost naked pilgrim who chooses the wrong trail have to disrupt our lives? Even the Sherpas had no interest in risking the trip to help him beyond a certain point."

Stephen calmly rebutted, "I wonder what the Sherpas would have done if the sadhu had been a well-dressed Nepali, or what the Japanese would have done if the sadhu had been a well-dressed Asian, or what you would have done, Buzz, if the sadhu had been a well-dressed Western woman?"

"Where, in your opinion," I asked instead, "is the limit of our responsibility in a situation like this?" . . .

Stephen said, "As individual Christians or people with a Western ethical tradition, we can fulfill our obligations in such a situation only if (1) the sadhu dies in our care, (2) the sadhu demonstrates to us that he could undertake the two-day walk down to the village, or (3) we carry the sadhu for two days down to the village and convince someone there to care for him."

The Individual vs. The Group Ethic

Despite my arguments, I felt and continue to feel guilt about the sadhu. I had literally walked through a classic moral dilemma without fully thinking through the consequences. My excuses for my actions include a high adrenaline flow, a superordinate goal, and a once-in-a-lifetime opportunity — factors in the usual corporate situation, especially when one is under stress.

Real moral dilemmas are ambiguous, and many of us hike through them, unaware that they exist. When, usually after the fact, someone makes an issue of them, we tend to resent his or her bringing it up. Often, when the full import of what we have done (or not done) falls on us, we dig into a defensive position . . . .

Among the many questions that occur to me when pondering my experience are: What are the practical limits of moral imagination and vision? Is there a collective or institutional ethic beyond the ethics of the individual? At what level of effort or commitment can one discharge one's ethical responsibilities?

Not every ethical dilemma has a right solution. Reasonable people often disagree; otherwise there would be no dilemma. . . .

The sadhu experience offers an interesting parallel to business situations. An immediate response was mandatory. Failure to act was a decision in itself. Up on the mountain we could not resign and submit our resumés to a headhunter. In contrast to philosophy, business involves action and implementation — getting things done. Managers must come up with answers to problems based on what they see . . . .

One of our problems was that as a group we had no process for developing a consensus. We had no sense of purpose or plan. The difficulties of dealing with the sadhu were so complex that no one person could handle it. Because it did not have a set of preconditions that could guide its action to an acceptable resolution, the group reacted instinctively as individuals. The cross-cultural nature of the group added a further layer of complexity. We had no leader with whom we could all identify and in whose purpose we believed. Only Stephen was willing to take charge, but he could not gain adequate support to care for the sadhu.

. . . .

The word "ethics" turns off many and confuses more. Yet the notions of shared values and an agreed-on process for dealing with adversity and change — what many people mean when they talk about corporate culture — seem to be at the heart of the ethical issue. People who are in touch with their own core beliefs and the beliefs of others and are sustained by them can be more comfortable living on the cutting edge. . . .

What would have happened had Stephen and I carried the sadhu for two days back to the village and become involved with the villagers in his care? In four trips to Nepal my most interesting experiences occurred in 1975 when I lived in a Sherpa home in the Khumbu for five days recovering from altitude sickness. The high point of Stephen's trip was an invitation to participate in a family funeral ceremony in

Manang. Neither experience had to do with climbing the high passes of the Himalayas. Why were we so reluctant to try the lower path, the ambiguous trail? Perhaps because we did not have a leader who could reveal the greater purpose of the trip to us.

Why didn't Stephen with his moral vision opt to take the sadhu under his personal care? The answer is because, in part, Stephen was hard-stressed physically himself, and because, in part, without some support system that involved our involuntary and episodic community on the mountain, it was beyond his individual capacity to do so. . . .

That is the lesson of the sadhu. In a complex corporate situation, the individual requires and deserves the support of the group. If people cannot find such support from their organization, they don't know how to act. If such support is forthcoming, a person has a stake in the success of the group, and can add much to the process of establishing and maintaining a corporate culture. . . .

For each of us the sadhu lives. Should we stop what we are doing and comfort him, or should we keep trudging up toward the high pass? Should I pause to help the derelict I pass on the street each night as I walk by the Yale Club en route to Grand Central Station? Am I his brother? What is the nature of our responsibility if we consider ourselves to be ethical persons? Perhaps it is to change the values of the group so that it can, with all its resources, take the other road.

NOTES

McCoy learned a valuable lesson about corporate ethics from his experience. Can the lesson be applied with equal force to the legal profession? What about the idea that even a highly moral individual, like McCoy's friend Stephen, is unlikely to be able to fulfill his perceived moral obligations without some support from the larger group? Is developing such a "group culture" important to finding ways to "do the right thing," or is this merely an excuse for our personal failures? Finally, what about the sadhu? How certain could McCoy and Stephen be that bringing the holy man down to the village was truly what the sadhu wished?

7.   Ethics and Cultural Differences

The story of the sadhu also illustrates that culture has a significant impact on our sense of morality and ethics. As you read the materials in this text, you will find opportunities to examine how cultural norms impact the decisions that lawyers make. Consider your own opportunities to develop a deeper understanding of how your own culture affects your approach to the problems in this book and those in the "real world" practice of law.

Many of us assume that we have "mainstream American" values, but are any of us sure what those are? Take two recent examples — the Justice Department's so-called "torture memos" — which we'll discuss at length later in this volume — and the use of on-line servers and browsers to track information. As to the first, did the memos from the Justice Department's Office of Legal Counsel "violate values key to our national identity" and "distort . . . laws to permit governmental conduct that is fundamentally un-American," as then Yale Law School Dean Harold Koh argued?[8]

Or are they acts of patriotism, made necessary in these perilous times, justified by a fight against a new kind of enemy, and an interpretation of laws permitted by the government's lawyers, as former White House counsel Alberto Gonzales claimed?

How one views the torture memos may relate to the background and culture of the observer as well as what the observer understands about what it means to be an "American" or a patriot. For example, do you think there is a national consensus on whether American soldiers should engage in torture? Or is it more complicated than "yes" or "no"? Do you agree with Koh that Justice Department lawyers stepped over a moral boundary? To some extent, your answers to these questions may be dependent on cultural perceptions of the meaning of "torture" or the proper emphasis on the duty to always "follow orders."

What about lawyers representing private entities or individuals? Does it matter if the private entity is doing business in a country with very different standards of morality or ethics? Several years ago, the Chinese government requested Yahoo to provide communications from Shi Tao, a Chinese journalist for the newspaper *Contemporary Business News*. After Yahoo complied, presumably after consulting its attorneys, Shi Tao was sentenced to 10 years in prison for "illegally providing state secrets abroad" based on the information Yahoo turned over. One commentator observed that on the one hand, it is understandable that while Yahoo "may have a moral obligation to criticize the practices of the host state [it is] not directly liable for the human rights violations of the state . . . ." But on the other hand, "the lawyer should be candid to her client about the economic, political, and moral effects of the client's actions when following a local law that may violate human rights."[9]

8. When the Individual Alone Chooses to Act

As we will see later in this volume, lawyers are focusing more and more frequently on the idea of a group or law firm culture as an important component of ethical behavior. In the following story, however, one aspiring lawyer chose to act with little, if any, support from the others around him.

Mike Comeaux, *Bar Exam: He Saved a Life, Got No Extra Time*
THE LOS ANGELES DAILY NEWS (February 26, 1993)[10]

While others kept taking their state bar exam, one aspiring lawyer put aside his papers to give cardiopulmonary resuscitation to a stricken test-taker until paramedics arrived — and then was refused extra time to finish the test, officials said.

---

[8] Harold Hongju Koh, *Can the President Be Torturer in Chief?*, 81 IND. L.J. 1145, 1165, 1166 (2005).

[9] James Heffernan, *An American in Beijing: An Attorney's Ethical Considerations Abroad with a Client Doing Business with a Repressive Government*, 19 GEO. J. LEGAL ETHICS 721, 728 (2006).

[10] Copyright © 1993 by the Los Angeles Daily News. Reprinted by permission.

More than 6,000 people were taking the timed, three-hour test — to qualify to be lawyers — in the Pasadena Convention Center on Tuesday when a 50-year-old man taking the exam suffered a seizure, officials said yesterday. Witnesses said only a handful dared to interrupt their test to help the man, who survived the seizure. But four witnesses and a state bar official confirmed that one of the test-takers administered CPR to the victim until paramedics arrived.

Jerome Braun, the state bar's senior executive for admissions, said that the incident did not reflect poorly on the legal profession. "I don't think lawyers are that hard-hearted as a group," Braun said. He said the test supervisor acted properly by refusing to give the good Samaritan extra time to make up for the minutes lost giving CPR. "If he or she asked for additional time, additional time probably would not be given because under those circumstances we could not determine how much people were affected by the situation," Braun said.

"The fairest way of all is to deal with the situation after the exam," he said. "That could be done by a post-exam analysis of scores, and if appropriate to do so by making such adjustments as seem necessary." . . .

Other would-be lawyers present — who will learn in May whether they passed the bar exam — said they were sobered by their own reactions to the incident and the refusal of bar officials to grant extra time for the hero to complete his test.

"A man sitting behind me was a paramedic, and he really felt the need to go to the assistance of this person, but he knew if he did that he risked blowing the entire exam," said Kim Enriquez of Ojai. "He really felt bad about that." "It really upset me, but I had to keep taking the test," Enriquez said. "It made me feel like a real cold person." Enriquez said that she compared notes with others and discovered many with similar feelings.

The seizure was heard by many, although not all, of the people in the room, said Mark Smith of La Verne, who also was taking the exam. "All of a sudden you heard a loud groan or a scream," Smith said. "You could hear a commotion at the back (of the convention hall). A lot of proctors went to the back."

He said that the pressure to continue taking the test uninterrupted was enormous. "We're so pressed for time that even 10 or 15 minutes makes a difference here," Smith said. "One or two missed issues could be the difference between passing and failing."

Two others taking the test — a 30-year-old West Los Angeles woman who was taking the test for the second time, and a 28-year-old Los Angeles woman — declined to give their names, fearing retribution by bar officials. "If these people aren't willing to give an extra 30 minutes to someone who gave CPR and saved someone's life, can you imagine what they'd do to us for bad-mouthing them?" the West Los Angeles woman said.

. . . .

Braun said the state bar officials administering the exam are trained in CPR and first aid. If the good Samaritan had not rushed to the victim's aid, one of the proctors could have aided him, he said. . . .

A decision to adjust the good Samaritan's score will be made by a 19-person committee of bar examiners, consisting of 10 lawyers and nine lay people, Braun said. "The person may pass the exam as given, so we may have to do nothing."

NOTES

The good news is that this good Samaritan did pass the bar; the bad news is that he remained anonymous in this story, not singled out for approbation. He chose to act as he did despite the lack of support from the group, and despite the personal risk involved. The spokesperson for the State Bar, arguably the entity that should lead the way in creating an ethical environment for lawyers, seems to make the case that what the good Samaritan did was not that significant: He notes that the proctors acted properly, defends those who did not respond, and argues that the proctors themselves were CPR trained and would have assisted the man.

What would have happened if the entire room full of exam-takers had stopped and organized a concerted effort to help the distressed man? Would this have caused the State Bar to take a more sympathetic position? Would it have protected the risk-taker, by forcing the proctors to extend the time of everyone in the room? We will never know.

9. Going the Whole Nine Yards

Lawyers are much more than advocates. Many lawyers live productive lives outside their professional lives. One appellate justice of our acquaintance volunteered weekly in a local soup kitchen and encouraged his clerks and students to join him. We all know lawyers who "pay it forward" on a daily basis. One of the many ways you can learn more about lawyers who go above and beyond is to visit the Lawyers and Settlements site — http://www.lawyersandsettlements.com/blog/category/lawyers-giving-back. You do not have to be an extraordinary lawyer in order to accomplish extraordinary things. Any lawyer willing to infuse his or her lawyering with humanity — or morality, if you will — can achieve this. A lawyer friend of ours once wrote:

> I represent people, not cases. If I just stopped after the case was over, I'd be leaving my client out in the cold. It goes back to the old days when I did criminal defense work. Clients came to me with more than just their criminal case. Their families were on welfare, or they'd lose their job if they couldn't make bail. I'd spend time with mothers, girlfriends, aunts, and uncles. One time, my client came to court with her three-year-old child, and the judge rolled her up into jail on some technicality. We got her out on a writ, but I couldn't leave the child there, so I took her with me.

> You've got to go the whole nine yards for your clients. If you don't, you're really not meeting their needs. I had a poor client with a big products liability case. She had almost no clothes and had never been in a courthouse, so we went out and bought her a whole wardrobe for trial. When we won big, we gave her financial advice even though we're not financial advisors. Common sense stuff, like put money in trust for the kids, and buy a nice home for cash so you don't have monthly payments.

Otherwise, the money could have been gone in a year. If that was risky for us to do, so be it.

I don't want to take over their lives or force them to do something they don't want, but I never want to abandon my clients at the courthouse door. I guess that means getting emotionally involved in your clients' lives, something I remember professors in law school telling me not to do: 'You're a lawyer, not a social worker.' But that's a price I'll gladly pay to try to help the *person*, not just the case.

Does this philosophy make sense, or is it asking for trouble?

B. SUPPLEMENTAL READINGS

1. PHILLIP B. HEYMANN & LANCE LIEBMAN, THE SOCIAL RESPONSIBILITIES OF LAWYERS (1988). This excellent soft-cover classic contains a series of interesting case studies on significant ethical and moral dilemmas that face practicing lawyers in today's society.

2. The battle over Lord Brougham continues to this day, almost two centuries later. Did Brougham truly set the standard of defending a client regardless of guilt or innocence? Not necessarily, say ethics professors Bruce A. Green and Fred C. Zacharias. In their article, *Reconceptualizing Advocacy Ethics*, 74 GEO. WASH. L. REV. 1 (2005), these two well-known ethics professors claim that Brougham repudiated his statement in Queen Carolyn's case. Poppycock, says one of the deans of legal ethics, Monroe Freedman, who in his brief piece *Henry Lord Brougham, Written by Himself*, 19 GEO. J. LEGAL ETHICS 1213 (2006), argues that Brougham actually reiterated his position even more strongly.

3. W. Bradley Wendel has written many important articles and you'll see his name again and again in this book. The first piece we mention here is *Public Values and Professional Responsibility*, 75 NOTRE DAME L. REV. 1 (1999). Professor Wendel attacks the "regulatory model" of legal ethics as one that does less to regulate than to instruct lawyers in how to avoid blame. Wendel insists on moral accountability in lawyering and a "values centered" method of teaching the discipline while at the same time recognizing that there is more than one set of acceptable moral values.

4. HOWARD LESNICK, BEING A LAWYER: INDIVIDUAL CHOICE AND RESPONSIBILITY IN THE PRACTICE OF LAW (1992). This classic raises many issues similar to those in this chapter. Included are discussions of the lawyer as advocate, the autonomy of clients and the related issues of attorney detachment and paternalism, and the meaning of a legal education.

5. Lisa G. Lerman, *Professional and Ethical Issues in Legal Externships: Fostering Commitment to Public Service*, 67 FORDHAM L. REV. 2295 (1999). This practical assessment of legal issues that students may encounter while working as externs is broken into professional and moral issues (supervisor misconduct, competency/diligence/neglect, unauthorized practice of law, billing fraud, confidentiality and client relations, conflicts of interest, and substance abuse).

6. Jeffrey M. Lipshaw, *Law as Rationalization: Getting Beyond Reason to Business Ethics*, 37 U. TOL. L. REV 959 (2006) examines how law, ethics, economics, and philosophy interrelate when lawyers advise clients and make decisions. The author distinguishes between a lawyer's moral choices when the law is neutral (such as a tobacco company buying a fast food chain) and others when it is not, such as representing a corporation that is doing risk assessment on products known to be defective.

7. Richard Wasserstrom, *Lawyers as Professionals: Some Moral Issues*, 5 HUMAN RIGHTS 1 (1975). This ground-breaking analysis of what the author calls the "role-differentiated morality" of lawyers is an important reading on lawyer professionalism and morality.

8. The late Fred C. Zacharias's *Coercing Clients: Can Lawyer Gatekeeper Rules Work?*, 47 B.C. L. REV 455 (2006) has an abstract that describes the article well:

> Recent federal regulations and amendments to the Model Rules of Professional Conduct — most of which have responded to lawyer involvement in corporate scandals — rest on the assumption that lawyers have a role to play in forcing clients to act legally, morally, or appropriately. Lawyers are distinctive, perhaps even unique among professionals, in that they are sometimes legally authorized to force clients into obeying the lawyers' advice. This Article reviews the rules that empower lawyers in this way, with a focus on the corporate context.

9. Marvin E. Frankel, *The Search for Truth: An Umpireal View*, 123 U. PA. L. REV. 1031 (1975), and Monroe Freedman, *Judge Frankel's Search for Truth*, 123 U. PA. L. REV. 1060 (1975). A debate between two of the most articulate thinkers on these issues. Judge Frankel argues that the legal system pays too little attention to the truth, and Professor Freedman replies that our justice system, in context, must govern the lawyer's professional obligation, even if that sometimes results in the "subordination" and "distortion" of truth.

10. When the advocacy debate was subjected to renewed scrutiny in the 1970s, a vast number of law review articles and studies have expanded on and modified these ideas. Among the most interesting are: Stephen Gillers, *Can a Good Lawyer Be a Bad Person?*, 84 MICH. L. REV. 1011 (1986); Theodore J. Schneyer, *Moral Philosophy's Standard Misconception of Legal Ethics*, 1984 WIS. L. REV. 1529 (1984); William H. Simon, *Ethical Discretion in Lawyering*, 101 HARV. L. REV. 1083 (1988); and Simon's *The Ideology of Advocacy: Procedural Justice and Professional Ethics*, 1978 WIS. L. REV. 29 (1978).

11. Another instance of the advocacy debate was a "call and response" series beginning with Elliot Cohen's *Pure Legal Advocates and Moral Agents: Two Concepts of a Lawyer in an Adversary System*, 4 CRIM. JUST. ETHICS 38 (1985). The response is from Memory and Rose, *The Attorney as a Moral Agent: a Critique of Cohen*, 21 CRIM. JUST. ETHICS 28 (2002) and at http://faculty.irsc.edu/faculty/ecohen/memory-rose1.pdf. In response, Cohen wrote *Pure Legal Advocates and Moral Agents Revisited: A Reply to Memory and Rose*, 21 CRIM. JUST. ETHICS 39 (2002), and at http://faculty.irsc.edu/faculty/ecohen/cohen.pdf. This is a full-on debate about legal advocacy and moral agents, analyzing the justifications and consequences of winning a case by all available means short of violating the law versus injecting considerations of justice and morality into one's practice.

PART TWO

THE LAWYER-CLIENT RELATIONSHIP

"[My client has] made his decisions consciously, temperately, and not in the heat of passion, but based on his true and sincere and honest beliefs about what is right for him. I stand with him 100 percent."

—Ronald Lee Deere's public defender, refusing to abide by a court order that would have forced him to act against his client's wishes, as quoted by the California Supreme Court

Chapter 2

UNDERTAKING A CASE

PROBLEM 1: HANGING OUT YOUR SHINGLE

A. INTRODUCTION

What standards must a lawyer meet in order to take a case? Does a presumption of competence come with admission to the bar? If not, what more is required? How much depends on the kind of case the lawyer is asked to undertake? And how does an inexperienced lawyer get the necessary training? Think about these questions as you read Problem 1.

B. PROBLEM

I

Arthur Hollins has been practicing law for eight years, emphasizing advice and incorporation of small businesses, though he also litigates some business disputes. Long-time client Ann Wilson consults Arthur about her son, whose leg was severely injured in a train collision apparently caused by a switching error or malfunction. She wants Arthur to represent her son in a suit against the railroad for damages.

Hollins is inexperienced in personal injury cases, though he believes he has done enough business litigation to be generally competent to handle a trial. But he has two concerns: first, he has never presented medical evidence before at trial; and second, he knows almost nothing about the workings of railroads.

Hollins has two old law school friends, Fred and Mary. Both are, in his opinion, top-notch personal injury attorneys, and he knows that Mary has been plaintiff's counsel in more than one train accident case. Hollins also knows that Mary would refuse to pay him a "referral fee" if he sends the case to her because she considers the practice "unethical."

QUESTIONS

1. Would it be ethical of Arthur to keep the case? Even if he felt Fred and Mary could perform better than he can?

2. Can Arthur justify taking the case by pointing out that Ms. Wilson told him: "I know this isn't right up your alley, but I really trust your judgment and ability"?

3. If Arthur refers out the case, can he accept a referral fee? May he choose Fred instead of Mary because of Mary's unwillingness to split fees? Even if he

believes Mary is better qualified than Fred?

4.   If Arthur does take the case, may he ask Ann to sign a letter waiving his competence?

II

You have recently been admitted and have just rented space from Hollins to open your own practice. After a few weeks waiting for the phone to ring, you get calls from two prospective clients. One is an old friend who wants you to incorporate his small boutique, "Very Vegan Cuisine." Another is a referral from an attorney acquaintance — a domestic relations case involving two children, a house, and a few other assets. In law school you took classes in both corporations and domestic relations law, but this would be your first experience of actual practice in those areas. Arthur has said, however, "I'll point you in the right direction on the incorporation but I don't do much domestic relations work."

QUESTIONS

1.   Should you take the incorporation matter? Should you take on the marital case? How is your decision affected by the differences between the two cases?

2.   Because you are just starting your practice, your hourly fee will be lower than what Arthur charges his clients. You expect the incorporation will take between 15 to 25 hours. A more experienced attorney would expect to spend roughly 10 hours. It is not possible for you to estimate how long the domestic relations case will take. If you take either matter, how should you bill your client?

3.   If you decide to take these cases, are you obligated to tell your prospective clients that you have no experience in these kinds of matters? If so, what should you tell them?

C.   READINGS

1.   Asking Questions About "Competence"

As you read these next pages, consider the following questions. What constitutes competence? Every lawyer has a first case; does inexperience with a particular type of matter necessarily render an attorney incompetent to handle it? Is it enough that the attorney studied the subject in law school? Or that the lawyer can consult a more experienced colleague? What other criteria should be considered?

Suppose a lawyer is competent, but perhaps not as talented as the lawyer next door. Must the matter be referred to the "better" lawyer? If so, how does that attorney ever get to the point where he or she can undertake any representation? Under what circumstances is an attorney ethically obligated to refer a matter to a specialist?

What if a lawyer is competent, but does not have the staff or other resources adequate to handle a complex matter? May the lawyer still take the case?

Finally, how do ethical standards of "competence" compare with the public's notion of what this term means? And with "competence" as a negligence or malpractice standard?

2. Sleeping Lawyers and Measuring Standards of Competence

How do we measure competence? How low a bar may it be? What about using the concept "ineffective assistance of counsel"? The Supreme Court defined ineffective assistance of counsel in the landmark criminal case of *Strickland v. Washington*, 466 U.S. 668, 686 (1984), holding that an attorney's assistance is ineffective if it "so undermined the proper functioning of the adversarial process that the trial cannot be relied on as having produced a just result." Is this standard limited to criminal cases?

If a lawyer sleeps during a client's trial, isn't this failure to even be present, at least mentally, the worst form of incompetence? In the last few years, the Internet and the press have shone the light of public scrutiny on a series of what we'll call the "Sleeping Lawyer Cases," involving lawyers who have actually fallen asleep during trial. More than one judge has found that even if the lawyer slept through portions of the trial the defendant would, in the words of one court, "still need to establish that he was prejudiced by that conduct, i.e., that there is a some possibility that, but for the fact that [counsel] slept, the outcome of [the defendant's] trial would have been different." *Williams v. United States*, 2007 U.S. Dist. LEXIS 59983 (N.D.N.Y. Aug. 15, 2007). Similarly, defendant "Tippins failed to demonstrate that he suffered any prejudice by reason of [counsel] Tirelli's sleeping." *Tippins v. Walker*, 77 F.3d 682, 684 (2d Cir. 1996).

Are these lawyers *per se* incompetent, even if their incompetence didn't affect the result? What standard do we apply? Do these sleeping lawyers have the requisite "legal knowledge and skill" that ABA Model Rule 1.1 requires? Knowledge and skill are the issues facing Arthur Hollins and the young lawyer in Problem 1 above — that is, do they know enough to do the job? These sleeping attorneys, however, may well have had plenty of *experience*, and all the specific skills and specialized knowledge they needed. They just appear to have completely, well, fallen asleep on the job. Rather than lack of knowledge and skill, their failures may relate more to a lack of "thoroughness and preparation," the other articulated (but sometimes under-appreciated) requirements of MR 1.1, or a lack of "diligence," as defined by MR 1.3.

Competence can be measured in several different ways, even in the same case. Thus, a lawyer may fail to meet the ethical duty of competence but still not be liable for malpractice if there are no *damages* to the client that are *caused* by the lawyer's failures. That means, in the case of a sleeping lawyer, that a malpractice case is likely to fail unless the client can prove not "just" incompetence but that a conviction was the result of that incompetence. The same standard applies in a civil context: *e.g.*, if the lawyer sleeps through a divorce case. The question the court asks is whether the incompetence affects the result. Moreover, the *but for* standard is the same whether the case is litigation or transactional.[1]

As we have seen, even falling asleep during trial does not mandate reversal of a conviction. Ineffective assistance of counsel also requires that a court believe a different result would have happened but for the lawyer's errors — or, as the United States Supreme Court has put it, that prejudice to the client resulted from those errors.[2]

3. Fiduciary Duty

When a lawyer agrees to take a client's case, that lawyer takes on a fiduciary responsibility to the client. Like "competence," the term "fiduciary duty" (sometimes referred to in the plural as "duties") has both an ethical and a tort usage. As with the term "competence," the meaning of the term "fiduciary duty" is much the same whether it describes a professional standard of conduct or a tortious breach of the duty. But unlike "competence," the term "fiduciary duty" is not itself mentioned in specific ethics rules. Rather, to understand fiduciary duty one must consider the component parts including: diligence, loyalty, candor to the client, duty to keep the client informed, and the duty to maintain inviolate a client's confidences. While it's somewhat of an oversimplification, we like to think of "fiduciary duties" as comprising "the Four C's":

- Competence;

- Confidentiality;

- Candid Communication; and

- Loyalty. (Yes, we know that "Loyalty" doesn't begin with a "C" but we prefer it to its inverse, "conflict of interest." We'll discuss loyalty in detail in Problems 7 through 12.)[3]

Together, the concept of fiduciary duty is larger than the sum of its parts. It is that highest duty under the law that a lawyer owes to each client by virtue of the lawyer's special position of trust over the client's affairs. It requires the lawyer to place the client's interests above the lawyer's own individual interests, and always to act on the client's behalf in utmost good faith. Here is how the California Supreme Court has long evaluated the fiduciary relationship in matters of lawyer discipline:

> The relationship between an attorney and client is a fiduciary relationship of the very highest character. All dealings between an attorney and his client that are beneficial to the attorney will be closely scrutinized with the

---

[1] For a thorough discussion of why the *but for* test for causing damages must always be applied, see the California Supreme Court's discussion in *Viner v. Sweet*, 70 P.3d 1046 (Cal. 2003).

[2] The Supreme Court refined the *Strickland* standard in *Padilla v. Kentucky*, 559 U.S. 356 (2010), which held that the failure of counsel to advise a criminal client as to possible deportation was *prima facie* "constitutionally deficient," and thus incompetent.

[3] Prof. Zitrin has long used "the Four C's" as a mnemonic in teaching both law students and lawyers in continuing education programs.

utmost strictness for any unfairness.[4]

In most jurisdictions, a lawyer's fiduciary duty to a client begins only after the attorney-client relationship is established, not before.[5]

Think about what the effect would be if a lawyer's fiduciary duties began before accepting the client, or as soon as the prospective client walked into the lawyer's office. We will see later why confidentiality is generally an immediate obligation, but does it make sense that a lawyer must take on all other fiduciary duties before s/he agrees to take the case?

4. "Trust me"?

"Arthur," says Ann Wilson in our problem above, "I really trust your judgment and ability." Even more than "ability" or skill, a client's trust in a lawyer's *judgment* may be the most valuable currency the attorney has. As one recent commentator put it, "Trust in a relationship — as opposed to trust [in a lawyer's competence] — presumes a relationship of sufficient breadth and depth to provide a baseline of mutual knowledge, familiarity, and confidence."[6]

That trust, though, is rarely earned easily, and almost never earned superficially; just saying "trust me" is not likely to work for lawyers any better than it does for politicians. Here's one view about the importance of trust and how to develop it.

Richard Zitrin, *Don't Just Talk About Trust — Earn It*
THE [S.F.] RECORDER, March 9, 2012[7]

A client's trust in a lawyer's judgment may be the most valuable currency the lawyer has — more than legal skills, experience, intelligence or knowledge. And yet a few months ago, when I wanted to share with my ethics students some thoughts about developing trust between client and lawyer, I couldn't find a good, common-sense article that summed it up. So I wrote this piece.

We are all the products of our own experiences. In my case, my first law job was working on a prison case where our client was accused of several counts of murder and aggravated assault. I was a total newbie, but even then I knew that I couldn't very well go into San Quentin State Prison, visit our client in a tiny, roach-infested visiting "room" smaller than a water closet and say to him, "Trust me!"

I was lucky to be in a situation where it was so obvious that trust had to be earned. Trust is rarely earned easily, and almost never earned superficially. No

---

[4] Hunniecutt v. State Bar of California, 748 P.2d 1161, 1167 (Cal. 1988), *quoting* Clancy v. State Bar, 454 P.2d 329, 333 (Cal. 1969).

[5] *See, e.g.,* In re Marriage of Pagano, 607 N.E.2d 1242, 1247 (Ill. 1992).

[6] Robert K. Vischer, *Trust and the Global Law Firm: Are Relationships of Trust Still Central to the Corporate Legal Services Market?*, U of St. Thomas Legal Studies Research Paper No. 10-19 (2010), *available at* http://ssrn.com/abstract=1666973 or http://dx.doi.org/10.2139/ssrn.1666973.

[7] Copyright © 2012 by American Law Media and Richard Zitrin. Reprinted by permission of the author.

matter who the client is, just saying "trust me" is not likely to work for lawyers any better than for politicians. Most members of the public are skeptical of lawyers. Compared to other "learned professions," lawyers have long fared poorly when it comes to public perception. Why? First, there's the common view that lawyers too rarely adhere to the truth or morality, cut corners, and sometimes even cheat. While the client is often perceived as the beneficiary of this behavior, these attributes, if true, hardly make lawyers more *trustworthy*. Second, many individual clients who need lawyers are meeting an attorney for the first (and possibly last) time, while institutional clients, led by increasingly sophisticated in-house legal teams, have become more and more skeptical of the value of their outside counsel at last with regard to the fees they charge.

In short, the lawyer who wants the client to develop authentic trust will have to earn it the old-fashioned way. How can lawyers accomplish this? First, they must recognize that this will take some time and patience; abiding trust is a product of experience. Here are some other thoughts:

• *Set ground rules* from the very beginning of the representation that make it clear what you can do and can't do. Managing expectations is essential. Many years ago a criminal defense lawyer told us that she told her clients, "No matter what, you will *never* get back to even. I can never make you whole as if this business never happened." This is good advice for any lawyer talking to a client.

• Echoing Abe Lincoln, *turn down* cases that really don't benefit the prospective client — those that are too small or too expensive, or where the clients will spend too much for too little return, resulting in a case will only benefit the lawyer's pocketbook.

• Communicate verbally *in English* (or whatever is the client's language of comfort). Clients don't speak "legalese." They will like it when you talk in a language they can easily understand, especially if you are explaining something necessarily written in legalese, starting with your retainer agreement.

• During the representation, try to be gentle but also *tough* and *honest*. Try to *avoid* telling clients what they want to hear, and focus on what they need to know. If the case is not going well, say so and don't pull your punches. Clients need — and most want — to hear the truth, not "don't worry, it's under control" (much as we often say this to ourselves). This is particularly true with clients who have unrealistic expectations about resolving the case, though this is preferably an issue you dealt with from the first day of your representation.

• Keep in mind your client's personal needs and emotions, not just the monetary ones. It is *not* all about the money. But it's sometimes all about the emotions. We lawyers measure most litigation and business deals in monetary terms, not to mention our fees. But there is almost always a bigger picture.

• Approach your clients as intelligent decision makers, and remember: *It's their case*, not yours. And while they will appreciate your confident judgment, a dash of humility won't hurt.

> • Perhaps most important, never presume to walk in the client's shoes. We are all tempted to say "I know exactly how you feel." Don't, because you *don't* know. You can empathize, "get it" intellectually, and appreciate their circumstances and their pain. But you have not been where the client has been, and your acknowledgement of this truth will serve you well in gaining your client's trust.

In short, building client trust is all about relationship building, not quite like a close personal friendship, because having clear boundaries between attorney and client is also necessary, but perhaps like two business partners. And remember, developing trust takes time and effort, and also good deal of *listening* before you do the telling.

Why, anyway, is trust so important? Because when push comes to shove and the client has a crucial decision to make and needs your advice, you will be able to call on your "trust reserves." Your client has confidence that your advice is both wise and respectful of the client's needs. You will not have to say, "Trust me!" if you have built your relationship of trust, because, having earned the client's trust, your insight and perspective will speak for itself.

With trust comes considerable responsibility, because trust can be a double-edged sword. When a client says she trusts you, you have the power of persuasion readily at hand. But you also have a heightened responsibility to not abuse that trust. The more vulnerable the client is, the more the client may tend to rely on your sound judgment; at the same time, the more easily the client may be swayed by what you say no matter what its validity. Perhaps the worst thing a well-meaning attorney can do with a trusting client is to persuade without being confident about what is actually in the client's best interests.

Trust is a powerful tool, and the more powerful it is, the more wisely and judiciously it must be used.

5. Does the Current Law School Environment Nurture Competence?

Do future lawyers really need to attend three years of law school before they are allowed to take a bar exam? Once you graduate will you be competent to represent clients? Are some students competent to practice while still in law school? Until the 1920s most aspiring American lawyers apprenticed themselves to other attorneys, studied the law as they worked, and then took the (often oral) law exams. It was only in the early 1950s that the balance tilted and there were more practicing lawyers who had gone to law school than had "read for the law."

How did this come about? Some observers believe that one major impetus for the mandatory three-year law school education model was a high-visibility ABA report by a committee chaired by Elihu Root in 1921 that reflected the belief that more needed to be done to protect both the public and the reputation of the profession, which was being damaged because of the actions of incompetent and unscrupulous lawyers.[8]

Other commentators have noted, however, that the desire to rid the profession of "unscrupulous" lawyers was, for some, a veiled attempt to justify the exclusion of those of non-Northern European stock from the profession. The reasoning went that if "would-be lawyers" were required to complete extensive education at an accredited law school before being allowed to take a bar exam, the profession could maintain its homogeneity.

In much of the Western world, lawyers can qualify to practice after completing their undergraduate legal studies, and then, in some countries, apprenticeships. Few in the U.S. suggest moving to that system; certainly, students gain a more sophisticated and specialized knowledge of the law in their post-graduate years. But do we need three years? The-three-year-long, classroom-based model of legal education has been criticized almost since it was implemented and calls for a shorter time in law school are now heard from many quarters.[9]

In 1998, well-respected appellate judge and former law professor Richard Posner wrote an article criticizing the three-year curriculum.[10] Posner criticized "the growing estrangement between academia and law practice. This estrangement is nicely captured in the following statement by a professor at the Yale Law School. 'Law professors are not paid to train lawyers, but to study the law and teach their students what they happen to discover.' "

Posner went on to suggest a two-year J.D. program modeled on the two-year M.B.A. program given at business schools, noting that two years would make it easier for law grads to "recoup their investment in legal education [without] working ridiculously long hours." Posner noted that what he describes as "elite" law schools would have little difficulty making this adjustment, while also suggesting an optional third-year curriculum for "elite" schools. The two-year program could return to old the LL.B. "bachelor of laws" degree common until the 1970s, while a J.D. would be awarded only to three-year students. But the dangers of such a two-tiered system are palpable. Do we really want to develop two "classes" of lawyers, "elite" J.D.s and non-elite LL.B.s?

Another possibility for the future is the feasibility of allowing non-attorneys to provide legal services to the poor on "simple" civil matters. New York's Chief Judge, Jonathan Lippman, is determined to study this possibility. But here, do we really want to develop a situation where "simpler" matters taken away from lawyers altogether?

On another point, however, commentators from across the political spectrum may be in closer accord with Posner. Lurking under the radar in Posner's observations about the high cost of law school and the fact that "elite" schools will

---

[8] Christopher T. Cunniffe, *The Case for Alternative Third-Year Program*, 61 ALB. L. REV. 85 (1997). *See* Elihu Root, *Report of the Special Committee to the Section of Legal Education and Admissions to the Bar of the American Bar Association*, 1921 A.B.A. Sec. Legal Educ. & Admissions to the Bar. 679, n.6, at 680.

[9] Jerome Frank, *Why Not a Clinical Lawyer-School*, 81 U. PENN. L. REV. 907–923 (1933).

[10] Richard Posner, *Law School Should Be Two Years, Not Three*, HARV. L. REC., Jan. 16, 1998.

not be in jeopardy by cutting back to two years is an acknowledgement that some law schools wouldn't survive without the additional income they derive from three years of tuition. Indeed, the Recession of 2008 made it clear that law schools are now churning out far more graduates than there are available jobs. Despite that recession, on average one new ABA-accredited school opens each year. Yet by 2011, about two dozen law schools from nationally known to local, had begun plans to cut back their student bodies. For example, UC Hastings, one of the first, set a goal of reducing its number of students by 20%. By 2012, most schools experienced huge drop-offs in applications, requiring "lower tier" schools to either take smaller classes or students they would not previously have considered.

Some critics have pointedly accused some law schools as maintaining or even increasing their student population as being "in it for the money," promising a degree with little or no prospects of a job.[11]

Others have sued some law schools (though so far without much success), alleging that they created an unfounded belief among applicants that there were many high paying legal jobs open to graduates of their institutions. There is no doubt that it is universally recognized that the entire climate for law graduate hiring has changed.

During this same recent time period, there's been parallel pressure for our law schools to teach competence. But how, and what should the requirements be? For example, should all students be required to pass an examination testing oral advocacy skills? What if a student wants to be a transactional lawyer who will never go to court?

While schools debate how to fulfill these needs, in recent years, many state bars have demanded that basic competency requirements be met before a new attorney may practice. Many bar examinations now include a "practical" or "performance" component. Almost two thirds of state tests now include a "skills" component to the bar exam often using the Multi-State Performance test. And the ABA's law school accreditation standards include a requirement that "(a) a law school shall require each student receive substantial instruction in: . . . (4) other professional skills generally regarded as necessary for effective and responsible participation in the profession; . . . and (b) a law school shall offer substantial opportunities for live-client or other real-life experiences . . . ."[12]

---

[11] See two of David Segal's articles for the NEW YORK TIMES: *Law School Economics: Ka-Ching!*, July 16, 2011; and *Is Law School a Losing Game?*, January 8, 2011.

[12] Note, however, that these standards have not been interpreted to require live-client experiences, nor must a law school provide opportunities for *every* student. This leaves law schools under little compulsion to require meaningful experiential programs. Students interested in significant changes in ABA standards can follow proposed changes at http://www.americanbar.org/groups/legal_education/resources/standards.html.

6.   Can — and Should — Students Count on Law School to Make Them Competent?

Given these circumstances, an increasingly important issue is whether practice-focused training should be required in law school curricula, or whether the tradition of doctrinally-focused courses and advanced, specialized seminars remains the better route. Should courses emphasizing simulation and role-playing, field placement courses, and law school based clinical work be required in our schools?

Most law students today appreciate that a well-rounded legal education means integrating traditional classroom-based doctrinal classes with on-the-job legal experiences. Those range from purely volunteer work, through pro bono work required for graduation, to paid law firm and other legal work, to apprenticeships for academic credit, to direct client service supervised by members of the law school faculty or adjunct professors. Should the mission of such law school offerings be skills training of law students or providing legal service to under-represented populations as well as or even in lieu of some doctrinal classroom work?

And more importantly, is this the path to competence? Randall Shepard, chair of the ABA's task force on the future of legal education, put it this way in August 2012:

> [T]he most dramatic change in the American legal education in the last 15 years has been expanding the opportunities students have for real life experiences in clinics and internships. Everyone I know thinks that's a good thing and it has made a difference.[13]

Two recent works, *Best Practices for Legal Education: A Vision and a Road Map*[14] and *The Carnegie Report — Educating Lawyers*,[15] reflect some of the current thinking among those who feel that law schools must implement significant changes to make the American model of legal education more practical. *The Carnegie Report* concludes that the goal of legal education to provide analytical knowledge alone is not sufficient. The report concludes that three apprenticeship goals — to learn conceptual knowledge, practical competence, and professional identity and purpose — should each be addressed during law school. While neither of the 2007 publications were greeted with the enthusiasm their authors hoped for, change is now slowly beginning.[16]

---

[13] http://blogs.wsj.com/law/2012/08/10/law-blog-fireside-chairman-of-aba-task-force-on-legal-education/.

[14] Roy Stuckey et al., *Best Practices for Legal Education: A Vision and A Road Map* (Clinical Legal Education Association, 2007).

[15] William M. Sullivan, Anne Colby, Judith Welch Wegner, Lloyd Bond & Lee S. Shulman, *Educating Lawyers: Preparation for the Profession of Law* (Jossey-Bass/Carnegie Foundation for the Advancement of Teaching, 2007).

[16] It sometimes appears to us that these periodic reports, many with the same focus, such as the earlier MacCrate Report referenced in the Supplementary Readings, reach similar conclusions but have not yet substantially changed the basic law school curriculum.

Even if there is general agreement that clinical teaching is valuable, "live-client" clinics have a lower faculty student ratio than the 100-student lecture hall delivery model, and are often seen as expensive. In spite of the changes of the past decade, very few law schools have enough openings in clinics to allow all interested students — much less *every* student — to take even one clinic. In addition to the financial pressures from on campus, there are also political pressures on law schools from elected officials, especially regarding state schools.

And there are other issues. For example, what if your law school offers a clinic but others try to shut it down? In recent years:

Maryland clinic students representing clients concerned about the environmental impact of chicken farming practices prompted legislators to move to seek information about the clinic's clients and withhold further clinic funding. Timber industry donors at the University of Oregon threatened to withhold funding from the entire university if legal challenges to lumbering practices were pursued by clients represented by the law school's clinic. The University of North Dakota School of Law Civil Rights Project was sued by a state legislator after the clinic filed a suit against a municipality challenging a display of the Ten Commandments on public property, the lawmaker suggesting that the clinic and its students were out of control and needed to be "reined in." The justices of the Louisiana Supreme Court enacted new regulations that severely tightened the rules for student legal clinics at the state's law schools, using regulations that appeared to apply across the board, but which were adopted immediately after the Tulane Environmental Law Clinic challenged, on environmental grounds, the building of a several hundred-million-dollar plant. Louisiana Governor Mike Foster, a supporter of the plant, had taken a strong stand against the clinic, calling the participants "a bunch of outlaws.[17]

A less political, but possibly even more troubling obstacle to students developing competence is the development of restrictions placed on student practice. In Tennessee, only students who are attending law schools in the state may get a student bar card, required before students can make supervised experiences in court. In Florida, students who want to appear in court must complete the same expensive and time consuming background checking process required of lawyers applying to practice in Florida after graduation.

7. Legal "Internships" After Graduation, Continuing Education, and "Mini-Law-Firms"

Would it be better to require post-graduate apprentice programs such as those in Canada, England, and Germany? What if lawyers, like physicians, were required to serve a "residency" after passing the bar examination and before independent practice? Many states have discussed implementing such a program. For example,

---

[17] Stories about clinics facing these problems are contained in Robert R. Kuehn & Bridget M. McCormack, *Lessons from Forty Years of Interference in Law School Clinics*, 24 GEO. J. LEGAL ETHICS 59 (2011). A list of these incidents has been compiled by the American Association of University Professors at http://www.aaup.org/article/publicized-instances-interference-law-school-clinics#. UaoYaJwUOQ0.

in 1989, a California State Bar consortium on competence recommended a series of proposals, which the consortium's chairman acknowledged were "hotter than a firestorm." These included: "internships" of up to 600 hours, supervised by law schools and taken either during school or as a post-graduate course; and "residencies" of two years which would limit new lawyers to practice under defined programs. But these ideas, facing objections from both young lawyers' associations and local bars, never got off the ground. More recently, New York Chief Judge Jonathan Lippman pushed through a proposal that graduates perform 50 hours of pro bono legal work before admission to the New York bar.[18] This program, which appears to be designed to help address the unmet legal needs of many low and middle income New Yorkers, focuses on the benefits to clients but does not address how law students would obtain the expertise necessary to become competent advocates.

Every state offers, and many states now require, new graduates to complete a "basic skills course" within 12 months of being admitted to the bar as part of a Continuing Legal Education program. In Illinois, which started its requirement in 2005, the course cover topics such as local court rules, government agency filing requirements, drafting pleadings, practice techniques, procedures under the Illinois Professional Responsibility Code, client communications, trust accounts, and record keeping, among other practice-based topics. Do such Basic Skills programs in the first year after law school make sense? If you were designing the requirements for such a program, what would you include?

Finally, several law schools have upped the ante in their efforts to teach their students practical practice skills, mostly by opening up their own "law firms" or associating with other existing law firms. Arizona State, inspired by the law dean's trip to the Mayo Clinic, opened its own non-profit "law firm" in 2013, with 30 graduates trained to provide low cost legal services. UC Hastings, California's oldest law school, started a third-year training program that places students fulltime into existing law firms, including the local public defender. A half-dozen other schools have recently developed similar on-the-job-training programs.[19]

Are new graduates the only ones who need to improve their competence and skills? Should education and training stop once a lawyer graduates from law school and is admitted to the bar? Does more experience equate with more competence or should experienced lawyers be required to participate in formal training events to improve and update their skills as well as their knowledge of the law. Only a few states no longer require some form of mandatory continuing legal education ("MCLE") for practicing lawyers. Should such requirements be uniform for all lawyers, or should it depend on the nature of their practice? How many hours of continuing education per year do you believe would be reasonable?

---

[18] http://www.legal-aid.org/en/mediaandpublicinformation/inthenews/ chiefjudgeannouncesprobonorequirementforadmissiontothebar.aspx. We discuss this further, and other efforts to provide legal services to the underserved poor, in Problem 32.

[19] For a thorough summary, see Ethan Bronner, *To Place Graduates, Law Schools Are Opening Firms*, N.Y. TIMES, March 7, 2013.

Will changes in legal education lead to improved competence? Perhaps like the Root report of almost 100 years ago, Carnegie and Best Practices will stimulate significant changes in how and when law students develop competence, increased third-year and post-graduate programs will require practice skills, bar exams will test for those skills, and state high courts will require *pro bono* practice. Obviously, only time will tell.

8.   Law Firm "Mentoring"

Can the law firms do it? What if lawyers and law firms, rather than law schools, were to bear the responsibility for training new lawyers? The author of the following article believes that there remains an important place for lawyer-to-lawyer mentoring. In Ms. Oseid's case, as the title of her article implies, her mentor was her older, more experienced brother. As you read this, how important do you believe mentoring is to a young lawyer learning competent legal practices?

Julie Oseid, *When Big Brother Is Watching [Out for] You: Mentoring Lawyers, Choosing a Mentor, and Sharing Ten Virtues from My Mentor*
59 S.C. L. Rev. 393 (2008)[20]

American legal education has passed through four phases: apprenticeship followed by a bar exam; law school as an alternative to apprenticeship; mandatory law school with no apprenticeship alternative; and, finally, our current system . . . .

[T]his dramatic change from apprenticeship to law schools ultimately eliminated the practitioner from a teaching role for prospective lawyers. . . . Many may be tempted to long for the time when all lawyers served apprenticeships [but] unfortunately, not all apprenticeships were ideal, and in some cases, the apprentice spent much time copying documents. . . . In the good-old days, several classes of people were excluded not only from mentoring but from the legal profession itself. The good-old days certainly would not have benefited me, a woman. Even today, a lack of mentoring for female lawyers is seen as a major impediment to their advancement.

Despite the potential downside of mentoring, the current use of mentoring as a supplement to a formal legal education has several positive benefits. Every lawyer should be on a lifetime journey to embrace professionalism, and mentoring is one way to help lawyers develop professionalism.

. . . .

Mentoring helps the prospective attorney learn ethics in part because it gives the new attorney an opportunity to discuss ethics in an informal setting. There is some debate about the relative value of formal mentoring programs versus informal mentoring relationships, but the empirical data suggests that both informal and formal mentoring are preferable to no mentoring.

. . . .

Through mentoring, new lawyers . . . obtain all the intangibles necessary for success: they are drawn into the loop of career development; they learn the stated and unstated practices and policies of the legal profession and of the firm or government office where they practice; they receive better and more challenging work; they are included in social events that can lead to professional opportunities; and they acquire marketing skills.

. . . .

Three common features have made my mentoring relationships successful: sharing values with a mentor, choosing a mentor with only a few more years of experience, and selecting a mentor who can keep confidences.

. . . .

My Mentor's Best Advice — Ten Virtues

. . . I want to share my mentor's best advice and wisdom in the form of the ten virtues he taught me.

If followed, the virtues and habits will help anyone become a successful lawyer and person. The first five virtues discussed are personal virtues: diligence, initiative, efficiency, reflection, and enjoyment. The second five virtues discussed are relationship virtues: simplicity, equality, civility, honesty, and sharing.

A. Personal Virtues

I call the first five virtues "personal" because they are the virtues that will help a lawyer develop the individual qualities for moral excellence. These virtues capture the essence of the lawyer as she works independently, which will be a significant part of her professional life. When no one is looking, these are the virtues that will be the measure of the lawyer.

1. Diligence — "You might not be able to outthink them, but you can outwork them."

2. Initiative — "Get out of the starting blocks as fast as possible at every single stage of your career."

3. Efficiency — "Your stock will increase if you do great work in a minimum amount of time."

4. Reflect — "Reflect on the big story of your life and all the short stories along the way."

5. Enjoy — "You will spend a major part of your life working, so find delight in the legal profession."

. . . .

B. Relationship Virtues

The virtues discussed in this section help a lawyer in the relationship aspect of the profession. In its most elemental form, the law is a service profession.

1. Simplicity — "A good lawyer is a good teacher who can simplify difficult concepts."

2. Civility — "Respect all the people, all the time."

3. Honesty — "Be trustworthy."

4. Share — "Find some way to give back."

5. Equality — "Hold your head level."

. . . .

A great legal mentor is one who has traveled the path ahead, but who takes the time to look over his shoulder, stretch out his arm, and beckon you to follow. He is not too far ahead of you; you can hear his advice about how to navigate the obstacles you might face as you make your own way along the path. He listens to all of your questions, confessions, and insecurities with confidentiality. He tells you about the roads that might diverge from the main path, recognizing that you might choose a different path. He urges you to practice law with morality and integrity. He helps you adopt the ten virtues that have made his journey successful and meaningful. An acronym for the ten virtues of diligence, initiative, efficiency, reflection, enjoyment, simplicity, civility, honesty, sharing, and equality is SEED RICHES. He plants the seeds of the virtues, which yield not monetary riches but rather the riches of character, professionalism, and service. He suggests ways to make your journey easier, but he warns you that the study and practice of law sometimes will be difficult, scary, and uncertain. Still, he urges you to take the journey because being part of the noble legal profession is a privilege and honor worth every stumble and sacrifice.

9. Competence and Negligence

How is competence measured after the fact? Every jurisdiction has ethical rules that make competence a requirement. As we mentioned in section 2, the Model Rules specifically address both competence (Rule 1.1) and its cousin, diligence (Rule 1.3). Nevertheless, it is too often true that only egregious examples of incompetent lawyering result in attorney discipline. For example, in 2003, the Supreme Court of South Dakota disbarred a lawyer who practiced out of her home with no computer, no staff, an outdated library, one bank account for both her practice and her personal finances, and no malpractice insurance. By the time of her disbarment she had six previous complaints with more pending. Several judges testified that she was "not competent." Among the conclusions of the court:

- Laprath does not understand how to commence an action, venue an action, give notice prior to hearing, or appeal administrative matters;

- Laprath is unable to diagnose and analyze even the most common legal problem and solve it within applicable rules;

- Laprath's written documents are error laden, poorly written, illogical or incomprehensible;

- Laprath's oral communication is poor. She fails to lay the proper foundation for evidence, objections are not made or are inappropriate, and evidence is presented in a disjointed, rambling fashion; and

- Laprath is chronically late in filing documents and court appearances.[21]

Clearly grounds for disbarment, right? But what took them so long? Should matters descend to this extreme level before disbarring an incompetent lawyer?

What standards should courts use in disbarring or otherwise disciplining lawyers for incompetence? The court in *People ex rel. Goldberg v. Gordon*, 607 P.2d 995, 998 (Colo. 1980), made an impassioned statement that the "license to practice law is a proclamation to the public that . . . the lawyer will perform the basic legal tasks undertaken, competently, ethically, and in accordance with the highest standards of professional conduct." But the court in fact only disciplined the lawyer for "lack of minimal professional competence," a very low threshold that Arthur Hollins would undoubtedly meet, and nowhere close to the "highest standards" mentioned by the court. Should the bar be set higher? Should lawyers be required to have more than "minimal professional competence" in order to avoid discipline? And should practice-based training be mandated in law schools or continuing education? Do you think that would make a difference?

Even cases that discipline lawyers recognize that "competence" is seen more as a negligence standard. Thus, in *Office of Disciplinary Counsel v. Henry*, 664 S.W.2d 62, 64 (Tenn. 1983), the Tennessee Supreme Court disciplined a lawyer for "mishandling four cases in a relatively short period of time," but noted: "There are problems inherent in using disciplinary proceedings to punish an attorney for the incompetent handling of a client's affairs, or for negligence."

If competence is indeed addressed more frequently in legal malpractice cases than in disciplinary matters, should we improve the way in which malpractice cases are handled in order to provide the assurance of competent representation? The author of the following article believes so.

Manuel R. Ramos, *Legal Malpractice: Reforming Lawyers and Law Professors*
70 Tul. L. Rev. 2583 (1996)[22]

In a Reebok ad shown during the 1993 Super Bowl, viewers were reminded that on a " 'perfect planet' there would be no lawyers." However, in our most imperfect world, there will always be lawyers. Both the number of lawyers and the incidents of legal malpractice will continue to increase. Getting rid of the ineffective systems of lawyer or judicial self-regulation and putting greater pressure on the existing criminal and consumer justice system to do more comprise only part of the answer. What about the breach of ethical and competency standards by lawyers that do not rise to the level of violations of criminal or consumer protection statutes? What about aggrieved clients who have been damaged?

In theory, many, including lawyers, would agree with the former Dean of the Harvard Law School, James Vorenberg, that legal malpractice claims and lawsuits

---

[21] *In re Laprath*, 670 N.W.2d 41 (S.D. 2003).

[22] Copyright © 1996 by Tulane Law Review. Reprinted by permission.

put pressure on lawyers to maintain high professional standards. Even the ABA, in its McKay Report, acknowledged that legal malpractice litigation is an option for aggrieved clients but that only those with large claims would find lawyers willing to take on the delays and expenses involved with litigating against other lawyers. Many scholars also complain that legal malpractice is not an effective form of lawyer regulation.

Legal malpractice, despite its current shortcomings, is still, by far, the predominant way in which lawyers are regulated. For instance, while insurance carriers, and lawyers, through their insurance premiums, spent $4 billion a year to resolve legal malpractice claims and lawsuits, only $100 million is spent collectively by all jurisdictions to discipline lawyers. Both figures may be higher today, but it is unlikely that the proportion or the 2.4% comparison of the disciplinary funding compared to legal malpractice funding has changed. The $100 million being spent on lawyer discipline could be better spent on hiring more white collar prosecutors or strengthening consumer protection sections in district attorneys' offices to keep an eye on lawyers. These prosecutors would be better paid, more competent, and more highly motivated than any discipline counsel.

Similarly, the $4 billion per year spent on legal malpractice, like other forms of tort compensation, could be better structured to favor the aggrieved clients. Many smaller claims, usually those under $100,000, fall through the cracks because clients are too unsophisticated to pursue the claims with insurance companies. Plaintiffs' lawyers do not find claims under $100,000 to be cost effective. Insurance companies seemingly do not mind paying for exorbitant defense fees that erode policy limits.[23]

. . . .

[I]nsurance claims that eventually mature into lawsuits handled by plaintiffs' lawyers tend to be successful, but the majority of claims remain claims and are easily disposed of by insurance companies. Add to these unsuccessful insurance claims the significant number of potential claims against uninsured and underinsured lawyers that are never paid by an insurance carrier, and the existing tort system of compensating aggrieved clients looks like a pyramid with the overwhelming majority of aggrieved clients left uncompensated.

Even those at the top of the pyramid, the clients or nonclients who receive compensation from the existing $4 billion annual fund of insurance monies, are second in line, taking their share only after the plaintiff and defense attorneys are paid their compensation. . . . Extrapolat[ing the numbers], the $4 billion annual cost to insurance carriers roughly means that only $1.824 billion is received by aggrieved clients . . . . Clearly, something is wrong when the plaintiff and defense lawyers end up getting more than the aggrieved client.

Litigation [via] the traditional tort system, however, is basically the only game in town. Legal malpractice litigation suffers from the same shortcomings that any other type of tort-based compensation system has when clients must pay plaintiffs'

---

[23] [88] All legal malpractice policies now have "eroding" policy limits. For instance, it would not be unusual on a $300,000 policy for it to be reduced to $200,000 after defense costs through trial.

attorneys on a contingency fee basis and insurance carriers must pay defense lawyers at an hourly rate.

The inherent conflicts found in any disciplinary system for lawyers and by lawyers make that model a nonstarter. Regulation by the existing tort system of legal malpractice offers greater potential. There are highly motivated actors. The aggrieved client wants justice, but obviously is looking for some type of compensation. Moreover, there is the plaintiff's legal malpractice lawyer, who, after sifting through hundreds of cases, acts as the gatekeeper and takes the best ones against insured lawyers for a contingency. . . .

Where the motivation, however, breaks down in legal malpractice litigation is on the defense side. As a former defense lawyer, I am convinced that there is no motivation to settle the case early. "Complicated" legal malpractice files "justify" even more time and attorneys' fees. The "case within a case" defense attorney's mentality is to settle as late as possible and wring out, on an hourly fee basis, the greatest amount possible per case. Indeed as seen in the Florida and California data, in legal malpractice cases, defense lawyers actually get more than plaintiffs' lawyers.

Insurance carriers, who should be highly motivated to save costs by quickly evaluating and settling "bad" cases early, instead defer to defense counsel to set the budgets. Insurers focus on marketing their policies; claims handling is almost an afterthought, especially when costs are simply passed through premiums to the insured lawyers.

Only recently have legal malpractice insurance carriers become receptive to contingency fees and flat fees by defense counsel. For instance, Richard Bush, a prominent Florida legal malpractice defense lawyer, is now paid on a "bulk" flat or contingency fee basis by legal malpractice insurance carriers looking to settle cases early and reduce defense costs. These carriers have finally discovered that hourly fees, and not contingency fees, are major obstacles to tort reform.

[Ramos then recommends mandatory malpractice insurance as a way of assuring that aggrieved clients get compensated and that complaints against lawyers would be more efficiently handled. His section on malpractice claims as being the best way to monitor lawyer competency concludes with the following:]

Despite its problems, legal malpractice litigation continues to be the overwhelming way in which the legal profession regulates itself. There is nothing else, particularly the lawyer or judicial disciplinary systems, that even comes close. So, why not just improve the handling of legal malpractice claims and lawsuits?

NOTES

While clients may waive confidentiality and certain conflicts of interest, almost every jurisdiction holds that clients cannot waive their own attorney's competence. But is malpractice litigation really the best way to assure lawyer competence, as Professor Ramos asserts? Or will the vast majority of "smaller" cases continue to fall through the cracks?

What about Ramos's assertion that the disciplinary system operates poorly? Can the disciplinary system be improved to better regulate the practice of law? And if the profession truly relies on malpractice insurance to protect clients, can lawyers be forced to buy insurance?[24]

Should insurance companies be required to provide it even to "high risk" attorneys? And what about at least requiring lawyers to disclose to clients and to the bar whether or not they carry malpractice insurance? Several states including California require this disclosure.

Finally, there may be many ethical situations where malpractice simply won't apply. While the tort of "breach of fiduciary duty" is available in most states, will those situations be sufficiently addressed through civil litigation alone? What happens, for example, when a lawyer breaches the duty of loyalty? Because the direct cause of damages is rarely the conflict of interest itself (as opposed to other breaches: of competence, confidentiality, etc.), there may be no malpractice claim even if the unethical behavior is clear.

Malpractice claims don't arise only between clients and their attorneys; we will address some other situations in greater detail in Problem 3. Is it possible that a lawyer could be sued for negligent referral? Assuming that Arthur Hollins knows of a qualified specialist, is he obligated to refer the case to that lawyer? What circumstances, if any, are there in which a general practitioner has a duty to refer a matter to a specialist? If the client refuses the lawyer's referral to a specialist, may the original lawyer perform the services without assistance?

Horne v. Peckham, 97 Cal. App. 3d 404, 414 (1979), took a strong stand on this question by upholding a trial court's use of a form jury instruction that said:

> It is the duty of an attorney who is a general practitioner to refer his client to a specialist or recommend the assistance of a specialist if under the circumstances a reasonably careful and skillful practitioner would do so.
>
> If he fails to perform that duty and undertakes to perform professional services without the aid of a specialist, it is his further duty to have the knowledge and skill ordinarily . . . used by specialists in good standing in the same or similar locality and under the same circumstances.
>
> A failure to perform any such duty is negligence.

While violation of rules of professional conduct does not automatically create a cause of action for malpractice, a breach of such a rule may be evidence of a failure to meet a standard of care. Frequently these days ethics "experts" are being called on to opine whether an attorney accused of malpractice met or failed to meet the standard of care. Do you see a clear distinction between malpractice and a breach of one's ethical duties?

---

[24] Currently, while many states require lawyers to notify clients of whether they carry malpractice insurance, only one, Oregon, actually requires lawyers to be insured.

10. Malpractice and the Wrong Client

A skill almost as important as developing client trust and being able to attract good cases is the ability to "red-flag" clients to be avoided. This skill is particularly crucial for new lawyers who are driven by the need to earn fees to support themselves and their families and pay off law school loans. Consider the following advice from an insurance claims director who oversees the defense of legal malpractice claims.

Katja Kunzke, *The Hazard: Failure to Screen Cases, in* WHY BAD THINGS HAPPEN TO GOOD LAWYERS, A SYMPOSIUM 84 A.B.A. J. 57 (1998)[25]

One of the best things lawyers can do to reduce their legal malpractice exposure is screen cases and clients in efforts to avoid, or at least be aware of, the ones that present the greatest risks for producing malpractice claims.

Certainly, lawyers must screen cases to make sure that they have sufficient time and resources to give to the matters they take on. But effective screening also seeks to identify three major risk factors: Expectations, communication and control.

Expectations. In a way, all malpractice claims are the result of unmet expectations, some reasonable and some not. If the expectations that clients have for their matters and for the lawyers they retain cannot be adjusted to attainable levels, a high malpractice claim risk exists.

If the lawyer discovers that the client wants an outcome that the legal system does not provide or that cannot be achieved under the circumstances, the lawyer must seriously consider rejecting the representation.

Motives play an important role in creating expectations. A client motivated by greed, vengeance or some lofty sentiment will expect you to further that motive, and that expectation should be discerned as early in the representation as possible.

. . . .

Communication. Effective communication between lawyer and client is critical to keeping expectations in line. But some clients require special handling to assure accurate communication and avoid unmet expectations.

[C]lients who communicate an unwillingness to understand their matters should be avoided. If a client shows no respect for your need to spend adequate preparation time or sufficient money to assure proper representation, warning bells should go off.

Control. Beware of the client who wields too much control. The evidence of this is lawyer switching, avoidable delays, insistence on knowing everything or doing parts of the lawyer's job, telling the lawyer how to do his or her job, balking at retainers or fees, impatience, or simple refusal to comprehend the lawyer's cautions about associated risks and costs.

---

[25] Copyright © 1998 by the American Bar Association. All Rights Reserved. Reprinted by permission.

Equally as dangerous are clients who cannot control themselves. A client's personal history of serious drinking or drug problems, employment terminations or criminal activity may evidence self-denial, dishonesty or an entitlement perspective that places a lawyer in the position of being the next logical target of the client's destructive tendencies.

NOTES

While Kunzke emphasizes discovery of these problems "early in the representation," the best and most sophisticated attorneys are those who develop ways of divining these difficulties *before* representation begins. It is much easier to walk away from a case or client before committing than after the case starts. As you will see in Problem 14 on cross-cultural lawyering, good lawyers develop sophisticated insights about whether potential clients are difficult and problematic or just "different" — for cultural, disability, or many other reasons. In those instances, the question becomes whether the lawyer can bridge the cultural (or other) barriers and effectively represent the client.

Kunzke ties her good advice to avoiding malpractice claims. Would you suggest anything different if Kunzke were evaluating a lawyer's ethics?

11. Referral Fees

There are rules governing fee arrangements for referrals, but do they work? Are there circumstances in which a referring attorney might end up in conflict with the putative client? What duties does the referring attorney owe the client? Referral fees can create several thorny issues, and debate persists on whether and to what extent referral fees are ethical. There are good arguments on both sides. Following the ABA, most states don't permit referral fees without the referring lawyer taking on a portion of the responsibility. But individual states differ, with some, such as California, allowing a "pure" referral with client consent. Read the following article focusing on referral practices in one such state, Michigan.

Sheryl M. Vassallo, *Practitioners Explore Issues of Referring Cases and Mastering the Fine Art of Referral Fees*
Michigan Lawyers Weekly, October 3, 2005[26]

Practitioners tell Michigan Lawyers Weekly that the judiciary's ability to administer justice is greatly enhanced by the legal community's time-honored and time-tested system for referring cases. Through a careful mixture of ethical rules, referral fees and dedication to doing what's best for the client, a successful redistribution of talent, skill and experience plays out on a daily basis where clients' needs are matched with attorneys' abilities. For many firms, the practice of making and accepting referrals along with the payment of referral fees is their bread and butter. For others, it may be just one of several revenue sources.

---

[26] Copyright © 2005 by Michigan Lawyers Weekly. Reprinted by permission.

More than competent

Employment lawyer Deborah L. Gordon of Bloomfield Hills [notes] "An attorney should refer a case whenever it's not in a field that you feel you're intimately familiar with," she stated. "If you don't have the expertise in that field, you better refer it out pretty quickly." Meanwhile, Detroit attorney Brian I. McKeen, who specializes in medical-malpractice law, observed that, even in those cases where the answer to the competency question is not cut and dried, referral may still be the best thing to do. "There's a difference between being competent to handle something and being the best person for the job," he explained. "While someone may be competent within the meaning of the rules of ethics to handle something, it doesn't mean they're the best person for the job. That's an important distinction."

For the money

Grandparents' rights expert and family law practitioner Richard S. Victor of Bloomfield Hills explained the economic benefit that comes from referring cases i.e., the referral fee helps ease the pain of "turning away business," which can seem quite unnatural to most attorneys. "Having referral fees allows the system to help both attorneys who are able to secure clients, and attorneys who are better able to handle and represent clients work together to improve the practice of law," he stated.

Moreover, auto no-fault expert Steven M. Gursten of Southfield said he believes clients are the ones benefiting the most from referral fees. "Clients are best served because the referring attorney has a direct financial interest in making sure his client gets to the best attorney possible," he declared. "This allows the client to obtain a better result and the referring attorney has an interest that is directly aligned with the client."

Meanwhile, [Professor Lawrence] Dubin pointed out the devil's advocate position. "The ethics rules state that if a lawyer is not competent to handle a representation, the lawyer may not accept that representation," he stated. "If a lawyer followed that ethics rule, then the argument is there is no need for a referral fee that provides an economic incentive to refer the case to another lawyer rather than handling the matter in an incompetent way."

Choosing a 'referee'

Criminal defense specialist Steven Fishman of Detroit advised that long-standing relationships are often the way to go when referring, but cautioned against allowing the strength of the relationship to be a substitute for staying informed about how that attorney has been performing. "If you're going to refer cases, make sure you keep up with the notion of how he or she is performing," he asserted. Fishman emphasized that practitioners cannot forget that, while they have referred the case out, it's still their reputation with the client that's on the line.

McKeen agreed, noting that referring attorneys "should look at what the attorney's track record has been in terms of their success at trial, in terms of their success in resolving cases."

Finally, Dubin stated that, in addition to competence and trustworthiness, another quality a referring attorney looks for in a lawyer is whether he "will honor any referral agreement entered into between the parties."

How much?

While the rules are silent as to how much a referral fee should be, the legal community has grown accustomed to certain standards. "There is no set amount that a referring lawyer is entitled to," Dubin said. "It seems to me the most common referral I've seen is one-third of the legal fee earned as a result of performing the legal services for the client."

Any more obligations?

Finally, assuming a referring lawyer has answered all the necessary competence questions, found the right attorney to represent the client and put the important issues in writing, is there anything else the referring attorney must do in order to collect her referral fee?

Dubin said, according to the MRPC, the answer is no. He pointed out that nowhere in the MRPC 1.5(e) is there a requirement that a referring attorney must assume any portion of responsibility for the case in order to collect a referral fee from the lawyer who ends up handling it.

However, Dubin noted that Michigan's liberal rule stands in stark contrast to the American Bar Association's Model Rule 1.5(e) which requires that the division of a fee among lawyers from different firms be "in proportion to the services performed by ach lawyer or each lawyer assumes joint responsibility for the representation."

NOTES

This article argues that referral fees benefit clients because they get better, more qualified lawyers. But is this always the case? What if the best lawyers, like Mary in our problem, don't agree to give referral fees? What are the downsides to liberalizing the ABA rule as Michigan has done? Do the benefits outweigh the negatives? Finally, some of those interviewed for this article not only say that lawyers who get a case in an area of practice other than their own should refer it out, but imply that they *must* do so. One states that a lawyer should refer any case in a field the lawyer is not "intimately familiar with," while another implies that lawyers should refer cases to "the best person for the job." Do you agree with these comments?

D. SUPPLEMENTAL READINGS

1. Scott Turow, *Why Competence Isn't Enough*, 17 STUDENT LAWYER 46 (1988). The author of this article, a well-known attorney-turned-novelist, was an early advocate of more practical training in law school, as expressed in this piece.

2. Bruce Shapiro, *Sleeping Lawyer Syndrome; Murder Case in Texas, During Which the Defendant's Lawyer Was Observed Sleeping*, THE NATION, April 7, 1997, is about an early "sleeping lawyer" case. This article details the 7-2 decision of the Texas Court of Criminal Appeals sustaining George McFarland's conviction despite McFarland's trial counsel reportedly sleeping through much of the trial. The court reasoned that McFarland's second trial counsel may have had a tactical reason for letting his co-counsel sleep.

3. *Strickland v. Washington*, 466 U.S. 668 (1984), and *Kimmelman v. Morrison*, 477 U.S. 365 (1986), are the two leading United States Supreme Court cases that define competence of counsel in criminal cases, in terms of what a criminal defendant must show in order to gain a reversal of a conviction or sentence based on the conduct of counsel. Contrast these cases with *New Jersey v. Davis*, 561 A.2d 1082 (N.J. 1989), which takes a broader view of attorney incompetence in criminal cases.

4. In *Padilla v. Commonwealth of Kentucky*, 559 U.S. 356 (2010), the U.S. Supreme Court held that the Sixth Amendment requires criminal defense counsel to affirmatively and competently advise their clients of the immigration/deportation consequences of criminal charges and criminal pleas and that failure to do so constitutes ineffective assistance of counsel, a significant change to criminal defense lawyer's understanding of competence under *Strickland*.

5. Russell G. Pearce, *Teaching Ethics Seriously: Legal Ethics as the Most Important Subject in Law School*, 29 LOY. U. CHI. L.J. 719 (1998). Professor Pearce bemoans the state of the ethical conduct of today's lawyers. He advocates more active involvement of law schools, including that they take teaching legal ethics more seriously. His solution is to require a three-credit first semester course, at least one advanced upper level course, and "pervasive" ethics teaching in all other classes.

6. Before Carnegie and Best Practices, there was the MacCrate Report. Robert MacCrate, et al., Section of Legal Education and Admissions to the Bar, Am. Bar Ass'n, *Legal Education and Professional Development — An Educational Continuum, Report of the Task Force on Law Schools and the Profession: Narrowing the Gap* (1992). He later wrote *Yesterday, Today and Tomorrow: Building the Continuum of Legal Education and Professional Development*, 10 CLINICAL L. REV. 805 (2004), about his recommendation to shift legal education from content-focused to outcome-focused instruction in order to ensure more competent and capable graduates. Follow the work of the American Bar Association's Task Force on the Future of Education at http://www.americanbar.org/groups/legal_ education.

7. Michelle Craven & Michael Pitman, *To the Best of One's Ability: A Guide to Effective Lawyering*, 14 GEO. J. LEGAL ETHICS 983 (2001), offers a comparison between competence and negligence and examines many ethical issues surrounding both. The authors focus on the varying approaches taken by different state bars to protect clients from inadequate legal representation, and eventually conclude that all rules must be written to protect client interests.

8. Robert Kehr, *Lawyer Error: Malpractice, Fiduciary Breach, or Disciplinable Offense?*, 29 W. ST. U. L. REV. 235 (2002), speaks about the fiduciary duty of competence. Kehr contrasts negligence and fiduciary duty breaches as torts. He argues that the difference is most apparent in the contrast in remedies: In negligence, remedies serve to make whole those adversely affected by conduct falling below minimum standards; in breaches of fiduciary duties remedies are used to assist those injured by acts that go beyond simple negligence.

9. Robert R. Kuehn & Bridget M. McCormack, *Lessons from Forty Years of Interference in Law School Clinics*, 24 GEO. J. LEGAL ETHICS 59 (2011). This article documents the effects of interference on law clinic representation and identifies lessons that can be drawn from this extended history. It examines both the sources and types of interference and the ways university and law school officials have reacted to efforts of those outside the legal academy to restrict the activities of clinics; provides empirical support for the negative effects of this interference on the attitudes and actions of law clinic attorneys; and suggests ways to help avoid or minimize future efforts to interfere in the cases handled by law school clinics as well as the effects of those efforts within an institution. The authors conclude that the profession and legal educators can and should do more to ensure that the important role of clinics in legal education and access to legal assistance is not hampered by the continuing specter of interference.

PROBLEM 2: MUST WE TAKE THIS CASE?

A. INTRODUCTION

Does a lawyer have an obligation to represent every person who walks in the door? Can law firms pick and choose their clients based on their personal preferences, or do they have an obligation from time to time to accept representation of those whom they disagree with or even find repugnant? Can a law firm reject representing such a client merely on a cost/benefit analysis? Finally, what about the law firm's associates? Should they have any say on the kinds of cases or clients the firm takes? After all, they will do the bulk of the day-to-day work. The general ethical guidelines which address these questions can be difficult to apply in practice, as the John law firm of University City finds out.

B. PROBLEM

John, John, John & Badou is a fast-growing 50-lawyer firm in University City, fourth largest city in the state, and home of the largest campus of State University. Senior partner Mitchell John has, since founding the firm 18 years before, tried to change its image from a small town law office to a full-service firm which can compete for clients with the firms in the state's largest cities.

In order to improve its image, the law firm has done a substantial amount of public interest work, including pro bono work in the area of civil liberties. This, the partners believe, gives the firm an enhanced reputation in the state's legal community, and increases the firm's attractiveness to the best law students in the state, and even students from the big eastern schools.

Mitchell John's younger brother Dean John heads up the pro bono and civil liberties effort. He spends a majority of his time, both paid and unpaid, on first amendment issues, and often works as a volunteer attorney with local civil liberties agencies. Dean chairs a bar association committee on free speech issues.

The biggest news story of the year in this college town has been the University's attempt to dismiss Professor of History Ernestine Hemp. Almost from her arrival at SU several years before, Hemp created controversy by lecturing on what she called "Euro-ism," her theme that Protestants of European ancestry are, on average, superior in abilities and morals to other groups, especially blacks and Jews. The controversy was largely limited to the academic community until the publication, two years ago, of her second book, *The Myth of the Holocaust*. This book claims that the vast majority of events surrounding the extermination of six million Jews and others never took place. Hemp's book blames "Jewish propagandists and self-victimizers." She also implies that the American enslavement of blacks was "largely the fault of black Africans themselves." As Hemp's book gained more notoriety and she began to attract more publicity for her off-campus speeches, SU instituted proceedings to dismiss her for cause from her tenured professorship.

Dean John has a close working relationship with the local university teachers' union, and has frequently represented its members. One day, he gets a call from

Wilfred Allen, president of the union. "Dean," says Allen, "we need your help with Professor Hemp. You know we always turn to you for the tough ones. You did a helluva job three years ago with Laurence Jerrold, and the issue is really the same: academic freedom. We want you to take Hemp's case, and we're hoping you'll scale down your fee like you did for Jerrold."

"Wilfred," says Dean, "I'm going to have to think about this one and get back to you. I've got to discuss it with my partners."

At the partnership meeting, the following issues are raised:

> • Chief law firm recruiter Andrea Badou points out that unlike typical free speech and public interest litigation, this case could substantially hurt recruitment among top law students.

> • Mitchell John argues that his brother's political aspirations — Dean plans to run for Congress in the next election — could be seriously damaged by his association with "extremist views" like those of Professor Hemp, even if Dean is acting only as her attorney. "By advocating the academic freedom of a racist," argues Mitchell, "Dean will be arguing for the end of his political career even before it begins."

> • Managing partner Tom John argues that taking the case will cost the firm clients. He expresses particular concern about two of the firm's largest clients, Burt & Jonah's, a nationally known confection company which has taken strong stands against ethnic and racial bias, and Pathways, the largest regional pharmaceutical chain, privately owned by two Jewish families.

Partner Alice Arnold points out, however, that three years ago, Dean John successfully represented Professor Jerrold in an appeal of his dismissal as head of the SU African Studies Department. Jerrold had written a number of papers that argued that African-Americans were superior to whites, and claimed that people with a high level of melanin pigment in their skin (primarily those of African ancestry) are more intelligent and physically stronger than others. "That's no less racist than this," says Arnold, and, echoing the union president, asks, "doesn't this case raise precisely the same issues as the Jerrold case?"

"Maybe," says Mitchell, "but Dean wasn't about to run for Congress then."

"Yes, and Jerrold didn't directly attack a particular ethnic group in a way that would cost us clients," Tom John points out.

"Besides," notes Andrea Badou, "you know our diversity goals and how important we decided they are. Representing Jerrold didn't hurt us attracting minority associates; since Jerrold himself is black, the free speech issues somehow seemed clearer. But with Hemp," Badou continues, "what do we say to racial and ethnic minority students?"

"Wait a minute, Andrea" says Dean John, "are you seriously arguing that because Jerrold is African-American, he's less racist than Hemp?"

"No," replies Badou, "I'm simply saying that representing him didn't have the cost to the firm — or to you — that representing Hemp would have."

Finally, the partners ask the advice of the firm's two Jewish and two African-American partners. One of the Jewish partners strongly objects to taking the case, noting that he had many relatives who died in the Holocaust. But the other Jewish partner and both black partners say they would support Dean if he chose to take the case.

QUESTIONS

1.   Are any of the objections voiced by the firm's partners sufficient, in and of themselves, to reject Hemp's case? Are the objections cumulatively sufficient to cause the John law firm to decline the case?

2.   What is the significance of the fact that although Dean and the law firm are not on retainer to the teachers' union, they have a close working relationship with the union and that Wilfred Allen's expectation is that the firm is available to assist?

3.   If the issues in the Hemp and Jerrold cases are truly the same, can the firm justify turning down Hemp after having represented Jerrold, solely for the reasons articulated here?

4.   What if it were acknowledged that Dean John and the John law firm are clearly the best lawyer and law firm in the area to handle this case? Does that increase their obligation? What if, finally, the union sought other counsel from the area and even went to the state's biggest cities, but couldn't find an experienced firm willing to take on Hemp's case? Would the John firm then be obligated to take on Professor Hemp?

5.   Suppose you are an associate at this firm and personally felt strongly opposed to working on Hemp's behalf. Do you think you and other associates should have a say in deciding to take the case? If the firm does take the case and you are asked to work on it, should you have the right to refuse?

C. READINGS

1. Ethical Rules and Their Limited Utility

It has long been said that "One of the highest services the lawyer can render to society is to appear in court on behalf of clients whose causes are in disfavor with the general public."[1]

But when is a lawyer ethically obligated to accept employment? Strong aspirational statements exist in both the ABA Model Code and the Model Rules[2]

---

[1] *Professional Responsibility: Report of the Joint Conference*, 44 A.B.A.J. 1159, 1216 (1958).

[2] The Code, Ethical Consideration 2-27, states strongly that "a lawyer should not decline representation because a client or a cause is unpopular or community reaction is adverse," while Paragraph 6 of the Preamble of the Model Rules and Model Rule 6.1 both have language encouraging lawyers to provide access and representation to those who have economic and social barriers that prevent them from hiring a lawyer.

but there is nothing in either the Code or the Rules that requires a lawyer to accept unpopular cases.

Some states, however, appear to be more explicit in mandating that their attorneys accept unpopular causes. California has perhaps the strongest such statement, stating it is "the duty" of every attorney "never to reject, for any consideration personal to himself or herself, the cause of the defenseless or the oppressed." Calif. Bus. & Prof. Code § 6068(h).

But how successfully can states legislate this kind of rule? What if a lawyer's personal feelings interfere with the lawyer's duty to be a vigorous advocate? What if undertaking a case would have serious financial considerations for the law firm? On the other hand, can we realistically expect lawyers always to "believe" in their clients' causes in order to vigorously represent those clients?

Ethical issues often are not easily resolved by general rules. Consider how you would apply these rules to guide you in your practice. Can such rules truly give rise to a duty? Or should they be viewed as merely aspirational? And how would they affect you as a working attorney at a small, mid-sized, or large law firm?

2.   The Courageous Stand of Anthony Griffin

The consequences of representing an undesirable client can be severe. Anthony Griffin was a Texas civil rights lawyer who in 1993 agreed through the A.C.L.U. to represent the grand dragon of the Texas Knights of the Ku Klux Klan against the efforts of Texas to obtain the Klan's membership list. Griffin is African-American, and was at that time Chief Counsel to the Texas branch of the NAACP. He made it clear that he found his new client personally repugnant. But, he told the *New York Times* in 1993, "people forget." Texas's arguments were the same as those "always used against every organization 'We' do not like. It was used against the N.A.A.C.P., . . . the Black Panther Party." Indeed, Griffin based his defense of the Klan on the case which first established an organization's right to privacy of its information, Alabama's attempt to get the membership lists of the NAACP. *N.A.A.C.P. v. Alabama,* 357 U.S. 449 (1958).

Most of Griffin's NAACP colleagues strongly disagreed with him, and believed that he could not represent both the Klansman and the NAACP. Griffin was soon discharged from his NAACP post, and as the Klan litigation proceeded, the NAACP filed an amicus brief supporting the State of Texas and opposing the applicability of *N.A.A.C.P. v. Alabama.*

Eventually, however, Griffin and his Klansman client prevailed both in and out of court. In June 1994, the Texas Supreme Court sided with Griffin on First Amendment grounds. Griffin himself received the first annual William Brennan Award for upholding freedom of expression. Perhaps more important, Griffin felt he had regained his reputation in the black community. When he addressed a Texas NAACP meeting after his dismissal, few in the audience would look at him in the beginning, he told writer Nat Hentoff, but by the end "200 people lined up to tell me, 'Now we understand, and we will tell others!' " And though he was dismissed as Texas NAACP general counsel, he took on a reverse discrimination case for its sister organization, the NAACP Legal Defense Fund.

No redemption is unanimous, of course, and not everyone was persuaded that Anthony Griffin did the right thing. Harvard Professor David Wilkins, who has written extensively and thoughtfully on law and the African American experience, and whose writings we will get to later in this volume, has argued that it made an important difference that Griffin, a black lawyer, was acting against the group he was identified with — and thus owed an obligation to.

But from the beginning, Griffin maintained that he was doing the right thing. "In our role as lawyers, we're not God," he told the *New York Times*. "If lawyers backed off because someone is unpopular or hated, then our whole system of justice would just fall apart."

Years after the event, Griffin told criminal defense lawyer Amy Porter that he strongly disagreed with the criticism that because he is black he should not have taken the Klan's case. Porter wrote that Griffin believes that " 'saddling black attorneys' with Wilkins' obligation thesis does a disservice to those who confront racism in the courts and in their practice daily. To limit black attorneys' client choices would paralyze their ability to practice."[3]

Griffin explained to Porter why he did not believe his representation of the Klan conflicted with his representation of the NAACP. Simply put, not all his clients like his other clients. Griffin noted that while he was representing the Klan, he was also representing several black student organizations as well as participating on behalf of the NAACP Legal Defense Fund in the important case of *Hopwood v. State of Texas*.[4]

3. Representing the Unpopular in a Politically Polarized World

The post 9/11 world has brought us lawyers representing accused terrorists whose cases have come under important appellate scrutiny regarding their basic rights, including their very right to counsel; *unaccused* detainees at Guantanamo who have never been charged but for whom representation is both difficult and unpopular; and one lawyer, Lynne Stewart, now serving a 10-year sentence for "felonious" disclosures she made after post-conviction visits to her client, the "blind sheikh," Omar Abdel Rahman, convicted of being the leader of a terrorist organization that masterminded the 1993 bombing of the World Trade Center. Many analysts argue that Stewart would never have been charged, much less convicted, had the events of September 11, 2001 not occurred. These analysts would also argue that her conviction was fueled by restrictive changes in government policy that were applied unduly harshly. But that doesn't change the wide disapprobation that the public had towards Stewart's representation. And those Anthony Griffin-like lawyers who have taken on cases for "terrorists" have suffered similar disapprobation. Clearly the stakes have been raised when it comes to representing the unpopular client.

---

[3] Amy Porter, *Representing the Reprehensible and Identity Conflicts in Legal Representation*, 14 TEMP. POL. & CIV. RTS. L. REV. 143 (2004).

[4] 78 F.3d 932 (5th Cir. 1996). See further discussion of this and similar cases in Chapter 13.

Like Griffin, though, the Guantanamo lawyers eventually won considerably broader support with the inadvertent help of a senior Defense Department official, Charles "Cully" Stimson, then in charge of detainee affairs and himself a lawyer. In 2007, Stimson chose the fifth anniversary of the opening of Guantanamo to go on a widely-broadcast radio show and state he found it "shocking" that some of America's largest and most prestigious law firms were representing detainees. He rattled off the names of several of these firms and then implied that corporate America should boycott them: "I think quite honestly when corporate CEOs see that those firms are representing the very terrorists that hit their bottom line in 2001, those CEOs are going to make those law firms choose between representing terrorists or representing reputable firms."

Reactions from all quarters came quickly. Stimson was not only condemned in the press, but by the ABA president and, within a week, by 100 law school deans. The Pentagon and the Bush administration were forced to apologize. "[A]t the time of the Boston Massacre, the British soldiers who shot the American citizens were charged, and John Adams represented them," said Boston College Dean John H. Garvey to the Boston *Globe*. "It's a very American thing to do."

Long before 9/11, some law firms had gone so far as to conceal their involvement in unpopular causes on both sides of the political spectrum. *The American Lawyer*'s Alison Frankel found a wide disparity in how firms dealt with representation on perhaps the most difficult and emotionally charged issue of its time — abortion.[5]

One Boston firm that represented several dozen protestors associated with Operation Rescue emphasized the First Amendment nature of its representation and took the position that recruitment concerns would not color its judgment about what cases to take. At the other extreme was a Chicago firm which handled a "hot potato" case by filing its briefs "anonymously," omitting the firm's name.

More recently, shortly after the Obama administration announced in early 2011 that it would not defend the Defense of Marriage Act in court, a House of Representatives coalition hired the large international firm of King & Spalding at discounted prices to defend "DOMA." Media and Internet reaction was swift and in some quarters strongly negative. Within a week, King & Spalding retreated, dropping the case and claiming that taking it had not been sufficiently "vetted." This in turn caused the immediate resignation of K&S partner Paul Clement, former US Solicitor General, who released a statement that said:

> I resign out of the firmly-held belief that a representation should not be abandoned because the client's legal position is extremely unpopular in certain quarters. Defending unpopular positions is what lawyers do. The adversary system of justice depends on it.

Can the business of law be incompatible with a law firm's ethics? Is keeping the firm's name off the brief a proper solution, or does it simply beg the question? Is backing out of a representation because of negative repercussions ever appropriate? What if a law firm's recruitment or bottom line is directly affected? Finally, do you

---

[5] *Handling the Abortion Hot Potato*, Am. Law. January/February 1990.

think it's easier for a large firm or a sole practitioner to stand against the tide?

4. Law Firm Associates, Credit Suisse, and the Decision to Take a Case

Usually, a law firm's partners, or simply its "new business committee," have authority to accept or reject a new case or client. But who should have this authority when a firm considers taking on a highly controversial matter? Should associates ever be asked their opinions? If they are not, how do they handle working for what to them may be reprehensible causes or unsavory clients? After all, it is the associates, not the partners who landed the client, who will do the bulk of the day-to-day work on most cases. Consider the different responses of associates and their firms in the Credit Suisse and other Holocaust reparations cases.

Credit Suisse and other Swiss banks were accused in a class action case of denying payments to the survivors of Holocaust victims. Credit Suisse in particular had been widely accused of stealing gold belonging to those who died in concentration camps. In early 1997, Washington D.C.'s Wilmer, Cutler & Pickering and New York's Cravath, Swaine & Moore were asked to represent Credit Suisse.

Despite the horrific implications of the allegations against Credit Suisse, Wilmer, Cutler accepted Credit Suisse as a client in the routine manner: The firm's "new business" committee approved it, and the new client then simply appeared on the periodic "new business" memo the firm circulates to all its lawyers. There was no indication that the firm's new business committee contacted all the firm's partners, much less its associates, for their input or to consider their opinions.

Cravath, Swaine & Moore, on the other hand, took pains to claim that its role would be advisory only. Cravath then had about a thousand employees, about a third of whom were Jewish. Although the firm insisted that it was simply providing strategic advice to help the bank determine its proper course of conduct, 12 associates challenged the decision in a written memorandum. The partner in charge of the representation admitted that these objectors "felt very strongly that the bank acted improperly in some of the vilest acts in memory and should not be represented," but overruled the associates' objections.

It is impossible to know what motivated Cravath and Wilmer, Cutler to take on Credit Suisse. Everyone, Credit Suisse no less than the worst criminal defendant, is entitled to representation. However, unlike the typical criminal defendant, the Swiss banks can and will pay whatever they must to get the best possible counsel. But, unlike the typical criminal defense attorney, an associate in a large firm is not likely to be given a say in deciding what clients the firm will represent.

However, another Washington D.C. law firm took an approach very different from that of Wilmer, Cutler. Arent, Fox, Kintner, Plotkin & Kahn was asked to represent one of the European insurance companies accused of wrongfully denying life insurance claims of relatives of people who had died in the Holocaust. The plaintiffs charged that when they tried to collect on the policies, the companies denied their claims for reasons such as not having original policies or proper death certificates, impossibilities given the realities of the death camps. Instead of approving the client, the Arent, Fox partners held a firm-wide meeting open to *all* who wanted to attend. After a vigorous debate at the meeting, the firm's management committee unanimously turned down the case.

What is remarkable about this inclusive decision-making is that it occurred in an environment in which large law firms have become big businesses first and associations of professionals second. The economics of large modern American law firms virtually require a conscious decision to focus on the bottom line first, not the feelings of associates, no matter how strong. Profitability is an important law firm issue — one that involves competition among law firms, not just money.

5. Happy, Healthy, and Ethical?

While law firms are subject to the same ups and downs as the American economy as a whole, even with the restructuring of big firms in the years after the 2007 Recession, salaries for first year associates at large law firms remain near the top of the economic ladder. In "hot" legal marketplaces, those salaries are higher than the salaries of some of the judges who will decide the motions they have drafted. Do these enormous salaries for associates give the firms that employ them *carte blanche* to force them to work on any case for any client, no matter how personally repugnant?

The culture of wealth among big firms has been soundly criticized by many. Before becoming a law professor and then a federal judge, Patrick Schiltz was a big firm associate and partner in Minneapolis. Schiltz clearly believes that decisions such as those made by Wilmer, Cutler and Cravath, Swaine & Moore are motivated by a "big firm culture" that pays homage to little beyond the bottom line. As you read this excerpt from his article, consider whether associates' soaring incomes make it easier for them to compromise their moral beliefs. And what about Dean, now Judge, Schiltz? His admonishments may sound a bit patronizing, but he has a cautionary tale to tell. Does he overstate the problem or correctly evaluate the dangers of this culture to the future health and happiness — and ethics — of today's law students?

Patrick J. Schiltz, *On Being a Happy, Healthy, and Ethical Member of an Unhappy, Unhealthy, and Unethical Profession*
52 Vand. L. Rev. 871 (1999)[6]

Dear Law Student:

I have good news and bad news. The bad news is that the profession that you are about to enter is one of the most unhappy and unhealthy on the face of the earth — and, in the view of many, one of the most unethical. The good news is that you can join this profession and still be happy, healthy, and ethical. I am writing to tell you how.

---

[6] Copyright © 1999 by Patrick J. Schiltz. Reprinted by permission.

I. *The Well-Being of Lawyers*

If one looks hard enough, one can scratch up some information about the health and happiness of attorneys. And this information — although rather sparse and, in some cases, of limited value — strongly suggests that lawyers are in remarkably poor health and quite unhappy.

Lawyers seem to be among the most depressed people in America. In 1990, researchers affiliated with Johns Hopkins University studied the prevalence of major depressive disorder ("MDD") across 104 occupations. They discovered that, although only about 3% to 5% of the general population suffers from MDD, the prevalence of MDD exceeds 10% in five occupations [including] lawyers. . . . The researchers did not know whether lawyers were depressed because "persons at high risk for major depressive disorder" are attracted to the legal profession or because practicing law "causes or precipitates depression." They just know that, whatever the reason, lawyers were depressed.

. . . .

Depression is not the only emotional impairment that seems to be more prevalent among lawyers than among the general population. [A 1996] Washington study found indicia of anxiety, social alienation and isolation, obsessive-compulsiveness, paranoid ideation, interpersonal sensitivity, phobic anxiety, and hostility in "alarming" rates among lawyers — rates many times the national norms.

Lawyers appear to be prodigious drinkers. . . . One researcher conservatively estimated that 15% of lawyers are alcoholics. The study of Washington lawyers found that 18% were "problem drinkers," a percentage "almost twice the approximately 10 percent alcohol abuse and/or dependency prevalence rates estimated for adults in the United States."

. . . .

The extremely limited information that is available indicates that the physical health of lawyers may not be much better than their emotional health. . . . In sum, attorneys seem to be an unhealthy lot.

People who are this unhealthy — people who suffer from depression, anxiety, alcoholism, drug abuse, divorce, and suicide to this extent — are almost by definition unhappy. It should not be surprising, then, that lawyers are indeed unhappy, nor should it be surprising that the source of their unhappiness seems to be the one thing that they have in common: their work as lawyers. "Work satisfaction affects life satisfaction." Almost a century ago, Russian playwright Maxim Gorky wrote: "When work is a pleasure, life is a joy! When work is a duty, life is slavery."

. . . .

II. *Explaining the Poor Health and Unhappiness of Lawyers*

Why are lawyers so unhealthy and unhappy? Why do so many lawyers, in the words of Judge Laurence Silberman, "hate what the practice of law has become"?

Lawyers give many reasons. They complain about the commercialization of the legal profession — about the fact that practicing law has become less of a profession and more of a business. They complain about the increased pressure to attract and retain clients in a ferociously competitive marketplace. They complain about having to work in an adversarial environment "in which aggression, selfishness, hostility, suspiciousness, and cynicism are widespread." They complain about not having control over their lives and about being at the mercy of judges and clients. They complain about a lack of civility among lawyers. They complain about a lack of collegiality and loyalty among their partners. And they complain about their poor public image. Mostly, though, they complain about the hours. . . . Lawyers are complaining with increasing vehemence about "living to work, rather than working to live"— about being " 'asked not to *dedicate*, but to *sacrifice* their lives to the firm.' "

. . . .

III. *The Ethics of Lawyers*

. . . [L]aw students do not think that they will become unethical lawyers. Students think of unethical lawyers as the sleazeballs who chase ambulances (think Danny DeVito in *The Rainmaker*) or run insurance scams (think Bill Murray in *Wild Things*) or destroy evidence (think Al Pacino's crew in *The Devil's Advocate*). Students have a hard time identifying with these lawyers. When students think of life after graduation, they see themselves sitting on the 27th floor of some skyscraper in a freshly pressed dark suit (blue, black, or gray) with a starched blouse or shirt (white or light blue) doing sophisticated legal work for sophisticated clients. Students imagine — wrongly — that such lawyers do not have to worry much about ethics, except, perhaps, when the occasional conflict of interest question arises.

If you think this — if you think that you will not have any trouble practicing law ethically — you are wrong. Dead wrong. In fact, particularly if you go to work for a big firm, you will probably begin to practice law unethically in at least some respects within your first year or two in practice. This happens to most young lawyers in big firms. It happened to me, and it will happen to you, unless you do something about it.

A. *Practicing Law Ethically*

Let's first be clear on what I mean by practicing law ethically. I mean three things.

First, you generally have to comply with the formal disciplinary rules . . . . In many other ways, subtle or blatant, you will be encouraged to think that conduct that does not violate the rules is "ethical," while conduct that does violate the rules is "unethical."

I don't have anything against the formal rules. Often, they are all that stands between an unethical lawyer and a vulnerable client. You should learn them and follow them. But you should also understand that the formal rules represent nothing more than "the lowest common denominator of conduct that a highly self-interested group will tolerate." . . . [C]omplying with the formal rules will not make you an ethical lawyer, any more than complying with the criminal law will make you an ethical person. Many of the sleaziest lawyers you will encounter will be absolutely scrupulous in their compliance with the formal rules. In fact, they will be only too happy to tell you just that. Complying with the rules is usually a necessary, but never a sufficient, part of being an ethical lawyer.

The second thing you must do to be an ethical lawyer is to act ethically in your work, even when you aren't required to do so by any rule. To a substantial extent, "bar ethical rules have lost touch with ordinary moral institutions." To practice law ethically you must practice law consistently with those institutions. For the most part, this is not complicated. Being an ethical lawyer is not much different from being an ethical doctor or mail carrier or gas station attendant. Indeed, long before you applied to law school, your parents had probably taught you all that you need to know to practice law ethically. You should treat others as you want them to treat you. Be honest and fair. Show respect and compassion. Keep your promises. Here is a good rule of thumb: If you would be ashamed if your parents or spouse or children knew what you were doing, then you should not do it.

The third thing you must do to be an ethical lawyer is to live an ethical life. . . . [B]eing admitted to the bar does not absolve you of your responsibilities outside of work — to your family, to your friends, to your community, and, if you're a person of faith, to your God. To practice law ethically, you must meet those responsibilities, which means that you must live a balanced life. If you become a workaholic lawyer, you will be unhealthy, probably unhappy, and, I would argue, unethical.

B. *Big Firm Culture*

It is hard to practice law ethically. Complying with the formal rules is the easy part. The rules are not very specific, and they don't demand very much. . . . Acting as an ethical lawyer in the broader, non-formalistic sense is far more difficult. . . . To understand why, you need to understand what it is that you will do every day as a lawyer. Most of a lawyer's working life is filled with the mundane.

Because practicing law ethically will depend primarily upon the hundreds of little things that you will do almost unthinkingly every day, it will not depend much upon your thinking. You are going to be busy. The days will fly by. When you are on the phone negotiating a deal or when you are at your computer drafting a brief or when you are filling out your time sheet at the end of the day, you are not going to have time to reflect on each of your actions. You are going to have to act almost instinctively.

What this means, then, is that you will not practice law ethically — you *cannot* practice law ethically — unless acting ethically is *habitual* for you. You have to be in the habit of being honest, of being fair, of being compassionate. These qualities have to be deeply ingrained in you, so that you can't turn them on and off — so that acting honorably is not something you have to *decide* to do — so that when you are at work, making the thousands of phone calls you will make and writing the thousands of letters you will write and dealing with the thousands of people with whom you will deal, you will *automatically* apply the same values in the workplace that you apply outside of work, when you are with family and friends.

Here is the problem, though: After you start practicing law, nothing is likely to influence you more than "the culture or house norms of the agency, department, or firm" in which you work. If you are going into private practice — particularly private practice in a big firm — you are going to be immersed in a culture that is hostile to the values you now have. The system does not *want* you to apply the same values in the workplace that you do outside of work (unless you're rapaciously greedy outside of work); it wants you to replace those values with the system's values. The system is obsessed with money, and it wants you to be, too. The system wants you — it *needs* you — to play the game.

. . . .

[Y]ou will absorb big firm culture — a culture of long hours of toil inside the office and short hours of conspicuous consumption outside the office. You will work among lawyers who will talk about money constantly and who will be intensely curious about how much money other lawyers are making. . . .

Big firm culture also reflects the many ways in which lawyers who are winning the game broadcast their success. . . . When lawyers speak with envy or admiration about other lawyers, they do not mention a lawyer's devotion to family or public service, or a lawyer's innate sense of fairness, or even a lawyer's skill at trying cases or closing deals, nearly as much as they mention a lawyer's billable hours, or stable of clients, or annual income.

It is very difficult for a young lawyer immersed in this culture day after day to maintain the values she had as a law student. Slowly, almost imperceptibly, young lawyers change. They begin to admire things they did not admire before, be ashamed of things they were not ashamed of before, find it impossible to live without things they lived without before.

. . . .

[N]either big firms nor big firm lawyers are all alike. But what you need to understand is that they are *becoming* more alike. One of the most consistent findings of the social scientists involved in a recent ABA study of the ethics of big firm litigators was that the cultures of individual firms are weakening, leaving a "void of guidance to junior lawyers." This void, in turn, is being "filled by other powerful systemic or environmental influences," especially influences from outside the firm. In other words, the distinctive cultures of individual big firms are influencing young lawyers less and less, while a generic big firm culture is influencing young lawyers more and more. That is why, no matter which big firm you join, there is a good chance that working at the firm will make you unhealthy, an even better chance it will make you unhappy, and an almost 100% chance that it will make you unethical . . . .

IV. *On Being a Happy, Healthy, and Ethical Lawyer*

This is the best advice I can give you: Right now, while you are still in law school, make the commitment — not just in your head, but in your heart — that, although you are willing to work hard and you would like to make a comfortable living, you are not going to let money dominate your life to the exclusion of all else. And don't just structure your life around this negative; embrace a positive. *Believe* in something — *care* about something — so that when the culture of greed presses in on you from all sides, there will be something inside of you pushing back. Make the decision now that *you* will be the one who defines success for you — not your classmates, not big law firms, not clients of big law firms, not the *National Law Journal*. You will be a happier, healthier, and more ethical attorney as a result.

NOTES

Is Schiltz right that almost all big firms have similar unhealthy cultures? Do you believe that lawyers' successes are inevitably measured in money, not, for example, by their public service? Or is Schiltz perhaps overstating a bit for emphasis?

What about the demands placed on associates? Can a firm justify its decision to take on a disagreeable client because it has to meet the higher payrolls resulting from the higher salaries it pays? While Schiltz does not directly mention the lack of control over the selection of clients or cases as a major factor leading to associates' unhappiness with their jobs, many associates certainly feel they have the worst of both worlds: No power to decide whom they represent, but the clear expectation that they will summon all the vigor necessary to further the interests of clients they may find repugnant. Much of life is about making sound choices. Think of ways in which self-respecting young associates might still make good choices even where they have little if any control over the clients they represent.

6. Appointments by the Court

What are a lawyer's obligations to accept representation when requested to do so by a court? ABA Model Rule 6.2 requires a lawyer to accept appointment unless there is good cause to withdraw, such as the representation would result in a violation of the rules or other law; the representation would impose an unreasonable financial burden on the lawyer; or the client or the cause is "so repugnant to the lawyer as to be likely to impair the client-lawyer relationship or the lawyer's ability to represent the client."

Are there clients so repugnant that the lawyer simply cannot be a vigorous advocate? What if the John law firm and Dean John were appointed by a court to represent Professor Hemp, or the grand dragon of the Ku Klux Klan? Or the convicted sheikh represented by Lynne Stewart? Could the firm successfully argue that the repugnance of these individuals is so great that the attorney-client relationship would be impaired? The comment to Rule 6.2 notes that a lawyer's freedom to select clients is "limited," and that all lawyers are required to accept "a fair share of unpopular matters or indigent or unpopular clients."

Could the law firm successfully argue that representation of these individuals would create an "unreasonable financial burden" because two major clients might leave? Or would it first have to show that the clients will in fact leave? And what constitutes an *unreasonable* financial burden? What if the clients leaving will reduce profits by 5%? Is that sufficiently "unreasonable"? On the other hand, what if the firm's biggest "rainmaker" states that he will resign and take his book of business elsewhere?

In England, barristers, the bar's trial attorneys theoretically don't have their choice of clients at all. They operate under what Professor David Mellinkoff has called the "taxi-cab" rule, meaning that if a client requests the barrister, the barrister can no more decline employment than a cab driver can decline a fare. "The rule is explicit," says Mellinkoff in *The Conscience of a Lawyer.* "Personal predilections" are not considered, and the rule "exists on paper and in practice." Could you envision such a rule in the United States?

Stateside, the ethical dilemmas of representing a client the lawyer does not want to take on come up most often in the context of clients who cannot pay. The Ninth Circuit once noted that the bar's duty to represent indigents upon court order is "an ancient tradition of the legal profession" that dates back to the 15th century. In requiring a lawyer to represent an indigent criminal defendant without compensation, the court said:

> An applicant for admission to practice law may justly be deemed to be aware of the traditions of the profession which he is joining, and to know that one of these traditions is that a lawyer is an officer of the court obligated to represent indigents for little or no compensation upon court order. Thus the lawyer has consented to, and assumed, this obligation and when he is called upon to fulfill it, he cannot contend that it is a 'taking of his services.'[7]

7. Mr. Mallard Goes to Washington

Here is the story of one lawyer "called upon to fulfill" his obligation: a young Iowa bankruptcy lawyer who was "asked" by the federal District Court to take on, without compensation, a civil rights case on behalf of a group of prisoners, and, famously, found himself before the United States Supreme Court.

Linda Greenhouse, *The Law; Can Lawyers Be Forced to Represent the Poor?*
THE NEW YORK TIMES (March 3, 1989)[8]

WASHINGTON, March 2— When a Federal District Court in Iowa asked a young member of its bar to handle a civil rights suit on behalf of two state prisoners, the lawyer, John E. Mallard, assumed he was free to decline.

He was wrong, at least according to the United States Court of Appeals for the Eighth Circuit, which interprets a 97-year-old Federal law as giving district judges in its seven Midwestern states the power to assign lawyers to represent indigent civil litigants without compensation.

Two years later Mr. Mallard's refusal to donate his time has set off waves far

---

[7] United States v. Dillon, 346 F.2d 633, 635 (9th Cir. 1965).

[8] Copyright © 1989 by The New York Times Company. Reprinted by permission.

beyond Fairfield, Iowa, a town of 9,500 people where he practices corporate and securities law with a three-member firm.

The 34-year-old lawyer argued his appeal before the United States Supreme Court this week. At a moment of heightened debate throughout the legal profession over how to address the legal needs of the poor, *Mallard v. United States District Court* presents the Justices with a vehicle for shaping the mandatory public service concept now taking root in bar associations and Federal and state courts.

Bar Associations Divided

The case has divided bar associations around the country, highlighting the lack of consensus within the profession as to whether lawyers should be required to devote a certain number of hours each year to those who cannot afford legal representation.

The Association of the Bar of the City of New York filed a brief urging the Supreme Court to view the duty of lawyers to donate their services "for the public good" — lawyers use the Latin phrase pro bono publico — as an obligation that comes with the power and privilege of bar membership.

The State Bar of California, by contrast, warned that "to compel unwilling attorneys to render uncompensated services" promised "incompetent representation" and might well be unconstitutional. "A solution to the unmet legal needs of the least among us cannot rest solely on the backs of private attorneys," the California bar's brief said.

The American Bar Association, which has been split for years over the issue of donated services, did not file a brief.

In the hourlong argument on Tuesday, the Justices appeared intensely interested in the case and troubled by the implications of the arguments.

Challenging Question

Responding to Mr. Mallard's assertion that Federal judges might request but not order a lawyer to donate services on a civil case, Justice Sandra Day O'Connor asked:

"What if every lawyer in the district is like you? What if they all say, 'No, we just don't want to do it'?" Referring to her own days of law practice in Arizona, Justice O'Connor said, "In my day it would have been unthinkable to tell the judge that I wouldn't do it."

Mr. Mallard said the prospect of an indigent litigant being left unrepresented, while troubling, was highly unlikely. "As a practical matter," he said, lawyers who had continuing relationships with Federal judges would be unlikely to refuse.

In his own case, he said, he had almost no Federal court experience and little desire to develop any. A Federal civil rights case, with multiple plaintiffs and defendants, was outside his expertise. His counteroffer to help an unrepresented person with a bankruptcy case or other financial matter was refused, he said.

The Federal court in Iowa has one of the country's most active civil pro bono programs. All attorneys admitted to practice before the court, who have appeared as counsel in a non-bankruptcy case in the last five years, are held available for assignment. Lawyers are reimbursed for their expenses but do not receive a fee.

At the simplest level, Mr. Mallard's case requires the Supreme Court to interpret a Federal statute, Section 1915(d) of Title 28 of the United States Code. The law, which dates to 1892, provides that a Federal court in a civil case "may request an attorney to represent" a person "unable to employ counsel." There is confusion among the lower Federal courts on what this language means.

Mr. Mallard urged the Court to interpret the law according to its "plain meaning."

Perception of Justice

"Request does not mean require," he said, noting that in other statutes, including the Criminal Justice Act, which provides lawyers for indigent criminal defendants, Congress was unambiguous about authorizing mandatory appointments. (The criminal program does not pose a pro bono issue, however, since lawyers are assigned to criminal defendants as a matter of constitutional right and are paid from $40 to $75 an hour from Federal funds.)

But even if the Court agrees with Mr. Mallard on the statutory language, the case does not necessarily end there. Gordon E. Allen, a Deputy Attorney General of Iowa, who argued on behalf of the district court, said a judge could require a lawyer to take such a case as "an expression of the inherent power of the court." He added, "What is at stake today is really the perception of justice."

Several Justices appeared interested in that approach, which has formed the basis for some mandatory programs of donated services at the state level. In New York, where the issue is under study by a special committee appointed by Chief Judge Sol Wachtler of the State Court of Appeals, the State Supreme Court in Westchester County has invoked its "inherent power" to require lawyers to handle divorce cases for the poor without compensation. . . .

Making his first Supreme Court appearance, Mr. Mallard, a graduate of Harvard College and Vanderbilt University Law School, turned in a capable if stilted performance. He started by referring, in formal Supreme Court style, to "the petitioner."

"That's you, is that right?" Justice O'Connor asked. Yes, Mr. Mallard said, and switched to the first person for the rest of his argument.

He did so well, in fact, that Justice John Paul Stevens was openly skeptical of his argument that he was "not competent" to handle the civil rights case. "Before this case came up, how many cases had you had in this Court?" Justice Stevens asked. "Did you think you were competent to come here? You must have. You picked yourself."

NOTES

Mr. Mallard was so effective before the United States Supreme Court that he won his case, by a 5-4 vote, on precisely the basis he argued — that "request" meant just that, and not, as Justice Stevens argued in dissent, "respectfully command."[9]

Nevertheless, since the district court did not rely on its "inherent authority" in making the appointment, the Supreme Court expressly declined to answer the larger question before it: Does a court have the inherent power to order a lawyer to serve without compensation? This question remains unclear to this day. Meanwhile, we return to the question of a lawyer's obligation to serve without compensation when we examine pro bono work in Problem 32.

D. SUPPLEMENTAL READINGS

1. DAVID MELLINKOFF, THE CONSCIENCE OF A LAWYER (1973). Professor Mellinkoff's study of an 1840 English case, excerpted briefly in the Introduction, remains a compelling treatise. Mellinkoff describes the struggle of barrister Charles Phillips in deciding whether he could continue to defend a man he knew to be guilty, *and* whom he had particular reason to strongly dislike. This issue may be clear to the criminal defense lawyers of today, but in its time had many parallels to the questions raised in Problem 2.

2. Amy Porter, *Representing the Reprehensible and Identity Conflicts in Legal Representation*, 14 TEMP. POL. & CIV. RTS. L. REV. 143 (2004). This article, referred to in section 2, above, contains a thorough review of the Griffin-Wilkins discussion on reprehensible clients and the question of "which side are you on," as well as a series of models to describe how lawyers approach — and should approach — these issues.

3. There are a large number of interesting articles about representation of clients despite moral opposition. In her thoughtful piece on morality-centered thinking, *Lawyers, Justice, and the Challenge of Moral Pluralism*, 90 MINN. L. REV. 389 (2005), Professor Kate Kruse argues that lawyers should be permitted to evaluate their own "moral conflicts of interest" in deciding whether or not to represent a client, even if they are "the last lawyer in town." Larry Cunningham, *Can a Catholic Lawyer Represent a Minor Seeking a Judicial Bypass for an Abortion? A Moral and Canon Law Analysis*, 44 J. CATH. LEG. STUD. 379 (2005), argues that pursuant to Catholic moral values and Canon law, a Catholic lawyer should not take on the representation.

4. Many articles have been written about the Lynne Stewart case. Alissa Clare, *Note: Current Development 2004–2005: We Should Have Gone to Med School: In the Wake of Lynne Stewart, Lawyers Face Hard Time for Defending Terrorists*, 18 GEO. J. LEGAL ETHICS 651 (2005), is particularly compelling because of the chilling effect the author believes the Stewart case will have on lawyers representing alleged terrorists or other unpopular criminal defendants.

---

[9] Mallard v. United States District Court, 490 U.S. 296 (1989).

5. Charles W. Wolfram, *Selecting Clients: Are You Free to Choose?* 34 TRIAL 21 (1998). Wolfram criticizes a decision by the Massachusetts Commission on Discrimination for sanctioning a female divorce lawyer who only handled women's cases. The lawyer rejected a male potential client who had been the homemaker and secondary bread-winner to his physician wife. Professor Wolfram argues that the lawyer had a constitutional right to limit her practice to representing women, since she did so on political and moral grounds. This particular case is also discussed in the Porter article above. For a defense of the commission's decision see Samuel Stonefield, *Lawyer Discrimination Against Clients: Outright Rejection — No; Limitations on Issues and Arguments — Yes*, 20 W. NEW ENG. L. REV. 103 (1998). Professor Stonefield's says that lawyers must be able to choose, including representing only people of one sex.

6. Carrie Johnson, *Arent Fox Rejects a Client*, LEGAL TIMES, April 14, 1997, at 14. This article describes in greater detail the decision-making process at Arent, Fox that led it to reject the case of one of the European insurers that had been denying claims of relatives of Holocaust victims.

7. Consider former U.S. Solicitor General Paul Clement's April 25, 2011 letter to his law firm, King & Spaulding, in which he resigned after the firm decided to drop its (and Clement's) representation of U.S. House Republicans in their efforts to support the Defense of Marriage Act. Clement's letter said that his personal views about DOMA were "irrelevant," but that a law firm should not abandon a client "because the client's legal position is extremely unpopular in certain quarters. Defending unpopular positions is what lawyers do." The letter is available on a few websites including the HUFFINGTON POST at http://www.huffingtonpost.com/2011/04/25/law-firm-doma-house-republicans-vetting-inadequate_n_853226.html. Interestingly, many liberal commentators such as Huffington who were opposed to DOMA agreed with Clement about his maintaining representation. As Dahlia Lithwicki wrote on slate.com ("Why even opponents of DOMA should want it to get a vigorous defense," April 26, 2011), "the legal system requires zealous advocacy on *both* sides of unpopular causes."

8. *Yarbrough v. Superior Court*, 702 P.2d 583 (Cal. 1985). Yarbrough was a prisoner convicted of murder and then sued civilly for wrongful death arising from the murder. The California Supreme Court reaffirmed its previous view that indigent prisoners are entitled to access to the courts, including appointment of counsel in appropriate cases. But the court declined to affirm the appellate court's view that counsel could be appointed without compensation. Rather, as in *Mallard*, the *Yarbrough* court consciously avoided the issue.

9. The National Legal Aid & Defender Association (NLADA), founded in 1911, is America's oldest and largest nonprofit association "devoted to excellence in the delivery of legal services to those who cannot afford counsel." The section of their home page titled Defender Resources often includes reports on the status of issues of importance to the criminal defense community. In a 2011 report they note that Pennsylvania and North Dakota have *no* state funding of indigent defense services. For lawyers in those states, as well as in the states where the funding is insufficient for defender services, the decision in *Madden v Township of Delran* (below) is more striking.

10. *Madden v. Township of Delran*, 601 A.2d 211 (N.J. 1992). New Jersey's highest court strongly criticized a system that does not require local governments to provide counsel to all defendants other than by relying on the bar. Nevertheless, the court upheld the right of the town of Delran to appoint a lawyer to represent an indigent defendant on a driving-while-intoxicated charge without compensating the attorney. Interestingly, after the attorney's law firm submitted a bill, had it denied, and brought suit, the town paid the bill. The law firm refused payment in order to bring the issue before the state Supreme Court, which commended the firm for acting in "the best traditions of the bar."

PROBLEM 3: TAKING ON A CLIENT AND GETTING PAID

A. INTRODUCTION

Getting a new client can be much more complicated than just meeting someone with a legal problem in your office and opening a new file. On some occasions whether the lawyer has taken on a new client is ambiguous. It's actually possible for lawyers to get new clients without knowing it. There may be duties the lawyer owes to non-clients. Even once it is clearly understood that the lawyer does have a new client, there remain many issues about how the lawyer is retained. Is the fee reasonable and appropriate to the representation? Are there other features of the representation agreement that are unfair or adhesive or unethical? To what extent may the lawyer be paid in stock, stock options, or the rights to the client's life story?

In addition: how is the *scope* of representation defined? Are the tasks to be performed by the lawyer sufficiently explained? Are they sufficiently narrow and discussed in a way that a client would clearly understand? That is, is it clear what the lawyer is *not* responsible for? In cases of limited and what are now termed "unbundled" representations, are those limits of a lawyer's duties clearly set forth?

Getting a new client is one of the most exciting moments of a case. But it is also a moment filled with ethical traps for the unwary. This problem explores those pitfalls.

B. PROBLEM

I

Alice Tennant is the junior partner at the small real estate law firm Land, Lord & Tennant. Her practice has emphasized real property law for seven years. At the request of the local realty board, she gives a speech to a group of business people on negotiating commercial real property leases. There is a cocktail reception after the speech.

Olive Martini, an old college friend, comes up to Alice and tells her how much she enjoyed the speech. Olive also tells Alice that she is intending to start a furniture business and is in the process of negotiating a lease. Olive explains that she is concerned because the lease states that the landlord is not responsible for any water or plumbing leaks from any of the residential units above the commercial unit. She tells Alice that when she inspected the premises, she noted numerous water spots in the ceiling and along the walls. She asks Alice how she can protect herself.

"Look," Alice tells Olive, "you really ought to call me at my office on Monday to discuss this further. But whatever else you do, make sure you're not underinsured. Come in to see me next week and we'll discuss the lease in more detail."

Olive, however, apparently satisfied with the information she has already gotten, never makes an appointment with Alice. A month later, Alice notices an announcement for the opening of Olive's business and assumes Olive went ahead and signed the lease.

QUESTIONS

1.   Was there an attorney-client relationship between Alice and Olive?

2.   When Olive asked for advice was Tennant's reply appropriate? If not, how should she have replied?

3.   Should Alice have done anything when Olive did not make an appointment?

4.   Suppose a few months later, the plumbing in one of the residential units above Olive's shop bursts, and water floods the store causing extensive damage to the furniture. Assume the insurance company denies Olive's claim, arguing that because she had prior knowledge of the leaks, her loss was not covered.

   a. If Alice is subpoenaed to a deposition in a case between Olive and her insurance company, must Alice testify that Olive admitted she knew of the leaks?

   b. Can Olive sue Alice for malpractice? Might she win?

5.   If Olive asked her question in the Q&A period during the talk, would any of your answers change?

II

Jeremiah Hamilton is an experienced and well-known business entrepreneur. Three years ago, Joan Goebel represented him in the purchase of a small business. Now Hamilton is back with a new matter — the purchase of a boat marina in Ocean City. The marina berths boats, rents boats and jet skis, and has a bar and restaurant.

Jerry and Joan meet in Joan's office, where Jerry tells Joan that he only wants Joan to deal with the marina purchase itself. Jerry says that he will take care of the transfer of the bar's liquor license, and obtaining necessary title to the boats, jet skis, and the like. "I probably know more about that stuff than you do anyway," he says.

Joan and Jerry sign a brief fee agreement, part of which looks like this: "3. Services to be rendered: Lawyer shall represent Client in a matter regarding: *Purchase of Handleby's Boat Marina, Ocean City.*"

Since Jerry is short on cash, he proposes that Joan be paid only $80 per hour, one-quarter her ordinary rate, in return for receiving a 10% interest in the closely-held corporation being formed to own the Marina. Jerry will own the other 90% of the stock. Later, Jerry further suggests that instead of the $80 per hour portion of the fee, he is willing to pay Joan a contingency fee of 25% for every dollar below $3 million he saves on the marina's sales price, including the extras. Joan is tempted, thinking that she can negotiate a better price. Pushed by Jerry, she finally agrees.

The marina deal closes a few months later, at $2.7 million, and Goebel, who has spent only 60 hours on the case, is feeling very good about her fee/stock arrangement.

QUESTIONS

1.   Is it appropriate for Goebel to negotiate for stock in lieu of some of her ordinary fees?

2.   Is the contingency fee charged by Goebel ethical? Even given her per-hour recovery for 60 hours of work, and the fact she is also getting stock?

3.   Suppose that the liquor license transfers without a hitch, and Hamilton assures Goebel that he obtained all the necessary UCC-1 forms for the boats and jet skis. Three months after close, however, Jerry is contacted by Carlo DiCredit, who says that he holds a $112,000 promissory note from the marina's previous owner, that the note is now due, and that it is secured by Department of Motor Vehicles "pink slips," which manifest title to the marina's boats and jet skis. Jerry, who didn't know that the boats and skis even had pink slips, calls Joan in a rage. Meanwhile, he is refusing to pay Goebel her $75,000 contingency fee or issue her stock.

What was the scope of Goebel's representation? Is *she* responsible for what happened with the boats and jet skis? Is she liable for malpractice? If so, what could she have done to avoid this? Finally, will she ever see her fees or her stock?

III

Read the fee agreement in section 5. Does it pass muster? If you believe it does not, briefly list the problems you find.

C. READINGS

1. When Does the Attorney-Client Relationship Begin?

Sometimes, lawyers can find themselves representing a client without even knowing it. When representation begins — and what the scope of that representation is — are not bright line tests, but they are particularly important issues. Their importance comes from the fact that the existence of an attorney-client relationship is usually the trigger for a lawyer's fiduciary duty.

Courts and ethics authorities take a variety of approaches in determining when someone becomes a client. But most agree with the Iowa Supreme Court that neither a retainer nor a formal agreement is required to establish the attorney-client relationship. *Kurtenbach v. TeKippe*, 260 N.W.2d 53, 56 (Iowa 1977). Many courts and experts believe that the attorney-client relationship may be inferred by the conduct of the lawyer, including what one commentator has called "casually rendered advice."[1]

In *Kurtenbach*, the Iowa Supreme Court developed the following test to examine the existence of a lawyer-client relationship: (1) Did the client seek advice from the lawyer? (2) Was it within the lawyer's area of competence? and (3) Did the lawyer, either directly or implicitly, agree to give the requested advice? The reasonable expectations and reliance of the putative client are important to courts evaluating this issue. One Massachusetts case, *DeVaux v. American Home Assurance Company*, 444 N.E.2d 355 (Mass. 1983), held that an attorney-client relationship could possibly result from the client talking to the lawyer's secretary:

> The plaintiff claims that the attorney placed his secretary in a position where prospective clients might reasonably believe that she had the authority to establish an attorney-client relationship. There is a question of fact for the jury whether the attorney permitted [this], thereby creating the appearance of authority.

Not all courts have gone this far. But the use of contract law concepts, including detrimental reliance, reasonable belief, and express and implied agreement, is common in most jurisdictions.[2]

What do these contract principles say about Tennant's casual conversation with her old college chum? What is the significance of these standards in determining malpractice liability? If a lawyer can get a client without knowing it, what if the lawyer doesn't perform the services the client expects — even if those services are no more than making a phone call or citing a single legal principle or case? The *Togstad* case described in the Supplemental Readings sets perhaps the highest known malpractice benchmark. But it is clear that once "clienthood" is conferred on the Olive Martinis of the world — and many states look to the reasonable belief of the putative client as evidence — the lawyer who fails to perform competently could be liable for malpractice.

2. "Client for Purposes of Confidentiality"?

If Olive Martini had simply asked her old friend Alice some questions and Alice had declined to answer, would the lawyer have any responsibility to Olive if Olive discussed confidential information about her situation? Does a lawyer in such circumstances have any duty to hold the prospective client's communication in confidence, even if she never becomes a client? We address issues of confidentiality in greater detail in the next three problems, but suffice it to say here that the almost universally accepted answer is "yes." Yet until the last decade, with the approval of the Restatement (Third) of the Law Governing Lawyers, section 15, and ABA Model Rule 1.18, the rules and regulations were less than clear. Now, with the ABA's recent approval of Model Rule changes suggested by the Ethics 20/20

---

[1] Ronald I. Friedman, *The Creation of the Attorney-Client Relationship: An Emerging View*, 22 CAL. W. L. REV. 209, 220 (1986). Friedman warns against giving advice "at cocktail parties, in building corridors, over the backyard fence . . . ."

[2] *See, e.g.*, Atkinson v. Haug, 622 A.2d 983, 986 (Pa. Super. Ct. 1993); Miller v. Metzinger, 91 Cal. App. 3d 31 (1979).

Commission, the concept of confidentiality owed a "prospective client" has been clarified and more fully codified.

Both the Restatement and the ABA Rule support the proposition that not only are verbal communications in such circumstances confidential, but so are any documents received by the lawyer. A few published cases in the 1990s dealt directly with this issue, usually in a manner consistent with the more-recent rules changes. For example, Nevada attorney Samuel Bull was approached by Todd, a criminal defendant in a jail where Bell had gone to meet with his own client. Todd gave Bell his own handwritten notes explaining his defense. Bell not only didn't consider the notes confidential — he turned them over to a judge — but gave his own assessment that Todd should be sentenced heavily. When Bull's actions came to light, Todd's sentence was reversed and the case was remanded for a new trial.[3]

And in *Commonwealth v. Mrozek*, 657 A.2d 997 (Pa. Super. Ct. 1995), Mrozek called a lawyer looking to hire him. The lawyer was meeting with other clients, and despite Mrozek's entreaties, the secretary was unable to interrupt the lawyer until Mrozek said, "Honey, I don't think you understand. I've just committed a homicide." That message finally got the lawyer's attention. However, even though the communication was made by a non-client to a secretary, the statement was suppressed on appeal as confidential.[4]

If a lawyer must maintain confidentiality even with non- or prospective clients, issues relating to conflicts of interest may also arise. After all, if the lawyer cannot reveal a confidence, even of a non-client, that confidence may be significant in evaluating whether the lawyer may subsequently represent a third party against that non-client if the confidence comes into play.[5]

Consider these interesting facts in *Flatt v. Superior Court*, 885 P.2d 950 (Cal. 1994): a prospective client spoke to a lawyer about suing his own former lawyer, but that former lawyer turned out to be a *current* client of the firm the prospective client consulted. The California Supreme Court held that the consulted lawyer had to maintain the prospective client's confidential communications, but did *not* have to tell the prospective client about the pending statute of limitations because of her firm's duty to its current client. While this case is of primary importance in California, it is valuable everywhere for its discussion of the interrelationship of confidentiality and conflicts of interest.

Does it make sense that a lawyer will be responsible for any *advice* given, even if she never sees the prospective client again? Do you think that a lawyer who not only receives information but also gives advice means the mere "prospective client" has morphed into a "limited, narrow-scope client"?

---

[3] Todd v. State of Nevada, 931 P.2d 721 (Nev. 1997).

[4] There are limits to this presumptive confidentiality. According to one California court, when the lawyer affirmatively states in advance that he is *not* willing to represent the prospective client, the client can no longer have an expectation of confidentiality, and the subsequent statements are neither confidential nor privileged. People v. Gionis, 892 P.2d 1199 (Cal. 1995).

[5] We address issues of conflicts of interest in more detail in Problems 7 through 11.

3. Accidental and Limited Clients, and Others Who May Be Owed a Duty

As the previous section intimates, a prospective client may become an actual client if the lawyer is not scrupulously careful. In addition to giving advice, this could happen in some of the following ways:

• *"Accommodation clients."* The Restatement, section 132, used this new term to mean an added person or entity being represented by the lawyer along with the lawyer's regular client, usually for a limited scope and no extra charge, because working for both clients avoids "duplication." But what does that mean? Is the person or entity accommodated a "real" client? Are the usual fiduciary duties owed? The Restatement hedges, concluding that "circumstances might warrant the inference that the 'accommodation' client understood and impliedly consented" not only to the lawyer's ongoing representation of the regular client, but to waivers of both confidentiality and conflicts of interest. Courts and commentators have for the most part not agreed with this conclusion, reasoning that a "client" is not a first- or second-class client, but just a "client" in all respects.[6]

• *Self-Help Services.* There exist a number of "self-help" websites that charge money to assist clients — if they *are* clients — in resolving their legal claims. Among the sites are those calling themselves SettlementCentral.com and 4MyClaim.com. On one such site, the computer walks the consumer through the writing of a demand letter in a personal injury case, complete with attached supporting information, creating what the site calls a "Settlement Demand Package (SDP)." This SDP, trumpets the site, "will forcefully inform the [insurance claims] adjuster that you know what you're doing and that this may be his or her last chance to settle without getting attorneys involved." But *if attorneys are* involved in running such sites, have they taken on clients to whom they owe fiduciary duties — including the duty of competence — and who may sue *them* in the event of professional negligence?[7]

• *Unbundled Services.* One lawyer who owns and operates a self-help website describes his site as providing "unbundled" services, a term increasingly used by those involved in delivery of legal services to the poor and those of modest means. *Unbundling* refers to providing limited legal services that cover only part of a client's overall needs, often without the lawyer formally appearing in the proceedings. The legal services are sometimes rendered in addition to using non-lawyer resources.

Is that the case with such a website? The website's owner claims that none of his site's consumers are clients, just transitory users of forms and information. Is that possible? Under traditional definitions of "client," such as the *Kurtenbach* standard, is it reasonable to conclude that these consumers are indeed clients? If they are, what duties are they owed? What standards of care need to be met to

---

[6] We'll address this issue more in Problem 10, when we discuss advance waivers in cases of limited-scope multi-client representations.

[7] One site trumpets, "Our Experienced Personal Injury Attorneys and Insurance Claims Adjusters Make it SIMPLE AND EASY to Settle Your Injury Claim: DO IT YOURSELF AND SAVE."

reach a level of competent representation?

Although the term "unbundled" is now widely accepted, this website owner's use of the term is odd at best. There is no question that "unbundling" has become a widely accepted practice, especially when it relates to poor or otherwise unrepresented persons. Recent changes in the ethics rules of some states explicitly allow for unbundling in situations such as preparing papers but not going to court. We'll return to this topic in Problem 32, which discusses legal services for indigent persons. We mention it here because we wonder if this term is overused, particularly in the context of non-indigent representation. This overbroad use may mean unscrupulous lawyers are claiming they are mere "scriveners" and not responsible for the substance of their work, an issue we will briefly examine in Problem 7.

• *Ghostwriting.* A closely related issue concerns "ghostwriting" pleadings for *pro se* litigants. This is not an uncommon procedure; it might occur, for example, when a prospective client arrives on the lawyer's doorstep with a claim whose statute of limitations is about to run. One federal district court criticized lawyers who accepted a flat fee for drafting a *pro se* employment discrimination complaint for a group of plaintiffs. Not only did the judge find this conduct ethically objectionable, but also questioned whether the lawyers had violated Fed. R. Civ. Proc. 11, which requires that pleadings be "nonfrivolous" and presented only after a "reasonable inquiry" has been conducted into the facts and law.[8]

Although the court did not discipline the lawyers, in *Laremont-Lopez* (see the last footnote), many saw this case as putting counsel on notice of the dangers of ghostwriting pleadings. One issue that perturbed the judge was that the lawyers did not make their ghostwriting known to the court, in accordance with the holdings of several state ethics opinions. On the other hand, ghostwriting, which could be considered a type of unbundled service, can be used to help those otherwise unable to gain access to the court system. As Fordham ethics Professor Bruce Green, who served as Co-Chair of the ABA Litigation Section's ethics committee, commented, while a court might understandably be "annoyed" with the lawyers' failure to disclose, "requir[ing] lawyers who provide drafting assistance to sign the pleading, enter an appearance on that party's behalf, or refrain from providing any assistance whatsoever" may prevent them from serving those who need legal assistance. The ABA ethics committee chimed in Formal Opinion 07-446 (2007). It modified an earlier position and reasoned that lawyers need not disclose their involvement because "the fact that a litigant submitting papers to a tribunal on a *pro se* basis has received legal assistance behind the scenes is not material to the merits of the litigation, ..."

What of the potential malpractice consequences of a partial representation? In *Laremont-Lopez*, the plaintiffs, who paid for drafting the complaint, seem clearly to have been clients, albeit with a "limited scope of representation." However, several courts have denied malpractice claims where the claims were not directly within a clearly defined limited scope. Thus, in *Flatow v. Ingalls*, 932 N.E.2d 726

---

[8] Laremont-Lopez v. Southeastern Tidewater Opportunity Project, 968 F. Supp. 1075 (E.D. Va. 1997), *aff'd*, 172 F.3d 44 (4th Cir. 1999). We will examine Rule 11 in detail in Problem 16.

(Ind. Ct. App. 2010), a lawyer representing plaintiff only as to a defamation cause of action, a limitation clearly spelled out in the retainer agreement, had no duties as to other parts of the case. Similarly, *Dunn v. Westbrook*, 971 S.W.2d 252 (Ark. 1998) affirmed a summary judgment in favor of a lawyer in a legal malpractice case because the lawyer was specifically hired only to clarify ownership of a life insurance policy in a partnership agreement, and not to review the entire agreement.

What level of competence should be required of these limited-scope lawyers? Should the standard of care be lower because of the limited representation, or should it be the same as if the lawyers had put their names on the complaint? What are counsel's fiduciary duties to the plaintiffs? *Must* they investigate the claim, if not under Rule 11, then to protect themselves from malpractice liability? What of the good Samaritan lawyer who drafts a complaint *pro bono* in order to preserve an individual's claim? Has this lawyer taken on a client? Can such a lawyer avoid taking on fiduciary responsibilities? We'll discuss "scope of representation" issues further in the next section.

•   *Duties to Third Party Non-Clients.* A number of cases in various jurisdictions have addressed the issue of whether attorneys may owe duties of care to third parties who are, unarguably, *not* their clients. The issue has come up most frequently in cases involving the beneficiaries of a will who want to file a malpractice suit against the lawyer who drafted the will for the decedent, and cases of derivative liability based on a lawyer's false or negligent opinions on behalf of a financial client directed towards prospective investors. The leading early case is *Lucas v. Hamm*, 364 P.2d 685 (Cal. 1961), which upheld the beneficiaries' right to sue. Since that case, a growing number of jurisdictions have taken an increasingly liberal view of the ability of intended beneficiaries to sue for malpractice in spite of the continued importance of the concept "privity" in New York and a few other jurisdictions.[9]

4.   Retainer Agreements and "Scope of Representation"

Many states now require written fee contracts between lawyers and their clients, especially since the ABA Rules began requiring them after the Ethics 2000 Commission recommended a change. But some states still do not require written agreements. Are they required in the state where you intend to practice? Even where ethics rules don't currently require it, the advantages of such agreements are clear for both lawyer and client, while the disadvantages are not substantial. It is hard to imagine many circumstances in which a written memorialization of the fee arrangements is not a good idea. Such memorializations protect the client, by putting the understandings in writing and by clarifying ambiguous points, and also protect the lawyer, since in most jurisdictions, ambiguities in the agreement — and most "swearing contests" between lawyer and client — are likely to be resolved against the attorney.

Such agreements do not have to be complex. Often a simple "engagement letter" can suffice: a "Dear Client" missive that sets forth the agreement and asks for a

---

[9] *See* Supplemental Readings, #3.

signature acknowledgement in reply. But even if very basic, the agreement should clearly state the rate or other manner of compensation, the way in which the costs of suit are to be handled, and the *scope of the representation.*

By "scope of representation," we mean a clear delineation of which tasks are being performed by the attorney, and which are not. Clearly defining this scope is as — if not more — important as, a clear description of the fee itself. For instance, is the lawyer handling the incorporation responsible only for the incorporating documents, or for holding a first meeting of shareholders as well? Will the lawyer be considered general counsel? And how is the term "general counsel" defined? What services are covered, and which are subject to special arrangements?

When these matters are set out from the beginning, the parties — lawyer and client alike — have the clearest possible understanding of the lawyer's role. Without this, the lawyer's expectations about what legal services will be performed may differ materially from the client's expectations about what legal services have been promised. Fees are usually simply a matter of money. But a misunderstanding about the limits of the engagement can affect the entire case itself, leading to ill will at a minimum and a malpractice suit and even discipline at worst.

Since many states follow the general principle that for malpractice purposes, the reasonable expectations of the client are at least a factor in determining the duties of the lawyer, a clearly defined scope of representation becomes crucial. However, even where that scope of representation may appear to be clearly narrow, the lawyer may still have duties to at least inform the client of other remedies in other forums. In *Nichols v. Keller*, 15 Cal. App. 4th 1672 (1993), a lawyer retained to file a workers' compensation claim for Nichols failed to advise Nichols that Nichols might also have a third party personal injury claim. When the statute of limitations ran on the third party claim, Nichols sued for malpractice. The lawyer won a summary judgment motion in the trial court, but the court of appeals reversed. The higher court held that the lawyer was in a far better position to know of another remedy available to the client and thus had a duty to tell the client about that:

> Generally speaking, a workers' compensation attorney should be able to limit the retention to the compensation claim . . . . However, even when a retention is expressly limited, the attorney may still have a duty to alert the client to legal problems that are reasonably apparent, even though they fall outside the scope of the retention.

As we saw in the preceding section, however, where the scope of representation is limited to only a *portion* of the case, courts have more frequently denied malpractice claims.

There are several other issues that a good fee agreement should address. Are people other than the client involved? If a third party is paying the fee (even if it's a parent paying for a child) the lawyer would be well-advised to specify who the client is, and who it is not. Most states' ethics codes have strong regulations about ensuring the independent professional judgment of the lawyer. The ABA Model Rules have affirmed this important concept in three separate places. Comment 10 to MR 1.7 says that, "A lawyer may be paid from a source other than the client, if the client is informed of that fact and consents and the arrangement does not compromise the lawyer's duty of loyalty to the client." MR 1.8(f) explicitly requires that accepting compensation from another can only be done when "there is no interference with the lawyer's independence of professional judgment or with the client-lawyer relationship." Were that not enough, MR 5.4(c) is even broader: "A lawyer shall not permit a person who recommends, employs, or pays the lawyer to render legal services for another to direct or regulate the lawyer's professional judgment in rendering such legal services." An organized crime kingpin may buy a lawyer's services and try to influence the defense of his lieutenant, but it is clearly unethical for the lawyer to go along.

What about other provisions a lawyer might want in an engagement agreement? May counsel require mandatory arbitration of any fee dispute? How about mandatory arbitration of any malpractice claim? States differ on these issues, and conflicting viewpoints exist even within states. The development of the law on these matters — and how to apply the law to principles of legal ethics — is very much in flux. So, too, is the legality of "retaining liens," or the ability of the lawyer to "lien," or, retain possession of the client's file until paid. We discuss these more fully in Problem 9.

There is a broad national consensus on the invalidity of fee agreement provisions that forbid the client from settling the case without the lawyer's permission, or to settle only if it is understood that the lawyer will get paid what he or she "would have" gotten paid had only the client followed counsel's advice. Most states agree with this language from Nebraska Advisory Opinion 95-1 (1995): "[T]he client may not be asked to agree to . . . surrender the right to settle litigation that the lawyer may wish to continue." Citing a 1916 Minnesota case, the opinion concludes that "a contractual provision removing a client's ability to compromise, settle or negotiate his own claim would be void as against public policy." Lawyers also face limitations on withdrawing from an engagement, and ethics rules define the grounds that permit or in some situations mandate withdrawal. Restrictions are particularly clear in litigation where the withdrawal is subject to judicial approval. We will examine this issue more closely in Problems 10 and 25.

One final point about fee agreements: They should be set forth in a language understood by both attorney and client. That language is usually English, but can be Spanish, Korean, Arabic, or scores of other languages. The one language that should be avoided is "legalese." Fee agreements, as well as other communications with the client, should be written in terms the client can clearly understand.

In other words, we're confident that you can do better than the fee agreement printed below, now about 15 years old. It was proffered proudly to one of us by a California lawyer at a malpractice avoidance seminar who asked whether this exemplar, which he got from a friend in New York, would fill the bill. Our answer? "Not so much."

> Further to our discussions with regard to the submissions attached, the following when countersigned by you will constitute this the agreement between us with respect to legal services to be rendered by me and my law firm on your behalf. You have requested and I hereby agree to render legal representation and counseling on your behalf as and when requested by

you in connection with making submissions to specified publishers and production companies. Such representation shall include but not be limited to submissions, general trade and business information, contract negotiation and document revision, and counseling . . . .

With respect to the legal services to be rendered in accordance with this Agreement and on your behalf, we bill matters such as this monthly, on a reasonable fee basis . . . . The fee to be charged — as mutually agreed — for the services to be rendered by me hereunder shall be 10% percent of all ("net") gross income (including fees, advances, royalties and other remuneration) earned by or paid to you, anyone on your behalf, and any of your corporate affiliates or entities for which I may render services hereunder with respect to the submitted work . . . . For the purpose of this Agreement, the term "net" gross income shall be defined as all gross income less distribution fees, and telephone service company charges. The fee to be charged for any additional, specific service shall be billed at an hourly rate of between $135.00–$175.00 per hour depending on the reasonability of the fee . . . based on the overall circumstances and your need.

Before you move on, think about the effect such confusing, even unintelligible, language could have on the attorney-client relationship.

5. Contingency Fees

Are contingency fees necessary to provide litigants access to the courts? Or is the contingency fee largely responsible for creating conflicts of interest between clients and their lawyers, as so-called "tort reformers" claim? While they have now been around for some time, contingency fees are still a relatively new form of payment. Most European countries forbid such fees, while Great Britain has only permitted them since 1995. Indeed, allowing such fees requires an exception to the long-standing ethical precept that in order to maintain independent professional judgment on behalf of the client, a lawyer must not acquire a proprietary interest in the client's case.[10]

A lawyer is generally prohibited from having a "proprietary interest" in the client's case because it can be harder to advise the client objectively when the lawyer has a "piece of the action." And yet, this is clearly what happens with contingency fees. Were this not enough, modern fee arrangements might have lawyers receiving hybrid contingency fees, such as a reduced hourly sum plus a smaller contingency in the event of a substantial recovery, or a combination of contingency and statutory fees, in which the attorney gets the greater of the two. These hybrid fees put even more pressure on the lawyer's ability to maintain independent professional judgment, especially since the more complicated the fee arrangement, the harder it will be, particularly for unsophisticated clients, to understand it clearly.

---

[10] See MR 1.8(j) and DR 5-103(A), which specifically exempt certain contingency fees.

The fee agreement below, the subject of litigation after the law firm entered bankruptcy (and the subject of Part III of our Problem above), purports to be a contingency fee agreement. Is it? Note the difference between the contingency fee and the "Enhanced Fee" described in this agreement, and when the lawyers may elect which type of fee to receive.

BROBECK, PHLEGER & HARRISON LLP CONTINGENCY FEE CONTRACT

JULY 20, 2001

Tickets.com

Attn: W. Thomas Gimple

Co-Chairman and Chief Executive Officer

Re: Contingency Fee Arrangement

This letter agreement . . . sets forth our mutual understanding regarding the continuation of the representation of Tickets.com, Inc., a Delaware corporation ("Tickets"), by Brobeck, Phleger & Harrison LLP ("Brobeck") in connection with the case captioned Ticketmaster Corporation [et al.] v. Tickets.com, Inc.

Tickets has requested that we consider continuing to represent Tickets in the Litigation on a contingency fee basis. As we discussed, contingency fee arrangements shift the risk of success in the Litigation, at least in part, from the client to the lawyer. We have discussed the terms of this Agreement and the compensation Brobeck may be entitled to receive for that risk shifting. . . . Tickets has confirmed that it has sought and obtained the advice of independent counsel with respect to this agreement.

As we have discussed, Brobeck would not normally be willing to undertake the arrangements contemplated by this Agreement . . . . Brobeck is concerned, as you know, about Tickets' solvency and ability to compensate Brobeck for its services through the trial date . . . .

Given all of this, Tickets and Brobeck agree as follows:

1. *Control of Litigation.* Tickets, as client, will retain ultimate authority to decide all issues that materially affect its cause . . . .

. . . .

6. *Contingent Fee.* Tickets shall pay to Brobeck, and Brobeck will be entitled to receive as attorneys' fees for the "contingent work" (defined below) . . . a fee which is contingent upon the outcome achieved at any Resolution ("Contract Contingent Fee"). The amount of the Contract Contingent Fee shall be . . . fifty percent (50%) of the "Case Recovery" . . . .

. . . .

7. *Costs.* Tickets shall pay all costs, disbursements and out-of-pocket expenses associated with the Litigation . . . . If Tickets fails to make any required deposit of

Trial Costs (to a maximum of $2.5 million . . .) set forth [herein], Brobeck, in its sole and unfettered discretion, may withdraw as counsel in the Litigation . . . .

8. Compensation in the Event of Withdrawal. If Tickets fails to make any required deposit of Trial Costs, and Brobeck elects to withdraw as counsel in the Litigation, Tickets shall pay, and Brobeck, in its sole and unfettered discretion, shall be entitled to receive, as compensation for the legal services provided in the Litigation, either (a) the amount of Contract Contingent Fee or (b) the aggregate timekeepers' fees incurred by Brobeck in connection with the Litigation . . . , calculated at 250% of Brobeck's guideline hourly rates in effect from time to time (the "Enhanced Hourly Fee").

   . . . .

10. *Settlement Authority.* Brobeck shall not settle the Litigation except with the consent of Tickets, and Tickets agrees that its consent will not unreasonably be withheld. If Brobeck or Tickets desires to settle the Litigation after receipt of a settlement proposal, and the other party objects to such settlement proposal, . . . then whether Tickets shall accept the settlement proposal shall be referred to the Arbitrator [a specific retired federal judge in San Francisco] within the next ten (10) days for determination. Tickets and Brobeck shall present their respective positions with respect to the settlement proposal in such form and at such time as determined by the Arbitrator. If the Arbitrator determines that the settlement proposal should be accepted in light of all circumstances known to him, then Tickets and Brobeck shall accept the settlement proposal. If the Arbitrator determines that the settlement proposal should not be accepted in light of all the circumstances known to him, then Tickets shall not accept the settlement proposal.

If Tickets takes some action with respect to the acceptance or rejection of a settlement proposal which impairs the operation of the terms of this paragraph 10 with respect to cooperation in developing and responding to settlement options or opportunities and to which Brobeck objects, Brobeck, in its sole and unfettered discretion, may withdraw as counsel in the Litigation . . . . In the event that Brobeck withdraws as counsel under this paragraph 10, Brobeck shall be entitled to elect between the Enhanced Fee, calculated as set forth in paragraph 8 above, or the Contract Contingent Fee.

   . . . .

14. *Right to Discharge Brobeck and Brobeck's Right to Withdraw.* Tickets shall have the unfettered right during the course of the Litigation to terminate the Brobeck representation. If Brobeck is discharged by Tickets, Brobeck shall elect in writing, before or within thirty days of its receipt of written notice from Tickets of terminating the representation, whether it selects Enhanced Fee or Contract Contingent Fee recovery as its fee. Similarly, and any other provisions of this Agreement notwithstanding, Brobeck shall have the unfettered right during the course of the Litigation to withdraw without cause in accordance with this Paragraph 14.

If Brobeck elects to withdraw under this Paragraph 14, as opposed to being discharged by Tickets or to withdrawing in accordance with other rights of withdrawal set forth in other provisions herein, the . . . parties will submit the question of the amount due Brobeck as and for its fees to an expedited arbitration, and the arbitrator's award for Brobeck's contingency work, which award will be binding and final, shall be for not less than 50% of Brobeck's guideline rates or more than the greater of 250% of Brobeck's guideline rates or the Contract Contingency Fee.

16. *Change of Control.* If [a change in control in Tickets occurs], Brobeck, in its sole and unfettered discretion, shall have the right to withdraw as counsel in the Litigation.

If there is a Change of Control and Brobeck elects to withdraw as counsel in the Litigation, Tickets shall pay, and Brobeck shall be entitled to receive as compensation for the legal services provided in the Litigation, either (a) the amount of Contract Contingent Fee or (b) the Enhanced Hourly Fee . . . .

Very truly yours,

BROBECK, PHLEGER & HARRISON LLP
By: /s/ Stephen M. Snyder

_____

Stephen M. Snyder
Partner

ACCEPTED AND AGREED TO:

TICKETS.COM INC.

NOTES

Because you are to evaluate this fee agreement under Part III of the Problem, we will not do so here. Suffice it to say that the panoply of improprieties in this agreement makes it one of the worst we have seen.

6.   Structured Settlements and Other Contingency Fee Issues

"Structured settlements" are often used in larger personal injury claims. Such settlements usually involve the purchase of an annuity by the paying party, such as an insurance company, which allows the plaintiff to be paid periodically over a term of years. There can be advantages to an annuity for plaintiffs who are minors and need protection of their settlement funds, or who have serious, permanent injuries, such as paralysis, which require continual ongoing medical care, that the periodic payments could be "structured" to cover.

But in a "structured settlement," how does the lawyer get paid? Lawyers are not generally happy to accept their fees in small payments over time. Recognizing this, defendants and insurance companies will often offer a substantial portion of the settlement in "up front" money, to cover the payment of those fees. Is this method fair to the client? Does such a proposal create an overt conflict between lawyer and client, making it even more difficult than in the ordinary fee situation to exercise *independent* judgment on behalf of the client?

One California ethics opinion stated that a lawyer could not appropriately insist on being paid the entirety of the legal fee "up front" because that might excessively diminish the client's portion of the recovery. The opinion based its reasoning not just on the California rule on excessive fees but "because Attorney's ongoing fiduciary duty to Client prohibits Attorney from collecting her fees in a way that defeats the very purpose of Client's willingness to settle."[11]

Other issues that arise with contingency fees that can have important financial implications include how costs are computed in relation to the fees. If costs are deducted from the gross amount awarded, before fees are computed, they come out of both the client's and the lawyer's shares of the recovery. But if *fees* are computed first, the costs wind up coming from the *client's* portion of the recovery alone. In *Baker v. Whitaker*, 887 S.W.2d 664 (Mo. Ct. App. 1994), a client agreed to pay a percentage of "amounts paid to me." When the client got a $1 million settlement, the existence of $200,000 in medical costs meant that how this phrase was interpreted — and whether the lawyer computed the fee as a percentage of the gross of $1 million or the net of $800,000 — had a substantial financial impact. The *Baker* court remanded the case, but strongly suggested the contract should be construed against the lawyer drafting the agreement.

Why, given all the potential problems, do all of our jurisdictions allow contingency fees in personal injury and other similar cases? The biggest argument in favor is access: the ability to go to court for those who don't have the money to fund litigation, but who have a legitimate complaint against someone, often an adversary with far more power and money. It is a valid argument, and though tort reformers argue that it opens the courts' floodgates to frivolous litigation, contingency fee lawyers don't get paid unless the client does, giving attorneys a disincentive for filing weak cases. And while contingency fees give a lawyer a "proprietary interest" in the client's case, that interest is usually closely aligned with the client's interest. The more money the lawyer can recover for the client, the more the lawyer gets paid. Finally, proponents argue that even if the lawyer gets more than an average hourly fee with a favorable outcome, the lawyer has assumed from the client most of the risks of the costs of litigation.[12]

On balance, given the importance of access and that few cases are sure things, contingency fees seem not only necessary but valuable to the client, but they do place an added burden on lawyers' shoulders to make sure their judgment is exercised in the client's best interests, not their own. There remain plenty of opportunities for abuse.

---

[11] California Formal Opinion 1994-135 (1994).

[12] Tort reformers disagree, claiming that too often, such as when liability is clear in a personal injury case, "contingency" fees are hardly contingent at all. They also argue that while there may be incentives for lawyers to work hard in "big" cases, there are disincentives for hard work and solid preparation in cases of lower value. *See, e.g.*, Lester Brickman, *Contingent Fees Without Contingencies: Hamlet Without the Prince of Denmark?*, 37 UCLA L. REV. 29 (1989). See also Problem 9, Part III.

7.   Excessive Fees?

Every jurisdiction in the country has an ethical rule that prohibits excessive or unreasonable fees. Most rules, like ABA Model Rule 1.5, which states that "A lawyer shall not make an agreement for, charge, or collect an unreasonable fee or an unreasonable amount for expenses," are accompanied by a laundry list of factors to be considered in determining whether the fee in question is "excessive" or "reasonable." But these are just words until they are applied. Since state bars and other lawyer regulatory agencies have only rarely imposed discipline for charging an excessive fee, the most frequent forum for discussing the reasonableness of fees is either a request for fees or a lawsuit arising from a fee dispute. How do courts interpret the reasonableness of a fee? The answer, not surprisingly, is "It depends." Here are two very different views from courts at opposite ends of the country.

BROBECK, PHLEGER & HARRISON v. TELEX CORP.
602 F.2d 866 (9th Cir.), *cert. denied*, 444 U.S. 981 (1979)[13]

Per Curiam.

This is a diversity action in which the plaintiff, the San Francisco law firm of Brobeck, Phleger & Harrison ("Brobeck"), sued the Telex Corporation ("Telex") to recover $1,000,000 in attorney's fees. Telex had engaged Brobeck on a contingency fee basis to prepare a petition for certiorari after the Tenth Circuit reversed a $259.5 million judgment in Telex's favor against International Business Machines Corporation ("IBM") and affirmed an $18.5 million counterclaim judgment for IBM against Telex. Brobeck prepared and filed the petition, and after Telex entered a "wash settlement" with IBM in which both parties released their claims against the other, Brobeck sent Telex a bill for $1,000,000, that it claimed Telex owed it under their written contingency fee agreement. When Telex refused to pay, Brobeck brought this action. Both parties filed motions for summary judgment. The district Court granted Brobeck's motion, awarding Brobeck $1,000,000 plus interest. Telex now appeals. . . .

Having had reversed one of the largest antitrust judgments in history, Telex officials decided to press the Tenth Circuit's decision to the United States Supreme Court. To maximize Telex's chances for having its petition for certiorari granted, they decided to search for the best available lawyer. They compiled a list of the preeminent antitrust and Supreme Court lawyers in the country, and Roger Wheeler, Telex's Chairman of the Board, settled on Moses Lasky of the Brobeck firm as the best possibility.

[Eventually, the following fee agreement between Lasky and Telex was signed.]

MEMORANDUM

1. Retainer of $25,000.00 to be paid. If Writ of Certiorari is denied and no settlement has been effected in excess of the Counterclaim, then the $25,000.00

---

[13] The use of another case involving the former Brobeck firm is entirely coincidental.

retainer shall be the total fee paid; provided, however, that

. . . .

3. Once a Petition for Writ of Certiorari has been filed with the Clerk of the United States Supreme Court then Brobeck will be entitled to the payment of an additional fee in the event of a recovery by Telex from IBM by way of settlement or judgment of its claims against IBM; and, such additional fee will be five percent (5%) of the first $100,000,000.00 gross of such recovery, undiminished by any recovery by IBM on its counterclaims or cross-claims. The maximum contingent fee to be paid is $5,000,000.00, provided that if recovery by Telex from IBM is less than $40,000,000.00 gross, the five percent (5%) shall be based on the net recovery, i.e., the recovery after deducting the credit to IBM by virtue of IBM's recovery on counterclaims or cross-claims, but the contingent fee shall not then be less than $1,000,000.00.

. . . .

[Telex president] Jatras signed Lasky's proposed agreement, and on February 28 returned it to Lasky with a letter and a check for $25,000 as the agreed retainer. To "clarify" his thinking on the operation of the fee agreement, Jatras attached a set of hypothetical examples to the letter. This "attachment" stated the amount of the fee that would be paid to Brobeck assuming judgment or settlements in eight different amounts. In the first hypothetical, which assumed a settlement of $18.5 million and a counterclaim judgment of $18.5 million, Jatras listed a "net recovery" by Telex of "$0" and a Brobeck contingency fee of "$0."

Lasky received the letter and attachment on March 3. Later that same day he replied: "Your attachment of examples of our compensation in various contingencies is correct, it being understood that the first example is applicable only to a situation where the petition for certiorari has been denied, as stated in paragraph 1 of the memorandum."

No Telex official responded to Lasky's letter. . . .

Lasky, as agreed, prepared the petition for certiorari and filed it in July 1975.
. . .

[A Telex settlement] meeting was held on September 5. Lasky told the assembled Telex officials that the chances that the petition for certiorari would be granted were very good. Wheeler, however, was concerned that if the petition for certiorari was denied, the outstanding counterclaim judgment would threaten Telex with bankruptcy. Wheeler informed Lasky that Telex was seriously considering the possibility of a "wash settlement" in which neither side would recover anything and each would release their claims against the other. Lasky responded that in the event of such a settlement he would be entitled to a fee of $1,000,000.

. . . .

On October 2 IBM officials . . . contacted Telex and the parties agreed that IBM would release its counterclaim judgment against Telex in exchange for Telex's dismissal of its petition for certiorari. On October 3, at the request of Wheeler and Jatras, Lasky had the petition for certiorari withdrawn. Thereafter, he sent a bill to

Telex for $1,000,000.

. . . .

Telex contends that the $1 million fee was so excessive as to render the contract unenforceable. Alternatively, it argues that unconscionability depends on the contract's reasonableness, a question of fact that should be submitted to the jury.

Preliminarily, we note that whether a contract is fair or works an unconscionable hardship is determined with reference to the time when the contract was made and cannot be resolved by hindsight.

There is no dispute about the facts leading to Telex's engagement of the Brobeck firm. Telex was an enterprise threatened with bankruptcy. It had won one of the largest money judgments in history, but that judgment had been reversed in its entirety by the Tenth Circuit. In order to maximize its chances of gaining review by the United States Supreme Court, it sought to hire the most experienced and capable lawyer it could possibly find. After compiling a list of highly qualified lawyers, it settled on Lasky as the most able. Lasky was interested but wanted to bill Telex on an hourly basis. After Telex insisted on a contingent fee arrangement, Lasky made it clear that he would consent to such an arrangement only if he would receive a sizable contingent fee in the event of success.

In these circumstances, the contract between Telex and Brobeck was not so unconscionable that "no man in his senses and not under a delusion would make on the one hand, and as no honest and fair man would accept on the other." This is not a case where one party took advantage of another's ignorance, exerted superior bargaining power, or disguised unfair terms in small print. Rather, Telex, a multi-million [dollar] corporation, represented by able counsel, sought to secure the best attorney it could find to prepare its petition for certiorari, insisting on a contingent fee contract. Brobeck fulfilled its obligation to gain a stay of judgment and to prepare and file the petition for certiorari. Although the minimum fee was clearly high, Telex received substantial value from Brobeck's services. For, as Telex acknowledged, Brobeck's petition provided Telex with the leverage to secure a discharge of its counterclaim judgment, thereby saving it from possible bankruptcy in the event the Supreme Court denied its petition for certiorari. We conclude that such a contract was not unconscionable.

NOTES

What do you think of Lasky's response to Telex president Jatras' note on hypothetical fee situations? By saying the hypothetical was "correct," was Lasky misleading Jatras? Or was Lasky's explanation of what he meant by "correct" sufficient? What obligations should counsel have to make their fee agreements clear and unambiguous? On whom should the burden of an ambiguous agreement fall? Lest you think lawyers are given complete *carte blanche* by courts, read this next case. Can you reconcile *Brobeck* and the *Fordham* decision, below, or do they appear to be inconsistent?

IN RE FORDHAM
668 N.E.2d 816 (Mass. 1996)

This is an appeal from the Board of Bar Overseers' dismissal of a petition for discipline filed by bar counsel against attorney Laurence S. Fordham. On March 11, 1992, bar counsel served Fordham with a petition for discipline alleging that Fordham had charged a clearly excessive fee . . . for defending Timothy Clark in the District Court against a charge that he operated a motor vehicle while under the influence of intoxicating liquor . . . .

After five days of hearings, and with "serious reservations," the hearing committee concluded that Fordham's fee was not substantially in excess of a reasonable fee and . . . recommended against bar discipline. Bar counsel appealed from that determination. . . . We direct a judgment ordering public censure be entered in the county court.

We summarize the hearing committee's findings. On March 4, 1989, the Acton police department arrested Timothy, then twenty-one years old, and charged him with OUI, operating a motor vehicle after suspension, speeding, and operating an unregistered motor vehicle. At the time of the arrest, the police discovered a partially full quart of vodka in the vehicle. After failing a field sobriety test, Timothy was taken to the Acton police station where he submitted to two breathalyzer tests which registered .10 and .12 respectively.

Subsequent to Timothy's arraignment, he and his father, Laurence Clark (Clark) consulted with three lawyers, who offered to represent Timothy for fees between $3,000 and $10,000. Shortly after the arrest, Clark went to Fordham's home to service an alarm system which he had installed several years before. While there, Clark discussed Timothy's arrest with Fordham's wife who invited Clark to discuss the case with Fordham. Fordham then met with Clark and Timothy.

At this meeting, Timothy described the incidents leading to his arrest and the charges against him. Fordham, whom the hearing committee described as a "very experienced senior trial attorney with impressive credentials," told Clark and Timothy that he had never represented a client in a driving while under the influence case or in any criminal matter, and he had never tried a case in the District Court. The hearing committee found that "Fordham explained that although he lacked experience in this area, he was a knowledgeable and hard-working attorney and that he believed he could competently represent Timothy." Fordham described himself as 'efficient and economic in the use of [his] time.' . . .

"Towards the end of the meeting, Fordham told the Clarks that he worked on [a] time charge basis and that he billed monthly. . . . He also told the Clarks that he would engage others in his firm to prepare the case. Clark had indicated that he would pay Timothy's legal fees." After the meeting, Clark hired Fordham to represent Timothy. [Fordham eventually won an innovative motion to suppress the blood alcohol results obtained by a breathalyzer. Then he gained acquittal for Clark at trial before a judge sitting without a jury.]

. . . .

Fordham [billed] Clark $50,022.25, reflecting 227 hours of billed time, 153 hours of which were expended by Fordham and seventy-four of which were his associates' time. Clark did not pay the first two bills when they became due and expressed to Fordham his concern about their amount. Clark paid Fordham $10,000 on June 20, 1989. At that time, Fordham assured Clark that most of the work had been completed "other than taking [the case] to trial." Clark did not make any subsequent payments. . . .

Bar counsel and Fordham have stipulated that all the work billed by Fordham was actually done and that Fordham and his associates spent the time they claim to have spent. They also have stipulated that Fordham acted conscientiously, diligently, and in good faith in representing Timothy and in his billing in this case.

. . . The board noted that "[a]lthough none of the experts who testified at the disciplinary hearing had ever heard of a fee in excess of $15,000 for a first-offense OUI case, the hearing committee found that [Clark] had entered into the transaction with open eyes after interviewing other lawyers with more experience in such matters."

In reviewing the hearing committee's and the board's analysis of the various factors, as appearing in DR 2-106(B), which are to be considered for a determination as to whether a fee is clearly excessive, . . . we are persuaded that [the fee was] clearly excessive.

The first factor listed in DR 2-106(B) requires examining "[t]he time and labor required, the novelty and difficulty of the questions involved, and the skill requisite to perform the legal service properly." Although the hearing committee determined that Fordham "spent a large number of hours on [the] matter, in essence learning from scratch what others . . . already know," [t]he hearing committee reasoned that even if the number of hours Fordham "spent [were] wholly out of proportion" to the number of hours that a lawyer with experience in the trying of OUI cases would require, the committee was not required to conclude that the fee based on time spent was "clearly excessive." . . . We disagree.

Four witnesses testified before the hearing committee as experts on OUI cases. One of the experts, testifying on behalf of bar counsel, opined that there were no unusual circumstances in the OUI charge against Timothy and that it was a "standard operating under the influence case." The witness did agree that Fordham's argument for suppression of the breathalyzer test results, which was successful, was novel and would have justified additional time and labor. He also acknowledged that the acquittal was a good result; even with the suppression of the breathalyzer tests, he testified, the chances of an acquittal would have been "[n]ot likely at a bench trial." . . . [A second expert testified similarly.]

An expert called by Fordham testified that the facts of Timothy's case presented a challenge and that without the suppression of the breathalyzer test results it would have been "an almost impossible situation in terms of prevailing on the trier of fact." He further stated that, based on the particulars in Timothy's case, he believed that Fordham's hours were not excessive . . . . The fourth expert witness, called by Fordham, testified [similarly]. . . .

Based on the testimony of the four experts, the number of hours devoted to Timothy's OUI case by Fordham and his associates was substantially in excess of the hours that a prudent experienced lawyer would have spent [:] several times the amount of time any of the witnesses had ever spent on a similar case. We are not unmindful of the novel and successful motion to suppress the breathalyzer test results, but that effort cannot justify a $50,000 fee in a type of case in which the usual fee is less than one-third of that amount.

The board determined that "[b]ecause [Fordham] had never tried an OUI case or appeared in the district court, [Fordham] spent over 200 hours preparing the case, in part to educate himself in the relevant substantive law and court procedures." Fordham's inexperience in criminal defense work and OUI cases in particular cannot justify the extraordinarily high fee. It cannot be that an inexperienced lawyer is entitled to charge three or four times as much as an experienced lawyer for the same service. A client "should not be expected to pay for the education of a lawyer when he spends excessive amounts of time on tasks which, with reasonable experience, become matters of routine."

. . . .

In charging a clearly excessive fee, Fordham departed substantially from the obligation of professional responsibility that he owed to his client. . . . Accordingly, a judgment is to be entered in the county court imposing a public censure.

NOTES

Does it matter that Lasky's fee was contingent and Fordham's fee hourly? (Note that contingency fees are almost universally prohibited in criminal cases.) What other factors distinguish these two cases? One is the difference between representing individuals and representing sophisticated corporations, especially when juries are the final arbiters of fact. Thus in November 1999, Houston's Piro & Lilly suffered a $6.3 million award against them and in favor of their client, the ex-wife of a billionaire who had challenged her prenuptial contract. The lawyers had charged a contingency fee that the client claimed was unconscionably excessive. The client's new lawyer claimed that "you can put the entire client file in two file boxes," and that the fee charged gave Piro $47,379 per hour for his 67 hours of billed time, while his partner received $8,079 per hour. The lawyers argued that the great result they had obtained for their client more than justified their fees, an argument not unlike Lasky's and Fordham's claims.[14]

Should the sophistication of the client clearly be a factor underlying all of these decisions? What about using the standard in the community as a barometer for determining excessive fees? Is this reasonable, or could it lead to unjust results if all lawyers in the locality charge what most people would consider unfair?[15]

---

[14] *See* Margaret Cronin Fisk, *Two Texas Lawyers Hit with $6.3M Overcharging Verdict*, Nat'l L.J., Dec. 6, 1999.

[15] Note that using the community standard has its limits. In *Goldfarb v. Virginia State Bar*, 421 U.S. 773 (1975) the Supreme Court held that a bar association could not set minimum fees without violating the Sherman Anti-Trust Act. California has eliminated the community standard factor entirely from its fee-evaluation rule. Cal. Rule of Prof'l Conduct 4-200.

Limits on excessive fees are not uniformly applied, even when the client is an individual. In yet another case involving a wealthy couple's divorce, a Tennessee appeals court upheld a lawyer's fee of $175,000, even though billings at an hourly rate totaled under $58,000. The court noted that while the hourly fee was set at $185 an hour, the contract stated that the client's "ultimate fee may vary depending on [factors including] the skill requisite to perform the legal service properly, or the amount involved and the results obtained," basically repeating some of the factors in the Tennessee rule on unreasonable fees. In an unpublished but well-circulated opinion, the court reasoned that this language put the client on notice that "the agreement provided for a fee in addition to [the lawyer's] customary hourly fee."[16]

Finally, under the category of "nothing lasts forever," a Washington State appeals court ruled that where a law firm's fee, set in 1972, for helping two entrepreneurs develop a shopping mall was discounted initially in return for 5% of the cash distribution from the mall in perpetuity, resulting in the original approximate $8,000 fee blossoming into a total of $380,000, the fee was unreasonable. The court took the position that a fee contract, generally evaluated at the time it is made, could be reevaluated in the face of subsequent altered circumstances such as these.[17]

8. Must Reasonable Fees Be Proportional to a Case's Dollar Value?

What fees may a court deem "reasonable" when measured against the amount of the client's recovery? *City of Riverside v. Rivera*, 477 U.S. 561 (1986), concerned allegations against the city of Riverside, California that police officers unlawfully entered people's homes and committed other violations of the Bill of Rights, and also engaged in racial and ethnic slurs against the mostly Latino plaintiffs. A federal district court ordered payment of almost $250,000 in legal fees in a case where the plaintiffs' recovery was only $33,350. A sharply divided Supreme Court held that the amount of attorneys' fees awarded in a civil rights action need not be proportional to the monetary recovery. Justice Brennan, writing for the Court, said that barring such fee recoveries would substantially diminish the incentive of lawyers to take on civil rights cases.

The dissents of both Chief Justice Burger and Justice Rehnquist, however, found both the fee and the amount of time spent flatly unreasonable. Rehnquist noted that the two plaintiffs' lawyers spent almost 2,000 hours on a case in which the jury awarded a mere $13,300 in damages for the violation of plaintiffs' federal constitutional rights. Despite the public benefit of the litigation, Rehnquist analogized to a lawyer who charges a client $25,000 to protect title to "Blackacre," a piece of real property worth only $10,000, and found the fee award unreasonable *per se*.

---

[16] Silva v. Buckley, Tenn. Ct. App. No. M2002-00045-COA-R3-CV (12/31/03).

[17] Holmes v. Loveless, 94 P.3d 338 (Wash. Ct. App. 2004).

Justice Powell provided the swing vote, noting that "the court may consider the vindication of constitutional rights in addition to the amount of damages," and noted that the district court had "made an explicit finding that the 'public interest' had been served by the jury's verdict."

The point of *Riverside v. Rivera* appears to be that a determination of the reasonableness of a lawyer's fee need not turn solely on the *economic* benefit received by the lawyer's clients, but it must be tied to *some* benefit, in this case to the public interest. On the other hand, in *Evans v. Jeff D.*, 475 U.S. 717 (1986), heard in the same term as *Rivera*, the Court determined that a settlement involving non-economic relief could be conditioned on a *waiver* of attorneys' fees. This time Brennan dissented, concerned that this could result in a disincentive to lawyers otherwise willing to take on cases involving non-economic public interests. Several states tried to find ways around this by allowing clients to agree in advance *not* to waive the attorneys' fees at settlement without that agreement waiving the clients' right to control settlement.[18]

What about circumstances not involving injunctive or other equitable relief, where a lawyer, knowing that a case is not likely to be financially viable, nevertheless undertakes the representation? Take, for example, a small business dispute over the payment of $10,000, where there is no provision for the payment of attorneys' fees and the lawyer will charge between $7,500 and $15,000 to perform the work. Do lawyers owe any duties to their prospective clients to warn them that such cases are likely to result in only one winner — the lawyer? Is undertaking such a case at least arguably a breach of fiduciary duty, in that the client's interests are subordinated to the lawyer's fee?

In *In re Taxman Clothing Co.*, 49 F.3d 310 (7th Cir. 1995), counsel for a bankruptcy trustee was denied fees when the court determined that his pursuit of the bankruptcy estate's claims cost more than the probable revenue to the estate. Even if the lawyer had not intentionally acted merely to generate work for himself, to plunge ahead without adequately evaluating the financial viability of the claims breached the lawyer's fiduciary duty.

9. Business Relationships, "IPOs," and Lawyer-Client "Deals"

Agreements for the payment of fees are hardly the only financial circumstances that can create conflicts between lawyer and client. According to the *National Law Journal*, one of the frequent complaints about high-powered entertainment lawyers is that they "don additional hats as business or personal managers, lenders or investors." The suspicion is that they "risk . . . placing their personal or financial interests above those of their clients." Because a lawyer has a fiduciary relationship with the client — one in which the client should be entitled to repose trust — all business transactions between lawyers and their clients should be closely scrutinized.

---

[18] *See, e.g.*, California State Bar Formal Ethics Opinion 1994-136 (1994).

While it's clear that entering into a real estate partnership with a client or lending or borrowing a client's money is a business transaction, what if the client assigns the lawyer the rights to her life story in return for representation? The ABA Model Rules address this issue in the conflict rules rather than under fee arrangements. Does this organization of the Rules make sense to you? Where does the interest of the lawyer lie in that circumstance — to get the client off, or to have the rights to a best-selling book?

One of the problems in evaluating the responsibilities of lawyers who enter business relationships with clients is the issue of when an attorney's fiduciary duty begins. In many states, while the attorney's fiduciary duty exists from the moment the lawyer has a client (as we saw earlier in discussing the *Kurtenbach* case), the contract for fees is considered an "arms-length transaction" in which the lawyer is free to negotiate as any businessperson would — at arm's length. While this view may make some sense from the point of view of the lawyer, it would appear to endanger unsophisticated clients who may be seeking representation for the first time.

This accusation is one that has often been hurled at Silicon Valley law firms that invest in their start-up clients. Firms such as Wilson, Sonsini, Goodrich & Rosati and the Venture Law Group have earned well-deserved reputations both as entrepreneurs and lawyers. So long as their investment is made at the inception of the relationship, they would argue that they owe no fiduciary duty at the time that investment is agreed to. Lawyers still have to meet the requirements of their state's rules on engaging in business transactions with a client. But when a start-up with a great idea, a great product, but no money comes to a big, powerful law firm, the start-up's principals may feel they have little choice but to accede to the firm's demands.

Investing in clients is an increasingly common occurrence, no longer limited to a few parts of the country. It is clear that if one properly follows all the safeguards involved in doing business with clients, the practice is presumptively ethical. But are there so many pitfalls along the road that prudence, if not ethics, should make law firms forbear from this practice? Read the following article.

Jonathan Ringel, *Investing in Clients: Sunny Gains, But Others See Ethics Cloud*

FULTON COUNTY DAILY REPORT (February 7, 2000)[19]

Atlanta law firms are discovering what their counterparts in Silicon Valley have known for years — investing in clients may be the best idea since the billable hour.

The practice, which has helped Internet start-ups raise capital and save legal fees, also has raised tricky ethics questions. . . . Some see conflicts of interest when lawyers who own a piece of their clients give advice that will directly affect the value of the lawyers' investment. Others say stock ownership, when limited, doesn't enhance a lawyer's temptation for misconduct.

Atlanta Firms Jump In

As legal ethicists debate, Atlanta firms are getting into the act . . . . A two-year-old firm called The Red Hot Law Group has opened an adjacent mentoring program for start-up clients who pay for their legal services with warrants allowing the law firm to own 5 percent of the company . . . .

Not New in Silicon Valley

Silicon Valley firms have been investing in their clients for 30 years, says Craig W. Johnson, chairman of the Venture Law Group in Menlo Park, Calif.

"The only reason this is interesting now is because the returns have been astronomical," says Johnson. For example, Johnson notes, the firm invested $30,000 in Yahoo! while helping the Internet giant go public. Yahoo! is worth more than $90 billion today.

Asked how the firm did, Johnson says only, "We sold too early."

. . . .

Lawyers say limiting a firm's investment in clients is key to avoiding ethics problems. But Andrew L. Kaufman, who teaches professional responsibility at Harvard Law School, is uncomfortable with the prospect that a lawyer's advice might affect the value of his or her investment. "As a lawyer you might be thinking to give cautious advice," he says. "As an entrepreneur, you might be more of a risk taker."

Stanford Law School legal ethics professor William H. Simon takes a different view. He says ethics fears surrounding lawyers investing in their clients are "unwarranted," although he acknowledges that lawyers obviously should not compromise their legal responsibility because they are too invested in the value of the company. He points out, in the interest of full disclosure, that his wife practices law at a Silicon Valley firm that invests in its clients.

Simon says a lawyer can be just as tempted to bend rules to keep its client afloat when the client's demise will mean the end of a major source of legal fees as it is to protect a stock investment. "You don't want the lawyer to compromise her ethics because she's too invested in the success" of her client, whether the client represents too much of a lawyer's client base or stock portfolio, he says. For that reason, Simon suggests that firms investing in their clients have, at the most, no more than 5 percent of a client's stock.

Harvard's Kaufman disagrees that the ethics problems presented by investments are the same as those related to fees. When lawyers are paid in cash, he says, as opposed to in stock, "what you get isn't determined by the advice you give."

. . . .

A Potential Problem

W. Pitts Carr, a shareholder lawsuit expert at Atlanta's Carr, Tabb & Freeman, says he sees nothing wrong with lawyers owning stock in corporations and representing those corporations in litigation or writing their contracts.

Carr does suggest a potential problem, even if he adds he's never seen it happen. If lawyers approve press releases or Securities and Exchange Commission disclosures, he says, "to me that would be a rock-solid conflict of interest" since those disclosures will have a direct effect on investors' valuation of the company.

That scenario doesn't bother Evelyn A. Ashley, founder of the Red Hot Law Group, which has two public securities lawyers. "If you have the highest standard, that's not something that's going to enter your mind," she says. When preparing documents for public companies, "We don't say, 'My God, how is that going to affect my investment?' "

NOTES

The foregoing article addresses only some of the troubling issues involved in investing in clients. Malpractice insurers are increasingly worried about the practice, often requiring that law firm investment in the client not exceed five percent. Even then, some malpractice carriers are uncomfortable, as they are with the related practice — also increasingly prevalent — of members of a company's outside law firm sitting on the company's board of directors. "It's clear that an outside lawyer who is also a director is much more likely to be sued for malpractice," Robert E. O'Malley told *Legal Times* a few years ago. O'Malley was vice chairman of ALAS, or, more formally, Attorneys' Liability Assurance Society, Inc., one of the country's largest malpractice insurers. "If there are two alternative courses of action before the board, and one of them would produce a big fee for the lawyer's firm while the other would not, it is difficult to imagine how the lawyer/director could offer disinterested advice," said O'Malley.

Even Wilson, Sonsini general counsel Donald Bradley acknowledges that "there is no no-risk way" to invest in a client.[20]

Bradley points out that individual Wilson, Sonsini lawyers are not allowed to invest in clients and a separate investment corporation makes the investment, rather than the firm itself. But the effect of this separation is questionable: The separate corporation's list of shareholders is virtually identical to the list of the law firm's shareholder attorneys.

Some of the troubling issues are relatively subtle and sophisticated in nature. For instance, Joseph F. Troy, a California attorney who has written and spoken often about investing in clients, believes that an independent third party should be brought in to evaluate the transaction, although he acknowledges that no rule of professional conduct requires this. Other issues include the inherent tension as to how the value of the shares will be negotiated, when and under what conditions stock options will vest, and to what extent stock issuance can be the sole, or principal, means of compensation.

---

[20] Remarks of Donald Bradley, Annual Ethics Symposium of the State Bar of California's Committee on Professional Responsibility and Conduct, June 2000.

There is also an important distinction between accepting stock or options from a start-up with little cash, and the practice of some firms of making ongoing investments in ongoing clients. Start-ups often have little power to resist the entreaties of the firms that they hire to do their initial public offerings (or IPOs). But they also have little to lose, and little cash with which to hire counsel. Ongoing investing, however, seems to be more directly about making money with little justification from a client-needs point of view. Should ethics rules make any distinctions in what kinds of law firm investments are appropriate?

D.   SUPPLEMENTAL READINGS

1. *Togstad v. Vesely, Otto, Miller & Keefe*, 291 N.W.2d 686 (Minn. 1980). In this action for legal malpractice, the court found an attorney-client relationship existed and that malpractice arose from an office visit, where the attorney advised that he did not think the client had a case, but would discuss it with his partner. The lawyer failed to contact the client again, and the client did not consult another lawyer until a year later. This case may provide the broadest definition of attorney-client tort liability, since the lawyer made it clear he had not agreed to take the case in question.

2. Susan R. Martyn, *Accidental Clients*, 33 HOFSTRA L. REV. 913 (2005). Even when lawyers make it clear they will not take on a representation, to the extent a lawyer offers legal advice or gains information from such a person, two duties attach to such an encounter: competence as to any advice offered and confidentiality that cloaks anything the lawyer learns or advises.

3. Larry R. Spain, *Collaborative Law: A Critical Reflection on Whether a Collaborative Orientation Can Be Ethically Incorporated into the Practice of Law*, 56 BAYLOR L. REV. 141 (2004) provides a thorough discussion of ethics and "collaborative law," which includes "unbundled" services.

4. Rachel Brill and Rochelle Sparko, *Limited Legal Services and Conflicts of Interest: Unbundling in the Public Interest*, 16 GEO. J. LEGAL ETHICS 553 (2003), is a valuable article that engages in an extensive discussion of the effect of unbundled legal services on representation of the limited-scope client and other prospective clients.

5. The number of non-clients to whom lawyers owe duties seems ever-increasing. Paul C. Peterson and Ryan P. Meyers, *Will the Real Intended Third-Party Please Stand Up?*, 80 DEF. COUNS. J. 11 (2013), discusses the erosion of the traditional "privity" requirement governing standing to sue lawyers. The article notes that courts are developing a sliding-scale standard for determining if a non-client has standing to sue. "[I]n a growing number of contexts, a lawyer's work product, representations, and conduct in representing a client may provide a basis for third-party liability." This article explores various cases in which the courts "tinker with the balance to be struck between lawyers' professional obligations to their clients and affording justice to aggrieved non-clients."

6. *White v. McBride*, 937 S.W.2d 796 (Tenn. 1996), concerned a lawyer who had a contingency fee contract with a husband to get one-third of the amount recovered from his wife's estate. Here, not only did the court find the contingency fee contract excessive and unenforceable, but also denied the lawyer's claim for *quantum meruit* fees, finding that here, the percentage was clearly excessive, especially given that there was little if any contingency about the husband eventually receiving funds. The court's holding on *quantum meruit* fees turned on public policy grounds: "To permit an attorney to fall back on the theory of quantum meruit when he unsuccessfully fails to collect a clearly excessive fee does absolutely nothing to promote ethical behavior."

7. Tort reformers have written many articles attacking contingency fees and suggesting, at a minimum, that percentages should be substantially curtailed where the risk of no recovery is small. Perhaps the most prolific tort reformer is Lester Brickman of Cardozo Law School. In addition to the 1989 article cited in section 5, the following are of interest: *The Market for Contingent Fee-Financed Tort Litigation: Is It Price Competitive?*, 25 CARDOZO L. REV. 65 (2003), examines the factors that inhibit the emergence of a price competitive market. The factors include

> asymmetrical knowledge with respect to the value of claims; the lack of sophistication of most purchasers of tort claiming services; the utility of uniform pricing in misleading consumers as to the risk being assumed by the lawyer; and the signaling functions of uniform pricing including the branding of price cutters as slackers or as inferior in quality.

Brickman argues that while contingency fees are subject to both ethical rules and fiduciary principles that limit such fees to "reasonable" amounts, regulatory regimes are do little and actually displace more effective regulation from outside the bar. He suggests that instead of standard contingency fees, variable contingency fees should be applied only to the amount of recovery added to the value of the claim that results from the lawyer's efforts. In another 2003 article, *Effective Hourly Rates of Contingency-Fee Lawyers: Competing Data and Non-Competitive Fees*, 81 WASH. U. L. Q. 653 (2003), Brickman argues that the uniform contingency pricing structure is a "heads-I-win-tails-you-lose" fee-setting practice. Cases that are too risky are rejected and lucrative cases are accepted and a standard contingency fee is charged regardless of litigation risk; he sees the return on investment as unjustifiable relative to the cost of the service.

8. Court cases and ethics opinions differ substantially from state to state as to whether and under what circumstances an attorney may take and keep an advance retainer. Some jurisdictions distinguish an advance fee, which even if termed non-refundable may be refunded if the lawyer doesn't do the work, and a "true" retainer, payable in advance to secure a particular lawyer's availability on behalf of a client. *Baranowski v. State Bar*, 593 P.2d 613 (Cal. 1979), discusses the distinction between these two types of retainers. *Federal Savings & Loan Ins. Corp. v. Angell, Holmes & Lea*, 838 F.2d 395 (9th Cir. 1988), holds that even where the fee agreement between the lawyers and the S&L provided that the retainer was earned upon receipt, this was *not* binding on the S&L's eventual receiver. In *Jacobson v. Sassower*, 489 N.E.2d 1283 (N.Y. 1985), the New York Court of Appeals refused to allow a discharged lawyer to keep the unearned portion of a retainer since the notice to the client about what is meant by "non-refundable" was not entirely clear and should be construed against the lawyer.

9. A great deal has been written about taking stock for legal services. Many of the best articles have been in the colloquial legal press. Two of these are Debra Baker, *Who Wants to Be a Millionaire?*, ABA JOURNAL, February 2000, and *From the Epicenter: A Discussion of Clients, Culture, and Competition*, a roundtable "special report" on "dot.com practices" published by LEGAL TIMES, October 4, 1999. *See also* Sharon Mary Mathew, *Comment: Stock-Based Compensation for Legal Services: Resurrecting the Ethical Dilemma*, 42 SANTA CLARA L. REV. 1227 (2002).

10. ABA Formal Opinion 00-418 (July 7, 2000) concludes that lawyers may acquire ownership interests in their clients either by obtaining stock in lieu of fees or by developing investment opportunities, and that "no inherent conflict of interest" exists. While the opinion warns about possible conflicts and the need to comply with ABA Rules 1.8(a) regarding business transactions and 2.1 regarding independent professional judgment, the opinion is an affirmation of the legitimacy of such arrangements.

11. What about third parties who acquire an ownership interest in their lawyer's case? The June 2011 CNN MONEY BLOG, *Have You Got a Piece of this Lawsuit?*, written by Roger Parloff (http://features.blogs.fortune.cnn.com/2011/06/28/have-you-got-a-piece-of-this-lawsuit-2/), discusses the controversy about how the environmental suit against Chevron in Ecuador was financed — by multiple third party investors. Burford, a private investment company, "invested $4 million in the Ecuadorians' case against Chevron in exchange for a 1.5% stake in any recovery, with the stated goal of increasing its outlay to $15 million, and its recovery percent 5.5%." The author of the blog is particularly concerned with the lack of transparency involved with litigation investment.

12. Jonathan Molot, *Litigation Finance: A Market Solution to a Procedural Problem*, 99 GEO. L.J. 65 (2010), highlights the *benefits* of litigation financing: Through access to the financial market, financially strapped plaintiffs gain an alternative to negotiation settlements with access to sufficient funding for litigation. This additional bargaining chip usually allows plaintiffs to be much more successful in the settlement negotiation process.

Chapter 3

COMMUNICATION AND CONFIDENTIALITY

PROBLEM 4: ROGER EARL RECEIVES SOME EVIDENCE

A. INTRODUCTION

Confidentiality is a vitally important aspect of the attorney-client relationship. The nature and extent of that confidentiality can create difficult issues for the attorney confronted by conflicting obligations — to the legal system and society as a whole. The dilemma of Roger Earl, the attorney in the following problem, is complicated by the fact that physical evidence — both the fruits and instrumentalities of crimes — is involved.

We first look at confidentiality, both by examining its broad parameters and by examining and evaluating many of its exceptions.

B. PROBLEM

I

Roger Earl is a well-known criminal defense lawyer. One afternoon four individuals consult him.

Adams, whose murder trial is to begin the next week, comes into Earl's office and says, "I was lying when I told you I didn't kill my wife. I did it, and here's the gun I used. I don't know what to do with it; I only know that I don't want the DA to get hold of it." Adams then places the gun on Earl's desk.

Then Baker comes in. She informs Earl that the money she took in the robbery for which Earl is defending her is buried in a plastic bag in the woods behind her home. She specifies the location. Earl knows that the prosecution's case against Baker is weak unless the DA can produce the money. The case is scheduled for trial in three weeks.

By now Earl is inundated with work; the last thing he needs is a new client. But Carlton, whom Earl has never met, barges in, and before Earl can say he is too busy, Carlton blurts out: "I just killed my partner. I used this gun. I don't want the gun found, and I don't want to get caught. I am prepared to pay for your advice, and if I am arrested I want you to represent me." Carlton then places the gun on Earl's desk.

While contemplating the events of the day, Earl gets a phone call from Dunn, a longstanding client. Dunn informs Earl that he has been organizing "the heist of the decade," a burglary of the Philadelphia mint. He also tells Earl that the burglary will occur the following Wednesday. He wants to retain Earl in advance in case anything goes wrong.

QUESTIONS

1. Earl — and our discussion — focuses on Adams. What should Earl do in Adams's case? Specifically, consider the following:

    a. How should Earl advise him?

    b. Should Earl inform the authorities of the existence of the physical evidence? If so, by what means?

    c. What, if anything, should Earl do with the physical evidence? What about fingerprints, serial numbers, etc.?

    d. To what extent is the communication confidential? May giving Earl the gun be construed as a "communication"?

    e. May Earl continue to represent Adams?

    f. Would it make any difference if Adams placed his wife's purse on the desk and told Earl he had taken it after he killed her?

2. What if after Adams had admitted killing his wife he placed a sealed, wrapped parcel on Earl's desk and said, "keep this for me until after the trial." What may, should, or must Earl do with the parcel?

3. How, if at all, does Baker's case differ from Adams's?

4. How are Carlton's and Dunn's situations different from Adams's? Are their communications confidential? Does it matter whether Earl takes on Carlton as a client? Does it matter that Dunn has long been Earl's client?

II

Examine the hypotheticals in Professor Zacharias's article in section 6 below. Using his third hypothetical and picking one other, decide what you would do if confronted by such a situation. Explore whether the ethics rules have changed with respect to the examples you choose.

C. READINGS

1. Mr. Garrow, His Lawyers, and Two Buried Bodies

Consider the circumstances confronting lawyers Francis R. Belge and Frank Armani. In this case, there was physical evidence — bodies, the victims of murders committed by their client. The following article describes the terrible dilemma these lawyers faced, and the gruesome decision they made. Following the article are excerpts from the opinions of two courts — the first setting aside Belge's criminal indictment, the second upholding that ruling, pointedly without reaching ethical issues. Last is a partial quote from the New York State Bar Association's ethics committee's opinion on whether Belge's conduct was subject to discipline. Are the trial court's conclusions correct? What about the appellate court's distinctions between the evidentiary rule of "privilege" and the ethics rule of "confidentiality"? Are the appellate court and the ethics committee in essential agreement or disagreement?

Does protection of the client's interests result in abandonment of "human standards of decency"? Are the client's interests and fundamental notions of justice mutually exclusive?

Slayer's 2 Lawyers Kept Secret of 2 More Killings
THE NEW YORK TIMES (June 20, 1974)[1]

Lake Pleasant, N.Y., June 19— Two lawyers for a man on trial here for murder did not disclose for six months that they had seen the bodies of two other people killed by their client because, they said, they were bound by the confidentiality of a lawyer-client relationship.

The court-appointed attorneys said today that their client had told them where to find the bodies of two missing women. They photographed the bodies, they said, but did not report the discoveries to authorities searching for the murder victims.

The lawyers also said they had kept their discovery from the father of one of the women, who had visited them in the hope that they could shed some light on the disappearance of his 20-year-old daughter.

"The information was so privileged — I was bound by my lawyers' oath to keep it confidential after I found the bodies," said Francis Belge, one of the two lawyers representing Robert Garrow. Mr. Garrow, a 38-year-old mechanic for a Syracuse bakery, is accused of fatally stabbing Philip Domblewski, an 18-year-old Schenectady student who was camping in the Adirondacks last July.

From what his lawyers said in a news conference today, as well as from what Mr. Garrow has — sometimes incoherently — blurted out in court, the defendant may be connected to at least four murders.

Mr. Belge and his associate on the case, Frank Armani, told of the secret they had kept at a news conference in this Adirondack village. They indicated that they could come forth now, released from their obligation by Mr. Garrow's own testimony yesterday. . . .

The Police Chief of Syracuse . . . said he would ask the Onondaga District Attorney to bring obstruction of justice charges against the lawyers. . . .

According to Mr. Belge, Mr. Garrow told him of raping and killing a woman in an abandoned mine shaft near Mineville, NY. The lawyer said this information was provided by Mr. Garrow a few weeks after the suspect was wounded and captured last Aug. 9 following a manhunt involving 200 state troopers and others.

---

[1] Copyright © 1974 by The New York Times Company. Reprinted by permission.

Some three weeks later Mr. Belge said, he discovered the body of Susan Petz, a 20-year-old woman from Skokie, Ill. She had been missing since July 20, when the body of her camping companion, Daniel Porter, a Harvard student, was found near Weavertown.

"We passed the shaft 10 times before I found it with a flashlight at twilight," Mr. Belge said. "Frank lowered me into the shaft by my feet and I took pictures."

The finding of Miss Petz's body was reported to the state police four months later by two children who had been playing in the mine.

Meanwhile, Mr. Belge said, Miss Petz's father visited him because his client, Mr. Garrow, had been unofficially linked to killings in the area.

"I spent many, many sleepless nights [over] my ability to reveal the information, especially after Mr. Petz came in from Chicago and talked to me," Mr. Belge said.

The lawyer found the second body at the end of September. He said that while Mr. Garrow provided a rough diagram locating Miss Petz's body, in the second instance he gave only a general description of an area in Syracuse near Syracuse University.

There, in Oakwood cemetery, Mr. Belge said, he found the body of Alicia Hauck, a 16-year-old high school girl who disappeared from her home in Syracuse nearly two months earlier, on July 11.

Concern for Parents

Miss Hauck's body was ultimately found and reported by a Syracuse University student on December 1. In the intervening months, her father, the owner of a bowling alley in Syracuse, and the police were treating the case as that of a runaway and were advertising pleas for the girl to come home.

"We both, knowing how the parents must feel, wanted to advise them where the bodies were," Mr. Belge said. "But since it was a privileged communication, we could not reveal any information that was given to us in confidence."

Both lawyers had apparently felt the weight of the confidence they honored until today. "Death is difficult enough to accept," Mr. Armani said, "but worrying and wondering, it'll drive you insane."

Two Obligations Seen

Professor David Mellinkoff of the University of California at Los Angeles' Law School, the author of a book, "The Conscience of a Lawyer," and a specialist in matters of legal ethics and confidentiality, said after being told of the case that in general the lawyers seemed to be under two conflicting obligations.

On one hand, he said, a lawyer is committed to keeping his clients' confessions of a completed crime in confidence. On the other, the lawyer cannot hide physical evidence, such as a weapon, or in this case, bodies, from the prosecution.

PEOPLE v. BELGE
83 Misc. 2d 186 (N.Y. County Ct. 1975)

[D]iscovery [of the bodies] was not disclosed to the authorities, but became public during the trial of Mr. Garrow in June of 1974, when to affirmatively establish the defense of insanity, these three other murders were brought before the jury by the defense in the Hamilton County trial. Public indignation reached the fever pitch; statements were made by the District Attorney of Onondaga County relative to the situation and he caused the Grand Jury of Onondaga County, then sitting, to conduct a thorough investigation. As a result of this investigation Frank Armani was No Billed by the Grand Jury but Indictment No. 75-55 was returned as against Francis R. Belge, Esq., accusing him of having violated § 4200(l) of the Public Health Law, which, in essence, requires that a decent burial be accorded the dead, and § 4143 of the Public Health Law, which, in essence, requires anyone knowing of the death of a person without medical attendance, [sic] to report the same to the proper authorities. Defense counsel moves for a dismissal of the Indictment on the grounds that a confidential, privileged communication existed between him and Mr. Garrow, which should excuse the attorney from making full disclosure to the authorities.

The National Association of Criminal Defense Lawyers, as Amicus Curiae, citing *Times Publishing Co. v. Williams*, 222 So. 2d 470, 475 (Fla. App. 1970) succinctly state the issue in the following language:

If this indictment stands,

> The attorney-client privilege will be effectively destroyed. No defendant will be able to freely discuss the facts of his case with his attorney. No attorney will be able to listen to those facts without being faced with the Hobson's choice of violating the law or violating his professional code of Ethics.

. . . .

In the most recent issue of the New York State Bar Journal (June 1975) there is an article by Jack B. Weinstein, entitled "Educating Ethical Lawyers." In a sub-caption to this article is the following language:

> The most difficult ethical dilemmas result from the frequent conflicts between the obligation to one's client and those to the legal system and to society. It is in this area that legal education has its greatest responsibility, and can have its greatest effects.

. . . .

Our system of criminal justice is an adversary system and the interests of the state are not absolute, or even paramount. . . .

A trial is in part a search for truth, but it is only partly a search for truth.

. . . .

The effectiveness of counsel is only as great as the confidentiality of its client-attorney relationship. If the lawyer cannot get all the facts about the case, he can only give his client half of a defense. This, of necessity involves the client telling his attorney everything remotely connected with the crime.

Apparently, in the instant case, after analyzing all the evidence, and after hearing of the bizarre episodes in the life of their client, they decided that the only possibility of salvation was a defense of insanity. For the client to disclose not only everything about this particular crime but also everything about other crimes which might have a bearing upon his defense, requires the strictest confidence in, and on the part of, the attorney.

When the facts of the other homicides became public, as a result of the defendant's testimony to substantiate his claim of insanity, "Members of the public were shocked at the apparent callousness of these lawyers, whose conduct was seen as typifying the unhealthy lack of concern of most lawyers with the public interest and with simple decency." A hue and cry went up from the press and other news media suggesting that the attorneys should be found guilty of such crimes as obstruction of justice or becoming an accomplice after the fact. From a layman's standpoint, this certainly was a logical conclusion. However, the constitution of the United States of America attempts to preserve the dignity of the individual and to do that guarantees him the services of an attorney who will bring to the bar and to the bench every conceivable protection from the inroads of the state against such rights as are vested in the constitution for one accused of crime. Among those substantial constitutional rights is that a defendant does not have to incriminate himself. His attorneys were bound to uphold that concept and maintain what has been called a sacred trust of confidentiality.

. . . In this type situation the Court must balance the rights of the individual against the rights of society as a whole. There is no question that Attorney Belge's failure to bring to the attention of the authorities the whereabouts of Alicia Hauck when he first verified it, prevented bringing Garrow to the immediate bar of justice for this particular murder. This was in a sense, obstruction of justice. This duty, I am sure, loomed large in the mind of Attorney Belge. However, against this was the Fifth Amendment right of his client, Garrow, not to incriminate himself. . . .

It is the decision of this Court that Francis R. Belge conducted himself as an officer of the Court with all the zeal at his command to protect the constitutional rights of his client. Both on the grounds of a privileged communication and in the interests of justice the Indictment is dismissed.

PEOPLE v. BELGE
50 A.D.2d 1038 (N.Y. App. Div. 1975)

We believe that an attorney must protect his client's interests, but also must observe basic human standards of decency, having due regard to the need that the legal system accord justice to the interests of society and its individual members.

We write to emphasize our serious concern regarding the consequences which emanate from a claim of an absolute attorney-client privilege. Because the only question presented, briefed and argued on this appeal was a legal one with respect to the sufficiency of the indictments, we limit our determination to that issue and do not reach the ethical questions underlying this case. *Order Affirmed.*

NOTES

Three and one-half years after Belge and Armani made their revelations, the committee on professional ethics of the New York State Bar Association exonerated Belge. The committee did, however, criticize him for taking pictures of Alicia Hauck's body in the Syracuse cemetery, and especially for moving her body parts to fit them within the frame of his photos:

"Such conduct should be avoided to prevent even the appearance that there might have been an intent to tamper with or suppress evidence."

However, the Bar committee's overall perspective strongly supported the primacy of confidentiality:

> The relationship between lawyer and client is in many respects like that between priest and penitent. Both lawyer and priest are bound by the bond of silence . . . . Proper representation of a client calls for full disclosure by the client to his lawyer of all possibly relevant facts, even though such facts may be the client's commission of prior crimes . . . . To encourage full disclosure, the client must be assured of confidentiality. Frequently, clients have a disposition to withhold information from lawyers. If the client suggests that his confidences will not be adequately protected or in some way be used against him, he will be far more likely to withhold information which he believes may be to his detriment or which he does not want generally known.

> The client who withholds information from his lawyer runs a substantial risk of not being accorded his full legal rights. . . . Thus, the interests served by the strict rule of confidentiality are far broader than merely those of the client, but include the interests of the public generally and of effective judicial administration.[2]

Do you agree that "a strict rule of confidentiality" best serves the client's interests as well as the interests of the public and the judicial system? It is noteworthy that at least one study has shown that even a strong rule of confidentiality won't assure truthful disclosure by a client. It is common knowledge among public defenders that clients withhold from them more information than from paid attorneys because they see the public defenders as part of the system rather than as advocates. As few as a third of criminal clients are aware of confidentiality rules.

If you had never been to law school, what would you do if someone gave you a gun that had been used in a crime? Or told you the location of a body? How would you have acted when confronted with the dilemma faced by Messrs. Belge and Armani?

---

[2] The Bar committee was quoted, *inter alia*, in Tom Goldstein, *Bar Upholds Lawyer Who Withheld Knowledge of Client's Prior Crimes*, N.Y. Times, March 2, 1978.

2. Future and "Continuing" Crimes and the ABA Model Rules

Two cases decided within six weeks of each other in the late 1990s brought the buried bodies case back to mind. In one, another case from Onondaga County, NY, the trial judge cited *Belge* in holding that a lawyer could not be compelled to testify before a grand jury about the whereabouts of a client who had disappeared with her child in violation of a custody order. The court concluded that even if a crime had been committed it could not be deemed a "continuing" one, and upheld the attorney-client privilege.[3]

The Texas Court of Criminal Appeals came to a very different result under facts not that dissimilar from the Garrow case.[4] Babysitter Cathy Lynn Henderson admitted to her lawyer, Nona Byington, that she had kidnapped and killed a 3-month-old baby boy. Henderson eventually drew two maps indicating the boy's location, and gave them to her lawyer. The local grand jury subpoenaed the maps, and the trial court, ruling that kidnapping was a continuing crime, compelled Byington to produce them. Texas law enforcement officers used the maps to locate the body of the boy. Byington's motion to suppress the maps and the evidence gained from them — the baby's body and evidence of a fatal blow to his head — was denied. Henderson's death sentence was upheld by the appeals court, which noted that "the attorney-client privilege was legitimately required to yield to the strong public policy interest of protecting a child from death or serious bodily injury." Yet there seemed to be only a theoretical issue about the child still being alive; Henderson had admitted to police that the boy had died, but claimed it was the result of an accidental fall.

3. The *Ryder* and *Meredith* Cases

Is there a difference between active concealment of evidence and simply not disclosing information? Read the brief excerpts from *In re Ryder*, 263 F. Supp. 360 (E.D. Va.), *aff'd*, 381 F.2d 713 (4th Cir. 1967) (*per curiam*), below. *Ryder*, a seminal case, is still often cited and analyzed, and helps answer this question.

In *Ryder*, Cook, a client of attorney Richard Ryder, told Ryder that he had robbed a bank and rented a safe deposit box in which he had placed stolen money and a sawed-off shotgun he had used in the robbery. Ryder moved the shotgun and stolen money to his own safe deposit box in order to remove them from his client's possession. The appellate Court made it clear that Ryder had crossed the line, saying he had "made himself an active participant in a criminal act, ostensibly wearing the mantle of loyal advocate, but in reality serving as an accessory after the fact."

---

[3] In re Grand Jury Investigation, 175 Misc. 2d 398 (N.Y. County Ct. 1998).

[4] Henderson v. State, 962 S.W.2d 544 (Tex. Crim. App. 1997).

IN RE RYDER
263 F. Supp. 360 (E.D. Va.), *aff'd*, 381 F.2d 713 (4th Cir. 1967)

PER CURIAM.

We reject the argument that Ryder's conduct was no more than the exercise of the attorney-client privilege. The fact that Cook had not been arrested or indicted at the time Ryder took possession of the gun and money is immaterial. Cook was Ryder's client and was entitled to the protection of the lawyer-client privilege.

Regardless of Cook's status, however, Ryder's conduct was not encompassed by the attorney-client privilege.

. . . .

It was Ryder, not his client, who took the initiative in transferring the incriminating possession of the stolen money and the shotgun from Cook. Ryder's conduct went far beyond the receipt and retention of a confidential communication from his client.

. . . .

Ryder also . . . intended that his actions should remove from Cook exclusive possession of stolen money, and thus destroy an evidentiary presumption. His service in taking possession of the shotgun and money, with the intention of retaining them until after the trial, unless discovered by the government, merits the "stern and just condemnation" the canon prescribes.

. . . .

Ryder's action is not justified because he thought he was acting in the best interests of his client. To allow the individual lawyer's belief to determine the standards of professional conduct will in time reduce the ethics of the profession to the practices of the most unscrupulous.

NOTES

Ryder involved a lawyer's active participation in the secreting of evidence. What is the difference between active participation and passive participation? Can a lawyer advise a client to destroy evidence as long as the lawyer does not participate in the act of destruction? Can counsel hint at such destruction in the context of explaining the law? What about physical alteration of evidence? Or removal from its original location? The following case — again, older but oft-cited and analyzed — addresses several of these issues.

PEOPLE v. MEREDITH
631 P.2d 46 (Cal. 1981)

Defendants Frank Earl Scott and Michael Meredith appeal from convictions for the first degree murder and first degree robbery of David Wade. Meredith's conviction rests on eyewitness testimony that he shot and killed Wade. Scott's conviction, however, depends on the theory that Scott conspired with Meredith and a third defendant, Jacqueline Otis, to bring about the killing and robbery. To support the theory of conspiracy the prosecution sought to show the place where the victim's wallet was found, and, in the course of the case this piece of evidence became crucial. The admissibility of that evidence comprises the principal issue on this appeal.

At trial the prosecution called Steven Frick, who testified that he observed the victim's partially burnt wallet in a trash can behind Scott's residence. . . . Frick served as a defense investigator. Scott himself had told his former counsel that he had taken the victim's wallet, divided the money with Meredith, attempted to burn the wallet, and finally put it in the trash can. At counsel's request, Frick then retrieved the wallet from the trash can. Counsel examined the wallet and then turned it over to the police.

The defense acknowledges that the wallet itself was properly admitted into evidence. The prosecution in turn acknowledges that the attorney-client privilege protected the conversations between Scott, his former counsel, and counsel's investigator. . . . The issue before us, consequently, focuses upon a narrow point: Whether under the circumstances of this case Frick's observation of the location of the wallet, the product of a privileged communication, finds protection under the attorney-client privilege.

This issue, one of first impression in California, presents the court with competing policy considerations. On the one hand, to deny protection to observations arising from confidential communications might chill free and open communication between attorney and client and might also inhibit counsel's investigation of his client's case. On the other hand, we cannot extend the attorney-client privilege so far that it renders evidence immune from discovery and admission merely because the defense seizes it first.

Balancing these considerations, we conclude that an observation by defense counsel or his investigator, which is the product of a privileged communication, may not be admitted unless the defense by altering or removing physical evidence has precluded the prosecution from making that same observation. In the present case the defense investigator, by removing the wallet, frustrated any possibility that the police might later discover it in the trash can. The conduct of the defense thus precluded the prosecution from ascertaining the crucial fact of the location of the wallet. Under these circumstances, the prosecution was entitled to present evidence to show the location of the wallet in the trash can.

. . . .

We now recount the evidence relating to Wade's wallet, basing our account primarily on the testimony of James Schenk, Scott's first appointed attorney. . . . Scott told Schenk . . . that he picked up the wallet, put it in the paper bag, . . . and then tried to burn the wallet in his kitchen sink. He took the partially burned wallet, Scott told Schenk, placed it in a plastic bag, and threw it in a burn barrel behind his house.

Schenk, without further consulting Scott, retained Investigator Stephen Frick and sent Frick to find the wallet. Frick found it in the location described by Scott and brought it to Schenk. After examining the wallet and determining that it contained credit cards with Wade's name, Schenk turned the wallet and its contents over to Detective Payne, investigating officer in the case. Schenk told Payne only that, to the best of his knowledge, the wallet had belonged to Wade.

The prosecution subpoenaed Attorney Schenk and Investigator Frick to testify at the preliminary hearing. When questioned at that hearing, Schenk said that he received the wallet from Frick but refused to answer further questions on the ground that he learned about the wallet through a privileged communication. Eventually, however, the magistrate threatened Schenk with contempt if he did not respond "yes" or "no" when asked whether his contact with his client led to disclosure of the wallet's location. Schenk then replied "yes," and revealed on further questioning that this contact was the sole source of his information as to the wallet's location.

At the preliminary hearing[,] . . . [o]ver objections by counsel, Frick testified that he found the wallet in a garbage can behind Scott's residence.

. . . .

The fundamental purpose of the attorney-client privilege is, of course, to encourage full and open communication between client and attorney. . . .

Judicial decisions have recognized that the implementation of these important policies may require that the privilege extend not only to the initial communication between client and attorney but also to any information which the attorney or his investigator may subsequently acquire as a direct result of that communication. In a venerable decision involving facts analogous to those in the instant case, the Supreme Court of West Virginia held that the trial court erred in admitting an attorney's testimony as to the location of a pistol which he had discovered as the result of a privileged communication from his client. That the attorney had observed the pistol, the court pointed out, did not nullify the privilege: "All that the said attorney knew about this pistol, or where it was to be found, he knew only from the communications which had been made to him by his client confidentially and professionally, as counsel in this case. And it ought therefore, to have been entirely excluded from the jury. It may be, that in this particular case this evidence tended to the promotion of right and justice, but as was well said in *Pearce v. Pearce*, 11 Jar. 52, in page 55, and 2 De Gex & Smale 25–27: 'Truth like all other good things may be loved unwisely, may be pursued too keenly, may cost too much.'" (*State of West Virginia v. Douglass* (1882) 20 W.Va. 770, 783.)

. . . [T]he attorney-client privilege is not strictly limited to communications, but extends to protect observations made as a consequence of protected communications. We turn therefore to the question whether that privilege encompasses a case in which the defense, by removing or altering evidence, interferes with the prosecution's opportunity to discover that evidence.

. . . .

When defense counsel alters or removes physical evidence, he necessarily deprives the prosecution of the opportunity to observe that evidence in its original condition or location. As the Attorney General points out, to bar admission of testimony concerning the original condition and location of the evidence in such a case permits the defense in effect to "destroy" critical information; it is as if, he explains, the wallet in this case bore a tag bearing the words "located in the trash can by Scott's residence," and the defense, by taking the wallet, destroyed this tag. To extend the attorney-client privilege to a case in which the defense removed evidence might encourage defense counsel to race the police to seize critical evidence. (See *In re Ryder* (E.D.Va. 1967) 263 F. Supp. 360, 369. . . .)

We therefore conclude that whenever defense counsel removes or alters evidence, the statutory privilege does not bar revelation of the original location or condition of the evidence in question. We thus view the defense decision to remove evidence as a tactical choice. If defense counsel leaves the evidence where he discovers it, his observations derived from privileged communications are insulated from revelation. If, however, counsel chooses to remove evidence to examine or test it, the original location and condition of that evidence loses the protection of the privilege. Applying this analysis to the present case, we hold that the trial court did not err in admitting the investigator's testimony concerning the location of the wallet.

NOTES

Consider these questions: If the state agreed in *Meredith* that defendant Scott's conversations with his former counsel and investigator were protected, then why were both required to testify at Scott's preliminary hearing? And why did the Supreme Court refer to this testimony? Since the preliminary hearing testimony was used to tie the wallet to Scott, why did the defense acknowledge that the wallet was admissible evidence? Finally, how much is *Meredith* about confidentiality and how much about the evidentiary, or testimonial, rule of attorney-client privilege? We'll reflect on some of these issues in section 5, below.

4. How Much Disclosure Is Required?

Peter A. Joy and Kevin C. McMunigal, two professors expert in criminal law, suggest in a recent article that *Ryder* and *Meredith* should be seen as limited to the fruits and instrumentalities of crimes, not *any* evidence: "Federal and state statutes differ greatly on . . . the potential relevance of the destroyed or concealed material. Fruits and instrumentalities of a crime typically meet the relevance requirement of such statutes, but evidence that is neither a fruit nor an instrumentality may not."[5]

Joy and McMunigal cite to *dicta* in *Ryder* supporting this view. Although *Meredith* refers to altering or removing "physical evidence," the actual evidence in question was the instrumentality of a crime. Joy and McMunigal note that a few states have adopted a broader requirement, such as in *Morrell v. State*, 575 P.2d 1200 (Alaska 1978), which held that "no distinction should be drawn in the privilege context between physical evidence obtained by a criminal defense attorney which is 'mere evidence' of a client's crime and that which may be said to be either a fruit or an instrumentality of the crime."

---

[5] Peter A. Joy & Kevin C. McMunigal, *Incriminating Evidence — Too Hot to Handle?* 24 [ABA] CRIM. JUST. 42 (2009).

The Restatement (Third) of the Law Governing Lawyers, § 119 (2000), implies a similar but slightly different take in requiring "evidence" to be turned over once the defense has had an opportunity to forensically test that evidence.

However, this remains an open and debatable issue. Several recent articles side with a narrower interpretation of what evidence must be disclosed. Professor Rodney Uphoff has an extensive and thorough review of case law and secondary sources in an article we cite further in our Supplemental Readings.[6]

He argues that the Restatement's view requires too much disclosure, and expresses preference for the narrower position taken in section 4-4.6 of the ABA Criminal Justice Standards for Prosecution and Defense Functions: "Unless required to disclose, defense counsel should return the item to the source from whom defense counsel received it." But those standards have not been revised for a generation. Uphoff does cite to other sources that agree with the principle he espouses, at least in California, that "while California law requires lawyers to disclose or to deliver fruits or instrumentalities of a crime to the authorities sua sponte, ordinary materials with evidentiary significance need not be disclosed sua sponte, but only if required by a court order or subpoena."

Soon after *Meredith*, California criminal defense attorney Milton J. Silverman made a strong case for this narrower interpretation by discussing both *Meredith* and its predecessor *People v. Lee*, 3 Cal. App. 3d 514 (Cal. Ct. App. 1970). *Lee* was an attempted murder case in which the instrumentality of the crime — a pair of boots with blood matching the victim's — was turned over to defense counsel by the defendant's wife, and then in turn by defense counsel to a judge and eventually to the prosecution. When the DA attempted to introduce the boots *and* testimony from the first defense counsel as to how he obtained them, the court allowed it, and the appellate court affirmed. Silverman agreed that "defense counsel has the obligation to surrender contraband, fruits or instrumentalities of the crime which he has taken into his possession." But, he argued:

> [In] the *Lee* case . . . [l]et's say that instead of the shoe being the issue, it is a *shoe print*. Let's say that this crime occurs in an open field, and the police secure it, do their investigation and release the scene. When the defense does its investigation, the defense lawyer notes that there is a shoe print in the ground. He makes a cast of it and has the ground cut out so that the print can be preserved. Can the prosecution then demand the evidence? Will the defense lawyer be required to turn it over?
>
> If the answer is yes, then the effective assistance of counsel protection of the constitution is meaningless. The defense counsel cannot be told on the one hand that his job is to zealously determine the *facts* in the case and acquire *evidence*, and on the other that the fruit of his labor must be turned over to the prosecution on demand.[7]

---

[6] Rodney J. Uphoff, *The Physical Evidence Dilemma: Does ABA Standard 4-4.6 Offer Appropriate Guidance?*, 62 HASTINGS L.J. 1177 (2011).

[7] Milton J. Silverman, *Fundamentals of Crime Scene Investigation: What Can a Lawyer Do?* CALIFORNIA ATTORNEYS FOR CRIMINAL JUSTICE FORUM (October/November/December 1983).

5. Confidentiality and Privilege: Not the Same

In the three principal cases we have discussed thus far, courts and several commentators have referred to both "confidentiality" and "privilege." But the two, while clearly closely related, are not the same, nor should they be evaluated and analyzed in the same way.

Confidentiality is a principle of legal ethics, embodied in the ethics rules (*see* ABA Model Rule 1.6). The attorney-client privilege is, like all privileges, a rule of *evidence*, relating to the admissibility of information before a court or tribunal. The concept of evidentiary privilege is thus considerably narrower than that of confidentiality. "Privilege" only protects an in-court revelation; "confidentiality" applies at all times and in all circumstances. That is, confidentiality requires a lawyer to remain silent or even refrain from using confidential information in any manner that would harm the client. Privilege applies only to the required after-the-fact revelation in a formal proceeding.

There is one more important distinction: the wider breadth of confidentiality. It is true, as *Meredith* notes, citing a 19th century West Virginia court, that "attorney-client privilege is not strictly limited to communications, but extends to protect observations made as a consequence of protected communications." But that definition still is far narrower than the definition of confidentiality. Confidentiality encompasses not just communications from the client to the lawyer, but *anything* the lawyer learns during the course of the representation. Most states follow the modern ABA Rule in this regard, though several, California among them, continue to use the concept of "secrets," usually defined as matters the lawyer learns *other than* through client communications, the revelation of which could be embarrassing or detrimental to the client.

Thus, the Garrow affair is best seen as turning on the ethical principle of confidentiality: Could the lawyers, having learned of the buried bodies, reveal that information to third parties? *Meredith*, on the other hand, ultimately turns on a question of evidentiary privilege: Must the communication from client to lawyer of the location of the wallet be revealed in a court proceeding? In this light, have the *Ryder* and *Meredith* cases understood this distinction clearly? Or have they mixed and matched these two closely-related but clearly distinct concepts?

These concepts are easy to confuse, even for sophisticated analysts. For example, California had no *de jure* exception to the seemingly absolute rule, under § 6068(e) of its Business & Professions Code, that lawyers "maintain the confidence, and at every peril to himself or herself, preserve the secrets" of the client. The California legislature, which "controlled" changes to both this confidentiality statute and its Evidence Code privileges, did not amend the statute governing absolute *confidentiality* until 2003. Yet over a decade earlier, the legislature changed the *Evidence Code* to allow limited exceptions under the *privilege*.[8]

Thus, for over a decade, lawyers in California lived with this basic anomaly, at least under its statutes: Lawyers could not reveal a confidence even to *warn*

---

[8] CALIF. EVI. CODE § 956.5.

someone of an imminent murder, but could, *after the fact*, be compelled to testify about what the client had said before the crime. This, of course, was an absurd position for any lawyer to be in, fortunately now corrected.

One more interesting variation is worth noting: While the ethical requirements of confidentiality may be broader than the privilege in almost all instances, it can occasionally work the other way around. In *Purcell v. District Attorney for Suffolk District*, 676 N.E.2d 436 (Mass. 1997), attorney Purcell was consulted by a client named Tyree about an eviction. After hearing Tyree threaten to burn down his building and deciding the threat was serious, Purcell informed the Boston police. When police went to Tyree's apartment, they found incendiary devices and other evidence of a planned arson. Tyree was charged with attempted arson. His first trial ended in a hung jury. Purcell had been subpoenaed to testify, but successfully quashed his subpoena. At the retrial, however, the judge ordered Purcell to testify. Purcell then filed his own appellate action to quash.

The Massachusetts Supreme Court agreed with Purcell. They noted that even though Purcell was justified in breaking his duty of *confidentiality before* the arson because of the potential danger to others, that did not break the attorney-client *privilege after* the fact. The court acknowledged the existence of a "crime fraud exception" to the privilege — that a client who uses an attorney's representation to further a crime or fraud loses the right to claim the privilege. But here, the lawyer was consulted about an eviction case, and none of Purcell's advice related to Tyree's planned crime.

6. Other Exceptions to Confidentiality?

As we mentioned in our Introduction, the Kutak Commission, charged with drafting the ABA Model Rules eventually approved in 1983, had proposed broad exceptions to the rule of confidentiality when a lawyer learns of the client's intent to commit a dangerous act. The ABA House of Delegates did not accept this approach, however, and by the time the rules were passed, both MR 1.6, and MR 1.13, relating to corporations, had become even more protective of attorney-client confidentiality than they had been under the old Code. Not until the Ethics 2000 Commission rules were approved in 2002 and 2003 did the ABA swing back towards the Kutak intent of broader exceptions to confidentiality, which most states have now adopted. How does your state deal with attorney-client confidentiality?

Not long after the Kutak proposals and the ABA's retrenchment, Professor Fred Zacharias, wrote an important law review article that posed in its appendix "hypothetical" exceptions to a strict rule of confidentiality based on true events. Zacharias, a frequent contributor to the literature in this field, was an advocate for liberalizing the exceptions to confidentiality. As you read these hypotheticals, consider the possible consequences of each. How many of his hypothetical exceptions to the rule of confidentiality would now be accepted under the most modern version of the ABA Rules?

Fred C. Zacharias, *Rethinking Confidentiality*
74 IOWA L. REV. 351 (1989)[9]

[I]n extreme situations calling for intervention, strict confidentiality rules often reduce lawyers' ability and desire to act.

Allowing lawyers some leeway to reveal client information would not destroy our legal order. Other well-developed legal systems circumscribe confidentiality more narrowly than we. Their continued viability suggests that our system, too, would survive limited exceptions.

At root, whether to adopt exceptions is a balance of countervailing costs and benefits. But the balance inevitably depends on facts. Only by determining how well strict confidentiality serves its intended purposes, and how much exceptions would undermine those goals, can code drafters put the normative question into proper perspective.

This Article's theoretical analysis and the data it presents are a first step toward providing that perspective. The Article unashamedly raises more questions than it answers. It is intended as a bridge to further study, and to show that empirical analysis of confidentiality rules is possible. . . .

Appendix — Hypotheticals

1. A client tells a lawyer the location of a "missing child" or kidnapping victim. The client is not implicated in the person's disappearance, but does not want the lawyer to disclose the information because the client "doesn't want to get involved." The client will not accept the lawyer's assurance that the lawyer could act without naming the client.[10]

2. An attorney obtains information from a client that would prove that another person falsely accused of a crime, is innocent. The attorney could reveal the information without implicating the client in the crime. The client refuses to disclose the information voluntarily.[11]

3. In a civil suit involving a serious automobile accident, the plaintiff is examined by defendant's doctor. The doctor discovers a life threatening aneurism. Although the aneurism was probably caused by the accident, plaintiff's own physician has not discovered it. The condition is curable, but if defendant's lawyer does not reveal the

---

[9] Copyright © 1989 by Iowa Law Review. Reprinted by permission.

[10] [278] In Subin, *supra* note 26, at 1103–04, Professor Subin discusses the even more dramatic situation in which the kidnap victim may die if the lawyer does not act promptly.

Numerous interesting "disclosure" situations beyond this Article's scope arise when a lawyer represents a client who is or may become a criminal defendant. . . . At one time or another, most criminal lawyers must consider whether to tell the authorities about (1) the whereabouts of a client who has skipped bail, (2) the possibility that the client has committed perjury, see *Nix v. Whiteside*, 475 U.S. 157 (1986) and authorities cited therein, and (3) client admissions or information that might lead to the discovery of additional evidence or crimes.

[11] [279] Cases have arisen in which lawyers learn from a criminal client that he or she, rather than the accused, has committed a crime. The courts uniformly have held that these communications are privileged and confidential. . . .

danger — against the client's wishes — plaintiff may die.[12]

4. The general counsel to a firm that produces a metal alloy used in the manufacture of airplanes learns of a company study that suggests that in some high-altitude flight patterns the alloy might weaken and cause a plane to explode. The alloy does, however, meet the minimum safety standards set by the government. The lawyer urges the Board of Directors to recall the alloy or at a minimum to inform users of its potential danger. The Board decides that the study is too inconclusive to warrant action in light of the dire financial consequences of disclosure to the company.[13]

5. From information given by and conversations with a client, an attorney becomes convinced that the client is mentally imbalanced, out of control, and will injure someone in the near future. The client has, however, not expressed any specific intention . . . . [Footnote citing *Tarasoff*, see section 7 below, omitted.]

6. X negotiates directly with Y and agrees to buy Y's house. Y agrees to provide "owner financing," subject to the contingency that X supply certain information concerning X's ability to pay. The only role X's attorney is to play in the transaction is to write the final sale contract and preside over the closing. Right before the closing, X's attorney learns from X's accountant that the financing information X supplied to Y contained inaccurate information. If any fraud was committed, it occurred before the attorney became involved.[14]

7. A client fortuitously receives an undeserved payment from the government (e.g., a duplicate welfare check or tax refund) and deposits it in a savings account. The client then contacts his/her attorney who advises the client to return the money. The client refuses.[15]

. . . .

10. A lawyer for a political organization learns that the client is secretly a Nazi front.

11. There are rumors that a former Vice President who resigned after pleading nolo contendere to tax evasion charges plans to run for public office again. He publishes a book in which he asserts that he at all times protested his innocence of any wrongdoing to his attorney. The attorney remembers that, in fact, the Vice President admitted accepting graft.[16]

12. President Nixon announces publicly that the Watergate tapes show he knew

---

[12] [280] *Spaulding v. Zimmerman*, 263 Minn. 346, 116 N.W.2d 704 (1962), discussed in G. Hazard, Jr. & W. Hodes, *supra* note 105, at 114; Luban, *The Adversary System Excuse* in D. Luban, *supra* note 25, at 83, 115.

[13] [281] The position of the CPR on various manifestations of this hypothetical is discussed in Ferren, *The Corporate Lawyer's Obligation to the Public Interest*, 33 Bus. Law. 1253 (1978).

[14] [283] Callan and David discuss a variant of this hypothetical in Callan & David, *supra* note 26, at 388–89. In a similar securities context, the Securities and Exchange Commission has taken the position that attorneys aware of proxy misinformation must disclose. See *S.E.C. v. National Student Mktg. Corp.*, 457 F. Supp. 682, 713 (D.D.C. 1978). The S.E.C. rule has fostered much debate.

[15] [284] Arguably, this scenario too involves an ongoing fraud. See *supra* note 283.

[16] [285] See *Agnew v. State*, 51 Md. App. 614, 649–56, 446 A.2d 425, 44–54 [sic] (1982).

nothing about any potentially illegal activities. Nixon's lawyer listens to the tapes and urges Nixon to disclose its contents "in the national interest." Nixon refuses and tells the press that he will not disclose anything about them because of his "duty to protect the presidency."

13. A car manufacturer knows that the placement of the gas tank on its compact car will cause the vehicle to burst into flames in 5% of rear end collisions. Its accountants determine that moving the gas tank will cost more than the company would have to pay in tort liability for injuries caused by the car's design. The company's attorney concludes that the company would not violate any criminal statute by continuing to produce the car, but nevertheless urges recall and redesign of the "defect." The company declines.[17]

NOTES

Note that the changes in ABA Model Rule 1.6 do not *mandate* disclosures but rather *permit* them. Some states have gone farther, requiring disclosure in cases of substantial bodily injury, and a few have even done so with respect to the relatively new exceptions for substantial financial harm to others that involve use of a lawyer's work product. We will look at these more expansive exceptions to MR 1.6 in Problems 25 and 27.

Finally, we should note before moving on that while the debate about broadening the narrow limits of disclosure has focused on these specific rules changes, there have long been other procedural (some lawyer-protective) exceptions to confidentiality, such as where a lawyer must defend against accusations brought by another, or even to enable a lawyer to press for payment of outstanding fees, both widely-accepted "self defense" exceptions in most jurisdictions.

7. *Tarasoff*, the Duty to Warn, and Its Consequences

In 1976, the California Supreme Court decided the case of *Tarasoff v. Regents of the Univ. of California*, 551 P.2d 334 (Cal. 1976). *Tarasoff* was a wrongful death case filed by the family of a woman who was killed by a University of California psychiatric patient after the patient had made direct threats on the woman's life to his therapist. The court upheld the family's right to sue the university, established an exception to the patient-psychotherapist privilege, and created a legal duty to warn potential victims when a patient presents a serious danger of violence.

Tarasoff quickly caused an enormous stir in both legal and medical circles, and has since become standard fare in law school and medical school texts on both ethics and torts. Psychiatrists argued that it could mark the end of psychiatry as they knew it, since patients would no longer be willing to disclose their true feelings in therapy, similar reasoning to that used by the New York State Bar Association in refusing to discipline attorney Francis Belge. For their part, lawyers worried that the *Tarasoff* standard would be applied to them, thus eroding the attorney-client relationship.

---

[17] [286] See generally D. Luban, *supra* note 25 (discussing the Ford Pinto case).

But the *Tarasoff* case presented an issue of civil liability and evidentiary privilege, and did not directly address a therapist's ethical duties. While this distinction might appear to be a fine one, the question in *Tarasoff* was, strictly speaking, not whether the therapist had an ethical duty to warn, but whether the university could be sued after he did not. Years later, the case has seemed to have little practical effect on the attorney-client relationship, while psychiatrists continue to practice without much visible change in the treatment of their patients.

Yet some psychiatrists — and some lawyers — now keep fewer records of their clients' confidences. One who still kept records was the psychiatrist in the highly publicized *Menendez* case in Los Angeles. That physician kept notes and tapes describing what both Eric and Lyle Menendez told him about killing their parents. The doctor also claimed that the brothers had threatened violence to others — including the doctor himself and his family. These threats became the focus of debate after the District Attorney got a search warrant to seize the psychiatrist's files and tapes in what was called a "*Tarasoff* raid." In a pre-trial proceeding, the California appellate court held that the evidence seized could be used at trial. *Menendez v. Superior Court*, 7 Cal. App. 4th 147 (Cal. Ct. App. 1991). The doctor's tapes and notes then became a principal focus in the explosive *Menendez* trial.

Tarasoff raises more questions than it answers. How much guidance does the case provide, since it is rooted in civil liability issues, not ethical ones?

Should attorneys have a *Tarasoff* duty to warn? Why or why not? How, if at all, do attorneys' obligations differ from those of psychiatrists? Every jurisdiction has rules that provide exceptions where confidentiality may be waived, but interestingly, there was *no* disclosure exception at all under California law when *Tarasoff* was decided. Does this mean that in these unusual circumstances the ethics rules are irrelevant to the analysis of duty? Finally, how should ethics rules and tort principles be integrated on such issues?

8.   Balancing the Duty to Warn: Pulling the Trigger vs. Jumping the Gun

At the least, most would argue that a lawyer should persuade the client not to act wrongly or violently. But is this always wise? What if that conversation spurs the client to violence? On the other hand, perhaps a bit of remonstration would persuade the lawyer that no real danger of violence exists. David McLaughlin, would certainly take this view. He made remarks to his lawyer that could have been construed as a threat to kill a judge who had ruled against him. The attorney elected to inform authorities, and McLaughlin found himself on trial. McLaughlin told the jury he was "just letting off steam," when he threatened to get his 9mm semiautomatic pistol and shoot the judge. The jury, several of whom acknowledged having made angry statements they later regretted, found McLaughlin not guilty. McLaughlin's next court case was his suit against his former lawyer for violating the attorney-client confidential relationship.[18]

---

[18] David McLaughlin, Plaintiff v. James T. Proctor, and DOES 1-10, Defendants, Marin County, CA Superior Court, No. 147546.

What would you have done if you were in this attorney's shoes? Is the lawyer "between a rock and a hard place" in deciding the right course of action? How do you determine when the threat is idle, and when a judge could end up dead? What standards should you apply? How sure must you be? Did his attorney jump the gun by failing sufficiently to investigate whether the situation was as dangerous as he had thought? Should he have at least discussed the matter with his client first? Did this lawyer unnecessarily violate his client's confidence?

9.   Confidentiality and Moral Imperative

What should a lawyer do with knowledge that a client has AIDS? Can the lawyer disclose that fact on the basis of danger to others? Read the following digest of an opinion by the Delaware Bar Association Professional Ethics Committee. Do you agree with this opinion? Are you comfortable that the Delaware Bar draws a distinction between a lawyer's ethical requirements and a "moral code"? How far should the ethical obligation to keep confidences extend in the face of what many would consider a moral imperative? Should there be a "moral compulsion" exception in the ethics rules?

DELAWARE BAR ASSOCIATION PROFESSIONAL ETHICS COMMITTEE, OPINION 1988-2
as digested in ABA/BNA's Lawyers' Manual on Professional Conduct, Vol. 5, No. 12 Ethics Opinions 901:2203 (1989)[19]

The lawyer's client has revealed that he has acquired immune deficiency syndrome. The woman with whom the client has lived for the last six months is a client of the lawyer's partner. This medical information was revealed to the lawyer in the course of representing the client, and the client has asked the lawyer not to reveal this to anyone. The lawyer is uncertain if the client has told the woman, but inquires whether he may properly disclose this fact to her if the client has not and does not choose to reveal it himself.

Rule 1.6 provides, in pertinent part, that a lawyer may not reveal information learned during the course of a representation unless the client has consented or unless it is necessary "to prevent the client from committing a criminal act that the lawyer believes is likely to result in imminent death or substantial bodily harm."

There is no Delaware statute that clearly makes criminal the transmission of AIDS to an unknown victim. Moreover, here it is not at all certain that the client will actually transmit AIDS to the woman with whom he lives, and therefore, the likelihood of imminent death or substantial bodily harm is less than in the situation where the client informs his lawyer that he intends to commit murder. Furthermore, under existing Delaware laws, the lawyer is not faced with a certain risk of civil or criminal liability if he maintains silence. Delaware law presently imposes no duty to warn a potential victim that AIDS may be contracted.

According to the letter of the ethics rules, the lawyer must maintain silence if his

---

[19] Copyright © 1990 by The American Bar Association/The Bureau of National Affairs, Inc. Reprinted by permission.

client requires it. But the lawyer may appropriately confront his client and under any moral code should do so. He should also point out the potential dangers in not disclosing. For example, it is not a crime, under current law, to fail to make disclosure, but a test case could be made. A prosecutor might argue that the client's conduct constitutes reckless endangering under 11 Del.C. 603 or 604. Also the lawyer should point out that there may be possible civil liability to the woman for failure to warn although existing law imposes no such obligation.

If, following confrontation with the client, the client still refuses to disclose his condition to the woman, then the lawyer's duty is non-disclosure. If the lawyer's moral code is such that he cannot abide by this duty, he may be pressed to the point of civil disobedience because obeying the letter of the law may require him to sacrifice more of his principles than he can bear. If so, the lawyer should inform his client of the decision to disclose and then be prepared to accept discipline if he cannot convince the disciplinary authorities to read a "moral compulsion" exception to the letter of Rule 1.6.

10.   A Terrorist Exception to Confidentiality?

In the aftermath of September 11, 2001, the United States government implemented the USA PATRIOT Act, and by the end of October 2001 the federal Bureau of Prisons (BOP) had adopted a new rule permitting the monitoring of otherwise confidential attorney-client communications.

The new rule authorized the Attorney General to order the BOP to monitor these communications when law enforcement had reasonable suspicion to believe that a prisoner was using attorney-client communications to facilitate acts of terrorism. Monitoring did not require judicial approval, and the Attorney General was given authority to review claims of privilege. The rule required the Attorney General to set up a separate team to investigate and monitor attorney-client communications. Although the team was to act separately from the office of the Attorney General and generally disclose material to law enforcement only by court order, communications could be disclosed without court approval if the team concluded that acts of violence were imminent.[20]

The government justified these measures on grounds of national security, noting that the Attorney General would only monitor where "inmates who have been involved in terrorist activities will pass messages through their attorneys for the purpose of continuing terrorist activities."[21]

Others saw the rule as direct interference with the attorney-client confidential relationship, claiming that the government's reliance on the crime fraud exception to the attorney-client *privilege* should not justify a preemptive interference with lawyer-client *confidentiality*.

---

[20] It was largely this rule and attendant BOP regulations that resulted in the criminal prosecution of attorney Lynne Stewart, referred to in Problem 2.

[21] *Prevention of Acts of Violence and Terrorism*, 66 FED. REG. at 55,064 (Oct. 31, 2001), as quoted in Avidan Y. Cover, *A Rule Unfit for All Seasons: Monitoring Attorney-Client Communications Violates Privilege and the Sixth Amendment*, 87 CORNELL L. REV. 1233, 1236 (2002).

The National Association of Criminal Defense Lawyers (NACDL) took a strong position against the rule, claiming that it prevented *any* conversations between lawyers and their prisoner clients, at least where the BOP had given the required written notification of monitoring. Some NACDL leaders argued that lawyers should refuse even to represent such prisoners. (The NACDL also argued that no lawyer should represent detainees in Guantanamo and thereby tacitly sanction the lack of due process afforded those detainees.)

Other government agencies also were accused of "spying" on lawyers and their terrorism-related clients. In New York City, Legal Aid lawyers appointed to represent detainees came up with a novel Fourth Amendment argument to protect *the lawyers' rights* to an attorney-client privilege, and seemed to gain some acceptance from the court.

John Caher, *Lawyers' Suit Proceeds over Taping of Conversations with Clients*
New York Law Journal, June 26, 2006[22]

Legal Aid lawyers claiming the government violated their rights by secretly recording attorney-client communications with 9/11 detainees won a major battle last week when a federal judge permitted the bulk of the action to proceed. The case is unusual in that it centers on the rights and privileges of lawyers operating behind the attorney-client shield, rather than the rights of the clients.

Eastern District of New York Judge Nina Gershon rejected nearly all of the arguments for dismissal, including qualified immunity, and said the attorneys raised a viable complaint under both the Wiretap Act and the Fourth Amendment. She dismissed a Fifth Amendment claim alleging violations of substantive due process rights, but only because that claim arose from the same alleged injuries and seeks the same remedy as the Fourth Amendment claim.

"The oldest privilege for confidential communications recognized by law, the attorney-client privilege, is intended to encourage full and frank communications between attorneys and their clients and thereby promote broader public interests in the observations of laws and the administration of justice," Judge Gershon wrote in Lonegan v. Hasty, 04-CV-2743. "That an individual is held in connection with an investigation of terrorist acts does not render that individual — or his or her attorney — ineligible for the protections of the Fourth Amendment."

Gershon's 36-page opinion and order is rooted in the terrorist attacks of Sept. 11, 2001, and the nation's response. In the aftermath, 84 individuals were arrested on immigration charges and detained at the Metropolitan Detention Center [MDC] in Brooklyn. None was ever charged with terrorist activity and most were simply deported.

Between Oct. 23, 2001, and Dec. 31, 2001, lawyers with the Legal Aid Society of New York conducted about 30 interviews with detainees. Officers at the MDC assured the lawyers that the meetings were not being taped. However, an investigation connected to another case led to the discovery of 308 videotapes proving that authorities had recorded meetings between attorneys and their clients.

A probe by the Justice Department's Office of the Inspector General found that meetings between attorneys and their clients were routinely recorded, despite the assurances the plaintiffs claim they were given by officials at the MDC.

. . . .

Gershon termed "misplaced" the defendant's reliance on cases holding that a convicted prisoner does not have a reasonable expectation of privacy within a prison cell. She observed that the plaintiffs in this case are defense attorneys, not convicted criminals, and that the interviews took place in an area designated for attorney-client communications, not in a cell.

NOTES

There are many issues related to the PATRIOT Act and other anti-terrorism measures, but here we focus on the following questions: Should national security ever trump the attorney-client confidential relationship? Is the distinction between privilege and confidentiality still viable when national security is at stake? Or should it remain inappropriate for the Attorney General — the prosecuting arm of the government — to make the decision about when that security is at issue? Would advance court approval help protect attorney-client confidentiality, or would requiring that protection simply be too slow in light of the threat of terrorism?

D. SUPPLEMENTAL READINGS

1. *Spaulding v. Zimmerman*, 116 N.W.2d 704 (Minn. 1962), is a case as unique — and as important — as the buried bodies case. This case, the basis for Professor Zacharias' third hypothetical, sets forth the balancing of confidentiality against public policy in the most dramatic possible fashion.

2. *People v. Meredith* has some distinct similarities to the earlier appeals court opinion in *People v. Lee*, 3 Cal. App. 3d 514 (Cal. Ct. App. 1970). *Lee* was an attempted murder case where the crime was committed by kicking the victim. The issue concerned the instrumentalities of the crime: bloody boots, hidden by the defendant, which his wife delivered to the Public Defender's Office. The PD in turn gave the boots to a judge when private counsel replaced the PD as counsel. The district attorney subsequently obtained the boots through a search warrant, and then introduced them at trial *along with* testimony from the Public Defender's Office testifying about the "chain of custody" of the boots. The court ruled, as in *Meredith* later, that the testimony was not protected under the attorney-client privilege.

3. *State v. Green*, 493 So. 2d 1178 (La. 1986). After shooting someone, the defendant met with an attorney to discuss how he might turn himself in. The defendant collected several items from his car and left them in the attorney's care. Rummaging through the items, the attorney found the gun involved in the

shooting, turned it over to the authorities, and then resigned from the case. In the subsequent murder trial appeal, the Louisiana Supreme Court ruled that the gun could be admitted into evidence, but *barred* the lawyer's testimony on attorney-client privilege grounds. John Randall Trahan, writing about this case in *A First Step Toward Resolution of the Physical Evidence Dilemma:* State v. Green, 48 LA. L. REV. 1019 (1988), analyzes the Louisiana Supreme Court's reasoning and reviews how different jurisdictions and courts have handled the "physical evidence dilemma."

4. *State v. Olwell,* 394 P.2d 681 (Wash. 1964). This case set forth a balancing test between the prosecution's right to introduce evidence, here a knife, and the lawyer's obligation to protect the source of the evidence. The knife was allowed into evidence, though the Washington Supreme Court reversed the lawyer's contempt citation, citing the attorney-client relationship and noting that the lawyer was entitled to hold the evidence for a reasonable period for testing purposes.

5. Jennifer Hodgkins, *Note: Attorney Compelled to Produce Kidnapper's Maps to Location of Baby's Body: Attorney-Client Privilege Yields to Policy Interests Embodied in State Ethical Rules of Confidentiality,* 29 TEX. TECH L. REV. 885 (1998) is a thorough, well-written review of the *Henderson* case discussed in section 2 above, the disapprobation and other pressures directed at the defense lawyer, and the ethical, public policy, and political decisions made by the court.

6. Monroe Freedman, *Where the Bodies Are Buried: The Adversary System and the Obligation of Confidentiality,* 10 CRIMINAL LAW BULLETIN 979 (1974). One of the leading thinkers on this issue concludes that the obligation of the attorney to the client and to the system of justice prevents the attorney from divulging information contrary to the client's interests.

7. GERALD F. UELMEN, LESSONS FROM THE TRIAL: THE PEOPLE V. O.J. SIMPSON, (1996). Professor Uelmen, an expert on ethics in criminal defense and former dean at Santa Clara School of Law, was a member of the team that defended O.J. Simpson. In this fascinating discussion of the defense of Simpson, he discusses, among many other items, how the team decided what to do with a knife discovered by the team.

8. Rodney J. Uphoff, *The Physical Evidence Dilemma: Does ABA Standard 4-4.6 Offer Appropriate Guidance,* 62 HASTINGS L.J. 1177 (2011) explores three scenarios that present variations on the physical evidence conundrum. He concludes that ABA Standard's more nuanced return-to-the-source rule strikes a better balance between defense counsel's duty to the court and the duties as an advocate, as opposed to the mandatory turnover rule championed by most courts and by § 119 of Restatement (Third) of the Law Governing Lawyers.

9. John M. Burman, *Lawyers and Domestic Violence: Raising the Standard of Practice,* 9 MICH. J. GENDER & L. 207 (2003), proposes that when it comes to issues of domestic violence, a lawyer should disclose. Burman reviews *Tarasoff* and surveys the status of the law in all 51 jurisdictions after the Ethics 2000 changes.

10. *In re Goebel,* 703 N.E.2d 1045 (Ind. 1998) is another case involving almost unique facts. Goebel, under physical threat from his indicted client, gave that client information about another client of the firm, whose husband was a witness against

Goebel's client. The information — an envelope that had been returned by the Postal Service due to a wrong address — contained a similar address from which the client deduced the correct address. The client in fact tracked down the witness and killed him. The lawyer could have revealed to the authorities the client's threat to himself and to the witness, but did not. Nevertheless, despite the breach of confidentiality and the obvious conflict of interest between the firm's clients, Goebel was punished with only a reprimand.

PROBLEM 5: WHEN DOES A LAWYER TALK TOO MUCH?

A. INTRODUCTION

In this chapter, we look at confidences from both ends of the spectrum. In Problem 4, we looked at when ordinarily protected confidential information must — or at least *may* — be revealed. Here, we examine the inopportune and unwise disclosure of confidences that otherwise are protected, the effects on confidentiality when an attorney consults another lawyer, and a few other unusual but important confidentiality issues. (We discuss inadvertent disclosures of confidences in Problem 6.)

What may a lawyer say about a client? What is permissible to reveal and what is "talking out of school"? If a confidence is revealed, either deliberately or unwisely, may opposing counsel use the information? What if circumstances make it difficult to engage in confidential communications at all? What limits are there, if any, on using the confidential information given by a consult*ing* lawyer to a consult*ed* attorney? Are there some matters, like a client's identity or whereabouts, which a lawyer *must* reveal because they don't rise to the level of confidential information? Consider the following scenarios involving three lawyers in Oil City.

B. PROBLEM

I

Attorney Matt Gold has a general practice in Oil City. He represents Anthony Verdi in a bitter divorce case. Discovery has been extensive, centering on the value of Verdi's business, and Gold has been having a lot of difficulty getting Verdi's cooperation. Verdi is an emotional sort, and argues about producing documents for far more time than he spends looking for them. In the last few weeks, he has called Gold at home several times to complain about his handling of the case.

Every Thursday afternoon, Matt joins Bruno Bianco and Joan Silver, good friends from their days together as associates, for a couple of hours of what they call "happy hour shop talk." Lately, Gold has taken to telling stories about Verdi, whom he's dubbed "the client from Hell." Last Thursday, Gold told his friends how Verdi called him at home at 10:30 p.m. and started yelling about Gold's having produced a document that was clearly discoverable. "This guy is such a pain in the keister," said Matt. "He's driving me nuts, and he's unpleasant on his best days. And he insists on telling me how to run the case. Besides," adds Matt, "I'm not so sure he's telling me the truth anyway about what his business is worth."

QUESTIONS

Is this reasonable discourse between friends or the improper revelation of the confidences or secrets of a client? Would it make a difference if Gold referred to a "client from Hell" without revealing his actual identity?

Which among Gold's statements breach confidentiality?

II

Samantha Redfern is a family law practitioner currently representing Serge Popnik, the owner of a chain of high-end men's clothing stores, in a contested divorce proceeding. Redfern learns from Popnik that he has hidden some assets, arguably community property or joint marital property, through questionable transfers to relatives. Redfern is concerned about certain tax aspects of Popnik's dealings. She calls tax attorney James T. McGuire for advice. Redfern meets with McGuire. In order to ask McGuire for his thoughts on solutions for Popnik's tax problems, she discloses to McGuire some of the confidential information that Popnik revealed to her.

QUESTIONS

1. May Redfern reveal Popnik's confidential information to McGuire without letting her client know? What if it is necessary to reveal Popnik's secrets in order to get adequate advice from McGuire?

2. Does Redfern need an advance promise or guarantee of confidentiality from McGuire before discussing Popnik's case with him? Or should she conceal Popnik's identity, and speak to McGuire only "hypothetically"?

3. Suppose that two weeks after Redfern's chat with McGuire, Mrs. Popnik's attorney calls McGuire to hire him as an expert consultant in the divorce. May McGuire accept the engagement? If McGuire works for Mrs. Popnik, may he disclose the information he learned from Redfern about Mr. Popnik? Must he? How would these answers change if Redfern had spoken to him only hypothetically?

III

David Grey is an Oil City general practitioner. One of his oldest clients is Armand Varady, a businessman who owns the city's only Hungarian restaurant. Early one morning, Varady is arrested for driving under the influence. After he is released on his promise to appear, Varady meets with Grey and makes a confession. "David, I got to tell you, Varady is not my real name. See, 15 years ago I got in trouble in Ohio, and I ran away from a work furlough house before I served my whole sentence. Armand Varady is the name of my cousin in Cleveland who died back in '92. But if I give my real name, everything I've accomplished here, my business, my family, is for nothing." After Varady leaves, Grey sits down to think about what to do.

QUESTIONS

1. Does Grey have an obligation to the court to reveal Varady's true identity, or at least the fact that his client is using a false name? Or must Grey protect Varady's confidence at all costs?

2. *When*, if ever, that is at what point in the proceedings from arraignment to trial, must Grey reveal the true identity?

C. READINGS

1. Do "Loose Lips Sink Ships"?

In dealing realistically with the confidences of a client, how tight-lipped must an attorney be? Consider the actions of the criminal defense lawyer in the highly publicized Polly Klaas case. On October 1, 1993, 12-year-old Polly Klaas was abducted from her bedroom in the small, semi-rural town of Petaluma, California. Two months later, her body was found in a wooded area 50 miles north of her home. Polly's case attracted enormous national media attention, and an 8,000-member volunteer army that circulated millions of flyers nationwide. Her memorial service was attended by 2,000 people, and was broadcast live on CNN. Her father, Marc Klaas, became a national spokesperson for parents of child victims.

Parolee Richard Allen Davis was arrested and charged with Polly's abduction and killing. The police reported that Davis had confessed to the crime and led them to the girl's body.

Public Defender Marteen Miller was appointed to represent Davis. After the arraignment, Miller held a sidewalk press conference in an atmosphere of intense media attention. Miller told the press Davis had admitted abducting and strangling Polly while under the influence of drugs and alcohol. Miller also said that Davis was not using his drugged state as an excuse and quoted Davis as saying, "I am responsible for this and I deserve any punishment I get." Miller said that Davis "just doesn't care about his fate" and might plead guilty.

Miller's press interview provoked considerable controversy. Some legal experts were concerned that Miller's statements laid the groundwork for an inevitable appeal, and others called for his removal. Dennis Riordan, whose clients have included Barry Bonds, San Quentin Six prisoner Johnny Spain, and the "West Memphis Three" released from prison in 2011, told the *National Law Journal* he was stunned that Mr. Miller "would apparently walk out of the interview with his client and announce what his client had said." Other lawyers were more tolerant. Davis was "already on the bus to the gas chamber," one well-known lawyer told the *National Law Journal*.

What do you think? Were Miller's public remarks ethical? Or did they improperly disclose client confidences? If confidential material was disclosed, does it matter whether the remarks helped or hurt Davis? The Davis case also raises another question: Would it be ethical for a defendant's trial lawyer, seeing no viable defense, to purposely create error by revealing confidences, thus jeopardizing a conviction and possibly postponing the client's execution date?

In practice, the revelation of attorney-client confidences may be far more common than most attorneys would like to think. Nevertheless, most ethical rules are broadly prohibitive of such revelations, and most courts adopt a strict "loose lips sink ships" attitude. Indeed, that attitude may extend even to matters learned by the lawyer that may be public. Many jurisdictions hold that these matters too are confidential, at least unless the matter is "generally known."[1]

2.   Is "Absolute" Confidentiality Truly Absolute?

Writing in 2004, Professor Abbe Smith, co-director of Georgetown's Criminal Justice Clinic, decries the words of another loose-lipped lawyer, quoted in the 2003 documentary *Capturing the Friedmans*, and then sets forth her outspoken philosophy as a "confidentiality absolutist."

Abbe Smith, *Telling Stories and Keeping Secrets*
8 D.C. L. Rev. 255 (2004)[2]

I. *A Storyteller and Confidentiality Absolutist*

In the course of writing this article, I saw the documentary Capturing the Friedmans, a powerful and disturbing film about . . . the father Arnold Friedman and the youngest son Jesse . . . charged with multiple counts of child sexual abuse. Although both Arnold and Jesse pleaded guilty, the charges seem questionable at best. . . .

For me, one of the most distressing things about the film was the appearance of Jesse's lawyer, Peter Panaro. . . . Clearly not among those lawyers who believe there is a professional obligation to preserve client confidences and secrets in the broadest sense, Panaro feels free to talk about everything from his revulsion toward Jesse's father to his belief that Jesse must have been guilty. . . .

Worse is Panaro's account of Jesse's tearful "confession." . . . In the film, Jesse denies his lawyer's account, and clearly did not give Panaro permission to say such a thing. The lawyer's conduct in the film is appallingly unethical.

. . . .

There is a growing concern . . . about telling client stories, mostly because of the potential exploitation of clients and, secondarily, because it encroaches on client confidentiality. . . .

I confess that I can sometimes be glib about this. I have even been known to refer to the "Good Story Exception" to confidentiality. . . . Of course, this is a narrowly drawn exception: If the story is run-of-the-mill, workaday, or otherwise not very compelling, the exception would not apply. This exception is in keeping with the increasing call for lawyers to violate client confidences in furtherance of the greater social good. But does protecting innocent human life necessarily have more social value than a really good story well told?

Glibness aside, how . . . can I — someone who makes her living by talking to judges and juries, clients and witnesses, students and fellows — accommodate a professional requirement to keep my mouth shut? Odd combination though it is, I

---

[1] *See, e.g.,* Iowa Sup. Ct. Attorney Disciplinary Bd. v. Marzen, 779 N.W.2d 757 (Iowa 2010).

[2] Copyright © 2004 by the University of the District of Columbia, David A. Clarke School of Law, Law Review. Reprinted by permission.

believe in both telling stories and keeping secrets. I believe that doing both is what good lawyers do . . . . Lawyers who believe that the ethical duty to protect client confidences is inviolable, no matter the social cost, are "confidentiality absolutists." To these lawyers — and I am one — client trust is sacrosanct; all other values must give way to the principle of maintaining client trust and confidence.

. . . .

Confidentiality absolutists believe that attorney-client confidentiality, unlike doctor-patient confidentiality and/or psychotherapist-client confidentiality, is inviolate. In this regard, it is more like priest-penitent confidentiality. It is not that attorneys, like priests, are stand-ins for God, but that confidences shared in a lawyer's office, police office, or jail cell should be treated as if they were shared in the confessional.

The concept of confidentiality has a long history dating back (ignominiously) to ancient Rome, where slaves were prohibited by law from revealing their master's secrets, and (not so ignominiously) attorneys were not allowed to give testimony against clients. The attorney-client privilege was first recognized in England in the late sixteenth century, and . . . in the United States at least by the middle of the nineteenth century. Under the Field Code of Procedure, adopted in 1848 in New York, lawyers were required to "maintain inviolate the confidence and at every peril to himself, to preserve the secrets of . . . clients." Under the influential 1887 Alabama Code of Ethics, the first formally adopted body of ethical rules, lawyers had "not only a legal duty to maintain the client's confidences under the attorney-client privilege, but . . . an absolute duty to maintain the secrets and confidences of the client at all costs as a matter of professional ethics." The ABA's Canons of Professional Ethics, adopted in 1908, expressly protected clients' "secrets or confidences" in Canon 6.

. . . .

Trust between lawyer and client has been called the "cornerstone of the adversary system and effective assistance of counsel." Just as the Bill of Rights protects individual freedom, lawyers who maintain client confidences protect individual privacy, dignity, and autonomy.

. . . .

II. *The Hard Cases*

There are always hard cases. Law practice wouldn't be nearly as interesting if there weren't hard cases raising difficult moral dilemmas. For me, the hard cases are (1) the hypothetical client who confesses to a murder for which the wrong man is about to be executed; (2) the real-life client who confides in his lawyer about judicial corruption; and (3) corporate clients who confide in lawyers about wrongful and/or criminal conduct that will likely pose danger to others . . . .

A. The Wrong Inmate About to be Executed

I became a criminal lawyer because, among other reasons, I wanted to help make sure that no innocent people (at least on my watch) are convicted and imprisoned or put to death. My commitment to this goal — and my life-long opposition to the death penalty — make the "execution of the wrong man" hypothetical especially difficult for me. It would be painful if I ever had to confront this situation in the flesh.

Still, if a client came to me and revealed that he had committed a crime for which an innocent man had been sent to death row, [i]f the client refused, . . . resisted all entreaties, and I were forced to conclude that he could not be moved, I would leave him be and keep his trust. It would not be easy, but I would manage it. In the aftermath, I would do what I could not to take it all on myself — though I imagine I would feel aggrieved and guilt-ridden.

In order to soothe my guilty conscience, I would likely point out that there is no guarantee, if I divulge such a confidence, that it would have any effect on the fate of the wrongly convicted man. The criminal justice system is deeply flawed, and this would be just one more wrongful conviction and punishment. . . .

B. Judicial Corruption

In 1992, Douglas Schafer, a lawyer in Tacoma, Washington, had a conversation with a client named William Hamilton. Hamilton told Schafer that Grant Anderson, who was about to become a Superior Court judge, was going to engage in improprieties as the trustee of a decedent's estate. Soon afterward, Hamilton bought a bowling alley owned by the estate at a below-market price, and, at around the same time, gave Judge Anderson a Cadillac. Hamilton shared this information with Schafer, who, outraged by such blatant judicial corruption, disclosed it to the authorities. Schafer's disclosure had impact. In 1999, in response to the information Schafer conveyed, the Washington Supreme Court removed Judge Anderson from the bench for "a pattern of dishonest behavior unbecoming a judge."

In 2003, attorney Schafer . . . was suspended from law practice for six months for the "willful, unnecessary and repeated violation of his ethical duty not to betray his client's trust." The ruling by the Washington Supreme Court prompted outcry on the order of "no good deed goes unpunished."

This is a hard case for me because, to my mind, there is no greater problem in our justice system than judicial corruption. Judicial corruption strikes at the heart of our system of justice. . . .

When judges are found to have engaged in corrupt conduct — whether as judges or lawyers — they ought to be brought down, and brought down hard.

Still, whatever Schafer's motive, I have no problem with his being disciplined. Schafer should not have divulged his client's confidences, no matter what sort of shenanigans his client was involved in. . . .

It is important to remember that the client confidences Shafer divulged put his client in jeopardy as well as a corrupt judge. Hamilton's insider deal with his

Cadillac quid pro quo was surely not lawful.

C. Corporate Clients

A number of legal scholars distinguish between corporate lawyers and criminal defense lawyers when it comes to confidentiality. I am sympathetic to this view and wish I could agree that a principled line can be drawn. Corporate clients are wealthy and bent on becoming wealthier. The dignity and autonomy interests of corporations and their CEO's are less compelling to me than those of individual criminal defendants. . . .

On the other hand, there is a compelling argument that lawyers ought to balance their professional obligations more heavily on the side of the public interest in a corporate context. Corporations are powerful entities. They can do real harm, whether we are talking about product safety, environmental hazards, tax evasion, or fraud. The traditional concern about individual rights is not an effective rejoinder to the claim that confidentiality has been used to shield organizational misconduct.

Still, I believe that lawyers can use their powers of persuasion and more [in the] long tradition of the corporate lawyer as "wise counselor." Corporations . . . choose their counsel based on many attributes, including the lawyer's value system. This is all the more reason for these lawyers to engage in moral as well as legal counseling with their clients. They should do everything they can to get these clients to do the right thing.

Conclusion

. . . [I]n the end, I don't have much faith in lawyers . . . exercising their own moral discretion about whether to disclose client confidences. I don't want to give lawyers the authority to determine when it is in the public interest to divulge confidences, even if they were allowed to do so only under limited circumstances, such as "where necessary to avoid 'substantial injustice.' "

NOTES

Professor Smith raises a series of issues we'll address later on in this volume, from the innocent man convicted of murder to an examination of corporate confidentiality in the new millennium.[3]

Smith's "absolutist" perspective raises several interesting questions, among them: Is there a point where "the interests of justice" must trump lawyer-client confidentiality to avoid the corruption of the judicial system? Are corporate entities entitled to the same principles of confidentiality that arose as an *individual* right? And finally, should lawyers ever be complicit, even by their silence, in the death of an innocent person?

As to the first question, the timing of this article — and many others focusing renewed scrutiny on confidentiality — is hardly coincidental. As we mentioned in

---

[3] *See* Problem 25 and elsewhere.

Problem 4, in 2002 and 2003, the ABA modified two important rules — MRs 1.6 and 1.13 in order to create several exceptions to strict confidentiality. Many if not most observers attributed some of these modifications, especially in Rule 1.13, to the fallout over Enron and similar scandals, and the effect of the so-called Sarbanes-Oxley legislation which, coupled with new SEC regulations addressing the duties of attorneys confronted by wrongdoing on the part of their "issuer" clients, materially increased the scope of attorney whistleblowing.[4]

3. The "Wrong Murderer" Cases

As to the last question, there have been several relatively recent cases in which lawyers have come forward after years of silence with information that exonerated prisoners on death row or serving a life sentence. Each of these cases has its own idiosyncratic features. The recurring theme in these cases is that the lawyers felt duty-bound by client confidentiality not to speak until some event — these events vary — came to pass. In chronological order:

• *Daryl Atkins, Virginia, January 2008*: Leslie P. Smith represented William Jones on murder charges. Jones and co-defendant Daryl R. Atkins forced a man to make a withdrawal from an ATM machine and then killed him. Both were convicted, but Atkins was sentenced to death while Jones received "LWOP" — life in prison without possibility of parole. (Under Virginia law only the actual perpetrator may get the death penalty.)

In his taped statement to the DA, Jones clearly identified Atkins as the shooter, but Smith knew that the prosecutors had stopped and started the interview tape and coached Jones to straighten out his inconsistent facts. Knowing that Jones — his own client — had been coached into saying that Atkins, not he, fired the gun, Smith asked Virginia's ethics counsel whether he could reveal this. They told him to remain silent. After all, he was bound by the duty of confidentiality.

After Jones' appeals were exhausted and his case final over, Smith again sought permission from the Virginia ethics authorities to speak. This time they told him to go ahead, since speaking would have no adverse effect on Jones. He did, disclosing the perceived prosecutorial misconduct and his belief that Atkins should be taken off death row. Atkins was eventually resentenced.

• *Alton Logan, Illinois, Spring 2008*: In 1982, Chicago lawyers Dale Coventry and W. Jamie Kunz represented Andrew Wilson on charges of killing two police officers. Wilson was eventually convicted and sentenced to prison for life. At about the same time, a man named Alton Logan was convicted of killing a McDonald's security guard, and he too was convicted and sentenced to life. Coventry and Kunz knew that Logan was innocent because Wilson had committed that killing too, and told his lawyers about it, unabashedly and almost gleefully. Logan was simply the victim of a case of mistaken identity.

Both Coventry and Kunz felt that they could reveal nothing. They did write an affidavit stating what they knew and placed it in a safety deposit box. When they

---

[4] We'll return at some length to Sarbanes-Oxley and other new corporate whistleblowing standards in Problem 25.

learned that Wilson had died in prison in November 2007, feeling no longer bound by confidentiality, they came forward. Alton Logan was exonerated and released in April 2008, 26 years after his incarceration.

• *Lee Wayne Hunt, North Carolina, May 2008*: In 1986, North Carolina lawyer Staples Hughes represented Jerry Cashwell on murder charges. Cashwell and his co-defendant, Lee Wayne Hunt, were both convicted of murder. But Cashwell told Hughes that Hunt had nothing to do with the murder, and that Cashwell, angered by his neighbors' television being too loud, had argued with the neighbors and killed them both.

But Hughes too said nothing, even after Cashwell's 2002 suicide in prison. It wasn't until 2007 that he determined to come forward, haunted by an innocent man serving a life sentence.

In this case, however, others were less than appreciative. Judge Jack A. Thompson excoriated Hughes, telling him, "If you testify I will be compelled to report you to the State Bar." Hughes was undeterred. But after his testimony, Thompson accused Hughes of "professional misconduct" and would not even consider new testimony relating to Hunt's innocence. Hughes then fought disciplinary charges, although these were eventually dropped. Hunt remains in prison.

• *Bill Macumber, Arizona, 2012*: This case has received a good deal of press because Governor Jan Brewer refused to release Macumber in 2009, despite much public pressure and the unanimous recommendations of Arizona's clemency board, and then replaced the majority of the clemency board in 2012 before denying Macumber's release once again.

Factually, Bill Macumber's case may be the strangest. The killings for which Macumber was convicted were a double homicide in 1962. Macumber's wife, now known as Carol Kempfert, was the accuser, telling her superiors in the local sheriff's office in 1974 that her husband had confessed to her. Based primarily on her testimony, Macumber was convicted.

But at the time of Macumber's trial over 35 years ago, a young lawyer named Thomas W. O'Toole had come forward, stating that his former client, already dead, had confessed to these very murders. His client, Ernesto Valenzuela, had been convicted of two very similar murders. His testimony was never heard by the jury after the trial judge ruled it inadmissible.

Years later, a lawyer for a university "justice project" told Macumber and Kempfert's son Ron that his father was almost surely innocent, framed by the mother during an ugly divorce. O'Toole, who by this time had been a judge for a quarter-century, reiterated his proposed testimony. But the sick and elderly Macumber remained in prison.

Finally, in November 2012, at age 77 and after 37 years in prison, Bill Macumber was freed, after accepting a political compromise: a no contest plea in return for his release. This was not exoneration, however. The local district attorney, for example, maintains Macumber is guilty.[5]

Each of these cases is different, but they raise several distinct questions and illustrate several distinct points:

First, when does attorney-client confidentiality give way in the face of grave harm to an innocent person? Does it have to be the imminent implementation of the death penalty? One wonders what Virginia attorney Leslie Smith would have done if Atkins were on the verge of having his death sentence carried out. Would he have been able to remain silent, as Abbe Smith says she would do? Should he have?

Second, can an argument be made that even sitting on death row or in prison for life is in and of itself "substantial bodily harm" as defined in MR 1.6(b)? After all, that's a brutal life.

Third, when does attorney-client confidentiality end? At death? When no further harm can befall the client through revelation? Or never?

Monroe Freedman, long a scholar of ethics, confidentiality, and criminal defense, told *New York Times*'s Adam Liptak that he'd "draw the line at the life-and-death situation" before reveling a confidence, noting that "extend[ing] it to incarceration in general" would make it far too broad. But later in the same article, Freedman acknowledges that Virginia's Smith may have acted properly "[i]f there is no threat of civil action against the client's estate and there are no survivors who continue to believe in the client's innocence."

The trigger for each of the attorneys in these four cases — including those where the client died — was slightly different. In Illinois, the lawyers said that their client had agreed they could reveal the truth after his death; in Arizona, Judge O'Toole got permission from his client's personal representative, his mother; and in North Carolina, attorney Hughes acted without additional permission, perhaps explaining some of the judge's ire.

Smith's client in Virginia was still alive, however. Here, with State Bar imprimatur, Smith of Virginia, resorted to the "no-more-possible-harm" criterion suggested by Freedman: "What reputational interest did Jerry have?" he asked. "He had pleaded guilty to killing two people . . . . His estate was a pair of shower shoes and two paperback books."

But the rule in most states as to when confidentiality ends is "never."[6]

In *Swidler & Berlin v. United States*, 524 U.S. 399 (1998), sometimes called "the Vince Foster case," Chief Justice Rehnquist upheld a posthumous attorney-client

---

[5] Adam Liptak writes regularly on legal issues for the NEW YORK TIMES. A few of his stories about wrongful conviction include: Adam Liptak, *No Way Out: The Changing Rules to More Inmates, Life Term Means Dying Behind Bars*, N.Y. TIMES, Oct. 2, 2005; Adam Liptak, *When Law Prevents Righting a Wrong*, N.Y. TIMES, May 4, 2008; and Adam Liptak, *A Potent Mix of Crime, Punishment and the Elusiveness of Freedom*, N.Y. TIMES, June 15, 2010. There was a lot of coverage of the *Macumber* case. One succinct summary was found on line: Richard Ruelas, *Arizona Man Convicted in 1962 Murders Freed*, THE REPUBLIC, azcentral.com, Nov. 9, 2012.

[6] HLC Properties, Ltd. v. Superior Court, 105 P.3d 560 (Cal. 2005), however, held that the attorney client privilege passes to the personal representative and when that person has discharged all duties, the privilege terminates.

privilege. This case came about when Kenneth Starr, the Clinton administration independent counsel, wanted to question White House counsel Vincent Foster regarding Hillary Clinton's role in the firing of seven employees of the White House travel office. Nine days later, before Starr could question him, Foster killed himself. Starr then sought Foster's lawyer's notes, claiming that the attorney-client privilege does not extend beyond a client's death. The Court disagreed:

> there are weighty reasons that counsel in favor of posthumous application [of the privilege]. Knowing that communications will remain confidential even after death encourages the client to communicate fully and frankly with counsel. . . . Clients may be concerned about reputation, civil liability, or possible harm to friends or family. Posthumous disclosure of such communications may be as feared as disclosure during the client's lifetime.

The Court also disagreed with Starr's assumption that the privilege rests in criminal law, similar to the Fifth Amendment self-incrimination protection:

> Clients consult attorneys for a wide variety of reasons, [beyond] possible criminal liability.

> This is true of disclosure before and after the client's death. Without assurance of the privilege's posthumous application, the client may very well not have made disclosures to his attorney at all, so the loss of evidence is more apparent than real. In the case at hand, it seems quite plausible that Foster, perhaps already contemplating suicide, may not have sought legal advice from [his lawyer] if he had not been assured the conversation was privileged.

Although death doesn't destroy an attorney's duty to keep a client's secrets, what about concealing a client's death. For example, New Jersey explicitly forbids lawyers from concealing personal injury clients' deaths in order to get better settlements,[7] while other courts have held that there is no duty to reveal the death of a client or a witness.[8]

4. Lawyer-to-Lawyer Consultations, Client Confidences, and a Dense ABA Opinion

Lawyers frequently consult with other lawyers to get specific advice or ideas on how to handle difficult or unfamiliar situations. In fact, as we learned in Problem 1, sometimes a lawyer *must* consult with an attorney more knowledgeable about the subject of the representation in order to competently take on the case. However, if the consulting attorney discloses client confidences to the consulted attorney, does the information lose its confidentiality? If so, what steps may, or must, the consulting attorney take to protect the client's secrets?

---

[7] *See* Eleanor Barrett, *Concealing Client's Death Gets Lawyer Suspended*, AMERICAN LAW MEDIA online services (July 9, 1999).

[8] See *People v. Jones*, 375 N.E.2d 41 (N.Y. 1978), which we excerpt in Problem 18, where we discuss more about such concealment.

On the other hand, what must the *consulted* attorney consider before giving advice? Is there information the consulted attorney should obtain before agreeing to the consultation? May the consulted attorney use the information received to the detriment of the client of the consulting attorney?

The ABA Standing Committee on Ethics and Professional Responsibility addressed these questions in one of its more convoluted opinions, Formal Opinion 98-411. This opinion concluded that the consulting attorney has only limited authority to disclose client information for certain matters "impliedly authorized" without express client authorization. "Hypothetical or anonymous consultations thus are favored where possible," says the opinion, because client secrets may best be protected that way. However, if the consulted attorney is able to divine either the client's identity or the specific case from the facts given, the consulting attorney will have violated client confidentiality, making anonymity at best a double-edged sword.

Moreover, the opinion concluded that merely being consulted does not give the consulted attorney any duty to the client of the consulting attorney, except if the consulted lawyer voluntarily takes on a duty to protect the new client's confidences *or* whenever "a reasonable attorney would know that confidentiality is assumed and expected." Whatever that phrase means. Absent any express agreement or "assumed or expected" understanding about confidentiality, the consulted attorney could use the client's information or disclose it to third persons.

Cautioning that giving advice could compromise the consulted lawyer's loyalty to existing clients, the opinion suggests that the consulted attorney get as much information about the consulting attorney's case and client as possible in order to do a thorough conflicts check (something we'll address at length in Problem 10). Additionally, the opinion recommends that the consulted attorney ask the consulting attorney to waive any conflicts of interest, or have the consulting lawyer's client agree to an ethical screen (another subject we discuss in Problem 10). The opinion does not address what happens if a conflict occurs after-the-fact, when the consulted attorney is *later* hired by the other side, *particularly* when the first consult was "hypothetical."

Understandably, Formal Opinion 98-411 has been the subject of considerable debate and substantial criticism, much of it justified. In an attempt to shine a light on a sticky subject that raises a wide range of issues, it may raise more questions than it answers. Southern Methodist University ethics Professors Frederick Moss and William Bridge set forth their criticism of this opinion in a 1999 law review article that warned that the Opinion's "main tactic is to establish, if only by repetition, that a client-lawyer relationship does not arise between the consulting lawyer's client and the consulted lawyer. Thus, if a consulted lawyer makes no promise, he is free of any ethical obligation to the consulting lawyer's client."[9]

Moss and Bridge note that Opinion 98-411's use of what they call the "quickie consult," i.e., "when a lawyer calls a colleague at another firm or a former law

---

[9] Frederick C. Moss & William J. Bridge, *Can We Talk?: A "Steele-Y" Analysis of ABA Opinion 411*, 52 SMU L. REV. 683 (1999). The "down-home" aphorisms contained in the article are in honor of their mentor, Professor Walter Steele.

professor to pose a hypothetical situation . . . from a real case, but [with] no identifying information," makes some sense. There, at least, they believe the lack of an attorney-client relationship between the consulted attorney and the consulting attorney's client seems "beyond dispute." They are more troubled with the Opinion's argument about "implied authorizations" by the client that enable the lawyer to consult with an outside counsel, which they describe as "as leaky as a bad bait bucket":

> We are left to guess exactly how the client is protected by her "reasonable expectation" of confidentiality.

> As for the consultation which becomes "un-anonymous" [n]o client-lawyer relationship exists, and therefore there is no duty. . . .

> The Committee's solution to the problem of the consultation that later becomes "un-anonymous" is, of course, prevention.

This prevention, they note, is to advise, anomalously in their view, that the consulted attorney check for conflicts of interest even though the Opinion actually "endorses hypothetical consultations" and acknowledges that no attorney-client relationship is thereby formed. And, as we've noted and even the opinion notes, hypothetical consultations are problematic, especially should they become "un-anonymous." Finally, the implication in the opinion that the consulted attorney may take on duties if "a reasonable lawyer" would know confidentiality is "assumed" opens up a troubling Pandora's box.

What should be made of all this? Some authorities posit that a client's confidences are protected so long as the consulting attorney seeks advice for the benefit of the client. Others are concerned that if lawyers must take such elaborate precautions to protect their respective clients (and guard against malpractice claims), they may simply take a pass on seeking advice, even when their lack of expertise or knowledge puts them at a disadvantage.

Do similar problems arise when a client replaces one attorney with another? May the old attorney disclose to the new attorney the client secrets he or she gained during the representation? Analyst Marla B. Rubin[10] believes that in general the old attorney may not divulge the client's secrets to the new lawyer without client consent, unless the client will benefit by such a disclosure.

5. When the Lawyer (Not the Client) Needs the Consultation

Another important issue is what happens when Attorney *A* wants to consult Lawyer *B* not for the benefit of *A's* client, but for the protection of *the attorney*. For instance, attorney *A* may have become privy to information about a client's possible future crime, or may be worried about an emerging conflict of interest. Here, the attorney wants to consult with a lawyer to protect the *attorney's own* rights, not the client's. Even though the need for such lawyer-to-lawyer help seems

---

[10] Marla B. Rubin, *Not Unless It Would Be to Their Benefit: Can You Disclose Clients' Confidences to New Counsel?, in* Law Firm Partnership and Benefits Report 10 (1997).

obvious, ethical rules had traditionally not dealt with this issue, until the relatively recent amendment to Model Rule 1.6, subsection (b)(4) added language authorizing attorneys to "reveal information relating to the representation of a client to secure legal advice about the lawyer's compliance with the Rules." This goes a long way towards enabling lawyers to get appropriate advice before making decisions — possibly ill-advised or ill-considered ones — on their clients' behalf.

What about where a lawyer may have committed malpractice? May the lawyer confidentially consult with others in the firm — the "loss prevention" partner, the ethics committee, or the managing partner — or may the others consult confidentially about the problem among themselves? These questions are beyond the scope of MR 1.6(b)(4), but not beyond the scope of recent analysis by several courts and commentators. They generally arise in the context of *privilege*: when a law firm claims in a later malpractice suit that its internal conversations were privileged as internal attorney-client communications.

It makes perfect sense that ordinarily, lawyers in a firm should be able to maintain a privilege when consulting others in the firm. The Restatement, § 73, comments (c) and (i) and ABA Formal Opinion 08-453 (2008) say as much. But when a law firm's representation of a client is ongoing when the firm's possible malpractice of that client arises, most courts have held that internal consultations on this topic are *not* privileged. They reason that even if the firm itself is a client, so too is the existing client, and those conflicting interests vitiate any internal privilege. Some have gone so far as to say that these discussions are not *confidential* — i.e., that the duty of candid communication requires revealing the malpractice to the client.[11]

Most opinions on this issue have come from federal courts, several from the Northern District of California. This 2011 order from a California magistrate judge proffers a succinct summary of the situation that reflects what appears to be the current consensus:

E-PASS TECHNOLOGIES, INC. v. MOSES & SINGER, LLP
2011 U.S. Dist. LEXIS 96231 (N.D. Cal. Aug. 26, 2011)

Order re Motion to Compel

The question here is whether and to what extent privileges apply to communications within a law firm regarding potential claims against a firm arising from its representation of an outside client. . . . In *Thelen Reid & Priest, LLP v. Marland*, No. 06-2071, 2007 U.S. Dist. LEXIS 17482, . . . (N.D. Cal. Feb. 21, 2007), . . . the court concluded that where there was a potential conflict of interest between the firm and its client the firm had to produce any communications 1) discussing claims that the client might have against the firm, 2) discussing known errors in the firm's

---

[11] ABA Formal Opinion 08-453 is strangely unclear on this issue. The opinion concludes that in-house consultation is confidential and appropriate where a lawyer consults internally to avoid acting unethically on a client's behalf, even where client confidences are revealed. But while the opinion concludes that "ethics counsel's" client is the firm as a whole, it doesn't directly address vitiating either confidentiality or the privilege.

representation of the client, and 3) discussing any known conflicts between the firm and the client. As another court held: "a law firm's communication with in-house counsel is not protected by the attorney client privilege if the communication implicates or creates a conflict between the law firm's fiduciary duties to itself and its duties to the client seeking to discover the communication." *In re Sunrise Securities Litigation*, 130 F.R.D. 560, 597 (E.D. Pa. 1989). "[W]here conflicting duties exist, the law firm's right to claim privilege must give way to the interest in protecting current clients who may be harmed by the conflict." *In re SonicBlue, Inc.*, No. 03-51775, 2008 Bankr. LEXIS 181, . . . (N.D. Cal. Bkrtcy. Jan. 18, 2008) . . . .

It is undisputed that Moses & Singer represented E-Pass in on-going litigation through at least some time after November 14, 2007, the date the district court decided the pending attorneys' fees motion. . . . The Court finds that the relationship was terminated, at the latest, on May 8, 2008. . . . The majority of the communications that took place during the attorney-client relationship, that is, before May 8, 2008, relate to the attorneys' fees motion brought against both E-Pass and Moses & Singer. Moses & Singer cannot credibly dispute that it owed a fiduciary duty to E-Pass during the time it represented E-Pass on this attorneys' fees motion. Rather, it is making the unprecedented argument that notwithstanding its fiduciary duty, at the same time it was representing E-Pass on the motion it could engage in intra-firm communications relating to how to protect itself from liability on the motion and then withhold those communications from E-Pass. Moses & Singer's interests were in conflict with those of E-Pass to the extent its interests were not fully aligned with E-Pass. . . .

If it intended to separately — and confidentially — represent itself on the fees motion it had a duty to disclose this conflict and obtain E-Pass's consent to continued representation. Because it failed to do so, it cannot claim that internal communications discussing or implicating such a conflict are privileged. . . .

As discussed above, the attorney-client relationship ended May 8, 2008 at the latest.

Communications between Moses & Singer attorneys after this date, even those which discuss E-Pass, are protected by the attorney-client privilege. . . .

For the foregoing reasons, Plaintiff's Motion to Compel is GRANTED IN PART.

Within 14 days from the filing date of this Order, Defendants shall provide Plaintiff with copies of the nonprivileged communications as set forth in this Order.

NOTES

This view, while not unanimous, seems to be the clear direction of the decisional law in those jurisdictions that have addressed the issue.[12]

---

[12] *See, e.g.,* Cold Spring Harbor Lab. v. Ropes & Gray LLP, 2011 U.S. Dist. LEXIS 77824 (D. Mass. July 19, 2011).

6. "MDPs," Unbundling, and Confidentiality

Many consumers would like to see "one-stop shopping" for legal and other related services. At the high, monied end, such services are often called "multidisciplinary practices," or "MDPs" while as we've seen in Problem 3, limited legal services are often described as "unbundled." Whether for big corporations or the poor, multidisciplinary and limited services raise the issue of how and to what extent confidentiality can be maintained when non-lawyers become involved. We'll revisit these issues of multidisciplinary practice in the last chapter of this volume, but meanwhile, this article provides food for thought on the issue of confidentiality.

Stacy L. Brustin, *Legal Services Provision Through Multidisciplinary Practice — Encouraging Holistic Advocacy While Protecting Ethical Interests*
73 U. Colo. L. Rev. 787 (2002)[13]

Barbara Davis has three kids [and] receives public assistance to support herself and her three children. She attends a job training program sponsored by a community college and is three courses away from receiving her certification in child development. She hopes to find a job and get off of public assistance within a year. The program is full time, five days a week.

Ms. Davis found out about the job training program from her case manager at The Community Center, a neighborhood organization located a few blocks from her apartment. Ms. Davis first went to The Community Center to get medical care for her kids. She could make an appointment with a doctor rather than waiting for hours as she had done in other clinics and emergency rooms.

As a patient of the medical clinic, she was entitled to use all of the services offered at The Community Center. She obtained two large bags of food once a month. She selected clothes and shoes from the second-hand clothing donations available on site, and she met with a caseworker. She expressed concerns to the caseworker about the difficulties her son, Michael, was having in school. She had requested that the school evaluate him to see if he had some type of learning problem, but school officials did not respond to her request. The caseworker sent her upstairs to make an appointment with someone in the legal clinic. She met with a lawyer at The Community Center who handles special education cases and the lawyer has been advocating on her behalf with the school system. . . .

Multiservice organizations such as The Community Center provide holistic, one-stop shopping to clients who face problems that require a multidisciplinary solution. Clients at these organizations are often struggling financially as well as emotionally. Rather than going from one non-profit agency to another in search of medical, legal, or social work services, they are able to access the services they need in one convenient location. . . .

The recent push to expand the rules regarding multidisciplinary practice (MDP)

---

[13] Copyright © 2002 by the University of Colorado Law Review. Reprinted with permission of the University of Colorado Law Review and the author.

is often associated with the "Big Five" accounting firms. These firms are interested in offering a package of services, including legal services, to customers in the United States, and they have vigorously advocated for rules changes. While the impetus for change has come from the heights of the corporate business world, the ramifications of such changes on legal services practice for those living in poverty are significant.

. . . .

The first major effort to change the prohibitions against MDPs took place in the early 1980s [from t]he Kutak Commission of the American Bar Association. In 1983, the ABA House of Delegates rejected the Kutak proposal and adopted the current version of Model Rule 5.4 banning [such] partnerships.

In 1998, [s]purred by fears that the world's largest accounting firms were providing legal services and engaging in the unauthorized practice of law, the ABA created the Commission on Multidisciplinary Practice to make recommendations about whether and how such multidisciplinary enterprises should be regulated. . . .

There is concern that non-lawyers in MDPs might be compelled by law or subpoena to divulge information that a lawyer would be prohibited from divulging. Clients who are the victims of domestic violence or elder abuse, for example, might disclose the situation to an attorney believing that the information will remain confidential. A social worker partnering with the attorney in an MDP might discover such information and be obligated by state statute to report the information. Others voice concern that MDP will erode the attorney-client privilege. Once information is disclosed to other professionals, the client may no longer be able to claim the attorney-client privilege (although other privileges may apply, i.e. doctor-patient, clergy-parishioner, social worker- or psychologist-patient) or the exception for agents of the attorney.

Opponents also fear that the independence lawyers have to make judgments and devise strategies for their cases will be compromised by the involvement of other professionals. Some believe that the sharing of fees, for example, may allow the bottom line to control, rather than concern for clients. . . .

After two years of public hearings and investigation, the Commission recommended, in its July 2000 report, that the ABA revise the Model Rules of Professional Conduct to allow lawyers and nonlawyers to engage in limited forms of multidisciplinary practice. Once again, however, the ABA rejected the proposal. The ABA House of Delegates urged jurisdictions around the country to resist the move toward MDP and to revise their ethical rules so as to "preserve the core values of the legal profession."

NOTES

A decade after the ABA rejected MDP for the second time, not much has changed. However, the press to allow law firms to have non-lawyer shareholders continues. The District of Columbia is the first American jurisdiction with a rule permitting non-lawyers to hold a financial or managerial position in a law firm. Under that rule, non-lawyers must abide by the rules of professional conduct and the lawyers must accept responsibility for the actions of the non-lawyers.

Elsewhere, especially in Australia and the UK, non-lawyer shareholders are now permitted in law firms under some limited circumstances. However, the ABA's Ethics 20/20 Commission, which focused particularly on globalization, stated in 2012 that "there does not appear to be a sufficient basis for recommending a change to ABA policy on nonlawyer ownership of law firms." At the moment, the confidentiality/MDP problem remains largely a future one.

7.   Does Confidentiality Extend to a Client's Whereabouts?

Must lawyers reveal either their clients' whereabouts or their clients' identities? Few recent cases have directly dealt with these issues. We briefly review here some of the important cases addressing whether a client's location may be confidential or privileged, and then look at identity in the next section.

One of the better known cases about location is that of Barry P. Wilson, who went to jail after refusing to testify as to the whereabouts of a client who was charged with drug smuggling. During the prosecution's investigation, federal prosecutors were seeking a "Mr. Tucker", whom Mr. Wilson had represented during the spring of 1982 and served as a reference for when "Tucker" rented an apartment. Wilson, however, refused to testify to the grand jury about "Tucker's" whereabouts. He was held in civil contempt and sentenced to the federal prison in Danbury, where he served time until the end of the grand jury's term. The sentencing judge acknowledged Wilson's refusal was "because of moral convictions," but Wilson himself had stated "I don't believe I'm above the law," and the judge agreed, saying Wilson could not "openly disobey" a law because he felt it "unjust."[14]

On the other hand, the New Jersey Supreme Court has held that an attorney could not be held in contempt for failing to disclose his client's whereabouts to a grand jury investigating the client. In *In re Joseph Nackson, on Contempt*, 555 A.2d 1101 (N.J. 1989), the client had consulted with Nackson about a fugitive warrant. The Court reasoned that an attorney should not be made to disclose information received from the client that concerned the continuing aspects or effects of past criminal conduct. But in *Commonwealth v. Maguigan*, 511 A.2d 1327 (Pa. 1986), the court held that an attorney had to disclose his client's location because the client had violated a court order.

However, where an attorney does more than merely withhold client information, the attorney will likely get into trouble. Consider the case of attorney Dennis Sieg, who aided his client in avoiding three traffic citations by helping the client represent to the court that the client was really his own brother. *In re Disciplinary Proceedings of Sieg*, 515 N.W.2d 694 (Wis. 1994). Sieg found out that his client had forged a letter ostensibly from the client's brother that said the brother consented to having the tickets on his record. Knowing it could further incriminate the client, Sieg then denied having known about the letter when the police requested a copy.

---

[14] *See* Tracy Breton, *Moral Decision Sends Lawyer into U.S. Prison*, THE NAT'L L.J., Sept. 30, 1985. Ultimately, the Massachusetts courts censured but did not suspend Wilson. Wilson has been in the public eye on more than one occasion. In 2012, he was sentenced to 90 days in jail for contempt, an event we discuss in Problem 21.

He also failed to disclose his client's true identity to the court when he discovered it. Sieg was suspended for 60 days.

Substantial disagreement remains on whether a client's whereabouts are privileged against disclosure, even when sought by a court. "Neither the ABA Code, the Model Rules, nor the ABA Defense Function Standards contain a specific rule directly answering the question when — or whether — an attorney is permitted or required to divulge a client's address or whereabouts," writes Professor John Burkoff in the September 2005 edition of his *Criminal Defense Ethics: Law and Liability* (*see* Supplemental Readings). Burkoff notes that the ABA and the Association of American Trial Lawyers published ethics opinions that come to opposite conclusions. Professor Burkoff's monograph contains an extensive list of cases and secondary authorities decided in both directions.

8.   Is a Client's Identity Confidential?

As we've noted, there is a close relationship between whereabouts and identity. Read the following article by noted ethics Professor Charles W. Wolfram, discussing a famous case involving disclosing a client's identity.

Charles W. Wolfram, *Hide and Secrets: The Boundaries of Privilege*
LEGAL TIMES, April 3, 1989[15]

Does the [attorney-client] privilege cover the name of a client, one who killed a pedestrian in a hit-and-run accident? If it does, does it also provide tactical advantages? For example, can a lawyer keep the client's name secret if he tries to plea-bargain with the police and prosecutor — attempting to cut a deal for the anonymous client but leaving a safe, protected route of retreat if he cannot? Can he hold the name secret if the personal-injury lawyer for the surviving relatives of the victim, learning of the plea bargaining, tries to subpoena the defense lawyer to force him to reveal the name?

In Florida last October, tentative answers to these questions emerged, then disappeared. The first answer came in *Baltes v. Doe* when West Palm Beach lawyer Barry E. Krischer persuaded state Circuit Judge Timothy P. Poulton to reject such a subpoena. Instead, Poulton entered a protective order against any attempt to coerce Krischer into giving up his client's name. But the parents of the 28-year-old victim, Mark Baltes, persisted. . . . At stake was a $5 million wrongful-death suit
. . . .

Krischer's moves had been careful and elaborate. Copying the procedure successfully employed by a California lawyer in *Baird v. Koerner*, 279 F.2d 623 (9th Cir. 1960), Krischer first went to a second lawyer, Scott N. Richardson. . . . Allegedly without mentioning the name of the secret client, Krischer filled Richardson in on the facts that he had learned and asked Richardson to open plea talks. Knowing that the Balteses would have to be involved in any plea arrangement, the prosecutor eventually notified [the Baltes'] lawyer Farish. Richardson's efforts foundered when the Balteses would not agree to an anonymous plea. But Farish still had no name — although he now knew who did.

Farish had little else to go on beyond some tantalizing details. Baltes, an electrician, was killed as he staggered into a road — drunk, as a post-mortem blood test would show — during the night of March 9, 1986. The driver never paused and was gone from the scene before anyone could identify the car. Pieces of the car left on the road by the force of the collision and paint chips from Baltes' skull indicated that the hit-and-run vehicle was a 1984 or 1985 white Buick Riviera. A search of auto records and interviews led nowhere. A reward offer brought only false leads.

All that changed dramatically on Election Eve 1988, when the local Florida prosecutor, with whom Richardson had been negotiating and who was up for reelection, publicly announced a sleuthing breakthrough — the driver was a local car salesman named William D. Morser. State Police established that a chip from the [Morser] car matched the chip from young Baltes' skull.

In February, Morser pleaded no contest to the criminal charges against him and was sentenced. . . . The Baltes' civil suit has been reinvigorated. . . . [O]nce Morser's name became public, the question whether the attorney-client privilege applies to a client's name became moot in the Baltes litigation. But the issue remains very much alive in legal circles.

The question of the confidentiality of a client's name actually rarely arises, but for many lawyers the issue seems to evoke strong protective instincts. . . . Several courts . . . have held that a client's identity is never protected by the privilege. Those courts reason that the privilege safeguards only client communications and that a name is not a communication but a fact, just like the fact that a client has red hair or a facial tattoo.

A few other courts, following one of the lines of reasoning in *Koerner*, protect client identity as privileged in some instances under a concept that seems to misapply the self-incrimination protection: Identity is protected if revealing it would supply the "last link" of evidence necessary to convict the client of a crime . . . . The last-link theory is also problematic because its application depends on the incriminating force of other evidence in the case — a consideration that has nothing to do with confidentiality of the original communication. . . .

Yet to conclude that client identity is never privileged might be too facile. While the analysis of the majority of courts is sound as far as it goes, it does not follow that confidential client communications will never be put at risk by forcing a lawyer to reveal a client's identity. Such a risk might have been what motivated the court in *Koerner*. The lawyer there had sent the Internal Revenue Service a letter with a large check, explaining that the check was to pay past-due taxes owed by an anonymous client. The government convened a grand jury and sought to compel the lawyer to identify the delinquent taxpayer. In the circumstances, revealing the client's name might also have revealed a confidential communication — the client's statement admitting owing overdue taxes.

But even with a reworked *Koerner* test, two problems remain. In both *Koerner* and *Baltes*, the risk of disclosure was self-inflicted because the web of incriminating evidence was self-constructed. The clients were exposed to no risk until their lawyers tried to have the cake of negotiating with the government while enjoying the culinary pleasure of asserting the privilege.

NOTES

Do you agree with Professor Wolfram that clients rarely expect confidentiality when they disclose their identities to lawyers? What about his assertion that "self-incrimination is irrelevant"? And why couldn't the fact that the client had red hair or a distinctive tattoo be confidential? If revealing them would be detrimental to the client, such as by identifying him as a perpetrator, wouldn't those identifying characteristics be "secrets" of the client learned during the course of the representation?

Perhaps part of the answer for Wolfram is that his article discusses the boundaries of *privilege*, focusing on the evidentiary rather than the ethical issue. But when a lawyer's conduct is evaluated by ethical standards, many states, through their ethics committees, have held that a client's identity may well be *confidential*. For example, several state bar opinions hold that lawyers cannot reveal their clients' identities to banks when their law firms seek loans based on receivables owed by the clients. *See, e.g.*, Arizona Opinion 92-4 (1992); Maryland Opinions 91-54 (1991), 93-8 (1993); Michigan Opinion RI-77 (1991); Texas Opinion 479 (1991).

Other cases and opinions discuss circumstances closer to those of Armand Varady. Several discuss the lawyer's dual responsibilities of protecting the confidentiality of a client's identity on the one hand while avoiding misrepresentations to the court on the other. Sometimes, navigating between these two duties can be like walking a tightrope. When a lawyer appears in court for a client, is referring to the client by an alias protecting the client's identity or a misrepresentation? Or perhaps both?

Among the several cases and ethics opinions with varying views of this tightrope is the oft-cited case of *State v. Casby*, 348 N.W.2d 736 (Minn. 1984). There a client gave police a relative's name, and the lawyer used that false name during plea negotiations with the prosecutor. The lawyer herself was convicted of misdemeanor misconduct, and also disciplined. But in *D'Alessio v. Gilberg*, 205 A.D.2d 8 (N.Y. App. Div. 1994), the court held that an attorney could not be compelled to reveal the name of a client who had consulted with the attorney regarding his possible past commission of a crime, where the crime was already committed, there was no possibility of further criminal acts if the individual was not identified, and the disclosure would expose the client to possible criminal prosecution. On almost the same facts as *Casby*, North Carolina Opinion 33 (1987) holds that a lawyer *cannot* reveal a client's identity if it will hurt the client (such as by revealing a prior record), until it comes time for the client to testify falsely at trial. The reality is that lawyers may find themselves between a rock and a hard place — either revealing a confidence or facing contempt. There are few safe harbors for those confronted with this dilemma.

Until the use of false social security numbers by illegal immigrants became a serious identity issue, client identity issues come up perhaps most frequently in tax payment situations such as *Koerner*. Businesses (including law firms) that receive $10,000 or more in cash must report these transactions to the Internal Revenue Service. Filling out the required Form 8300 presents problems for criminal defense attorneys, since the transfer of large amounts of cash is frequently a signal to prosecutors and police that the person paying the money may be dealing in drugs or other contraband. The form requires the recipient to list not only the amount of money received, but also identifying information about the payer.

A series of federal cases in the 1990s addressed this issue. In *United States v. Gertner & Newman*, 873 F. Supp. 729 (D. Mass. 1995), a federal district court held that an attorney could *refuse* to provide the identifying information on the form when the person paying was a current client with a pending case. But in *United States v. Ritchie*, 15 F.3d 592 (6th Cir. 1994), a lawyer's refusal to provide identifying information about the client because the lawyer had adequately reported on *his own* tax liability was held insufficient; the court refused to quash a subpoena. Two Ninth Circuit cases bookmark the issue. In *Ralls v. United States*, 52 F.3d 223 (9th Cir. 1995), the court held that identifying a client who had paid the lawyer's fee was inherently part of the client's privileged communications. On the other hand, *United States v. Blackman*, 72 F.3d 1418 (9th Cir. 1995) required an attorney to disclose the client information where there was no ongoing investigation, the information would not incriminate the client, and the information constituted corporate records that had no 5th Amendment protection.

9. Confidentiality and Problems at Guantanamo

Finally, the problems confronting lawyers representing Guantanamo detainees form an excellent case study of what confidentiality is all about. The reading below, excerpts a brief prepared by Philadelphia ethics guru Lawrence J. Fox on behalf of lawyers suing the government because of restrictions on their ability to maintain a viable confidential relationship with their clients.[16]

The brief touches on a number of "real world" practical consequences when confidentiality cannot easily be maintained. We find it a cogent summation of the important concept of "confidentiality."

Brief of Amici Professors of Ethics and Lawyers Practicing in the Professional Responsibility Field,
Center for Constitutional Rights v. Bush
Case No. 06-cv-313 (S.D.N.Y.) (July 13, 2006)

Lawyers at the Center for Constitutional Rights and affiliated lawyers represent a number of foreign nationals detained at Guantanamo and considered "enemy combatants" by the United States government, [and] their next friends, primarily family members of the detainees. The NSA program of electronic eavesdropping raises serious ethical issues for these lawyers, who have both an ethical obligation

---

[16] We must note that all of this volume's authors were signatories on the brief.

to communicate with their clients and other individuals concerning these cases and an ethical obligation to ensure the confidentiality of those communications. The criteria announced by government officials for targets of the NSA eavesdropping program are so open-ended that they would include many, if not all, of those clients, family members and others these lawyers must contact. . . .

A. The Fiduciary Obligation to Assure Confidentiality

Lawyers are fiduciaries of their clients. Lawyers' fiduciary obligations to their clients were originally recognized in the common law, and now they are codified in the rules of professional ethics. One of these fiduciary obligations requires lawyers to protect the confidentiality of their clients' information. This fiduciary obligation is recognized in three distinct doctrines of law: The lawyer's ethical duty of confidentiality; the evidentiary privilege for attorney-client communications; and the evidentiary privilege for attorney work-product. Analysis of these three doctrines demonstrates that the law has been robust in protecting the confidentiality of client information.

1. The Duty of Confidentiality

The first aspect of the lawyer's fiduciary obligation is the duty to ensure the confidentiality of information learned in the course of a representation. The confidentiality obligation is two-fold, consisting of both a prohibition and an affirmative duty. First, it prohibits the lawyer from disclosing confidential information about the client without client consent. . . . Second, the confidentiality obligation imposes on lawyers an affirmative duty to take steps to ensure the secrecy of client information. When communicating with clients or in pursuit of a client case, the lawyer must ensure that the communication is private, whether the communication is in person, on paper or electronic. No client matters are discussed in public locations, such as elevators or courthouse corridors, where they can be overheard. "A lawyer must act competently to safeguard information relating to the representation of a client against inadvertent or unauthorized disclosure. . . ." ABA MR 1.6, cmt. 16 (2005).

Client information must be kept away from prying eyes and ears. Client files must be kept secure. Lawyers must instruct and supervise their employees to preserve confidentiality. A lawyer must take reasonable steps so that law-office personnel properly handle confidential client information with care. . . .

2. Attorney Client Privilege

The rules of evidence recognize clients need to consult lawyers in confidence, and those rules provide a virtually absolute bar on discovery of confidential lawyer-client communications that are for the purpose of seeking or providing legal advice. To ensure that such communications will be covered by the privilege, the lawyer must make sure that only the lawyer and the client are privy to the communication. The attendance of a client's accountant [or child] at a meeting between the lawyer and client can destroy the privilege.

Similarly, written communications are treated with special care. All confidential client information must be acquired, stored, retrieved, and transmitted under systems that are reasonably designed and managed to maintain confidentiality, and therefore it is up to lawyers to take necessary affirmative steps to put those systems in place. Lawyers are also obliged to label written communications with an appropriate description. Copies are not sent to anyone whose knowledge of the information would waive the privilege. . . .

Electronic communications also must be protected to maintain the privilege. Telephone conversations are not conducted in public places or with individuals on the line who could break the privilege. Faxes are sent with appropriate identification of their privileged content. And bar associations have spent endless hours debating (and largely resolving) to what extent lawyers may employ e-mail and cell phones when communicating with clients consistent with maintaining the privilege.[17]

Finally, lawyers are bound to resist — to the greatest extent legally permissible — the attempts by others to access privileged information. Lawyers are required to refuse to testify, to argue that their refusal is consistent with the privilege and, if the lawyer is subject to an adverse decision on the issue, to seek if at all possible appellate review, including suffering a possible contempt citation to force a further adjudication of the privilege claim.

3. The Attorney Work Product Privilege

Evidence law also protects the confidentiality of client information through the attorney work product privilege. This doctrine applies to all work undertaken by or at the direction and control of the lawyer either in anticipation of or in actual litigation, as these lawyers here are so engaged. . . . The work product privilege is intended to preserve a zone of privacy in which a lawyer or other representatives of a party can prepare and develop legal theories and strategy "with an eye toward litigation," free from intrusion by their adversaries. *Hickman v. Taylor*, 329 U.S. 495, 510–511 (1947)

But the privilege is only available, and the ability to prevent the review of the lawyer's work product will only succeed, if, again, the lawyer takes the precautions to ensure the confidentiality of the work product. . . . This requires the lawyer to conduct these activities in a careful manner. No one participates who is not essential to the task. All who participate are required to maintain confidentiality.

B. The Public Policy Foundation

Why do the legal profession and courts go to such great lengths to maintain confidentiality and the privileges? Because courts have determined that " 'full and frank communication between attorneys and their clients . . . promote[s the] broader public interests in the observance of law and the administration of justice.' " *Swidler & Berlin v. United States*, 524 U.S. 399, 403 (1998) (quoting *Upjohn Co. v.*

---

[17] [Editor's Note: We will look at this debate in Problem 6.]

United States, 449 U.S. 383, 389, 101 S. Ct. 677, 682, 66 L. Ed. 2d 584 (1981)). We must encourage our clients to trust us and share their innermost secrets with us. Otherwise [i]f we do not know what our clients did or what they plan to do, we cannot provide them with the legal advice they require. . . .

For this reason, a lawyer who knows that his or her conversations are subject to surveillance, even if the surveillance were by someone other than an adversary, has no choice. "Given the objectives of the attorney-client privilege, a communication must be made in circumstances reasonably indicating that it will be learned only by the lawyer, client, or another privileged person. The circumstances must indicate that the communicating persons reasonably believed that the communication would be confidential." Restatement (Third) of the Law Governing Lawyers § 71 (2000). . . .

For example, if a lawyer thinks there might be a listening device in a room, the lawyer should meet with the client elsewhere. If telephone calls are being monitored, the lawyer should not use the telephone. If the lawyer has reason to believe that emails are being reviewed or mail read by persons other than the client, the lawyer must find an alternative confidential means of communication. Even if the client is at some distance, the lawyer must take appropriate precautions and, if necessary, only communicate face-to-face.

What is described here is not simply a best practice, one that is recommended if at all possible. Rather it is an obligation. Lawyers have an uncompromising duty to be competent. Model Rules of Prof'l Conduct R. 1.1 (2005). This includes a duty to . . . assure the client that the fact-gathering process remains confidential and protected from inadvertent disclosure or waiver. The lawyer must protect not only information gathered but the sources of the information, *i.e.* witnesses the lawyer has interviewed or sources the lawyer has consulted.

Lawyers also have a duty to communicate with their clients. Model Rules of Prof'l Conduct R. 1.4 (2005). Without such communication the lawyer cannot know the client's lawful goals and concerns, nor can the client learn the results of the lawyer's diligent work and the advice the lawyer must provide the client. And, again, the two-way communication process must be kept confidential or the lawyer will be in breach of the duty of confidentiality owed to the client.

C. The Effect of Surveillance Here

It is easy to understand how a threat of surveillance could compromise and undermine the ability to represent the client in a profound way when the lawyer resides near next friends, witnesses and others. Avoiding telephone calls and e-mail exchange would force all communications — not just those with the client — to be carefully planned and scheduled with follow-up communication and spur of the moment inspiration or inquiry giving way to an obligation to engage in the stilted and time-consuming task of rescheduling yet another meeting. Cutting off electronic communication in this scenario does not just place a burden on the lawyer-client relationship[;] it erodes the relationship in a fundamental way.

This is particularly so given the fact that we live in a world where otherwise instantaneous conversations — with clients not incarcerated, witnesses and other sources — on a whim or a breakthrough are the norm. When lawyers are forced to deviate from that norm, the result is a dramatically unbalanced playing field. An adversary with all the power and resources of the government is free, without any fear of surveillance, to take advantage of every form of modern electronic communication — telephone, facsimile, e-mail and the internet. . . .

If the situation is virtually impossible when the individuals with whom the lawyer must communicate are geographically close and easily accessible so that the lawyer has the capability to work around the surveillance, it is truly impossible to conjure how much more difficult it would be for a lawyer, required by a real threat of surveillance, to avoid traditional methods in dealing with clients and their next friends, potential witnesses and other sources of information who reside across the seas. Just the act of making appointments, if subject to surveillance, invades the attorney-work product privilege, reveals confidential information and perhaps, in and of itself, discloses attorney-client privileged information as well. A fortiari, no substantive conversation can take place if it is possibly subject to surveillance. . . .

The burden this places on the lawyer-client relationship is without precedent and in effect destroys the relationship entirely. Government surveillance of electronic communications [means that these lawyers] cannot do their job and their clients cannot have effective representation when 6,000 miles, huge expense and two or more airplane flights, a train and a taxicab ride, separate the lawyer from his or her clients and others who must be contacted. Simply posing the required follow-up question becomes an expensive multi-week ordeal. . . . And heaven forefend that the contacted individual — like every other individual in the history of the modern world — forgets to tell the lawyer something and needs to communicate yet again.

NOTES

Before we move on, one area we have not touched on is the work product doctrine, shaped largely by the Supreme Court in *Hickman*, a case mentioned in the above brief.[18]

"Work product" covers lawyers' impressions, conclusions, and strategies during the preparation of a case. These matters, even if memorialized, are immune from discovery by the other side. This material need not come from the client, and indeed is often originated by the attorney. In fact, in almost all jurisdictions, the claim of immunity from discovery is held not by the client but by the lawyer. In his concurrence in *Hickman*, Justice Jackson succinctly articulated the reason for the doctrine: "Discovery was hardly intended to enable a learned profession to perform its functions . . . on wits borrowed from the adversary."

---

[18] While the brief describes this as a "privilege," it is more commonly and most accurately referred to as a "doctrine."

D. SUPPLEMENTAL READINGS

1. *Commonwealth v. Chmiel*, 889 A.2d 501 (Pa. 2005) held that the fee arrangement between a client and attorney is not privileged. The case involved a murder trial in which the prosecutor attempted to prove that part of the motivation for the murder was the defendant's need for money to pay a prior attorney's fee. The Supreme Court of Pennsylvania rejected defendant's arguments that his attorney-client privilege had been violated when his former attorney testified about their fee arrangement. See also *In re Nassau County Grand Jury Subpoena Duces Tecum*, 830 N.E.2d 1118 (N.Y. 2005), which also held that identity and fees were not protected by the attorney-client privilege. Note, however, that by statute, attorneys' fees agreements are confidential in California. Calif. Bus. & Profs. Code § 6149.

2. Clark D. Cunningham, *How to Explain Confidentiality?*, 9 CLINICAL L. REV. 579 (2003), Professor Cunningham's article is best captured in this quote from the article:

> One of the most critical, yet inadequately explored, issues in lawyer client communication is the problem of explaining confidentiality, especially exceptions which permit or require the lawyer to disclose confidential information. Failure to disclose these exceptions results in misrepresentation to the client (*e.g.*, "everything you tell me is confidential"), yet an accurate and complete explanation of the exceptions may inhibit the very trust that the right of confidentiality is intended to create.

This article reports on the use of simulated interviews in the classroom to model an empirical approach to analyzing this problem that can be applied to law school clinics.

3. John Burkoff, *Criminal Defense Ethics: Law and Liability* (September 2005 edition), Chapter 5, and especially section 5.13, contains an extensive review of case law and secondary opinions on the propriety of revealing a client's whereabouts, and the reasoning of some courts in dealing with the issue on a case-by-case basis.

4. The requirements of public disclosure by a candidate can conflict directly with ethical duties. Thus, Dean Erwin Chemerinsky of UC Irvine, a longtime ethics maven, wrote an Op Ed in the L.A. TIMES on May 1, 2009 with the heading: "No room for a covert client list in city attorney race." His argument: a Los Angeles area attorney running for elective office had no grounds on which to base his refusal to make public his client list. The lawyer-candidate claimed, understandably, that the list was *confidential* even if in the normal case the name of the client is not *attorney-client privileged*.

5. *In re Marriage of Decker*, 562 N.E.2d 1000 (Ill. App. Ct. 1990). In a domestic relations case, the husband's attorney was properly held in contempt for refusing to obey the trial court's order that she disclose her client's whereabouts and his intent to abscond with his child.

6. In *State v. Gonzalez*, 234 P.3d 1 (Kan. 2010) the court refused of confirm contempt of a public defender for failure to reveal her client's identity. The court approached the issue from a privilege (rather than confidentiality) perspective but still found that non-disclosure was justified: "McKinnon invoked the attorney-client privilege to prevent her compelled disclosure of what she believed to be confidential client information." If the defender had revealed her client's identify it would have revealed the client's intention to commit perjury.

7. For a lengthy and thorough analysis of the *Nackson* and *Maguigan* cases and an attorney's duty to inform the courts as to a fugitive client's whereabouts, see Shelly Hillyer, *The Attorney-Client Privilege, Ethical Rules of Confidentiality, and Other Arguments Bearing on Disclosure of a Fugitive Client's Whereabouts*, 68 Temple L. Rev. 307 (1995).

PROBLEM 6: TECHNOLOGY + CONFIDENTIALITY = TROUBLE

A. INTRODUCTION

Cell phones, e-mail, voicemail, wireless Internet, websites, chat rooms, hypertext links, integrated work servers, outsourcing, blogging, social networking, technology-assisted document review and virtual law offices. What do these changes have to do with practicing law? Plenty, when you consider that the majority of lawyers utilize most of this technology in their practices. Yesterday this technology was cutting-edge; today it's routine. And tomorrow? Who knows what changes new technological inventions and improvements will bring?

What is technology? One of our favorite definitions comes from computer genius Alan Kay, who says technology is anything that wasn't around when you were born.[1] Considering that the age differences between law students and senior lawyers can be 40 or 50 years, that leaves a lot of room to debate what is technology, and what is not.

As you consider the ethical issues raised by technological advances, keep in mind the larger context: how technology has fundamentally changed the way lawyers do business — physically, interpersonally, and professionally. The profession of law, never the quickest to change, has done reasonably well in recognizing these fundamental realities. For instance, in 2012 the ABA's Ethics 20/20 Commission twice proposed changes to the ethics rules prompted by modern technology and globalization that were adopted virtually in their entirety. One question to keep an eye on in this Problem is whether ethical issues associated with the use of technology are simply the same issues with a new face, or whether the use of the technology itself creates new ethical problems.

In examining these questions, this problem focuses primarily on attorney-client relations, especially confidentiality, security, and privilege issues. For the most part we look at these issues viewed through the prism of modern technology, though we address inadvertent disclosure from a somewhat broader perspective.

B. PROBLEM

I

Frank Tecchi is a newly-minted partner who's considered a rising star by his law firm. Tecchi grew up in the electronic age, and he loves it. He's always the first in his firm to have the latest in cellular technology, "smart phones," iPads, and other hand-held computers, infrared and Wi-Fi interfaces, and he's up to date on all the

---

[1] http://en.wikiquote.org/wiki/Alan_Kay#A_Conversation_with_Alan_Kay.2C_2004-05. As reported by Kevin Kelly in his TED talk — http://www.tedxamsterdam.com/2009/video-kevin-kelly-on-what-technology-wants/ — Kay famously stated that "the best way to predict the future is to invent it."

latest apps. He likes to say that he carries "all my 'key docs' " from his current cases on his ever-present 128 GB flash drive.

Many of Frank's clients are start-ups whose executives share his passion for technology. It's not surprising then, that many of Frank's communications with his clients occur not just by email and cell phone, but often by email sent from his cell phone, and even occasionally by responding to a client's text. As often as not, documents are transmitted as attachments sent directly from his firm's work server, or downloaded either from a secure area on Frank's state-of-the-art website or from his own storage on "the Cloud."

QUESTIONS

Tecchi is not particularly concerned about the use of these communications, but the issue hasn't escaped the notice of the firm's managing partner, Jeanette Glanville. Glanville, worried about breaches of confidentiality, asks Tecchi to evaluate several issues:

- Must the firm's e-mails to its clients be encrypted to ensure confidentiality? What about e-mails from a smart phone? Or from a coffee shop with a wireless connection?

- Are cellular phone transmissions confidential, or does the ease with which they can be intercepted make them open to all who may be listening?

- The website's "clients only" area requires each client to have an individual "username" and password, but is that sufficient security to allow clients to download information left for them by Tecchi, and to ensure that no client can access another client's area?

- The firm is growing and Tecchi and others have recommended storing documents on "the Cloud," but is that safe? What if a Cloud company goes out of business? Or somehow loses data? Are there enough assurances in place?

Glanville makes it clear that she is concerned about ethical requirements generally and confidentiality especially, the potential for waiver of the attorney-client privilege, and potential malpractice liability.

If you were Tecchi, how would you respond to your managing partner in light of her concerns?

While Tecchi is responding to Glanville on his laptop, he realizes he left his flash drive on the table and his iPhone at the cash register of the coffee shop. He looks for them, but they're gone. What should he do? What *must* he do?

II

Susan Browning and her client were exchanging drafts of a contract. They decided to send opposing counsel Russ Bluestone the latest draft of their proposed contract by e-mail. When Bluestone opened the proposed contract, he turned on a feature of his word processing software that displayed the text of all "embedded data," including previous drafts exchanged between Browning and her client, and all of the comments that Browning and her client exchanged, some of which dealt with their strategy in redrafting the contract.

QUESTIONS

1.   May Bluestone read the edits and comments in the document? *Must* he? What other obligations, if any, does he have?

2.   What difference would it make if Bluestone had received the document with the edits, "tracked changes," and comments already displayed in the text without him having to do anything other after opening the document?

3.   If Browning realizes her mistake later the same day and calls Bluestone to ask him to delete the document without looking at the embedded data, must he do so?

4.   What if Bluestone had received an email from Browning discussing strategy that was clearly directed to her client, but was mistakenly sent to Bluestone's office? Should he read it? Why (or why not)?

5.   What difference would it make, if any, if the email were accompanied by this disclaimer at the bottom?

ATTORNEY-CLIENT CONFIDENTIAL AND PRIVILEGED COMMUNICATION. If you are not a client of this law firm, or one specifically authorized to receive this electronic mail by a client of this firm, you may not read, copy, use, or distribute this privileged attorney-client communication. If you received this e-mail in error, PLEASE DELETE THIS EMAIL AND ITS ATTACHMENTS from any instrument on which you have received this, and from any work-station and all e-mail servers. Please then reply to the sender or contact the firm at [PHONE] to advise us that you received and have deleted the email. THANK YOU.

C.   READINGS

1.   How Safe is E-Mail?

The use of e-mail came late to the legal profession and was soon followed by a spate of ethics opinions about whether e-mail communications with clients were sufficiently secure to be deemed confidential. Most of the early opinions — those in 1994 through 1996 — determined they were not. Iowa's Board of Professional Responsibility made this call twice in the space of a few months.[2]

First, Iowa Opinion 95-30 concluded that in order for e-mails containing "sensitive material" to meet the ethical standard of confidentiality, they must be encrypted, or coded in a special way like wartime messages sent in code, to prevent anyone but the intended recipient from reading them. Opinion 95-30, which also covered webpages and Internet advertising, received a great deal of publicity,

---

[2] Iowa Opinions 95-30 (May 16, 1996) and 96-1 (August 29, 1996).

enough so that a few months later, the Board reconsidered its position. But its second opinion, 96-1, adhered to the idea that e-mails with sensitive material were not sufficiently secure. This opinion offered more alternatives: Get the client's consent to the communication, or in the alternative, encrypt, create a password firewall, or otherwise ensure security. Other states with early opinions, including Colorado and North and South Carolina, also concluded that encryption was necessary.

Many cyberlaw experts disagreed, arguing that e-mail was no less secure than the U.S. mail or overnight couriers (all of which reserve the right to open packages sent through their services). Others pointed out that the federal Electronic Communications Privacy Act (ECPA) made it a felony to intercept e-mail, just like with "snail mail," and argued that it requires no technological know-how to take a letter out of a mailbox or mailroom, a much easier task than stealing an e-mail. By 1997, the tide had turned in favor of the confidentiality of e-mails without encryption. A few states, including Illinois and New Jersey, declined to require encryption, and then South Carolina and Iowa reversed themselves.[3]

That is not to say that the security of email will never become an issue again. For today's lawyer, the issue has shifted to the practical: What steps should be taken to comply with the best practices to protect email confidentiality? Encryption is now just one possible strategy for protecting client confidences.[4] Erik Mazzone, Director of the Center for Practice Management for the North Carolina Bar, writing on his blog, Law Practice Matters, notes that the *contents* of the email could affect whether to use encryption:

> A few days ago, a lawyer friend of mine asked if I meet a lot of lawyers who use encrypted email. I told him I hadn't — that apart from the lawyers whose clients (banks, mostly) required the use of encrypted email, I hadn't come across many other lawyers using it . . . .
>
> A Google search on "is email secure?" reveals a torrent of articles over the years on the topic, most of which conclude that email is not a terribly secure technology . . . . That said, with the continued clash of ethical self-regulation and technology, it won't surprise me when some unsuspecting lawyer somewhere has a client communication intercepted and becomes the ethics test case for encrypted email. All lawyers are required to maintain the confidentiality of their clients' information. If you, in the course of your practice, also have occasion to email trade secrets like, say, the recipe for Coca Cola, it's probably a good idea to have some passing familiarity with encrypted email.[5]

As issues about encryption faded, several other issues came to the fore, many having to do with location and, thus, security. Emails sent through a law firm's

---

[3] South Carolina Advisory Ethics Opinion 97-08; Iowa Opinion 97-01 (September 18, 1997).

[4] See the website of the ABA's Law Practice Management Section — here the ABA provides support for lawyers interested in encryption: http://www.americanbar.org/groups/departments_offices/legal_technology_resources/resources/charts_fyis/FYI_Playing_it_safe.html.

[5] Erik Mazzone, *Should Lawyers Use Encrypted Email?*, LAW PRACTICE MATTERS, July 27, 2012 http://www.lawpracticematters.com/home/2012/07/27/should-lawyers-use-encrypted-email.html.

secure server are one thing, but those sent from an open-channel "hot-spot" at an airport or the local coffee shop are quite another. Even if these common areas have WPA or other secure password protection, such protection does little when the password is given out to everyone sitting in the airport lounge or having a cappuccino. Similarly, emails sent through hotel servers, many sent by smart phones, iPads, and other portable devices, may to one extent or another be compromised.

Then there is the issue of the address the email correspondent is using. A lawyer who emails a client at the client's email provided by the employer may have vitiated confidentiality. In Washington, the federal district court in *Sims v. Lakeside School* found that public policy requires recognition of privilege notwithstanding employer policy.[6] In New York, however, e-mail messages between the chairman of the orthopedics department of Beth Israel Hospital and his personal counsel sent through Beth Israel's server were held not privileged.[7]

In *Beth Israel*, the hospital's email policy stated that the e-mail system should be used for business purposes only, and that no employee had a right of privacy with respect to messages sent or received over the hospital's systems. Significantly, the court rejected the claim that the standard confidentiality legend on the lawyer's in-bound e-mails prevented any waiver stemming from Beth Israel's policy. California came to a similar conclusion in *Holmes v. Petrovich Development Company, LLC*, 191 Cal. App. 4th 1047 (Cal. Ct. App. 2011), which held that e-mails from an employee to her lawyer were not protected by the lawyer-client privilege where she used a computer of defendant company to send them.

The ABA addressed this decisional disparity in Formal Opinion 11-459: Duty to Protect the Confidentiality of E-mail Communications with One's Client, which states that a lawyer using email with a client "ordinarily must warn the client about the risk of sending or receiving electronic communications using a computer or other device, or e-mail account, where there is a significant risk that a third party may gain access [especially] in the context of representing an employee, . . . where there is a significant risk that the communications will be read by the employer or another third party."

A similar issue arises with notifying clients about risk when the locus of the communication from the lawyer's end is not entirely secure. As the North Carolina Bar's Mazzone notes, a lot has to do with the importance of the content of the communication. If "secret trial strategy" is the subject of the email, the lawyer exchanging that information had better reconsider two or three times. Why is content so important? Because while emails from an airport lounge may still give both lawyer and client a reasonable expectation of privacy under the ECPA[8], the interception of sensitive information like trial strategies or the "formula for Coke"

---

[6] Sims v. Lakeside School, 2008 U.S. Dist. LEXIS 4140, at *20–*22 (W.D. Wash. Jan. 17, 2008).

[7] Scott v. Beth Israel Medical Center, Inc., 17 Misc. 3d 934 (N.Y. Sup. Ct. 2007).

[8] *See* David Hricik & Amy Falkingham, *Lawyers Still Worry Too Much About Transmitting E-mail Over the Internet*, 10 J. Tech. L. & Pol'y 265 (2005), in which Professor Hricik updates other work that had become widely cited for the proposition that e-mail was secure for purposes of attorney-client communications, and thus a reasonable expectation of privacy existed.

rings a bell that can't — and *won't* — be unrung by the other side.

2. Land Lines and Mobile Devices

Many lawyers have sensitive, even confidential information including photos stored on their phones. If lawyer's e-mails are deemed safe, even though few of us understand how they get from the sender to the recipient, what about smart phones, iPads, and other mobile devices? The answer has to do with both law and technology — and ultimately again, whether the participants to the communication have a reasonable expectation of privacy. Thinking about telephones helps clarify how changing technology results in changes in reasonable expectations, as the following excerpted article, by David Hricik, the law professor cited many times in this Problem, explains:

David Hricik, *Lawyers Worry Too Much About Transmitting Client Confidences by Internet E-Mail*
11 GEORGETOWN JOURNAL OF LEGAL ETHICS 459 (1998)[9]

The legal protections afforded land-based phone calls are strong. Such calls are subject to Fourth Amendment protection against unreasonable search and seizure. In addition, the Federal Wiretap Act protects land-based telephone calls, making interception of an oral phone call a crime. Finally, federal law provides a civil damage remedy for any person whose oral communication is intercepted, disclosed, or intentionally used in violation of federal law, and illegally intercepted oral communications may not be admitted as evidence even if they are not privileged.

Despite the actual risk of misdirection or interception, discussion of client confidences during land-based telephone calls does not violate the duty of confidentiality — even though phones are easily tapped. The required expectation of confidentiality need *not* be absolute. It only needs to be a *reasonable* expectation.

Confidentiality and Cordless Telephone Calls

The objective facts regarding the ease with which cordless phone calls (not cellular phones — *cordless* phones) may be intercepted vary dramatically from those underlying land-based phone calls; the current legal rules governing interception do not.

As a factual matter, the broadcast of a cordless telephone call can far more readily be intentionally intercepted or inadvertently overheard than a land-based call. "Inadvertent interceptions have occurred frequently with cordless phones, which transmit on a normal FM frequency within radio range. Using a cordless phone is like operating a radio station and broadcasting your message. Anyone within range could receive the communication."

Merely because people know that the cordless broadcast might be intercepted does not mean they do not expect the landline-based transmission of their call to be protected. The critical issue, then, is whether the fact that a cordless phone *broadcasts* the conversation over FM radio frequencies destroys any objective expectation of confidentiality.

The legal protection afforded to the broadcast portion of a cordless phone call has, since 1994, been identical to a land-based phone. [T]he 1994 amendments to ECPA § 2512(A) protect cordless telephone broadcasts as a matter of federal law in the same manner as land-based telephone calls. However, the criminalization of interception "does not, of course, make it technologically more difficult for someone to intercept" or inadvertently receive them. Thus, although it is now illegal to intercept cordless broadcasts, it is still more common for inadvertent interception to occur, and such unintended interception can occur through devices which are legal and common for the general public to own — namely, other cordless phones, FM radios, and baby monitors.

Consequently, whether a lawyer should use a cordless phone to discuss confidential information — even though privilege is almost certainly not waived and any interception or subsequent disclosure or use of the message would be unlawful — probably depends on whether the disclosure of the transmitted information would likely be detrimental to a client.

Confidentiality and Cellular Telephone Communications

Like cordless phones, cellular phones *broadcast* conversations over the airwaves to receiving stations, which then transmit the calls over land-based phone lines.

While cordless phones may still be intercepted or inadvertently overheard through common household appliances, the same is not true for cellular phones, however. While they use part of the spectrum for transmission, they do not transmit within a range or frequency capable of inadvertent interception by commercial users of the air waves or listeners." Since April 1994, it has been illegal to market the scanners that can intercept cellular communications in the United States.

. . . .

Sensitive communication over a cellular phone, still, may be overheard. While most lawyer-client conversations could safely take place on a cellular phone, because interception could cause no harm, some information may be so sensitive that it should not be transmitted by cellular phone. Consequently, disclosure of identifiable confidential information that would likely be detrimental to the client should be avoided during cellular phone calls, absent client consent or the use of technology that is particularly difficult to intercept.

NOTES

One issue not addressed in this article is the high incidence of lost or stolen smart phones and iPads, not to mention laptops. This may be just the loss of property and some personal photos to many, but to lawyers who use their phones and iPads for business, a lost or stolen phone may mean that confidential information is in great jeopardy. Most lawyers have by now password-protected their laptops, and increasingly do so with encryption. But many lawyers' cell phones and iPads have little if any protection, despite the fact that they are linked to their own laptops and, often, the law firm's server. The importance of maintaining control over such items is obvious. We have included in the Supplementary Readings two articles that address what to do both to prevent and to ameliorate the loss of a sensitive computing device.

Hricik's older article does not focus on "texting," and while that's a medium used largely by young people for interpersonal connections, many lawyers have found themselves texting, if for no reason other than to return communications texted by clients. What implications these texts have may extend beyond the issue of confidentiality. For one thing, it is far more difficult (although not impossible) to maintain an organized record of texts, should the lawyer require them later. Little has been written on this issue and the possible consequences for lawyers whose texts are far from clear.

3. The Cloud and Virtual Law Offices

Lawyers with cell phones, a laptop, and access to a wireless Internet source can do much of what a lawyer in a paneled office with support staff and a large library can do. Why not go all the way, avoid the expense of running an office, and open a virtual law office? The ability to access files stored on a server in "the Cloud" from almost anywhere makes this possible. While there are significant concerns about this sort of virtual practice, many lawyers, especially in the current economic climate, are opening practices that depend on the Cloud for file storage.[10]

Cloud computing is a "sophisticated form of remote electronic data storage on the internet. Rather than storing data on a computer server at a law office or other place of business, data stored 'on the Cloud' is kept on large servers located elsewhere and maintained by the vendor,"[11] a third party who has control over the management of information stored on the Cloud. The Cloud acts like an external hard drive that is accessible from any remote location.

Moving your practice, including client confidences, onto the Cloud and out into the world raises a host of problems. Are attorneys sufficiently tech-savvy to evaluate whether a prospective Cloud service provider (CSP) provides a standard of confidentiality that meets MR 1.6? Who is liable if data is stolen? Or lost?[12] Does the CSP reserve the right to modify any content put in the Cloud? What if the CSP goes bankrupt and sells the remote server without completely scrubbing any data on the server? Is this in any way different from the law firm copier that is recycled and replaced with a more modern machine? Copiers have hard drives, often with sensitive data on them. What if a subpoena issues to the CSP? Will lawyers be able

---

[10] Stephanie Kimbro is one of the leaders in the field of virtual practice and now writes and speaks about compliance with ethical and other issues. In addition to her Internet presence, she publishes "how to" hints with the ABA Law Practice Management Section. *See, e.g.*, Stephanie Kimbro, *Virtual Law Practice: How to Deliver Legal Services Online*, ABA LAW PRACTICE MANAGEMENT SECTION (2010).

[11] Richard Acello, *Get Your Head in the Cloud*, ABA JOURNAL, 28–29 (Apr. 2011) (adopting the definition from the Alabama State Bar Disciplinary Commn., Op. 2010-02.

[12] Joe Dysart, *The Trouble with Terabytes*, ABA JOURNAL 35 (Apr. 2011), notes that "while any reputable cloud providers makes continual backups of your data, law firms should also negotiate for additional, physical copies to be provided for storage either at the law firm or with another third party."

to rely on the CSP to alert them and give them an opportunity to object?[13]

Over the past decade, a number of state ethics committees have wrestled with the ethical issues presented when lawyers use Cloud computing in their law practices. As of this writing seven formal opinions have been issued,[14] all of which have determined that it is ethical for lawyers to use Cloud computing, with most concluding that lawyers must take reasonable steps to ensure that their law firm's confidential data is protected from unauthorized third party access. Of at least equal importance has been passage by the ABA of Ethics 20/20 rules revisions, including to both Model Rules 1.6 and 5.3, that address Cloud computing specifically and electronic communications more generally.

Is Cloud computing covered by the ECPA? Yes, according to the First Circuit, which twice heard an appeal in *U.S. v. Councilman*, 245 F. Supp. 2d 319 (D. Mass. 2003), *aff'd*, 373 F.3d 197 (1st Cir. 2004) 418 F.3d 67 (1st Cir. 2005), and upon rehearing *en banc* concluded as follows:

> Although the text of the statute does not specify whether the term "electronic communication" includes communications in electronic storage, the legislative history of the ECPA indicates that Congress intended the term to be defined broadly. Furthermore, that history confirms that Congress did not intend, by including electronic storage within the definition of wire communications, to thereby exclude electronic storage from the definition of electronic communications.

4. The Problem with Websites

Problems with websites fall into two categories — lawyers with websites and non-lawyers with websites (including self help web sites that could make the user believe they are getting legal help). We'll look at non-lawyer sites first.

Self-Help Services. " Self-help" websites charge money to "assist" clients — while claiming they are *not* clients — in resolving their legal claims. Among the sites are those calling themselves SettlementCentral.com and 4MyClaim.com. On one such site, a computer program walks the consumer through the writing of a demand letter in a personal injury case, complete with attached supporting information, creating what the site called a "Settlement Demand Package (SDP)." This SDP, trumpeted the site, "will forcefully inform the [insurance claims] adjuster that you know what you're doing and that this may be his or her last chance to settle without getting attorneys involved."

The SettlementCentral site states, "Our Experienced Personal Injury Attorneys and Insurance Claims Adjusters Make it SIMPLE AND EASY to Settle Your

---

[13] See this report by the Electronic Frontier Foundation for an overview on CSP's. https://www.eff.org/pages/when-government-comes-knocking-who-has-your-back.

[14] North Carolina State Bar Council 2011 Formal Ethics Opinion 6, Massachusetts Bar Association Ethics Opinion 12-03, Oregon State Bar Formal Opinion No. 2011-188, Professional Ethics Committee of the Florida Bar Op. 10-2 (2011), New York State Bar Association's Committee on Professional Ethics Op. 842 (2010), Pennsylvania Bar Association Ethics Opinion No. 2010-060 (2010), and Iowa Committee on Practice Ethics and Guidelines Ethics Opinion 11-01 (2011).

Injury Claim: DO IT YOURSELF AND SAVE." The site trumpets a disclaimer with the large-print headline "No Legal Advice Regarding Personal Injury Claims." Do you think that is enough to protect the lawyers working on the site from malpractice claims from their "non-clients"?[15]

The My Lawyer site says it offers "A new kind of legal service" and "Easy-to-prepare documents PERSONALIZED FOR YOUR CIRCUMSTANCES." LegalZoom's television ads claim: "Over a million people have discovered how easy it is to use LegalZoom for important legal documents, and LegalZoom will help you incorporate your business, file a patent, make a will and more. You can complete our online questions in minutes. Then we'll prepare your legal documents and deliver them directly to you."[16]

Is any of this the practice of law? Some courts have said that it is. If attorneys are involved running such sites, have they taken on clients to whom they owe fiduciary duties — including the duty of competence — and who may sue them in the event of professional negligence? A Missouri federal court found that LegalZoom, with three attorney and one non-attorney partners, was illegally practicing law in the state of Missouri by selling Missouri consumers do-it-yourself wills and other legal documents online. In California, in a case where LegalZoom was accused of creating a flawed living trust, requiring the estate to spend more than $10,000 on an outside attorney to fix the problems, the case settled when LegalZoom agreed to change a number of their advertising practices.[17]

What protection is there for users of self-help sites when there are *no* attorneys involved? These sites can't be regulated as easily by state bars, nor will legal malpractice claims be available. Not long ago, *Consumer Reports* examined three will-preparation self-help sites and concluded "all three are better than nothing if you have no will. But unless your needs are very simple — say, you want to leave everything to your spouse with no other provisions — none of them is likely to meet your needs. And we found problems with all three."[18]

What about lawyers who simply want to use websites to help bring in business and work more effectively with clients? The author of the following article is Senior Vice President of the Texas Lawyers' Insurance Exchange. The article was written from the perspective of malpractice issues in Texas, but it is applicable elsewhere — a valuable treatment of a wide variety of issues relating to attorney websites.

---

[15] To read the entire disclaimer go to http://www.settlementcentral.com/page0027.htm, and if you like, explore the site from there.

[16] An advertisement that appeared on television, as quoted in a class action brought against LegalZoom, Inc., in Janson v. LegalZoom.com, Inc., 802 F. Supp. 2d 1053, 1055 (W.D. Mo. 2011).

[17] *See* Webster v. LegalZoom.com, Inc., No. BC 438637 (Los Angeles Super. Ct. filed May 27, 2010).

[18] Consumer Reports Money Adviser issue: July 2011 http://www.consumerreports.org/cro/money/retirement-planning/write-your-own-will/overview/index.htm.

Jett Hanna, *Attorney Liability for Internet Related Activity: An Early Analysis*

http://www.texasbarcle.com/Materials/Events/574/39963_01.pdf, reprinted in *Spring 2000 ABA Legal Malpractice Conference Program Materials* (New York, Apr. 6–7, 2000)[19]

Current Online Legal Services

A number of form and kit services are now operating on the web, such as Nolo Press at www.nolo.com and US Legal Forms at www.uslegalforms.com. Nolo's site simply functions as an order point, while US Legal Forms actually lets you download forms immediately. What is truly an innovation is a number of sites now offering kits and forms that are clearly lawyers or law firms.

The home page of Richard S. Granat, a Maryland attorney, at www.granat.com, illustrates one of the primary innovations in marketing that the Internet makes possible. On the front page, there is a link that says "self help divorce form kits." That link takes you to a listing of divorce kits available in not only Maryland, but other states as well, from www.divorcelawinfo.com, which Granat's home page discloses is an "affiliated site." Granat's home page also states that the only legal service his firm performs is to assist pro se parties. Document drafting services are available if the consumer (client?) cannot fill out the forms in the kits offered. Email and phone consultations are available at a fixed rate of $30 per phone call. For more complicated matters, the Granat home page states that a referral will be made to another attorney. Mediation services can also be arranged.

. . . .

It is unlikely that all legal services will be provided on the Internet in the near future, but certainly significant aspects of law practice can be transferred to the web or other software efficiently. The web can be your paralegal. It is very easy to create a web site that takes information from a client and then generates a document utilizing the client's responses. Imagine clients simply logging on to your website, answering the questionnaire you used to have to fill out with them during an appointment, and generating legal documents for them instantly.

Liability for Kits and Forms

There is no law directly on point in Texas regarding liability for "kits" or forms" of which I am aware. In the past, kits and forms were generally printed as books. In all cases found in Texas, there has been no finding of liability for providing a defective book to someone.

The new cyberworld of kits and forms may lead to different results, however. The way in which Texas has defined legal services with regard to publications indicates that failure to warn someone that a kit or form is not a substitute for representation by an attorney could lead to liability.

---

[19] Copyright © 2000 by Texas Lawyers' Insurance Exchange. Reprinted by permission of TLIE and the author.

If a lawyer providing a kit or form with instructions is rendering legal advice, do all of the characteristics of an attorney client relationship attach to the situation? That would certainly appear [to be] the case. . . . A "client" who has chosen a kit may not be choosing the right kit, and thus providing the kit or form may not be part of "competent and diligent" representation. . . . The possibility of imposition of liability on an attorney for a defective kit or form that is either prepared by or recommended by the attorney thus seems high.

Mistakes by the Client

Clients will make mistakes when filling out forms or providing information to attorneys. When they do, they may claim that the attorney should have investigated the situation further and realized the client's mistake.

If clients are filling out forms to create automated legal documents, review of the document by an attorney or paralegal may avoid problems. For example, legal descriptions on deeds might be something that should be reviewed by a professional. Other types of information that are simply misspelled or omitted, however, are probably going to be a problem regardless of whether the information is gathered automatically or not. It is possible to force a web page user to respond to a particular question, but situations in which a blank answer is acceptable or where multiple responses might be appropriate could be overlooked.

. . . .

Confidentiality

One of the basic foundations of the attorney client relationship is confidentiality. Recent events have demonstrated that some of the best web sites have had significant security problems. In one case, a hacker appears to have stolen a large list of credit cards from an online merchant and distributed them to a large number of people.

Security must be analyzed on several levels. Secure transmission for the client to the attorney's web server is required. Secure transmission of the legal document is required. Any information about the client that remains on the attorney's web server or on the attorney's computer system needs to be secure from hacking. While the ABA opinion on e-mail encryption may be a basis for arguing that client interactions with a secure web site are entitled to similar presumptions of privacy, the security issues for a web site and secure storage of client information are more complex than those of e-mail security.

Conflicts of Interest

Automated generation of legal documents creates some significant conflict of interest questions. . . . Consider the following scenario: Husband and wife decide to generate wills online; each working separately with the same automated system. The husband leaves his share to his girlfriend, while the unsuspecting wife leaves her share to her husband.

Conclusion

The Internet will definitely give attorneys new ways to practice their profession . . . . Even lawyers who do not utilize the Internet themselves may have clients, partners, associates or employees who use the Internet to perform their duties, and should stay abreast of the changing nature of ethical and malpractice issues associated with Internet use.

NOTES

Note the thread that underlines much of Hanna's discussion — the fine line between providing information and giving advice, an issue we've already examined in Problem 3. Another issue familiar from Problem 3 is the importance of defining the scope of representation. Hanna makes a significant point in this regard: Texas specifically forbids lawyers from making the scope of representation so narrow as to preclude competent representation. Think about how this might affect some of the issues, such as ghost-writing pleadings and providing unbundled services, as we discussed in Problem 3.

Who is going to enforce ethical rules regarding websites? Although a 2010 ABA opinion has provided some guidance on web sites,[20] its opinion is dense and not easily understood. The opinion does note, properly, the danger of "expectations created by the website," and warns that lawyers who "invite inquiries" through the site "may create a prospective client-lawyer relationship." To fix this problem, many lawyers and law firms now carry explicit website disclaimers about not forming attorney-client relationships, and many others do not allow direct email communications with the firm's attorneys.

Finally, while websites cover the world, discipline operates state-by-state. Model Rule 8.5 provides that the website and its lawyers are subject to discipline in the jurisdiction in which they are admitted. How hard will that make it for someone in Alabama to complain about the conduct of a lawyer in Beverly Hills? We'll return to the topic of websites and advertising in Problem 31.

5. Metadata or Embedded Data

These terms, while distinct, are now generally lumped together either as "metadata," or "embedded data." Many, including Professor Hricik, call this "data about data." Metadata includes "information stored in electronic documents that can show changes made to the document and comments made electronically to the document."[21] It shows when the document was created and by whom, who has accessed or worked on the document, when the document was printed, what changes were made, and on the like. Significantly, in programs like Microsoft Word, it also shows all comments made during the drafting of the document. Other

---

[20] ABA Formal Opinion. 10-457 (2010).

[21] David Hricik and Chase Edward, *Metadata: The Ghosts Haunting e-Documents*, 13 GEORGIA BAR J. 5, 16 (2008) (citing to Definition of Metadata, http://wordnetweb.princeton.edu/perl/webwn?s= metadata&sub=Search+WordNet&o2=&o0=1&o8=1&o1=1&o7=&o5=&o9=&o6=&o3=&o4= &h=).

embedded data is created not by the user but by the program itself, and may be unknown to the user. These may be even harder to see, but can cause equal damage if seen by the wrong eyes.

Professor Hans Sinha, writing in the Maine Law Review,[22] explains that the ethical issues associated with metadata contain

> two distinct and intertwined acts. The first is the failure on the part of the sending lawyer to ensure that the document he or she electronically transmitted to opposing counsel did not contain confidential and privileged information within the document's metadata. This step involves the attorney's [competence] and above all, the attorney's duty to preserve the confidentiality of information . . . . Second is the conscious act on the part of the receiving lawyer to actively seek out and review, or 'mine,' metadata embedded in the electronically received document. This step involves the attorney's duty to respect the rights of third parties, his duty not to engage in fraudulent conduct, as well as the attorney's duty to zealously represent his client.

Professor Sinha examined fourteen ethics opinions and concluded that "two predominant views have emerged." The first is that the mining of metadata is unethical, an "impermissible attempt by the receiving attorney to breach what the profession holds dearest: the confidentiality between an attorney . . . and his client." The second view is equally important: "the duty to protect the confidentiality between the sending attorney and his client falls on the shoulders of the sending attorney . . . ." Sinha then argues that "absent a clear prohibition of metadata mining in the rules of professional conduct, . . . the mining of metadata is not ethically prohibited."

Do you agree? Can't *both* views articulated by Sinha work together? That is, don't lawyers have both an ethical duty to avoid transmitting metadata *and* a duty to avoid "mining" it?[23]

Tech-ethics expert Hricik has a different view than Sinha: "a lawyer who transmits a document knowing that it contains embedded client confidences violates the duty of confidentiality," but nevertheless that transmission of embedded data is "inadvertent," and that the lawyer receiving and tempted to examine it may not do so if "the recipient should know that the transmission was inadvertent."[24]

The DC Bar has developed a more narrow prohibition against "mining": "a receiving lawyer is prohibited from reviewing metadata sent by an adversary only where he has actual knowledge that the metadata was inadvertently sent. In such instances, the receiving lawyer should not review the metadata before consulting

---

[22] Hans P. Sinha, *The Ethics of Metadata: A Critical Analysis and a Practical Solution*, 63 MAINE L. REV. 175 (2010).

[23] We will discuss the duties that attend on both lawyers' sides when unconcealed information is inadvertently transmitted, an area where the case law is more developed, in Section 8 below.

[24] David Hricik, *I Can Tell When You're Telling Lies: Ethics and Embedded Confidential Information*, 30 J. LEGAL PROF. 79 (2006). Note that Hricik uses the term "embedded data" to cover both data generated by the user and by the program.

with the sending lawyer" to determine confidentiality issues.[25]

ABA Model Rule 1.6(c) specifically avoids addressing the issue of whether lawyers can take a look at that metadata: "[W]hether the lawyer is required to take additional steps, such as returning the document or electronically stored information, is a matter of law beyond the scope of these Rules, as is the question of whether the privileged status of a document or electronically stored information has been waived." Perhaps more helpful is a map and table from the ABA's Law Practice Management Section showing the rules (or lack thereof) on metadata in each state.[26]

Given the confusion about the law, and even exactly what comprises "metadata" or "embedded data," Professor Hricik's 2006 article, cited in footnote 24, is particularly valuable. Hricik goes through most of the major software programs used by lawyers to point out where the embedded data can be found, and then provides a primer on "How to Remove or Avoid Creating Embedded Data." What should a lawyer's ethical duties be to avoid creating such data and then to "scrub" the files of embedded data before transmitting them? This is still largely an open issue, though the trend — as we've seen above — is to set a standard that lawyers provide only "clean" files to the opposition — a standard that may require lawyers to call for technical assistance.

6. Electronic Communication and Malpractice

As we have pointed out before, ethical violations and malpractice are not the same thing, and while the existence of the former may be some evidence of the latter, an ethical violation is insufficient in and of itself to prove malpractice. Here, however, the question seems to be the reverse: Can a malpractice action be maintained even where the attorney has acted entirely ethically?

As one example, the Attorneys' Liability Assurance Society, or ALAS, which insures many larger firms, has taken the position that attorneys need not encrypt e-mail in order for their clients to have an expectation of privacy. No communication is perfect, argues William Freivogel, at the time one of ALAS's principal spokespersons. Even in face-to-face communications, "many people read lips," he told Wendy R. Leibowitz of the *National Law Journal* in 1997.

The reality is that cell phones, laptops, and other devices, because they are portable, are easier to lose, easier to steal, and easier for police to search. Might a lawyer's failure to password protect a personal mobile device grounds for malpractice, even if it's not "unethical"? Richard Granat recently wrote in the *ABA Journal* that "if you are a litigation lawyer and you don't use automated litigation support methods, you may be guilty of malpractice."[27]

---

[25] www.dcbar.org/for_lawyers/ethics/legal_ethics/opinions/opinion341.cfm.

[26] http://www.americanbar.org/groups/departments_offices/legal_technology_resources/resources/charts_fyis/metadatachart.html.

[27] *Tracking Techies: Finding the Footprints of America's Switched-on Lawyers*, ABA JOURNAL, April 2012.

Professor Mary Dunnewold, writing in the ABA Student Lawyer Magazine,[28] points to another danger area: a lawyer's failure to use Internet resources in conducting research or investigation. She discusses *Cajamarca v. Regal Entertainment Group*[29] in which a federal judge sanctioned and reprimanded a lawyer both for failing to adequately investigate his client's case using social media, and for failing to advise her to maintain her "proof" on her hard drive. During discovery in this sexual harassment lawsuit, material facts emerged showing that the lawyer's client had lied about the incidents that led to the claim, her symptoms, and her personal history — lies the lawyer could have discovered by visiting his client's Facebook page.

Much of this discussion may sound like a steady drumroll of concern about ethical traps waiting to open beneath the unsuspecting lawyer. That is the reality of practicing in this modern technological age. No matter how convenient the tools technology provides, when an attorney *can* be overheard, or a computer screen can be seen, or metadata exposed, lawyers must avoid these pitfalls. Long ago, when the authors were in law school, we were told never to discuss a case in an elevator because the walls have ears. Now, so do the airwaves, the means of oral and written communications, and the great world-wide web.

7.   Tweeting, Friending, Social Networking, and More

In case you think we have exhausted all the ethical or malpractice issues of cyberspace, consider these:

May a lawyer tweet about a case she's handling? Lurk on an opposing party's Facebook page?[30] Or "friend" a judge on Facebook? The same ethics issues are involved — confidentiality, competence, loyalty, vigorous advocacy — but whether it's Facebook, LinkedIn, Twitter, or a hundred other places, the venue is very different.

Court decisions and ethics opinions, still in their nascent stage, are not always consistent. For example, in Florida a court held that lawyers and judges could not be "friends" on Facebook (and other related sites) if that lawyer might appear before the judge, on the theory that it conveys the impression that a lawyer is in a special position.[31] In New York on the other hand the ethics committee stated, "a judge generally may socialize in person with attorneys who appear in the judge's court, subject to the Rules Governing Judicial Conduct."[32] New York requires their judges to avoid impropriety and promote public confidence in the integrity and impartiality of the judiciary online and in public. The committee did not see why

---

[28]   41 ABA STUDENT LAWYER MAGAZINE (2012).

[29]   863 F. Supp. 2d 237 (E.D.N.Y. 2012), further order of August 31, 2012, at 2012 U.S. Dist. LEXIS 124485 (E.D.N.Y. Aug. 31, 2012).

[30]   Almost all states' ethics opinions now say "no," because this would be communicating with an adverse represented party.

[31]   Judicial Ethics Advisory Committee, Florida Supreme Court. Opinion Number: 2009-20, November 2009. As judges are elected in Florida, it is interesting to note that this opinion does permit fan pages for judge elections.

[32]   Judicial Ethics Committee, New York. Opinion 08-176, January 2009.

lawyers and judges could not conduct themselves similarly on online social media.

The ABA's recent Opinion 452 (February 21, 2013) seems to agree. "Social interactions of all kinds, including ESM [electronic social media], can be beneficial to judges to prevent them from being thought of as isolated or out of touch," states the opinion, which analyzed the issue under the ABA Model Code of Judicial Conduct. "When used with proper care, judges' use of ESM does not necessarily compromise their duties under the Model Code any more than use of traditional and less public forms of social connection such as U.S. mail, telephone, email or texting."

As for some other tech-related issues, we offer the following:

Networks, Hard Drives, Copiers, and Work Servers. Almost all law firms, even small ones, have computer networks, and DSL and wireless connections. Even if not using "the Cloud," these are still direct portals to the Internet. Many networks operate in a way that requires the computers to remain on, and the networks open. This means that remote access to a law firm's computer network is often available around the clock.

This access, of course, is extremely desirable. It enables lawyers to telecommute from home while using files located at the office — in the firm's computer system. A lawyer can draft emergency pleadings to be filed in New York while in trial in Texas, communicate with branch offices in Anchorage and Salt Lake City from a skybox at Giants Stadium, and send files to their clients all across the country while sitting in an airport lounge in Philadelphia. But with access comes risk.

While firewalls and passwords generally protect law firm work servers, the non-law firm portals at airports, hotels, and coffee shops may be far less secure. Computer hackers still seem to have too easy a time breaking through many firewalls, breaking down passwords, and accessing computer networks. Once the computer hard drive or network server is accessed, confidential client information is jeopardized. Even files that have been deleted, including those that have been emptied from the "recycle bin," may be recoverable. They will still exist on the hard disk if they are located on a part of the disk that has not actually been overwritten by another file. And remember, modern printers have hard drives too, which may well contain sensitive information.[33]

Even without a virtual practice, law firms are storing and backing up files electronically. Law firms that suffered through the devastation caused by storms like Hurricanes Katrina, Irene, or Sandy are acutely aware of how easily both primary and back-up data can be lost if they are stored in the same location. Off-site legal storage seems now to be a necessity. Companies are doing a booming business providing electronic off-site storage in addition to keeping physical files.

---

[33] In addition to hackers, hard disks can become the focus of discovery battles. In that arena, there is a reasonable argument to be made that, like garbage, a deleted file has been abandoned, and if the law firm does not do the equivalent of "shredding," the file is still subject to discovery. This creates the possibility that opposing counsel could be permitted to bring in a computer expert to attempt to recover these files.

Cookies. Most people know by now that when talking cyberspeak, "cookies" doesn't refer to Oreos, but to the little text files placed on your computer when you access a new web site. These files help speed up access time and can be used to identify you (or, more accurately, your computer) when you re-access the site at a later date. But in the wrong hands, and with the increased use of "surveillance cookies," your hard drive could be used to trace where your computer has traveled on the net, which could result in the discovery of confidential information.

Legal Briefing Services. These concerns may be of particular significance for those lawyers and (mostly small) firms who have taken to using research and briefing services to alleviate some of their workload. This work is usually done by licensed attorneys, in the US or abroad, though whether the lawyers are admitted to practice in the particular state where the work will be used is open to serious question. More significantly, these services, including research, memoranda, and even briefs ready for filing with a court, don't consider either the attorney who hires them or the end-user — the attorney's client — to be their own client. Accordingly, they generally do not perform conflict of interest checks. At least theoretically, these briefing services could be writing the papers filed on both sides of the same case.

Websites and Disclaimers. The possibility that people could consider themselves clients of a law firm simply by submitting a question on the firm's website has led law firms to include disclaimers that the information contained there is not intended as legal advice, and does not result in the formation of an attorney-client relationship. But just saying this doesn't necessarily make it so. First, in order to be effective, the disclaimers have to be both complete and accurate. Second, if they are placed anywhere other than prominently on the home page, a visitor may not see the disclaimer until after a fair amount of site exploration. Third, once the visitor does encounter the disclaimer, the guest should be required to "click" on or otherwise accept the notice before proceeding. Fourth, disclaimers that state, for example, that the firm is not giving legal advice are unlikely to override the actual receipt of legal advice. And finally, if the website provides hypertext links to other locations over which it has no control, inaccuracies at those linked sites may be attributable to the law firm. In other words, disclaimers may say whatever they say, but the true test will be what information was imparted to a prospective client, under what circumstances, and with what expectations.

Chat Rooms, Blogging, and Solicitation. Of course, the Internet doesn't only provide opportunities for law firm websites, but for a myriad of consumer-based and -run sites. Sites for victims of mass torts, plane crashes, or defective products are venues for opportunistic lawyers to lurk and troll in real-time chat rooms for new clients. Lawyers want potential clients to know about their successes. While we mention chat rooms here, we discuss blogging and e-solicitation in some detail in Problem 31.

8. Inadvertent Disclosure

Whether email error, mistaken replies "to all," mass electronic faxes, or old-fashioned hard-copy errors, what to do with inadvertent disclosure issues has become an increasingly important and heavily-litigated subject.

To review just some of the issues: What should a lawyer do with confidential information that is inadvertently disclosed by the opposing side? Does it make a difference whether the disclosure is completely accidental, the result of imprudence, or intentionally leaked by a disgruntled employee? Does it matter whether the lawyer who receives the information is aware of its confidentiality? What about notice to the disclosing lawyer? Is there a difference between transmission of *confidential* information vs. *privileged* data?

One of the earliest opinions to directly address the issue of inadvertent disclosure is excerpted below.

AEROJET-GENERAL CORP. v. TRANSPORT INDEMNITY INSURANCE
18 Cal. App. 4th 996 (Cal. Ct. App. 1993)

Sometime between July 1988 and August 1989, . . . [Attorney Scott] DeVries received a packet of documents concerning the Aerojet litigation from David Strode, an Aerojet employee.

According to DeVries, the only item he was interested in was a memorandum revealing the existence of a witness, Warren Michaels. Michaels was a Sacramento-based independent insurance adjustor who investigated a prior industrial accident at the Aerojet facility. The memorandum by an attorney with Bronson, Bronson & McKinnon (Bronson), opposing counsel herein, described an interview with Michaels and contained the attorney's assessment of Michaels' "witness potential" in the litigation. DeVries initially contacted Michaels by telephone and spoke with him about the case.

Curiosity developed about how DeVries had learned of Michaels' existence because his name had not been divulged during the discovery process. . . . DeVries revealed that he learned of Michaels from a document that had originated from the Bronson firm, which represented a number of the defendant insurers.

Almost a year later, Bronson searched its records to find the document naming Michaels. At this point it was discovered that the memorandum naming Michaels was part of a larger packet of documents that had presumably been sent to Bronson's client, Crum & Forster, the parent corporation for the insurers represented by Bronson.

When deposed in connection with respondents' motion for sanctions, DeVries acknowledged that he had no reason to believe that Bronson or their clients had consented to the disclosure of the documents. Nevertheless, he reviewed them, and did not immediately notify any opposing counsel, the special discovery master, or the trial court that he had received them. . . . He kept the documents for a period of "weeks to months" on his desk or credenza, and did not put them in the Aerojet case file. The documents were ultimately destroyed "during a routine housecleaning."

. . . .

The [trial court's] sanction order was not based on DeVries' failure to advise opposing counsel of his receipt of the documents, but for his failure to do so in a timely fashion. It recites that the documents given to DeVries were "undeniably a privileged communication between opposing counsel and his client detailing pretrial and trial strategies." Furthermore, "neither the Bronson office nor Crum & Forster had knowledge of or had consented to Aerojet's possession of these documents." The court summarized the conduct that it found to be "unethical and in bad faith . . . . Upon receipt of the documents, Mr. DeVries failed to contact opposing counsel. Mr. DeVries failed to investigate how his client obtained the documents. Mr. DeVries failed to tell his partners he had received the documents from Aerojet. Mr. DeVries looked at the documents and used the information contained therein to his own advantage. Finally, Mr. DeVries destroyed the documents."

It was further ordered that Warren Michaels be precluded from testifying during any phase of the trial.

DeVries did not violate any laws, statutory or decisional, or any rules of court or rules of professional conduct in the manner by which he obtained the subject information. It is undisputed that DeVries is free of any wrongdoing in his initial receipt of the documents.

The issue concerns the duty of an attorney who, without misconduct or fault, obtains or learns of a confidential communication (Evid. Code § 952) among opposing counsel, or between opposing counsel and opposing counsel's client. Assuming there to be such a duty, it becomes more difficult to define when the confidential communication reveals a relevant and potentially helpful witness, such as occurred here, regardless of whether the witness should have been revealed through discovery. There is no State Bar rule of professional conduct, no rule of court nor any statute specially addressing this situation and mandating or defining any duty under such circumstances.

In response to respondents' argument that DeVries should not even have read the documents at issue, which they support with an American Bar Association ethics opinion, we note that this complex litigation involves hundreds of insurance policies and parties, numerous law firms, scores of individual attorneys and a great number of documents. The files were voluminous — the attorneys were swamped with pleadings, correspondence, discovery and other documents. Their job entailed careful review and cataloguing of the documents coming across their desks, and one cannot identify, let alone analyze, many of these documents until they have been reviewed. . . . Given the number of attorneys and documents involved in this case, DeVries cannot be faulted for examining this memorandum.

. . . .

The attorney-client privilege is a shield against deliberate intrusion; it is not an insurer against inadvertent disclosure. Further, not all information that passes privately between attorney and client is entitled to remain confidential in the literal sense. The most obvious example is information that is required to be disclosed in response to discovery, such as the identification of potential witnesses. Consequently, whether the existence and identity of a witness or other nonprivileged information is revealed through formal discovery or inadvertence, the end result is the same: The opposing party is entitled to the use of that witness or information. This fundamental concept was lost in the skirmish below.

"The attorney-client privilege only protects disclosure of communications; it does not protect disclosure of the underlying facts upon which the communications are based . . . ."

If the underlying information which respondents sought to prevent plaintiffs from using is not privileged, and if such information was revealed to plaintiffs' counsel through no fault or misconduct of his own, plaintiffs and their counsel were entitled to use it. . . . In the instant case, the existence of witness Warren Michaels was not privileged. Michaels was not unknown to Aerojet in the literal sense — he had previously adjusted a workers' compensation claim by an Aerojet employee, and he had knowledge relevant to the litigation.

We think that the manner in which DeVries obtained the information in this case — through documents inadvertently transmitted to his client — is irrelevant to resolution of the issue. Assuming no question of waiver, the problem would be no different if DeVries had obtained the same information from someone who overheard respondents discussing the matter in a restaurant or a courthouse corridor, or if it had been mistakenly sent to him through the mail or by facsimile transmission. Once he had acquired the information in a manner that was not due to his own fault or wrongdoing, he cannot purge it from his mind. Indeed, his professional obligation demands that he utilize his knowledge about the case on his client's behalf.

In the absence of any clear statutory, regulatory or decisional authority imposing a duty of immediate disclosure of the inadvertent receipt of privileged information, we conclude the sanction order cannot stand.

NOTES

What do you think of the assertion in *Aerojet* that it doesn't matter whether witness Michaels' name was revealed during discovery or from inadvertently disclosed confidential communications, since "the end result is the same"? Does this "end result" analysis justify all lawyers' use of all material no matter how it is obtained?

What of the court's final assertion that how DeVries obtained the witness' name is "irrelevant"? The court argues that had the information come by mail or by fax, DeVries could still use it, and indeed *must* use it. But most confidential faxes come with cover-sheet notices that the fax is a lawyer-client confidential communication. Would a lawyer receiving such a fax have as legitimate a justification for reading it as DeVries had to read the Bronson memo? Wouldn't such a lawyer know the fax was intended to be confidential? Is this argument of the court pure *dicta*, since DeVries did not know the memo was confidential as he read it? Finally, how does that *dicta* square with the court's earlier reasoning that DeVries was blameless because he didn't know what he was reading?

9. The ABA's Changing View

The ABA opinion referred to in passing by the *Aerojet* court is ABA Formal Opinion 92-368 (November 10, 1992). That opinion comes to a very different conclusion than *Aerojet*, or at least *Aerojet*'s *dicta*. It holds that when a lawyer receives information that appears confidential and not intended for that lawyer, the recipient should *not* look at the materials, but rather should notify the sending attorney and abide by that attorney's further instructions. The opinion further says that a lawyer's zeal in pursuing the client's cause must be tempered by "doing the right thing." But the ABA cites little direct authority in support of this proposition. The opinion does offer an analogy between inadvertent disclosures of confidences and inadvertent *waivers* of the evidentiary privilege.

The ABA ethics committee's willingness to reach a do-the-right-thing conclusion squares with the views of many ethics experts and commentators — that lawyers who use information they know is not meant for them provide a sad commentary on the state of the profession and its lack of comity. But for years, there was a dearth of hard authority supporting this position. It was clear that many attorneys closer to the reality of the daily practice of law are more sanguine about the profession's rougher edges. These lawyers might ask whether we really expect a Scott DeVries *not* to look at all the material he received. Or, for that matter, can we really expect Russ Bluestone, our lawyer in this Problem, *not* to read the entire electronic file, and to use the information it provides?

In 2005, in Formal Opinion 05-437, the ABA withdrew Formal Opinion 92-368 to be consistent with the 2002 version of Model Rule 4.4, which only requires notification to the opposing, inadvertently disclosing party. Neither Rule 4.4 nor Opinion 05-437 require that the receiving lawyer will forego looking at the document.

Nevertheless, put yourself in the shoes of the lawyer whose support staff replies to "all" and sends an email message to the opposition as well as to the client. A lawyer of our acquaintance tells us this story:

> It was my first year as an associate for a large urban law firm. I was the junior person on a massive litigation matter, and the senior partner told me to send a letter to certain defense counsel and not to others. I wasn't sure exactly who he meant, so I asked him again. But he got impatient and said it too quickly, then stalked off. I was afraid he'd think I wasn't smart enough, but I guess I was still confused. The letter was about defense strategy. I sent it out, but I sent it to one lawyer who wasn't part of the strategy, whose client we were pointing the finger at. I admit it; it was a big mistake. When the partner found out, he was livid. He was a powerful partner and I knew I would be finished at that firm, but a friend of mine in the mailroom figured out a way to blame it on a messenger who had just quit.

> I look at inadvertent disclosure this way: If you left your purse in the subway, wouldn't you hope someone would return it? If you found someone's purse in the subway, would you take all the money or give it back? I see it as, "There but for the grace of God go I."

This argument is persuasive, but is it enough to convince you? Or do you still feel not only that you must look inside the purse, but *use* what you find there?

10.   *WPS, Rico,* Notice to Counsel, and Beyond

In 1999, a different district of the California Court of Appeals than the *Aerojet* court decided what has become known as the "WPS" (appropriately pronounced "Whoops") case.[34]

WPS's lawyer received boxes of trial exhibits from the State Compensation Insurance Fund's lawyer, including litigation summaries that were clearly marked in bold capital letters at the top "Attorney-Client Communication/Attorney Work Product," and "Do Not Circulate or Duplicate." The word "CONFIDENTIAL" appeared around the perimeter of each page. Despite this, WPS's attorney showed the documents to his expert, who in turn gave them to another lawyer who was involved in a separate case against the Fund. The trial court determined that the documents were privileged and should have been returned by WPS's lawyer. Relying substantially on ABA Opinion 92-368, the court sanctioned WPS's lawyer $6,000.

The appeals court agreed that the documents were privileged, and held that their inadvertent disclosure did not waive any privilege:

> The conclusion we reach is fundamentally based on the importance which the attorney-client privilege holds in the jurisprudence of this state. Without it, full disclosure by clients to their counsel would not occur, with the result that the ends of justice would not be properly served. We believe a client should not enter the attorney-client relationship fearful that an inadvertent error by its counsel could result in the waiver of privileged information or the retention of privileged information by an adversary who might abuse and disseminate the information with impunity. In addition, it has long been recognized that " '[a]n attorney has an obligation not only to protect his client's interests, but also to respect the legitimate interests of fellow members of the bar, the judiciary, and the administration of justice.' "

Despite this language, the appeals court reversed the sanctions against the attorney, noting that California, whose rules are not based on either the ABA's Model Rules or Model Code, does not generally rely on American Bar Association opinions. More significantly, however, the *WPS* court set forth guidelines to be followed in future instances of inadvertent disclosure. First, the lawyer should examine the materials without reading them to ascertain whether they are privileged and if they are, refrain from further examination. Second, the recipient should notify the sender that the privileged material was received. Third, the sending and receiving lawyers should meet and confer to resolve what to do with the material, or in the absence of an agreement, seek guidance from the court.

At least one knowledgeable California ethics authority, Ellen Peck, who served as both a State Bar Court judge and principal staff to California's ethics and rules

---

[34] State Compensation Insurance Fund v. WPS, Inc., 70 Cal. App. 4th 644 (Cal. Ct. App. 1999).

revision bodies, believes that *WPS* and *Aerojet* are easily reconciled with each other. *WPS*, in Peck's view, explains what to do with the receipt of what is "patently attorney-client privileged or confidential information or is clearly marked [as such]," while *Aerojet* deals with information that is not privileged or confidential.[35] But is it so clear that *Aerojet* involves discovery that both sides agreed is not privileged or confidential? And how does the recipient attorney know whether material is "patently" privileged merely because of its label? The label may raise a presumption or at least provide notice, but the issue of privilege and confidentiality is often in substantial disagreement between the parties. Besides, facsimile cover sheets and e-mails with confidentiality admonitions are routinely used for non-confidential purposes — including dinner reservations, requests for tee times, and, in our experience, communications to opposing counsel.

One final issue raised by *WPS*: How can the recipient attorney comply with the court's first requirement, to refrain from examining the materials, and then knowledgeably attempt to resolve the issue with the other side — or, indeed, test the claim of privilege itself? Peck leaves it to the recipient attorney to "analyze the content of the document and the circumstances of its release to determine whether you have one of three independent grounds for usage of the information. . . ." Clearly, this is necessary, as she puts it, to fulfill "your duties of competence and loyalty to your client." But if a lawyer must make this analysis later, what sense does it make to refrain from doing this when the document is first received?

One thing the *WPS* case makes clear is the necessity in California to notify opposing counsel. In 2007, in *Rico v. Mitsubishi Motors Corp.*, the California Supreme Court upheld the disqualification of a lawyer who, after obtaining confidential documents, did not alert opposing counsel, claiming it would be disadvantageous to his client. The court strongly re-affirmed the *WPS* principle that an attorney in these circumstances may not read a document any more closely than is necessary to ascertain that it is privileged. Once it becomes apparent that the content is privileged, counsel must immediately notify opposing counsel and try to resolve the situation.

Moreover, the fact that the document was not "clearly flagged as confidential" was immaterial: " '[T]he absence of prominent notations of confidentiality does not make them any less privileged' " [quoting the lower court opinion]. "The *State Fund* rule is an objective standard. In applying the rule, courts must consider whether reasonably competent counsel, knowing the circumstances of the litigation, would have concluded the materials were privileged, how much review was reasonably necessary to draw that conclusion, and when counsel's examination should have ended." The court also found a new ground to disqualify counsel: the lawyer's review of confidential documents, which created what the court called "unmitigable damage."[36]

The fact that the California high court has spoken does not a uniform national policy make. Still, because California has been in the forefront of the case law since

---

[35] *Walking the Ethics Tightrope: What to Do About Inadvertent Disclosure*, 14 LAWYERS' MUTUAL INSURANCE CO. BULLETIN 1 (1999).

[36] Rico v. Mitsubishi Motors Corp., 171 P.3d 1092, 1098–1099 (Cal. 2007).

Aerojet, that state's Supreme Court carries with it even more weight than usual. The trend seems clear: At the least, the inadvertently disclosing lawyer is entitled to notice. ABA Rule 4.4(b) states: "A lawyer who receives a document relating to the representation of the lawyer's client and knows or reasonably should know that the document was inadvertently sent shall promptly notify the sender." What is less clear is what happens after giving notice. May the receiving lawyer then take advantage of the inadvertently disclosed information? *Rico*, with its "unmitigable damage" references, implies that lawyer would have been disqualified even if he had given notice.

Nor is California the only state to use disqualification as a remedy. A 1999 Florida state court opinion goes even further than *Rico*:

> The receipt of privileged documents is grounds for disqualification of the attorney receiving the documents based on the unfair tactical advantage such disclosure provides. Moreover, contrary to plaintiffs' argument, on certiorari review a movant is "not required to demonstrate specific prejudice in order to justify disqualification."

> While recognizing that disqualification of a party's chosen counsel is an extraordinary remedy and should be resorted to sparingly, we believe the prudent course in this case is to disqualify counsel. . . . [P]erceptions are of the utmost importance. Thus, how much of an advantage, if any, one party may gain over another we cannot measure. However, the possibility that such an advantage did accrue warrants resort to this drastic remedy for the sake of the appearance of justice, if not justice itself, and the public's interest in the integrity of the judicial process.[37]

11.   Does Inadvertent Disclosure Waive the Client's Privilege?

In recent years, there has been a definite trend away from having inadvertently disclosed material constitute a waiver of the attorney-client privilege. Even though the basic principles of privilege and waiver have not changed too much since Wigmore's day, the increased use of technology, especially the routine and heavy use of electronic communications, has played a clear part in this trend to relax strict application of Wigmore, and is often mentioned in court and ethics committee opinions as a reason not to hold inadvertent disclosures to be waivers of the privilege. A couple of examples follow.

After discussing older, stricter authorities, including *Wigmore on Evidence* and *Wright & Graham on Federal Practice & Procedure*,[38] one federal judge in *Berg Electronics, Inc. v. Molex*, 875 F. Supp. 261, 262 (D. Del. 1995) wrote the following:

---

[37] ABAMAR Housing and Development, Inc. v. Lisa Daly Lady Decor, Inc., 724 So. 2d 572, 573–74 (Fla. Dist. Ct. App. 1998).

[38] More precisely, JOHN H. WIGMORE, EVIDENCE, § 2325, at 633, and CHARLES ALAN WRIGHT & KENNETH W. GRAHAM, JR., FEDERAL PRACTICE AND PROCEDURE § 5726, at 543, n.75, the latter stating that inadvertence can only be claimed if the holder "did not bother to look at [the documents] before turning them over," and even then, "it is difficult to see why courts should come to his rescue when he realizes he should have been more careful."

A disadvantage of this traditional approach is that it divests the client of the opportunity to protect communications he or she intended to maintain confidential. The privilege for confidential communications can be lost if papers are in a car that is stolen, a briefcase that is lost, a letter that is misdelivered, or in a facsimile that is missent. This approach takes from the client the ability to control when his or her privilege is waived, and is inconsistent with the Supreme Court's admonition that courts should apply the privilege to ensure a client remains free from apprehension that consultations with a legal advisor will be disclosed.

In *Van Hull v. Marriott Courtyard*, 63 F. Supp. 2d 840 (N.D. Ohio 1999), the judge went beyond holding that inadvertent disclosure did not waive the privilege and required return of the document in question.[39] He warned that "willful or deliberate noncompliance" with the order to return the document would result in "the customary sanctions" *and* "may lead to dismissal with prejudice of the plaintiff's complaint and an award of attorneys' fees and costs."

While the overall trend is to relax the rules on waiver, *perhaps* to be more forgiving of those who disclose and *possibly* to be harsher to those who read what is disclosed, the debate about this issue is not yet over. After all, the fact that there is no privilege waiver does not necessarily lead to a complete bar against receiving counsel using any of the material. And when a court rules that disqualification of counsel is an appropriate remedy even without a showing of prejudice, one suspects that the war over inadvertent disclosures is still being waged. *Aerojet* and similar opinions continue to make sense to many, particularly those who argue that the burden should not be on the innocent recipient of information to figure out what is truly confidential.

12.   "Geek-ifying" Law School

When the ABA adopted comment 8 to MR 1.1, one commentator on the EDiscoveryResourceDatabase website said: "This officially terminates the world of ediscovery ignorance in which many lawyers have been choosing to live in for the past years. It's the end of the world as we know it."[40] Comment 8 simply says: "To maintain the requisite knowledge and skill, a lawyer should keep abreast of changes in the law and its practice, *including the benefits and risks associated with relevant technology*, engage in continuing study and education and comply with all continuing legal education requirements to which the lawyer is subject." (Emphasis ours).

Roland Trope and Sarah Jane Hughes' 160 page treatise *Red Skies in the Morning: Professional Ethics at the Dawn of Cloud Computing*[41] provides a detailed, cautionary look at the sunny new world of technology-supported practice.

---

[39] The same result occurred in Maine. *See Corey v. Norman, Hanson & De Troy,* 742 A.2d 933 (Me. 1999).

[40] *It's the "End of the World" as We Lawyers Know It,* February 1, 2013 by "alejoesq" http://ediscoveryresourcedatabase.com/2013/02/01/its-the-end-of-the-world-as-we-lawyers-know-it/.

[41] Roland L. Trope & Sarah Jane Hughes, *Red Skies in the Morning - Professional Ethics at the Dawn of Cloud Computing,* 38 WM. MITCHELL L. REV. 111 (2011).

The authors attempt to define broad areas of risk created by the new technologies and offer guidance to counsel on identifying such risks, assessing whether they can be mitigated by reasonable precautions, and if not, what counsel may need to do to fulfill their professional ethical obligations. They conclude that "the development and adoption of new communications technologies will seldom require significant changes to the long standing professional ethical rules, however surprising, rapid, and disruptive the technologies prove to be upon their emergence." But they offer no guarantees.

Throughout this problem we have highlighted some of the issues technology creates for all practitioners, especially as it affects confidential communications between attorney and client. The goal has been to heighten awareness of these special challenges, so they bring few surprises when they occur. In Problem 18, we'll return to some of these issues in the context of e-discovery.

D. SUPPLEMENTAL READINGS

1. Since this is an extremely fluid and shifting area of the law, we recommend that you begin any research by looking at the ABA Legal Technology Resource Center Website, available at: www.abanet.org/tech/ltrc/home.html.

2. Many law review articles do an excellent job covering the territory of cyberethics. Here are several of particular note:

• Catherine J. Lanctot, *Attorney-Client Relationships in Cyberspace: The Peril and the Promise*, 49 DUKE L.J. 147 (1999), is a scholarly treatment that points out how using the telephone for confidential communications was treated with considerable caution by lawyers when it first arrived on the scene — much like the wariness about the Internet today;

• J. Clayton Athey, then a third year law student at Georgetown, wrote an excellent comment for his school's law journal, *The Ethics of Attorney Web Sites: Updating the Model Rules to Better Deal with Emerging Technologies*, 13 GEORGETOWN J. LEG. ETHICS 499 (2000);

• Peter R. Jarvis & Bradley F. Tellam, *Competence and Confidentiality in the Context of Cellular Telephone, Cordless Telephone, and E-Mail Communications*, 33 WILLAMETTE L. REV. 467 (1997), is a thorough discussion of ethics, confidentiality, and these communication mechanisms;

• Eric Friedberg and Michael McGowan, *Lost Back-Up Tapes, Stolen Laptops and Other Tales of Data Breach Woe*, THE COMPUTER & INTERNET LAWYER (Oct. 2006) is a technical article that discusses encryption and data back-up method; and

• Michael W. Loudenslager, *E-Lawyering, the ABA's Current Choice of Ethics Law Rule & the Dormant Commerce Clause: Why the Dormant Commerce Clause Invalidates Model Rule 8.5(b)(2) When Applied to Attorney Internet Representations of Clients*, 15 WM. & MARY BILL RTS. J. 587 (2006) is a long article with in-depth analyses of the rise of e-lawyering and jurisdiction over the attorney giving advice.

3. David Hricik & Amy Falkingham, *Lawyers Still Worry Too Much About Transmitting E-mail Over the Internet*, 10 J. TECH. L. & POL'Y 265 (2005). Tech

expert Hricik and his co-author update other Hricik work that had become widely cited for the proposition that e-mail was secure for purposes of attorney-client communications, and thus there was a reasonable expectation of privacy. Since those articles were published, a few others have taken issue with his conclusions. Say the authors: "In a rather Quixotic fashion, this Article presents a very careful inquiry into the factual risks and an analysis of the legal protections associated with e-mail, with the hope of ending this debate." This carefully researched article is worth reading, and has a happy ending: the authors' belief that lawyers can meet their obligation of confidentiality when sending e-mail transmissions.

4. Armen Keteyian, *Digital Photocopiers Loaded with Secrets*, CBS NEWS INVESTIGATIVE REPORT, April 20, 2010, *available at* http://www.cbsnews.com/8301-18563_162-6412439.html. How dangerous can copier hard drives be? Investigative reporter Keteyian bought four from a New Jersey warehouse for $300 apiece, plugged them in, and found all kinds of hard-drive information, including sensitive documents from the sex crimes and narcotics units of the Buffalo, N.Y. police department, with the names of targets of a drug raid; a New York construction company's design for a building near Ground Zero, with names and addresses and social security numbers of employees; and 300 pages of individual medical records that should have been protected by HIPAA, including blood tests, drug prescriptions, and one cancer diagnosis.

5. RICHARD SUSSKIND, THE END OF LAWYERS? RETHINKING THE NATURE OF LEGAL SERVICES (2008). Susskind applies his IT background to develop an extremely broad and often negative assessment of the legal landscape at the beginning of the 21st century, and describes what he believes that will replace it. Chapter 7, "Access to Justice and the Law," is especially valuable for its insights into a far more pressing issue: the unmet legal needs of millions of people, and the social cost this unmet need extracts.

6. Andrew M. Pearlman, *Untangling Ethics Theory from Attorney Conduct Rules: The Case of Inadvertent Disclosures*, 13 GEO. MASON L. REV. 767 (2005), gives a comprehensive overview of the ethical issues surrounding inadvertent disclosure, and offers both practical and normative ideas on the ethical consequences of an attorney's receipt and choice to read or to not to read inadvertently disclosed materials.

7. David Hricik, *I Can Tell When You're Telling Lies: Ethics and Embedded Confidential Information*, 30 J. LEGAL PROF. 79 (2006), cited in the Readings above, is a valuable review of embedded data, its confidentiality, transmission, and use, and the duties that impact the lawyers who transmit and receive that information. Hricik also wrote another useful article that explains metadata for the practicing lawyer. David Hricik & Chase Edward, *Metadata: The Ghosts Haunting e-Documents*, 13 GEORGIA BAR J. 5 (Feb. 2008).

8. Michael Lewis, *Attack of the Masked Cyberdudes!*, N.Y. TIMES MAGAZINE, July 15, 2001. The best-selling author tells the incredible story of Marcus Arnold, who, using a "pseudonym on top of a pseudonym," became the highest-rated legal expert on AskMe.com, a heavily-trafficked Internet "knowledge exchange," despite the facts that he wasn't an attorney and was, in fact, only 15 years old.

9. In *Competent Computing: A Lawyer's Ethical Duty to Safeguard the Confidentiality and Integrity of Client Information Stored on Computers and Computer Networks*, 19 GEO. J. LEGAL ETHICS 629 (2006), John D. Comerford promotes the approach taken by a 2005 Arizona ethics opinion for safeguarding electronic client information. Ariz. Formal Opin. 05-04 states that attorneys who do not possess the expertise necessary to safeguard their systems are "ethically required to retain an expert consultant who does have such competence." Comerford argues that the Arizona approach should serve as a model for both the ABA and other state bars to protect the confidentiality and integrity of electronically stored client information. The years since have seen a move in this direction.

10. In the quickly-moving world of electronic ethics, Audrey Rogers' 1995 article is "ancient" but it provides an important — and at the time, much needed — review of the traditional and new tests of attorney-client privilege waivers and their ramifications in light of the modern reality of frequent inadvertent disclosures. *New Insights on Waiver and the Inadvertent Disclosure of Privileged Materials: Attorney Responsibility as the Governing Precept*, 47 FLA. L. REV. 159 (1995); reprinted at 46 DEFENSE L.J. 363 (1997).

11. Lawyers and social networking is the latest big topic. Professor Kathleen Vinson has written *The Blurred Boundaries of Social Networking in the Legal Field: Just 'Face' It*, 41 U MEMPHIS L. REV. 355 (2010). Helen W. Gunnarsson, *Friending Your Enemies, Tweeting Your Trials; Using Social Media Ethically*, 99 ILL. BAR J. 500 (2011), warns lawyers that social media permeates society and attorneys should be cautious of how much information they give out. Gunnarsson helps distinguish between people attorneys can friend and others, like opposing counsel, they should consider and reconsider. A student told one of us that "I think you should include this because it is very relevant to the average 20-something who will accept a friend request from most anyone on Facebook without batting an eye."

12. Because change is so rapid when it comes to technological change, we also recommend following journals and individual lawyer blogs that discuss technology:

- The website of the ABA Commission on Ethics 20/20, which focused on technology issues, is at http://www.americanbar.org/groups/professional_responsibility/aba_commission_on_ethics_20_20.html;

- www.legalethics.com, a site emphasizing cyberethics, Internet ethics, and legal ethics and technology;

- The Pew Internet and American Life Project's August 2011 report on social networking usage is available at http://pewinternet.org/Reports/2011/Social-Networking-Sites.aspx;

- Brian Tannebaum's blog *My Law License*, is at http://www.mylawlicense.blogspot.com/;

- Daniel A. Schwartz's, *Connecticut Employment Law Blog*, is at http://www.ctemploymentlawblog.com/;

- Peter Olson's blog, *Solo In Chicago*, is at http://soloinchicago.com/;

- Washington, D.C. solo Carolyn Elefant, blogs at MyShingle.com, and has posted extensively about social media and lawyer ethics. More about

Elefant in Problem 31.

Chapter 4

LOYALTIES AND CONFLICTS OF INTEREST

This chapter, the longest in the book, focuses on a critical aspect of the lawyer-client relationship — loyalty. In the previous chapter, we discussed an important corollary of that duty: preserving the client's confidences and secrets. These duties are two of the "Four C's," the four fiduciary duties we outlined in Problem 1. It is sometimes said that lawyers owe their clients "undivided" loyalty. This means that lawyers must serve their clients' needs without interference or impairment from *any* other interests.

Such so-called "conflicts of interest" can arise in a wide variety of circumstances. Before we examine those circumstances in the next six Problems, we want to emphasize our belief that thinking about "loyalty" — an affirmative concept — may provide a better understanding than "conflicts of interest," a negative expression.

Problem 7 begins our inquiry by illustrating several of the circumstances in which loyalty can easily become compromised. Few lawyers, of course, represent only one client at a time. Conflicts of interest can arise whenever the lawyer represents multiple parties in the same matter, or whenever the interests of other clients might impair the lawyer's loyalty and judgment on behalf of the client.

But conflicting loyalties involving one lawyer and two separate clients are just the tip of an increasingly complex iceberg. In the following several problems, we'll dig beneath this iceberg's surface. For instance, lawyers' duties of loyalty may be affected by their own legal fees, how they invest their money, who they know, even what positions they have taken in other cases. Their loyalty may be impaired not because of their other clients, but because of their relationship to witnesses or to non-clients who have an interest in the outcome of their work. Loyalty is increasingly difficult to evaluate when the client is an entity, such as a corporation or partnership, which speaks through its principal constituents, because lawyers must divine which constituents speak for the entity. And businesses sometimes merge and undergo changes in control, which can create its own set of challenges. Indeed, sometimes identifying exactly *who* the client is can be the biggest challenge.

There are several other significant issues to be discussed in this chapter. First, there is an important distinction to be made between concurrent representations and successive ones (that is, one current and one former representation). We will examine the extent to which loyalty has "legs" after the representation is over such that a "conflict of interest" still exists. Second, we will look at whether and to what extent a conflict analysis must be "imputed" to all members of a lawyer's firm. This is particularly important given the modern-day mobility of lawyers moving "laterally" from one firm to another. For example, when lawyers change firms, do they impair their new firm's ability to work against the lawyer's former client, or the lawyer's *former firm's* client? Third, we will look at several specific areas of law in which impairment of loyalty is common and particularly troublesome. Several of these examples appear in Problem 7, but we will devote Problems 11 and 12 to the special issues that arise in, class actions, multi-district consolidated litigation and insurance defense work.

Finally we will examine what remedies are available when a lawyer or law firm's loyalty becomes impaired. Among the remedies we discuss are the willingness of all affected clients to waive any conflicts of interest; exempting law firms from some imputed conflicts; and the possibility of "screening" the "tainted" lawyer from any knowledge of the current case. We will also examine a remedy available to the former client: disqualifying a law firm from appearing against it.

PROBLEM 7: WHEN ARE TWO CLIENTS TOO MANY?

A. INTRODUCTION

Returning to Problem 7, examine each of the following scenarios. It is important for lawyers always to be vigilant in looking for actual and, less obvious but of equal and perhaps greater importance, *potential* conflicts of interest, and to recognize these conflicts early in the representation. That is, *when is the universe of the lawyer's loyalty to one client impaired by his or her duties to another?* Once the client is clearly identified, lawyers should consider two related issues: Whether their loyalty is compromised such that conflicts of interest exist; and whether it is possible to represent more than one client even where loyalty is compromised, if the clients give their informed consent.

B. PROBLEM

I

Sam and Irma Hammond want to dissolve their marriage. They believe that they can do it on a friendly basis. Both trust Margaret Healy, a lawyer who has done work for both of them before. The Hammonds tell Healy that they have sat down and discussed it seriously, and that they have agreed on child custody, how much child support would be paid, and how the property should be divided. Neither one wants to consult another lawyer. "We trust you, Margaret," says Irma. "All two lawyers would do is argue with each other and add to the expense."

QUESTIONS

1. May Healy represent both parties? If so, should she place any conditions on her representation?

2. What can and/or should Healy say to the Hammonds about matters told to her in confidence by one or the other? What if one party knows information which that party does not want to disclose to the other?

3.   Assume that the child support money Mr. Hammond is prepared to pay his wife is 50% higher than the local court's guidelines for such payments. Should Healy inform the parties of this fact? Should Healy advise Sam to pay less? If Healy does, what are her duties to Irma? What happens if the Hammonds don't know that Sam's pension is jointly owned, or community property, which means that under the law of their state, it should be shared between them? Should Healy tell them or remain silent?

4.   What happens if both parties fail to agree on a complete settlement?

5.   What happens if the parties agree? Who goes to court to ratify the agreement before the judge?

II

Tyler Plevin is an experienced attorney who specializes in representing small businesses and their owners. He has represented Tom Quan and Emerald and Joe Huen, the owners of Quan Huen Graphics, for many years, both regarding their business partnership and on other matters. One day, Tom Quan calls Tyler and says, "Since Joe Huen's death, Emerald and I have decided that she should sell her interest in the business to the company. We've discussed the terms of the sale and we've worked it all out. We're each 50% owners now, so it shouldn't be too complicated. We want you to draft the papers."

QUESTIONS

1.   May Plevin draw up the papers on behalf of both parties? Does the size of the company matter? Or the direct involvement of each principal? What other considerations might make a difference?

2.   Does Plevin have a duty to inform both Tom and Emerald that there may be a conflict of interest? If so, what must he say?

III

Faye Stern represents Ted and Esther Vandiver. They are plaintiffs in a personal injury action against a taxicab company and the driver of another car for injuries sustained in a traffic accident while they were passengers in the taxi. Mr. Vandiver suffered a broken arm, while Mrs. Vandiver sustained a severe spine injury, requiring surgery and long-term rehabilitation.

QUESTIONS

1.   Do Mr. and Mrs. Vandiver have common or conflicting interests? Describe them. May Stern nevertheless represent both? *Should* she?

2.   Would it make a difference if one of the Vandivers had been driving the car?

3.   What happens if just before trial, the defendant offers what Stern believes to be a good settlement, but the Vandivers can't agree on what to do? Could Stern have done something to prevent this problem?

4. Suppose the stress of the litigation takes its toll on the Vandivers, and they file for divorce. How will this affect Stern's representation of the couple?

IV

Arturo Ziegler represents brothers Joe and Billy Brown on robbery charges. They tell Ziegler, "We totally trust each other, and we're afraid that two lawyers might drive us apart."

QUESTIONS

1. May Ziegler represent both brothers? What if Billy is accused of merely driving the getaway car, while Joe is accused of pulling a gun on the store owner?

2. Assume that during plea negotiations, the DA offers to drop charges against Billy, but only if Joe will plead guilty. How does this affect Arturo's representation?

C. READINGS

1. Conflicts of Interest and Impaired Loyalty

Any time a lawyer or law firm acts on behalf of more than one individual whose interests are intertwined — be it in litigation, a business transaction, or family, estate, and probate matters — the danger of a conflict of interest exists. That's true when there is more than one client in the same litigation (adverse or not) or more than one client in the same negotiation or enterprise, or simply when more than one client seeks the attorney's advice. In many situations this never becomes a problem. But it is usually difficult, and often impossible, to predict at the outset which matters will go smoothly and which will not.

Although every state's ethical rules preclude a lawyer from representing conflicting interests, these general rules are rarely definitive about the subtleties of such conflicts. It is easy enough to spot an obvious conflict — a lawyer or law firm[1] representing opposite sides in the same litigation matter — but how do lawyers identify more subtle (many would say "potential") conflicts of interest? Does the distinction between "actual" and "potential" even make sense?

ABA Model Rule 1.7 moves away from the term "conflict of interest" in favor of a discussion of when a lawyer's ability to represent a client "may be materially limited" by the lawyer's other responsibilities. As we've already noted, this concept, focusing on the lawyer's unimpaired loyalty to each client, makes sense. But what does "materially limited" mean?

Consider the following brief article about a nationally known lawyer who didn't see a potential conflict of interest and found himself criticized for it. Before 9-11, one of the most significant terrorist attacks on American citizens was the bombing of Pan American Airlines Flight 103 while over the town of Lockerbie, Scotland.

---

[1] Loyalty is imputed from a single lawyer to that lawyer's firm, an important concept that forms the bulk of the discussion in Problem 10.

And one of the most flamboyant lawyers of his time, F. Lee Bailey, turned up right in the middle of the story.

Andrew Blum, *Lockerbie Lawyer Advises Libya*
THE NATIONAL LAW JOURNAL, November 29, 1993[2]

F. Lee Bailey, who has represented Patty Hearst, the Boston Strangler and other famous clients, traveled to Libya in August and was paid to advise that nation on procedures and options in turning over two suspects in the Pan Am 103 bombing, The National Law Journal has learned.

Mr. Bailey's trip made him the latest in a line of lawyers the Libyans have either contacted or asked to represent them in the aftermath of the Lockerbie bombing. But in Mr. Bailey's case, his New York law firm also represents five clients in the civil litigation.

Although Mr. Bailey said he saw no conflict of interest, at least one client wondered otherwise, and officials of Pan Am families' groups criticized him both for the trip and for not telling his clients about it. Word of his trip surfaced among the families in recent weeks.

. . . .

Mr. Bailey went to Libya under a Treasury Department license required for Americans who do business with, travel to, or accept payments from Libya. Mr. Bailey declined to say how much the Libyans had paid him but said Treasury officials had a full accounting of his fees.

In an interview from Florida, where he is in a trial, Mr. Bailey said he went to Libya to advise "upper-level" members of the government "as to what the comparative options would be for surrendering the two [suspected] bombers in the Pan Am 103 case."

Libya intelligence agents Abdel Basset Ali Al-Megrahi and Lamen Khalifa Fhimah have been indicted in both the United States and Scotland on charges that they planted and detonated the bomb that killed 270 people in 1988.

Mr. Bailey said his advice included information on U.S. and other justice systems, and whether surrender in a particular country could lead to a resolution of all the criminal charges. While ruling out representing the suspects, Mr. Bailey said he saw no conflict in advising the Libyans on "what the means of surrender should be. The families would be in favor of that. The purpose of my going there was to facilitate their return to somewhere." Mr. Bailey said he was prepared to inform clients of his trip but did not because the visit did not become public.

. . . .

Elizabeth Phillips, former president of Victims of Pan Am 103, said none of the families Mr. Bailey represents "would want to have him represent Libya. It's our understanding our State Department represents us in these matters."

---

[2] Copyright © 1993 by The New York Law Publishing Company. Reprinted with the permission of The National Law Journal.

. . . .

A sobbing [client] said she was "uptight" and declined to talk further. Another victim family member was upset with Mr. Bailey: "I'm finding it difficult to believe he would do something that would jeopardize the victims he represents.

"But I just don't know why he didn't contact us to ask how we felt before he went," the relative said, noting that because Mr. Bailey was paid, it "sounds like it's a conflict somewhere there."

. . . .

NOTES

What of the conduct of F. Lee Bailey? Are you persuaded that there is no conflict between representing the families of victims of the crash, and advising the Libyan government about the terms of surrender of the alleged perpetrators? Is advising Libya insufficient to rise to "responsibilities to another client or to a third person"? What of Bailey's comments expressing concern about how his colleagues (as opposed to his clients) would feel about his Libyan connection?

Interestingly, in April 1994, the *National Law Journal* provided a postscript to Bailey's possible conflict when it obtained documents through a Freedom of Information Act request. The paper learned that Bailey's State Department request for a travel license to Libya was *not* to consult with the government, but rather because he had been "requested to take on the defense" of the two accused. When confronted with this, however, Bailey claimed that he ultimately never met with the defendants, and argued he had no conflict with his civil clients. Indeed, he remained on as counsel for all his Lockerbie victim families.

2. Multiple Conflicts and Billy Joel

In the Fall of 1992, singer Billy Joel filed a malpractice lawsuit against his lawyers, the high-profile New York law firm of Grubman, Indursky & Schindler. The suit rocked both the entertainment world and the entertainment law community. The issues presented by the Billy Joel suit have both similarities to and differences from F. Lee Bailey's representation. Read the following article.

Jeffrey Jolson-Colburn, *Joel Suit Has Music Lawyers Deeply Divided*
THE HOLLYWOOD REPORTER, October 14, 1992[3]

The legal slugfest between pop singer Billy Joel and his former attorney has brought to a head the highly charged conflict-of-interest issue that is bitterly dividing major music industry attorneys.

"Some attorneys have forgotten what they learned in law school about ethics," said prominent music lawyer Don Engel. He referred to the increasingly common practice of counsel representing multiple sides in a negotiation. "The sleaze factor

---

[3] Copyright © 1992 by The Hollywood Reporter. Reprinted by permission.

is getting worse in the industry," he believes.

To the alarm of some observers, a number of powerful attorneys have increasingly become the wheeling-dealing superagents of the music business. Like the biggest Hollywood film agencies, these lawyers often package deals while collecting from all parties involved, sometimes representing a label, artist and manager simultaneously.

"The ethics in the music business are between weak and none, and hopefully this suit will be able to do something about that," said Joel's attorney, Leonard Marks, after filing the $90 million suit against Allen Grubman.

A survey of the industry's most powerful lawyers revealed a deep rift, even in the ranks of those who benefit most from representing multiple sides in a deal. The attorneys are violently torn on whether this is an acceptable practice or not. Some said it's all right, assuming clients sign a waiver, while others dismiss it as unethical and a clear conflict of interest.

Nonetheless, it has become quite commonplace in the industry and observers said the Joel suit against Grubman is shining a bright light into this dark region of horse-trading and incestuous backroom bedfellowing.

In the current case, Joel says Grubman was representing his label, CBS Records (now Sony), at the same time he represented Joel. The suit says Grubman never informed Joel of this, never explained the potential conflict nor had him sign a conflict-of-interest waiver. Grubman's reply to the suit says that there was no conflict of interest as Joel "handsomely benefitted" from Grubman's good relations with CBS and that CBS did not formally retain Grubman until well after Joel's recording contract was signed.

Whatever the merits of this particular case, it has brought the issue to the forefront. Most major attorneys agreed that a waiver could be sufficient in certain friendly negotiations. But they differed widely in their views of the ethics of multilateral practice.

"It is an obvious conflict of interest and it's gotten worse in the last few years," said attorney Owen Sloane, whose clients include Elton John, Kenny Rogers, Frank Zappa and Motown. "In negotiations, every single point is adverse. Either you are violating record company confidences or you are not getting the best deal for the artist."

On the other side of the coin, most attorneys in the music industry viewed the present standards as acceptable.

Bert Fields, a key industry attorney whose clients include Michael Jackson as well as Allen Grubman in the Billy Joel suit, said, "99 percent of the time a client wants to go ahead with a certain lawyer because he has terrific contacts at the label. If you get income from a label, it's all right to them because they believe they can get a better deal from someone connected. The client says, 'I realize you may be influenced, but I'll take that risk.' That is nothing unethical."

Other attorneys pointed out that a lawyer's strong ties to a label only increased the conflict-of-interest potential for a young band.

"If a lawyer is paid every year from a label, the attorney may worry that pushing too hard on a deal will hurt, and that's a conflict," said Don Passman, who represents Janet Jackson and Quincy Jones, among others. "You have to take conflict of interest on a case-by-case basis, but generally, it's being done too much by some people and we need to pull back from it a little bit."

"Who's going to turn down millions a year because of a little conflict of interest?" asked Engel.

. . . .

"Even more insidious and pervasive is when artist attorneys do not represent the label, but are looking to the labels as a future source of business," Sloane observed. "Even though they don't represent the label, they make a sweetheart deal because they want the label to know they are their type of lawyer, so they get referrals and otherwise benefit from the largesse of the record companies."

Veteran industry attorney Jay Cooper explained that "it's hard for young lawyers to get in the business. It takes years to get the contacts and the power, so there are fewer law firms handling more artists and companies. The business has been becoming somewhat incestuous for some time."

. . . .

Another legal superpower in the music industry is John Branca and his firm of Ziffrin, Brittenham and Branca, who have brokered many of the recent megadeals for artists like Prince, the Rolling Stones and Aerosmith, and who shared in the Michael Jackson deal.

Branca said his firm was meticulous about informing clients of potential conflict and obtaining waivers. "We are very sensitive and aware in this area, and follow the letter and spirit of the law. We have specific guidelines."

But are waivers enough? Some attorneys don't think so, especially in the case of young bands who are hungry for a deal.

"I don't know if it's totally waivable," Cooper said. "If you have a waiver is the attorney home free? I don't know." He added, in a note that could chill the attorneys whose income relies on the waiver, "Soon, the waiver will be challenged."

"Can you ever really get informed consent?" Sloane asked. "We'll soon find out."

NOTES

When the *Billy Joel* suit was first filed, Fields, Grubman's lawyer, was quoted in the Hollywood *Reporter* as saying "I don't think there is a conflict of interest involved here. I haven't investigated it yet, but if they disclosed it to his manager, that was disclosing it to Joel. And then it's no impropriety." Does this explanation hold up? Or should Joel, the client, himself be entitled to notice? Fields' remarks were particularly unusual in light of the fact that part of Joel's complaint alleged the malfeasance of that same manager and the collusion of the manager and attorney Grubman.

A year after the *Joel* lawsuit was filed, the parties announced a settlement, although the terms were kept highly confidential. Some speculated that Grubman paid Joel nothing, while others estimated a settlement figure as high as $10 million. The questions about conflict of interest remained. Among them were these: Is a lawyer ever justified in not disclosing potential conflicts of interest? Is Grubman's nondisclosure justified where he can demonstrate his presence works to the benefit of both clients? Or does this beg the question?

A few more questions about multiple interrelated representations: What happens when a lawyer like Allen Grubman or Bert Fields represents so many people or entities in the same field that the clients may be competitors in any individual case? The highly visible Fields, in his 80s still a major Hollywood player, has a law firm web page that states that he's "represented virtually every major Hollywood studio and talent agency."[4]

What if among the studios and producers among his listed clients — DreamWorks, MGM, United Artists, The Weinstein Company, Jeffrey Katzenberg, David Geffen, and Jerry Bruckheimer — two or three are competing to distribute the hottest new hot movie? Whom does he help, DreamWorks or Weinstein? Or Katzenberg vs. Geffen? Similarly, what happens when a sports lawyer represents a dozen pro quarterbacks, all of whom are compared to each other in salary negotiations? Or more directly, when two are interested in the same job, such as in the Spring of 2012, when the San Francisco 49ers expressed an interest in signing new free-agent star Payton Manning. His agent, Tom Condon, handled the negotiations. But Condon also represented then current 49er QB Alex Smith. Manning eventually signed elsewhere. But could Condon have promoted Manning to the team that was planning to re-sign Smith?

What about a law firm specializing in private adoptions that provides the birth parents with the pictures and files of only one, or two, of the firm's 80 prospective adoptive couples? See *In re Petrie*, 742 P.2d 796 (Ariz. 1987), which disciplined an attorney for choosing one adoption client couple over another.

3. Lawyers "for the Situation"

The justification offered by entertainment and sports lawyers — that everyone benefits from having the lawyers' hands on all sides of a deal — harkens back to early in the last century, when during his confirmation hearing, future Supreme Court Justice Louis D. Brandeis espoused his concept of a "lawyer for the situation" — that is, a lawyer acting to resolve all the issues among all parties to best achieve common goals.[5]

Some estate-planning attorneys have long considered themselves lawyers "for the situation" by representing an entire family, or at least husband and wife, in coordinating an estate plan that makes sense for everyone. But in this role they

---

[4] http://www.greenbergglusker.com/people/attorneys/fields as of April 3, 2012.

[5] Much has been written about Brandeis's statement. Professor Geoffrey C. Hazard, Jr. has taken a particular interest in this concept. *See Lecture: Lawyer for the Situation*, 39 VALPARISO L. REV. 377 (2004), as well as GEOFFREY C. HAZARD, W. WILLIAM HODES & Peter R. Jarvis, THE LAW OF LAWYERING § 2.2:102 (updated annually).

would be inevitably challenged by questions of impaired loyalty. May the lawyer even ask husband and wife their ultimate bequest desires without careful conflict waivers? How are "mirror wills" or mirror trusts done without shared confidences? What if one spouse has secrets, such as a lover? What if one partner wants to make a change and not tell the other? And what about working with the children of the family, particularly adult children with their own families, who may not only have their own estate planning issues — ones that may be dependent at least in part on knowing their parents' plans — but who also may be prospective executors and trustees, and, of course, beneficiaries? Other lawyers may see themselves as lawyers for the situation when they represent a divorcing couple. One noted scholar with a Christian perspective has suggested that the family unit effectively creates a situation, rather than a client, that the lawyer can properly "represent."[6]

But can one truly consider a situation, or even a family, to be a "client"? Or must attorneys recognize that they represent *clients*, whether singly or multiply? Does calling oneself a lawyer for the situation beg the question and allow the lawyer to avoid the ordinary conflict analysis required of others? After all, to echo the question asked at the end of the Billy Joel article, how effectively can a lawyer represent the "situation" when one relatively weak client — like a "young band hungry for a deal" — is negotiating with another client who is much stronger?

There are many other situations in which being a "lawyer for the situation" is tempting and, some argue, almost inevitable. Transactional business formation is one such area. We'll focus on representing organizations in the next problem, but what about when the organizations are formed? That is: If George and Georgette want Lawyer Larry to form JoJo, LLC, who does Larry represent before the business is formed? The business? That would be akin to representing the "situation," as the business doesn't yet exist. What if G or G tells Larry not to go forward? Does he reply that he represents the entity and therefore must continue? Clearly not. What happens if G and G both go forward, argue about terms, and after the LLC is formed sue each other?

There are surprisingly few cases that address these issues. In *Jesse by Reinecke v. Danforth*, 485 N.W.2d 63, 67 (Wis. 1992), the Wisconsin Supreme Court argued that if an individual (or, presumably, several people) retains a lawyer to form an entity and the entity eventually becomes the lawyer's client, that would result in "automatic dual representation," but once the entity is incorporated, "the entity rule applies retroactively such that the lawyer's pre-incorporation involvement with the person is deemed to be representation of the entity, not the person."

But viewed contemporaneously rather than in hindsight, does it make sense for the lawyer, in "real time," to represent something that may or may not come to exist? What if the incorporating attorney never serves the entity after formation? The law on this question remains unclear in most jurisdictions.

---

[6] *See* THOMAS SHAFFER, AMERICAN LEGAL ETHICS 302 (1985); Shaffer, *The Legal Ethics of Radical Individualism*, 65 TEX. L. REV. 963 (1987).

4. Multiple Clients and Informed Consent

Are there some situations in which multiple clients not only can but *should* have the same lawyer, because of convenience, economy, or trust? Are some of the hypothetical scenarios set forth in this problem appropriate for a single lawyer to handle? Both subsections of Model Rule 1.7 allow for representation if the lawyer "reasonably believes" it is workable, and if the client consents. But when are clients well advised to give this consent? And what is it they are really consenting to? Don't clients expect their lawyers to protect every confidence, even if they are co-represented? One of the authors of this course book wrote the following analysis.

Richard A. Zitrin, *Risky Business . . . Representing Multiple Interests*
I [Cal. State Bar] Ethics Hotliner (Winter 1992–1993)[7]

A San Francisco attorney represents the driver-husband and passenger-wife in a simple auto accident. Now the couple is divorcing, and it's not amicable. A small Los Angeles law firm has represented an International Union and several of its Southern California locals for years; now there's a dispute between the international and one of the locals that may lead to litigation. A Riverside lawyer negotiates a contract for the sale of a business between two of his biggest clients; a year later they're accusing each other of negotiating in bad faith.

By the time these lawyers — composites based on real cases — sought help out of their conflict of interest dilemmas, it was too late.

Indeed, where a lawyer's loyalty to a particular client is any way impaired by that attorney's other loyalties or interests, withdrawal — and the loss of a valued client — may be the least that can happen. At worst is the possibility [of] a malpractice lawsuit or even potential discipline.

Recognizing the Problem

The everyday practice of most firms, large and small, is replete with potential conflicts of interest. Careful practitioners must learn to spot these situations and anticipate potential problems before they occur. I advise lawyers who consult me to follow these rules:

First, think not of conflicts of interest, but of *potential* conflicts. Look at any representation situation from the point of view that there *is* — or could be — a conflict of interest, rather than from the perspective that there's not.

Second, think beyond "conflicts"; think in terms of *"impaired loyalty."* This phrase, taken from rule 1.7 of the American Bar Association Model Rules of Professional Conduct, suggests the lawyer ask not "Do I have a conflict of interest?" or even "Do I have a potential conflict?" The question becomes "Is there *any* way — through my representation or *anything else* — in which my loyalty to Client may be impaired?"

Third, remember that, although in perhaps 99 of 100 cases a conflict will never ripen, it is impossible to predict with certainty *which* case is the 100th. The only way to protect the interest of all clients — and the law firm itself — is if preventive measures are undertaken at the inception of representation, and in *all* 100 cases.

There are many situations in which multiple clients not only can but should have the same lawyer. . . . But situations where the lawyer's ability to represent a client is impaired should trigger a full explanation to the client(s). A disclosure of divided loyalties will rarely, if ever, be meaningful if it merely recites the existence of the problem. At a minimum, the lawyer must also advise the client of "the actual and reasonably foreseeable adverse consequences." (Rule 3-310(A)(1), California Rules of Professional Conduct.)

[These suggestions may help:]

(1) memorialize all communications, not just the clients' consents;

(2) specifically address what happens to attorney-client confidences in the multiple representation situation;

(3) spell out specific ramifications of multiple representation in an "if/then" format; and

(4) specifically address the ground rules of what will happen in the event a conflict arises, including withdrawal.

One point — too often overlooked — which should always be a part of any disclosure, is how client confidentiality will be treated. Clients have come to expect that lawyers will strictly protect every confidence, and they will still expect it, even if they are co-plaintiffs in a personal injury case, or both sides in a contract negotiation, or the parties to an "uncontested" dissolution. But allowing such parties to tell their mutual lawyer anything which can be held in confidence vis-á-vis the other party inevitably asks for trouble. It is almost impossible to maintain, for example, "his" secrets as against "her," and "hers" as against "him," with the parties feeling mistrust, knowing that the lawyer may know something they don't. This may doom efforts to cooperate before they've begun. The best solution is to agree — in advance — that, among multiple clients, there shall be no confidences. Should the client insist on blurting out a "confidence," however, the lawyer may be required to withdraw.

Explaining the multiple representation from an "if this happens, then here's what happens next" point of view may make the ramifications clearer to the client. The if/then approach is also valuable in explaining confidences, and in delineating when the lawyer must withdraw from representation.

One final point: client consent can't cure conflicts in every — or even most — situations. The lawyer should adopt the standards suggested by rule 1.7 of the American Bar Association Model Rules of Professional Conduct: agree to conflict waivers only where the clients' consents, viewed objectively, are reasonable; and make certain no consent is obtained where the lawyer is unable to make full disclosure.

These suggestions for preventive, anticipatory communications are neither new, nor particularly sophisticated, nor difficult to carry out. But the dangers of ignoring such communications can be severe. The rewards are ample: clients who are more efficiently served with quality legal help, and lawyers who are free to serve the needs of all their clients without fear of the consequences.

NOTES

Is the approach taken in the previous article really workable? How effective can such client consents really be? For example, suppose the clients agree that anything one client tells the lawyer will be told to the other client. Suppose further that some time down the road, one client inadvertently discloses something that he or she doesn't want the other party to know, and tells the lawyer that notwithstanding their prior agreement, the lawyer may not reveal it. May the lawyer simply rely on the earlier consent and tell the other party? Or may that first client now revoke the earlier consent? If the first client can't change his or her mind, does that mean that right at the beginning of the case, the client has consented to a *permanent* waiver of a fundamental part of the lawyer-client relationship — confidentiality? But if the client *may* change the agreement, how effective was that agreement in the first place?

Will *one* waiver always suffice? What happens when a lawyer represents 15 homeowners who receive a lump sum settlement for defective construction from the subdivision developer? Or three clients, each alleging sex discrimination by their employer, who are offered a lump sum in settlement? ABA Model Rule 1.8(g) says that the clients must consent to an aggregate settlement. Assuming that the clients, fully informed, consented to a carefully drafted waiver of loyalty back in the beginning of the case, how does the attorney now divide up the pot? Is the original prospective conflicts waiver enough? What about the fact that by the end of the case, after discovery and investigation has been conducted, the relative values of each homeowner's claim, or the fact that two of the former employees easily found new jobs while the third remains unemployed, are materially different than when the waiver was executed?

In short, sometimes a single "conflicts waiver" may not be enough. As circumstances during the course of a case change, another waiver — more specifically, consent to a particular settlement split — will likely be necessary.

5. Confidentiality and Joint Representation

Those relatively few authorities that have directly addressed the issue are not unanimous that waiving confidentiality is necessarily a part of a waiver of conflicts of interest. Take, for example, the common occurrence of one lawyer representing both husband and wife in estate planning matters. As in some of our problem's examples, it is understandable that many couples will want one attorney handling the affairs of both spouses. But one can easily imagine situations in which one spouse is hiding something — money, perhaps, or a secret relationship — from the other. Should a waiver of confidences be necessary for joint representation?

Opinions go both ways. No, says Florida Ethics Opinion 95-4 (May 1997). The facts posited are that "Husband, Wife, and Lawyer have always shared all relevant asset and financial information," but there was never an understanding about whether or not the lawyer would maintain separate confidences. When the husband reveals that he has executed a codicil in favor of a woman with whom he has had an extra-marital affair, the lawyer is precluded from revealing either the affair or the codicil to the wife. The lawyer, according to the opinion, can only withdraw from representing both parties, citing a conflict of interest. The drawbacks to the lawyer's taking such a course may seem obvious. (How would you feel if you were the wife and *your* lawyer withheld this information?) Indeed, the opinion acknowledges that while a prior agreement about confidences is "not ethically required," such an understanding might have avoided the situation that occurred. And there is certainly the possibility that, from the point of view of civil liability, the wife could maintain a cause of action for professional negligence and breach of fiduciary duty based on the lawyer's failure to inform her of highly significant matters relating to the representation.

On the other hand, in *A. v. B. v. Hill Wallack*, 726 A.2d 924 (N.J. 1999), the New Jersey Supreme Court faced an unusual fact pattern involving the Hill Wallack law firm, which represented both husband and wife in estate planning matters. The lawyers wanted to reveal their knowledge of the existence of the husband's illegitimate child to the wife, even though there was no explicit agreement between them to waive confidentiality. They reasoned that this information was significant to the wife's estate planning, as part of what she devised to the husband could eventually go to the illegitimate child. The Supreme Court reversed the appellate court and agreed that the law firm could tell the wife, relying in part on the unusually broad exceptions to confidentiality contained in New Jersey's version of Model Rule 1.6. Also, however, under the unique facts of this case and in an interesting conflicts of interest twist, the law firm had learned of the illegitimate child when it represented the child's mother in a paternity action against the husband without being aware of the conflict (and without the husband raising it). When the firm learned of the conflict, they withdrew as counsel to the mother, but felt obligated to reveal the existence of the child to the husband's wife. The court used the fact that the lawyers had not learned of the child from the husband as one reason to permit that circumstance to be disclosed to the wife.

Should there be at least a presumption of a waiver of confidentiality? Again, authorities differ. For example, the Restatement Third of the Law Governing Lawyers, § 60, describes sharing confidentiality between clients is "normal and typically expected." But D.C. Legal Ethics Opinion No. 296 (2000) disagrees, at least in part: The lawyer has the duty to inform the clients of how confidentiality will be dealt with, and absent that, confidentiality is presumed. Moreover, one size may not fit all on this issue. Thus, in a toxic tort case with multiple plaintiffs represented by the same lawyer, each client's medical history will directly affect that person's recovery. If confidentiality is waived, does that mean that all clients' medical records must be shared with *all other clients*? We'll examine this question in Problem 11.

6.   Adequate Disclosure, Reasonable Consent, and "Unwaivable" Conflicts

Is it realistic to expect attorneys to go through the kind of analysis and disclosure suggested above in the "Risky Business" article each time more than one party is involved, even where there is no direct conflict?

Posit this situation, which we have used for many years in our continuing education seminars for lawyers. Joan Black, a potential client, comes in to see you. She has been harassed continually at her job for the past three years, ever since her new supervisor, Tom Nemo, arrived. The harassment has included suggestive remarks and asides sent through e-mail, and offensive notes placed on her desk in Nemo's handwriting. You believe she has an excellent case, with unusually good documentation.

After Joan meets with you, she calls you to say that, upon discussing it with her husband and family, she has decided not to file suit. "It's just too emotionally expensive," she tells you. "I found a comparable job at another company, and I just want to put all this behind me."

Two months later, Dora Brown comes in to see you. She discusses a sexual harassment case, and you soon realize that it too relates to Nemo. Unfortunately, Dora doesn't have any of the documentation that Joan had. "I was disgusted," she tells you, "so I threw it away." After Dora leaves, you call Joan and ask whether she would be willing to be a witness and have her documentation used. "No!" she tells you emphatically. "I put all that behind me and that's where I want it to stay." Can you take Dora's case?

Though they recognize that they can't reveal what former client Joan told them, most lawyers still believe at first that they can take Dora's new case. After all, they reason, they are no worse off than any other lawyer who doesn't know about Joan or her documentation. But doesn't the inability to reveal what Joan told you — evidence which would now be extremely helpful to Dora — interfere with how vigorously you can represent Dora? For example, how would you know to subpoena Joan and her documents except from her confidential communications? Finally, the Catch-22: how effective would Dora's waiver of conflict be, since you can't tell Dora what it is that you know but can't use, for to do so would violate Joan's trust? That is, because you can't fully disclose, Dora can never give fully *informed* consent.[8]

The language of the Comment to ABA Rule 1.7, paragraph (8), is illuminating: Where "the lawyer's ability to recommend or advocate all possible positions that each [client] might take because of the lawyer's duty of loyalty to the others," consent may be impossible, since "[t]he conflict in effect forecloses alternatives that would otherwise be available to the client." Thus, we have what ethics experts call an unconsentable or unwaivable conflict.

---

[8] A similar situation occurred in *Selby v. Revlon Consumer Products*, 6 F. Supp. 2d 577 (N.D. Tex. 1997). There a lawyer had represented two plaintiffs in a sexual harassment case. One client dropped out. The lawyer continued to represent the other client, and set his former client's deposition. The district court agreed with the former client that the lawyer was barred from taking the deposition. Another similar situation is described in Illustration 7 of the Comment to the Restatement (Third), § 132.

7. Prospective or "Advance" Waivers

Recent ethics opinions have trended significantly towards increasing the use of advance or prospective waivers of a lawyer's conflicting loyalties. Until recently, that approval had usually been either guarded or limited, and sometimes, as in the case of ABA Formal Opinion 93-372, both. First, Opinion 93-372 concludes that any potential conflict of interest would have to be described "with sufficient clarity" for the client's consent to be considered fully informed. Second, even if all clients were so informed and consented, the waiver would have to be reevaluated later if circumstances changed, to see whether a further waiver was necessary, or indeed whether the representation could continue at all. Clearly, prospective waivers of conflicts that are unknown, can't be sufficiently described, or — as we saw above — can't be adequately disclosed, would not pass muster under this ABA opinion.

A California case allowing a limited prospective waiver, *Zador Corp. v. Kwan*, 31 Cal. App. 4th 1285 (1995), tracks the ABA opinion's reasoning. *Zador* held that when a law firm got the agreement of co-defendant clients that if they wound up in a dispute with each other, the firm could withdraw as to one "notwithstanding any adversity that may develop," and remain as counsel to the other, its longtime client. A dispute soon occurred, and the law firm actually filed a cross-complaint on behalf of its ongoing client against its former client. Nevertheless, since the waiver anticipated precisely the situation that occurred, the court upheld its validity and allowed the firm to continue its representation. While the court didn't expressly rely on this, it is of no small consequence that the dropped former client had expressly asked to be taken in by the firm, which was already representing its ongoing client and which made it clear it did not want to jeopardize that longstanding relationship.

Some contemporaneous cases developed similar limitations. Thus, in *Worldspan v. Sabre Group Holdings, Inc.*, 5 F. Supp. 2d 1356 (N.D. Ga. 1998), a six-year-old open-ended advance waiver was not considered an effective prospective consent that would allow the law firm to represent otherwise conflicted clients. That waiver stated that in matters not substantially related to the law firm's representation of Worldspan, the firm "will not be precluded from representing clients who may have interests adverse to Worldspan." The court cited both this waiver's lack of specificity and its age in voiding it.

The Restatement (Third) of The Law Governing Lawyers is broader than the 1993 ABA opinion and the *Zador* waiver, although still somewhat circumscribed. Section 122, Comment (d) states that "a client's open-ended agreement" is ineffective "unless the client possesses sophistication in the matter in question and receive[s] independent legal advice about the consent." The concept of the "sophisticated client" has gained much purchase in the decade since.

Thus, in 2005, the ABA issued Formal Opinion 05-436, which effectively overruled a large portion of the 1993 opinion and liberalized prospective waivers substantially, particularly where the client is a sophisticated user of legal services. In 2006, a New York City ethics opinion, citing "the need" for advance waivers and noting the dangers of "an overly broad interpretation of the duty of loyalty," went even further. The opinion begins by concluding that lawyers may ask clients "to allow the law firm to bring adverse litigation on behalf of another current client . . . ." But for a "sophisticated client," such consent could also (1) allow a law firm to sue its own client even where the lawsuit is "substantially related" to the firm's representation of that first client, and (2) consent to a "blanket advance waiver" — i.e., an open-ended waiver where the future adverse party may not be a current client of the firm or even currently in existence.[9]

A proposed California rules change — not approved or yet considered by that state's Supreme Court as of this writing — is similar, allowing open-ended advance waivers if made by sophisticated clients, even if they involve "future facts and circumstances that to a degree cannot be known when the consent is requested." That is, waivers would be permitted even when there could not be completely informed consent as to future conflicts. The proposal would even "permit[] the lawyer to be adverse to the client in the current . . . litigation."[10]

As of the date of this volume's publication, few states' rules have gone nearly as far as the New York opinion, and the California rule change was still only a controversial proposal. But it is clear to us from our own observations and experiences that in the day-to-day "real-world" practice of law, many law firms with "sophisticated clients" have jumped the gun on the rules and are requesting and getting broad, even "blanket," advance waivers from their clients. In California, we ourselves have seen many examples of such blanket advance waivers notwithstanding that the California rules, as of the Spring of 2013, clearly do not and have never permitted this practice.[11]

The issue of advance waivers remains highly controversial. Many "lawyers' lawyers" and large-firm general counsel strongly favor these waivers for reasons of business retention and expansion, and they also may ease bringing in new partners from other firms. Many consumer advocates and public-interest lawyers oppose these waivers, arguing that they are unfair to the average client, and that even "sophisticated" clients should not be allowed to waive conflicts where they can't do so knowingly and intelligently.

8. Conflicts and Criminal Defense

What happens when a lawyer's ethical obligations are viewed in the context of a criminal defendant's Sixth Amendment right to the effective assistance of counsel? Read the following excerpt of a case decided by the United States Supreme Court.

---

[9] Assoc. of the Bar of the City of New York, Formal Opinion 2006-1 (2006). In addition, this opinion does not necessarily require written consent "if informed consent can be found under the circumstances."

[10] Proposed rules revision approved by the State Bar of California, July 2011, Rule 1.7, Comment paragraph 22. Compare this paragraph to Comment 22 of ABA MR 1.7.

[11] While the advance waiver issue is one that affects (and is advocated by) law firms more than individual attorneys, the issue applies across the board. As we've noted, we will focus on law *firms* rather than single lawyers — and the important issue of "imputing" conflicts from one lawyer to the entire firm — in Problem 10.

CUYLER v. SULLIVAN
446 U.S. 335 (1980)

Mr. Justice Powell delivered the opinion of the Court.

Respondent John Sullivan was indicted with Gregory Carchidi and Anthony DiPasquale for the first-degree murders of John Gorey and Rita Janda. The victims, a labor official and his companion, were shot to death in Gorey's second-story office at the Philadelphia headquarters of Teamsters' Local 107. Francis McGrath, a janitor, saw the three defendants in the building just before the shooting. They appeared to be awaiting someone, and they encouraged McGrath to do his work on another day. McGrath ignored their suggestions. Shortly afterward, Gorey arrived and went to his office. McGrath then heard what sounded like firecrackers exploding in rapid succession. Carchidi, who was in the room where McGrath was working, abruptly directed McGrath to leave the building and to say nothing. McGrath hastily complied. . . . The victims' bodies were discovered the next morning.

Two privately retained lawyers, G. Fred DiBona and A. Charles Peruto, represented all three defendants throughout the state proceedings that followed the indictment. Sullivan had different counsel at the medical examiner's inquest, but he thereafter accepted representation from the two lawyers retained by his codefendants because he could not afford to pay his own lawyer.[12] At no time did Sullivan or his lawyers object to the multiple representation. Sullivan was the first defendant to come to trial. The evidence against him was entirely circumstantial, consisting primarily of McGrath's testimony. At the close of the Commonwealth's case, the defense rested without presenting any evidence. The jury found Sullivan guilty and fixed his penalty at life imprisonment.

. . . .

DiBona and Peruto had different recollections of their roles. . . . Peruto recalled that he had been chief counsel for Carchidi and DePasquale, but that he merely had assisted DiBona in Sullivan's trial. . . . DiBona said he had encouraged Sullivan to testify even though the Commonwealth had presented a very weak case. Peruto remembered that he had not "want[ed] the defense to go on because I thought we would only be exposing the [defense] witnesses for the other two trials that were coming up." . . . Carchidi claimed he would have appeared at Sullivan's trial to rebut McGrath's testimony about Carchidi's statement at the time of the murders.

. . . .

The Pennsylvania Supreme Court affirmed both Sullivan's original conviction and the denial of collateral relief. The court saw no basis for Sullivan's claim that he had been denied effective assistance of counsel at trial. It found that Peruto merely assisted DiBona in the Sullivan trial and that DiBona merely assisted Peruto in the

---

[12] [1] DiBona and Peruto were paid in part with funds raised by friends of the three defendants. The record does not disclose the source of the balance of their fee, but no part of the money came from either Sullivan or his family. *See United States ex rel. Sullivan v. Cuyler,* 593 F.2d 512, 518, and n.7 (3d Cir. 1979).

trials of the other two defendants. Thus, the court concluded, there was "no dual representation in the true sense of the term."

The Court of Appeals . . . held that the participation by DiBona and Peruto in the trials of Sullivan and his codefendants established, as a matter of law, that both lawyers had represented all three defendants. The court recognized that multiple representation "'is not tantamount to the denial of effective assistance of counsel. . . .'" But it held that a criminal defendant is entitled to reversal of his conviction whenever he makes "'some showing of a possible conflict of interest or prejudice, however remote. . . .'" The court found support for its conclusion in Peruto's admission that concern for Sullivan's codefendants had affected his judgment that Sullivan should not present a defense.

. . . .

Sullivan's claim that he was denied the effective assistance of counsel guaranteed by the Sixth Amendment because his lawyers had a conflict of interest . . . raises two issues expressly reserved in *Holloway v. Arkansas*, 435 U.S., at 483–484. The first is whether a state trial judge must inquire into the propriety of multiple representation even though no party lodges an objection. The second is whether the mere possibility of a conflict of interest warrants the conclusion that the defendant was deprived of his right to counsel.

In *Holloway*, a single public defender represented three defendants at the same trial. The trial court refused to consider the appointment of separate counsel despite the defense lawyer's timely and repeated assertions that the interests of his clients conflicted. This Court recognized that a lawyer forced to represent codefendants whose interests conflict cannot provide the adequate legal assistance required by the Sixth Amendment.

Holloway requires state trial courts to investigate timely objections to multiple representation. But nothing in our precedents suggests that the Sixth Amendment requires state courts themselves to initiate inquiries into the propriety of multiple representation in every case. Defense counsel have an ethical obligation to avoid conflicting representations and to advise the court promptly when a conflict of interest arises during the course of trial. Absent special circumstances, therefore, trial courts may assume either that multiple representation entails no conflict or that the lawyer and his clients knowingly accept such risk of conflict as may exist. Indeed, as the Court noted in *Holloway*, trial courts necessarily rely in large measure upon the good faith and good judgment of defense counsel.

. . . .

Holloway reaffirmed that multiple representation does not violate the Sixth Amendment unless it gives rise to a conflict of interest. [A] possible conflict inheres in almost every instance of multiple representation. . . . But . . . a reviewing court cannot presume that the possibility for conflict has resulted in ineffective assistance of counsel.

. . . .

The Court of Appeals granted Sullivan relief because he had shown that the multiple representation in this case involved a possible conflict of interest. We hold that the possibility of conflict is insufficient to impugn a criminal conviction. In order to demonstrate a violation of his Sixth Amendment rights, a defendant must establish that an actual conflict of interest adversely affected his lawyer's performance. Sullivan believes he should prevail even under this standard. He emphasizes Peruto's admission that the decision to rest Sullivan's defense reflected a reluctance to expose witnesses who later might have testified for the other defendants. The petitioner on the other hand, points to DiBona's contrary testimony and to evidence that Sullivan himself wished to avoid taking the stand. [J]udgment is vacated and the case is remanded for further proceedings consistent with this opinion.

MR. JUSTICE MARSHALL, concurring in part and dissenting in part.

[T]he potential for conflict of interest in representing multiple defendants is "so grave," see ABA Project on Standards for Criminal Justice, Defense Function, Standard 4-3.5 (b) (App. Draft, 2d ed. 1979), that whenever two or more defendants are represented by the same attorney the trial judge must make a preliminary determination that the joint representation is the product of the defendant's informed choice. . . . If the Court's holding would require a defendant to demonstrate that his attorney's trial performance differed from what it would have been if the defendant had been the attorney's only client, I believe it is inconsistent with our previous cases. Such a test is not only unduly harsh, but incurably speculative as well. The appropriate question under the Sixth Amendment is whether an actual, relevant conflict of interests existed during the proceedings. If it did, the conviction must be reversed. . . . An actual conflict of interests negates the unimpaired loyalty a defendant is constitutionally entitled to expect and receive from his attorney.

NOTES

The Supreme Court's opinion in *Cuyler* was hardly the last word on the issue. For defendant Sullivan, his case returned to the court of appeals, where his claim that he was denied effective assistance of counsel was upheld. Meanwhile, Federal Rule of Criminal Procedure 44(c), pending at the time of *Cuyler*, soon became law. It provides that:

> The court shall promptly inquire with respect to such joint representation and shall personally advise each defendant of his right to the effective assistance of counsel, including separate representation. Unless it appears that there is good cause to believe no conflict of interest is likely to arise, the court shall take such measures as may be appropriate to protect each defendant's right to counsel.

Wheat v. United States, 486 U.S. 153 (1988), presented the inverse circumstance to *Cuyler*. Justice Rehnquist's 5-4 opinion upheld the conviction of a criminal defendant who *sought* to have the same counsel as two codefendants, and was expressly willing to waive any conflicts of interest. The district court, in the words of Rule 44(c), "inquire[d] with respect to joint representation," and found what was, in its view, an irreconcilable conflict. The lower court then took "measures as may be appropriate to protect [the] right to counsel," and denied the defendant counsel of choice based on the conflict.

Interestingly, while Rule 44(c) serves on its face to protect criminal defendants, it has come to be used in conjunction with *Wheat* as a tactic to disqualify a defendant's attorney of choice, such as where counsel has represented potential adverse witnesses. See *United States v. Moscony*, 927 F.2d 742 (3d Cir.), *cert. denied*, 501 U.S. 1211 (1991) in which the court disqualified counsel who had represented four targets of a federal investigation, one of whom was indicted while the others became probable witnesses. A similar tactic was used by the prosecutors in the John Gotti case to disqualify Gotti's attorney of choice, Bruce Cutler, even after the pair had been through two "hung juries" together.[13]

Gotti was convicted in that third trial. And in August, 1994, another New York court disqualified famed attorney William Kunstler from representing any of the World Trade Center bombing defendants, because he had originally spoken to three different defendants, causing the judge to conclude that he could not represent any of them without harming the others. THE NEW YORK TIMES said that the court's decision meant that "the lawyers who have been most in demand by various defendants, and have been the most visible public advocates of those accused, have now been entirely squeezed out of the case in what has to be seen as a major victory for the Government."[14]

The basis for such disqualifications largely comes down to the same issue we discussed earlier — whether the client's waiver of a conflict of interest must be objectively reasonable in order to be effective. The difference in the criminal setting, of course, is that *courts*, rather than the clients and their attorneys, are now making these determinations.

9. Criminal Defense Conflicts, Waivers, and Effective Assistance of Counsel

Where have the Supreme Court cases left the issue of jointly representing criminal defendants? Courts have looked at this issue in both *Cuyler* and *Wheat* contexts, that is, direct or collateral attacks on conviction itself, and pre-trial prosecutorial claims of "unwaivable" joint representations. Meanwhile, some observers and ethics experts continue to see an inherent underlying conflict of interest between any two criminal defendants, and claim that joint representation should never be undertaken, at least during trial or plea negotiations.[15]

In trial, the inherent problems seem clear: Joint representation affords no opportunity for any inconsistencies in the defense of the respective clients. In *Griffin v. McVicar*, 84 F.3d 880 (7th Cir. 1996), the court reversed a conviction where one lawyer represented both co-defendants in the same trial. The lawyer,

---

[13] United States v. Locascio, 6 F.3d 924 (2d Cir. 1993). Here, the alleged conflict dealt with tapes of conversations between Cutler and Gotti that could be interpreted as involving planning illegal acts. The prosecution asserted the tapes could make Cutler a witness and at the least would put the lawyer in the position of defending his own conduct as well as Gotti's as he dealt with the tapes.

[14] Aug. 26, 1994, at 1.

[15] *See* Peter R. Jarvis & Bradley F. Tellam, *Conflicts About Conflicts*, [ABA] PROFESSIONAL LAWYER, May 1996, at 22–23, in which sophisticated ethics experts were informally surveyed and agreed overwhelmingly that such circumstances "should" amount to an unwaivable conflict.

Goldenhersh, had presented a joint defense of an alibi and faulty eyewitness identification. But in pre-trial motions, Goldenhersh had essentially admitted that conflicts of interest existed between his two clients. He moved to sever the two trials both because Griffin had made admissions that could prejudice co-defendant Smith, and because Smith's serious prior record could prejudice Griffin. Fifteen years after trial, on habeas corpus, the appellate court agreed that prejudice had indeed occurred.[16]

In *U.S. v. Newell*, 315 F.3d 510 (5th Cir. 2002), an attorney for two defendants ended up with a defense for one that pointed the finger at the other. The existence of a conflict waiver didn't prevent reversal of a conviction because the conflict that occurred was not foreseeable by that defendant. And in a broader defendant-protective case, *U.S. v. Schwarz*, 283 F.3d 76 (2d Cir. 2002), one of the police assault cases stemming from the highly publicized attack on Abner Louima in New York, the defendant officer's waiver of conflict of interest was held ineffective as to the defense lawyer, who was under contract to the police union, in that working for the union, the PBA handicapped the lawyer in his ability to blame one of the other involved officers for the assault. The policeman's conviction was reversed.

However, that same year, the U.S. Supreme Court spoke again and in another closely divided opinion held in *Mickens v. Taylor*, 535 U.S. 162 (2002), that defense counsel's conflict of interest, because he had represented the murder victim on other charges at the time of the homicide, was *not* enough for a new trial under *Cuyler* unless there was a demonstrable effect on the representation.

In plea bargaining, prosecutors are often inclined either to offer "package deals" to resolve the entire case, or agreements that require one defendant to testify against others. This would seem necessarily to set off one defendant against another. Thus, in *Thomas v. Foltz*, 818 F.2d 476 (6th Cir. 1987), one attorney represented all three co-defendants in a murder case. The DA offered a package deal to reduce charges if, and only if, all three pled guilty. Thomas was reluctant to do so, but eventually did knowing that his plea was a predicate to the co-defendants getting their plea bargains. The court found a conflict of interest existed. The co-defendants had competing interests which the attorney could not protect due to the "all or nothing" group offer. In contrast, in *Hanna v. Indiana*, 714 N.E.2d 1162 (Ind. Ct. App. 1999), prosecutors attempted to disqualify two law firms jointly representing six co-defendants, police officers charged with abuse of their office. The DA argued that joint representation would interfere with the state's ability to negotiate with individual defendants to cooperate in return for leniency. The court, after analyzing *Wheat*, held that the lawyers should not be disqualified. Not only had defense counsel explained the waivers of conflict to the defendants, but so had both a magistrate and independent outside counsel.

How do the standards applied to pre-trial *Wheat* disqualifications compare to the showing required to reverse a conviction? Compare two similar cases in which a lawyer first represented one criminal defendant in a trial, then the co-defendant

---

[16] It is worth noting that before trial, the prosecution challenged whether Goldenhersh could represent both co-defendants because their defenses could become "antagonistic to each other." This argument, made in 1981, several years before *Wheat*, went nowhere.

in a subsequent case. In one case, the Ninth Circuit upheld the pre-trial disqualification of counsel when she moved on to represent Defendant #2. During her representation of the Defendant #1, the attorney had disparaged and even pointed the finger at Defendant #2. But Defendant #2 wanted the lawyer because she knew the case and had successfully gotten a reduced sentence for the first defendant. Besides, none of her arguments, most of which took place at sentencing, could have been admitted against Defendant #2.[17]

In the other case, the Eleventh Circuit refused to reverse the murder conviction of Defendant #2 after the same law firm had represented Defendant #1.[18] The majority of the court, sitting *en banc*, noted that the defendant claimed an insanity defense, and interpreted *Cuyler* as requiring direct and specific "inconsistent interests" before reversal was required.

NOTES

This Problem and its readings have examined numerous practice areas in which conflicts can and often do arise, and several practice situations that provide difficult recurring issues of conflicting loyalties. We will discuss other practice areas in the other problems in this chapter, particularly Problems 8, 11, and 12, and other loyalty issues throughout, especially in Problems 9 and 10.

Loyalty is not only a core fiduciary duty but one that has engendered more than its share of attention, modification, and controversy. While full treatment of all loyalty issues and every practice area is not possible in this volume, it *is* possible for us all to recognize the systemic issues that exist in different forms in many, many venues.

D. SUPPLEMENTAL READINGS

1. May a lawyer represent both sides in a divorce case? In *Klemm v. Superior Court*, 75 Cal. App. 3d 893 (1977), an attorney friend represented both the husband and wife in an uncontested divorce. The parties were in agreement on all issues. Both signed written consents to the joint representation. The court found that "with full disclosure to and informed consent of both clients," the attorney could represent both. But the court sounded a "note of warning," reminding lawyers that they "owe the highest duty to each [client] to make a full disclosure of all facts and circumstances which are necessary to enable the parties to make a fully informed decision. . . . Failing such disclosure, the attorney is civilly liable [and] lays himself open to charges, whether well founded or not, of unethical and unprofessional conduct."

2. Several jurisdictions have both malpractice and disciplinary cases in which lawyers representing both sides in a real estate deal — even the simple purchase of

---

[17] United States v. Stites, 56 F.3d 1020 (9th Cir. 1996). Note the implication this case has for so-called "positional conflicts," which we discuss in Problem 9.

[18] Freund v. Butterworth, 165 F.3d 839 (11th Cir. 1999). This case is discussed further in the Supplemental Readings.

a home — face a conflict of interest. In those situations where consent is not clear and unambiguous, courts tend to find against the attorneys. See *Colorado v. Bollinger*, 681 P.2d 950 (Colo. 1984), and *In re Lanza*, 322 A.2d 445 (N.J. 1974), both involving sales of single family homes. This trend has continued through more recent case law. *Baldasarre v. Butler*, 625 A.2d 458, 467 (N.J. 1993), noting "the disastrous consequences of dual representation convinces us that a new bright-line rule prohibiting dual representation is necessary" in complex real estate transactions.

3. Thomas D. Morgan, *Suing a Current Client*, 9 GEO. J. LEGAL ETHICS 1157 (1996). This noted ethics professor argues the interesting and rather unusual proposition that law firms should not be prevented from suing their own clients on entirely unrelated matters. Analyzing the history of conflicts rules, concluding that the current rule "snuck up on the bar," and reducing the importance of loyalty by using a test of "whether a reasonable client in the circumstances of the case would perceive a breach of loyalty," Morgan favors a rule that would allow an adverse lawsuit unless it would have a " 'material' adverse effect on representation" of one of the firm's clients.

4. Then-Georgetown student Alice Brown wrote a helpful Note, *Advance Waivers of Conflicts of Interest: Are the ABA Formal Ethics Opinions Advanced Enough Themselves*, 19 GEO. J. LEGAL ETHICS 567 (2006). Brown evaluates both the 1993 and 2005 ABA opinions and the then-current state of Model Rule 1.7, and suggests and describes additional standards that she believes are warranted.

5. Peter R. Jarvis & Bradley F. Tellam, *When Waiver Should Not Be Good Enough: An Analysis of Current Client Conflicts Law*, 33 WILLAMETTE L. REV. 145 (1997). This is a valuable review of when current conflicts should be nonwaivable. The authors focus on the conflicts rules of Oregon and the District of Columbia to compare, contrast, and conclude. A more recent valuable treatment of waivable or "consentable" conflicts is Kevin H. Michels, *What Conflicts Can Be Waived? A Unified Understanding of Competence and Consent*, 65 RUTGERS L. REV. 109 (2012).

6. For further analysis of lawyers representing family members in divorces or estate planning, see Russell Pearce, *Family Values and Legal Ethics: Competing Approaches to Conflicts in Representing Spouses*, 62 FORDHAM L. REV. 1253 (1994) and Teresa S. Collett, *Disclosure, Discretion, or Deception: The Estate Planner's Ethical Dilemma from a Unilateral Confidence*, 28 REAL. PROP. PROB. & TRUST J. 683 (1994). Professor Pearce argues that ethical guidelines should allow lawyers to represent families as a group to mediate among the members. While this was a hot topic in the 1990s, with the onset of widespread family law mediation, the bulk of the analysis has shifted to that forum. We will look at this again in Problem 22. Professor Collett criticizes the fundamental unfairness of one spouse in a joint representation being able to maintain unilateral confidences in a manner that hurts the other spouse.

7. Catherine Houston Richardson, *A "Rest in Peace" Guide of Estate Planning Ethics*, 28 J. LEGAL PROF. 217 (2003–04), explores potential conflicts of interest for attorneys in estate planning such as representing spouses and multiple family members; being named as beneficiary for a will the attorney is drafting; and being named as the fiduciary of the probate estate. The author, an Alabama estate planning lawyer, suggests that the ABA Model Rules do not adequately address the problems faced by estate planners, and highlights guidelines created by ACTEC, an organization of trust and estate lawyers, to illustrate steps such lawyers can take to avoid conflicts of interest.

8. Simone A. Rose & Debra R. Jessup, *Whose Rules Rule? Resolving Ethical Conflicts During Simultaneous Representation of Clients in Patent Prosecution*, 44 IDEA 283 (2004), discusses the specific conflicts faced by patent attorneys, particularly the inconsistencies between the ABA Model Rules and the United States Patent and Trademark Office Code of Professional Responsibility. The authors argue that the duty of confidentiality must "dominate the practice of all law, including patent law," and assert that when an attorney simultaneously represents two clients and discovers information from one relating to the other that would be required to be disclosed under the PTO duty of candor, the duty of confidentiality supersedes the PTO duty of candor and disclosure should not be required.

9. *Freund v. Butterworth*, 165 F.3d 839 (11th Cir. 1999), was decided *en banc* after its initial panel opinion (117 F.3d 1543 (1997)). In both decisions, the court refused to overturn Freund's murder conviction, even though the same law firm had earlier represented his co-defendant. While the majorities reasoned that the test of *Cuyler v. Sullivan* had not been met, particularly because Freund sought an insanity plea, Judge Tjoflat, writing in dissent, called the case "a classic example of how a conflict of interest can prevent a law firm from adequately representing a criminal defendant." Tjoflat (and other dissenters *en banc*) noted that by undertaking the exceptionally difficult course of seeking a finding of not guilty by reason of insanity, the law firm essentially admitted that Freund had actually committed the homicide. The firm's disinclination to attempt to shift the blame to the co-defendant, or attempt to plea bargain for leniency in return for testimony against the co-defendant, demonstrated to the dissenters a direct conflict of interest requiring reversal.

10. What happens where the criminal law conflict between the defendant and a *witness*? *Castillo v. Estelle*, 504 F.2d 1243 (5th Cir. 1974), which was widely cited, concerned a lawyer appointed to represent a criminal defendant while also representing one of the principal prosecution witnesses, the owner of the company that had been the victim of a theft. Though the lawyer's representation of the witness was unrelated to the criminal charges, the court reversed the conviction, noting that the lawyer had not disclosed the situation to the defendant, and that the lawyer "is likely to be restrained in the handling of that client/witness," making the situation "so inherently conducive to divided loyalties as to amount to a denial of the right to effective representation."

11. More recently, witness cases have gone both ways. Compare *Rivera v. State*, 58 A.3d 171 (R.I. 2013), denying disqualification, with *Heidt v. State*, 736 S.E.2d 384 (Ga. 2013), where a lawyer was disqualified because the lawyer had represented the defendant's girlfriend, a potential witness whose own criminal case was ongoing.

PROBLEM 8: WHO IS MY CLIENT?

A. INTRODUCTION

In the last problem, we examined several typical conflicts of interest. Before specific conflicts are evaluated, however, we must always first ask: Who is the client? "Isn't that obvious?" you might ask. "Isn't the client the person who walked into my office asking for help?" Often it is, especially when the client is a single individual. But when the client is an organization, it gets complicated. Remember to think in terms of "divided loyalty": "Do I know to whom I owe my duty as a lawyer?" If the answer is not a clear and unequivocal "yes," there may be a question about the identity of your client. And, if your client is an organization, through whom do you communicate to that client? Consider the situation facing attorney Esperanza Dejos.

B. PROBLEM

I

Esperanza Dejos represents HiFly Realty. HiFly was started by Gary Lavin, a real estate broker and developer with whom Dejos had worked on previous projects. Lavin organized HiFly as a limited partnership. Lavin and his two co-developers became the three general partners. Lavin then brought in seven airline pilots as investors and limited partners. Lavin was installed as managing general partner and began receiving a monthly salary for managing the business. HiFly purchased commercial real estate in a new industrial park at the edge of town and leased out the space. The partnership has recently been looking at acquiring another similar property.

Dejos has handled several matters for HiFly, including leases and leasebacks, a few eviction matters, and a property damages lawsuit. She's also recently been asked by Lavin to help renegotiate HiFly's bank loan to fund the new acquisition. Dejos finds Lavin always to be cooperative, and HiFly pays its bills promptly. Though she is not on retainer, Dejos considers herself the partnership's counsel, and considers HiFly to be one of her best clients.

One day, Dejos gets a call from Andy Arthursen, the accountant who is examining the books to put HiFly's financial papers in order for the new bank loan. "Esperanza, something's come up and I'm worried," he tells Dejos. "I've got to see you right away."

At a meeting that afternoon, Andy tells Esperanza that "I think someone's been cooking the books. Not only can't we show this to the bank, but it looks like the partnership has failed to make distributions to the pilots. It's like Gary's set up his own slush fund."

"Andy, are you saying Gary is stealing from the pilots?" asks Dejos.

"Not exactly, Esperanza. Technically, the partnership is, since the money is still in partnership accounts. But Gary's the one who controls the money, and it looks to me like it's being concealed from the investors."

"How sure are you about this, Andy?" asks Dejos.

"Well . . ." Andy says, then pauses. "I guess I'm pretty darn sure."

QUESTIONS

1.   What are Esperanza's obligations? What advice should she give, and to whom? What disclosures should she make, and to whom? For example, should she advise the limited partners, even though she has never even met most of them?

2.   Suppose Eddie O'Neill calls Esperanza, introduces himself as one of the investors, and says, "Gary's been talking about a new acquisition, and I want to know what you think. I've been looking at buying a new Cessna with Red Farber, one of the other limited partners, and I've only got so much to invest. Is buying another property a good idea?" How does Esperanza answer O'Neill? What, if anything, does she say about what the accountant has learned? Are her obligations to O'Neill different than under Question 1? Are her obligations to O'Neill different than to the other limited partners?

3.   Would it make a difference if Esperanza actually helped Lavin put the original deal together and drafted the partnership agreement?

4.   Finally, assume that it is the president and treasurer of a local union chapter who may be "cooking the books," and that Dejos represents the local. Since a union is generally defined as an association of its members, would Dejos have an obligation to disclose the problem to every rank and file member? If not, what should she do?

II

Assume now that Hi-Fly is a corporation that Lavin had recently sold to a threesome named John, Paul, and Jones. These three bring in Benedict Banker as counsel. Banker's initial review of the files makes him suspicious about what appears to him to be the over-inflated value of the company. Banker contacts Dejos and asks for all the HiFly corporate files. Must she turn them over? Will she be ordered to turn them over in a lawsuit?

C. READINGS

1. Whom Do You Represent?

The question "Who is my client?" would be relatively straightforward if it could simply be answered by saying, "It's the entity or organization." But saying that the client is the entity is the beginning, not the end, of the inquiry. The lawyer for the entity must also ask several other questions. We'll start with these: Who within the entity speaks for it? With whom does the attorney have confidential and privileged communications? Is the attorney sure whom he or she does *not* represent?

Let's focus for a moment on this last issue. Representing an entity is usually complicated by the fact that a lawyer may have close relationships with many of the organization's management and directors. Particularly in a closely-held organization like HiFly, those individuals, in turn, may seek to consult the attorney about personal issues including their own potential personal liability, and they may have expectations that communications with "their lawyer" are confidential. What should the lawyer tell these individuals? What confidentiality may the lawyer maintain with them?

In 1992, William Aramony, the former president of United Way of America, was indicted for stealing hundreds of thousands of dollars by diverting United Way funds for his own personal use. Aramony eventually was sentenced to seven years in prison. Before his trial, his criminal defense lawyers accused "his" former civil attorneys — or were they only counsel for the entity United Way?— of violating their duty of confidentiality. Here is the report from *Legal Times*, Washington D.C.'s legal newspaper.

Eva M. Rodriguez, *Indicted Ex-United Way Chief Says Lawyers Ratted on Him*
LEGAL TIMES, January 16, 1995[1]

WASHINGTON— "Three of William Aramony's former counsel have betrayed him."

So begins a motion submitted by the current legal team for the indicted former president of United Way of America. Using quasi-biblical terms, Aramony's attorneys allege that their client was stabbed in the back by the three lawyers at Washington's Verner, Liipfert, Bernhard, McPherson and Hand who Aramony once believed looked after his legal interests.

Aramony says his former lawyers breached a "sacred" attorney-client relationship when they disseminated highly personal — and perhaps damning — information about him. The Verner, Liipfert partners vigorously dispute Aramony's conflict-of-interest charge and say their loyalties were with their client — United Way, which Aramony headed until he was fired in 1992.

Unfortunately for Aramony, U.S. District Judge Claude Hilton ruled Jan. 6 that he couldn't have been betrayed because the Verner, Liipfert partners — Lisle Carter Jr., Berl Bernhard and James Hibey — were never his counsel: They were hired and paid by United Way. And although Aramony was president of the organization and dealt frequently with the Verner, Liipfert team, the lawyers' legal obligations were to the organization, not to him.

[Aramony's] allegation . . . offers a cautionary tale for association executives never to confuse their own interests with those of the organization they serve.

"There's a potential difficulty at a human level because the real relationships are with a person, not with an abstraction called an entity," says Robert Boisture, a

---

[1] Copyright © 2013 ALM Media Properties, LLC. Reprinted by permission from the January 16, 1995 edition of Legal Times. All rights reserved. Further duplication without permission is prohibited.

partner at Washington's Caplin & Drysdale and outside counsel to Independent Sector, the country's largest coalition of charities and nonprofit organizations.

"So, you may feel a sense of loyalty to the individual," he continues. "But you're paid and hired by the organization . . . ."

But according to Aramony's current attorneys, William Moffit and John Cline, the situation for their client was anything but clear. . . . Moffitt and Cline filed a motion asking Judge Hilton to suppress any evidence that the government may have gleaned from interviewing the Verner, Liipfert lawyers — evidence that Aramony considers confidential.

Moffitt and Cline lay out examples of how Aramony could have believed that he had an attorney-client relationship — or at the very least, an implied attorney-client relationship — with Verner, Liipfert.

For starters, Carter had represented Aramony personally in 1984 or 1985 for about one month when Aramony was engaged in contract negotiations with United Way. According to Moffitt and Cline, Carter or other Verner, Liipfert lawyers also represented Aramony in personal matters on other occasions.

Aramony hired Carter as general counsel for United Way in 1988. When Carter retired in 1991, Kathryn Baerwald took over as general counsel to United Way and recommended to Aramony that the organization hire outside counsel. Aramony, in turn, recommended to Baerwald that she hire Verner, Liipfert, which she did in January 1992.

Moffitt and Cline claim . . . in their 32-page motion that both Bernhard and Hibey told Aramony that if his interests diverged from those of the organization, they would represent him and drop United Way as a client.

In separate affidavits, Verner, Liipfert's Hibey and Carter insist that their "sole and exclusive" client was United Way, even though they had handled some personal matters for Aramony in the past.

Bernhard, in an affidavit and in an interview, also strongly denies that he ever told Aramony that he considered himself the executive's lawyer or that he would represent Aramony should he and the organization's interests conflict.

Bernhard calls the allegations made by Moffitt and Cline "offensive, appalling, and inaccurate."

"In a desperate attempt to save their client from trial, [Aramony's current lawyers] have made personal and scurrilous attacks on three reputable attorneys, even to the point of baldly accusing [Bernhard and Hibey], two of the most honorable and respected attorneys in the District of Columbia, of selling out their client for money," wrote [prosecutor Randy] Bellows.

Moffitt and Cline's arguments were of no avail. On Jan. 6, Judge Hilton . . . dismissed Aramony's motion out of hand. "I find from the submissions and the affidavits presented, that there is not a sufficient issue presented to require an evidentiary hearing," Hilton said.

NOTES

First, note the danger of corporate counsel representing the CEO or personal matters as Carter and Hibey acknowledge they did. By doing so, they walked on a slippery slope, though in this instance they managed not to slide down it.

As for Aramony, he was convicted, and the court of appeals, in *United States v. Aramony*, 88 F.3d 1369 (4th Cir. 1996), *cert. denied*, 520 U.S. 1239 (1997), affirmed both the conviction and the trial judge's ruling that the lawyers in question represented the organization and not its president. The appellate court also addressed a related issue worth mentioning here — Aramony's claim of a "joint defense privilege" with *United Way*:

> The joint defense privilege, also known as the common interest rule, 'has been described as an extension of the attorney client privilege.' To be entitled to the protection of this privilege the parties must first share a common interest about a legal matter.

> Although the district court did not explicitly address this issue, we conclude that the joint defense privilege did not protect Aramony's communications with [counsel] because Aramony and UWA clearly did not share a common interest about a legal matter.

Here, of course, Aramony's and United's interests actually conflicted.

That the lawyer represents the entity is the easy part. As we move on, think about these two other questions: What individuals within the entity speak for it? And with whom may the *attorney* speak under the umbrella of a confidential and privileged attorney-client relationship? It is very difficult — perhaps impossible — for a lawyer to evaluate the role as attorney for the entity without answering these two questions. It's clear, however, that lawyers generally cannot communicate to the entire entity at once any more than they can sit down and have lunch with it; they must do so through its appropriate representatives or constituents. Similarly, attorney-client confidentiality must have some limits, or it would extend to every employee of the organization, and make the job of corporate counsel impossible. Keep these issues in mind as you examine the rest of the readings for this problem.

2.   Whom Do You Tell in the Organization?

In representing an organization against an outside entity, traditionally there was no question to whom you owed your professional responsibilities; you would protect the organization's interests as against the outsider. With Enron and other scandals and the Sarbanes-Oxley regulations, this simplistic view is changing rapidly. We will study the post-Enron era at length later in this volume, and evaluate the sometimes difficult issue of when lawyers *can't* shut the door on outside regulators. We will also examine further what happens when there is internal conflict, as with Hi-Fly. Any organization is merely a structural entity that acts through its constituents.

Here, we begin by focusing on who the client is and whom the client speaks through. What should be the lawyer's relationship to the CEO, or to the governing board as an entity? If individual members, officers, or employees take unauthorized actions that are adverse to the organization, what do you do then? Who do you talk with? How do you determine what is adverse to the organization, the test set forth in Model Rule 1.13? And when, if at all, is there an obligation to "blow the whistle"?

When the organization is small and anything other than a solely-owned entity, conflicting interests may become more severe because of the more personalized and intimate service the lawyer has given in what may appear superficially to be a "family-type" atmosphere. It may be even more important in such situations for a lawyer like Dejos to have clear answers to these questions.[2]

A generation before Enron, the Securities and Exchange Commission had already entered this debate by suspending well-known Wall Street lawyers William Carter and Charles Johnson from practice before the SEC for failing to force its client, the National Telephone Co., to disclose its true financial condition or reveal the truth themselves: that it was near bankruptcy in 1974 and 1975, while it was attempting to find new capital. Carter and Johnson were not parties to the obfuscation; indeed, after they found out about it, they advised the company's CEO to fully disclose the company's true finances to the SEC, but he refused. Eventually, the board of directors, sensing something in the air, asked the lawyers what was going on, and the lawyers responded with the full story.

But were the lawyers wrong to wait for the Board to ask "the right question"? An administrative law judge at the SEC thought so and suspended them. On appeal, the reviewing commission called it "a close judgment," but reinstated the lawyers by finding the evidence "insufficient to establish that either respondent acted with sufficient knowledge and awareness or recklessness. . . ."

Even back in 1981, this was hardly a ringing endorsement. Now, as we'll see later in Problems 25 and 26, the duties of lawyers have changed materially and Carter and Johnson likely would have had a different result to their appeal.

3. The *Garner* Case

The following Fifth Circuit case, *Garner v. Wolfinbarger*, provides a historical background for understanding the genesis of ABA Model Rule 1.13. *Garner* was often cited and relied on during the debate over that rule. Note the absolutist positions advanced by the shareholders, the corporation, and, notably, the American Bar Association as amicus on behalf of the corporation. Note also the court's reliance on *Wigmore on Evidence*. Of what significance is it that the issue of corporate attorney-client confidentiality has been joined here not in the context of the lawyer's ethical obligations, but on the issue of evidentiary privilege in a litigation matter?

What do you think of the *Garner* court's conclusion? Does the case-by-case balancing test employed by the court offer a reasonable solution between the extreme positions of the litigants? Or is the court splitting the baby in half in order to avoid setting forth a more concrete standard of conduct for corporate counsel?

---

[2] Even with solely-owned entities, lawyers should be careful lest they mix their representation of the entity with the representation of the individual.

GARNER v. WOLFINBARGER
430 F.2d 1093 (5th Cir. 1970)

This case presents the important question of the availability to a corporation of the privilege against disclosure of communications between it and its attorney, when access to the communications is sought by stockholders of the corporation in litigation brought by them against the corporation charging the corporation and its officers with acts injurious to their interests as stockholders.

Stockholders of First American Life Insurance Company of Alabama (FAL) brought, in the Northern District of Alabama, a class action alleging [securities violations], seeking to recover the purchase price which they and others similarly situated paid for their stock in FAL. The defendants are FAL and various of its directors, officers and controlling persons. The plaintiffs also claim that FAL was itself damaged by alleged fraud in the purchase and sale of securities, and they assert against various individual defendants a derivative action on behalf of the corporation.

FAL filed a cross-claim against all other defendants, asserting in its own behalf the rights the plaintiff shareholders had claimed in the derivative aspect of their complaint.

R. Richard Schweitzer served as attorney for the corporation in connection with the issuance of the FAL stock here involved. After the transactions sued upon were complete he became its president. On deposition Schweitzer was asked numerous questions concerning advice given by him to the corporation about various aspects of the issuance and sale of the stock and related matters. Other questions went into the content of discussions at meetings attended by him and company officials and information furnished to him by the corporation. All questions related to times at which Schweitzer acted solely as attorney, before he became an officer of the company and before the filing of suit. Objections were made by counsel for the corporation and by Schweitzer himself that the attorney-client privilege barred his revealing both communications to him by the corporation and the advice which he gave to the corporation. . . .

The District Judge held that the privilege is not available to the corporation as against these plaintiff stockholders.

. . . .

[Plaintiffs'] argument is that the privilege is not available to FAL in the circumstances of this case against the demands of the corporate stockholders for access to the communications. The corporation says that its right to assert the privilege is absolute and of special importance where disclosure is sought in a suit brought by the shareholders against the corporation. The American Bar Association appears as amicus curiae and supports the view of an absolute privilege.

The privilege does not arise from the position of the corporation as a party but its status as a client. However, in this instance plaintiffs deny the availability to the corporation of the otherwise existent privilege because of the role of the corporation as a party defending against claims of its stockholders.

We do not consider the privilege to be so inflexibly absolute as contended by the corporation, nor to be so totally unavailable against the stockholders as thought by the District Court. We conclude that the correct rule is between these two extreme positions.

. . . .

The Availability of the Privilege

Professor Wigmore describes four conditions, the existence of all of which is prerequisite to the establishment of a privilege of any kind against the disclosure of communications.

. . . .

The problem before us concerns Wigmore's fourth condition, a balancing of interests between injury resulting from disclosure and the benefit gained in the correct disposal of litigation. We consider it in a particularized context: Where the client asserting the privilege is an entity which in the performance of its functions acts wholly or partly in the interests of others, and those others, or some of them, seek access to the subject matter of the communications.

It is urged that disclosure is injurious to both the corporation and the attorney. Corporate management must manage . . . . Part of the managerial task is to seek legal counsel when desirable, and, obviously, management prefers that it confer with counsel without the risk of having the communications revealed at the instance of one or more dissatisfied stockholders. The managerial preference is a rational one . . . .

But in assessing management assertions of injury to the corporation it must be borne in mind that management does not manage for itself and the beneficiaries of its action are the stockholders. . . . For example, it is difficult to rationally defend the assertion of the privilege if all, or substantially all, stockholders desire to inquire into the attorney's communications with corporate representatives who have only nominal ownership interests, or even none at all.

. . . .

The ABA urges that the privilege is most necessary where the corporation has sought advice about a prospective transaction, where counsel in good faith has stated his opinion that it is not lawful, but the corporation has proceeded in total or partial disregard of counsel's advice. The ABA urges that the cause of justice requires that counsel be free to state his opinion as fully and forthrightly as possible without fear of later disclosure to persons who might attack the transaction.

. . . .

In summary, we say this. The attorney-client privilege still has viability for the corporate client. The corporation is not barred from asserting it merely because those demanding information enjoy the status of stockholders. But where the corporation is in suit against its stockholders on charges of acting inimically to stockholder interests, protection of those interests as well as those of the corporation and of the public require that the availability of the privilege be subject to the right of the stockholders to show cause why it should not be invoked in the particular instance.

Good Cause

There are many indicia that may contribute to a decision of presence or absence of good cause, among them the number of shareholders and the percentage of stock they represent; the bona fides of the shareholders; the nature of the shareholders' claim and whether it is obviously colorable; the apparent necessity or desirability of the shareholders having the information and the availability of it from other sources; whether, if the shareholders' claim is of wrongful action by the corporation, it is of action criminal, or illegal but not criminal, or of doubtful legality; whether the communication related to past or to prospective actions; whether the communication is of advice concerning the litigation itself; the extent to which the communication is identified versus the extent to which the shareholders are blindly fishing; the risk of revelation of trade secrets or other information in whose confidentiality the corporation has an interest for independent reasons. The court can freely use *in camera* inspection or oral examination and freely avail itself of protective orders, a familiar device to preserve confidentiality in trade secret and other cases where the impact of revelation may be as great as in revealing a communication with counsel.

The order relating to availability of the attorney-client privilege is Vacated. The cause is Remanded for further proceedings not inconsistent with this opinion.

NOTES

Although *Garner* was decided over 40 years ago, it is a case that has often been discussed by other courts and used by ethics authorities. Some courts have formally adopted the *Garner* reasoning and some or all of the nine factors it cites as relevant to "good cause." Others have criticized the "good cause" test as vague and overbroad, or have limited corporate privilege only through the crime fraud exception. Most often, though, courts have accepted the *Garner* concepts in principle that the best interests of the corporation are not congruent with the best interests of management, and that the fiduciary duties owed to those such as shareholders mean there is no absolute privilege. See one example of such a case in Section 6, *below.*

After the *Upjohn* case (our next reading) was decided, some predicted the demise of the *Garner* doctrine. The contrary has proved to be the case, as courts have sought to carve out public policy exceptions for corporate privilege. Interestingly, *Upjohn* was the first Supreme Court case to directly affirm that a corporate attorney-client privilege even *existed.*[3]

As recently as 1962, only eight years before *Garner,* an Illinois federal judge had held that the privilege was "historically and fundamentally personal in nature," something that could only "be claimed by natural individuals." In his opinion, the

---

[3] In 1906, the high court had held that corporations did not have a privilege against self-incrimination. Hale v. Henkel, 201 U.S. 43 (1906).

judge wondered who, among all the corporate employees, would be able to claim the privilege, and noted that with corporations, "with their large number of agents, masses of documents and frequent dealings with lawyers, the zone of silence grows large." The Court of Appeal reversed the trial court, noting that "certainly, the privilege would never be available to allow a corporation to funnel its papers and documents into the hands of its lawyers for custodial purposes and thereby avoid disclosure."[4]

4. Upjohn

Upjohn Co. v. United States remains the single most important case defining the scope of the corporate attorney-client privilege. The United States government was investigating possible illegal payments by Upjohn Company, the pharmaceutical manufacturer, to foreign governments. Upjohn instructed its general counsel, Gerard Thomas, to conduct an internal investigation, which produced interviews with and answers to questionnaires from Upjohn employees throughout the world. The government subpoenaed the files "relative to the investigation conducted under the supervision of Gerard Thomas." The lower court held that communications between counsel and the company's "control group" were privileged, but communications with lower level Upjohn employees were not. The Supreme Court reversed, with Justice Rehnquist writing an opinion that the privilege applies to more than just a "control group." The following is an excerpt from that opinion.

UPJOHN CO. v. UNITED STATES
449 U.S. 383 (1981)

In the case of the individual client the provider of information and the person who acts on the lawyer's advice are one and the same. In the corporate context, however, it will frequently be employees beyond the control group as defined by the court below — "officer and agents . . . responsible for directing [the company's] actions in response to legal advice" — who will possess the information needed by the corporation's lawyers. Middle-level — and indeed lower-level — employees can, by actions within the scope of their employment, embroil the corporation in serious legal difficulties, and it is only natural that these employees would have the relevant information needed by corporate counsel if he is adequately to advise the client with respect to such actual or potential difficulties.

The control group test adopted by the court below thus frustrates the very purpose of the privilege by discouraging the communication of relevant information by employees of the client to attorneys seeking to render legal advice to the client corporation. The attorney's advice will also frequently be more significant to noncontrol group members than to those who officially sanction the advice, and the control group test makes it more difficult to convey full and frank legal advice to the

---

[4] Radiant Burners, Inc. v. American Gas Association, 207 F. Supp. 771 (N.D. Ill. 1962), *rev'd*, 320 F.2d 314 (7th Cir. 1963). Interestingly, at the time of the appeals court opinion, this kind of concealment had already been in place in the tobacco industry, although the revelations did not occur until the 1990s. We will tell something of this story in Problem 18.

employees who will put into effect the client corporation's policy.

The narrow scope given the attorney-client privilege by the court below not only makes it difficult for corporate attorneys to formulate sound advice when their client is faced with a specific legal problem but also threatens to limit the valuable efforts of corporate counsel to ensure their client's compliance with the law. In light of the vast and complicated array of regulatory legislation confronting the modern corporation, corporations, unlike most individuals, "constantly go to lawyers to find out how to obey the law," particularly since compliance with the law in this area is hardly an instinctive matter. . . . The test adopted by the court below is difficult to apply in practice . . . . An uncertain privilege, or one which purports to be certain but results in widely varying applications by the courts, is little better than no privilege at all.

The communications at issue were made by Upjohn employees to counsel for Upjohn acting as such, at the direction of corporate superiors in order to secure legal advice from counsel. As the Magistrate found, "Mr. Thomas consulted with the Chairman of the Board and outside counsel and thereafter conducted a factual investigation to determine the nature and extent of the questionable payments *and to be in a position to give legal advice to the company with respect to the payments.*" Information, not available from upper-echelon management, was needed to supply a basis for legal advice concerning compliance with securities and tax laws, foreign laws, currency regulations, duties to shareholders, and potential litigation in each of these areas. The communications concerned matters within the scope of the employees' corporate duties, and the employees themselves were sufficiently aware that they were being questioned in order that the corporation could obtain legal advice. The questionnaire identified Thomas as "the company's General Counsel" and referred in its opening sentence to the possible illegality of payments such as the ones on which information was sought. . . . Consistent with the underlying attorney-client privilege, these communications must be protected against compelled disclosure.

The Court of Appeals declined to extend the attorney-client privilege beyond the limits of the control group test for fear that doing so would entail severe burdens on discovery and create a broad "zone of silence" over corporate affairs. Application of the attorney-client privilege to communications such as those involved here, however, puts the adversary in no worse position than if the communications had never taken place. The privilege only protects disclosure of communications; it does not protect disclosure of the underlying facts by those who communicated with the attorney. . . . Here the Government was free to question the employees who communicated with Thomas and outside counsel. Upjohn has provided the IRS with a list of such employees, and the IRS has already interviewed some 25 of them . . . .

NOTES

Upjohn concerns the evidentiary privilege in Rule 501 of the Federal Rules of Evidence. Some state courts have adhered to the control group test. *See, e.g., Consolidation Coal Co. v. Bucyrus-Erie Co.*, 432 N.E.2d 250 (Ill. 1982) (rejecting *Upjohn*'s approach because it has the "potential to insulate so much material from the truth-seeking process"). Is it so clear that the *Upjohn* questionnaires were "confidential communications" protected by the attorney-client privilege? Would there have been a different result if someone other than counsel had sent out the questionnaires? After *Upjohn*, the Supreme Court held in *United States v. Arthur Young & Co.*, 465 U.S. 805 (1984), that a certified public accountant firm, the independent auditor responsible for reviewing the corporation's financial statements, was required to release its tax work papers in response to an IRS summons.

5. Whither the Privilege After *Upjohn*?

Does *Upjohn* mean a corporation may keep internal investigations private simply by asking its legal department to handle them? Or that any documents prepared with litigation in mind will be covered by a privilege? Is the breadth of corporate attorney-related privileges getting broader or narrower? Like the answer to many questions, it depends on whom you ask. In 1970, the same year as *Garner* and a decade before *Upjohn*, the federal court in the District of Columbia held that the minutes of a hospital's meetings investigating the death of a patient could remain confidential so that the hospital would feel free to conduct a candid inquiry.[5]

This so-called "self-critical analysis" privilege was later approved by several other courts, while rejected by others. Still other courts have debated about whether there should be an attorney "work product" privilege not merely for documents prepared "primarily or exclusively for litigation," but those which are simply prepared with the expectation they *may* be used in litigation.[6]

The New Jersey Supreme Court tackled these issues in a 1997 opinion excerpted below, in a case dealing with the plaintiffs' efforts to discover the employer-defendant's internal investigation of sexual harassment charges.

PAYTON v. NEW JERSEY TURNPIKE AUTHORITY
691 A.2d 321 (N.J. 1997)

The privilege of self-critical analysis exempts from disclosure deliberative and evaluative components of an organization's confidential materials. According to one court, "[t]he primary justification for this privilege is the encouragement of candor and frankness toward the ends of discovering the reasons for past problems and preventing future problems." Although some courts have rejected the privilege, others have adopted it.

Several lower courts in this State have adopted the privilege and granted seemingly absolute protection to evaluative and deliberative portions of organizations' files. Others have accommodated the confidentiality concerns arising from potential disclosure of deliberative and evaluative processes by employing a balancing test instead of a more rigid privilege.

---

[5] Bredice v. Doctors Hospital, Inc., 50 F.R.D. 249 (D.D.C. 1970), *aff'd*, 479 F.2d 920 (D.C. Cir. 1973).

[6] *See, e.g.*, United States v. Adlman, 134 F.3d 1194 (2d Cir. 1998), broadening this privilege in a 2-1 decision.

We decline to adopt the privilege of self-critical analysis as a full privilege, either qualified or absolute, and disavow the statements in those lower court decisions that have accorded materials covered by the supposed privilege near-absolute protection from disclosure. Instead, we perceive concerns arising from the disclosure of evaluative and deliberative materials to be amply accommodated by the "exquisite weighing process."

Although trial courts should accord significant weight to self-critical analysis and although confidentiality concerns about such information at times may outweigh competing interests in disclosure (especially if the information is obtainable through other sources), certain interests in disclosure are strong enough, in their reflection of important public policies, to outweigh such confidentiality concerns under most, if not all, circumstances.

We recognized one such public policy in *Dixon* [*Dixon v. Rutgers, the State University of New Jersey*, 541 A.2d 1046 (N.J. 1988)], where we stressed the paramount public interest in the eradication of discrimination, an interest that outweighed the interest in confidential communications in the tenure process. [W]e believe that the balance, assuming a valid claim and relevance, is normally best struck in favor of disclosure. As we described in *Dixon*, however, acknowledging the need to order disclosure does not end the inquiry. Instead, [a court can use] "a protective order that limits access to persons directly involved in the case." Consequently, we reject the privilege of self-critical analysis in favor of a case-by-case balancing approach.

Defendant maintains that the attorney-client privilege protects the entire investigatory process because attorneys employed by defendant participated in the investigation. We disagree with that blanket contention.

While an organization or corporation like defendant can be a "client" for purposes of the privilege [citing, *inter alia*, *Upjohn*], a fine line exists between an attorney who provides legal services or advice to an organization and one who performs essentially nonlegal duties. An attorney who is not performing legal services or providing legal advice in some form does not qualify as a "lawyer" for purposes of the privilege. Thus, when an attorney conducts an investigation not for the purpose of preparing the litigation or providing legal advice, but rather for some other purpose, the privilege is inapplicable.

NOTES

Payton contains a thorough analysis of the law in many jurisdictions. The case is also part of what may be a growing trend to focus on public policy as an important enough goal to curtail certain aspects of corporate attorney-client protections. But *Payton* also concerns a defendant that is a public agency. Do the public policy arguments apply with equal force to private corporations? What *should* the trend be regarding institutional confidentiality and privilege?

6. Parents and Subsidiaries

What constitutes a separate corporation? Is an affiliated subsidiary always the same as the parent corporation for purposes of conflicts of interest? What about a *wholly-owned* subsidiary? And who holds the attorney-client privilege and confidentiality? This issue has long been the subject of ethics opinions, scholarly articles, and, increasingly, case law, particularly since ABA Ethics Opinion 95-390 (January 25, 1995).

That opinion is one of the ABA's most factionalized. The committee's majority concluded that lawyers were not "necessarily barred" from undertaking representation adverse to corporate affiliates of their current clients. Only if the affiliate is an actual client, or if the new representation "will materially limit" the law firm's duties to the original client, will conflict of interest rules prevent representation. The majority opinion contains good advice about what "prudence and good practice" may dictate, but leaves it at that: advice.[7]

It is rare when an ABA opinion has written dissents. This opinion had three. Lawrence J. Fox, a partner in a prestigious Philadelphia law firm and a longtime advocate of client-protective conflicts rules, wrote one. After commending the opinion's "laudable practical advice," Fox wrote that the "advice" would have been a mandate "if the majority had not strained the meaning of Model Rule 1.7 to permit what everyone on this Committee agrees is ill-advised: suits against corporate affiliates of corporate clients."

We look at two issues: First how does the parent/subsidiary relationship play out in disqualifying a law firm, and second, how holds the privilege when the parent and the "sub" no longer are acting in concert?

In *GSI Commerce Solutions, Inc. v. BabyCenter, LLC*, 618 F.3d 204 (2d Cir. 2010) the trial court disqualified a law firm that was representing Johnson & Johnson on several ongoing matters while undertaking representation of another client against BabyCenter LLC, a wholly owned subsidiary of "J&J." The Second Circuit conducted a thorough review of the particular facts, the case law, secondary sources, and ABA Opinion 95-390. The court recognized that the BabyCenter case was unrelated to the firm's J&J representations, and evinced agreement with the ABA opinion that parent and affiliate corporations "should not be considered a single entity for conflicts purposes based solely on the fact that one entity is a wholly-owned subsidiary of the other . . . ." However, the court upheld the disqualification based on two key factors: there was "substantial operational commonality" between BabyCenter and J&J, and both entities "rel[ied] on the same in-house legal department to handle their legal affairs." This met the court's test that the law firm's representation would have the effect of diminishing "the level of confidence and trust in counsel" that J&J was entitled to.

---

[7] Comment 34 to Model Rule 1.7, added in 2002, reaches a similar conclusion: "A lawyer who represents a corporation or other organization does not, by virtue of that representation, necessarily represent any constituent or affiliated organization, such as a parent or subsidiary . . . . Thus, the lawyer for an organization is not barred from accepting representation adverse to an affiliate in an unrelated matter."

Note both the use of the word "necessarily" in both the opinion and the rule comment, and note further — even though the *GSI* court says this was not determinative — that the subsidiary in *GSI* was wholly-owned, not merely an "affiliate." Where does this leave things? Decidedly up in the air. What do you think the standard should be? Should there be an absolute ban against representing at least a wholly-owned subsidiary?

If it makes a difference in evaluating conflicts that parents and subsidiaries share legal counsel, does it matter in determining whether they also share confidentiality and the attorney-client privilege? This too remains an open question. We summarize one court's extensive analysis: the third Circuit's opinion in *In re Teleglobe Communications Corp.*, 493 F.3d 345 (3d Cir. 2007), in which the court applied the law of Delaware, where many corporations legally reside.

In *Teleglobe*, the court found that a parent ordinarily controls the privilege when a subsidiary is wholly-owned because the subsidiary exists only for the parent's benefit: "[T]he directors of the subsidiary are obligated only to manage the affairs of the subsidiary in the best interests of the parent and its shareholders." But when, as in *Teleglobe*, the parent [here "BCE"] decides to spin off (and thus cut off) the subsidiary, the rules change. At that point, the court held, the parent has fiduciary duties to the *shareholders of the subsidiary*. When Teleglobe went into bankruptcy after being spun off, Teleglobe shareholders sued BCE. Closely following *Garner* as a guide, the court held that the Teleglobe shareholders could maintain a derivative shareholder suit against BCE and seek discovery of information that BCE argued was privileged.

So do the subsidiary's shareholders get the parent's documents? It still depends. First, the court adopted the prevailing view — that when joint clients sue each other, the attorney-client privilege is waived — in the parent-subsidiary context. The court cited to Restatement (Third) of the Law Governing Lawyers § 75(2) and noted that "[t]his rule has two bases: (1) the presumed intent of the parties, and (2) the lawyer's fiduciary obligation of candor to both parties." Then, the court acknowledged the validity of BCE's position that this general rule should be "flipped" in the case of a parent and subsidiary, since "no parent would want its subsidiary to be able to invade the privilege in subsequent litigation, and so courts should not presume that intent."

But the court explicitly declined to fashion even a "default" test: "[B]ecause parent subsidiary relationships often change, having opposite default rules for wholly owned, solvent subsidiaries, and not-wholly owned or insolvent subsidiaries, seems unwieldy." Rather, the court, as the *Garner* court did decades before, remanded the case to the district court for further findings. It did note, however, that "[f]inding that BCE and Teleglobe were jointly represented is not enough" to require BCE to produce the disputed documents, and the district court should examine whether BCE and the Teleglobe shareholders were jointly represented "on a matter of common interest that is the subject-matter of those documents."

Confused? Join the crowd. And *Teleglobe* represents just one court's view, although an important one.

7. What Constituents of the Corporation Get a Confidential Relationship?

We now flip around the issue answered in *Upjohn* — how broad is the *corporation's* privilege? — and ask what corporate *individuals* may expect their communications to be confidential and privileged. Here are two takes, the first a piece by practicing lawyers evaluating employees' confidentiality and privilege in light of an important 2005 case, the second a more tongue-in-cheek but no less compelling effort by a lawyer-writer discussing what to do about confidentiality with corporate higher-ups.

Ivonne Mena King & Nicholas A. Fromherz, *Getting the Upjohn Warning Right in Internal Investigations*
17 PRACTICAL LITIGATOR 59 (2006)[8]

What is an *Upjohn* warning, and what purpose does it serve? In essence, an *Upjohn* warning is a disclaimer issued by an attorney for a company to an employee of the company, wherein the employee is advised that the attorney does not represent the employee, but rather the company as legal entity.

When the third-party employee knows that she is not the client, the privilege clearly belongs to the company alone.

From the company's perspective, a finding that an employee also holds the attorney-client privilege with respect to certain communications can pose a serious dilemma. Any holder of the attorney-client privilege can block disclosure of privileged communications by another holder. Thus, potential conflicts can arise when the company-holder wishes to disclose, and the employee-holder does not. The gravity of this problem is magnified by the fact that companies now have a very strong incentive to disclose the findings of internal investigations, because disclosure of such discoveries is one of the main ways that companies can avert more serious government action. On the other hand, employees who have communicated wrongdoings will often have a strong disincentive to disclose if it is their personal action that lies at the heart of the wrongdoing. Naturally, the wrongdoing employee, who may face serious criminal and civil charges, has no interest in being the proverbial sacrificial lamb that saves the company from harm at his own expense.

[M]any of these pitfalls can be avoided by a properly given *Upjohn* warning, which ensures that the attorney-client privilege belongs only to the company, enabling it to waive or hold the privilege at will.

In re Grand Jury Subpoena: Under Seal

The importance of a properly-given *Upjohn* warning was recently affirmed by the Fourth Circuit case of *In re Grand Jury Subpoena: Under Seal*, [415 F.3d 33 (4th Cir. 2005)]. Although the court ultimately held that the *Upjohn* warning issued was adequate to preclude the relevant employees from asserting the attorney-client privilege, . . . this opinion offers a stern warning to those attorneys who would not

---

[8] Copyright © 2006 by The American Law Institute. Reprinted with permission of ALI-ABA.

take seriously the exact protocol of delivering these warnings.

The pertinent facts: . . . AOL Time Warner began an internal investigation into its relationship with another firm. [AOL] hired outside counsel to assist in the investigation, and over the next several months, outside and in-house counsel interviewed three Company employees (hereinafter the "Employees"). . . . [W]hen the company agreed to waive the attorney-client privilege and disclose the contents of these interviews pursuant to a grand jury subpoena, . . . [p]resumably to serve their own (diametrically opposed) interests, the Employees moved to quash the interview disclosures on the grounds that they, too, held the attorney-client privilege with respect to the interviews.

Counsel's *Upjohn* warning stated:

> We represent the company. These conversations are privileged, but the privilege belongs to the company and the company decides whether to waive it. If there is a conflict, the attorney-client privilege belongs to the company. . . . You are free to consult with your own lawyer at any time.

When conducting the interviews, however, outside counsel told the Employees that it "could" represent them "as long as no conflict appear(ed)." Other similar statements were made to the Employees as well, such as "(w)e can represent (you) until such time as there appears to be a conflict of interest," and "we represent AOL, and can represent (you) too if there is not a conflict." These latter statements were the basis of the Employees' argument that they reasonably believed, at the time of the interviews, that the investigating attorneys represented both them and the Company.

Nevertheless, considering these facts, the court explained that . . . the attorney-client privilege as to these communications was solely possessed by the Company. In particular, the court noted that:

> There is no evidence of an objectively reasonable, mutual understanding that the (Employees) were seeking legal advice from the investigating attorneys or that the investigating attorneys were rendering personal legal advice.

The Trouble With Watered-Down Warnings

However, notwithstanding the Company's success in the case, the court offered a strong critique of the *Upjohn* warning practice used by the investigating attorneys. Indeed, explaining that its opinion should not be construed as an affirmation of "watered-down" *Upjohn* warnings, the court stated that the attorneys' practice represented a "potential legal and ethical mine field." In the court's view, the stakes were high:

> Had the investigating attorneys, in fact, entered into an attorney-client relationship with (the Employees), as their statements . . . professed they could, they would not have been free to waive the (Employees') privilege when a conflict arose. It should have seemed obvious that they could not have jettisoned one client in favor of another. Rather, they would have had to withdraw from all representation and to maintain all confidences.

This would have surely complicated the Company's ability to cooperate with the government.

[A]s the *In re Grand Jury Subpoena* case demonstrates, many dangers accompany a careless *Upjohn* warning practice. For the corporation's sake, counsel should make it abundantly clear that the corporation is the client, not the employee.

NOTES

Note the significant practical change in the way corporate investigations are handled today as opposed to 1980, as in *Upjohn*.[9]

And now we continue this serious issue in a lighter vein. In light of Enron and other corporate scandals that have occurred since this article was written, the issue of "Miranda warnings" for those who consider corporate counsel *their own* lawyers has become only too real. This article focuses on the tension for corporate counsel between wanting all the information from the corporate players but having to "Mirandize" them first.

Joel Cohen, *Warning Your Client That You're Not His Lawyer*
NEW YORK LAW JOURNAL, November 5, 1993[10]

PICTURE THIS: Armed with a search warrant, a team of FBI agents raid company headquarters of Graftco, Inc. (Graftco) to establish proof of payoffs made to gain subcontracting work on military contracts. They seize boxes of records and interview several senior executives, including the chief executive officer — Jim Upcreek. At the opening volley, some of the executives make incriminating statements. Others lie. Still others, panicked by the unfolding events, implicate the company and top management, including Upcreek.

When the dust begins to settle, Upcreek, a lawyer by training who has never practiced law, telephones Graftco's outside counsel whom he had actually retained for Graftco years before. With criminal law expert in tow, outside counsel arrives shortly after the FBI has left. After sizing up the warrant and talking to Upcreek and other executives, they get a better fix on what occurred and quickly try to define the parameters of the FBI's investigation.

Upcreek's longstanding relationship with outside counsel, coupled with a mounting case of nerves, leads Upcreek to blurt out, "the FBI asked pointed questions about me." After that comment, the lawyers decide that it is imperative to debrief Upcreek as fully as they can. After everyone else is gone, they quiz him thoroughly, emptying out *every* possible bit of information, incriminating to him or not.

The lawyers don't want to frighten Upcreek by telling him that, in truth, they represent Graftco, not him. Indeed, to warn Upcreek now that anything he says

---

[9] We'll examine "modern" corporate duties to investigate and government disclosures further in Problems 25 and 26.

may someday be divulged to the government (if outside counsel's true client, Graftco, later decides that it suits its purpose to do so) would devastate him. In what might be called Machiavellian altruism, they decide not to advise him who their real client is.

Thus, this law-trained Upcreek, drawing on the widely held belief that any communications between an individual and the attorney he perceives to be representing him are privileged, tells all. He begins by saying that he lied to the FBI to limit his own criminal exposure, which, it turns out, is substantial.

. . . .

The belief, largely held by the public, that any conversation with a lawyer is sacrosanct — that it cannot be repeated, or re-uttered in testimony by the lawyer — is incorrect. The mere fact that a corporate employee, however high a position he or she occupies, was interviewed by the company's counsel will not automatically spread the protective umbrella of the attorney-client privilege. . . . The determination . . . will depend on the employee's "reasonable" belief that he or she, in addition to the corporation, was actually a client.

[M]uch depends on the words exchanged between the participants before the employee's interview substantively begins. So, if the lawyer tells the employee the following, there is little risk that the employee will mistakenly conclude that the conversation is safeguarded.

- "I do not represent you. I represent the company;

- "If you tell me that you have done something wrong, I must report it to my client and perhaps recommend to my client that action be taken against you;

- "If you feel more comfortable in talking to your lawyer before talking to me, I would encourage you to do so;

- "In fact, just so you understand, there may come a time when the company may want me to repeat to a prosecutor what you tell me today. That statement could conceivably be used against you;

- "All right? Having heard all of that, are you willing to talk to me now?"

NOTES

Before we move on, one brief note on an issue we don't mention elsewhere. Lawyers are sometimes asked to become members of the board of directors they or their firms represent. There is no prohibition against doing this, but the potential conflicts — and issues about whether the individual is serving as a director or lawyer or both — should be obvious. ABA Formal Opinion 98-410 (February 27, 1998), addresses this, and warns that the lawyer must make clear to the corporation from the outset the differences between the two roles, that some matters discussed with the lawyer in the role as director may not be confidential, and that conflicts of interest can and do occur.

8. Side-Switching and Changing Loyalties

What happens when control of the organization changes, whether the take-over is hostile or as a result of a sale? What happens to the attorney-client privilege? And may the original lawyers still represent the original owners?

In *Goodrich v. Goodrich*, 960 A.2d 1275 (N.H. 2008), the New Hampshire Supreme Court examined what should happen when a father sold the controlling shares of his business to his sons and they later litigated a dispute. The court adopted the "practical consequences" test articulated by the U.S. Supreme Court in *Commodity Futures Trading Commn. v. Weintraub*, 471 U.S. 343, 348 (1985). In *Weintraub*, the high court held that "when control of a corporation passes to new management, the authority to assert and waive the corporation's attorney-client privilege passes as well. New managers . . . may waive the attorney-client privilege with respect to communications made by former officers and directors."

In *Goodrich*, the company changed control with the sale of stock. The New Hampshire court noted the important distinction between an asset sale and a sale of a business' entire operations, such as a sale of stock:

> A pure asset sale transfers only ownership over property, not control of the establishing corporation itself, and, accordingly, does not transfer the attorney-client privilege. If, however, an entity acquires control of the . . . business operations, rights and liabilities, it is generally accepted that it also acquires authority over the attorney-client privilege. Transfer of the privilege allows the acquiring entity to pursue pre-existing rights or defend against pre-existing liabilities, in keeping with the corporation's best interests.

In *Goodrich*, after the stock transfer changed control, the company "continued to operate as a New Hampshire corporation in good standing." It was, thus, the same corporate entity, although its business plan soon changed substantially. Thus, "[w]hether old T & M continues to exist 'as it did' under prior ownership is not the linchpin of the 'practical consequences' standard. Rather, the proper focus is upon whether control of old T & M passed with the transfer of ownership."

The trial court in *Goodrich* tried to rule in conformity with a leading New York Court of Appeals case, which the higher court extensively analyzed in its opinion. That case, *"Tekni-Plex,"* which in turn relied on *Weintraub*, is quite complex, but its importance nationwide is substantial. We excerpt it here.

TEKNI-PLEX v. MEYNER AND LANDIS
674 N.E. 2d 663 (N.Y. 1996)

KAYE, CHIEF JUDGE.

Central to this appeal, involving a dispute over a corporate acquisition, are two questions. First, can long-time counsel for the seller company and its sole shareholder continue to represent the shareholder in the dispute with the buyer? And second, who controls the attorney-client privilege as to pre-merger communications? We conclude that counsel should step aside, and that the buyer controls the privilege as to some, but not all, of the pre-merger communications.

Facts

Tekni-Plex, Inc., incorporated under the laws of Delaware in 1967, manufactured and packaged products for the pharmaceutical and other industries. In 1986, Tang became the sole shareholder of Tekni-Plex. From that time until the corporation's sale in 1994, Tang was also the president, chief executive officer and sole director of Tekni-Plex.

Appellant Meyner and Landis (M&L), a New Jersey law firm, was first retained as Tekni-Plex counsel in 1971. During the ensuing 23 years, M&L represented Tekni-Plex on various legal matters, including environmental compliance. . . . Additionally, during this period M&L represented Tang individually on several personal matters.

In March 1994, Tang and Tekni-Plex entered into [a] Merger Agreement with TP Acquisition Company (Acquisition), whereby Tang sold the company to Acquisition for $43 million. M&L represented both Tekni-Plex and Tang personally. The two instant lawsuits grow out of that transaction.

Acquisition was a shell corporation created by the purchasers solely for the acquisition of Tekni-Plex. Under the Merger Agreement, Tekni-Plex merged into Acquisition, with Acquisition the surviving corporation, and Tekni-Plex ceased its separate existence. Tekni-Plex conveyed to Acquisition all of its tangible and intangible assets, rights and liabilities. Acquisition in return paid Tang the purchase price "in complete liquidation of Tekni-Plex," and all of Tang's shares in Tekni-Plex — the only shares outstanding — were canceled . . . .

Following the transaction, Acquisition changed its name to "Tekni-Plex, Inc." (new Tekni-Plex). In June 1994, new Tekni-Plex commenced an arbitration against Tang, alleging breach of representations and warranties contained in the Merger Agreement regarding the former Tekni-Plex's (old Tekni-Plex) compliance with environmental laws.

Tang retained M&L to represent him in the arbitration. New Tekni-Plex moved . . . against M&L (1) enjoining the law firm from representing Tang in any action against new Tekni-Plex, (2) enjoining M&L from disclosing to Tang any information obtained from old Tekni-Plex, and (3) ordering M&L to return to new Tekni-Plex all of the files in the law firm's possession concerning its prior legal representation of old Tekni-Plex.

[Discussion]

[I]n the circumstances presented, M&L should be disqualified from representing Tang in the arbitration. As for confidential communications between old Tekni-Plex and M&L generated during the law firm's prior representation of the corporation on environmental compliance matters, authority to assert the attorney-client privilege passed to the corporation's successor management . . . .

New Tekni-Plex, however, does not control the attorney-client privilege with regard to discrete communications made by either old Tekni-Plex or Tang individually to M&L concerning the acquisition — a time when old Tekni-Plex and Tang were joined in an adversarial relationship to Acquisition. Consequently, new Tekni-Plex cannot assert the privilege [as to the acquisition]. Nor is new Tekni-Plex entitled to the law firm's confidential communications concerning its representation of old Tekni-Plex with regard to the acquisition.

Here, . . . Acquisition was merely a shell corporation, created solely for the purpose of acquiring old Tekni-Plex. Following the merger, the business of old Tekni-Plex remained unchanged. . . . As a practical matter, then, old Tekni-Plex did not die. To the contrary, the business operations of old Tekni-Plex continued under the new managers. Consequently, control of the attorney-client privilege with respect to any confidential communications between M&L and corporate actors of old Tekni-Plex concerning these operations passed to the management of new Tekni-Plex. An attorney-client relationship between M&L and new Tekni-Plex necessarily exists.

Indeed, M&L's earlier representation of old Tekni-Plex provided the firm with access to confidential information conveyed by old Tekni-Plex concerning the very environmental compliance matters at issue in the arbitration. M&L's duty of confidentiality with respect to these communications passed to new Tekni-Plex; yet its current representation of Tang creates the potential for the law firm to use these confidences against new Tekni-Plex in the arbitration.

[However,] to grant new Tekni-Plex control over the attorney-client privilege as to communications concerning the merger transaction would thwart, rather than promote, the purposes underlying the privilege. . . . Where the parties to a corporate acquisition agree that in any subsequent dispute arising out of the transaction the interests of the buyer will be pitted against the interests of the sold corporation, corporate actors should not have to worry that their privileged communications with counsel concerning the negotiations might be available to the buyer for use against the sold corporation in any ensuing litigation.

NOTES

Tekni-Plex has too often been misunderstood and sometimes misapplied. Its analysis is more complicated than *Goodrich* in part because there was no stock transfer. But Justice Kaye, in evaluating the practical consequences of this situation, found that since "old Tekni-Plex" had sold "all of its tangible and intangible assets, rights and liabilities," those included the relationship with the lawyers and the privilege for everything *except* the issue in which "New" and "Old" were adverse — the acquisition. Is this a brilliant application of a practical standard given the realities of business transfers in a modern fluid economic climate? Or a decision too dependent on formulaic technicalities?

Before we move on, we want to make two points. First, there is a common thread running through almost all these cases, from *Garner*, to *Payton, GSI, Teleglobe, Goodrich*, and *Tekni-Plex*: the "exquisite weighing process," as Payton called it, of fact-specific inquiries. This makes it extremely difficult to identify unifying themes. On the other hand, one might also call this case-specific approach an effort by each of these courts to reach a result that makes *common sense* under the circumstances. Viewed in that way, the paucity of bright line tests may be more understandable, as these courts grapple their way to appropriate practical resolutions, as the Supreme Court suggested in *Weintraub*.

Second, changes of control are not limited to corporations. Trusts, especially in litigation, often change control if the party challenging the existing order successfully shows bias on the part of the original trustee. In most states including California, the new neutral trustee steps into the shoes of the former trustee — the "CEO" of the trust if you will — and takes on all privileged and confidential lawyer information that "runs" with the trust, which is the client. This could mean that any nefarious dealings by the former trustee known to the lawyer will now become an open book to the new trustee.

9. "Thrust-Upon" Conflicts

What happens where the corporate conflict arises from a merger outside the law firm's control, creating a conflict that is "thrust upon" the lawyers? Must they now withdraw from all representation? The law in this area is still in relatively nascent development.

A 2005 opinion of the New York City Bar set forth two typical scenarios and then analyzed thoroughly and in considerable detail the rules and case law bearing on this issue. We briefly excerpt from the Introduction and Conclusion of that opinion:

THE ASSOCIATION OF THE BAR OF THE CITY OF NEW YORK COMMITTEE ON PROFESSIONAL AND JUDICIAL ETHICS, FORMAL OPINION 2005-05

Conflicts that arise through no fault of the lawyer may develop in the course of representing two or more clients in unrelated matters as a result of corporate acquisitions or other unforeseeable circumstances. In those situations, lawyers typically seek conflict waivers from the affected clients, but in some instances a client may withhold consent to the multiple representation. This opinion examines the lawyer's ethical duties when confronted with such so-called "thrust upon" conflicts, which are illustrated by the following two scenarios.

Scenario 1: A law firm represents Client A in a breach of contract suit against Company B. During the pendency of that suit, Client C, a longtime ongoing client of the law firm, acquires Company B in a stock sale, and Company B becomes a wholly owned subsidiary of Client C . . . .

Scenario 2: A law firm has advised Client A for several years regarding various intellectual property licensing issues. The law firm has also advised Client B for several years on general corporate transactional matters not involving intellectual property licensing, including current negotiations with Company C to form a joint venture. During the course of those negotiations, Client A acquires Company C
. . . .

Conclusion

When, in the course of continuing representation of multiple clients, a conflict arises through no fault of the lawyer that was not reasonably foreseeable at the outset of the representation, does not involve the exposure of material confidential information, and that cannot be resolved by the consent of the clients, a lawyer is not invariably required to withdraw from representing a client in the matter in which the conflict has arisen. The lawyer should be guided by the factors identified in this opinion in deciding from which representation to withdraw. In reaching this decision, the overarching factor should be which client will suffer the most prejudice as a consequence of withdrawal. In addition, the attorney should consider the origin of the conflict, including the extent of opportunistic maneuvering by one of the clients, [and] the effect of withdrawal on the lawyer's vigor of representation for the remaining client . . . .

NOTES

Note that this opinion assumes that the law firm finds itself with concurrent but *unrelated* representations with no substantial relationship between them, and no need to disclose confidences of either client. Note also that if the conflict is caused a *law firm* merger or its hiring of a conflicted lawyer, the results would be quite different. We will discuss much more about that issue in Problem 10.

10.   The United Mine Workers Litigation

And what about organizations other than corporations? To whom do attorneys representing unions or trade consortiums owe their duty of loyalty? *Yablonski v. United Mine Workers of America*, 448 F.2d 1175 (D.C. Cir. 1971), was one of several cases that came out of the struggle to control the UMW between Tony Boyle and Joseph Yablonski. Yablonski, a reformer, brought suit under the Labor-Management Reporting and Disclosure Act, more commonly known as the Landrum-Griffith Act or the LMRDA. The Yablonski forces had strong evidence that the leadership of UMW President Boyle was corrupt, and that it had stolen both union funds and union elections. They believed that honest elections would have installed Yablonski as union President. The LMRDA action was brought to examine Boyle's conduct in running the union, and to demand an accounting of union and pension funds.

LMRDA actions are brought by union members against the union as well as its individual leaders. The UMW was represented in the Yablonski matter by the same law firm that represented Boyle on other matters. Yablonski objected, arguing that *he*, not Boyle, actually represented the best interests of the union, and that the union's law firm, one clearly loyal to Boyle personally, should be replaced. The court agreed, likening Yablonski's suit to a shareholder derivative action. The court evaluated the proper role of union counsel in this way:

> We are not required to accept at this point the charge of the appellants that the "true interest" of the union is aligned with those of the individual appellants here; this may or may not turn out to be the fact. But in the exploration and the determination of the truth or falsity of the charges

brought by these individual appellants against the incumbent officers of the union and the union itself as a defendant, the UMWA needs the most objective counsel obtainable.[11]

After Boyle's private law firm was disqualified, the union's in-house general counsel, also beholden to Boyle, took over the Yablonski case on behalf of the union. Again the Yablonski group objected, and again the Court of Appeals agreed.

The matter ended favorably for the Yablonski side, but tragically for Yablonski himself. In 1969, during the pendency of the litigation, Yablonski and his wife and child were murdered during a break-in at their home. Eventually, "Tough Tony" Boyle was convicted of conspiracy to murder Jock Yablonski, and sent to prison. During the pendency of the ongoing Yablonski litigation, the Yablonski forces gained control of the union, and the union petitioned to switch sides. Interestingly, the Boyle defendants then made the same claim about new union counsel that Yablonski had previously made, but this time, the Court of Appeals — making perhaps a largely political decision that the best interests of the union were now being served — denied Boyle's motion.[12]

Once again, it seems that practical case-specific considerations ruled the day.

11. Lawyers for Partnerships

Last but not least — and vital to Esperanza Dejos — what about partnerships? Despite the widespread existence of partnerships, and the common use of limited partnerships which, like HiFly, are ordinarily created for the ownership and development of real estate, there is very little authority — and even less agreement — defining whom the lawyers for those partnerships represent, and with whom they may share confidential information.

ABA Formal Opinion 91-361 (July 12, 1991) addresses these issues. It concludes that Model Rule 1.13 applies to partnerships, and that a lawyer for the partnership represents the entire entity. "There is no logical reason to distinguish partnerships from corporations or other legal entities in determining the client." The opinion recognizes that individual partners — unlike corporate officers, for example — continue to have individual rights and to carry personal liability for partnership acts. Nevertheless, the ABA concludes that a lawyer does not necessarily have an attorney-client relationship with any of the individual partners. Whether this relationship exists will depend on "the specific facts" of the situation.

What about confidences? Generally, says Opinion 91-361, they are gained by the lawyer on behalf of the partnership, and thus shared among all partners. On this point too, however, the ABA hedges in a footnote excepting from this general rule situations in which the lawyer is representing the partnership in a dispute against one of its partners. But how is "dispute" defined? Do Gary Lavin's actions create a dispute between him and the partnership, at least once Esperanza Dejos is aware of the situation?

---

[11] Yablonski v. United Mine Workers, 454 F.2d 1036 (D.C. Cir. 1971).

[12] Weaver v. United Mine Workers, 492 F.2d 580 (D.C. Cir. 1973).

To support both its proposition that the entity is the client, and its view that the individual partners are not necessarily clients, ABA Opinion 91-361 cites *Margulies v. Upchurch*, 696 P.2d 1195 (Utah 1985). But *Margulies* also holds that the reasonable beliefs of partners that the lawyer represented them individually must be considered in determining whether an attorney-client relationship existed. Couldn't Lavin harbor such a belief?[13]

Moreover, the ABA opinion specifically notes that for a *limited* partnership, application of Model Rule 1.13 might be different. Since limited partnerships are quite common, more complex structurally, and at least as likely to wind up in litigation as general partnerships, one wonders why the ABA chose to consider limited partnerships the exception to the rule. Perhaps it was recognition of the difficulty in developing clear guidelines for limited partnerships.

The case law on these issues is not consistent. For example, three California cases each come out differently: first, that a partnership lawyer does not necessarily represent the individual partners: see *Responsible Citizens v. Superior Court*, 16 Cal. App. 4th 1717 (1993), which is described further in the Supplemental Readings. Second, that confidences imparted by one partner to the attorney must be *shared* with all partners, even limited partners; see *McCain v. Phoenix Resources, Inc.*, 185 Cal. App. 3d 575 (1986), another case cited by Opinion 91-361. Third, whether or not the limited partners are considered clients "is of no great moment," since the lawyer for the general partner necessarily owes a fiduciary "duty to the partnership to look out for all the partners' interests," a quote from *Johnson v. Superior Court*, 38 Cal. App. 4th 463, 479 (1995).

Note that the ABA opinion and most of the case law is a generation old. Little has been said or done since to clarify these issues, and there continues to be even less *de jure* guidance when it comes to limited partnerships. To a point, the imprecision and lack of uniform authority about entity representation shows that this issue has simply not been thoroughly treated. But it is also true that this dearth of authority emphasizes the difficulties inherent in grappling with this issue. We can't say how much comfort this might be to Esperanza Dejos as she tries to resolve her dilemma, but we are confident she is not alone.

D. SUPPLEMENTAL READINGS

1. *Fassihi v. Sommers, Schwartz, Silver, Schwartz & Tyler, P. C.*, 309 N.W.2d 645 (Mich. Ct. App. 1981). Defendant attorneys represented a closely-held corporation with two officers and shareholders, both radiologists and employees of the corporation, each with 50% ownership. When one physician, the corporation's president, ousted the other, the ousted doctor sued, and the attorney claimed attorney-client privilege and confidentiality. The court held that the attorney for

---

[13] Consideration of the putative client's reasonable belief in personal representation is not unique to *Margulies*. For example, see *Rosman v. Shapiro*, 653 F. Supp. 1441 (S.D.N.Y. 1987), using this standard for a closely-held corporation. And in *Westinghouse Elec. Corp. v. Kerr-McGee Corp.*, 580 F.2d 1311 (7th Cir. 1978), Kirkland & Ellis represented a trade association. The court considered the "reasonable belief" of the association's members that they had confidential relationships with "K&E," held that K&E had a professional obligation to maintain those confidences, and disqualified the law firm.

the corporation had a fiduciary relationship with both shareholders and a duty to advise the ousted shareholder of his individual representation of the president, and that no privilege could be asserted against the ousted shareholder because, as a member of the corporate board, he was part of the entity's "control group." The court also cited the *Garner* case for the proposition that disclosure is warranted where a corporation seeks to defraud one of its shareholders.

2. Ellen A. Pansky, *Between an Ethical Rock and a Hard Place: Balancing Duties to the Organizational Client and Its Constituents*, 37 S. TEX. L. REV. 1165 (1996), is a good, brief, and readable survey of the problems faced by organizational attorneys. This article remains an excellent summary on this issue.

3. Sherman L. Cohn, *The Organization Client: Attorney-Client Privilege and the No-Contact Rule*, 10 GEO. J. LEG. ETHICS 739 (1997), is an interesting and frank critique of the common policy of organizational lawyers advising organizational employees in a way that may be in the best interests of the organization but stretches the bounds of the relationship between those employees and the attorney.

4. Richard W. Painter, *Ethics in the Age of Un-incorporation: A Return to Ambiguity of Pre-Incorporation or an Opportunity to Contract for Clarity?*, 2005 U. ILL. L. REV. 49. One of the primary authors of Sarbanes-Oxley-related regulations suggests that relationships between lawyers and unincorporated entities, including scope of representation, should be determined by contract between them, rather than reliance on rules and case law that often do not apply to the unique circumstances involved.

5. Darian M. Ibrahim, *Solving the Everyday Problem of Client Identity in the Context of Closely Held Businesses*, 56 ALA. L. REV. 181 (2004), proposes a new model rule for closely held corporations that would allow an attorney to represent the entity on external matters and one of the shareholders on internal matters. An interesting discussion of what would be a substantial departure from the existing norm.

6. Ronald D. Rotunda, *Conflicts Problems When Representing Members of Corporate Families*, 72 NOTRE DAME L. REV. 655 (1997), is a valuable article on this difficult subject.

7. Jessica Taylor O'Mary, *When Business Decisions of a Client Create A Current Client Conflict of Interest: Implications in a Complex Ethical Landscape*, 43 B. C. L. REV. 1203 (2002), discusses what happens when client makes a business decision to merge, thus creating "thrust-upon" conflicts for lawyers in current litigation.

8. Most cases and materials on partnerships are a generation old. One leading case is *Responsible Citizens v. Superior Court*, 16 Cal. App. 4th 1717 (1993). The court cited four factors in determining whether the lawyer for a partnership represented the individual partners: the type and size of the partnership; the nature and scope of the lawyer's representation; the amount of contact between the lawyer and the partner in question; and the lawyer's access to information relating to the specific partner's interests.

9. Professor Roy Simon, writing in the N.Y. PROFESSIONAL RESPONSIBILITY REPORTER (September 2010) provides a helpful overview of the question, "Does the Lawyer for a Partnership Represent the Partners?" While Simon notes that most cases looking at this topic were written in the mid-1990s, soon after the Uniform Partnership Act was adopted by most states, he discusses recent developments in New York.

10. Two older New York City ethics opinions take the position that lawyers for limited partnerships not only may, but *must* disclose a general partner's malfeasance to the limited partners. Ass'n Bar City of N.Y. Opinion 1986-2 allows disclosure, while Opinion 1994-10 requires it; even though the limited partners are not clients, disclosure is required to protect the interests of the partnership.

11. Are individual members of trade associations all clients of the association's lawyers? *Westinghouse Electric Corp. v. Kerr-McGee Corp.* 580 F.2d 1311 (7th Cir. 1978), cited above in a footnote, provides one valuable perspective and an interesting read, answering the question "yes." Compare D.C. Ethics Opinion 305 (2001), which says "no."

12. An excellent analysis of the duties of union counsel is contained in Russell G. Pearce, *The Union Lawyer's Obligations to Bargaining Unit Members: A Case Study of the Interdependence of Legal Ethics and Substantive Law*, 37 S. TEX. L. REV. 1095 (1996).

13. *United States v. International Brotherhood of Teamsters*, 119 F.3d 210 (2d Cir. 1997), was decided in the aftermath of a hotly contested — and government-supervised — election for Teamsters' president between Ron Carey and James Hoffa, Jr., son of the notorious former Teamster boss. When Carey won, Hoffa objected to the union's court-appointed Election Officer. Although Carey cooperated with the Election Officer's investigation and waived any attorney-client confidentiality between him and his campaign's lawyers. Carey's campaign manager, Jere Nash, refused to do so. When Nash did not accede to the Election Officer's demands, the government took the issue to court. Both the district court and the Second Circuit Court of Appeal agreed that Nash had no independent rights of privilege and confidentiality. (Though Carey cooperated, his election was eventually invalidated, and Hoffa wound up winning a new election from which Carey was barred from being a candidate.)

14. Dennis P. Duffy of the Baker & Botts law firm has done a paper, *Selected Ethics and Professionalism Issues in Labor and Employment Cases*, that he updates periodically (*see, e.g.*, SN 020 ALI-ABA 689 (2008)) that is a first-rate overview of recent development in conflicts of interest issues in representing labor and unions.

PROBLEM 9: WHAT HAPPENS WHEN YOUR PERSONAL INTERESTS GET IN THE WAY?

A. INTRODUCTION

An attorney's loyalty to a client and independence of professional judgment may be compromised whenever the lawyer's own interests are affected by the representation. Most apparent among these interests is financial gain. Charging clients a fee comes with the territory, but lawyers must make sure their own financial interests don't interfere with their clients' cases. There are myriad other interests that may affect a lawyer's actions on behalf of a client: an attorney's personal relationships; the desire to withdraw from a case that's lost its luster; the desire for an intimate relationship with the client; and a lawyer's personal positions or beliefs that are antithetical to a client's legal position. This problem addresses these situations and some issues that flow from them, such as a lawyer's desire to withdraw from a case.

B. PROBLEM

I

Melanie Cameron is a sole practitioner. Consider these two scenarios:

1. Cameron represents William Simons. He is accused of stealing a car. Cameron has agreed to represent Simons for $3,500 if the case resolves before trial, and $10,000 (an additional $6,500) if the case goes to trial.

The DA has offered a plea bargain that both Melanie and Will think is far too stiff. Cameron advises him that he might want to take his chances at trial. He says, "I'd like to, you know, but I'm worried about the extra bucks for you. You deserve it, but my folks are just barely making it as it is, and I work at McDingle's for nine bucks an hour. I guess it's just too expensive for us to go to trial. So I better plead guilty."

What should Cameron do?

2. Cameron also represents Lola Lipp in a contingency-fee case concerning injuries Lipp received in an auto accident. Cameron has taken her case on the understanding that Lipp will pay all costs incurred along the way, including deposition fees, investigation, and experts. Cameron's written agreement reflects this, and Melanie also has written Lipp a letter outlining these costs and advising that "while I think that beyond a few depositions, costs will be modest, I cannot be certain of this. It is possible that significant investigation or expert advice will be necessary."

Unfortunately, discovery has revealed that there are potential eyewitnesses, necessitating extensive investigation, and questions about liability arise for which an accident reconstruction specialist would be most helpful. Costs will be substantially greater than anticipated. But when Cameron approaches Lipp about this, the client seems taken aback, and says she doesn't have the money. What should Cameron do? Specifically:

(a) If Cameron wants to continue to represent Lipp, must she provide the funds for these unexpected expenses?

(b) Suppose on the other hand that Cameron determines that it is impossible for her to fund the extra expenses and also that the new issues about liability make the case far less attractive by substantially reducing the settlement value. May Cameron withdraw from the case?

(c) What if Lipp, frustrated by Cameron's refusal to pay for the additional costs, fires her and hires another lawyer? What rights (if any) does Cameron have?

II

Arnie Berkowitz is a sole practitioner. Arnie has a stock portfolio, which he manages himself. He owns 500 shares of stock in Globetrotting Airways, Inc., which represents about 9% of his portfolio. He is asked by the Airline Pilots Association to head the negotiating team for their new contract with "Globie." Money, of course, is a big concern, but the pilots are also concerned with the safety of the airline's fleet of BX-15s. While the pilots' association has so far said nothing about these aircraft, they have unreleased documentation that they believe shows the planes are unsafe. They don't want to reveal the information, but have threatened privately to do so if their demands for a full BX-15 repair and recall program are not met in the new collective bargaining agreement.

QUESTIONS

Setting aside the issue of "insider trading," how do you answer these questions?

1. May Arnie undertake this representation? Should he? What, if anything, must he do beforehand? Does the size of his holdings in Globetrotting make a difference? Why (or why not)?

2. Suppose Arnie did not own stock in Globie at all, but was a golfing partner of the company's chief financial officer. Is this the kind of relationship that creates a conflict? Could Arnie represent the pilots in this circumstance?

3. What if Arnie's wife worked for Globie in a non-managerial capacity? Could Arnie represent the pilots? What if the Globie employee were his brother-in-law?

III

Sam Shade has been in sole practice for 25 years. One day, Bernard Bentley comes in with a personal injury case. Shade agrees to take the case for one-third of the gross recovery if the case does not go to trial and 40% if the case is tried. Shade looks at jury verdicts and settlements in comparable cases and determines that the estimated value of this case is $70,000 to $120,000. He also estimates that the case will require about 200 hours of preparation plus four days in trial. He thinks that if he does the prep work there's a good chance that the case could settle shortly before trial for $60,000 to $70,000.

Instead of filing a complaint, Shade telephones the defendant's insurance carrier. After the medical information is verified, the carrier's adjuster offers Shade $18,000 to settle the case now. Since Bentley does not have any residual injury, Shade decides to recommend settlement now. This way, he reasons, he can get a $6,000 fee for ten hours of work, rather than the larger fee he would hope to get, but may not get, if the case goes to the day of trial. "After all," he advises his client, "jury awards are unpredictable." And so, of course, are settlements. Is this proper?

C.   READINGS

1.   When Lawyers Have Something to Gain

What happens when a lawyer develops a close relationship with a client, even becoming like a surrogate relative, particularly when the client has no other family? American Bar Association guidelines specifically prohibit lawyers who practice estate planning from preparing trusts or wills in which they are beneficiaries, and those guidelines have been adopted by a majority of states. Moreover, many question the propriety of an attorney serving as a trustee managing trust assets.

The conflict dangers of such dual roles are obvious, and the temptations can be great. Not all stories are as extreme — nor as highly publicized — as Francis X. Morrissey's, but Morrissey's dramatic fall from grace provides an cautionary tale about how strong those temptations can be. Morrissey is best known as the lawyer for the estate of Brooke Astor, the extraordinary wealthy society doyenne, philanthropist, and recipient of the Presidential Medal of Freedom, who died at the age of 105 in 2007. Mrs. Astor's son Anthony Marshall had hired Morrissey to help Marshall steal millions from his mother's estate. Rumors about this persisted during Mrs. Astor's last years, and within months after her death, both Marshall and Morrissey had been indicted.

Morrissey, however, was not a one-time defrauder. According to numerous published accounts, with the help of another estate planning attorney, Warren J. Forsythe, he had a pattern of having himself named as beneficiary in a series of elderly rich people's estates. According to these accounts, Forythe would prepare the documents leaving substantial sums to Morrissey, who had been acquainted with the victims. Until the Astor affair, he had gotten away with this by reaching secret settlements with the families of the decedents, thus avoiding any scrutiny more serious than occasional rumors.

With the Astor affair, however, Morrissey reached the end of the line. He and Marshall were both convicted in October 2009 and sentenced to prison, and Morrissey was disbarred shortly thereafter. In March 2013, those convictions were upheld.[1] As for Forsythe, he died in 2012 with no record of discipline.

---

[1] *See, inter alia,* Stefanie Cohen and Dareh Gregorian, *Attorney Inherits the Windfall — Astor-Case*

2.   Can We Expect Lawyers to Act "Better"?

No, says Professor Leonard E. Gross, an "economic behavioralist" who has done empirical research to determine if the existing conflicts rules square with what economic behaviorists predict about how lawyers and clients will behave.

Leonard E. Gross, *Are Differences Among the Attorney Conflict of Interest Rules Consistent with Principles of Behavioral Economics?*
9 GEORGETOWN JOURNAL OF LEGAL ETHICS 111 (2006)[2]

Lawyers' Behavior in Assessing Conflict of Interest Situations will be Largely Self-Motivated

Do lawyers behave like other people when it comes to determining whether to conform their behavior to ethical norms? . . . This data confirms the hypothesis that lawyers will be inclined to behave in ways that are consistent with their self-interest, and that clients will generally defer to their attorney's suggestion to waive conflicts of interest.

. . . .

Empirical Results

A survey concerning behavior in conflict of interest situations was sent to 439 graduates of Southern Illinois University School of Law (all the alumni for which we have e-mail addresses), and 157 people responded. The demographics of the attorneys who responded to the survey were similar to those in Illinois as a whole. Illinois is reasonably representative of the country, though it has more large firms than does the nation as a whole. The results of the survey reveal some interesting information about how lawyers and clients behave (or at least how lawyers say they behave). The results were inconclusive with respect to how frequently lawyers discussed conflicts of interest with their clients, [from] one to two times per month or more [to] less frequently than once a year.

When lawyers do identify conflicts and inform their clients about them, they overwhelmingly indicate that they believe the conflicts are waivable. . . . A follow-up question asked how often attorneys told their clients that they could do a good job notwithstanding the conflict . . . . Both small firms and medium sized ones were much less likely to tell clients that they could do a good job notwithstanding the conflict than were large firms.

Legal Eagle Weasels His Way Into Wills of the Rich and Elderly, NEW YORK POST, Aug. 8, 2006; Serge F. Kovaleski & Colin Moynihan, *Many Clients of Astor Lawyer Left Him Bequests in Their Wills*, N.Y. TIMES, Jan. 4, 2008; *New York Probate Litigation blog*, available at http://www.nyprobatelitigation.com/archives/news-former-brooke-astor-lawyer-in-the-news-once-more.html; Lou Ann Anderson, *Astor attorney's disbarment: little too little, little too late*, www.EstateofDenial.com, March 1, 2010, available at http://www.estateofdenial.com/2010/03/01/; and Julia Marsh, *Brooke Astor's Son Anthony Marshall Loses Appeal, Faces Up to Three Years in Prison*, NEW YORK POST, March 26, 2013.

[2] Copyright © 2006 by Georgetown Journal of Legal Ethics. Reprinted by permission.

[This] may be explained in a number of ways. One possibility is that many lawyers and firms may make calculated business decisions that they will gain more clients than they will lose by adopting self-interested definitions of conflicts and obtaining broad consents to future conflicts while revealing as little as possible to clients.

Clearly, it is easier to hide the ball from the client when the client lacks sophistication. Survey results reveal that clients almost invariably consent to waiving conflicts. . . . Furthermore, clients very rarely raise conflicts sua sponte. Seventy-two percent of lawyers reported that clients never raised possible conflicts that the lawyer had not first raised with them.

One possible explanation for the relative absence of discussion between lawyers and clients about conflicts of interest is that lawyers rarely have conflicts of interest . . . . Another perhaps more plausible explanation is that because of self-interest, lawyers do not reveal many conflicts to their clients . . . .

An outstanding case study by Susan P. Shapiro based on interviews with lawyers in Illinois supports the notion that lawyers, when faced with conflicts of interest, act in self-interested ways. . . . Shapiro observes that . . . [w]hen confronted with conflicts, lawyers reacted in a number of ways. A few would decline to represent a client for fear that a conflict of interest would preclude them from subsequently accepting a more lucrative client. Shapiro observed, however, that for every respondent who indicated that his firm declined to take a case because of a potential conflict, several others described identical situations in which they would take the case, explaining that they would deal with the conflict later if and when it arose.

Principles of Behavioral Economics do not Support Disparate Treatment of Certain Kinds of Conflicts of Interest

The ethics rules permit clients to waive some attorney conflicts of interest but not others. . . . [W]e must address why Rule 1.8(a) permits lawyers to have business dealings with clients (subject to disclosure and waiver and provided that the transaction is "fair") and why Rule 1.8(c) permits lawyers to draft documents on behalf of clients who are relatives, thereby leaving themselves substantial bequests. One cannot plausibly argue that there is little danger of the lawyer taking advantage of the client in those situations. The cases are legion in which attorneys have exerted undue influence over relatives while drafting wills or inter vivos bequests which leave them or other relatives substantial amounts of money. Likewise there are many cases in which attorneys who engaged in business dealings with their clients put their own interests ahead of those of their clients.

. . . .

One might argue that contingent fees are needed to enable clients to hire lawyers in situations in which they could not otherwise afford them or in which they were unwilling to assume the risk of the litigation. However, the same argument could be made with respect to advancement of medical costs and living expenses. Clients may fall victim to low ball offers from insurance companies if they are unable to obtain money to pay their medical bills and living expenses. Although one might argue that clients will be less inclined to fire lawyers in whom they have lost confidence if they would still owe them money from the advancement of living expenses or medical bills, the same issue arises when clients consider firing lawyers whom they have retained on a contingent fee basis. In many jurisdictions, they still owe the lawyer a reasonable fee for his services on a quantum meruit basis, regardless of whether the contingency ultimately occurs. Thus, we are still left struggling for an explanation for the disparate treatment [under Rule 1.8(e)] between permitting contingent fees generally but not permitting the advancement of living expenses and medical bills.

. . . .

Although one could argue that permitting a greater degree of latitude in contingent fee situations is a necessary tradeoff for encouraging lawyers to handle cases, this justification of the rule is incomplete. It does not explain the failure to adequately inform clients of the conflict, which would be necessary if the rule is truly designed to benefit clients in obtaining representation . . . .

NOTES

Do Professor Gross' conclusions sound too harsh? Or is there a reasonable likelihood that lawyers are that self-interested? Even in the face of their so-called "fiduciary duty" to always put the client's interest ahead of themselves? What part of Gross' conclusions resonate with you? Do you agree, for example, that lawyers should be absolutely forbidden to do business with clients, as he suggests? Or are the protections of 1.8(a), if followed, adequate? And if contingency fees are necessary to provide litigants access to the courts, is Gross correct that contingency fees and living expenses should be treated in the same way?

3. Fee Arrangements and Conflicts of Interest

What about more subtle financial conflicts than the grossly self-interested overreaching of attorney Morrissey in Section 1? The following article argues that almost *any* fee arrangement can create a conflict between the interests of the lawyer and those of the client. Is this true? If it is, what can the attorney do to avoid such a conflict? Are such conflicts inherent in the practice of law, or are there ways of charging fees that would avoid or at least minimize the problem?

Richard Zitrin, *When Fees Are Unethical*
CALIFORNIA LAWYER (November 1989)[3]

Abby Perkins, a young lawyer who's been passed over for partner, decides to go out on her own. She struggles financially; she's behind in her rent and hasn't paid her secretary in two weeks. When the defense offers to settle a contingency fee case, she's tempted to take the first offer.

Abby asks her friend Stuart Markowitz, a partner at her former firm, to help evaluate the case. Markowitz tells her she's settling for too little, but she recommends the offer to her client anyway. Only after her client refuses to settle

---

[3] Copyright © 1989 by Richard Zitrin. Reprinted by permission of the author.

and fires her does Abby realize she's acted unethically. She's allowed her own financial problems to interfere with the interests of her client.

This story, straight out of an old *L.A. Law* episode, is too true to life. Real lawyers know that, as the California Supreme Court put it in *Maxwell v. Superior Court* (1982) 30 C3d 606, "Almost any fee arrangement between attorney and client may give rise to a 'conflict.'" This doesn't mean attorneys should stop getting paid. It simply means lawyers must always consider the effect their fees have on their clients.

. . . .

[M]any potential conflicts have been subject to very little comment. The court in *Maxwell* mentioned three:

- Either the attorney or the client in a contingency fee arrangement "needs a quick settlement while the other . . . would be better served by pressing on."

- A lawyer receiving a flat fee may have an incentive "to dispose of the case as quickly as possible, to the client's disadvantage."

- An attorney paid by the hour might be tempted to "drag the case on" without real benefit to the client.

Contingency fees aren't just necessary, they're desirable. They increase access to the courts for those who can't otherwise afford it.

Theoretically an identity of interest exists between attorney and client in a contingency fee case: The higher the recovery, the larger the fee. But most plaintiffs attorneys know that a lawyer can make far more money per hour by turning cases over quickly than by doing the preparation necessary to maximize recovery for each client. "The vagaries of a contingency fee practice don't always lend themselves to even cash flow," says Oakland plaintiffs litigator David W. Rudy.

Early disposition may be best for some clients, such as an accident victim with relatively minor injuries. But in more complex contingency fee cases, the responsible plaintiffs attorney will usually need to conduct discovery before fully evaluating the case.

How a specific case should be litigated always involves judgment calls and matters of strategy difficult to second-guess. But the client must come first. "You simply make your judgments based on the client's best interests. That's just part of the job," says Rudy.

Sometimes it is in the client's interest to settle. A San Francisco sole practitioner recalls winning a multimillion-dollar verdict, then being ready to litigate the appeal against the defendant's offer to settle for about 50 percent of the verdict. "I was sure we were going to prevail, and I couldn't help thinking I could retire on the fee I'd receive," says the lawyer.

Then he realized that his client, who was destitute, would do very well with the amount offered in settlement and would remain impoverished during the years of appeal. "I was looking at the appeal from my economic perspective, not my client's. When I put myself in my client's shoes, I had to resolve the case."

On the other side is the defense lawyer, who generally bills at an hourly rate. The longer the case goes on, and the more work done, the larger the fee.

"I try to make our work as efficient as possible," says Peter E. Romo, a partner in the San Francisco office of Adams, Duque & Hazeltine. That means ongoing communications with clients and a balancing of the need for discovery against the opportunity for quick case resolution.

Principles can get in the way of a settlement that makes economic sense, as when a defendant refuses to settle because it would seem an admission of wrongdoing. It's then, notes Romo, the ethical defense lawyer takes the size of his fee into consideration by advising the client of the likely costs.

Sometimes the lawyer should ask if it's ethical to represent the client at all when the vast majority of the recovery will be spent on hourly fees even if the client wins. "I think it's important to be right up front with my client," says Ronald S. Smith of Beverly Hills. "I ask, 'Do you want to give Ron Smith $7,500 to pursue a $10,000 claim?'"

Most criminal law practitioners in California's major metropolitan areas charge flat fees for representing criminal defendants. However, because it's often impossible to determine how much work a case will require — in particular, whether it will actually go to trial — this fee structure gives the lawyer three uncomfortable choices: Assume the case will go to trial and charge a larger sum, to the detriment of the client; assume it will not, to the lawyer's potential financial detriment; or split the difference, which may average out over time but doesn't serve the needs of either the client or the lawyer in any particular case.

James Larson, of the San Francisco criminal defense firm of Larson & Weinberg, no longer sets his fees this way. He says it is fairer to charge one fee for preparation until trial — work that almost always must be done — and a second fee for the trial itself. Larson's clients don't pay for trials that never take place, and Larson has eliminated the conflict that might tempt him to encourage a questionable guilty plea.

Unfortunately, other problems may arise with this type of fee structure. Criminal clients often don't have the funds to pay the entire fee in advance and may be unable on the eve of trial to pay the trial fee. Larson says courts themselves sometimes look favorably on his request to be appointed and paid by the court if an incarcerated client is indigent. Otherwise, he says, "My job is to try the case anyway, with or without the rest of the fee."

Surprisingly, nowhere do the California Rules of Professional Conduct say that legal fees can cause a conflict of interest. Rule 3-300 says a lawyer "shall not . . . knowingly acquire an ownership, possessory, security, or other pecuniary interest adverse to a client." But the "discussion" appended to this rule explains that it was not intended to apply to most fee agreements, including contingency fees . . . .

The clearest words yet may be those of U.S. Supreme Court in *Evans v. Jeff D.* [, 475 U.S. 717 (1986)]. The court permitted a settlement in a civil rights action that required the plaintiff's attorney to waive his fee. While this result is harsh, Justice John Paul Stevens' description of a lawyer's ethical obligation sounds like hornbook law: The lawyer "must not allow his own interests, financial or otherwise, to influence his professional advice." Thus a lawyer should "evaluate a settlement offer on the basis of his client's interests, without considering his own interest in obtaining a fee."

4. The Problem of Determining the Attorney's Fee Independently of the Client's Recovery

What happens when opposing counsel, or even the judge, drives a wedge between a client's recovery and a lawyer's fee? On the other hand, in cases where the attorney's fees are awarded separately from the client's recovery, how can a lawyer manage to negotiate one without it conflicting with the other? Read the excerpt from this most appropriately titled case.

IN RE FEE
898 P.2d 975 (Ariz. 1995)

Respondents' client gave birth to a severely brain-damaged boy. In 1987, after unsuccessfully seeking representation from three other attorneys, she retained respondents [Attorneys Fee and Montijo] on a 40% contingent fee. They filed a medical malpractice suit against the State of Arizona and Pima County.

The medical negligence claim was admittedly weak. Respondents' success in developing a colorable racketeering theory, however, prompted negotiations. After an unproductive initial settlement conference, a second was scheduled for January 21, 1991, the day before trial. On Friday the 18th, the defense offered a structured settlement consisting of a cash lump sum followed by periodic payments. This proposal designated a separate amount for attorneys' fees. After consulting an annuities expert, respondents and their client decided that her needs would likely be greater than those contemplated by the offer.

The following Monday at 3:30 P.M., the parties, attorneys, and annuities experts met with the settlement judge. In a private conference with respondents' group, the judge brought up the latest proposal. This prompted a discussion about the "common defense tactic" of making separate offers of attorneys' fees. Respondents and the judge agreed that such a move frequently had the effect of "driving a wedge" between a plaintiff's lawyer and his or her client by causing fees to become a source of discomfort, disagreement, and potential conflict.[4]

Despite his recognition of this strategy, however, and respondents' argument that the reasonableness of their fee was an issue for the trial court at the conclusion of the case, the settlement judge indicated that, in his opinion, the contingent fee being charged here was excessive.

Respondents asserted at the disciplinary hearing that during these negotiations they spoke with their client about the insufficiency of the attorneys' fees being offered by the defense. They claimed that she authorized them to demand more

---

[4] [2] Indeed, the defense here has since acknowledged that this was its purpose in making a separate offer of fees.

money for the care of her son, thereby possibly securing an increase in fees as well. Although he was not technically a party to these proceedings, the record shows that the son's interests were important to all participants, particularly the court. Consequently, following respondents' pleas, the judge agreed to seek more money from the defendants.

Late in the day, the settlement judge called both sides into the courtroom to discuss a new offer, consisting of $175,000 in cash, annuities [long-term periodic payments] for both mother and son, $400,000 in attorneys' fees, and $55,000 in costs. According to the judge, this offer was higher than the previous one because of respondents' representations that the client needed, among other things, better housing and "specially equipped transportation" for her son, as well as additional funds for his possible future surgeries.

After conferring briefly, respondents met privately with the client and proposed that she pay them an additional $85,000 in attorneys' fees from her share of the cash proceeds. During this discussion, the judge approached the trio and asked if they needed his help. Respondent Fee testified that he felt pressed by the judge's presence and told him, "I don't want you here." Fee also told the client that she should not allow herself to feel coerced by her attorneys or the judge and that she could refuse the offer or take additional time to consider it.

After repeatedly advising the client of her right to seek independent advice and obtaining numerous assurances from her that she was satisfied with the arrangement, Fee prepared a handwritten agreement concerning the additional fees.

The three then returned to the courtroom where respondents informed their annuities expert about the new agreement. They asked the expert to review the proposed settlement with the client one final time to ensure that the available funds would be sufficient to meet her needs and that the overall agreement was fair.

Respondent Fee announced that they agreed "in principle" to the settlement. However, when the judge repeated the terms previously discussed, nobody disclosed the existence of the newly-enacted fee agreement. Both the [disciplinary] committee and the commission found that respondents, not wanting to upset the settlement and believing it was not this judge's role to determine reasonableness of fees, planned to reveal the separate agreement to the trial judge in connection with the formal approval of attorneys' fees . . . .

Ten days after the conference, the client telephoned the settlement judge, informed him of the separate agreement and asked whether she was required to comply with it. The judge obtained a copy of the agreement, held a hearing during which he removed respondents from the case, appointed pro bono counsel to complete the settlement, and provided for the proceeds to be relayed through the clerk of the court for "proper" distribution. He then initiated these disciplinary proceedings.

A majority of the disciplinary commission recommended 60-day suspensions.[5]

---

[5] [7] Two commissioners dissented, finding the recommended penalty overly harsh for what they considered a technical violation.

We agree that respondents breached ER 3.3(a)(1), which states: "A lawyer shall not knowingly . . . make a false statement of material fact or law to a tribunal." . . . Respondents knowingly failed to disclose the separate agreement to the settlement judge in violation of this rule. At the same time, they engaged in "conduct involving dishonesty, fraud, deceit or misrepresentation" in violation of ER 8.4(c).

There are remarkably few cases applying the rules of professional conduct in a settlement contest and none that we can find directly on point.

. . . .

Respondents did not want to lose a favorable settlement for their client. At the same time, they neither wished to permit the defense to dictate the amount of their fees, nor felt comfortable with pressure from the judge to reduce them. Moreover, respondents clearly attempted to ensure that their client fully understood and concurred in the separate agreement. Both the committee and commission specifically found the modification was fair and that the client understood it. The uncontradicted evidence also suggests that respondents thought they were not obligated to disclose the arrangement to the settlement judge.

Nevertheless, we cannot condone their conduct. In our judgment, respondents should have either disclosed the complete arrangement or politely declined any discussion of fees. Fear that this might have jeopardized the settlement, while understandable, does not excuse their lack of candor with the tribunal. The system cannot function as intended if attorneys, sworn officers of the court, can lie to or mislead judges in the guise of serving their clients. "Zealous advocacy" has limits. It clearly does not justify ethical breaches.

Although we adopt the factual findings of both the committee and the commission, we are compelled to agree with the dissenting commissioners that the recommended sanction "exceeds the misconduct." [Thus, censure is imposed instead of suspension.] Nothing in the record suggests that respondents pose any threat to the public. Moreover, they already have suffered a considerable penalty by virtue of the extensive negative publicity surrounding this case.

We wish to discourage the previously-described tactic of "driving a wedge" between lawyer and client in negotiations.

CORCORAN, JUSTICE, dissenting:

I respectfully dissent.

I view the facts in this case differently from the majority. The respondents Fee and Montijo lied to the settlement judge so that they would get more money and their client would get less money. It is especially egregious for a lawyer to lie to a judge for the purpose of increasing his own fees at the direct expense of his client. I cannot agree with the committee, the commission, and the majority that respondents lacked dishonest or selfish motives. *Res ipsa loquitur.* Such conduct warrants at least a suspension and not a mere censure.

NOTES

In contrast, in December 1997 California's State Bar Court unanimously suspended attorney Stephen Yagman for one year for pocketing not only the $378,000 in attorneys' fees awarded by the court, but also insisting on his percentage of his clients' jury award of about $44,000.[6]

His insistence on this additional fee, just under $20,000, was enough for the court to conclude Yagman acted with "moral turpitude" towards his clients. The decision on Yagman, a well-known Los Angeles gadfly who will reappear later in this volume, may have been influenced, pro and con, by his reputation for both his willingness to take on tough police misconduct cases and his abrasive demeanor that many consider uncivil and some find offensive. However, it appears that the *Fee* court was influenced by its acceptance of the good faith of the two attorneys.

One way the issue of fees vs. recoveries can be avoided is for the lawyer and client to agree among themselves to put all monies received — both client recovery and fees — in one pot and divide that. Theoretically this could be interpreted as a lawyer splitting fees with a non-lawyer (the client), but we know of no jurisdiction that has prohibited it. The *Evans v. Jeff D.* problem (see the Zitrin article above), where the "wedge" issue is not fees vs. recovery but non-monetary victory for the client and *no* fees for the lawyer, would, however, not necessarily be solved by the "one pot" strategy.[7]

Read the following California ethics opinion that addresses the limits on balancing fees v. recovery, and some common-sense ideas about how to make this balance more workable:

CALIFORNIA STATE BAR FORMAL OPINION NO. 1994-135 (1994)

The contract between Attorney and Client will ordinarily govern the extent to which Attorney's fee shall be paid at time of settlement . . . . Thus, if the written agreement is silent as to when and to what extent Attorney shall be paid her percentage fee in the event of a structured settlement, she could not receive her entire fee at time of settlement, and would instead receive payment only on a pro rata basis. That is, she would receive her agreed-upon percentage of Client's first payment and all subsequent payments. Given the administrative headache such an arrangement might cause, Attorney and Client would be free to contract further between them at or near the time of settlement to "cash out" Attorney, so long as . . . Client's informed consent is obtained.

. . . .

Merely reciting that Attorney's fees shall be paid entirely at settlement is not

---

[6] In re Yagman, 3 Cal. State Bar Ct. Rptr. 788 (1997), *review denied*, 1998 Cal. LEXIS 6210 (Cal. Sup. Sept. 16, 1998). We will examine another *Yagman* case in Problem 21.

[7] In reaction to *Jeff D.*, Calif. Formal Opinion 1994-136 offers that a client could contract away the right to accept a settlement that waives fees in civil rights cases, if the lawyer complies with both conflicts rules and the rule about business relationships between lawyer and client.

sufficient to meet [ethical and fiduciary] requirements. Rather, the agreement must specify how paying all of Attorney's fees at settlement could affect Client's recovery. In the case of a structured settlement, the likely effects on Client's recovery include diminishing the amount available for an annuity, and deferring some or all of Client's compensation for a period of time so that Attorney is paid first, before any monies go to Client. Unless the agreement contains a candid appraisal of these effects, the requirements of Business and Professions Code section 6147 (a)(2) have not been met. For example, circumstances exist where Attorney's fees, should they be fully paid in advance of any recovery to Client, would amount to more than the entirety of the first several years of Client's annuity payments . . . .

When Settlement is Negotiated

When a possible structured settlement is eventually discussed and negotiated, the relative positions of Attorney and Client become more complex. No longer is the situation simply a matter of determining the theoretical apportionment of a recovery. In settlement negotiations, it is likely that the issues of the amount and timing of Attorney's fee payment will be raised by opposing counsel. Even if these issues are not directly raised by the opponents, Attorney will be obligated to raise them with Client . . . .

[P]resentation of a structured offer of settlement creates a clear potential for a de facto conflict of interest between Attorney and Client. Perhaps the most obvious problem occurs where the initial down payment offered is small, but the overall annuity is substantial . . . .

An offer of a structured settlement may be accompanied by opposing counsel's specific assurance that Attorney's fees will be paid in full "up front." But even counsel's specific offer of front-loaded fees does not change the requirement that Attorney may receive the fees only on a pro rata basis unless the fee agreement makes specific other provision . . . . If such a subsequent agreement between Attorney and Client is entered into, particular attention must be paid . . . that the terms of the transaction be "fair and reasonable to the client."

[Thus], in the event settlement is accepted, even where all other requirements are met, Attorney may not accept the immediate payment of her entire fee unless such payment comports with rule 4-200. Rule 4-200 requires that the fee collected shall not be unconscionable . . . . Take, for example, a wheelchair-bound Client who wants the substantial structured annuity allocated in such a way as to provide the cost of living, care, and human assistance on an ongoing annual basis to last for Client's lifetime. Here, the structure most advantageous to Client is likely to involve an initial payment of only a small percentage of the total, far less than Attorney's fee. Yet if Attorney insists on payment of the entirety of her fees before Client receives anything, the fees could eat up not only the entire downpayment but the first several years of structured annuity as well.

In such a circumstance, Attorney would have to alter her receipt of fees to avoid a unconscionable result . . . because Attorney's ongoing fiduciary duty to Client prohibits Attorney from collecting her fees in a way that defeats the very purpose of Client's willingness to settle.

The best protection for both Attorney and Client against the anomalies presented by a settlement offer that may put Client and Attorney at odds may be the inclusion, per Business and Professions Code section 6147 (a)(2), of language which recognizes and anticipates these situations and discusses how they will be dealt with when they arise, thus fully amplifying in the fee agreement how Attorney's fee and Client's recovery are interrelated.

5.   Contingency Fees in Criminal Cases?

All American jurisdictions forbid contingency fees in criminal cases. The reasons most often advanced are first, that there is no economic recovery from which to take a fee (an argument also heard with regard to contingency fees in divorce cases); and second, that paying lawyers a premium for acquittal would cause them to encourage their clients to turn down "favorable" plea bargains and go to trial. But many criminal defense lawyers charge their clients "flat fees," receiving the same amount whether the case goes to trial or not. Doesn't this practice cause lawyers to encourage their clients *not* to go to trial and to accept possibly *unfavorable* plea bargains?

William Simons doesn't have what is traditionally thought of as a contingency fee. Yet, since he must pay $6,500 in the event the case goes to trial, couldn't it be argued that this is a kind of contingent payment? Is William's fee any less contingent than paying a premium for "winning"? Is it fair to argue that in each of these three situations, the contingent premium for winning, the flat fee, and the bifurcated fee for William, the lawyer's interests are potentially placed at odds with the client's interests? There is a dearth of reported appellate cases on this issue, though the second and third types of fee arrangements are rather common in many jurisdictions.

There are anecdotal reports, however, of the issue being raised by appellate lawyers trying to overturn a conviction. For example, in 1997, a Georgia lawyer was accused of ineffective assistance of counsel by the convicted defendant's appellate attorneys because he accepted a $25,000 fee but promised — in a handwritten note on the bottom of the fee contract — to refund $15,000 "should all charges against [defendant] be dismissed and another perpetrator either arrested or identified." This arrangement appears to show little more than the lawyer's willingness to receive less should it be discovered before trial that the authorities were prosecuting the wrong man. But the defendant's expert witness, a member of the state bar's board of governors, testified that "the fact that the ultimate fee is contingent on something makes it a contingency contract." The expert also testified that this contingency created an "incentive" for the lawyer to take the case through trial rather than "work[ing] towards early termination."[8]

This seemingly ignores the requirement that another perpetrator be found before the fee is refunded, a circumstance that no lawyer (except perhaps Perry Mason in his prime) is likely to accomplish. It also underscores the point that almost any fee can be interpreted as creating a lawyer-client conflict.

------

[8] *See* Lolita Browning, *Assault Case Deal Labeled Contingency Fee*, Fulton County (Ga.) DAILY REPORT, April 14, 1997.

6. Failure to Pay Fees and Withdrawal

If a client doesn't make agreed-upon payments, may the lawyer then withdraw from representation? Virtually every jurisdiction has a rule of professional conduct that would allow a lawyer to seek withdrawal if the client fails to meet agreed-upon financial obligations. But seeking withdrawal and obtaining it can be two different things. ABA Model Rule 1.16 specifies several grounds that would permit a lawyer to withdraw so long as the client's interests are not adversely affected. But that withdrawal is *permissive*, not mandatory. Subsection (c) of the rule notes that when a court orders the lawyer to remain on the case, "a lawyer shall continue representation notwithstanding good cause. . . ."

Is $1.8 million in unpaid legal fees good cause? In 2011, plaintiffs won a $19 *billion* verdict against Chevron because of contamination related to oil drilling in the jungles of Ecuador. The case itself has been going on since 1993, when the original suit was filed against Texaco. Chevron, which acquired Texaco in 2001, refused to honor the Ecuadorian decision. Smyser Kaplan Veselka LLP, a Houston-based firm representing two of the plaintiffs, said it "cannot financially survive as a law firm without payment of the fees it is owed under its contract," and moved to withdraw.[9]

What would you do if you were the judge?

While it is perhaps not the most common occurrence, judges, vested with great discretion to permit or deny withdrawal for reasons relating to fees, do deny those requests fairly frequently. The more acute the problem and the closer to trial, the greater the possibility withdrawal will be denied.

7. Don't Slam the Door Behind You

While the failure of the client to fulfill a fee agreement is one common ground on which a request for withdrawal may be based, there are many other grounds considered appropriate in most states as well as under ABA Model Rule 1.16. These include when the lawyer believes that the client insists on doing something the lawyer sees as "repugnant" or simply something with which the lawyer has "fundamental disagreement," or where the client has made the lawyer's continued representation "unreasonably difficult." Indeed, a lawyer may withdraw for *any* reason at all if so long as the attorney "take[s] steps to the extent reasonably practicable to protect a client's interests," including giving reasonable notice. All these grounds are permissive only — not mandatory, as in the case of an emerging and direct conflict of interest — but leave lawyers with relatively wide latitude to withdraw, subject to the approval of the tribunal hearing the matter.

Some states' rules are more strict. For instance, a member of the State Bar of California may not withdraw at all, even *with* legitimate grounds, "until the member has reasonable steps to avoid reasonably foreseeable prejudice to the

---

[9] *See, e.g., Daniel Gilbert, Plaintiffs' Lawyers in Chevron Case Seek to Withdraw*, WALL St. J., May 4, 2013.

rights of the client," considerably stronger language than in ABA MR 1.16.[10]

How can a lawyer successfully get out of a case without endangering the client's position? What does it mean to "avoid reasonably foreseeable prejudice" to the client? Obviously, courts will insist on a lawyer demonstrating adequate grounds for withdrawal. But may an attorney file a declaration in support of a motion to withdraw that lays out, chapter and verse, exactly how the client has been "unreasonably difficult" or insists on a "repugnant or imprudent course"? Or must lawyers be careful not to slam the door behind them as they leave the case? Read the different approaches and views expressed in the following article.

Abdon M. Pallasch, *Breaking Off the Attorney-Client Relationship*
CHICAGO LAWYER (June 1996)[11]

Edward M. Genson of Genson, Steinbeck, Gillespie & Martin stood before Cook County Circuit Judge Fred G. Suria Jr.

"Why do you want to drop your client?" the judge asked.

"'Ethical, moral' reasons," Genson replied.

Would he elaborate? No, Genson would not. Then I'm not letting you off the case, said Suria, unless your client agrees. The client didn't.

And with that, Genson went right back to zealously defending U.S. Rep. Mel Reynolds, D-Dolton. Reynolds is under indictment for allegedly sleeping with underage girls and offering them money to lie to the government.

Dropping a client can be a gut-wrenching decision for the attorney who can't stomach his client for any of a number of reasons. Convincing a judge the withdrawal is warranted can be equally trying. Professional model codes and court rules may conflict. Case law and a lawyer's own personal code make the process even more complex. Nevertheless, decisions to withdraw — and questions about how to do it — are becoming more and more common.

. . . .

Requests for withdrawal affect more than high-profile cases. Examples? My client owes me money — can I withdraw? . . . My client might be planning to do something terrible here, but I don't want to broadcast it. What can I do?

. . . .

But every now and again comes a situation that forces an attorney to make a tough call on whether to seek leave to withdraw — and leaves a judge with a difficult choice of whether to grant it. Ethics rules, case law and opinion all clash over whether an attorney's first duty is to his client's confidentiality, the integrity of the court, or the attorney's conscience.

The bind Genson finds himself in with Reynolds — according to prosecutors —

---

[10]   Cal. R. Prof'l Conduct 3-700(A)(2).

[11]   Copyright © 2013 Law Bulletin Publishing Co. Reprinted by permission.

is that while Genson was defending Reynolds against the initial indictments, Reynolds allegedly tampered with witnesses and fabricated documents that he gave to Genson to use in his defense. Those charges against Reynolds were included in the second round of indictments, handed down the day Genson asked to withdraw.

But were Genson's two words — "ethical, moral" — uttered in open court too much? At least one expert says Genson violated his client's confidence by saying as much as he did. . . . Professor Monroe Freedman argues that attorney-client privilege is paramount and should never be compromised, even if the attorney suspects his client may commit perjury. "The lawyer has no business revealing that kind of information to the judge in the first place; and once that has happened, there certainly cannot be an appropriate lawyer-client relationship," Freedman said.

Defense attorney E. Michael Kelly of Hinshaw & Culbertson agreed with Freedman that the attorney-client privilege is paramount but said Genson did not reveal too much.

"Genson was quite prudent and moderate in his approach," Kelly said. "You have to say something to make the claim for withdrawal meritorious and Genson has done it the right way. God only knows what the ethical, moral problem is — and that's the way it should be. Genson's a pro."

. . . .

The closeness to trial is often a deal-breaker, judges said, no matter how meritorious the request for withdrawal.

Jack J. Carriglio of Fran & Schultz remembers one case in which a trial-eve request for leave to withdraw was shot down. "It was a multi-defendant case, and another lawyer in the case came into the court the day before the trial, he had a conference with his clients, and they told him they would not be paying fees," Carriglio said. "We were working at a three-month trial. He said, 'I'm a sole practitioner, and I can't be here three months without being paid.' He said the court should consider getting substitute counsel and suggested the court delay the trial to allow them to do so.

"The judge said if he left the courtroom, the marshals would be sent to send him back. Once he filed papers in the case, it was not the court's concern that he was having fee problems. That lawyer stayed and represented the client and did a pretty good job. He was never paid."

NOTES

Whether one agrees with Professor Freedman that even using the words "ethical" and "moral" is stating too much, or with those who feel that this vague, generalized approach is appropriate when necessary, it is clear that the safest tactic is for the attorney to withdraw with considerable circumspection. The withdrawing lawyer is often between a rock and a hard place — being clear enough to convince the court to grant withdrawal, while not being so clear as to slam the door on the client's case while leaving the courtroom.

8. Who "Owns" the Case File?

Suppose a lawyer successfully withdraws from a case, and in a way that does no harm to the client. Who "owns" the case file, client or lawyer? Almost all jurisdictions agree that if the client has paid the lawyer's bills, the file belongs to the client. But that is only the beginning of the story. Two of the issues that arise most frequently are what happens when the client has *not* paid the legal fees, and to what extent a lawyer's work product should be included in the definition of "the file."

The ABA rules provide surprisingly little guidance on these issues. State ethics opinions and a few court cases have been more illuminating. Calif. Formal Opinion 1994-134 takes a strong pro-client view, making it clear that the file belongs to the client, and that clients are "entitled to constant access" to the file during the case. It concludes that even where the client discharges the attorney and demands the file before a formal substitution of counsel, "the attorney may not withhold the file from the client or successor counsel merely to await the technicality of formal withdrawal." The lawyer may "retain possession and control of the file only to the extent necessary to represent the client competently" until formally relieved. Finally, this opinion concludes that "a discharged attorney who wants to keep a copy of the file normally must bear the copying expense."

Most other states don't go quite this far, though more states now hold that where fees are still owed the lawyer, the attorney may not hold the file hostage, even if the fee agreement has a provision for a "retaining lien." A retaining lien is, simply, a contractual provision by which the client agrees the lawyer can retain the file until the fees are paid. Such liens are now considered to be void as against public policy in most states, including California, which was one of the first to so hold.[12]

Some states, including, most significantly, New York, continue to permit retaining liens. While New York rule 1.16(c)(5) requires that the non-payment be "deliberate," the burden seems to fall on the client to prove the lien should not be upheld. "An exception to the attorney's right to a retaining lien may be found, in the court's discretion, where the client has made a clear showing of: (1) a need for the documents, (2) prejudice that would result from the denial of access to the papers, and (3) inability to pay the legal fees or post a reasonable bond." *Shoe Show, Inc. v. Launzel*, 1993 U.S. Dist. LEXIS 5843, at *4 (E.D.N.Y. Apr. 30, 1993).

Other jurisdictions, such as the District of Columbia, fall somewhere in between. D.C. Rule 1.8(i) leaves the narrowest of retaining liens: only attorney work product, and only when withholding the work product poses no "significant risk to the client of irreparable harm." The Restatement (Third) of the Law Governing Lawyers (2000), § 43 rejects retaining liens in most situations, except that a client who does not pay for specific documents may not be entitled to receive those documents, according to comment (c) of § 43.

What about the general obligation of lawyers to produce their attorney work product? While the law is still far from clear in many jurisdictions, courts and

---

[12] *See, e.g.*, Academy of Calif. Optometrists v. Superior Court, 51 Cal. App. 3d 999 (1975).

ethics counsel are more and more frequently requiring law firms to turn over this work product as part of the "file." Perhaps the leading case, further discussed in the Supplemental Readings, is another New York case, *In re Sage Realty Corp. v. Proskauer Rose Goetz & Mendelsohn, LLP*, 689 N.E.2d 879 (N.Y. 1997), in which the New York Court of Appeals required the Proskauer firm to turn over all work product except material created only for internal law firm use.

9.   Close Relationships and Sex with Clients

Can personal relationships compromise your ability to be loyal to your client? It seems settled that spouses working on opposite sides of a case will be disqualified as counsel, while spouses' firms may sometimes still continue in the case with the informed consent of all clients. California is clear: CA Rule of Professional Conduct 3-320 provides that "A member shall not represent a client in a matter in which another party's lawyer is a spouse, parent, child, or sibling of the member, lives with the member, is a client of the member, or has an intimate personal relationship with the member, unless the member informs the client in writing of the relationship." Does defining which relationships must be disclosed and consented to in such formulaic terms make sense to you? Or should the real test include a subjective component? That subjective element could be defined as any relationship that the lawyer feels may have an effect on the representation, or even any relationship that the *client* reasonably believes *could* have such an effect. What is your view?

One very personal relationship obviously fraught with problems is a sexual relationship with a client. This will almost always create a professional conflict of interest to one degree or another. Many jurisdictions have laws that ban medical practitioners and psychotherapists from having sex with their patients. Should there be a *per se* rule prohibiting all lawyer-client sex? Should such rules be limited to certain types of representations, such as divorce? Or are more general ethical rules adequate to address any problems that could arise from such relationships? When we asked these same questions in 1995 for the first edition of this book, we noted that only two jurisdictions — California and Oregon — had explicit rules on the subject.

This has changed. Model Rule 1.8(j) forbids sexual relationships between lawyers and clients unless a consensual sexual relationship existed before the client-lawyer relationship commenced. But by 2008, Profession Craig Feiser reported, there was little uniformity among the states: "Many states have adopted something close to Rule 1.8(j). Some have adopted even stronger rules, while others still do not have any ethical prohibition on attorney-client sex."[13]

The theories behind the rules prohibiting sex focus on one or more of three concepts: the existence of a conflict of interest; questions about the ability of a sexually-involved attorney to perform legal services competently while exercising independent, objective judgment; and the potential for a lawyer's position of power over and responsibility for the client — in short, the attorney's fiduciary duty —

---

[13] Craig D. Feiser, *Strange Bedfellows: The Effectiveness of Per Se Bans on Attorney-Client Sexual Relations*, 33 J. LEGAL PROF. 53 (2008).

being used to unduly influence the client into having the relationship. Most of these rules, including ABA MR 1.8(j), prohibit using the attorney-client relationship as a launching pad for a sexual liaison, but don't prohibit representing clients where the relationship is pre-existing.

A word or several about civil liability: Even in those states where engaging in sex with a client is a *per se* violation of the ethical rules, it is important to remember that sexual behavior is not by itself tantamount to malpractice. In *Vallinoto v. DiSandro*, 688 A.2d 830 (R.I. 1997), for example, Rhode Island's highest court reversed a jury verdict against a lawyer who had a sexual relationship with his client during a divorce case. The *Vallinoto* court held that the client had not proven she had been damaged in the case by the lawyer's action, and that alone required reversal and a new trial. But the court went further, concluding that in order for the client to show that the lawyer's services departed from the standard of care, she would have to show more than the sexual relationship. Indeed, the court also concluded that the sexual conduct did not constitute a breach of the lawyer's fiduciary duty. *Id.* at 835.

In *Suppressed v. Suppressed*, 565 N.E.2d 101 (Ill. Ct. App. 1990), the court concluded that even if the sex was coerced by fear the lawyer would not otherwise do his job, legal malpractice and even breach of fiduciary duty claims did not lie where there was "no specific harm other than [the client's] own emotional distress."[14]

10. Lawyers' Personal and Political Agendas

ABA Model Rule 1.7(b) says that a lawyer may not represent a client if the lawyer's representation is "materially limited . . . by the lawyer's own interests." A "lawyer's own interests" can be interpreted broadly, relating to anything that could affect the attorney's ability to provide the client independent professional judgment. How broad? Although the following case was decided under California's ethics rules, including Rule 3-310 on conflicts of interest, the reasoning would seem to apply throughout the country, as the case's reference to the Restatement intimates.

OASIS WEST REALTY, LLC v. GOLDMAN
250 P.3d 1115 (Cal. 2011)

Oasis filed a complaint for breach of fiduciary duty, professional negligence, and breach of contract against [its former attorneys, Kenneth] Goldman and his law firm, Reed Smith, LLP.

As demonstrated below, we conclude that Oasis has stated and substantiated the sufficiency of its legal claims against its former attorneys.

In early 2004, plaintiff Oasis embarked on a plan to redevelop and revitalize a nine-acre parcel it owned in Beverly Hills by erecting a five-star hotel and luxury condominiums. A Hilton hotel was already on the property, and the project is often

---

[14] *But see* Tante v. Herring, 453 S.E.2d 686 (Ga. 1994), further described in the Supplemental Readings, for a somewhat different perspective.

referred to as the Hilton project. The Hilton project required the approval of the Beverly Hills City Council.

Oasis retained defendant Attorney Goldman and his law firm, defendant Reed Smith, to provide legal services in connection with the Hilton project . . . . Oasis has alleged that it hired Goldman "because, among other things, he was an attorney reputed to be an expert in civic matters and a well-respected, influential leader who was extremely active in Beverly Hills politics." Oasis said it believed that "Goldman's statements and opinions on City development matters bore significant influence on City Council members and the local citizenry," particularly on members of the Southwest Homeowners Association, of which he was the president.

During the representation, Goldman became "intimately involved in the formulation of the plan for Oasis'[s] development of the Property, its overall strategy to secure all necessary approvals and entitlements from the City and its efforts to obtain public support for the Project. Mr. Goldman was a key Oasis representative in dealing with Beverly Hills City Officials . . . ." Reed Smith, in turn, received about $60,000 in fees. In April 2006, Goldman advised Oasis that he and Reed Smith would no longer represent Oasis in connection with the Hilton project.

Oasis's development proposal was presented to the city council in June 2006, after the representation had ended . . . . In April 2008, the council certified the environmental impact report and adopted a General Plan Amendment Resolution . . . , which paved the way for final approval of the Hilton project.

Shortly thereafter, a group of Beverly Hills residents opposed to the general plan amendment formed the Citizens Right to Decide Committee, with the goal of putting a referendum on the ballot that would allow voters to overturn the city council's approval of the Hilton project. It was at this point that Goldman engaged in the conduct that is of concern in this proceeding.

According to the complaint, Goldman "lent his support" to the group opposing the Hilton project; "campaigned for and solicited signatures for a Petition circulated by said citizen's group" . . . ; and "distributed a letter seeking to cause residents of Beverly Hills to sign the Petition . . . ."[15]

---

[15] [2] The note read as follows:

"LORI AND KEN GOLDMAN

"Dear Neighbor:

"Sorry we missed you when we stopped by.

"We stopped by to see if you would sign the Referendum Petition to overturn the City Council's recent approval of the Hilton plans. The Council approved an additional 15-story Waldorf-Astoria Hotel (where Trader Vic[']s is now), a new 16-story condo tower on the corner of Merv Griffin Way and Santa Monica and a new 6-8 story condo tower on the corner of Wilshire and Merv Griffin Way. At the last minute, the Council also allowed the developer to remove one of the floors of parking that they had previously agreed to add! And all of this in addition to the 232 condos that the Council had just finished approving on the Robinson's-May site. And all of this at one of the busiest intersections on the entire Westside!

"And all this is in the name of more and more revenue. And they don't even make any plans to seriously correct the awful intersection and lines of waiting traffic that will grow and grow.

"So we will sign the Referendum Petition and urge you to do likewise. Please call us at (310) 552- . . . to figure out a convenient time to sign. We have only 2 weeks!

Goldman insisted that he at no time disclosed confidential information acquired during the representation of Oasis to anyone, and did not believe that he disclosed to anyone that he had ever represented Oasis in connection with the Hilton project.

The citizens' committee collected the necessary signatures to place the proposed general plan amendment on the ballot as Measure H. Measure H . . . passed . . . by a margin of 129 votes.

The Court of Appeal . . . acknowledged our oft-quoted warning in *Wutchumna Water Co. v. Bailey* (1932) 216 Cal. 564, 573–574 [15 P.2d 505] — that "an attorney is forbidden to do either of two things after severing his relationship with a former client. He may not do anything which will injuriously affect his former client in any manner in which he formerly represented him nor may he at any time use against his former client knowledge or information acquired by virtue of the previous relationship" — but decided that such a "sweeping statement" applied only "in the context of subsequent representations or employment" and did not govern "the acts an attorney takes on his or her own behalf." Although Goldman "unquestionably acted against the interest of his former client, on the issue on which he was retained," the Court of Appeal found that Oasis had not stated a claim for breach of duty or violation of professional ethics, inasmuch as Goldman had not undertaken a "second attorney-client relationship or second employment of any kind" with an adverse interest, was no longer representing Oasis as a current client, and had not disclosed confidential information acquired during the representation.

. . . .

Oasis contends that Goldman, as its lawyer, was "a fiduciary . . . of the very highest character" and bound "to most conscientious fidelity — *uberrima fides.*" Among those fiduciary obligations were the duties of loyalty and confidentiality, which continued in force even after the representation had ended. As we have previously explained, "[t]he effective functioning of the fiduciary relationship between attorney and client depends on the client's trust and confidence in counsel. [Citation.] The courts will protect clients' legitimate expectations of loyalty to preserve this essential basis for trust and security in the attorney-client relationship." [The Court then again quotes the *Wutchumna* language cited above at 573–4.]

Oasis contends that defendants violated this prohibition in a number of ways. Oasis asserts in particular that Goldman acquired confidential and sensitive information relating to the Hilton project through the course of the representation . . . and that Goldman then *used* this information when he actively opposed the precise project he had been retained to promote . . . . In light of the undisputed facts that Goldman agreed to represent Oasis in securing approvals for the project, acquired confidential information from Oasis during the course of the representation, and then decided to publicly oppose the very project that was the subject of the prior representation, it is reasonable to infer that he did so. Moreover, inasmuch as Goldman was obligated under rule 3-310(B) of the State Bar Rules of Professional Conduct to disclose to Oasis any personal relationship or interest that he knew or reasonably should have known could substantially affect the exercise of his professional judgment — but never did so — it is likewise reasonable to infer that

"Ken and Lori"

Goldman's opposition to the project developed over the course of the representation, fueled by the confidential information he gleaned during it . . . .

Defendants argue first that the duty we outlined in *Wutchumna* is overbroad and should be read to apply in only two specific circumstances: (1) where the attorney has undertaken a concurrent or successive representation that is substantially related to the prior representation and is adverse to the former client, or (2) where the attorney has disclosed confidential information. The Court of Appeal explicitly limited the duty to these two circumstances . . . . But [i]t is well established that the duties of loyalty and confidentiality bar an attorney not only from using a former client's confidential information in the course of "making decisions when representing another client," but also from "taking the information significantly into account in framing a course of action" such as "deciding whether to make a personal investment" — even though, in the latter circumstance, no second client exists and no confidences are actually disclosed. (Rest.3d Law Governing Lawyers, § 60, com. c(i), p. 464.)

Defendants' contention that they were somehow relieved of their duties of loyalty and confidentiality by section 125 of the Restatement Third of the Law Governing Lawyers is mistaken. A comment to that provision explains that "[i] *n general,* a lawyer may publicly take personal positions on controversial issues without regard to whether the positions are consistent with those of some or all of the lawyer's clients. . . . For example, if tax lawyers advocating positions about tax reform were obliged to advocate only positions that would serve the positions of their present clients, the public would lose the objective contributions to policy making of some persons most able to help. *However,* a lawyer's right to freedom of expression is modified by the lawyer's duties to clients."

. . . .

Defendants complain that a "broad categorical bar on attorney speech" would lead to a parade of horribles. They warn that a lawyer would be prevented even from voting in an election against the former client's interest and that the prohibition would necessarily extend to every attorney in an international law firm. It seems doubtful that a single vote in a secret ballot in opposition to a client's interest would offer "a reasonable prospect" of "adversely affect[ing] a material interest of the client." (Rest.3d Law Governing Lawyers, § 60(1)(a).) In any event, we are not announcing a broad categorical bar here . . . .

The absence of a "broad categorical bar on attorney speech" also disposes of defendants' attempt to interpose a First Amendment defense. Defendants assert that "preventing client suspicions that their former attorneys will use confidential information . . . is not a compelling state interest." But the claim before us does not propose a "broad prophylactic prohibition[] of political speech" to guard against a mere "suspicion without proof" that Goldman may have used confidential information. Rather, as demonstrated above, Oasis has presented a prima facie case that Goldman *did* use confidential information, to the detriment of his former client, with respect to the precise subject of the prior representation. Defendants have cited no authority to suggest the First Amendment would protect such duplicity.

The judgment of the Court of Appeal is reversed.

NOTES

Although the *Oasis West* court speaks somewhat interchangeably about confidential information and loyalty, it is still clear from the opinion and the twice-quoted portion of the 1932 *Wutchumna* case that loyalty lives on past the end of an attorney-client relationship and that this to some degree limits the abilities of lawyers to act on their own personal interests.

Here is another example in a different, more politicized, context. In 1995, noted Chicago personal injury lawyer Philip H. Corboy, Jr. withdrew from representing Illinois state senator Robert Raica on a medical malpractice claim because Raica had voted for "tort reform" that would limit damages of the very kind the politician was seeking with Corboy's help. Corboy acknowledged to *Chicago Lawyer* that he had first lobbied his client for his vote, a fact which Raica likened to "a surgeon [who] had me on the operating table [and] said, 'Well, Senator, how are you going to vote on tort reform?'" After Raica's vote, Corboy withdrew because Raica "took away the rights of people but retained them for himself. . . . Having devoted 40 years of my life to protecting the rights of victims, I did not feel I could represent him." In short, when his personal beliefs got in the way of his representation, Corboy got out of the case. But was his lobbying effort proper?

11. A Word About "Positional Conflicts"

Are lawyers permitted to take a legal position in one case and advocate an opposite legal theory in another? There is still relatively little law on this issue. Yet most authorities see no grounds on which to prevent this unless taking position #1 will have a direct and significant adverse effect on the client advocating position #2. Comment 24 to ABA Model Rule 1.7 now states this standard: A lawyer may take inconsistent legal positions in different courts at different times. But if taking position #1 creates "a significant risk" that client #2 will be seriously compromised, such as "when a decision favoring one client will create a precedent likely to seriously weaken the position taken on behalf of the other," a conflict exists.

Before the 2002 revision to the Model Rules, the comment in MR 1.7 on positional conflicts had stated that it was "ordinarily not improper to assert such positions in cases pending in different trial courts, but . . . may be improper to do so in cases pending at the same time in an appellate court." This is sometimes called the continuum approach. Some courts, Michigan being one example, have retained their continuum approach to positional conflicts, while others have adopted the ABA standard, seeing a significant risk that a lawyer's action on behalf of one client will materially limit the lawyer's effectiveness in representing another client in a different case.

May a lawyer take opposite positions in the same court if at significantly different times? Or in different jurisdictions at proximate times? Does the lawyer owe any duty to the court to make consistent legal arguments, at least where those arguments are in front of the same court? Does the fact that the area of law is novel, e.g., climate change, mean lawyers need to be especially alert to this type of conflict?[16]

Here's a straightforward example of a disabling positional conflict brought to the court's attention by the lawyer himself:

WILLIAMS v. DELAWARE
805 A.2d 880 (Del. Sup.Ct. 2002)

The appellant Joseph Williams filed these consolidated appeals from his conviction and death sentence for first-degree murder. Williams' lawyer, Bernard J. O'Donnell, has filed a motion to withdraw. The motion also requests that substitute counsel be appointed by this Court to represent Williams on appeal.

O'Donnell asserts that, on appeal, Williams could raise an arguable issue that the Superior Court erred when it concluded it was required to give "great weight" to the jury's 10-2 recommendation in favor of the death penalty for Williams. O'Donnell contends, however, that he may have a conflict in presenting this argument because he has advocated a contrary position on behalf of a different client in another capital murder appeal pending before this Court. In *Garden v. State*, O'Donnell argued in his opening brief that the Superior Court erred when it *failed* to give great weight to the jury's 2-10 vote rejecting the imposition of the death penalty for Garden.

O'Donnell is concerned that his representation of both clients on this issue will create the risk that an unfavorable precedent will be created for one client or the other. O'Donnell also is concerned that it may invite questions about his credibility with this Court and his clients' perception of his loyalty to each of them . . . .

O'Donnell's motion to withdraw must be granted and substitute counsel will be appointed. O'Donnell and the State are both commended for their recognition of and adherence to the highest standards of professional conduct.

D. SUPPLEMENTAL READINGS

1. *Maxwell v. Superior Ct.*, 639 P.2d 248 (Cal. 1982). An attorney agreed to represent a defendant facing robbery charges in exchange for the right to exploit the defendant's life story. The trial court ruled that an inherent conflict was created which demands the disqualification of the attorney. The California Supreme Court reversed, stating that the defendant's consent after extensive discussions with his attorney constituted an adequate waiver, which precludes counsel's removal.

2. DOUGLAS E. ROSENTHAL, LAWYER AND CLIENT: WHO'S IN CHARGE? (1974). This book retains vitality long after its publication. The author takes a strong view about how lawyers receive their fees, including blunt views about quick-recovery contingency fee cases that pay off for the lawyer but not the client.

3. Other helpful fees/conflicts resources include: a Florida Bar pamphlet on attorney's fees and the attorney-client relationship (*available at* http://www.

---

[16] *See, e.g.*, Christopher L. Colclasure, Denise W. Kennedy, & Stephen G. Masciocchi, *Climate Change and Positional Conflicts of Interest*, 40 COLO. LAW. 43 (2011), referenced further in the Supplemental Readings.

floridabar.org/tfb/TFBConsum.nsf/0a92a6dc28e76ae58525700a005d0d53/
afb630a0b709b85b85256b2f006c61d1?OpenDocument) and the Massachusetts bar
site on collecting fees (http://www.mass.gov/obcbbo/Ethics%20of%20Charging%
20and%20Collecting%20Fees.pdf).

The ABA has a helpful newsletter on fees as well: (https://www.americanbar.org/
newsletter/publications/gp_solo_magazine_home/gp_solo_magazine_index/solo_
lawyer_ethics_fee_client_relationship.html).

4. *People v. Barboza*, 627 P.2d 188 (Cal. 1981). The county's contract with the
public defender specified that $15,000 will be deposited in an account to pay for
defense counsel who is appointed when the public defender is disqualified from
representing a defendant. The public defender was to pay for any deficiencies in the
account, but at the end of the year any remaining balance was returned to the public
defender's office. The court ruled that this contract created a conflict of interest
between the county and the public defender, because it gives the public defender a
disincentive to declare himself disqualified for a case.

5. *In re Sage Realty Corp. v. Proskauer Rose Goetz & Mendelsohn, LLP*, 689
N.E.2d 879 (N.Y. 1997). Sage Realty hired the Proskauer firm in a complex real
estate restructuring for which Proskauer billed — and Sage paid — about $1 million
in fees. After a falling out, Sage fired Proskauer and hired another firm. Proskauer
resisted giving Sage a large number of documents including internal memos, drafts
of instruments, research, and lawyers' notes written on contracts, transactions and
charts. The New York Court of Appeal held that this information, even though work
product, must be turned over to Sage, except internal law office memos intended
solely "for lawyers to be able to set down their thoughts." Sage's payment of its legal
fees seems critical to the decision, the court noting that Sage had paid for the
creation of the documents it sought. Also, the court determined that copying the
material, which amounted to fourteen volumes containing over 500 documents, was
properly chargeable to the client.

6. Allison Rhodes & Robert Hillman, *Client Files and Digital Law Practices:
Rethinking Old Concepts in an Era of Lawyer Mobility*, 43 SUFF. U. L. REV. 897
(2010). This article evaluates the issue of lawyers controlling their clients' *digital*
files. Although written before the Ethics 20/20 changes in 2012, the article is a useful
and thorough summary of the development of the issue of digital file control — one
that varies materially from state to state. From the article: "The digitization of
client files and law firm intellectual property, however, severely tests the existing
framework for defining the relative rights and interests of law firms, lawyers, and
clients."

7. Stephen W. Simpson, *From Lawyer-Spouse to Lawyer-Partner: Conflicts of
Interest in the 21st Century*, 19 GEO. J. LEGAL ETHICS 405 (2006), discusses the
history of family law conflict of interest rules and examines the impact of same sex
marriage laws on those rules. He then proposes an alternative scheme of rules that
would avoid the issues created by same sex marriage laws.

8. In *In re Lewis*, 415 S.E.2d 173 (Ga. 1992), the Georgia Supreme Court
suspended a lawyer from practice for three years even though his sexual relationship with his divorce client was uncoerced, did not adversely affect his representa-

tion, and predated the representation. The court held that the lawyer's professional judgment could or might reasonably have been affected by the relationship: "Every lawyer must know that an extramarital relationship can jeopardize every aspect of a client's matrimonial case — extending to forfeiture of alimony, loss of custody, and denial of attorney fees." Two years later, the same court, in *Tante v. Herring*, 453 S.E.2d 686 (Ga. 1994), decided that the lawyer's adulterous relationship with his client may have been a violation of legal ethics, but "a satisfactory result . . . by necessity precludes a claim for legal malpractice." However, the court sustained the client's claim for breach of fiduciary duty, since this claim included the allegation that the lawyer had misused confidences about the client's medical and emotional condition to persuade her to engage in a sexual relationship. The court noted it might have taken a stronger pro-client stance had the matter been a divorce case.

9. Compare the *Tante* case with *In re Ashy*, 721 So. 2d 859 (La. 1998) which dealt with a client in a criminal matter. There, the Court recognized that some individuals could be particularly susceptible to unacceptable sexual advances by their attorney when pressured by a criminal investigation. A satisfactory result should not be considered.

10. *In re Maternowski*, 674 N.E.3d 1287 (Ind. 1996), presents an interesting twist on the potential conflict caused by a lawyer's personal principles. Two criminal defense lawyers had long taken the position, as a policy matter, not to represent clients who cooperate with the government. They nevertheless continued to represent a client who was indecisive about whether he wanted to cooperate with the authorities. This continued representation, in the face of their stated beliefs, coupled with the fact that their fees were being paid by third parties who were alleged accomplices of the defendant, resulted in the two lawyers being suspended from practice for 30 days for having a personal conflict of interest with their client that could interfere with their ability to exercise independent professional judgment.

11. Christopher L. Colclasure, Denise W. Kennedy & Stephen G. Masciocchia, *Climate Change and Positional Conflicts of Interest*, 40 THE COLORADO LAWYER (October 2011). This article reviews positional conflicts — those that arise when a lawyer asserts a legal or factual position that is or may be adverse to a client in an unrelated matter — in the context of climate change, an area of law where lawyers need to be particularly aware of the potential for conflict between positions taken for different clients.

12. Note, *The Plaintiff As Person: Cause Lawyering, Human Subject Research, and the Secret Agent Problem*, 119 HARV. L. REV. 1510 (2006), describes the "cause lawyer's" conflicts of interest between advocating for the client in the traditional sense and advocating for the principled cause. The author presents a middle ground approach where the lawyer advocates primarily for the client, discloses any potential conflicts of interest arising from the cause for which the lawyer is advocating, and allows the client to make an informed decision mindful of the risks and benefits of representation by a lawyer who focuses on a cause.

PROBLEM 10: LOYALTY, IMPUTATION, AND THE BUSINESS OF BEING A PROFESSION

A. INTRODUCTION

Thus far, we have framed the loyalty issues in this chapter in terms of a single lawyer representing more than one client. But life in the legal fast lane is rarely that simple. Most lawyers work as part of a law firm, many in megafirms of increasing size and complexity. And, as we saw in our examination of organizational clients, relationships between lawyers and clients can be far more complex than a simple one-on-one.

During the last quarter century the old patterns of law practice have changed dramatically. The legal market place has a fluidity that has increased exponentially. Law firms expand and diversify by merging or acquiring whole practice sections of other firms. "Lateral transfers" move from one firm to another. These partners or senior associates bring "books of business" — that is, their own stable of clients when they change firms. Many law conglomerates have grown to over 1000 lawyers in cities across the country and around the globe.

These developments create increasingly complex issues for both lawyers and clients. Nowhere is this more clearly manifested than in the explosion of litigated motions to disqualify law firms, and the backlash by those firms as they attempt to limit such motions. The issues center not just on traditional notions of client loyalty but on the fact that an individual lawyer's representation of a client has long been "imputed" to the entire firm, in order (for example) to preserve confidentiality within the four walls of the firm. But today, with "four walls" often more figurative than a physical reality, the question has become to what extent loyalty — and thus disqualifying conflicts of interest — must also be imputed to the firm.

An enormous body of case law and much recent proposed rule-making is devoted to these issues. This is an area of the law currently in great flux. This problem explores from a variety of angles the modern realities of the duty of loyalty owed by a *law firm*.

B. PROBLEM

I

Meeker, Reynolds, and Stearns began as an intellectual property law "boutique" that catered to high tech and other start-up companies. But the downturn in dot.coms led to the loss of some of Meeker, Reynolds' biggest clients and a slowdown in new business. The partners eventually decided to expand into other areas, including real estate litigation. They have had some serious discussions about merging with ten to twelve lawyers from the litigation department of Burton & Barrows across town.

Talks between Meeker, Reynolds, and Burton & Barrows litigators heat up. Before their firm's monthly partnership meeting, Leonard Meeker and Elizabeth

Reynolds meet to discuss presenting their expansion proposal to the firm.

"Beth," says Meeker, "I just learned that B&B has sued Royster Homes on behalf of Hoosier Trust over that joint venture agreement with Royster a few years ago. Their guy Pete Markovich is taking the case with him when he comes over here. Didn't we represent Royster on its initial public offering just before it entered into that joint venture?"

"Yeah, we did, Len," says Reynolds. "In fact, we had to learn about Royster's assets, its earning potential, its board of directors, everything. They had to pass muster with the SEC, and we had to arrange with Arbenz Accounting to get their books in order. It was quite a job, and we earned quite a fee. Does that give us a conflict with the B&B litigators?

"I don't know, Beth," replies Meeker. "Not everyone who worked on the case would be joining our firm. Besides, we only represented Royster in its IPO. Isn't that OK? I mean, putting together an IPO has nothing to do with a lawsuit over a joint venture agreement. Right?"

"Maybe so, Len," concludes Reynolds, "but we'd better check it out before we pitch our partners on this deal."

QUESTIONS

1. If Meeker, Reynolds absorbs the Burton & Barrows litigators, will any conflict exist if their new partners continue to represent Hoosier in its lawsuit against Royster? Does Meeker, Reynolds have confidential information about Royster Homes that would be of use to Hoosier in its lawsuit against Royster? Does that make a difference?

2. Does it matter whether Meeker, Reynolds is continuing to represent Royster on other intellectual property and securities matters unrelated to the lawsuit? Why or why not?

II

At the partnership meeting Meeker and Reynolds inform the other members of the firm about the merger details and their would-be new partners' potentially troublesome representation of Hoosier in the lawsuit against Royster. Ed Stearns suggests that the firm simply set up an ethical wall around the litigators in the Hoosier/Royster lawsuit. " 'Screening' is done all the time these days. Can't we do it here?"

QUESTIONS

1. Can the new lateral transfers to Meeker, Reynolds continue to represent Hoosier if Royster moves to disqualify them?

2. If Meeker, Reynolds establishes an ethical screen, what would it look like?

3. Assume that Royster moves to disqualify the former Burton & Barrows attorneys from representing Hoosier. Should Royster prevail, or will the screen surrounding the former B&B attorneys be sufficient to allow them to continue representing Hoosier? If the former B&B attorneys are disqualified, should the disqualification apply to the entire Meeker, Reynolds firm?

C. READINGS

1. Conflicts, "Imputation," and Motions to Disqualify Counsel

What happens when a law firm has lawyers representing conflicting interests? And what happens when lawyers move from firm to firm, or when two firms merge? A few ethics rules address the conduct of lawyers as members of firms, including ABA Model Rules 1.7, 1.9, and 1.10. These rules have undergone some substantial recent changes, especially MR 1.10, that focus more directly on law firms. But generally speaking, at least formalistically, "disciplinary rules" are designed to punish individual lawyers, not law firms.[1]

In the following pages, we will examine how each individual lawyer's representations are "imputed" to, or adopted by, that attorney's law firm, and what standards are used in determining whether law firms may engage in those representations when loyalty issues arise. No problem discussed in this book is more complex. We begin with the simplest situation in which a law firm has two clients in the same matter. The scenarios in Problem 7 exemplify these situations; these issues may be resolved by obtaining client consent, and indeed, this is the way law *firms* must also resolve such conflicts. No other mechanism works.

But what happens when one member of a law *firm* represents X in a lawsuit against Y, while another member of that same firm currently represents Y in another venue in an entirely unrelated matter? When the conflict is *concurrent*, courts and ethics rules almost uniformly forbid this.[2]

The reasons for this rationale are threefold. First, because confidences and access to information are shared within law firms, with cases often discussed and worked on in teams, that firm is considered like a single entity for purposes of confidentiality. Second, the single-entity concept acknowledges that financial interests are shared by firm members. Thus, when a single lawyer represents a client, that representation — and the duty of loyalty — is "imputed" to the entire firm, and it is the entire firm that is considered to be the client's "lawyer." Put another way, the question of whether a law firm may represent X and Y becomes almost identical to whether an individual attorney may do it, all other things being the same (which they are not, as we shall soon see).

---

[1] In 1993, the Committee on Professional Responsibility of the Association of the Bar of the City of New York published a report recommending that New York State's disciplinary rules be revised to permit disciplining law firms. This controversial report has not spawned a vast movement. While there are Sarbanes-Oxley and other newer regulations open more avenues for such discipline, ethical sanctions are rare. Thus, our focus on the most common sanction — disqualification.

[2] The lone exception is Texas, which under its Rule 1.06(b) *allows* a law firm to represent client X against current client Y if the X v. Y representation is not related to the firm's other representation of Y. Texas thus applies the ABA *former client* test, see *infra*, section 4 ff., to *current* clients.

The third part of the analysis is whether the clients — usually the issue is with Y, the firm's client who is also adverse in *X v. Y* — are willing to consent. To the extent ethics rules prohibit a lawyer from representing one client in a matter directly adverse to another current client without both clients' consents, the same is true of law firms regardless of whether there is a relationship between the two matters. Where consent is given, the representation may continue. Where it is not, the next step is ending at least one representation and sometimes both.

A law firm's conflict of interest may be addressed in an after-the-fact malpractice lawsuit, but in actual practice the issue is most often joined in a motion to disqualify counsel. Motions to disqualify have become so common that many firms argue they are not really ethical matters, but legal and tactical ones. Indeed, an enormous body of case law has developed setting standards and tests for disqualification, and the issue of whether the motion to disqualify is a litigation tactic rather than an issue of loyalty arises frequently. Still, no matter how much a law firm might want to avoid it, at the heart of the matter is the basic issue of conflicts of interest. Keep this in mind as we examine loyalty issues through several motions to disqualify.

First, we go to the Second Circuit Court of Appeals, which developed a substantial body of law on this and related issues in the 1950s through 1980s. Posit a large law firm with several offices, two lawyers who have nothing to do with each other, and two clients, each represented by one of the lawyers, who also have nothing at all to do with each other. Why shouldn't the representations of each client be allowed? The Second Circuit answered that question in *Cinema 5, Ltd. v. Cinerama, Inc.* In *Cinema 5*, a New York City law firm was disqualified from representing Cinema 5 against Cinerama because one of its partners, Fleischmann, was also a partner in a separate Buffalo firm which was already representing Cinerama in another matter. Even though two law firms were involved, the only common thread being attorney Fleischmann, the court treated the two firms as one, and upheld the disqualification of the New York City firm. The reason was not the relationship between the two cases, but the right of each client to the undivided loyalty of its attorney.

CINEMA 5, LTD. v. CINERAMA, INC.
528 F.2d 1384 (2d Cir. 1976)

One firm in which attorney Fleischmann is a partner is suing an actively represented client of another firm in which attorney Fleischmann is a partner. The propriety of this conduct must be measured not so much against the similarities in litigation, as against the duty of undivided loyalty which an attorney owes to each of his clients . . . . Cinerama . . . was entitled to feel that at least until that litigation was at an end, it had [Fleischmann's] undivided loyalty as its advocate and champion . . . and could rely upon his "undivided allegiance and faithful, devoted service. . . ." Needless to say, when Mr. Fleischmann and his New York City partners undertook to represent Cinema 5, Ltd., they owed it the same fiduciary duty of undivided loyalty and allegiance. . . . [T]he professional judgment of a lawyer must be exercised solely for the benefit of his client, free of compromising influences and loyalties, and this precludes his acceptance of employment that will adversely affect his judgment or dilute his loyalty.

[T]he lawyer who would sue his own client, asserting in justification the lack of "substantial relationship" between the litigation and the work he has undertaken to perform for that client, is leaning on a slender reed indeed. Putting it as mildly as we can, we think it would be questionable conduct for an attorney to participate in any lawsuit against his own client.

Where the relationship is a continuing one, adverse representation is prima facie improper. . . . [S]o long as Mr. Fleischmann and his Buffalo partners continue to represent Cinerama, he and his New York City partners should not represent Cinema 5, Ltd. in this litigation.

NOTES

Cinema 5 is a case that stands in strong opposition to bending the rule prohibiting law firm conflicts. Thus, a conflict can't be cured by screening off the offending lawyer, creating an "ethical wall," a "firewall," or "cone of silence"[3] around one attorney so that no confidences or secrets are revealed or received. Note the repeated reference to "Mr. Fleishman *and his partners*," because the whole law firm is in play. According to *Westinghouse v. Kerr-McGee Corp.*, 580 F.2d 1311 (7th Cir. 1978), this is true even where a national law firm had offices in different cities, and representation was indirect through a trade association.

The *Cinema 5* court holds that the lack of a "substantial relationship" between the two cases is no justification for dual representation. The phrase "substantial relationship" is a term of art that developed to help evaluate when a lawyer or law firm may sue a *former* client, which we will address presently.

2. The "Hot Potato" Doctrine

What if a law firm tries to avoid a direct conflict of interest by withdrawing from representing the less interesting (or less lucrative) client? Suppose X wants the law firm to sue Y, and Y is a minor client of the firm in an unrelated case. May the firm withdraw its representation of Y in order to take X's case? According to several courts, the answer in these so-called "hot potato" cases is "no." Thus, in *Truck Ins. Exch. v. Fireman's Fund Ins.*, 6 Cal. App. 4th 1050, 8 Cal. Rptr. 2d 228 (1992), Oakland's then-largest law firm, Crosby, Heafey, Roach & May, wanted to represent Truck Insurance, a major client, against Fireman's Fund, but already represented Fireman's Fund on a small matter. Crosby asked for consent, but Fireman's Fund refused. The firm then dropped Fireman's Fund as a client and undertook the representation of Truck against Fireman's Fund. The court had little difficulty in disqualifying Crosby.

The "hot potato" doctrine is now almost universally applied by courts. These legal finesses often occur because of the pressure on large firms caused by the mobility of today's modern lawyer. When firms merge or take on additional "lateral hires," these problems are common.

---

[3] We prefer to avoid the now appropriately discredited term "Chinese wall."

Thus, in *Picker Int'l, Inc. v. Varian Assocs.*, 869 F.2d 578 (Fed. Cir. 1989), the firms of Jones, Day, Reavis & Pogue and McDougall, Hersh & Scott merged. At the time of the merger, Jones, Day was representing long-time client Picker in a suit against Varian. Varian was a client of the McDougall firm in unrelated matters. McDougall asked Varian for consent to have Jones, Day continue to represent Picker after the merger, but Varian refused. At that point, McDougall purported to withdraw as Varian's counsel, just before the merger. The court rejected this withdrawal on the same grounds as if only one law firm were involved, and instead required Jones, Day to withdraw as Picker's counsel. *Picker* reaffirms the idea that a law firm cannot drop a client like a "hot potato," even where a major merger is at stake. The same holds true for lateral hires.

3. Lawyer Mobility and Client Loyalty

Another slightly more complicated situation occurs when a law firm finds itself with a conflict of interest through a merger or lateral hire and tries to "screen off" the new lawyer(s) from any involvement in order to retain its ongoing client. What should happen then? The Montana Supreme Court's opines:

KRUTZFELDT RANCH, LLC v. PINNACLE BANK
272 P 3d 635 (Mont. 2012)

JUSTICE BETH BAKER delivered the [Unanimous] Opinion of the Court.

Appellants Krutzfeldt Ranch, LLC, William Krutzfeldt, and Julie Krutzfeldt appeal the Thirteenth Judicial District Court's order denying their motion to disqualify and to permanently enjoin the Crowley Fleck law firm from representing Appellee Pinnacle Bank in this action. We reverse.

PROCEDURAL AND FACTUAL BACKGROUND

In June 2008, the Krutzfeldts and Pinnacle Bank entered a loan agreement in which the Bank agreed to lend the Krutzfeldts $5 million to develop a subdivision in Billings, Montana. Pinnacle Bank retained the Crowley Fleck law firm ("Crowley") to represent it in connection with the transaction. In August 2009, Pinnacle Bank refused to disburse further funds under the loan, asserting the Krutzfeldts had not satisfied certain obligations under the agreement. In February 2010, the Krutzfeldts, represented by Don Harris, sued Pinnacle Bank . . . . Crowley continued to represent Pinnacle Bank in the litigation.

In June 2010, Harris retained attorney Lance Hoskins of Brekke & Hoskins, PLLC, to advise Harris and the Krutzfeldts . . . . Harris stated that Hoskins's involvement in that matter, while dormant for intermittent and lengthy periods, ultimately extended over several years of litigation.

Prior to retaining Hoskins in the Krutzfeldts' suit, Harris informed Hoskins that Pinnacle Bank was represented in the litigation by Jeff Oven of Crowley . . . . On July 13, 2010, Hoskins sent Harris an e-mail that addressed liability issues and indicated Hoskins had conducted some preliminary research on the tax issues.

Hoskins stated, "I have some theories that may have some merit after further research. I hate to scorch the earth yet. Let's talk via phone or in person."

On July 19, 2010, Harris and Mr. Krutzfeldt met with Hoskins and discussed the liability claims, defenses, damages, settlement options, and the results of Hoskins's initial tax research. On July 21, 2010, Hoskins sent Harris an engagement letter which set forth the terms of Hoskins's work. The document appeared to be a standard engagement form and indicated the continuing nature of Hoskins's involvement in this matter:

> Thank you for asking Brekke & Hoskins PLLC (the "Firm") to represent and advise your firm regarding income tax issues for Butch Krutzfeldt discussed below . . . .
>
> *Services.* Our engagement is to assist your firm in reviewing income tax issues related to Butch Krutzfeldt's lawsuit against Pinnacle Bank and for such other matters as are agreed to in the future . . . .

Although not offered into evidence, the parties agreed the letter was sent with a bill of $2,375.00 for Hoskins's services thus far in the Krutzfeldt case. Both parties acknowledged the document did not say "final bill" or otherwise indicate Hoskins had completed his services in the matter.

On December 20, 2010, the parties conducted a settlement conference. Harris called Hoskins more than once the week before the conference and left a message informing Hoskins his help would be necessary if the parties neared resolution of the lawsuit. Hoskins did not return the call.

On January 5, 2011, Harris received a "Dear Client" letter from Brekke & Hoskins announcing that the two partners had joined Crowley effective January 1, 2011. . . . Harris sent Oven an e-mail stating the conflict could not and would not be consented to or waived, and Crowley thus would need to withdraw as counsel for Pinnacle Bank . . . . Crowley responded by letter that same day, stating, "[p]ursuant to Rule 1.10(c), we have established an ethical screen" to prevent both Hoskins and Brekke from having any involvement in the Krutzfeldt case or receiving any fee earned by the firm in that matter.

On January 14, 2011, the Krutzfeldts moved to disqualify Crowley from representing Pinnacle Bank . . . . Crowley opposed the motion on the ground that, when Brekke and Hoskins moved to Crowley on January 1, 2011, all of their clients, including the Krutzfeldts, became "former clients" governed by M.R. Pro. C. 1.9. The trial court heard argument on the matter and subsequently denied the Krutzfeldts' motion . . . . The Krutzfeldts appeal . . . .

DISCUSSION

Application of the Rules of Professional Conduct in this case turns on whether the Krutzfeldts were current or former clients of Hoskins at the time he joined Crowley. [While Montana ethics rule 1.10(c)] prohibits a lawyer from representing an adverse party against a former client, the lawyer's disqualification is not imputed to other members of the firm if . . . the personally disqualified lawyer is timely screened from any participation in the matter and is apportioned no part of the fee therefrom . . . . Since the District Court found the Krutzfeldts were former clients, it concluded Crowley's screen of Hoskins and Brekke satisfied the Rule.

Crowley argued in the District Court that the Krutzfeldts were former clients because all of Hoskins's current clients necessarily became former clients when Hoskins joined Crowley. The District Court rejected this contention, [and we] agree. The attorney-client relationship is not automatically terminated when a lawyer joins another firm. . . . An attorney "cannot avoid the automatic disqualification rule applicable to concurrent representation by unilaterally converting a present client into a former client prior to the hearing on the motion for disqualification." *State Farm Mut. Auto. Ins. Co. v. Fed. Ins. Co.*, 72 Cal. App. 4th 1422, 1431, 86 Cal. Rptr. 2d 20 (1999) . . . .

The critical fact here is that . . . . Hoskins did not withdraw from his representation of the Krutzfeldts prior to accepting his new position. . . . The "Dear Client" letter gave no indication the Krutzfeldts were no longer Hoskins's client. To the contrary, the letter contemplated future legal services: "We feel we will be more responsive and efficient to your needs and the ever changing tax and regulatory world by utilizing the resources that Crowley Fleck has to offer." . . . In the absence of any affirmative steps by Hoskins prior to his transition, if the Krutzfeldts were Hoskins's current clients on December 31, 2010, they remained in an attorney-client relationship at the time he signed on as a member of the Crowley team.

[W]e conclude Hoskins had a concurrent conflict of interest at the time he took the job with Crowley. After the July 19 meeting, Hoskins sent Harris a formal engagement letter indicating the prospective nature of his services. Hoskins's bill for his services did not indicate it was a "final" bill, nor did he take any steps to conclude his relationship with the Krutzfeldts. That he was not consulted for the next several months was simply a matter of timing. Following Harris's call to advise Hoskins of the upcoming settlement conference, Hoskins did nothing until sending Harris the form letter . . . . At no time did Hoskins advise Harris of any notice or intent to withdraw as counsel . . . .

Crowley makes much of the fact that Hoskins had only a limited involvement in the Krutzfeldt matter. It points out that Hoskins did not participate in many important stages of the litigation, including an argument on a motion for summary judgment, the depositions of critical witnesses, and a settlement conference. We find this distinction irrelevant. Hoskins had been retained for a limited purpose, as stated in his engagement letter . . . . An attorney's duty to his client, however, is not dependent on the purpose for which he has been engaged . . . . His limited specific role in the case does not diminish his professional obligations to the Krutzfeldts.

. . . .

The Krutzfeldts have made a sufficient showing of prejudice in this case. They lost the time and money they invested in Hoskins. They lost their trial date because Hoskins's abrupt move rendered them without expert assistance just weeks before trial and prompted the need for their motion to disqualify. Without prior notice of Hoskins's move, they did not have an opportunity to elect to seek new tax counsel or to determine how to address the impending conflict. Aside from these setbacks, the Krutzfeldts assert the most damaging loss was that of their attorney's loyalty. They argue that to ignore a lawyer's duty of loyalty in this case effectively would sanction the opportunistic hiring of an adverse party's attorney to weaken and derail the adverse party's claim against the hiring client.

So inviolate is the duty of loyalty to an existing client that not even by withdrawing from the relationship can an attorney evade it. . . . Nor does it matter that the intention and motives of the attorney are honest. The rule is designed not alone to prevent the dishonest practitioner from fraudulent conduct, but as well to preclude the honest practitioner from putting himself in a position where he may be required to choose between conflicting duties, or be led to attempt to reconcile conflicting interests, rather than to enforce to their full extent the rights of the interest which he should alone represent.

In addition to the dangers posed to clients, allowing attorneys to switch sides in the middle of litigation threatens the public's trust in the legal profession . . . . When lack of observance leads to breach of the duty of loyalty and resulting prejudice, disqualification is required.

We acknowledge that disqualification has a significant effect on litigation and should be imposed sparingly. Disqualification burdens the judicial system with delays and it burdens the party that must retain and reeducate new counsel in the proceedings . . . . [However,] there is no course short of disqualifying Crowley which would respect Hoskins's duty of loyalty to the Krutzfeldts. Disciplinary action, which occurs subsequent to the violation and resulting harm, is an inadequate remedy for a party who, like the Krutzfeldts, had no prior notice and acted diligently under the circumstances.

Crowley nonetheless asserts the prejudice to the Krutzfeldts, if any, is minimal compared to Pinnacle Bank losing Crowley as counsel. The hardship to Crowley's existing client is most regrettable, particularly since it could have been avoided. However, once it is determined that Rule 1.7 applies, the Rules do not contemplate a balancing of hardships. "Rule 1.10 imposes imputed disqualification automatically . . . without requiring any showing of either actual leakage or even actual access to confidential information; these are conclusively presumed." [Cites] Forcing a client to resort to the courts when the Rules compel withdrawal of counsel only adds to the client's litigation costs, increases delay in the proceedings, and furthers dissatisfaction with the profession and the system of justice.

NOTES

In *Krutzfeldt*, the *concurrent* nature of Hoskins' conflict meant that screening him at the new firm was unavailable as a remedy. This, as the court noted, was a matter of "inviolate" loyalty. But is the same duty, or the same degree of loyalty, owed to *former* clients when a lawyer migrates to a new firm? What is the "substantial relationship" test, and how does it relate to confidentiality and loyalty? What is "screening," and how do "ethical screens" work?

Before we jump into these important questions, let's examine for a moment the underlying realities that cause these issues to be so hotly debated and widely litigated. Clients want, perhaps above anything else, their lawyer's undivided loyalty — to know that their lawyers are watching their backs. But many law firms increasingly want to act like other business institutions, a desire they must counterbalance against their professional and fiduciary duties. Firms don't want to be limited in their client bases by what many see as an over-inflated sense of loyalty. And they want to be able to merge together, to take on "free agent" lawyers and grow, much as other businesses do. They want to act unhampered by what they see as residual vestiges of loyalty to long-gone clients. It is this tension between the loyalty that clients want and the business that law firms want to develop that has fueled this area of law.

4. Former Representations and the "Substantial Relationship" Test

What happens where a law firm wants to take on representation that is adverse not to a current client, but to a *former* one? The standards used in both ethics rules and case law are significantly different from the almost blanket prohibitions that have traditionally applied to current clients. The threshold test is commonly called the "substantial relationship" test: that is, is there a substantial relationship between the subject matter of the current representation ($X v. Y$) and the former engagement (involving ex-client Y)? In most jurisdictions, if the answer is yes, it is presumed that the law firm received confidential information *from* the former client that is material to the current case *against* that former client. The test was first articulated in *T.C. Theatre Corp. v. Warner Bros. Pictures, Inc.*, 113 F. Supp. 265, 268–69 (S.D.N.Y. 1953), and has been used in countless cases since. A line of Second Circuit cases refined the test, which also became embodied in ABA Model Rule 1.9, and interpreted at length in the Comment to that rule. The purposes of the test are to assure attorney loyalty and protect confidentiality, while still allowing clients counsel of choice when possible. As Judge Weinfeld wrote in *T.C. Theatre*, "a lawyer's duty of absolute loyalty to his client's interests does not end with his retainer." Moreover, the lawyer has the continuing obligation to preserve the client's confidences and secrets *after* the representation. The presumption that the lawyer received material confidences avoids making the former client state its case for disqualification by revealing the very confidence it told its former lawyer and doesn't want used.

While the substantial relationship test may sound simple on the surface, in its application it is anything but. Among the questions raised about this test are these:

• *What constitutes a former client?* Is an actual case necessary? Is it sufficient that the client consulted the lawyer even if counsel was never retained? We already have seen in *Krutzfeldt* and the "hot potato" cases that a lawyer can't make a client "former" by dropping the client or switching firms.

• *What does "matter" mean?* Is it required that the "matter" be litigation? How about a lawyer who represents one client against a former client in a business negotiation? Or an attorney who provides ongoing business advice to a company that is a competitor of the former client? The weight of authority does not limit "matter," although whether the matter is in litigation may make some difference in the analysis as to confidentiality, as we'll see in a moment.

• *What constitutes "adversity"?* Is "adversity" limited to direct representation of one client against the former client, or can the "adverse" relationship be more subtle or indirect? Courts have disagreed broadly on this question. Some cases have interpreted the term literally, while others have held that "adverse" can mean "differing" or even "not exactly aligned."[4]

• *What constitutes a "substantial relationship" between the current and former representations?* This is the very core of the test. It is subject to the most analysis and scrutiny by the courts, but at the same time remains the most difficult concept to define. Some courts look to the facts of each representation. Others examine the common legal issues. A few courts seem, strangely, to invert the presumption about confidences by arguing that a substantial relationship turns on whether the lawyer has obtained confidential information that can be used against the former client.

A number of cases decided under California law illustrate some of the more nuanced issues. In *Trone v. Smith*, 621 F.2d 994 (9th Cir. 1980), the first review of the test applying California law, the court concluded that among the determining factors in finding a substantial relationship was the knowledge the lawyer had gained of the "policies, practices and procedures" of the former client. To many, this seemed to make sense. After all, shouldn't a court's inquiry focus on whether the attorney has learned *anything* that could be used against the former client? What could be more useful than "inside" knowledge about how the former client thinks — how litigation decisions are made, or settlement postures are taken?

However, a decade later, *H. F. Ahmanson & Co. v. Salomon Bros., Inc.*, 229 Cal. App. 3d. 1445 (1991), developed an oft-cited and somewhat more limited three-part test relating more directly to the underlying facts of the two cases: (1) whether the cases are similar factually; (2) whether they are similar legally; and (3) the extent of the lawyer's involvement.

More recent California cases seem to have broadened the *Ahmanson* test. In *Jessen v. Hartford Casualty Insurance Co.*, 111 Cal. App. 4th 698 (2003), the court held that if the former representation "placed the attorney with respect to the prior client" in a "direct and personal" relationship, the third *Ahmanson* factor was determined as a matter of law, and "the only remaining question is whether there is a connection between the two successive representations. . . ." Then, in *Farris v. Fireman's Fund Insurance Co.*, 119 Cal. App. 4th 671 (2004), an insurance company sought to disqualify a law firm prosecuting a bad faith case against it because former coverage counsel for the insurer now worked for the plaintiff's firm. *Farris* discussed *Jessen* and *Ahmanson* at length, cited *Trone v. Smith* with approval, and disqualified the lawyer despite acknowledging that "the services [in the two cases] are distinct."

• *"Playbooks" and "poker tells."* Some commentators criticized *Jessen* and *Farris* as they had *Trone* — for advocating the generally disfavored "playbook" approach to former client relationships. As ABA Formal Opinion 99-415 put it, a lawyer's general knowledge of the strategies, policies, or personnel of the former employer, without more, is not enough to establish a substantial relationship. *See also* the Restatement Third of the Law Governing Lawyers, § 132. But the *Farris*

---

[4] *See* In re Blinder, Robinson & Co., 123 B.R. 900 (Bankr. Colo. 1991).

court argued strongly that *Jessen* was not a "playbook" case, because it "mandates that the information acquired during the first representation be . . . directly at issue in, or have some critical importance to, the second representation." *Farris* cites favorably the portion of the Restatement § 132 that states that if a lawyer performed work and "there is a substantial risk that [the present representation] will involve the use of information acquired" while doing that first work, a substantial relationship exists.

What about "poker tells"? All good lawyers know that the more personal the knowledge — how to "push the client's buttons," or the personal idiosyncrasies of the client, such as what it means when the client scowls, or giggles, in deposition, or even more significant, how the client rubs her nose when she's telling less than the whole truth — the more valuable that knowledge is. If the idea behind the substantial relationship test is truly to avoid harm to the former client, these factors are crucial ones. Do they amount to the kinds of information that is barred by the case law discussed above, or by the Restatement? At this juncture, despite the substantial body of law on this issue, the answer is less than clear, though several courts have ordered disqualification in similar circumstances.

• *The presumption of confidentiality.* If there exists a substantial relationship, the next element of the test is the presumption that the attorney received confidences from the former client. While jurisdictions generally agree on this presumption, they disagree as to whether it may be rebutted. The Restatement (Third) of the Law Governing Lawyers, § 132, Comment (d)(iii), for example, states that "when the prior matter involved litigation, it will be conclusively presumed that the lawyer obtained confidential information," but non-litigated matters should be considered case by case.

A second issue is what is meant by "confidentiality"? Does it include those things we have sometimes referred to as "secrets," matters the lawyer learns about the client during the course of the representation? Under the *Trone, Jessen,* and *Farris* cases, the answer is clearly "yes."

5. So What About Loyalty?

Although the substantial relationship test discusses confidences extensively, the significance of loyalty may not be immediately apparent. Nevertheless, the concept of loyalty forms the underlying basis of the test. Thus, ABA Model Rule 1.9 on former clients states that "the client previously represented . . . must be reasonably assured that the principle of loyalty to the client is not compromised."

Several cases also turn on the issue of loyalty. Thus, in *Casco Northern Bank v. JBI Associates, Ltd.*, 667 A.2d 856 (Me. 1995), actual transmission of confidential information was not required to disqualify a firm once a substantial relationship between past and present representations had been established. The Maine Supreme Court disqualified an attorney for a limited partnership in litigation against a general partner whom the attorney had previously represented in setting up the partnership. The court held that even if the former client had no reasonable expectation that the information the lawyer received was confidential; the client still had a reasonable expectation of *loyalty.* Here's how another court put it:

[W]e adhere to our precedents in refusing to reduce the concerns underlying the substantial relationship test to a client's interest in preserving his
confidential information. The second fundamental concern protected by the
test is . . . the client's interest in the loyalty of his attorney.[5]

Trone, Jessen, and *Farris* all point generally to "information acquired" during
the representation as sufficient to create a substantial relationship. These cases all
"sound" in loyalty as much as confidentiality. Similarly, in *Cardona v. General
Motors Corp.,* 942 F. Supp. 968 (D.N.J. 1996), GM claimed that a lawyer who had
defended many "lemon law" cases for GM could not join a plaintiffs' lemon law firm
adverse to GM even if there was no similarity between the facts of the cases. GM
argued that the lawyer's new job involved a breach of loyalty. The court agreed: "At
the heart of every 'side-switching attorney' case is the suspicion that by changing
sides, the attorney has breached a duty of fidelity and loyalty to a former client, a
client who had freely shared with the attorney secrets and confidences with the
expectation that they would be disclosed to no one else." Id. at 975. The court thus
directly tied together loyalty and the concept of client "secrets."

6. Migrating Lawyers, Imputation, and the Substantial Relationship Test

The most difficult issues regarding the substantial relationship doctrine arise
when more than one law firm is involved and the analysis must consider the
"migrating" lawyer, an issue we are now ready to address. Assume that Lawyer L
is moving from Firm A to Firm B, that Firm A used to represent X, and that Firm
B is currently adverse to X in the case of X v. Y. We again take this step by step.

• *Is there a substantial relationship?* If there is no substantial relationship
between Firm A's representation of X and the current matter of X v. Y —
remember that this issue will likely to be fact-specific and depend on the
jurisdiction in which L is practicing — then Firm B will not be precluded from
taking on L or staying in the X v. Y case. If there is a substantial relationship, we
must address to what extent L's experience at Firm A results in a disabling conflict
of interest being imputed to Firm B upon L's arrival there.

• *Did the migrating lawyer receive material confidential information at the old
firm?* Here, in most jurisdictions, this is a *rebuttable* presumption as it relates to
the particular lawyer. That is, if L can show that s/he acquired no confidential
information about X at the old firm, L and firm B are in the clear, especially if L is
"screened off" from any involvement in that case, an issue we are getting closer to
discussing. Most jurisdictions now follow the Second Circuit's materiality standard,
first articulated in *Silver Chrysler Plymouth, Inc. v. Chrysler Motors Corp.,* 518
F.2d 751 (2d Cir. 1975), an older but oft-cited case from the court that developed
the substantial relationship test, that a lawyer who performed only minimal tasks
and who never shared in any of the former client's confidences would not be
presumed to have acquired those confidences:

---

[5] In re American Airlines, Inc., 972 F.2d 605, 616 (5th Cir. 1992).

[T]here is reason to differentiate for disqualification purposes between lawyers who become heavily involved in the facts of a particular matter and those who enter briefly on the periphery for a limited and specific purpose relating solely to legal questions. . . . Under the latter circumstances the attorney's role cannot be considered "representation" within the meaning of *T.C. Theatre Corp.*

This was a relatively new concept when *Silver Chrysler* was decided. Now, ABA Model Rule 1.9 lends support to this position, distinguishing between whether *the lawyer* or only the lawyer's *former firm* received material confidential information from the old firm's client. The Model Rule 1.9 comments discuss this liberalized rule and the competing interests involved when lawyers migrate from one firm to another, including the business realities of modern law firm mobility.

• *Must confidences be imputed to the lawyer's new firm?* Once it has been determined that the migrating lawyer has (or is presumed to have) confidential information from the former client of the old law firm, the next question is whether the receipt of that information is now imputed to the lawyer's new firm. Fifteen years ago, almost all jurisdictions held that there was an *irrebuttable* presumption that the new firm was tainted with the former client's confidential information.

This presumption had a great deal to do with the duty of loyalty. Migrating lawyer L may have *formerly* felt a strong duty of loyalty to X, the old client. But now, at the new firm, L is working with, hanging out with, and sharing profits with the lawyers at Firm B. And B represents Y, X's opponent, not X. It's natural for L to feel a great deal of pressure — business, financial, and simply collegial — to help the new firm and *its* clients, to whom L will now develop loyalty.

Look at it from the former client's perspective. Why should the former client trust that its former lawyer will remain silent at the new firm? And why should client X trust that Firm B, *the very law firm opposing it*, will refrain from tapping into L's information? When it comes to lawyers who claim only "peripheral" involvement at the old firm, how does the client know that L had not actually been more involved, and had received confidences and secrets? By trusting L? Clearly not.

The District of Columbia bar has twice taken the former client's point of view. First, in Opinion 212 (1990), it held that a law firm must be disqualified unless *all* lawyers who worked on the former client's matter have left the firm, and no remaining lawyer has ever received confidences about the matter. Then, the D.C. bar amended its version of Model Rule 1.10(b) to require imputed law firm disqualification when there is *either* (rather than both) a substantially related matter *or* any remaining lawyer who had material confidential information.

The Nebraska Supreme Court has adopted a "bright line" rule of disqualification: If the lawyer's prior firm represented the former client in a way in which confidential information was transmitted to that firm, then those confidences are imputed to all other lawyers of that firm, no matter how peripheral their participation in the former representation. *Creighton Univ. v. Hickman*, 245 Neb. 247, 512 N.W.2d 374 (1994). Indeed, here the disqualification related to a paralegal and her new law firm. Most jurisdictions, however, are more flexible than D.C. and Nebraska.

  • *How may a law firm rebut its receipt of confidential information?* Almost all jurisdictions still impute confidences to the new firm, B, and without more will generally disqualify new firm B from representing Y against X.[6] But in many jurisdictions, the presumption of imputation to the firm is no longer irrebuttable.[7]

And so we come at last to the principal rebuttal: screening, or creating "ethical walls" around the "tainted" lawyer. Outside of client consent or a broad, open-ended advance waiver (which we have discussed at length elsewhere), screening that shields the attorneys working on the case from receiving any information from the migrating attorney is the only way a law firm can both grow and take on otherwise conflicted business.

Not surprisingly, a great ongoing debate rages over whether such ethical walls or screens should be permitted, and how effective they will be. Courts, rules, and commentators are widely split on the issue.

7. Screening: A Brief History

When a former client's confidences are imputed to a lawyer who moves to another firm, does creating a wall around the lawyer — to prevent both the lawyer's involvement in the *new* case and the new firm finding out what the lawyer knows about the *old* case — sufficiently protect the former client's interests? A growing number of jurisdictions, while still in the minority, have approved some form of screening mechanism beyond those that historically have been afforded former government employees.

Under the old ABA Model Code, DR 5-105 supported the position now taken by the Nebraska "bright line" rule: No attorney can "switch sides" against a client, even if the lawyer switching sides personally had little or nothing to do with that client.

The first exception to this prohibition against screens was ABA Formal Opinion 342 (1975), which applied to former government attorneys. The old code provided that a lawyer should not accept employment in a matter for which "he had substantial responsibility while he was a public employee." The committee interpreted this rule liberally, noting weighty policy reasons why it should not be applied to broadly limit a lawyer's new employment after government service: The imposition of harsh restraints on future private practice would impair the government's ability to recruit attorneys. Subsequently, most jurisdictions that prohibited screening for private attorneys eventually accepted the government

---

[6] Disqualification will *not* always follow in the wake of a court finding a current conflict, if the court believes the conflict is almost over, only slight, or one that will not cause prejudice. For a list of what he calls these "no-harm-no-foul conflicts," see William Freivogel's excellent website www. Freivogelonconflicts.com.

[7] Many but not all. A fair number of states have maintained an irrebuttable presumption requiring disqualification (and not allowing screening) where the migrating lawyer had substantial involvement in the matter at the previous law firm. Among them: Arizona, Colorado, Massachusetts, Nevada, New Mexico, and Ohio. Other states have yet to determine exactly where they stand.

lawyer exception, now embodied in MR 1.11.

Not long after Opinion 342 was issued, various commentators and private firms began pushing for ethical screens for private attorneys who had changed firms. Soon, the Seventh Circuit took a broad stand in applying the substantial relationship test, but also fashioned a liberal screening test that allowed law firms to rebut the previously irrebuttable presumption of imputed confidences. *Schiessle v. Stephens*, 717 F.2d 417 (7th Cir. 1983) developed this test:

> [T]he presumption of shared confidences could be rebutted by demonstrating that "specific institutional mechanisms" . . . had been implemented to effectively insulate against any flow of confidential information from the "infected" attorney to any other member of his present firm. Such a determination can be based on objective and verifiable evidence presented to the trial court and must be made on a case-by-case basis. Factors appropriate for consideration by the trial court might include, but are not limited to, the size and structural divisions of the law firm involved, the likelihood of contact between the "infected" attorney and the specific attorneys responsible for the present representation, the existence of rules which prevent the "infected" attorney from access to relevant files or other information pertaining to the present litigation or which prevent him from sharing in the fees derived from such litigation.

Schiessle began as an outlier, but in the years since, screening has gained ground. An ABA Ethics 2000 Commission proposal liberalizing screening was defeated in the ABA's House of Delegates, but at during that same time, the American Law Institute approved a Restatement provision, § 124(2), that narrowly allowed for screening "when there is no substantial risk" of using confidential information against the former client. Three conjunctive prongs were necessary before the "no risk" test could be met: the unlikelihood that significant confidential information was known; "screening measures" that were "adequate"; and notice to all clients of the screen.

In February 2009, the ABA House narrowly passed (after a tie vote the previous summer) major modifications to MR 1.10 that allow for broad screening. The new rule requires that the "disqualified lawyer is timely screened from any participation" in the case, written notice is given to affected clients along with a description of the screening procedures, and "certifications of compliance" are provided the former client by both the screened lawyer and the lawyer's new firm.

Meanwhile, case law in some states has also moved towards more liberal screening. Thus, in *Kirk v. First American Title Ins. Co.*, 183 Cal. App. 4th 776 (2010), the California appellate court expressly found that the presumption of confidences imputed to a firm was now considered "rebuttable." The *Kirk* court set forth five general requirements:

> [(1)] physical, geographic, and departmental separation of attorneys; [(2)] prohibitions against and sanctions for discussing confidential matters; [(3)] established rules and procedures preventing access to confidential information and files; [(4)] procedures preventing a disqualified attorney from sharing in the profits from the representation; and [(5)] continuing

education in professional responsibility.

Id. at 810–11.

As this book goes to publication, it is still unclear to what extent the screening train has left the station. Clearly, the more screening and the less imputation the happier law firms will be. But client advocates continue to speak with strong voices on behalf of limited screening and greater imputation. Sometimes it seems that the two sides in this debate are talking past each other. Those arguing for a screen claim that no one has produced evidence that ethical walls have ever been breached; those arguing against screens claim there is no way for the former client to know if such breaches ever occurred, since the attorneys benefitting by such breaches would never voluntarily admit it, and because business pressure is so great that "peep holes" in the wall may occur without a conscious decision to cheat. As long-time ethics professor Thomas Morgan put it years ago and reiterates today, "no one outside a firm — indeed, often leadership inside a firm — can ever be sure what has transpired behind the law firm's closed doors."[8]

It seems that the only area of agreement between the two sides is that screening exists to promote the business of practicing law. Where the disagreement comes in is whether this is desirable and at what cost. If maximizing business opportunities for lawyers is more important than the principles of loyalty and client confidentiality, one must ask what possible interest the new firm has in protecting the tainted lawyer's former client, now the opposing party? Is it ever fair to ask the former client to trust the word of the tainted lawyer's new firm, now vigorously opposing the former client on the other side? Finally, is screening an idea whose genesis is in the reality of law as a business rather than a profession? Can ethical precepts and client obligations come first if screening is allowed?

Perhaps because of these questions, despite all the discussion about the implementation of ethical screens, and despite the reality of law as a big business, the number of jurisdictions allowing screening (except for government lawyers) has increased only modestly in recent years. The count is ever-changing.[9]

One final point: It remains unclear how the extent of screening changes will directly affect those cases that turn more directly on loyalty rather than confidences, such as *Casco, Cardona,* and the three California cases cited above. For example, the presumption now found rebuttable in *Kirk* with respect to confidences may not apply to the reasoning in *Jessen* and *Farris,* also relatively recent decisions. And another California case, *Stanley v. Richmond,* 35 Cal. App. 4th 1070 (1995) held that a lawyer in a domestic case who had entered into negotiations with opposing counsel to join him in a partnership could be liable in malpractice to her client for breaching the duty of *loyalty.*

---

[8] Thomas D. Morgan, *Screening the Disqualified Lawyer: The Wrong Solution to the Wrong Problem,* 10 U. OF ARKANSAS LITTLE ROCK L.J. 37, 48 (1987–88), quoted in his and his co-authors' PROFESSIONAL RESPONSIBILITY: PROBLEMS AND MATERIALS (11th ed. 2011).

[9] www.freivogelonconflicts.com, cited in our Introduction as a key website, keeps good track of the current status of screening, as well as most conflicts issues.

8. What Does the Future Hold for the Duty of Loyalty?

As we have seen, many judges and commentators have waxed eloquent about the duty of loyalty as a fundamental principle of the attorney-client relationship. Yet in the new millennium, attorneys in some quarters are arguing that "loyalty" has largely become an obsolete concept, especially in a large law firm setting. During the Ethics 2000 rules revisions, the business law section of the ABA presented a proposal that would have allowed screening *in current cases* if no substantial relationship existed between the matters.[10]

To many, it makes little sense to apply the substantial relationship test to current clients, since the doctrine was clearly designed to balance interests of clients and their *former* lawyers so that lawyers did not forever have to be precluded from any taking case against any past client. But in March 2011, a group of attorneys — almost all general counsel — from 33 of the largest American law firms proposed applying the substantial relationship test to current clients and several other changes to the ABA Model Rules that go well beyond that.[11]

These proposals might have seemed outrageous a decade ago, but while still far-fetched, are less surprising today, given the growth of large international conglomerate law firms and the increasing trend for law firms to look more like any other business. Among the proposals, which would apply only to so-called "sophisticated clients," are these:

- New representation adverse to a law firm's current client *without that client's consent* if the matter has no "substantial relationship" to the current client's matter, so long as screens are set up;

- Continuing current representation of *both* clients when a law firm representing one client brings in a laterally-hired lawyer representing an adverse client, again with screens in place, and *again without client consent;*

- Unfettered open-ended advance waivers including those that would allow "direct adversity" even during the current engagement;

- A basic switch that "presumptions under the conflict rules and certain other rules would be reversed, *unless the parties specified otherwise.*"[12]

There are several other parts to the proposal, including that clients could agree to limit their lawyers' own liability for mistakes, something now expressly prohibited by specific rule.

The authors of this proposal use a broad "irrebuttably presumed" definition of "sophisticated clients," to include: any entity that is a "repetitive user of legal

---

[10] For a more recent take, see Daniel J. Bussel, *No Conflict*, 25 GEORGETOWN J. OF LEGAL ETHICS 207 (2012), described further in the Supplemental Readings. As mentioned, Texas Rule 1.6 allows screening in cases against current clients.

[11] *Proposals of Law Firm General Counsel for Future Regulation of Relationships Between Law Firms and Sophisticated Clients*, addressed to ABA Commission on Ethics 20/20, March 2011.

[12] James W. Jones & Anthony E. Davis, *In Defense of a Reasoned Dialogue About Law Firms and Their Sophisticated Clients*, 121 YALE L.J. ONLINE 589 (2012), http://yalelawjournal.org/2012/03/27/jones&davis.html. Jones and Davis are principal authors of the proposals.

services" if it has the opportunity to consult with independent counsel (whether or not it did so); any entity operating in "at least five jurisdictions"; any publicly traded company, no matter the size; and any government entity that could consent to conflicts waivers (though under these proposals such consent would not be required).

We examine some of the points and counterpoints of these proposals:

• *A lack of uniform regulation.* The general counsel argue that their work is "made frustratingly difficult not only by the lack of a single, uniform set of rules governing professional conduct across the country — a lack that often results in conflicting, inconsistent, and unpredictable results from one jurisdiction to another — but also by a prevailing set of regulatory norms that simply do not match the realities of the world in which they live."[13]

But lack of uniformity is not new in our federalist system. And even if there is a lack of uniformity, why is the solution to allow concurrent representations of conflicting interests?

• *Is Loyalty vital or obsolete?* In a November 2011 follow-up to their March proposal, the collective general counsel wrote:

> The imputation rules . . . are not well-suited to maintaining the integrity of the profession . . . . Moreover, the impact of the imputation rules has been profoundly transformed by the evolution of the modern law firm . . . . [W]here law firms have hundreds or thousands of lawyers practicing in different disciplines, offices, cities, and, with increasing frequency, even countries, they are likely to share a firm name but little else of consequence . . . . To say that the loyalty of a lawyer engaged on a matter requires as well the loyalty of the hundreds or thousands of far-flung strangers who happen to be in business with that lawyer is a fiction that no longer serves a purpose.[14]

However, generally speaking, these "far-flung strangers" still are closely connected because they share both profits and attorney-client confidentiality and privilege within one law firm.

Among others, Philadelphia ethics maven and former big-firm managing partner Lawrence Fox, whose brief on confidentiality and Guantanamo we read in Problem 5, was quick to attack these proposals.[15]

Fox strongly defends the duty of loyalty as "quite simply . . . the most fundamental of all fiduciary duties . . . , a duty that is recognized in the common law of every jurisdiction of the United States and codified in every American code of legal ethics ever promulgated." In Fox's view, MR 1.7 is "intentionally unbounded

---

[13] *Id.*

[14] November 30, 2011 letter from General Counsel to Co-Chairs, ABA Commission on Ethics 20/20.

[15] Lawrence Fox, *The Gang of Thirty-Three: Taking the Wrecking Ball to Client Loyalty*, 121 YALE L.J. ONLINE 567 (2012), http://yalelawjournal.org/2012/03/27/fox.html. Fox has garnered some criticism for his impolitic (although often amusing) language, which he acknowledged when he said "Extremism in the defense of loyalty is no vice." (A close paraphrase of Barry Goldwater's famous paraphrase of Cicero: "extremism in the defense of liberty is no vice.")

. . . [e]ven if the conflicting matter [is] tiny or totally unrelated."

Jones and Davis disagree: "The lynchpin of Fox's strident rejection of the Law Firm Proposals is an extreme view of client loyalty that is simply unworkable when wedded to the extreme view of imputation that he also embraces. While no one would dispute that a lawyer owes an unwavering duty of loyalty to his or her client, the nature of that duty is not as universally agreed upon — or nearly as unbounded — as Fox suggests."

Jones and Davis note that their proposal is "fully consistent with the English common law . . . . Indeed, [under] the so-called 'English rule' . . . loyalty is interpreted to mean that a lawyer . . . should not represent two different clients *in the same matter.*"

Fox is not persuaded. He notes that in the GC's view, "any one of these exalted law firms should be free, without the courtesy of picking up the phone, to sue its present 'sophisticated' clients for any claim (including RICO, fraud, or antitrust violations) . . . so long as the conflicting matter is not substantially related to the law firm's representation of the client."

• *Sophisticated clients.* The general counsel argue that sophisticated clients gain from their proposals, by more often being able to have their ongoing law firm of choice. They note that while the presumptions about conflicts would be largely reversed, "no client would be forced to accept any of these results and could easily avoid them simply by stipulating to the contrary . . . ."

But this requires "sophisticated" clients to affirmatively stipulate to protections other clients get automatically. Why? Fox puts it bluntly: "because it drives [firms] crazy that their intake committees are forced to turn down literally millions of dollars of business each year, maybe even each month, because of conflicts of interest."

Fox calls the GCs' definition of the "sophisticated client" a "myth." In his view, these clients' "sophistication relates to finding new drugs, designing electric vehicles . . . , running a restaurant, selling automobiles, or providing valuable services such as actuaries and accountants. It has little or nothing to do with our profession, our skill sets, or our rules of professional conduct. In order to be sophisticated about those matters we say you need three years of law school, passage of a bar examination [and so on].

"If you are a 'repetitive user of legal services,' whatever that means, you are a sophisticated client. Name any business and that criterion will be met. A little incorporation, one liability lawsuit, family succession and estate planning, and (before you know it) you are a repetitive user . . . ."

Indeed, one of us is a minority owner of a "mom-and-pop" restaurant formed as an LLC. Because the LLC had lawyers for business formations, bringing in new partners, and lease negotiations, it is a "repetitive user" under the GCs' standards, though its owner, born in another country and not conversant with the American legal system, clearly should not be deemed "sophisticated."

• *Do prospective waivers allow choice of counsel or destroy the lawyer-client relationship?* The General Counsel argue that advance waivers allow sophisticated clients a major plus: choosing their counsel so long as they accept that the full-service firm they pick may have other clients adverse to them (if they are unrelated to the firm's representation of them). Fox, not surprisingly, takes strong issue:

> [T]he GCs . . . actually have the temerity to give the sophisticated client 'the right' to consent to an open-ended, undefined-in-any-way, prospective waiver of any current or future client conflict uncabined as to (a) the nature of the matters involved (RICO, treble damages, bet-the-company litigation), (b) when in the future the conflict might arise, [and] (c) whether the conflict is even waivable under [current] rules . . . . Again, how lucky are those sophisticated clients?

• *The fundamental dispute.* The law firm GCs say that modifying these rules not only conforms to reality but helps big clients by giving them more legal options. Many others believe, as Fox puts it, that the profession as we know it may be at stake: "[For] the firms who are offering these proposals, . . . if the cost of increasing profits is a fundamental compromise of what we thought it was that made us professionals, that is a result they are willing to embrace. . . . Whether these proposals are ever adopted, . . . the damage to the profession's public image has already occurred . . . ."

What do you think about these proposals: grossly overbroad deregulation, or the natural consequence of the evolution of the business of law? Do you agree with Fox that loyalty should remain paramount, or with the general counsel, who say they represent today's reality? Would clients be giving away too much if these proposals were enacted? For example, does a prospective client's ability to "stipulate to the contrary" sufficiently protect clients if the current presumptions about conflict are "reversed"? Finally, do these proposals, and the strong reaction, mean that law practice has gotten increasingly polarized over the last quarter-century? To what end?

9. Corporate Subsidiaries, Client Interests, and Disqualification

What happens in the world of corporate conglomerates, where a parent may own several subsidiaries, some of which are far-flung and have little connection to the parent? May a firm represent a client against the parent (or subsidiary) of a former corporate client? This is another emerging issue, and the courts that have considered it have not agreed on how to analyze the situation. One question is whether courts will look beyond corporate organizational charts to the practical effect on the client.

In *Teradyne, Inc. v. Hewlett-Packard Co.*, 20 U.S.P.Q.2d 1143 (N.D. Cal. 1991), Teradyne sued Hewlett-Packard for patent infringement. One law firm representing Teradyne in the litigation also represented H-P's wholly owned subsidiary, Apollo Computer, in related trademark matters. The court found that there was an "identity of interests" between H-P and Apollo, and that the firm had a conflict of interest by simultaneously representing Apollo while representing Teradyne against H-P. The court disqualified the firm from representing Teradyne.

Two other courts reached different results based on the same facts in lawsuits brought in New York and California: *Brooklyn Navy Yard Cogeneration Partners LP v. PMNC* (N.Y. Super. Ct. 1997)[16] and *Brooklyn Navy Yard Cogeneration Partners LP v. Superior Court*, 60 Cal. App. 4th 248 (1997). The far-reaching opinion below discusses the California version of *Brooklyn Navy Yard*, bucks the law-as-a-business trend, provides a thoughtful analysis of corporate-subsidiary conflicts focusing on the *interests* of a party, and finds a logical extension of the substantial relationship test to third parties holding confidences.

MORRISON KNUDSEN CORP. v. HANCOCK, ROTHERT & BUNSHOFT
69 Cal. App. 4th 223 (1999)

HANLON, P. J.

This is an appeal from a preliminary injunction preventing the law firm of Hancock, Rothert & Bunshoft (Hancock) from representing the Contra Costa Water District (District) in any dispute with Morrison Knudsen Corporation (Morrison), or Morrison's wholly owned subsidiary, Centennial Engineering, Inc. (Centennial) concerning the Vasco Road or Los Vaqueros construction projects in Livermore.

Hancock seeks to represent the District in proceedings on a cross-complaint against Centennial [called "the Unimin sand dispute"], and the alleged conflict stems primarily from Hancock's ongoing representation of Morrison's [third party] insurance underwriters in matters involving Morrison, rather than from representation of Morrison itself or of Centennial. We conclude: (1) that the court could consider the information Hancock received as underwriter's counsel in determining whether there was a conflict; (2) that this information could be deemed to create a conflict if it was "substantially related" to the District's dispute with Centennial; (3) the court could reasonably find that the information was substantially related to the Centennial dispute; (4) the court could reasonably find that there was a sufficient "unity of interest" between the Centennial and Morrison to treat them as one entity for purposes of the alleged conflict; and (5) the determination that Hancock should be disqualified was not an abuse of discretion under all of the circumstances.

. . . .

Hancock had never represented Centennial, but Centennial's parent, Morrison, had retained Hancock on various matters until about 1990. Beginning in the 1980s, and continuing up to the time of the District's dispute with Centennial herein, Hancock was retained by the underwriters of Morrison's primary comprehensive insurance policy to monitor the defense attorneys Morrison retained on errors and omissions claims. In its capacity as "monitoring counsel," Hancock received detailed confidential communications from Morrison's defense counsel concerning the progress of cases and Morrison's potential liability.

---

[16] See a report in *ABA/BNA Manual on Professional Conduct*, 319 (1997) for a discussion of the opinion.

. . . .

This case is "a square peg which does not fit into the round holes of the rules most commonly applied in attorney disqualification cases." . . . The [trial] court wrote, with italics added, that "[Hancock's] prior direct representation of Morrison, *coupled with its current status as monitoring counsel for [Morrison's] underwriters*, supports the conclusion that [Hancock] has acquired substantial knowledge of the policies, attitudes and practices of [Morrison's] top management with respect to litigation of this type."

Two issues not generally presented in former representation cases are raised here. First, could the court properly consider the information Hancock obtained as counsel for Morrison's underwriters in determining whether Hancock should be disqualified herein? Second, if the answer to the first question is "yes," was the information Hancock gained from its prior representation of Morrison and its present representation of Morrison's underwriters sufficiently relevant to the Unimin sand dispute to create a conflict of interest?

. . . .

[A]n attorney's receipt of confidential information *from a nonclient* may lead to the attorney's disqualification. In this case, Morrison's declarations testified to an understanding that its communications with Hancock in Hancock's capacity as "monitoring counsel" for Morrison's underwriters would be kept confidential, even if Morrison was not Hancock's "client" in those matters. This was a reasonable expectation. Hancock's own declarations acknowledged that it treated information received from Morrison "confidentially, given the Underwriters' good faith obligations to their insured." Accordingly, we conclude that the court could properly take into account the confidential information Hancock received as "monitoring counsel". . . . While Morrison had a reasonable expectation that this information would be kept confidential, it could not expect "fidelity" from Hancock as if Hancock were an attorney sitting on its board of directors. Hancock's loyalty ran to its client, the underwriters, not to Morrison. . . . Like a case of successive representation, the primary consideration for the (non)client in this instance is one of confidentiality rather than loyalty.

We therefore conclude that the proper standard for assessing whether the information Hancock received as the underwriters' counsel disqualified it from representing the District is . . . the "substantial relationship" test ordinarily applied in successive representation cases.

. . . .

Application of the Substantial Relationship Test

As for the nature and extent of Hancock's involvement in Morrison's cases, the evidence established that the involvement was substantial, even in Hancock's capacity as monitoring counsel for the underwriters. The declarations averred that in those matters, attorneys at Hancock discussed litigation strategy with Morrison's officers and defense counsel, conducted defense research, and participated in settlement discussions and mediations. Morrison personnel declared that from 1990 to 1996, they had received advice from Hancock on the "value" of cases [and], "the upside and downside of settlement alternatives. . . ."

[T]here was substantial evidence that as monitoring counsel Hancock had considerable exposure to Morrison's litigation policies and strategies.

. . . .

A final factor militating in favor of a "substantial relationship" finding, and one not present in the usual successive representation case [is that], Hancock was privy by virtue of this continuing role to information about Morrison's financial condition which could be useful to a Morrison adversary. As counsel put it to the court, a monitoring attorney at Hancock could potentially report to a Hancock attorney for the District that [Morrison is] "going to settle quickly because we've already exhausted certain amounts within their policy. . . ."

The Unity of Interests Test

It is undisputed that Hancock had never represented Centennial, or monitored any claim against Centennial on behalf of the underwriters. Since any conflict of interest arose solely from Hancock's dealings with Morrison, the remaining question is whether Morrison and Centennial are to be treated as separate entities for purposes of the alleged conflict.

The court disqualified Hancock based on the "close relationship" it found between Morrison and Centennial. In support of this finding, the court cited among other things the District's tender of PG&E's $12.4 million Unimin sand claim to Morrison as well as Centennial. . . . The court also cited . . . evidence confirm[ing] that as counsel for Morrison's underwriters, Hancock had ongoing communications about litigation matters with Richard Edmister and Edwin Appel, the in-house attorneys at Morrison who would be managing Centennial's defense.

. . . .

[California State Bar Ethics Opinion 1989-113] opined, in the context of its hypothetical involving a suit against a client's subsidiary, that "if the attorney has obtained confidential information directly from the nonclient subsidiary under circumstances where the subsidiary could reasonably expect that the attorney had a duty to keep such information confidential, the attorney might be precluded from acting adversely to the subsidiary in matters related to the subject on which the attorney had obtained such confidential information."

. . . .

The *Brooklyn Navy Yard* court referred extensively to the State Bar Opinion, and conceded it stated that corporations could be treated as one entity for conflict purposes if they were either alter egos or had a unity of interests. However, the court thought that the "unity of interests" standard was too uncertain to provide any useful guidance. . . . *Brooklyn Navy Yard*'s analysis conflicts with formal ethics opinion No. 95-390 of the American Bar Association's Committee on Professional Ethics.

The ABA Committee addressed "whether a lawyer who represents a corporate client may undertake a representation that is adverse to a corporate affiliate of the client in an unrelated matter, without obtaining the client's consent." The ABA Opinion concluded that while corporate affiliation alone did not necessarily create an attorney-client relationship, there were "particular circumstances" in which an affiliate could be considered an additional client. "This would clearly be true," the ABA Committee thought, "where one corporation is the alter ego of the other. It is not necessary, however, for one corporation to be the alter ego of the other as a matter of law in order for both to be considered clients."

[Here, the court summarizes the factors favoring disqualification.] First, as previously discussed, in the course of the firm's work involving the parent corporation, it received confidential information.

[Second,] the parent in this instance controls the legal affairs of the subsidiary.

A third set of considerations stems from the evidence of Morrison's participation in the construction project at issue. Here the record shows that Morrison personnel administered Centennial's contract, that Centennial had no contractual authority independent of Morrison, and that the District was aware of Morrison's controlling role.

. . . .

In light of all of the foregoing considerations, the trial court could reasonably find that Morrison and Centennial were, in the court's word, "closely" enough related to be treated as one entity for purposes of the conflict herein.

Centennial and Morrison do not claim to be alter egos, and the question is whether the absence of such a relationship is dispositive. We conclude that it is not.

. . . .

The "unity of interests" test will continue to develop on a case-by-case basis, and take more definite and useful shape in the process. . . . [H]ere, the principal focus should be the practical consequences of the attorney's relationship with the corporate family. If that relationship may give the attorney a significant practical advantage in a case against an affiliate, then the attorney can be disqualified from taking the case. [T]hat is as close as we can come to defining a "bottom line."

NOTES

Does this opinion make good solid common sense, or is the decision simply unfair to the District, which lost a lawyer that had never represented the other side?

10. Shared Space and Non-Lawyer Migration

As if lawyer migration and imputed law firm disqualification were not complicated enough, several other "twists" on these issues exist. Two bear brief mention here. Many lawyers who keep separate law firms and separate books share office space, receptionists, phone systems, and sometimes computers. These shared space situations present difficult issues of imputed conflicts of interest.

When lawyers conduct themselves as a firm or even hold themselves out to the public or to a client in a way that suggests that they are a firm, they will be treated as one law firm for conflicts purposes. This is also often true when it comes to disqualification, responsibility to work on a case, and, ultimately, malpractice liability. The comment to Model Rule 1.10 recognizes shared space arrangements and emphasizes the issue of whether confidences are shared as well. But what about those situations where it is reasonably possible that information will be shared unintentionally or by proximity? Many state ethics opinions, as well as a few cases, address these issues. The majority seem to turn on how much a lawyer protects against inadvertent disclosure of confidences. When attorneys in the same suite keep their separate files sacrosanct, use a separate telephone, computer system, and fax machine, have different support staff, and make it clear they are in separate practices, they are far more likely to be permitted to represent adverse interests than if these protections are not in place. Even then, however, with close proximity of lawyers within a suite of offices, representing adverse interests will always be somewhat problematic.

We have discussed lawyers who change firms, but what about migrating non-lawyer personnel or temporary "contract" lawyers? These personnel serve under the law firms "umbrella," and the lawyers who supervise them must ensure that they respect attorney-client confidences just as the attorney does.[17]

But does a change of employment lead to the same disqualification standard that confronts law firms that take on migrating attorneys? Does it make sense to have a different standard for support staff than for lawyers? What might justify such different treatment? While the case law remains split, most courts applied similar confidentiality standards to nonlawyer personnel as to attorneys, while possibly being more lenient on the use of screens.

Perhaps the first case to deal with this issue is *In re Complex Asbestos Litigation*, 232 Cal. App. 3d 572 (1991). A paralegal moved from a firm that handled asbestos defense work to a plaintiff's asbestos firm, reviewing many of his former firm's files before he left. Although the court found that the paralegal's new firm was tainted by his knowledge, it nevertheless set up a *future* test less stringent than the substantial relationship test in one respect, and much like the *Schiessle* test in another. First, the court held that since a paralegal, and not a lawyer, was involved, the usual presumption of confidences didn't apply; rather, the burden was on the former client to show that the employee had obtained material confidences. Second, the receipt of confidences could be rebutted by showing that the paralegal did not disclose them to the new law firm due to screening measures, or what the court termed a "cone of silence" employed by the new firm.

Does it make sense that paralegals are presumed *not* to have confidential information, given their wide access to files? The *Creighton* case, discussed in § 6 above, used the opposite presumption and even came up with a "bright line" disqualification rule. And most recent cases have generally not made a distinction

---

[17] Non-lawyers, of course, are not subject to discipline under rules of professional conduct. But they can, for example, be contractually bound to maintain confidences as a condition of employment and lawyers are responsible for supervising their non-lawyers.

between lawyer and paralegal. For example, *In re American Home Products*, 985 S.W.2d 68 (Tex. 1998), concerned a legal assistant who had formerly worked for a defense firm representing one of the defendants. She spent significant time interviewing potential witnesses and investigating plaintiffs, meeting with counsel, and preparing memoranda about the evidence. Thereafter, she went to work for a plaintiffs' lawyer who failed to screen her. The lawyer was disqualified.

In *Ciaffone v. Eighth Judicial District Court*, 945 P.2d 950 (Nev. 1997), a plaintiff's firm hired a secretary who had worked for two months for the opposing law firm in a case the plaintiff's firm was handling. Although she was not assigned to a lawyer working on the case, the firm did not screen her. The court applied the confidentiality rule to nonlawyer employees and disqualified the plaintiff's firm. And in a series of cases in Florida in 2000, 2001, and 2002, lawyers hiring paralegals who had worked for the other side were uniformly disqualified.[18]

What about temporary lawyer hires? Do conflicts rules apply to these admitted attorneys who are not part of the firm? DC Bar Assoc. Opinion 352 (2010) concluded that a fact-specific analysis should be used in such cases. Factors to consider include whether the "temp" worked on a single issue or on multiple matters, used the firm's offices, could access confidential information, or used law firm email. At a minimum, a law firm would be foolish not to screen this lawyer.

Finally, how might this issue apply to *you* as a law student working for one law firm one summer and another the next? The Restatement, § 123, Comment *f*, draws a somewhat artificial distinction between "summer associate" students and those "who have completed their legal education and are waiting admission." Whether this makes sense to you or not, you should be forewarned that a loyalty/disqualification analysis *may*, in some jurisdictions, apply to *you*.

D. SUPPLEMENTAL READINGS

1. Committee on Professional Responsibility, *Discipline of Law Firms*, 45 RECORD OF THE ASSOCIATION OF THE BAR OF THE CITY OF NEW YORK (June 1993). This report, which advocated extending disciplinary rules to govern the conduct of law firms, was an early signal of changes finally being considered preliminarily in several jurisdictions. Noting that certain disciplinary rules such as advertising regulations already apply to law firms, the committee advocated applying conflict of interest rules to law firms as a whole and to require their participation in avoiding conflicts, rather than keeping the disciplinary focus solely on individual attorneys.

2. *IBM v. Levin*, 579 F.2d 271 (3d Cir. 1978), involved an interesting and important issue, one of the few in this area *not* frequently litigated: A law firm that had represented IBM over the years on various labor matters filed an antitrust suit against IBM, and IBM sought its disqualification. The law firm was disqualified even though it was not on retainer to IBM and had no specific open file at the time

---

[18] In a December 31, 2002 article in the MIAMI DAILY BUSINESS REVIEW, *Costly Lesson: Miami Lawyer Ordered Off Big Negligence Case Because He Hired a Paralegal Who Had Worked for the Opposing Law Firm*, reporter Laurie Cunningham reviews several of these Florida cases.

the antitrust action was filed. The court held that "the pattern of repeated retainers, both before and after the filing of the complaint, supports the finding of a continuous relationship."

3. *Hartford Acc. & Indem. Co. v. RJR Nabisco, Inc.*, 721 F. Supp. 534 (S.D.N.Y. 1989). This case is a twist on the "hot potato" scenario described in the readings. Here, instead of "firing" its client, the law firm fired the "tainted" lawyer. A law firm sued RJR Nabisco on behalf of the Hartford. The law firm then fired its lawyer, who represented RJR. That lawyer took RJR with him. Even though the conflict arose during concurrent representation, the court allowed the law firm to remain as counsel for Hartford, reasoning that RJR had only been with the firm because of the departed lawyer.

4. James M. Altman, *A Young Lawyer's Nightmare*, N.Y. L.J., Feb. 16, 2001, describes the sad story of a young would-be associate who lost his job because of a previous representation, and discusses how transient lawyers' allegiances have become and the difficulties of navigating conflicts rules.

5. Douglas J. Hoffer, *Navigating Conflict-Interest Disqualification Motions*, 84 WISCONSIN LAWYER, Sept. 2011, is an article helpful for understanding conflicts and disqualification motions. The article argues that objections to an attorney's involvement in a case on conflict grounds can be raised by non-client parties as well as clients. The author describes *Foley-Ciccantelli v. Bishop's Grove Condominium Ass'n, Inc., Foley-Ciccantelli v. Bishop's Grove Condominium*, 797 N.W.2d 789 (Wis. 2011), an unusual and dense disqualification case raising these issues that produced three separate state high court opinions.

6. *Chrysler Corp. v. Carey*, 5 F. Supp. 2d 1023 (E.D. Mo. 1998), approves the chilling prospect that lawyers who switch sides in a case may not only be subject to disqualification, but may be sued for malpractice as well. The case holds that either a breach of the duty of confidentiality or the duty of loyalty would support a finding of professional negligence. On the other hand, in *Beal Bank, SSB v. Arter & Hadden, LLP*, 167 P.3d 666 (Cal. 2007), the California Supreme Court ruled that while a lawyer who moved from Arter to another law firm could still be sued for malpractice, the statute of limitations against former firm Arter ran from the date of the lawyer's departure.

7. Two opposing views about the expansion of the "substanatial relationship test" are as follows: Professor Daniel Bussell engages in a thorough and readable review of current law in *No Conflict*, 25 GEO. J. OF LEG. ETHICS 207 (2012). He argues that the "substantial relationship" test should be applied to current clients, thus allowing suits against current clients on "unrelated" matters. On the other hand, Milas Markovic uses Sullivan & Cromwell's representation of Lehman Brothers during the recent financial crisis as a case study demonstrating that attorney conflicts of interest can undermine the representation of even extremely sophisticated corporate clients: *The Sophisticates: Conflicted Representation and the Lehman Bankruptcy*, 2012 UTAH L. REV. 903.

9. *Hitachi, Ltd. v. Tatung Co.*, 419 F. Supp. 2d 1158 (N.D. Cal. 2006), contains a thorough review of the California case law on screening as it existed at the time of the 2009 ABA rule changes then being considered by California, and prior to the decision in *Kirk v. First American Title Ins. Co.*, 183 Cal. App. 4th 776 (2010). *Kirk* lays down a detailed prescription for a permissible California screen, allowed in part because the facts — a one-time 17-minute consultation years earlier — showed the lawyer's minimal involvement.

10. California State Bar Formal Opinion 1997-150 lays out the parameters for shared space arrangements among lawyers to avoid problems among their clients. Although the opinion focuses mostly on the confidentiality of communications and not on conflicts of interest, it notes how such conflicts can arise particularly from shared staff, advertising, or the inadvertent or careless sharing of confidences.

PROBLEM 11: CLASS ACTION AND MASS-PLAINTIFF CASES

A. INTRODUCTION

We have seen in the several problems in this chapter first how conflicts of interest affect a single lawyer's representation of single clients, and then, in Problem 10, how law firms are affected. But the ethical rules describing both conflicts of interest and the duty of loyalty were designed for a traditional paradigm of legal representation: one lawyer and one client. While the rules and case law have been broadened to address multiple lawyers taking on multiple clients, there are situations in which the rules lag farther behind the reality of actual practice. In class action cases, either the existing rules don't seem to apply in the same way as in other situations, or other considerations, including public policy ones, create exceptions to the usual rules. Yet there are no special ethics rules, and not much agreement, on how class action situations should be handled. The result is often concern, confusion, and sometimes collusion. In other instances where a class action is not an appropriate vehicle despite the presence of a multitude of clients, lawyers can find themselves representing literally hundreds of individual clients, with little help from the ethics rules, and with often troubling results.

B. PROBLEM

I

Stephanie Nyala is a partner in the class action firm of Nyala, Jones & Samuel. One day over dinner, Joella Winston, a friend of Nyala's, complained that she had purchased a computer from Great Guys/Great Buys, a regional electronics store, expecting to get a free printer. The store had advertised that anyone buying a new computer and monitor would get the printer free-of-charge. "I knew the printer was a bottom-of-the-line model," said Joella, "but it had to be better than what I had. I ended up buying two computers, one for the office, and one for my daughter, but I never did get a printer."

Nyala investigated and discovered that when GG/GB ran out of stock of the giveaway printers, they simply told customers that they would have to call back later. Since the printers were a discontinued model, the store was never able to restock them. Those customers who called back were eventually told that the offer had expired.

Nyala smelled a good class action suit, based on GG/GB's deceptive advertising. Since the store had advertised the printer as "a $189 value," a class action could be quite remunerative. But Nyala's friend Joella made it clear she wanted no part of being a class representative. So Nyala found herself in need of some GG/GB customers to become her "named plaintiffs," or class representatives.

QUESTIONS

1. What can Nyala do to solicit the store's customers to become her clients? May she contact friends whom she knows shop at the store, even if they have never been her clients? May she have someone hand out flyers in front of the store's branches?

2. What if after filing the case, Nyala discovers that three computer purchasers from one of GG/GB's suburban stores are suing one of her partner Sherman Jones's clients in a serious auto accident? Does Nyala have a conflict of interest unless these claimants "opt out" of the class action? Or may she continue to represent the class as a whole and the named class representatives?

3. After filing, Nyala conducted discovery and learned that during the ad campaign, Great Guys/Great Buys sold 14,000 computers but gave away only 3,200 printers. Nyala receives a settlement offer from GG/GB's attorneys: For customers of GG/GB's four city and five suburban locations, the store will give each customer who has proof of purchase $10.00 and a coupon for a $90.00 store credit. However, the customers of GG/GB's four "remote," or more rural, locations — about 2,000 in all — will receive only the $10.00 check. The store's attorneys claim that these stores, run by independent franchisees, simply couldn't afford the store credit. Still, with an arguable "settlement value" of $1,220,000 ($100 for 12,000 customers and $10 for 2,000 customers), the defense lawyers are offering Nyala a fee of $305,000, representing 25% of the total "recovery," a most generous sum given the amount of legal work done.

May Nyala accept the offer? What about those who are getting only $10.00? Is this settlement fair to them? Does it matter? Does it matter whether any of Nyala's "class reps" shopped at a rural store?

II

Julie Samuel gets a phone call from her cousin Martha, who lives in a small semi-rural subdivision near a large Cavalier Oil refinery. A recent refinery fire caused considerable air pollution, and many of the subdivision's residents suffered respiratory harm. Some needed hospital care for severe asthma and bronchial symptoms, while others more fortunate suffered runny noses, teary eyes, or skin irritations. Martha tells Julie that many of her friends want to sue the refinery. Julie attends a meeting at the subdivision clubhouse and encounters 104 people who sign a sheet asking her to represent them. But she knows that the case can't be filed as a class action, because the medical conditions and damages for each prospective plaintiff are different and distinct.

QUESTIONS

1. May Samuel take on individual law suits for over 100 plaintiffs? If she does, what should she put in her retainer agreements about conflicts of interest?

2. What other issues must or should she address in those agreements?

3.   What structure or plan can Samuel set up to avoid having to deal with a small handful of naysayers in the event a good settlement is offered?

C. READINGS

1. A Brief Class Action Introduction

Representing a class presents among the most complicated, and most multifaceted, issues of loyalty a lawyer is likely to face. Class counsel must address many of the same issues discussed in this chapter, including: identifying the client; representing multiple clients; conflicts of interest among clients; and conflicts between the attorney's own interests, including fees, and those of the clients. And that's just for starters.

Class actions are lawsuits in which lawyers represent a "class" of similarly-situated people whose interests are protected by one or more "class representatives," or "named plaintiffs," who themselves have fiduciary duties to the passive members of the class — many of whom do not even know they are class members.[1]

Filing a class action case creates a putative class. Only after a class is "certified" by a court are the passive class members given notice of the class' existence, and the opportunity to "opt out" of the class should they wish to pursue their claims individually. Historically, though, few chose to opt out since the damages for such things as defective toasters or bank overcharges were too small for people to pursue individually. Indeed, the very point behind class actions was to provide a remedy for these "little" wrongs by banding people together in a "class."

Class actions increased dramatically in popularity in the 1960s, when a change in the Federal Rules of Civil Procedure allowed individual members of a class to collect money damages. With increasing popularity came increasing difficulty in applying ethical rules designed with individual clients in mind. The use of class actions to litigate mass tort and employment claims raised the stakes substantially, changing the traditional class action into a major, "big ticket" item, often in complex and multi-jurisdictional litigation.

As we saw in Problem 7, in multiple-plaintiff cases, each individual remains a separate client, entitled to the lawyer's loyalty to his or her particular case. Class actions don't — indeed, *can't* — work that way. The sheer number of potential class members means that if each were considered an individual client, with the full right to settle only upon individual approval, it would be impossible to ever pursue, much less resolve a case. And running a conflicts check — or obtaining a conflicts

---

[1] Fed. R. Civ. P. 23(a) defines a class action as follows:

    (1) the class is so numerous that joinder of all members is impracticable;

    (2) there are questions of law or fact common to the class;

    (3) the claims or defenses of the representative parties are typical of the claims or defenses of the class; and

    (4) the representative parties will fairly and adequately protect the interests of the class

waiver — would be impossible, as often, the *number* of individual class members is not known, much less the name of each class participant.

2.   Embarking on a Class Action Case

Lawyers often begin a class action themselves, creating the class, defining its scope and objectives, and finding representative class members. Class action lawyers thus have far more power than attorneys in traditional litigation. In many jurisdictions, they even have the power to settle the case themselves, subject to court approval. How do these cases get started? The ethical answer is, "very carefully." While class actions still sometimes begin with one plaintiff, or a small group, who find themselves with a problem and seek out legal help, in modern class actions, it's more often the other way around, with lawyers finding people, often "acquaintances" or those discovered during preliminary investigation, to serve as representative class members. Not surprisingly, some law firms "troll" for class action clients through advertising that in some cases borders on or even crosses the line into direct solicitation.

We'll look at advertising and solicitation more thoroughly in Problem 31. But as a general rule, an attorney or firm may send written notices of intended or existing class actions as long as the notices comport with Fed. R. Civ. P. 23 and the general ethical limitations on lawyer advertising, especially Model Rule 7.3. Subsection (c) of that rule requires the words "Advertising Material" on any written communication sent to non-clients "known" to the attorney to be in need of legal services. Are potential class members "known" to an attorney to be in need of legal services?

In *Coles v. Marsh*, 560 F.2d 186, 189 (3d Cir. 1977), the court held that "the district court lacked power to impose any restraint on communication for the purpose of preventing the recruitment of additional parties plaintiff or of the solicitation of financial or other support to maintain the action." In *Gulf Oil Co. v. Bernard*, 452 U.S. 89 (1981), the United States Supreme Court cited *Coles* with approval. Plaintiffs in *Gulf* had claimed racial and sex discrimination in a claim before the EEOC, and Gulf entered into an agreement with the government to cease its discriminatory practices and to implement affirmative action programs to rectify its prior conduct. It also agreed to offer back pay to alleged victims of the discrimination, and sent out notices to these claimants offering that back pay if the claimants would agree to waive all their claims against Gulf. When plaintiffs' attorneys proposed sending a letter to these claimants suggesting that they decline the proffered settlements, Gulf requested and obtained an order from the court prohibiting such communications between plaintiffs' attorneys and the potential class members.

The Supreme Court held that the order unnecessarily interfered with the claimants' ability to obtain information about whether they should accept Gulf's offer, and it interfered with the attorneys' attempts to gather facts about the case. However, in a footnote, the Court also noted the "heightened susceptibilities of non-party class members to solicitation amounting to barratry as well as the increased opportunities of the parties or counsel to 'drum up' participation. . . ."

One way *not* to start a case is to hire "professional lead plaintiffs," a technique that led to the downfall, disbarment, and imprisonment of several high profile class action lawyers beginning in 2006. That year, a federal grand jury in Los Angeles indicted the well-known plaintiffs' securities class action firm Milberg Weiss Bershad & Schulman and two named partners, David Bershad and Steven G. Schulman, for allegedly participating in a conspiracy to pay secret kickbacks to individuals who repeatedly appeared as Milberg's lead plaintiffs in different cases.

Next came the indictments of star class action counsel Mel Weiss, Milberg's leader in New York, and his former partner, William Lerach of San Diego. They too were accused of secretly paying kickbacks to other "professional lead plaintiffs." After pleading guilty in 2007, Lerach was sentenced to two years in a federal prison, fined $250,000, ordered to pay another $7.75 million in forfeitures. Weiss pled guilty in 2008 and was sentenced to 30 months in prison and fines and restitution of $10 million. Both were disbarred.

Another concern in commencing a class action is abandoning a pre-existing individual client. In a traditional class action such as the one brought by Ms. Nyala, no one individual has an effective remedy, since the recovery is too small to warrant bringing a lawsuit. But in today's modern, complex, high-stakes class-action world, individual class members may have millions of dollars at stake. The long history of the Nestlé Poland Springs litigation offers an example of what can happen when a lawyer shunts aside an individual client in favor of commencing a class action.[2]

In 2002, attorneys Garve Ivey, Thomas Sobol, and Jan R. Schlichtmann (of *A Civil Action* fame) "approached a number of bottled water companies with information that Nestlé had misrepresented the source and quality of its Poland Springs brand of bottled water." Glenwood Farms hired Ivey and Sobol to represent it individually against Nestlé, while Schlichtmann found an "acquaintance" to serve as a potential class representative. The lawyers attempted to negotiate a settlement with Nestlé before filing suit, but ultimately disagreed on whether to accept it. With Schlichtmann ready to file a class action, Sobol and Ivey filed class action cases of their own on behalf of two representatives that they had found, and Nestlé withdrew its settlement offer.

Glenwood then sued Ivey and Sobol for abandoning it as an individual client in order to bring the potentially more lucrative class actions. Ivey settled before trial, but Sobol and his law firm did not, resulting in a jury award against them of $3.9 million. Before Glenwood could proceed on its punitive damages claim against Sobol, he and his firm settled.

The litigation did not end there, but continued through suits by Schlichtmann and others for claimed compensation (denied in 2011), claims by Glenwood that Sobol and Ivey had fraudulently suppressed evidence in their trial (also denied), and claims involving a fourth lawyer and law firm and another plaintiff water-producer. But the "take-away" is clear: Once a lawyer has an individual client, loyalty to that

---

[2] The following narrative is based on court opinions and memoranda in Glenwood Farms Inc. v. Garve Ivey, Docket No. 03-CV-217-P-S (D. Me., filed Aug. 3, 2003), Glenwood Farms, Inc. v. O'Connor, et al., 09-CV-2050P-S (D. Me., Order of Oct. 14, 2009), Ehrlich v. Stern, 908 N.E.2d 797 (Mass. Ct. App. 2009), and Bartle v. Berry, 953 N.E.2d 243 (Mass. Ct. App. 2011), which is the case quoted.

client means that the lawyer can't switch to creating a class action without the client's consent.

3.   Who Is the Lawyer's Client in a Class Action?

Beyond the central client, the class itself, who is, or are, the clients, and what power (if any) do they have? The individual named plaintiffs, or class representatives, are generally considered to be clients of the lawyer. In the reading below, we will see that even class representatives may not be accorded the usual privileges of being a client.

Karen Donovan, *Huh? I'm the Lead Plaintiff?*
THE NATIONAL LAW JOURNAL, May 24, 1999[3]

His question was simple enough.

"I would specifically like to know if I am your 'client' according to your records," Charles D. Chalmers asked in a May 28, 1998, e-mail to Barrack, Rodos & Bacine, a Philadelphia law firm that specializes in filing securities fraud class actions.

He didn't get a yes or no answer. But meanwhile, Barrack Rodos was busy putting him forth as a "lead plaintiff" in a class action that settled without his knowledge, input or consent.

At the time, Mr. Chalmers, a San Francisco lawyer, also had no idea what it meant to be a "lead plaintiff." But he did some research.

Mr. Chalmers' strange relationship with Barrack Rodos stems from his investment in Digital Lightwave Inc., a Clearwater, Fla., maker of test products for high-speed telecommunications networks. On Jan. 22, 1998, the company announced that it would restate revenues sharply downward, citing the "discovery of certain errors in the timing of revenue recognition and a review of accounting policies and procedures."

The next day, the first of 23 class actions alleging securities fraud was filed in federal district court in Tampa. Mr. Chalmers monitors his investments on the Internet. . . . After Digital Lightwave dropped its bombshell announcement, Mr. Chalmers noticed a slew of press releases from law firms notifying investors of class actions. A Jan. 26, 1998, release from Barrack Rodos was among the first.

"I wanted to follow it," recalls Mr. Chalmers, who lost about $39,360 on his investment. He e-mailed Barrack Rodos on Sunday, March 1, 1998, inquiring how he could "monitor" the suits. Several hours later, he got an e-mail response, a form letter from Maxine S. Goldman, "shareholder relations manager" at the law firm. "Please be advised that we would be delighted to have you join our action," it began, urging him to send back information on how much stock he had purchased "as soon as possible."

When Congress passed the Securities Litigation Reform Act, the debate centered on "lawyer-driven" class actions, which often had nominal plaintiffs. Lobbyists pushing to pass the law invariably cited a quote from William S. Lerach, the most successful class action lawyer and the prime target. He said, according to Forbes magazine, "I have the greatest practice in the world. I have no clients."

The law's "lead plaintiff" provision was supposed to take control away from the law firms and put it in the hands of the investor with the largest financial stake, which would then select counsel. It provides for a 60-day notice period, after which anyone can move to be a lead plaintiff. In practice, it has led to a 60-day scramble by law firms to solicit investors like Mr. Chalmers.

E-mailing Maxine

By March 16, [Maxine Goldman] forwarded a letter with papers to sign. "Our intention is to join you in the litigation," she wrote. The letter asked him to sign and return an enclosed "Sworn Certification" the next day. The certification, another requirement of [a] 1995 law, states that Mr. Chalmers will not accept payment for being a "representative party."

When he signed the form, Mr. Chalmers says, he thought that being a representative party meant that he had agreed to be deposed and to show his investment record to assist the case. Of lead plaintiffs, he admits, "I didn't know from bupkis."

When Mr. Chalmers asked Ms. Goldman if he was, indeed, the law firm's client, she responded, "An agreed order has been submitted which would appoint our group of plaintiffs the lead plaintiff and us as lead counsel."

Mr. Chalmers e-mailed Ms. Goldman on July 22 with a list of nine questions, asking her to identify the named plaintiffs in the case and whether discovery had begun. She replied that the firm had sent out the "Digital Lightwave newsletter" earlier that month, and she asked whether he had received his copy.

Mr. Chalmers sent back a curt e-mail on July 23, telling her that the newsletter contained "very little 'news.'"

Mr. Chalmers got no response from Ms. Goldman.

"We are having a strange correspondence," Mr. Chalmers wrote back, reminding her that he was a lawyer.

That's when Mr. Chalmers had his first contact with a lawyer from Barrack Rodos. Ms. Goldman referred him to M. Richard Komins. Mr. Chalmers claims that he also got the run-around from Mr. Komins, who finally forwarded a copy of the settlement stipulation in early December, after U.S. District Judge Susan C. Bucklew said from the bench that she was inclined to approve the deal. When Mr. Chalmers got the document on Dec. 12, he says, he was stunned to see his name referenced as a "lead plaintiff" in the case. "They wanted to be sure that I didn't find out who I was until after they had obtained her preliminary approval," he surmises.

Mr. Chalmers sprang into action once he discovered what the 1995 law had to say about lead plaintiffs, demanding to contact the other nine investors listed as lead plaintiffs. He got little satisfaction.

In February he addressed his concerns with Judge Bucklew in a lengthy letter. By then, he had tracked down two other "lead plaintiffs," who said they had never been told that they were being proposed for such a role and that settlement had never been discussed with them. One of them was Bob McMurtry, of Depew, Okla., who says that he first learned of the proposed settlement when Mr. Chalmers called.

Judge Bucklew took up Mr. Chalmers' objections at a day-long hearing on March 12. When Mr. Chalmers related his first conversation with Mr. Komins, when the Barrack Rodos lawyer told him that he could not look at the evidence in the case because it was subject to a protective order, the judge became alarmed. She had never issued a protective order.

[I]t was clear that Barrack Rodos never consulted with Mr. Chalmers before cutting a deal with Digital Lightwave.

Lawyers on both sides suggested that increased participation by plaintiffs in these settlements would amount to an annoyance. Glen DeValerio, of Boston's Berman, DeValerio & Pease, concedes that the 1995 law demands increased participation by investors in these suits. But, he says, "the language is one thing, and the practicalities are another."

Digital Lightwave's defense counsel, Michael D. Torpey, says that the 1995 law envisioned one lead plaintiff. "Glen's right, we do a better job of settling without them." Judge Bucklew said "there was a very poor job of communication" with Mr. Chalmers, but she approved the settlement.

NOTES

Comment 1 to ABA Model Rule 1.4 states: "The client should have sufficient information to participate intelligently in decisions concerning the objectives of the representation and the means by which they are to be pursued, to the extent the client is willing and able to do so." Is there a justification for suspending this rule in class actions? Is it true that having actual plaintiffs participate in settlement negotiations will only interfere with the negotiating process? If so, do the plaintiffs' lawyers have a real client?

4. Are Passive Class Members Clients?

What about the absent members of the class, those who may qualify as class members but do not even know yet that the class exists? Fed. R. Civ. P. 23(a)(4) says that those who represent the class must "fairly and adequately protect the interests of the class." Most commentators, and most cases that have addressed the issue, agree this means that even if only the named plaintiffs are accorded the full-service status of "clients," the class lawyer nevertheless undertakes certain fiduciary duties to all class members. It also means that class counsel generally may not settle a case on behalf of the named plaintiffs alone while leaving the class out while class certification is pending.[4]

---

[4] *See, e.g.*, Roper v. Consurve, Inc., 578 F.2d 1106 (5th Cir. 1978).

Is there a meaningful distinction between a "client" and a passive class member to whom fiduciary duties are owed but who may not be anointed with full client status?

Interestingly, several courts have held that even passive class members have an attorney-client relationship with class counsel, at least when it comes to whether opposing counsel is communicating with a represented party when contacting *any* member of a certified class. In a leading case, *Kleiner v. First National Bank of Atlanta*, 751 F.2d 1193, 1207, n.28 (11th Cir. 1985), the court said that "at a minimum, class counsel represents all class members as soon as a class is certified." *Fulco v. Continental Cablevision*, 789 F. Supp. 45, 47 (D. Mass. 1992), states it bluntly and broadly: " 'Once the court enters an order certifying a class, an attorney-client relationship arises between all members of the class and class counsel.' "

In *Janik v. Rudy, Exelrod & Zieff*, 119 Cal. App. 4th 930, 939–40 (2004), a California appellate court closely examined this relationship in holding that class counsel may have duties to class members beyond the four corners of the class certification order. That court, noting that class members have the right to sue class counsel for negligence, went on, explaining and expanding *Kleiner*:

> In *Kleiner*, the court held that unauthorized communication with class members by the defendant's attorneys was a violation of the rules of professional conduct. In discussing whether an attorney-client relationship had been formed between the plaintiff's attorney and absent class members at the time of the communication, the *Kleiner* court noted, "Once a class has been certified, some but not all aspects of the relationship are present. A lawyer who represents the named plaintiff in a class which has been certified immediately assumes responsibility to class members for the diligent, competent prosecution of the certified claims. However, it cannot truly be said that he fully 'represents' prospective class members until it is determined that they are going to participate in the class action." The court there was focusing on the point in time at which the attorney-client relationship arises, not the scope of that relationship. Clearly the court did not hold, as defendants suggest, that class counsel's obligation to absent class members does not extend beyond the diligent prosecution of class members' claims as they are literally described in the class certification order.

One issue that case law has barely touched on directly is conflicts of interest. If a million member class means a law firm has a million "clients" upon certification, how does the firm run a conflicts check to ensure, for example, that the firm is not adverse to any of the million clients in any firm cases? The answer, of course, is that it cannot. Does this mean that courts that call the passive class members "clients" are naive or unsophisticated? Or should different rules about client conflicts be applied as to passive class members? Indeed, ordinary rules *cannot* apply, because even after class certification, the identities of all individuals comprising the class are not known until their claims are submitted, processed, and accepted. Even then, processing is done by an independent claims manager usually not part of the plaintiff law firm.

When it comes to settlement authority, courts generally take a narrow view of client involvement. For example, in *Kincade v. General Tire and Rubber Company*, 635 F.2d 501 (5th Cir. 1981), the court refused to interfere with class counsel's authority to settle, despite an appeal brought by several named representatives as well as passive class members:

> Appellants' argument that the settlement cannot be applied to them because they did not authorize their attorneys to settle the case or otherwise consent to the settlement is also easily disposed of. Because the "client" in a class action consists of numerous unnamed class members as well as the class representatives, and because "[t]he class often speaks with several voices . . . , it may be impossible for the class attorney to do more than act in what he believes to be the best interest of the class as a whole . . . ." Because of the unique nature of the attorney-client relationship in a class action, the cases cited by appellants holding that an attorney cannot settle his individual client's case without the authorization of the client are simply inapplicable.

5. Other Class Action Conflicts Issues

Not only do class actions generally have more than one named plaintiff, but conflicts can also arise between these plaintiffs and the absent class members. For example, what happens if a lawyer finds potential class representatives and decides to pursue claims that fit their situations, while ignoring others? Has the attorney failed to act on behalf of the whole class? Other classes are so large that it is impossible for all class members to have the same interests in settlement. Can a class attorney adequately represent all the members of the class when the interests of the class members are diverse and potentially adverse to each other? The Supreme Court addressed this in *Amchem Products, Inc. v. Windsor*, 521 U.S. 591 (1997), excerpted below.

Conflicts can exist among segments of a class, some members getting a smaller measure of recovery than others or, as in *Amchem*, potentially no recovery at all. As class actions become more common in mass tort cases, ethical issues become more dicey and difficult. How much attention must plaintiffs' class action attorneys pay to each segment, or sub-class? May they settle for the greater good rather than get something for everyone?

What if a favorable settlement is offered to the class as a whole that excludes the named plaintiffs? While the lawyer works with the class representatives and not individual class members, the named plaintiffs' obligations to the class under Rule 23(a)(4) still apply. And courts have consistently held that class representatives cannot act in a way that holds the absent members of the class hostage against the class' best interests.

Unfortunately, the Ethics 2000 Commission chose not to deal with these and other uniquely class action-related issues in a special rule, and not much has changed since in terms of ethical guidance. That means that class action lawyers remain governed — and guided — only by the ordinary rules regarding conflicts of interest, Federal Rule 23, and a body of case law that lacks uniformity.

Sometimes, of course, the existing rules *can* be helpful. For example, in some cases, settlement can turn a class action into a massive series of individual cases. Take, for example, an employment discrimination claim where the settlement involves individual hearings to see whether particular class members would have received specific jobs or promotions had discrimination not taken place. In these situations, it would appear that the class character of the individual members is gone; they are no longer absent, no longer anonymous, and no longer all similarly situated. Rather, they have developed what are, in effect, individual claims. At this point, the law firm representing the class may find itself engaged in the individual representation of several (or several hundred) plaintiffs, each of whom is a client, and each of whom is entitled to the lawyers' undivided loyalty. We will address such cases at greater length beginning in section 7.

Finally, although conflicts can occur over the scope and objectives of the representation, or the actual certification of a class, the largest area for conflict is, of course, fees. Class actions are expensive to litigate and prepare. Today they often involve committees of lawyers who each pledge to "front" specific sums of money to help fund the litigation. As a result, when settlement is at hand, lawyers feel that they have earned their sometimes very substantial fees. But no less true than in simpler fee situations is the concept we have addressed at length before — the conflict between the client and the lawyer who wishes to receive fees. We examine that issue in the next section. But first, *Amchem*.

AMCHEM PRODUCTS, INC. v. WINDSOR
521 U.S. 591 (1997)

JUSTICE GINSBURG delivered the opinion of the Court.

This case concerns the legitimacy under Rule 23 of the Federal Rules of Civil Procedure of a class-action certification sought to achieve global settlement of current and future asbestos-related claims. The class proposed for certification potentially encompasses hundreds of thousands, perhaps millions, of individuals tied together by this commonality: each was, or some day may be, adversely affected by past exposure to asbestos products manufactured by one or more of 20 companies. Those companies, defendants in the lower courts, are petitioners here.

The United States District Court for the Eastern District of Pennsylvania certified the class for settlement only, finding that the proposed settlement was fair and that representation and notice had been adequate. That court enjoined class members from separately pursuing asbestos-related personal-injury suits in any court, federal or state, pending the issuance of a final order. The Court of Appeals for the Third Circuit vacated the District Court's orders, holding that the class certification failed to satisfy Rule 23's requirements in several critical respects. We affirm.

. . . .

The class action thus instituted was not intended to be litigated. Rather, within the space of a single day, January 15, 1993, the settling parties — CCR defendants [defendant asbestos companies joining forces under the name Center for Claims

Resolution] and the representatives of the plaintiff class described below — presented to the District Court a complaint, an answer, a proposed settlement agreement, and a joint motion for conditional class certification.

. . . .

More than half of the named plaintiffs alleged that they or their family members had already suffered various physical injuries as a result of the exposure. The others alleged that they had not yet manifested any asbestos-related condition. The complaint delineated no subclasses; all named plaintiffs were designated as representatives of the class as a whole.

A stipulation of settlement accompanied the pleadings; it proposed to settle, and to preclude nearly all class members from litigating against CCR companies, all claims not filed before January 15, 1993, involving compensation for present and future asbestos-related personal injury or death.

Class members, in the main, are bound by the settlement in perpetuity, while CCR defendants may choose to withdraw from the settlement after ten years. A small number of class members — only a few per year — may reject the settlement and pursue their claims in court. Those permitted to exercise this option, however, may not assert any punitive damages claim or any claim for increased risk of cancer.

. . . .

Objectors raised numerous challenges to the settlement. They urged that the settlement unfairly disadvantaged those without currently compensable conditions in that it failed to adjust for inflation or to account for changes, over time, in medical understanding. They maintained that compensation levels were intolerably low in comparison to awards available in tort litigation. . . . And they objected to the absence of any compensation for certain claims, for example, medical monitoring, compensable under the tort law of several States.

. . . .

Objectors maintained that class counsel and class representatives had disqualifying conflicts of interests. In particular, objectors urged, claimants whose injuries had become manifest and claimants without manifest injuries should not have common counsel and should not be aggregated in a single class.

. . . .

Rule 23(a) states four threshold requirements applicable to all class actions: (1) numerosity (a class [so large] that joinder of all members is impracticable"); (2) commonality ("questions of law or fact common to the class"); (3) typicality (named parties' claims or defenses "are typical . . . of the class"); and (4) adequacy of representation (representatives "will fairly and adequately protect the interests of the class").

. . . .

In setting out these factors, the Advisory Committee for the 1966 reform anticipated that in each case, courts would "consider the interests of individual members of the class in controlling their own litigations and carrying them on as they see fit."

. . . .

As the Third Circuit observed in the instant case: "Each plaintiff [in an action involving claims for personal injury and death] has a significant interest in individually controlling the prosecution of [his case]"; each "has a substantial stake in making individual decisions on whether and when to settle."

While the text of Rule 23(b)(3) does not exclude from certification cases in which individual damages run high, the Advisory Committee had dominantly in mind vindication of "the rights of groups of people who individually would be without effective strength to bring their opponents into court at all."

. . . .

Among current applications of Rule 23(b)(3), the "settlement only" class has become a stock device. . . . Although all Federal Circuits recognize the utility of Rule 23(b)(3) settlement classes, courts have divided on the extent to which a proffered settlement affects court surveillance under Rule 23's certification criteria.

. . . .

We granted review to decide the role settlement may play, under existing Rule 23, in determining the propriety of class certification. We agree with petitioners to this limited extent: settlement is relevant to a class certification. The Third Circuit's opinion bears modification in that respect. But the Court of Appeals in fact did not ignore the settlement; instead, that court homed in on settlement terms in explaining why it found the absentees' interests inadequately represented.

Confronted with a request for settlement-only class certification, a district court need not inquire whether the case, if tried, would present intractable management problems, for the proposal is that there be no trial. But other specifications of the rule — those designed to protect absentees by blocking unwarranted or overbroad class definitions — demand undiluted, even heightened, attention in the settlement context. Such attention is of vital importance, for a court asked to certify a settlement class will lack the opportunity, present when a case is litigated, to adjust the class, informed by the proceedings as they unfold.

. . . .

The Third Circuit highlighted the disparate questions undermining class cohesion in this case:

> Class members were exposed to different asbestos-containing products, for different amounts of time, in different ways, and over different periods. Some class members suffer no physical injury or have only asymptomatic pleural changes, while others suffer from lung cancer, disabling asbestosis, or from mesothelioma. . . . Each has a different history of cigarette smoking, a factor that complicates the causation inquiry. The [exposure-only] plaintiffs especially share little in common, either with each other or with the presently injured class members. It is unclear whether they will contract asbestos-related disease and, if so, what disease each will suffer. They will also incur different medical expenses because their monitoring

and treatment will depend on singular circumstances and individual medical histories.

Differences in state law, the Court of Appeals observed, compound these disparities.

. . . .

Nor can the class approved by the District Court satisfy Rule 23(a)(4)'s requirement that the named parties "will fairly and adequately protect the interests of the class."

As the Third Circuit pointed out, named parties with diverse medical conditions sought to act on behalf of a single giant class rather than on behalf of discrete subclasses. In significant respects, the interests of those within the single class are not aligned.

The settling parties, in sum, achieved a global compromise with no structural assurance of fair and adequate representation for the diverse groups and individuals affected. Although the named parties alleged a range of complaints, each served generally as representative for the whole, not for a separate constituency.

The Third Circuit found no assurance here - either in the terms of the settlement or in the structure of the negotiations — that the named plaintiffs operated under a proper understanding of their representational responsibilities. That assessment, we conclude, is on the mark.

Impediments to the provision of adequate notice, the Third Circuit emphasized, rendered highly problematic any endeavor to tie to a settlement class persons with no perceptible asbestos-related disease at the time of the settlement. Many persons in the exposure-only category, the Court of Appeals stressed, may not even know of their exposure, or realize the extent of the harm they may incur. Even if they fully appreciate the significance of class notice, those without current afflictions may not have the information or foresight needed to decide, intelligently, whether to stay in or opt out.

Family members of asbestos-exposed individuals may themselves fall prey to disease or may ultimately have ripe claims for loss of consortium. Yet large numbers of people in this category — future spouses and children of asbestos victims — could not be alerted to their class membership.

Affirmed.

NOTES

The Supreme Court followed its decision in *Amchem* with another asbestos case, *Ortiz v. Fibreboard Corp.*, 527 U.S. 815 (1999). In *Ortiz*, the Court again rejected a proposed global settlement, holding that there were significant disparate interests within the class that called for the establishment of subclasses with their own representatives. This settlement was especially vulnerable because it included a "no-opt-out" provision, which would have prevented asymptomatic "exposure-only" class members from preserving their own individual claims. Given the Supreme Court's two pronouncements, is there any room for plaintiffs' class action attorneys to ethically represent an entire class in large mass tort cases? How can attorneys settle such wide-ranging cases without bringing in other counsel to ensure representation of each subdivision of the class? Finally, while the Supreme Court did not answer the question, what is the future of classes created for settlement purposes only? The Supreme Court reversed the Third Circuit's absolute prohibition of such "settlement classes." But is there any scenario in which such timing would *not* at least raise suspicion?

6.   Collusion, Attorneys' Fees, and Settlements of Dubious Value

In 1994, an Alabama state court judge approved a settlement in a class action against the Bank of Boston. The case charged the bank with holding escrow account interest that belonged to its borrowers, rather than paying it to them as it was earned. The 715,000 class members each had had mortgages issued through the bank at one time or another. Plaintiffs' and defense counsel told the judge that their settlement was worth over $40 million. But according to The New York *Times*, the maximum individual recovery was only $8.76.[5]

Besides, there was no dispute that the money belonged to the class members; the only question was *when* it would be paid. The court also approved $8.5 million in class counsel's fees, despite the fact, according to Illinois federal judge Milton I. Shadur, that the bank had offered essentially the same settlement two years earlier, *except* that the plaintiffs' lawyers' fees were then only $500,000. To make matters worse, under the first offer, the bank would pay the fees, but under the final settlement, the fees were to be paid out of the *class'* recovery. Since class members who no longer had mortgages had no funds left in the bank, the entire attorneys' fees bill had to be paid by those who still had their mortgages.

This gave the case the unique feature of charging some class members far more in fees than they "won" in back interest. One Maine couple "recovered" $2.19 from the class action, but had to pay out $91.33 in attorneys' fees. Many claimed they never even knew they were members of a class until they had "miscellaneous deductions" used to pay the lawyers charged to their escrow accounts. Eventually, some of these class members filed their own class action against the plaintiffs' attorneys and the bank for fraud. This case, however, was dismissed, barred by the statute of limitations.

The Bank of Boston settlement aroused the ire of many, including Judge Shadur, and the Attorney General of Florida, where the bank's principal mortgage company was located, who undertook an investigation. But lawyers for both the plaintiffs and the bank pointed out that the bank did change its accounting practices as part of the agreement.[6]

---

[5] *See* Barry Meier, *Math of a Class Action Suit: Winning $2.19 Costs $91.33*, N.Y. TIMES, Nov. 21, 1995.

[6] Barry Meier, *Math of a Class Action Suit: Winning $2.19 Costs $91.33*, N.Y. TIMES, Nov. 21, 1995; *see also* Hon. Milton Shadur, *The Unclassy Class Action*, 23 LITIGATION; Kimberly Blanton, *Class-action Suit Winners Sue Lawyers*, BOSTON GLOBE, Nov. 22, 1995.

While not quite as onerous, fees being paid by defendants also create conflicts of interest. In 2003, Joseph Rice, a leading class-action lawyer from South Carolina, accepted a $20 million fee from an asbestos class defendant's parent company as well as from the class settlement. At the same time, he was being criticized for creating a settlement trust that worked to the disadvantage of more seriously ill plaintiffs. Despite significant criticism from many, his fees were approved.[7]

In recent years, courts have been more willing strike down collusive fee awards in cases that do little for the class but provide substantial rewards for the lawyers. Read this brief excerpt of a 2011 Ninth Circuit opinion.

IN RE BLUETOOTH HEADSET PRODUCTS LIABILITY LITIGATION
654 F.3d 935 (9th Cir. 2011)

The settlement agreement approved in this products liability class action provides the class $100,000 in *cy pres* awards[8] and zero dollars for economic injury, while setting aside up to $800,000 for class counsel and $12,000 for the class representatives — amounts which the court subsequently awarded in full in a separate order. . . . Objectors challenge the fairness and reasonableness of the settlement . . . . We agree that the disparity between the value of the class recovery and class counsel's compensation raises at least an inference of unfairness, and that the current record does not adequately dispel the possibility that class counsel bargained away a benefit to the class in exchange for their own interests. We therefore vacate both orders.

. . . .

Collusion may not always be evident on the face of a settlement, and courts therefore must be particularly vigilant not only for explicit collusion, but also for more subtle signs that class counsel have allowed pursuit of their own self-interests and that of certain class members to infect the negotiations. A few such signs are:

(1) "when counsel receive a disproportionate distribution of the settlement, or when the class receives no monetary distribution but class counsel are amply rewarded";

(2) when the parties negotiate a "clear sailing" arrangement providing for the payment of attorneys' fees separate and apart from class funds, which carries "the potential of enabling a defendant to pay class counsel excessive fees and costs in exchange for counsel accepting an unfair settlement on behalf of the class"; and

(3) when the parties arrange for fees not awarded to revert to defendants rather than be added to the class fund.

Here, the pre-certification settlement agreement included all three of these warning signs. As discussed earlier, the settlement's provision for attorneys' fees is

---

[7] Alex Berenson, *Lawyer Cashes in on Both Sides*, INT'L HERALD TRIBUNE, March 13, 2003.

[8] [Editors' Note: *Cy pres* awards in class actions refer to funds used for the abstract "benefit" of the class, often through contributions to social or legal causes or agendas aligned with the class goals. Such awards are often made in lieu of returning unclaimed settlement funds to the defendants.]

apparently disproportionate to the class reward, which includes no monetary distribution. The settlement included a "clear sailing agreement" in which defendants agreed not to object to an award of attorneys' fees up to eight times the monetary *cy pres* relief afforded the class. Moreover, the settlement also contained a "kicker": all fees not awarded would revert to defendants rather than be added to the *cy pres* fund or otherwise benefit the class.

NOTES

While it is impossible to undertake here an exhaustive study of all the nuances of unfair and arguably unethical class action practices, coupon settlements are a particularly sensitive issue. When coupons or discounts become the class' compensation, the actual money paid is both indirect and uncertain, making an accurate determination of the value of the settlement problematic at best. For example, in the 1990s a class action suit against major airlines involved over 4,000,000 people and attorneys' fees of $14 million. While these fees totaled less than four percent of the claimed recovery, none of the settlement was "paid" in cash but in coupons good for $10 or $25 off future fares. Restrictions on these coupons limited their use; most significantly, the coupons couldn't be "stacked," or all used at one time for one flight. Since they were usable only in small increments ($10 maximum on any fare under $250, and $25 on any fare under $500), most customers found the coupons not worth the trouble.

7. Representing Large Numbers of Individual Parties

What happens when lawyers find themselves with cases that *look like* class actions, with scores, even hundreds, of individual plaintiffs, but that aren't eligible for class action treatment, usually because each case is unique on its facts and/or has unique damages? Mass cases — usually but not always tort claims, especially allegations about toxic pollution or defective drugs — have become more and more common, but the ethical rules that govern them remain the same. That is, despite multiple parties with similar complaints, these cases are *individual representations*, not group or class ones, and the same ethical rules that apply to the lawyers in Problem 7 who represent two clients will apply equally to lawyers representing hundreds.

Take, for example, a toxic tort case: A large number of people on the east side of town sue for damages, alleging that a local company deposited toxic waste into the town's groundwater. Given the scientific sophistication of most such cases and the specialized area of law, it would be almost impossible for each individual plaintiff to find a separate lawyer. Besides, plaintiffs without serious symptoms or prognoses might not be able to find lawyers at all.

So, as with class actions, it makes sense for plaintiffs to band together in a single lawsuit. Even if they don't, their suits may eventually become consolidated before one court for the sake of judicial economy, where they are often called "multi-district litigation," or "MDLs." But each plaintiff's circumstances remain different, from how close to the "plume" of toxicity the plaintiff lives to how severe the damages, from the sniffles or a rash to cancer. And with disparate damages come disparate proof problems.

In class actions, as we've seen, the lawyers represent the class itself, and cases are settled without individual class members' approval. But mass tort cases are made up of large numbers of *individual* lawsuits, and the lawyers represent individual clients, no matter how many there are. Each of those individuals has the autonomous right to settle, the right to have his or her lawyers negotiate the best possible resolution or go to trial, and the right to have the lawyers give their considered advice about what is best for that one individual.

But if a lawyer or group of lawyers represents 300 individual plaintiffs, how can they possibly do their best job for each, fulfill their fiduciary duties to each, and advise each what's best for that particular person, without it getting in the way of their representation of everyone else? The answer is "with great difficulty." Here are some practical realities:

• Defendants like to settle claims by "buying global peace," which means that if all or at least the vast majority of plaintiffs don't settle, a defendant will simply take the offer off the table.

• Defendants are not in the business of partitioning their settlements. They offer a lump sum and leave the division to plaintiffs' counsel.

• Some plaintiffs or groups of plaintiffs inevitably have higher damages and better likelihoods of high settlement values than others, depending, say, on location in the "plume" of toxicity, degree of harm or illness, and likelihood of being able to prove that the toxicity caused the harm.

• If the cases don't settle and go to trial, it is common for both sides to choose some exemplar or "bellwether" cases to try or arbitrate first: typical cases that may help define a global settlement after, say six, ten, or 15 trials.

These realities create a plethora of pitfalls for even the most ethical lawyer. The disparate hierarchy of case values puts counsel in a dicey position when advising people whose claims seem to be *de minimus* versus those whose claims are more serious or provable. How can counsel be loyal to Plaintiff #1, Plaintiff #300, and every plaintiff in between if she suggests more money go to one person rather than another?

A lawyer can't just simply divide up the lump sum offered by the defendant, at least not under the ethics rules. Settlements require the individual consent and approval of each client, as we'll discuss in the next section.

Even more troubling may be what happens when the defendant makes a substantial offer to settle but only if, say, 85% of the plaintiffs agree. If an insufficient number of plaintiffs sign up to settle, may the lawyer try to persuade the minority to climb on board because the settlement offer is good for the vast majority of plaintiffs? Or must the lawyer advise those few only according to what's right for *them*, which might be *not* to settle, because the deal, while good for most, is not good for them? That is, can lawyers ever give a true, honest opinion to *all* clients in these circumstances?

And if trial is necessary, how does the plaintiff's lawyer choose her "guinea pigs" for the bellwether cases? Those cases may well involve greater rewards, but these plaintiffs face an all-or-nothing risk.

Finally, we have yet to address whether lawyers can avoid the conflicts of interest that face them personally. Cases like mass toxic tort or defective drug claims are often extremely expensive to litigate and frequently remain problematic as to proof. Rewards are high, but so are risks, After investing millions, it's understandable that lawyers may take sides on whether to settle, may tend to favor big-damages clients over small, and may be tempted to take short-cuts around the ethics rules.

8.   The Current State of the Law

Current ethics rules and case law offer little in the way of a comfort for lawyers faced with the problems discussed above. For one thing, every jurisdiction in the country has a rule that states that the client alone decides whether to settle. What case law has addressed this issue has generally considered this to be an *unwaivable* right.[9]

Moreover, ABA Model Rule 1.8(g) states that "[a] lawyer who represents two or more clients shall not participate in making an aggregate settlement of the claims of or against the clients." These two closely-related concepts mean that plaintiffs' lawyers trying to figure out an ethical way to represent hundreds of clients cannot do it by majority rule, super-majority rule, electing a "litigation steering committee," or any other mechanisms that might seem to make intuitive sense — and that many plaintiffs' lawyers have tried.

In *The Tax Authority, Inc. v. Jackson-Hewitt, Inc.*, 898 A.2d 512 (N.J. 2006), 154 individual plaintiffs signed separate agreements to be bound by a settlement upon the recommendation of a plaintiffs' steering committee and subsequent affirmation by "a weighted majority of plaintiffs." The New Jersey Supreme Court undertook a thorough review of the case law, including *Eagle-Picher*, and several differing academic perspectives (including Professor Nancy Moore's, discussed below). It upheld the appellate court's reasoning that even *one client* out of 154 who objected to a settlement between the franchisees and a franchisor could veto the entire deal. As the lower appellate court put it:

> While it is indeed regrettable that one of 154 plaintiffs may possibly upset a settlement as to which all others have now agreed, we see no principled basis upon which to require [it] to settle when it does not wish to do so . . . .[10]

However, because the plaintiffs' attorney had taken reasonable steps to ensure a degree of fairness — the steering committee and "weighted" majority — the Supreme Court decided to apply its decision prospectively only, even though the

---

[9] Usually the rule is embodied in MR 1.2 or its equivalent, and the comment to the rule. And see the early leading case of *Hayes v. Eagle-Picher Indus., Inc.*, 513 F.2d 892 (10th Cir. 1985), among others cited below.

[10] The Tax Authority, Inc. v. Jackson-Hewitt, Inc., 873 A.2d 616, 630 (N.J. Super. Ct. 2005).

state ethics rules had been on the books for some time. That court also recommended that the state Commission on Ethics Reform examine possible changes in the ethics rules. As of March 2013, however, the New Jersey rules remain the same.

This strict reading of the ethics rules is hardly an outlier position. It is in accord not only with *Eagle-Picher*, but with other similar cases. For example, in *In re Hoffman*, 883 So. 2d 425, 433 (La. 2004), the Louisiana Supreme Court insisted that "[u]nanimous informed consent by the lawyer's clients is required before an aggregate settlement may be finalized. The requirement of informed consent cannot be avoided by obtaining client consent in advance . . . ."

ABA Formal Opinion 06-438 (February 10, 2006) reaffirmed that MR 1.8(g) "protects a client's right in all circumstances to have the final say in deciding whether to accept or reject an offer of settlement." Further, "Rule 1.8(g) deters lawyers from favoring one client over another in settlement negotiations by requiring that lawyers reveal to all clients information relevant to the proposed settlement." That means that each client must be told "the total amount or result of the settlement or agreement, the amount and nature of every client's participation in the settlement or agreement, the fees and costs to be paid to the lawyer from the proceeds or by an opposing party or parties, and the method by which the costs are to be apportioned to each client." Other sources, including a 2009 New York City opinion and several law review articles, are in accord.[11]

One final note: The one point that the ABA opinion and most cases and other sources do *not* explicitly make is that the lawyer has an independent fiduciary duty to give each client the *best possible advice* about what to do, not just to disclose the facts about settlement or ensure the client's right to settle. While giving this independent advice would seem to go without saying, this ultimate test of loyalty is often not explicitly affirmed in cases or opinions. Does that mean that it is somehow less important? Or ignored? Or simply assumed?

9. Do the Current Rules Foster Toxic Settlements?

Perhaps because the rules and cases provide so little flexibility, there are far too many examples of lawyers cutting corners, ignoring client rights, and even getting disbarred and going to jail by playing fast and loose with mass tort cases.

First, take the Fen-Phen cases. In Kentucky, lawyers William Gallion and Shirley Cunningham were disbarred and then jailed for abusing their clients' trust in distributing $200 million in Fen-Phen aggregate settlements. The "Special Judge" appointed over the case stated that the lawyers passed out settlement funds "like it was theirs to do with as they wish," including $95 million that went into their own pockets. The Kentucky lawyers were eventually jailed, and the judge first assigned the case was removed. Noted third-party "neutral" Kenneth

---

[11] NYC Formal Ethics Opinion 2009-6; *See also* Nancy J. Moore, *The Case Against Changing the Aggregate Settlement Rule in Mass Tort Lawsuits*, 41 S. Tex. L. Rev. 149 (1999), referred to further in the Supplemental Readings. Professor Moore was the "Reporter" or chief staff counsel, for the Ethics 2000 Commission.

Feinberg, who initially approved the settlement, had to disown his own fairness opinion.[12]

Read the case below regarding attorneys Leeds, Morelli, & Brown (LMB).

JOHNSON v. NEXTEL COMMUNICATIONS, INC.
660 F.3d 131 (2d Cir. 2011)

[A]ppellants and some 587 individuals hired LMB to pursue employment discrimination claims against Nextel . . . . The agreement specified a one-third contingency fee to go to LMB. The complaint alleges that LMB never intended to bring, and never brought, any discrimination actions against Nextel. Instead, LMB intended to follow a prior LMB practice of seeking direct payments, including payments as a legal consultant, from putative defendant-employers, in this case, Nextel. On September 28, 2000, LMB and Nextel met in New York and signed an agreement styled the Dispute Resolution and Settlement Agreement ("DRSA"). Under the DRSA, LMB was to be paid $2 million if it persuaded the claimants to: (i) drop all pending lawsuits and administrative complaints against Nextel within two weeks . . . ; and (ii) sign within ten weeks individual agreements in which each claimant agreed to be bound by the DRSA.

The DRSA . . . was designated as the exclusive means of settlement for all claimants then represented by LMB. The first stage consisted of an interview and direct negotiation between Nextel and each individual claimant. The second stage called for non-binding mediation [and] the third stage called for binding arbitration . . . .

The DRSA provided that Nextel would pay another $1.5 million to LMB upon the resolution of half of the claimants' claims and a final $2 million upon resolution of the remaining claims. LMB also promised not to accept any new clients with claims against Nextel . . . . Finally, the DRSA provided that Nextel would retain LMB as a legal consultant [for] two years following the resolution of all claims for an additional consultancy fee of $83,333.35 per month, or $2 million, bringing the total value of the DRSA to LMB to $7.5 million.

The complaint alleges that, in the weeks following the execution of the DRSA, LMB approached the claimants to obtain signed Individual Agreements and Pledges of Good Faith. In the Individual Agreement, the particular claimant had to state that he or she "reviewed the [DRSA]; had the opportunity to discuss that Agreement with [LMB] or any other counsel of [his or her] choosing; and agree to comply fully with the terms of that Agreement." With respect to the payment of legal fees, the Individual Agreements stated only that "I acknowledge and understand that . . . Nextel has agreed to pay an amount of money to [LMB] to cover the attorneys' fees and expenses, other than expert fees, that Claimants might otherwise pay to [LMB] . . . ."

The six appellants, along with all but fourteen of the claimants, signed Individual Agreements and Pledges of Good Faith. The complaint alleges that, notwithstanding the statements in the Individual Agreements and Pledges of Good Faith, LMB

---

[12] *See* Cunningham v. Abbott, 2011 Ky. App. LEXIS 24 (Feb. 4, 2011).

did not allow the claimants to review the full DRSA, but rather provided only the signature page of the DRSA, the Individual Agreements, and a document entitled "Highlights of Settlement Agreement" . . . .

. . . .

The existence of a fiduciary duty between LMB and appellants is beyond dispute. It is also plain that, if there was a breach, it could not have been due to negligence but rather, given the nature of the DRSA and the complaint's allegations, had to be knowing and intentional on LMB's part.

Appellants contend that LMB breached its fiduciary duty to the claimants by signing the DRSA because the terms of the DRSA created a conflict of interest between LMB and its claimant clients — a conflict that was not consentable, that is, one that could not be obviated by procuring the clients' consent. Moreover, they allege that even if the conflicts were consentable, LMB failed to properly disclose them. Appellants further argue that as a result of LMB's undisclosed conflicts of interest, their settlement awards were "unreasonably low and did not approximate the true value of the[ir] claims."

The DRSA created overriding and abiding conflicts of interest for LMB and thoroughly undermined its ability to "deal fairly, honestly, and with undivided loyalty to [appellants]." The DRSA on its face created enormous incentives on LMB's part to obtain from each and every one of its clients waivers of important rights. If LMB were to cause all claimants to waive [those] rights . . . LMB would be paid $2 million by Nextel even though not a single claimant had recovered anything.

The overriding nature of the conflict is underscored by the fact that, when fourteen of the 587 clients failed to agree, Nextel's final, but pre-consultancy, payment to LMB was reduced from $2 million to $1,720,000, or $20,000 per non-agreeing client.

It cannot be gainsaid that, viewed on its face alone, the DRSA created an enormous conflict of interest between LMB and its clients. Such a conflict is permissible only if waivable by a client through informed consent. However, there may be circumstances in which a conflict is not consentable. For two reasons, this is such a case. First, because LMB was not lead counsel in a class action, the class-protective provisions of Fed.R.Civ.P. 23 were not triggered. Therefore, LMB's clear duty as counsel to the parties seeking relief from Nextel was to advise each client individually as to what was in his or her best interests taking into account all of the differing circumstances of each particular claim. The DRSA was flatly antagonistic to that duty . . . .

By entering the DRSA, agreeing to be bound by its terms and accepting the financial incentives available therein, LMB violated its duty to advise and represent each client individually, giving due consideration to differing claims, differing strengths of those claims, and differing interests in one or more proper tribunals in which to assert those claims . . . . LMB was being paid by Nextel in effect to ignore its duty to represent clients as individuals with differing claims and interests that might require differing amounts of time and preparation vigorously to pursue a recovery.

. . . .

Second, . . . given the conflicts described above, any advice from LMB to its claimant clients could not possibly be independent advice untainted by the counter-incentives of the DRSA such that the resulting consent would be valid.

NOTES

In light of this law firm's behavior, perhaps the most surprising feature of this opinion is that it reversed a trial court that had *dismissed* the plaintiffs' claims.

It seems to have taken a while for mass plaintiffs' litigators to appreciate the difference between their class action cases and their individual representations. Or perhaps many just stuck their heads in the sand. As Professor Nancy Moore recently wrote, "mass tort lawyers often treat their clients as if they were members of a class without affording them the judicial protections given to actual class members."[13]

Indeed, that may be the biggest problem. More than one case has crossed our field of vision in which experienced mass plaintiffs' lawyers — while not overtly stealing from clients or taking millions from the other side — have nevertheless seem to have forgotten that they represent individual clients. The features of some mass individual representations are marked by:

- Brief retention agreements that make no mention of conflicts of interest despite the hundreds of plaintiffs involved;

- Retainer agreements in which clients expressly give up both the right to settle and the right to avoid aggregate settlements, ostensibly appointing their lawyers as "attorneys-in-fact";

- Settlements that are forged by counsel's agreement with defendants, with minimal or no discussion with or full disclosure to plaintiffs;

- Plaintiffs asked to sign "ratifications" of settlement agreements without being shown the settlement agreements themselves, even being told by their lawyers that the settlement agreements that they are ratifying are "confidential" so they may not see them; and

- Settlement agreements that state that if a sufficient percentage of plaintiffs agree to (or "ratify") the settlement, plaintiffs' counsel agrees to defend *the defendants* against the non-settling plaintiffs — essentially plaintiffs' counsel's agreement to switch sides and become adverse to their own clients.

In short, it seems that some lawyers representing large numbers of plaintiffs believe that their ability to act entirely within the bounds of the current ethics rules is beyond "with great difficulty," and approaches "impossible." This is hardly an excuse for unethical behavior, but there is a disconnect between abiding strictly

---

[13] Nancy J. Moore, *The Absence of Legal Ethics in the ALI's Principles of the Law of Aggregate Litigation: a Missed Opportunity — and More*, 79 GEO. WASH. L. REV. 717, 728–9 (2011).

by the current rules and managing a case with huge numbers of plaintiffs, even among the most ethical of lawyers.

10. A Problem in Need of a Solution?

No ethical lawyer would think that the methods described above "solve" anything other than making things easy and profitable for the lawyers who engage in them. But isn't some kind of solution necessary to bridge the gulf between the current inflexible rules and the reality of practice: that mass torts and other large multi-plaintiff cases are here to stay?

Several authorities have suggested solutions from both plaintiffs' and defense counsel's perspectives. The solutions, among others, include:

- Getting clients' prior authorization to a *minimum* settlement amount;
- Getting clients' agreement to an *minimum aggregate* amount;
- Permitting "damages averaging," or allowing a settlement that minimizes differences between the strongest and weakest claims in order to satisfactorily accommodate the vast majority of plaintiffs;
- Developing "matrixes" based on objective standards such as the degree of harm, proximity to harm, causation, and damages of each client, and then placing each client into a "matrix group" that gets a particular settlement level;
- Combining the above with administration, placement, and distribution of all matrix claims by independent third-party special master or "claims supervisor"; and
- Allowing individual plaintiffs who don't agree to simply "opt out" of participation.

None of these solutions quite does the job. Defendants like minimum aggregate sums but for plaintiffs' counsel that's like giving away the "bottom line." Plaintiffs are most comfortable with being able to opt out of a settlement that doesn't get them what they want, but defendants don't like the possibility of not buying the peace they seek. And none of these rules square entirely with MR 1.8(g) as it now stands, a rule that was not developed with mass plaintiffs' cases in mind.

In 2010, the American Law Institute, promulgated a series of "Principles of the Law of Aggregate Litigation."[14] Among those principles:

§ 3.17 Circumstances Required For Aggregate Settlements to Be Binding

(a) A lawyer or group of lawyers who represent two or more claimants on a non-class basis may settle the claims of those claimants on an aggregate basis provided that each claimant gives informed consent in writing . . . .

---

[14] AMERICAN LAW INSTITUTE, PRINCIPLES OF THE LAW OF AGGREGATE LITIGATION (2010). These principles are not part of the RESTATEMENT (THIRD) OF THE LAW GOVERNING LAWYERS (2000), also the work-product of the ALI.

(b) In lieu of the requirements set forth in subsection (a), individual claimants may, before the receipt of a proposed settlement offer, enter into an agreement in writing through shared counsel allowing each participating claimant to be bound by a substantial-majority vote of all claimants concerning an aggregate-settlement proposal . . . . An agreement under this subsection must meet each of the following requirements:

(1) The power to approve a settlement offer must at all times rest with the claimants collectively and may under no circumstances be assigned to claimants' counsel. Claimants may exercise their collective decisionmaking power to approve a settlement through the selection of an independent agent other than counsel.

(2) The agreement among the claimants may occur at the time the lawyer–client relationship is formed or thereafter, but only if all participating claimants give informed consent . . . .

(3) The agreement must specify the procedures by which all participating claimants are to approve a settlement offer . . . .

(4) Before claimants enter into the agreement, their lawyer or group of lawyers must explain to all claimants that the mechanism under subsection (a) is available as an alternative means of settling an aggregate lawsuit under this Section.

Unfortunately, the four requirements the ALI sets forth are somewhat diluted by the language of the actual proposals. The power to settle only "remains with the claimants" if they do not hire a third-party, supposedly "independent," agent. Such an agent would violate MR 1.8(g) as currently drafted, and does not seem to vest power in the plaintiffs as claimed, but to vitiate it and hand it to someone else.

Similarly, the ALI says that "the amount of information required for informed consent depends on the facts of the case," hardly a clear standard. And disclosure of alternatives is something the ALI says can be undertaken at any time prior to settlement. But if it is not part of the retainer agreement *ab initio*, can it ever be fair to all clients when they are asked to consent after-the-fact? Moreover, the proposal "does not prevent counsel from refusing to represent claimants who chose [not to settle]." That is, those plaintiffs are likely to be left without representation.

In short, as Professor Moore has noted, "the Principles offer a view of mass representation that is unduly rosy. They not only ignore the application of ethics rules to various aspects of nonclass aggregations, but also affirmatively downplay the risks of such representation and the role that ethics rules play in protecting the individual clients against such risks."[15]

Are there solutions, then, that are more workable? Some commentators, including Professor Moore, recommend full disclosure. But even full disclosure may not be enough unless it's accompanied by *advice* tailored to the needs of each individual client — a real stumbling block considering the inherent conflicts in the circumstances of various clients.

---

[15] Moore, *The Absence of Legal Ethics, supra,* at 728.

Others, including senior federal judge Jack B. Weinstein, a pioneer in handling mass tort "MDLs," and Judge Alvin K. Hellerstein, the judge in charge of perhaps the most challenging mass claim case ever, flowing from the events of 9-11, argue forcefully that such cases require judicial oversight.

Over the years, Judge Hellerstein has issued a number of orders, opinions, and decisions in the 9-11 case, formally known as *In re World Trade Center Disaster Site Litigation*, 834 F. Supp. 2d 184 (S.D.N.Y. 2011). The judge recognized early on that a case with over 9,000 individual, disparate plaintiffs would have "numerous potential conflicts among them and between them and their law firm." He appointed an independent ethics counsel, Hofstra law professor Roy Simon, to oversee the plaintiffs' lawyers. When in 2010, the lawyers proposed dismissing some non-responding plaintiffs "with prejudice," meaning that their cases could never be refiled, he hired a "special counsel" to try to contact those plaintiffs and ascertain their wishes.

In a 2011 order, Judge Hellerstein wrote that this case "fit[] neither paradigm — individual or class" but that it had many similarities with class actions. These included "a mass settlement in an aggregate amount," "the settlement amount subject to subdivision among sub-classes," a settlement "negotiated and executed not with Plaintiffs . . . but with the law firm representing the large majority of the Plaintiffs," and plaintiffs who did not "have choice about terms, conditions, or amounts. Their assent was to be manifested, as in class settlements, by an after-the-fact ratification . . . ."

The judge also noted the "compelling" conflict between the principal plaintiffs' law firm and the plaintiffs: "[S]ince a normal attorney-client relationship cannot function where one lawyer represents so many clients, each with varying and diverse interests, judicial review must exist to assure fairness and to prevent overreaching . . . . Faced with difficult and complicated choices, the Plaintiffs needed unconflicted attorneys with whom to consult and be advised. [Plaintiffs' counsel] itself had a compelling interest to settle, [having] carried on eight years of strenuous litigation and two appeals without any compensation. It had borrowed heavily, and incurred a large interest expense. The prospect of settlement and a fee of $250 million gave the firm an interest that may not have been in line with many of its clients' interests."

Thus, he concluded, when "[t]he parties to a lawsuit, if all are involved, may dismiss or settle their own lawsuit; in general, a judge does not have to be involved. In a class action, in contrast, a dismissal or settlement is not effective unless, after hearing the parties and any appearing members of the class who object, a judge finds settlement fair and reasonable, in the interests of the settling class. For the same reasons requiring a judge to review and approve class settlements for fairness, a district judge must review a mass tort settlement such as that now before me.[16]

Judicial oversight might work reasonably well in these circumstances, where a knowledgeable judge experienced in multi-district litigation is involved. But is judicial oversight enough? What happens with 500 plaintiffs in a state court case

---

[16] In re World Trade Center Disaster Site Litigation, 834 F. Supp. 2d 184 (S.D.N.Y. 2011).

that doesn't have a coordinating MDL mechanism or particular mass-tort case experience?

Ultimately, perhaps, a solution may rest with the extent of the disclosure. While courts, ethics opinions, and commentators have noted that full disclosure should include all the elements of the settlement for the individual plaintiff in question and the group of plaintiffs generally, there can be and perhaps should be disclosure beyond this. Professor Moore suggests as much, asking "what ensures that the clients have been adequately informed of both the advantages and the risks of proceeding as part of a 'litigation group'? What ensures that the decisions are truly consensual?" She then answers her own question:

> Under rules of professional conduct, individual clients must be fully informed, at the outset of the representation, of any significant risk that the representation may be materially limited by the lawyer's duty to other clients. With that information, individual clients might decide that they want to become part of a litigation group represented by this particular lawyer. But some clients might refuse, or they might decide that they prefer to be represented by a lawyer who represents a more narrowly tailored group.

Taking this disclosure even one step further, if prospective clients are informed *at the outset* that if they join the litigation group, their lawyers may make decisions that will be in the interests of the overall group of plaintiffs and not necessarily in the best interests of that individual, and, going yet another step further, that their lawyers will recommend settlement based on a broad consensus of plaintiffs, say 75% or more, this disclosure may be enough to allow the prospective plaintiffs to give informed consent. This disclosure is more likely to be found "consentable" if the plaintiffs are ensured that regardless of whether they join in the eventual settlement, their lawyers will continue to represent them to the best of their abilities.

Would such a disclosure comport with MR 1.8(g)? Perhaps, but probably not. If the disclosure allowed for a carefully-thought-out decisionmaking process involving, say, 75% or more of plaintiffs, this doesn't pass muster under the current rule. But it may make the most sense to revise this rule slightly, not to *broadly* allow aggregate settlements decided on by lawyers with big loyalty conflicts and huge fees at stake, but to *narrowly* allow fully-informed clients to knowingly and intelligently abrogate a degree of their settlement autonomy in the interests of becoming represented plaintiffs in a mass-plaintiff case.

D. SUPPLEMENTAL READINGS

1. Nancy Moore is likely the nation's foremost academic expert on class action ethics. Two of her most important articles about regulating class action ethics bookend each other, and are an invaluable analyses of the issues confronted by class action lawyers and those who would regulate them. They are *Who Should Regulate Class Action Lawyers?*, 2003 U. ILL. L. REV. 1477 (2003), and *Who Will Regulate Class Action Lawyers?*, 44 LOY. U. CHI. L.J. 577 (2012). Note the slightly different titles.

2. *The Future of Class Action in Mass Tort Cases: A Roundtable Discussion*, 66 FORDHAM L. REV. 1657 (1998), provides a good explanation of the claimed abuses of class actions and discusses the effects of *Amchem*. Participants include plaintiffs' and defense counsel and judges.

3. David J. Kahne, *Curbing the Abuser, Not the Abuse: A Call for Greater Professional Accountability and Stricter Ethical Guidelines for Class Action Lawyers*, 19 GEO. J. LEGAL ETHICS 741 (2006), states that Fed. R. Civ. P. 23 is not an adequate "procedural safeguard for class claimants," and that the Model Rules are "inapplicable in the eyes of the courts" and have "stalled any effort to introduce meaningful alternative ethical guidelines." The author argues that "clear ethical boundaries for the professional behavior of lawyers" involved in mass tort litigation are sorely needed.

4. Martha Matthews, *Ten Thousand Tiny Clients: The Ethical Duty of Representation in Children's Class Action Cases*, 64 FORDHAM L. REV. 1435 (1996), is a thorough explication of the problems and suggested solutions faced by those representing children in class actions. Matthews believes that children in class actions are rarely, if ever, consulted and their feelings are usually ignored by generally well-meaning but paternalistic lawyers. Matthews favors consultation with the children, their parents or guardians and others who are claiming to speak for them before determining the goals of a class action.

5. Perhaps the most controversial coupon case involved General Motors pickup trucks with side-mounted gas tanks. In July 1993, a federal district court in Philadelphia approved a class settlement covering roughly 5.7 million owners of these trucks. The owners would get coupons good for $1,000 off their next light duty truck; the coupons, however, were neither "stackable" nor transferable other than to family members. The plaintiffs' lawyers fees were set at $9.5 million. In *In re General Motors Corp. Pick-Up Truck Fuel Tank Products Liability Litigation*, 55 F.3d 768 (3d Cir. 1995), the court reversed the settlement, which Judge Edward R. Becker called "a GM sales promotion device." The court found that the settlement "provided absolutely nothing to those unwilling or unable to purchase another GM truck." A similar class action later settled in Louisiana. This settlement allowed fully transferrable and "stackable" coupons, creating a "secondary market" that gave the coupons an actual street value, and also allocated $5 million to fire safety research, including $1 million of the attorneys' fees.

6. Jack B. Weinstein, *Ethical Dilemmas in Mass Tort Litigation*, 88 NW. U. L. REV. 469 (1994). The federal judge who pioneered mass tort cases, from Agent Orange 40 years ago (see several opinions in *In re "Agent Orange" Product Liability Litigation*, (E.D.N.Y.) from 1982 to 2004) to the *Zyprexa* case in the new millennium (*see In re Zyprexa Prods. Liab. Litig., 451 F. Supp. 2d 458 (E.D.N.Y. 2006)*), writes about his belief that lawyers must act in the public interest in such cases. "It is my impression," he writes, "that few of the groups of plaintiffs I have dealt with in Agent Orange, asbestos, or DES were helped systematically or sympathetically as communities by lawyers handling their cases. Most lawyers were focused on getting cash for the individual client, obtaining a large fee, and closing the file." An interesting article by an outspoken, activist judge and, according to some, the person who coined the term "quasi-class action."

7. Howard M. Erichson, *A Typology of Aggregate Settlements*, 80 Notre Dame L. Rev. 1769, 1781 (2005) is a vitally important work that evaluates and analyzes various forms of aggregate settlements in an attempt to better define and describe them. Erichson's work is considered by many to be the "go to" discussion of what "aggregate settlements" actually are.

8. A duo of late-1990s articles by leading academic writers on tort practice come to very different conclusions. Nancy J. Moore, *The Case Against Changing the Aggregate Settlement Rule in Mass Tort Lawsuits*, 41 S. Tex. L. Rev. 149, 165 (1999), referenced in the text, takes the view that an individual client should be treated as any individual, with client autonomy to settle, and an aggregate settlement rule should be maintained. Charles Silver & Lynn A. Baker, *Mass Lawsuits and the Aggregate Settlement Rule*, 32 Wake Forest L. Rev. 733 (1997) asks the question "What settlement-related behaviors should be encouraged in mass lawsuits? And why?" Silver & Baker are prepared to be far more sanguine with liberal waiver and non-unanimity if it leads to practical results for most clients.

9. Both Professor Moore, in articles cited above, and Professor Silver have written more recently on this issue. In Professor Silver's case, this includes Charles Silver & Geoffrey Miller, *The Quasi-Class Action Method of Managing Multi-District Litigations: Problems and a Proposal*, New York University Law and Economics Working Papers 174 (2009); *The Allocation Problem in Multiple-Claimant Representations*, 14 (U. Chi.) Sup. Ct. Econ. Rev. 95 (2006), with Paul H. Edelman and Richard A. Nagareda; and *Merging Roles: Mass Tort Lawyers as Agents and Trustees*, 31 Pepp. L. Rev. 301 (2003).

PROBLEM 12: A DAY IN THE LIFE OF LYNCH, DAHL & WONG

A. INTRODUCTION

We have viewed many aspects of loyalty and conflicting interests in this chapter. Now, in the chapter's last problem, we look at the unique issues facing the insurance defense lawyer. This is the shortest but one of the more important problems in this book. We find each year that a healthy percentage of our students will do some amount of insurance defense work.

In doing that work, lawyers must grapple with these issues: How does a lawyer serve two masters: one who pays the bill, hires counsel, and has an ongoing relationship the law firm, and the other who is often a one-time user of legal services but who is the "officially" represented client? If there are two "clients," the existing rules can't fully apply, but other considerations, including public policy ones, may excuse what would otherwise be an untenable situation. But what if there's a direct conflict between insurer and insured? Are they both "clients" then? If so, all clients are to be treated equally, aren't they? Or may one client be more "equal" than another?

B. PROBLEM

Lynch, Dahl & Wong is a 25-lawyer litigation firm. The firm's bread-and-butter practice is its insurance defense work, where it is hired by an insurance carrier client to represent one of its insureds. Firm founder Leonard Lynch and managing partner Danielle Dahl have worked hard to cultivate their insurance carrier clients, and have formed close working relationships with their best clients' senior executives. Recently, New States Insurance Company, one of the firm's largest clients, announced a new policy: All defense lawyers' fees and costs will be subject to billing guidelines and audits. Part of this new program requires firms to obtain advance approval for the hiring of any expert where the anticipated cost would exceed $750, or for videotaping a deposition.

I

Dahl has been defending 18-year-old Midge Trasky in an auto intersection accident case for Secured Home and Life Insurance, another of the firm's best clients. The complaint claims Midge struck a pedestrian in a crosswalk with her father's car, causing the pedestrian to suffer a compound fracture of the leg.

Lynch, Dahl provides periodic reports on each Secured Home file, including the lawyer's summary of the facts, information on the latest discovery, and an estimate of case value. To provide current information, and because Midge's deposition is to be taken in a few weeks, Dahl has just interviewed Midge for the first time since the beginning of the case. During the interview, Midge hesitated and then asked Dahl if there would be a problem if someone else had been driving the car, someone who shouldn't be driving. Danielle was immediately concerned that Midge was on the verge of admitting that someone else had been driving at the time of the accident, a fact which, if known by the insurance company, could cause it to potentially drop the defense. Nevertheless, Danielle reassured Midge that telling her the truth was the best course. Midge then admitted that she was not driving after all, because shortly before the accident, she had allowed her 15-year-old cousin, Carrie, to get behind the wheel. Carrie is unlicensed and uninsured.

QUESTIONS

1. Dahl knows that Midge's admission means that Secured Home very likely would have no responsibility to pay for the accident. What should Danielle advise Secured?

2. Did Dahl have a duty to give Midge advice about the ramifications to her coverage if someone else was driving before Midge divulged that Carrie was driving? Does she have that duty *after* the disclosure? May Danielle give Midge such advice in view of her relationship with the insurance company?

3. What should Dahl do if Midge repeats at deposition what she told Danielle privately? Must she tell Secured? *May* she?

4. May Danielle stay in the case and attempt to settle it before Midge's deposition?

5. May she stay in the case if it does not settle quickly?

II

At a partner's meeting to discuss what to do about New States' new policy, senior partners Dahl and Lynch seemed resigned, albeit uncomfortable about having an insurance company dictate what they could do to work up a case. But Malcolm Wong, the youngest and most outspoken of the three, was outraged: "Come on! This amounts to practicing law without a license, or at the least a direct interference with our ability to represent our insureds. How can they make the decision on what's necessary for a case and what isn't? We'd be violating our ethical duties to agree to this!"

QUESTIONS

1. Do Wong's concerns make sense or is he out of line? If New States thought that a particular expert was unnecessary to defend an insured, but the insured wanted the company to hire one and Lynch, Dahl agreed, whose preferences should control?

2. Is Wong right that the firm's lawyers might be violating ethical duties by agreeing to New States' billing and auditing requirements? What rules of professional conduct could be involved?

C. READINGS

1. Coverage Counsel and Liability Counsel

Insurance is one of the few industries that is in the business of litigating cases. Not surprisingly then, insurance carriers can be highly desirable clients. Insurance practice includes coverage work, in which a law firm determines whether an event involving a particular insured is covered under the policy; and subrogation cases, after-the-fact claims among insurance companies to resolve the relative liabilities of their insureds. But the bread and butter of most insurance practices is the litigation of liability claims, or insurance defense work, in which the insurer hires an attorney to represent the insured under its policy.

It is now well-established in almost all jurisdictions that "coverage counsel," those who determine whether the insured is covered under the policy, should come from a different firm than "liability counsel," or the lawyers defending the insured in the litigation. When coverage counsel determines that the insured might not be covered, the carrier often agrees to defend the case but only under a "reservation of rights letter," which is issued to put the insured on noticed that the carrier reserves the right to not cover the settlement of the claim. But what if the litigator learns something vital to the issue of coverage? Read the following excerpt from this leading case decided some years ago by the Arizona Supreme Court.

PARSONS v. CONTINENTAL NATIONAL AMERICAN GROUP
550 P.2d 94 (Ariz. 1976)

We accepted this petition for review because of the importance of the question presented. We are asked to determine whether an insurance carrier in a garnishment action is estopped from denying coverage under its policy when its defense in that action is based upon confidential information obtained by the carrier's attorney from an insured as a result of representing him in the original tort action.

. . . .

[T]he Parsons filed a complaint alleging that Michael Smithey [age 14] assaulted the Parsons and that Michael's parents were negligent in their failure to restrain Michael and obtain the necessary medical and psychological attention for him. . . .

[Insurance carrier] CNA's retained counsel undertook the Smitheys' defense and also continued to communicate with CNA and advised. . . .

"The above referred-to confidential file shows that the boy is fully aware of his acts and that he knew what he was doing was wrong. It follows, therefore, that the assault he committed on claimants can only be a deliberate act on his part."

After CNA had been so advised they sent a reservation of rights letter to the Smitheys stating that the insurance company, as a courtesy to the insureds, would investigate and defend the Parsons' claim, but would do so without waiving any of the rights under the policy. The letter further stated that it was possible the act involved might be found to be an intentional act, and that the policy specifically excludes liability for bodily injury caused by an intentional act. This letter was addressed only to the parents and not to Michael.

. . . .

Appellants contend that CNA should be estopped to deny coverage and have waived the intentional act exclusion because the company took advantage of the fiduciary relationship between its agent (the attorney) and Michael Smithey. We agree.

. . . .

The attorney in the instant case should have notified CNA that he could no longer represent them when he obtained any information (as a result of his attorney-client relationship with Michael) that could possibly be detrimental to Michael's interests under the coverage of the policy.

The attorney representing Michael Smithey in the personal injury suit instituted by the Parsons had to be sure at all times that the fact he was compensated by the insurance company did not "adversely affect his judgment on behalf of or dilute his loyalty to [his] client, [Michael Smithey]." Ethical Consideration 5-14. Where an attorney is representing the insured in a personal injury suit, and, at the same time advising the insurer on the question of liability under the policy it is difficult to see how that attorney could give individual loyalty to the insured-client. "The standards of the legal profession require undeviating fidelity of the lawyer to his client. No exceptions can be tolerated."

. . . .

The attorney in the present case continued to act as Michael's attorney while he was actively working against Michael's interests. When an attorney who is an insurance company's agent uses the confidential relationship between an attorney and a client to gather information so as to deny the insured coverage under the policy in the garnishment proceeding we hold that such conduct constitutes a waiver of any policy defense, and is so contrary to public policy that the insurance company is estopped as a matter of law from disclaiming liability under an exclusionary clause in the policy.

NOTES

Reservation of rights issues are most often resolved at or near the beginning of a case. In many jurisdictions, when an insurance company reserves its rights, the insured may be entitled to an independent lawyer, at company expense, to ensure fairness to the insured. See *San Diego Navy Fed. Credit Union v. Cumis Insurance Society*, 162 Cal. App. 3d 358 (1984), described more fully in the Supplemental Readings.

2.   Loyalty and the Insurance Defense Lawyer

To whom does an insurance lawyer owe loyalty: the insured or the insurance carrier? Or both? The insured is the subject of the litigation and the one who indirectly pays for representation as part of the insurance policy. But the carrier retains the attorney and is responsible for direct payment. It is the carrier whose claims personnel form personal relationships with the lawyers, and that determines how many cases to send to the law firm. Finally, it is usually the carrier that decides on a settlement value after receiving reports from the attorney. Many cases and commentators have described insurance defense as a "dual representation." The issue almost always comes up in the context of a lawyer who failed to protect the interests of the *insured* as against the insurance carrier. In *Parsons*, for instance, the court addresses this dual representation in passing, noting that "[t]he attorney in the instant case should have notified CNA that he could no longer represent them. . . ." The excerpted analysis in the following case, upholding the insured's malpractice liability claim against the insurance defense lawyer, describes that dual representation.

BETTS v. ALLSTATE INSURANCE CO.
154 Cal. App. 3d 688 (1984)

In accepting employment to render legal services, an attorney impliedly agrees to use such skill, prudence and diligence as lawyers of ordinary skill and capacity commonly possess, and he is subject to liability for damage resulting from failure so to perform. Furthermore, it is an attorney's duty to "protect his client in every possible way," and it is a violation of that duty for the attorney to "assume a position adverse or antagonistic to his client without the latter's free and intelligent consent given after full knowledge of all the facts and circumstances." The attorney is "precluded from assuming any relation which would prevent him from devoting his entire energies to his client's interest."

These traditional obligations of an attorney are in no way abridged by the fact that an insurer employs him to represent an insured. Typically, in such a situation, the attorney in effect has two clients, to each of whom is owed a "high duty of care." To the insured, the attorney owes "the same obligations of good faith and fidelity as if he had retained the attorney personally." (*Lysick v. Walcom* (1968) 258 Cal. App. 2d 136, 146 [65 Cal. Rptr. 406].)

Provided there is full disclosure and consent, an attorney may undertake to represent dual interests. However, whether in the insurer-insured context or otherwise, the attorney who undertakes to represent parties with divergent interests owes the "highest duty" to each to make a "full disclosure of all facts and circumstances which are necessary to enable the parties to make a fully informed decision regarding the subject matter of litigation, including the areas of potential conflict and the possibility and desirability of seeking independent legal advice."

The loyalty owed to one client by an attorney "cannot consume that owed to the other." Thus a lawyer who, while purporting to continue to represent an insured and who devotes himself to the interests of the insurer without notification or disclosure to the insured breaches his obligations to the insured and is guilty of negligence. (*Lysick v. Walcom, supra.* . . .)

NOTES

Lysick, a case that has been cited in many jurisdictions, concerned an insurance defense lawyer who failed to inform the insured of a plaintiff's demand above the limits of the policy and rejected the demand without consulting with the insured or asking the insurer to pay more. The case held that abiding by the *insurer's* wishes regarding settlement without considering the *insured's* position constituted representing "two parties with divergent interests, insofar as the settlement of the case was concerned." This breach of the duty of loyalty to the insured meant that the insured could maintain a negligence action against the attorney when the original case went to trial and resulted in a verdict much larger than the policy.

Several other courts have followed the language from an early leading New York case with a similar holding: "The attorney may not seek to reduce the company's loss by attempting to save a portion of the total indemnity in negotiations for the settlement of a negligence action, if by so doing he needlessly subjects the assured to judgment in excess of the policy limit."[1]

3. Is Dual Representation Realistic? Is the "Unique" Relationship Workable?

More recently, some authorities have recognized that the special problems of this "tripartite" relationship have to be addressed in special ways. The *Third Restatement of the Law Governing Lawyers*, section 134 reaffirms the *Parsons* holding on confidentiality and the duty of a lawyer to exercise independent professional judgment.

But recall our discussion in Problem 7 about the effectiveness of certain consents, particularly where the parties do not have equal power. Can the insured's consent truly be "free and intelligent" in the insurance situation, when a refusal of consent might be tantamount to refusing legal counsel? When an insured signs an insurance contract, does that include a consent to joint representation? Does the insured have any real choice other than to consent? Some argue that most of the time, consenting to dual representation is not a problem, since conflicts between insurer and insured occur only rarely. Here's how one court put it: "[T]he attorney has two clients whose primary, overlapping and common interest is the speedy and successful resolution of the claim and litigation."[2]

But is this really true? Does "successful resolution" mean the same to the insurer and the insured? The insurer's primary goal is usually to resolve the case as inexpensively as possible, minimizing both the costs of defense and the cost of settlement. The insured's goal may be very different: to have minimal intrusion on the insured's time or minimal disruption of his or her life, or to avoid the traumatic experiences of being deposed or sitting through trial as the named defendant.

The ostensibly common interests of insurer and insured may suddenly diverge at the moment of settlement, as in *Lysick*. Most insurance policies don't give the insured a "vote" on settlement. On the other hand, several cases have held that where a client refuses to settle, the lawyer hired by the carrier may not be able to settle the case, *even if* the insurance policy does not require the insured's consent. For example, in *Rogers v. Robson, Masters, Ryan, Brumund & Belom*, 407 N.E.2d 47, 49 (Ill. 1980), the Illinois Supreme Court held that a physician could maintain

---

[1] American Employers Ins. Co. v. Goble Aircraft Specialties, Inc., 205 Misc. 1066 (N.Y. Sup. Ct. 1954).

[2] American Mut. Liab. Ins. Co. v. Superior Ct., 38 Cal. App. 3d 579 (1974).

an action against the lawyers who represented him in a malpractice case and settled without his consent:[3]

> Although defendants were employed by the insurer, plaintiff, as well as the insurer, was their client . . . and was entitled to a full disclosure of the intent to settle the litigation without his consent and contrary to his express instructions. . . . Defendants' duty to make such disclosure stemmed from their attorney-client relationship with plaintiff and was not affected by the extent of the insurer's authority [under the insurance policy] to settle.

Some other cases take an opposite view. For example, *Teague v. St. Paul Fire and Marine Ins. Co.*, 10 So. 3d 806 (La. Ct. App. 2009), also concerned a physician who objected to a settlement made without his consent. After the case went to the Louisiana Supreme Court, which remanded with instructions, the appellate court held that the doctor had *no right* to participate in the settlement because the contract of insurance didn't provide that right. The court did criticize the lawyer for not informing Dr. Teague about the mediation of the case, but in a disciplinary case, the Louisiana Attorney Disciplinary Board exonerated the doctor's attorneys of all charges *including* diligence and conflict of interest except one: an admonition for failing to communicate adequately with the doctor.[4]

It is interesting to note that *Rogers*, *Teague*, and even the *Zuber* discipline matter, all refer to dual representation, as does most case law. As we have learned, this representation means that the highest duty of care is owed to both clients. It also means that the confidences of both must be either shared or carefully guarded. It means that the lawyer must maintain the balancing act of protecting one client's confidences and vigorously representing the other. But as these and other circumstances show, is this balancing act truly feasible for the insurance defense lawyer?

4. More Dual Representation Problems, and a Florida Solution

In 2002, the Florida Supreme Court approved a "Statement of Insured Client's Rights," codified as Florida Rule 4-1.8(j): "Conflicts of Interest; Prohibited and Other Transactions." A few other states, including Ohio, have since developed similar guidelines. Read the following story about that rule, and note the author's recitation of a series of bullet-point issues to which dual representation gives rise.

Robert A. Clifford, *Sunshine State Enlightens Clients' Rights*
CHICAGO LAWYER 13 (January 2003)[5]

Lawyers hired by insurance companies to defend policyholders in Florida must give them a Statement of Insured Client's Rights under a new mandatory disclosure rule adopted last year by the Florida Supreme Court. It is believed to be the first

---

[3] Typically, although not in the cases cited here, professional liability policies, including for attorneys, are much more likely to give the insured veto power on consent.

[4] In re Zuber and Nobile, Louisiana Attorney Discipline Board No. 09-DB-060 (2011).

[5] Copyright © 2013 by Law Bulletin Publishing. Reprinted by permission.

of its kind in the country, and I believe it should be more widespread.

The Statement informs the client of possible conflicts of interest faced by his or her lawyer. The document spells out the policyholder's rights and, in the case of an insurance contract, explains the three-way relationship between the lawyer, the policyholder and the insurance carrier that often can lead to competing loyalties.

Initially, it had been reported that the insurance industry resisted these new rules; but, after increasing support from other factions, insurance representatives participated in the drafting of the document. The effort to adopt these rules was instigated by lawyers who formed a special committee in 1999 to examine a number of insurance defense ethics issues including these questions:

> • When an insurance company hires a lawyer to defend a policyholder, can the company's claims adjuster tell the lawyer how to conduct the defense?

> • Can the company require the lawyer to sacrifice independent professional judgment in favor of cost-cutting guidelines imposed by the company?

> • Can the law firm hired by the insurance company send an itemized bill containing confidential client information to the insurer's outside auditor?

> • What happens when the insurance company agrees to pay for the policyholder's lawyer but reserves the right not to pay any judgment if it decides that the claim wasn't covered?

> • Does a policyholder have any greater say in his legal defense when he faces a judgment that exceeds his policy limits?

Following a year of study and hearings, the committee found it was unable to definitively answer these and other questions.

There's no bright line. What the insurance industry calls "controlling the litigation," many attorneys call "treading on the attorney's professional conduct," the committee said. . . .

The Statement is a breakthrough in professional conduct involving representation in insurance coverage disputes in that it contains 10 paragraphs of information to the client about the lawyer-client relationship, fees, confidentiality, conflicts of interest and risks. It also addresses who has the right to direct the lawyer, the right to hire independent counsel and the right to report disciplinary violations to the bar.

. . .

Frankly, I think the Statement doesn't go far enough. Defense lawyers often don't advise their clients of the inherent conflicts in insurance matters; and this Statement is a step toward informing a client, which is paramount in any representation.

. . . .

Although many defense lawyers recognize that the client is their priority, too often lawyers are conflicted because of the dueling loyalties to those who are signing their paychecks. Privately, many will admit to this ethical dilemma.

It is difficult to make these conflicts disappear, but it is wise to disclose as much as possible to the client so that s/he is well-informed and can make decisions based upon accurate and full information.

And, it is heartening to see, as in Florida, that the insurance industry finally is embracing this effort.

5.   Two Clients or Just One? Does the Ability to Sue Provide the Solution?

As we've seen, it's by now well-established that the insured can sue an insurance defense lawyer for negligence, including for breaches of loyalty. Few if any would disagree that the insured is the lawyer's client; after all, it's the insured whose name appears in the case caption, and who the lawyer represents as a client before the court.

But what about the insurer? It is clear that the concept of "dual representation" breaks down when the insurer/insured relationship does not go smoothly. Does today's thinking on the "tripartite" relationship still allow for the insurer to be denominated a client? One issue that could shed light on this question is whether the insurer may sue the defense lawyers for malpractice, since with rare exceptions the carrier has to pay the damages. Read the brief excerpt from this leading opinion on this issue from the Michigan Supreme Court.

ATLANTA INTERNATIONAL INSURANCE CO. v. BELL
475 N.W.2d 294 (Mich. 1991)

A rule of law expanding the parameters of the attorney-client relationship in the defense counsel-insurer context might well detract from the attorney's duty of loyalty to the client in a potentially conflict-ridden setting. Yet to completely absolve a negligent defense counsel from malpractice liability would not rationally advance the attorney-client relationship. Moreover, defense counsel's immunity from suit by the insurer would place the loss for the attorney's misconduct on the insurer. The only winner produced by an analysis precluding liability would be the malpracticing attorney. . . .

The defense counsel-insurer relationship is unique. The insurer typically hires, pays, and consults with defense counsel. The possibility of conflict unquestionably runs against the insured, considering that defense counsel and the insurer frequently have a longstanding, if not collegial, relationship.

In a malpractice action against a defense counsel, however, the interests of the insurer and the insured generally merge. The client and the insurer both have an interest in not having the case dismissed because of attorney malpractice. Allowing recovery for the insurer on the basis of the failure of defense counsel to adhere to basic norms of duty of care thus would not 'substantially impair an attorney's ability to make decisions that require a choice between the best interests of the insurer and the best interests of the insured.' [ ] The best interest of both insurer and insured converge in expectations of competent representation.

. . . .

To hold that an attorney-client relationship exists between insurer and defense counsel could indeed work mischief, yet to hold that a mere commercial relationship exists would work obfuscation and injustice. The gap is best bridged by resort to the doctrine of equitable subrogation to allow recovery by the insurer.

NOTES

Other courts, such as the Minnesota Supreme Court in *Pine Island Farmers Coop v. Erstad & Riemer, P.A.*, 649 N.W.2d 444 (Minn. 2002) have adopted the "equitable subrogation" reasoning in *Bell*. But these courts have actually *avoided* the dual representation trap by coming up with a practical solution that relies on a doctrine that some would call a "legal fiction," justified by the social reality of the usefulness of insurance. *Bell* makes it clear that while it may sue, the insurance carrier is *not* a client in Michigan. Similarly, in Arizona, the court that authored *Parsons*, while not adopting "equitable subrogation," nevertheless made it clear that the insurer could sue for malpractice, but that the issue did not depend on whether or not the insurer was denominated a "client."[6]

California, among other states, has refused to follow this path. In *Unigard Insurance Group v. O'Flaherty & Belgum*, 38 Cal. App. 4th 1229 (1995), the court noted that a previous California court had rejected equitable subrogation, and instead found that both insured and insurer were clients:

> *The O'Flaherty Law Firm Owed An Independent Duty of Care to Unigard.* We must first address the threshold issue of whether an insurer can bring a legal malpractice action against counsel hired by the insurer to represent an insured . . . .
>
> In *Fireman's Fund Insurance Co. v. McDonald, Hecht & Solberg* (1994) 30 Cal. App. 4th 1373, 36 Cal. Rptr. 2d 424, the court rejected equitable subrogation as a basis for such an insurer's legal malpractice action. However, Unigard does not rely on that doctrine. Unigard claims an independent right to assert a malpractice claim against the O'Flaherty law firm arising out of its allegedly negligent representation of Wilkinson, Unigard's insured . . . .
>
> We conclude that where the insurer hires counsel to defend its insured *and does not raise or reserve any coverage dispute, and where there is otherwise no actual or apparent conflict of interest between the insurer and the insured that would preclude an attorney from representing both*, the attorney has a dual attorney-client relationship with both insurer and insured. This relationship provides a sufficient basis for Unigard's legal malpractice action against the O'Flaherty law firm.[7]

Note the large caveat in *Unigard*, however. Joint clienthood only applies where there is no possible conflict of interest, a point the *Unigard* court saw fit to italicize. Thus, the ability to sue, while important in its own right, does not appear to directly

---

[6] Paradigm Ins. Co. v. the Langerman Law Offices 24 Pac.3d 593 (Ariz. 2001).

[7] Unigard Ins. Group v. O'Flaherty & Belgum, 38 Cal. App. 4th 1229, 1236–7 (1995).

answer the question of whether the law firm has one or two clients.

6.   Two Clients, One Client, or Perhaps One-and-a-Half?

Much has been written and debated in the past 20 years among insurance industry stakeholders, members of the insurance defense bar, and law professors about whether the insurance defense counsel represents two clients — the traditional view — or one client, the insured — a "trending" view in many jurisdictions. Here are two early examples of the sides of this debate:

Denver law professor Stephen L. Pepper, has long argued for a "single client model" in which lawyers have only one client, the insured. Pepper postulates that the single client model is necessary to act "as a substantial counterbalance to the lawyer's self-interest," since lawyers face "the bias created by the economic power of the insurance companies which pay them on the one hand, and the arguable ethical obligation to assist the insured *against* the company, on the other."[8] In contrast, Texas law professor Charles Silver, a frequent writer on this subject, believes that the opposite is true: The insurance defense lawyer can have two *equal* clients at all times, as envisioned by the insurance contract.[9]

The consensus on the one- vs. two-client model is not clear, either among commentators or in state case law. Indeed, a number of recent commentators, particularly among insurance defense counsel, disagree even about how many states fall into the "one-" or "two-client" category.[10]

Case law seems to be turning increasingly to what we might call the "two clients unless . . ." solution — as in *Unigard*, where dual representation can exist only in cases where no conflict exists between insurer and insured — or the "one-and-a-half-client" model, in which the insured is the "primary" client and the insurer is a client only until a conflict of interest arises. This is the conclusion reached in a 2011 Minnesota appellate decision that evaluated the tripartite relationship in light of the standards set in *Pine Island*. The case involved a coverage issue: The lawyer hired by the insurer to represent the insured, RDI, failed to ask the arbitrator for an explanation of the arbitration award, thus making it impossible to tell whether RDI was covered under its policy. Read this excerpt.

---

[8] Stephen L. Pepper, *Applying the Fundamentals of Lawyers' Ethics to Insurance Defense Practice*, 4 CONN. INS. L.J. 27 (1997–1998).

[9] See especially, and most pungently, Charles Silver & Kent Syverud, *The Professional Responsibilities of Insurance Defense Lawyers*, 45 DUKE L.J. 255 (1995), and Charles Silver & Michael Sean Quinn, *Are Liability Carriers Second-Class Clients? No, But They May Soon Be: A Call to Arms Against the Restatement (Third) of the Law Governing Lawyers*, 6 COVERAGE (March/Apr. 1996).

[10] *See, e.g.*, PATRICIA A. BRONTE, KEY DEVELOPMENTS: ETHICS AND THE TRIPARTITE RELATIONSHIP (2008); and WILLIAM T. BARKER & CHARLES SILVER, THE PROFESSIONAL RESPONSIBILITIES OF INSURANCE DEFENSE COUNSEL (2012). Bronte, an insurance coverage lawyer, writes that 15 states hold to the single client rule, while 16 allow dual representation. Barker and Silver, both insurance lawyers, have a recent book that has a chart showing 38 states allowing dual representation and only four forbidding it. That is obviously a wide disparity. *See* also William Freivogel's notable site, in this case http://www.freivogel.com/insurancedefense.html, for his more neutral and perhaps more nuanced "scorekeeping."

REMODELING DIMENSIONS, INC. v. INTEGRITY MUTUAL INS. CO.
806 N.W.2d 82 (Minn. Ct. App. 2011)

The supreme court has described this set of inter-relationships as a "tripartite relationship" [citing *Pine Island*]. The supreme court has recognized that when the interests of the insurer and the insured are adverse, an attorney "will tend to favor the interests of the insurer at the expense of those of the insured." . . .

The existence of a tripartite relationship, however, does not displace the enduring fundamental principle that . . . an attorney retained by an insurer to represent an insured "owes a duty of undivided loyalty to the insured and must faithfully represent the insured's interests." Accordingly, "an attorney retained by an insurer to defend its insured . . . is under the same obligations of fidelity and good faith as if the insured had retained the attorney personally."

Nonetheless, dual representation of an insured and an insurer is permissible in limited circumstances, if the interests of an insured and an insurer are not adverse so that an attorney does not have a conflict of interest. In that situation, the attorney may represent both the insured and the insurer, so long as two conditions are satisfied: first, the insured must consult with an attorney who explains "the implications of dual representation and the advantages and risks involved," and, second, the insured must expressly consent to the dual representation after the consultation. *Id.*; cf. Minn. R. Prof. Conduct 1.7(b)(4).

In this case, [u]ndoubtedly, RDI's interests and Integrity Mutual's interests were aligned while the arbitration proceeding was pending to the extent that each had an interest in avoiding liability or minimizing damages. Accordingly, while the arbitration proceeding was pending, the attorney could have shared information with Integrity Mutual, or Integrity Mutual could have contributed toward the attorney's defense strategy. But RDI's interests and Integrity Mutual's interests would not have been aligned to the extent that either of them desired an explanation of the arbitration award. As illustrated by this lawsuit, an explanation of an arbitration award may determine whether an insurer has a duty to indemnify an insured. RDI's attorney would have had a conflict of interest if he had represented both RDI and Integrity Mutual and had been called upon to request an explanation of the arbitration award. Thus, *Pine Island*'s precondition for proper dual representation — the absence of a conflict of interest — is not satisfied.

NOTES

Interestingly and perhaps ironically, while the *RDI* appeals court accepted the "one-and-a-half client" solution — that is, the lawyer started out with two joint clients, but wound up with only one — that meant that by the end of the case, RDI's attorney did *not* represent the insurer any longer, and thus the insurer was *not* responsible for the lawyer's failure to act.[11]

---

[11] After this segment was written and edited for publication, the authors learned that the Minnesota Supreme Court, in *Remodeling Dimensions, Inc. v. Integrity Mut. Ins. Co.*, 819 N.W.2d 602 (2012), had reversed the appeals court. The high court found that "the question is whether a principal-agency

Courts have understandably been reluctant to declare insurance carriers mere third party payors who do not enjoy the status of clients. This might cost them rights and remedies to which they feel entitled, without which the insurance system as we know it might not exist. Nevertheless, if insurance carriers are clients, the weight of authority suggests their rights may be secondary to the rights of insureds. Can there be such a thing as a "second class" client? Increasingly, it appears so in some limited circumstances.

7. Limiting Defense Costs vs. Insureds' Confidentiality

In recent years insurance companies have undertaken two measures to limit their own defense costs, and have earned themselves scorn and enmity from many, including some of the "panel" attorneys the companies have traditionally hired to defend their insureds. One measure involves instituting billing guidelines and audits, discussed here; the other involves using in-house or "captive" counsel to defend their cases, discussed in the next section.

Sylvia Hsieh, *Billing Guidelines and Fee Audits of Defense Lawyers Struck Down*
2000 LAWYERS WEEKLY USA 435, May 15, 2000[12]

Where insurance defense lawyers have to comply with insurance companies' billing guidelines and submit to third-party audits, this violates the Rules of Professional Conduct unless the insured consents, says the first state supreme court to address this issue. . . .

"This is very hot news," says Lloyd Milliken, Jr. of Indianapolis, president of the Defense Research institute (DRI). "This is going to change the way the defense business is being run," says Gary M. Zadick of Great Falls, Mont., one of the lawyers who brought the case.

The guidelines have become a standard feature in defense work and typically require pre-approval before a lawyer can take a deposition, hire an expert or spend money on other litigation costs. In addition, lawyers are often required to submit detailed billing statements to third-party auditors who oversee the expenses.

But the Montana Supreme Court unanimously held that a defense lawyer's sole client is the policyholder, not the insurance company. Therefore, the pre-approval process interferes with lawyers' independent judgment and the use of outside auditors violates client confidentiality, the court said.

Thirty-two state ethics committees have already reached the same conclusion. However, the insurance industry has largely ignored them as non-binding, says Great Falls, Mont. attorney Robert James, a co-petitioner in the case who says he has received calls from lawyers in every state about it. . . .

---

relationship existed between Integrity and the attorney, not whether the attorney represented Integrity." Finding that the insurer had "a duty to notify RDI of RDI's interest in an explanation of the arbitration award," the high court thus found the attorney-representation analysis unnecessary to answer.

[12] Copyright © 2000 by Lawyers Weekly USA. Reprinted by permission.

[D]efense lawyers and insurance companies will be trying to fashion agreements to avoid similar litigation in other states, including ways to seek the insured's "informed consent" to the billing guidelines, says Michael Aylward, a Boston defense attorney and vice chair of DRI's insurance committee.

Milliken says third-party auditing is already "on its way out," judging from recent meetings between DRI and insurance industry representatives, many of whom said they are dropping their outside auditors. . . .

The insurance companies argued that the lawyers represent two clients — the insured and the insurance company that foots the bill. Courts in other jurisdictions have held this way in other contexts. But the Montana court said that none of those decisions addresses whether they are clients for purposes of the Rules of Professional Conduct.

"[T]he stark reality [is] that the relationship between an insurer and insured is permeated with potential conflicts. . . . In cases where an insured's exposure exceeds his insurance coverage, where the insurer provides a defense subject to a reservation of rights, and where an insurer's obligation to indemnify its insured may be excused because of a policy defense, there are potential conflicts of interest," the court said.

The insurance companies argued that the pre-approval process is necessary to control litigation costs.

But the court said that "the requirement of prior approval fundamentally interferes with defense counsel's exercise of their independent judgment."

. . . .

The court next addressed a requirement in the insurer-imposed guidelines that defense lawyers submit detailed descriptions of their work to independent auditors hired by the insurance companies. The defense lawyers argued that this practice violated a professional conduct rule that bars a lawyer from revealing information to third parties unless the client consents.

The insurance companies argued that auditors fell within the "magic circle" of people with whom information can be shared, such as secretaries, interpreters and computer technicians.

But the court disagreed, finding that the auditors don't have a common interest with the insured.

"Their mission . . . is to find fault with legal charges, not to further the representation of insureds. Further, unlike secretaries and computer technicians who are engaged to assist defense counsel, third-party auditors are not employed by defense counsel and . . . they are potential adversaries of defense counsel. . . ."

One question is whether the insured can consent by signing a provision in the policy agreeing to the billing guidelines and third-party auditing.

Defense lawyers say this won't fly. "Putting it in a policy where there's no negotiation would not be 'fully informed consent.' It would be a contract of adhesion," says Zadick.

NOTES

In this instance, not only did Montana lead the nation, but the nation reacted swiftly. By 2001, the ABA had joined the Montana court and the dozens of state ethics committees cited in the article in condemning the auditing practice as violative of the insured's confidential relationship with the assigned attorney.[13]

Note that the Montana court expressly used a "one-client" model in reaching its conclusion. But given the widespread acceptance of this court's position and the ABA's supportive opinion, the issue does not appear to turn on the one- vs. two-client analysis.

If auditors can't be used to limit insurance defense costs, what about the insurer itself setting restrictive guidelines? Would such rules interfere with a lawyer's competent representation on behalf of the insured, as Malcolm Wong worries? The ubiquitous Professor Silver argues "no."

"The doctrinal foundation of the practice of insurance defense is endangered as never before . . . because liability insurers sought to manage litigation costs. In other words, it happened because they tried to do their job," Professor Silver wrote in *When Should Government Regulate Lawyer-Client Relationships? The Campaign to Prevent Insurers from Managing Defense Costs*, 44 Ariz. L. Rev. 787 (2002). "The problem that rankles defense lawyers is that insurers do the job too well. They place significant pressure on defense lawyers to become more efficient. This is purely a matter of economics; it raises no problems of ethics," because "tripartite relationships are contractual."

One must question, however, whether Silver's pro-industry view ignores the defense lawyers' claims that they cannot competently perform their jobs for their principal clients — the insureds — with a heavy lid on costs and time spent. Or, perhaps, Silver's point merely brings us back full circle to the one- vs. two-client debate.

8. Insurance Company Employee and Defense Counsel: Another Dual Role?

Can an insurance company employee serve as counsel for the insured, or is the conflict of interest so direct that it simply is not permissible? What about other issues, such as the insurer's unauthorized practice of law? Cases and ethics opinions go both ways. Here is one view.

AMERICAN INSURANCE ASS'N v. KENTUCKY BAR ASS'N
917 S.W.2d 568 (Ky. 1996)

In this consolidated action, Complainants [all insurance companies] timely filed a motion seeking review by this Court of Advisory Ethics Opinion E-368 which was issued by the Board of Governors of respondent, Kentucky Bar Association. . . . In addition, State Farm requests that this Court review that portion of Unauthorized Practice of Law Opinion U-36 which proscribes the use, by insurance companies, of

---

[13] ABA Formal Ethics Op. No. 01-421 (2001).

salaried attorneys to provide defense services under the insurers' policies of insurance. . . .

[W]e hereby approve and adopt E-368 as written, and choose not to disturb U-36. At issue is the following question presented in E-368: (1) May a lawyer enter into a contract with a liability insurer in which the lawyer or his firm agrees to do all of the insurer's defense work for a set fee?

The Board of Governors answered "no" to this question. . . . The Board, indicating that the lawyer's duty to the insured client was a function of the attorney-client relationship and not governed by or limited by the terms of the insurance contract, expressed concern that this set fee arrangement would result in the loss of control of the insured client vis-a-vis actions taken by counsel. . . . The Board characterized [this] as but the latest issue to arise from attempts by insurers to cut costs. One such cost-cutting measure . . . involved the practice of insurers to provide defense services directly through salaried attorney employees, a practice, the Board concluded, that "is not permitted in Kentucky, for in addition to the obvious conflicts of interest . . . the practice would violate the law governing unauthorized practice."

The opinion relied upon . . . long-standing Kentucky case law which proscribes a corporation from being licensed to practice a learned profession, such as law. Ethical rules and legal precedent were merged in the opinion to reach the conclusion that in the typical action on an insurance contract, the insured, and not the insurer, was the party-defendant, and that, therefore, "the insurance company must hire members of the private bar to undertake representation of their insured."

Notwithstanding the trends of other jurisdictions, [t]he age-old adage of "if it ain't broke, don't fix it" seems appropriate in disposing of Complainants' argument herein. . . .

In fact, no situation is more illustrative of the inherent pitfalls and conflicts therein than that in which house counsel defends the insured while remaining on the payroll of the insurer. "No man can serve two masters," regardless here of either any perceived "community of interest," or Complainants' Pollyanna postulate that house counsel will continue to provide undivided loyalty to the insured.

. . . .

[W]e do not wear the blinders that Complainants apparently have in place, for we view the situation surrounding the set fee agreement as ripe with potential conflicts. Respondent was able to cite to nineteen such conflicts, including representation of the insured which becomes more complex than anticipated, resulting in financial hardship for the attorney; policy and/or coverage defenses asserted by the insurer against the insured; and disagreement between the insured and the insurer with regard to settlement negotiations. . . . Inherent in all of these potential conflicts is the fear that the entity paying the attorney, the insurer, and not the one to whom the attorney is obligated to defend, the insured, is controlling the legal representation.

NOTES

The sometimes salty Kentucky court opinion adopts a position quite similar to that espoused by Professor Pepper. It is a perspective resting on two largely unrelated legal principles: a corporation's unauthorized practice of law, and the conflicts of interest such representation implies. But it by no means reflects a unanimous view, as the court itself recognizes. For example, in *Cincinnati Ins. Co. v. Wills*, 717 N.E.2d 151 (Ind. 1999), the Indiana Supreme Court cited the Kentucky opinion but came to a different conclusion. The Indiana case began somewhat differently, with *plaintiffs* moving to disqualify defense counsel who were "captive" insurance company employees, arguing that the insurers were engaged in the unauthorized practice of law. The trial court agreed, but the Indiana Supreme Court reversed, holding that the companies may represent insureds so long as counsel were mindful of their ethical duties to their insureds/clients. The court did ban the lawyers from using a law firm name, since it misled the public by not clearly acknowledging their captive status.

Such decisions have been the rule rather than the exception. In 2011, however, the trend toward allowing "captive" law firms to represent insureds took a step back in *Brown v. Kelton*, 380 S.W.3d 361 (Ark. 2011), which also involved a plaintiff's attempt to disqualify the lawyer. *Kelton* agreed in principle with the dual reasoning of the Kentucky court. A 2012 survey of state court decisions in light of *Brown v. Kelton* found the score to be 11 state courts in favor of "captive" law firms, and three that have ruled against.[14]

In Formal Opinion 03-430 (July 9, 2003), the ABA ethics committee firmly took sides. Not only did this opinion support the concept of insurance company staff lawyers representing insureds, but it favored the use of law firm style names instead of requiring that the "firm" state that "XYZ Insurance" was defending. And while the opinion stated that the insured client would have to be advised of the lawyers' employee status, the plaintiffs and their counsel could be left in the dark.

D. SUPPLEMENTAL READINGS

1. There are a number of excellent discussions of the tripartite relationship including: WILLIAM T. BARKER & CHARLES SILVER, PROFESSIONAL RESPONSIBILITIES OF INSURANCE DEFENSE COUNSEL (2012), referenced in section 6 above, Amber Czarnecki, *Ethical Considerations Within the Tripartite Relationship of insurance Law — Who is the Real Client?*, 74 DEFENSE COUNSEL J. 172 (2007); and the ever excellent William Freivogel, http://www.freivogel.com/insurancedefense.html.

2. *San Diego Navy Fed. Credit Union v. Cumis Insurance Society*, 162 Cal. App. 3d 358 (1984). This extremely important case set the stage for what nationally became known as "*Cumis* counsel." The plaintiff's insurer, Cumis, provided counsel to defend its insured San Diego Federal Credit Union in an action for general and punitive damages for tortious wrongful discharge. Cumis nonetheless sent notice to

---

[14] Dwayne D. Hedges, Case Note: Brown v. Kelton: *The Arkansas Prohibition on the Use of Employee Attorneys to Defend the Insured*, 65 ARK. L. REV. 953 (2012).

the credit union reserving its right to assert at a later date that the credit union was not covered for certain damages. The credit union retained independent counsel to protect its interests. The court found that under these circumstances there is a conflict of interest between the insurer and the insured, and the insured thus has a right to independent counsel paid for by the insurer.

3. The first number of Volume 4 of the CONNECTICUT INSURANCE LAW JOURNAL (1997–1998) contains not only the article by Professor Stephen Pepper mentioned in section 6 above on the single client model of insurance defense, but articles by professors Charles Silver, Nancy J. Moore, Thomas Morgan, and others.

4. Eugene R. Schiman & Michelle J. Benycar, *Tripartite Relationship: Who Protects the Rights of the Insured?*, N.Y.L.J., April 30, 2003, deals with New York's version of a written engagement letter, referred to in the notes at the end of section 2 of the Readings. The New York letter, unlike the Florida letter described above, does *not* ensure the primacy of the insured. The authors criticize the New York rule, explain why they feel it is inappropriate, and suggest what can be done.

5. The insurer's desire to save costs is exemplified by the efforts of Allstate Insurance Company, which was accused of penalizing claimants who hired their own attorneys to pursue claims on their policies. For example, if an uninsured motorist caused an accident injuring someone insured by Allstate, Allstate would send their own insured a notice suggesting that it was not in their interest to hire an attorney to try to obtain the fullest possible coverage under the Allstate policy. A Washington trial court found that these practices amounted to the unauthorized *and negligent* practice of law by Allstate, which was also found to have breached its fiduciary duties to its insureds. Similar claims were made against Allstate in California, Illinois, Indiana, West Virginia and Florida. Reporter Mark Ballard has been following the Allstate story for some time. Two of his reports can be found in THE NATIONAL LAW JOURNAL: *Allstate's Master Plan?*, Nov. 9, 1998 and *Allstate Tactics Under Fire*, Jan. 31, 2000. See also Deborah Lohse, *Insurer's Anti-Counsel Stance Gains Enemies*, DAILY J., July 29, 1998, describing the West Virginia Bar's unauthorized practice decision.

6. Gail Diane Cox, *Captive Firms of Insurers Get Stung in Court*, NAT'L L.J., May 15, 2000, reports that Kentucky is no longer alone in condemning the practice of having insurance company in-house or employee attorneys represent the companies' insureds. Montana strictly forbids such a practice, and the Florida State Bar Board of Governors gave preliminary approval to a measure acknowledging the potential for conflict between insurers and their insureds when the insurers use employee attorneys.

Chapter 5

WHO CONTROLS THE CASE? HOW SHOULD LAWYERS AND CLIENTS SHARE DECISIONMAKING?

PROBLEM 13: IS THE LAWYER THE CLIENT'S SAVIOR OR MOUTHPIECE?

A. INTRODUCTION

What should a lawyer do when the client doesn't want to follow the lawyer's advice? What if the client insists on a course of conduct that the lawyer is convinced is not in the client's best interests? The answers to these questions are even more difficult when the client is not a mature, reasonably objective adult, when the client is mentally impaired, or when the client is under extraordinary pressure, such as facing a potential death sentence. In many respects, we see these issues as the most difficult lawyers ever have to face. Almost no lawyer is immune from being put in these difficult circumstances. In the following problem the lawyer is confronted with difficult choices while representing a juvenile offender with a mind of his own.

B. PROBLEM

I

You are a sole practitioner with considerable juvenile court experience. One day, the parents of 14-year-old Joseph Umberto come in to see you. Joseph has been charged in juvenile court with robbery and assault with a deadly weapon, charges stemming from an incident in which a young woman was shot in the leg and her purse was taken. You talk to Joe, who says he was so shaken by the incident he can't remember anything other than his and two friends' presence at the scene. You agree to take the case and reach an agreement for fees with Joe's parents, first explaining that even though they will pay you, your responsibility is to Joe, not to them. They agree, saying, "We only want what's best for Joe."

In talking to Joe and checking school records, you learn that while he has no previous record, he has a history of learning difficulties and of some psychological abnormalities which have only, to this point, been vaguely diagnosed. You find Joe pleasant enough, though decidedly withdrawn. Joe agrees to a psychiatric examination done by a doctor you trust. This doctor reports that Joe is in need of intensive psychiatric counseling to avoid more serious problems. He believes that without this intensive program, the boy's withdrawal is likely to become more pronounced and potentially irreversible.

You and Joe contest the charges, but at the hearing the juvenile court referee finds that Joe is guilty. The DA now intends to argue for placement either at the Youth Authority ("YA") or at the new Juvenile Hall "secure facility," where there is little in the way of psychiatric counseling. You believe that with the help of the doctor and a sympathetic probation officer, you could still persuade the referee to grant probation, with placement at home and therapy under the doctor's direction.

You discuss these alternatives with Joe. Although you question him closely about how much he knows about YA or the local lock-up, he expresses a clear preference for those alternatives: "I don't like talking to these guys about what's going on inside my head, anyway." You know how tough the Hall can be, much less YA, and you are concerned that what Joe may now consider an adventure he could eventually strongly regret.

How should you advise Joe? Specifically:

QUESTIONS

1. How hard should you push Joe to adopt your view? Gentle persuasion, firm advocacy, or (figurative) strong arm-twisting?

2. To what extent should the views of Joe's parents be taken into account? How much power should they have in the ultimate decision of what Joe should do?

3. Does Joe's age or maturity matter? How much?

4. If you can't persuade Joe to your point of view, should you override his wishes and make the decision for him?

Ultimately, who decides "what's best for Joe" — you, the parents, or Joe?

II

Consider *People v. Deere* below, and the Smith case in the note that follows. What is your duty to a client who tells you to abandon all efforts to mitigate a possible sentence of death, or even argue *in favor* of a death sentence?

III

Choose one of the examples in section 3 and evaluate what you would do, both to what extent you would persuade the client, and how you would ultimately act?

C. READINGS

1. Two Extremes of Lawyering

Who makes the decisions, the lawyer or the client? Are there some issues that are solely for the attorney to decide? Are there issues that the client must decide? What about the vast area in between? How will decisionmaking authority be established in the attorney-client relationship? Some years ago, Oklahoma law professor Judith Maute came up with a somewhat simplistic but effective way of dividing lawyer-client decisionmaking patterns into two broad models on either extreme, the "paternalist" and the "instrumentalist."[1]

"[T]he paternalist lawyer," offered Maute, "presumes to know what the client wants and pursues those ends without regard for what the client may actually desire." Along the way such a lawyer "assumes moral responsibility for the representation." An "instrumentalist" lawyer, on the other hand, will do exactly what the client asks, without providing much in the way of advice or input. Maute suggests, and we agree, that neither of these extremes encourages good lawyering. Lawyers who don't discuss courses of conduct with their clients but act paternalistically are failing to ascertain what their clients' needs really are. On the other hand, the instrumentalists act, as Maute puts it, "purely as technicians, awarding their clients too much authority and abdicating responsibility."

Maute is clearly critical of both extremes, and most lawyers generally find themselves somewhere in between. But is a balance always the correct approach, or are there circumstances in which one extreme may be the correct choice? Can you posit circumstances in which clients force lawyers to adopt one or the other extreme? Are some of the circumstances we posit in this problem and these readings possible candidates for a lawyer to take a more extreme role?

Recall the reading in Problem 1 on developing trust between you and your client. It seems self-evident that the more trust the client has in the lawyer, the more likely the lawyer's ability to persuade or dissuade, and thus avoid some of the Scylla-and-Charybdis problems that these readings focus on. Of course, no matter how much the client trusts the lawyer, it's not going to be enough all the time.

2. Balanced Decisionmaking

Balancing the decisionmaking between lawyer and client is often a delicate task. It is generally accepted that lawyers have control over purely "tactical" considerations, while clients control the "ultimate issues." But what constitutes tactics in one case may be an ultimate issue in another. Ethical rules have generally resorted to rather ambiguous standards. EC 7-7 of the old ABA Model Code allocates authority as follows:

> In certain areas of legal representation not affecting the merits of the cause or substantially prejudicing the rights of a client, a lawyer is entitled to make decisions on his own. But otherwise the authority to make decisions is exclusively that of the client and, if made within the framework of the law, such decisions are binding on the lawyer.

Model Rule 1.2 describes settlement and the "objectives of representation" as matters for the client to decide, while the attorney decides other matters. Thus, as we saw in Problem 11, the decision to settle the case belongs to the client. But is this language always clear? Does "affecting the merits of the cause" arguably limit the lawyer's role to little more than ministerial duties? How do lawyer and client

---

[1] Judith L. Maute, *Allocation of Decisionmaking Authority under the Model Rules of Professional Conduct*, 17 U.C. DAVIS L. REV. 1049 (1984).

determine what actions will "substantially prejudice the rights of clients"? How does one evaluate what are and are not the "objectives of representation"?

For example, in most litigation matters, lawyers ordinarily decide what discovery should be conducted. The client does not consent to each and every set of interrogatories or document requests, and often doesn't even know when they are sent. But is this always the case? What if the client has clearly made cost a factor? What about where granting opposing counsel an extension of time, ordinarily appropriate, would result in a calendaring consequence that may be important to the client? Ordinarily, the lawyer decides most questions of trial strategy, but this may be subject to a client's power to preempt some lawyer decisions. And what of the client who, out of anger at the other side, instructs the lawyer not to give anything "extra" to the other side beyond the minimum required? Does the client have the power to preempt the lawyer's decisions for less commendable reasons?

What information is an attorney obligated to provide the client? Is an attorney in a position to manipulate the client's decision by selecting the information that is given the client? And finally, consider these questions, which will repeat themselves in various iterations throughout these readings: If the client seeks an end that the lawyer considers imprudent, to what extent must the attorney follow the client's stated choices? Under what circumstances should, or may, the attorney override the client's wishes? As you've undoubtedly guessed, the nuances suggested by these questions rarely have clearly defined answers.

3. Three Client Circumstances and the Temptations of Paternalism

A lawyer may have additional responsibilities depending upon the maturity, intelligence, experience, mental condition, or age of a client. But does the attorney always know better than the client what is in the client's "best interests"? When does "helping" become controlling or masterminding people's lives? While these readings focus most heavily on representing children and those facing the death penalty, there are many other, unfortunately too common, situations in which these issues play a major role. Consider what you would do in the following circumstances:

a. You represent a pregnant teenager who doesn't want to live at home anymore. She wants you to petition the court for an order emancipating her from her parents. If the petition is granted, the teenager, who has no financial resources of her own, will be living in a tenement in the worst part of town, or, even worse, might wind up homeless.

b. You represent a client who has Down Syndrome. The client lives off income from a trust fund left by his deceased parents. You believe that the client's brother, who manages the fund, is making highly imprudent investments and wasting assets. Your client adores his brother and will hear nothing of your concerns.

c. Your client is a ninety-one-year-old widow. She recently has been befriended by her gardener. She calls you and tells you she wants to change her will, leaving her house all of her substantial financial assets to the gardener. You know that her current will leaves everything to her two children.

4. Life or Death for David Mason

There are no more graphic examples of the tug-of-war of client autonomy than death-penalty cases. We now discuss in some detail three such cases: In the first, competing attorneys fought over the client's desire to be executed; in the second a lawyer stood by his client's decision not to present mitigating evidence at trial even when ordered to do so by the state's Supreme Court; in the third and most famous, the defendant, Unabomber Ted Kaczynski, claimed he was forced to accept plea bargain because his lawyers insisted on presenting a defense he could not abide and did not want.

First, David Mason. In many cases, most lawyers would consider the filing of motions and the creation of other pleadings "tactical" or "technical" issues where decisionmaking rests with the attorney. But in the case of David Mason and his two competing attorneys, filing a motion or appeal took on a life-or-death significance, addressing the ultimate point of the representation itself. While reading the following article, consider the difficult choices that the attorneys for this death row inmate faced.

Richard Barbieri, *A Fight to the Death*
THE RECORDER (SAN FRANCISCO), April 17, 1993[2]

For the last nine years, Charles Marson has been trying to get David Edwin Mason out from under a death sentence. In January, Marson filed a 106-page *habeas corpus* petition in federal court seeking a new trial.

Meanwhile, his client was trying to get him fired. The condemned prisoner no longer wishes to fight his execution and believes he has found the right lawyer to smooth the way to his own demise — Sacramento's Michael K. Brady.

Mason and the 41-year-old trial lawyer, who says he handles mostly death penalty trials and drunken-driving cases, seem well suited to each other in one significant way: They both believe that executions are appropriate in certain cases.

"Dave has asked me to perform a particular task - that is to help him waive his appellate rights," Brady said in an interview last week.

Mason is seeking a judge's permission to fire Marson, a Remcho, Johansen & Purcell partner who was appointed to represent him in 1984. Marson is not following his wishes, Mason charges, because the former American Civil Liberties Union attorney is personally opposed to capital punishment.

By agreeing to help Mason in his unusual pursuit, Brady finds himself in a high-stakes dispute with Marson, who by his actions remains as committed to saving Mason's life as Brady is to helping end it.

Marson informed Brady in a March 16 letter he would no longer send him copies of any court papers he files on Mason's behalf. "I hope you have reconsidered your

---

involvement in the effort to rush Mr. Mason into the gas chamber," Marson added
. . . .

Mason was sentenced to death in 1984 for murdering four elderly Oakland residents over eight months in 1980, and then fatally strangling a fellow inmate in jail two years later. The California Supreme Court has already unanimously affirmed Mason's sentence and denied two state *habeas* petitions.

Marson filed a new *habeas* in San Jose federal court Jan. 7. It claims Mason should be granted a retrial because of new evidence he has turned up. But the *habeas* petition has become a sidelight in the case.

U.S. District Judge Ronald Whyte has scheduled a May 13 hearing to consider Mason's competence. And while he's not formally appointed Mason's lawyer, Brady is waiting in the wings.

If Mason is deemed mentally fit, he'll immediately fire Marson and stop all appeals, Brady said. And there's little in the law to stop him.

The U.S. Supreme Court has held that condemned prisoners judged sane enough to make an intelligent decision about their fates can forgo their appeals.

. . . .

"I become his lawyer, and we withdraw the *habeas* petition and [Mason] goes to the top of the list," Brady said . . . .

For his part, Mason, 36, says he knows what he's doing. "I'm sure it has crossed your mind that anyone who wants to die has to be a fool," Mason wrote to Brady on Jan. 26. "I disagree with that thought, I'm no fool. I am pro-death penalty, always have been, more since my years here. So now that I'm caught up in it, I can't exclude myself."

Although most condemned prisoners fight to the end, Mason's position is not unique. The states have carried out nearly 200 executions nationwide since 1973, with 21 involving so-called volunteers — prisoners who seek out their own executions by waiving their appeals.

Brady is not threatening to take such extreme measures on Mason's behalf. But his role in the case, which had not been widely known until it surfaced in press reports last week, is likely to draw increasing attention from other lawyers.

"A lawyer's job is to represent his client effectively, and you don't represent your client effectively by seeking his execution," said James Thomson, a Sacramento criminal defense lawyer and former death penalty committee chairman of the California Attorneys for Criminal Justice. "There's already a prosecutor in the picture," he said.

Boalt Hall professor Franklin Zimring added: "He's going to become the Jack Kevorkian of San Quentin's death row."

But Brady defends himself, saying he's just carrying out his client's wishes.

. . . .

In a letter dated Feb. 23, Mason charges that Marson is "not counsel for petitioner, he is counsel and lobbyist for the anti-death penalty movement. . . . I would ask you to appoint [Brady] as counsel for petitioner, allowing Mr. Marson to pursue his objective without censoring my own."

. . . .

Marson, 50, who was legal director of the ACLU Northern California chapter between 1972 and 1977, is well known among capital defenders. "He's a real good lawyer and highly respected by everybody in the defense bar, one lawyer said.

Brady says he views his task as a defense lawyer as giving clients "fair and vigorous representation." "That doesn't mean that when some of my clients are convicted I'm sorry to see them go to jail. They deserve it, in some cases."

In an interview on Friday, Brady said he had just spoken to Mason, who informed Brady that he had chosen the method of execution he prefers - gas chamber. Brady said he had told Mason that lethal injection was a less painful way to die.

"He said, 'My mind is made up.' He doesn't want to die lying on his back and wants to take his punishment like a man."

NOTES

In the Spring of 1993, David Mason finally fired Charles Marson and hired Michael Brady, but that did not end the controversy. While Brady filed papers requesting the abandonment of appeals and habeas petitions on Mason's behalf, other attorneys continued to file numerous pleadings trying to save the life of David Mason. Most prominent among these was Charles Marson, who, though he had been fired, "filed one appeal after another to try to save the condemned inmate's life — until the final hours," according to the San Francisco *Chronicle* of August 24, 1993.

Marson and others argued to the last that because of Mason's history of childhood abuse, mental illness and attempted suicide, Mason was not competent to decide for himself whether he should live or die. Ultimately, Judge Whyte disagreed, lifting all stays, and Mason died just after midnight on the morning of August 24, 1993. That morning's San Francisco *Chronicle* said this about attorney Michael Brady:

> With the execution only moments away, Brady stood waiting for a signal from Mason to stop the execution and refile a federal appeal the inmate had chosen to withdraw in January. Prison officials and state prosecutors said they would honor any decision by Mason to pursue that appeal, even if he changed his mind while sitting in the gas chamber.

> But the signal never came.[3]

Who was right, Michael Brady or Charles Marson? Was Brady "the Kevorkian of death row," or merely advocating his client's position? Was Marson a hero trying to

---

[3] *Mason Put to Death*, CHRONICLE (San Francisco), Aug. 24, 1993, at 1.

save a man's life, or presumptuously inserting his own set of beliefs for those of his client? From Brady's perspective, Mason was a clearheaded individual who had the right to decide his own fate. From Marson's perspective, Mason was a severely mentally disabled person, and part of the proof of that disability was his "volunteering" to die.

To what extent did these two lawyers allow their personal preferences to interfere with their lawyering? Marson was a well-known death-penalty opponent, but Brady was an avowed death-penalty supporter. Is it fair to ask whether Brady carried out Mason's wishes or his own?

This question of so-called "death volunteers" has hardly abated in the years since Mason's execution. There have always been and still are death row "volunteers." We'll look at a very different example in section 6 below.

5. Is It Possible for a Lawyer to Act Objectively About the Client's Desires?

How difficult is it for a lawyer whose client is facing a death sentence to evaluate the client's needs objectively? How much is the lawyer's perception of the client's ability to make decisions slanted by the counsel's strong disagreement with the client's stated desires? Or by the lawyer's concern that the client, faced with the ultimate penalty, may be less capable than the typical client to make reasoned decisions on his or her own behalf? In the following case, a lawyer struggles to make the most objective determination possible, a very different approach than the certitude that drove Michael Brady and Charles Marson.

PEOPLE v. DEERE
808 P.2d 1181 (Cal. 1991)

Defendant Ronald Lee Deere was convicted of one count of first degree murder and two counts of second degree murder . . . . The penalty was fixed at death. The penalty judgment was subsequently reversed by this court in *People v. Deere* (1985) 41 Cal. 3d 353, 222 Cal. Rptr. 13, 710 P.2d 925 (*Deere I*).[4]

Following a remand for retrial of the penalty phase, the sentence was again fixed at death. This appeal is automatic.

I. *Factual and Procedural Background*

Because defendant does not deny responsibility for the three killings, we need not dwell unduly on the evidence linking him to the crimes. Apparently despondent over the termination of his relationship with Cindy Gleason, defendant shot and killed the husband and two young children of Ms. Gleason's sister, Kathy Davis. Defendant had previously threatened to kill "everyone" in Ms. Gleason's family if she stopped seeing him. . . .

Defendant initially pleaded not guilty but later moved to withdraw his plea. The

---

[4] [Eds.: All further citations to *Deere I* have been omitted.]

trial court appointed a psychiatrist, Dr. Tommy Bolger, to examine him. Following the examination and a report confirming defendant's competence, the court found defendant competent to plead guilty, waive jury trial and cooperate with counsel in the event his plea was withdrawn. The court then permitted defendant to withdraw his plea of not guilty, waive his rights, and plead guilty to each count and admit the special circumstance allegation. His counsel concurred in the change of plea. Based on the transcript of the preliminary hearing, the court then found defendant guilty of one count of first degree murder in the killing of Don Davis, and two counts of second degree murder in the killings of Michelle and Melissa Davis. The court also found true the multiple-murder special circumstance allegation.

Thereafter, defendant also waived jury on the penalty issue. Pursuant to stipulation, the court considered the testimony at the preliminary hearing and an earlier hearing to suppress evidence. While defendant offered no mitigating evidence, he made a brief statement voicing remorse for his crimes and announcing that he deserved to die. Counsel argued that the aggravating circumstances did not outweigh those in mitigation and therefore that the penalty should not be death.

Counsel also explained to the court the reasons which impelled him to agree to the guilty plea, the waiver of jury trial and the failure to offer mitigating evidence. According to counsel, he argued with defendant over each of these decisions, but ultimately grew to appreciate and concur in his client's point of view. Defendant, counsel explained, believed that to call mitigating witnesses would " 'cheapen' his relationship with his family and remove 'the last vestige of dignity he has.' " The decision not to offer evidence, counsel stated, was " 'made . . . in close consultation with [defendant]. It has been based on his desires and my conclusion that I have no right whatsoever to infringe upon his decisions about his own life.' "

In his first appeal, defendant claimed, inter alia, that counsel had been deficient in failing to offer any evidence in mitigation during the penalty phase apart from defendant's testimony at the preliminary hearing. A majority of this court agreed, holding that a defense counsel's failure to present any mitigating evidence in the penalty phase of a capital trial deprives the defendant of effective assistance of counsel. The judgment was, accordingly, reversed as to penalty, but affirmed in all other respects.

At the penalty retrial (to be discussed more fully below) defendant again waived jury trial. The prosecution offered no evidence in aggravation beyond that already presented at the first trial. Defense counsel, at defendant's insistence, failed to present any mitigating evidence apart from certain testimony at the preliminary hearing. The trial court, in response, held counsel in contempt for refusing to obey its order to present any available mitigating evidence, in conformity with this court's decision in *Deere I* . . . .

II. *Discussion*

A. *Ineffective Assistance of Counsel*

    . . . .

[D]efendant contends that counsel rendered ineffective assistance in failing to present evidence in mitigation. The claim is totally without merit, if not specious.

As noted earlier, we held in *Deere I, supra* that defendant was denied adequate representation at the penalty phase as a result of counsel's failure to present evidence in mitigation, notwithstanding defendant's unequivocal desire that no such evidence be presented. Defendant was represented at the penalty retrial by the same deputy public defender who had appeared on his behalf at the first trial. Defendant's views with respect to the presentation of mitigating evidence also remained unchanged; defendant was adamant, in counsel's words, that "[h]e does not want any evidence presented on his behalf because in his heart that is his private life and to bring that evidence into court would violate his relationships with everybody he holds dear and respects in this world. And to him, those relationships are more important than anything else, including his life."

Thus, counsel was confronted with the unenviable and wrenching choice of obeying the law as defined by this court in *Deere I*, or honoring his client's deeply held convictions. To make the dilemma even more acute, the trial court ordered counsel to present whatever mitigating evidence was available in accordance with our decision, or be held in contempt.

Forced to choose between the Scylla of his duty to his client and the Charybdis of his obligation to the law, counsel chose his client. As he explained: " . . . I think I am obligated to argue for [defendant] in this situation. If the Court — if I were to follow the Court's order and present mitigating evidence, assuming for the purpose of argument it is available, [defendant] would object to the very depth of his soul. He's told me that. I know he would do that." Counsel explained that his client's clear and unequivocal wishes simply left him no choice: "I feel under the unique circumstances of this case I must make this decision. . . . [Defendant] has never once altered his position. . . . His position today is the same as it was the first day I met him. And although we argued vigorously on many occasions concerning what we should do in this case, . . . slowly but surely he convinced me his position is the correct one. He's made his decisions consciously, temperately, and not in the heat of passion, but based on his true and sincere and honest beliefs about what is right for him. I stand with him 100 percent. And to accede to the Court's order to either offer mitigating evidence or state for the record that there is none available would be the most gross conflict of interest I can imagine for an attorney in a case like this. So I cannot do it. I hope the Court doesn't feel that denial is contemptuous, but if the Court sees it that way, so be it."

Thus, under severe legal constraints, and at personal risk, counsel courageously performed the duty owed to his client. The trial court, as it had warned, thereupon held counsel in contempt for willful failure to comply with its order. The court then weighed the evidence before it, found that the aggravating outweighed the mitigating circumstances, and sentenced defendant to death. Subsequently, however, the court stayed the sentence for the purpose of obtaining additional mitigating evidence. . . .

At the continued hearing, the prosecution presented no additional evidence. Defense counsel reiterated that it was defendant's desire not to present any mitigating evidence. Thereafter, defendant, through [newly appointed] Attorney Landau, presented six witnesses in mitigation. . . . [and] an example of defendant's art work, which he had obtained from defense counsel pursuant to a subpoena duces tecum. In argument, Landau stressed defendant's artistic talent and the work he could accomplish in prison if his life were spared. Defense counsel also argued in favor of life, stressing the absence — in his view — of aggravating circumstances, and the psychological stress defendant was under at the time of the offenses.

In light of the foregoing, we find defendant's assertion that he was denied effective assistance of counsel to be totally without merit. [Death penalty affirmed.]

. . . .

MOSK, J., concurring:

To permit a defendant convicted of a potentially capital crime to bar his counsel from introducing mitigating evidence at the penalty phase . . . would . . . prevent this court from discharging its constitutional and statutory duty.

. . . .

"To allow a capital defendant to prevent the introduction of mitigating evidence on his behalf withholds from the trier of fact potentially crucial information bearing on the penalty decision no less than if the defendant was himself prevented from introducing such evidence by statute or judicial ruling. In either case the state's interest in a reliable penalty determination is defeated." (*People v. Deere, supra,* 41 Cal. 3d at pp. 363-364, citations omitted.)

. . . .

I turn now to the case at bar. In my view, no *Deere* error occurred or, if it did, it was effectively cured. To be sure, at defendant's request counsel again declined to present available evidence in mitigation. By so doing, he violated his obligation to the court and the adversarial process. But this time, the court . . . appointed special counsel.

NOTES

Defendant Deere's deputy public defender made impassioned speeches "on behalf" of his client at the penalty phase of both trials. When he spoke at the second trial of arguing "for" his client, and "stand[ing] with him 100%," Deere's attorney really meant arguing *against* the introduction of mitigating evidence and in favor of his client's expressed desires. What do you think of this lawyer's actions under what he himself called these "unique circumstances"? Did he perform his client a service by being the one person in the "system" to express his client's deeply held wishes, or did he abrogate his role as counsel by becoming his client's "mouthpiece"?

Although the propriety of defense counsel's conduct was not directly before the court, the *Deere* justices themselves disagreed on the issue. While the court's majority lauded the lawyer's ethics for "courageously" performing his duty to his client "at personal risk," the concurrence, by a former California Attorney General, saw this same behavior as a clear ethical breach — the failure of an attorney to perform his duty to the court under the Constitution.

In a 1998 Arizona case, the trial lawyers for Douglas Alan Smith went even further than the public defender in *Deere*. At their client's request, they affirmatively argued for a death sentence, even though the prosecution sought only imprisonment. Unlike Michael Brady, Jamie McAlister, Smith's lawyer, was an avowed death penalty opponent. Arguing for a death sentence was "difficult," McAlister told the *ABA Journal*, "but when my client makes a careful, rational, legal decision, I have an obligation to be a vigorous advocate on his behalf." McAlister's advocacy failed to get Smith what he wanted; he received a sentence of 62 years in prison. But the lawyer left the case "at peace with myself," confident she had made the right call. "What would bother me more would be to see somebody stripped of his right to make his own decisions about the course of his life."[5]

What would you have done if you were the defendant's lawyer in *Deere*? Would you be "at peace" with yourself if you had argued in favor of a death sentence for your own client? Can any trial lawyer, who often must make ethical judgment calls in the heat of battle, ever be sure what the right decision is?

When considering what to do in such extraordinarily difficult circumstances, two relatively recent U.S. Supreme Court decisions have weighed in on both sides of the issue. In *Florida v. Nixon*, 543 U.S. 175 (2004), defense counsel conceded guilt at trial without express client consent. The defendant's lawyers felt that the only chance to avoid the death penalty was to make this concession and argue sentence, but the defendant was unresponsive each time the strategy was explained. The Florida court found the lawyers' acts were "the functional equivalent of a guilty plea," and reversed. The Supreme Court disagreed, called the decision, though made without clear client consent, strategic, and reinstated the death penalty.

On the other hand, in *Rompilla v. Beard*, 545 U.S. 374 (2005), a 5-4 majority held that defense counsel had a duty to investigate what mitigating evidence might be available to present — here, what turned out to be the horrific childhood of the defendant — rather than merely rely on the defendant's understated representations. This defendant, however, did not refuse to have mitigation testimony presented.[6]

---

[5] *See* Mark Hansen, *Death's Advocate*, ABA J., Dec. 1998, at 22.

[6] There are other similar though distinct cases involving life-or-death issues, particularly "right to die" cases, where a terminally ill patient wants to cease life-prolonging measures. These, of course, are also important, though we have chosen to focus on other cases here.

6.   When a Client's Ability is "Impaired"

ABA Model Rule 1.14(a) provides that when a client's ability "to make adequately considered decisions" is impaired (whether because of minority, mental disability, or for some other reason) "the lawyer shall, as far as possible, maintain a normal client-lawyer relationship with the client." What does this rule mean in practice? What does "as far as possible" mean? Who decides whether the client has the ability to make an "adequately considered decision"? What if, as in the case of Theodore Kaczynski, the man convicted as the Unabomber, his two lawyers believe that he is substantially impaired even though a court found him "competent" to stand trial? Is a lawyer permitted in those circumstances to determine, over the client's explicit objection, the defense to be presented at trial?

Richard A. Zitrin, *The Kaczynski Dilemma, A Defense Lawyer's Ethical Duty to a Self-Destructive and Mentally Ill Client*
LEGAL TIMES (Washington, D.C.), February 2, 1998[7]

The Kaczynski case is over, . . . achieved only after Theodore Kaczynski had been denied the ability to decide the course of his own defense.

Kaczynski's counsel, Quin Denvir and Judy Clarke, faced what might be the toughest ethical dilemma any lawyer can have: How to represent your client when the strategy you firmly believe is in your client's best interests is totally unacceptable to the client. Making this situation worse was their belief that Kaczynski was seriously mentally ill, if not legally insane . . . .

First, a somewhat oversimplified summary: Kaczynski wanted nothing to do with any defense that suggested he was mentally ill. Whatever consideration Denvir and Clarke gave to actually presenting an insanity defense was effectively stymied by the client's refusal to submit to a psychiatric evaluation. The lawyers continued to insist, over Kaczynski's objections, that they would present a "mental defect" defense, although it remained unclear exactly how.

Judge Garland Burrell Jr. agreed to allow the defense team to raise the issue of Kaczynski's mental state, but the government filed an unusual document objecting to the use of Kaczynski's mental illness as a defense, and demanding a hearing on the issue. Judge Burrell then ordered a competency evaluation. After Kaczynski was found competent, Burrell denied Kaczynski's request to conduct his own defense [and allowed his lawyers to present their mental disease defense], and the plea of guilty and sentence of life imprisonment soon followed.

On the surface, the plea arrangement seems to have gotten most people what they wanted. Kaczynski's brother, David, and his mother were grateful that Ted's life had been spared. Prosecutors avoided the growing criticism over their insistence on the death penalty for one so obviously mentally ill. And Judge Burrell got off the horns of several legal dilemmas: Had he correctly ruled that Denvir and Clarke could use Kaczynski's mental condition in court? Should he have allowed Kaczynski to hire San Francisco defense lawyer Tony Serra to come in and put on

---

a political defense, a move that would have delayed the trial for several months and created a possible circus? Was he justified in denying Kaczynski, now found competent, the right to represent himself?

Who Decides Best Interests?

It's likely that no one was more relieved by the guilty plea than Kaczynski's dedicated attorneys. Their care for their client and concern for his welfare were manifest, and helped them avoid a complete breakdown in their relationship, even when they were completely at odds with him. This undoubtedly contributed to the successful plea negotiations. But did Ted Kaczynski get what *he* wanted from this plea bargain? And ultimately, did his attorneys act in his best interests, not as they saw those interests, but as *he* saw them?

We will never know, and even the participants may never know, what would have happened had Denvir and Clarke acted as Kaczynski's "mouthpieces" by representing his views in court as strongly as they could. Perhaps they would have gone to trial and their client would have received the death penalty, although this seems unlikely. Perhaps Judge Burrell's refusal to allow Kaczynski to represent himself would have led to conviction but would have been reversed on appeal. Or perhaps Serra would have been allowed to represent Kaczynski, or advise him in his self-representation, presenting a political defense. Perhaps the very nature of that defense would have convinced a jury that Kaczynski was indeed crazy and did not deserve to die.

All this, of course, is rank speculation. But it's based on what could have happened had Kaczynski's lawyers chosen to do his bidding - acting in what *he* thought were his best interests, rather than what they thought. By never presenting their client's view of his case, they may have put Kaczynski in the position of accepting a plea he really didn't want — an offer he couldn't refuse.

How much of a mouthpiece must a lawyer be, particularly where the client is mentally impaired?

. . . .

It's difficult to be critical of Kaczynski's lawyers in making this hard, almost impossible, decision — especially under such trying circumstances. But I must disagree with their choice. Who in the courtroom spoke for what Ted Kaczynski wanted, crazy as that may have sounded to us? The answer is no one. It's obvious that no defense lawyer would have voluntarily presented the case Kaczynski's way or advocated his "strategy." But ultimately, it was Kaczynski's life at stake, and his call to make. As members of the criminal law community often say, "We don't do the time."

. . . .

[T]he predicament of defense counsel representing a mentally impaired defendant is ultimately everyone's problem, judge and prosecution included. Everyone should focus on assuring the defendant that his voice will indeed be heard, not by what Kaczynski felt forced to resort to — tossing a pencil across a table or making a speech during jury selection — but from the very beginning of the case.

NOTES

After his conviction, Kaczynski continued to maintain that he was sane and to try to set aside his guilty plea because it was based on his own lawyers' threats to use a "mental defect" defense. Indeed, while he ultimately lost in the Ninth Circuit Court of Appeals, he got a vote for reversal on this ground from the homonymous Judge Alex Kozinski. But sometimes, when clients of questionable competence *are* given the right to decide the course of their defense, it doesn't turn out at all the way the client intended, as in the case of Daniel Colwell.

Trisha Renaud, *Killer's Demand to Die Changes to Plea for Life*
FULTON COUNTY DAILY REPORT, July 14, 1999[8]

From the beginning, Daniel Morris Colwell said he wanted to die.

When he appeared at the Americus police station in 1996 to confess gunning down two strangers only minutes before, he told police he had killed because he wanted to die in the electric chair.

And, at his 1998 sentencing trial, he said the same thing repeatedly to his lawyers who tried to save his life by arguing that his death wish was a manifestation of mental illness. He said the same thing to the judge who told his lawyers they should accede to his wishes that they argue for death. The Sumter County Superior Court jury obliged him by sentencing him to die.

To celebrate the verdict, Colwell asked his lawyers to bring him a steak dinner.

Now, however, Colwell wants to live.

His lawyer says Colwell changed his mind because, for the first time in years, he is receiving the medication and dosage needed to treat his mental illness. . . .

Colwell, diagnosed by the state's doctors as a schizophrenic and manic depressive . . . "now realizes what happened to him," [his lawyer Michael] Mears says.

He says the judicial and mental health systems failed a mentally ill man, adding, "a very sick individual was allowed to try to commit suicide."

Colwell, says Mears, wants to withdraw his guilty plea and plead not guilty by reason of insanity. His client, he adds, now has "tremendous remorse for what he did."

Mears filed a motion for a new trial . . . Colwell "realizes that the decision which he made before and during his trial were decisions which were not the acts of a sane and rational human being," the motion says, adding that the sentencing trial "was a proceeding fundamentally tainted by Mr. Colwell's mental illness" and should be set aside.

Attached to the motion is a June 28th letter Mears received from Colwell. Colwell wrote his lawyer to say "Mears, I very much want to go to a state mental hospital to get help to save my life. I am very sorry for killing those people."

Those were very different words from those Colwell used at his trial.

In a booming voice, he told jurors that "God is ordering you jurors to give Daniel Colwell the death penalty." He also gave them a warning. "How do you know I won't escape and torture your loved ones?" he said. "Jurors, why take the risk?"

NOTES

The Colwell case is thoroughly laced with irony. Colwell's lawyers strongly resisted his efforts to control his own defense; his guilty plea was entered over their objection. Eventually the trial judge ordered the lawyers to follow Colwell's demands. But at trial, Colwell ultimately decided to allow his lawyers to present a defense because he feared that their failure to do so might result in a reversal of his conviction and a delay of his death sentence.

Almost the opposite situation occurred in the case of Andrew Goldstein, who admitted that he had killed a woman he did not know by pushing her in front of a subway train. This case received widespread publicity because Goldstein had a long and thoroughly-documented psychiatric history that included his efforts on over a dozen occasions to voluntarily hospitalize himself so he would get treatment. An overcrowded hospital system repeatedly discharged him, even though there was clear evidence he was dangerous.

Goldstein's first trial resulted in a hung jury on the issue of insanity, drawing only two "NGI" votes. Several jurors commented afterwards that Goldstein's demeanor in court appeared to be normal. So Goldstein's lawyers suggested that he go off his anti-psychotic medication in order to enable the second jury to see him in a mentally ill, "insane" state. His lawyers told David Rohde of the New York *Times* that Goldstein was "very comfortable" with this strategy and wanted to testify while off the medication.[9]

The judge hearing the Goldstein trial said she would allow him to stop taking his medication so long as he remained sufficiently competent to stand trial.

Rohde reported that the lawyers' "unusual tactic" was strongly opposed by the doctors treating Goldstein at Bellevue's psychiatric hospital. But Rohde also quoted Dr. E. Fuller Torrey, an expert on schizophrenia, as saying that if he were Goldstein, he would "want the jury to see how psychotic I could be."

Within a week of the start of his trial, Goldstein had indeed begun to show signs of psychotic behavior, twice assaulting the social worker who accompanied him to court. The judge ordered that Goldstein's medication be offered to him twice a day in case he changed his mind. Dr. Torrey had predicted to the *Times*' Rohde that a return to a psychotic state would be harrowing for Goldstein: "I've never seen anyone with schizophrenia who enjoyed being in a psychotic state," Indeed, he eventually chose to take his medication, unable to handle the increasing mental illness that his abstinence had brought on.

---

[9] David Rohde, *For Retrial, Subway Defendant Stops Taking His Medication*, N.Y. TIMES, Feb. 23, 2000, which thoroughly reviews this case.

Goldstein was then convicted. "The tragedy," wrote Jonathan Gregg in *Time*, "is that in repeatedly seeking help, Andrew Goldstein behaved more responsibly than the state that is now prosecuting him."

The advances made in recent years in administering powerful psychotropic drugs have materially complicated the already difficult ethical issues that lawyers face. The Supreme Court has ruled that no death sentence can be carried out unless the defendant is competent. *Ford v. Wainwright*, 477 U.S. 399 (1986). That leaves open the issue of forced medication, on which state courts differ. And it leaves the lawyer (as well as doctors ordered to medicate) with a near-impossible situation: Allow a client to become or remain incompetent in order to avoid a life-or-death trial or, worse, to prevent a sentence of death from being carried out. Or permit medication, restored mental health, and, potentially, execution.

7.   How Impaired Must a Client Be for the Lawyer to Trump the Client's Desires?

A lawyer's personal belief about what is in the client's "best interests" might interfere with more than the lawyer's vigorous representation and desire to make decisions for the client. It may also have a substantial effect on counsel's determination whether the client has the capacity to make his or her own decisions in the first place. May or should an attorney try to establish a client's incompetence where the client disagrees and wants to be found competent? Should the lawyer hire an independent expert to examine that competence? May or should counsel reveal information communicated in confidence in order to establish the client's incompetence?

This situation is never easy for the thoughtful lawyer. The client doesn't want action taken, and Rule 1.14 makes it clear that a normal relationship should be maintained as much as possible. Nevertheless, what if it appears clear that the client needs immediate protection? May the lawyer step in to save the client from him- or herself?

In contrast to the narrow language of ABA Rule 1.14(a), Rule 1.14(b)'s language was broadened in 2002, and now says an attorney may seek a guardian or "other protective action" where the lawyer "reasonably believes" the client is not able to act in his or her own interest. Rule 1.14(c) was added to reiterate the importance of confidentiality but to allow that under narrow circumstances "the lawyer is impliedly authorized" to protect the client.

Clearly, the seeking of a guardianship or conservatorship, the assistance of an expert to determine the necessity of such action, or similar intervention by the lawyer may intrinsically involve the disclosure of information that the lawyer is usually not entitled to reveal. Comment 9 to MR 1.14, also added in 2002, explicitly recognizes the danger that disclosure could "adversely affect the client's interests," then re-emphasizes the narrow scope when client protection necessitates "implied authorization," and ends by acknowledging the clear reality: "The lawyer's position in such cases is an unavoidably difficult one." No one envies a lawyer in this position.

ABA Formal Opinion 96-404 paved the way for these changes. That opinion acknowledges that there are times when maintaining an ordinary lawyer-client relationship may be difficult, even impossible. But the opinion cautions that the lawyer's independent intervention is not authorized when *the lawyer believes* the client's actions are "ill-considered" or against the client's best interest. Rather, the lawyer can only act when *the client cannot* "act in his own interest." Even then, the lawyer must take the "least restrictive action under the circumstances." Thus, appointing a guardian, a "serious deprivation of the client's rights," ought to occur only when no "other less drastic, solutions are available."

Several states, in ethics opinions and court decisions, have addressed the question of what a lawyer should do because of the client's perceived mental incompetence. For the most part, they have been in accord with a "least restrictive" approach. For example, Michigan Informal Opinion CI-882 (1983) holds both that a lawyer must resolve all doubt in favor of the client's competence before seeking a guardianship and that, even if that doubt is resolved, the attorney must still avoid the use of any confidential information.

Several other authorities remind us of the importance of speaking for the client's own wishes, even in cases of incompetence. Alaska Ethics Opinion 94-3 (1994) requires that even where a guardian exists, "it is the lawyer's duty to make his client's wishes known to the court. The disabled client has no one but his attorney to speak for him." And in *Matter of M.R.*, 638 A.2d 1274 (N.J. 1994), described further in the Supplemental Readings, an acknowledged incompetent woman wanted to choose one parent as guardian over another, and when her attorney did not represent *her* wishes, the court admonished an attorney to "advocate the decision that the client makes" unless it is "patently absurd" or "pose[s] an undue risk of harm."

California stands alone as having no equivalent to MR 1.14(b), either by statute or rule. Among the rules pending before the California Supreme Court in March 2013 is a version of 1.14, but that version, if approved, would be significantly narrower than the ABA rule. It would allow attorneys "to notify an individual or organization that has the ability to take action to protect the client," but not permit lawyers to take action themselves. The inability of the lawyer to take action in any circumstances has been the consistent California view. Three existing albeit older California ethics opinions each conclude that a lawyer may not under *any* circumstances abrogate confidentiality by petitioning the court for a conservator or other similar action.[10]

That confidentiality includes the lawyer's observations of the client's behavior, which under California law are deemed "secrets" of the client. Moreover, the lawyer cannot act on behalf of an interested relative, for example, because that would create a conflict of interest with the unwilling client, and no waiver of conflict of interest is possible if the client is not competent.

What if the client is severely delusional and cannot possibly assist the lawyer in the preparation of a defense, including an insanity defense? This is the situation that confronted the lawyer in the following case, which demonstrates that even in

---

[10] California Formal Opn. 1989-112; L.A. Bar Opin. 450; San Diego Co. Bar Opin 1978-1.

California, there are limits to client autonomy.

PEOPLE v. BOLDEN
99 Cal. App. 3d 375 (1979)

Samuel Othello Bolden, Jr., appeals the order finding him mentally incompetent to stand trial based upon a jury verdict of incompetence. Bolden contends he was denied due process by Penal Code section 1368 which requires his attorney to give an opinion of his client's competence, and was denied effective assistance of counsel when his counsel offered evidence of his incompetence although Bolden desired to be found competent.

Bolden was charged with robbery, two counts of assault with intent to murder, and two counts of assault with a deadly weapon. Criminal proceedings were suspended to determine if Bolden was competent to stand trial. . . . Two psychiatrists testifying for the People said Bolden was not competent to stand trial, as he was suffering delusions. He believed the people he was charged with assaulting, his father and brother, were actually aliens from outer space who were inhabiting the bodies of his father and brother.

Out of the jury's presence Bolden's counsel explained to the court his client wanted to testify in his own behalf and wanted to be found competent to stand trial. While counsel felt he had a duty to pursue his client's desires, he also felt he had a duty to represent his client's best interests. He had been told by professional people a not-guilty-by-reason-of-insanity defense was available for his client. He felt he needed his client's cooperation to pursue this defense. Bolden's current mental state interfered with such cooperation. Counsel's solution to this dilemma was to place Bolden on the witness stand to testify to his competence, and then to offer his own psychiatric witness who testified Bolden was not competent to stand trial.

After 10 minutes of deliberation, the jury returned a verdict of not competent to stand trial. Bolden was committed to Patton State Hospital for treatment.

Penal Code section 1368 requires a judge who doubts the mental competence of the defendant to "inquire of the attorney for the defendant whether, in the opinion of the attorney, the defendant is mentally competent." Bolden contends this section violates the attorney-client privilege by requiring the attorney to reveal knowledge gained in the course of his relationship with his client.

This statute does not, however, require the disclosure of a confidential communication. "What the attorney observes of or hears from his client is not always privileged. It is apparent that some ingredient of disclosure or revelation is essential to the element of communication." Although an attorney's opinion of his client's competence may be principally drawn from confidential communications he has had with that client, merely giving the opinion does not reveal any protected information.

. . . .

No complaint is made about the skill of his attorney or the attorney's dedication to his client. Bolden's contention is the attorney was acting in what he felt was the best interest of his client rather than as an *advocate* of his client's position. By his attorney "siding" with the People in offering evidence of incompetence, Bolden contends, his desire to be found competent went unrepresented.

Diligent advocacy does not require an attorney to blindly follow every desire of his client. An attorney can ordinarily make binding waivers of many of his client's rights as to matters of trial tactics. When the attorney doubts the present sanity of his client, he may assume his client cannot act in his own best interests and may act even contrary to the express desires of his client. To do otherwise may cause prejudicial error.

Bolden's attorney provided effective assistance to his client.

NOTES

Is Bolden's lawyer's acting parentally — following his view of his client's best interests — more justified here by the clear disability of his client than it was in the *Deere* or *Kaczinski* cases? Is disability a matter of degree, as ABA Model Rule 1.14 suggests, or a matter of ascertainable fact, such as an in-court determination of competence? What do you make of the lawyer's decision in *Bolden* to let his client testify in support of a claim of competence, while the expert testified against this finding? Was this "splitting the baby in half," or was it no more than a gesture from a lawyer who was taking a position at odds with his client's wishes?

Note that despite the strict California law and absence of 1.14 or its functional equivalent, the appellate court had little difficulty in determining Bolden's lawyer acted properly. But what about the appellate court's reasoning? This court states flatly that "what the attorney observes of or hears from his client is not always privileged," and that "merely giving [an] opinion" is not revealing confidential information. Perhaps, but haven't we learned such observations are confidential as "secrets" learned during the course of the representation?

One material difference between *Bolden*, where the issue is the competence of a criminal defendant to stand trial, and most of the other cases we've seen, is that constitutional rights are in play. If a Bolden is not competent, he cannot meaningfully confront his accusers, testify in his own defense, or provide assistance to counsel to allow counsel to competently represent him. Perhaps the *Bolden* court could have focused on these constitutional requirements in creating an exception to the privilege instead of the approach it did take.

8. Representing Children

A lawyer's responsibility to a child presents yet another issue of particular difficulty. Some children's advocates take the position that a lawyer is always obligated to advocate for the child's point of view, no matter what the lawyer thinks is in the child's best interest. Do you agree? If not, where would you draw the line? When are children old enough to have the capacity to make their own "adequately considered decisions"? The following article, while a generation old, provides an excellent example of this dilemma, and also points out the difference between being a child's guardian and the child's lawyer.

Jan Hoffman, *When a Child-Client Disagrees with the Lawyer*
THE NEW YORK TIMES, August 28, 1992[11]

When a client gives marching orders to a lawyer about the course the client wants to pursue, the lawyer generally has to obey or risk getting dismissed. But if that client is a child, and the marching orders strike the lawyer as dangerous, does the lawyer still have to obey the client?

Just such a question has been posed in a Chicago juvenile court. It goes to the heart of a lawyer's responsibility to a client who is a child, and it would probably stump King Solomon. The case involves a 13-year-old girl in foster care who is eager to return home and who is being fought over by two lawyers who want to represent her.

The lawyer that the girl wants to drop is her court-appointed guardian, who is obligated to argue for what he determines to be in the girl's best interest. But his plan collides with what she wants. So another lawyer has stepped forward. This lawyer would be willing to be a traditional advocate for her, representing her marching orders in court. Hearings on which lawyer will be able to speak for her are set for Sept. 4.

The girl wants to resume overnight visits with her mother and stepfather, but the stepfather recently completed four years in prison after being convicted of sexually assaulting her. The guardian insists that the visits take place during the day and that they be supervised, and that the stepfather undergo therapy for sex abuse before the family can be reunited.

"This fight is not about the child's right to have her wishes granted; that's up to the judge," said Barry A. Miller, the lawyer the girl wants to retain. "It's about the right to have her voice heard in the legal process. The question is whether a child can be considered adequately represented by a court-appointed attorney who refuses to advocate for what she wants."

The clash over the lawyers' role is emblematic of the internal conflict faced by many lawyers and lay volunteers who represent children: Should they perform in the traditional role of a lawyer, arguing for their client's point of view, or be more of a third parent, presenting to a judge what they think would be best for the child?

. . . Children were rarely seen and almost never heard in the courts until 1967, when the Supreme Court gave the right to counsel to juveniles charged with crimes. In the 70s, children's advocates, like Hillary Clinton, argued that children should be heard in cases that significantly affected their well-being.

Certainly children's voices have been growing louder in a number of legal arenas. Twenty-seven states now permit lawyers or guardians, who may or may not be lawyers, to be assigned to children in custody disputes.

. . . .

And in July, a Florida juvenile court judge ruled for the first time that Gregory K, a 12-year-old boy in foster care, could sue to terminate the parental rights of his

---

[11] Copyright © 1992 by The New York Times Company. Reprinted by permission.

natural mother so that he can be adopted by his foster parents.

The Chicago girl is fighting for exactly the tool that Gregory K. had: A lawyer to represent her position.

Lawyers in Conflicting Roles

In Chicago, virtually all children in neglect and abuse proceedings are represented by the Cook County Office of the Public Guardian, a brigade of 71 lawyers who work with 25,000 children. The office is supervised by Patrick T. Murphy, a high-profile figure among children's rights advocates. The Public Guardian's office has a two-pronged role: As a guardian ad litem who argues for what the guardian thinks is in the best interests of a child, and the child's lawyer, who represents the child's point of view in legal matters.

The Chicago office is one of the few that combine these roles. The roles are at odds in this case because of the objection raised by the girl, so Mr. Miller and Barbara S. Shulman of Miller, Shakman, Hamilton & Kurtzon argue that they should now step in on her behalf, a move Mr. Murphy opposes.

Since [her stepfather's incarceration] the girl has been living with her maternal grandmother and permitted frequent visits with her mother, who was declared unfit by the state's Department of Children and Family Services because she refused to acknowledge that her husband had abused her daughter. The stepfather was released from prison last year and has rejoined his wife. Now the girl wants overnight visits and to rejoin her family eventually.

Warning Signals Raised

Mr. Murphy said his office initially allowed the girl to have overnight visits with the couple. But last March, he said, he learned that the stepfather, supported by the mother, had recanted his confession, proclaimed his innocence and, although he was in counseling, said he had not sought specific therapy for sex abusers. Mr. Murphy complained to the juvenile court judge, who ordered that visits to the home be stopped.

At a recent court hearing, the girl's therapists said the girl had grown despondent about not seeing her family, so the therapist suggested the girl get a new lawyer. The Legal Assistance Foundation of Chicago, which handles suits on behalf of children, contacted Ms. Shulman and Mr. Miller.

Associate Judge Stephen V. Brodhay of Cook County Circuit Court, Juvenile Division, who has been presiding at hearings in this case, will decide whether the girl was manipulated into substituting lawyers. "Just because a young incest victim decides she wants to go home, does that mean her attorney has to go along with that decision?" asked Miriam Soloveichik, an assistant public guardian who is active in the case. "Can she make a reasoned, adult decision? The answer has to be no."

At the bar convention a few weeks ago, a number of positions on the role of children's lawyers was staked out by a panel. While legal experts agree that representing very young children poses its own set of difficulties, children who are about 7 to 14 years old offer baffling ethical and practical obstacles. They are old enough to talk about whether they want to go back to a neglectful home or why they want to live with mom or dad, but their reasons may seem immature and ill-advised to the lawyer.

"Where does your job end?" said Sara D. Eldrich, a New Haven lawyer who is chairwoman-elect of the family law section of the Connecticut Bar Association, which is trying to write its own guidelines. If a lawyer asks a psychologist for an opinion in a custody case, she said, and the psychologist's recommendation is at odds with what the child wants, "have you breached your responsibility?"

These questions have reached a boiling point, in part because more courts are allowing children to have some sort of advocate speak on their behalf. But a 1990 study sponsored by the United States Department of Health and Human Services concluded that among the states requiring guardian ad litems for abused and neglected children, there was little consistency over who could serve as a child's representative, what the responsibilities entailed, and how ethical conflicts should be handled.

NOTES

More states now afford guardians and representation than at the time this article was written, but in many states the role of guardian — and whether a guardian may also act as the child's counsel — remains a muddled issue. Today, many states now have child abuse reporting statutes that require a wide variety of professionals, sometimes lawyers, to disclose suspected instances of child abuse. But these reporting statutes may directly conflict with the ordinary requirements of a confidential lawyer-client relationship. The result of this conflict can be a difficult balancing test. Formal Opinion 1997-2 of the Association of the Bar of the City of New York holds that even if a social services lawyer has a confidential relationship with an abused child, the lawyer's physical observation of abuse may be revealed. Other states, however, have held that lawyer-client confidentiality trumps the duty to reveal without consent. Just one more tough issue among many in this challenging area.

D.   SUPPLEMENTAL READINGS

1. David Luban, *Paternalism and the Legal Profession*, 1981 WISC. L. REV. 454 (1981). This article, oft-cited even today, is an excellent academic and philosophical discussion of the paternalistic model of decisionmaking. Professor Luban begins his article with seven hypotheticals which set forth circumstances similar to those confronting the attorney for Joe Umberto.

2. Paul Tremblay, *On Persuasion and Paternalism: Lawyer Decisionmaking and the Questionably Competent Client*, 1987 UTAH L. REV. 515 (1987). This article discusses six alternative strategies for the lawyer who deals with a client of questionable competence. These alternatives range from acceding to the client's wishes regardless of the consequences, to using persuasion, to seeking a guardian, acting as a de facto guardian, or allowing a family member to do so.

3. Professor William Simon's recent take on paternalism and Professor Luban's perspective is *Lawyer Advice and Client Autonomy: Mrs. Jones's Case*, 50 MD. L. REV. 213 (1991). Interesting thinking from one of the ethics world's most interesting thinkers.

4. PHILIP HEYMANN & LANCE LIEBMAN, *"RITA'S CASE,"* THE SOCIAL RESPONSIBILITIES OF LAWYERS 2-21 (1988). This is a compelling account of an attorney working on a child custody case in a public interest setting who must balance the duty to represent the client's best interest and her stated desires. This account also provides a glimpse into the world of public interest law and how the legal and social service needs of the clientele often intertwine.

5. Rebekah Denn, *Dispute Embroils Killer's Request to Die*, SEATTLE POST-INTELLIGENCER, July 7, 2001, tells the sad and compelling story of James Elledge, another "volunteer" for death who insisted his appeals be abandoned. Elledge suffered from mental illness, committed his crimes while under the influence of alcohol, and had a horrific home life as a child. While in prison he educated himself, risked his life to save a prison guard in a racially motivated riot, and informed prison officials about a planned breakout. Yet he insisted on dying: "I don't look at this as an execution, I look at it as a separation. There's a dirty part of my soul, and I want it destroyed."

6. Adam Liptak, assisted by other staff reporters, wrote a compelling series of articles in the NEW YORK TIMES in October 2005 called *No Way Out* on the plight of both adults and juveniles who were sentenced to "LWOP," or "life without possibility of parole." Given the hopelessness of their situations and the dismantling of prison rehabilitation programs, many defendants were ready to choose the death penalty over life in prison without parole. Among the articles are: Adam Liptak, *No Way Out: The Changing Rules to More Inmates, Life Term Means Dying Behind Bars*, NEW YORK TIMES, Oct. 2, 2005, Adam Liptak, *No Way Out: The Youngest Lifers Locked Away Forever After Crimes as Teenagers*, NEW YORK TIMES, Oct. 3, 2005, and Adam Liptak, *No Way Out: Dashed Hopes, Serving Life, With No Chance of Redemption*, NEW YORK TIMES, Oct. 5, 2005.

7. MICHAEL MELLO, THE UNITED STATES OF AMERICA VERSUS THEODORE JOHN KACZYNSKI: ETHICS, POWER AND THE INVENTION OF THE UNABOMBER, CONTEXT BOOKS (1999), is written by a lawyer who consulted with Ted Kaczynski's defense team and was Kaczynski's self-described friend. Mello is critical of the defense counsel's decision to push the Unabomber to enter a guilty plea to avoid the death penalty, thus keeping the defendant from getting his day in court. Mello argues that Kaczynski was denied all his legal options because his lawyers kept him in the dark about the details of their strategy. He does, however, engage in a strange comparison between Kaczynski and John Brown and his abolitionist crew.

8. *In re the Conservatorship of Rooney*, Los Angeles Superior Court case No. 126970 (first filed 2011), in which the elderly former child actor and frequent Judy Garland co-star Mickey Rooney first placed himself under a conservatorship and then sued his stepson for elder abuse, breach of fiduciary duty, and misappropriation. The case is a textbook example of what can happen to elderly people when their will is overborne by others. Here, fortunately, Rooney was able to understand the benefits of a conservatorship and placed himself in the conservatorship for his own protection. The pleadings, available on line, make compelling reading. The case is still active.

9. *Matter of M.R.*, 638 A.2d 1274 (1994), involved a young adult with Down's Syndrome whose parents were divorced and who had expressed the desire to move from her mother's home to her father's. The trial court appointed a lawyer to represent the woman. The New Jersey Supreme Court engages in an excellent discussion about the attorney's role as advocate even where "incompetency is uncontested." The court concludes, *inter alia*, that "with proper advice and assistance," generally incompetent people are capable of making their own decisions on certain matters, and that the role of the attorney is to "protect [the client's] right to make decisions," and "to advocate the decision that the client makes."

10. *In re K.M.B.*, 462 N.E.2d 1271 (Ill. 1984). In contrast, in this case, a delinquent juvenile violated probation. Prior to the disposition hearing, K.M.B. informed her court-appointed attorney that she wanted to be placed in her mother's home. Upon recommendation of her counsel, the court placed K.M.B. in a children's home. K.M.B. appealed, alleging that she was denied the right to counsel because counsel did not follow her wishes at the hearing. The court affirmed, finding that unlike other court-appointed counsel, juvenile court-appointed counsel must not only protect the juvenile's legal rights but must also act in his or her best interests, even when the juvenile does not agree.

11. Marvin R. Ventrell, *Rights & Duties: An Overview of the Attorney-Child Client Relationship*, 26 Loy. U. Chi. L.J. 259 (1995) contains a historical review of the legal rights of children and a worthwhile review of the duties of attorneys for children, including a valuable section on how to deal with circumstances when the child's objectives differ from the lawyer's.

12. A series of articles at 64 Fordham L. Rev. 1379 *et seq.* (1996), grew out of a symposium on conflict of interest issues relating to the representation of children. One of the principal conflicts discussed is the tension between a lawyer acting as advocate for what a child wants vs. advocating what the attorney believes is in the child's best interests. Of particular interest are articles by Christopher N. Wu, the managing partner of a public interest law firm that represents children, on representing children in dependency cases (at pages 1857 *et seq.*) and Professor Nancy J. Moore's article at page 1819, especially her analysis at 1844 *et seq.* of the effect of parents as "interested third persons."

PROBLEM 14: PRACTICING LAW IN A MULTI-CULTURAL WORLD

A. INTRODUCTION

Sometimes "differences" make a difference and sometimes they don't. Regardless of who we are or where we use your legal skills, we will undoubtedly be working with people with whom we share some common traits and with others whom we *perceive* as very different because of culture, class, race, gender, sexual orientation, economic, and family background, as well as myriad other reasons. A lawyer's learning and decisionmaking preferences may affect the ability to communicate the information a client needs as well as that lawyer's effectiveness at aiding the client in making a decision. Not surprisingly then, because of the developing recognition that these differences can impact a lawyer's ability to deliver services, several states now require lawyers to learn about "multi-culturalism" as part of their Continuing Legal Education requirements. In this problem we focus on whether and when "differences" become a professional or ethical issue, and how lawyers can deal with these differences to provide competent and diligent representation to all their clients.

Whether lawyers work domestically or globally, they and their clients will inevitably be addressing cross-cultural issues. The US Census projects that minorities (defined as all but the single-race, non-Hispanic white population), now 37% of the U.S. population, are projected to comprise 57% of the population in 2060. The total minority population would more than double, from 116.2 million to 241.3 million over the period.[1] The next and future generations will reflect a very different world. This changing demographic landscape is demonstrated in the dramatic increase in the number of same-sex households, an increase in the number of Americans identifying themselves as multi-racial, and the fact that Latinos now surpass African Americans as the largest minority segment.[2]

One thing we can guarantee: All this *will* have an effect on the way we all practice law.

B. PROBLEM

I

JoAnne Bronson represents a battered woman, a relatively recent immigrant, now separated from her husband. The woman tells JoAnne she wants to dissolve her marriage because she is afraid for her safely but refuses to prosecute her husband or seek a restraining order because the husband has threatened her with serious

---

[1] (*U.S. Census Bureau Projections Show a Slower Growing, Older, More Diverse Nation a Half Century from Now*, United States Census Bureau, December 12, 2012, *available at*, http://www.census.gov/newsroom/releases/archives/population/cb12-243.html.

[2] *See, e.g.*, Velma E. McCuiston, Barbara Ross Wooldridge & Chris K. Pierce, *Leading the Diverse Workforce: Profit, Prospectus and Progress*, LEADERSHIP & ORG. DEV. J., Sept. 30, 2004, at 173.

bodily harm if she does. She also insists she will not seek custody of her two children, including an infant, because of fears of retribution against her and her family in the "old country." Her religious leader suggests that she use an informal system to "resolve this problem because the American system does not understand our values."

JoAnne knows that the circumstances of her client's case make it very likely that the client would be awarded custody, and there are available legal remedies that would serve to protect her, but those remedies are not, of course, infallible.

QUESTIONS

What should JoAnne do? What would *you* do if this were your client? Would it make a difference if the client's husband is abusive to the children as well as his wife? What if she were in love with another man? Or another woman? What other things could make a difference?

II

Kayla Hotchkiss works for a large firm whose main office is in a major metropolitan area in the United States but has offices all over the world. She grew up in the city in which she practices, knows people from a wide range of ethnic and cultural backgrounds, has traveled widely, and sees herself as a "global" citizen. She is meeting with a client who has asked her to finalize negotiations on an import contract with a small Japanese firm that produces unique silks. The client explains that he is frustrated because the person with whom he has been negotiating does not seem to be able to make independent decisions and does not seem to understand that time is of the essence in coming to closure on the transaction.

QUESTIONS

What, if any, role should Kayla take in helping her client understand differences in culture? What should Kayla do to prepare herself to engage in the negotiations with the Japanese firm? Whose cultural norms should be followed?

C. READINGS

1. Lawyer-Client Dialogues Across Cultural Lines

One of the questions raised after Barack Obama's election was "aren't we now living in a post racial society"? One of the clear answers during President Obama's first term was "no." There are still vestiges of overt racism, sexism, and religious and other biases in many pockets in the United States, but for most lawyers and law students, these overt issues have faded. Most see themselves as pretty savvy and fair-minded. While we believe the "isms" of the past may be fading, they are certainly not gone.[3] Perhaps more significantly in today's world are the less overt

---

[3] One need not look far for support. For one person's story see, Nicolas Peart's *Why Is the N.Y.P.D.*

"isms." We as lawyers and law students are too often not aware of the more subtle or indirect effects cultural differences have on our own perceptions and behaviors.

In the excerpt that follows, a group of clinical law professors attempt to show through two dialogues how difficult bridging cultural gaps can be - and why it is of paramount importance not to make assumptions, since superficial similarities can easily turn out to be differences. Read the two scenarios described below and the professors' comments. See if they help you gain a better understanding of how the two lawyers in our problem might approach their clients.

Robert Dinerstein, Stephen Ellmann, Isabelle Gunning, & Ann Shalleck, *Connection, Capacity and Morality in Lawyer-Client Relationships: Dialogues and Commentary*
10 CLINICAL LAW REVIEW 755 (2004)[4]

In the following dialogue, Allen Anderson, an employment discrimination attorney, is a white male in his 40's who, due to a shooting, cannot walk and uses a wheel chair. His client, Anthony Braxton, is also a white male and in a wheel chair, but in his late 20's. The encounter between Anderson and Braxton reflects that there can be even more challenging divisions for lawyers searching for ways to connect with their clients - despite profound similarities that lawyer and client may also share:

L1:   Hello, Mr. Braxton. Come in. Ah! I see I don't have to offer you a chair since you like me have brought your own. Get comfortable here.

C1:   Mr. Anderson, I hadn't realized when I called to make an appointment that you were in a wheelchair too. Call me Tony.

L2:   Tony it is and I am Al. And yes, I was the victim of a shooting in my teens. Wrong place at the wrong time. But I didn't let that stop me from finishing college and going on to law school.

C2:   I respect that a lot. I was in a car accident. I would have been a pro football player but for it. I had been picked in the draft and everything. But with a lot of prayer and help from friends and family and God, I got through and have recreated my life as a stock broker. I work for a large company . . . where I have had my troubles.

L3:   My staff told me that this was an employment discrimination case. Does your boss know nothing of the Americans with Disabilities Act?

C3:   It's not that, Al. At least I don't think so. The head of our firm is a born-again Christian. He is a member of Pat Robertson's church, and he hates gays and lesbians. He thought I was great, wheelchair and all, when I was hired because he saw me as a church-going former football player. Which of course is exactly what I am. But I

After Me?, N.Y. TIMES, Dec. 17, 2011. For a broader approach, see MICHELLE ALEXANDER, THE NEW JIM CROW: MASS INCARCERATION IN THE AGE OF COLORBLINDNESS (2010). See also our Problems 20 and 29, especially section 3 of Problem 20.

[4] Copyright © 2004 by Clinical Law Review, Inc. Reprinted by permission.

am also gay and when he found that out . . . well, everything changed and my work life became hell.

L4:   Uh, well . . . Mr. Braxton. I think it only fair to tell you that I too am a member of Reverend Robertson's church. My religious views on homosexuality are separate from my job in helping you make sure that your boss follows the law.

Here Al Anderson starts out assuming that he and his client, Tony Braxton, could identify very closely as physically challenged men who, through faith, have overcome difficulties to create successful careers, only to discover that other differences - their different sexual orientations and different moral and religious views on this - may cause them to be quite distant. These differences alone may make Anderson feel that Braxton is in the "we have nothing in common" category, although clearly as a factual matter that is not true. Anderson will have to think carefully and honestly about whether his religious beliefs will allow him to zealously represent his client. . . .

This aspect of the Anderson-Braxton relationship highlights the reality that while lawyers can and should work to bridge differences with their clients, they must also be prepared for the possibility that some differences are unbridgeable. Just as Braxton may be unable to trust Anderson, so Anderson may be unable to fully commit himself to representing Braxton. Again, self-awareness and honesty are key.

Here, Anderson has not revealed the details of his religiously based moral code other than to implicitly confirm that it views homosexuality in some kind of negative light. Whether Anderson should politely refuse to represent Braxton is highly contextualized — as the specifics of any attorney-client relationship are. The key issue for the lawyer is not what outside observers might conclude about the fundamental tenets of his church, but how Anderson understands whatever those tenets are. While there may be some church doctrine that reflects a disapproval of gay and lesbian people or homosexual behavior, there probably are also tenets on the connection between all people in the eyes of God and the primacy of love as a moving force in one's life. How Anderson understands and balances these two broad moral approaches will be decisive for his ability to represent Braxton. If Anderson's disapproval of homosexual behavior means that he, personally, dislikes anyone he discovers is gay or lesbian and feels a discomfort with and disrespect for them, then he needs to let Braxton find an attorney who can represent him with zeal. On the other hand, Anderson, who is a civil rights attorney, may find that his religious views are more focused on the aspects of brotherly love. He could decide that their shared physical challenges and the ways in which both men have relied on God and faith to succeed constitute a much greater connecting force than their differences around their sexual orientations. . . .

You are, of course, always "getting to know the client" as an interview progresses, and part of what you may get to know is about difference, as in the following conversation, which takes place in the office of attorney Bryan Culbert in Seattle, Washington, sometime in late November or early December of 1999:

L1:   (After greetings and small talk) Ms. Yamashita, how can I help you?

C1:   Well, Mr. Culbert, I was arrested. It is an absolute outrage! And frankly I may want to sue the Seattle police.

L2:   I see. You have been arrested and feel that this was unjust. Do you have a lawyer for the criminal matter? And by the way, what were you arrested for?

C2:   Destruction of property, assault, resisting arrest. I was arrested near the World Bank meetings during the demonstrations downtown. And the cops just went wild! I don't have a lawyer for the arrest; that's why I came to you but I want to sue as well. I mean what happened to the First Amendment?

L3:   Okay. Well, let's start with the criminal matter first since that will move faster than any civil matter we might choose to bring and, frankly, the outcome of the criminal case may well affect our civil case.

C3:   What?! You mean I can't sue the cops for beating me because they made up these charges?

L4:   No. But if we don't "beat" the criminal charges, so to speak, while you can sue, a judge or jury may, I stress may, feel that whatever injuries you suffered were within the officer's line of duty because you assaulted him or her or were destroying property. So we can sue, but our case is harder. Remember there was a good deal of publicity around the demonstrations opposing the World Bank and International Monetary Fund economic policies in third world countries. Some people already believe that the Seattle cops lost it with the protestors. And that will help us. But others think that the protestors got out of line, but even here we can focus in on you and your behavior and your right to protest peacefully and be treated with respect and dignity regardless of how others were behaving. But let's get back to the criminal situation - you were arrested demonstrating against the World Bank and the cops roughed you up. Tell me exactly what you were doing in the demonstration when the cops approached you and what they said and did.

C4:   And here is my problem again! I was not demonstrating! I'm a reporter for . . . .

[Here,] Culbert is confronted with a client who is quite upset about her criminal case and the circumstances of her arrest. Culbert immediately starts using active listening (L2); he mirrors his client's statement of fact by restating the substance ("you were arrested") and he identifies the feelings she expressed ("and you feel that this was unjust"). His client, Yamashita, is so angry that she is focused on a civil case rather than the more pressing criminal matter. Culbert, in his attempt both to calm her down and to redirect her attention to the criminal case, makes some logical assumptions about what happened. If she was arrested during the demonstrations against the World Bank and IMF policies, it's likely that she was participating in the demonstrations. But in fact this didn't have to be the case. The effects of demonstrations, and police action directed at them, can involve local residents and bystanders as well as demonstrators (and this was true in Seattle in 1999).

In this case, the logical but incorrect assumption has managed to offend the client because, unbeknownst to the lawyer, the client feels that the crux of her case rests on inappropriate stereotyping and racial assumptions. You could imagine, too, that if Yamashita had not had a legitimate reason for being out past curfew — if she was neither lawfully working nor engaged in civil disobedience — the lawyer could have missed an opportunity to explore what she in fact was doing out on the streets. What if Yamashita were a drug dealer and was working, but not lawfully so? Culbert's defense might still focus in on all the confusion of the Seattle demonstrations but if he had not asked his client about her activities in an open and nonjudgmental manner, he would not be prepared for any "surprises" about his client's history. He would generally be better off if he explored carefully whether or not his client really was on the street for the demonstrations rather than making even plausible, but premature, assumptions. Having made this mistake, however, he now must try to recover from it:

L5:   Ms. Yamashita, I am sorry. I shouldn't have assumed. You said First Amendment and I heard right to protest when you were talking about freedom of the press. Both important rights. Again I'm sorry. Let's back up. What were you doing that night exactly?

C5:   I was downtown at about 8 PM. It was after curfew but it was clear there were protestors out and I wanted to . . . well, do my job. Observe what actions they were engaged in. Maybe interview people. Some were obviously our own homegrown petty criminals out looting, but some people were mad and were able to tell me about their issues.

L6:   And that means you were doing what . . . walking or in a car? On the streets or inside stores or what?

C6:   I was walking. I had left my car so that I could really see what people were doing. I did not go into any stores because they were all closed. I just talked to people I saw on the street.

L7:   What happened right before the police approached you?

C7:   I was talking with some people who were real protestors when some other people came and broke a store window. I was trying to call to my photographer who was with me but way down the street. And then I started to shout to the people going in. Saying things like, "What are you doing? Is this part of your protest? How does breaking into a store help your cause?" And then the police came.

L8:   Did you say who you were as soon as you saw them?

C8:   Why? I'm black so I have to identify myself as legitimate?

L9:   No, but you were out past curfew and as you said, you were near people who had broken into a store. The cops could make an honest mistake given the heat of the moment.

C9:   Yeah, well. . . . I didn't see them right away. I was trying to stop the looters from going in and the cops came from behind and grabbed me and threw me to the ground. And that is when I said "Hey! I'm a reporter! I'm not with them!"

L10:   Did they hear you?

C10:   Of course they heard me! I was screaming as one would if your arms were twisted and you had been thrown down. They didn't care!

L11:   Okay, I'm sorry. I'm just trying to get a sense of what it was like out there. And these are questions — how easily able the cops were to hear you — that will come up and we have to be ready for them. What did they say to you when you said that you were a reporter?

C11:   Well there were two on me. One guy, the older one, was saying "Shut up, bitch!" And the other guy was trying to cuff me. The one who said shut up, hit me too. And I screamed again that I was a reporter and the younger guy pulled out my press badge which was on a chain around my neck and started to say something like "It does say she's a reporter" and the older cop said "what!" and looked at the badge for . . . less than a second and said "Yamashita! Her! She stole that to sneak through. Take her and let's get her friends." And then they took me to the police van.

L12:   Did either of these officers hit you again or say anythi ng to you as they took you to the van?

From the conversations, we can tell that Yamashita is mixed race, African American and Asian American, and we can infer that she "looks" black. Culbert's race is unknown, but it is apparent that he is not black. That is clear from Yamashita's reaction to his question about identifying herself to the police (C8), a reaction whose heat suggests that she does not feel she is talking to someone who can identify with the problem of being presumptively perceived to be "up to no good" rather than an "upright citizen." Had Culbert been African American, he might have been able to ask the same question about identifying herself without getting quite the same reaction of anger and resentment. Then Yamashita might have assumed that he knows law enforcement shouldn't be that way but that he himself has had to endure such questions just to ensure his own safety when stopped by the police. Context matters. But it is important to note that non-black Culbert uses other skills in the face of his client's misunderstanding of his intent. He freely apologizes for his initial mistaken assumption about her involvement in the demonstration (L5), and apologizes again for another question that annoys her, even though he thinks he had a good reason for the question (L11). And in each case he also provides the legitimate explanation for his questions without resentment. These kinds of reactions can go a long way in encouraging a client, over time, to trust you even if your initial interactions have been less than ideal.

NOTES

In the cultural "global village" of our nation, and in the many situations in which lawyers find themselves with clients or opposing parties from other cultures and other countries entirely, it is all too easy to find oneself in circumstances where communications break down because the other person is using different analytical tools and may be affected by unconscious biases and assumptions, while you may be affected by your own different biases and assumptions.

2. Decisionmaking in the "Global Village"

How should lawyers approach their decisionmaking tasks? How do your own pre-law school experiences and background help you understand the law? How about your own sense of morality? What else will you utilize in helping to make decisions for those whose background, experience, and means of communicating are very different from your own?

One of the most significant obstacles to working across differences is the perception that our own way is the "right" way. In the past few decades however, in the world of learning and brain science, and now in the broader world of practice, a consensus is developing that people are actually smart in different and equally valuable ways. Howard Gardner's 1983 work *Frames of Mind: The Theory of Multiple Intelligences* pioneered this thesis using the term "multiple intelligences."

Legal education as a whole has been slow to recognize the concept of multiple intelligences, but in the world of clinical law teaching, a number of people have explored this in cross-cultural work and written about it. Susan Bryant and Jean Koh Peters were the first. In the seminal work *The Five Habits: Building Cross-Cultural Competence in Lawyers*,[5] they observe that anyone communicating with a lawyer will naturally convey intent through words and behavior. They suggest that instead of interpreting the speaker through the *listener's* cultural lens that when the listener can focus on the *speaker's* intent and perspective, the listener's understanding improves dramatically.

The previous reading provided some good examples of this in situations of significant but modest cultural differences. Imagine how much more difficult this active listening is when the cultural differences are more magnified — *and* how much more important the listener's ability to understand.

Professor Angela Olivia Burton writes about the theory of multiple intelligences in the context of legal practice.[6] She observes that MR 2.1 and its comments "[a]uthoriz[e] the lawyer to refer to concerns such as "moral, economic, social and political factors" when advising a client. Because such concerns "may decisively influence how the law is applied," advice premised entirely upon a technical interpretation of legal rules "may be of little value to a client." She suggests an approach based on multiple intelligences to help students and lawyers more effectively communicate with clients.

Do you believe that lawyers need to engage in difficult discussions about complex and contentious issues such as the law's relationship to matters of race, culture, and gender as a necessary part of lawyering? Does sensitivity to and

---

[5] Susan Bryant & Jean Koh Peters, *The Five Habits: Building Cross-Cultural Competence in Lawyers*, 8 CLINICAL L. REV. 33 (2001).

[6] Angela Olivia Burton, *Cultivating Ethical, Socially Responsible Lawyer Judgment: Introducing the Multiple Lawyering Intelligences Paradigm into the Clinical Setting*, 11 CLINICAL L. REV. 15 (2004).

understanding of cultural differences rise to the level of an ethical issue in your mind?

3. Client-Centered Lawyering and Abuse Cases

In the following piece, the authors passionately argue that the lawyer's job is to empower the client to make decisions and then defer to the client's choices, something we focused on in Problem 13. The authors assume paternalism on the part of the lawyer is always a bad thing, but are there circumstances in which the lawyer should substitute his or her own judgment? Think also about the lawyer's function as advisor. What obligation does the lawyer have to directly explain these client- vs. lawyer-centered dynamics to the client? How does the client's level of sophistication and ability to comprehend affect your own analysis?

In Problem II, should Kayla insist her American client comply with the Japanese norm or vice versa? What distinguishes Problem I from Problem II in terms of the lawyer's role in deferring or controlling the client's decisionmaking?

V. Pualani Enos & Lois H. Kanter, *Who's Listening? Introducing Students to Client-Centered, Client-Empowering, and Multidisciplinary Problem-Solving in a Clinical Setting*
9 Clinical Law Review 83 (2002)[7]

The client-centered advocate works to understand the client's perspectives regarding the substance and context of the client's problem(s). This approach also involves addressing the client as a whole person, recognizing her place within the community and her relationships with family, friends and others. It necessitates seeing the abuse in the context of the client's life, rather than defining the client in terms of the abuse.

A client-centered approach involves addressing the multitude of issues facing each client and recognizing that legal relief such as restraining orders, criminal prosecution, custody and visitation orders, or immigration benefits typically address only a few of the client's needs. Additionally, legal relief may further the client's legal goals but have a negative impact on the client's emotional recovery from abuse or her economic, educational, employment or health care goals. While the services and resources available to her are important issues to discuss, her alternatives do not always turn on using services. A client-centered approach focuses on the client's articulated desires, . . .

Empowering a client involves an effort by her advocate, reaffirmed in every stage of the relationship between them, to ensure that the client has the information, capacity and opportunity to articulate her needs, determines what course of action will best meet those needs, and obtains from others the resources and cooperation necessary to keep herself and her children safe. Client empowerment, therefore, begins with a client-centered analysis of the problem presented, so that the advocate — whether a lawyer or other provider — sees the problem through the client's eyes and is therefore in a position to assist the client in addressing her

---

[7] Copyright © 2002 by Clinical Law Review, Inc. Reprinted by permission.

problem the way she deems best. Once the problem is defined from the client's perspective, the advocate's role can best be viewed as partnering with a client to exchange information, assisting the client in prioritizing her needs and desires, and strategizing with her to devise alternatives that best address the client's priorities. The advocate can then support the client in analyzing alternatives by weighing the benefits and risks of each alternative carefully and honestly, including the potential time and resources to be expended by the client and the impact of any action taken on the client's long term goals. To maintain a true partnership throughout this process, the advocate must accept and respect the client's right to make and execute decisions, no matter whether, or how slowly, she is prepared to act.

This model of client-centered and client-empowering advocacy shifts the power dynamic inherent in traditional lawyer/client roles with the intent of equalizing power and status between an attorney and client and tapping into the strengths and knowledge of the client as well as the attorney. It emphasizes information sharing and joint problem-solving, as opposed to limiting the client's understanding and directing the client toward service-based solutions. Using this approach, the empowering advocate works to provide the client with the opportunity to form her own relationships with other helping professionals, and supports her in maintaining these relationships, rather than representing the client in all of her dealings with others. Moreover, limiting the preeminence of the attorney in speaking on behalf of the battered client can increase her safety. . . . Co-opting the client's power, even if intended to further the best interests of the client, is dangerous because it mirrors the power and control dynamic central to abusive relationships. Repeating this pattern, even if it feels familiar and appealing to the client, can only be harmful. We have found that attorneys who have been trained through traditional legal methods find this approach particularly challenging, even when they are obviously committed to assisting victims of violence. However, we have personally experienced the increased client satisfaction that accompanies this shift from a hierarchical power relationship to an empowering partnership, and believe that client satisfaction can provide even the most skeptical lawyer with the incentive to achieve competency in this method. . . .

Most importantly, however, this approach avoids the most dangerous and unhelpful thing an advocate can do, which is to give a victim of domestic violence advice and instructions about how best to ensure her safety and that of her children. Advocates do not have enough time to learn all the facts and do not have enough control over enough factors to predict with reliability the results of any particular action or course of conduct. While the client herself may not have all the facts, and certainly cannot control all of the factors vital to her continued safety, she has greater access to the facts and control over her environment than does her advocate. Also, in the end, it will be the client who must live with the consequences of all decisions.

NOTES

Do you agree that the lawyer should defer to the client in the domestic abuse problem described above? Has this article changed your views in any way?

This is an article that contains some radical ideas. We in the United States are taught to believe that abuse is bad. We have professional reporting requirements for social workers, teachers, and the like. Abuse is a criminal offense, increasingly whether or not the victim cooperates. In this context, there is much to be said for the brave position taken in this article. The authors' argument for client-centered lawyering, as they term it, makes a lot of sense in such very personal matters. As the authors note, paternalistic lawyering may repeat and reinforce some elements of the abusive situation.

But do you agree that the highly client-centric approach suggested here is *always* the right one? The authors say that a more traditional approach "can only be harmful." Moreover, the authors state that their client-centric approach "focuses on the client's articulated desires." But this assumes that we lawyers can accurately understand those desires as articulated, which we saw in section 1 is not always easy. Moreover, the authors state that "the most dangerous and unhelpful thing an advocate can do . . . is to give a victim of domestic violence advice" about her and her children's safety. Do you agree? Perhaps by "advice" the authors mean "do-this/do-that" solutions, as opposed to what options and alternatives are available to her. Does a lawyer have a duty of competence to advise the client to the extent of making sure the client understands what options exist, so that she might *consider* them?

Finally, some clients prefer that the lawyer be more directive and assertive, perhaps to the point of making the decisions for the client. The authors want both client-directed results and an end to paternalistic relationships. But what if the result the client wants is paternalistic direction? Might this depend on both the client and the circumstances? Or the cultural background of the client, as Part I of the Problem suggests? Might it even depend on the relationship between the particular lawyer and the particular client?

4.   White Lawyers and Culturally Diverse Clients

In the next article, Fordham ethics Professor Russell Pearce, long a leading thinker on the relationship of race and culture, acknowledges the difficulties all white lawyers have dealing with — and getting over — being part of the predominating group in this country.

Russell G. Pearce, *White Lawyering: Rethinking Race, Lawyer Identity, and Rule of Law*
73 FORDHAM LAW REVIEW 2081 (2005)[8]

This Essay will explore what it means to be a white person in the legal profession and how recognition of whiteness as racial identity requires a dramatic rethinking of professional norms.[9]

---

[8] Copyright © 2005 by Russell G. Pearce. Reprinted by permission of the author.

[9] [FN3] This Essay focuses on whiteness; it makes no claims — and indeed rejects the notions — that race is the only significant identity in lawyering or that racial identity does not intersect and interact with other identities. A number of scholars have discussed how nonracial identities influence lawyering.

As white people, we too often view racial issues as belonging to people of color. We tend to do that in one of two ways. Some whites believe that race generally does not matter except in the rare case of an intentional racist. Other whites view whites generally as racists and look to people of color to tell them how to understand issues of race. This Essay rejects both of these approaches. The Essay argues that for white lawyers, as well as lawyers of color, increased "competence [in] dealing with racial matters" and "speak[ing] openly, frankly, and professionally about relations" is necessary both to competent client representation and equal justice under law.

. . . [W]hether they view themselves as color-blind or racist, white lawyers understandably have a tendency to treat whiteness as a neutral norm or baseline, and not a racial identity, and tend to view racial issues as belonging primarily to people of color, whether lawyers or clients. This approach is consistent with, and reinforces, the prevailing professional norm that lawyers should "bleach out" their racial, as well as their other personal, identities.

As this Essay explains, this unfortunate symbiosis of whiteness and professionalism undermines the work of lawyers both in their representation of clients and in their systemic efforts to promote the rule of law. The latest research in the field of organizational behavior suggests that the assumption of lawyer neutrality so central to lawyer professionalism is not only wrong descriptively, but that it also undermines the very goals it seeks to promote. In particular the pathbreaking research of Robin Ely and David Thomas demonstrates that in a diverse society and legal profession an integration-and-learning perspective that openly acknowledges and manages racial identity would far better promote excellent client representation and equal justice under law than the currently dominant commitment to color blindness. . . .[10]

. . . .

As a general descriptive matter, white people are the dominant racial group in legal organizations. They represent 83.2% of judges, 89.2% of lawyers, and 79.5% of law students, percentages which exceed the 75.1% of the American population that is white. In elite legal jobs, the white domination is even greater. Whites represent almost 98% of partners in the 100 top law firms.

As the dominant racial group, whites can view ourselves as having no particular racial identity. An African-American friend recently described his impression that newspaper stories describing lawyers usually identified the race of lawyers of color but mentioned no race for white lawyers. As a member of the dominant group in the legal profession, the white lawyer is the norm. With regard at least to our race, we start by looking around the room and feeling like we belong, as is so often the experience of white students, particularly the men, in my seminar who do not see race as a useful way to discuss their experience. . . .

[Eds.— Here, Professor Pearce sets forth an extensive bibliography of related articles.]

[10] [FN10] Robin J. Ely & David A. Thomas, Cultural Diversity at Work: The Effects of Diversity Perspectives on Work Group Processes and Outcomes, 46 Admin. Sci. Q. 229, 260-65 (2001) [hereinafter, Ely & Thomas, Cultural Diversity]; Robin J. Ely & David A. Thomas, Team Learning and the Racial Diversity-Performance Link 23-35 (2004) (Harvard Business School Working Paper No. 05-026) [hereinafter Ely & Thomas, Team Learning].

The experience of law students and lawyers of color is quite different. As a minority group in the legal profession, they have "no choice except to learn about white culture if they are to survive." When people of color look around the room, they know they are not the dominant culture and do not necessarily assume the same fit and the same authority. Enhancing this effect is the congruence of white dominance in the legal profession with white dominance in a society where whites have a greater share of wealth and power. When white lawyers, judges, and court personnel assume my students of color are tenants and not legal representatives, or assume a summer associate of color is a member of the support staff, they are applying generalizations about race relations congruent with the relative distribution of racial power found in society in general. The incongruence of the authority position of being a lawyer, or of having a position of authority within the legal profession, complicates the organizational tasks of lawyers of color.

While race makes a significant difference in our experiences as lawyers, intergroup theory reminds us that it is not determinative. These experiences, like those relevant to organizational groups and other identity groups to which we belong, provide us with data. How we manage that data — whether we acknowledge it consciously and how we respond to it — is a matter of choice on both an individual and group level. One way I choose to manage my white identity is to acknowledge and discuss issues of race with my students and colleagues and, indeed, to write this Essay as a way of communicating with a broader group of legal academics, lawyers, and law students. Although this Essay represents a preliminary account of the white experience in the legal profession, this part offers at least two conclusions: White racial identity exists and whites tend to avoid acknowledging their identity.

NOTES

Professor Pearce's postulate is proposed not to engender sympathy but to underscore the difficulty in bridging the cultural gap that whites — especially straight white males — have never had to deal with in much of their practice of law. While he describes the challenge, he's a little short on solutions. Before we look at a few suggested solutions, read the next section about a white lawyer dealing with a group of Cuban refugees who not only brought different cultural and linguistic barriers to their representation but an enormous political/cultural issue — their loyalty, above all else, to their bosses at the CIA.

5. The Watergate "Foot Soldiers" Plead Guilty

If there was one seminal event that first focused the attention of the American legal system on ethics, that event was the Watergate break-in in 1972. The debacle of Watergate included the infamous "Saturday night massacre," in which one lawyer, President Richard M. Nixon, ordered another lawyer, then-Attorney General Elliot Richardson, to fire a third, Watergate Special Prosecutor Archibald Cox. When Richardson refused, he too was fired, and Nixon moved down the Department of Justice chain of command until he found someone willing to carry out his orders. The fall of lawyers, from the President, who resigned in disgrace in August 1974, to a United States Attorney General (John Mitchell), to the White House counsel (John Dean), to the creator of the campaign of "dirty tricks" against political opponents (Donald Segretti), focused our country on the ethics of lawyers as never before.

One lawyer who did not fall was Washington, D.C. criminal defense attorney Henry Rothblatt, Jr. who played a small though fascinating and important role in the Watergate case as defense counsel for his four clients Messrs. Barker, Martinez, Sturgis, and Gonzalez, four of the seven defendants in the original Watergate break-in case. Almost every lawyer would agree that whether a criminal defendant pleads guilty or not guilty is a decision ultimately controlled by the client. Yet, under the unusual circumstances in which he found himself in early 1973, Rothblatt refused to accede to the guilty pleas of his four clients, and instead withdrew from the case.[11]

These four, the "Watergate foot soldiers," were all Cuban refugees and veterans of the abortive "Bay of Pigs" invasion, in which the CIA attempted to invade Cuba to eliminate Castro in 1961. They all were intelligence operatives for the CIA willing to do almost anything to bring the Castro government down. They were charged along with their three Anglo superiors, E. Howard Hunt, G. Gordon Liddy, and James McCord, with the burglary of Democratic National Committee headquarters at the Watergate apartments in June 1972, during Nixon's reelection campaign.

The "foot soldiers" had all worked for Hunt, one of the chief CIA agents involved in the "Bay of Pigs" invasion, and were extraordinarily loyal to him and "the Agency." After their arrest, the four "foot soldiers" maintained that they engaged in the Watergate operation at the behest of Hunt, carrying out the break-in in the belief that Hunt was operating under authority of the CIA.

The trial of the seven Watergate defendants began in Washington in January 1973, before United States District Court Judge John J. Sirica. In his opening statement, Rothblatt outlined his clients' defense as that of four soldiers with no criminal intent following the orders of superiors. Immediately after opening statements, however, E. Howard Hunt changed his plea to guilty. This, the four "foot soldiers" would later argue, was a signal from their superior that they too were to plead guilty. As defendant Barker later put it in an affidavit:

> After we came to Washington for our trial . . . I was told by Mr. Hunt that he had decided to plead guilty and that we did not have any defense. This represented to me a final decision that there would be no disclosure at the trial as to the true nature of the operation we had engaged in and that the plan which was to be followed was for us to plead guilty. . . .

Right after Hunt's guilty plea, the four soldiers wrote a letter to Rothblatt insisting that they be allowed to change their pleas to guilty. But Rothblatt believed his clients had legitimate defenses and were being duped into not using them. He believed that the CIA had had *no* authority to conduct the break-in, and that the "foot soldiers" were being used as pawns in a yet-unknown and dangerous high-stakes political game. Having failed in his attempts to convince his clients,

---

[11] We do not here address the propriety of Rothblatt representing multiple defendants. See our discussion in Problem 7.

Rothblatt then refused to participate in their guilty pleas. He gave the letter to Judge Sirica, and told the court he "couldn't in good conscience, as a member of the bar, knowing my professional responsibilities," participate in his clients' efforts to plead guilty.

After ascertaining that each of the four defendants still wished to plead guilty, the judge replaced Rothblatt with another attorney. Within a few days, and with the concurrence of new counsel and after extensive *voir dire* by the court, the four guilty pleas were accepted. In September, 1973, however, before their final sentences were imposed, the foot soldiers had come to understand and agree with Rothblatt's perspective — they had been duped by Hunt and never should have pled guilty. They moved to withdraw their guilty pleas, which Judge Sirica denied. The circuit court of appeals, sitting *en banc*, in a highly factionalized decision, affirmed that ruling, the majority noting that the defendants had knowingly overruled Rothblatt's advice and pled guilty with the competent assistance of successor counsel.[12]

As for Rothblatt, who had taken the highly unusual step of refusing to accede to what is clearly a client decision, his paternalism was proved correct — at least on this particular occasion. Were his actions justified? Perhaps, at least with 20/20 hindsight. Besides, his clients were allowed to plead guilty after his withdrawal, and so were not harmed by that withdrawal. Not much is known about the manner in which Rothblatt approached his clients, so it is difficult to speculate what he did to bridge the gap between his experiential and cultural view of the world and his clients'. His clients were from two different cultures than Rothblatt: one their ethnicity and anti-Castro fervor, the other their devotion to the CIA and an almost slavish adherence to a master who, as it turned out, was selling them out.

6. Multi-Cultural Lawyering

We have learned much about multi-cultural lawyering in the 40-plus years since Watergate, but we are still in an embryonic stage. What are some of the issues a lawyer from a Christian or Jewish background might face when considering Muslim clients? What about vice versa? In the movie Philadelphia a homophobic lawyer represents a lawyer with AIDS. Is today's equivalent the transgendered lawyer or client? In the following article, a clinical professor attempts to come up with some answers for how lawyers can bridge experiential, cultural, and perceptual gaps today, with one more perspective on "client-centered" lawyering.

Carina Weng, *Multicultural Lawyering: Teaching Psychology To Develop Cultural Self-Awareness*
11 CLINICAL LAW REVIEW 369 (2005)[13]

Crafting a good solution to a client's problem could require familiarity with more than just the relevant legal facts; indeed, familiarity with more facts about the client's situation could determine whether the lawyer even is thinking about the

---

[12] United States v. Barker, 514 F.2d 208 (D.C. Cir. 1975).

[13] Copyright © 2005 by Clinical Law Review, Inc. Reprinted by permission.

right legal claim. . . . [C]lient-centered models of lawyering have [been] developed. The first model, promulgated by Binder and Price,[14] recognizes that the client has superior knowledge about her values, goals and situation, which will enable her to better choose a satisfactory resolution. . . .

However, [c]ritics noted that the Binder-Price model conceptualized the client as a copy of the lawyer, minus the legal know-how. This copy shared the lawyer's socioeconomic status, perspective, organizational modes, etc. — for example, related his situation in clear, chronological order — and thus was ready, willing, and able to participate in the lawyering model promulgated by Binder and Price. Other clients, who might ramble, evince reluctance to discuss certain topics or to commence an interview, lie, or display anger or hostility were, in the Binder-Price parlance, "difficult" and "atypical."

The early Binder-Price model does offer some explanation as to why clients might be 'difficult,' but the reasons do not take into account culture, whether based on race, socioeconomic status, or other factors, except age[, that] affect the client's participation in the lawyering relationship . . . .

In *Constructions of the Client within Legal Education,* Ann Shalleck points out that this undifferentiated model of client-centered lawyering in fact maintains the lawyer as the dominant player . . . .[15]

Concerns about a "one-size-fits-all" training model arose among mental health professionals before they arose among law clinicians. Derald and David Sue warned that an 'ethnocentric' model of counseling teaches students to practice in a way that can harm their clients. The model views the experiences of clients of color "from the 'White, European-American perspective.' " For example, a counselor might view a patient's reluctance to self-disclose as paranoia, when in fact that reluctance might be "a healthy reaction to racism" from the counselor. . . .

Small wonder, then, that Michelle Jacobs should find the Binder-Price client-centered model troubling when applied to the primary consumer at her clinic, namely poor, black clients. Jacobs reminds us that clients labeled difficult by textbooks espousing client-centered lawyering might be resisting the lawyer's invitation to participate in the lawyering process. Rather than dismiss the client as difficult, lawyers need to ask ourselves why the client might be resisting our invitation. Might the client's response be a reaction to behavior by the lawyer who fails to recognize "the real client in her full context — culturally, politically and economically"? Or based on the client's perception of a lawyer who is culturally different from her?

. . . Jacobs' and Shalleck's critiques raise questions about how well the standard model of client-centered lawyering works with clients who are disenfranchised and often economically and racially/ethnically diverse from their lawyers. Even though client-centered lawyering focuses on respecting and empowering the client, it does

---

[14] [FN27] David A. Binder & Susan C. Price, *Legal Interviewing and Counseling: A Client-Centered Approach* (1977).

[15] [FN35] Ann Shalleck, *Constructions of the Client Within Legal Education*, 45 Stan. L. Rev. 1731, 1742–48 (1993).

not address the dynamics of power and subordination (historical, actual, or perceived) in the attorney-client interaction. Thus, suggestions to improve client-centered lawyering also draw on the theory of rebellious lawyering. . . . With rebellious lawyering, the emphasis is on the client: How the client's life — including her membership in an outsider group and her group's history of subordination — defines the legal problem, generates the solutions, and determines the course of action. With this emphasis, the client might more effectively participate as an equal in the decisionmaking process.

. . . .

Building this bridge is not an easy task. Empathy and active listening may elicit more details from the client, and questioning the premises of the American legal system may help the lawyer consciously to avoid its biases. But the lawyer's cultural lens will operate automatically to filter this information and to create expectations about the lawyer-client interaction. So, unless the lawyer understands her own culture and the ways it affects her interactions with others, she risks perpetuating the status quo of discrimination.

. . . .

Training in multicultural lawyering brings together [many] approaches. . . . As a starting point, multiculturalists focus on a broad understanding of culture as "unstated assumptions, shared values, and characteristic ways of perceiving the world that are normally taken for granted by its members." Multicultural lawyering training teaches the student to be aware of the cultural basis for his own behavior and champions using "'cultural lens' as a central focus of professional behavior . . . recogniz[ing] that all individuals including themselves are influenced by different contexts, including the historical, ecological, sociopolitical, and disciplinary." Thus, the student develops a "personal-cultural orientation" toward lawyering in which she considers how her and others' behavior is guided by culturally learned expectations and values. With such knowledge and regular practice, the student is better equipped to develop more accurate decision making that is less biased by the cultural backgrounds of either the lawyer or the client or by the complexity of the problem presented. . . .

For practical guidance to develop cultural self-awareness, student "lawyers" can turn to the five habits for cross-cultural lawyering that Bryant and Jean Koh Peters have devised. . . . For example, Habit 1, Degrees of Separation and Connection, . . . asks students to identify similarities and differences between the student and the client and to consider how these aspects affect information gathering/processing and professional distance/judgment. By deliberately identifying similarities and differences, the lawyer can challenge assumptions about himself and the client, probe for facts, and lawyer based on fact. Habit 5, The Camel's Back, encourages cultural self-awareness, specifically with regard to bias and stereotype. First, the student identifies factors like stress, lack of control, and burn out that disrupt the lawyer-client interaction and make bias and stereotype more likely to intrude. That identification permits proactive efforts to minimize future interference. Second, and in conjunction with Habit 1, the student identifies client traits and personal traits that cause the lawyer to treat the client with insensitivity. . . .

Why is some understanding of cognitive and social psychology necessary? Because, currently in our society, we typically do not discriminate intentionally against people who differ from ourselves. So, lawyers treat clients in culturally insensitive ways due to "unconscious or aversive racism," which can stem from categorization errors that characterize cognitive functioning and from unconscious tendencies to favor members of social groups similar to themselves over members of other groups. Learning more about these psychological processes provides a basis for understanding how lawyers behave in ways that cause discrimination and, therefore, how to assess their own beliefs and lawyering practices.

A lawyer who understands that he has subconscious cognitive categories - called schemas — . . . might be less defensive about acknowledging that his behavior is discriminatory. In addition, awareness of how a schema is created might enable a dominant-culture lawyer to understand how that culture influences the contents of his schemas and to make conscious efforts to diversify his interactions and to question the contents of his schemas in an effort to act with more accuracy regarding members of different cultures. Such a change could more easily allow the client's life, including her membership in an outsider group and that group's history of subordination, to define the legal problem, generate the solutions, and determine the course of action.

NOTES

The adjectives "difficult" and "atypical," as much as anything else, bring home the point of the last article that client-centered lawyering is not nearly enough to succeed in providing lawyering that is both client-sensitive and culturally sensitive and sophisticated. We provide our own personal example. Some years ago, one of us, hired as an ethics and malpractice avoidance speaker on behalf of an insurance company, was touring California giving presentations with a colleague about the need to get conflict of interest waivers and fee agreements in writing. All went well until we got to a town in California's central valley, where, ten minutes into our presentation, one lawyer stood up and asked this question: "That's all well and good if you're dealing with Western culture. But we have many Hmong clients and it simply doesn't work this way in their culture. How do we make our ethical requirements conform to their cultural needs?" This thoughtful and caring question took over the entirety of our three-hour program, and while we can't say that we answered it, the attempt to address client needs on the client's own home ground made better lawyers of us all.

7. The Arrival of Global Law

As attorney Kayla Hotchkiss struggles with how to get a frame of reference to assist her in helping her client, she will not be alone. Professor Laurel S. Terry, our foremost expert on ethics and globalization, has looked at the history of American legal ethics and sees a strong movement towards international comparative analysis because of the growing number of lawyers working globally. Read the brief excerpt below.

Laurel S. Terry, *U.S. Legal Ethics: The Coming of Age of Global and Comparative Perspectives*
4 WASHINGTON UNIVERSITY GLOBAL STUDIES LAW REVIEW 463 (2005)[16]

In order to understand why there may have been a sea change in the nature of the U.S. legal ethics dialogue, it is useful to examine the current practice context for lawyers. Recent U.S. trade statistics help explain the importance of global and comparative legal ethics discussions because they reveal a significant amount of both inbound and outbound international trade by clients. . . . International trade has increased significantly over the past few decades, with a forty-three-fold increase in exports between 1960 and 2004 and a seventy-seven-fold increase in imports during this period. . . .

Another important development that affects the practice context in which lawyers work is the dramatic increase in the foreign-born U.S. population. . . . Since the last census . . . a 57% increase . . . This increase has affected large states and small states, states on the coasts and states such as Missouri, that are in the middle of the country. . . .

Logic and the data . . . suggest that individual clients, as well as business clients, are increasingly likely to need the services of both U.S. and foreign lawyers. Some of these foreign born individuals may need to handle family matters in their home country at some point in their lives, such as inheritance or custody matters. In a business context, foreign born residents may be more likely to set up joint ventures, distributorship relationships, or other business relationships, with individuals in their home countries. When they do so, U.S. lawyers may find themselves working with lawyers from other countries.

Given the dramatic increase in international trade of goods and services and the movement of individuals across borders, it should come as no surprise that there also has been a dramatic increase in the amount of international trade in legal services. For example, U.S. statistics show $3.37 billion in outbound U.S. legal services trade in 2003 and $879 million in inbound U.S. legal services trade. . . .

Moreover, the increase in international legal services trade has not been limited to the United States. . . . Trade in legal services has also been significantly growing in other countries [including, significantly] Hong Kong, China . . . and Australia. . . . Because of the dramatic increase in legal services trade, it should come as no surprise to learn that foreign offices of law firms have grown dramatically, even within the past five years. For example, Carole Silver recently reported that for a group of forty-seven U.S. law firms with foreign branch offices in London, the average firm size in 1999 was twenty lawyers; five years later, in 2004, it was forty-four lawyers. In the two years between 1998 and 2000, U.S. law firms opened forty-one new foreign offices.

What is even more striking is the degree to which law firms are truly global. Of the ten largest law firms in the world, all had offices in ten or more countries. Strikingly, six of the world's ten highest-grossing law firms had more than 50% of their lawyers working in countries outside of the firm's home country.

---

[16] Copyright © 2005 by Washington University. Reprinted by permission.

8. The Impact of U.S. Foreign Policy

Not only does young attorney Hotchkiss need to be mindful of cultural differences, developing new communication skills, especially the listening ones, culturally-biased thought processes on both sides, culturally diverse business practices, and long-distance communication in the global marketplace (among many other issues), she may also need to be sensitive to American and Japanese treaty and trade regulations and — like it or not — American foreign policy itself. The following cites but one example of the problem.

Clayton Collins, *Now, Being a Yankee Isn't Dandy*
CHRISTIAN SCIENCE MONITOR, June 28, 2004[17]

After 14 years of regular travel to Brazil, Andrew Odell was thunderstruck by what he found there on a trip last month. "I have never run into such a consensus view on US politics," says the contract negotiator and partner at Bryan Cave, a New York law firm. "People condemn the US (for its Middle East policy), and are frightened by the US."

In subtle and not-so-subtle ways, America's troubled world standing is beginning to color its business relationships abroad. So far, the practical impact seems minimal. Many executives, including Mr. Odell, see their foreign counterparts distinguishing politics from business — especially when a cheap dollar makes American goods and services attractive overseas.

On the other hand, perceptions count. In what many view as an era of bold political unilateralism by the United States, negotiators working cross-border deals for US firms in Latin America, Europe, and Asia now find themselves facing a precipitous shift in their homeland's image abroad. And they're struggling with whether and how to adjust to it.

"I would say it creates a backlash for everybody in an interdependent world," says Bruce Patton, deputy director of the Harvard Negotiation Project in Cambridge, Mass. "If you're a really big kid and you don't lean over backward not to be coercive, people think you're a bully. . . . If you get what you want just because you can, they hate you for it."

That's what appears to be happening with America's image abroad. For example, only 15 percent of Indonesians felt somewhat favorable or very favorable toward the US, down from 61 percent a year earlier. The Roper survey of 30,000 people in 30 countries also found declines in non-Muslim countries: Russia, down 25 percentage points; France, down 20 points; Italy, down 10.

"Overseas, they perceive Americans as being aggressive and uncompromising," says Sheida Hodge, managing director of the cross-cultural division for Berlitz International in Princeton, N.J. Ms. Hodge spent the last half of 2003 on the road. "Everywhere I went I heard the same thing: 'Americans want to have their way.' The Japanese tell you; the Chinese tell you; the French tell you."

---

[17] Copyright © 2004 Christian Science Monitor. Reprinted by permission. All rights reserved.

. . . .

Some observers say overseas companies are simply pessimistic about whether the US can sustain its recovery, with crude-oil prices at historic highs, and don't see the US as a place to invest serious money. Others attribute it to a less hospitable US stance toward foreign business since 9/11.

But a Harvard Business School study released early this year suggested only minimal effects from overseas anger at the US. In 12 countries, only 12 percent of consumers preferred a local brand to a global (often US) brand. One reason the backlash is minimal, experts suggest, is that many US multinationals, such as Eastman Kodak, have worked hard to establish a local identity in the countries where they operate.

The question is whether consumer antipathy will grow - and how American business should react.

Instead of a softer stance, one emerging school of negotiating calls for tougher tactics. According to this view, the US is losing business because its win-win approach fails overseas.

"So often, especially where culture is used as a barrier, the excuse is that 'Well, it's our culture, so you have to give us something. It's our culture, so in order for you to do business here, you're going to have to compromise,'" says Jim Camp, a negotiating coach in Vero Beach, Fla., and author of the contrarian new book "Start with No."

Mr. Camp, who has worked with nearly 200 public- and private-sector clients, cites a major American supplier to the photographic-instruments industry. "That American supplier has not had one year of profitability in the past nine years," he says. "They've had a win-win mind-set, and they've compromised away their margins of profit. . . . They'll cut their price trying to get someone to like them."

But other dealmakers aren't panicked. Experts say that it's still about individual relationships built on mutual respect and trust. And anecdotes suggest that America may still have some goodwill to draw upon.

. . . .

"People can separate what they feel about the current administration's politics from their desire to do a deal," says [another American lawyer].

NOTES

While the attitude of American administrations can change markedly — witness the foreign policy differences between the administrations of Presidents Jimmy Carter and Ronald Reagan, or George W. Bush and Barak Obama — it is important to keep people's attitudes, sometimes ever changing, about their own country and ours in mind. Do you think that if America is unpopular in the eyes of much of the world that unpopularity can materially hurt international negotiations, or is it still, as one commentator put it, a matter of personal relationships? While a negotiating attitude of "Start With No" would seem to perpetuate the "bully" image of Americans and be antithetical to bridging cross-cultural gaps, is it possible that Americans *do* start by giving away too much? Is it possible that "Start With No" is a viable principle for American lawyers? Or would we be better off sticking with increased cross-cultural understanding and better communication skills?

Finally, do you agree with the ubiquitous Lawrence Fox, who says, "We need to think about how to export our legal values rather than import legal values from other places."[18]

There are many countries that are attempting, to one extent or another, to implement an American-style legal system, Interestingly, Japan, despite the cultural differences between there and the United States, as suggested by the problem, is one such country. So are Korea and several former Soviet bloc countries in southeastern Europe. The world is a smaller and constantly-changing place today, and only time will tell how our legal system affects others and how we are affected by theirs.

D. SUPPLEMENTAL READINGS

1. Howard Gardner wrote the book that brought the concept of "multiple intelligences" into the mainstream of education and practice. He observed that rather than a single type of intelligence; human beings have several — most of which are neglected by standard testing and educational methods. His book, FRAMES OF MIND: THE THEORY OF MULTIPLE INTELLIGENCES (1983), has directly and indirectly influenced generations of teachers and practitioners.

2. Hundreds of articles have been written about lawyering across differences. In addition to the Bryant and Burton articles referenced in section 2, we mention some of the most recent that we have found most valuable:

• Antoinette Sedillo Lopez, *Making and Breaking Habits: Teaching (and Learning) Cultural Context, Self-Awareness, and Intercultural Communication through Case Supervision in a Client-Service Legal Clinic*, 28 WASH. U. J. L. & POL'Y 37 (2008), focuses on supervision and education for effective representation of clients from different cultures;

• M. McCary, *Bridging Ethical Borders: International Legal Ethics with an Islamic Perspective*, 35 TEX. INT'L L.J. 289 (2000), discusses what she sees as a cultural failure to address specific ethical issues resulting from religious-based doctrines;

• Nelson P. Miller, et al., *Equality as Talisman: Getting Beyond Bias to Cultural Competence as a Professional Skill*, 25 T.M. COOLEY L. REV. 99 (2008), offers a model for professional cultural competence in five areas: communication, cognition, relationship, resources, and references;

• Paul Tremblay, *Interviewing and Counseling Across Cultures: Heuristics and Biases*, 9 CLINICAL L. REV. 373 (2002), explores some of the challenges and opportunities of bringing cross-cultural issues into a law

---

[18] James Podgers, *20/20 Eyes Global Change*, ABA JOURNAL, March 2010.

school classroom and some of the issues raised in consciously creating a more professional and culturally sensitive law school culture;

• Christine Zuni Cruz shares personal reflections on reflections on "firstness" on the occasion of being the first tenured Pueblo Indian on the faculty of the University of New Mexico School of Law (*Toward A Pedagogy and Ethic of Law/Lawyering for Indigenous Peoples*, 82 N.D. L. REV. 863 (2006));

• Leigh Goodmark, *Transgender People, Intimate Partner Abuse, and the Legal System*, 48 HARV. C.R.-C.L. L. REV. 51 (2013), the first law review article to specifically concentrate on the intimate partner abuse of transgender people.

3. For two extremely valuable pieces that are helpful for thinking through the issues of cross-cultural lawyering in domestic violence cases, see Kimberley Crenshaw, *Mapping the Margins: Intersectionality, Identity Politics, and Violence Against Women of Color*, 43 STAN. L. REV. 1241 (1991), and Leslie Espinoza Garvey, *The Race Card: Dealing with Domestic Violence in the Courts*, 11 AM. U. J. GENDER SOC. POL'Y & L. 287 (2003), Crenshaw's article, now 15 years old, was an important groundbreaking work and is still valuable.

4. Blanca M. Ramos, *Acculturation and Depression among Puerto Ricans in the Mainland*, 6/1/05 Soc. WORK RESEARCH 95 (2005), describes the distinctive manner in which depression manifests itself for Puerto Ricans who have moved to the mainland. Although it is written for social workers, it discusses the challenges all professional service providers face in understanding how their clients are experiencing their services.

5. Client-centered lawyering is often offered as a tool to help work across cultures. Leslie Espinoza challenges the "client-centered" model of interviewing and counseling, arguing for a more contextualized approach to lawyer-client interaction that helps clients construct their own narratives (Leslie Espinoza, *Legal Narratives, Therapeutic Narratives: The Invisibility and Omnipresence of Race and Gender*, 95 MICH. L. REV. 901 (1997)), while Kate Kruse understands moral philosophy as providing a deep, rich version of what autonomy means, an understanding that can help guide lawyers to the nuances of an engaged client-centered approach to determining clients' objectives. (*Engaged Client-Centered Representation and the Moral Foundations of the Lawyer-Client Relationship*, 39 HOFSTRA L. REV. 577 (2011)).

6. Robert E. Lutz, Philip T. von Mehren, Laurel S. Terry, Peter Ehrenhaft, Carole Silver, Clifford J. Hendel, Jonathan Goldsmith & Masahiro Shimojo, have written an ambitious and comprehensive work, *Transnational Legal Practice Developments*, 39 INT'L LAW. 619 (2005), that attempts to provide an up to date review of international and domestic regulatory schemes that affect lawyers engaged in international multijurisdictional practice. This report, written for the American Bar Association, explains the history and development of WTO negotiations designed to liberalize "trade in services," or the work lawyers do across international lines. The United States is not included in these various agreements because our individual states insist on regulating the practice of law within their jurisdictions. The article points out that while the ABA supports the federalistic regulation of legal services in the United States, it also urges all states to adopt rules permitting foreign lawyers to open offices to practice as "foreign legal consultants" (FLCs) without taking a U.S. qualification examination. By the beginning of 2005, states that have by the ABA's reckoning 80 percent of the U.S. "market for legal services" overseas, including New York, California, Illinois, and Texas, had FLC rules in place.

7. Catherine A Rogers, *Lawyers Without Borders* (Sept. 9, 2008), Bocconi Legal Studies Research Paper No. 1265410. Available at SSRN: http://ssrn.com/abstract= 1265410 or http://dx.doi.org/10.2139/ssrn.1265410), describes how professional regulation of attorneys is still attempting to catch up with the rapid growth in international legal practice, which until recently has been wholly unregulated. She sees the primary effort toward regulation as having been through revisions to Model Rule 8.5 to extend the reach of the rule to international cases and professional activities in foreign countries. She believes that resolving the problems with Rule 8.5 is only a first step in the difficult but important task of developing a coherent regulatory regime for international legal practice

8. Mauro Zamboni asks a question not often asked by American lawyers: Whether it is actually possible and/or "right" to export ones legal concepts and legal models to other legal communities. *Rechtsstaat, In Pluralism and Law: Proceedings of the 20th IVR World Congress, Amsterdam 2001 — International Association for Philosophy of Law and Social Philosophy*, World Congress, Vol. 2.

PART THREE

BALANCING THE DUTY OF ADVOCACY WITH THE DUTY TO THE LEGAL SYSTEM

"The most difficult ethical dilemmas result from the frequent conflicts between the obligation to one's client and those to the legal system and to society. It is in this area that legal education has its greatest responsibility, and can have its greatest effects."

—Jack B. Weinstein, 1975

411

Chapter 6

WHAT PRICE TRUTH? WHAT PRICE JUSTICE? WHAT PRICE ADVOCACY?

PROBLEM 15: HOW FAR SHOULD RICHIE GO TO GET HIS CLIENT OFF?

A. INTRODUCTION

May a lawyer represent a client he or she firmly believes committed the crime charged? Or knows is in fact guilty? How far should or must the lawyer go in representing such a client? What if the lawyer finds the client to be personally distasteful, even repugnant? In the following hypothetical, a lawyer who represents such a criminal client must decide how far to go in presenting a defense in which the lawyer does not believe, in cross-examining a truthful witness, and in arguing the case. As you reflect on this situation, consider how much you would or should do for such a client. If you provide vigorous representation to a client who is "bad" or "guilty," are you then aligned with that client? What if there are "legal technicalities" that you can use even if they belie the truth? Do you abdicate your role as a seeker of justice? Or should the client's conduct and personality not make any difference, because of the job you have to do? Finally, what does the word "guilty" mean?

B. PROBLEM

It is the question perhaps most frequently asked of lawyers: "How can you justify representing someone you're convinced is guilty?" Richie Richewski has heard it hundreds of times, at friends' cocktail parties, his kids' soccer games, wherever he goes in his life away from the courthouse. To Richie, the answers are clear, but many lawyers are themselves uncomfortable with these questions, and would never do what Richie Richewski does for a living.

Simeon "Richie" Richewski is one of the most respected criminal defense lawyers in River City. Although he is a private lawyer, not a public defender, he accepts more than his share of "assigned cases" where he's appointed by the court. These cases don't pay very well, but Richie likes the work more than defending wealthy clients accused of drunk driving, or white-collar embezzlement cases. Richie often says that assigned cases are "what doing criminal defense work is all about."

Not all of Richie's cases are a walk in the park however, and Kirk Hopman is a case in point. Richie has been appointed by the court to represent Hopman on three counts of child abuse with great bodily injury. The indictment charges that on several occasions, Hopman struck his girlfriend Rowena Soo's three-year-old child, and once threw the child against the walls of their apartment, causing brain damage. Soo is also accused and faces the same charges, though the deputy D.A. assigned to the case has made it clear that she considers Hopman the perpetrator and Soo only an aider and abettor.

In a jail conference room, Hopman denies he did anything wrong, but tells a story that includes several factual inconsistencies. Richie is almost certain that Hopman is guilty, but can't be absolutely sure, since Hopman denies everything. Richie finds the allegations repugnant. Besides, though he likes most of his clients, Richie finds Hopman manipulative and demanding. Nevertheless, Richie knows that there are "winning chances" if the case goes to trial, because the witnesses against his client — especially the one witness who claims to have seen Hopman actually "tossing that kid around" — are "flaky," not exactly model citizens, the type of witnesses Richie knows he has an excellent chance of impeaching successfully.

QUESTIONS

1. At the settlement conference, should Richie convince Hopman to accept a guilty plea? May he go to trial with a client whom he is convinced has committed the crime? Or whom he finds personally repugnant?

2. Assume that at the settlement conference, Hopman insists on going to trial, but Soo pleads guilty and agrees to testify against Hopman. Since the district attorney has a policy of only accepting "packaged deals," allowing a plea bargain only if both defendants agree to it, she refuses to negotiate with Soo. The judge, however, tells Soo that she will consider probation after the trial if Soo pleads guilty. Given no alternative other than trial, Soo "pleads to the sheet" — that is, she pleads guilty to all of the charges, including that Soo personally committed great bodily injury on her own child, even though she has steadfastly denied this, and even though the DA herself believes the perpetrator was Hopman.

Richie realizes that although Soo will testify against Hopman, her guilty plea could help create a reasonable doubt defense that Soo, not Hopman, committed the injuries. After all, reasons Richie, he can use Soo's plea to the sheet as an admission that she herself caused her son's injuries. May Richie use this defense? Should he? *Must* he? Should he come out "with both guns blazing" in cross-examination of Soo even if he believes Hopman, not Soo, caused the injuries? How vigorously can he argue to the jury that Hopman is not guilty?

3. Assume that on the eve of trial, Hopman admits to Richie that he took Soo's child in a fit of rage and threw him against the wall, and that he had "hit the child a few other times pretty hard" in the past. Does this change how Richie deals with the plea bargain? If Richie and Hopman decide that Hopman will not testify at trial, may Richie still try the case? Or vigorously cross-examine the independent witnesses? What about the cross-examination of Soo and the argument that Soo committed the acts? Is there a difference in how vigorously Richie may argue to the jury that Hopman is not guilty?

4. After you read the Subin and Mitchell readings in Section 9 below, decide who is correct about their closing arguments about stealing the "Christmas star."

Would Subin's argument meet Justice White's standard (see Section 10)? Would Mitchell's? What argument would you give to the jury?

C. READINGS

1. The "Adversary Theorem" Revisited

We began Part III of this book by reprising the quote from New York federal judge Jack B. Weinstein that we first encountered in one of the *Belge* opinions in Problem 4. Judge Weinstein's remark was as accurate today as when it was written almost 40 years ago. In Chapter One, we suggested that balancing advocacy for our client on one hand and our duty to society and the legal system on the other is "the central ethical question." Weinstein takes this one step further, describing this "dilemma," in essence, as the most important issue in legal education.

In the 1960s and 1970s, how lawyers struck a balance between the traditional adversary role of lawyers — including the traditional concept that lawyers best act in the public interest when they diligently and vigorously serve the needs of their clients — came under particular scrutiny. Beginning in the 1960's, the Warren Supreme Court brought crucial reforms to criminal law advocacy by broadening defendants' rights and requiring that all criminal defendants be afforded counsel.[1]

The idea of "zealous" advocacy — we prefer the term "vigorous" — was trumpeted by lawyers in court and in best-selling books, such as Louis Nizer's *My Life in Court*, first published in 1962. Then in the early and mid-1970s a pitched battle was waged over the legal system: on one side there were reformers such as Ralph Nader and "Nader Raider" and legal commentator Mark Green, who twenty years later became Ombudsman for the City of New York. These lawyers attacked this "zeal above all" concept. On the other side were traditional establishment leaders who, like Simon Rifkind, excerpted in the next section, extolled the virtues of "zealous" advocacy and believed that a lawyer should never be identified with his or her client or that client's cause, just with good lawyering. This was also the era of Watergate, a time when lawyers in the Nixon administration were being accused of highly unethical conduct, adding further fuel to the debate.

The most telling criticisms of the profession, however, have come not from journalists, commentators, or consumer spokespersons, but from the public itself — the legal consumer who sometimes values the services of lawyers and sometimes feels victimized by them. Not surprisingly, to the average member of the public, the O.J. Simpson trial, the Casey Anthony case, and others in which the defense is seen as particularly zealous on the client's behalf, define the American justice system.

Some new and well-publicized work by lawyers involves lawyers committed to freeing innocent prisoners, such as the "Innocence Project," has softened some of the criticism. But the negative image of the legal profession has not abated very much in the decades since the '70s. The average layperson continues to ask pointed

---

[1] Most importantly, see *Gideon v. Wainwright* 372 U.S. 335 (1963); *Escobedo v. Illinois*, 378 U.S. 478 (1964); and *Miranda v. Arizona*, 384 U.S. 436 (1966).

questions about the behavior of lawyers. Many of these questions are the ones we address in this critical part of this volume: Are lawyers ever justified in helping their clients lie? Can they justify hiding the truth? Do they ever have a duty to reveal the truth? How much trickery can they use and then justify in the name of "strategy," "tactics," or legal technicalities"? How nasty or "hardball" can they be in representing their clients, even if it means hurting innocent people? Is the analysis the same or different when comparing the lawyer who represents a corporation that is stealing money from its shareholders or worse, promoting cigarettes to minors, as opposed to the lawyer who represents the factually guilty criminal defendant? And, of course, how can lawyers vigorously and aggressively represent criminal defendants whom they know to be guilty?

2.   Is Advocacy a Search for Truth?

Mark Green's 1975 book *The Other Government*, helped further the overt attack on the adversarial system. He argued that when influential Washington law firms lobbied against the public interest on behalf of powerful clients such as the Tobacco Institute or major car manufacturers, the lawyers did so as "a matter of personal choice, not professional compulsion." Green argued that these lawyers should be held morally responsible for assisting such clients. He wanted these lawyers to "make a judgment about the likely impact on the public" of their representation, and to withdraw their representation if the client wanted to act in a way which would create a "demonstrable though avoidable public harm." Among the lawyers he criticized was the highly-respected Lloyd Cutler (20 years later President Cllinton's chief White House counsel), who lobbied on behalf of General Motors to postpone automobile safety regulations, and whose offices were picketed, spawning the debate between Monroe Freedman and Michael Tigar we refer to in Problem 2.

Among the lawyers responding to attacks like Green's was Simon Rifkind, a highly respected attorney, political advisor, and observer of the legal scene, and the guiding force of one of New York's most powerful law firms. He articulated a cogent and thought-provoking counterattack, a portion of which is reproduced below.

Simon H. Rifkind, *The Lawyer's Role and Responsibility in Modern Society*
30 THE RECORD OF THE ASSOCIATION OF THE BAR OF THE CITY OF NEW YORK 534 (1975)[2]

"How could you represent so-and-so?" is a question frequently put to me. . . . The tone of voice which accompanies the question sufficiently discloses that the questioner has consigned the client to some subhuman category of untouchables.

As you know, there are fashions in untouchability. One season it is a sharecropper in Mississippi, the next season it is a multi-million share corporation in Detroit. From the viewpoint of the adversary system, the applicable principle is the same.

. . . .

---

[2] Copyright © 1975 by The Association of the Bar of the City of New York. Reprinted by permission.

Recently, a group of law students picketed a prominent Washington lawyer [Cutler] in order to give expression to their disapproval of his representation of a large corporation. Had they mastered the meaning of the adversary system they would have known that their conduct was subversive of the central tenet of the profession they were about to enter.

. . . .

Experience tells me that the adversary system has been good for liberty, good for peaceful progress and good enough to have the public accept that system's capacity to resolve controversies and, generally, to acquiesce in the results.

Those who have voiced [contrary] views have not taken account of the operation of the adversary process. The utility of that process is that it relieves the lawyer of the need, or indeed the right, to be his client's judge and thereby frees him to be the more effective advocate and champion. Since the same is true of his adversary, it should follow that the judge who will decide will be aided by greater illumination than otherwise would be available.

Lord MacMillan in his famous address on the ethics of advocacy delivered in 1916 quotes this exchange:

Boswell: "But what do you think of supporting a cause which you know to be bad?"

Johnson: "Sir, you do not know it to be good or bad till the judge determines it. You are to state facts clearly; so that your *thinking*, or what you call *knowing*, a cause to be bad must be from reasoning, must be from supposing your arguments to be weak and inconclusive. But, sir, that is not enough. An argument which does not convince yourself may convince the judge to whom you urge it; and if it does convince him, why then, sir, you are wrong and he is right. It is his business to judge; and you are not to be confident in your opinion that a cause is bad, but to say all you can for your client, and then hear the judge's opinion."

. . . .

This change in the professional wind has caused to bloom a body of lawyers who call themselves public interest lawyers. Instead of advancing the cause of a client who has selected the lawyer as his advocate, the public interest lawyer selects the client and advances his own cause. He pretends to serve an invisible client, the public interest. . . . Inevitably the lawyer is driven to identify his predilections with the public interest. That is unctuous.

. . . [T]he most baffling problem of substance is how to locate the public interest. It simply will not do to accept a set of simplistic labels and to decide, a priori, that in a contest between an employer and an employee the public interest demands that the employee shall always prevail; or that in a landlord-tenant controversy, the latter is always to be preferred. . . . Oh, if only life were that simple!

The traditional relationship of lawyer to client does not contemplate that the lawyer will be a hired hand or a hired gun. He is a professional counsel and not a menial servant. He takes instructions only in those areas in which it is appropriate for the client to give them. In other respects the lawyer is in command. To the client he owes loyalty, undivided and undiluted, zeal and devotion. . . . His object is to achieve for his client the best which is available within the law by means compatible with the canons of ethics.

. . . .

In general terms, truth commands a very high respect in our society. No one can be heard to challenge judges when they pay homage to truth.

With some trepidation I should like to tender the suggestion that in actual practice the ascertainment of the truth is not necessarily the target of the trial, that values other than truth frequently take precedence, and that, indeed, courtroom truth is a unique species of the genus truth, and that it is not necessarily congruent with objective or absolute truth, whatever that may be.

. . . [T]he object of a trial is not the ascertainment of truth but the resolution of a controversy by the principled application of the rules of the game. In a civilized society these rules should be designed to favor the just resolution of controversy; and in a progressive society they should change as the perception of justice evolves in response to greater ethical sophistication.

NOTES

In one sweeping statement, Rifkind not only defended the traditional advocacy system that to this day dominates our conduct as lawyers, but also took a strong swipe at Mark Green's concept that lawyers have an obligation to serve consistent with a clearly defined public interest. He even suggests that lawyers like Green were conflating their own personal interests into what *they* decided was "the public interest." And by quoting Samuel Johnson, he also made the telling point that the job of an advocate is not to judge the client, but to advocate the client's cause, perhaps echoing Charles Phillips' defense of Courvoisier. Nevertheless, in the 40 years since, largely because of public opinion, the underlying controversy has deepened rather than gone away.

3. "Cause Lawyers": The Opposite of the "Neutral" Advocate?

In the following article, a longtime public defender, now a law professor, argues in favor of "cause lawyering" and suggests that the major ethical problem for criminal defense attorneys is the conflict between the interests of one client and another, not between the individual client and the lawyer's interest in a cause.

Margareth Etienne, *The Ethics of Cause Lawyering: An Empirical Examination of Criminal Defense Lawyers as Cause Lawyers*
95 JOURNAL OF CRIMINAL LAW & CRIMINOLOGY 1195 (2005)[3]

In 1990, Jose Orlando Lopez retained a prominent criminal defense attorney, Barry Tarlow, to represent him on serious narcotics charges. Mr. Tarlow's understanding with his client was that Tarlow would "vigorously defend and try" the case but that he would not negotiate on Lopez's behalf if Lopez decided to turn over State's evidence and become an informant in exchange for a reduced sentence. For moral and ethical reasons, it was Tarlow's general policy "not to represent clients in negotiations with the government concerning cooperation." . . . According to Tarlow, such cooperation negotiations were "personally, morally and ethically offensive" and he would no sooner represent a snitch than he would represent "Nazis or an Argentine general said to be responsible for 10,000 'disappearances.' "

Whatever one thinks of Tarlow's policy, this case highlights an important truth. For Barry Tarlow and many other defense attorneys, the practice of criminal defense is about much more than helping individual clients achieve their individual goals. Criminal defense attorneys are often motivated by an intricate set of moral and ideological principles that belie their reputations as amoral (if not immoral) "hired guns" who, for the right price, would do anything to get their guilty clients off. Some of the collateral causes advanced by these attorneys are laudable while others are not. But almost all of them raise ethical concerns that the rules . . . are not well-equipped to resolve. . . .

The cause-motivated approach to lawyering contradicts the traditional view of those in the legal profession as rights-enforcers or as neutral advocates of their clients' interests. Weighing the virtue of neutrality in an advocate versus that of activism, the ethics and professional responsibility literature seems to embrace the former as the more appropriate of the two. Lawyers are strongly advised to be zealous but neutral advocates of their clients' interests. They also have a duty of loyalty to clients that may prohibit them from representing clients in cases where the attorney feels the pull of professional, personal, or political interests distinct from those of the client.

These conflicts raise significant ethical concerns for cause lawyers — activist lawyers who use the law as a means of creating social change in addition to a means of helping individual clients. These lawyers are known by many names in the legal and sociological literature, including . . . public interest lawyers. . . . The worry for the cause lawyer is that the pursuit of her "cause" may at times conflict with the client's interest. A lawyer's professionalism is measured in part by her ability to keep her personal and political agendas apart from (and secondary to) her clients' agendas. . . . Tarlow's particular policy of not representing snitches is open to criticism on this ground, but is merely one example of an overall approach to criminal defense lawyering in which the attorney's moral and political values play centrally in her advocacy decisions.

In this Article — the first to seriously evaluate whether criminal defense lawyers are cause lawyers — I consider several examples of cause lawyering as described by defense lawyers during the course of forty interviews. Through their discussions, I explore the types of values or commitments that animate defense lawyers' approaches to the practice of law and the impact of such "cause lawyering" on the criminal defendant. I consider whether the cause lawyering approach in the criminal context is compatible with ethical and professional rules, and argue that it should be. Sometimes criminal defendants are better represented by defense attorneys who are "cause lawyers" passionately seeking to advance their political and moral visions through the representation of their clients than by attorneys who have no overriding "cause" other than the representation of the individual client. Ethical and professional norms should be more adaptive to these instances.

My conclusion provides no quarrel with the notion that the defendant's goals should take priority over the attorney's personal or political goals. Rather, [t]his paper challenges the well-established view that neutrality (or at least client-centrality) is the only ethical approach to lawyering. I provide empirical evidence supporting the contention that in many instances the cause lawyer's approach is not only defensible but preferable.

NOTES

Do you find it interesting that the term Rifkind uses so disparagingly — "public interest lawyer" — is one Etienne refers to so favorably? Is this just a semantic disconnect or do these two perspectives really embody irreconcilable differences about what it is to be a good lawyer? And who is correct: Etienne, who sees honorable lawyers acting based on "an intricate set of moral and ideological principles," or Rifkind, who finds "unctuous" lawyers who "pretend to serve an invisible client, the public interest," "identify[ing their own] predilections with the public interest"? At the least, it seems that these two perspectives are worlds apart.

4. Defending "Terrorists"

Since Rifkind's day, it seems that more and more "traditional" lawyers have come to argue that some degree of moral imperative is a consideration in their legal representation. Many others continue to excoriate lawyers for the people they choose to represent. One graphic example of such criticism came from the Defense Department official in charge of "detainee affairs," Cully Stimson, who lashed out at 14 large law firms for representing Guantanamo detainees *pro bono*. Calling this "shocking," Stimson stated:

> I think, quite honestly, when corporate CEOs see that those firms are representing the very terrorists who hit their bottom line back in 2001, those CEOs are going to make those law firms choose between representing terrorists or representing reputable firms.[4]

---

[4] Federal News Radio interview with Charles "Cully" Stimson, January 11, 2007.

Anant Raut, a young litigator for one of those firms, Weil, Gotshal & Manges, replied to Stimson in an open letter:[5]

> I practice general corporate litigation. I also represent, on a pro bono basis, five men who are being held as "enemy combatants" at the U.S. detention center in Guantnamo Bay, Cuba. "How can you defend terrorists?" is a question I'm sometimes asked when people learn about my pro bono work. On Jan. 11, in your capacity as the deputy assistant secretary of defense for detainee affairs, you asked the same question of every lawyer representing detainees in Guantnamo . . . .

> Mr. Stimson, I don't defend "terrorists." I'm representing five guys who were held or are being held in Guantnamo without ever being charged with a crime, some of them for nearly five years . . . .

> The second most common question [I'm asked] is, "Why do you do it?"
> . . . .

> There is a widespread belief, as well as a need to believe, that the men we're holding in Guantnamo must be bad people. They must have done something to end up there. They couldn't just be, in large part, victims of circumstance, or of the fact the U.S. government was paying large bounties in poor countries for the identification and capture of people with alleged ties to terror. If the bulk of the detainees are guilty of nothing but being in the wrong place at the wrong time, if there's no evidence that some of them did the things of which the government has accused them, then it would mean that we locked innocent people in a hole for five years.

> It would mean not only that our government wrongfully imprisoned these men but that the rest of us stood idly by as they did it. It would mean that we have learned nothing from *Korematsu v. United States* that we have learned nothing from the McCarthy-era witch hunts, and that when we wake up from this national nightmare, once again we will marvel at the extremism we tolerated in defense of liberty. It would mean that even as we extol the virtues of fairness and due process abroad, we take away those very rights from people on our own soil.

> The Rev. Martin Luther King Jr. once wrote, "Injustice anywhere is a threat to justice everywhere." It is my belief that the true test of a nation's commitment to liberty occurs not when it is most readily given, but rather when it is most easily taken away.

> Mr. Stimson, that is why I do what I do.

NOTES

After a day or two to digest it, reaction to Stimson's interview was strongly negative, and there was no measurable effect on the law firms who had taken on the Guantanamo representations.

---

[5] Anant Raut, *Why I Defend Terrorists*, reported on Salon.com, January 17, 2007. Reprinted with permission of salon.com and the author.

5. Representing the Guilty Client

One of the most difficult issues for the public understanding of the legal profession is how the criminal defense lawyer justifies representing the guilty client. Almost all of us have been brought up with one generation or another of Perry Mason, a lawyer who uses all the tricks in the book, but only for his seemingly limitless stable of innocent clients. Going back almost a hundred years, the West Coast's first great criminal defense attorney, Earl Rogers, claimed that he only represented people he believed innocent, at least according to his biographer and daughter, the noted journalist Adela Rogers St. Johns.[6]

TV shows and movies make heroes of lawyers who, like Atticus Finch in *To Kill a Mockingbird*, do their level best to get justice for their falsely accused clients.

But often, the reality of the criminal defense lawyer at trial (as opposed to the frequent pretrial job of negotiating the best possible plea for a client) is the use of skill and persuasion to convince the jury to acquit a *guilty* client. The public may be asking, "How can you try to get that guilty person off?" But to most experienced criminal defense lawyers, that question is old news, as old as the Courvoisier case we discussed in the first chapter.

We have a long history of such representation, including the legal career of Clarence Darrow, whose impassioned defense of the guilty Leopold and Loeb, among others, is the stuff of legend. But we also have the explicit requirements of the Fifth Amendment, to due process of law, and of the Sixth Amendment, that criminal defendants be afforded "the *effective* assistance of counsel." And, as innumerable cases from *Powell v. Alabama*[7] on have held, "effective" means far more than sitting around waiting for something to happen. So when we turn on the television of the new millennium, we see not Perry Mason, but the lawyers on "The Practice" or "Suits" using the strategy they call "Plan B": pointing the finger at someone else — anyone else — so that their client, innocent or guilty, might avoid conviction.

Let's return for a moment to the idea espoused by Dr. Samuel Johnson — that the lawyer must avoid judging the client. Wouldn't it be impossible for criminal defense lawyers to perform their functions if they sat in judgment of their clients as well as defended them? Representing criminal defendants is not everyone's cup of tea; many lawyers choose not to do it. But those who do undertake a serious and often difficult responsibility.

6. True Evidence, False Defense

Effective assistance of counsel is one thing, even if it means doing your best for a client whom you do not believe. But how far does a lawyer have to go in that representation? May an attorney, knowing the client is guilty, put on evidence that, though truthful in itself, misleads the jury into thinking that the client did not commit the crime? *Must* a lawyer put on such evidence? The State Bar of Michigan

---

[6] ADELA ROGERS ST. JOHNS, FINAL VERDICT (1962).

[7] 287 U.S. 45 (1932).

addressed these questions in a 1987 opinion.

MICHIGAN OPINION CI-1164
(1987)

Client is charged with armed robbery. He proposes to call some friends as witnesses at trial, who will give truthful testimony that he was with them at the time of the crime. At the preliminary examination the victim had testified that the robbery occurred at the same hour and time to which the friends will testify. Client has confided to attorney that he robbed the victim; his theory on the time mix-up is that he stole the victim's watch and rendered him unconscious so that the victim's sense of time was incorrect when relating the circumstances of the robbery to the investigating detectives. Months later, at the preliminary examination, the victim relied on the detectives' notes to help him recall the time. Client and attorney have decided that client will not testify at trial. Would it be ethical for attorney to subpoena the friends to trial to testify that client was with them at the alleged time of the crime?

DR 7-101 requires counsel to represent the client zealously. A defense attorney can present any evidence that is truthful; if the ethical rule were otherwise it would mean that a defendant who confessed guilt to his counsel would never be able to have an active defense at trial.

The danger of an opposite approach is that sometimes innocent defendants "confess guilt" to their counsel or put forth a perceived "truthful" set of facts that do not pass independent scrutiny. Many crimes have degrees of guilt, as in homicide, where the "true facts" go to the accused's intent; something a jailed defendant may not be in a reflective mood to assess. Criminal defense counsel are not sent to the jail's interview room to be their client's one person jury and they certainly are not dispatched to court to be their client's hangman. Our society has made the decision to permit a person charged with crime to make full disclosure to his counsel without fear that, absent the threat of some future conduct (such as a threat to kill a witness), the lawyer will not disclose the information so provided.

The role of criminal defense counsel is to zealously defend the client within the boundaries of all legal and ethical rules. Therefore, if the information confidentially disclosed by the client were to prevent counsel from marshaling an otherwise proper defense, the client would, in effect, be penalized for making the disclosure. Such a policy, over a longer run, would tend to cause future defendants to fail to disclose everything to their lawyer; the result would be that they would receive an inadequate defense. Such an approach would be fundamentally inconsistent with the implicit representation made to defendants as a part of procedural due process that they may disclose everything to their lawyer without fear of adverse consequence.

It is the prosecution's responsibility to marshal relevant and accurate testimony of criminal conduct. It is not the obligation of defense counsel to correct inaccurate evidence introduced by the prosecution or to ignore truthful evidence that could exculpate his client. Although the tenor of this opinion may appear to risk an unfortunate result to society in the particular situation posed, such an attitude by defense counsel will serve in the long run to preserve the system of criminal justice envisioned by our constitution.

DR 7-102(4) prohibits counsel from using perjured testimony or "false evidence," but it is perfectly proper to call to the witness stand those witnesses on behalf of the client who will present truthful testimony. The testimony of the friends will not spread any perjured testimony upon the record. The client indeed was with the witnesses at the hour to which they will testify. The victim's mistake concerning the precise time of the crime results in this windfall defense to the client. . . .

NOTES

In contrast, in the 2009 case of *Torres v. Donnelly*, 554 F.3d 322 (2d Cir. 2009), defense counsel "inadvertently elicited [trial] testimony counsel personally knew to be inaccurate" — that the eyewitness stated she had failed to identify the defendant in a pre-trial photo spread when in fact she had. According to the court's opinion: "Subsequently, to avoid becoming a witness himself and to comply with his ethical obligations to the court to correct false testimony, counsel agreed to stipulate that, contrary to [the witness'] testimony during cross-examination, [she] had identified Torres." The defendant's later habeas petition for ineffective assistance of counsel was denied.

Is there a difference between the Michigan opinion and the *Torres* case? Both involve incorrect testimony. In both cases, the testimony was innocently mistaken, not perjurious. But in *Torres*, the court's cites to this New York ethics rule: "[i]n the representation of a client, a lawyer shall not: (4) knowingly use perjured or false evidence."

These are subtly but significantly different cases, however. Tellingly, once the prosecutor had pressured him in chambers, the lawyer in *Torres* thought he could be a witness to the photo ID. More significantly, the lawyer proffered the wrong testimony himself, albeit inadvertently. Most importantly, the *Torres* court "merely" determined on habeas that there were insufficient grounds for reversible error, *i.e.*, that the result of the case would not have changed. What if the lawyer had simply stayed silent? Would the court have sanctioned him for doing so given the reasoning of the Michigan Opinion and the defendant's Fifth Amendment rights? We think not.

7. Criminal Defense Justifications

One can readily understand that to the public, the use of the "true testimony — false alibi" suggested by the Michigan opinion is not justice served but justice denied. Yet for those who do this work, techniques like this are not only accepted, they are taught, practiced, polished, and even applauded. Defense lawyers learn how to "try someone, anyone, other than the defendant," or to point the finger at a person or persons unknown (sometimes called the "dude done it" defense).

Since in a criminal trial the state must be put to its proof and proof must be beyond a reasonable doubt, criminal defense lawyers reason, cogently, that their job — their sworn duty — is to do anything within the bounds of ethical rules to raise such a doubt in the minds of the jurors. Put another way, truth must be measured not by whether the accused is guilty, but by whether the state has met its constitutional burden. That, these lawyers argue, is truly justice served, since justice, to paraphrase legendary federal appeals court judge Learned Hand, should be measured by how well we treat the worst members of our society, not the best. Thus, for lawyers to do less than *their* best would truly be justice denied.

Do you agree? Or is this kind of defense beyond the appropriate role of a lawyer, even in a criminal case? Consider where you fit on this spectrum as you review the rest of the readings for this problem.

Are there other reasons criminal defense lawyers use to justify their defense of guilty clients? We've read Margareth Etienne's views above. Briefly excerpted here are several justifications suggested many years ago by a Stanford law professor and former public defender that still apply today.

Barbara Babcock, *Defending the Guilty*
32 CLEVELAND STATE LAW REVIEW 175 (1983)[8]

The Garbage Collector's Reason. It is dirty work but someone must do it. We cannot have a functioning adversary system without a partisan for both sides. . . . The civil libertarian tells us that . . . [i]n protecting the constitutional rights of criminal defendants, we are only protecting ourselves.

The Legalistic or Positivist's Reason. Truth cannot be known. Facts are indeterminate, contingent, and in criminal cases, often evanescent. . . . [T]here is a difference between legal and moral guilt; the defense lawyer should not let his apprehension of moral guilt interfere with his analysis of legal guilt. The example usually given is that of a person accused of murder who can respond successfully with a claim of self-defense. The accused may feel morally guilty but not be legally culpable. . . .

The Political Activist's Reason. Most people who commit crimes are themselves the victims of horrible injustice. This statement is true generally because most of those accused of rape, robbery and murder are oppressed minorities. . . . Moreover, the conditions of imprisonment may impose violence far worse than that inflicted on the victim. . . .

The Social Worker's Reason. Those accused of crime, as the most visible representatives of the disadvantaged underclass in America, will actually be helped by having a defender, notwithstanding the outcome of their cases. Being treated as a real person in our society and accorded the full panoply of rights and the measure of concern afforded by a lawyer can promote rehabilitation. . . .

The Egotist's Reason. Defending criminal cases is more interesting than the routine and repetitive work done by most lawyers, even those engaged in what passes for litigation in civil practice. . . . Actual court appearances, even jury trials, come earlier and more often in one's career than could be expected in any other area

---

of law. And winning . . . has great significance because the cards are stacked for the prosecutor. . . .

NOTES

Are the reasons offered by Babcock valid ones? Are some more persuasive than others? Which appear to you to be more ethical? More moral? How do these reasons compare to Etienne's, Anant Raut's, or with the other ideas articulated in these Readings?

8.   Taking Advantage on Cross-Examination

We now spend some time with two cross-examination scenarios — the elderly witness or victim whose ability to recall is questioned, and the rape victim who is known by the lawyer to be telling the truth. First, consider the elderly woman in the next article. Is the described cross-examination justified? Does the witness' age make any difference? Does it matter that the witness is also the victim? Or what further damage or humiliation is inflicted on her? Does the nature of the crime make a difference? What about the potential penalty to the client? Or should zealous representation of the client be the lawyer's only concern in all cases, no matter what?

E.R. Shipp, *Fear and Confusion in Court Plague Elderly Crime Victims*
THE NEW YORK TIMES, March 13, 1983[9]

An 89-year-old woman sat in a wheelchair next to the witness stand in State Supreme Court in Manhattan and, during questioning over two days, pleaded with the judge and the defense attorney to let her go home.

"I was never in a mix-up like this in my life," she said. "I feel as though I am just sitting here being persecuted for nothing, absolutely nothing."

Thousands of New York City's elderly citizens are the victims of crime each year. For the woman on the witness stand, Eleanor Cosgrove, the attempt to describe her case - in which a lawyer was charged with stealing from her — was made difficult by poor health, a faltering memory and fear. "I am scared to death," she repeatedly said.

The police and prosecutors say they are increasingly concerned about the physical or psychological barriers that prevent elderly victims from becoming witnesses and that make it difficult to prosecute those who prey upon them. . . .

Both the police and the District Attorneys' offices say they are spending more time working with the elderly, teaching them how to prevent crime and encouraging them to come forward to report it.

But in preparing cases for trial, they say, three main hurdles must be overcome:

---

[9] Copyright © 1983 by The New York Times Company. Reprinted by permission.

the victim's fear, deliberate delay by the defense and, if the case progresses that far, rigorous cross-examination during trial.

"They're afraid," said Acting Justice Francis N. Pecora of State Supreme Court in Manhattan. "They're intimidated, and they are then more or less browbeaten by the defense attorney. It's like being assaulted a second time."

. . . .

Linda A. Fairstein, chief of the Sex Crimes Bureau of the Manhattan District Attorney's office, estimated that 10 percent to 20 percent of the victims of sexual crimes prosecuted by her office were 65 or older.

Sherry Roman, the chief of the Major Offense Bureau of the Bronx District Attorney's office, said, "A very significant portion of our cases involves the elderly as victims."

But because of such physical disabilities as failing eyesight, these elderly victims "generally make poor witnesses," said Sgt. Michael W. Gerhold, who heads one of Manhattan's two senior robbery units.

. . . .

"A major problem is stalling tactics by defense lawyers to delay the trial," said Judge Irving Lang of the city's Criminal Court. "Everybody's memory fades with time, but older people have particular problems in that regard."

Finally comes the trial and the sometimes grueling cross-examination by the suspect's attorney.

Many defense attorneys, Miss Fairstein said, try to show that the elderly witness does not really know what went on.

"They do that," Miss Fairstein said, "by asking so many detailed questions that will have to result in an 'I don't know' or 'I don't remember' answer, trying to shake the foundation of the case and give the impression of faulty memory, obtuseness and senility. They prey on mistakes."

A defense lawyer, Donald O. Weinberger, gave another view: "There's a responsibility you take on when you become a defense attorney. You've got to cross-examine that witness and make sure that witness is correct about what he's saying. That's not so easy, whether or not it's an old person."

At the age of 89, Mrs. Cosgrove was one of the oldest witnesses to appear in recent cases, and the defense tried to show that, because of her advanced age and uncertainty about so many details, the jury should not believe any of her testimony.

The defendant, Erich Reisch, had been her attorney and was charged with stealing $129,000 from her and using the money for such things as a 1981 Cadillac, certificates of deposit listed in his and his wife's names, and real-estate investments, also in his wife's name.

Mr. Reisch maintained that he was not guilty. He contended that Mrs. Cosgrove had wanted "a greater yield" than she was receiving on her savings accounts and thus he had made investments for her, even though some were in other names. He further said that Mrs. Cosgrove had lent him money for the car and other items, and that he had given her promissory notes but that he had neglected to keep copies for himself. Mrs. Cosgrove did not recall such notes.

On cross-examination, Mr. Reisch's attorney, Bruce H. Goldstone, immediately began to raise doubts about her memory. He asked, "Have you found that as you get older your memory perhaps is not as good as it was years ago?" She answered: "I wouldn't say so. I'm pretty keen."

That led to a dispute about her birthdate. After Mrs. Cosgrove said that she was born on April 22, 1893, Mr. Gladstone read from the transcript of a February 1982 hearing — one of three previous proceedings at which Mrs. Cosgrove had been required to give testimony — showing her saying: "I was born in 1903."

"Oh, no, I never said that," Mrs. Cosgrove replied. "I never said 1903. I was in school then. So I had no occasion to use 1903."

The longer the questioning proceeded, the more confused Mrs. Cosgrove appeared to become.

The assistant district attorney in the case, Seth Rosenberg, urged the jury to focus upon what Mrs. Cosgrove did clearly recall — that she had not authorized Mr. Reisch to use her money for investments or his personal affairs.

. . . .

After deliberating several days, the jury deadlocked 11 to 1 in favor of conviction, leading Justice Clifford A. Scott to declare a mistrial. A new trial, at which Mrs. Cosgrove will again have to testify, is set to begin April 5.

9.   How Far Should One Go With a Guilty Client?

Years ago, for the first volume of the Georgetown Journal of Legal Ethics, a noted criminal law professor, Harry I. Subin, analyzed a case he had encountered as the director of a law school criminal law clinic. The client, charged with rape, had at first denied his guilt. While Subin doubted this story of innocence, he also recognized "some strength to [his client's] arguments, and that there were questionable aspects to the complainant's story." Eventually, though, the client confessed to Subin that his alibi was false and he was guilty. Years later, and with ethical hindsight, Subin analyzed how he had behaved upon learning of his client's guilt. Troubled by his actions, he proposed a far less adversarial role for the criminal defense lawyer that would have avoided presenting a "false defense" for a client known to be guilty.

Harry I. Subin, *The Criminal Defense Lawyer's "Different Mission": Reflections on the "Right" to Present a False Case*
1 GEORGETOWN JOURNAL OF LEGAL ETHICS 125 (1987)[10]

II. Truth Subversion in Action: The Problem Illustrated

[When my client finally admitted guilt] I did not pause very long to ponder the problem, however, because I concluded that knowing the truth in fact did not make a difference to my defense strategy, other than to put me on notice as to when I might be suborning perjury. Because the mission of the defense attorney was to defeat the prosecution's case, what I knew actually happened was not important otherwise. What did matter was whether a version of the "facts" could be presented that would make the jury doubt the client's guilt.

Viewed in this way, my problem was not that my client's story was false, but that it was not credible. . . . To win, we would therefore have to come up with a better theory than the alibi, avoiding perjury in the process. Thus, the defense would have to be made out without the client testifying. . . .

There were two possible defenses that could be fabricated. The first was mistaken identity. . . . [But] it seemed doubtful that the mistaken identification ploy would be successful. The second alternative, consent, was clearly preferable. . . . To prevail, all we would have to do would be to raise a reasonable doubt as to whether he had compelled the woman to have sex with him. The doubt would be based on the scenario that the woman and the defendant had met before, and she voluntarily returned to his apartment. . . .

The consent defense could be made out entirely through cross-examination of the complainant, coupled with argument to the jury about her lack of credibility on the issue of force. I could emphasize the parts of her story that sounded the most curious. . . . [An] allegedly stolen watch was never found, there was no sign of physical violence, and no one heard screaming or any other signs of a struggle.

. . . .

How all of this would have played out at trial cannot be known. Predictably, the case dragged on so long that the prosecutor was forced to offer the unrefusable plea of possession of a gun. As I look back, however, I wonder how I could justify doing what I was planning to do had the case been tried. I was prepared to stand before the jury posing as an officer of the court in search of the truth, while trying to fool the jurors into believing a wholly fabricated story: that the woman had consented, when in fact she had been forced at gunpoint to have sex with the defendant. I was also prepared to demand an acquittal because the state had not met its burden of proof when, if it had not, it would have been because I made the truth look like a lie. If there is any redeeming social value in permitting an attorney to do such things, I frankly cannot discern it.

. . . .

---

[10] Copyright © 1987 by The Georgetown Journal of Legal Ethics and Georgetown University. Reprinted by permission.

III. *Can Lawyers "Know" the Truth?*

. . . .

The argument that the attorney cannot know the truth until a court decides it fails. Either it is sophistry, designed to simplify the moral life of the attorney, or it rests on a confusion between "factual truth" and "legal truth." The former relates to historical fact. The latter relates to the principle that a fact cannot be acted upon by the legal system until it is proven in accordance with legal rules. . . .

Given that the attorney is not the trier of fact in the case but the representative of the defendant, it seems appropriate that the lawyer be directed to apply a burden of proof in favor of the client. Because there is a strong societal interest in providing the defendant the opportunity to state a case, the presumption should be strong. It would seem, therefore, that the attorney should be permitted to offer a defense unless he or she knew" beyond a reasonable doubt that the defense was false.

Applying this standard to the case under discussion, I would conclude that I "knew" beyond a reasonable doubt that the proposed consent defense was false. . . .

IV. *Does the Truth Matter? Appraising the Different Mission*

[One cannot sensibly] defend the utterly arbitrary line we have drawn between deliberately offering perjured testimony and deliberately attempting to create false "proof" by offering truthful but misleading evidence, or by impeaching a truthful witness. Instead [one should] recognize that the right to put forward a defense is limited, not absolute. . . .

V. *Accomplishing the Defense Attorney's Different Mission — Morally*

I propose a system in which the defense attorney would operate not with the right to assert defenses known to be untrue, but under the following rule:

"It shall be improper for an attorney who knows beyond a reasonable doubt the truth of a fact established in the state's case to attempt to refute that fact through the introduction of evidence, impeachment of evidence, or argument."

In the face of this rule, the attorney who knew there were no facts to contest would be limited to the "monitoring" role. Assuming that a defendant in my client's situation wanted to assert his right to contest the evidence against him, the attorney would work to assure that all of the elements of the crime were proven beyond a reasonable doubt, on the basis of competent and admissible evidence. This would include enforcing the defendant's right to have privileged or illegally obtained evidence excluded: The goal sought here is not the elimination of all rules that result in the suppression of truth, but only those not supported by sound policy. It would also be appropriate for the attorney to argue to the jury that the available evidence is not sufficient to sustain the burden of proof. It would not, however, be proper for the attorney to use any of the presently available devices to refute testimony known to be truthful. I wish to make clear, however, that this rule would not prevent the attorney from challenging *inaccurate* testimony, even though the attorney knew that the defendant was guilty. . . .

Applying these principles to my rape case, I would engage fully in the process of testing the admissibility of the state's evidence, moving to suppress testimony concerning the suggestive "show-up" identification at the precinct, and the gun found in the defendant's apartment after a warrantless search, should the state attempt to offer either piece of evidence. At the trial, I would be present to assure that the complainant testified in accordance with the rules of evidence.

Assuming that she testified at trial as she had at the preliminary hearing, however, I would not cross-examine her, because I would have no good faith basis for impeaching either her testimony or her character, since I "knew" that she was providing an accurate account of what had occurred. Nor would I put on a defense case. I would limit my representation at that stage to putting forth the strongest argument I could that the facts presented by the state did not sustain its burden. . . .

NOTES

Noting that evidence rarely falls into neatly wrapped packages labeled "true" and "false," attorney and law professor John B. Mitchell, writing in the same ethics journal that published Subin's article, tested the practical difficulty of Subin's proposal by trying to present a closing argument that both provided a defense to the accused and avoided resting on falsehoods.

Mitchell hypothesized that he was defending a young woman accused of shoplifting a Christmas tree star. The store manager stopped the defendant when she walked straight through the store and out the door with the star in her hand. When stopped, the woman burst into tears. Just as the manager was about to take her to the store's security office, a small fire broke out in the camera section, and he rushed off to help put it out. When he returned five minutes later, the woman was still sitting where he had left her. Back in the security room, the manager asked her to empty her pockets. He found that the woman had nothing else belonging to the store, but did have a ten-dollar bill. The star cost $1.79.

Mitchell's fictitious client admitted her guilt to him: "[The star] was so pretty. . . . I would have bought it, but I also wanted to make a special Christmas dinner for Mama and didn't have enough money to do both. . . . But that star . . . I could just see the look in Mama's eyes if she saw that lovely thing on our tree."

First, Mitchell describes how he would defend the case. Then we read a final excerpt: Subin's response to Mitchell's proposed defense.

John B. Mitchell, *Reasonable Doubts are Where You Find Them: A Response to Professor Subin's Position on the Criminal Lawyer's "Different Mission"*
1 GEORGETOWN JOURNAL OF LEGAL ETHICS 343 (1987)[11]

My defense is not that the defendant accidentally walked out, but rather that the prosecution cannot prove the element of intent to permanently deprive beyond a reasonable doubt. Through this theory, I am raising "doubt" in the prosecution's case. . . . In my effort to carry out this legal theory, I will *not assert* that facts known by me to be true are false or those known to be false are true. As a defense attorney, I do not have to prove what *in fact* happened. That is an advantage in the process I would not willingly give up. . . . Thus, in this case I will not claim that my client walked out of the store with innocent intent (a fact which I know is false); rather, I will argue:

> The prosecution claims my client stole an ornament for a Christmas tree. The prosecution further claims that when my client walked out of that store she intended to keep it without paying. Now, maybe she did. None of us were there. On the other hand, she had $10.00 in her pocket, which was plenty of money with which to pay for the ornament without the risk of getting caught stealing. Also, she didn't try to conceal what she was doing. She walked right out of the store holding it in her hand. Most of us have come close to innocently doing the same thing. So, maybe she didn't. But then she cried the minute she was stopped. She might have been feeling guilty. So, maybe she did. On the other hand, she might just have been scared when she realized what had happened. After all, she didn't run away when she was left alone even though she knew the manager was going to be occupied with a fire inside. So, maybe she didn't. The point is that, looking at all the evidence, you're left with "maybe she intended to steal, maybe she didn't." But, you knew that before the first witness was even sworn. The prosecution has the burden, and he simply can't carry any burden let alone "beyond a reasonable doubt" with a maybe she did, maybe she didn't case.
>
> . . .

Is this a "false defense" for Professor Subin? Admittedly, I am trying to raise a doubt by persuading the jury to appreciate "possibilities" other than my client's guilt. Perhaps Professor Subin would say it is "false" because I know the possibilities are untrue. But if that is so, Professor Subin will have taken a leap from defining "false defense" as the assertion that true things are false and false things are true, for I am doing neither of those things here. . . .

Another perspective from which to look at the function of a defense attorney involves understanding that function in the context of the nature of evidence at trial. Professor Subin speaks of facts and the impropriety of trying to make "true facts" look false and "false facts" look true. But in a trial there are no such things as facts. There is only information, lack of information, and chains of inferences therefrom.

. . . .

In a system where factual guilt is not at issue, Professor Subin's "falsehoods" are, in fact, "reasonable doubts."

Harry I. Subin, *Is this Lie Necessary? Further Reflections on the Right to Present a False Defense*
1 GEORGETOWN JOURNAL OF LEGAL ETHICS 689, 691-692 (1988)[12]

John B. Mitchell has written a thought-provoking response to my argument. While there is much in his presentation with which I disagree, I think that he has stated as well as anyone can the case for what I have called the "false" defense. He has not persuaded me. But he has demonstrated a flaw in my formulation, which I would like to correct here. In essence, Mitchell has convinced me that precluding the defense attorney from attacking a truthful case against the defendant may be incompatible with the defense attorney's responsibility to assure that the prosecution meets its high burden of proof at trial. I shall therefore offer this modification of my original proposal: when the defense attorney knows that the prosecution's evidence is true, he or she may nonetheless suggest to the jury alternative explanations of the facts, for the purpose of assisting the jury to measure the weight of the evidence. The jury must, however, be instructed as to the limited purpose for which these alternative explanations, made without a good faith basis, are being offered.

. . . Mitchell's presentation is, however, flawed in two respects. In the first place, the closing argument which he offers, with its intimations that the defense theory is not dependent upon the facts, is much more forthright than those which most attorneys would give. What they would actually say would be more cryptic with respect to what the jury should conclude about the truth, something like:

> The prosecution claims that my client walked out of the store intending not to pay. I ask you, members of the jury, why would this young lady, with $10.00 in her pocket, steal a $1.79 Christmas tree ornament? Isn't it more likely that in the hustle and bustle of Christmas shopping she saw the ornament, focused for a second on the beautiful Christmas tree she was decorating, picked it up and then forgot she had it when she left the store? At the very least, don't you believe that possibility creates a reasonable doubt about whether she intended to steal the ornament?

> Moreover, even if Mitchell's sanitized closing was given, it is still designed to persuade the jury of the existence of facts he knows to be not true: here, that the woman in fact left the store accidentally (i.e., "maybe she did (leave accidentally). None of us was there."). That is not a lie, but it certainly creates a false impression, which amounts to the same thing.

---

[12] Copyright © 1988 by The Georgetown Journal of Legal Ethics and Georgetown University. Reprinted by permission.

10. The Supreme Court Speaks

Subin is concerned with adhering to the truth, and Mitchell with not creating falsehoods. But Justice Byron White famously stated, in the Supreme Court's seminal eyewitness identification case, that it the job of criminal defense lawyers to argue what they know to be false, so long as it is testing the prosecution's case. Read this brief excerpt.

UNITED STATES v. WADE
388 U.S. 218, 256–57 (1967)

[D]efense counsel has no . . . obligation to ascertain or present the truth. Our system assigns him a different mission. He must be and is interested in preventing the conviction of the innocent, but . . . we also insist that he defend his client whether he is innocent or guilty. . . . If he can confuse a witness, even a truthful one, or make him appear at a disadvantage, unsure or indecisive, that will be his normal course. Our interest in not convicting the innocent permits counsel to put the State to its proof, to put the State's case in the worst possible light, regardless of what he thinks or knows to be the truth. . . . In this respect, as part of our modified adversary system and as part of the duty imposed on the most honorable defense counsel, we countenance or require conduct which in many instances has little, if any, relation to the search for truth.

11. Cross-Examining the Truthful Witness

Professor Monroe Freedman has long been one of the most controversial but articulate and enlightening commentators on the adversary system. Beginning with a 1966 law review article[13] and continuing through numerous other articles and two books,[14] Freedman has evaluated the role of lawyer - especially the criminal defense lawyer — as advocate, and the limits that law and ethics place on that role. Like Subin, Freedman begins by questioning how the rules of ethics can justify — even require — the cross-examination of a known truthful witness. Freedman even concludes that this cross-examination is more onerous ethically than putting on perjured testimony. But Freedman reaches a very different conclusion than Subin.

To make his points, Freedman uses as a factual vehicle a rape case not unlike Professor Subin's, a scenario which was originally used in a 1966 Washington, D.C. symposium on legal ethics that included former Chief Justice (then appeals court judge) Warren Burger. Professor Freedman has discussed this scenario in different contexts and various forums, including in his 1975 book, *Lawyers' Ethics in an Adversary System*, which has been called both the most controversial and the most important volume on the ethics of legal advocacy, in which he underscores his differences with the future chief justice.

---

[13] *Professional Responsibility of the Criminal Defense Lawyer: The Three Hardest Questions*, 64 MICH. L. REV. 1469 (1966).

[14] LAWYERS' ETHICS IN AN ADVERSARY SYSTEM (1975); UNDERSTANDING LAWYERS' ETHICS, first published in 1990 and now in its fourth edition.

In this scenario, the defendant has admitted to his lawyer that he committed forcible rape. However, the lawyer has found a witness, Jones, a "rejected and jealous suitor" (remember this symposium occurred in 1966!), who reported that he had known the victim to flirt with and even have sex with other men while she and Jones were a couple. Of course today, this evidence would be inadmissible almost everywhere, but it still serves well for purposes of graphically illustrating whether a lawyer should — or even must — cross-examine the truthful witness.

MONROE FREEDMAN & ABBE SMITH, UNDERSTANDING LAWYERS' ETHICS 207-12 (4th ed. 2010)[15]

Should the defense lawyer use the information supplied by Jones . . . and, if necessary, call Jones as a witness?

One of the panelists who spoke to that question was former Chief Justice Warren Burger. Burger first discussed the question in terms of "basic and fundamental rules." One of those rules, which he characterized as "clear-cut and unambiguous," is that "a lawyer may never, under any circumstances, knowingly . . . participate in a fraud on the court." That rule, he said, "can never admit of any exception, under any circumstances," and no other consideration "can ever justify a knowing and conscious departure" from it. Moreover, only the "naive and inexperienced" would take a contrary position, which is a "perversion and prostitution of an honorable profession." Indeed, Burger held any other view to be "so utterly absurd that one wonders why the subject need even be discussed among persons trained in the law."[16]

Despite his powerful rhetoric and assertion of absolute principles, Burger's response to the question of cross-examining the truthful witness was similar to ours. The function of an advocate, he declared, and "particularly the defense advocate in the adversary system," is to use "all legitimate tools available to test the truth of the prosecution's case." . . .

That, of course, is sanction for a deliberate attempt to perpetrate a fraud upon the finder of fact. The lawyer knows that the client is guilty and that the victim is truthful. In cross-examining her, the lawyer has one purpose only: to make it appear, contrary to fact, that [she] is lying in testifying that she was raped.

There is only one difference in practical effect between presenting the defendant's perjured alibi - which the Chief Justice considered to be clearly improper — and impeaching the truthful [victim]. In both cases the lawyer participates in an attempt to free a guilty defendant. In both cases, the lawyer participates in misleading the finder of fact. In the case of the perjured witness, however, the attorney asks only non-leading questions, while in the case of impeachment, the lawyer takes an active, aggressive role, using his professional training and skills, in a one-on-one attack upon the client's victim. The lawyer thereby personally and directly adds to the suffering of the victim. In short, under the euphemism of

---

[15] Copyright © 2010 by Matthew Bender & Company, Inc., a member of LexisNexis. Reprinted by permission.

[16] [1] Burger, *Standards of Conduct for Prosecution and Defense Personnel: A Judge's Viewpoint*, 5 AM. CRIM. L.Q. 11-15 (1966).

"testing the truth of the prosecution's case," the lawyer communicates a vicious lie to the jury and to the community.

. . . .

We agree [with Professor David Luban] that the question of cross-examining witnesses known to be telling the truth is most difficult in the rape context. Insofar as Luban's position is an endorsement of rape shield statutes . . . we agree with him. However, we do not share his view that it is better that an innocent man go to jail than that a woman be called a "whore."

. . . Still, the authors have chosen different responses to the ethical question of advocacy in a rape case. Freedman . . . stopped taking rape cases [while] Smith has represented many indigent adults and juveniles accused of rape, and continues to do so . . . .

In answering hard questions of legal ethics, Burger . . . answered questions of lawyers' ethics by uncritical application of legalistic norms, regardless of . . . context . . . . Lying is wrong. It follows, therefore, that no lawyer, under any circumstances, should knowingly present perjury. Cross-examination, however, is good. It follows, therefore, that any lawyer, regardless of context and consequences, can properly impeach a witness through cross-examination.

. . . .

Let us return, then, to the case involving the street robbery at 16th and P Streets.[17]

The defendant has been wrongly identified as the criminal by one witness, but has been correctly identified by another witness — a nervous, elderly woman who wears eyeglasses — as having been only a block away five minutes before the crime took place. If the woman is not cross-examined effectively and her testimony shaken, it will serve to corroborate the erroneous evidence of guilt. On the other hand, the lawyer could take the position that since the woman is doing her civic duty by testifying truthfully and accurately, she should not be made to appear to be mistaken or lying.

If the latter position were to be adopted as a rule applicable to all cases . . . we would do serious harm to the administration of justice. As soon as clients learned that confiding in their lawyers would result in less effective representation, such confidences would rarely be given. The result would be intentional ignorance, the practice in which the client is put on notice that he is not to tell his lawyer anything that might cause the lawyer to be less vigorous in her advocacy . . . .

More to the present point, a . . . lawyer, in ignorance of the truth, would conduct the most effective possible cross-examination in virtually every case . . . . From the point of view of the impact on the truthful and accurate witness, however, the result would be identical . . . .

The rape is much harder, because the injury done to the complaining witness there is more severe than the more limited embarrassment of the truthful robbery

---

[17] [Eds. — We will examine this "case" further in the next Problem.]

witness. In addition, in the rape case, the lawyer is ultimately relying upon the illogical and sexist inference that the complainant would voluntarily have sex with a stranger because she had sexual relations with [others] . . . . Nevertheless, we come to the same conclusion in the case of cross-examining the rape victim.

NOTES

Interestingly, despite the language in *Wade*, Freedman has long held that cross-examining a truthful and accurate witness in order to make the witness appear mistaken or lying is more difficult to accept even than presenting known perjury. In fact, in his 1975 book, he ended his excerpt of the above section with this sentence: "Unlike the Chief Justice, however, I find [the cross-examination] a far more difficult and painful choice than that of client perjury." We will examine his views on perjury in the next Problem. Note, also, the co-authorship of "confidentiality absolutist" Abbe Smith, who is more sanguine about taking the rape client than her colleague.

D. SUPPLEMENTAL READINGS

1. Randy Bellows, *Notes of a Public Defender*, in PHILLIP B. HEYMANN & LANCE LIEBMAN, THE SOCIAL RESPONSIBILITIES OF LAWYERS (1988), in which then-public defender Bellows grapples compellingly with his obligation to represent his clients to the best of his ability, while finding himself increasingly uncomfortable, even appalled, by his role as their advocate.

2. In 1911, the infamous Triangle Shirtwaist fire killed over 100 sweatshop workers, mostly immigrant women, and created an atmosphere which helped revolutionize the rights of workers and conditions of the workplace. In the aftermath of the fire, famed criminal defense lawyer Max D. Steuer defended the factory owners on criminal charges, successfully getting them acquitted by cross-examining a young survivor of the fire who spoke little English, and proving her direct testimony had been rehearsed and memorized word for word. Steuer's efforts have been extolled as the best example of zealous advocacy and pilloried as the worst example of an advocacy system run amok. Steuer and the Triangle trial have been the subject of many treatments over the years. A few of those are: AARON STEUER, MAX D. STEUER, TRIAL LAWYER (1950); LEON STEIN, THE TRIANGLE FIRE (1962) and, more recently, on the 75th anniversary of the fire, Daniel J. Kornstein, *A Tragic Fire - A Great Cross-Examination*, NEW YORK LAW JOURNAL, March 28, 1986. Most of these treatments have justified Steuer's actions.

3. Thomas L. Shaffer, *Serving the Guilty*, 26 LOY. L. REV. 71 (1980). This article explores, from a moral and religious perspective, whether a lawyer may represent a guilty client.

4. *Johnson v. U.S.*, 360 F.2d 844 (D.C. Cir. 1966). There, in a concurrence, Warren Burger further articulates his views about the role of the criminal lawyer as a "highly important but nonetheless limited function" of "put[ting] the prosecution to its proof, to test the case against the accused."

5. Nothing served to galvanize the American public on the behavior of criminal defense lawyers as much as the O.J. Simpson trial. For two worthwhile books on the subject from very different perspectives, we suggest GERALD F. UELMEN, LESSONS FROM THE TRIAL (1996), and BIRTH OF A NATION 'HOOD (Toni Morrison, ed., 1997). Professor Uelmen was part of the Simpson "dream team" and is a former dean of Santa Clara Law School and a frequent commentator on the ethics of criminal defense lawyers. The Morrison volume focuses on sociology and race, not law, from a variety of interesting individual perspectives and includes a valuable piece by the late Federal Court of Appeals Judge A. Leon Higgenbotham.

6. The Washington University Journal of Law and Policy contains a debate regarding the role of lawyers as zealous advocates, as opposed to adopting more of the traits of social workers. One might term it a modernized version of the famous Subin-Mitchell debate in the readings. The three pieces of particular note are: Jane Aiken & Stephen Wizner, *Law as Social Work*, 11 WASH. U. J.L. & POLICY 63 (2003), Abbe Smith, *The Difference in Criminal Defense and the Difference It Makes*, 11 WASH. U. J.L. & POLICY 83 (2003), and Katherine R. Kruse's response, *Lawyers Should be Lawyers, but What Does that Mean? A Response to Aiken & Wizner and Smith*, 14 WASH. U. J.L. & POLICY 49 (2004).

PROBLEM 16: WHEN THE CLIENT INSISTS ON LYING

A. INTRODUCTION

This problem concerns one of the most difficult and dicey ethical dilemmas that can arise in practice — what to do when your client lies, or you suspect your client is going to lie? Should you remain silent and do nothing? Urge your client to correct the lie? Withdraw from the representation? Tell the court? The perjurious client pits two important ethical obligations directly against each other: the duty to the client to preserve confidences and provide loyal, vigorous representation versus the lawyer's obligation to society and the system of justice to avoid untruthfulness. Layered on this dichotomy, one oft-cited thesis cites a third component: the duty to ascertain as best as you can the client's true story. There are no easy answers, as you will find when you consider the following problem and the accompanying readings.

B. PROBLEM

I

Review Professor Monroe Freedman's scenario about the 16th and P Streets robbery case, in Problem 15.

QUESTIONS

1. What would you do if your client insisted on testifying falsely in the manner described by Freedman?

2. Of the suggested solutions to the "perjury trilemma," which would you adopt, and why?

3. Does it make a difference in how you would handle the situation that you know, as Professor Freedman tells you, that your client is actually not guilty?

II

Review the dialogue of the movie *Anatomy of a Murder* in Section 10, below, and Professor Freedman's description of the book in the pages following.

QUESTIONS

1. Does the defense lawyer in *Anatomy of a Murder* suborn perjury by the way in which he advises the defendant, or is this the legitimate tactic of a hard-nosed trial lawyer who is informing his client of the law?

2. Compare the *Anatomy of a Murder* scenario to Professor Freedman's description in the reading that follows of the defendant who is asked how often he carries a penknife. Would you make a distinction between the two scenarios? Is there a distinction in the propriety of the advice given in each scenario? Why, or why not?

C. READINGS

1. A Brief Regulatory History

No debate on ethical issues arouses more emotion or causes more controversy than what a lawyer — especially a criminal defense lawyer — should do about a client's perjured testimony. The modern history of this debate can be traced to a series of law review articles by Professor Monroe Freedman in the mid-1960s. Before we turn to the writings of Professor Freedman and his scenarios, which form the basis of Problem 16, it is useful to review the history of the prevailing ABA rules in the last several decades.

By 1969, the ABA had passed the Model Code. But to some, the Code seemed to add fuel to the perjury debate rather than resolve it. DR 4-101(C) set forth an exception to the rule of confidentiality: a lawyer *may* reveal a client's intention to commit a crime. But under DR 7-102(A)(4) a lawyer *shall not* knowingly *use* perjured testimony. When first passed, DR 7-102(B) said that a lawyer who learns that a client has "perpetrated a fraud" on a tribunal must call on the client to rectify the fraud and if the client does not, *shall* reveal the fraud to the tribunal.

Many felt that these disciplinary rules were inherently inconsistent and that none fully addressed the issue at hand. How, for example, did one reconcile the mandatory language of DR 7-102 with the permissive language of DR 4-101? Is perjury a crime within the meaning of 4-101, or — since the perjury relates directly to the underlying case for which the lawyer is giving representation — should the client's intent to lie at trial *not* be considered as part of the "future crime exception" to the rule of confidentiality? What is meant by "knowingly using" perjury? In 1975, DR 7-102(B) was amended to provide an exception to revealing the fraud "when the information is protected as a privileged communication." But many felt this exception swung the pendulum too far in the other direction, essentially swallowing the rule.

In the early 1970s, the ABA developed a set of standards for prosecutors and criminal defense lawyers. Standard 7.7 called upon lawyers faced with a perjurious client to allow the testimony to occur, but only in the narrative, as opposed to the usual question-and-answer format. The lawyer was then to refrain from arguing this testimony to the jury. This method found some favor with institutionalized criminal defense organizations, such as public defenders' offices, which were searching for a way to take a position that walked the tightrope between "snitching off" one's client and permitting outright perjury. It also found favor with some appellate courts, several of which upheld trial court orders requiring that defense lawyers act in accordance with this standard.

The problem with the narrative method, however, is that it fools absolutely no one, especially the jury. Many, including the U.S. Supreme Court, have criticized it[1], some feeling it is tantamount to hanging a sign around the defendant's neck that says "LIAR."

When it revised the criminal law standards, the ABA first reaffirmed but then abandoned Standard 7.7 and its narrative approach, preferring to rely on Model Rule 3.3, created in 1983 and amended substantially in 2002.

Under MR 3.3(a)(3) a lawyer *shall not knowingly* offer evidence "that the lawyer *knows* to be false," (our emphasis), while the "lawyer *may* refuse to offer evidence, other than the testimony of a defendant in a criminal matter, that the attorney *reasonably believes* is false."[2]

No longer is this prohibition limited to a "material" falsehood, as it was in the 1983 version. Comments 7 and 9 of the new Rules attempt to clarify both this change and the ABA's position on this oft-debated issue. Comment 7 states that while the ABA's position — and its rule — do not permit testifying in the narrative, it acknowledges that in jurisdictions in which courts have approved this method, lawyers should follow those courts. And Comment 9 reinforces that the permissive portion of MR 3.3(a)(3) does *not* apply to testimony by a criminal defendant. The Restatement (Third) of the Law Governing Lawyers, § 120, reaches a similar conclusion.

2. The Perjury "Trilemma"

When he first articulated the "perjury trilemma" in the 1960s, Professor Freedman's views were sufficiently controversial that the District of Columbia Bar sought (unsuccessfully) to take disciplinary action against him. Now, we excerpt at some length Freedman's ideas about "the perjury trilemma," and explore his best known and most controversial thesis — that if necessary, a lawyer in a criminal case must present the client's perjurious testimony before the court, even when the lawyer knows it is perjury. We excerpt a brief expostulation of the "trilemma" in its most recent form: the fourth edition of Professor Freedman and Professor Abbe Smith's current book. We will provide the factual scenario we use as the foundation for our problem above in section 5.

---

[1] See *Nix v. Whiteside*, 475 U.S. 157, at 170, fn 6, which described this method as "a signal at least to the presiding judge that the attorney considered the testimony to be false and was seeking to disassociate himself from [it]." We examine *Nix v. Whiteside* in detail in Section 3.

[2] Note that in *civil* cases, the anomaly between these two phrases of Rule 3.3(a)(3) is more pronounced.

Monroe H. Freedman & Abbe Smith, Understanding Lawyers' Ethics
207-12 (4th ed. 2010)[3]

Is it ever proper for a criminal defense lawyer to present testimony that she knows is perjurious? Our answer is yes.[4]

. . . .

Underlying proposed solutions to the problem of client perjury are two sharply different models of the lawyer-client relationship. The traditional model . . . is one of trust and confidence between lawyer and client. The client is urged to confide in the lawyer and is encouraged to do so by a pledge of confidentiality.

The other model is one referred to in the literature as selective ignorance (or, sometimes, intentional ignorance). That is, the lawyer puts the client on notice that the lawyer would prefer not to know certain kinds of facts, and/or that the lawyer can be expected to pass on to the judge or the other party information that the client would prefer to keep confidential. The burden is then on the uncounseled client to speculate about whether to entrust potentially harmful facts to the lawyer — to decide, that is, what is relevant and what is irrelevant, what is incriminating and what is exculpatory. . . .

The problem for the client is illustrated by a case related by a lawyer who practiced intentional ignorance. The client was accused of stabbing her husband to death with a kitchen knife. In conferences with her lawyer, she consistently denied committing the crime. The facts, however, were damning. The killing had taken place in the couple's kitchen; only her fingerprints were on the knife; she was in the apartment at the time; and she had no other suspect to offer. An investigator informed the lawyer, however, of reports from neighbors that the husband had had a habit of getting drunk and brutalizing the wife. Confronted with that information by her lawyer, the defendant broke down and "confessed." Her husband had been drunk and was about to attack her again. As she backed away, her hand fell upon the knife and, in her terror, she stabbed him.

Why, expostulated the lawyer, had she not volunteered the information to him in the first place? Because, explained his client — who was unsophisticated about the law of self-defense — "it proved I did it."

Apart from the practical problems of requiring clients to do their own lawyering, we question whether intentional ignorance is a moral resolution of the lawyer's ethical problem. Certainly, lawyers who practice intentional ignorance have the comfort of saying that they have never knowingly presented a client's perjury. On the other hand, by remaining ignorant, these same lawyers have disabled themselves from being in a position to dissuade their clients from committing the perjury.

---

[3] Copyright © 2010 by Matthew Bender & Co., Inc., a member of LexisNexis. Reprinted by permission.

[4] [1] An overwhelming proportion of trial lawyers agree . . . . [W]e have discussed this question at countless professional meetings around the country and have found that litigators — both civil and criminal — tend to share our view.

. . . .

The Trilemma

The lawyer's ethical difficulty has been called a trilemma, because it derives from three obligations. First, in order to give clients the effective assistance of counsel to which they are entitled, lawyers are required to seek out all relevant facts. Second, in order to encourage clients to entrust their lawyers with embarrassing or possibly harmful information, lawyers are under a duty of confidentiality with regard to information obtained in professional relationships. Third, lawyers are expected to be candid with the court.

A moment's reflection makes it clear, however, that one cannot do all three of those things — know everything, keep it in confidence, and reveal it to the court over the client's objections. To resolve this trilemma, therefore, one of the three duties must give way.

If we forgo the first duty (seeking all relevant information), we would be adopting the model of intentional ignorance. If we sacrifice the second duty (maintaining confidentiality), clients would quickly learn that their lawyers could not be trusted and would withhold damaging information; again, the result is intentional ignorance. Only by limiting the third duty — by allowing lawyers to be less than candid with the court when necessary to protect clients' confidences — can we maintain the traditional lawyer-client model.

NOTE

Professor Freedman's model has never achieved widespread *de jure* support, even if anecdotally it may be more common in everyday practice. Our review of *de jure* perspectives next returns us to the Supreme Court's *Nix v. Whiteside*, decided on quite a different basis than the principles articulated by Freedman.

3. *Nix v. Whiteside*

First some facts: Whiteside, facing murder charges, claimed he acted in self-defense. He told his lawyer, Robinson, that he believed the deceased was coming at him with a gun. About a week before trial, however, Whiteside told Robinson for the first time that he had not actually seen something metallic in the deceased's hand. Robinson questioned Whiteside closely, and when pressed, Whiteside admitted that "[i]f I don't say I saw a gun, I'm dead." Robinson then took very strong steps to dissuade Whiteside from testifying to having seen a metallic object. He threatened to tell the court of the presumed perjury, and to impeach the testimony himself, and also threatened to withdraw.

Ultimately, this dissuasion was successful. Whiteside testified, but only that he believed the deceased had a gun, not that he had seen it. He was convicted, and brought a habeas corpus action alleging ineffective assistance of counsel due to Robinson's admonitions. The Court decided 9-0 against Whiteside, but split 5-4 in its discussion of what Robinson should have done had he not dissuaded his client from testifying.

NIX v. WHITESIDE
475 U.S. 157 (1986)

We must determine whether, in this setting, Robinson's conduct fell within the wide range of professional responses to threatened client perjury acceptable under the Sixth Amendment.

. . . .

Although counsel must take all reasonable lawful means to attain the objectives of the client, counsel is precluded from taking steps or in any way assisting the client in presenting false evidence or otherwise violating the law. This principle has consistently been recognized in most unequivocal terms by expositors of the norms of professional conduct since the first Canons of Professional Ethics were adopted by the American Bar Association in 1908.

. . . .

Indeed, both the Model Code and the Model Rules do not merely *authorize* disclosure by counsel of client perjury; they *require* such disclosure. See Rule 3.3(a)(4) [now 3.3(a)(3)]; DR 7-102(B)(1); *Committee on Professional Ethics and Conduct of Iowa State Bar Association v. Crary*, 245 N.W.2d 298 (Iowa 1976).

These standards confirm that the legal profession has accepted that an attorney's ethical duty to advance the interests of his client is limited by an equally solemn duty to comply with the law and standards of professional conduct; it specifically ensures that the client may not use false evidence. . . .

Whether Robinson's conduct is seen as a successful attempt to dissuade his client from committing the crime of perjury, or whether seen as a "threat" to withdraw from representation and disclose the illegal scheme, Robinson's representation of Whiteside falls well within acceptable standards of professional conduct. . . .

. . . .

Robinson's action, at most, deprived Whiteside of his contemplated perjury. Nothing counsel did in any way undermined Whiteside's claim that he believed the victim was reaching for a gun. . . . On this record, the accused enjoyed continued representation within the bounds of reasonable professional conduct and did in fact exercise his right to testify; at most he was denied the right to have the assistance of counsel in the presentation of false testimony. . . .

The rule adopted by the Court of Appeals, which seemingly would require an attorney to remain silent while his client committed perjury, is wholly incompatible with the established standards of ethical conduct. . . .

NOTES

While the justices unanimously agreed Whiteside did not receive ineffective assistance of counsel, Justices Brennan, Blackmun, and Stevens, in their concurrences, became the first of many to criticize the Chief Justice's conclusions in *dicta* about the lawyer's mandate to reveal the perjury. Wrote Brennan:

[I]t is not surprising that the Court emphasizes that it 'must be careful not to narrow the wide range of professional conduct acceptable under the Sixth Amendment so restrictively as to constitutionalize particular standards of professional conduct and thereby intrude into the State's proper authority. . . .' Unfortunately, the Court seems unable to resist the temptation of sharing with the legal community its vision of ethical conduct. But let there be no mistake: the Court's essay regarding what constitutes the correct response to a criminal client's suggestion that he will perjure himself is pure discourse without force of law. . . . Lawyers, judges, bar associations, students and others should understand that the problem has not now been 'decided.'

Justice Stevens wrote the following:

[T]he post-trial review of a lawyer's pre-trial threat to expose perjury that had not yet been committed — and, indeed, may have been prevented by the threat — is by no means the same as review of the way in which such a threat may actually have been carried out. Thus, one can be convinced — as I am - that this lawyer's actions were a proper way to provide his client with effective representation without confronting the much more difficult questions of what a lawyer must, should, or may do after his client has given testimony that the lawyer does not believe.

4. The Aftermath of *Whiteside*

Professor Freedman was also quick to criticize his old adversary the Chief Justice.[5] But this time, he was joined by a loud chorus of others who criticized both Burger's use of Supreme Court dicta to set attorneys' ethical standards and his conclusion that lawyers *must* disclose client perjury. Many pointed to Burger's use of the *Crary* case, which deals with civil perjury at deposition, a decidedly different issue with no Fifth or Sixth Amendment implications.

In Opinion 87-353 (1987), however, the ABA ethics committee firmly agreed with the *Whiteside* majority's analysis of a lawyer's ethical duties. There, the committee reconsidered its previous Opinion 287 in light of Model Rule 3.3.

Opinion 287 dealt with how a criminal defense lawyer should respond when the judge inquires about a client's prior criminal record. It held that even if the lawyer knows the client has a record, he or she should not reveal it to the court in any of three situations: when the records custodian erroneously informs the court that the defendant has no record; when the lawyer is asked directly by the judge (in which case the lawyer should remain silent); *and* where the client falsely replies in the negative when asked by the court. The new opinion concluded that under Rule 3.3, this last situation "imposes a duty on the lawyer, when the lawyer cannot persuade the client to rectify the perjury, to disclose the client's false statement to the tribunal. . . ."

---

[5] *The Aftermath of* Nix v. Whiteside: *Slamming the Lid on Pandora's Box*, 23 CRIM. L. BULL. 25 (1987).

Opinion 87-353 then discussed the *Whiteside* case, noting that Rule 3.3 was written to apply to both civil and criminal cases except as the Fifth and Sixth Amendment rights of an accused might limit that application. *Whiteside*, concludes the opinion, stands for the proposition that these rights do not in fact interfere with applying Rule 3.3.

Citing Freedman, Opinion 87-353 then discusses whether its holding interferes with an effective attorney-client relationship. It answers this question with a resounding "no": "neither the adversary system nor the ethical rules permit the lawyer to participate in the corruption of the judicial process by assisting the client in the introduction of [false] evidence. . . ." Indeed, "implicit in the promise of confidentiality is its nonapplicability where the client seeks the unlawful end [of giving] false evidence."

Clearly, however, the Fifth and Sixth amendments and the duty of confidentiality *versus* the duty to prevent the presentation of false evidence to the court *are* inconsistent in those rare instances of client perjury. The Opinion appears to beg this question, in two ways. First, it claims that the lawyer's professional relationship to the client remains unchanged. (Freedman might suggest you imagine yourself in the client's place; how would you feel about the relationship with your lawyer if he or she went to the court and told it you had lied?)

Second, the Opinion closes with the admonition that it is strictly limited to a situation "where the lawyer *knows* that the client has committed perjury." This parallels the last sentence of today's Rule 3.3, which allows lawyers not to present testimony they *believe* is perjurious *except* in criminal cases.

This brings us right back to the third prong of Freedman's trilemma — the duty to learn the facts of the case — and the danger of what he used to call "selective ignorance," and now describes as "intentional ignorance."

5. Freedman's Client's Perjury Described and His Solution Offered

Now, for the questions set forth in our problem above. Freedman and Smith describe the facts that result in perjury, which Freedman first described in his initial work in the 1960s and 1970s, along with his conclusions about how he would handle the perjury, well before *Whiteside* was decided. We again use the 2010 edition of his and Professor Smith's current book.

Monroe H. Freedman & Abbe Smith, Understanding Lawyers' Ethics
(4th ed. 2010)[6]

Your client has been erroneously accused of a robbery committed at 16th and P Streets at 11:00 p.m. He tells you at first that at no time on the evening of the crime was he within six blocks of that location. You are able to persuade him that he must tell you the truth and that doing so will in no way prejudice him. He then reveals to you that he was at 15th and P Streets, one block away from the scene of the crime, at 10:55 that evening, but that he was going east, away from the scene of the crime, and by 11:00 p.m., he was six blocks away.

There are two prosecution witnesses. The first mistakenly, but with some degree of persuasion, identifies your client as the criminal. The second witness is an elderly woman who is somewhat nervous and who wears glasses. She testifies truthfully and accurately that she saw your client at 15th and P Streets at 10:55 p.m. She has corroborated the erroneous testimony of the first witness and made conviction extremely likely. On cross-examination, however, her reliability is thrown into doubt through demonstration that she is easily confused and has poor eyesight. . . .

Your client insists on testifying, which is his right as a matter of due process. He believes that he is more likely to be found not guilty if he takes the stand . . . . However, he is convinced that he cannot afford to admit that the second prosecution witness correctly placed him one block from the scene of the crime at 10:55 pm., because that would rehabilitate both the elderly witness and the prosecution's case. You try to dissuade him . . . but he is adamant.

The most obvious way to avoid the ethical difficulty appears to be withdrawal from the case, if that can be done without prejudice to the client. The client will then find another lawyer and will probably withhold the incriminating information from her. In systemic terms, withdrawal under such circumstances is difficult to defend, since the new lawyer will be in no position to attempt to dissuade the client from presenting it. Only the original attorney, who knows the truth, has that opportunity, but loses it in the very act of evading the ethical problem.

Moreover, the lawyer should be forbidden to withdraw if doing so would prejudice the client in any way. Prejudice cannot ordinarily be avoided if the case is near to trial or the trial has begun . . . . The court will require the lawyer to give extraordinary reasons for withdrawal, which would require the lawyer to reveal [too much] to the judge. Since the judge will be sentencing the client in the event of a conviction, the prejudice to the client would be severe.[7]

[The authors then discuss the narrative solution then suggested by Section 7.7 of the ABA Standards Relating to the Defense Function long ago abandoned by the

---

[7] In his *Lawyer's Ethics in an Adversary System*, Freedman pointed out that "[t]he difficulty is all the more severe when the client is indigent. In that event, the client cannot retain other counsel, and in many jurisdictions it is impossible for appointed counsel or a public defender to withdraw from a case except for extraordinary reasons." This appears to inform his and Professor Smith's current thinking.

ABA but, as they note — and as we will see in Section 7 — far from dead in many states.]

Neither of us has ever heard of a case in which the prosecutor objected to a defense lawyer's asking a defendant to testify in narrative [a standard evidentiary objection]. Why should the prosecutor object, when the defendant's own lawyer is signaling to everyone in the courtroom that the defendant is guilty and trying to lie his way out of it?

. . . .

In the relatively small number of cases in which the client who has contemplated perjury rejects the lawyer's advice and decides to proceed to trial, to take the stand, and to give false testimony, the lawyer should go forward in the ordinary way. That is, the lawyer should examine the client in a normal professional manner and should argue the client's testimony to the jury in summation to the extent sound tactics justify doing so . . . .

We are not completely comfortable with this position. Indeed, one of the reasons that client perjury has produced such a substantial body of literature since 1966 is that no one has been able to resolve the trilemma in a way that is wholly consistent either with general norms of morality or with professional standards of ethics.

. . . [However, w]e cannot find — in terms of personal morality — a more acceptable course. We find deep moral significance in the dignity of the individual and in the way that dignity is respected in the American constitutional adversary system.

The argument is sometimes raise that a lawyer who knowingly presents perjured testimony is suborning perjury. However, subornation of perjury is "the crime of procuring another to commit perjury . . . ." Clearly, that is not what happens when the idea of perjury originates with the client.

NOTES

A few observations about both Freedman/Smith excerpts before moving on: First, note Freedman and Smith's antipathy towards withdrawal, on the grounds that it will foster lack of candor from the client in discussions with the succeeding lawyers, thus resulting in *those* lawyers' ignorance. Freedman is hardly the only commentator who has criticized the withdrawal solution. Norman Lefstein, a former law school dean, wrote soon after *Whiteside* that "withdrawal from a defendant's case should never be viewed as a solution to the perjury dilemma."[8]

Second, Freedman and Smith use the term "intentional ignorance." This is an intentional change from Freedman's previous phrase, "selective ignorance." Undoubtedly, this change was made to underscore the responsibilities of lawyers to find out the truth for all the reasons the authors state. However, many lawyers employ the method described by a criminal defense attorney of our acquaintance in the next section, on knowledge. After you read that, ask whether it is so clear, as

[8] *Client Perjury in Criminal Cases: Still in Search of an Answer*, 1 GEO. J. LEGAL ETHICS 521 (1988).

Freedman claims, that "selective" ignorance is "intentional," and whether this strategy is so abhorrent. There seems to be a wide gulf between the lawyer "putting the client on notice" not to be candid, and recognizing that the client will likely not tell the lawyer "the whole truth" no matter what. After all, why are the authors so sure that clients will be willing to tell their lawyers, strangers until they appear in the holding cell, the truth in any event?

Third, it appears that Freedman has to an extent, albeit a modest one, softened his stand on putting on perjured testimony, or at least softened the language with which he described his conclusions in his 1966 law review article and 1975 book. While space does not permit a comparison here, that is our impression.

Finally, we ask you whether Freedman's conclusion that putting on perjured testimony should be distinguished from "subornation" resonates with you. Do you agree, or does he take an overly narrow view of subornation in order to justify his conclusions?

6. When Do You Know You *"Know"*?

In the current version of ABA Rule 3.3 the determination of whether the lawyer "knows" the evidence is false is critical. By their very narrow definitions of "knowing," both *Whiteside* and ABA Opinion 87-353 in effect provide a *de facto* "solution" to the perjury trilemma. Opinion 87-353 explicitly says that knowledge will ordinarily be based on a client's own admissions, and that "[t]he lawyer's suspicions are not enough." Both the ABA opinion and Justice Blackmun's *Whiteside* concurrence cite *United States ex rel. Wilcox v. Johnson*, 555 F.2d 115 (3d Cir. 1977), for the proposition we have seen espoused by Dr. Samuel Johnson — that lawyers should not assume "the role of the judge or jury to determine the facts."

As we've seen, this narrow view is bolstered by rule's distinction between the first sentence of § 3.3(a)(3), which *requires* disclosure only where the lawyer "knowingly" offers false evidence "the lawyer knows to be false" (note the double use of the verb "to know"), and the last sentence, which *permits* the lawyer to refuse to offer what the attorney *reasonably believes* is false evidence (except in a criminal case).

Courts since *Whiteside* have largely agreed with a narrow vision of knowledge. Thus, in *United States v. Long*, 857 F.2d 436, 444 (8th Cir. 1988), a lawyer "concerned" about the testimony of his client did not put the client on the stand. The court reversed the conviction, stating that a lawyer cannot act against the client's interests unless the client gives "a clear expression of intent to commit perjury." More recently, in *United States v. Midgett*, 342 F.3d 321 (4th Cir. 2003), a lawyer believed that his client was going to testify falsely about a third person in a vehicle who could have committed the robbery. The lawyer had no corroborating evidence, and advised the court, which gave the defendant the choice of having his lawyer withdraw, representing himself and being permitted to testify, or agreeing not to testify. The defendant didn't testify. The Fourth Circuit Court of Appeals reversed the conviction, and distinguished *Whiteside* by noting that unlike that case, this defendant "never told his lawyer or otherwise indicated to him that his intended testimony was perjurious." Another 2003 case, in Wisconsin, went even further: requiring an affirmative admission by the client in order for a lawyer to know his client will commit perjury.[9]

Others, including some ethics professors, have been critical of this narrow definition of knowing. Samuel Dash, former chief of staff to the Senate Watergate Committee and later a Georgetown ethics professor, argued that the Wisconsin rule directly undermined Rule 3.3. In a 2003 article, South Carolina ethics professor Nathan Crystal argued for a "factual inconsistency test." Perjury, for Crystal, would be known "if the defendant's testimony will be inconsistent with facts that defendant has admitted (the factual admission test) or with facts known to the lawyer through independent investigation (the factual inconsistency test)".[10] But what if the lawyer's investigation is incomplete?

Crystal claims that his test is consistent with the "firm factual basis" test adopted by the Restatement of the Law Governing Lawyers. But the Restatement states that a "firm factual basis" only exists "when facts known to the lawyer or the client's own statements indicate to the lawyer that the testimony or other evidence is false."

On the other hand, Brent R. Appel, who argued *Whiteside* before the Supreme Court for the State of Iowa, also adopts the narrow view of "knowing." In a 1988 law review article, Brent R. Appel, *The Limited Impact of Nix v. Whiteside on Attorney-Client Relations*, 136 U. PA. L. REV. 1913 (1988), he argues that *Whiteside* will rarely have a direct impact on actual cases. The duty to take affirmative action to prevent perjury arises "only when an attorney 'knows' that the client intends to testify falsely. Only rarely will a lawyer know both that proposed testimony is false and that the client is determined to offer the false testimony at trial."

This narrow definition of "knowing" wouldn't make Professor Harry Subin happy.[11] Nor, of course, does it please Professor Freedman, for whom "intentional ignorance" is an ethical affront. It works well, however, for many criminal defense lawyers, one of whom expressed his methodology to us as follows:

> I try not to ask my clients to tell me what they did. Instead, at the first interview, I ask "what do *they say* you did?" Let's face it; clients are changing their stories all the time. Sometimes, the "facts" just get in the way. Anyway, how do I know what version is the truth and what's not? I once had a client who was a notorious liar. One time, when I asked him to tell me what occurred, he looked me right in the eye and said, "do you want the truth, or do you want the *whole* truth? Or do you really want to know what happened?" Look, my job is to defend my client; I have to know enough about the case to be able to put together the best possible defense. But it's not my job to give my clients lectures about trusting me with the

---

[9] State v. McDowell, 669 N.W.2d 204 (Wis. Ct. App. 2003).

[10] Nathan Crystal, *False Testimony by Criminal Defendants: Still Unanswered Ethical and Constitutional Questions*, 2003 U. ILL. L. REV. 1529 (2003).

[11] See Subin's discussion of "knowledge" in the Problem 14 readings.

truth, or to give them the third degree every time they tell me a story.[12]

Freedman has decried the "tell me what they said you did" method as a victory of tactics over ethics, calling it "sophistry . . . produced by unrealistic rules." Indeed, he clearly believes that presenting perjured testimony is preferable to avoiding the truth.

7.   Is There a Solution to the "Trilemma"? Is There a Majority Rule?

No commentator has yet offered an entirely satisfactory solution to the perjury trilemma. When David A. Kaplan of the *National Law Journal* sought the reactions of ethics experts to the case of an innocent man held in prison because another man's lawyers felt bound by confidentiality not to reveal their own client's perjury, then Yale Law School Dean Guido Calabresi told Kaplan that there are no rules capable of governing all situations. "Any system breaks down in the extreme case," he said, "and one never knows what one will do."[13]

Almost all lawyers recognize the potentially conflicting duties to client and court that make up two-thirds of the "trilemma." Professor Freedman tries to solve this conflict by the way he treats the third trilemma component — full and complete knowledge of the relevant facts, followed by "continuing, good faith efforts to dissuade the client" from perjury. If the client is successfully dissuaded, both the client's and society's needs are served.

But what if the lawyer fails to dissuade the client? Ultimately, Freedman's solution puts him at odds with the majority of other commentators. Here's how one court put it:

In our system the courts are almost wholly dependent on members of the bar to marshal and present the true facts. . . . When an attorney adds or allows false testimony . . . he makes impure the product and makes it impossible for the scales [of justice] to balance.[14]

Yet Freedman would argue that based on his anecdotal surveys of actual practitioners, *his* view, not the ABA's in Rule 3.3 nor the Supreme Court's in *Whiteside*, is truly the majority view. As a practical matter, criminal defense lawyers would find their jobs far more difficult if they had to place their duties to the court above their "loyalties" to their clients, who frequently start out mistrustful, are scared throughout, and in the end are often sent to prison with only their lawyers to take their side.

---

[12] According to NYU law professor Steven Gillers, Alan Dershowitz once told television interviewer Charlie Rose "I never ask a client whether he did it or not," in order to avoid having the client lie to him. *See* STEPHEN GILLERS, REGULATION OF LAWYERS 394 (8th ed. 2009).

[13] David A. Kaplan, *What Would Ethics Experts Do?*, NAT'L L.J., Jan. 25, 1988. So difficult is this issue that at least one state ethics opinion failed to resolve it, pointing not only to a conflict in the ethics rules but between those rules and decisional law. *See* Maine Professional Ethics Commission Opinion 140 (1994). Recall from Problem 5 several examples of those innocents imprisoned because lawyers for other clients felt they could not reveal the truth.

[14] Dodd v. Florida Bar, 118 So. 2d 17, 19 (Fla. 1960).

In his second book, Freedman is still less than fully comfortable with presenting perjured testimony, but he is more comfortable with the morality of his choice: "I find deep moral significance in the dignity of the individual and in the way that dignity is respected in the American constitutional adversary system." Thus, with the exception of a situation involving an even higher moral value — such as acting to save the life of an innocent person on death row — he could not, "consistent with my own sense of morality," break his pledge to his client, even if the client insists on testifying falsely.

Could Freedman be right that his is at least the *de facto* "majority view"? Whether he is or not is a matter of anecdotal information and remains a solution that departs significantly from almost all *de jure* authorities. But it appears to us that as we write this edition, the MR 3.3 solution and the requirements of *Whiteside* are likely *not* the majority rule.

Surprisingly, allowing the defendant to testify in the narrative and then not arguing that testimony continues to have enormous vitality in state courts, to the point where it appears to us to represent the majority rule under decisional law. District of Columbia Rule 3.3 actually lays out a specific procedure for narrative testimony, and decisions in at least these states — California, Colorado, Florida, Illinois, Indiana, Kentucky, Mississippi, Massachusetts, New York, Pennsylvania, and West Virginia — endorse the procedure and in some cases (notably California) appear to require it.[15] The court in *People v. Johnson*, 62 Cal. App. 4th 608 (Cal. Ct. App. 1998), engaged in an extensive discussion of the right of a criminal defendant to testify, and then evaluated six possible solutions to the perjury problem, everything from Professor Freedman's position to refusing the defendant the opportunity to take the stand, and concluded that the narrative approach was "the best accommodation of the competing interests" involved.

Almost all commentators would agree that the narrative solution is at best only a compromise. Some compromises provide the lowest common denominator, but to us, this one provides the worst of both worlds: the presentation of the false story *and* the breach of client confidentiality. Moreover, this concept was twice expressly rejected by the ABA, not accepted in the Restatement, offensive to Professor Freedman and his adherents, and inappropriate under the Supreme Court's holding in *Whiteside*. Nevertheless, it remains the solution of choice in decisional law.

---

[15] *See* People v. Jennings, 70 Cal. App. 4th 899 (1999); People v. Gadson, 19 Cal. App. 4th 1700 (Cal. Ct. App. 1993); People v. Guzman, 45 Cal. 3d 915, 248 Cal. Rptr. 467 (1988); Commonwealth v. Mitchell, 781 N.E.2d 1237 (2003); People v. Andrades, 828 N.E.2d 599 (N.Y. 2005); Pennsylvania v. Jermyn, 652 A.2d 821 (Pa. 1995); State v. Layton, 432 S.E.2d 740 (W. Va. 1993). At least one state, Connecticut, has a 1992 ethics opinion approving the narrative but a more recent case, State v. Chambers, 994 A. 2d 1248, 1258 n. 12 (Conn. 2010), expressly declined to approve any procedure, though it cited neutrally the narrative approach in *People v. Johnson, infra*. We emphasize that we have not done a full state-by-state search; cases from other states referenced are cited in Richmond, Faughnan and Matula, *Professional Responsibility in Litigation* (ABA TIPS section, 2011), at 548, fn 152. We thank Brian Faughnan for alerting us to this information.

What, then, of ABA Model Rule 3.3? Almost every state has adopted the post-2002 version of rule 3.3.[16] Nevertheless, as we've noted, Comment 7 to rule 3.3 expressly defers to a state's decisional law if it differs from the rule.

Can we do any better? Perhaps the best solution is to allow criminal defendants to "tell their story." Freedman notes that this is the rule in most European countries, where criminal defendants are not sworn at all, but merely tell their stories. Some commentators have suggested that juries should be advised that the defendant might present perjurious testimony. Apart from enormous constitutional problems, such instructions are probably not necessary. Juries are not easily fooled, and experienced prosecutors know that full well. When they argue the motives of witnesses to lie, the most obvious is the defendant's. It is partly for this reason that many defense lawyers are reluctant to have their clients testify, regardless of the perjury issue. Indeed, the vast majority of criminal defendants are convicted at trial. Given these circumstances, it is reasonable to conclude that the jury already views a defendant's with skepticism, as "telling a story" rather than the truth told under oath.

8. Perjury in Civil Cases

Most of the debate on client perjury — as with the issues we raised in Problem 15 — has occurred in the context of criminal cases, with all of the constitutional components those cases bring. But what about perjury in civil cases? Unlike perjury in criminal cases, civil perjury is most likely to occur before trial, in responses to discovery, either by written interrogatories or at or just before deposition. Because of this, there is both more time to rectify the perjury and more time to allow the lawyer to withdraw if the client refuses to rectify.

There are surprisingly few cases directly addressing civil perjury, perhaps because the circumstances usually lack the drama of the criminal/constitutional venue, and perhaps because of the greater opportunity for counsel to rectify pre-trial perjury. We discuss rectification in the next section.

Perhaps the most oft-cited case — the one cited by Chief Justice Burger in *Whiteside* - has an unusual, even idiosyncratic, set of facts. In *Committee on Prof. Ethics v. Crary*, 245 N.W.2d 298 (Iowa 1976), Crary, a lawyer who was his client's lover, did not attempt to prevent or correct her false testimony that she was in Chicago for a period of time when she was actually with Crary. Crary was disbarred. Similarly, the court in *In re Attorney Discipline Matter*, 98 F.3d 1082 (8th Cir. 1996), had little difficulty upholding a lawyer's disbarment where an in-court tape machine, inadvertently left running, recorded the lawyer actively suggesting that the client lie.

In *Doe v. Federal Grievance Comm.*, 847 F.2d 57 (2d Cir. 1988), the court reversed a lawyer's suspension by following *Whiteside*'s narrow definition of knowledge. *Doe* involved an underlying civil case but concerned an *adverse witness*,

---

[16] We note that at least four states, Florida, Georgia, Oklahoma, and South Dakota, have eliminated the phrase excluding criminal cases from those in which a lawyer may refuse to put on testimony if counsel *believes* it to be false (an omission that may raise constitutional questions).

not the lawyer's own client. Still, its adherence to the narrow definition of knowledge is significant.

Finally we examine the interesting case history of *Breezevale Ltd. v. Dickinson*, which concerns a District of Columbia civil case and subsequent malpractice action.[17] Again, however, the case is more an analogy than direct, in that the witness in question ultimately did not lie in deposition.

Breezevale was represented by the national firm of Gibson, Dunn & Crutcher in a lawsuit against Firestone. A custodian of records was subpoenaed to testify about documents. Before the deposition she admitted to the GDC lawyer that she had forged the documents relating to one of Breezevale's three principal claims. The lawyer allowed the deposition to begin, but Breezevale's representative at deposition asked the lawyer to halt the proceedings once it became clear the forgeries would be disclosed. The lawyer did not do so, and the witness testified and admitted the forgery.

Breezevale then sued for malpractice. The jury returned a $3.3 million verdict in favor of Breezevale, because although documents had been forged, it found that the lawyer should have attempted to prevent or at least forestall the deposition. The trial court, however, threw out the verdict, saying that it was the forgeries, not the lawyer's conduct, that caused any damages, and granted GDC a $5.3 million "bad faith" award.

On appeal, first to an appellate panel and then *en banc*, the malpractice verdict was reinstated and the bad faith award set aside. In its view, the two appeals panels agreed that despite the fraud the lawyer could have and should have taken further interlocutory steps to protect the client rather than merely submit the witness to deposition. The *en banc* court rejected the proposition that "a client who engages in wrongdoing in connection with any aspect of litigation thereby as a matter of law forfeits all rights of recovery against the attorney."[18]

In civil discovery, as before a criminal trial, dissuasion is the name of the game. We believe that telling the client the consequences of falsehood, including the possible perjury charge, is legitimate even if actual perjury prosecutions are generally saved for presidents or baseball stars. As the deposition day approaches, many lawyers, would agree with what Illinois trial lawyer William McErlean wrote 25 years ago: It's time for "unsubtle, high-powered tactics," so go ahead with the "heavy artillery."[19]

When that fails? New Hampshire attorney Steven E. Feld could have benefitted from McErlean's advice. In *Feld's Case*, 737 A.2d 656 (N.H. 1999), when Feld learned the full extent of a client's false deposition testimony over the lunch recess,

---

[17] There are three published D.C. appeals court opinions on this case: 759 A.2d 627 (D.C. 2000), 783 A.2d 573 (D.C. 2000), and 879 A.2d 957 (D.C. 2005).

[18] Breezevale Ltd. v. Dickinson, 783 A.2d 573 at 574. Ultimately, however, the law firm prevailed. On remand, GDC prevailed on its bad faith claim, the trial court found that Breezevale had based its malpractice claim primarily on forgeries and denied the malpractice award, while awarding GDC attorneys' fees. In *Breezevale Limited v. Dickinson*, 879 A.2d 957 (D.C. 2005), the appellate court upheld the trial court's decisions.

[19] William R. McErlean, *What Do You Do When Your Client Lies?*, Litigation (Winter 1989).

he failed to advise his client to correct the falsehood and did nothing to clarify it himself. While Feld did not help create the perjury, he compounded his conduct by later allowing the client to respond inaccurately to interrogatories on a similar subject. The New Hampshire Supreme Court punished Feld, but interestingly, despite his double violation, *only* by public censure

9.   Rectification, and *Jones v. Clinton*

What if the client still lies at deposition? McErlean describes lawyers who "react as if poked with a cattle prod, rise up, and demand a break. After some time, they come back with the client, who sheepishly says that he didn't really understand the question or was confused . . . ." We too have seen this dozens of times. What about lawyers who admit outright that the client has lied? Again our observations square with McErlean's: "Never have I heard counsel come in after a break and say this: 'My client wants to correct testimony he gave this morning because he lied.'"

Is this "ethically suspect," as McErlean suggests? Perhaps, as the lawyer cannot lie any more than the client or witness. Nevertheless, rectification appears to be far more important than the reasons the lawyer gives on the record. It seems almost like a legal fiction: If rectification occurs, the lawyer has performed adequately, if not entirely truthfully.

This brings us to perhaps the best-known example of possible perjury in a civil discovery context: the January 17, 1998 deposition given by President Bill Clinton in the lawsuit brought against him by Paula Jones. The deposition came ten days after Monica Lewinsky's affidavit, which she later admitted was partly false, that denied sexual involvement with the President. At his deposition, Clinton denied having sex with Lewinsky and testified that he had never been alone with her. Most damning may have been his answer to his own lawyer Robert Bennett's question referring to Lewinsky's affidavit: "In paragraph eight of her affidavit, she says this, 'I have never had a sexual relationship with the President, he did not propose that we have a sexual relationship. . . .' Is this a true and accurate statement as far as you know it?" Clinton's answer: "That is absolutely true."

Given that Bennett himself asked this question, it's reasonable to conclude that the President's lawyer did not know the truth of the situation until later, perhaps not until shortly before the August 17, 1998 grand jury testimony of his own client. Indeed, after learning from special prosecutor Kenneth Starr's report that Lewinsky had disavowed parts of her own affidavit, Bennett wrote Judge Susan Webber Wright, who presided over the *Jones* case, that "portions of her affidavit were misleading and not true. Therefore, pursuant to our professional responsibility, we wanted to advise you that the court should not rely on Ms. Lewinsky's affidavit." Interestingly, Bennett did *not* advise the judge not to rely on the President's testimony, including Clinton's answer regarding the very part of Lewinsky's affidavit she had disavowed.

Was Bennett's failure to rectify the President's deposition testimony disingenuous? Self-serving? Unethical? One argument made in opposition to Clinton's impeachment — that the President's deposition statements about Lewinsky were not "perjury" because they were not material to the *Jones* suit —

might support Bennett. But how would Bennett explain attempting to rectify the status of Lewinsky's affidavit while remaining silent on his own client's deposition? Interestingly, Judge Wright had no trouble seeing the fallacy in this distinction. In her ruling holding the President in contempt for "giving false, misleading and evasive answers," she cited Bennett's letter in concluding that Clinton's answer about Lewinsky's affidavit had been just as "misleading and not true" as Lewinsky's affidavit itself.[20]

There is no unanimity of authority on a civil lawyer's duty to rectify false statements. For example, the *Feld* court, while noting in passing that "[o]f course, a lawyer always has a duty to correct errors created by his client when the attorney learns of them," based its decision more on the attorney's failure to stop his client's falsehoods rather than correct them after-the-fact. Numerous state ethics opinions have addressed what a lawyer must do upon learning that the client has given a false response in a civil matter. Most, but not all (see the Supplemental Readings), require that the lawyer at least advise the client to rectify the false statements and, if that is not done, then withdraw.[21] Other states go further, requiring that the lawyer actually reveal the perjury if the client refuses to correct it.[22]

On the surface, ABA Formal Opinion 93-376 (August 6, 1993) seems to agree with the latter view. But the language of the opinion equivocates, further clouding the issue: "If all else fails, direct disclosure to the court *may* prove to be the only effective remedial measure. . . ." (Emphasis added.) Formal Opinion 98-412 (September 9, 1998) continues the ABA's tightrope walk by noting that rectification is necessary only where the court or opposing party may rely on the false statement. How are these opinions affected by the amendments to Rule 3.3? Is it possible that Robert Bennett could justify his silence about President Clinton's statements at deposition because by August, no one was likely to rely on them?

10.   Witness Preparation and Its Limits: "The Most Difficult Question"

The one area of almost universal agreement among commentators is that a lawyer should do all things possible to dissuade a client from testifying falsely. In "real world" terms, this dissuasion solves the perjury problem far more often than it fails.

But what about witness preparation? In "going to the woodshed," or coaching, to prepare a client's testimony, how does the lawyer draw the line between giving valid legal advice and information that suggests false testimony? Judge John D. Voelker, who served on the Michigan Supreme Court in the 1950s, provided one of the most famous examples of the fine line between advising a client and assisting in a fraud. It comes not from one of Voelker's opinions, but from his novel *Anatomy of*

---

[20]   Jones v. Clinton, 36 F. Supp. 2d 1118, 1130, n.15 (E.D. Ark. 1999).

[21]   *See, e.g.*, Alabama Opinions 83-61 (April 7, 1983) and 84-54 (April 5, 1984), Calif. Formal Opinion 1983-74 (1983), North Carolina Opinion 203 (1995).

[22]   *See, e.g.*, Maryland Opinion 85-67 (Feb. 11, 1985), Michigan Opinion CI-1103 (Aug. 4, 1985), New Jersey Opinion 520 (Oct. 6, 1983), Virginia Opinion 1451 (1992).

a Murder, which he wrote under a pseudonym, and which became both a best-seller and a blockbuster movie. In the novel, the defense attorney narrator describes "the Lecture" he gives his clients:

> [C]oaching clients, like robbing them, is not only frowned upon, it is downright unethical and bad, very bad. Hence the Lecture, an artful device as old as the law itself, and one used constantly by some of the nicest and most ethical lawyers in the land. "Who, me? I didn't tell him what to say," the lawyer can later comfort himself. "I merely explained the law, see."[23]

Here is the crucial dialogue from the award-winning movie, which differs somewhat from the book. An army lieutenant, played by Ben Gazzara, is accused of murdering a man named Barney Quill, shortly after Quill raped Gazzara's wife. Jimmy Stewart, representing Gazzara, tells his client that of all the defenses to murder, only one — that Gazzara had a "legal excuse" — might apply. Stewart tells Gazzara that he is just explaining the "letter of the law," but Gazzara thinks Stewart has something more in mind:

> Ben Gazzara: Go on.
>
> Jimmy Stewart: Go on with what?
>
> Ben: With whatever it is you're getting at.
>
> Jimmy (smiling): You're bright, Lieutenant. Now let's see how really bright you can be. Ben: Well, I'm working at it. Jimmy: Now because your wife was raped, the sympathy will be with you. What you need is a legal peg so the jury can hang up their sympathy on your behalf, you follow me? (Pause while Gazzara thinks hard.) What's your legal excuse, Lieutenant? What's your legal excuse for killing Barney Quill?
>
> Ben (thinking): Excuse. Just excuse. (Stands up and walks to window, back to Stewart.) Well, what excuses are there?
>
> Jimmy: How should I know? You're the one who plugged Quill.
>
> Ben (staring out window, thinking): I must have been mad.
>
> Jimmy: No, bad temper's no excuse.
>
> Ben (walking back towards Stewart): Well, I mean I must have been crazy. (Pause.) Am I getting warmer? (Jimmy walks to door, starts to open it.)
>
> Ben (insistently): Am I getting warmer?
>
> Jimmy: I'll tell you that after I talk to your wife. In the meantime, see if you can remember just how crazy you were.[24]

Eventually, Gazzara comes up with the legal "excuse" of killing under an "irresistible impulse," a kind of temporary insanity defense discovered by Stewart's

---

[23] Robert Traver, (John D. Voelker), Anatomy of a Murder (1958).

[24] Anatomy of a Murder (Columbia Pictures 1959, renewed 1987, 8 Otto Preminger Films, Ltd.). All rights reserved. Courtesy of Columbia Pictures.

law associate in the dark recesses of an old Michigan case.

To evaluate "the Lecture" and other coaching, we return to the writing of Monroe Freedman, this time from one of his original formulations of this debate, from his seminal 1975 book.

MONROE H. FREEDMAN, LAWYERS' ETHICS IN AN ADVERSARY SYSTEM
59–75 (1975)[25]

When I first attempted to analyze problems of professional responsibility several years ago, I suggested that the question of interviewing and counseling the client prior to trial is probably the most difficult of all. As I have thought about issues of legal ethics and discussed them with others over the ensuing years, I have become more and more persuaded that it is indeed the most difficult question. . . .

If people do respond to suggestion, and if the lawyer helps the client to "fill in the gaps" and to avoid being "tripped," by developing "new ideas" in the course of repeated rehearsals, it is reasonably clear that the testimony that ultimately is presented in court will have been significantly affected by the lawyer's prompting and by the client's self-interest. Whether the end product is "well within the truth, the whole truth and nothing but the truth" is therefore subject to considerable doubt

. . . .

[I] might seem to suggest that the conscientious lawyer should avoid giving a client or other witness an understanding of what is relevant and important and should rely only upon narrative statements unassisted by questions that seek to elicit critical facts. However, anyone who has conducted interviews will immediately recognize that such a procedure would be highly impractical. An untrained and perhaps inarticulate person cannot be expected to relate all that is relevant without a substantial amount of direction. That is why one of the most important functions of the lawyer is to provide an awareness of what is legally relevant. . . . [I]f we rely only upon unprompted narrative, many important facts will be omitted, facts which can be accurately reported if memory is prompted by recognition, such as through leading questions. Obviously, therefore, we are faced with another dilemma. On the one hand, we know that by telling the client that a particular fact is important, and why it is important, we may induce the client to "remember" the fact even if it did not occur. On the other hand, important facts can truly be lost if we fail to provide the client with every possible aid to memory. Furthermore, since the client's memory is inevitably going to be affected by reconstruction consistent with self-interest, a client who has a misunderstanding of his or her own legal interest could be psychologically inclined to remember in a way that is not only inconsistent with the client's case, but also inaccurate.

[I]ssues of judgment or degree [may] be colored by the client's understanding

---

[25] Copyright © 1975 by Monroe H. Freedman. Reprinted by permission. Professor Freedman has updated and expanded his analysis in FREEDMAN & SMITH, UNDERSTANDING LAWYERS' ETHICS (4th ed. 2010), excerpted elsewhere here. Although he and Professor Smith have updated his analysis, Professor Freedman has kindly permitted us to continue to use this earlier formulation.

(whether correct or incorrect) of his or her own interest. For example, assume that your client, on trial for his life in a first-degree murder case, has killed another man with a penknife but insists that the killing was in self-defense. You ask him: "Do you regularly carry the penknife in your pocket, do you carry it frequently or infrequently, or did you take it with you only on that particular occasion?" He replies: "Why do you ask me a question like that?" It is entirely appropriate to inform him that his carrying the knife only on that occasion, or infrequently, might support an inference of premeditation, while if he carried the knife invariably, or frequently, the inference of premeditation would be negated. Thus, your client's life may depend upon his recollection as to whether he carried the knife frequently or infrequently. Despite the possibility that the client or a third party might infer that the lawyer was prompting the client to lie, the lawyer must apprise the defendant of the significance of his answer. There is no conceivable ethical requirement that the lawyer trap the client into a hasty and ill-considered answer before telling him the significance of the question. As observed by Professor John Noonan of Boalt Hall (in an article otherwise generally critical of my position): "A lawyer should not be paternalistic toward his client, and cannot assume that his client will perjure himself." Professor Noonan continued: "Furthermore, a lawyer has an obligation to furnish his client with all the legal information relevant to his case; in fulfilling this duty to inform his client, a lawyer would normally not violate ethical standards."

Up to this point, the analysis presented in this chapter parallels that in my earliest article. . . . I now believe, however, that I erred in going on to conclude that the *Anatomy of a Murder* situation is "essentially no different from that just discussed" . . . I concluded that it should not be unethical for the lawyer to give the advice. Although I did not articulate it at the time, I also had in mind the "I am a law book" rationale, that is, that the attorney would be doing no more than informing the client of what is in the applicable statutes and court decisions. After considerable reflection, I now consider that decision to have been wrong . . . (It is the same as if, in the penknife case, the defendant had in fact bought the knife the very day of the killing, and the lawyer had advised him to say instead that he had been carrying it daily for several months.)

. . . .

Referring specifically to the *Anatomy of a Murder* case, I suggested . . . [that t]o withhold the advice would not only penalize the less well-educated defendant, but would also prejudice the client because of his initial truthfulness in telling his story in confidence to the attorney.

The fallacy in that argument is that the lawyer is giving the client more than just "information about the law," but is actively participating in — indeed, initiating — a factual defense that is obviously perjurious. To suggest that the less well-educated defendant is entitled to that extent of participation by the attorney in manufacturing perjury carries the "equalizer" concept of the lawyer's role too far. Moreover, even though the client has initially been truthful in telling his story to the attorney in confidence, it does not follow that there is any breach of confidentiality if the lawyer simply declines to create a false story for the client.[26]

---

[26] [*] That is a very different matter from accepting a client's decision to commit perjury, and

NOTES

This isn't just the stuff of movies. In 1997, a well-known Dallas plaintiffs' asbestos firm, Baron & Budd, accidentally turned over to the defense a memo entitled "Preparing for Your Deposition" that read to many observers like a primer in how to stretch the truth in litigation. The memo advises clients to "STOP TALKING IMMEDIATELY" if their lawyer interrupts, because "your attorney is trying to fix something you said wrong. . . ." It instructs clients to listen closely to any "suggestion" made in their lawyer's questions, and offers examples that sound like much more than hints: "You meant that insulating cement was used on steampipes, didn't you?" or "You didn't see the product before the 1960s, right?" Trial judges in both Texas and Ohio were sufficiently upset to order the document disclosed in discovery and to sanction the firm's conduct. We will look at the results of the Ohio case upholding sanctions in Problem 18. Baron & Budd fared better in its home state of Texas, where a divided appeals court held that the memorandum was privileged. One Texas trial judge referred the matter to the grand jury, but no action was ever taken. Named partner Fred Baron remained until his death one of the highest-profile plaintiffs' asbestos lawyers in the nation.

D. SUPPLEMENTAL READINGS

1. There were an enormous number of articles on client perjury in Freedman's wake. Among the commentators, Charles W. Wolfram is among the most prolific and significant. He has written several articles on the issue. *Client Perjury*, 50 S. CAL. L. REV. 809 (1977), is one of the few treatises which focuses on perjury in civil cases. *Client Perjury: The Kutak Commission and the Association of Trial Lawyers on Lawyers, Lying Clients, and the Adversary System*, 921 AMER. BAR FOUND. RES. J. 964 (1980), addresses the varieties of client perjury and various proposals under consideration for dealing with client perjury at the time the Model Rules were being considered.

2. Norman Lefstein has also written frequently and cogently on perjury. In addition to the 1988 article mentioned in the readings, see *The Criminal Defendant Who Proposes Perjury: Rethinking the Defense Lawyer's Dilemma*, 6 HOFSTRA L. REV. 665 (1978), in which Professor Lefstein responds to Professor Freedman's writings with his own approaches for handling client perjury; and *Reflections on the Client Perjury Dilemma and* Nix v. Whiteside, CRIM. JUSTICE (Summer 1986), in which he took a stand strongly critical of the majority opinion analysis in *Whiteside.*

3. Monroe Freedman has an excellent newer piece about the tensions between the tradition under which it was ethically unthinkable for a lawyer to disclose a client's fraud on the court and Model Rule 3.3's requirement that lawyers take remedial action with known perjury. 21 GEO. J. OF LEGAL ETHICS 133 (2008). Freedman argues that because lawyers who choose to know about perjury are almost always court-appointed attorneys representing poor criminal defendants,

---

presenting that perjury to the court, recognizing that to do otherwise would undermine the confidential relationship.

that has produced a race- and class-based double standard, resulting in a *de facto* denial of equal protection.

4. Among the early criticisms of Justice Burger's mandatory disclosure requirement in *Nix v. Whiteside* is Carl A. Auerbach, *What Are Law Clerks For?: Comments on* Nix v. Whiteside, 23 SAN DIEGO L. REV. 979 (1986), which strongly criticizes the opinion for its errors of law and analysis.

5. Peter J. Henning, *Lawyers, Truth, and Honesty in Representing Clients*, 20 NOTRE DAME J.L. ETHICS & PUB. POL'Y 209 (2006), is part of a Symposium on Law and Politics as Vocation. In this piece, Professor Henning suggests that the lawyers should strive to be "honest" and that the focus in the ethics literature on "truth" is misplaced. He contends that requiring lawyers to ensure that the truth is revealed undermines their duty of advocacy. A focus on honesty is a better approach because it strikes a balance between the lawyers competing duty to the court and his or her client.

6. A few ethics opinions on perjury in civil cases come to surprising outcomes. N.Y. County Opinion 712 (1996) holds that an attorney who cannot persuade the client to recant false testimony not only may conceal the perjury, but *may not* disclose it. Moreover, the lawyer need not withdraw "if the attorney reasonably believes that he can argue or settle the case without using the false testimony." Philadelphia Ethics Opinion 95-3 (1995) holds that an attorney who knows a client testified falsely at deposition need not reveal it if the testimony is not material, and may continue as counsel, so long as the lawyer doesn't offer the deposition in court, which would trigger the prohibition against presenting false evidence.

7. Ruth Marcus, in a March 1998 article in the WASHINGTON POST, *Prosecuting Civil Perjury Is Unusual, but It Can Mean Prison*, provides a good summary of when civil perjury is prosecuted. She quotes NYU ethics expert Stephen Gillers as saying he had never heard of such a case but concluded after doing research that were a fair sampling of examples. "We were conveying the message that perjury is tolerated as part of the game [of civil litigation] and it's not. It's dangerous and it's wrong."

8. Erin K. Jaskot & Christopher J. Mulligan, *Witness Testimony and the Knowledge Requirement: An Atypical Approach to Defining Knowledge and its Effect on the Lawyer as an Officer of the Court*, 17 GEO. J. LEGAL ETHICS 845 (2004). This student note provides a good summary of the current case law in which courts have attempted to create a knowledge standard under Rule 3.3.

9. Richard Zitrin, *The Narrative Form Is an Untenable Solution in Criminal Cases*, [S.F.] RECORDER, March 29, 2013. Professor Zitrin reviews in detail the dialogue between the court and counsel in California's *People v. Johnson*, mentioned in the readings, and the six proposed solutions the *Johnson* court examines before settling on the narrative as the best solution. Zitrin offers his own critique of *Johnson*'s choices.

10. Among the many articles on the Baron & Budd memorandum are Bob Van Voris, *Client Memo Embarrasses Dallas Firm*, NAT'L L.J., Oct. 13, 1997, which first gave the memo national attention, and Michael Higgins, *Fine Line*, 84 A.B.A. J. 52 (1998), which analyzes the line between preparing a witness and suborning perjury in light of the Baron & Budd memo and the *Jones v. Clinton* case.

PROBLEM 17: PUSHING THE ENVELOPE AND COMING CLEAN TO THE COURT

A. INTRODUCTION

This problem explores the tension between the duties of candor to the court on the one hand, and diligent and vigorous representation of the client's cause on the other. As you contemplate the quandaries faced by lawyers Gabrielle Yetzi and Annette Friel, below, ask yourself whether disclosure of the complete "truth" is the ultimate goal of litigation. Also consider these questions, and where you might draw the line: How much knowledge of the truth is necessary in order to pursue a case? Should an affirmative duty be imposed on all lawyers to investigate the facts *before* taking a position? What if the purpose of filing a complaint is merely to delay or harass? May the complaint still be filed so long as there is a legitimate legal justification? Does the amount of candor depend on whether the lawyer is grappling with disclosure of the law on point, as opposed to the probative facts? Does it make sense to have different standards for disclosing the law as opposed to the facts?

B. PROBLEM

I

Attorney Gabrielle Yetzi is an environmental lawyer. She represents Save Our Land ("SOL"), an environmental group dedicated to preserving open space. A developer is planning to build a large shopping mall on the only remaining undeveloped commercially-zoned land within the city. The massive project will require, among other things, the cutting of 1,000 mature oak trees. SOL wants the site to be converted to public park land, but the site is already zoned commercial/retail and the local planning commission has already approved the project since it conforms to the city's master plan.

SOL wants Yetzi to file a lawsuit on its behalf to stop the project. SOL knows that the developer is in a precarious financial condition, and that if development doesn't proceed quickly, the project may die. SOL President Ernest Green tells Yetzi "we don't really care if we win or not, but our lawsuit could tie up this project. You don't have to be aggressive. You don't have to get the case on the active trial list. Just buy us some time. Maybe we can find a public funding source to acquire at least some of the land. And maybe in the meantime the developer goes bankrupt."

QUESTIONS

1. Would it be proper for Yetzi to file the suit requested by SOL? Is it sufficient if the sole justification for filing is delay? Or that the land would be permanently altered once development begins?

2. Suppose Yetzi finds a city ordinance requiring a hearing before the Parks Commission before any tree 100 years old or more may be cut down. She asks

Green whether there were any such hearings. Green checks with his staff and reports back to Yetzi that no one at SOL could recall. Are there sufficient grounds for Gabrielle to file the lawsuit based on a failure to have a hearing? Even if SOL's sole goal remains simply to delay development?

3. Suppose, instead, the most Yetzi can find is the possibility that there was not a quorum at one of the many City Council and Planning Committee meetings where pieces of the development plan were on the agenda. Would this alone be a sufficient basis for filing the complaint?

4. Assume Yetzi files the lawsuit. Must she follow her client's instructions about using various delay tactics? Are there times when *inaction* could amount to inappropriate delay or harassment under Rule 11 of the Federal Rules of Civil Procedure or other relevant standards?

II

Annette Friel is a plaintiff's personal injury attorney. On behalf of client Daniel Hathaway, she is defending against a summary judgment motion in state court in a products liability case that turns on the definition of what constitutes a "defective product design." Friel's research showed that, while it is a close question, the law supports her client's position, and she has filed a strong brief. She feels that oral argument went very well, and that the judge is inclined to deny the defendant's motion. At the conclusion of the hearing, the judge stated that she would take the matter under submission and render a decision within one week.

The next day, Friel spends some time reviewing the stack of recent opinions which has been accumulating on her desk. She sees a case in these "advance sheets" which is directly against her client's position. Neither she nor opposing counsel had cited this case.

QUESTIONS

1. Does Friel have a duty to disclose the new case's holding to the judge before a decision is rendered? Would doing so cause her to violate any duty to her client?

2. Suppose that upon rereading the case carefully, Friel concludes that harmful language redefining the meaning of "design defect" is not absolutely necessary to the case's holding. May she now avoid raising the issue with the court because the bad language is merely *dicta*?

3. What if Friel learns of the new case only after the court clerk has posted a "tentative ruling" in her favor, which under the local court rules will become final unless her opposing counsel gives notice that he intends to argue the matter further the following day?

III

In another state court case, Friel represents Mary Cooper, who has been injured in a car accident. Cooper claims that the defendant drove through a stop sign at a four-way stop, hitting her and causing her injury. There are no independent witnesses. Although the police were called and their report tends to corroborate

Mary, Friel knows that the report only represents one officer's opinion based largely on the client's statement. So the week before trial, Friel sends her investigator back to the scene to canvass the neighborhood for eyewitnesses one last time. To her surprise, the investigator turns up an eyewitness who had been out of the country for some months after the accident. Unfortunately, the witness, who appears entirely credible, clearly recalls that it was Mary, not the defendant, who ran the stop sign.

QUESTIONS

1. Assume that the discovery deadline has passed and (as is the law in many states) there is no order for the exchange of "ongoing discovery." Must Friel disclose this information to the court or opposing counsel? May she?

2. May she have Mary testify at trial? May she then argue that there is no evidence other than the driver's testimony to refute her client's story?

3. In closing argument, may Annette say the following: "Unfortunately, no one witnessed the accident except the parties, so we have to rely on Mary's recollection and the defendant's, and the statements of the police officer, to piece together what happened."

C. READINGS

1. Rule 11

While the rules of ethics speak to the issues raised here, of equal and perhaps greater practical importance are the effects of a variety of court-imposed sanctions, and the dangers of liability for malpractice or malicious prosecution. Most lawyers who are accused of abusing the court system by the use of a frivolous pleading will not face disciplinary charges, but rather a court's threatened imposition of sanctions. Federal courts employ several methods to control litigation by imposing sanctions against errant lawyers and their clients. The most important has been Fed. R. Civ. Proc. 11. Many states have similar provisions. *See, e.g.*, Calif. Code of Civ. Proc. § 128.5. Here is an article giving a brief history of Rule 11, and offering some thoughts about the relationship of Rule 11 and discipline under the ethics rules.

Peter A. Joy, *Happy (?) Birthday Rule 11*
37 LOYOLA OF LOS ANGELES LAW REVIEW 765 (2004)[1]

Rule 11's Role in Controlling Lawyers' Litigation Conduct

Rule 11 was a little used federal rule until it was amended in 1983 to provide for a more meaningful system of sanctions for frivolous filings. Under the pre-1983

---

[1] Copyright © 2004 by Loyola Law School of Loyola Marymount University. Reprinted by permission.

Rule 11, a lawyer's signature on a pleading certified that there was good cause for the pleading and that it was not brought for the purpose of delay. This earlier version of Rule 11, in effect from 1938 until the 1983 amendments, was criticized "on the grounds that 'good cause' was poorly defined and that other abuses, such as litigation intended to harass or to force the opposing party to incur unnecessary expenses, were not prohibited."

In response to these concerns, as well as growing complaints among lawyers, judges, and the public over frivolous litigation, the [federal courts'] Advisory Committee amended Rule 11 in 1983. The 1983 version of Rule 11 expanded the significance of the lawyer's signature to require an affirmative duty upon the lawyer to conduct a "reasonable [prefiling] inquiry" demonstrating that the filing "is well grounded in fact and is warranted by existing law or a good faith argument for the extension, modification, or reversal of existing law." In addition, the signature certified that the filing "is not interposed for any improper purpose, such as to harass or to cause unnecessary delay or needless increase in the cost of litigation."

The changes to Rule 11 proved to be significant. First, a "reasonable inquiry" or objective standard replaced the "good faith" or subjective standard of the old version of Rule 11. Second, the amended version of Rule 11 expanded the improper purposes for filing to include "any improper purpose" and not just delay. Third, the 1983 version of Rule 11 required the judge to sanction the offending lawyer for violating Rule 11 rather than leaving discretion with the judge. . . . These changes combined to expand the scope of Rule 11 violations to make them easier to prove, and to require a sanction for every violation. . . .

As Professor Georgene Vairo has pointed out, at least one thing is certain about the 1983 version of Rule 11 — every empirical study showed that the amended version caused lawyers to "stop and think" and engage in "significantly more prefiling research than they had before Rule 11 was amended." The 1983 version of Rule 11 also began to take up a significant portion of lawyers' energies and court deliberations. One multi-circuit study found that in a one-year period nearly 25% of lawyers who practiced in federal court had been involved in cases in which Rule 11 motions or show cause orders had been filed but did not lead to sanctions, and nearly 8% had been involved in cases where judges imposed sanctions. In addition, this study found that during the same one-year period over 30% of lawyers had received out-of-court threats of sanctions and nearly 25% had received in-court threats of sanctions in cases where no formal Rule 11 sanctions requests or procedures were initiated.

Understandably, the threats and sanctions took a toll on lawyer relations. A Federal Judicial Center study in 1991 demonstrated that over 50% of the 483 federal judges responding to the survey believed that Rule 11 motions "exacerbate unnecessarily contentious behavior of counsel toward one another." Similarly, a 1992 study by the American Judicature Society (AJS) found that 64% of the lawyers surveyed thought that Rule 11 had caused a decline in lawyer civility.

Responding to these and other studies and complaints about Rule 11, the Advisory Committee . . . concluded that in many ways the 1983 version was counterproductive to promoting efficient and ethical litigation conduct, and it proposed amendments designed to correct some of the problems and inefficiencies.

Among its changes, the 1993 version of Rule 11 provided that the purpose of Rule 11 sanctions is solely the deterrence of objectionable filings, made the imposition of sanctions discretionary, provided a "safe harbor" against sanctions for filings that are withdrawn, permitted the filing of factual allegations without evidentiary support at the time of filing provided they were likely to have evidentiary support after discovery, and removed discovery activity from the scope of the rule. The Advisory Committee's note emphasized that a "court has available a variety of possible sanctions to impose for violations, such as striking the offending paper; issuing an admonition, reprimand, or censure; requiring participation in seminars or other educational programs; ordering a fine payable to the court; [and] referring the matter to disciplinary authorities."

A few years after the 1993 amendments to Rule 11, the Federal Judicial Center surveyed judges and lawyers for their views on the effects of the amendments. Among the issues surveyed, the questionnaires asked whether Rule 11 should be modified to better deter groundless filings, and whether sanctions should be mandatory rather than discretionary. Of those responding, the largest percentages — 52% of judges, 41% of plaintiffs' attorneys, 37% of defendants' attorneys, and 40% of other attorneys — stated that Rule 11 "is just right as it now stands."

. . . .

The Use of Rule 11 and Subsequent Professional Discipline

Several challenges exist to investigating the use of Rule 11 sanctions. There are no reporting requirements for the federal courts to track and report the use of Rule 11, so researchers must use surveys of lawyers and judges, research actual court dockets, or rely on electronic database searches to understand the uses of Rule 11. [Here, Professor Joy discusses at length the methods he used for his empirical research to correlate Rule 11 cases and disciplinary cases under ethics rules.]

Despite the difficulties of using electronic databases for researching issues concerning the use of Rule 11 sanctions, the data from those searches do tell a story that is useful in understanding the interplay between Rule 11 sanctions and lawyers' discipline for the same conduct. . . .

Of the 1473 district court cases citing to Rule 11 [during 1993-2003], trial judges imposed sanctions on lawyers or lawyers and parties in only 274 cases and imposed sanctions solely on parties in ninety-two additional cases. Further analysis of the cases reveals that the circuit courts affirmed sanctions against lawyers in 170 cases and against parties in fifty-eight cases. . . .

The foregoing analyses of reported Rule 11 cases involving lawyer sanctions tell a partial story. The data illustrate the frequency of Rule 11 sanctions against lawyers, but they do not provide us with information about disciplinary referrals under Rule 11, nor professional discipline against lawyers for the conduct underlying their Rule 11 sanctions. . . .

[T]he data reveal a very low number — only four cases — of disciplinary referrals in [Rule 11] cases reported to computer databases. After discipline was referred in these cases, disciplinary authorities could either decide not to take action, to issue private discipline, or to issue public discipline. Because only the public discipline cases appear as reported cases, correlating Rule 11 sanctions that include referrals to disciplinary authorities with resulting discipline captures only the public discipline cases, which comprise slightly less than sixty percent of all lawyer discipline cases.

. . . .

As a final step to uncover the relationship between reported Rule 11 sanctions against lawyers and discipline against these lawyers for that same conduct, I reviewed published discipline cases against the lawyers after the date of their Rule 11 sanctions. I read each discipline case to see if the basis for the discipline explicitly referred to the Rule 11 sanction.

As discussed previously, trial judges imposed Rule 11 sanctions against lawyers in 274 district court cases, and circuit courts affirmed sanctions against lawyers in 170 cases. In searching subsequent discipline cases involving the lawyers from the combined total of 444 district and circuit cases, . . . only three of the lawyers were disciplined in whole or in part for the same conduct that triggered their Rule 11 sanctions.

. . . .

The foregoing analysis of reported cases demonstrates very little correlation between reported state discipline cases based upon the same conduct triggering Rule 11 sanctions since the 1993 amendments. This data is consistent with a survey of lawyer disciplinary authorities in 1992 and 1993 revealing that "few, if any, Rule 11 violations had been reported" under the 1983 version of Rule 11. Although this investigation demonstrates little empirical evidence of a relationship between Rule 11 sanctions and subsequent lawyer discipline, it begs the question, advanced by some commentators, of whether there should be such a relationship.

2. Should the Rule 11 Pendulum Swing Again?

As Professor Joy notes, the Rule 11 pendulum has swung back and forth from mild (1938-1983), to stringent (1983–1993) to more moderate (1993 onward). There are always some who want to amend Rule 11 yet again to eliminate the safe harbor provision under which otherwise sanctionable pleadings may be withdrawn. The following article reviews and argues in favor of one recent example of pending federal legislation that would have again made Rule 11 more strict. Do you agree that this would be a reform? Or is this legislation little more than client (or defendant) protectionism?

Sandra Davidson, *FRCP 11: A Wounded Remedy for Unethical Behavior*

62 JOURNAL OF MISSOURI BAR 16 (2006)[2]

The argument for eliminating the 21-day grace period is not only an ethical one concerning the current law's failure to deter, but also an economic one. Forcing the wrongfully sued defendant to have to challenge the frivolous charges or misrepresentations, but then denying any financial recovery to that defendant, deprives him or her of funds. Thus, the defendant suffers an irretrievable loss. This loss constitutes an injury that the federal rule on sanctions should not permit. (Of course, it may also be that a plaintiff must attack a frivolous defense or misrepresentation, so this problem of loss is not just an issue for defendants. This article will, however, for convenience only, argue in terms of defendants having to challenge frivolous claims or misrepresentations made by plaintiffs.)

The Lawsuit Abuse Reduction Act of 2004, H.R. 4571, targeted Rule 11 for change. Introduced by Rep. Lamar Smith (R-Tex.), the bill supported both mandatory sanctions for frivolous suits and elimination of nationwide forum shopping. Under that proposed legislation, Rule 11 sanctions would become mandatory instead of discretionary, and the 21-day "safe harbor" period would be eliminated. The bill passed the House on a 229 to 174 vote, but the legislation was not introduced in the Senate.

[Now, current proposed legislation] is garnering both support and opposition. Among supporters is a newly formed coalition called the Lawsuit Abuse Reform Coalition (LARC) [, c]omprised of more than 70 member organizations from the business world. . . . Another supporter of the legislation is the American Tort Reform Association.

The Judicial Conference of the United States opposes the Lawsuit Abuse Reduction Act. Also opposing that law is the American Judicature Society. In part, their opposition seems to be a classic battle over the separation of powers. Judges may well be opposed philosophically to legislators trying to become too intimately involved in courtroom procedure.

According to the 2005 survey of federal district judges released by the Federal Judicial Center, more than 80% of the 278 district judges indicated that "Rule 11 is needed and is just right as it now stands." In evaluating the alternatives, 87% of the respondents preferred the current Rule 11, 5% preferred the version in effect between 1983 and 1993, and 4% preferred the version proposed in H.R. 4571. . . .

Also, the American Association of Trial Lawyers' web site has harsh words about the Lawsuit Abuse Reduction Act. But this article, "Proposal Unfairly Targets Civil Rights Plaintiffs and Chills Meritorious Claims," which appears under the hearing of "Factsheets & Resources," says that "[i]n 1993, the U.S. Congress amended Rule 11 . . . in large part because it was being abused by defendants in civil rights cases. . . ." That language is perhaps misleading. . . .

The battle over Rule 11 will continue. Of course, whatever one thinks about the

---

[2] Copyright © 2006 by Sandra Davidson. Reprinted by permission.

current Rule 11 may well be colored by personal experiences. Fairly recently, I received payment of my attorney fees as a result of Rule 11 sanctions. But I held my breath during the 21-day waiting period. Had the other side simply withdrawn its complaint, either my client would have paid my bill or I would have written the time and effort off as a pro bono contribution to a conscientious client who should never have been put through the ordeal of a federal lawsuit. Not surprisingly, my view is that the safe harbor of Rule 11 can have a dual effect of tolerating arguably unethical behavior by attorneys and depriving wronged defendants from the ability to recover their economic loss caused by such behavior.

Perhaps more important than making up our own minds about Rule 11 is that we attorneys be aware that this debate is ongoing. The future of Rule 11 may, in effect, be controlled by legislators, not judges. And even we who do not particularly like Rule 11 can have qualms about that potential turn of events.

NOTES

Despite the 1993 amendments, the current Rule 11 is hardly toothless, as one might suspect from the wide judicial support the current rule enjoys. No one, even "tort reformers," considered the liberalized amendments to be a return to the pre-1983 days of a largely symbolic rule. Take the case of *U.S. Bank National Ass'n, N.D. v. Sullivan-Moore*, 406 F.3d 465 (7th Cir. 2005). There, a federal trial court sanctioned an entire law firm, Fisher and Fisher, P.C., a "high volume operation" dealing in real estate closings, foreclosures, and other similar matters, for mishandling a foreclosure action against an elderly woman named Mattie Sullivan-Moore, who, as the court noted, " 'never received proper notice of the proceedings." Fisher and Fisher eventually discovered her address was wrong, but aside from moving to correct "a scrivener's error," did nothing to stop the eviction from proceeding.

"Instead of exploring at that point whether Sullivan-Moore had received adequate process," noted the appeals court, "Fisher and Fisher pressed forward. . . . [A]lthough she had never received the requisite notice of the proceedings, Sullivan-Moore was evicted." The trial court identified numerous Rule 11 violations, including failing to reasonably review the complaint and repeatedly exacerbating or failing to correct the error. The trial court concluded that the initial mistake as to Sullivan-Moore's address "was an honest one" for which Fisher and Fisher should not be faulted. But, it nevertheless sanctioned the entire firm by requiring all the lawyers to attend a 16-hour course on civil procedure. Neither the finding of Rule 11 violation nor the nature of the sanctions was erroneous, concluded the court of appeals: "Neither the firm's caseload nor its practice of shuffling cases from one attorney to another within the firm excuses the type of negligent action that caused Sullivan-Moore to be evicted."

3. Adequate Investigation and Relying on the Client

In addition to the "safe harbor" provision discussed above, another significant softening of Rule 11 in the 1993 amendments is the language in Subsection (3) affording lawyers the opportunity to identify certain contentions for which they may not yet have discovered evidentiary support, and in Subsection (4) allowing denials based on "lack of information and belief."

Courts have split over whether to use a subjective or objective test to determine sanctions. In *Garr v. U.S. Healthcare*, 22 F.3d 1274 (3d Cir. 1994), a divided appeals court upheld sanctions where the pleadings turned out to be meritorious, but the majority described the lawyer's pleading as a "shot in the dark [that] somehow hits the mark." *In re Keegan Management Co. Securities Litigation*, 78 F.3d 431 (9th Cir. 1996), came out the opposite way in another 2-1 vote: Even if the lawyer hadn't adequately investigated, sanctions were reversed where it turned out the claim was not objectively frivolous. The key difference between these cases may be that *Garr* was based on Rule 11 before the 1993 amendments, while *Keegan* was based on the more liberal post-1993 rule.

The following case, focusing on the extent to which a lawyer may rely on the representations of a client rather than conducting an independent investigation, was also decided under the post-1993 changes. Would the censure of famed left-wing New York "movement lawyer" William Kunstler have come out differently if the case had been based on the 1983 version of the rule?

HADGES v. YONKERS RACING CORP.
48 F.3d 1320 (2d Cir. 1995)

BACKGROUND

This appeal concerns the most recent dispute arising out of the efforts of plaintiff-appellant Hadges to compel various racetracks and state agencies to permit him to pursue his career as a harness racehorse driver, trainer and owner. We set forth below the factual background. . . .

Hadges was first licensed by the New York State Racing and Wagering Board (Racing Board) in 1972. His license was suspended and revoked in 1974 because he failed to disclose the full extent of his criminal arrest record in his initial license application. Hadges was relicensed in 1976.

In early 1989, the Racing Board again suspended Hadges's license for six months after determining that Hadges had illegally passed wagering information to a member of the betting public at Roosevelt Raceway in 1986. According to the Racing Board, as Hadges approached the starting gate, he trailed behind the other horses and shouted, "Get the '7,'" to someone in the stands. The number seven horse did in fact win, and Hadges's horse, number two, drove erratically and interfered with the other horses.

In September 1989, although the Racing Board had reissued Hadges's license, YRC denied Hadges the right to work at its racetrack, Yonkers Raceway. In response, Hadges [who throughout was represented by attorney William M. Kunstler] filed an action against YRC in the district court under 42 U.S.C. § 1983, which resulted in the decision in Hadges I. In March 1990, the district court granted YRC's motion for summary judgment, finding that YRC's practices were not state action and thus could not give rise to liability under § 1983. In two footnotes, the district court indicated its apparent understanding that Hadges was not barred from racing at other facilities but "that proof that other tracks in the state followed YRC's decision could establish state action."

. . . .

Hadges brought the instant Rule 60(b) action in the Southern District of New York. He sought to vacate the court's decision in Hadges I on the ground that YRC had [claimed] that Hadges could continue to work at other tracks despite the YRC ban. [T]he district court ruled against Hadges and granted YRC's motion for summary judgment. In response to a request by YRC, the court also imposed sanctions under Fed.R.Civ.P. 11 on both Hadges and Kunstler.

FACTS UNDERLYING RULE 11 SANCTIONS

In support of his claim for relief in the Rule 60(b) action, Hadges submitted a sworn statement that 1993 was his "fifth year . . . out of work, with the boycott by Yonkers still in effect." Plaintiff's memorandum of law, signed by Kunstler, also asserted that Hadges "has not worked for more than four years." Hadges claimed that he had applied to race at other tracks in New York State, but that these tracks refused to act upon the applications, thereby barring him from racing. . . .

In response, YRC produced documents revealing that Hadges had in fact raced at Monticello Raceway five times in 1991 and seven times in 1993. The most recent race took place less than one month before Hadges submitted his affidavit stating that he had been banned from racing by all tracks in New York State for more than four years. YRC also submitted letters of current and former Racing Secretaries from race tracks in Saratoga, Batavia Downs, Fairmount Park, Vernon Downs and Buffalo who asserted that Hadges had not applied (or they had no recollection of his having applied) for racing privileges at their respective tracks in the relevant time period.

. . . .

After YRC requested sanctions, Hadges submitted an affidavit dated December 28, 1993, admitting that he had raced in Monticello in 1991 and 1993, but explaining that he considered the races insignificant because he had earned less than $100 in the two years combined. That affidavit also described a so-called "scratching incident" that Hadges claimed had taken place at Yonkers Raceway on October 31, 1989. He stated that although his state racing license had been restored in 1989, New York State Racing Board judges "scratched" him from that race, in which he was to have ridden the horse "Me Gotta Bret." . . . Hadges submitted to the court a "scratch sheet," purporting to document his version of the event.

YRC then submitted what the district court later described as "overwhelming proof" that the scratch sheet did not refer to an October 1989 race, but rather to a November 1987 race.

[T]he district court . . . was "quite concerned" that Hadges and Kunstler had attempted "to indicate that [Hadges] had not raced in four years when, in fact, he had privileges at Monticello in both 1991 and 1993." The court stated that Hadges had "made matters worse by attempting to strengthen his claim of state involvement alleging that he was scratched from driving Me Gotta Bret on October 31, 1989 by the judges of the racing board." The court further found that submission of the undated scratch sheet was a "flagrant misrepresentation . . . suggesting the need for sanctions, certainly against the plaintiff and possibly against his counsel." The judge invited Hadges and Kunstler to submit papers opposing the imposition of sanctions.

Thereafter, Hadges submitted an affidavit admitting that he had made a misstatement about the scratching incident but expressing his objection to sanctions. He stated that this error was the result of a simple memory loss, and that the scratch sheet involved was bona fide proof of his having been scratched in 1987 rather than in 1989.

Kunstler also submitted a sworn response, which stated that he "had no idea" that the scratch sheet was from 1987 rather than 1989 . . . . Regardless of its date, he argued, the scratch sheet was evidence that YRC was acting as an agent of the state Racing Board and could therefore be held liable in a § 1983 action. Thus, he maintained that submission of the document was not sanctionable. Kunstler's affidavit did not describe the efforts he had undertaken to verify his client's factual claims.

[T]he judge imposed a Rule 11 sanction of $2,000 on Hadges [and] also censured Kunstler under Rule 11 for failing to make adequate inquiry as to the truth of Hadges's affidavits. . . . In the course of his opinion, the judge stated:

"Mr. Kunstler is apparently one of those attorneys who believes that his sole obligation is to his client and that he has no obligations to the court or to the processes of justice. Unfortunately, he is not alone in this approach to the practice of law, which may be one reason why the legal profession is held in such low esteem by the public at this time."

Rule 11 Sanctions

[A]n amended version of Fed.R.Civ.P. 11 came into effect on December 1, 1993, five days before Hadges filed his complaint. . . . The 1993 amendment to Rule 11 is "intended to remedy problems that had arisen" under the 1983 version of the Rule and is expected to "reduce the number of motions for sanctions presented to the court." The new Rule liberalizes the standard for compliance and provides procedural safeguards to enable parties to avoid sanctions. Of particular relevance here, the 1993 amendment establishes a "safe harbor" of 21 days during which factual or legal contentions may be withdrawn or appropriately corrected in order to avoid sanction.

If Hadges had received the benefit of the safe-harbor period, the record indicates that he would have "withdrawn or appropriately corrected" his misstatements, thus avoiding sanctions altogether. Hadges did in fact correct one of his misstatements by admitting in an affidavit, sworn to on December 28, 1993, just 12 days after YRC asked for sanctions, that he had raced at Monticello in 1991 and 1993. Thus, this misstatement is not sanctionable.

Hadges also explained and corrected his misstatement about the 1989 date of the first scratching incident and described another scratching incident in 1989 involving another horse (Dazzling GT). This correction was supported by his own affidavit sworn to on March 17, 1994, and the affidavit of Erik Schulman, sworn to on March 16, 1994. Both were filed with the district court on March 21, 1994, just one week after the court issued its order stating that it was considering imposition of sanctions. . . . We note that Kunstler also filed an affidavit making similar retractions.

Kunstler did not receive the benefit of the safe-harbor period. The district court imposed sanctions on Kunstler for failing to adequately investigate the truth of Hadges's representations prior to submitting them to the court. . . .

[We have held] that "an attorney is entitled to rely on his or her client's statements as to factual claims when those statements are objectively reasonable." Calloway v. Marvel Entertainment Group, 854 F.2d 1452, 1470 (2d Cir. 1988), rev'd in part on other grounds sub nom. Pavelic & LeFlore v. Marvel Entertainment Group, 493 U.S. 120, 110 S. Ct. 456, 107 L. Ed. 2d 438 (1989). This interpretation is in keeping with the advisory committee notes on former Rule 11, which indicates that the reasonableness of an inquiry depends upon the surrounding circumstances, including

> such factors as how much time for investigation was available to the signer; whether he had to rely on a client for information as to the facts underlying the pleading . . . ; or whether he depended on forwarding counsel or another member of the bar. Advisory committee note on 1983 amendment to Fed.R.Civ.P. 11.

In Calloway, at least one of the plaintiff's claims "was never supported by any evidence at any stage of the proceeding," and we affirmed the district court's imposition of sanctions. Calloway, 854 F.2d at 1470 & 1473. However, we went on to set forth a procedure for district courts to follow in analyzing whether an attorney has conducted a reasonable inquiry into the facts underlying a party's position.

> In considering sanctions regarding a factual claim, the initial focus of the district court should be on whether an objectively reasonable evidentiary basis for the claim was demonstrated in pretrial proceedings or at trial. Where such a basis was shown, no inquiry into the adequacy of the attorney's pre-filing investigation is necessary. *Id.* at 1470.

The new version of Rule 11 makes it even clearer that an attorney is entitled to rely on the objectively reasonable representations of the client. No longer are attorneys required to certify that their representations are "well grounded in fact." Fed.R.Civ.P. 11 (1983) amended 1993. The current version of the Rule requires only that an attorney conduct "an inquiry reasonable under the circumstances" into whether "factual contentions have evidentiary support." Fed.R.Civ.P. 11(b) & (b)(3). Thus, the new version of Rule 11 is in keeping with the emphasis in Calloway on looking to the record before imposing sanctions.

In its first sanction decision in April 1994, the district court here stated:

> There is nothing to indicate that, on the serious factual misrepresentations made in plaintiff's papers, Mr. Kunstler had independent knowledge

of their falsity. However, it is equally clear that he made no attempt to verify the truth of the plaintiff's representations prior to submitting them to the court.

Apparently, the district court did not focus, as Rule 11 now requires, on whether the pretrial proceedings provided "evidentiary support" for the factual misrepresentations with which the court was concerned. It is clear that the record before the district court contained evidentiary support for Kunstler's incorrect statements. . . . We reverse the Rule 11 sanction of Hadges and the censure of Kunstler.

NOTES

The *Hadges* court combined the post-1993 "safe harbor" provision and liberalized standard for alleging facts with the Second Circuit's rule that an attorney may rely on "objectively reasonable" evidence. While liberalization of Rule 11 was seen by many as necessary to allow reasonable access to the courthouse, particularly in such matters as civil rights cases, does *Hadges* swing the pendulum too far back, allowing lawyers too much leeway? Or did it work fairly for Kunstler, who claimed he knew of no falsehoods, moved quickly to correct them, and had supporting evidence of his client's claims? It still is somewhat unclear the extent to which a duty to investigate is required by attorneys to meet Rule 11.

4. Continuing Investigation, Continuing Duty?

Note that the recognition of the continuing nature of investigations can cut both ways. Since a lawyer's advocacy is *continuing*, this may buy the lawyer time to investigate, but not the option to hide behind a shield of ignorance forever. What of the lawyer who learns later that the claim filed turns out to be frivolous? In the words of an Oklahoma appeals court that acknowledged the lawyer's subjective good faith under its state version of Rule 11, "if at any point in this inquiry we find either that [counsel] had no reasonable basis in fact or law to initially file the claim, or that after filing the claim he could not produce evidence which would reasonably support the continuation of the claim, we will not hesitate to affirm the trial court's imposition of proper sanctions."[3]

Similarly, in *Zamos v. Stroud*, 87 P.3d 802 (Cal. 2004), an unanimous California Supreme Court resolved a split in its circuits this way:

> Previously, this court has characterized one of the elements of the tort of malicious prosecution as *commencing, bringing, or initiating* an action without probable cause . . . . Defendants contend *continuing* to prosecute a lawsuit discovered to lack probable cause does not constitute the tort of malicious prosecution. . . . Continuing an action one discovers to be baseless harms the defendant and burdens the court system just as much as initiating an action known to be baseless from the outset . . . . For the reasons stated, we conclude an attorney may be held liable for malicious prosecution for continuing to prosecute a lawsuit discovered to lack probable cause.

---

[3] Warner v. Hillcrest Medical Center, 914 P.2d 1060 (Okla. Civ. App. 1996).

5. Tort Claims for Frivolous Lawsuits

In addition to sanctions under Rule 11 and ethical rules that can result in discipline, parties and their lawyers who pursue frivolous claims may also be liable to the opposing party for the common-law tort of malicious prosecution. That tort requires substantially more than a favorable finding on the original case. In most states, there must be both malicious intent and a lack of probable cause to file or continue the action. Probable cause in a civil context has generally been defined as an honest belief after a reasonable investigation that the client has a tenable claim, and that a reasonable attorney after a reasonable investigation would have thought it tenable. It does not mean, however, that the client must prevail, even on summary judgment.

Liability for malicious prosecution and sanctions for Rule 11 under the 1993 amendments have some distinct similarities. Some courts will continue to invoke Rule 11 for meritorious actions taken for an "improper purpose" — not unlike the malicious intent standard required for malicious prosecution. Also, courts in both Rule 11 and malicious prosecution cases continue to examine what weight should be given to the adequacy of the lawyer's investigation and reliance on the statements of a client, and the question of whether subjective or objective standards — or both — should apply.

For example, *Tool Research & Engineering Corp. v. Henigson*, 46 Cal. App. 3d 675 (Cal. Ct. App. 1975), holds that where the lawyer erroneously relied on the client, "the attorney's reasonable and honest belief that his client has a tenable claim" is sufficient to defeat the malicious prosecution cause of action, at least "after a reasonable investigation and industrious search of legal authority" by counsel. The Michigan Supreme Court studied *Henigson* in a malicious prosecution and abuse of process action arising out of an underlying medical malpractice claim, and concluded that the investigation bar set by *Henigson* was too high: [T]he lawyer risks being penalized for undertaking to present the client's claim to a court unless satisfied, after a potentially substantial investment in investigation and research, that the claim is tenable. . . . Time will not always permit 'a reasonable investigation and industrious search of legal authority' before the lawyer must file a complaint to preserve the client's claim."[4] And in California, that state's Supreme Court, in *Sheldon Appel Co. v. Albert & Oliker*, 765 P.2d 498 (Cal. 1989), pushed the *Henigson* test as well, not allowing a subjective evaluation of malice unless the case filing was objectively untenable:

> [I]f the court finds that the prior action was in fact tenable, probable cause is established — and the malicious prosecution action fails — without regard to the adequacy or inadequacy of the attorney's legal research efforts.[5]

---

[4] Friedman v. Dozorc, 312 N.W.2d 585 (Mich. 1981).

[5] Note that California courts have applied the *Sheldon Appel* standard to find some claims objectively untenable. For example, in *Arcaro v. Silva*, 77 Cal. App. 4th 152 (Cal. Ct. App. 1999), a collection company that brought an action against someone who had advised the collection company that the supposed signature was a forgery lost the subsequent malicious prosecution action when the court held that the

What happens in the opposite situation? Suppose that a lawyer *refuses* to undertake an action desired by a client — for example, by joining a particular party in a lawsuit — because counsel personally believes it to be unwarranted under Rule 11 standards. Should an objective test be used in this situation when the lawyer's client sues for professional negligence? The answer appears to be "no," at least according to *Mills v. Cooter*, 647 A.2d 1118 (D.C. 1994). Here, the attorney's subjective belief that a filing is unwarranted will control — at least where it occurs well before the statute of limitations runs and the client is informed: "[T]he second-guessing after the fact of Cooter's professional judgment was not a sufficient foundation for a legal malpractice claim. . . . An attorney is under no obligation to maintain a position which the attorney does not believe that he can honorably defend."

To what extent are law suits against attorneys an abusive tactic designed to create a conflict? In *Creating Conflicts of Interest: Litigation as Interference with the Attorney-Client Relationship*, 43 Am. Bus. L.J. 173 (2006), T. Leigh Anenson discusses this practice and argues that it can violate Rule 11 and create a cause of action for tortious interference with attorney client relationship. Does this mean that lawyers could spiral into an endless cycle of suits against each other?

6. Other Rules, Statutes, and Methods of Sanctions

Rule 11 and its state equivalents do not form the only bases for sanctions for a lawyer's improper use of a judicial forum. Several other mechanisms exist in federal law, and in most states. Fed. R. Civ. Proc. 26, also amended in 1993, has become perhaps the most important of these rules. Rule 26(a)(1) now *requires* each party to affirmatively disclose information to the other side "without waiting for a discovery request." Moreover, Rule 26(g) mandates that these disclosures be both signed and certified by the lawyer in the same manner as Rule 11 certification, while Rule 37 specifically authorizes sanctions. 1993 changes to several other federal discovery rules have served to require both a more open exchange of discovery and increased scrutiny of attorneys who make frivolous or over-extensive discovery demands. 28 U.S.C. § 1927 provides authority for monetary sanctions against lawyers who act unreasonably or vexatiously. Various federal rules of appellate procedure have been invoked to discipline lawyers, as the *Hendrix* case, which we excerpt in a few pages, demonstrates.

Another method of deterrence is anti-SLAPP legislation, a new concept 30 years ago that has increased in popularity across the country as an effective means of protecting individuals' rights to speak, assemble, and petition by providing special and speedy adjudication for those who are sued for speaking out. The following Houston *Chronicle* editorial advocated for strong anti-SLAPP legislation in Texas.

---

company "had no objective, reasonable basis in the facts known to it for a belief Arcaro's purported signature was genuine." *Id.* at 159.

Editorial: Yes to Nosy Questions: Coercive Lawsuits Shouldn't Keep People from Exercising their Constitutional Rights
HOUSTON CHRONICLE, March 20, 2011[6]

They're called SLAPP suits. The punchy acronym stands for strategic lawsuits against public participation. They are legal pre-emptive strikes designed to put terror in the hearts of those with nosy questions, suspicions of wrongdoing or the urge to stir their fellow citizens to action. Their targets range from journalists to whistle-blowers to ordinary citizens engaged in the routine workings of our democracy — whether this is researching news stories, speaking out against abuses in public agencies or merely organizing petition drives.

"Short of a gun to the head, a greater threat to the First Amendment can scarcely be imagined," New York Supreme Court Judge J. Nicholas Colabella observed in describing SLAPP suits in 1992.

Was Judge Colabella overstating the dangers of SLAPPs? We don't believe so. Over the years, SLAPP suits have been brought against individuals and groups for circulating petitions, testifying at public hearings, lobbying, peaceful demonstrations — even for writing letters to the editor, say law professors George Pring and Penelope Canan, whose 1996 book, SLAPPs: Getting Sued for Speaking Out, is considered a ground-breaking work on the subject.

Here are some examples of the harm done by SLAPP suits in Texas: In Austin, a women who had filed a complaint against a doctor before the Texas State Board of Medical Examiners and later complained to a television station was sued for defamation by the doctor. Defendants were eventually granted a summary judgment, but not before the doctor was able to run up legal costs needlessly. In Dallas, a developer of a low-income housing project and the principal of the developer sued a local newspaper for news gathering activities prior to publication of any article, claiming that the investigation was intended to defame them and interfere with their business relationships. In Houston, former HISD administrator Robert Kimball made complaints to the school district against a private company that contracted with HISD to teach troubled children and the company sued Kimball for defamation.

Lawsuits such as these are a clear threat to processes that perform an overriding public good by protecting individuals from possible professional malpractice, tracking the expenditure of tax dollars and watchdogging the performance of those chosen to perform services for the benefit of the community. SLAPP suits strike at the heart of our democracy - citizen participation. Whether that comes in the form of writing a newspaper article, voicing a criticism or signing a petition, this participation without fear of legal retaliation is a cornerstone of our system. These voices must continue to be heard without the threat of multimillion dollar damages acting as a giant, heavy-handed mute button available only to individuals and corporations with fat wallets.

Two anti-SLAPP bills have been filed for consideration in the current session of the Texas Legislature . . . . Together these bills form the Texas Citizen Participa-

---

tion Act, which is modeled after similar acts passed in 27 states and the District of Columbia. If approved, the Texas act would allow defendants to seek dismissal of SLAPP suits earlier in the legal process, thus avoiding excessive litigation costs and fees. It would also allow defendants who are sued as a result of exercising their right of free speech or their right to petition the government to file a motion to dismiss the suit. At this point, the plaintiff would be required to provide clear evidence of a genuine case for each essential point of his claim. If the motion to dismiss is granted, the plaintiff may be required to pay the defendant's legal fees.

These protections are basic tools to help protect citizens in their free exercise of fundamental, constitutionally derived rights of speech and petition. Over time, exercise of these rights has been openly threatened and visibly curtailed by SLAPP suits intended to intimidate and bully. In a crowded legislative agenda in Austin, likely to get more crowded as lawmakers' attention shifts to matters such as redistricting, these bills must not be forgotten. Defending citizens against this kind of intimidation deserves a priority. SLAPP suits are the bully's chosen weapon against democracy. The bullies must not be allowed to prevail any longer in Texas.

NOTES

Texas' legislature had considered proposed anti-SLAPP rules for 15 years before this legislation passed, *unanimously*, and became law. Minnesota and California, one of the first states to pass an anti-SLAPP law, in 1992, are considered to have the strongest laws. In 1996, the number of states with such laws was eight; in 2013, the number of states with such legislation stands at 28 plus the District of Columbia.

Beyond specific statute and rule authority, some courts have relied on their "inherent powers" to sanction unwarranted attorney conduct. The U.S. Supreme Court has acknowledged this "inherent power." In *Alyeska Pipeline Co. v. Wilderness Society*, 421 U.S. 240 (1975), the Court said that assessing attorneys' fees was justified when a party "has acted in bad faith, vexatiously, wantonly, or for oppressive reasons." And in *Chambers v. NASCO, Inc.*, 501 U.S. 32 (1991), the Court held that federal courts have the inherent power to sanction bad faith conduct and award attorneys' fees whether or not the conduct is subject to a specific federal sanctioning provision.

Do federal and state practice rules regulating attorney conduct constitute supplementary ethical requirements over and above the rules of professional conduct? What about judicial decisions based on the "inherent power" of courts? Are these efforts on the part of our courts attempts to legislate morality without changing the rules of ethics themselves? The answers to these questions are not simple. Lawyers in all jurisdictions are bound by applicable rules of professional conduct. But it would be overly simplistic to claim that ethical codes, and *only* those codes, govern attorney conduct.

7. Disclosure of Adverse Authority

When an attorney finds direct authority against a client's position and fails to disclose it to the court, the lawyer does so at his or her peril, in addition to violating Model Rule 3.3(a). But while the court may require full disclosure of adverse authority, a client may be quite unhappy with a lawyer who is completely honest with the court, perceiving that lawyer as less than a vigorous advocate. Is it possible to be a diligent and effective advocate and fully disclose adverse authority? And what exactly constitutes "directly adverse authority"? Many courts have addressed these issues.

One might think that big firms working for big clients might be the most likely violators of this rule, as here, in *Amoco Oil Co. v. United States*, 234 F.3d 1374 (Fed. Cir. 2000):

> By failing to cite controlling adverse authority, the conduct of appellant's counsel was inappropriate and potentially a violation of counsel's duty of candor toward the court. *See* Model Rules of Prof'l Conduct R. 3.3(a)(3) . . . . The appeal should wisely have been abandoned after this court's [controlling] *Carnival* decision was handed down. At the very least, recognizing that an *en banc* rehearing or Supreme Court review was theoretically possible, although not likely, appellant's counsel could have either submitted a motion to stay the appeal, or included in its opening brief a frank citation of the *Carnival* decision along with plausible grounds for distinguishing the case. But ignoring such precedent and raising new issues in a reply brief are not acceptable.

On the other hand, lawyers for rock bands may be subject to similar disapprobation. When Led Zeppelin's Robert Plant and Jimmy Page tried to get injunctions against alleged copyright thieves, their lawyer did not help their cause by his lack of candor on adverse authority:

> At oral argument, the Court asked Plaintiffs' counsel whether he knew of any cases denying injunctions of this type, and if so, why he did not disclose them. Counsel responded that three judges of the Southern District of Florida had granted such injunctions, but that he had "heard" from a lawyer friend that there may have been such a case denying injunctive relief. He emphasized, however, that he had never personally been denied such an injunction and could not direct the Court's attention to a single case in which such an injunction was denied. Plaintiffs' counsel thus contended that he was not obligated to disclose the adverse authority because he was not personally involved in those adverse cases. This Court's humble understanding of the ethical obligation of attorneys, however, is that they must disclose adverse case authority whether or not they are personally involved in the adverse cases. Otherwise, the majority of attorneys would be exempt from the requirement of citing the relevant Supreme Court case law on a given legal issue. While the Court can certainly understand an attorney's desire to reach a resolution most favorable to his client, higher than the requirements of zealous advocacy

are the obligations of truth, honesty, and ethical virtue.[7]

How direct does the adverse authority have to be? Is an adverse decision in another circuit "directly adverse"? *In Employers Insurance of Wausau v. United States*, 815 F. Supp. 255, 258 (N.D. Ill. 1993), the court took a middle view, but was not terribly happy with the lawyer involved:

> It is true that such nondisclosure does not violate Rule 3.3(a)(3) of this District Court's Rules of Professional Conduct (because the directly adverse authority from another Circuit does not bind this Court), but the lawyers' responsibility of candor to the tribunal should have caused Wausau's lawyers at least to point out the existence of the adverse authority in their memorandum (of course making clear their disagreement with its ruling).

To what extent are there continuing duties to reveal adverse information? The extent of such duty is unclear, and such a rule may be difficult to enforce if nothing is before the court when the lawyer learns of the adverse authority. As a practical matter, will attorneys like Annette Friel be willing to make such revelations on their own after the issue has been resolved — albeit without prejudice? After all, how would the court ever know if the lawyer fails to provide the appropriate law?

8. Failure to Disclose and Sanctions

How does the failure to reveal controlling authority get applied in practice? Read this brief excerpt from a Seventh Circuit court that took a very dim view of the failure to cite the controlling case, and a very broad view of the possible consequences.

IN RE HENDRIX
986 F.2d 195 (7th Cir. 1993)

This appeal concerns the effect of a discharge in bankruptcy on litigation against the debtor's liability insurer outside of bankruptcy. *In re Shondel*, 950 F.2d 1301 (7th Cir. 1991), decided well before the appeal briefs were filed yet cited by neither party, dooms the appeal, but we shall not stop with that observation, as there are a few new wrinkles in this case.

. . . .

We [address] the parties' failure to cite *Shondel*. Although the cases are not identical, this appeal could not succeed unless we overruled *Shondel*. Needless to say, the appellant failed to make any argument for overruling *Shondel*, for it failed even to cite the case. This omission by the Atlanta Casualty Company (the real appellant) disturbs us because insurance companies are sophisticated enterprises in legal matters, *Shondel* was an insurance case, and the law firm that handled this appeal for Atlanta is located in this circuit. The Pages' lawyer, a solo practitioner in a nonmetropolitan area, is less seriously at fault for having failed to discover *Shondel* — and anyway his failure could not have been a case of concealing adverse

---

[7] Plant v. Does, 19 F. Supp. 2d 1316 (S.D. Fla. 1998).

authority, because *Shondel* supported his position. At all events, by appealing in the face of dispositive contrary authority without making arguments for overruling it, Atlanta Casualty filed a frivolous appeal.

. . . .

There is a further point. Although as we noted in *Thompson v. Duke*, 940 F.2d 192, 196 n.2 (7th Cir. 1991), the circuits are divided (and we have not taken sides) on whether a failure to acknowledge binding adverse precedent violates Fed. R. Civ. P. 11, if Atlanta Casualty's counsel knowingly concealed dispositive adverse authority it engaged in professional misconduct. ABA Model Rules of Professional Conduct Rule 3.3(a)(3) [now 3.3(a)(2)] (1983). The inference would arise that it had filed the appeal for purposes of delay, which would be an abuse of process and thus provide an additional basis for imposition of sanctions under Fed. R. App. P. 38 ("damages for delay"). A frivolous suit or appeal corresponds, at least approximately, to the tort of malicious prosecution, that is, groundless litigation; a suit or appeal that is not necessarily groundless but was filed for an improper purpose, such as delay, corresponds to — indeed is an instance of — abuse of process.

We are not quite done. Rule 46(c) of the appellate rules authorizes us to discipline lawyers who practice before us. In deciding whether a lawyer has engaged in conduct sanctionable under that rule, we have looked not only to the rules of professional conduct but also to Rule 11 of the civil rules, which makes it sanctionable misconduct for a lawyer to sign a pleading or other paper, including a brief, if he has failed to make a reasonable inquiry into whether his position "is well grounded in fact and is warranted by existing law or a good faith argument for the extension, modification, or reversal of existing law." Reasonable inquiry would have turned up *Shondel.* The lawyer who signed Atlanta Casualty's briefs in this court is therefore directed to submit a statement within 14 days as to why he should not be sanctioned under Rule 46(c).

Affirmed, with order on sanctions.

9.   Arguing for "Extension of Existing Law"

If the rule about citing adverse authority is to be strictly applied, what may a lawyer do in making "a good faith argument for an extension, modification or reversal of existing law," as expressly permitted by Model Rule 3.1? (With the exception of substituting the word "nonfrivolous" for" good faith," Rule 11 uses the identical language.) In *Golden Eagle Distrib. Corp. v. Burroughs Corp.*, 801 F.2d 1531 (9th Cir. 1986), a three-judge appellate panel examined this question. The district court judge had sanctioned the law firm of Kirkland & Ellis under Fed. Rule Civ. Proc. 11 for failure to cite three adverse cases. Even though California does not have either Model Rule 3.3 or DR 7-102, the court found that Rule 3.3 was a "necessary corollary" to interpreting Rule 11.

The appeals court reversed the sanctions order. On appeal, the law firm claimed, among other things, that its brief was a good faith argument for an extension or reversal of existing law. The appeals panel held that it was not necessary for the law firm to "identify" its argument in that manner:

It is not always easy to decide whether an argument is based on established law or is an argument for the extension of existing law. . . . In even a close case, we think it extremely unlikely that a judge, who has already decided that the law is not as a lawyer argued it, will also decide that the loser's position was warranted by existing law.

Then, in excusing the failure to cite adverse authority, the court said the following:

Were the scope of the rule to be expanded as the district court suggests, mandatory sanctions would ride on close decisions concerning whether or not one case is or is not the same as another. . . . The burdens of research and briefing by a diligent lawyer anxious to avoid any possible rebuke would be great. And the burdens would not be merely on the lawyer. If the mandatory provisions of the Rule are to be interpreted literally, the court would have a duty to research authority beyond that provided by the parties to make sure that they have not omitted something.

. . . .

[N]either Rule 11 nor any other rule imposes a requirement that the lawyer, in addition to advocating the cause of his client, step first into the shoes of opposing counsel to find all potentially contrary authority, and finally into the robes of the judge to decide whether the authority is indeed contrary or whether it is distinguishable. It is not in the nature of our adversary system to require lawyers to demonstrate to the court that they have exhausted every theory, both for and against their client. Nor does that requirement further the interests of the court. It blurs the role of judge and advocate. . . .

A substantial minority of the Ninth Circuit court was unhappy with these views and requested *sua sponte* to rehear the case *en banc*. That request was denied (*Golden Eagle Distrib. Corp. v. Burroughs Corp.*, 809 F.2d 584 (9th Cir. 1987)). Five judges joined in a strongly worded dissent, which contained the following paragraph:

How can a brief be warranted by existing law if its argument goes in the face of directly contrary authority from the highest court of the jurisdiction whose law is being argued? How can a brief be warranted to be a good faith argument for the extension, modification, or reversal of existing law when there is not the slightest indication that the brief is arguing for extension, modification or reversal?

Just as the Ninth Circuit court split on this issue, so too have other circuits, with the Seventh and Eleventh Circuit siding with the dissenters in *Golden Eagle*. For example, in *De Sisto College, Inc. v. Line*, 888 F.2d 755 (11th Cir. 1989), counsel was sanctioned for failing adequately to research the relevant law, which would have prevented unnecessary litigation, and for citing law in another circuit. The court concluded that a lawyer arguing for modification of existing law must first articulate what that existing law is.

10. Disclosing Facts

Failing to disclose adverse authority is an issue that has been widely litigated and thoroughly analyzed. But what of Annette Friel's *factual* dilemma? What ethical obligations does a lawyer have to disclose a witness not subject to ordinary discovery? Model Rule 3.3 is clear about a lawyer's duty to take remedial measures, including disclosure to the tribunal, when the lawyer knows a person is engaging in criminal or fraudulent conduct. It is far less clear when it comes to witnesses and information that adversely affect a client's case. Rule 3.3(a)(1) states that the lawyer shall not knowingly "make a false statement of fact or law to a tribunal or fail to correct a false statement of material fact or law" to the court. Does arguing to the judge or jury in the manner suggested in the problem violate this rule? What about Model Rule 3.3(a)(3), which permits (but does not require) a lawyer to refuse to offer evidence she believes to be false? While it might be a major leap to call it perjury, does Mary Cooper's testimony now fall into this "false evidence" category? Note the difference between the "believes to be" standard here, and the "knows" standard we discussed with respect to client perjury.

What if Mary Cooper had been drinking on the day of the accident? Paragraph 9 of the Comment to Rule 3.3 states that a lawyer may refuse to offer testimony that the lawyer "reasonably believes is false." The reason given is that "[o]ffering such proof may reflect adversely on the lawyer's ability to discriminate in the quality of evidence and thus impair the lawyer's effectiveness as an advocate." But is this reasoning likely to be persuasive to Annette Friel? Or is it more likely that her *failure* to present Mary Cooper's testimony as effectively as possible will call into question Ms. Cooper's role as victim and Ms. Friel's role as an advocate?

A lawyer in Friel's position may also consider the possible malpractice consequences of revealing factually strong information that is not subject to discovery and that hurts the client's case. It may be quite difficult for a lawyer to justify revealing adverse facts. Might it also breach confidentiality by revealing a "secret" learned during the course of the representation? Contrast this with the attorney who, in *Mills*, above, refused to file claims he honorably believed were not reasonable. Realistically, when it comes to facts, isn't there a greater danger that the aggrieved client, if the case is lost, will see counsel as disloyal and sue for malpractice and breach of fiduciary duty?

A brief note about disclosure of facts by prosecutors, a subject we will address more fully elsewhere. In *Brady v. Maryland*, 373 U.S. 83 (1963), the Supreme Court held that as a matter of constitutional right, a prosecutor is required to disclose evidence favorable to a criminal defendant, an issue we discuss more fully in Problem 23. Anomalously, in *People v. Jones*, 375 N.E.2d 41 (N.Y. 1978), there was no denial of due process when the prosecutor failed to disclose during plea negotiations that the complaining witness had died. We will look more closely at this case in Problem 19.

D. SUPPLEMENTAL READINGS

1. Phillip B. Heymann and Lance Liebman, *When to Give Up a Law Suit, in* THE SOCIAL RESPONSIBILITIES OF LAWYERS 336–54 (1988). This is an excellent case study of a close call, on the border between frivolous filing and dedicated and loyal advocacy.

2. For a liberal extreme on the lawyer's duty to investigate in light of a client's assertions, see *Driskill v. Babai*, Summit Co. Appellate Dist. No. 17914, 1997 Ohio App. LEXIS 1162 (Mar. 26, 1997). *Driskill* was a wrongful death medical malpractice action in which plaintiff's lawyer filed a complaint relying solely on "plaintiff's description of the medical care [the decedent] received," and then voluntarily dismissed the case before trial. The defendants sought sanctions under Ohio's Rule 11, but the appellate court upheld the trial court's denial: While "it might be preferable practice for attorneys to acquire the injured party's medical records and have an expert review them before filing, . . . [a]ttorneys do not act in bad faith or engage in 'frivolous conduct' if they reasonably rely on the representations of the injured party and/or his or her family. . . ."

3. David H. Taylor, *Filing With Your Fingers Crossed: Should a Party Be Sanctioned for Filing a Claim to Which There Is a Dispositive, Yet Waivable, Affirmative Defense?*, 47 SYRACUSE L. REV. 1037 (1997). This is an important and dicey issue that arises frequently. Professor Taylor covers the territory well, evaluating the difficult balance between meeting the procedural burden to assert defenses while still avoiding frivolous filings.

4. Andrew Ross Sorkin, *Dubious Case Found Lawyers Eager to Make Some Money*, N.Y. TIMES, October 30, 2012. Sorkin, the TIMES' financial columnist, exposes how law firms, including the nation's largest, DLA Piper, lined up to represent Paul Ceglia, who claimed that Mark Zuckerberg had stolen his idea for Facebook when at Harvard. Ceglia produced supposed contracts and emails that were rather transparently fraudulent if seriously examined. But according to Sorkin, blinded by hundreds of millions of dollar signs, several law firms "not only took on the case, they argued volubly that they had vetted Mr. Ceglia's evidence." The house of cards soon fell apart, the U.S. Attorney indicted Ceglia for fraud, and the law firms quickly left the sinking ship.

5. Lauren A. Weeman, *Bending the (Ethical) Rules in Arizona: Ethics Opinion 05-06's Approval of Undisclosed Ghostwriting May Be a Sign of Things to Come*, 19 GEO. J. LEGAL ETHICS 1041 (2006). Should lawyers be able to avoid Rule 11 Sanctions by "ghostwriting" a brief for a *pro se* litigant? This student note examines a recent Arizona opinion approving the practice.

6. Daisy Hurst Floyd, *Candor Versus Advocacy: Courts' Use of Sanctions to Enforce the Duty of Candor to the Tribunal*, 29 GA. L. REV. 1035 (1995). This article contains a good review of post-1993 standards on what constitutes reasonable inquiry, and good faith arguments for modification or extension of existing law.

7. Several United States Supreme Court cases have addressed the issue of what happens when appointed criminal appellate counsel concludes that there are no nonfrivolous issues that can be addressed on appeal. *Anders v. California*, 386 U.S. 738 (1967), required that even if counsel felt there were no nonfrivolous issues, counsel could not withdraw without setting forth in a brief to the court "anything in the record that might arguably support the appeal." More recent cases have narrowed *Anders*. In *Jones v. Barnes*, 463 U.S. 745 (1983), Barnes' appellate attorney raised some issues on appeal that his client insisted on, but rejected others. Chief Justice Burger's majority opinion held that "counsel's professional evaluation" of the merits of various claims was sufficient. In *McCoy v. Court of Appeals*, 486 U.S. 429 (1988), the Court upheld Wisconsin's rule requiring that the appellate attorney's "*Anders* brief" discuss the principal facts and law that led the attorney to believe that an issue was meritless, in effect forcing the lawyer to argue against the client. Finally, in *Smith v. Robbins*, 528 U.S. 259 (2000), the Court, in a 5-4 vote, approved the California Supreme Court's own modification of the *Anders* procedure: A lawyer need not file an *Anders* brief or a *McCoy* discussion, merely a brief reciting the case's "procedural and factual history," and then ask the appellate court to review the record to see if it found any issues worth briefing, while remaining available to brief those issues should the court request. The *Robbins* dissenters argued that this abrogated counsel's role as an advocate. The majority maintained that they were not overruling *Anders*, and that those states that chose to require an *Anders* brief could still do so.

8. Barbara Arco, *Comment: When Rights Collide: Reconciling the First Amendment Rights of Opposing Parties in Civil Litigation*, 52 U. MIAMI L. REV. 587 (1998). This Comment offers a good analysis of the important competing First Amendment issues that arise in SLAPPs and anti-SLAPP legislation.

9. Christopher W. Deering, *Candor Toward the Tribunal: Should an Attorney Sacrifice Truth and Integrity for the Sake of the Client?*, 31 SUFFOLK U. L. REV. 59 (1997). This Comment offers a first-rate history on the development of the duty to disclose adverse authority.

10. *Commonwealth v. Pavao*, 423 Mass. 798 (Mass. 1996), suggests that the duty to disclose law adverse to the client is at least more ambiguous when it comes to constitutional rights in criminal cases. In *Pavao*, a judge failed to conduct a personal colloquy with the defendant before accepting a waiver of the right to a jury. Defense counsel knew that the failure was grounds for automatic reversal, yet he said nothing to correct this error of law as it occurred. The appellate court said that this deliberate omission "exceeded the bounds of acceptably zealous representation," and refused to reverse the conviction. The Massachusetts Supreme Court disagreed as to the conviction, since the defendant should not be saddled with counsel's strategy where the point of the waiver was that it must come personally from the accused. The higher court also stopped short of calling the lawyer's conduct unethical: "We express no opinion on the propriety of defense counsel's inaction but do suggest to the [disciplinary powers] that they consider whether such conduct should be subject to an explicit disciplinary rule."

11. Other states have disciplined lawyers for failure to cite adverse controlling authority in criminal cases. *See Tyler v. State of Alaska*, 47 P.3d 1095 (Alaska Ct. App. 2001) and *In re Thonert*, 733 N.E.2d 932, (Ind. 2000).

12. Chenise S. Kanemoto, *Bushido in the Courtroom: A Case for Virtue-Oriented Lawyering*, 57 S.C. L. REV. 357 (2005). In this piece, a practicing attorney recommends that lawyers adopt the virtues of the Samauri including politeness, honor, humility, integrity, and courage. The author argues that adherence to these principles would greatly enhance law practice. It is possible that they might, if followed, eliminate the need for such sanctions as Rule 11.

Chapter 7

TACTICS, FREE SPEECH, AND PLAYING BY THE RULES

PROBLEM 18: IS DISCOVERY SURVIVAL OF THE FITTEST?

A. INTRODUCTION

The place where most of the modern "advocacy game" is played is not the courtroom, but the discovery arena. In recent years, much of the analysis of lawyer overzealousness has focused on abuses in the discovery process. Attorney Clancy Garrett's methods can and should be analyzed in light of the black letter rules; one's conclusions would be fairly subjective, with reasonable lawyers differing significantly in opinion. But also think about Clancy Garrett's actions in the larger sense — whether certain tactics, assuming they're technically "ethical," might nevertheless not be moral.

We ask again whether there should be a difference between morals and ethics. Can or should a technical definition of what is "ethical" be used as a sword? We also pose this question: Is discovery part of the adversarial system itself, or a means of exchanging information that facilitates the adversarial process? And whatever you think it is, what *should it be*?

B. PROBLEM

Clancy Garrett is a senior litigation partner with Williams, Ruth, Foxx, Mantle & Henderson, a 250-lawyer firm in the southern part of the state. He is in charge of training first through fourth year associates in litigation techniques. Here are some of the views he espouses.

- "We *do not* give away discovery. We do not give them *anything*. If you can argue with a straight face that you don't understand *exactly* what they mean, then object on grounds of ambiguity. If you can think of a claim to make, then make it. Your job is to get in their way, not to give them information. Make them go to the expense of filing a motion to compel us to produce."

- "If you are ordered to turn everything over, try to back up the truck and bury the important stuff. Even when we have to give discovery, we don't have to provide a road map."

- "We will ask for every conceivable piece of information, and go to the mat on it. We want personal stuff, voluminous stuff, the stuff that will wear the other side down. Let them have second thoughts about whether they want to stay the course."

- "So in employment termination cases, insist on every scrap of paper to every prospective employer to make them prove what they've done to mitigate damages. And concentrate on getting medical records if they so much as whisper the words 'emotional distress.'"

- "We must hold our discovery to the eleventh hour, and our settlements until the day of trial. Our job is to protect our clients, not to dole out money to lightweights who can't stay the course. Litigation is a war of attrition. We have the resources here, and our clients have the resources to back us up."

- "If we litigate every case to the nth degree, giving no quarter and offering nothing, we will see our opponents fold nine out of ten times. The tenth time, they may roll the dice and go to trial, but even then, their chances are no better than even. And there's always an appeal. So give no quarter."

Clancy also tells the associates how he manipulates opposing counsel in the discovery process. For instance, although he is known by his friends to be very supportive of gender equality issues, he purposely calls female attorneys "honey" during deposition and has been heard to make such remarks as, "You know, you're beautiful when you're angry!" when they object to his questions. "This way," he explains, "I get the upper hand even before trial!"

Consider these views. Which practices do you think are ethical and which are not? Why? When do tactics that are merely "hardball" become unethical?

C. READINGS

1. Discovery "Hardball": Bogle & Gates and the "Dear Doctor" Letters

How far can a law firm go in stonewalling discovery? And how far must young firm associates play along silently or put their jobs in jeopardy? The pressures on law firm associates can, of course, be considerable, and each firm's "culture" is important in determining how its lawyers are "supposed" to act. Take the case of Bogle & Gates, described at length in the Stuart Taylor article *Sleazy in Seattle*, cited in the Supplemental Readings, and reported in part in *Washington State Physicians Ins. Exch. & Assoc. v. Fisons Corp.*, 858 P.2d 1054 (Wash. 1993).[1]

In 1986, Bogle & Gates began representing the drug company Fisons in a case filed by the parents of a three-year-old girl named Jennifer, who was permanently brain damaged from a dose of theophylline, the active ingredient in Fisons's Somophyllin Oral Liquid. The parents also sued the girl's pediatrician for prescribing the drug. Theophylline can be toxic when given to children like

---

[1] In the account below, we have drawn on our treatment of this case in THE MORAL COMPASS OF THE AMERICAN LAWYER 62–65 (1999).

Jennifer who are also suffering from a viral infection. Though Fisons knew of this problem, the pediatrician did not, because the company had never warned him. The doctor filed a counter-claim against Fisons, saying he never would have prescribed the drug had he been told.

During discovery, Jennifer's lawyers requested "all documents pertaining to any warning letters including 'Dear Doctor' letters or warning correspondence to the medical profession regarding the use of the drug Somophyllin Oral Liquid." The pediatrician's lawyers asked Fisons for "any letters sent by your company to physicians concerning theophylline toxicity in children." The law firm knew of at least two documents fitting these descriptions: a 1981 letter addressed "Dear Doctor" on the subject of "Theophylline and Viral Infections" sent to 2,000 physicians, but not Jennifer's doctor; and a 1985 memo warning of an " 'epidemic' of theophylline toxicity." However, Bogle & Gates advised Fisons not to produce either document.

Eventually, with no proof that Fisons had misled him, the doctor settled with Jennifer's parents. The parents' lawsuit against Fisons continued until, in March 1990, the pediatrician's lawyer received in the mail from an anonymous source a copy of the 1981 "Dear Doctor" letter. A month later, with this document now the cornerstone of Jennifer's case, Fisons settled for $6.9 million. The pediatrician, wanting to clear his name, kept alive his lawsuit against Fisons, and also complained of discovery abuse. At trial, the pediatrician won a million dollar verdict against Fisons, and another $450,000 in attorneys' fees.

The doctor was less successful on his plea for sanctions for discovery abuse. Rather than conceding it had erred, Bogle & Gates defended its position, arguing, as to the "Dear Doctor" letter, that the firm had interpreted this request as being limited to the "term of art referring to a warning letter mailed at the FDA's request to all physicians," and not merely to *any* letter addressed "Dear Doctor." As for the 1985 memo, they argued that they had simply limited their response to information about Fisons's Somophyllin *brand name*, even though the request referred to theophylline. Bogle produced the sworn declarations of 14 experts, including eminent ethics authorities and two past presidents of the Washington State Bar. Typical of the declarations was one that said, in part: "Practitioners' see discovery as a part of, not an exception to, the adversary system. . . . Tendentious, narrow, and literal positions with regard to discovery are, in my opinion, both typical and expected. . . ."

Faced with this array, the trial judge refused to sanction Bogle for discovery abuse, finding that Bogle's conduct was "consistent with the customary and accepted litigation practices in the bar of this community and this state."

On appeal, the Washington Supreme Court unanimously reversed the trial court. "It appears clear," wrote Chief Justice James Anderson, "that no conceivable discovery request could have been made by the doctor that would have uncovered the relevant documents." The higher court remanded the case with instructions to punish Bogle in an amount "severe enough to deter these attorneys and others" from engaging in such conduct again.

Bogle agreed to pay $325,000, made a public admission of its mistake, and said it had "taken steps to ensure that all attorneys at Bogle & Gates understand that the rules . . . must be complied with in letter and spirit." Yet less than two years after the *Fisons* opinion, in the view of federal Judge Robert Bryan, litigators from Bogle & Gates obfuscated, stonewalled, and "gave answers that were just plain wrong" while defending Subaru of America on charges that the driver's seatbacks in Subaru's Justy could collapse in a rear-end accident. In one request, plaintiffs had asked for National Highway Traffic Safety Administration records that showed the collapse of driver's seats from a rear-impact "force" of 30 miles per hour. Bogle's response was that the request was "vague, confusing and unintelligible. . . . Specifically, 30 miles per hour is a velocity, not a force, and due to this confusion of technical terms, no meaningful response can be given." Judge Bryan called this "lawyer hokum," and forced Bogle to pay the other side's attorneys' fees.

Was this a repeat performance or a legitimate objection? In any event, it's impossible to know for certain why Bogle would risk more judicial wrath. It is possible that Bogle's sanction, even at $325,000, was seen merely as the cost of doing business. Perhaps a stronger signal than the *Fisons* court opinion was the signal sent by the firm when the two lawyers primarily responsible for the Fisons discovery remained with Bogle in good standing, with one promoted to partner.

Was Bogle & Gates, a firm that ceased to exist in the late 1990s, an isolated case? We think it unlikely. One more brief example: Atlanta's powerful Alston & Bird and its client, chemical giant Du Pont. They were accused by judges in Florida, Hawaii, and Georgia of concealing test results that would have helped plaintiff growers prove that their crops were damaged by herbicide after they used Du Pont's product, Benlate. Georgia federal judge J. Robert Elliott called the misrepresentations in the case he tried the worst instance of discovery abuse he had ever seen. He sanctioned Du Pont and Alston & Bird *jointly* for $114 million, saying he would forgive $100 million if Du Pont publicly admitted wrongdoing. Du Pont appealed and won, ironically, on the basis of an appeals court finding that a full due process hearing was required because "Du Pont and its counsel may very well have engaged in criminal acts."[2]

After remand, Alston & Bird ultimately settled the sanctions issue by agreeing to pay $250,000 to the Georgia Supreme Court's Commission on Professionalism. Alston attorneys remained adamant in justifying their actions, and it seemed unlikely that the Benlate controversy would dissuade the firm from similar behavior in the future.

Consider what you would do if you were a young associate in a firm and were asked to engage in a discovery tactic that you believed was wrong. Should you, or may you, refuse a partner's instructions if the practice is technically "ethical," i.e., within the four corners of the ethics rules? How can you at least educate yourself about such conduct and its potential consequences? When you become a partner, will you be able to avoid the same practices?

---

[2] *Bush Ranch, Inc. v. E.I. Du Pont de Nemours & Co.*, 918 F. Supp. 1524 (M.D. Ga. 1995), *rev'd, In re E.I. DuPont De Nemours & Co. (Benlate Litigation)*, 99 F.3d 363 (11th Cir. 1996).

2. Sources of Discovery Abuse

Is abusive discovery inevitable? In 1981, Wayne Brazil, a young law professor who soon became a longtime federal magistrate judge in California, participated in creating a report on a study undertaken by the American Bar Foundation that evaluated the civil discovery system and found it replete with abuses, problems, and a marked lack of judicial decisiveness. Brazil wrote an article for the ABA Journal about that report that reads, remarkably, as if it could have been written last week. In the years since Judge Brazil's article, federal discovery has undergone several changes: the Civil Justice Reform Act of 1990, and changes to Federal Rule of Civil Procedure 26, governing discovery, in 1993, 2000, and 2006. Yet to many, little seems to have changed.

Later studies, including two in the late 1990s — by the Rand Institute for Civil Justice on the effects of the 1990 Act, and the ABA Litigation Section's Special Task Force on Ethics: Beyond the Rules — reached conclusions similar to the 1981 study, including that larger cases involve much greater discovery abuse. Studies since the 2006 amendments to Rule 26 are scant, but many observers feel that the most recent amendments have not solved and may even have exacerbated some of the problems, as we'll see later in these readings.

Can the failings of the discovery system be rectified? Consider who is more responsible for the problems of the discovery system — lawyers or judges. Is the blame equal on both sides? How can lawyers monitor themselves or their clients to avoid discovery abuses, or is discovery so embedded at the core of litigation that only closer judicial activism will help?

Wayne D. Brazil, *Civil Discovery: How Bad are the Problems?*
67 ABA Journal 450 (1981)[3]

During the last few years many practicing lawyers, judges, and legal scholars have criticized the way pretrial discovery is working in civil litigation. . . . In 1979 the American Bar Foundation began sponsoring a study whose purpose was to meet this need.

We . . . [interviewed] 180 lawyers who practice in the Chicago area. Because we interviewed lawyers from a wide range of civil practices, we were able to compare the experiences and complaints of groups of quite differently situated attorneys.

. . . The data show that there are great differences between the character of discovery in large cases and in smaller cases and that in larger lawsuits the system is plagued with severe problems that prevent it from effectively serving the purposes for which it was designed. The interviews also produced a dramatically intense and consistent chorus of criticism of the role the courts play in the discovery arena. An overwhelming majority of the lawyers we interviewed blame the judiciary for many of the discovery system's most severe problems. Four of every five respondents believe the courts should impose sanctions more frequently. And

---

[3] Copyright © 1981 by American Bar Association. Reprinted by permission.

litigators who primarily handle large matters call in loud and remarkably united voices for more help from the courts in controlling what appears to be a runaway system.

. . . .

[B]ig case lawyers portrayed a system whose most salient characteristic is gross inefficiency. Among the sources of that inefficiency, none plays a more pervasive, troublesome role than evasion. Evasive responses to discovery requests have become a ubiquitous feature of the system in sizeable lawsuits. . . . Providing evasive or only partly responsive answers to discovery requests is not the only form of "foxholing" that plagues larger lawsuits. Another widely used avoidance technique is delay. . . . Doctrinal shields of information — the attorney-client privilege, the work product doctrine, and rules protecting trade secrets — also are significant sources of friction and inefficiency in the discovery stage of major lawsuits.

. . . .

These deficiencies or limitations, however, by no means are always self-imposed. The big case litigators we interviewed made it quite clear that they spend considerable time and creative energy trying to increase the odds that opposing counsel will fail to discover damaging information from their clients. As one declared, "Most attorneys still see discovery as a game and play it to the hilt to avoid disclosure."

. . . .

Several lawyers admitted that only a small percentage of the information their own discovery efforts produce is really useful. Many also reported that to uncover key information they had to develop elaborate systems of discovery probes, employing different kinds of discovery devices in carefully orchestrated sequences, and that they had to commit substantial resources not only to sifting through immense amounts of material produced by their opponents but also to framing careful follow-up inquiries.

. . . .

Some of this inefficiency is attributable, of course, to the complex legal theories on which some large cases turn and to the large data bases the theories sometimes require. The lawyers we interviewed, however, left us with no doubt that whatever inefficiency is inherent in the development of big cases is substantially aggravated by adversarial maneuvering that intensifies through cycles of mutual mistrust. The kind of attitude that both reflects and generates mistrust was succinctly articulated by one interviewed litigator. "In the adversarial system it's one group's job to get information and the other's not to give it to them."

The inefficiency of the discovery process in larger cases might be tolerable if it regularly accomplished the goal of distributing all the important information about a case among all the parties. Unfortunately, the system as it operates in larger cases has no such redeeming feature. . . . [I]n half of the larger, more complex lawsuits that are closed by settlement, at least one of the attorneys believes he knows something of significance about the case that counsel for other parties have not discovered. [Moreover,] in half of the cases they settle they believe that another party still has [undiscovered] relevant information.

. . . .

As a group, lawyers who primarily handle smaller cases [$25,000 or less in dispute] are measurably less dissatisfied with how the discovery system works than are their larger case counterparts. . . . In smaller matters there is less money available to support elaborate tactical plans, there tends to be less data to process, and the existence and sources of relevant evidence tend to be more predictable.

. . . .

The lawyers interviewed readily acknowledged that lawyers and ways of lawyering are responsible for many of the defects of the discovery system. Despite these concessions, however, many lawyers feel that the principal culprits in the discovery system's failings are judges. The only partly articulated theory supporting this belief seems to be that irresistible economic and adversarial pressures will compel attorneys to adopt evasive and sometimes abusive tactics unless the courts impose a system of predictably tight and telling restraints.

. . . .

[T]here is one aspect of judicial behavior that provoked far more complaints than any other. Eighty per cent of *all* the interviewed lawyers believe that the courts should more frequently sanction discovery abuse. . . . Many litigators are intensely angry about what they perceive as the courts' failure to provide the discipline the system requires.

. . . .

We should report one additional result of our study that has important implications for reform efforts. Contrary to some assumptions, there is no broad support for the notion that the scope of discovery should be narrowed. While among all the lawyers we interviewed 30 per cent favored cutting back the scope of discovery, twice as many (60 per cent) favored leaving the scope as it is and 10 per cent favored broadening it. . . .

At least according to the lawyers in our sample, it would be a mistake to focus efforts to reform discovery on the formal descriptions of its proper scope. Instead, litigators believe the real need is to devise a system of restraints and rewards that will combat the pervasive problem of evasion and curb misuse of the system's tools.

NOTES

Before we move on, consider a few additional questions. Does how discovery is conducted in a particular case depend on the tone that's set in that case? If so, who sets that tone? Some academics have argued that plaintiffs' lawyers typically are, to paraphrase one of the lawyers Brazil quotes, those whose job is to get the information, while defense counsel are those whose job is to not give it up. If this is so, is it defense counsel who generally sets the discovery tone? Many plaintiffs' lawyers feel this way, and claim to be ready for an open and friendly exchange until a Clancy Garrett type appears in opposition. Others argue that the tone is really set by plaintiff's counsel, who determines the case's breadth and thus how much resistance is necessary.

Brazil's article makes it clear that most lawyers are comfortable with broad discovery and upset the most about insufficient judicial control of abuses. Do you think lawyers still feel the same way today? If so, does that mean that discovery, while a two-way street, is not equally wide in each direction?

3.   Is Access to Discovery an Ethical Issue?

The following article, while it refers to e-discovery in its title, is primarily focused on limits on access to information through changes in the discovery rules. It has a clear point of view — not surprising from a lawyer who ran a think tank largely funded by plaintiffs' lawyers. Nevertheless, as we've seen from the Brazil article, James Rooks is not the only one with this perspective. Is his point of view justified? And if it is, and narrower discovery is further obfuscated by the likes to Clancy Garrett, does access to information itself become an ethical issue?

James E. Rooks, Jr., *Will E-Discovery Get Squeezed?*
40 TRIAL 18 (2004)[4]

For at least the past 15 years, the ability of requesting parties — which, in products liability cases, usually means the plaintiffs — to use the broad discovery rights originally envisioned in the Federal Rules of Civil Procedure, and the notice-pleading regime they complement, has been steadily curtailed. Similar developments have been seen in state courts, owing to the trickle-down effect of the federal rules on their state counterparts.

In major part, discovery rights have been truncated through neither the intransigence of opposing parties nor the rulings of judges — but through amendments to the rules themselves by the federal courts' own official rule-makers, urged on by the lobbying of tort "reform" advocates. During that period, federal court litigants have lost at least the following:

- the right to obtain information through lawyer-managed discovery, not through mandatory, limited disclosure requirements;

- the right to determine how many interrogatories and depositions are necessary to develop adequate proof;

- the right to depose a witness for as long as it takes to get answers to relevant questions;

- the right to get all relevant information, not merely what the opposing party decides is supportive of claims and defenses;

- the right to complete discovery without repeated hearings before judges or discovery masters, with the attendant cost in time and money.

Throughout this period, for every de jure right lost, an opposite de facto right has

---

[4] Copyright © November 2004 by the Consumer Lawyers of America. Reprinted by permission.

been created for defendants. Most of this occurred in the rule amendment cycles of 1993 and 2000.

The 1993 discovery amendments. The 1993 amendments established the federal courts' current system of initial disclosure, which relieved federal judges of some of their discovery workload. The amendments also established presumptive limits of 25 interrogatories and 10 depositions per side in each case. Escape from the presumptive limits requires at least one motion by a requesting party and a decision by a judge, magistrate judge, or discovery referee. The net effect has been increased time and money spent on discovery — a change that has benefited defendants more than plaintiffs.

The 2000 discovery amendments . . . . The rule-makers made initial disclosure mandatory for nearly all cases, in all courts; limited the required disclosure to information supporting the disclosing party's claim rather than requiring disclosure of all information relevant to the case; established a presumptive limit of "one day of seven hours" for depositions; and — most critically — narrowed the scope of discovery defined in Rule 26(b)(1) from "the subject matter involved in the action" to "the claim or defense of any party."

What — or who — drives this curtailment of discovery rights? The public comments on the 2000 amendments show clearly the interests that promote this kind of rule-making: A number of the proposals that led to the 2000 amendments were supported by officers of, or advocates for, business and defense bar organizations. Among them: [Rooks lists here a number of corporations and defense bar organizations.]

Several proposals were opposed by consumer, public interest, and trial lawyer organizations, and by academics. Among the groups were the Lawyers' Committee for Civil Rights Under Law, the NAACP Legal Defense Fund, the National Association of Consumer Advocates, the New York State Bar Association's Commercial and Federal Litigation Section, and ATLA. And both the scope-of-discovery amendment and a cost-shifting proposal (which the Judicial Conference later rejected) were opposed by the U.S. Department of Justice.

NOTES

The most dramatic 1993 and 2000 changes in the federal discovery rules were to Federal Rule of Civil Procedure 26, although Rule 34 was also significantly impacted. The further 2006 revision to Rule 26, primarily affecting electronic discovery, is discussed in Section 7, below.

4.   Are Depositions Incubators for Abuse?

The deposition room has long been the place where young lawyers cut their teeth. Some observers feel it has too often become the place where lawyers cut up each other, try their best to offend the other side, or make frivolous objections that at best muddy the record the deposing attorney is attempting to create. Some of the worst examples follow.

Answer by Obfuscation: Some years ago, the young Dallas firm of Bickel & Brewer made itself a national reputation when the firm's witness preparation and deposition methods became an issue in a Texas case resulting in a $15,000 sanction. As reported by *Texas Lawyer* and later by the *New York Times*, part of the testimonial exchange between an Akin Gump associate and a Bickel & Brewer client went like this:

Attorney: When did you review those documents?

Witness: What do you mean by "when"?

Attorney: The documents that were reviewed, where were they located?

Witness: They were located . . . what do you mean by "where"?

Partner William Brewer was quoted in the *New York Times* saying he encourages witnesses to challenge deposition questions by telling them "to interrogate the interrogator . . . . The question 'Did you review the document?' could mean anything from acknowledging the existence of the document to memorizing it."

Objection ad absurdum: In 2012, the Ohio Supreme Court held that the Ohio Public Records Act required county recorder's offices to limit their charges for electronic documents such as CDs to their actual costs. The Recorder had attempted to charge $2 per page under the statute governing photocopying of recorded instruments such as deeds. During a deposition of the head of IT for the Country Recorder, plaintiffs' lawyer Marburger attempted to ask the witness about photocopying vs. copying electronic records, with the following result:

MARBURGER: During your tenure in the computer department at the Recorder's office, has the Recorder's office had photocopying machines?

CAVANAGH [defense counsel]:   Objection.

MARBURGER: Any photocopying machine?

THE WITNESS: When you say "photocopying machine," what do you mean?

MARBURGER: Let me be — let me make sure I understand your question. You don't have an understanding of what a photocopying machine is?

THE WITNESS: No. I want to make sure that I answer your question correctly.

          . . . .

CAVANAGH: There's different types of photocopiers, Dave.

MARBURGER: You're speaking instead of — you're not under oath. This guy is.

CAVANAGH: I understand that, but I understand what his objection is. You want him to answer the question, but I don't think it's fair.

MARBURGER: It's not fair?

CAVANAGH: It's not a fair question. A photocopy machine can be a machine that uses photostatic technology, that uses xerographic technology, that uses scanning technology.

          . . . .

MARBURGER: Not in my judgment. Do you have photocopying machines at the Recorder's office?

. . . .

CAVANAGH: Dave, the word "photocopying" is at issue in this case, and you're asking him whether something is or isn't a photocopy machine, which is a legal conclusion —

MARBURGER: This isn't a patent case. There's no statute that defines — where I'm asking him to define technology for me. I'm asking — I want to find out from a layperson's perspective, not an engineer's perspective, not a technician's perspective, but from — I have an idea.

MARBURGER: How about this: Have you ever heard the term "photocopier" or "photocopy" used in the Recorder's office by anybody?

THE WITNESS: Photocopy? I'm sure in the time I've been there someone has used the term . . . .[5]

Inappropriate and offensive comments: This is a brief excerpt from widely-reported transcript of famed Texas lawyer Joe Jamail defending a witness in the Delaware case of *Paramount Communications, Inc. v. QVC Network, Inc.*[6]:

[Opposing Counsel] JOHNSTON: No, Joe —

MR. JAMAIL: He's not going to answer that. Certify it. I'm going to shut it down if you don't go to your next question.

MR. JOHNSTON: No. Joe, Joe —

MR. JAMAIL: Don't "Joe" me, asshole. You can ask some questions, but get off of that. I'm tired of you. You could gag a maggot off a meat wagon.

While the Delaware Supreme Court criticized Jamail, who was not a member of the Delaware bar, it did not attempt to discipline him.

In *Principe v. Assay Partners*, 154 Misc. 2d 702 (N.Y. Sup. Ct. 1992), a young associate from a New York law firm had to put up with these comments from a less-than-politic male attorney: "I don't have to talk to you, little lady"; "Tell that little mouse over there to pipe down"; "Be quiet, little girl"; and "Go away, little girl."

The court reviewing this behavior called the offending lawyer's conduct unprofessional and "offensive," "a paradigm of rudeness, [to] condescend, disparage, and degrade a colleague upon the basis that she is female." The court then ordered a fine

---

[5] State ex rel. Data Trace *Information Services, L.L.C. v. Cuyahoga County Fiscal Officer*, 131 Ohio St.3d 255 963 N.E.2d 1288 (Ohio, 2012). Deposition transcript excerpts were reported in the plaintiffs' brief to the court, and in the media, including in the Cleveland Plain Dealer (on-line), *Identifying photocopy machine poses problem for Cuyahoga County official*, bylined by "Plain Dealer staff," March 17, 2011, and updated March 24, 2011, 2:22 PM

[6] 637 A.2d 34 (Del. 1994).

of $1,000; whether this was enough to serve as disincentive or small enough to act as an invitation is open to question.[7]

Finally, in the 1970s, tens of thousands of lawsuits were filed over the Dalkon Shield, an intrauterine birth control device made by A.H. Robins & Co that caused many different injuries to both women and their babies, including pelvic inflammatory disease, or "PID." Robins argued that certain sexual practices and hygiene issues could "enhance the environment for pelvic inflammatory disease," in the words of Morton Mintz, who wrote a book on these cases.[8] But, wrote Mintz, these issues "do not *cause* PID." Robins' lawyers fought a battle over how personal and intimate their questions could be without stepping over the line. One example: An Iowa woman who lost her womb and ovaries to PID was required to testify in front of her husband about her sexual history for ten years prior to her ever being fitted for the IUD, questions Mintz described as "demeaning" and her own lawyer called "disgusting."

In the Dalkon Shield case, the judge spoke out strongly. The appendix to Mintz's book quotes Judge Miles W. Lord, who presided over the principal Dalkon Shield litigation in Minnesota, Robins's home, addressing A.H. Robins's CEO, chief of research and development, and general counsel in his Minneapolis courtroom in 1984:

> [W]hen the time came for these women to make their claims against your company, you attacked their characters. You inquired into their sexual practices and into the identity of their sex partners. You exposed these women — and ruined families and reputations and careers — in order to intimidate those who would raise their voices against you. You introduced issues that had no relationship whatsoever to the fact that you planted in the bodies of these women instruments of death.

Consider these questions about taking depositions: What will be expected of new associates at a law firm when it comes to behavior in this arena? Is there hope for a view that honorable lawyers can act in good faith, or are obfuscation, game-playing, and stonewalling more likely to be part of the task demanded of the new associate?

Do the rules apply in the same way for men and women? Do our images and expectations about women and how they act vary from our images and expectations of men? Despite all efforts to create a "level playing field," do most of us still expect men to take a more "macho" approach while women are expected to be "kinder and gentler"?

Whatever one's answers to these questions, hopefully you will never be involved in a dispute that descends to the level this one described in federal judge Gregory A. Presnell's brief order.

---

[7] See a reference to this case in the *Wunsch* case in Problem 21.

[8] MORTON MINTZ, AT ANY COST: CORPORATE GREED, WOMEN AND THE DALKON SHIELD (1985).

AVISTA MANAGEMENT, INC., d/b/a Avista Plex, Inc., v. WAUSAU UNDERWRITERS INSURANCE COMPANY
United States District Court Middle District of Florida Orlando Division

ORDER

This matter comes before the Court on Plaintiff's Motion to designate location of a Rule 30(b)(6) deposition. Upon consideration of the Motion, the latest in a series of Gordian knots that the parties have been unable to untangle without enlisting the assistance of the federal courts it is

ORDERED that said Motion is DENIED. Instead, the Court will fashion a new form of alternative dispute resolution, to wit: at 4:00 P.M. on Friday, June 30, 2006, counsel shall convene at a neutral site agreeable to both parties. If counsel cannot agree on a neutral site, they shall meet on the front steps of the Sam M. Gibbons U.S. Courthouse, 801 North Florida Ave., Tampa, Florida 33602. Each lawyer shall be entitled to be accompanied by one paralegal who shall act as an attendant and witness. At that time and location, counsel shall engage in one (1) game of "rock, paper, scissors." The winner of this engagement shall be entitled to select the location for the 30(b)(6) deposition . . . .

DONE and ORDERED in Chambers, Orlando, Florida on June 6, 2006.

GREGORY A. PRESNELL, Judge

5. One Solution: "Issue" Sanctions and Dismissal

If discovery sanctions such as the $325,000 fine Bogle & Gates received in the *Fisons* case or Alston & Bird's quarter million dollar "contribution" are viewed by law firms as part of the cost of doing business, abusive discovery behavior is unlikely to be cured by limiting the penalties imposed on these firms to "mere" money. "Stonewalling" may be seen as cost-effective.

But courts have a powerful alternative to monetary fines: the ability to use "issue sanctions," which can be tailored to respond to the particular discovery abuse found by the court. Issue sanctions raise the stakes significantly for law firms caught stonewalling in discovery, since they materially limit the law firm's *client* from presenting or defending its case. In the extreme situation, a case can be dismissed, a course of action ratified by the United States Supreme Court in *National Hockey League v. Metropolitan Hockey Club, Inc.*, 427 U.S. 639 (1976). There, the plaintiffs in an antitrust suit failed to respond fully and timely to hundreds of interrogatories over a period of seventeen months. The trial court finally sanctioned the plaintiffs by dismissing their case entirely. After the court of appeals modified the trial court's order, the high court reaffirmed the dismissal.

The Court noted the "natural tendency . . . to be heavily influenced by the severity of outright dismissal as a sanction for failure to comply with a discovery order." Nevertheless, to "deter those who might be tempted" to abuse the discovery process, the district court's dismissal was upheld. The Court concluded "that the extreme sanction of dismissal was appropriate in this case by reason of respondents' 'flagrant bad faith' and their counsel's 'callous disregard' of their responsibilities."

National Hockey League raised questions as well as answering them: Is it fair to punish discovery violators for the sake of example? How much discretion should a judge have to impose a "death penalty" sanction? Of what import is the judge's perception of the merits of the case? The stage of the litigation? How high the stakes are? Should the judge's discretion be limited by strict guidelines? And what if the fault lies only with the lawyers — what remedy does their client have?

In the years since *National Hockey League*, there were few discovery-induced dismissals and no more than a trickle of significant "issue sanctions" — at least until the 1990s. Since then, courts have seemed to be somewhat more willing to consider issue sanctions, perhaps increasingly frustrated with the non-responsiveness of law firms not only to the discovery requests of opposing counsel, but to the courts' own orders.

In the late 1990s, General Motors and its counsel ran afoul of more than one court in cases relating to gas tank fires in various GM vehicles. The following article describes how one Georgia judge dealt with discovery abuse by imposing a series of issue sanctions that seriously interfered with GM's ability to defend the case.

Bill Rankin, *Did GM and its Lawyers Suborn Perjury in Georgia Case?*
THE NATIONAL LAW JOURNAL, October 26, 1998[9]

ATLANTA— Recently sanctioned by a Georgia Judge, General Motors Corp. and its legal team from Chicago's Kirkland & Ellis and Atlanta's King & Spalding must now defend themselves at an upcoming hearing against allegations that GM suborned perjury and obstructed justice in court cases across the country.

On October 27 here, GM and its attorneys are expected to refute accusations that a key GM witness gave false pretrial testimony on numerous occasions and that knowing GM lawyers sat mute during the depositions and allowed it to happen.

The allegations were filed by Jim Butler, [who] filed a wrongful-death lawsuit against GM on behalf of a woman whose husband died from burn-related injuries after a May 21, 1997 auto accident. His 1985 Chevrolet Chevette was clipped in the rear by a Volvo, causing the Chevette's fuel tank to leak gasoline and the car to burst into flames, the lawsuit contends.

"Better Boxes"

Repeated discovery violations by GM and its attorneys in the case led to a scathing Oct. 8 order by Fulton County State Judge Gino Brogdon.

In it, Judge Brogdon said the last straw involved 81 boxes of documents he had ordered GM to produce for Mr. Butler by June 19. Instead GM's lawyers sent 71 boxes, explaining that they had consolidated the documents in "better boxes."

But during an Oct. 5 hearing, King & Spalding's Philip Holladay admitted that GM lawyers had removed, without the judge's permission, 2,300 documents from the boxes because they were, he said, "nonresponsive" to Mr. Butler's discovery requests . . . . "Despite heartfelt admonishment from the court as to questionable discovery tactics and plain misconduct, GM has engaged in perhaps the most bold and flagrant discovery abuse and defiance of its kind," Judge Brogdon wrote.

Judge Brogdon struck GM's defenses and skipped over jury questions by finding that GM's Chevrolet Chevette had a defectively designed fuel system which caused it to become engulfed in flames; that the fuel tank was susceptible to puncture in foreseeable collisions; and that the car was made in a way that created an "unreasonable risk" of fuel leakage and post-collision fuel-fed fires. All a jury must do now is determine whether the Chevette, already found to be defective, caused the driver's injuries and death and the amount of damages needed to compensate them.

The severe sanctions were necessary, the judge said, to prevent the abuse from continuing. "A Swahili proverb provides 'When two elephants struggle, it is the grass that suffers,' " he wrote. "Similarly, where litigants and their lawyers engage in this type of reprehensible misconduct, the integrity of the judicial process suffers." General Motors said that it believed Judge Brogdon's ruling was "in error."

NOTES

The war over this General Motors case escalated for the next year. In March 1999, Judge Brogdon held a crime fraud hearing on the issue of perjury by the witness described in the article, former GM engineer Edward Ivey. Ivey had done a cost-benefit analysis of how much GM would have to spend to prevent post-collision fuel fires. Ivey claimed that he had done this analysis on his own, rather than under the direction of his GM superiors, and had so testified in many depositions. Plaintiffs claimed to have proof he did the cost-benefit analysis under GM directive.

Judge Brogdon did not conclude whether GM's in-house or outside lawyers overtly suborned Ivey's perjury, but he found that there was "a shameful scheme by GM to defraud and mislead several courts, to thwart and obstruct justice and to enjoy the ill-gotten gains of likely perjury," including the GM lawyers' refusal to provide Ivey-related documents in a series of cases. In September 1999, the judge ordered further issue sanctions — the loss of GM's attorney-client and work-product privileges for documents relating to the Ivey report and testimony. Three weeks later, rather than produce the documents now required by Judge Brogdon's order, GM settled the case.[10]

Although the evidence is largely anecdotal, courts have seemed to pick up the pace of issue sanctions. In 1996, for example, when federal district court judge

---

[10] Bampoe-Parry v. General Motors Corp., Fulton Co. (Ga.) No. 98VS138297.

Gladys Kessler found that Union Oil of California (Unocal) had hidden its own highly damaging test results from plaintiffs, she ruled that Unocal was forbidden to claim that its product contained lower levels of dangerous benzene.[11]

A few years earlier, Suzuki Motors was fighting numerous lawsuits claiming that their Samurai sports utility vehicle was prone to roll over. In 1991, when Suzuki was asked in a written interrogatory whether General Motors had turned down an offer to market the Samurai in the United States because GM had safety concerns, Suzuki's lawyer, Atlanta's Joe Freeman, Jr., claimed Suzuki was "unaware of any decision by General Motors not to market the Samurai." When plaintiffs' attorneys proved this false by subpoenaing GM's own records, including correspondence between GM and Suzuki showing that GM had specifically mentioned safety problems in backing away from marketing the Samurai, federal judge B. Avent Edenfield described the lawyers' actions as a "cover-up" having "the same result as an outright lie." In addition to fining the lawyers, Edenfield also entered a judgment against Suzuki on liability, leaving the company to fight only about damages.[12]

Finally, recall the Baron & Budd witness preparation memorandum we examined in Problem 16. Word of that memo spread from Texas, where it was first uncovered, to other states where Baron & Budd was engaged in litigation, including Ohio. There, after the memo was brought to the attention of state trial court judge George Elliott, he ordered Baron & Budd to disclose witness preparation documents in the case before him, stating that any claim of work product or attorney-client privilege should be submitted to the judge for his *in camera* review. The Ohio Supreme Court, in its opinion upholding the issue sanctions eventually levied by Judge Elliott, picks up the story from there.

STATE EX REL. ABNER v. ELLIOTT, JUDGE
706 N.E.2d 765 (Ohio 1999)

Despite Judge Elliott's September and October 1997 orders, appellants did not provide the defendants in the asbestos cases with any witness preparation documents and, although claiming that all of these materials were protected from disclosure by the attorney work product and attorney-client privileges, appellants did not submit the materials to Judge Elliott for an *in camera* inspection. In addition, at a November 1997 deposition, after Judge Elliott overruled appellants' objections, appellants' counsel instructed the deponent not to answer questions concerning witness preparation based on work-product and attorney-client privileges.

As a result of the foregoing actions by appellants, defendant North American Refractories Company filed a motion for sanctions. In December 1997, after a hearing, Judge Elliott issued an order in which he found that the Texas deposition preparation document constituted evidence of improper coaching of prospective

---

[11] Richardson v. Union Oil Company of California, 167 F.R.D. 1 (D.D.C. 1996) 170 F.R.D. 333 (D.D.C. 1996).

[12] Malautea v. Suzuki Motor Corp., 148 F.R.D. 362 (S.D. Ga. 1991), *aff'd*, 987 F.2d 1536 (11th Cir. 1993).

deponents, that it was reasonable to infer that similar deposition materials had been used to coach clients and witnesses in asbestos litigation in Butler County [Ohio] that had been filed by the same law firm that prepared the Texas document, that the court thereby issued its September and October 1997 discovery orders, and that appellants had not complied with those orders. Judge Elliott consequently ordered the following:

"Therefore, at the trial of this case, upon request of defense counsel, the jury will be instructed to accept and consider the following as being conclusively proved facts established by the greater weight of the evidence, viz.:

"1. Prior to trial plaintiff and his co-workers met with plaintiff's attorneys and paralegals to prepare for this lawsuit.

"2. At least one such meeting occurred before (a) the preparation of plaintiff's answers to written interrogatories, (b) the deposition of plaintiff by defendants' counsel, and (c) the deposition of each co-worker.

"3. During each of those meetings, plaintiffs' attorneys or paralegals either gave to or showed plaintiff and the co-workers certain lists, photographs, or other items which disclosed the product name, manufacturer name, product type, product description, packaging description, location of use, time of use, and typical trade or job of the Armco workers who used numerous products manufactured by defendants.

"4. Before, during, or immediately after the disclosure of that information to plaintiff and, or, the co-workers, plaintiff's attorneys informed plaintiff and, or, the co-workers that it would be to their advantage for them to name as many of the defendants' products as possible during their depositions.

"The foregoing instruction shall also be given to the jury in any other asbestos-related personal injury action in this county wherein court-ordered discovery of improper witness coaching techniques either has been or will be prevented by the objections of plaintiffs' counsel."

NOTES

Dismissal and/or judgment are the most extreme sanctions possible. Under Rule 37 of the Federal Rules of Civil Procedure, a "willful" abuse is required before such sanctions can be imposed. But what does "willful" mean? What is the necessary degree of culpability required for dismissal or judgment? Should the same standards apply to a finding of liability? And who is responsible for sanctions? What conflicts of interest may arise between lawyers and clients over who should pay for monetary sanctions? Could a client successfully argue a law firm's malpractice liability for issue sanctions by claiming that it refused to produce important documents only because it relied on the firm's advice?

6. An Extreme Example of Discovery Abuse

When lawyers feel that they are beyond the power of courts to sanction their conduct, they can too easily be sucked into the vortex of injurious advocacy — protecting the client regardless of cost, the rules, or ordinary morality. For 40 years starting in the 1950s, lawyers for tobacco companies provided an extreme example of this concealment.

In the late 1990s, Minnesota Attorney General Hubert H. Humphrey III had prepared and filed a lawsuit against a number of tobacco companies claiming that their suppression of evidence that cigarettes caused cancer had cost his state billions of dollars in health care. In December 1997, Minnesota federal judge Kenneth J. Fitzpatrick's signed a broad disclosure order that the Supreme Court refused to overturn. Thus, in April 1998, the tobacco companies were forced to turn over 39,000 documents to Humphrey that for the first time revealed to the public how much those companies had hidden from public view — and how their lawyers had participated in the cover-up. The excerpt from the following article, published right after the 39,000 documents were disclosed, describes the behavior of some of the lawyers.

Milo Geyelin & Ann Davis, *Big Tobacco's Counsel Accused of Conspiracy*
THE WALL STREET JOURNAL, April 23, 1998[13]

Tobacco lawyers are in the hot seat.

Thus far, the conduct of the $45 billion tobacco industry has been the focus of both civil lawsuits and the government's criminal inquiries. But now anti-tobacco forces are mobilizing on a new front: war with the industry's hired guns . . . .

The documents released Tuesday for example include a 1985 report prepared by outside lawyers for R.J. Reynolds Tobacco Co. that suggests that they were aware of the company's efforts to suppress and destroy research that could have hurt their client in lawsuits. . . .

[T]he anti-tobacco camp is energized. "I find it extremely offensive that the companies and their lawyers say this is what lawyers do," said Richard Daynard, a Northeastern University law professor. "It's not what lawyers do. It's not the normal work of corporate counsel to help their clients defraud their customers." He adds that he is encouraging plaintiffs to name law firms as defendants in civil suits.

"The lawyers are likely to continue fighting the release of documents by invoking the privilege shielding communications between lawyers and clients from disclosure. That privilege can be breached only after a judicial finding that there is evidence of a crime or fraud."

. . . Depositions of lawyers aren't likely to go smoothly either. When lawyers for Oklahoma, which has named Shook, Hardy & Bacon as a defendant, tried to take the deposition of former Shook partner William Shinn last year, he refused to

---

[13] Copyright © 1998 by The Wall Street Journal. Reprinted by permission.

answer any questions. He did so on the advice of his lawyers at the high-powered criminal defense firm Williams & Connelly.

Still, there is growing evidence that since the first public health alarms linking cigarettes to lung cancer were sounded in the early 1950s, lawyers have cautioned the industry against conducting internal research to get to the bottom of the public health debate to avoid negative results that could hurt in court.

The 1985 Jones Day report released Tuesday depicts widespread involvement by Reynolds's outside lawyers in editing and, in some cases, suppressing scientific research reports. The report noted "very strong interaction" between scientists and the law department saying that lawyer involvement went beyond mere "word-smithing" of research reports to "efforts to prevent the distribution or production of certain reports."

After the Surgeon General's report linking smoking to cancer in 1964, lawyers' "influence" over "research objectives" at Reynolds increased, the document said. The lawyers, it explains, "did not want anyone performing research that would appear to acknowledge that cigarettes or cigarette smoke contained harmful constituents or posed a health problem."

The law firm with the deepest ties to the tobacco industry — and the one that has come under the most scrutiny — is Shook Hardy in Kansas City, Mo. Since successfully representing Philip Morris in a smoker's suit in 1954, it has represented four of the six major tobacco companies. In the process, it has emerged as the industry's top trouble shooter.

More than a half-dozen judges have found that industry documents the firm claimed were shielded by the attorney-client privilege could be turned over to plaintiffs because they contained evidence of a crime or fraud. Plaintiffs have accused the firm of working behind the scenes to generate junk science for the tobacco industry's independent research arm, the Council for Tobacco Research, and of abusing the attorney client privilege to keep negative research results from reaching the public. . . . And at a meeting with Brown & Williamson in 1981, Shook lawyer Richard Northrip recommended doing testing of tobacco additives in house, rather than contracting with outsiders, so the company could terminate any research that yielded negative results, remove the additive and "destroy the data," according to a document describing the meeting. Brown & Williamson maintains it ignored the advice.

Shook declined to comment.

NOTES

After the disclosure of the documents, the Minnesota case was soon settled for $6.6 billion. As for the attorney-client privilege, it was relied on by tobacco lawyers for far more than refusing to answer deposition questions. It was the primary reason for the creation of the so-called "special projects" unit of the Council for Tobacco Research. According to documents uncovered in 1992 during litigation in New Jersey federal court, the "special projects" unit was supervised by lawyers rather than scientists, and lawyers had decision-making authority over both the hiring and firing of scientific employees and the selection of research projects.

Hon. H. Lee Sarokin, the judge who presided in that case, quoted a CTR participant as saying, "When we started CTR Special Projects, the idea was that the scientific director of CTR would review a project. If he liked it, it was a CTR special project. If he did not like it, then it became a lawyers' special project. . . . We wanted to protect it under the lawyers. We did not want it out in the open." "No evidence," wrote Sarokin in his opinion overruling all claims of privilege, "could be more damning. . . . [E]ven more disturbing is defendants' announced practice of using the 'special projects' division in order to shield damaging research results from the public and the FTC."[14]

7. An Electronic Discovery Primer

The following piece summarizes the components of electronic discovery in the modern age. It is not unusual today for first and second-year associates at many firms to spend the vast majority of their time doing document review. They accordingly are often the gatekeepers for the kinds of "e-discovery" described below. It's important, then, to understand what these "documents" may include. This article, by its own reckoning already out of date when written, is nevertheless a succinct and cogent summary of the territory.

Mark E. Borzych, *Avoiding Electronic Discovery Disputes: Practice Questions Answered*
41 ARIZONA ATTORNEY 36 (2005)[15]

In a partnership dispute, plaintiff's attorney requested from opposing counsel electronic files of accounting records, contracts, e-mail and other correspondence for a specific period of time. This information was copied onto a CD and turned over to her.

Unfortunately, her discovery request did not demand imaging of the computer hard drives on which those files had originally resided. Subsequently, those computers were forensically examined, and when the contents of the hard drive were compared to the material on the CD, it became apparent that the production was incomplete, in part because important electronic evidence was missing.

When most attorneys think of "documents" as they prepare or respond to discovery requests, they probably think of paper — hard-copy — documents. Unfortunately, an attorney who applies such a limited scope to the discovery process risks either overlooking important information or not producing crucial evidence. "Moreover," said one court in stating the common view, "it is a well accepted proposition that deleted computer files, whether they be e-mails or otherwise, are discoverable." A requesting party also may miss an important opportunity to obtain possibly relevant information in the form of metadata,

---

[14] Haines v. Liggett Group, Inc., 140 F.R.D. 681 (D.N.J. 1992), *rev'd*, 975 F.2d 81 (3d Cir. 1992). For more on this fascinating case, see the reference in the Supplemental Readings, below.

[15] Copyright © 2005 by the Arizona Attorney magazine, State Bar of Arizona, January 2005. Reprinted by permission.

residual or "inaccessible" data, and other operating system artifacts.

"Document" Definition in Flux

One court recently explained that computerized data and "other electronically-recorded information" includes, but is not limited to, the following:

Voice mail messages and files, back-up voice mail files, e-mail messages and files, backup e-mail files, deleted e-mails, data files, program files, backup and archival tapes, temporary files, system history files, web site information stored in textual, graphical or audio format, web site log files, cache files, cookies, and other electronically-recorded information.[16]

Unlike paper documents, however, electronic documents or data may be compromised, destroyed or lost as new files or data are created, saved to or deleted from a hard drive. This is the case because new information continuously overwrites old data. Simply turning on a typical Windows-based computer can alter hundreds of files and potentially destroy relevant electronic evidence.

Preservation Letters and the Duty To Preserve

Due to the volatile nature of electronic data, the timing of a preservation request may be critical. To protect the integrity of electronic evidence, the preservation letter should also include a request for the computer to be taken out of service until a forensically accurate mirror image of the hard drive can be created. That last step may require more specialized knowledge.

Specialized neutral experts can [obtain] forensically accurate hard drive "mirror images" to preserve electronic evidence and to analyze the computer data properly. A forensic mirror image is a "byte-for-byte copy of everything on the hard drive," including deleted files and unused disk space. In contrast, a "functional copy" only duplicates disk structures and active files . . . .

When forensically imaging a hard drive, a computer forensic specialist's objective is to establish that the image is identical to the original. The accuracy of the image is determined by calculating the "hash value" of the contents of the hard drive using an "algorithm known as MD5 (Message Digest 5). This algorithm computes a unique hexadecimal alphanumeric identifier for the data on the hard drive." Once the hash value of the data in the image is determined, it is compared to the hash value of the data on original media. The image is considered forensically accurate if the two hash values are the same.

. . . .

As technology continues to advance, lawyers must be prepared to confront and address electronic discovery issues. Not long ago, there was virtually no case law addressing these issues. Now, case law in this area is evolving rapidly. With that evolution, the learning curve for lawyers is starting to diminish as more published

---

[16] [4] *Super Film of America, Inc. v. UCB Films, Inc.*, 219 F.R.D. 649, 657 (D. Kan. 2004) (quoting *Kleiner v. Burns*, No. 00-2160-JWL, . . . (D. Kan. Dec. 15, 2000)).

opinions emerge, and judges' expectations continue to rise regarding electronic discovery matters.

NOTES

In the years since this article, almost every lawyer has become aware that "documents" do not refer to just pieces of paper. But most would still be intimidated by the technical terms Borzych uses: "hash value," "algorithm MD5," "hexadecimal alphanumeric identifier." How much knowledge is necessary today for a lawyer to be able to handle e-discovery competently? Think about this question particularly in light of the *Zubulake* cases below, in which a federal judge places lawyers on notice of what she expects them to do — *and* understand.

8. Two Events that Shaped Electronic Discovery

First, in 2003 and 2004, a series of related decisions from noted federal court judge Shira Scheindlin helped shape the course of modern e-discovery. These decisions all came in the same employment discrimination case, *Zubulake v. UBS Warburg* (S.D.N.Y.).[17]

The opinions, taken together, provide a roadmap of requirements for the parties and, significantly, the parties' attorneys, in dealing with e-discovery. *Zubulake* has often been used since as a template in other cases and other venues, and was also influential in shaping the second event: the December 2006 amendment to F.R.C.P. 26, which specifically addresses e-discovery.

After holding in *Zubulake I* that the plaintiff had the right to e-discovery, when the defendant still balked at the cost of producing data, Judge Scheindlin ruled in *Zubulake III* that existing data must be produced at the producing party's cost, and that the cost of restoring erased or inaccessible data should be shared between the parties depending on a number of factors. When the defendant still didn't produce documents because they had been destroyed, Scheindlin ruled in *Zubulake IV* that a "litigation hold" must be placed on the destruction of any documents once litigation begins *or is anticipated*.

Finally, when depositions of defendant's witnesses showed that some e-documents had been destroyed despite defense counsel's instructions to preserve them, Scheindlin reacted strongly, ordering an issues sanction: She instructed the jury it could draw an adverse inference from the fact that documents had been destroyed. Plaintiff Zubulake received a huge jury verdict.

In *Zubulake V*, Judge Scheindlin made it clear that when attorneys advise their client to implement a litigation hold, "that is only the beginning." Then, under the headings "Counsel's duty to locate relevant information" and "Counsel's continuing duty to ensure preservation," Scheindlin laid out details of her expectations, and made this statement:

---

[17] These cases are commonly called — and referred to by the court as — *Zubulake* ["Zoo-boo-lah-kee"] *I, II, III, IV,* and *V.* Their citations are, respectively, *I:* 217 F.R.D. 309; *II:* 230 F.R.D. 290; *III:* 216 F.R.D. 280; *IV:* 220 F.R.D. 212; and *V:* 229 F.R.D. 422. All are 2003 opinions except the last, which is in 2004. *Zubulake II* dealt only with a collateral issue.

[I]t is *not* sufficient to notify all employees of a litigation hold and expect that the party will then retain and produce all relevant information. Counsel must take affirmative steps to monitor compliance so that all sources of discoverable information are identified and searched. This is not to say that counsel will necessarily succeed in locating all such sources . . . . But counsel and client must take *some reasonable steps* to see that sources of relevant information are located.

The same affirmative duty, she wrote, is required to preserve that information: "The *continuing* duty to supplement disclosures strongly suggests that . . . a 'duty to preserve' connotes an ongoing obligation."

The revisions to Rule 26 address some of these same issues. Documents produced must be in a format usable by the requesting party. E-documents should be produced if "relevant, not privileged, and reasonably accessible." Producing parties may object to production due to cost or undue burden. Production may nevertheless be ordered in such circumstances, but requesting parties are advised to attempt to obtain the information in other ways prior to making burdensome requests.

How *Zubulake* and Rule 26 on e-discovery will affect the behavior of lawyers is not yet clear. How do lawyers see it? Not surprisingly, it depends on what side of the fence they sit. In his article above, James Rooks worried that the e-discovery amendments would further narrow plaintiffs' discovery opportunities. Meanwhile, corporate litigation counsel William Barnette[18] worries that e-discovery rules now require companies to preserve absolutely everything and put them in danger of spoliation charges should an e-document be missing.

9.   E-Discovery and Failure to Disclose

We now come to *Qualcomm Inc., v. Broadcom Corp.*, at the intersection of two important concepts — electronic discovery and attorneys' failure of to disclose. Several years ago, Qualcomm filed a patent infringement suit against Broadcom that eventually went to trial. During discovery, Qualcomm concealed two key patents, and also its participation in a "Standards Setting Organization" ("SSO")— participation that would have meant its patent rights as to Broadcom were completely waived.[19]

During trial, a Qualcomm witness truthfully testified on cross-examination that she knew Qualcomm had participated in the SSO, and she possessed 21 emails that verified this. After trial, the judge asked a magistrate judge to conduct an inquiry into why this information only came to light at the end of trial. In the first two in a series of four cases, each called *Qualcomm Inc., v. Broadcom Corp.*,[20] the magistrate judge found, among other things, that:

---

[18] See his 2012 article further summarized in the Supplemental Readings.

[19] Such "SSOs" determine an industry baseline standard that others can follow without paying royalties. Any participant must disclose to the "SSO" any patents "reasonably necessary" to practice that standard. The Qualcomm cases are important for patent law reasons as well as for its discussion of e-discovery breaches.

[20] "Qualcomm I," 539 F. Supp. 2d 1214 (S.D. Cal.2007); "Qualcomm II," 2008 U.S. Dist. LEXIS 911

- In preparing the witness, both inside and outside counsel learned of numerous emails that proved that Qualcomm had participated in the SSO;

- After the witness was examined, counsel nevertheless asserted to the court, falsely and on the record, that no emails existed that were responsive to Broadcom's discovery requests;

- There were "over two hundred thousand pages of emails and electronic documents that were finally produced four months after trial containing direct evidence that multiple representatives of Qualcomm participated in the [SSO]";

- Outside counsel not only failed to produce emails but failed to investigate the existence of other electronic evidence; and

- "Qualcomm intentionally withheld tens of thousands of decisive documents," and could not have done so "without some type of assistance or deliberate ignorance from its retained attorneys."

In *Qualcomm I*, the court issued an Order to Show Cause why Qualcomm and its attorneys should not be sanctioned. In *Qualcomm II*, the magistrate judge held that Qualcomm's discovery failures justified a finding of an "exceptional case," allowing her to order Qualcomm to pay Broadcom's attorneys' fees of over $8.5 million. She also ordered 19 lawyers, each of whom she named, to forward her order to the State Bar for investigation.[21]

In *Qualcomm III*, the district court judge permitted the outside lawyers to waive attorney-client privilege in order to defend themselves against sanctions at a further hearing in front of the magistrate. The opinion in *Qualcomm IV* was the result of that hearing:

> There still is no doubt in this Court's mind that this massive discovery failure resulted from significant mistakes, oversights, and miscommunication on the part of both outside counsel and Qualcomm employees. . . . [A] number of Qualcomm employees, including legal counsel, knew that Qualcomm [participated in the SSO] during the relevant time period and yet no one informed [outside counsel].

While the court was "dismayed that none of the attorneys considered the larger discovery picture" after they learned of documents that "clearly proved that the prior document collection had been inadequate," and while none lawyers followed up on "several discovery paths that seem obvious, at least in hindsight," the magistrate judge found that "the involved attorneys did not act in bad faith," and thus declined to sanction outside counsel.

What is the lesson of the *Qualcomm* litigation? Is it that the failure of counsel to investigate what e-discovery needs to be done may be sanctionable if only by a

---

(S.D. Cal. Jan. 7, 2008); "Qualcomm III," 2008 U.S. Dist. LEXIS 16897 (S.D. Cal. Mar. 5, 2008); and "Qualcomm IV," 2010 U.S. Dist. LEXIS 33889 (S.D. Cal. Apr. 2, 2010).

[21] In *Qualcomm Inc., v. Broadcom Corp.*, 548 F.3d 1004 (Fed. Cir. 2008), the appeals court upheld the trial court's "exceptional case" ruling: "[T]he litigation misconduct findings were sufficient standing alone to support the exceptional case determination here." This appellate decision also addressed the breadth of important patent sanctions against Qualcomm.

court's public censure? Or is it that outside counsel can still "get away with it" by hiding behind the shield of what they say the client did not reveal? The *Qualcomm* opinions were issued after the 2006 amendments to FRCP 26. How long will counsel continue to be able to claim that they were oblivious to "several discovery paths that seem obvious, at least in hindsight"?

10.   Discovery, Making Money, and a Kinder Approach

Many observers of modern American litigation believe that discovery — and the increased importance at many law firms of litigation *support* — that is, the machinery of the discovery process — is regarded by these firms as a major profit center. Is money driving the discovery engine? As long ago as 1995, one consultant at a legal administrators' conference estimated that litigation discovery alone, at $45 billion a year, made up close to half of the revenues of legal services "industry."[22]

Since 1995 the trend in litigation support has been towards outsourcing and the use of e-discovery, but that doesn't mean discovery is less important as a way for law firms (especially the largest firms) to make money. In a 2012 survey of the AmLaw 200 and other major corporate firms, The Cowan Group reports that 40% of BigLaw firms still call "litigation support" a profit center.[23]

Charles R. Morgan, former vice president, general counsel, and secretary of Chiquita Brands International Inc., and senior corporate counsel of Kraft Foods, tells this story: "When I was thinking about going back to private practice, I interviewed some very big firms. I was talking to the head of the litigation department at a very large firm and explained that I had an interest in helping companies settle or resolve cases early on. He told me that it was a terrible idea. I asked, 'Why? And he said, 'Because we make all of our money at this law firm in discovery practice.' "[24]

Horace Green doesn't see it that way, as this article notes, paraphrasing Green's own words.

Richard Zitrin, *Five Who Got It Right*
13 Widener Law Journal 209 (2003)[25]

Horace Green, The Gentleman Lawyer

The pressures on lawyers to turn litigation into war remain great. When the lawyer is a litigation partner in a large nation-wide firm, those pressures are magnified. Many lawyers swear they will not engage in war games despite the adversarial culture they work in. But it's quite another thing to live up to this

---

[22] Rebecca Morrow, *Bottom Line Changes*, Legal Assistant Today (May-June 1995).

[23] https://cowengroup.com/documents/survey.2012.tcgms.pdf.

[24] Corporate Legal Times, June 1997, at 1.

[25] Copyright © 2003 by Richard Zitrin. Excerpted from *Five Who Got it Right*, 13 Wid. L.J. 209 (2003). Used Reprinted by permission of the author and the Widener Law Journal. All rights reserved.

promise. The reality is that lawyers who insist on always acting in a manner consistent with their personal beliefs can lose business and opportunities for promotion, even, as happened to Horace Green, their largest clients. It's an unfortunate truth about the legal profession that lawyers like these, who should be the rule, remain the rare exception.

Why did I become a lawyer? It sounds corny, but I used to watch Perry Mason. I thought that Perry Mason was cool because he didn't use his fists, he didn't use a gun, he didn't use a knife. He solved cases by the power of his intellect. That was much more impressive than taking up a gun.

My philosophy of being a lawyer is simple: My clients deserve my best. If I give them less, I'm cheating them. But I also believe that the advocacy system is set up to be fair to both sides. That only works if *I* am as fair and reasonable as I can be. I can't control how other people litigate. The only thing I can control is how *I* litigate. If I do something that is unfair and inconsistent with my values, then it's my fault that the system doesn't work. If I do what I should and somebody else doesn't, the system may not work, but not because of something I could change.

I consider myself a member of an honorable profession. I don't want to be a lawyer at the cost of losing who I am as a person. I'm a lawyer when I'm working, but I'm always Horace Green the person.

Some battles have to be fought; there are legitimate disputes. But I don't believe it helps the system to create disputes where none need exist. It makes cases more expensive for my client, and then I'm not serving my client's interests. I work for businesses, and businesses work on a fundamental principle: bring as much money in as you can and pay out as little as possible. I'm an expense to them. Being fair and reasonable with the other side won't conflict with my client's interests. It is *consistent* with those interests.

I know many lawyers disagree because they see litigation as a war of attrition. If you kill 10,000 of theirs and they kill 10,002 of yours, that's a good day for them because the numbers work out in their favor. But they are not keeping the big picture in mind. I won't fight over every piece of paper I give to the other side. If there's a document that should be turned over, ultimately you're going to have to do it. If you fight about it, you magnify its importance. You can't wish bad documents away, so you don't shred it, you don't hide it, you just deal with it.

Certain clients don't like this. They want their lawyers to use every trick in the book. One of my biggest clients fired me because they wanted me to do some things I wasn't comfortable with. I had discovered some documents at their plant that I felt had to be turned over to the other side. The client didn't agree. The documents weren't a "smoking gun," but they contradicted my client's position that their product had never behaved in this one particular way. Ultimately, we turned over the documents. I had trouble sleeping when I was working for this client, and for the first time in my life I had back problems. When they fired me, my billings took a nosedive and it took me about a year to recover. But all of a sudden my back problems went away and I was sleeping better. So whatever I lost in terms of hours, I gained more.

NOTES

Shortly after this article was written, Horace Green and a partner opened their own firm, where he continues to be dedicated to both his clients and to his principles. We have suggested along the way in this volume — and will examine more closely in Problem 30 — that one of the most important things law students can do for themselves is to choose a career that makes them happy. It sounds as if Horace Green has figured that out.

As you enter the practice of law and encounter the Clancy Garretts of your firm, how will you be affected if extensive, exhaustive, and contentious discovery appears to be one of the principal ways in which that firm makes money? Is it possible to determine whether the firm's clients approve of this? Most importantly, how will you behave during discovery wars?

D. SUPPLEMENTAL READINGS

1. Over a decade apart, here are two well-presented articles on discovery intimidation and game-playing. First, in *Rambo Depositions: Controlling an Ethical Cancer in Civil Litigation*, 25 HOFSTRA L. REV. 561 (1996), Jean M. Cary discusses the problem of attorneys who use rude, profane, and intimidating behavior, which she calls "Rambo tactics," to seize control of a deposition. Cary examines and then disputes the claim that these lawyers are simply zealously representing their clients and are behaving no differently than other attorneys. She highlights three court rulings finding this behavior unacceptable and resulting in various sanctions including case dismissal.

2. Second, in *Common Discovery Abuse Games: Who Said Lawyers Don't Like to Have Fun?*, 8 ABI COMMITTEE NEWS (American Bankruptcy Institute, June 2011), Emily C. Taube discusses discovery abuses caused by what she perceives as a process "subject to minimal judicial control." She believes that bad discovery abuse is once again increasing, but that today this may more commonly result, at least in bankruptcy court, in default judgments against the offenders.

3. Stuart Taylor, Jr., *Sleazy in Seattle*, AMERICAN LAWYER, April 1994, describes the Bogle & Gates/Fisons affair in detail and with considerable style. An excellent "read" about an amazing discovery story.

4. Bradley F. Wendell wrote *Rediscovering Discovery Ethics*, 79 MARQ. L. REV. 895 (1996), while an associate at Bogle & Gates. Wendell provided an interesting and often provocative analysis of discovery in an adversary system, sanctions as the means of policing abuses, and whether it is possible to infuse lawyers with sufficient morality so they can begin to "take their public responsibilities seriously."

5. Ellington, C. Ronald, *Discovery Abuse in the State of Georgia — Just How Bad Is It?*, POPULAR MEDIA, Paper 11 (2004), http://digitalcommons.law.uga.edu/cgi/viewcontent.cgi?article=1014&context=fac_pm&sei-redir=1&referer=http%3A%2F%2Fwww.bing.com%2Fsearch%3Fq%3DEllington%252C%2BC.%2BRonald%252C%2BDiscovery%2BAbuse%2Bin%2Bthe%2BState%2Bof%2BGeorgia%2B%25E2%2580%2594%2BJust%2BHow%2BBad%2BIs%2BIt%253F%252C%2BPOPULAR%2BMEDIA%252C%2BPaper%2B11%26src%3DIE-SearchBox%

26Form%3DIE8SRC#search=%22Ellington%2C%20C.%20Ronald%2C%
20Discovery%20Abuse%20State%20Georgia%20%E2%80%94%20Just%20How%
20Bad%20It%3F%2C%20POPULAR%20MEDIA%2C%20Paper%2011%22 is a
survey of abuses according to 4,500 surveyed Georgia lawyers. The top abuses
sound familiar: (1) boilerplate objections; (2) overly broad and burdensome requests
of marginal relevance; (3) failing to produce documents or redacting documents on
"relevance" grounds; (4) making "speaking objections" to coach deponents; (5)
delaying the production of critical documents (or producing in waves); (6) asserting
privileges without proper basis; and (7) parsing document requests so narrowly so
as to avoid production of documents that are fairly comprehended by a request.

6. In two interesting law review articles, Professor Linda S. Mullenix has
debunked what she considers the "myth" of discovery abuse, and the link between
our society's supposed litigiousness and such abuse. She suggests that the reforms
of the past decade were likely unnecessary. *Discovery in Disarray: The Pervasive
Myth of Pervasive Discovery Abuse and the Consequences for Unfounded Rule-
making*, 46 STAN. L. REV. 1393 (1994), and *The Pervasive Myth of Pervasive
Discovery Abuse: The Sequel*, 39 B.C. L. REV. 683 (1998).

7. In *Cincinnati Bar Ass'n v. Statzer*, 800 N.E.2d 1117 (Ohio 2003), a lawyer was
disciplined for intentionally misleading a witness in deposition by placing a series of
audio cassettes before the witness, each labeled to make it appear they contained
conversations between the witness and the lawyer. The tapes were all blank. The
lawyer contended the subterfuge was necessary to draw out truthful testimony, but
the court disagreed: When the lawyer resorts to "subterfuge that intimidates a
witness," the deception is no more likely to induce the truth than a lie based on the
threat.

8. *Haines v. Liggett Group, Inc.*, 140 F.R.D. 681 (D.N.J. 1992), *rev'd*, 975 F.2d 81
(3d Cir. 1992). The trial court opinion in *Haines* makes for fascinating reading. It is
the first such opinion that in effect accuses tobacco company lawyers of collusion by
intentionally assisting in hiding cigarette dangers and using the attorney-client
privilege to do so. Judge H. Lee Sarokin overruled his own magistrate in voiding all
privileges, finding that the hearings before a special master had disclosed numerous
instances of improper behavior by both the tobacco industry and its lawyers.
Despite what appears in hindsight to be a clear case for disclosure, Sarokin's order
was reversed by the Third Circuit Court of Appeals, and Sarokin was removed from
the case, tainted, said the appeals court, by his presiding over an earlier cigarette
case, *Cipollone v. Liggett*, 683 F. Supp. 1487, 1490–93 (D.N.J. 1988), which he had
referred to in his *Haines* opinion. However, Sarokin's detailed published opinion,
including some specifics of the information uncovered before the special master,
remained available to be used by others attacking the tobacco industry's discovery
shield.

9. *Chrysler Financial Services Americas LLC v. Hecker (In re Hecker)*, 53 BCD
76 (Bankr. D. Minn. 2010) involved an obfuscating debtor who frustrated discovery
(and the judge) to the point where the judge issued a $83 million default judgment
of non-dischargability.

10. Panel Discussion, *Sanctions in Electronic Discovery Cases: Views from the
Judges*, 78 FORDHAM L. REV. 1 (2009), is an excellent discussion of this increasingly

important issue among an illustrious group of judges, including Judge Scheindlin of *Zubulake* fame.

11. Gretchen Morgenson, *All That Missing E-Mail . . . It's Baaack*, N.Y. TIMES, May 8, 2005, describes how emails claimed to have been lost by Morgan Stanley as a result of September 11 terrorist attack resurfaced in a lawsuit against Morgan brought by wealthy financier Ronald Perelman. The re-discovery of the e-mails "may force Morgan Stanley to defend itself against countless investor cases it had previously won." Morgenson takes the view that Morgan did not make sufficient effort to locate the information in response to discovery requests.

12. Thomas Y. Allman, *Conducting E-Discovery after the Amendments: The Second Wave*, 10 SEDONA CONF. J. 215 (2009) is a look at the "second wave" of case law after the 2006 amendments on e-discovery, including an evaluation of the significance of the *Qualcomm* case and the extent to which documents need to be preserved.

13. William P. Barnette, *Ghost in the Machine: Zubulake Revisited and Other Emerging E-Discovery Issues under the Amended Federal Rules*, 18 RICHMOND J.L. & TECH. 11 (2012). This extensive article by in-house litigation counsel for a large company (Home Depot) is a thorough review of the *Zubulake* series of cases, the 2006 amendments to Rule 26 on electronic discovery, and subsequent federal case law. Barnette concludes that the Rule 26 amendments have made e-discovery more expensive and broader rules on spoliation claims have resulted in requiring all parties to preserve all e-documents and discourage cooperation between the sides of a dispute.

PROBLEM 19: THE FINE LINE BETWEEN
POSTURING AND LYING IN NEGOTIATION

A. INTRODUCTION

Whether they do transactional work or litigation, or handle civil, criminal, or administrative matters, most lawyers find that they negotiate as a daily part of their professional lives. Negotiation by its very definition involves providing something less than "the truth, the whole truth, and nothing but the truth." But is there a difference between a direct misstatement and one that is less direct but ultimately no less misleading? When does a misrepresentation become a lie, and when is it merely a legitimate negotiation tactic — "puffing," or "playing poker"? And is there ever a time when an attorney is obligated to either volunteer information or share with the other side the hidden weaknesses of his or her position? Read how negotiator Ross Davids deals with these issues, and, after reading a selection of other viewpoints decide where you stand.

B. PROBLEM

I

Ross Davids is a lawyer with a statewide reputation for artful negotiating. In a recent seminar he gave on negotiation, Ross described a few of his methods.

> I want to protect my client. One of the simplest ways is by answering a question with another question. When opposing counsel in a small business purchase asked how solvent my client was, I just replied, 'Do you really think he'd be doing this deal if he wasn't?' Later, when my client's finances came up again, I pretended to get angry, and objected to all those 'personal' questions. In actuality, my client's balance sheet was not as clean as we'd like it, but it was a pretty small deal, and the other lawyer never did check it out.

> I never want to lie, but stretching the truth is not lying. Let me tell you what I mean. We just did a mediation in a construction defect case. I told them that we had architectural, framing and soils experts all lined up. Actually, we'd put the architect to work already, and I'd talked to the soils expert, but I didn't want to be wasting thousands on him or a framer if the mediation was successful. So I just took what the architect and I *thought* they'd say, and told the mediator 'that's what we're gonna prove at trial.' I figure it's no harm, no foul, since we almost definitely would get that testimony anyway.

> In that same case, we told them we had a corroborating witness who heard our client twice ask the general contractor about earth movement and get told that it was 'no problem.' Actually, we do have the name of this person, but we've had some problems tracking her down. We believe she's a Mexican citizen who's back in Mexico. But sometimes, your strongest case

519

is the one you can present at a mediation or settlement conference, since that's the time you can 'tell a little white lie,' or 'play poker' and run a bluff. After all, that contractor knows exactly what he said to our client.

I always want to use my client as a shield to deflect committing to a deal when I may be able to get a better one. Sometimes, when I have my client's authority to settle, I'll pretend to conspire with the other lawyer. I'll say something like, 'Tell you what, if you and I can agree that X dollars is fair, I'll sell it to my client if you do the same with yours.' That gets me off the hook of being the one to blink. At other times, I'll say I really can't move forward without getting my partner — a real 'tough guy'— to agree, even if I'm running the show.

Or say an insurance company client evaluates a case at $50,000. That doesn't mean I can't say to a weak opponent that the company won't pay more than twenty. In negotiating a deal, it's the same idea. Say my client gives me authority to purchase at $500,000. Of course, I'll try to close the deal for a lot less. If opposing counsel is foolish enough to come down to five hundred right away, I'll say something like, 'I'll tell my client, but frankly, no way will she go for anything that high.' I know my client would pay the five hundred, but why shouldn't I find out how good a deal I can get? After all, if they're already down to 500, isn't it true that my client will *no longer* pay that much in order to get the best deal she can? I mean, that's why she hired me, right?

Evaluate each of Ross Davids' tactics.

II

Take two of the examples in the negotiation ethics roundtable article in Section 3, below, and evaluate how you would behave, and why.

III

Assume a deputy district attorney is going to trial with an eyewitness who is a drug addict and has several "failures to appear" on his record, that is, failing to make a scheduled court appearance. Must the DA share this information with the defense during a plea negotiation session in the DA's office? What if the plea-bargaining takes place in chambers in the presence of the judge? What if the deputy DA knows that the witness "temporarily" cannot be found?

C. READINGS

1. Squaring Negotiation with Candor

It all seems so simple: ABA Model Rule 4.1, titled "Truthfulness in Statements to Others," says that a lawyer may not "make a false statement of material fact" to a third party. And yet, even the strongest proponents of full and candid disclosure acknowledge that negotiation, by its very nature, involves misleading the opponent, concealing one's true position, and — to use the poker parlance often adopted to describe the process — running a bluff. In short, negotiation is not, and will never be, a matter of "putting all our cards on the table."

Indeed, paragraph 2 of the Comment to Rule 4.1 acknowledges that "puffing" in negotiation is a fact of life: "Whether a particular statement should be regarded as one of fact can depend on the circumstances. Under generally accepted conventions in negotiation, certain types of statements ordinarily are not taken as statements of material fact [such as] estimates of price or value . . . and a party's intentions as to an acceptable settlement of a claim . . . ."

The requirement of being truthful to the tribunal is a long-established ethical precept. But lawyers — litigators and transactional attorneys alike — inevitably have difficulty squaring principles of fairness and candor with the give and take of negotiation. Perhaps it is not surprising that negotiation is governed by relatively vague and equivocal rules of professional conduct, since it generally occurs behind closed doors, under conditions that would make it difficult in any event to enforce a bright line disciplinary standard. Thus, in discussing negotiation ethics, we will also revisit an increasingly familiar issue — whether conduct that may be technically "ethical," in the sense that one can "get away with it," is nevertheless "wrong," in the sense that one should not do it.

Iowa law professor Gerald B. Wetlaufer is a proponent of this last view.[1] He submits that lawyers should own up to the fact that they lie, and do so under his broad definition: any effort "to create in some audience a belief at variance with one's own." Citing the Random House Dictionary, which goes beyond direct falsehoods to define "lie" as "something intended or serving to convey a false impression," Wetlaufer argues that concealments and omissions are also lies. He catalogues the ways in which lawyers lie — and fool themselves into believing either that they don't, or that the lies don't "count." Many sound familiar. We summarize:

- *"I didn't lie,* which includes "My statement was literally true" (though misleading), "I was speaking on a subject about which there is no Truth," and "I was merely putting matters in the best light."

- *"I lied, if you insist on calling it that, but it was . . .":* "ethically permissible" (and thus OK); "legal" (and thus OK); "just an omission"; or ineffectual, because it was just a white lie, or was simply not believed.

- *"I lied but it was justified by the very nature of things."* This includes situations where lying is considered part of the rules of the game, such as negotiations, where most lawyers feel that candor defeats the very purpose of the exercise.

- *"I lied but it was justified by the special ethics of lawyering,"* especially the duties owed clients: loyalty, confidentiality, and, of course, so-called "zealous" representation.

- *"The lie belongs to someone else,"* usually the client, so that the lawyer is "just the messenger."

- *"I lied because my opponent acted badly."* This includes "self-defense," or

---

[1] Gerald B. Wetlaufer, *The Ethics of Lying in Negotiations,* 75 Iowa L. Rev. 1219 (1990).

"having to lie" before the opponent does, and lying to teach the opponent a lesson, or because bad behavior means the opponent has forfeited any right to candor.

- *"I lied but it was justified by good consequences,"* that is, ends justifying means, justice triumphed.[2]

As we examine lying vs. negotiating and misleading vs. posturing, consider Wetlaufer's perspective. Whether one agrees with his conclusions, it's hard not to agree that these phrases ring true. Does he ask too much of lawyers to avoid these excuses?

2. Candor, the "Prisoner's Dilemma," and Judge Rubin's Views

Although there are various versions of what has been described as the "prisoner's dilemma," the basic scenario is the same: Two defendants are accused of committing a serious crime. The prosecutor, looking to strengthen the state's case, promises each prisoner that informing on the co-defendant will result in probation for the informant, while the other defendant will receive a very heavy sentence, perhaps life. Each prisoner, thinking alone, will be tempted to inform. But they can cooperate with each other if they choose to. They know that if they *both* inform, the prosecutor's case is made and both will be sentenced heavily to, say, 20 years, while if *neither* informs, the prosecutor's case will remain weak and they will be convicted of lesser crimes and serve only a year or two. For any individual, the best obtainable result is immediate freedom, but this result requires betrayal by one, and trust by the other. The best result for the prisoners in the long run would be to cooperate with each other. But this cooperation requires trust, and therein lies the dilemma. Can either trust the other to follow through and not inform, knowing that the other could inform and gain freedom?[3]

There are many similarities between the prisoners' dilemma and litigation. Litigation, played out to its conclusion through trial — and then appeals — will result in a loser, a "winner," and the enormous expenditure of resources, both in money and the time and labor of lawyers (who are often the *only* ones who win in extensive litigation). When one party believes it can win while the other side will lose, it will either not negotiate, or negotiate in bad faith. However, if both sides trust each other to cooperate, including the candid revelation of the strengths, and especially the weaknesses, of their positions, they may engage in a successful negotiation.

---

[2] We have adopted this summary from ZITRIN & LANGFORD, THE MORAL COMPASS OF THE AMERICAN LAWYER 163-64 (1999).

[3] Game theorists have written extensively about the prisoners' dilemma. (We've moved the apostrophe for grammatical reasons.) See for an early example, ROBERT D. LUCE & HOWARD RAIFFA, GAMES AND DECISIONS, 94-102 (1957). There are literally hundreds of Internet sites focused on studying this dilemma. Or watch a DVD of the very first season of the television show *Survivor*, in which alliances and trust played a central theme in Richard Hatch's winning strategy. Countless reality-show participants have faced the prisoners' dilemma since.

Judge Alvin Rubin would certainly agree with this last sentence. Numerous commentators have written about the ethics of negotiation. Perhaps the first significant modern commentary is that of Judge Rubin, then a federal district judge in Louisiana, and later a member of the court of appeals for the Fifth Circuit. Concerned about the lack of guidance provided by the ABA Code, then the prevailing standard, Judge Rubin raised many questions about how lawyers should negotiate, and developed two principles for lawyers to live by. His thoughts, excerpted here, stimulated a great deal of critical thinking on the subject.

Alvin B. Rubin, *A Causerie on Lawyers' Ethics in Negotiation*
35 LOUISIANA LAW REVIEW 577 (1975)[4]

[T]here are few lawyers who do not negotiate regularly, indeed daily, in their practice. . . . There are a few rules designed to apply to other relationships that touch peripherally the area we are discussing. A lawyer shall not:

- knowingly make a false statement of law or fact.

- participate in the creation or preservation of [false] evidence. . . .

- counsel or assist his client in conduct that [is] illegal or fraudulent, or

- knowingly engage in *other illegal conduct.*

. . . .

But nowhere is it ordained that the lawyer owes any general duty of candor or fairness to members of the bar or to laymen with whom he may deal. . . .

Is the lawyer-negotiator entitled, like Metternich, to depend on "cunning, precise calculation, and a willingness to employ whatever means justify the end of policy" Few are so bold as to say so. Yet some whose personal integrity and reputation are scrupulous have instructed students in negotiating tactics that appear tacitly to countenance that kind of conduct. In fairness it must be added that they say they do not "endorse the *propriety*" of this kind of conduct and indeed even indicate "grave reservations" about such behavior; however, this sort of generalized disclaimer of sponsorship hardly appears forceful enough.

. . . .

The professional literature contains many instances indicating that, in the general opinion of the bar, there is no requirement that the lawyer disclose unfavorable evidence in the usual litigious situation . . . . [T]ales [abound] of how the other side failed to ask the one key question that would have revealed the truth and changed the result, or how one side cleverly avoided producing the critical document or the key witness whom the adversary had not discovered . . . . Judge Marvin Frankel, an experienced and perceptive observer of the profession, comments, ". . . advocates freely employ time-honored tricks and stratagems to block or distort the truth."

. . . .

---

[4] Copyright © 1975 by Louisiana Law Review. Reprinted by permission.

[In negotiation,] counsel for a plaintiff appears quite comfortable in stating, when representing a plaintiff, "My client won't take a penny less than $25,000," when in fact he knows that the client will happily settle for less; counsel for the defendant appears to have no qualms in representing that he has no authority to settle, or that a given figure exceeds his authority, when these are untrue statements. . . . [E]stimable members of the bar support the thesis that a lawyer may not misrepresent a fact in controversy but may misrepresent matters that pertain to his authority or negotiating strategy because this is expected by the adversary.

To most practitioners, negotiations are merely, as the social scientists have viewed it, a form of game; observance of the expected rules, not professional ethics, is the guiding precept. But gamesmanship is not ethics.

. . . .

[First,] *The lawyer must act honestly and in good faith.* Another lawyer, or a layman, who deals with a lawyer should not need to exercise the same degree of caution that he would if trading for reputedly antique copper jugs in an oriental bazaar. . . . Good conduct exacts more than mere convenience.

. . . .

While some difficulty in line-drawing is inevitable when such a distinction is sought to be made, there must be a point at which the lawyer cannot ethically accept an arrangement that is completely unfair to the other side, be that opponent a patsy or a tax collector. So I posit a second precept: *The lawyer may not accept a result that is unconscionably unfair to the other party.*

. . . .

The unconscionable result in these circumstances is in part created by the relative power, knowledge and skill of the principals and their negotiators. . . . The imposition of a duty to tell the truth and to bargain in good faith would reduce their relative inequality, and tend to produce negotiation results that are within relatively tolerable bounds.

[P]art of the test must be in result alone: . . . [T]here certainly comes a time when a deal is too good to be true, where what has been accomplished passes the line of simply-a-good-deal and becomes a cheat. . . . This duty of fairness is one owed to the profession and to society; it must supersede any duty owed to the client.

. . . Surely if its practitioners are principled, a profession that dominates the legal process in our law-oriented society would not expect too much if it required its members to adhere to two simple principles when they negotiate as professionals: Negotiate honestly and in good faith; and do not take unfair advantage of another — regardless of his relative expertise or sophistication. This is inherent in the oath the ABA recommends be taken by all who are admitted to the bar: "I will employ for the purpose of maintaining the causes confided to me such means only as are consistent with truth and honor."

NOTES

Was Judge Rubin's view that of a bench-bound Pollyanna, or a realistic visionary? Whatever view you might have, his reasoning, and some of his aphorisms — "gamesmanship is not ethics"; "good conduct exacts more than mere convenience" — struck a chord with attorneys, law professors, and his colleagues on the bench, who cited his article in several opinions. There is no question that the increased scrutiny of the lawyer as negotiator, and the existence of Model Rule 4.1, owe more than a little to Rubin's strong and articulate stand.

3. A Roundtable on Negotiation Ethics

In the years since Rubin framed the issue, commentators have continued to be interested in the ethics of negotiation, perhaps because of the anomaly of how to tell the truth in a process that inherently involves deception, perhaps because there is so little clear authority that governs a lawyer's conduct. In 1988, one writer gathered many major academic commentators, seasoned the mix with a number of practicing attorneys, sprinkled in a couple of judicial officers, including Judge Rubin, and surveyed the 15-member group on four hypothetical negotiation problems that today, a quarter century later, continue to have resonance. The results show a wide variety of opinions even among those who have devoted much thought to the issue.

Larry Lempert, *In Settlement Talks, Does Telling the Truth Have Its Limits?*
INSIDE LITIGATION (March 1988)[5]

Law professor Charles Craver, who teaches courses and workshops on legal negotiation and settlement, likes to begin by saying, "I've never been involved in legal negotiations where both sides didn't lie." It tends to get some "shocked responses," he admits.

Craver, a former litigator and labor law practitioner, does not stop there. He goes on to defend some lies in the course of settlement talks as perfectly proper.

To U.S. Magistrate Wayne Brazil, on the other hand, lying is anathema, and nothing about the settlement setting excuses it. "My opinion is, no lying," he says, adding, somewhat wryly, "Strike one blow for naivete."

Whether naive or not, Brazil does seem to be in a minority. Not all lawyers are as unapologetic as Craver, but interviews with experts who have focused on negotiation and ethics, plus several litigators and judicial officers, indicate that most believe lying in settlement talks is not always prohibited (and that volunteering the truth is not always required).

In the 15 interviews, *Inside Litigation* asked what a lawyer ought to do in each of four hypothetical settlement situations. The hypotheticals were elaborations on suggestions made by Craver, who teaches at George Washington University's National Law Center.

---

[5] Copyright © 1988. Reprinted by permission of the author.

Participants included nine law professors who have written on ethics, negotiation, or both; five experienced litigators; a federal circuit court judge; and a U.S. magistrate. . . . Most specified what they believed prevailing ethics rules would allow. A few answered in terms of what they would do but did not venture opinions on the formal ethics rules. In several instances, some noted that ethics rules might permit lying but that, personally, they would not do it. The lawyers also volunteered suggestions on tactics.

. . . .

[Model Rule 4.1 implies] the lawyer would not be lying because according to well-established custom, he or she would be speaking in a context where puffing is part of the game. Of course, says Craver, "It's easy to characterize your own statement as puffing, and the other's as mendacity."

SITUATION NO. 1: LYING ABOUT AUTHORIZED LIMITS

Your clients, the defendants, have told you that you are authorized to pay $750,000 to settle the case. In settlement negotiations, after your offer of $650,000, the plaintiffs' attorney asks, "Are you authorized to settle for $750,000?" Can you say, "No, I'm not"?

(Two of the litigators well-known for representing plaintiffs were asked essentially the same question with the roles reversed . . . .)

Of those willing to give a straight yes or no answer, six say no, you cannot say that. Seven say yes, you can - but all but one of these add that as a matter either of personal ethics or strategy, they would not give such an answer.

"Outright lying always is out of bounds," according to David Luban of the University of Maryland. It's not that one can never be misleading in the admittedly adversarial game of negotiation, he explains. But the way the process works, when one side makes an evasive statement, the other side can ask a question to clarify that position. A flat, declarative statement sends no signal that clarification is needed. "People have to be able to rely on flat-out declarations," Luban says, or the process breaks down or, at best, becomes "incredibly time-consuming."

Geoffrey Hazard Jr., the author of the ABA Model Rules, agrees that "you're allowed to make an evasive statement." He too says that an outright lie in Situation No. 1 would violate Rule 4.1.

STATEMENTS OF MATERIAL FACT?

Litigator Jacob Stein, however, argues that this is one of those statements, referred to in the comment to Rule 4.1, that "ordinarily are not taken as statements of material fact." If the opponent says he or she is not authorized to pay more, "I don't rely on that," says Stein. "In the realm of negotiation, the issue is whether there's reliance."

Several participants contend that the ethics rules would permit the lie but their personal standards would not. Stein is in this camp. So is James White of the University of Michigan: "A flat denial of that sort" — although permissible —

"makes me uncomfortable. It's questionable morally," White says.

Craver, on the other hand, not only believes that lying is permissible in Situation No. 1 but says "I don't have any hesitancy in lying about my authorized limits"; he has done it before and would do it again, he says. Lying is an acceptable response to the inquiry, in his view, because "the other side has no right to that information."

Avoiding the Problem

Most of those interviewed point out that a negotiator who is asked about authorized settlement limits can dodge the question or deflect it in a variety of ways. "The way to avoid [the problem] is to think ahead and have answers ready," says White. He recalls, for example, negotiators who would simply laugh and say, "You don't think I'm going to tell you answers to questions like that."

. . . .

A no-lying rule, Craver complains, means that the negotiator would always have to swear off the "limited authority" technique — a Mutt and Jeff kind of approach that casts the negotiator as a nice guy whose flexibility is limited by a tough-minded client. The negotiator could never say, "I'm sorry, I'm just not authorized . . . ," even when the statement is true, because he or she would be forced to tell the truth — and cut off a possible better deal for the client — when the opponent probes further and hits on the actual authorized figure. Yet, "limited authority" is a "very, very common technique," Craver says. And saying, "No, I'm not authorized," he notes, is much more forceful than saying, "You know you can't ask me that."

Some experienced practitioners, however, eschew that technique anyway. For one thing, they say, it would imply a lack of influence with the client that the opponent would not find credible. Says plaintiffs' lawyer Leonard Ring, "I don't use the word authorize. . . . I have a lot of persuasion with my client."

Situation No. 2: Lying About an Injury

You represent a plaintiff who claims to have suffered a serious knee injury. In settlement negotiations, can you say your client is "disabled" when you know she is out skiing?

The score: no, 14; yes, one. This question was the only one of the four that yielded a solid consensus. Actually all 15 participants agree that a negotiator cannot lie about the client's injury — he or she cannot say a leg has been broken when an X-ray shows the contrary. The only disagreement is over the possible interpretation of "disabled." (Told that this one question produces a nearly unanimous response, Hazard chuckles. "Thank heaven for small blessings," he says.)

The principle, adhered to by all, is that negotiators cannot misrepresent specific, verifiable facts. Not only is it wrong, but many of the lawyers add that it is, to use Ring's characterization, "dumb."

. . . .

SITUATION NO. 3: EXAGGERATING AN INJURY

You are trying to negotiate a settlement on behalf of a couple who charge that the bank pulled their loan, ruining their business. Your clients are quite upbeat and deny suffering particularly severe emotional distress. Can you tell your opponent, nonetheless, that they did?

The score: no, eight; yes, five (with two not answering directly).

. . . .

[S]everal lawyers who find the assertion of disability in No. 2 to be unethical do not object to the assertion of emotional distress in No. 3. Obviously, some distress has occurred — "if they didn't care at all, there wouldn't be a legal matter," says Craver. "I'm embellishing the concern." White agrees that exaggeration of the degree of pain experienced by a client is "well within the range of puffing . . . ."

Explaining further, White draws an analogy to sales law[:], "It's like two car dealers negotiating the sale and purchase of a car." (Independently, [Professor Ronald] Rotunda arrives at a similar analogy but draws a different conclusion. Contending that the exaggeration in Situation No. 3 is improper, Rotunda observes, "If lawyers want to be like used car salesmen, this is a good place to start.")

. . . .

Several who say the lawyer in No. 3 cannot make an outright assertion about emotional distress do acknowledge that the issue can be raised in a more oblique way. Hazard, for example, would let the negotiator say that cutting off a loan is the kind of act that can produce serious distress. . . . Or you can ask a rhetorical question, says Luban: "Wouldn't *you* feel as though the world has caved in on you?"

. . . .

SITUATION NO. 4: A MISTAKEN IMPRESSION

In settlement talks over the couple's lender liability case, your opponent's comments make it clear that he thinks the plaintiffs have gone out of business, although you didn't say that. In fact, the business is continuing, and several important contracts are in the offing. You are on the verge of settlement; can you go ahead and settle without correcting your opponent's misimpression?

The score: no, four; yes, nine (with two not answering directly).

The participants agree that you cannot say anything to further or ratify the misimpression. But beyond that point, disagreement sets in.

Hazard says no on the ground that the ethics rules incorporate the law of fraud — "and the law of fraud," adds Hazard, "is more exacting than most lawyers think." The opponent's belief that the client is out of business is "a manifest misapprehension that goes to the bargain itself," Hazard says. . . .

Interestingly, Craver, outspoken in his support for lying in Situation No. 1, finds No. 4 so difficult a situation that he cannot give a definite answer. If he thought that correcting the misimpression would not hurt the client, he says, he would do it. But if it looked like the settlement would fall apart on that issue alone, he's not so sure. By contrast, Luban — who flatly says no to the outright lie in No. 1 — generally approves keeping quiet in No. 4.

The difference for Luban lies in his rule that flat-out declarations have to be true — No. 4, obviously, involves no such declaration. "It's not my job to do their job for them," Luban says of the opponent in No. 4, "as long as my word isn't on the line."

. . . .

Luban cites a Minnesota Supreme Court case from 1962 to show what he means about consequences. In *Spaulding v. Zimmerman* (116 N.W.2d 704)[6] a car crash had led to a personal injury suit. The defense doctor examined the plaintiff and discovered a potentially fatal medical problem that neither the plaintiff, the plaintiff's lawyer, nor the plaintiff's doctor knew about. The defense doctor revealed his finding to the defendant's lawyer, who settled the case without mentioning that the plaintif' could drop dead any second (presumably, that fact would have affected the settlement value adversely from the defense point of view). The defendant's lawyer was not responsible for the plaintiff's misimpression about the value of the case. "But it's perfectly clear that any lawyer with a grain of conscience would tell the plaintiff he had to see a doctor. You don't let somebody drop dead to save your client some money," Luban says.

. . . .

In *Spaulding v. Zimmerman*, the Minnesota court did not say the defendant's lawyer had acted unethically, but it did void the settlement, as the plaintiff had asked it to do. As a practical matter, that points to a problem with keeping quiet in Situation No. 4, as several interviewees emphasize — if an attack on the settlement ensues once the opponent learns the facts, your client might not have the peace he thought he was buying. "That's one practical reason for taking the ethical high road," says Brazil.

But Stein, who says that correction of the misimpression is not required, believes that a well-crafted release would probably foreclose an attack on the settlement.

Not surprisingly, given the range of reactions to the hypotheticals, experts approach the issue of truth in the settlement process from a variety of perspectives.

"I don't see why the law should allow attorneys to tell a bald-faced lie," says Rotunda. As he sees it, the comments to Rule 4.1, which forgive certain lies because of "generally accepted conventions in negotiation," are an attempt to "slice the baloney [too] thin."

. . . .

At the same time, countervailing forces exist — and not just moral or religious ones — in favor of candor. One such force is reputation. Legal practice would be cumbersome indeed if other lawyers were never willing to take you at your word, Craver notes. "There has to be a level of candor if one is going to practice law," he says. Moreover, he observes, candor can be a good tactic. In this regard, he says a

---

[6] We looked at this case through the eyes of Professor Fred Zacharias in Problem 4.

possible approach to Situation No. 4 would be to correct the misimpression and build on the boost in credibility with the opponent that such a step would bring.

[Michigan attorney Thomas] McNamara has another reason to tell the truth — he knows he would not be a good liar. "I can't be my most convincing when I'm lying," he says.

NOTES

How do these different views square with your own? How did you feel about Professor White's equating negotiations between lawyers with negotiations between car salesmen? Is this an apt analogy, or do you agree with Professor Rotunda that this is exactly the comparison lawyers should attempt to avoid? And what about responses like rhetorical questions, or saying "you know I can't answer that"? Are these likely to be seen by opposing counsel as weak responses indicative of a weak case?

4.   The Corporate Lawyer's Perspective

Although the preceding article appeared in a litigation periodical, the negotiation principles discussed there are equally applicable to corporate transactional settings such as the purchase and sale of a business discussed in the next article by Stuart Fleishmann. In the second article, New York practitioner Barry Temkin looks at litigating for corporate clients, where the ability to pay is often an issue. Both examine the usual issues — lying and misleading — along with the lawyer's obligation, if any, to correct the other side's false impressions.

Fleischmann does an excellent job summarizing typical corporate transactional dilemmas. His hypotheticals often emphasize the conditions of the deal points rather than "just" the money. Then, Temkin argues that there should be a "safe harbor" for lawyers who *omit* telling the truth.

Stuart K. Fleischmann, *Contract Negotiating: How Much Truthfulness is Required*
The PROFESSIONAL LAWYER 123 (1999 ABA Symposium)[7]

The point of this outline is to raise consciousness about the limits on corporate lawyering or negotiating . . . . The "art" of negotiating is what some call it. The practice of lying — or tolerating inadequate disclosures or omissions — is what others call it.

. . . The lawyer is under several distinct duties to Client, including the duty of loyalty, the duty of confidentiality, the duty of obedience and the duty to exercise sufficient skill and care to best attempt to achieve Client's objectives. Obviously, Lawyer is not permitted to engage in illegal conduct in attempting to achieve Client's objectives. . . . Ethical considerations also affect the limits of negotiations. . . .

---

[7] Copyright ©1999. Reprinted by permission of the author.

Reading and taking to heart the Model Rule prohibitions, one would assume that it is *never* permissible to lie or condone outright lying in negotiations. Yet, as the literature and case law make clear, it all depends on what you mean by "lying."

Some Difficult Situations

It probably goes without saying that most lawyers would not knowingly tolerate fraud on the part of their clients and would seek to resign from the relationship if the client insists on perpetrating a fraud. This is the easy case. But there are a number of circumstances that arise in virtually all contract negotiations that raise questions about a client's behavior and the lawyer's response thereto that are much harder to deal with. Consider the following:

• *The Risk Allocation Situation* — Many Clients believe that since representations and warranties are in essence a risk sharing mechanism, truthfulness isn't necessarily required. Assume that Other Side requests a representation or warranty on a specific situation (*i.e.*, the non-existence of ERISA or environmental liabilities). Client is not aware of any problems, but feels it will be too expensive and one never knows what an internal investigation could uncover. Client decides instead to make a "flat" representation that no liabilities exist and to give an indemnity to Other Side for breach of this warranty. Other Side agrees to go ahead based on the flat representation. . . . Since Other Side thinks the indemnity is "belt and suspender" protection, it does not concern itself with whether the Client will financially be able to honor its indemnity or whether the possible existence of liabilities alone would cause it to cancel the deal. In this circumstance, is it acceptable for Lawyer to allow Client to give a false representation and agree to bear the consequences without so informing Other Side and letting Other Side decide if it is willing to bear the risk?

• *The Promissory Fraud Situation* — Clients are typically asked to agree to undertake certain activities in contracts and agreements (reporting obligations, information sharing, covenants not to compete, financial tests, etc.). . . . What does the Lawyer do if the Client tells you that it so badly needs the funds now that it doesn't care whether it can honor the covenants, preferring instead to renegotiate the covenants later on once its problems become known?

• *The "No Meeting of Minds" Situation* — Sometimes in legal and business negotiations there is a disconnect between what parties believe to be the "business understanding" and the particular legal language used in the final agreement to represent this "understanding." For example, some Clients may agree to make certain payments, yet it is often unclear whether the payments are to be made on a "before" or "after" tax basis. If the two sides actually discuss a provision that Lawyer has drafted and Lawyer feels Other Side is confused, does Lawyer have a duty to correct the misunderstanding? If Lawyer knows or believes that the provision is susceptible to different interpretation by Other Side, does Lawyer have a duty to raise the matter in a specific discussion and correct the possible misunderstanding? Is there any difference if . . . the Other Side (or its counsel) drafted the provision?

• *The Greater Expertise Situation* — If Lawyer believes that an independent accountant or other non-legal professional has made a mistake that will be relied on by Other Side, is Lawyer under any duty to raise the issue for Other Side? Can Lawyer and Client assume that Other Side is "on its own"? Does any of this change if, instead of accountants, Lawyer believes that the Other Side or its counsel is inexperienced or worse?

• *The Materiality Situation* — Any transaction will have its "material" points that both sides would agree go to the heart of the business arrangement or rationale for entering into a transaction. Just as obviously, there are innumerable details that, while interesting, are relatively unimportant to either side. . . . [I]s it up to the Lawyer to decide whether something is material and, if not, must a Lawyer correct all misstatements or omissions? Is there a duty to correct Other Side's misunderstanding?

• *The False Demands Situation* — In many negotiations, a Lawyer or Client may put forth a series of demands several of which may in fact be irrelevant to the Client and which, in fact, are nothing more than "bargaining chips." They are included nonetheless to give the impression that Client has a number of important points that must be addressed. In fact the real purpose is to afford the Client points that can be bargained away in hopes of getting the Client the deal it really wants. Is putting forth so-called "false demands" and claiming their importance under these circumstances appropriate behavior?

• *The Duty of Confidentiality Situation* — In all negotiations, there are issues that are sensitive to Client and may not be able to be disclosed due to confidentiality concerns and, therefore, an issue arises as to whether truthfulness is always required. For example, in attempting to settle a case or agree to a payment amount, Other Side may inquire about Client's ability to take an action or the amount of its insurance coverage. . . . In such cases, being truthful and responding fully to an inquiry or volunteering information could breach the Lawyer's duty of confidentiality and disclosure could be adverse to Client. Is Lawyer free to disclose information in these circumstances?

• *Lying vs. Misleading Situation* — In negotiations, there is often a distinction between lying and providing misleading information. It would seem to be inappropriate for Lawyer to say "I don't know" to a request for specific information when he in fact does have the information. But what about the Lawyer who responds (in a misleading way?) to a question about whether the Client has a long-term supply contract by saying "yes" when he knows the contract party has recently indicated an intention not to renew the arrangement at the end of the contract period?

Conclusions

It has been said that when one deals with the Lawyer in a contract negotiation, the Other Side should not have to approach the situation as if it were bargaining for copper pots in a sidewalk bazaar. The involvement of Lawyer in the process, a trained and licensed professional, is meant [to] and should convey that the negotiations are tempered by a code of reasonable conduct. In the absence of a judge, arbitrator or other independent party to monitor behavior, it must be up to lawyers individually and the profession itself to encourage full and fair dealing in corporate negotiations.

Barry R. Temkin, *Misrepresentation by Omission in Settlement Negotiations: Should There be a Silent Safe Harbor?*
18 GEORGETOWN JOURNAL OF LEGAL ETHICS 179 (2004)[8]

The commentary to Model Rule 4.1, as noted above, provides that a lawyer "generally has no affirmative duty to inform an opposing party of relevant facts." Yet the same comment also states that an impermissible misrepresentation "can also occur by partially true but misleading statements or omissions that are the equivalent of affirmative false statements."

Under the silent safe harbor proposal, as under comment 1 to Model Rule 4.1, a lawyer who does not introduce into settlement negotiations the topic of a client's ability to pay a judgment is under no obligation to disclose information that would be advantageous to the adversary, such as the existence of an insurance policy, assuming that there is no requirement of substantive or procedural law for that disclosure. However, once the lawyer departs from the safe harbor and elects to speak, what is said should not consciously and materially mislead. A lawyer who affirmatively introduces the concept of a client's ability to pay a judgment [or] who pleads poverty in settlement negotiations in order to place on the table the client's ability to pay a judgment should disclose the existence of the insurance policy.

The following hypotheticals illustrate possible scenarios in which the defendant's ability to satisfy a judgment comes into play:

Hypothetical 1: Defense counsel states "My client is going out of business." Defense counsel does not disclose the existence of a substantial liability policy which is available and sufficient to pay any resulting judgment.

The permissibility of this statement in settlement negotiations may depend on its context, whether elicited by the claimant or volunteered by the defense, and whether adduced to create the impression of the collectibility of a future judgment. For example, the following variations on this hypothetical illustrate a continuum of misdirection, ranging from simple avoidance to outright deception.

Hypothetical 1A:

Claimant's attorney: "Tell me a little about your client."

Defense counsel: "I don't want to talk about my client. Let's talk about how you think you are going to prove your case without a credible witness."

Hypothetical 1B:

Claimant's attorney: "Tell me a little about your client."

Defense counsel: "Well it's going out of business."

Hypothetical 1C:

Defense counsel: "I am offering you ten cents on the dollar. Take it or leave it, because my client is going out of business."

Hypothetical 1D:

Claimant's attorney: "I am a little concerned about whether a judgment would be collectible against your client."

Defense counsel: "My client is going out of business."

Hypothetical 1E:

Defense counsel: "I am offering you ten cents on the dollar on this case. You'd better take it because my client is going out of business and you will not be able to collect on your judgment."

In each of the five hypothetical examples, defense counsel omits the existence of insurance coverage, and in the last four, counsel tells the claimant that the defendant corporation is going out of business. On one end of the spectrum of responses, Hypothetical 1A is beyond reproach . . . . The defense attorney in that example remains in the safe harbor. Hypothetical 1B is ethically acceptable, as it is not clear from the context that defense counsel is attempting to create a false impression that the firm is without assets with which to pay a judgment. The plaintiff's attorney asked an open-ended question asking for general background information, and the defense attorney replied in kind. On the other end, Hypothetical 1E is manifestly false under the terms of the hypothetical, which postulate the availability of insurance coverage, and should subject the attorney to discipline for falsely stating that a judgment would be uncollectible.

Hypotheticals 1C and 1D are more interesting, as the attorney is implying without expressly stating that a judgment would be uncollectible, thereby creating a false impression without deliberately misstating the facts. In Hypothetical 1C, the defense attorney suggests that the offer may not be available in the future due to the defendant's plan to go out of business. Here, the question of collectibility is not explicit, as in the following two hypotheticals. The defense attorney, in this example, may argue that there are other issues at play beyond the collectiblity of a judgment. For example, the offer of ten cents on the dollar may have the advantage of timely payment, whereas a delay by the plaintiff may render a subsequent settlement subject to the whims of a bankruptcy trustee or insurance adjuster. The representation that a corporation is going out of business is not necessarily tantamount to the statement that it has no assets . . . . Accordingly, the incomplete information disclosed in Hypothetical 1C represents a permissible misdirection, and not an impermissible misrepresentation.

In Hypothetical 1D, the defense attorney is aware that the plaintiff's attorney is concerned with the collectibility of a judgment, and answers with a truthful statement that fails to disclose additional information useful to the other side. . . . [T]here is no general ethical duty to disclose insurance information to an adversary. Nor is there an ethical duty to answer an adversary's questions during settlement negotiations. Indeed, there are some circumstances in which the existence of insurance coverage, while generally discloseable in litigation, can be considered a secret or confidence of the client such that its disclosure could affect the settlement of other cases or encourage numerous additional suits. It could be argued that it is incumbent upon the plaintiff's attorney, in this example, to ask the follow-up question as to the existence of insurance. But, in the final analysis, it seems that Hypothetical 1D is a classic illustration of an intentionally misleading omission. The defense attorney deliberately contributed to the misconception of the adversary, thereby pouring gasoline on the fire. [Thus,] a misrepresentation by "partially true but misleading statements or omissions that are the equivalent of affirmative false statements" within the meaning of Comment 1 to Model Rule 4.1.

On the other hand a lawyer who discloses the existence of insurance in Hypotheticals 1A-C is not necessarily praiseworthy, as the client may have an interest in preserving the confidentiality of the insurance information, which its attorney had no duty to disclose . . . .

While it has long been apparent that an attorney may not make affirmative factual misrepresentations in settlement negotiations, a growing body of authorities and commentators has posited that an attorney is ethically obligated to correct misimpressions caused by half-truths or omissions which are relied upon by adversaries to their detriment.

. . . .

An explicit and fundamental premise of the safe harbor proposal is, as Professor Wetlaufer has pithily observed, that lying is endemic in the legal profession and in settlement negotiations in particular. The range of lying runs the full gamut, from Wetlaufer's curious definition of disingenuous arguments, or "a belief at variance with one's own," through misdirection, omissions, and half-truths right up through good old-fashioned, Mark Twain-style whoppers. The adversary system assumes and requires the zealous and vigorous advocacy of attorneys on behalf of their clients. The more aggressive negotiators, including the most ethically aggressive, often obtain optimal results for their clients and develop successful practices. The best bluffers frequently clean up at the poker table . . . .

Accordingly, the safe harbor proposal posits that absent court rule, principle of substantive law, or prior factual representation, an attorney should have no duty to make any affirmative factual representations in the course of settlement negotiations, subject only to the crime/fraud exception. Once an attorney speaks, what is said should be truthful.

NOTES

Fleischmann has obviously read Judge Rubin's article closely, even referring to buying copper pots at a bazaar. Is it equally apparent that he suffers from a similar rose-colored view? He doesn't directly answer his own hypotheticals, but he infers a high moral standard of lawyering. Is this laudable? Is it workable? Does Fleischmann's suggestion that lawyers' negotiation tactics be restricted by "a code of reasonable conduct" give any greater guidance than the existing rules of professional conduct? Before you move on, think about what the roundtable consensus would be on these issues, and how *you* would answer Fleischmann's questions.

Temkin takes quite a different perspective both in his answers and, unlike Fleischmann, his certitude. Do you agree with his conclusions? If so, do you see the answers as clearly as he seems to? Perhaps the difference between these two practitioners is in part the difference between a transactional lawyer and an aggressive litigator.

Note that both authors are aware of how *confidentiality* may affect disclosure, an issue that must always be remembered.

Recall our discussion of Monroe Freedman's *Anatomy of a Murder* and penknife scenarios in Problem 16, and the semantics the lawyer uses to inform the client of how the law and facts interrelate. Are the semantic distinctions we see in these two articles similar? How things are said once again seems to be a part of the ethical fabric of these issues.

5.   The Gulf Between Theory and Practice

It is clear from the "roundtable" results that many commentators see the issue of truth in negotiation as framed by one standard under a technical reading of the rules ("would it be ethical?" equates with "can I get away with it?"), and another standard based on "doing the right thing." But the average practicing lawyer likely has given little thought to this distinction. Rather, this practitioner is "in the field" day in and day out, closing deals, negotiating settlements, and, most likely, telling opposing counsel what he or she thinks the other side should hear in order to obtain the desired result, likely without too much thought about the ethical conundrum.

We talked with several lawyer-mediators of our acquaintance to find out their thoughts about what lawyers tell them in mediation caucus rooms. The majority felt they were not told the truth, even when the lawyers said that they were at the limit of their client's authority, or that their client "would not accept a dime less than (*X*)." "It would be ridiculous for me to expect that a lawyer is going to tell me, much less opposing counsel, the real bottom line, or the real limit of authority," says one highly skilled and successful lawyer-mediator. "I expect them to hold back, to run a bluff, to exaggerate. I have to be realistic; that's how the negotiation process works, and — for better or worse - most mediations work the same way."

What does this say about our justice system's methods of negotiation and dispute resolution? Perhaps it means that those few who have thought and written on the subject are more sophisticated in their thinking than the average practitioner in the trenches. Perhaps it means they are less realistic. Perhaps it also means the formal rules of ethics have not yet addressed these issues with sufficient specificity and clarity to tell those practicing lawyers not only what kind of behavior is *preferred* for them, but what kind of behavior is *required*.

6.   Civil Liability and Malpractice Concerns

There may be significant liability risks in making misrepresentations in negotiations. For example, if the lawyer/negotiator affirmatively misrepresents a material fact that induces the other party to rely on it, and if that reliance is justified, then the injured party may, in many jurisdictions, be able to void the contract. The lawyer who made the misrepresentations may be liable in tort to the injured party, unless the client has lied to the lawyer. In *Hansen v. Anderson, Wilmarth & Van der Maaten*, 587 A.2d 1346 (Iowa 2001), a client sued his lawyer for failing to ferret out the opposing party's misrepresentations. In turn, that lawyer sued her opposing counsel over the opponent's false representations. The court allowed the suit to go forward, noting that a "lawyer has a duty to the lawyer requesting the information to give it truthfully . . . . [A] breach of that duty supports a claim for equitable indemnity by the defrauded lawyer against the defrauding lawyer."

Additionally, a lawyer whose misrepresentations or other unethical conduct in negotiations lead to a void contract or damages assessed against the client may be subject to a malpractice action by the lawyer's own client. Lawyers who conceal their misconduct during negotiations have also been held to be liable to clients in malpractice lawsuits.[9]

However, there is an increasing body of case law, especially in California, that severely restricts when a "done deal" may be undone even if fraud exists, and that by extension limits when potential liability of the lawyer to third parties might exist. To illustrate, we turn to the famous Facebook-Winklevoss brothers dispute, the subject of the award-winning movie *Social Network*, and also of this Ninth Circuit case, decided under California law, with an opinion by Chief Judge Alex Kozinski.

FACEBOOK, INC. v. PACIFIC NORTHWEST SOFTWARE, INC.
640 F.3d 1034 (9th Cir. 2011)

[T]he Winklevosses claim that Mark Zuckerberg stole the idea for Facebook from them. They sued Facebook and Zuckerberg . . . . [A] mediation session [was set] so that the parties could reach a global settlement. Before mediation began, the participants signed a Confidentiality Agreement stipulating that all statements made during mediation were privileged, non-discoverable and inadmissible "in any arbitral, judicial, or other proceeding."

After a day of negotiations, ConnectU, Facebook and the Winklevosses signed a handwritten, one-and-a-third page "Term Sheet & Settlement Agreement." . . . The Settlement Agreement also purported to end all disputes between the parties. The settlement fell apart during negotiations over the form of the final deal documents, and Facebook filed a motion with the district court seeking to enforce it.

After signing the Settlement Agreement, Facebook notified the Winklevosses that an internal valuation prepared to comply with Section 409A of the tax code put the value of its common stock at $8.88 per share. The Winklevosses argue that

---

[9] *See* the oft-cited *Muhammed v. Strassburger, McKenna, Messer, Shilobod & Gutnick*, 587 A.2d 1346 (Pa. 1991). Note that *Muhammed* also held that short of fraud or misrepresentations, attorneys could *not* be sued for negligence when their clients agreed to settle the underlying case. This is by no means a universally held position. For a further discussion of this issue, see the Epstein article described in the Supplemental Readings.

Facebook misled them into believing its shares were worth four times as much. Had they known about this valuation during the mediation, they claim, they would never have signed the Settlement Agreement. The Winklevosses charge Facebook with violating Rule 10b-5 [and fraud] . . . .

The Winklevosses are sophisticated parties who were locked in a contentious struggle over ownership rights in one of the world's fastest-growing companies. They engaged in discovery, which gave them access to a good deal of information about their opponents. They brought half-a-dozen lawyers to the mediation. Howard Winklevoss — father of Cameron and Tyler, former accounting professor at Wharton School of Business and an expert in valuation — also participated.

Parties involved in litigation know that they are locked in combat with an adversary and thus have every reason to be skeptical of each other's claims and representations. They can use discovery to ferret out a great deal of information before even commencing settlement negotiations. They can further protect themselves by requiring that the adverse party supply the needed information, or provide specific representations and warranties as a condition of signing the settlement agreement. Such parties stand on a very different footing from those who enter into an investment relationship in the open market, where it's reasonable to presume candor and fair dealing, and access to inside information is often limited. . . .

The Settlement Agreement grants "all parties" "mutual releases as broad as possible"; the Winklevosses "represent and warrant" that "[t]hey have no further right to assert against Facebook" and "no further claims against Facebook & its related parties." . . . As sophisticated litigants, the Winklevosses or their counsel should have . . . understood that the broadest possible release includes both known and unknown securities claims. An agreement meant to end a dispute between sophisticated parties cannot reasonably be interpreted as leaving open the door to litigation about the settlement negotiation process . . . . The district court correctly concluded that the Settlement Agreement meant to release claims arising out of the settlement negotiations, and that the release was valid . . .

The Winklevosses are not the first parties bested by a competitor who then seek to gain through litigation what they were unable to achieve in the marketplace. And the courts might have obliged, had the Winklevosses not settled their dispute and signed a release of all claims against Facebook. With the help of a team of lawyers and a financial advisor, they made a deal . . . . For whatever reason, they now want to back out. Like the district court, we see no basis for allowing them to do so. At some point, litigation must come to an end. That point has now been reached.

NOTES

Note that Judge Kozinski makes a clear distinction between parties in litigation, where no holds are barred and formal information-gathering (i.e., discovery) exists, and transactional negotiation, where good faith and fair dealing are implied. Is Kozinski right about there being a material distinction regarding *caveat emptor*? Consider Fleischmann's "Risk Allocation Situation." Would Judge Kozinski thus have come out the other way when it comes to the "flat" representation in a transactional context?

What about malpractice for incompetent representation during negotiation that does not directly relate to settlement issues? A large number of courts have held that a client may establish a malpractice claim against an attorney arising out of negotiations when, for example, the lawyer fails to adequately investigate the other side's assets;[10] or on the narrow basis of when a lawyer fails to adequately prepare for trial, thus forcing the client to accept a low settlement or to pay more than the client otherwise would have had to pay had the attorney been prepared.[11]

However, in mediation settings at least, a number of states, again led by California, have developed such strong confidentiality and evidentiary privilege rules that they severely limit the ability of clients to sue even for clear mistakes made by their own lawyers. For instance, *Cassel v. Superior Court*, 244 P.3d 1080 (Cal. 2011) holds that client Cassel may not sue his own lawyer for malpractice that took place during mediation, *even if* that malpractice occurred during a private attorney-client conversation between the two. The court concluded, in essence, that mediation confidentiality in California trumps even the ability to use attorney-client confidential information to prove a lawyer's malpractice.[12]

7. The Duty of the Prosecutor

What about the prosecutor's behavior in plea negotiations? Are the rules that apply to prosecutors the same ones that apply to other advocates? Are they more stringent? When we discussed the necessity of disclosing material facts in Problem 15, we had occasion to cite to *Brady v. Maryland*, 373 U.S. 83 (1963), which held that as a matter of constitutional right, a prosecutor *must* disclose material evidence favorable to a criminal defendant. In our present problem, do the eyewitness' drug addiction and history of failures to appear constitute material evidence favorable to the defense? What about the possible unavailability of the witness?

In the following case, the New York Court of Appeals held that a prosecutor's silence during plea negotiations about the death of the complaining witness/victim did not violate either the defendant's due process rights or the prosecutor's ethical obligations.

PEOPLE v. JONES
375 N.E.2d 41 (N.Y. 1978)

Plea negotiations had been conducted before the complaining witness had been located, were continued after the case had been marked ready, and culminated on April 26, 1976 when defendant withdrew his prior plea of not guilty and pleaded guilty to robbery. . . .

---

[10] *See, e.g.,* Patrick v. Ronald Williams P.A., 402 S.E.2d 452 (N.C. Ct. App. 1991).

[11] *See* Fishman v. Brooks 487 N.E.2d 1377 (Mass. 1986).

[12] We excerpt this case in Problem 22 below.

When defendant appeared for sentencing, defense counsel moved to withdraw the plea of guilty on the ground that it had come to his attention the previous day that the District Attorney's office had been informed of the death of Rodriguez, the victim, on April 22, 1976, four days prior to the acceptance of the plea.

In support of the motion to withdraw the plea, counsel for defendant contended that "in the spirit of *Brady v. Maryland*" the prosecution was obliged to disclose the fact of Rodriguez' death to the defense and averred that had counsel . . . "been informed of that fact I would not have allowed, at least I would have advised my client not to make the plea . . . ." At no time did defendant assert, nor does he now, that he was innocent of having committed the criminal acts charged.

It advances analysis to focus on the precise nature of the matter which was not disclosed by the prosecutor during the plea negotiations — information with respect to the death of the complaining witness. The circumstance that the testimony of the complaining witness was no longer available to the prosecution was not evidence at all. Further to the extent that proof of the fact of the death of this witness might have been admissible on trial, it would not have constituted exculpatory evidence — i.e., evidence favorable to an accused where the evidence is material either to guilt or to punishment. Accordingly, it does not fall within the doctrine enunciated by the Supreme Court of the United States in *Brady v. Maryland*. . . .

The question remains as to the extent of the prosecution's obligation to disclose information in its possession which, as here, is highly material to the practical, tactical considerations which attend a determination to plead guilty, but not to the legal issue of guilt itself . . . [that] is whether the pretrial conduct of the prosecutor in the course of plea negotiation was such as to constitute a denial of due process.

. . . .

Counsel cite no reported case, nor has our independent research disclosed any, in which judicial attention has been focused on the failure of a prosecutor before trial or during plea negotiations to disclose nonevidentiary information pertinent to the tactical aspects of a defendant's determination not to proceed to trial. No particularized rule can or need be laid down; some comments may usefully be assayed, however. At the threshold we assume that, notwithstanding that the responsibilities of a prosecutor for fairness and open-dealing are of a higher magnitude than those of a private litigant, no prosecutor is obliged to share his appraisal of the weaknesses of his own case (as opposed to specific exculpatory evidence) with defense counsel. . . . All the reported instances of deceitful persuasion appear to have involved positive misstatement or misrepresentations; none has considered the effect to be accorded silence only. Consistent with legal principles recognized elsewhere in our jurisdiction, it would seem that silence should give rise to legal consequences only if it may be concluded that the one who was silent was under an affirmative duty to speak. . . .

NOTES

The ABA Standards Relating to the Administration of Criminal Justice, Standard 3-4.1(c), says: "A prosecutor should not knowingly make false statements or representations as to fact or law in the course of plea discussions with defense counsel or the accused."[13]

While the *Jones* court saw no duty to make an affirmative disclosure of a non-evidentiary fact under *Brady*, note that like Barry Temkin, the court seems to approve of silence as a "safe harbor" for the prosecutor. Should it be? What about the prosecutor's ethical duty? Didn't this prosecutor's silence clearly mislead defendant Jones by leaving him with an erroneous understanding of the strength of the case against him? And didn't Jones clearly rely on this erroneous understanding when pleading guilty? In this respect, the *Jones* facts seem quite close to Temken's Hypotheticals 1C and 1D. To what extent should similar standards apply to the DA here?

Or should there be a *higher* standard? Standard 3-3.11 relates to the prosecutor's duty to make *Brady* disclosures, but it also requires disclosure of information that "would tend to reduce the punishment of the accused." Does this standard apply in that if Jones had known of the death of the victim, he likely would have gotten a much better "deal," thus "reducing his punishment"? If the standard applied, should the court have considered prosecutorial ethics in its ruling and if so, should it have decided the opposite way?

People v. Jones continues to be a much-discussed case, even today, with opinions deeply divided about the propriety of the decision on ethical grounds. On *Brady* grounds, it would likely be decided the same way today, particularly in light of the Supreme Court's decision in *United States v. Ruiz*, 536 U.S. 622 (2002). *Ruiz* held that the prosecution had no duty to disclose impeachment information about prosecution witnesses during pre-trial plea bargaining, even though that information would have to be disclosed for trial. Justice Breyer's majority opinion reversed the Ninth Circuit, in significant part because he distinguished between fairness at trial on one hand and in a "factually justified" negotiated plea on the other. But this leaves open the ethical issue.

The question of where prosecutorial *ethics* lie, especially in a court's decision whether to overturn a plea-bargained conviction, remains largely unresolved, as courts tend to stop with an analysis of *Brady*. What do you think our commentators on negotiation ethics would say about the prosecutor's actions in *Jones*? Or the prosecutor in Part III of our problem? One thing is almost certain: There would be no unanimity of opinion.[14]

D. SUPPLEMENTAL READINGS

1. ROGER FISHER & WILLIAM URY, GETTING TO YES (1981). This seminal bestselling book on the keys to successful negotiation is not primarily about ethics, but it is referred to by many who specialize in mediation and negotiation techniques, and those who deal with the ethics of negotiation. It is must reading for anyone with a particular interest in the negotiation process.

---

[13] We note that these standards are undergoing long-overdue revision as we write this edition.

[14] Prosecutorial ethics is the subject of Problem 23, including a further reference to the *Jones* case, and a discussion of the extent to which a prosecutor's ethical duty exceeds the requirements of *Brady v. Maryland*.

2. James J. White, *Machiavelli and the Bar: Ethical Limitations on Lying in Negotiation*, 1980 AM. B. FOUND. RES. J. 921. Professor White, quoted at some length in the Lempert roundtable, wrote this interesting and valuable article, making the important point that negotiation has an "almost galactic scope," used not just in the legal system, but in business, labor disputes, family situations, even war and terrorism. White also points to significant community, ethnic, and other cultural variables that affect how different people negotiate. He provides an interesting example of a negotiation between two of his better students, one African-American, one Jewish, who — although from the same city — had assimilated very different negotiation patterns, which resulted in different approaches and reactions in their negotiation.

3. Sissela Bok, a philosopher and an acute observer of the legal system, wrote an oft-referenced book, LYING: MORAL CHOICES IN PUBLIC AND PRIVATE LIFE (1978), in which she states that "what the liar perceives as harmless or even beneficial may not be so." Bok examines lying in the context of our whole society, in which "the veneer of social trust is often thin." Lying, she argues, can damage or even destroy this trust. When trust is damaged, she argues, the whole community is damaged; when trust is destroyed, "societies falter and collapse."

4. CHARLES CRAVER, EFFECTIVE LEGAL NEGOTIATION AND SETTLEMENT (1986). This book, written by one of the "hardliners" of Lempert's negotiation roundtable (and the man who created the hypotheticals), is a complete study of the "art" of negotiation, with a specific chapter devoted to negotiation ethics.

5. Does it matter if a party dies? *Virzi v. Grand Trunk Warehouse & Cold Storage Co.*, 571 F. Supp. 507 (E.D. Mich. 1983) sets aside a settlement that was based on a negotiation consummated after the death of the plaintiff, because the plaintiff's attorney did not inform defense counsel of the death. ABA Formal Opinion 95-397 (September 18, 1995) addressed the same issue and also concluded that the attorney had to disclose the client's death. Upon that death the attorney is without a client, and the failure to disclose this fact is "tantamount to making a 'false statement of material fact'" to the opponent. *Virzi* and Formal Opinion 95-397 provide a contrast both to *People v. Jones*, above, and to Virginia State Bar Opinion 952 (1987), which holds that where a lawyer was preauthorized by both his deceased client and the client's estate to accept a settlement offer, the lawyer had no affirmative duty to advise the opposing insurance defense counsel of the client's death unless opposing counsel specifically inquired as to the health of the client.

6. *Chase Manhattan Bank, N.A. v. Perla*, 65 A.D.2d 207 (N.Y. Sup. Ct. 1978), held that an injured lender could sue the *debtor's* lawyer for fraud when the lawyer lied about how the debtor would act in the future. The *Perla* court held that if the lawyer had knowledge that the client would not act as promised, the lawyer's statement to the contrary was an actionable misrepresentation.

7. Gary T. Lowenthal, *The Bar's Failure to Require Truthful Bargaining by Lawyers*, 2 GEO. J. LEGAL ETHICS 411 (1988). This article examines the ABA's treatment of potentially dishonest behavior in negotiation. The author argues that while much exaggeration may be tactical posturing, the temptation to misrepresent or conceal information during negotiations is too great and requires stronger regulation. He concludes that unless the ABA seriously hopes to provide more than a guide on how to avoid civil liability, it should drop the pretense that it regulates bargaining behavior at all.

8. Michael H. Rubin, *The Ethics of Negotiation: Are There Any? A Look at Ethical Issues for Commercial Finance Attorneys*, ACFA paper presented January, 2009, considers how the current ABA Model Rules (and the incoming New York Rules), may relate to personal moral principles that can guide or restrict the options of attorneys during negotiations. The paper was adapted in part from the author's prior publications, including: *The Ethics of Negotiations: Are There Any?*, 56 LA. L. REV. 447 (1995).

9. Lynn A. Epstein, *Post-Settlement Malpractice: Undoing the Done Deal*, 46 CATHOLIC U. L. REV. 453 (1997). This article criticizes the willingness of courts to permit clients to sue their attorneys after they have settled a case. Professor Epstein bases her argument in part on the "type of gamesmanship" in negotiations supported by the Model Rules. The author acknowledges that the *Muhammed* case, which immunized lawyers from malpractice claims (other than fraud) after their clients had accepted settlements, has been soundly criticized by most other jurisdictions.

10. Art Hinshaw & Jess K. Alberts, *Doing the Right Thing: An Empirical Study of Attorney Negotiation Ethics*, 16 HARV. NEGOT. L. REV. 95 (2011). These dispute resolution professors surveyed 734 practicing lawyers and asked them what they would do "if a client asked them to assist in a fraudulent pre-litigation settlement scheme." Half said they wouldn't help, but a third said they'd help to at least some extent. "The data," say the authors, "reveal a pervasive cultural and structural problem arising from the way lawyers think about negotiation." They then propose a plan of greater truth-telling to "raise lawyer negotiation conduct to a level consistent with the Model Rules" by clarifying the rules and increasing enforcement.

11. STEVEN LUBET, LAWYER'S POKER (2006). There are so many references in this Problem to poker that it would be imprudent to leave out this Northwestern ethics professor's recent book, subtitled "52 Lessons that Lawyers can Learn from Card Players." While not just about negotiation, the book does say, at page 7, that "just like litigation, poker is all about winning."

PROBLEM 20: "HONEST ABE'S" TRIAL TACTICS

A. INTRODUCTION

The line dividing legitimate trial tactics from trickery and sharp practices can be a very thin one indeed. Although there are prohibitions against material misrepresentations (see, e.g., MR 3.6 and 3.7) and a requirement of candor to the tribunal (see, e.g., MR 3.3), the Model Rules — and the Model Code before it — provide little in the way of concrete guidance about the tactical tricks of a lawyer's trade. Read about the tactics used by "Honest Abe" Dennison and his law partner. On which side of the line do they fall, and why?

B. PROBLEM

Abe Dennison is one of the most successful trial lawyers in Port City. He and his law partner, Arthur McCabe, provide general litigation services for some of the greater Bay Area's wealthiest families, especially among the social elite. Dennison is president of the Marina Yacht Club, where he engages in lunchtime and "happy hour" rainmaking, and is quite often seen playing $100 "Nassaus" on the city's most exclusive golf course.

Although Dennison is smoother than silk out of the courtroom, in court he takes on a bumbling, "aw shucks" persona. This, he explains to clients and friends, gives jurors the impression he's just a "hick from the sticks," thus creating juror sympathy. He carries this persona right through the trial. He rarely objects without hesitating, starting over, and making a little speech, which he privately calls "my Jimmy Stewart Method." Instead of "objection, irrelevant," Dennison is inclined to say "I'm sorry, Your Honor, but I don't under . . . I can't put my finger on why . . . I just can't figure out why that question has anything to do with this case." Dennison's persona has earned him from his courthouse colleagues the sarcastic sobriquet "Honest Abe."

Dennison also tries to mask the sophistication of his clients, insisting they "dress down" in court by wearing off-the-rack discount store clothes rather than the stylish outfits they favor. He has even bought bus or subway passes for clients, and then placed them conspicuously in his clients' pockets or handbags. Dennison justifies these practices as "trial tactics" necessary to ensure winning verdicts.

One time in a personal injury case, he hired his secretary's sister for the sole purpose of sitting in the first row behind Dennison's table and acting as if she was the girlfriend of his client. The case was tried in a county where Dennison feared the presence of his client's gay lover would bias the jury against his client.

In a rare criminal case, Dennison was hired by a wealthy yacht club friend to represent his son, who had been accused of rape. Dennison knew that the jury would be acutely aware of the cross-racial nature of the alleged assault — Dennison's client being white, the alleged victim first generation Chinese-American. In order to diffuse this, Dennison recruited an attractive Chinese-American woman who had been his Trial Practice student the year before to act as his law clerk during the trial. He emphasized to her the importance of being friendly to the defendant during the course of the trial, "complete," as he put it, "with touching."

Arthur McCabe considers himself a mentor to the young associates at the firm. He advises them that they must manipulate the jury and use all available tricks of the trade to defend against large jury verdicts. McCabe tells the associates that "selecting a jury is the most important part of trial. In fact, a well selected jury will win your case." McCabe then recounts a case where he defended two wealthy immigrants from Mexico City in a breach of contract action brought by a real estate sales company. McCabe confides that it was very important to pack the jury with working class individuals and persons of Hispanic descent. "Having dressed my clients to look like immigrants who had scraped their life savings together to buy this property, it was important to get people on the jury who would readily accept the idea that these poor souls were struggling against a rich, white brokerage firm. Although we never mentioned the words 'race' or 'prejudice,' we made it very clear in other ways that this was an out-and-out case of racial and ethnic discrimination."

I

Evaluate these trial tactics. Are they ethical? Would you use them? Can tactics be devious and still be ethical?

II

Examine briefly the tactics of attorneys Darrow and Dodd and the "nerd defense," all described below in section 1. Especially, evaluate Max Wildman's strategy in the wrongful death case, also described below. Whether a plaintiff has a new girlfriend or even a new wife is considered irrelevant in wrongful death cases in most states. Does that influence your opinion of the ethics of Wildman's strategy?

III

After reading the *Thoreen* case and the synopses of the other "client-switching" cases that follow, answer these two questions:

1. What do you believe the ethical standard should be for a lawyer facing such an eyewitness issue? Do you think the court's pre-approval should be required? Why or why not?

2. Do you see a material difference between these identification cases and the tricks of Honest Abe? What is it?

C. READINGS

1. Courtroom Tactics and "Parlor Tricks"

A story is attributed to Clarence Darrow. Back in the early part of the 20th century, when everyone smoked and people smoked freely in the courtroom, Darrow was sitting at counsel table listening to the prosecutor's closing argument. He lit a big Havana cigar and started smoking it. As the DA's argument progressed, the cigar ash grew longer and longer. Darrow had placed a straight wire down the center of the cigar, which kept the ash attached. As time went by, the jury paid less and less attention to the prosecutor and more and more to the cigar. The defendant was ultimately acquitted.

It is said that famed Chicago insurance defense lawyer Max Wildman once hired an attractive young woman to sit behind the plaintiff in a case concerning the wrongful death of the plaintiff's wife. The woman's job was to make friendly small talk with the plaintiff during court recesses; the idea was that the jury would observe the plaintiff's "new relationship" and lose sympathy for his loss.

Famed left-wing "movement" lawyers William Kunstler and Lynne Stewart — both referenced elsewhere in this chapter — pioneered what became known in New York as "the nerd defense," in which the lawyers dress their clients to look "mousey" and harmless, complete with "nerdy" eyeglasses. It worked for them by helping to free a man accused of multiple murders of police in the late 1980's, and has actually been studied since by psychologists and social scientists. As recently as 2011, the "nerd defense," complete with bifocals, was cited by a New York lawyer as helping acquit his murder suspect at trial. "The nerdier the better," commented another New York defense lawyer.

Better, perhaps, but is it ethical? After the 2011 verdict, NYU ethics professor Stephen Gillers addressed the issue on the on-line Legal Ethics Forum: Is putting glasses on a defendant with perfect eyesight deceitful under ethics rules? He concluded "no," since "cleaning up" a client is standard operating procedure, like allowing an in-custody criminal defendant to shave and wear street clothes. But at least one blogger had more doubts: glasses, like crutches or a wheelchair, may convey false information about the client's "physical capabilities." Still the blogger also thought it was "too close a call" to permit discipline, noting that some people wear glasses for minor visual impediments or even as a fashion statement.[1]

Often, the tricks and devices used in the "trade" are told in "war stories" and set out like trophies to be admired. Take the following article, in which a practicing lawyer gleefully describes some of the devices he has used to persuade the jury. Written for the self-described "TV generation," it is equally relevant in the Internet era.

Roger J. Dodd, *Innovative Techniques: Parlor Tricks for the Courtroom*
TRIAL (April 1990)[2]

What happens in the courtroom is necessarily serious. That work requires and deserves respect. I mean no disrespect by referring to demonstrative evidence and other demonstrative techniques as parlor tricks. But I want to emphasize how important it is to stimulate, impress, and sometimes entertain during the trial of a case. This is the TV generation, and mere words from the witness may no longer be enough to persuade or convince.

---

[1] *See* http://ethicsalarms.com/2011/02/21/the-perplexing-nerd-defense/ for one report of this story. *See also* Professor Gillers' post, searchable at http://www.legalethicsforum.com/blog/.

[2] Copyright © 1990 by Association of Trial Lawyers of America. Reprinted by permission.

Creative Approach

. . . No matter how uncreative we think we are, each of us can bring a case alive for a jury by following a simple thought process.

- To begin the thought process, the trial lawyer must target the dominant emotion of the case - the emotion that the jury must feel in order to acquit.

- The lawyer must develop a theme that targets that emotion, and organize and present the case around that theme. A good theme will be a simple slogan, a few vivid words that will stick in the jurors' minds. . . .

- The trial lawyer must think through the emotion and theme to be targeted using the five senses: smelling, seeing, hearing, touching, and tasting. . . .

- If at all possible, the trial lawyer should be part of the demonstration. We lawyers have a public relations problem. We come across as holier-than-thou in attitude — particularly in our native habitat, the courtroom. By becoming a part of the demonstration, we lose that attitude and become human beings. Jurors relate to us. . . .

Sweet Smell of Success

Demonstrative evidence in one court-martial resulted directly in a verdict of acquittal of possessing and distributing cocaine and LSD. . . .

The "drunk" witness testified before the trial that he had consumed about a quart of Jack Daniels whiskey but that he still remembered the defendant possessing and distributing marijuana, cocaine, and LSD. We began thinking about how to convince the jurors that this witness was too drunk to see, to remember, or to be cognizant of what was going on around him.

Mental buzzers went off, lights flashed, and we decided that we would introduce into evidence a quart of Jack Daniels. We obtained the quart, placed an exhibit sticker on it, and leaned back to admire the brilliance of our work. Then we decided that we could easily buy another quart for an exhibit and we should sample this one. It was only when we opened the bottle and poured some into a glass that this fair idea became a much better one.

As soon as the bottle was opened, we realized that what stimulates most people about liquor is its smell, not just its taste. It is not the sight of the bottle. If you have a question about that, think back to your college days when you would enter a room where there had been a party the night before and smell the stale alcohol. Remember that impact?

We decided that we must open the bottle in the courtroom so the jury could actually smell the alcohol. Again, reverting back to the thought process, we decided that the most acceptable reason for opening the bottle was to pour it into cups to show how many cups of alcohol are in a quart.

Now we were targeting sight as well as smell. Of course we would have people testify; that would target hearing. We decided against going so far as to suggest that the jury should exercise their sense of taste.

. . . .

Once the alcohol was poured, the smell of Jack Daniels permeated the courtroom. The bourbon sat on the jury rail throughout the closing argument. We are confident of the effectiveness of this demonstration because after the verdict was announced the jury foreman told us, "That sure was one hell of a lot of bourbon."

2.   Contempt and Client Identification

One of the ways in which unethical conduct can be directly regulated by the court is by the court's use of its power to hold a lawyer in contempt. The following case concerns the appeal of a federal district judge's finding of criminal contempt against an attorney who appeared before him. The opinion attempts to draw the line between zealous advocacy and obstructing the administration of justice. Is it possible to establish a "bright line" test?

UNITED STATES v. THOREEN
653 F.2d 1332 (9th Cir. 1981)

I. *Introduction*

The issue before us is whether an attorney may be found in criminal contempt for pursuing a course of aggressive advocacy while representing his client in a criminal proceeding such that, without the court's permission or knowledge, he substitutes someone for his client at counsel table with the intent to cause a misidentification, resulting in the misleading of the court, counsel, and witnesses; a delay while the government reopened its case to identify the defendant; and violation of a court order and custom.

We affirm the district court's finding of criminal contempt.

II. *Facts*

By February 1980, Thoreen, an attorney, had practiced law for almost five years. He was a member of the bars of the State of Washington and of the Western District of Washington. He had made numerous court appearances and participated in one trial and several pretrial appearances before Judge Jack E. Tanner of the Western District of Washington.

In February 1980, he represented Sibbett, a commercial fisher, during Sibbett's non-jury trial before Judge Tanner for criminal contempt for three violations of a preliminary injunction against salmon fishing. In preparing for trial, Thoreen hoped that the government agent who had cited Sibbett could not identify him. He decided to test the witness identification.

He placed next to him at counsel table Clark Mason, who resembled Sibbett, and had Mason dressed in outdoor clothing denims, heavy shoes, a plaid shirt and a jacket-vest.

Sibbett wore a business suit, large round glasses, and sat behind the rail in a row normally reserved for the press.

Thoreen neither asked the court's permission for, nor notified it or government counsel of, the substitution.

On Thoreen's motion at the start of the trial, the court ordered all witnesses excluded from the courtroom. Mason remained at counsel table.

Throughout the trial, Thoreen made and allowed to go uncorrected numerous misrepresentations. He gestured to Mason as though he was his client and gave Mason a yellow legal pad on which to take notes. The two conferred. Thoreen did not correct the court when it expressly referred to Mason as the defendant and caused the record to show identification of Mason as Sibbett.

Because of the conduct, two government witnesses misidentified Mason as Sibbett. Following the government's case, Thoreen called Mason as a witness and disclosed the substitution. The court then called a recess.

When the trial resumed, the government reopened and recalled the government agent who had cited Sibbett for two of the violations. He identified Sibbett, who was convicted of all three violations.

On February 20, 1980, Thoreen was ordered to appear on February 27 and show cause why he should not be held in criminal contempt. At the hearing, Judge Tanner found him in criminal contempt.

. . . .

B. Contempt

Judge Tanner found Thoreen in criminal contempt for the substitution because it was imposed on the court and counsel without permission or prior knowledge; the claimed identification issue did not exist; it disrupted the trial; it deceived the court and frustrated its responsibility to administer justice; and it violated a court custom. He found Mason's presence in the courtroom after giving the order excluding witnesses another ground for contempt because Thoreen planned that Mason would testify when the misidentification occurred. . . .

Thoreen's principal defense is that his conduct was a good faith tactic in aid of cross-examination and falls within the protected realm of zealous advocacy. He argues that as defense counsel he has no obligation to ascertain or present the truth and may seek to confuse witnesses with misleading questions, gestures, or appearances.

He argues also that (1) in the absence of a court rule controlling who may sit at counsel table, his failure to give notice of the substitution is not misbehavior within 18 U.S.C. § 401(1) (1976); (2) he did not intend to deceive; and (3) the exclusion order was not directed at Mason.

1. Zealous Advocacy

While we agree that defense counsel should represent his client vigorously, regardless of counsel's view of guilt or innocence, we conclude that Thoreen's conduct falls outside this protected behavior. . . . When we review this conduct and find that the line between vigorous advocacy and actual obstruction is close, our doubts should be resolved in favor of the former. [But t]he latitude allowed an attorney is not unlimited. He must represent his client within the bounds of the law. As an officer of the court, he must "preserve and promote the efficient operation of our system of justice."

Thoreen's view of appropriate cross-examination, which encompasses his substitution, crossed over the line from zealous advocacy to actual obstruction because as we discuss later, it impeded the court's search for truth, resulted in delays, and violated a court custom and rule. Moreover, this conduct harms rather than enhances an attorney's effectiveness as an advocate.

. . . .

Making misrepresentations to the court is also inappropriate and unprofessional behavior under ethical standards that guide attorneys' conduct. These guidelines, in effect in Washington and elsewhere, decree explicitly that an attorney's participation in the presentation or preservation of false evidence is unprofessional and subjects him to discipline.

Substituting a person for the defendant in a criminal case without a court's knowledge has been noted as an example of unethical behavior by the ABA Committee on Professional Ethics. See Informal Opinion No. 914, 2/24/66.

. . . .

Making misrepresentations to the fact finder is inherently obstructive because it frustrates the rational search for truth. It may also delay the proceedings. . . .

To be held in criminal contempt, the contemnor must have the requisite intent.

"An attorney possesses the requisite intent only if he knows or reasonably should be aware in view of all the circumstances, especially the heat of the controversy, that he is exceeding the outermost limits of his proper role and hindering rather than facilitating the search for truth." Proof of an evil motive or of an actual intent to obstruct justice is unnecessary.

Good faith is a defense to a finding of intent, but it does not immunize all conduct undertaken by an attorney on behalf of a client. It requires only that a court allow an attorney great latitude in his pursuit of vigorous advocacy.

. . . .

Conclusion

Thoreen's error in judgment was unfortunate. The court's ire and this criminal contempt conviction could have been avoided easily and the admirable goal of representing his client zealously preserved if only he had given the court and opposing counsel prior notice and sought the court's consent.

Nonetheless, viewing the evidence in the light most favorable to the government, we find that there is sufficient evidence to find beyond a reasonable doubt that Thoreen violated 18 U.S.C. § 401(1) and (3). The district court's findings were not clearly erroneous. We AFFIRM the contempt conviction. . . .

NOTES

The opinion in *Thoreen*, while upholding the contempt citation as "not clearly erroneous," seemed to have some substantial sympathy for the attorney. A decade later, in another case involving a defendant/stand-in switch, Illinois attorney David Sotomayor had his state court criminal contempt upheld by a 4-3 Illinois Supreme Court decision, although this court also sounded sympathetic to the attorney. The dissenting justices noted that Sotomayor had a legitimate reason to show the unreliability of the witness' identification. By sanctioning the lawyer for providing an objective identification test, "[t]he case points out how arguably meaningless in-court I.D.'s are," Fordham ethics professor Bruce A. Green told the *New York Times*.

Unlike Thoreen, Sotomayor acted spontaneously on a single day, never misrepresented that the person sitting next to him at counsel table was the defendant, and didn't dress up the defendant or dress down the stand-in (both wore similar modest attire). Moreover, identification was not an irrelevant issue; indeed, the judge who made the contempt finding also dismissed all charges against Sotomayor's client.[3]

The big problem may have been Sotomayor's failure to inform the judge in advance of what he said was a lunchtime inspiration. But no rule existed requiring the defendant to be at counsel table, just in the courtroom. Indeed, in one of the few other published opinions on this issue that we have found, failure to seek the court's permission was the focus:

> We emphasize that the contemptuous conduct in this case was not merely the substitution of another person for a defendant. . . . [T]he appellant claims that such substitution is a well-recognized and much-used tactic in Oklahoma County; and this may well be true. However, the appellant does not claim that it is common practice to switch persons without the knowledge of the court. And this, in our opinion, is the source of the contempt finding. At the contempt hearing, Judge McFall testified that he would on occasion allow a defendant to be seated in the back of the courtroom. . . . We find no fault in an attorney wanting to insure a true test of a witness' identification. Nevertheless, the attorney must inform the court of his or her intentions.[4]

Interestingly, as in the Illinois case, the Oklahoma trial judge dismissed the defendant's case — after all, the eyewitness identification had failed — and the appellate court chastised the prosecutor for attempting to lead the witness

---

[3] See the report on this case in Jan Hoffman's article, *At the Bar*, N.Y. TIMES, July 29, 1994. This case is reported in *People v. Simac*, 641 N.E.2d 416 (Ill. 1994).

[4] Miskovsky v. State ex rel. Jones, 586 P.2d 1104 (Okla. Crim. App. 1978).

afterwards into correcting himself and reduced the defense lawyer's fine from $500 to $100.

> We do not believe an out-of-court attempt to reinforce a witness' identification in the manner [used by the District Attorney] is proper, and attorneys should refrain from conduct of this nature. It must also be noted that this opinion should not prevent defense counsel from testing the ability of a witness to identify a defendant when a true question of identity is presented.

Id. at 1110.

The *Thoreen* court says that in a close case, doubts should be resolved in favor of vigorous advocacy. Why, then, did Sotomayor suffer the same fate as Thoreen? "We ought to give the guy a medal," the incoming president of the National Association of Criminal Defense Lawyers told the *New York Times* referring to Sotomayor.

3.   Racial Issues in Court

Many of the most highly publicized trials in this nation continue to have a large racial component, starting with the most famous of recent times, the, O.J. Simpson murder case, with its allegations of a racially bigoted police investigator. After Simpson was acquitted, one of his own defense attorneys, Robert Shapiro, criticized lead counsel Johnnie Cochran on national television for "playing the race card" and "dealing it from the bottom of the deck." Many others in the mainstream media accused Cochran of achieving what to them seemed to be an unjust result by injecting the issue of race into the trial.

But was it the defense who placed race at issue in the Simpson case? Read the following article by the late A. Leon Higginbotham, Jr., a highly-regarded federal appeals judge, and his law clerks.

A. Leon Higginbotham, Jr., Aderson Bellegarde Francois & Linda Y. Yueh, *The O.J. Simpson Trial: Who Was Improperly "Playing The Race Card"?*

in Birth of a Nation'hood: Gaze, Script and Spectacle in the O.J. Simpson Case (Toni Morrison & Claudia Brodsky Lacour, editors, 1997)[5]

[The authors first describe the evidentiary rules on bias and credibility.]

The foregoing cases, statutes, and jury instructions represent a formal modern enactment of the ancient maxim *falsus in uno, falsus in omnibus* — originally construed as "he who speaks falsely on one point will speak falsely upon all" — and serve as means to enforce the Supreme Court's admonishment that "the exposure of a witness's motivation in testifying is a proper and important function of the constitutionally protected right of cross-examination." This plethora of unequivocal state and federal jurisprudential precedents sanctioned the defense team's efforts

---

to inquire about the racial bias of detective Mark Fuhrman.

Was Mark Fuhrman Biased?

The Simpson trial presented the case of an African-American man accused of killing his white ex-wife and her white male friend. Mark Fuhrman, the prosecution's main police witness, whom Mr. Cochran referred to as a "lying genocidal racist," once admitted that "when he sees a nigger driving with a white woman, he pulls them over" for no reason other than the fact that the man is African American and the woman is white. So strong was Mr. Fuhrman's bias toward African Americans that he wished "nothing more than to see all niggers gathered together and killed." So deep were Mr. Fuhrman's prejudices that he allowed himself to be taped using the word "nigger" at least forty-two times. Yet, when questioned on the stand about whether he harbored a bias toward African Americans, Mr. Fuhrman denied that he did so. Indeed, Mr. Fuhrman went on to emphatically deny having used the word "nigger" at all in the past ten years.

The jury, therefore, had at least four reasons to consider Mr. Fuhrman a less than credible witness against Mr. Simpson. First, the fact that Mr. Fuhrman lied about using the word "nigger" (*falsus in uno*) meant that he could have been lying about other aspects of his testimony (*falsus in omnibus*). Second, the jury had cause to disbelieve Mr. Fuhrman's testimony because Mr. Fuhrman perjured himself on the witness stand. . . . Third, the jury could have reasonably determined that Mr. Fuhrman was biased against Mr. Simpson for having been married to a white woman because Mr. Fuhrman held and acted upon a strong bias against interracial couples made up of African-American men and white women. Fourth, the jury could have reasonably found that Mr. Fuhrman's investigation and testimony against Mr. Simpson was tainted because it was Mr. Fuhrman's fervent wish to have "all niggers gathered together and killed." Thus, the Simpson defense team had a legal and professional obligation to introduce to the jury this very substantial and damning evidence of Mr. Fuhrman's lack of credibility.

This may seem to be an obvious point. However, during and after the trial, it appeared as if most Americans considered it morally wrong, socially irresponsible, and generally "unfair" for Mr. Cochran and his co-counsel to have "interjected" race into the trial.

Why was it unfair?

If Different Biases Had Been Involved, Would the Commentators Have Been as Critical of a Defense Counsel's Strategy to Raise the Issue of Race, or Gender, or Religion?

Any critical evaluation of the fairness of the commentary on the O.J. Simpson case should start with the assessment that there were several factors present during the trial that affected the public reaction to the verdict and that may have led commentators to claim that the defense improperly "played the race card": the race of the defendant, his fame and wealth, the race and gender of the victims, the race of the main police witnesses, the particular racial bias held by these witnesses, the race of lead counsel for the defense, and even the race of the judge. Since the interplay of these factors undoubtedly contributed to the incorrect perception that the defense had improperly played the race card, it then follows that changing one or more of these factors might also conceivably alter the perception that the defense improperly interjected race into the trial.

For example, if the main police witnesses had been African Americans with a history of hatred of and hostility toward whites, and if O.J. Simpson had been white, would the commentators have been as critical of any defense counsel who raised the "bias issue" as to the black police officers' prior conduct? Or, if Mr. Simpson's wife had been black, would these same commentators have been just as vehement in condemning the verdict as an outrage?

Underlying all these scenarios described below is the basic question of whether, assuming that the violence and the commission of the crime were precisely the same, the intensity of the criticism would have been the same, less or more, if the variables as to race, gender, or religion were different than those involved in the O.J. Simpson case.

If the defendant had been Jewish and the prosecution's main police witness had a history of calling Jewish individuals "kikes" and then lying about it on the witness stand, automatically stopping any motorist wearing a yarmulke, and wishing that "all kikes should be gathered together and killed," would the critics claim that it was unfair for the defense to introduce evidence that the witness was a lying, anti-Semitic neo-Nazi? Probably not.

If the defendant had been a woman, and the prosecution's main police witness had a history of calling women "bitches" and then lying about it on the witness stand, sexually harassing women at work, and wishing that "all bitches should be gathered together and killed," would the critics claim that it was unfair for the defense to introduce evidence that the witness was a lying, misogynistic harasser? Probably not.

If the defendant had been gay, and the prosecution's main police witness had a history of calling gays "faggots" and then lying about it on the witness stand, arresting any men seen holding hands, and wishing that "all faggots should be gathered together and killed," would the critics claim that it was unfair to introduce evidence that the witness was a lying, genocidal homophobe? Probably not . . . .

Under any of the above scenarios, would the defense be accused of unfairly playing the gender card, or the religion card, or the ethnicity card, or the sexual-orientation card? Probably not.

The Tensions Between the Rhetoric of Seeking a Color-Blind Society and the Reality of Living in a Race-Conscious Nation

Perhaps it is both inevitable and understandable that the Simpson case would be used as a metaphor for the seemingly intractable problem of race in America. In the larger scheme, the case did not really involve any major public policy issues. However, the public paid so much attention to the trial that by the time the verdict was finally announced, there seemed to be a need to infuse the case with a measure of deeper social importance in order to justify all of the time and money spent on it. Unfortunately, the lessons that most Americans took from the trial were wrong.

. . . The victims' graves were not the only ones that were disturbed by the public recrimination over the verdict. In the process, we also stirred up the shallow grave where is stored the vestiges of centuries of slavery, segregation, racial oppression, biases, and prejudices, also revealing in that ancient muddy racial pit corpses only half buried and souls only half put to rest. The trial was merely the shovel we used to dig up that grave.

The Simpson trial *did not create* the racial tensions that American society experiences and desperately attempts to conceal. To pretend to be shocked at the differences in racial attitudes in the reactions to the verdict is, therefore, more than a little disingenuous. The "racial divide" in public opinion over the verdict is not a phenomenon newly created by the Simpson trial; it has existed all along, and it took the tragic double murder of two innocent people to expose the hypocrisy of our collective consciousness. It is this same self-deception that Americans engage in when politicians and even the courts declare that race-conscious remedies in public policies are evils that keep us from reaching the promised land of a color-blind society.

NOTES

In a postscript to the article, Higginbotham noted ironically that the press paid little attention to officer Mark Fuhrman's plea of no contest and resulting conviction for perjury, or to the fact that, although he apologized to the police department, his family, and the general public, he never expressed any remorse for his diatribes against African Americans over the years.

"Playing the race card" is merely a catch phrase unless it is placed in context. Some cases necessarily involve issues of race, sex, or ethnicity. Racially and ethnically motivated incidents occur, as do sexual harassment and discrimination, and criminal sexual behavior. In these cases, no one seriously argues with lawyers who emphasize issues of race, ethnicity, or sex.

And it's not *inevitably* black-vs-white issues that cause outrage. For example, in the widely-reported murder trial of John Ditullio in December 2010, the public was outraged at defense counsel's request, granted by the judge, for a make-up artist to cover up the swastika tattoo on Ditullio's neck at the cost of $150 a day — perhaps not unlike the "nerd defense" described above.[6]

But what about playing the race card as Abe Dennison did with his law clerk when race itself is not directly an issue? After all, most racism in the United States is *indirect*. Experienced lawyers don't decide to raise race in a vacuum; they know that to make it an effective tool they must tie it to something in the case — what the police did, what a witness saw or said, what opposing counsel has charged. Does this justify Dennison's actions? Excuse them?

What about when race comes into play in how a lawyer selects a jury? Read what famed (or is it infamous?) trial lawyer Melvin Belli was quoted as telling the Association of Trial Lawyers of America in 1982: "The g_d_ Chinese won't give you

---

[6] *See, e.g.,* CBS news reports at http://www.cbsnews.com/8301-504083_162-20026011-504083.html; http://abcnews.go.com/US/neo-nazi-accused-hate-crime-murder-makeover/story?id=12324409;   Molly Moorhead, *Neo-Nazi John Ditullio Gets Life Sentence in 2006 Stabbings,* TAMPA BAY TIMES, Dec. 16, 2010.

a short noodle on a verdict. You've got to bounce them out of there. In the last case that I tried, I used all my challenges getting rid of those sons of the Celestial Empire."[7]

These remarks caused an uproar in Belli's hometown of San Francisco, where Asian-American civil rights groups were quick to demand an apology. But aside from the overt offensiveness of the remarks, is the *strategy* that underlies them justified? And how does this strategy compare to Arthur McCabe's in selecting a jury for his Mexican-American clients? We'll examine this issue more closely in section 6, below.

4. Courtroom Attire

How would you feel if opposing counsel, an African-American, presented his opening argument to a predominantly black jury wearing a Kente cloth scarf? Kente cloth has become a symbol of ethnic pride for many African-Americans. Does wearing it give opposing counsel an unfair advantage? And should that advantage be the test for whether the attorney's garb is suitable or his trial behavior unethical? D.C. attorney John T. Harvey III argued to Judge Robert M. Scott that he should be able to wear his Kente cloth during trial "for religious and cultural reasons." Despite a large number of supporters including the president of the local NAACP chapter, the judge refused to budge on his insistence that Harvey remove the cloth.[8]

What about other garb worn for religious reasons? What about a priest defending a criminally accused who is wearing a clerical collar? An observant Jew who wants to wear a yarmulke in court? Or a lawyer who wants to wear his turban and declines to explain the religious beliefs behind the attire? In *La Rocca v. Lane*, 338 N.E.2d 606 (N.Y. 1975), the New York Court of Appeals required a criminal defense lawyer priest to abandon his clerical collar because it might unduly prejudice the jury. But the same lawyer won the right to use the collar four years later in another reported case, where the court found no prejudice that could not be dealt with in voir dire.[9] And yet another New York appellate court required the removal of a yarmulke.[10]

Jensen v. Superior Court, 154 Cal. App. 3d 533 (1984) allowed a lawyer to retain his turban without explanation, holding that there was no showing of disruption or interference with the administration of justice. Finally, in *Ryslik v. Krass* 652 A.2d 767 (N.J. Super. Ct. 1995), the court found that a priest defendant in a vehicle accident case who testified in clerical garb did not unduly prejudice the jury. The court found that any potential bias for the priest (who was *not* found liable) was cured when the court addressed the problem during jury selection. Are there different standards for attorneys acting as lawyers, witnesses and parties? If so,

---

[7] As quoted in The National Law Journal, Aug. 2, 1982.

[8] *See* the discussion in Patrice Gaines-Carter, *D.C. Lawyer Told to Remove African Kente Cloth for Jury Trial*, The Wash. Post, May 23, 1992; *also see* Anita Womack, *Judge Tells Lawyer Not to Wear Kente Cloth in Court*, Wash. Times Daily, May 23, 1992.

[9] People v. Rodriguez, 101 Misc. 2d 536 (N.Y. Crim. Ct. 1979).

[10] Close-It Enters., Inc. v. Mayer Weinberger, 64 A.D.2d 686 (N.Y. App. Div. 1978).

why? Would curative jury instructions work with attorneys as well as non-attorneys?

Prejudice and disruption or interference also appear to be the test for non-religious attire. Thus, in a Florida case, a lawyer who had gone to jail for contempt when he refused to wear a tie and then took to wearing string ties. His case went to the Florida Supreme Court, which, in *Sandstrom v. State*, 336 So. 2d 572 (Fla. 1976), decided against him, but not without a strongly worded dissent that argued there had been no showing of disruption, interference with "the search for truth," or peril to the judicial system. A more egregious case occurred in *Florida Bar v. Burns*, 392 So. 2d 1325 (Fla. 1981), in which an attorney was disciplined for appearing in court on a stretcher, dressed in bedclothes, ostensibly because he had been advised by his doctors to have complete bed rest due to an illness. It did not help that the attorney walked to and from his doctor's appointment the previous day.

Women have suffered far more significant limitations on their attire than the kind of ties they may wear. For example, one superior court judge in Seattle (a woman) is reported to have insisted that women lawyers appearing before her wear skirts, not pants.[11] Gradually, the absence of disruption, distraction, and disrespect have been cited to justify a variety of women's attire, from slacks and a sweater to miniskirts.[12]

The new millennium has seen these issues fade. But others have arisen, such as the dress of Muslim women in the courtroom. Read the following excerpted article:

Anita Allen, *Veiled Women in the American Courtroom: Is the Niqab a Barrier to Justice?*
Scholarship at Penn Law, Paper 329 (Sept. 2010), *available at* http://lsr.nellco.org/upenn_wps/329/[13]

While most American Muslims dress in standard "western" secular clothing, some U.S. women who practice Islam dress modestly. A number wear hijab headscarves in everyday life, and keep their arms and legs covered. A few wear the niqab. The niqab is a garment worn outside the home or in the presence of unrelated men that cloaks a woman's head and neck, leaving only her eyes exposed. A very few US Muslim women don the burqa. The burqa is a full body mantle worn outside the home, cloaking the woman's entire body and face. . . .

In the U.S., there have been no sustained calls for local, state or federal government to ban the hijab, niqab or burqa from public places or schools. In fact, in contrast to the overwhelming majority of Europeans that support a ban against wearing the niqab, sixty five percent of Americans say they would oppose such a ban.

---

[11] Birkland, *No Skirting the Issue in This Courtroom*, SEATTLE TIMES, Sep. 30, 1999, at B1.

[12] *See* In re DeCarlo, 357 A.2d 273 (N.J. Super. Ct. N.J. 1976) and Peck v. Stone, 32 A.D.2d 506 ((N.Y. App. Div. 1969). In both cases, the appellate court overruled the trial court's contempt order, but on narrow vagueness grounds]

[13] Copyright © 2010 by Scholarship at Penn Law. Reprinted by permission.

. . . .

A noteworthy, bell-weather development because Michigan has the largest population of Muslims in the country, a recently adopted Michigan law allows judges to order Muslim women . . . to bare their faces in court or go home. Courtroom controls over attire are clearly warranted and necessary for the sake of security, order and decorum. Yet banning from the courtroom the niqab head-covering of a sincere, practicing Muslim woman of whose identity the court is certain, is intolerant and risks running afoul of the First Amendment principle of religious free exercise and other federal laws.

The Michigan Niqab Case

Michigan District Judge Paul Paruk dismissed Ginnah Muhammad's lawsuit against a car rental company when she refused to unveil. The rental company was seeking $3,000 to cover repairs on an auto mobile leased to Muhammad, an African American Muslim. Muhammad said the car had been damaged by thieves. Although she wanted access to small claims court to litigate her claim, Muhammad did not wish to show her full face. She wanted to wear her niqab, as she did in daily life. Because she refused to uncover her full face in his courtroom, Judge Paruk dismissed Muhammad's case. . . .[14]

The Supreme Court of Michigan appears to have sided with Judge Paruk. On June 17, 2009, by a vote of 5 to 2, the Supreme Court of Michigan adopted an amendment to Michigan Rule of Evidence 611 [which] provides that: "The court shall exercise reasonable control over the appearance of parties and witnesses so as to (1) ensure that the demeanor of such persons may be observed and assessed by the fact-finder, and (2) to ensure the accurate identification of such persons." This amendment would presumably allow a judge to ask a party or witness entering the courtroom wearing a ski-mask, nylon stocking stretched over his head or a Ku Klux Klan hood to remove it for the duration of the proceeding.

Yet Michigan Rule 611(b) was not adopted in response to ski masks, stockings or Klan hoods. It was adopted to provide positive legal authority for Michigan judges (like Judge Paruk), to order a woman wearing the niqab (like Ginnah Muhammad) to uncover her face or leave the courtroom. The niqab has been understandably reviled as a symbol of women's political oppression and subservience; but coercing a woman to remove an emblem of religious piety raises a specter of political oppression of another kind.

In a 1991 Memorandum addressed to his state's judges, New Jersey Chief Justice Robert N. Wilentz directed judges he supervised not to restrict litigants or witnesses from dressing as they choose: "I do not believe we should try to influence how litigants or witnesses dress, absent something that approaches the obscene. . . . I believe the fact finder, albeit the jury or the judge, should see the litigant or witness as the person wishes to appear and reach whatever conclusions flow from that 'fact.' "

Tolerance, sensitivity and pragmatism are not inherently inconsistent with the

---

[14] [21] Muhammad v. Paruk, 553 F.Supp.2d 893 (E.D.Mich.2008).

popular US emphasis on judges having control over their courtrooms. Judges should have substantial control over their courtrooms, including the power to ban clothing or nudity that disrupts, demeans or trivializes the forum of justice. Judges can exercise control and yet be highly tolerant of a person's style and religious preferences. . . .

[U]nlike [those wearing] Mickey Mouse ears, a Batman costume, a comically oversized sombrero, . . . [w]omen of Muslim faith wearing the niqab are neither disruptive nor an affront.

They have a right not to be observed, so long as they can be seen, heard and identified in other straightforward and appropriate available ways.

NOTES

Is attire, then, an ethical issue? Arguably yes, at least to the extent that religious garb clashes with "reasonable judicial control over appearance," as in Michigan, or is designed to prejudice either the jury or the court, like Mickey Mouse ears or a Batman costume. Thus, understandably, a lawyer was not permitted to appear in court wearing a World War II German officer's uniform, complete with Nazi insignia, because it was prejudicial to the administration of justice.[15]

5. Ethics, Trial Tactics, and Modern Techniques of Jury Selection

Trial tactics may not have travelled quite as far down the information superhighway as other technologies, but the last generation has seen an explosion of new techniques. Videotaped depositions, laser-assisted demonstrative evidence, and computer-modeled incident reconstruction have all become common. Other techniques focus on understanding the jury. Jury focus groups help lawyers determine in advance the kind of jury they want, and "shadow juries" are hired by the lawyers to follow the case moment by moment, available for debriefing every evening. More often than not, "big-ticket" cases use the services of an in-court jury consultant to help select the chosen few who will hear the case.

More subtle but perhaps no less manipulative of the fact-finding process are the books, articles, on-line programs, and seminars that teach the science — for it has become a science as much as an art — of storytelling. Psychologists and social scientists can develop the perfect storytelling profile for the average jury — extroverted, relaxed delivery, slightly rapid conversational mode of speech, and plenty of eye contact, hand gestures, and facial expression. They analyze racial, ethnic, and socioeconomic class distinctions between witnesses and jurors, to decide how best to bridge the gaps. And, of course, they make a scientific study of selecting the right jury to hear the particular story in question.

Significantly, many new techniques have emerged that are designed to evaluate the different physical demeanors of witnesses and prospective jurors — upright or

---

[15] In re Price, 709 P.2d 986 (Kan. 1985).

relaxed while seated, legs straight or crossed, and so on — and most recently, new studies and emerging software and computerization to evaluate the meaning of various facial expressions of both witnesses and prospective jurors.

Many of these techniques are both cost- and labor-intensive, making them difficult for the average small firm lawyer to access. But to many lawyers, these techniques are becoming part of what they see as their duties of competence and vigorous advocacy.[16]

But it is important to recognize that technological advances, when taken to the extreme, could affect the fact-finding process far more than just suggestion, persuasion and manipulation. What constitutes reasonable prying and what becomes unethical invasion of privacy? A 1999 law review article about the ethics of some of the more traditional invasions of privacy notes that "[m]any investigational procedures skirt the outer limitations of acceptable practices [and]may even constitute jury tampering, obstruction of justice or invasion of privacy or constitute ethical violations by the attorney. The authors cite to a "community network model" in which trial consultants use "non-professionals" to gather information — people who may overstep the bounds and make prospective jurors feel threatened or intimidated.[17]

In the years since that article, privacy invasions have become far more sophisticated and subtle with the use of the Internet and the popularity of social media. As we've seen in Problem 6, some investigative uses of social media have become unethically improper. It's not yet been determined, though, where the limits lie in the use of social media to investigate prospective jurors. We should note that the more sophisticated the computer modeling, the more difficult it may be to detect its fraudulent application. The more widespread and detailed the jury investigation, the more difficult it may be to discover an invasion of the privacy of members of the jury panel.

Modern techniques are here to stay, several of which we would use ourselves. Are those commentators who believe that jury selection has gotten too personal correct? Or as many trial lawyers would argue, do the parties' rights to a fair trial trump such privacy concerns in the interests of getting a fair and impartial jury? We merely suggest that, as with any other developments in the profession, understanding and using these techniques must be coupled and balanced with an understanding of their potential abuse.

6.   Jury Selection and Race

The extraordinary work of Alabama-based Equal Justice Initiative and its charismatic leader Bryan Stevenson has been lauded for its combination of advocacy and disciplined analysis in many quarters. In 2010, it published a scathing indictment of racially biased jury selection in the South. We excerpt here the

---

[16] We've seen in Problem 6 that competence now *requires* some significant technological awareness.

[17] Franklin Strier & Donna Shestowsky, *Profiling the Profilers: A Study of the Trial Consulting Profession, its Impact on Trial Justice and What, if Anything, to do about it*, 1999 WISCONSIN L. REV. 441 (1999).

Executive Summary and the Findings and Recommendations that make up the first several pages of this 60-page report.

Equal Justice Initiative, *Illegal Racial Discrimination in Jury Selection: A Continuing Legacy*
August 2010[18]

EXECUTIVE SUMMARY

Today in America, there is perhaps no arena of public life or governmental administration where racial discrimination is more widespread, apparent, and seemingly tolerated than in the selection of juries. Nearly 135 years after Congress enacted the 1875 Civil Rights Act to eliminate racially discriminatory jury selection, the practice continues, especially in serious criminal and capital cases.

The staff of the Equal Justice Initiative (EJI) has looked closely at jury selection procedures in Alabama, Arkansas, Florida, Georgia, Louisiana, Mississippi, South Carolina, and Tennessee. We uncovered shocking evidence of racial discrimination in jury selection in every state. We identified counties where prosecutors have excluded nearly 80% of African Americans qualified for jury service. We discovered majority-black counties where capital defendants nonetheless were tried by all-white juries. We found evidence that some prosecutors employed by state and local governments actually have been trained to exclude people on the basis of race and instructed on how to conceal their racial bias. In many cases, people of color not only have been illegally excluded but also denigrated and insulted with pretextual reasons intended to conceal racial bias. African Americans have been excluded because they appeared to have "low intelligence"; wore eyeglasses; were single, married, or separated; or were too old for jury service at age 43 or too young at 28. They have been barred for having relatives who attended historically black colleges; for the way they walk; for chewing gum; and, frequently, for living in predominantly black neighborhoods. These "race-neutral" explanations and the tolerance of racial bias by court officials have made jury selection for people of color a hazardous venture, where the sting of exclusion often is accompanied by painful insults and injurious commentary.

While courts sometimes have attempted to remedy the problem of discriminatory jury selection, in too many cases today we continue to see indifference to racial bias in jury selection.

Too many courtrooms across this country facilitate obvious racial bigotry and discrimination every week when criminal trial juries are selected. The underrepresentation and exclusion of people of color from juries has seriously undermined the credibility and reliability of the criminal justice system, and there is an urgent need to eliminate this practice. This report contains recommendations we believe must be undertaken to confront the continuing problem of illegal racial bias in jury selection. We sincerely hope that everyone committed to the fair administration of law will join us in seeking an end to racially discriminatory jury selection.

---

[18] Copyright © 2010 by Equal Justice Initiative. Reprinted by permission.

This problem has persisted for far too long, and respect for the law cannot be achieved until it is eliminated and equal justice for all becomes a reality.

Bryan A. Stevenson

Executive Director

FINDINGS

1. The 1875 Civil Rights Act outlawed race-based discrimination in jury service, but 135 years later illegal exclusion of racial minorities persists.

2. Racially biased use of peremptory strikes and illegal racial discrimination in jury selection remains widespread, particularly in serious criminal cases and capital cases.

3. The United States Supreme Court's 1986 decision in *Batson v. Kentucky* has limited racially discriminatory use of peremptory strikes in some jurisdictions, but the refusal to apply the decision retroactively has meant that scores of death row prisoners have been executed after convictions and death sentences by all-white juries, which were organized by excluding people of color on the basis of race. Moreover, dozens of condemned prisoners still face execution after being convicted and sentenced by juries selected in a racially discriminatory manner.

4. Most state appellate courts have reversed convictions where there is clear evidence of racially discriminatory jury selection. However, by frequently upholding convictions where dramatic evidence of racial bias has been presented, appellate courts have failed to consistently and effectively enforce anti-discrimination laws and adequately deter the practice of discriminatory jury selection.

5. EJI studied jury selection in eight states in the southern United States: Alabama, Arkansas, Florida, Georgia, Louisiana, Mississippi, South Carolina, and Tennessee. State appellate courts in each of these states — except Tennessee, whose appellate courts have never granted *Batson* relief in a criminal case — have been forced to recognize continuing problems with racially biased jury selection. The Mississippi Supreme Court concluded in 2007 that "racially profiling jurors and [ ] racially motivated jury selection [are] still prevalent twenty years after *Batson* was handed down."

6. Alabama appellate courts have found illegal, racially discriminatory jury selection in 25 death penalty cases in recent years and compelling evidence of racially biased jury selection has been presented in dozens of other death penalty cases with no relief granted.

7. In some communities, the exclusion of African Americans from juries is extreme. For example, in Houston County, Alabama, 80% of African Americans qualified for jury service have been struck by prosecutors in death penalty cases.

8. The high rate of exclusion of racial minorities in Jefferson Parish, Louisiana, has meant that in 80% of criminal trials, there is no effective black representation on the jury.

9. There is evidence that some district attorney's offices explicitly train prosecu-

tors to exclude racial minorities from jury service and teach them how to mask racial bias to avoid a finding that anti-discrimination laws have been violated.

10. Hundreds of people of color called for jury service have been illegally excluded from juries after prosecutors asserted pretextual reasons to justify their removal. Many of these assertions are false, humiliating, demeaning, and injurious. This practice continues in virtually all of the states studied for this report.

11. There is wide variation among states and counties concerning enforcement of anti-discrimination laws that protect racial minorities and women from illegal exclusion.

12. Procedural rules and defaults have shielded from remedy many meritorious claims of racial bias.

13. Many defense lawyers fail to adequately challenge racially discriminatory jury selection because they are uncomfortable, unwilling, unprepared, or not trained to assert claims of racial bias.

14. Even where courts have found that prosecutors have illegally excluded people of color from jury service, there have been no adverse consequences for state officials. Because prosecutors have been permitted to violate the law with impunity, insufficient disincentives have been created to eliminate bias in jury selection.

15. In some communities racial minorities continue to be underrepresented in the pools from which jurors are selected. When challenges are brought, courts use an inadequate and misleading measure of underrepresentation known as "absolute disparity," which has resulted in the voidable exclusion of racial minorities in many communities.

16. Under current law and the absolute disparity standard, it is impossible for African Americans to effectively challenge underrepresentation in the jury pool in 75% of the counties in the United States. For Latinos and Asian Americans, challenges are effectively barred in 90% of counties.

17. The lack of racial diversity among jurors in many cases has seriously compromised the credibility, reliability, and integrity of the criminal justice system and frequently triggered social unrest, riots, and violence in response to verdicts that are deemed racially biased.

18. Research suggests that, compared to diverse juries, all-white juries tend to spend less time deliberating, make more errors, and consider fewer perspectives.

19. Miami; New York; Los Angeles; Hartford, Connecticut; Jena, Louisiana; Powhatan, Virginia; Milwaukee, Wisconsin; and the Flordia Panhandle are among many communities that have seen unrest, violence, or destruction in response to non-diverse criminal jury verdicts.

20. The lack of racial diversity among prosecutors, state court judges, appellate judges, and law enforcement agencies in many communities has made jury diversity absolutely critical to preserving the credibility of the criminal justice system.

Recommendations

1. Dedicated and thorough enforcement of anti-discrimination laws designed to prevent racially biased jury selection must be undertaken by courts, judges, and lawyers involved in criminal and civil trials, especially in serious criminal cases and capital cases.

2. The rule banning racially discriminatory use of peremptory strikes announced in *Batson* v. Kentucky should be applied retroactively to death row prisoners and others with lengthy sentences whose convictions or death sentences are the product of illegal, racially biased jury selection but whose claims have not been reviewed because they were tried before 1986.

3. To protect the credibility and integrity of criminal trials, claims of illegal racial discrimination in the selection of juries should be reviewed by courts on the merits and exempted from procedural bars or technical defaults that shield and insulate from remedy racially biased conduct.

4. Prosecutors who are found to have engaged in racially biased jury selection should be held accountable and should be disqualified from participation in the retrial of any person wrongly convicted as a result of discriminatory jury selection. Prosecutors who repeatedly exclude people of color from jury service should be subject to fines, penalties, suspension, and other onsequences to deter this practice.

5. The Justice Department and federal prosecutors should enforce 18 U.S.C. § 243, which prohibits racial discrimination in jury selection, by pursuing actions against district attorney's offices with a history of racially biased selection practices.

6. States should provide remedies to people called for jury service who are illegally excluded on the basis of race, particularly jurors who are wrongly denigrated by state officials. States should implement strategies to disincentivize discriminatory conduct by state prosecutors and judges, who should enforce rather than violate anti-discrimination laws.

7. Community groups, civil and human rights organizations, and concerned citizens should attend court proceedings and monitor the conduct of local officials with regard to jury selection practices in an effort to eliminate racially biased jury selection.

8. Community groups, civil and human rights organizations, and concerned citizens should question their local district attorneys about policies and practices relating to jury selection in criminal trials, secure officials' commitment to enforcing anti-discrimination laws, and request regular reporting by prosecutors on the use of peremptory strikes.

9. States should strengthen policies and procedures to ensure that racial minorities, women, and other cognizable groups are fully represented in the jury pools from which jurors are selected. States and local administrators should supplement source lists for jury pools or utilize computer models that weight groups appropriately. Full representation of all cognizable groups throughout the United States easily can be achieved in the next five years.

10. Reviewing courts should abandon absolute disparity as a measure of

underrepresentation of minority groups and utilize more accurate measures, such as comparative disparity, to prevent the insulation from remedy of unfair under-representation.

11. State and local justice systems should provide support and assistance to ensure that low-income residents, sole caregivers for children or other dependents, and others who are frequently excluded from jury service because of their economic, employment, or family status have an opportunity to serve.

12. Court administrators, state and national bar organizations, and other state policymakers should require reports on the representativeness of juries in serious felony and capital cases to ensure compliance with state and federal laws barring racial discrimination in jury selection.

13. The criminal defense bar should receive greater support, training, and assistance in ensuring that state officials do not exclude people of color from serving on juries on the basis of race, given the unique and critically important role defense attorneys play in protecting against racially biased jury selection.

14. Greater racial diversity must be achieved within the judiciary, district attorney's offices, the defense bar, and law enforcement to promote and strengthen the commitment to ensuring that all citizens have equal opportunities for jury service.

NOTES

Not all criminal defense lawyers agree that *Batson* should be followed — at least on *their* side. Defense lawyers from perhaps the most legendary, Clarence Darrow, to today's most outspoken, Professor Abbe Smith, have argued that they should be able to pick biased juries — biased, that is, in favor of the criminal defendant.[19]

D. SUPPLEMENTAL READINGS

1. ROBERT E. KEETON, TRIAL TACTICS AND METHODS (1973). This seminal volume on the art of trying cases keeps a careful eye on the ethics of trial work.

2. Celia W. Childress, *An Introduction to Persuasion in the Courtroom: What Makes a Trial Lawyer Convincing?*, 72 AMJUR TRIALS 137 (2007 update). A broad-ranging article about all aspects of what makes trial lawyers effective. Of particular interest are the sections about styles of verbal delivery, non-verbal behaviors, mannerisms, and visual presentation (including clothing, makeup, etc). The article

---

[19] In a famous 1936 article, Darrow argued for choosing Englishmen over Irishmen, Catholics over Baptists, and agnostics over the religious, especially Lutherans, and to get rid of women, who are inclined to take the process too seriously. Clarence Darrow, *Attorney for the Defense: How to Pick a Jury*, ESQUIRE, May 1936, *reprinted in* ARTHUR AND LILA WEINBERG, CLARENCE DARROW, VERDICTS OUT OF COURT, 316–17 and reported in Mimi Samuel, *Focus on Batson: Let the Cameras Roll*, 74 BKLYN. L. REV. 95 (2008). And recall Melvin Belli's comments about Chinese jurors in the Notes in section 3. Abbe Smith, in her 1998 law review article cited in the Supplemental Readings, takes a higher road, noting questions of constitutional due process, effective assistance of counsel, and loyal advocacy, all of which may require counsel to choose her duty to the client over racial, cultural, or any other neutrality.

points out how all great trial lawyers understand and use these influencing factors in various ways, rather than relying solely on legal skills and logic.

3. Michael J. Brown, *The Effects of Eyeglasses on Mock Juror Decisions*, 23 AMERICAN SOCIETY OF TRIAL CONSULTANTS (March 2011), adapted from Brown, M. J., Henriquez, E., & Groscup, J., *The Effects of Eyeglasses and Race on Juror Decisions involving a Violent Crime*, AMERICAN JOURNAL OF FORENSIC PSYCHOLOGY, 26 (2008). This article and its more formal companion also focus on the "immaterial" but vitally important ways in which trial lawyers persuade juries, here from the psychologists' perspective.

4. W. LANCE BENNETT & MARTHA S. FELDMAN, RECONSTRUCTING REALITY IN THE COURTROOM: JUSTICE AND JUDGMENT IN AMERICAN CULTURE (1981). This book is an in-depth analysis of how best to tell a story in the courtroom that will be found believable by the jury. It discusses many of the psychological techniques and devices mentioned above.

5. *Hawk v. Superior Court*, 42 Cal. App. 3d 108 (1974), is a textbook case of all the trial tactics *not* to engage in. While defending Juan Corona on 25 counts of murder in a highly publicized trial, attorney Hawk amassed 14 counts of contempt, $3,000 in fines, and a 54-day jail sentence. Hawk's conduct ran the gamut from the most severe, such as advising his client to disobey an order of the court and making comments during jury voir dire that improperly attempted to influence jurors, to the seemingly innocuous — calling his client by his given name. All but two of the judgments of contempt were sustained.

6. D. A. Clay, *Race and Perception in the Courtroom: Nonverbal Behaviors and Attribution in the Criminal Justice System*, 67 TUL. L. REV. 2335 (1993). This interesting law review note discusses racial attitudes of jurors as they affect jury verdicts, and how racial bias can and cannot be controlled. It also provides a good summary of the literature in the field.

7. Stuart Taylor, Jr., *Selecting Juries: Dumb and Dumber*, LEGAL TIMES, April 14, 1997. Taylor reports on election campaign revelations by Philadelphia District Attorney Lynn Taylor that her Republican opponent, who was also a senior prosecutor, urged colleagues to exclude whole categories of African-Americans (among other groups) from juries. The prosecutor, Jack McMahon, also argued for keeping highly educated and well-informed people off juries because "they take those words, 'reasonable doubt,' and actually try to think about them."

8. Lonnie T. Brown, Jr., *Racial Discrimination in Jury Selection: Professional Misconduct, Not Legitimate Advocacy*, 22 REVIEW OF LITIGATION 209 (2003), is an article by a Georgia law professor who has written often about racial issues, that ties ethics and constitutional law together in evaluating racially discriminatory jury selection.

9. In a 2010 opinion piece for CNN, *Racism common in jury selection*, June 23, 2010, http://edition.cnn.com/2010/OPINION/06/23/lyon.racial.jury.selection/?fbid= RfOn6wNIT7j, Andrea Lyon, a DePaul law professor and death penalty defense attorney, describes two women, each married, a homeowner, with two or three children, and an elementary school teacher — one white, one black. The prosecutor peremptorily challenged the black woman, giving the "facially neutral" reason that she "wore her dress too tight."

10. Can religion properly be used as the sole reason for a peremptory challenge? Daniel Hinkle, *Peremptory Challenges Based on Religious Affiliation: Are They Constitutional?*, 9 BUFF. CRIM. L. REV. 139 (2005), which, as the title implies, discusses exclusion of jurors based on religion, where *Batson* standards have *not* been applied. Hinkle argues that *Batson* protections should be applied to bar peremptory challenges based solely on religion.

11. *Attorney for the Defense: How to Pick a Jury*, ESQUIRE MAG., May 1936, *reprinted in* ARTHUR AND LILA WEINBERG, CLARENCE DARROW, VERDICTS OUT OF COURT 316–17 (1989), gives this "greatest" trial lawyer's views — and biases — about selecting a winning jury, as referenced in the Readings.

12. Abbe Smith, *Nice Work if You Can Get It: "Ethical" Jury Selection in Criminal Defense*, 67 FORDHAM L. REV. 523, 531 (1998). Smith argues that an attorney's obligation to fight cultural stereotypes or to serve the interests of the broader community cannot conflict with the duty to the client. She states it is unethical for a criminal defense attorney to ignore the impact of race and sex on juror attitudes and that *Batson'* s prohibition against race-based peremptory challenges directly conflicts with an attorney's obligation to zealously advocate for his or her client.

13. Anthony V. Alfieri, *Race Prosecutors, Race Defenders*, 89 GEO. L.J. 2227 (2001). Contrary to Smith, Alfieri claims that criminal defense lawyers should use a socially-conscious approach which does not exploit stereotypes, and that claiming that the use of stereotypes is zealous advocacy is unfounded and inapt.

14. David C. Baldus et al., *The Use of Peremptory Challenges in Capital Murder Trials: A Legal and Empirical Analysis*, 3 U. PA. J. CONST. L. 3 (2001). The author presents an overview of the literature on peremptory challenges and an empirical study performed in the 1980s and 1990s in Philadelphia revealing that discrimination in the use of peremptory challenges on the basis of race and gender continues to be widespread despite Supreme Court decisions banning these practices. The study also found that prosecutors are more successful than defense attorneys at controlling the composition of the jury.

PROBLEM 21: CIVILITY, CONTEMPT OF COURT, FREE SPEECH, AND PUBLICITY

A. INTRODUCTION

This problem concerns two important facets of litigation: lawyers' relations with each other and the tension between free speech rights and protecting the goal of a fair trial. The lawyers in the Problem use various "tricks of the trade" to gain advantage. Consider whether these attorneys' actions are the effective strategies of smart, vigorous, but ethical advocates, or the sneaky tricks of unethical lawyers. Consider whether the behavior described here is prohibited by the letter of the rules, and whether and to what extent attorneys have free speech rights like every other citizen. Note also that more than purely "ethical" issues are involved: the notions of "civility" and "professionalism," the court's contempt powers, and constitutional law.

B. PROBLEM

I

Attorney E.Z. Boyette, a local sole practitioner who's been practicing in Suburban County for 30 years, and Samantha Tesk, a partner in a mid-sized firm in Urban City across the river, represent opposing parties in Suburban Superior Court. The trial date is 60 days off.

1. Boyette needs an order that would shorten the normal time for hearing a motion to compel production of documents sufficiently in advance of trial to avoid close of discovery. The local court rules state that such "orders shortening time" "shall, with appropriate accompanying declaration, be presented to the Presiding Judge, and if that judge is not reasonably available, then to any Superior Court Judge."

The current P.J. is a notorious stickler on procedure, and Boyette is concerned his excuse in support of the motion for shortened time may not be sufficient. So he decides to present his motion between 9:00 and 9:15, the one time in the day when the P.J. is unavailable since he sits as Master Trial Judge during that time. Sure enough, Boyette finds the P.J. unavailable, but does find Judge Braithwaite still in chambers. Braithwaite, never known for promptness or exacting procedure, signs the order shortening time.

Boyette, having gotten his order signed, now goes to the clerk's office to calendar the motion. The clerk tells him that all motions filed this date are being set for hearing on the following Tuesday. Recalling that motions judge Hickenlooper takes a very narrow view of discovery, and further that Hickenlooper will be at a judges' weekend retreat through Monday, Boyette tells the deputy clerk who calendars the motion, "If you can set this on Monday, it'll make my life a whole lot easier. It's gonna be real tough on me if I gotta be here on any other day." The clerk, who is on friendly terms with Boyette due to occasional shared coffee breaks and miscellaneous other pleasantries over the years, assumes that Boyette has genuine scheduling difficulties and agrees to calendar the hearing for Monday. Braithwaite will now hear the motion.

2. Braithwaite grants Boyette's motion. Boyette then serves Tesk with a request for production of documents, while readying to leave town for a week on a long-planned backpacking trip. He informs Tesk of his plans, and gives her an additional week to produce the documents. Tesk, however, decides to seek a protective order allowing her to redact, or "black out," a portion of the documents, on grounds of privilege. She knows this is a "long shot," but decides to give it a try, especially since she's now angry with Boyette.

Tesk now needs an order shortening time for a hearing on her motion for a protective order, but she knows that Boyette would oppose an OST. She realizes that, with Boyette's opposition, the court might not grant her request, since her motion is more tactical than substantive. So she waits two days until the first day of Boyette's vacation, when she calls Boyette's office, as required by the court's local rules, and leaves the following message with Boyette's secretary: "Will make ex parte request for OST tomorrow, Department 12 at 9:00 A.M."

Tesk's request for an OST is heard and, not surprisingly, is unopposed because Boyette is out-of-town. The hearing on the motion for the protective order is set for the day after Boyette returns from vacation.

QUESTIONS

1. Evaluate the conduct of attorneys Boyette and Tesk. Which conduct of these lawyers do you feel is unethical? Do some of these lawyers' actions, while they may not strictly violate ethical rules, nevertheless fail to meet a reasonable standard of conduct for an attorney? Which actions, and why?

2. Consider the two scenarios in the Notes after the Freedman article below. Are these two examples ethical? Sleazy? Might they be considered both ethical and sleazy?

II

Miles Bethea is one of the best-known plaintiffs' products liability lawyers in the state. He and his opposing counsel, the equally celebrated Michael Epstein, have been litigating the case of *McVie v. Reliable Motors* for the past two years. Plaintiff Doreen McVie claims the brakes on her new Reliable failed, causing her to crash into a light pole. She sustained a severe spinal injury and as a result is paralyzed below the waist. During the two months that she owned the car, she returned it to her dealer three times, complaining that the brakes felt "soft." The dealer's service mechanics checked the car each time and found nothing wrong.

The case is now in trial. Bethea believes that one of his most important pieces of evidence is that as of the date McVie bought her car, Reliable's zone service offices had received at least 13 complaints from car owners about braking problems and "soft" brakes. Although only three of the complaints involved accidents, Bethea believes that these reports show that even before McVie bought her car, Reliable was on notice that cars like hers may have had brake problems.

Unfortunately for Bethea, he and McVie have drawn Judge Marcia MacAboo, a jurist with a restrictive view of evidence in products liability and punitive damages cases. Bethea supports his offer to admit the complaints with several cases in which similar evidence had been received in courts in his state. On the second day of trial, when the admissibility of the complaints is argued, the following discussion takes place on the record:

BETHEA: We ask now that these documents be admitted into evidence as plaintiff's Exhibit numbers 4(a) through (m).

EPSTEIN: Objection, Your Honor, these reports. . . .

THE COURT: Sustained, counsel, the objection is sustained. These documents are completely irrelevant; no foundation.

BETHEA: Would the Court be more specific? I . . . .

THE COURT: I don't have to explain my ruling to your satisfaction. There will be no more said about this.

BETHEA: But refusing to admit these complaints will perpetuate a false impression about auto safety. It's absurd to have dangerous . . . .

THE COURT: Counsel!

BETHEA: It makes no sense at all to . . . .

THE COURT: That's enough, and that's contempt! Two days in jail at the close of this case.

Is this contempt or proper vigorous advocacy? Would this finding of contempt be affected by whether the jury was present at the time of this colloquy?

III

Mike Epstein's investigators have learned that McVie was in and out of three alcohol rehabilitation clinics over a five-year period ending a year before the accident. Records at the state's Motor Vehicles Bureau show that McVie has two convictions for driving under the influence, one eight years ago, and the other 15 months before the accident. The last conviction resulted in a year's suspension of McVie's license, which ended just 10 weeks before the accident.

McVie's case against Reliable Motors is both newsworthy and emotionally charged. Reliable is known for its "safe" yet economical cars. Local TV stations and newspapers have been following the progress of the case since McVie filed suit two years ago.

On the fourth trial day, McVie testifies before the jury and Epstein grills her on cross-examination, including about her alcohol consumption. At the end of the day, Epstein is bombarded by news people on the courthouse steps. "Look," he tells reporters, "in this case, *I* represent the good guys. A reasonable jury can't possibly find McVie credible," he continues. "There's nothing wrong with these cars. McVie caused her own injuries. She's a lush and shouldn't have been on the road. She took her life into her own hands and now she's looking for a deep pocket to pay her."

QUESTIONS

1. Did Epstein act within the bounds of propriety in making these statements to the press? How important is determining whether the statements are likely to prejudice the case or interfere with the plaintiff's ability to get a fair trial? What if Epstein had made these comments before trial?

2. Suppose Bethea, frustrated by Judge MacAboo's adverse rulings, lashed out at her in his after-court press conference: "If she knew how to apply rules of evidence, we wouldn't be trying this case with one hand tied behind our backs and one foot stuck in cement." Is this comment proper?

C. READINGS

1. Is There an Ethical Duty of Civility and Professionalism?

Besides their duties to clients, the courts, and the public, should lawyers have professional obligations to each other? Do those duties — or should they — include civility, respect, common courtesy, and fair play? Various organizations have tried to legislate "professionalism" and civility, with mixed success. In 1988, the ABA adopted a Creed of Professionalism that included the lawyer's responsibilities to the courts, the justice system, and opposing counsel and parties. The Creed was, however, only intended to be aspirational; indeed, a disclaimer explicitly stated that it was not intended to supersede or modify any disciplinary rule.

Nevertheless, aspirational "creeds" can serve a valuable purpose by creating a community standard that encourages a "kinder, gentler" way of thinking and, perhaps, some amount of peer pressure to conform to what have been defined as reasonable behavioral norms. "The Texas Lawyers' Creed" was formally adopted by the Texas Supreme Court in 1989. We quote briefly from it below. In reading this excerpt, ask yourself whether these aspirational guidelines are effective, or mere homilies.

TEXAS RULES OF COURT, TEXAS LAWYER'S CREED — A MANDATE FOR PROFESSIONALISM
(November 7, 1989)

The conduct of a lawyer should be characterized at all times by honesty, candor, and fairness. In fulfilling his or her primary duty to a client, a lawyer must be ever mindful of the profession's broader duty to the legal system.

. . . [A]busive tactics range from lack of civility to outright hostility and obstructionism. Such behavior does not serve justice but tends to delay and often deny justice. The lawyers who use abusive tactics instead of being part of the solution have become part of the problem.

. . . .

I know that professionalism requires more than merely avoiding the violation of laws and rules. I am committed to this creed for no other reason than it is right.

I. *Our Legal System*

A lawyer owes to the administration of justice personal dignity, integrity, and independence.

I am passionately proud of my profession. Therefore, "My word is my bond."

. . . .

II. *Lawyer to Client*

I will advise my client that civility and courtesy are expected and are not a sign of weakness. . . .

I will advise my client that we will not pursue conduct which is intended primarily to harass or drain the financial resources of the opposing party.

I will advise my client that we will not pursue tactics which are intended primarily for delay.

. . . .

I reserve the right to determine whether to grant accommodations to opposing counsel in all matters that do not adversely affect my client's lawful objectives. A client has no right to instruct me to refuse reasonable requests made by other counsel.

III. *Lawyer to Lawyer*

A lawyer owes to opposing counsel, in the conduct of legal transactions and the pursuit of litigation, courtesy, candor, cooperation, and scrupulous observance of all agreements and mutual understandings.

. . . .

I can disagree without being disagreeable. I recognize that effective representation does not require antagonistic or obnoxious behavior. . . .

I will not, without good cause, attribute bad motives or unethical conduct to opposing counsel nor bring the profession into disrepute by unfounded accusations of impropriety.

NOTES

The Texas Creed is informal and, on its face, aspirational only: It is explicitly "not a set of rules that lawyers can use and abuse to incite ancillary litigation." Obeying the Creed "depends primarily upon understanding and voluntary compliance, secondarily upon re-enforcement by peer pressure and public opinion," and only lastly on the courts' inherent powers. It is clear that certain standards of behavior are expected by Texas' highest court. But what happens if the standards aren't met?

Can the rules of ethics define lawyers' obligations to each other? Must the duty of vigorous representation be incompatible with maintaining professional courtesy? Or is there a "hierarchy" of professional duties? If a lawyer's overriding duty is to the client, does that obligation supersede any obligations that lawyers may owe each other?

2.   Can Ethics Rules Be Used to Enforce Courtesy or Civility?

To date, rules of courtesy and fair play have not been included in the disciplinary rules of most states. Even the few jurisdictions that have formally incorporated rules of civility and courtesy use primarily aspirational language. Could state ethics rules actually adopt civility or courtesy as a *requirement* of lawyer behavior, the abrogation of which would be punishable by discipline? Should lack of courtesy ever be subject to discipline? Is it possible to use a civility rule to punish a lawyer? Perhaps, but it wouldn't be easy. Read the following case and its discussion of § 6068(f) of the California Business & Professions Code, which reads in relevant part: "It is the duty of an attorney . . . to abstain from all offensive personality."

UNITED STATES v. WUNSCH
84 F.3d 1110 (9th Cir. 1996)

This matter arose during the course of a criminal tax prosecution brought by the United States against three defendants, William and Beverly Wunsch and their daughter, Teri Sowers. Shortly after Sowers' arrest by federal agents on March 18, 1993, Frank Swan telephoned Assistant United States Attorney Elana Artson, counsel for the United States. Swan identified himself as Sowers' lawyer and asked about the charges pending against his client including the conditions for her release.

. . .

On March 24, 1993, Artson moved to disqualify Swan . . . from representing Sowers, arguing that their representation of both Sowers and her parents, who at that time were the targets of a grand jury investigation, amounted to a conflict of interest. . . . On April 28, 1993, the district court granted the motion to disqualify them from representing the Wunsches, and denied Sowers' motion to reconsider.

On May 6, 1993, Artson received a letter from Swan. Appended to the letter was a single sheet of paper with the following photocopied words, all enlarged and in capital letters:

MALE LAWYERS PLAY BY THE RULES, DISCOVER TRUTH AND RESTORE ORDER. FEMALE LAWYERS ARE OUTSIDE THE LAW, CLOUD TRUTH AND DESTROY ORDER.

The district court cited as authority for its disciplinary action Local Rules 2.2.6, 2.5.1, and 2.5.2; section 6068(f) of California's Business and Professions Code; "and the Court's inherent power[.]" With respect to the court's inherent power, we note that an attorney admitted to a particular bar may be disciplined for conduct that violates the bar's local rules of professional conduct. This power to discipline is not limited to conduct that occurs within the course of litigation.

We begin by noting that, "Once a lawyer is admitted to the bar, although he does not surrender his freedom of expression, he must temper his criticisms in accordance with professional standards of conduct." No reference to any court or judge appears or is even hinted at in the letter of attachment. Moreover, Swan's criticism "cannot be equated with an attack on the motivation or the integrity or the competence of the judge."

Interference with the Administration of Justice

The district court cited to two published decisions in support of its conclusion that Swan's sexist communication constituted an interference with the administration of justice under Local Rule 2.5.2. See *Matter of Swan*, 833 F. Supp. at 798 (citing *In re Plaza Hotel Corp.*, 111 Bankr. 882 (Bankr. E.D. Cal.); *Principe v. Assay Partners*, 154 Misc. 2d 702, 586 N.Y.S. 2d 182 (N.Y. Sup. Ct. 1992)). Neither of these decisions supports the district court's conclusion.

[I]n *Principe*, the court sanctioned an attorney for unprofessional conduct in the litigation process, based on a series of demeaning remarks directed against a female attorney at deposition. The remarks, which included references to the female lawyer as "little lady," "little mouse," "young girl," and "little girl," were accompanied by rude hand gestures and had been made in front of other counsel, the witness, and a court reporter. . . .

In both cases the courts imposed sanctions based on facts showing that each attorney's sexist behavior was not only deplorable, but clearly interfered with the administration of justice. In the instant case, however, we have a single incident involving an isolated expression of a privately communicated bias. . . . While we decline to hold that a single egregious act of bigotry could never subject an officer of the court to disciplinary sanctions, . . . [e]qually clearly, however, the courts cannot punish every expression of gender bias by attorneys without running afoul of the First Amendment.

. . . Our review of the California case law dealing with "offensive personality" in the context of the administration of justice fails to reveal a single controlling decision — much less a clear line of authority — that either specifically discusses the scope of section 6068(f) or explicitly limits its applicability to, e.g., courtroom interactions.

To be sure, there are a few reported decisions which give some hint of the limits of section 6068(f). . . . Nevertheless, we are unable to discern from these cases any clearly delineated bounds to the reach of Cal. Bus. & Prof. Code § 6068(f).

. . . .

Clearly, "offensive personality" is an unconstitutionally vague term in the context of this statute. See, e.g., *Cohen v. California*, 403 U.S. 15, 25, 91 S. Ct. 1780, 29 L. Ed. 2d 284 (1971) ("disturbing the peace . . . through . . . offensive conduct" fails to give sufficient notice of what was prohibited). As "offensive personality" could refer to any number of behaviors that many attorneys regularly engage in during the course of their zealous representation of their clients' interests, it would be impossible to know when such behavior would be offensive enough to invoke the statute. For the same reason, the statute is "so imprecise that discriminatory enforcement is a real possibility[,]" *Gentile v. State Bar of Nevada*, 501 U.S. at 1051 (1991) (Kennedy, J., minority opinion), and is likely to have the effect of chilling some speech that is constitutionally protected, for fear of violating the statute.

. . . .

The question before us is not whether Swan displayed a deplorable lack of sensitivity, but whether the district court's decision to impose sanctions on Swan . . . can be upheld as a matter of law based on the authorities cited. For the reasons set forth above, we conclude that it cannot.

Reversed.

NOTES

Rules of court stating general prohibitions can only go so far in suspending a lawyer from practice. In *In re Snyder*, 472 U.S. 634, 105 S. Ct. 2874 (1985), the United States Supreme Court ruled unanimously that a North Dakota lawyer who wrote a mean-spirited, even nasty, note to the district court's secretary on the subject of the inadequacy of a court-appointed fee could not be suspended under federal practice rules prohibiting "conduct unbecoming a member of the bar" despite the strong, even offensive language of his letter. Said Chief Justice Burger, "even assuming that the letter exhibited an unlawyer-like rudeness, a single incident of rudeness or lack of professional courtesy — in this context — does not support . . . a finding that a lawyer is 'not presently fit to practice. . . .' "

3.   Are Courts Helpless in the Face of Uncivil and Discourteous Conduct?

Not entirely. In *Aspen Services, Inc. v. IT Corporation*, 583 N.W. 2d 849 (Wis. App. 1998), for example, the court found that although civility rules may not be enforceable in a bar disciplinary proceeding, they can be used to support a sanctions award in litigation. The most likely way such aspirational principles can become required modes of behavior is through their incorporation into local rules of court that govern the practice of individual jurisdictions. It may, then, come down to whether the courts themselves are ready to mete out discipline for bad behavior.

Other courts have, albeit rarely, sanctioned lawyers for uncivil conduct. In *Matter of Golden*, 496 S.E.2d 619 (S.C. 1998), a lawyer narrowly escaped suspension from practice but was publicly reprimanded for making gratuitously insulting, threatening, and demeaning comments in the course of two depositions. Golden asked a deponent if he was "cheap," and a "janitor." He then told the deponent he was "not smart enough to argue with" and referred to him as an "inmate" of a hospital. Finally, he called a female opposing party "a mean-spirited, vicious witch and I don't like your face and I don't like your voice. What I'd like, is to be locked in a room with you naked with a sharp knife."

However, reversal of discipline or sanctions for even the nastiest possible lawyer behavior may be as common as punishment. *Saldana v. Kmart Corp.*, 84 F. Supp. 2d 629 (D. V.I. 1999), disciplined a lawyer for repeated bad behavior including the ongoing use of the word "f-k" in deposition colloquy and conversations with opposing counsel. That ruling was later overturned by the appellate court, which reasoned that although it could not condone use of such language, no discipline was warranted since the attorney did not use the language in court or in her pleadings.[1]

Revson v. Cinque & Cinque, 70 F. Supp. 2d 415 (S.D.N.Y. 1999), involved a dispute between a client, Revson, and her former lawyers. Burstein, Revson's new lawyer, was sanctioned $50,000 by the trial court for numerous acts of bad behavior, among other things writing a letter to former attorney Cinque threatening to "tarnish" his reputation with the "legal equivalent of a proctology exam"; making a sham offer to settle by setting an unreasonable deadline and then immediately filing suit even though Cinque met that deadline; publicly accusing Cinque of fraud without any evidence; threatening to interfere with the lawyers' other clients; and contacting former clients to ask about "experiences, good or bad," about their billing practices. But the appellate court reversed the sanctions award based on its conclusion that the substance of the claims brought was not "so completely without merit as to require the conclusion that they must have been undertaken for some improper purpose."[2]

Finally, there is this extreme and more recent example from Florida, with a dialogue between two lawyers named Mooney and Mitchell in a suit by Mitchell's client against Volkswagen, represented by Mooney. The lawyers first could not agree on a date for a hearing, and then could not agree on scheduling a deposition. Their periodic email dialogue so offensive that we warn you of its offensiveness before reprinting it here:

May 2008: Mooney (defense counsel) to Mitchell (plaintiff's counsel):

"Please do not send me any more of these absurd emails. While I am happy to know that you are also the judge in this case, your continued unprofessional & juvenile behavior is not necessary."

Mitchell, to Mooney:

"Old Hack: Your unprofessional and otherwise asinine behavior is not necessary. Learn to litigate professionally and these issues will be avoided."

August 2008: Mooney to Mitchell:

"Hey Junior, Wow, you are delusional!!!! What kind of drugs are you on??? I can handle ANYTHING a little punk like you can dish out remember, I have been doing this for 20+ years and have not had a single heart attack as a prosecutor for 15 years, I have handled case loads in excess of 200 cases, many of which were more important /significant than these little Mag Moss claims that are handled by bottom feeding/scum sucking /loser lawyers like yourself. . . . otherwise, go back to your single

[1] Saldana v. Kmart Corp., 260 F.3d 228 (V.I. 2001).

[2] Revson v. Cinque & Cinque, *P.C.*, 221 F.3d 71 (2d Cir. 2000).

wide trailer in the dumps of Pennsylvania and get a life."

Mitchell to Mooney:

"Finally, God has blessed me with a great life; I work when I want to, I ride my dirt bikes with my kids . . ."

Mooney to Mitchell:

"This is the most horrifying email I have ever read — the fact that you are married means that there truly is someone for everyone, even a short/hairless jerk. Moreover, the fact that you have pro-created is further proof for the need of forced sterilization!!!"

October 2008: Mooney to Mitchell:

"Ahhh, yes, the continuing saga of scheduling with Sparky . . ."

From Mitchell to Mooney:

". . . Ahh, yes the joys of working with a lying, dilatory mentally handicapped person. By the way, I do not think I deserve the jerk comment, I was actually on the internet trying to what out what type of retardism you have by checking your symptoms e.g. closely spaced eyes, dull blank stare, bulbous head, lying and inability to tell fiction from reality, so I could donate money for research for a cure. However, apparently those symptoms are indicative of numerous types of retardism. Have a great day Corky I mean; Mr. Mooney."

Mooney to Mitchell:

"Thanks Sparky, more evidence of the jerk you are . . . the fact that I have a son with a birth defect, really shows what type of weak minded, coward you truly are. . . . If you need to find the indications of 'retardism' you seek, I suggest you look in the mirror, then look at your wife — she has to be a retard to marry such a loser like you . . . Then check your children (if they are even yours . . . . Better check the garbage man that comes by your trailer to make sure they don't look like him) . . . Unfortunately, it looks the better part of you was the sperm cells left on the back seat of the Ford Pinto . . . too bad they didn't have a rear end impact/explosion before you were born . . . that would have made the world a better place . . ."

Mitchell to Mooney:

"Three things Corky:

(1) While I am sorry to hear about your disabled child; that sort of thing is to be expected when a retard reproduces, it is a crap shoot sometimes retards can produce normal kids, sometimes they produce F***** up kids. Do not hate me, hate your genetics. At least you definitely know the kid is yours.

(2) You are confusing realities again the retard love story you describe taking place in a pinto and trailer . . .

(3) Finally, I am done communicating with you: your language skills, wit and overall skill level is a level my nine- year-old could successfully combat . . . and now I am bored. So run along and resume your normal activity of attempting to put a square peg into a round hole and come back when science progresses to a level that it can successfully add 50, 75 or 100 points to your I.Q."[3]

The Florida Supreme Court disciplined both lawyers in late 2010, but with mere slaps on the wrist — and quite oddly given the dialogue, gave the more serious punishment to plaintiff's lawyer Mitchell. Mitchell was suspended for ten days and ordered to take an anger management workshop, while Mooney received only a public reprimand and was required to take a "professionalism workshop."[4] And Mitchell's client's case against Volkswagen was dismissed by the trial judge.

Clearly, such conduct is grossly offensive. Also clear is that the Florida statute, quoted in the footnote, is not clearly unconstitutional as is the vague "offensive personality" prohibition in *Wensch*. Rules that punish acts that are "prejudicial to the administration of justice" have often been upheld in contempt proceedings. But what was punished here appears to have been the offensive language. Should that have been the basis for punishment? Could it be that Mooney's language was strategic: to goad Mitchell into joining in, in a manner that resulted in Mitchell's client's case being dismissed? After all, it was Mooney who reported Mitchell to the state bar.

4. *Should* Civility Be Regulated?

To give one view on the subject of civility we turn once again to the words of Professor Monroe Freedman.

Monroe Freedman, *Masking the Truth to Resolve Competing Duties*
LEGAL TIMES, September 11, 1995[5]

. . . [T]hose who proclaim a lack of civility disagree wildly as to what they are talking about. For an increasing number of judges, civility means that lawyers should sacrifice their clients' interests in order to protect "brother lawyers" from

---

[3] This dialogue has been reported in various places, including: Lee Logan, *Court Punishes Bay Area Lawyers Who Called Each Other "Hack" and "Loser" — and worse*, TAMPA BAY TIMES, December 30, 2010; Anayat Durrani, *When Lawyers Attack*, PLAINTIFF MAGAZINE, February 2011, and Heather M. Kolinsky, *Just Because You Can Doesn't Mean You Should*, 37 NOVA L. REV. 113 (2012).

[4] The Supreme Court opinions are unpublished but may be cited as *Florida Bar v. Mooney*, 49 So. 3d 748 (Fla. 2010) and *Florida Bar v. Mitchell*, 46 So. 3d 1003 (Fla. 2010). The court found both had violated Florida Rule of Professional Conduct 4-8.4(d), which states a lawyer shall not: "engage in conduct in connection with the practice of law that is prejudicial to the administration of justice, including to knowingly, or through callous indifference, disparage, humiliate, or discriminate against litigants, jurors, witnesses, court personnel, or other lawyers on any basis, including, but not limited to, on account of race, ethnicity, gender, religion, national origin, disability, marital status, sexual orientation, age, socioeconomic status, employment, or physical characteristic.

real practice claims — for example, not raising a statute of limitations counsel has missed. Most lawyers would agree that that kind of "civility" is inconsistent with the bar's traditional ethic of zealous representation of our clients' interests.

Nevertheless, when a survey was conducted in the 7th Circuit by a committee chaired by Judge Marvin Aspen, a majority of lawyers and judges agreed that there is a civility problem. But what type of conduct did those lawyers and judges agree was a problem? Were they talking about good manners, which might include such things as promptly returning telephone calls or being accommodating about scheduling? If that's what the fuss is about, it's hard to justify the enormous investment of time and effort that has been lavished on the issue. Or were they talking about more serious matters, like discovery abuse or willful misrepresentations in pleadings? . . .

The answer is that the Aspen committee respondents were talking about all of the above and a lot more. In defining civility, the Aspen committee's survey said that it means "professional conduct in litigating proceeding." It would be hard to get much broader or vaguer than that, but the committee contrived to do so; it went on to say that "civility" includes "good manners or social grace." I know that's hard to believe, but you can look it up.

. . . .

In view of the committee's all-inclusive definition of civility, it's hardly surprising that a majority of those surveyed answered yes when the committee asked: "As so defined, do you believe there is a problem of 'civility?' " Under the "social grace" definition, the respondents could have been referring to anything from slurping coffee to wearing large pinkie rings, mismatched socks, or garish lipstick. Others, of course, might have been referring to matters that go beyond the dictionary definition of civility, like suppressing documents in discovery.

In addition to meaningless (or overinclusive) definitions, there's a serious problem of perception when lawyers are asked about incivility. Consider a common enough situation. The plaintiff's lawyer attempts to ask a long series of questions, some of which are embarrassing to the defendant. The plaintiff's lawyer has a theory, and the questions might lead to relevant evidence to support her theory. The defendant's lawyer doesn't see the theory or doesn't consider it meritorious, views the questions as harassment, and advises her client not to answer. Both lawyers have acted in good faith to advance or protect their clients' interests. And both lawyers are likely to leave the deposition complaining that the other has engaged in discovery abuse, one by asking improper questions, the other by obstructing legitimate discovery. The result is that two of two lawyers concur that there's a problem of civility, each one referring to her adversary's conduct, and each one mistaken in her perception.

Competing Values

But there's a deeper problem with the perception of incivility in discovery. Our civil discovery rules have created an unresolved tension between competing values — on the one hand, disclosure requirements, and on the other hand, lawyer-client confidentiality and work product. A similar point was made by Justice Antonin

Scalia, dissenting from the Supreme Court's approval of the 1993 amendments to the Federal Rules of Civil Procedure. Joined by Justices David Souter and Clarence Thomas, Scalia warned that the new requirement of Rule 25(a), to give one's adversary information that is "relevant" to "disputed facts," is "potentially disastrous" to America's traditional adversary system. This new requirement, he explained, puts an "intolerable strain upon lawyers' ethical duty to represent their clients and not to assist the opposing side." Making a judgment about what is relevant, Scalia noted, "plainly requires [the lawyer] to use his professional skills in the service of the adversary."

. . . .

[T]here is an obvious tension between those policies that has not been resolved. The result is that lawyers have developed the practice of reading discovery requests extremely strictly (read disingenuously) and the courts have condoned that practice. . . .

Making Hard Choices

There is a way to deal effectively with this kind of unresolved tension, to deal with what Justice Scalia called the "intolerable strain" that is placed upon lawyers who are told by the discovery rules to serve their clients' adversaries. The way to do that is to make the hard choices[:] favor discovery over confidentiality, [which] would require [judges to] take discovery rules at face value and abandon the American lawyer's traditional ethic of client loyalty, [or] favor client loyalty and confidentiality over discovery, which would mean abandoning . . . discovery reform. . . .

The way not to resolve these kinds of tensions, however, is by dithering on about "civility" and calling upon lawyers to make the hard choices that the established bar and the bench are unwilling to make. That way, we are sure to continue to pay the price of widespread disingenuousness and dishonesty.

NOTES

Do you agree with Freedman's analysis? Does the focus on civility and professionalism detract from a focus on *ethics*? Or is civility an integral component of an ethical attorney? Would Freedman call the behavior of the two Florida lawyers a "mere" lack of civility, or would he agree with disciplining them for their ethical failures under the cited Florida rule?

Finally, consider this thought: Whatever protections are afforded by creeds and rules on civility, they do not regulate the cajoling and schmoozing that takes place between lawyers and court personnel, particularly by those lawyers who know their way around the local courthouse. Consider these two examples:

1. The court clerk's office closes at 5:00. Lawyer shows up at the clerk's office at 5:03 and begs to be let in to file a motion with today's date, absolutely the last date on which the motion may be filed. Using all of the force of her friendly personality, she tries to convince the clerk to let her file the motion. The last thing the clerks do before leaving is to change the "FILED" date stamp to tomorrow's date. They

haven't changed the stamp yet, and Lawyer begs to be allowed to file with today's date on her pleading.

2.   Attorney is in trial, and during cross-examination he obtains testimony that he would really like transcribed for his closing argument the next day. He goes to the court reporter after court and pleads with her to type up "just a real short piece of the transcript" for him overnight. He smiles and cajoles, and the reporter, who's known him for years as a friendly acquaintance, agrees to help, though she's under no obligation to do so.

Are such activities acceptable? Should they be regulated? Is it even possible to do so?

5. Speech as Contempt

Judges have wide latitude to deal with what they perceive as contempt. Contempt is vaguely defined as a disrespectful obstruction of justice. This definition applies equally to attorneys, clients, and trial spectators. Should a lawyer, however, be allowed more latitude than a party or a spectator? After all, mustn't the lawyer make sure that the trial court record is complete? Or is it true that in acquiring the privilege to practice law, an attorney waives some free speech privileges in return?

In *In re Kunstler*, 168 A.D.2d 146, 571 N.Y.S.2d 930 (1991), famed New York defense attorney William M. Kuntsler was held in contempt for the following colloquy with the trial court in what had become known as the Central Park Jogger Rape Case. The occasion was Kunstler's motion for a new trial.

> MR. KUNSTLER: It is outrageous. You will not have an evidentiary hearing despite all the law that calls for it?
>
> THE COURT: I will not hear oral argument. Call the next case.
>
> MR. KUNSTLER: You have exhibited what your partisanship is. You shouldn't be sitting in court. You are a disgrace to the bench.
>
> THE COURT: Sir, I hold you in contempt of court.
>
> MR. KUNSTLER: You can hold me in anything you wish. I am outraged.
>
> THE COURT: I am giving you an opportunity to be heard right now.
>
> MR. KUNSTLER: I am saying this, judge. Every case in the world says you should hold a hearing in order to determine whether outside influences affected a juror. Every case there is. I submitted them to you. Even when a juror falls asleep, the Second Department has held there should be a hearing. And for you to deny it without a hearing, I think it is outrageous. You are violating every standard of fair play.
>
> THE COURT: I am holding you in contempt of court. You are fined $250 or 30 days in jail.[6]

---

[6] Four of the five defendants in the widely-publicized Central Park Jogger case had confessed and later recanted. All were convicted. In 2002, after another person admitted the rape and DNA evidence

Contempt resulting from the words used by counsel is generally summary in nature — the order of contempt immediately follows the words, without hearing or due process. Kunstler was held in contempt because the judge found his words insulting and offensive. Should decorum be the standard which determines contempt? Or is that standard as vague as "offensive personality"? Should more be required, such as an obstruction of justice? In *Kunstler*, one appellate department jurist, Judge Wallach, wrote in dissent that offending a judge's sensibilities is insufficient: The test for summary contempt should be either that the lawyer disrupted the hearing or that his statements interfered with the court's calendar. "On this record," he concluded, "it would appear that the good ship Justice sailed serenely on, without a one-degree compass point deviation from its appointed course."

It appears that the United States Supreme Court is in substantial agreement with that dissent. Here's what the Court said in *In re McConnell*, 370 U.S. 230, 236, 82 S. Ct. 1288 (1962): "The arguments of a lawyer in presenting his client's case strenuously and persistently cannot amount to a contempt of court so long as the lawyer does not in some way create an obstruction which blocks the judge in the performance of his judicial duty." In an earlier case[7] the Court said that a trial judge should give "due allowance for the heat of controversy," even if the claim seems "far fetched and untenable," before summarily holding an attorney in contempt. Yet Kunstler's contempt was upheld.

Standards for what constitutes contempt based on the words spoken by counsel continue to vary by jurisdiction, court, and circumstance. One significant factor appears to be whether counsel is engaged in the good-faith albeit persistent efforts to make a clear record so that an appellate court can rule later on the disputed issue. But the manner and means of presentation to the court — respect or the lack of it, insult, or sarcasm — will undoubtedly have an effect on the trial court's decision to pull the contempt trigger.

When the language spoken in court amounts to what a judge can rationally call "disrupting the administration of justice," punishment for contempt is far more likely to stand. In May 2012, well-known Boston criminal defense attorney Barry P. Wilson went off to jail to serve 90 days for contempt of court. The grounds were exactly that: disruption of the administration of justice.

During jury selection the year before in the case of Garrett Jackson on charges of murder, Wilson vociferously objected to the removal of a woman from the jury whose two children had criminal records and the inclusion of a former Department of Homeland Security employee who had a lengthy law enforcement background. Here's what Wilson told Judge Patrick F. Brady:

> How can I look at my client and say he should think this is legitimate after you make a ruling like that and you excuse a woman who had two children. . . . No way I'm gonna try a case with that man. That's ridiculous. Fifteen years as a federal agent and he's gonna be unbiased? Are you kidding me? I can't do it, I won't do it.

---

supported his admission, all five of the defendants were exonerated and released.

[7] Sacher v. U.S., 343 U.S. 1, 78 S. Ct. 842 (1952).

Mr. Wilson, is there some reason why I should not hold you in contempt?" replied the judge.

Later, after Jackson was convicted and sentenced to life imprisonment, Brady returned to the contempt issue and eventually wrote a four-page opinion finding Wilson in contempt and sentencing him to 90 days. A pertinent part of that opinion is as follows:

> Mr. Wilson lost his temper at a ruling of the court and delivered a loud, abusive, insulting, and disruptive outburst in defiance of the court ruling. At least in part the outburst was likely motivated by a desire to force the court to excuse the juror because Mr. Wilson's screaming was so loud the juror may have heard him and concluded that Mr. Wilson 'did not like him.' Needless to say, the court cannot tolerate such behavior.

Indeed, Mr. Wilson had stated during his "speech" on the record that "the other thing is I think maybe if he's standing outside there you better go ask him if he heard me screaming because I think you gotta excuse him now cause I think he knows I don't like him."[8]

This remark surely made upholding the contempt sentence far easier, and is where it may depart from several other statements we've cited here. Is that enough to distinguish it as speech that truly disrupted the administration of justice? Or despite those comments, did "the good ship Justice sail serenely on," as the dissenting judge in the Kunstler matter noted? It was at least enough for the contempt sentence to be upheld.

6. Publicity and the *Gentile* Case

ABA Model Rule 3.6 was designed to limit a lawyer's free speech outside the courtroom to ensure a fair trial. Subsection (a) limited a lawyer's speech when the lawyer should know that it "will have a substantial likelihood of materially prejudicing" a proceeding. Subsection (c) of the rule offered several exceptions, including a so-called "safe harbor" allowing a lawyer to state "without elaboration . . . the general nature of the claim or defense."

In 1991, the United States Supreme Court decided *Gentile v. State Bar of Nevada*, 501 U.S. 1030, 111 S. Ct. 2720 (1991). Dominic Gentile was a well-known and well-regarded criminal defense lawyer in Southern Nevada. Within hours of his client, Sanders, being indicted on criminal charges, Gentile held a televised press conference. Below is a portion of his prepared remarks at that press conference, reproduced from Appendix A of the Supreme Court opinion.

> [T]his indictment is a significant event in the history of the evolution of sophistication of the City of Las Vegas, because things of this nature, of exactly this nature have happened in New York with the French connection

---

[8] *See, e.g.*, Travis Andersen, *Defense lawyer begins 90-day jail term*, BOSTON GLOBE, May 16, 2012, Travis Anderson, *Barry P. Wilson, fiery defense attorney, begins serving 90-day jail sentence*, BOSTON GLOBE, Boston.com, May 15, 2012; Brian R. Ballou, *Criminal defense lawyer ordered to jail on contempt charge*, BOSTON GLOBE, May 20, 2011; Noah Schaffer, *Defense counsel held in contempt*, MASS. LAWYERS WEEKLY, March 20, 2012.

case and in Miami with cases — at least two cases there — have happened in Chicago as well, but all three of those cities have been honest enough to indict the people who did it: the police department, crooked cops.

When this case goes to trial, and as it develops, you're going to see that the evidence will prove not only that Grady Sanders is an innocent person and had nothing to do with any of the charges that are being leveled against him, but that the person that was in the most direct position to have stolen the drugs and money, the American Express travelers' checks, is Detective Steve Scholl.

There is far more evidence that will establish that Detective Scholl took these drugs and took these American Express Travelers' checks than any other living human being.

And I have to say that I feel that Grady Sanders is being used as a scapegoat to try to cover up for what has to be obvious to people at Las Vegas Metropolitan Police Department and at the District Attorney's office.

Now, with respect to the . . . so-called other victims, . . . four of them are known drug dealers and convicted money launderers; three of whom didn't say a word about anything until after they were approached by Metro and after they were already in trouble and are trying to work themselves out of something.

Gentile went to trial on Sanders' case, and his client was acquitted. But the Nevada State Bar disciplined Gentile for his remarks, giving him a private reproval, the lightest form of punishment. Because of the importance of the issue, Gentile allowed his confidential discipline file to become public, and took his case first to the Nevada and then the United States Supreme Court.

Gentile's discipline was eventually overturned, though in the unusual circumstance of a divided court with two separate majority opinions, one by Chief Justice Rehnquist, the other by Justice Kennedy. The Rehnquist majority opinion held, 5-4, that the standard used in the disciplinary rule, the "substantial likelihood" of material prejudice, did not violate the First Amendment and was constitutionally justifiable. Kennedy's opinion dissented on this issue, arguing that the rule ought to require the higher standard of prejudice. But Kennedy's opinion was in the majority, 5-4, in holding that the safe harbor provision was void as unconstitutionally vague. Justice O'Connor, the swing vote, was a member of both majorities. We briefly excerpt first Kennedy's and then Rehnquist's opinion.

GENTILE v. STATE BAR OF NEVADA
501 U.S. 1030, 111 S. Ct. 2720 (1991)

Justice Kennedy [Majority opinion as to Part III and Judgment]:

Nevada Supreme Court Rule 177 is a rule governing pretrial publicity almost identical to ABA Model Rule of Professional Conduct 3.6. . . .

Nevada's application of Rule 177 in this case violates the First Amendment.

Petitioner spoke at a time and in a manner that neither in law nor in fact created any threat of real prejudice to his client's right to a fair trial or to the State's interest in the enforcement of its criminal laws. Furthermore, the Rule's safe harbor provision, Rule 177(3), appears to permit the speech in question, and Nevada's decision to discipline petitioner in spite of that provision raises concerns of vagueness and selective enforcement.

I

Model Rule 3.6's requirement of substantial likelihood of material prejudice is not necessarily flawed. Interpreted in a proper and narrow manner, for instance, to prevent an attorney of record from releasing information of grave prejudice on the eve of jury selection, the phrase substantial likelihood of material prejudice might punish only speech that creates a danger of imminent and substantial harm. A rule governing speech, even speech entitled to full constitutional protection, need not use the words "clear and present danger" in order to pass constitutional muster.

. . . .

Under those principles, nothing inherent in Nevada's formulation fails First Amendment review; but as this case demonstrates, Rule 177 has not been interpreted in conformance with those principles by the Nevada Supreme Court.

II

Even if one were to accept respondent's argument that lawyers participating in judicial proceedings may be subjected, consistent with the First Amendment, to speech restrictions that could not be imposed on the press or general public, the judgment should not be upheld. The record does not support the conclusion that petitioner knew or reasonably should have known his remarks created a substantial likelihood of material prejudice, if the Rule's terms are given any meaningful content.

. . . .

As petitioner explained to the disciplinary board, his primary motivation was the concern that, unless some of the weaknesses in the State's case were made public, a potential jury venire would be poisoned by repetition in the press of information being released by the police and prosecutors, in particular the repeated press reports about polygraph tests and the fact that the two police officers were no longer suspects. . . . Far from an admission that he sought to "materially prejudice an adjudicative proceeding," petitioner sought only to stop a wave of publicity he perceived as prejudicing potential jurors against his client and injuring his client's reputation in the community.

Petitioner gave a second reason for holding the press conference, which demonstrates the additional value of his speech. Petitioner acted in part because the investigation had taken a serious toll on his client. Sanders was "not a man in good health," having suffered multiple open-heart surgeries prior to these events. . . .

An attorney's duties do not begin inside the courtroom door. He or she cannot ignore the practical implications of a legal proceeding for the client. Just as an attorney may recommend a plea bargain or civil settlement to avoid the adverse consequences of a possible loss after trial, so too an attorney may take reasonable steps to defend a client's reputation and reduce the adverse consequences of indictment, especially in the face of a prosecution deemed unjust or commenced with improper motives. A defense attorney may pursue lawful strategies to obtain dismissal of an indictment or reduction of charges, including an attempt to demonstrate in the court of public opinion that the client does not deserve to be tried.

. . . .

Petitioner's judgment that no likelihood of material prejudice would result from his comments was vindicated by events at trial. While it is true that Rule 177's standard for controlling pretrial publicity must be judged at the time a statement is made, ex post evidence can have probative value in some cases. . . .

The trial took place on schedule in August, 1988, with no request by either party for a venue change or continuance. The jury was empaneled with no apparent difficulty. The trial judge questioned the jury venire about publicity. Although many had vague recollections [about the case,] not a single juror indicated any recollection of petitioner or his press conference.

At trial, all material information disseminated during petitioner's press conference was admitted in evidence before the jury, including information questioning the motives and credibility of supposed victims who testified against Sanders, and Detective Scholl's ingestion of drugs in the course of undercover operations (in order, he testified, to gain the confidence of suspects). The jury acquitted petitioner's client. . . .

III

As interpreted by the Nevada Supreme Court, the Rule is void for vagueness, in any event, for its safe harbor provision, Rule 177(3), misled petitioner into thinking that he could give his press conference without fear of discipline. Rule 177(3)(a) provides that a lawyer "may state without elaboration . . . the general nature of the . . . defense." Statements under this provision are protected "[n]otwithstanding," subsection 1 and 2(a-f). By necessary operation of the word "notwithstanding," the Rule contemplates that a lawyer describing the "general nature of the . . . defense" "without elaboration" need fear no discipline, even if he comments on "[t]he character, credibility, reputation or criminal record of a . . . witness," and even if he "knows or reasonably should know that [the statement] will have a substantial likelihood of materially prejudicing an adjudicative proceeding."

Given this grammatical structure, and absent any clarifying interpretation by the state court, the Rule fails to provide "fair notice to those to whom [it] is directed." A lawyer seeking to avail himself of Rule 177(3)'s protection must guess at its contours. The right to explain the "general" nature of the defense without "elaboration" provides insufficient guidance because "general" and "elaboration" are both classic terms of degree. . . .

Petitioner testified he thought his statements were protected by Rule 177(3). A review of the press conference supports that claim. He gave only a brief opening statement, and on numerous occasions declined to answer reporters' questions seeking more detailed comments. One illustrative exchange shows petitioner's attempt to obey the rule:

QUESTION FROM THE FLOOR: Dominick, you mention you question the credibility of some of the witnesses, some of the people named as victims in the government indictment.

Can we go through it and *elaborate* on their backgrounds, interests —

MR. GENTILE: *I can't because ethics prohibit me from doing so.*

Last night before I decided I was going to make a statement, I took a close look at the rules of professional responsibility. There are things that I can say and there are things that I can't. Okay?

. . . .

The judgment of the Supreme Court of Nevada is *reversed.*

CHIEF JUSTICE REHNQUIST [Majority opinion as to Parts I and II, dissent as to Part III and Judgment]: We conclude that the "substantial likelihood of material prejudice" standard applied by Nevada and most other states satisfies the First Amendment.

. . . .

The Southern Nevada Disciplinary Board found that petitioner knew the detective he accused of perpetrating the crime and abusing drugs would be a witness for the prosecution. It also found that petitioner believed others whom he characterized as money launderers and drug dealers would be called as prosecution witnesses. Petitioner's admitted purpose for calling the press conference was to counter public opinion which he perceived as adverse to his client, to fight back against the perceived efforts of the prosecution to poison the prospective juror pool, and to publicly present his client's side of the case. The Board found that in light of the statements, their timing, and petitioner's purpose, petitioner knew or should have known that there was a substantial likelihood that the statements would materially prejudice the Sanders trial.

. . . .

It is unquestionable that in the courtroom itself, during a judicial proceeding, whatever right to "free speech" an attorney has is extremely circumscribed. An attorney may not, by speech or other conduct, resist a ruling of the trial court beyond the point necessary to preserve a claim for appeal. Even outside the courtroom a majority of the Court in two separate opinions in the case of *In re Sawyer*, 360 U.S. 622, 79 S. Ct. 1376, 3 L. Ed. 2d 1473 (1959), observed that lawyers in pending cases were subject to ethical restrictions on speech to which an ordinary citizen would not be.

. . . .

Because lawyers have special access to information through discovery and client communications, their extrajudicial statements pose a threat to the fairness of a pending proceeding since lawyers' statements are likely to be received as especially authoritative. . . . We agree with the majority of the States that the "substantial likelihood of material prejudice" standard constitutes a constitutionally permissible balance between the First Amendment rights of attorneys in pending cases and the state's interest in fair trials.

NOTES

There are few post-*Gentile* cases delineating the permissible scope of attorney speech under the First Amendment. In *U.S. v. Cutler*, 58 F.2d 825 (2d Cir. 1995), the Second Circuit found that a showing of actual prejudice was not important, but that a showing of intent to counter prejudicial publicity is a crucial factor in deciding whether there is a reasonable likelihood that attorney speech interferes with a fair trial.

7. The Revised ABA Rule and Other Alternatives

In 1994, the ABA substantially modified Rule 3.6, significantly narrowing it and expanding its exceptions. Taking a page from Justice Kennedy's opinion in *Gentile*, Rule 3.6(c) allows a lawyer to make a statement that is reasonably required "to protect a client from the substantial undue prejudicial effect of recent publicity. . . ." It appears that this provision is not limited to counteracting prejudice to the jury, but could also be used to defend a client, to use Kennedy's words, "in the court of public opinion." And to solve the unconstitutionally vague provision allowing a public description of the "general nature" of a claim or defense, the ABA eliminated the offending phrases "without elaboration" and "general nature"; now, an attorney may simply describe the client's defense. Retaining this exception is understandable, since without it, a prosecutor could refer to available court documents, such as indictments and search warrants, while a defense lawyer could not respond with a client's defense unless and until some document about it was filed with the court. Clearly under this new rule, Dominic Gentile's press conference would not have subjected him to discipline.

Several states — and commentators — continue to question why a lower First Amendment standard should be used only for lawyers. The leading case decided under the Model Code, *Chicago Council of Lawyers v. Bauer*,[9] held that DR 7-107 was unconstitutionally vague and overbroad, and that only comments that pose a "serious and imminent threat" of interference with the fair administration of justice may be prohibited.

With California's joining the parade following the massive publicity in the O.J. Simpson case, every jurisdiction in the country now has a rule that limits lawyers' free speech in cases of prejudicial publicity. In most jurisdictions, however, remaining First Amendment protections and the realities of disciplinary agencies' enforcement priorities mean that such rules will likely only rarely be the source of attorney discipline. Many enforcement agencies simply find it too difficult to

---

[9] 522 F.2d 242 (7th Cir. 1975). See a further discussion of this case in the Supplemental Readings.

sustain a violation, and in most instances, the exceptions to MR 3.6 may effectively swallow the rule.

Moreover, since a violation turns on the likely prejudicial effect on the judge or jury, and a disciplinary hearing usually occurs after the fact of a trial, it is difficult to show any *actual* prejudice. Although Rehnquist's opinion makes it clear that no actual prejudice is necessary for the "substantial likelihood" standard to be violated, one must question why such a rule is necessary if careful jury voir dire successfully eliminates or cures the prejudice anyway. As the *Gentile* case and many studies[10] have shown, potential jurors rarely remember the details of pretrial publicity by the time trial rolls around, and even if they do, they view what they read in the press and see on television with healthy skepticism. Perhaps the emphasis on prejudicial *pretrial* publicity has been misplaced. Thus, the District of Columbia rule is limited to cases currently in trial, when curing the prejudice can be far more difficult.

Nevertheless, some courts have on rare occasions disciplined lawyers for violating Rule 3.6, and in one case dismissed a case as an issue sanction against the client of the offending attorney. Two notable cases ensnared prosecutors for improper pre-trial publicity. In *Attorney Grievance Comm'n v. Gansler*, 835 A.2d 548 (Md. 2003), prosecutor Gansler released a defendant's confession and the plea bargain offers he had made to the defendant. Noting that prosecutors "are held to even higher standards of conduct than other attorneys," particularly where it comes to expressing their opinions about a defendant's guilt, the court upheld the Grievance Commission's discipline, but only as to a wrist-slap public reprimand. And, as we will discuss at greater length in Problem 23, North Carolina district attorney Michael Nifong was disbarred in 2007 in part for his pre-trial statements to the press, many of which were false.

Finally, in *Maldonado v. Ford Company*, 719 N.W.2d 809 (Mich. 2006), the lawyer for plaintiff in sexual harassment case repeatedly disclosed to the press a previous sexual harassment conviction of the alleged perpetrator that had been expunged by the court, rendering it inadmissible. The repeated violation of the pre-trial publicity rule resulted in the trial court dismissing the case, a decision upheld on appeal.

8. Criticizing the Judge

Does lawyers' free speech narrow when it comes to criticizing a judge? The ABA has a specific rule covering the issue: Model Rule 8.2 prevents a lawyer from making a statement critical of a judge, either when the lawyer knows the statement is false, or when the lawyer recklessly disregards whether it is true or false.

Former Congresswoman Elizabeth Holtzman ran afoul of a similar New York rule. Holtzman was elected Kings County (Brooklyn) District Attorney, where she continued a highly visible political career that included a run for the United States Senate. When she read in a deputy DA's memo that a judge had asked a rape victim

---

[10] *See, e.g.*, Martin F. Kaplan, *Cognitive Processes in the Individual Juror*, *in* THE PSYCHOLOGY OF THE COURTROOM (N. L. Kerr and R. M. Bray eds., 1982). Kaplan's chapter cites numerous other studies.

to get down on the floor in chambers and show the position she was in at the time of the assault, Holtzman was outraged, and fired off a letter to the judge who chaired the state's Task Force on Women in the Courts. Then, she released her letter to the press in the form of a "news alert."

This press release resulted in a disciplinary investigation of Holtzman. Despite Holtzman fighting the matter to the United States Supreme Court, the private letter of admonition she received was upheld by the New York Court of Appeals,[11] which was unpersuaded by the fact that Holtzman thought the allegations were true. The sanction was warranted, said the court, because Holtzman did nothing to investigate the charges, not even talking to her staff attorney. The court rejected her argument that actual malice, such as that required for defamation of public figures, was required in order to sustain a disciplinary violation: "Accepting [Holtzman's] argument would immunize all accusations, however reckless or irresponsible, from censure as long as the attorney uttering them did not actually entertain serious doubts as to their truth."

What about lawyers who express opinions about a judge, rather than alleging particular "facts"? In *In re Westfall*, 808 S.W.2d 829 (Mo. 1991), a Missouri prosecutor went on television to criticize the opinion of an appeals judge who rejected a criminal prosecution. Westfall said the judge's opinion "distorted the statute . . . and convoluted logic to arrive at a decision that he personally likes." He characterized the judge as "a little bit less than honest." Westfall defended his statement by arguing first, that he was merely expressing his personal opinion about the judge, not stating facts, and second, that he was criticizing the judge's opinion, not the judge. In light of the words used, this last defense simply doesn't hold up. But Westfall's first argument also failed to impress both the majority of the Missouri Supreme Court (though the Chief Justice wrote a strong dissenting opinion), and the U.S. Supreme Court, which denied certiorari on the same day it was denied for Holtzman.[12]

More recently, in *Office of Disciplinary Counsel v. Gardner*, 793 N.E.2d 425 (Ohio 2003), the Ohio Supreme Court upheld a six month suspension of attorney Gardner for making accusations of judicial impropriety against a panel of appellate judges. Among other things, Gardner declared that the panel had issued an opinion so "result driven" that "any fair-minded judge" would have been "ashamed to attach his/her name" to it. The court found that this was not protected speech even though no malice was found, and adopted "an objective standard" based on whether a reasonable attorney, "considered in light of all his professional functions," would so act, and "whether the attorney had a reasonable factual basis for making the statements."

Other courts have been more lenient in allowing lawyers to express their opinions, blunt though they may be, about judges. Thus, where a Texas attorney called a judge "a midget among giants," a court refused to discipline the lawyer because he was merely expressing his own personal beliefs. *State Bar v. Semaan*, 508 S.W.2d 429 (Tex. 1974). In 1959, the Supreme Court decided *In re Sawyer*, 360

---

[11] *In re Holtzman*, 78 N.Y.2d 184, 573 N.Y.S.2d 39, 577 N.E.2d 30 (1991).

[12] 502 U.S. 1009 (1991).

U.S. 622, 79 S. Ct. 1376 (1959). Some commentators believe that *Gentile* effectively overruled much of this case. But others believe that part of the *Sawyer* holding still controls: that opinions about judges should be protected, even in a pending case, unless the lawyer's speech obstructs justice. But what constitutes obstruction of justice? Interestingly, the *Holtzman* court itself agreed that "obstruction of justice" was the appropriate standard, claiming that Holtzman's criticism did more than merely attack one judge's reputation. Was Holtzman's press release a broad attack on the administration of justice? Essentially, the court's finding was "yes."

Read the opinion of another court, in which noted jurist Alex Kozinski, widely considered both a conservative and an intellectual, carefully analyzed the over-the-top behavior of a well-known Los Angeles legal gadfly and came to an interesting result.

STANDING COMMITTEE ON DISCIPLINE, UNITED STATES DISTRICT COURT FOR THE CENTRAL DISTRICT OF CALIFORNIA v. YAGMAN
55 F.3d 1430 (9th Cir. 1995)

Never far from the center of controversy, outspoken civil rights lawyer Stephen Yagman was suspended from practice before the United State Distric Court for the Central District of California for impugning the integrity of the court and interfering with the random selection of judges by making disparaging remarks about a judge of that court. We confront several new issues in reviewing this suspension order.

The convoluted history of his case begins in 1991 when Yagman filed a lawsuit *pro se* against several insurance companies. The case was assigned to Judge Manuel Real, then Chief Judge of the Central District. Yagman promptly sought to disqualify Judge Real on grounds of bias. The disqualification motion was randomly assigned to Judge William Keller, who denied ityuyyy and sanctioned Yagman for pursuing the matter in an "improper and frivolous manner.:"

A few days after Judge Keller's sanctions order, Yagman was quoted [in the L.A. *Daily Journal* legal newspaper] as saying that Judge Keller "has a penchant for sanctioning Jewish lawyers: me, David Kenner and Hugh Manes. I find this to be evidence of anti-semitism." The district court found that Yagman also told the *Daily Journal* reporter that Judge Keller was "drunk on the bench." . . .

Around this time, Yagman received a request from Prentice Hall, publisher of the much-fretted-about Almanac of the Federal Judiciary, for comments in connection with a profile of Judge Keller. Yagman's response was less than complimentary.[13]

Soon after these events, Yagman ran into Robert Steinberg, another attorney who practices in the Central District. According to Steinberg, Yagman told him that, by leveling public criticism at Judge Keller, Yagman hoped to get the judge to

---

[13] [4] The portion of the letter relevant here reads as follows:

> It is an understatement to characterize the Judge as "the worst judge in the central district." It would be fairer to say that he is ignorant, dishonest, ill-tempered, and a bully, and probably is one of the worst judges in the United States.

recuse himself in future cases. Believing that Yagman was committing misconduct, Steinberg described his conversation with Yagman in a letter to the Standing Committee on Discipline. A few weeks later, the Standing Committee received a letter from Judge Keller [stating] "there is clear evidence that Mr. Yagman's attacks upon me are motivated by his desire to create a basis for recusing me in any future proceeding."

1. We begin with the portion of Local Rule 2.5.2 prohibiting any conduct that "impugns the integrity of the Court." As the district court recognized, this provision is overbroad because it purports to punish a great deal of constitutionally protected speech, including all true statements reflecting adversely on the reputation or character of federal judges.

To save the "impugn the integrity" portion of Rule 2.5.2, the district court read into it an "objective" version of the malice standard enunciated in *New York Times Co. v. Sullivan*, 376 U.S. 254 (1964) . . . to prohibit only false statements made with either knowledge of their falsity or with reckless disregard as to their truth or falsity, judged from the standpoint of a "reasonable attorney."

. . . .

Though attorneys can play an important role in exposing problems with the judicial system, false statements impugning the integrity of a judge erode public confidence without serving to publicize problems that justifiably deserve attention. . . .

Attorneys who make statements impugning the integrity of a judge are, however, entitled to other First Amendment protections applicable in the defamation context. To begin with, attorneys may be sanctioned for impugning the integrity of a judge or the court only if their statements are false; truth is an absolute defense. . . .

It follows that statements impugning the integrity of a judge may not be punished unless they are capable of being proved true or false; statements of opinion are protected by the First Amendment unless they "imply a false assertion of fact."

With these principles in mind, we examine the statements for which Yagman was disciplined.

2. We first consider Yagman's statement in the *Daily Journal* that Judge Keller "has a penchant for sanctioning Jewish lawyers: me, David Kenner and Hugh Manes. I find this to be evidence of anti-semitism." Though the district court viewed this entirely as an assertion of fact, we conclude that the statement contains both an assertion of fact and an expression of opinion.

Yagman's claim that he, Kenner and Manes are all Jewish and were sanctioned by Judge Keller is clearly a factual assertion: The words have specific, well-defined meanings and describe objectively verifiable matters. . . . Thus, had the Standing Committee proved that Yagman, Kenner or Manes were not sanctioned by Judge Keller, or were not Jewish, this assertion might have formed the basis for discipline. The committee, however, didn't claim that Yagman's factual assertion was false . . . . We proceed, therefore, on the assumption that this portion of Yagman's statement is true.

The remaining portion of Yagman's *Daily Journal* statement is best characterized as opinion; it conveys Yagman's personal belief that Judge Keller is anti-Semitic. As such, it may be the basis of sanctions only if it could reasonably be understood as declaring or implying actual facts capable of being proved true or false.

. . . .

3. The district court also disciplined Yagman for alleging that Judge Keller was "dishonest." This remark appears in the letter Yagman sent to Prentice Hall in connection with the profile of Judge Keller in the Almanac of the Federal Judiciary. The court concluded that this allegation was sanctionable because it "plainly implies past improprieties." Had Yagman accused Judge Keller of taking bribes, we would agree with the district court. Statements that "could reasonably be understood as imputing specific criminal or other wrongful acts" are not entitled to constitutional protection merely because they are phrased in the form of an opinion.

When considered in context, however, Yagman's statement cannot reasonably be interpreted as accusing Judge Keller of criminal misconduct. The term "dishonest" was one in a string of colorful adjectives Yagman used to convey the low esteem in which he held Judge Keller. The other terms he used — "ignorant," "ill-tempered," "buffoon," "sub-standard human," "right-wing fanatic," "a bully," "one of the worst judges in the United States" — all speak to competence and temperament rather than corruption; together they convey nothing more substantive than Yagman's contempt for Judge Keller. Viewed in context of these "lusty and imaginative expressions," the word "dishonest" cannot reasonably be construed as suggesting that Judge Keller had committed specific illegal acts . . . .

Were we to find any substantive content in Yagman's use of the term "dishonest," we would, at most, construe it to mean "intellectually dishonest" — an accusation that Judge Keller's rulings were overly result-oriented. Intellectual dishonesty is a label lawyers frequently attach to decisions with which they disagree. . . . Because Yagman's allegation of "dishonesty" does not imply facts capable of objective verification, it is constitutionally immune from sanctions.

4. Finally, the district court found sanctionable Yagman's allegation that Judge Keller was "drunk on the bench." Yagman contends that, like many of the terms he used in his letter to Prentice Hall, this phrase should be viewed as mere "rhetorical hyperbole." The statement wasn't a part of the string of invective in the Prentice Hall letter, however; it was a remark Yagman allegedly made to a newspaper reporter. Yagman identifies nothing relating to the context in which this statement was made that tends to negate the literal meaning of the words he used. We therefore conclude that Yagman's "drunk on the bench" statement could reasonably be interpreted as suggesting that Judge Keller had actually, on at least one occasion, taken the bench while intoxicated. Unlike Yagman's remarks in his letter to Prentice Hall, this statement implies actual facts that are capable of objective verification. For this reason, the statement isn't protected.

For Yagman's "drunk on the bench" allegation to serve as the basis for sanctions, however, the Standing Committee had to prove that the statement was false. This it failed to do; indeed, the committee introduced no evidence at all on the point. . . .

As an alternative basis for sanctioning Yagman, the district court concluded that Yagman's statements violated Local Rule 2.5.2's prohibition against engaging in conduct that "interferes with the administration of justice." The court found that Yagman made the statements discussed above in an attempt to "judge-shop" — i.e., to cause Judge Keller to recuse himself in cases where Yagman appeared as counsel.

The Supreme Court has held that speech otherwise entitled to full constitutional protection may nonetheless be sanctioned if it obstructs or prejudices the administration of justice. Given the significant burden this rule places on otherwise protected speech, however, the Court has held that prejudice to the administration of justice must be highly likely before speech may be punished.

In a trio of cases involving contempt sanctions imposed against newspapers, the Court articulated the constitutional standard to be applied in this context. Press statements relating to judicial matters may not be restricted, the Court held, unless they pose a "clear and present danger" to the administration of justice. The standard announced in these cases is a demanding one: Statements may be punished only if they "constitute an imminent, not merely a likely, threat to the administration of justice. The danger must not be remote or even probable: it must immediately imperil." . . .

. . . .

The question remains whether the possibility of voluntary recusal is so great as to amount to a clear and present danger. We believe it is not. . . . Judge Real, for example, despite receiving harsh criticism from Yagman, did not recuse himself in *Yagman v. Republic Ins.*, where Yagman was not merely the lawyer but also a party to the proceedings. . . .

We can't improve on the words of Justice Black in *Bridges [v. California*, 314 U.S. 252, 62 S. Ct. 190 (1941)] at 270–71 (footnote omitted):

The assumption that respect for the judiciary can be won by shielding judges from published criticism wrongly appraises the character of American public opinion. For it is a prized American privilege to speak one's mind, although not always with perfect good taste, on all public institutions. And an enforced silence, however limited, solely in the name of preserving the dignity of the bench, would probably engender resentment, suspicion and contempt much more than it would enhance respect.

Reversed.

D. SUPPLEMENTAL READINGS

1. Susan E. Davis, *Uncivil Behavior: The Tactics Lawyers Resort to When They're Not Restrained*, CALIFORNIA LAWYER (July 1999). This article is a pungent, to-the-point view of the lack of civil behavior in the profession, complete with a list of root causes, including: "because it works," "testosterone poisoning," and "it's contagious." Davis also offers some valuable proposed solutions.

2. Brenda Smith, *Civility Codes: The Newest Weapons in the "Civil" War Over Proper Attorney Conduct Regulations Miss Their Mark*, 24 DAYTON L. REV. 151

(1998). This article questions whether civility codes are really the best solution for improving the legal profession.

3. G.M. Filisko, *You're Out of Order! Dealing with the Costs of Incivility in the Legal Profession,* ABA JOURNAL (Jan. 2013). Filisko argues that the time for mandatory civility is long overdue, and that all state bars should follow the lead of the few jurisdictions that have made civility mandatory.

4. Christopher J. Piazzola, *Ethical Versus Procedural Approaches to Civility: Why Ethics 2000 Should Have Adopted a Civility Rule,* 74 U. COLO. L. REV. 1197 (2003), is another pro-civility article focusing on how rules commissions have yet to adopt ethical rules requiring civility or professionalism by attorneys. It cites the case of Lee Rohm, the lawyer in the *Saldana* case cited in section 3, among other interesting examples.

5. David A.Grenardo, *Making Civility Mandatory: Moving from Aspired to Required* CARDOZO PUBLIC LAW, POLICY AND ETHICS JOURNAL, (Oct. 26, 2012), *available at* http://ssrn.com/abstract=2188407. This article examines what civility is, and the problem of incivility. Grenardo discusses what he sees as the legal profession's limited response to incivility to date, and in most instances it falls short.

7. Two older cases that reached opposite results in explosive circumstances remain of interest. *In re Carrow,* 40 Cal. App. 3d 924 (1974). Attorney Carrow won reversal of an order of contempt in a highly politicized trial that the appeals court acknowledged had been difficult on both the judge and the lawyers. Carrow's comment about the trial becoming a "joke" was made in response to a witness' runaway narrative and couched in otherwise respectful terms. ("Your Honor, I submit this trial is becoming a joke.") In *In re Friedland,* 376 N.E.2d 1126 (Ind. 1978), by contrast, discipline was sustained against a lawyer who called the trial a farce. This was held to be "conduct prejudicial to the administration of justice," and a false accusation against the judicial officer. Here, however, the attorney was otherwise disrespectful.

8. Lonnie T. Brown Jr., *Civility and Collegiality — Unreasonable Judicial Expectations for Lawyers as Officers of the Court?* 2 ST. MARY'S (TX) J. ON LEG. MALPRACTICE AND ETHICS, 324, (2012). Professor Brown notes the Eleventh Circuit's recent unprecedented use of the term "officer of the court" to in effect, sanction an attorney for the purportedly uncivil act of failing to provide defendant attorneys with notice prior to a lawsuit. Brown expresses concern that this might force litigators to compromise important client-centered duties. Brown argues that courts should carefully define sanctionable officer-of-the-court conduct by reference to well-defined, existing procedural and ethical norms, thereby enhancing predictability.

9. Carla Messikomer, a non-lawyer writing in the Fordham Law Review, wrote *Ambivalence, Contradiction and Ambiguity: The Everyday Ethics of Defense Litigators,* 67 FORDHAM L. REV. 739 (1998). In this piece she studied lawyers' comfort levels with certain terms. She was struck by the way in which words like "rules" and "norms" were within attorneys' comfort zones, but terms like "ethics" and "misconduct" made them "uneasy." She noted the "soft, polite, rather amorphous" acceptance of terms like "incivility," a word she also called "euphemistic."

10. In *Free Speech for Lawyers*, 28 HASTINGS CONST. L.Q. 305 (2001), Professor W. Bradley Wendel analyzes and criticizes the disparate treatment of free speech in cases that don't deal with lawyers as opposed to those that do.

11. Lonnie T. Brown, Jr., *"May It Please the Camera, I Mean the Court" — An Intrajudical Solution to an Extrajudicial Problem*, 39 GA. L. REV. 83 (2004), re-examines pre-trial publicity after *Gentile* and suggests that in the modern era of high-visibility trials like Scott Peterson's and Michael Jackson's and the post-9/11 politicization of cases like that of the so-called "American Taliban," John Walker Lindh, we need rules that "equate the court of public opinion with courts of law for purposes of professional regulation."

12. *Chicago Council of Lawyers v. Bauer*, 522 F.2d 242 (7th Cir. 1975). An association of local lawyers sought declaratory relief and an injunction against the enforcement of a local criminal "no-comment" rule of court and disciplinary rule. The "no-comment" rule, in the criminal context, prohibited the extrajudicial comments by lawyers in connection with pending cases if there was a reasonable likelihood that the release of such information would interfere with a fair trial. The plaintiffs argued that the "no-comment" rules deprived lawyers of their freedom of speech under the First Amendment. The court agreed, holding that the "no-comment" rule in the criminal context may bar only those comments which pose a serious and imminent threat of interference with the fair administration of justice. The court also criticized rules which purported to sanction lawyers for criticizing judges, as violative of "pure" free speech.

PROBLEM 22: ADVOCATES' AND MEDIATORS' ETHICAL DILEMMAS IN MEDIATION

A. INTRODUCTION

This problem explores ethical issues relating to mediation, an ever-increasingly important method of resolving disputes. Many of these issues have been touched on elsewhere in this volume: confidentiality, conflicts of interest, and negotiation tactics among them. But mediation brings a new spin to these issues, particularly because of the lack of enforceable black-letter rules. We also address how both advocates and mediators engage in balancing acts, between the parties and, on occasion, between the client and the public welfare. For instance, sometimes a mediation settlement is offered only on the condition of secrecy. When a mediator sees a disparity in power between the parties or a litigator sees a danger in "secretizing" a settlement about an issue that endangers the public, mediators must reconcile personal morality and their professional obligations.

B. PROBLEM

I

Peter van Lund of Cooper, van Lund & Winters LLP, represents Benedict, Inc., a corporation with diverse pharmaceutical holdings. One of Benedict's most lucrative subsidiaries is KimPro, a company that manufactures *Annihilator*, a chemotherapy that drug trials have shown is particularly effective for treating ovarian cancer.

Marla Justice is a partner at Fisler & Nichols, a small firm that represents plaintiffs in injury cases. She has developed a niche doing products liability work. Justice represents Jacob Stephens, whose wife, Joy, unsuccessfully underwent *Annihilator* chemotherapy and died at age 38. Justice and her experts believe that the chemotherapy used on Joy was tainted, resulting in her death.

Justice and van Lund have engaged in constant discovery battles, so she is surprised when, shortly before the hearing on her latest discovery motion, van Lund suggests mediating the case. Though aware of Cooper, van Lund's adage, "Litigate and never blink!" she readily agrees. She suggests the names of a few lawyers whom she knows are skilled "neutrals" knowledgeable in products liability matters. Van Lund, however, demands Jimmy Springer, a recently-retired judge who has rejoined Emile & Springer, van Lund's former firm. Van Lund insists that "only Springer can get this done."

QUESTIONS

1. Does Justice have an ethical duty to suggest mediation to her client in the first place? What if Justice is opposed to mediation because she believes that individual plaintiffs are at a disadvantage when facing powerful mega-companies?

What about here, where van Lund has made the offer but will only mediate with Springer?

2. Does van Lund's previous employment with Springer's firm pose ethical concerns? How should they be resolved? Does van Lund's hand-picking Springer raise any ethical issues?

3. What duties, if any, do Springer or van Lund have to disclose their relationship? What if van Lund has used Springer as a mediator on 10 prior occasions? What if van Lund and Springer had a close, personal relationship instead of a professional one? *Who*, if anyone, should disclose?

II

At the mediation, after several difficult hours with little progress toward settlement, Springer calls Justice into the coffee room for a "private chat." Van Lund, he says, has just made a surprising one-time offer: Settle the case today for $3,000,000 or get ready to go to trial. Justice is shocked, especially since the offer is substantially higher than her own private evaluation. She asks Springer what's going on. Springer tells her he will only speak if she promises silence, even as to her client. He then tells her that her latest discovery motion will likely result in "smoking gun" documents revealing "adverse incidents" that show tainted *Annihilator* was directly responsible for the deaths of several women and the near-death poisoning of others.

Springer then meets with just the lawyers. Van Lund places two conditions on his offer: first, that the parties enter into a settlement agreement in which neither the amount nor the information about other adverse incidents may be revealed; and second that Justice may tell Stephens only of the existence of a problem without mentioning any specifics.

QUESTIONS

1. Was it ethical for Justice to meet Springer or van Lund without Stephens?

2. May Justice ethically recommend settlement while keeping the specifics about adverse incidents from her client? Would a totally "confidential" settlement be ethical if she *could* tell Stephens what she knows?

3. In considering the offer, would it be appropriate for Justice to tell Stephens her concerns about future harm to the public if secrecy shrouds the discovery? Could Justice recommend *against* settlement if the discoverable information must remain secret?

4. What, if anything, may Springer say about the mediation? May he write about it in his bi-monthly newsletter if he changes all the names? If this were court-ordered mediation and he were ordered to do so, could he write a report to the court detailing how he thought the case should be resolved?

III

Virginia Westport is a successful full-time lawyer-mediator. She is mediating a case with Lester Granot, who represents Al Pottman, a self-employed 48-year-old landscaper who was hit and injured by a Quick Cab taxi, and John Quincy, an experienced defense lawyer representing Quick Cab and its driver.

During an early "caucus" with Westport, Granot, who strikes her as having little litigation experience, confides that Pottman's medical bills are only $10,000 and that while Pottman is in great pain and can no longer handle the physical rigors demanded of his livelihood, he has only soft-tissue injuries, though his improvement is unlikely. Granot tells Westport that his demand is $50,000.

During a later caucus with Quincy, he notes the weakness of opposing counsel and makes it clear that he considers the case to be worth little. He offers to pay only a $15,000 "nuisance value." He pressures Westport to resolve matters "so we can all get back to more important things."

As Westport leaves that caucus she runs into Pottman, who had gone for a cup of coffee. He tells Westport that he is worried about his case, his attorney, and his future. He had been a landscaper for 20 years and is concerned about providing for his family. He says that even though the doctors say he won't be able to go back to landscaping, Granot told him his "medicals are too low" for a large settlement. He found Granot through a friend of a friend, and feels stuck because Granot's contingency fee contract, which calls for 40% of the recovery, contains a lien against any recovery should Pottman fire him. Pottman makes it clear he feels intimidated by the whole mediation process and does not know who to trust. He pleads for Westport's help.

QUESTIONS

1. What should Westport do? May she reply to Pottman at all? Suppose that given her experience, she believes that the true value of his case is $150,000 to $250,000. Should she tell either Granot or Pottman? Would your answer change if Quincy had told her "I'd offer $100,000 or more, but *not* against that lightweight lawyer"?

2. What if Westport believes that Granot is incompetent or that his fee is unethically high? May she tell Pottman to get a different attorney? Should she? May she simply stop the mediation?

C. READINGS

1. What Is Mediation?

As the world of litigation evolves, so does the way in which people respond to conflict. ADR, an acronym for Alternative Dispute Resolution, has become "part and parcel of the practice of law and constitutes a tool of equal rank with litigation to achieve, in the proper case, prompt and cost-effective dispute resolution."[1]

There are many types of ADR, including mediation, arbitration (where the "neutral" is a private decision-maker, acting as trier of both fact and law), judicial reference to a special master, early neutral evaluation, "med/arb" (unsuccessful mediation turns into binding arbitration), and "arb/med" (arbitrator attempts to get the parties to resolve the case consensually before arbitration). The use of ADR is likely to increase dramatically as more courts promote "fast track" timetables that discourage delay. Today, less than five percent of civil filings end up going to trial. That leaves 95% that resolve another way. Over 80% of cases that go to mediation settle at the mediation or shortly after. Why do you think this is so?

Mediation has changed greatly in the last 15 years. Even its very definition has changed. According to the Sixth edition of Black's Law Dictionary, used through most of the 1990s, mediation was defined as "the act of a third person who interferes between two contending parties with a view to reconcile them or persuade them to adjust or settle their dispute."

By the time the Preamble to the 2005 Model Standards (discussed extensively in the next section) was drafted, mediation was defined far more generally:

> Mediation is a process in which an impartial third party facilitates communication and negotiation and promotes voluntary decision making by the parties to the dispute. Mediation serves various purposes, including providing the opportunity for parties to define and clarify issues, understand different perspectives, identify interests, explore and assess possible solutions, and reach mutually satisfactory agreements, when desired.

Note the difference in tone between these two definitions. Note too the absence of the words "settlement," "resolution," and "persuasion" in the more modern definition.

In some ways, the "art" of mediation, and its use by artful mediators, is more than merely conveying information between disputants. Mediators listen carefully to both advocates and parties to be able to frame the case's issues and highlight particular strengths and weaknesses of each side. There are many techniques that mediators use to move parties from polarization to potential resolution. How they do this may raise ethical concerns for mediator and advocate. Ethical concerns are avoided when the mediators earn the one thing most important in their arsenal: *trust*. We know many experienced litigators who prefer to use a mediator chosen by the other side for precisely this reason.

The beauty of mediation is that it allows litigants and their lawyers control over the outcome of their disputes. No third party, whether judge, jury, or arbitrator, makes rulings or issues awards. The process generally saves time and money. More importantly, it can provide a measure of satisfaction to all, while allowing for more creative solutions than traditional litigation. Moreover, parties can resolve disputes without destroying ongoing relationships. And parties can achieve goals other than "merely" resolving a dispute. And because mediation is generally a voluntary process, there is no risk. In their writings and discussions, mediators often refer to

---

[1] New Jersey Joint Ethics and Advertising Opinion 676/18 (April 4, 1994).

"the process," and to "letting the process work." Many mediators say that preserving the process is their main goal, not settlement. Many others talk about the primacy of neutrality and "symmetry," a concept that is more than equality — a balance of fair dealing and equal treatment for all sides.

Some old-style advocates continue to criticize mediation as little more than a forum for a fishing exhibition, allowing free discovery without the hammer of the court. But with court-ordered mediation increasingly common, the parties and their counsel are required to make a "good faith" effort at settlement.[2]

Still, what information is provided and how it is ultimately used is largely dependent on the attorneys. Should a lawyer refuse to reveal information in an attempt to save the "smoking gun" for trial? Or is a client best served by a more open, candid approach? Over the years, more candor has become the norm, as the process works most of the time, and the adequate exchange of information is a necessary part of that process.

Once parties decide to mediate, their selection of the mediator is voluntary — unless a particular mediator is insisted on by a court. This decision usually based on the mediator's style, reputation, and relevant experience. There are times when some lawyers may insist on a specific mediator. This often occurs when a "repeat customer" — say an insurance carrier — has learned to trust a particular individual's style, approach, and — most important — word. Mediators have no actual power in forcing parties to settle, but they often have enormous informal influence over the disputants. Many are retired judges or attorneys with formidable reputations in the legal community.

Mediator selection criteria, whether based on real or perceived data, can raise ethical concerns. For instance, what if an attorney bases selection on the perception that the particular mediator has a reputation for extracting large settlements from insurance carriers? Or that the mediator is known to be close to one party or another? Or particularly tough-minded and tough-talking, even intimidating? Market forces may afford the best protection against mediator bias. After all, mediators would not stay in business long if their neutrality were frequently questioned.

2. Ethical Rules for Mediators

Historically, ADR was used by stipulation of the parties. As a result, formal rules governing the process of mediation were slow to develop. The ABA largely shied away from developing extensive rules about mediation, even during the Ethics 2000 revisions. But over the past dozen years and after some false starts during the 1990s, extensive rules of conduct for mediators have been developed and adopted by several organizations and some states.

Perhaps the biggest false start in mediation rule-making was lumping arbitration and mediation together as "ADR." Arbitration already had two

---

[2] "Court-ordered mediation" is something of an oxymoron, since one of the hallmarks of mediation has always been the voluntary nature of the process, something the 2005 standards include in the term "self-determination." Mandated good faith for an essentially voluntary process is difficult at best.

foundational statutes: the federal Arbitration Act of 1954 requires courts to recognize and enforce arbitration awards that are fundamentally fair, while the Uniform Arbitration Act, adopted in 49 states, outlines a series of arbitration requirements that make overturning an arbitration award nearly impossible.[3]

While it has long been generally accepted that the mediator should be a neutral third party with no vested interest in the outcome of a dispute,[4] perhaps because mediators are not judges and have no decisionmaking power, codified regulations were slower to develop. There were a number of ethics codes for ADR neutrals that promulgated by national ADR professional organizations, state-wide regulatory or judicial bodies, individual courts, and so on,[5] but many of these codes applied to both arbitrators and mediators alike, despite the fact that arbitrators act far more like judges than they act like mediators.

This problem also characterized the 2002 changes to the ABA Model Rules, which eliminated a rule addressing the lawyer as "intermediary" and added Rule 2.4, titled Lawyer Serving as Third-Party Neutral. This rule also drew no distinction between mediators and arbitrators, despite the vast differences in these neutrals' roles. MR 2.4 was only a relatively modest change that, even before it was approved, did not seem adequate to serve as the basis for a uniform, systematic approach to ethics for lawyer-mediators. Vital issues such as confidentiality, conflicts of interest, fees, court obligations, and competency standards were not specifically addressed. More specific rules were necessary.

Those more sophisticated rules came shortly after MR 2.4 was passed. First, the National Conference of Commissioners on Uniform State Laws and the American Bar Association's Section of Dispute Resolution drafted a Uniform Mediation Act (UMA), which culminated in final uniform legislation being approved in 2003. The UMA focuses primarily on the issue of confidentiality, which we will examine more thoroughly in the next section. The number of states approving the UMA or similar legislation has increased only slowly in the model statute's first decade. But by Spring 2013, 10 states and the District of Columbia had approved it, six states had similar legislation, and three states — Hawai'i, Massachusetts and New York — were considering it.[6]

In the early 1990s, a group of ADR organizations working together with the ABA's section on dispute resolution drafted and passed, in 1994, the first version of the Model Standards of Conduct for Mediators. These standards achieved some degree of acceptance within the "industry," but it was not until their extensive

---

[3] *See generally* William C. Smith, *Much to Do About ADR*, ABA J., June 2000, at 62.

[4] Many mediators say this lack of investment should extend even to the issue of whether the case settles — the only goal being to protect the neutrality of the mediation process itself.

[5] *See* the CPR-Georgetown Commission on Ethics and Standards of Practice in ADR monograph, *Principles for ADR Provider Organization*, June 2000, at 18.

[6] The states that have approved it or similar legislation are Delaware, Florida, Illinois, Indiana, Iowa, Montana, Nebraska, Nevada, New Jersey, Ohio, Oregon, South Dakota, Utah, Vermont, Washington, Wyoming, and the District of Columbia. *See* the Uniform Law Commission website at http://uniformlaws. org/Legislation.aspx, and The International Institute for Conflict Prevention & Resolution (CPR), *available at* http://www.cpradr.org/Resources/ALLCPRArticles/tabid/265/ID/239/Legislation-Where-the-Uniform-Mediation-Act-Stands-in-the-States-Web.aspx.

revision in 2005 that the Model Standards achieved widespread acceptance. Almost as soon as the revisions were completed, the American Bar Association House of Delegates formally approved them, and American Arbitration Association and the Association for Conflict Resolution immediately followed suit.[7]

Today, even ADR groups or state organizations that have not officially approved them suggest their use as guidelines. These guidelines, however, are just that. They don't have the force of law, though various mediator organizations may require compliance for all mediators who want to join that group.

The 2005 standards kept the same nine divisions they had had in 1994, but substantially updated the language, distinguished between mandatory ethics requirements and aspirational provisions by the use of "shall" and "should," and provided guidance for mediators to resolve conflicts among the standards. Here are brief comments about each of the first six Standards:

Standard I: Self-Determination. This standard, emphasizing the voluntariness of a mediation, makes it clear that self-determination governs all aspects of the mediation, not just the results, but the process, with the sole exception of a court-appointed mediator. Put another way by many mediators, it means that "the parties own the mediation."

Standard II: Impartiality. It goes without saying that a mediator *has to* be impartial. But that's just the start. They must appear impartial, and withdraw if they cannot be. However, as we've noted, there are mediators who are used regularly by one side or another. We believe that such familiarity does not equate to a lack of impartiality, but the standards themselves don't address this.

Standard III: Conflicts of Interest. As used here, this means that the mediator is bound to make a "reasonable inquiry" into actual and potential conflicts of interest, and disclose them to all parties. The definition of "conflicts of interest" is considerably more flexible than similar rules pertaining to lawyers or judges: "involvement by a mediator with the subject matter of the dispute or from any relationship between a mediator and any mediation participant, whether past or present, personal or professional, that reasonably raises a question of a mediator's impartiality." The key to mediation neutrality under this standard is disclosure.

Standard IV: Competence. This means exactly what it says, although no formal minimum standards are required. Rather, the question is whether after disclosure "the parties are satisfied with the mediator's competence and qualifications."

Standard V: Confidentiality. This standard makes specific reference to the UMA, which we'll discuss more in the next section on confidentiality. First, "a mediator shall maintain the confidentiality of all information obtained by the mediator in mediation, unless otherwise agreed to by the parties or required by applicable law." Second, anything told to the mediator in a private "caucus" with one side must be kept confidential absent the party's consent to disclose to the other side.

---

[7] These standards can be found in their entirety at http://www.americanbar.org/content/dam/aba/migrated/dispute/documents/model_standards_conduct_april2007.authcheckdam.pdf.

Standard VI: Quality of the Process. This standard, easily the longest and most detailed, was substantially revised in 2005 and is one of the most important, in that "process" is so central to mediation. "Quality of the process" means, among other things, "diligence," "procedural fairness," "mutual respect," and "honesty and candor." The standard defines "quality of the process" in ten separate paragraphs, including provisions that specify when the mediator may postpone or even terminate the mediation, or when the mediator may "explore . . . potential accommodations" for those who don't clearly understand the process.

More specifically, Standard VI permits a mediator to postpone or terminate the mediation or withdraw as mediator in the event of apparent criminal conduct, the disclosure of information about domestic abuse or violence, or, broadly, if any "participant conduct . . . jeopardizes conducting a mediation consistent with these Standards." Moreover, "[i]f a party appears to have difficulty comprehending the process, issues, or settlement options, or difficulty participating in a mediation, the mediator should explore the circumstances and potential accommodations, modifications or adjustments that would make possible the party's capacity to comprehend, participate and exercise self-determination."

These provisions are a far cry from earlier generations of ethical standards, which more strongly discouraged mediators from ever "putting their thumbs on the scales." Mediators under these earlier standards were observers as much as participants, with an abiding sense that it was not their place to change the equation. Indeed, the changes in Standard VI have not been met with universal acceptance, not just as to the issues raised in this paragraph, but also regarding "honesty and candor." Some mediators feel that at certain times, complete honesty and candor can destroy what would otherwise be a successfully concluded mediation. For example, mediators frequently present settlement proposals as their own, rather than a particular party's, to avoid that party being boxed into an unwanted position. In addition, strong confidentiality restrictions may at some point interfere with the greater liberality to stop mediations, if confidentiality requirements then prevent the mediator from advising appropriate authorities.

3. Confidentiality and "Fairness" Under the Uniform Act and California Case Law

Is the inviolate confidentiality of the mediation proceeding important? Undoubtedly. It is the touchstone of the desirability and success of mediation. In order to facilitate settlement, it is almost invariably necessary that parties share with the mediator information that would ordinarily be client confidences, trial strategies, and work product. The parties have a clear expectation that such discussions will be absolutely protected both as to the other side and — our focus in this section — to the outside world. Even though the mediator cannot disclose such information to the other side without consent, the mediator can and often does *use* the information without revealing it in suggesting solutions to the parties. But when it comes to the outside world, the confidentiality protections are not uniform.

The Federal Rules of Evidence provide a limited privilege for settlement discussions, while state laws offer widely varying degrees of protection. Some jurisdictions, such as California,[8] hold that all communications related to the mediation are confidential and can never be disclosed. The drafters of the UMA counted some *2,500* statutes around the country that deal in some way with confidentiality in mediation, but there was nothing close to uniformity prior to passage of the Uniform Act. The UMA was in large part an effort to move towards uniformity on confidentiality. Here is what the summary provided by National Conference of Commissioners on Uniform State Laws says about confidentiality in the uniform act:

National Conference of Commissioners on Uniform State Laws, *Meditation Act Summary*
http://www.uniformlaws.org/ActSummary.aspx?title=Mediation%20Act
(visited March 2013)

The UMA's prime concern is keeping mediation communications confidential. Parties engaged in mediation, as well as non-party participants, must be able to speak with full candor for a mediation to be successful and for a settlement to be voluntary. For this reason, the central rule of the UMA is that a mediation communication is confidential, and if privileged, is not subject to discovery or admission into evidence in a formal proceeding [see Sec. 5(a)]. In proceedings following a mediation, a party may refuse to disclose, and prevent any other person from disclosing, a mediation communication. Mediators and non-party participants may refuse to disclose their own statements made during mediation, and may prevent others from disclosing them, as well. Thus, for a person's own mediation communication to be disclosed in a subsequent hearing, that person must agree and so must the parties to the mediation. Waiver of these privileges must be in a record or made orally during a proceeding to be effective. There is no waiver by conduct.

As is the case with all general rules, there are exceptions. First, it should be noted that the privilege extends only to mediation communications, and not the underlying facts of the dispute. Evidence that is otherwise admissible or subject to discovery does not become inadmissible or protected from discovery by reason of its use in a mediation. A party that discloses a mediation communication and thereby prejudices another person in a proceeding is precluded from asserting the privilege to the extent necessary for the prejudiced person to respond. A person who intentionally uses a mediation to plan or attempt to commit a crime, or to conceal an ongoing crime, cannot assert the privilege.

Also, there is no assertable privilege against disclosure of a communication made during a mediation session that is open to the public, that contains a threat to inflict bodily injury, that is sought or offered to prove or disprove abuse, neglect, abandonment, or exploitation in a proceeding where a child or adult protective agency is a party, that would prove or disprove a claim of professional misconduct filed against a mediator, or against a party, party representative, or non-party participant based on conduct during a mediation. If a court, administrative agency, or arbitration panel finds that the need for the information outweighs the interest in confidentiality in a felony proceeding, or a proceeding to prove a claim of defense

---

[8] *See* Calif. Evidence Code § 1115 *et seq.* More about that shortly.

to reform or avoid liability on a contract arising out of the mediation, there is no privilege.

NOTES

The exceptions here make sense. Basic fairness would seem to require most of them. Note, however, the last phrase: that a court may choose to override confidentiality in a collateral proceeding to prove or disprove some element of the mediation agreement. Is this an exception that could swallow much of the rule?

California was perhaps the first state to become a hotbed of mediation, in the early 1990s. Calif. Evidence Code § 703.5 included mediators among quasi-judicial officers who could not "testify, in any subsequent civil proceeding, as to any statement, conduct, decision, or ruling, occurring at or in conjunction with the prior proceeding," with only narrow exceptions. In 1997, the legislature passed the California Mediation Act, which included a chapter on confidentiality and privilege in the Evidence Code, §§ 1115 *et. seq.* Three early California appellate court cases raised questions about the extent of mediation confidentiality. *Rinaker v. Superior Court*, 62 Cal. App. 4th 155 (1998), held that a mediator's testimony could be compelled if it would protect a party's constitutional rights by preventing perjury. In *Olam v. Congress Mortgage Co.*, 68 F. Supp. 2d 1110 (N.D. Cal. 1999), the plaintiff claimed to have signed a settlement agreement in distress. Later *all* the parties wanted the mediator to testify, and the court ordered that testimony to determine the plaintiff's capacity to contract. The settlement agreement was ultimately enforced.

Then came the third case, *Foxgate Homeowners' Association v. Bramalea California Inc.*, 78 Cal. App. 4th 653 (2000). There, an appointed hybrid mediator/discovery master required the parties to appear with their experts for five days of hearing. Defense counsel refused to bring his experts, saying he didn't want to respond to the plaintiff's frivolous claim. The mediator prepared a report to the court, a procedure the parties had agreed to, and based on that report's conclusion that counsel had delayed and obstructed the mediation process, the trial court sanctioned defense counsel. The appeals court wrote that "[w]hile confidentiality is essential to make mediation work, so too is the meaningful, good faith participation of the parties and their lawyers." Concluding that no privilege should be read so broadly as to immunize parties and their lawyers from sanctions for disobeying court orders, the court held the mediation privilege to be waived notwithstanding the clear statutory language. Most mediators were worried, if not appalled.

Foxgate was appealed and the strength of mediation confidentiality and privilege soon increased dramatically. In *Foxgate Homeowners Association v. Bramalea California, Inc.*, 25 P.3d 1117 (Cal. 2001), the California Supreme Court, saying that confidentiality is essential to effective mediation, pointed out that the Evidence Code provided for "no exceptions," and that the statute "unqualifiedly bars disclosure of communications" in the mediation. It reversed the appellate court and held that the mediator/referee could not report the conduct of defense counsel, even if the mediator thought counsel acted in bad faith. The two competing issues of good faith and confidentiality directly squared off in *Foxgate*, and confidentiality won.

Finally, in 2011, the same court went even further in *Cassel v. Superior Court*, which again reversed an appellate court ruling. *Cassel* concerned a client who filed a complaint against his lawyers for malpractice in giving the client advice below the standard of care prior to and at the mediation. As a result, the complaint alleged, the lawyers were liable for malpractice. At issue, among other things, was key testimony from the plaintiff at his deposition, and desired testimony from the client's own lawyers. Some brief case excerpts, beginning with the court's description of the client's claim:

CASSEL v. SUPERIOR COURT
244 P.3d 1080 (Cal. 2011)

[P]etitioner testified about meetings with his attorneys immediately preceding the mediation, at which mediation strategy was discussed, and about conversations with his lawyers, outside the presence of the other mediation participants, during the mediation session itself. Petitioner's deposition testimony was consistent with the complaint's claims that his attorneys employed various tactics to keep him at the mediation and to pressure him to accept [the opposing party's] proffered settlement for an amount he and the attorneys had previously agreed was too low.

The appellate court majority reasoned that the mediation confidentiality statutes are intended to prevent the damaging use *against a mediation disputant* of tactics employed, positions taken, or confidences exchanged in the mediation, not to protect attorneys from the malpractice claims of their own clients. Thus, the majority concluded, when a mediation disputant sues his own counsel for malpractice in connection with the mediation, the attorneys — already freed, by reason of the malpractice suit, from the attorney-client privilege — cannot use mediation confidentiality as a shield to exclude damaging evidence of their own entirely private conversations with the client. The dissenting justice urged that the majority had crafted an unwarranted judicial exception to the clear and absolute provisions of the mediation confidentiality statutes.

Though we understand the policy concerns advanced by the Court of Appeal majority, the plain language of the statutes compels us to agree with the dissent. As we will explain, the result reached by the majority below contravenes the Legislature's explicit command that, unless the confidentiality of a particular communication is expressly waived, . . . [it] extends beyond utterances or writings "in the course of" a mediation, and thus is not confined to communications that occur *between mediation disputants* during the mediation proceeding itself.

We must apply the plain terms of the mediation confidentiality statutes to the facts of this case unless such a result would violate due process, or would lead to absurd results that clearly undermine the statutory purpose. No situation that extreme arises here. Hence, the statutes' terms must govern, even though they may compromise petitioner's ability to prove his claim of legal malpractice.

. . . .

The obvious purpose of the expanded language is to ensure that the statutory protection extends beyond discussions carried out directly between the opposing parties to the dispute, or with the mediator, during the mediation proceedings themselves. All oral or written communications are covered, if they are made "for the purpose of" or "pursuant to" a mediation. It follows that, absent an express statutory exception, all discussions conducted in preparation for a mediation, as well as all mediation-related communications that take place during the mediation itself, are protected from disclosure. Plainly, such communications include those between a mediation disputant and his or her own counsel, even if these do not occur in the presence of the mediator or other disputants.

JUSTICE CHIN, concurring:

I concur in the result, but reluctantly. This holding will effectively shield an attorney's actions during mediation, including advising the client, from a malpractice action even if those actions are incompetent or even deceptive. Attorneys participating in mediation will not be held accountable for any incompetent or fraudulent actions during that mediation unless the actions are so extreme as to engender a *criminal* prosecution against the attorney. This is a high price to pay to preserve total confidentiality in the mediation process.

NOTES

Many felt as Justice Chin did, that in *Cassel*, confidentiality squared off against fairness, and fairness lost. No justice argued that the *Cassel* result was "fair," and all emphasized the clear statutory mandate. Justice Chin implied that the California legislature should re-examine what has become the virtually absolute nature of mediation confidentiality.

California is at one extreme here. Although Florida has a similar strong statute, it has not yet been interpreted as broadly as *Cassel*. Other states, if they do have statutes other than the UMC, keep their footing on a more moderate UMA-style confidentiality ground. But even the UMA's confidentiality provisions are quite strong. In the next section, we'll examine how they may conflict with an attorney's other obligations, and other conflicts lawyers may face in mediation.

4. Ethical Issues Facing Practicing Lawyers in Mediation

Strong confidentiality rules, even if they don't quite match California's, can create ethical problems for lawyers who are advised to do one thing under their state's applicable ethics code and quite another under the UMA or other governing mediation statutes. One issue is what notice is actually given by mediators who, remember, may not always be lawyers. Mediators who give notices that confuse confidentiality and privilege may be misleading the participants. Those that do not carefully state the law and the exceptions may create other misleading impressions. Lawyers representing clients must be assiduous in the care they exercise in advising their clients about these issues. In other situations, parties may not fully understand the interrelationship between potential criminal acts, self-incrimination, and the limits of mediation confidentiality.[9]

And lawyers in states like Illinois with strong requirements to report malfeasance by other attorneys may find these requirements are at odds with the confidentiality provision required by mediation.[10]

Lawyers *and* mediators who know that state mediation statutes require strong confidentiality may feel enabled to stretch the truth, lie, or even overtly mislead. Clearly, California seems currently to have given lawyers license to twist their clients' arms without any client recourse. ABA Formal Opinion 06-439 (2006) addressed the requirements of truthfulness in mediation and compared those requirements to negotiation tactics. We've examined the ethics of negotiation tactics in Problem 19. Should they be different in mediation?

In Opinion 06-439, the ABA notes that some argue that "lawyers involved in caucused mediation should be held to a more exacting standard of truthfulness because a neutral is involved. The theory underlying this position is that, as in a game of 'telephone,' . . . distortions tend to become magnified on continued retransmission." On the other hand, others assert that "less attention need be paid to the accuracy of information being communicated in a mediation — particularly in a caucused mediation — precisely because consensual deception is intrinsic to the process." The opinion accepts neither viewpoint, concluding that "the ethical principles governing lawyer truthfulness do not permit a distinction to be drawn between the caucused mediation context and other negotiation settings."

Finally, does today's lawyer have an ethical obligation to offer mediation to the client? Could a failure to advise about ADR ever fall below the standard of care and result in malpractice? Clearly, litigation is not always the best choice for every client's case. If a lawyer has a duty to effectively serve the client, does it follow that discussing mediation as a potential resolution should be mandated?

The ethical duty to inform clients of alternatives to litigation is referred to in several sections of the ABA Model Rules. Model Rule 2.1 Comment 5 says that "it *may* be necessary under rule 1.4 to inform the client of forms of dispute resolution that might constitute reasonable alternatives to litigation" (our emphasis). Is such a requirement reasonable? Or should it be made stronger by requiring or at least suggesting that a lawyer not wait until an issue is already in litigation before it is referred to an alternative means of resolution?

An increasing number of states have amended the model rules to specifically address lawyers suggesting ADR. For example, Colorado's rules imply an ethical duty, while Georgia's rule mandates a non-discretionary duty. Malpractice lawsuits are also based on such failures. To date no cases have been reported with a specific finding that the failure to offer a client mediation is malpractice, primarily because malpractice cases must prove *causation*, that is, that the client's result would have been better if the advice had been given. But such a case will happen. First, legal malpractice, like medical malpractice, often turns on informed consent, while

---

[9] *See* Maureen E. Laflin, *The Mediator As Fugu Chef: Preserving Protections Without Poisoning The Process*, 49 S. Tex. L. Rev. 943 (2008), which summarizes several cases touching on this issue.

[10] California, with no reporting requirement, does not face this particular problem.

litigation may be viewed as the legal equivalent to surgery: not always the most desirable means to resolution, and one for which the client should make the ultimate choice. The client, after all, bears most of the risk. Without being offered mediation, a client's choice to litigate may not be fully informed. Second, since lawyers have the inherent conflict that comes with receiving any fee, offering mediation — almost always more cost-effective and fee-reducing — may come to be seen as part of an attorney's fiduciary duty.

5. Lawyers as Mediators

When a lawyer serves as a mediator, different ethical issues pertain: Conflicts of interest between parties in mediation and the lawyer's own firm, the extent of necessary disclosures, and, finally, the question of whether the mediator is engaged in the practice of law. First, read this piece about the sometimes sad reality that law firms do not always provide the best environment in which to emphasize the benefits of mediation.

John G. Bickerman, *Leaving the Firm, Conflicts, Firm Economics and Issues of Culture can Stifle ADR Practice*
DISPUTE RESOLUTION MAGAZINE (Winter 1998)[11]

At first, I believed my former firm would embrace a meaningful dispute resolution practice. It seemed logical that such a practice could complement and enhance the firm's litigation department. After several years of generating hundreds of thousands of dollars in fees for the firm, I drafted a detailed business plan showing how the firm could develop a profitable dispute resolution practice area. The firm's response to the proposal was lukewarm. Over the next three years, I slowly realized that my vision of a full-time mediation practice could not be realized within a large national firm.

. . . .

Conflicts presented a daily concern for me. . . . Several attorneys in Florida approached me about mediating the litigation brought by the state's Attorney General against the major tobacco manufacturers. . . . [This case] could have generated considerable income for the firm if I had been selected. The response from several partners was swift and negative. Mediating this case would have foreclosed the firm representing any of the tobacco company participants in the pending litigation. Although no one at the firm was engaged in such representation, the possibility . . . posed a sufficient threat to potential business opportunity that I was discouraged from expressing further interest in this assignment. . . .

[Conflicts of interest are complicated, for example by such matters as what are called] "settlement facts" and how these facts are used after the mediation ends. Information learned during a mediation that may not go directly to the merits of the dispute may still be of strategic importance to the party. For example, a mediator may learn that a party is contemplating a merger or that a party is teetering on bankruptcy.

---

[11] Copyright © 1998 by Dispute Resolution Magazine. Reprinted by permission. All rights reserved.

Now fast forward several months and consider the dilemma whereby the firm and perhaps an attorney in the firm are engaged in a business transaction adverse to this mediation participant but that is not substantially related to the subject of the mediation. The knowledge of these settlement facts poses a very practical problem. Arguably, the attorney in possession of this information has an ethical obligation to share it with the firm's present client. Yet, sharing this information would breach the confidentiality of the mediation process.

. . . .

The driving force that predicts behavior in most firms is money or, less charitably, self-interest. . . . Litigators in my former firm saw themselves as dispute resolvers [but] because many lawyers had only a partial understanding of how mediation works, they underestimated its utility to clients, or, more cynically, worried that using effective dispute resolution processes might cut short a lucrative litigation.

More troubling, they viewed mediation as contrary to the business of litigation. Seeing themselves as true warriors who go to battle to vindicate the rights of their clients, they feared signaling to either clients or adversaries that they would prefer to settle instead of going to war. They had little interest or incentive to tinker with a business that had elevated them to the senior ranks of the firm.

Mediation cannot provide the leverage, and thus the profit margin per case, that large-scale litigation generates. Profits for most firms rest squarely on the pyramid of leverage. Litigation and most business transactions frequently require many layers of lawyers. The very efficiency that mediation seeks to achieve, eliminating the time and expense of litigation, strikes at the heart of a law firm profit model.

NOTES

This is not the first time we have seen lawyers' self-interest, particularly in generating income, conflict with the best interests of clients. Is there anything different about the mediation setting that makes this a more difficult conflict to deal with? Less difficult? How can this problem be solved so lawyers initiate mediation in those cases where it is truly in the client's best interests?

We'll address more about conflicts and disclosure for lawyer/mediators in the next section, but first a final question here: Are mediators engaged in the practice law while mediating? Most claim firmly that they are not, and most of the existing literature agrees. And yet, some parties and lawyers in mediation actively seek the substantive advice and knowledge of lawyer-mediators with expertise in a particular area of law. If the mediator gives this advice, doesn't that constitute the practice of law? Taking it a step further, what happens when the parties are not represented by counsel? Can a lawyer-mediator's statement that "nothing shall be construed as my practicing law or giving you legal advice" override the reality that the neutral does just that? We've seen in other situations that merely saying "I am not practicing law" does not inure the lawyer from being found to have done just that. Finally, how is malpractice insurance affected by whether or not the lawyer is "merely" mediating or is also giving legal advice?

There are no clear answers to these questions in this still-developing area. But something a leading mediator — an attorney with over 30 years' experience mediating family law cases, many without counsel — told us years ago still makes sense. This particular mediator routinely both advised litigants of the likely court outcome, and memorialized marriage settlement agreements himself, knowing that leaving these matters to the parties alone might result in guesswork or errors neither intended. As for whether he was practicing law, he saw the distinction between a "yes" or "no" answer as little more than semantic, a matter of form over substance.

6.   Dealing with Mediator Conflicts of Interest

Even with the implementation of the Uniform Mediation Act, how a mediator deals with conflicts issues in mediation is a matter of considerable debate with no clear consensus. Neither the UMA's Standard II (Impartiality) nor Standard III (Conflicts of Interest) contain particularly strong disqualifying statements. That makes some sense, as we've already observed: Unlike judges or arbitrators, mediators have no *de jure* power and are often used repeatedly by the same "customers," to everyone's benefit. After all, who better than someone known and trusted to tell parties the truth about the strengths and weaknesses of their case?

One of the biggest differences between a mediator's and an advocate's role is that the mediator has no duty of loyalty to the parties (or perhaps more accurately an equal duty of loyalty to all parties). As a result, even after the UMA was drafted, there has not been a uniformly perceived need for mediators to engage in a tightly-controlled system of conflicts checks and disclosures. Moreover, mediators often do not know the identity of all the actual parties in interest. They may never be actually aware of this until some time during the mediation session itself. For example, the only "named" parties may be the plaintiff and defendant; while the existence of an insurance carrier may be expected, there may be an "excess carrier," or another entity that has partially indemnified the defendant as the result of an assignment, an anticipated buy-out, or a merger. The party's desire for confidentiality may have led to this information being concealed from the opposing party and the mediator prior to the mediation. Since mediation is a party-driven process, the parties are the ones who determine what information they want to convey, and when.

Some lawyer-mediators believe that these factors, and their roles as facilitators, mean that conflict checking is not necessary to the extent it is for arbitrators — or lawyers and law firms. On the other hand, there is much to be said for the mediator making the fullest possible disclosure to the parties. It is hard to argue that *too much* disclosure is likely to be harmful to those participating in the mediation. And since one of the primary goals of the mediator is to build trust, disclosure of any prior relationship with the parties or counsel — usually not a disabling factor — can serve as a trust-builder. Moreover, when a mediator has an ongoing relationship with one side, such as an insurer who brings a particular neutral a good deal of repeat business, it seems the other parties clearly have a right to know this. The UMA standards could definitely use some clarification in this respect.

7. Power: An Ethical Issue?

One of the best and most interesting features of mediation is that no one comes to the process with *de jure* power. But while mediators may make no decision nor force the parties to agree to anything, they usually have substantial *de facto* power. They usually control — with the parties' consent — both the process and the flow of information between the parties. Even orchestrating the seating arrangement at the joint session may have significant repercussions, as can deciding how and when to break up into caucuses.

The very nature of the process is one in which the mediator selectively offers each side's view to the other in an effort to move towards settlement or other resolution. And, of course, a major hallmark of mediation is that each side can communicate with the mediator *ex parte* in confidence. This process gives the mediator much discretion in determining what information should, or should not, be conveyed to the other side, and when. Clearly, how the mediator determines these issues can have a large impact on the mediation.

Perhaps the most important ethical issue related to a mediator's use of power is how he or she deals with power imbalances among the parties and their representatives. The parties are the ultimate decisionmakers, but they often come to the table from inherently unequal bargaining positions. Such imbalances are heightened when parties are unrepresented. Concerns also exist where one lawyer is more knowledgeable or experienced or has more resources than the others. Issues relating to unequal power are particularly prevalent in domestic law mediation. However, race, gender, and economic disparities between the parties also can create power issues.

On one hand, mediators must guard against taking the easy path of siding with the more powerful party, or allowing that party's will to control the result. On the other hand, mediators must avoid the temptation to balance out power by "putting a thumb on the scales," or presenting facts, law, or negotiating positions slanted in favor of the weaker party. Such efforts undermine neutrality and "symmetry" and create the danger that the *mediator's* version of fairness will supplant that of the parties. Most mediators agree that good settlements are not only based on probable court results but also on people's own sense of fairness and justice.

Selecting a mediator for a particular case may also relate in part to power. Mediators are often chosen because of their expertise in a particular subject: employment law, intellectual property, or construction defects, for example. Parties and their attorneys frequently want and even expect mediators to be more than passive facilitators, and to offer advice and input based on their expertise in an area of law. Sometimes, mediators are chosen precisely because the parties and lawyers *want* them to exert power. While it is controversial among mediators, some adopt a style in which throwing their weight around is part of the ordinary course of business. Sometimes, a lawyer may select a mediator to serve as a "reality check" for a client who needs to hear about the weaknesses of a case from a neutral third party, or who wants the mediator to give a personal opinion of the value of the case.

Where should the ethical lines be drawn? Is it acceptable for mediators to "throw their weight around" or express a personal belief in the "right" amount for settlement? Should a mediator attempt to neutralize power discrepancies between the parties? Is this necessary to ensure fairness, or does it fly in the face of the true meaning of the word "neutral"? And, finally, is there an inconsistency between an effort to balance power and the duty of confidentiality? What happens when a lawyer acts unethically? Does that change the neutral's appropriate course of action? Should it?

In part, the answers to these questions are informed by Standard VI of the UMA. But once again, with the wiggle room built into the language supporting that standard, mediators will be hard-pressed to find a "blueprint" solution to these questions when and as they occur.

8.   Secret Settlements: Justice for Whom?

A lawyer's foremost loyalty is to the client. But what about when public safety is also at risk? Should advancing the client's interests always outweigh the rights of the public as a whole?

It is not uncommon that as part of a settlement agreement, key information remains "secret" to all but the parties to the initial dispute. By contract, parties can agree to prevent discovered evidence from ever being made public. This perhaps most frequently occurs in products liability cases or those involving high-profile or highly scrutinized individuals such as ministers, doctors, or teachers. When individual cases settle secretly, the public remains at risk.

Perhaps the most widely-publicized example of secret litigation in the last decade concerned defective Firestone tires that shredded during normal use.[12] What was not well-known was that Cooper tires suffered from similar defects but those remained secret for a longer period of time.[13] Some other examples of secrecy agreements involving products include: defective heart valves and other medical prostheses; prescription medicines with fatally adverse side effects; exploding automobile fuel tanks; toxic oil spills and chemically contaminated water; and dangerous cribs and playground equipment. The fatally defective Dalkon Shield intrauterine device was the subject of many secret settlements, to the point where some lawyers were asked to promise never to take another Dalkon Shield case.

Outside the products liability arena, private agreements have been made by a home for the mentally ill whose administrator had sexually abused a Down syndrome patient; the Catholic Church in resolving numerous child molestation cases; and law firms settling severe AIDS discrimination litigation in exchange for silence.

---

[12] Estimates of the number of people killed in crashes before the Firestone story was made public range from 88, see Bob Van Voris, *Lawyers Caught Between Clients and Public Safety in Tire Cases*, AMERICAN LAWYER MEDIA, Sept. 22, 2000 and NATIONAL LAW JOURNAL, Sept. 25, 2000, to almost 200, see Keith Bradsher, *S.U.V. Tire Defects Were Known in 1996 But Not Reported*, N.Y. TIMES, June 24, 2001, at 1.

[13] *See* testimony and colloquy at the hearing before the Subcommittee on Antitrust, Competition Policy and Consumer Rights of the U.S. Senate Judiciary Committee, December 11, 2007, particularly the testimony of Johnny Bradley, Jr.

"Secret settlements" actually injure individuals twice; though "compensated" for their injury, the aggrieved cannot share their stories with the world, forcing them to live with the knowledge that many others are placed at great risk. It is obvious that the ethical and moral implications for lawyers on both sides are substantial.

9.   What Is a "Secret Settlement"?

Secret settlements can come in several forms:

Protective orders are intended to legitimately restrict the use of discovery, such as where trade secrets are involved in litigation. These orders, especially when they are stipulated to by both sides and approved by a judge without close scrutiny, have sometimes been used to protect defendants from having to reveal a potentially dangerous situation to the public. Federal Judge H. Lee Sarokin, who handled several New Jersey tobacco cases in the early 1990s and who first revealed previously secret information that exposed "Big Tobacco" wrongdoing,[14] described how he routinely granted protective orders until the first litigated tobacco case, *Cipollone v. Liggett Group, Inc.*, 106 F.R.D. 573 (D.N.J. 1985): "I must confess that for a considerable period of time, as a routine matter I signed consent orders on the theory that since the parties agreed and the lawyers agreed, there was no reason for us to examine the agreement. But I slowly came to the realization that there were other interests involved."[15] Those interests, of course, belonged to the public.

Stand-alone secrecy agreements come in the form of either "private protective orders" or agreements to return discovery at the close of the case. Often the settlement offer seems "too good" for plaintiff to turn down, though some later regret accepting it when they realize the likely harm to others.[16]

Sealing court files and/or changing the names of the parties on court documents. These extreme measures, which seem to directly subvert the court processes, serve to deny the public access to ordinarily-public information in court records. They generally can be accomplished only by stipulation and court approval.

Stipulated reversals and depublication are two ways litigants who reach a settlement after trial can effectively change the decision of the trier of fact. Depublication, somewhat less onerous, avoids adverse precedent by permitting an opinion to stand as "unpublished," without affecting the case's actual result. Stipulated reversals, while rare, do occur: They involve agreements to wipe the trial court's judgment off the books by stipulating to reverse that judgment on appeal in return for immediate payment. For example, if a doctor lost a medical malpractice case in court, the physician might offer to settle now for 100 cents on the dollar in exchange for erasing a judgment that might affect the doctor's future

---

[14] See our further discussion of this in Problem 18.

[15] Quoted in Jaffe, *Public Good vs. Sealed Evidence*, STAR-LEDGER (Newark), Sept. 2, 1990.

[16] *See, e.g., 60 Minutes II* of October 10, 2000, depicting a lawyer who felt it necessary to enter a secrecy agreement on behalf of the mother of a man who died in a Firestone case, while the mother, knowing others had died, expressed regret at having ever agreed to secrecy, and felt that *she* was responsible.

insurability.[17] In this gold-from-dross procedure, the loser of the case becomes the *de jure* winner, and can trumpet that "victory."

10.   Is Secrecy an Ethical Issue?

One view, to which we acknowledge our adherence, says that it is. Lawyers — those on *both* sides — are indispensable participants in secrecy agreements. After all, they not only engage in secret settlements in the name of "zealous advocacy," they create the documentation. But given the stakes involved, the issue is whether zeal and loyalty to the client's interests outweigh the public's right to know of significant dangers to health or safety.

We have seen in our examination of confidentiality, how the rules, especially Model Rule 1.6, balance lawyers' abilities to protect their client's confidences with their duties to protect society. The fulcrum of that balance has moved somewhat in many states as a result of the 2002 and 2003 rules revisions. But "secretizing" information in settlements *does not* interfere with confidentiality at all, as it pertains only to matters subject to discovery during litigation.

One problem with the current lack of ethical standards relating to secrecy is that attorneys who believe it to be in their client's economic interests to enter into such agreements will do so; their perceived duty of advocacy will trump any possibility of disclosing, even if a lawyer believes disclosure is permitted under MR 1.6. So long as such agreements are "ethical," they will be entered into regardless of any danger to the public, on the theory that the client's interests (usually considered by lawyers to be financial ones) come first. A fair share of the blame lies with current ethics rules that, in the view of most lawyers, *require* their participation.

We know many plaintiffs' lawyers who would prefer not to feel compelled to accept secret deals. We know that many defense lawyers and in-house counsel would like nothing better than to say, "I can't help you hide the truth about a danger." But lawyers are doing exactly what they've been taught to do: put the client first. The Sarbanes-Oxley rules discussed elsewhere in this volume have given some lawyers pause about how far this "client first" attitude may go. But a sea change on the issue of secrecy is likely to occur only when lawyers are widely prohibited from contracting away their ability to disclose known, discovered dangers to the public so that their sole client may benefit.

Read the following excerpt, which explores some of the issues of ethics and responsibility that flow from secret settlements.

---

[17] See *Neary v. Regents of the Univ. of Calif.*, 834 P.2d 119 (Cal. 1992), which authorized stipulated reversals absent "extraordinary circumstances." Note that *U.S. Bancorp Mortgage Co. v. Bonner Mall Partnership*, 513 U.S. 18 (1994), disapproved of this practice.

Alan F. Blakley, *To Squeal or Not to Squeal: Ethical Obligations of Officers of the Court in Possession of Information of Public Interest*
34 CUMBERLAND LAW REVIEW 65 (2003-2004)[18]

One Clergy Sex Abuse Settlement

In October 1998, Paul J. Marcoux settled a claim against Archbishop Rembert Weakland and the Archdiocese of Milwaukee. The claim arose from Marcoux's allegations that he and the archbishop had an illicit sexual affair that began with Marcoux's being sexually abused by the archbishop. Marcoux claimed that at one time the archbishop had written him a "love letter, which Marcoux still possessed. The parties executed a settlement agreement prior to the initiation of any litigation. Among other things, the settlement agreement required Marcoux to return all originals and copies of any correspondence (including presumably the "love letter") or documents that he had received at any time from anyone concerning the Archdiocese of Milwaukee including, but not limited to, Archbishop Weakland. In return for Marcoux's compliance and agreement to refrain from further action, the archdiocese paid him $450,000.00. . . .

The sexual relationship between Archbishop Weakland and Marcoux began in 1979. During the time between 1979 and May of 2002, many people found some of Archbishop Weakland's views on a variety of sexual subjects inexplicably odd. For instance, it has been reported that in 1988, Archbishop Weakland wrote a column in which he said that, "[S]ome adolescent sex abuse victims were 'not so innocent' and were sexually active, street wise, and aggressive." . . . However, prior to the disclosure of the settlement did anyone have reason to suspect that Archbishop Weakland's . . . policies and practices concerning priests in his archdiocese accused of sexual abuse were influenced primarily by his own past . . .?

In 1990, prior to the Marcoux-Weakland settlement, but during the Marcoux-Weakland relationship, John Ramstack settled a lawsuit against the Reverend David Hanser of the Archdiocese of Milwaukee. . . . Ramstack claimed that Reverend Hanser had sexually abused John and three of his brothers. The resulting settlement for $65,000.00 included a confidentiality provision . . . .

Had the Hanser-Ramstack settlement received public notice, would someone have uncovered the Marcoux-Weakland affair in 1990? Would the Archdiocese of Milwaukee or the Catholic Church of the United States have developed a sexual abuse policy a decade earlier than it did? Would the revelations about a well-known archbishop have been sufficient to cause widespread change and saved countless victims? . . .

The example of the Archdiocese of Milwaukee typifies the ethical questions involved in settlements concerning underlying allegations of private matters having public interest. A plethora of additional questions arise. In 1990, how should the attorney representing John Ramstack have approached the competing interests of

---

[18] Copyright © 2003 by the Cumberland Law Review. Reprinted by permission.

his client and the interests of the public at large? Should attorneys ever have any obligation to consider those questions? How should the attorney for Reverend Hanser in 1990 have balanced his duty to the archdiocese to keep additional claims from awakening, his duty to help prevent additional abuse, and his duty to insure that Reverend Hanser received treatment and was prevented from being in contact with additional potential victims? . . . Similar questions arose at the time of the Marcoux-Weakland settlement. Finally, . . . [i]f the archdiocese had used the Ramstack-Hanser litigation as a catalyst of change and implemented a socially responsible policy for addressing sexually abusive priests, would the undisclosed settlement, protecting the parties' privacy, have been completely justified?

Products Liability Cases

Since 2000, Ford Motor Co., Bridgestone Tire Co., and Firestone Inc. have been involved in products liability litigation concerning the failure of tires installed on Ford sport utility vehicles that resulted in roll-over accidents. However, as early as 1991 lawsuits began, thus indicating that even then Firestone knew of the problems and was involved in settlements that included confidentiality provisions. In current litigation, many documents are kept in a "reading room," accessible only to the attorneys working on the case. Presumably, the court and the parties still wish their records to remain private.

On December 5, 2000, Bloomberg, LP and Dow Jones and Co., Inc. filed a motion to intervene for the purpose of having information in the Bridgestone/Firestone case removed from the confidential "reading room." Even though the court noted that 6.5 million tires were recalled on August 9, 2000, and that congressional hearings had been held concerning the tires, the court refused to allow public access to the documents. The court drew a distinction between documents filed with the court and documents that had simply been produced in discovery. While it held that a court has a special obligation to the public, it held that when the parties stipulate to secrecy, the intervening press should be allowed to argue for disclosure only if one of the parties seeks to have discovery information disclosed or seeks the intervention of the court.

Is this an abdication of responsibility by the court? What is the role of the court in a case of a defective or dangerous product when litigants have no incentive to disclose the information? . . . Who advocates for the public when the news media is not even aware of an issue? With increasingly busy court dockets, is this an additional task heaped on the courts that will further slow the judicial process? Should courts second-guess attorneys and litigants who know more about their disputes? . . . Didn't the companies have the right to try to fix the problems they discovered through these claims without being hounded by the press? Did the attorneys for the companies have an obligation to notice a trend . . .? If so, when did that obligation arise? After the tenth claim? The hundredth claim? Should the plaintiffs' attorneys, in an effort to recognize the public interest of the litigation, advise their clients not to accept a settlement because it has a confidentiality provision?

NOTES

Could a rule of professional responsibility solve these ethical quandaries? One of the authors of this volume thinks so, and has proposed a modification to the ABA Model Rules.[19]

On the other hand, shouldn't litigants have a reasonable expectation of privacy, particularly when they opt *voluntarily* to resolve a matter in mediation, without the assistance of the court system? One of the strongest benefits of alternative dispute resolution is that it assists parties in the resolution of their disputes while also affording them strict confidentiality of *all* proceedings. This provides a safe harbor for parties to take risks without fear of public exposure. Parties contractually bind themselves to arbitration to assure the highest degree of confidentiality, as well as more control over the triers of fact and the forum in which the case will be heard. Others voluntarily opt for mediation largely because of these same confidentiality considerations.

Some criticize the idea of forcing litigants to reveal information that they have stipulated be kept secret; they argue this will discourage early settlement of their disputes. How does involving the court system change this? Should parties' stipulations ever trump the public's right of access to court documents? How attenuated can health and safety issues be as a factor in making these determinations?

A generation ago, Harvard law professor Arthur Miller argued that "[l]itigants do not give up their privacy rights simply because they have walked, voluntarily or involuntarily, through the courthouse door." Describing some information that discovery compels being produced as "intensely personal and confidential," Miller claimed that discovery rules were never intended to destroy privacy or confidentiality rights by "promoting public access" to discoverable information: "Courts exist to serve private parties bringing a private dispute."[20] However, it seems clear in light of the two latest rounds of federal discovery reforms that those drafting changes to the Federal Rules of Civil Procedure do not consider either court disputes or the discovery information they generate to be private.[21]

Professor Miller also suggested that the need for greater public access had been exaggerated. He opposed reforms that allow greater public access, and argued that heightening this access would wreak havoc on the efficient functioning of the litigation process and jeopardize personal and commercial interests. Is this true? Or might there be efficiency *and* public access?

Few today maintain as Miller did a generation ago that evidence of dangers is "only" anecdotal. A few states have responded to secrecy by enacting "sunshine in

---

[19] The rule has been published in several articles. *See, e.g.*, Richard A. Zitrin, *The Case Against Secret Settlements (Or What You Don't Know Can Hurt You)*, 2 J. INST. FOR STUDY OF LEGAL ETHICS 115 (1999).

[20] Arthur R. Miller, *Confidentiality, Protective Orders and Public Access to the Courts*, 105 HARVARD L. REV. 427 (1991).

[21] *See, e.g.*, Mary Elizabeth Keaney, Note: *Don't Steal My Sunshine: Deconstructing the Flawed Presumption of Privacy for Unfiled Documents Exchanged During Discovery*, 62 HASTINGS L.J. 795 (2011).

litigation" laws: legislation or court rules that recognize the importance of public access. Florida, Texas, and Washington have the strongest laws, but only Washington's makes an attorney's failure to comply a disciplinary violation. The result in Florida has been that that strong law is routinely violated by lawyers who know they will not be disciplined for that violation. Legislation is now pending in the United States Senate, having achieved bipartisan Judiciary Committee support in 2011, but a new legislative term means that the legislation has to start essentially from scratch.[22]

Perhaps the strongest "sunshine in litigation" law is Texas Rule of Civil Procedure 76(a), which affects filed and *unfiled* court documents, including documents produced pursuant to discovery requests that never go to court. Passed in 1990 by a 4-3 vote of the Texas Supreme Court with the staunch support of then-associate justice Lloyd Doggett, the rule has been seen by some as a model for other jurisdictions interested in open court records.

"That judicial records should be open to public inspection is not a novel idea," wrote Justice Doggett in 1991.[23] "As expressed by Justice Tom Clark, 'The principle that justice cannot survive behind walls of silence has long been reflected in the Anglo-American distrust for secret trials.'" Doggett noted that "greater access to civil justice records promotes health and safety for the public," and argued that "by presuming open access by the public, the rule strengthens democracy." Concluded Doggett: "To close a court to public scrutiny of the proceedings is to shut off the light of the law."

What do you think about these widely divergent opinions?

D. SUPPLEMENTAL READINGS

1. R. Wayne Thorpe and Susan M. Yates, *An Overview of the Revised Model Standards of Conduct for Mediators*, 12 DISPUTE RESOL. MAG. 30 (2006), contains an excellent summary of the new model standards and a discussion of the most difficult and controversial provisions.

2. Pamela A. Kentra, *Hear No Evil, See No Evil, Speak No Evil: The Intolerable Conflict for Attorney-Mediators Between the Duty to Maintain Mediation Confidentiality and the Duty to Report Fellow Attorney Misconduct*, 1997 B.Y.U. L. REV. 715 (1997), and Monica L. Warmbrod, *Comment: Could an Attorney Face Disciplinary Actions or Even Legal Malpractice for Failure to Inform Clients of Alternative Dispute Resolution?*, 27 CUMB. L. REV. 791 (1997), are two excellent pieces analyzing this important issue during a time prior to the substantial increases in formal rules on confidentiality rules that came with the UMA and the 2005 Standards revisions.

3. Maureen E. Laflin, *The Mediator as Fugu Chef: Preserving Protections Without Poisoning the Process*, 49 S. TEX. L. REV. 943 (2008). The title of this piece

---

[22] S.623, "The Sunshine in Litigation Act," passed by Senate Judiciary in April 2011. Co-author Richard Zitrin was a principal drafter of this legislation and testified at the Senate Judiciary hearing referenced above.

[23] Lloyd Doggett & Michael J. Mucchetti, *Public Access to Public Courts*, 69 TEX. L. REV. 643 (1991).

comes from the fugu fish — delicious if perfectly prepared, poisonous if not. This article focuses on the ethical conflicts and conundrums lawyers face in trying to abide by both the ethics rules of their state and the confidentiality rules that govern mediations. It is one of a number of good articles in this symposium issue from South Texas School of Law.

4. James J. Alfini, *Mediation as a Calling: Addressing the Disconnect Between Mediation Ethics and the Practices of Lawyer Mediators*, 49 49 S. TEX. L. REV. 829 (2008), is a first-rate piece describing the disconnect between a lawyer's core values and duties and those of a mediator. Another article from the South Texas symposium.

5. Of the many articles on power disparities in mediation, perhaps the most important are those by Tina Grillo. Two of Grillo's pieces are *The Mediation Alternative: Process Dangers for Women*, 100 YALE L.J. 1545 (1991), and *Respecting the Struggle: Following the Parties' Lead*, 13 MEDIATION Q. 279 (1996). These articles evaluate the mediation process as it affects relatively unempowered women, especially in domestic cases.

6. Diversity awareness and recognition that cultural differences can profoundly affect a mediation's outcome are always important factors to consider. Two articles in the Summer 1999 MEDIATION QUARTERLY address this issue: Howard H. Irving, Michael Benjamin, and Jose San-Pedro, *Family Mediation and Cultural Diversity: Mediating with Latino Families*, Vol. 16, at 325 and Cherise D. Hariston, *African Americans in Mediation Literature: A Neglected Population*, Vol. 16, at 357.

7. Lloyd Doggett & Michael J. Mucchetti, *Public Access to Public Courts*, 69 TEX. L. REV. 643 (1991). This seminal article, referenced in the readings, was the first to bring the dangers of secrecy to public scrutiny. The anecdotal evidence laid out in this article has proved to be abiding, and virtually beyond challenge.

8. Opposite sides of the secrecy coin are represented by Richard J. Vangelisti, *Proposed Amendment to Federal Rule of Civil Procedure 26(c) Concerning Protective Orders: A Critical Analysis of What It Means and How It Operates*, 48 BAYLOR L. REV. 163 (1996), discussing the debate about the availability and scope of protective orders, and Wayne Brazil, *Protecting the Confidentiality of Settlement Negotiations*, 39 HASTINGS L.J. 955 (July 1988), which makes the case for why settlement negotiations should be protected as confidential. Two of the authors of this volume have written a chapter on secret settlements for their book THE MORAL COMPASS OF THE AMERICAN LAWYER (1999), and modified part of that chapter in two articles, one of which focused on an explosive case involving secrecy and Prozac. Richard Zitrin & Carol M. Langford, *The Moral Compass: Hide & Secrets II — The Louisville Prozac Trial*, LAW NEWS NETWORK (on-line magazine) and American Lawyer Media, April 1999. The proposed rule of professional conduct prohibiting secret settlements, discussed in section 11 is discussed in Richard A. Zitrin, *Why the Laudable South Carolina Rules Must Be Broadened*, 55 S.C. L. REV. 883 (2004), and *The Case Against Secret Settlements (Or What You Don't Know Can Hurt You)*, 2 J. INST. FOR STUDY OF LEGAL ETHICS 115 (1999), among other places.

9. An excellent objective review of the status of secrecy agreements in the courts is contained in Laurie Kratky Doré, *Secrecy by Consent: The Use and Limits of Confidentiality in the Pursuit of Settlement*, 74 NOTRE DAME L. REV. 283 (1999). For an excellent bibliography of the literature in the area and a catalogue of state regulations, see The Roscoe Pound Institute monograph, *Materials on Secrecy Practices in the Courts* (July 2000).

10. S. 623, *The Sunshine in Litigation Act of 2011*, at http://thomas.loc.gov/cgi-bin/query/z?c112:S.623.IS: or in legislative style at http://www.gpo.gov/fdsys/pkg/BILLS-112s623rs/pdf/BILLS-112s623rs.pdf. This is perhaps the "cleanest" effort to date to draft a bill that protects public safety while also protecting the rights of litigants, especially defendants, from excessive intrusion on their ability to defend their cases and their rights to protection of legitimate trade secrets.

Chapter 8

THE SPECIAL PROBLEMS OF THE GOVERNMENT LAWYER

PROBLEM 23: MUST A PROSECUTOR PLAY BY DIFFERENT RULES?

A. INTRODUCTION

Prosecutors have enormous power: discretion in deciding who to investigate; whether a case should be filed; under which criminal statutes it should be filed; whom it should be filed against (and what other individuals should be given immunity); and how certain criminal statutes should be applied. They also have discretion to determine when a case is appropriate for prosecution, and whether it warrants a plea negotiation. Eventually, at trial, they turn into advocates, whose ego drive and desire to win are every bit as strong as any other advocate's — and, generally, whose belief in the correctness of their position is honestly and deeply held.

The job of the prosecutor also comes with special responsibilities. Prosecutors have what many consider a quasi-judicial function, with a special obligation to balance their advocacy with their other role as seekers of justice. Every state has special rules that address prosecutors' conduct, and the ABA wrote a special set of standards to further analyze that conduct. With the seemingly ever-increasing power that prosecutors wield comes the need to use the power wisely — and the potential to abuse it.

B. PROBLEM

I

When Heather Hunt won election as District Attorney of the City and County of Metropolis, she did it with a pledge to concentrate on violent crimes. Part of her "priorities pledge" was a promise not to prosecute anyone on "simple loitering" charges. In the two years since Hunt's election, despite the increasing presence of the homeless in several areas of Metropolis, the district attorney's office has never prosecuted a loitering case. Police have done no more than occasionally moving or breaking up larger gatherings of homeless.

The Mission District is a pleasant middle class residential neighborhood. Recently, the Mission District Safe Neighborhood Coalition met with Hunt to complain about an influx of homeless in Mission Park and the nearby Town Square shopping mall. The coalition complained that the park is no longer comfortable for the families and kids who live in the neighborhood. The Town Square representatives claimed their businesses were losing money. Hunt orders her charging deputies to send out the word to police that her office will now enforce the loitering statute in Town Square and Mission Park but will continue its prior policy in all other areas of the city.

QUESTIONS

1.   Was Hunt's campaign promise to not prosecute loitering cases proper?

2.   Is prosecuting loitering only in the Mission District an appropriate exercise of prosecutorial discretion or an improper selective enforcement of the laws?

3.   What if the loitering statute was in disuse not because Heather chose to ignore it, but because it had not been enforced by anyone in the state for 35 years? May she now use it in the Mission District?

4.   Suppose again that the loitering statute has been in disuse for the last 35 years. Suppose, too, that Hunt receives a report that reputed drug lord Leonard Sheldon is in Metropolis to organize and take over much of the city's drug trade. May Hunt tell the police chief that her office would prosecute Sheldon for anything, including loitering, and for the police to "keep a close eye" on Sheldon?

5.   Suppose instead that Hunt wants the police department to watch Abu Nazir, a reputed terrorist who was reported to be in Metropolis, and to charge him with any available offense including loitering?

II

Michael Stone is a deputy in the district attorney's Serious Crimes Unit. Metropolis police robbery inspector Ronald Rico asks Mike to charge Benjamin Sisk for the robbery of Whit Moore. Last week, Moore was robbed by a young black male after he withdrew money from an ATM. Three days later, Moore was having a drink in a local bar across town, The Lucky 7, when Sisk walked in. Moore, sure that Sisk was the man who robbed him, called the police, and Sisk was arrested.

Rico puts Sisk in a lineup, at which Moore makes a positive identification. Moore is a 57-year-old white male who admits to having had two drinks in the bar before Sisk walked in. After the robbery, Moore had described the robber as a black male in his early twenties, muscular, short black hair, moustache, between 6'1" and 6'3" tall. This description fits Sisk, except that he is 5'10 1/2."

Stone knows he has enough to charge Sisk, but harbors doubts. First, he checks Sisk out, and finds that he is a longtime resident of the city, he has had one adult arrest, three years ago at age 19, for disturbing the peace, and no convictions. Sisk has held the same job for the past 18 months, as a supermarket checker. Second, Stone wonders about the size discrepancy in the description, which, though not enormous, could be significant. Third, although Metropolis has a large black population, Moore, who two years before moved from a small town in the Midwest, has apparently had little close exposure to African-Americans and has no black friends. Stone is concerned that Moore's "i.d." may possibly have been unintentionally motivated by the coincidence of seeing a black man of similar looks and attire to the robber in the bar just a few days later.

QUESTIONS

1. May Stone file robbery charges against Sisk? Should he? Which of Stone's musings, above, is appropriate for him to consider?

2. Suppose Rico had previously arrested Sisk's brother on similar robbery charges two years ago. Should Stone consider this fact in deciding whether to charge Sisk?

3. Assume that Rico unlawfully searches Sisk's apartment in violation of state and federal search and seizure laws, and finds Moore's driver's license inside the apartment. Stone is now convinced of Sisk's guilt, but may he take this evidence into account in deciding whether to charge Sisk, when he knows the evidence will be excluded at trial?

4. Assume that Stone has a witness statement taken by an officer at the Lucky 7 Bar from a friend of Moore's that states Moore has said on more than one occasion that "all those black people look alike." Must Stone, even if he is now convinced of Sisk's guilt, give this report to the defense? Does it matter whether Stone considers the report "material"?

5. Suppose Deputy DA Peter Sling is assigned the case for trial. After reviewing the file, Sling harbors significant doubts about Sisk's guilt. In light of this, would it be appropriate for Sling to dismiss the case? What about offering Sisk a better plea bargain? If Sisk turns down the deal, proclaiming his innocence, may Sling argue at trial the absolute accuracy of Moore's "i.d.," even if he himself is not convinced?

C. READINGS

1. Are a Prosecutor's Ethical Standards Different?

Prosecutors, we are often reminded, are not merely advocates but objective "ministers of justice."[1] As such, they should be held to a different — indeed, a *higher* — ethical standard than the average advocate. It has often been said that "the duty of a prosecutor is to seek justice, not merely to convict." The seminal case of *Berger v. United States*, 295 U.S. 78 (1935) defines the role of a prosecutor eloquently:

> The representative not of an ordinary party to a controversy, but of a sovereignty whose obligation to govern impartially is as compelling as its obligation to govern at all; and whose interest, therefore, in a criminal prosecution is not that it shall win a case, but that justice shall be done. As such, he is in a peculiar and very definite sense the servant of the law, the twofold aim of which is that guilt shall not escape or innocence suffer. He

---

[1] Model Rule 1.3, Comment 1.

may prosecute with earnestness and vigor — indeed, he should do so. But, while he may strike hard blows, he is not at liberty to strike foul ones. It is as much his duty to refrain from improper methods calculated to produce a wrongful conviction as it is to use every legitimate means to bring about a just one.

Id. at 88, 1321.

With this dual role come some special responsibilities, both of constitutional[2] and ethical dimension, such as Model Rule 3.8, which enumerates a series of special requirements for prosecutors. Some of those special responsibilities have been defined in the past by the ABA's specific standards for prosecutors, selected portions of which are set forth below. However, we note that while a task force is now at work revising these standards, the most recent published edition dates from 1992. The standards have always been largely hortatory, and have even less force of law with the passage of time. Nevertheless, the values set forth in the standards are worth our consideration. Among the most important are the following:

AMERICAN BAR ASSOCIATION STANDARDS FOR CRIMINAL JUSTICE
(3d ed. 1992)[3]

Standard 3-1.2 The Function of the Prosecutor

(a) The office of prosecutor is charged with responsibility for prosecutions in its jurisdiction.

(b) The prosecutor is an administrator of justice, an advocate, and an officer of the court; the prosecutor must exercise sound discretion in the performance of his or her functions.

(c) The duty of the prosecutor is to seek justice, not merely to convict.

Standard 3-3.6 Quality and Scope of Evidence Before Grand Jury

. . . .

(b) No prosecutor should knowingly fail to disclose to the grand jury evidence which tends to negate guilt or mitigate the offense.

(c) A prosecutor should recommend that the grand jury not indict if he or she believes the evidence presented does not warrant an indictment under governing law.

Standard 3-3.9 Discretion in the Charging Decision

(a) A prosecutor should not institute, or cause to be instituted, or permit the continued pendency of criminal charges when the prosecutor knows that the charges are not supported by probable cause. A prosecutor should not institute, cause to be instituted, or permit the continued pendency of criminal charges in the absence of sufficient admissible evidence to support a conviction.

---

[2] See *Brady v. Maryland*, 373 U.S. 83 (1963), and *United States v. Bagley*, 473 U.S. 667 (1985), on the requirement to turn over exculpatory evidence.

[3] Copyright © 1992 by American Bar Association. Reprinted by permission.

(b) The prosecutor is not obliged to present all charges which the evidence might support. The prosecutor may in some circumstances and for good cause consistent with the public interest decline to prosecute, notwithstanding that sufficient evidence may exist which would support a conviction. Illustrative of the factors which the prosecutor may properly consider in exercising his or her discretion are:

   (i)   the prosecutor's reasonable doubt that the accused is in fact guilty;

   (ii)   the extent of the harm caused by the offense;

   (iii)   the disproportion of the authorized punishment in relation to the particular offense or the offender;

   (iv)   possible improper motives of a complainant;

   (v)   reluctance of the victim to testify;

   (vi)   cooperation of the accused in the apprehension or conviction of others; and

   (vii)   availability and likelihood of prosecution by another jurisdiction.

(c) A prosecutor should not be compelled by his or her supervisor to prosecute a case in which he or she has a reasonable doubt about the guilt of the accused.

(d) In making the decision to prosecute, the prosecutor should give no weight to the personal or political advantages or disadvantages which might be involved or to a desire to enhance his or her record of convictions.

Standard 3-3.11 Disclosure of Evidence by the Prosecutor

(a) A prosecutor should not intentionally fail to make timely disclosure to the defense, at the earliest feasible opportunity, of the existence of all evidence or information which tends to negate the guilt of the accused or mitigate the offense charged or which would tend to reduce the punishment of the accused.

Standard 3-4.1 Availability for Plea Discussions

(a) The prosecutor should have and make known a general policy or willingness to consult with defense counsel concerning disposition of charges by plea.

(c) A prosecutor should not knowingly make false statements or representation as to fact or law in the course of plea discussions with defense counsel or the accused.

NOTES

These ABA standards certainly pay more than lip service to the notion that the prosecutor's role is special. But without legal force, how well is the conduct of prosecutors actually regulated? Are the admonitions of Model Rule 3.8 sufficient? Many have noted that, in the words of one commentator, disciplinary charges have been "brought infrequently under the applicable rules and . . . meaningful sanctions have been applied only rarely."[4]

---

[4] Richard A. Rosen, *Disciplinary Sanctions Against Prosecutors for Brady Violations: A Paper Tiger*, 65 N.C. L. Rev. 693 (1987).

Professor Bennett L. Gershman, a former deputy district attorney who served on the front lines and as special assistant to New York State's attorney general and has written frequently (and critically) about prosecutors, reported that he reviewed "[l]iterally hundreds of truly egregious instances of prosecutorial misconduct," none of which resulted in punishment of the prosecutor by either his superiors or the bar.[5]

2. Must Prosecutors Follow "Higher Standards" in Disclosing Information?

Surely, many prosecutors take seriously the requirements of Rule 3.8 and are mindful of the advice given in the ABA standards. But they also are aware that they can get away with a lot of corner-cutting if they choose not to abide by the rule, much less the standards. For example, in *Bagley*, cited above, the Supreme Court limited reversals based on *Brady v. Maryland* to those situations in which "there is a reasonable probability that, had the evidence been disclosed to the defense, the result of the proceeding would have been different." And, as we mentioned in Problem 19, courts have found that *Brady* disclosure does not include information about impeachment or even the death of a key witnesses if that disclosure relates to a plea negotiation rather than trial.

Bagley means that many, even most, convictions will stand even if there are some *Brady* violations, whether unintentional or intentional. This fact cannot be lost on prosecutors. Still, when read in conjunction with Rule 3.8, it seems that at the least, such prosecutors, by violating *Brady*, would also violate the ethical mandates of that rule.[6]

There are, of course, *Brady* violations that result in reversals. The most recent high profile case was the conviction of the Senator Ted Stevens of Alaska, accused of failing to report gifts in the form of renovations to a small house he owned. He was prosecuted in the fall of 2008 just as he was running for re-election, which he lost by a narrow margin. The *Brady* violations in this rather weak case were so great that U.S. Attorney General Eric Holder requested the dismissal of all charges against Stevens within six months of his conviction.[7]

But is that it? Is *Brady* the ceiling? Or does MR 3.8 extend beyond *Brady*? As we've noted in Problem 19, neither the *Jones* case from New York nor the Supreme Court's opinion in *Ruiz* addressed whether a prosecutor, bound "to seek justice,"

---

[5] BENNETT L. GERSHMAN, PROSECUTORIAL MISCONDUCT 13-2 n.4 (6th ed. 1991). Later studies, especially the work of Fred Zacharias, show that the paucity of discipline has continued into the new millennium.

[6] It is worth noting that only one Supreme Court case addressing *Brady* issues specifically cites to the disclosure requirements under MR 3.8(d): *Cone v. Bell*, 556 U. S. 449 (2009), at fn 15, which quotes the rule as requiring prosecutors to "make timely disclosure to the defense of all evidence or information known to the prosecutor that tends to negate the guilt of the accused or mitigates the offense, ..." In *Cone*, the issue was the failure to turn over mitigating evidence at the death-penalty phase in the trial of a Vietnam veteran with possible PTSD and various addictions. The death sentence was reversed and remanded.

[7] *See*, e.g., among the many articles written, Jeffrey Toobin, Annals of Law, *Casualties of Justice*, THE NEW YORKER, January 3, 2011, focusing on the suicide of the prosecutors. *See also* Nina Totenberg, *Justice Dept. Seeks To Void Stevens' Conviction*, April 1, 2009, *available at* npr.org.

must disclose information that the defense would want to know even if it's not part of either *Brady* or ordinary discovery.

In 2009, the ABA issued opinion 09-454 (July 2009), which in essence says that when it comes to disclosure of information, *Brady* is not the ceiling but the floor. The opinion created a hypothetical designed to distinguish between disclosure under *Brady* and disclosure under Rule 3.8(d): an eyewitness identification case in which two witnesses had identified the defendant but three others had not, with one naming another suspect. In the hypothetical, the prosecutors pursue other leads and find them not credible, and thus, in their view, not *material* under *Brady*. The question is whether the prosecutors nevertheless have the duty to turn over this information to the defendant. The opinion answers that question "yes," noting what some courts seemed to have ignored: that rule 3.8(d) has neither a "materiality" standard nor a "*de minimus*" threshold. Rather it requires, in the plain language of the rule, disclosure of "all evidence or information . . . that tends to negate the guilt . . . or mitigates . . . ."

Nevertheless, as we go through the readings for this Problem, we'll examine several forces at work that may serve to counteract the requirements of MR 3.8 when it comes to how prosecutors actually behave. These include the rare and then often-anonymous discipline of prosecutors, the broad civil immunity prosecutors enjoy, their required obedience to their superiors' dictates, right or wrong, and for federal prosecutors, the claim that local ethics rules don't apply to them.

We'll explore each of these forces further below. But first we examine prosecutorial discretion.

3.   Prosecutorial Discretion and Selective Prosecution

Prosecutorial discretion is necessary. It is impossible to prosecute every individual for every crime committed. And a certain amount of selective prosecution is appropriate as well — choosing to file charges against Smith while declining them against Jones, for articulable and judicious reasons.

But when does prosecutorial discretion become an abuse of power, and selective prosecution become discriminatory enforcement? Whens the ABA first codified Standard 3-3.9 governing discretion, it was subject to considerable and vigorous debate, and ultimately gave great leeway to the prosecutor's subjective evaluation of circumstances. Though the standards have faded in importance, broad discretion is still the rule of the day.

Should there be stricter guidelines regarding discretion? Some, like Monroe Freedman, have argued that the decision to prosecute should not be based on personal vendetta or bias, or as Justice Robert Jackson, a former United States Attorney General, said, "Picking the man and then searching the law books or putting investigators to work, to pin some offense on him." Freedman cited *Yick Wo v. Hopkins*, 118 U.S. 356 (1886), the constitutional law case read by practically every law student, noting that *Yick Wo* was about a law "fair on its face" but applied "by public authority with an evil eye and an unequal hand."[8]

---

[8] Lawyers' Ethics in an Adversary System 81–83 (1975).

On the other hand, other commentators from Professor Richard Uviller in the 1970s[9] to Kenneth Starr in the Whitewater controversy and the Martha Stewart and Barry Bonds prosecutors, have argued that prosecutors *should* be able to consider the particular individual being scrutinized. Uviller noted that all prosecutors would consider an individual's personal character and prior record in determining a plea bargain. Why not then, he argued, in deciding whom to investigate? Many who defended the lengths to which Starr went to investigate and seek prosecution of President Bill Clinton for the Monica Lewinsky affair make a similar argument: The fact that Clinton was the president made it especially important to the public interest that he be held accountable.

We will return to examine Starr's role as independent counsel more closely. For the moment, we remain focused on the "real world" problems of prosecutorial discretion and selective enforcement that occur every day in district attorneys' offices throughout the country. Below are four specific examples, the first involving broad policy questions and large numbers of people, the second involving selecting one particular person to investigate, the third involving selecting one particular person *not* to charge, and the final example being the compelling story of a 12-year-old murder defendant and the prosecutor who wanted both a conviction on the maximum charge and lenient sentence for a penalty.

Post 9/11 Scrutiny of Muslims and Arabs. Many have raised the issue of whether since September 11, 2001, individuals with Arab and Muslim backgrounds have been singled out for investigation, scrutiny, detention, and prosecution. Most of these issues relate not to allegations of terrorist activities, but to other endeavors facially irrelevant to terrorism. For example, *U.S. v. Alameh*, 341 F.3d 167 (2d Cir. 2003), involved a person of Arab ethnicity who claimed he was being selectively prosecuted for unlawful procurement of naturalization — marrying a citizen to get a green card. His lawyers argued that prior to 9/11, 85% of those prosecuted for this activity had non-Arab non-Muslim names, but after 9/11, the percentages were inverted — 85% of those prosecuted did have Arab or Muslim names. However, the court held that Alameh had failed to meet his burden of presenting sufficient evidence even to warrant conducting discovery on a selective prosecution claim. How close is this circumstance to that in *Yick Wo*? Similar tales abound, even over a decade after 9/11.

Celebrity Justice? Marion Barry, Martha Stewart, and Barry Bonds. Second, we examine whether celebrity can result in selective prosecution. In 1990, Washington, D.C. Mayor Marion Barry found himself the focus of federal agents who mounted a sting operation against him. The government went to substantial lengths to set its trap, including the use of a false "friend" who overtly encouraged him to use drugs. Barry was videotaped using "crack" cocaine, and then arrested. Many felt that had Barry been anyone other than the mayor, and a rather controversial one, the sting operation never would have occurred, or at least never would have gone to such lengths to encourage his criminal behavior. Some argued that the sting had more to do with the federal prosecutors' political dislike of Barry than his actual drug use. But federal authorities argued that any lengths within the

---

[9] *The Virtuous Prosecutor in Quest of an Ethical Standard: Guidance from the ABA*, 71 U. MICH. L. REV. 1145 (1973).

bounds of the law were appropriate when the alleged drug user is none other than the mayor of the nation's capital.

Barry eventually pled guilty to reduced charges.[10] By 1994, declaring himself rehabilitated, Barry, made a stunning political comeback, winning reelection as mayor. But was it fair to single him out for prosecution in the first place?

Then we have the case of Martha Stewart, sent to prison for crimes many felt were minor "theoretical" insider-trading offenses that would not have been prosecuted had she not been a celebrity. Did prosecutors use her as a "poster child" to warn off others? If so, did her name recognition justify making Stewart an example of what can happen when insider trading takes place, or was it selective and thus unfair?

Finally, we have baseball home run king Barry Bonds, indicted for lying to a federal grand jury about his use of performance-enhancing drugs. As with Stewart, many felt it was appropriate to single out a celebrity to serve as an example to us all. But others felt that this case was more about prosecutorial grandstanding at the expense of an unpopular superstar known for his irascible and egotistical demeanor.

Bonds was never charged with steroid use, but with lying about it. The jury failed to convict him of perjury, settling only on one charge of "obstruction of justice" for failing failed to answer a specific question directly. Many observers felt that this charge, on appeal as we go to press, was weak and indirect. Did either the Bonds or Stewart cases teach us the lesson that prosecutors say they were designed to do? Or were they largely a waste of time, money, and valuable resources?

"Butch" Hallinan and the Singleton *Case.* Should selective *avoidance* of enforcement be permitted as legitimate prosecutorial discretion? May a prosecutor let a criminal defendant free, or offer a sweet plea arrangement or sentence reduction in exchange for testimony? Clearly, this happens all the time. Supposedly, the deal is offered to someone whom the prosecutor sees as being less of a threat to society. But can this discretion also be abused? Take the widely-reported case of Patrick "Butch" Hallinan, a well-known San Francisco lawyer whose brother served as the city's district attorney.[11]

The U.S. Attorney in Reno, Nevada indicted Hallinan in 1993 for allegedly conspiring with his drug-lord client, Ciro Mancuso, to assist in Mancuso's criminal enterprise. The chief prosecution witness? Mancuso himself, who, facing a sentence of up to 60 years, gave his expertise and testimony to the government in return for a promise of leniency. The case against Hallinan collapsed embarrassingly at trial, but Mancuso was sentenced to only nine years in prison, a vastly reduced sentence. Had Hallinan been convicted, many observers speculated Mancuso would have

---

[10] This plea itself caused some controversy, in that it was conditioned on Barry's resignation as mayor.

[11] See, *inter alia*, the extensive series of articles by Howard Mintz in the Recorder (San Francisco) and by several reporters, especially Rob Haeseler of the San Francisco Chronicle, from August 1993 through mid-1997.

received little if any further time in custody.[12] Was it legitimate to argue that Mancuso posed less of a threat to society than did his lawyer?

For a brief moment in 1998, at least one court had concluded that inducing a prospective criminal defendant to become a witness by offering leniency or immunity was a violation of the federal bribery statute. "If justice is perverted when a criminal defendant seeks to buy testimony from a witness, it is no less perverted when the government does so," wrote the appeals court panel in *United States v. Singleton*, 144 F.3d 1343 (10th Cir. 1998). Within weeks, however, the Kansas prosecutors who made the leniency/immunity offers in a drug-trafficking case had successfully sought a stay. They soon got an *en banc* decision that decisively reversed the three-judge panel.[13]

The *en banc* court held that the anti-bribery statute refers to an individual offering the bribe and that an assistant U.S. attorney offering leniency is acting on behalf of the government itself. The court also implied that applying the anti-bribery statute could restrict the sovereign prosecutorial powers of the executive branch. Not everyone agreed. Georgetown law professor Paul Rothstein, who closely followed the case, told the *ABA Journal* that the original three-judge panel had correctly interpreted the bribery statute's plain meaning: "The majority opinion appears to give the words an illogical reading in order to preserve a practice it feels is necessary and desirable for law enforcement purposes."[14]

Lionel Tate and His Prosecutor. Finally, we come to the sad irony of Lionel Tate. Lionel's case raises the issue of whether a prosecutor may file a charge for which he thinks the penalty is too severe. The case, which got a great deal of publicity due to the youth of the defendant, also raises a collateral question: What happens when a prosecutor changes opinions about the initial charges midstream?

In March 2001 in Broward County Florida, Lionel Tate, then 14, was sentenced to life without possibility of parole for the murder of a six-year-old committed when Lionel was 12. At sentencing, the prosecutors requested leniency for Lionel, and even talked afterwards about joining the defense's appeal to the governor for leniency. But the judge, Joel T. Lazarus, who imposed the full adult sentence, took that opportunity to criticize the prosecution, saying that if the state did not believe the boy deserved a life sentence, prosecutors should have tried Lionel only on lesser charges: "To talk about travel to the governor to seek a reduction in charge or sentence, if accurate, is of tremendous concern to this court. It not only casts the prosecutor in a light totally inconsistent with his role in the criminal justice system, but it makes the whole court process seem like a game. . . ."[15]

The prosecutor defended his handling of the case by saying that the severity of the crime justified trying Lionel as an adult but should have included leeway in

---

[12] In fact, Mancuso complained in his appeal to the Ninth Circuit that he should have received a shorter sentence in light of his good efforts as an informant. See Mr. Mintz's RECORDER article of July 23, 1996, *Hallinan Witness Says He Got Less Than He Bargained For.*

[13] *United States v. Singleton*, 165 F.3d 1297 (10th Cir. 1999).

[14] The decision whom to prosecute can also be a significant issue in corporate cases, as we'll see below.

[15] *See, e.g.*, Dana Canedy, *A Sentence of Life Without Parole for Boy, 14, in Murder of Girl, 6*, N.Y. TIMES, March 10, 2001, at 1.

sentencing. He also noted that the defense had summarily dismissed a generous plea bargain.[16]

Should the prosecutor be allowed to seek a *conviction* resulting in the severest possible penalty and then turn around at *sentencing* to request leniency? Or was Judge Lazarus right that the prosecution should not speak out of both sides of its mouth, but go to trial only on a charge whose consequences it could accept at sentencing? Put another way, did the prosecution abuse its discretion by overcharging the case?

Finally, the issue of prosecutorial discretion in cases of corporate malfeasance has come of age in the new millennium, in several respects. Increasing government scrutiny of corporate entities have raised several issues that relate to prosecutorial discretion. Some questions to ponder:

- Should the entire entity be charged, such as Arthur Andersen in the Enron aftermath? Even if that results in the loss of thousands of jobs?

- Should the government offer immunity to mid-level employees, or even higher-ups in order to get evidence against the "biggest fish"?

- Should the government offer immunity to the corporation itself in return for evidence against the "big fish"? And perhaps most importantly:

- Should the government require corporations to engage in wholesale or even partial waivers of the attorney-client privilege or work-product doctrine as a condition of immunity to facilitate the government's prosecutions?

The DOJ's position on these issues, especially the last, has changed several times in the last few years and remains something of a moving target.

4. Abuse of Power? Inside the Beltway

There has undoubtedly been more written about the investigation and possible prosecution of President Clinton by special prosecutor Kenneth Starr — and Clinton's subsequent impeachment and acquittal — than any other event in American legal history. We do not intend here to add to the verbiage. We do feel it is important, however, to pause briefly and examine an issue that tens of millions of Americans debated daily: Did prosecutor Starr abuse his power by the manner in which he investigated the President concerning his relationship with White House intern Monica Lewinsky?

We begin by noting that Starr, as an independent prosecutor, had enormous power, virtually unfettered and unchecked. With one exception, we don't evaluate Starr's office's conduct from the perspective of his role as independent counsel; largely as a result of Whitewater, that office no longer exists, and is unlikely to reappear any time soon. Rather, we briefly review some of Starr's office's conduct

---

[16] Interestingly, particularly in light of our discussion in Problem 13, Lionel's mother, a Florida state trooper, seemed to have had decisionmaking power over Lionel's plea. She rejected several offers by the prosecutors to have her son plead guilty to second-degree murder and accept a sentence of three years in a juvenile detention center and 10 years of probation.

in light of the dichotomy we suggest above: Does prosecutorial discretion permit the targeting of an individual when that individual — here, a sitting President — is so vital to the public interest that higher scrutiny or broader discretionary leeway is justified? Or did the zeal applied amount to an attempt at selective prosecution — an abuse of prosecutorial discretion, under Justice Jackson's theory that it is simply wrong to be "picking the man and then searching the law books, or putting investigators to work, to pin some offense on him"?[17]

The first point to consider, and the one in which Starr's role as special prosecutor *is* relevant, is that Starr was appointed for the very purpose of focusing on President Clinton and his wife Hillary Rodham Clinton. This clearly vitiates the issue of singling out an individual. On the other hand, many observers argued that Starr focused on a collateral matter (Clinton's relationship to Lewinsky) and an offense for which few, if any, ordinary citizens would be prosecuted (alleged perjury by denying a sexual relationship in a deposition in a civil matter otherwise unrelated to the prosecutorial investigation). In this respect, Starr's office may well have violated Justice Jackson's admonition not to search to "pin an offense on him."[18]

Other than the very existence of an investigation on the collateral subject of the Lewinsky matter, Starr's office was perhaps most heavily criticized in three areas: the manner in which the investigation of Lewinsky was conducted, including her initial detention; the manner in which witnesses subpoenaed before the grand jury were treated; and the manner of Starr's testimony before Congress in the impeachment inquiry. This last issue — accusations that Starr's testimony before Congress, rather than being a neutral recitation of facts, was accusatory and prosecutorial in nature — while seemingly a reasonable interpretation, relates directly to Starr's brief as independent counsel and his and his staff's interpretation of what that meant. We accordingly leave it there.

The other two issues, the treatment of Lewinsky and the treatment of witnesses (whether considered unfriendly or neutral), both concern the question of whether Starr's zealous investigative practices, given the importance of his target, justified an abrupt and sometimes peremptory prosecutorial style. St. John's University law professor John Q. Barrett, a former member of special prosecutor Lawrence Walsh's staff, has often pointed out that every prosecutor's office allocates resources, and every prosecutor's office will be more vigorous in pursuing a key witness in an alleged crime lord's case than in a routine bank robbery. Barrett's point is not only well-taken, it is accurate and even necessary.

Assume for a moment a justifiable increased scrutiny in light of the importance of Starr's investigation. It is nevertheless difficult to see how the peremptory subpoenaing of a privately-owned bookstore, Kramerbooks, for records of Lewinsky's purchases, forcing that bookstore to defend its customer's rights of privacy at its own expense, is consistent with a proper understanding of the

---

[17] This is not unlike Marion Barry's case, albeit on a much grander scale.

[18] In this respect, the prosecution seems similar to Barry Bonds', although Bonds, more seriously, was in front of a grand jury, not merely at a deposition.

concept that the "duty of the prosecutor is to seek justice, not merely to convict."[19]

5. Abuse of Power? Outside the Beltway

Whatever one concludes about special prosecutor Starr and his staff in their handling of the Lewinsky matter, there can be little question that they had an extraordinary amount of power. This is true of most prosecutors; indeed, we will focus most of our remaining discussion on why this is so. In Starr's case, it made him, for a time, arguably the most powerful person in America.

Enormous power also is given local prosecutors, on a routine day-in-day-out basis. In the case of two prosecutors, one in Colorado and another in North Carolina, the power was more fleeting but no less overwhelming.

In April 2001, a veteran prosecutor in Jefferson County, Colorado was disciplined for posing as a public defender to persuade a suspected ax murderer, who soon confessed, to surrender. The prosecutor, Chief Deputy District Attorney Mark Pautler, was unrepentant after being put on 12 months' probation but not actually suspended from practice, and appealed the disciplinary committee's 2-1 vote against him to the state Supreme Court, which unanimously upheld the discipline.[20]

"Members of our profession must adhere to the highest moral and ethical standards," said Justice Rebecca Kourlis, writing for the court. "Those standards apply regardless of motive. Purposeful deception by an attorney licensed in our state is intolerable, even when it is undertaken as a part of attempting to secure the surrender of a murder suspect."

In July 1998, Pautler had posed as public defender "Mark Palmer" after William "Cody" Neal, suspected in a triple murder earlier the same day as well as several other crimes, had been on a cell phone with investigators and insisted on speaking with a public defender. Pautler told the disciplinary panel that he didn't trust the public defenders, and that providing one was out of the question because the defense lawyer would have had to advise Neal to say nothing more.

Instead, Pautler decided that he would pose as a public defender, reasoning that only a real attorney could pull off the deception. According to Denver's *Rocky Mountain News*, "When Neal asked Pautler what his rights were, the prosecutor-turned-defense attorney dodged the question."[21] Pautler told the disciplinary panel that he had checked with his boss before acting.

---

[19] The Kramerbooks subpoena was also widely reported. It is our understanding both from news accounts and our own unpublished sources that the bookstore was offered and accepted financial help from the American Booksellers Association, the primary association of independent booksellers, in fighting the subpoena, and that legal fees had reached several hundred thousand dollars when Lewinsky reached an immunity agreement with the special prosecutor and then consented to the bookstore's revealing a list of her purchases.

[20] *See* In re Pautler, 47 P.3d 1175 (Colo. 2002).

[21] Sarah Huntley, *Prosecutor Admits He Lied*, ROCKY MOUNTAIN NEWS (Denver), March 8, 2001. *See also* Marlys Duran, *Attorney Pautler appeals to state high court; He says he was right to lie to fugitive killer*, ROCKY MOUNTAIN NEWS (Denver), April 24, 2001.

Although it is certainly understandable why law enforcement officers would not want to leave a dangerous fugitive at large — Neal surrendered peacefully and many have written that Pautler deserved a medal — one wonders why the lawyers didn't let competent police officers do their job. One must also ask on what basis Pautler believed he had the authority or power to participate in such an overt lie. Indeed, the court made it clear that "noble motives" don't allow prosecutors to ignore the Rules of Professional Conduct. "[W]e are adamant that when presented with choices, at least one of which conforms to the rules, an attorney must not select an option that involves deceit or misrepresentation," wrote Justice Kourlis.

Nevertheless, Pautler remained unrepentant even after the Supreme Court ruling. "Lawyers are told not to do the right thing but to do the expedient thing to keep their license," Pautler was quoted as saying by the *Denver Post*. "I think it is more important to save lives. I think this slavish adherence to the code even though human lives are going to be lost doesn't make sense. Neal indicated he had killed literally hundreds of people, was armed and would kill again. . . . I don't know how you can minimize somebody who just killed three women."[22]

Phil Cherner, a lawyer speaking on behalf of the Colorado criminal defense bar saw it differently, telling the *Post* the ruling was an "emphatic statement that we are held to the highest responsibility and . . . [that] the rules apply to everybody, including prosecutors. I'm glad [Kourlis] put a stop to this nonsense."

It must be noted, however, that the state's high court, while critical of Pautler's conduct, placed him on probation without requiring actual suspension.

In 2006, North Carolina and the country witnessed the swift rise and even swifter fall of Durham County chief prosecutor Michael B. Nifong. Nifong first made the news in the spring of 2006 at a highly-publicized series of events during which he accused three Duke lacrosse players of raping a woman at a party. The cross-racial nature of the charges — the players are white, the alleged victim black — briefly made him something of a hero in the area's African American community; a white prosecutor willing to take on the students of hallowed Duke University. But Nifong's 15 minutes of fame were short-lived.

First, Nifong was criticized for trying his case in the press, assuring those who would listen that the players were guilty. Then he was accused of suppressing DNA evidence that would have exonerated the three players. In short order, he was facing ethics charges, then criminal charges, then removal from office, and by mid-2007, disbarment. Along the way, he eventually admitted that "there is no credible evidence" against the three athletes. Everyone in this case lost something, Nifong most of all. Nifong's is a case study in Lord Acton's famous aphorism that "power corrupts, and absolute power corrupts absolutely."[23]

---

[22] Howard Pankratz, *Deception By Lawyers Ruled Out Decision Stems From Attempt To Get Murder Suspect's Surrender*, DENVER POST, May 14, 2002.

[23] The Nifong matter was reported widely in the press. For an index of major stories, see http://topics.nytimes.com/topics/reference/timestopics/people/n/michael_b_nifong/index.html.

6. Abuse of Power at Trial

Saying that a prosecutor, even at trial, must be both advocate and seeker of justice is a lot easier than doing it. Famed death penalty defense attorney (and former prosecutor) Anthony Amsterdam put it this way: Two adversaries in trial are like two prize-fighters; "Consider how very difficult it is for any human being to stand in the ring getting pummeled by left jabs and right hooks from an adversary whose avowed, legitimate and obvious purpose is to knock the hell out of you . . . and in that atmosphere to remember that your goal is not to strike back . . . but rather to do justice. . . ." One's instinct, says Amsterdam, is "to hit back first and worry about doing justice later."[24]

While this may help us understand the difficult task a prosecutor faces, many observers believe that prosecutors' behavior in trial is directly due to the fact that their conduct is largely unencumbered by either court scrutiny or external ethical checks. Again, we confront the issue of virtually limitless power. "Prosecutors today wield greater power, engage in more egregious misconduct, and are less subject to judicial or bar association oversight than ever before," wrote Professor Gershman in 1992.[25] In many regards, not much has changed since then.

In the 1970s and 1980s, hard-charging Chicago prosecutor J. Scott Arthur had a great conviction record and had put a number of people on death row, including two of the defendants known as "the Ford Heights 4." He prosecuted one of the four, Dennis Williams, twice, once in 1978 and again in 1987 after the first conviction was overturned. During those trials, Arthur:

- Failed to reveal that the prosecution's star witness had made an initial statement to police at variance with his later statements;

- Offered a deal to an informant — protective custody in another state — to secure his testimony;

- Induced a supposed accomplice of Williams to testify against him in his second trial in return for releasing her from her 50-year sentence seven weeks after Williams was convicted in his second trial;

- Allowed that accomplice to lie on the witness stand when she denied getting a deal from the prosecutor;

- Removed every single black potential juror from the jury box; and most egregiously,

- Withheld during the first trial a statement from a witness who had identified the actual killers only five days after the events had taken place.

When confronted by Williams at a hearing on whether the state owed him damages for wrongful conviction, Arthur maintained despite it all that Williams,

---

[24] Amsterdam, now a New York University law professor, made these remarks at a December 1986 retreat of the Association of the Bar of the City of New York. The remarks were reported by ethics professor Stephen Gillers in *The Prosecution and Defense Functions: Do They Promote Justice?*, 42 The Record of the Ass'n of the Bar of the City of N.Y. 626, reprinted by Professor Gillers in his book Regulation of Lawyers: Problems of Law and Ethics, now in its fifth edition.

[25] *Tricks Prosecutors Play*, Trial, April 1992.

exonerated by the court and the governor, was guilty.[26]

Indeed, Arthur's conduct was, according to the Chicago Tribune, "so egregious that it became a touchstone used by appellate courts in evaluating other prosecutors' behavior . . . cited more than 100 times. . . ." Tellingly, even in the cases involving Scott Arthur's most egregious conduct, the courts not only did not discipline him but assiduously *avoided using his name* — an unfortunate practice but an all-too-common occurrence when courts address prosecutorial abuse.

For instance, Judge Alex Kozinski excoriated the conduct of Assistant United States Attorney Jeffrey S. Sinek, reversing a defendant's conviction because of Sinek's repeated failures to tell the truth about a plea agreement with an informant. Kozinski even quoted Justice Douglas: "'the function of the prosecutor under the Federal Constitution is not to tack as many skins of victims as possible to the wall. His function is to vindicate the right of people as expressed in the laws and give those accused of crime a fair trial.' "[27]

In the same case, Kozinski criticized the fact that the United States Attorney's office is often beyond public scrutiny and judicial review. But when it came to citing Mr. Sinek by name, the generally-outspoken Kozinski still the opinion's author, acceded to the request of Sinek's office and removed Sinek's name, describing him only as "the prosecutor" or "the AUSA."[28]

One example of discipline of a prosecutor who *was* named is *In re Zawada*, 92 P.3d 862 (Ariz. 2004). There, the Arizona Supreme Court suspended a prosecutor who had a history of misconduct for his actions in a trial involving an insanity defense. Without any basis in fact, Zawada attacked the testimony of six psychiatrists who testified on insanity, including the state's witnesses. Among other things, he accused the defense of fabricating testimony by paying off the experts. The defendant's conviction was reversed. The court described Zawada as "single-handedly responsible for much of the law in Arizona on . . . extreme prosecutorial misconduct." Zawada's actual suspension was for six months. Given the extraordinarily egregious nature of the misconduct and the prosecutor's history, do you think the six months suspension was adequate? What should courts do in such extreme situations?

And in *People v. Hill*, 952 P.2d 673 (Cal. 1998), the offending prosecutor, Rosalie Morton, was repeatedly named by the California high court, which reversed defendant Hill's conviction. "The most disturbing aspect of this case was the outrageous and pervasive misconduct on the part of the state's representative at trial: the public prosecutor," said the opinion. The court called Morton's misconduct "continual" and "constant." Though excoriated in a unanimous high court opinion, Morton received *no* public discipline for her behavior.

---

[26] *See* http://www.law.northwestern.edu/cwc/exonerations/ilWilliamsChart.pdf, which documents the specifics of the Williams case; and Ken Armstrong & Maurice Possley, *Reversal of Fortune, Trial & Error: How Prosecutors Sacrifice Justice to Win*, CHICAGO TRIBUNE, Jan. 13, 1999; *see also* James S. Liebman, *The Overproduction of Death*, 100 COLUM. L. REV. 2030 (2000).

[27] United States v. Kojayan, 8 F.3d 1315 (9th Cir. 1993).

[28] *Contrast* 8 F.3d 1315 *with* the November 1, 1993 version at 1993 U.S. App. LEXIS 28301.

Most prosecutors, to be sure, play it by the book. But the failure of courts to use a prosecutor's name when overturning a conviction surely adds to their sense of empowerment. Scott Arthur and Rosalie Morton were never disciplined; Pautler received no suspension, and Zawada only six months. Without more than verbal, often anonymous, chastisement, those prosecutors who take ethical risks feel that they are unlikely to be punished, or at least punished severely, by either the courts or disciplinary authorities. The rest of our discussion will explore this question, first by looking at whether prosecutors have to play by the same ethical rules as all other lawyers, and then by examining other ways in which prosecutors are held accountable for their actions, and to what extent.

7.   Must All Prosecutors Play by the Same Rules?

In 2002, then Assistant U.S. Attorney Anthony Kline failed to turn over to the defense notes a police officer made in interviewing a shooting victim — notes that indicated the accused might not be the shooter. When the case resulted in a hung jury, the prosecutor in charge of the second trial turned over the notes, though the defendant was nevertheless convicted. But the lingering question was whether Kline had a duty to turn over the notes, if not as *Brady* material then under the D.C. Rule 3.8, requiring prosecutors (as does the ABA rule) to turn over all information that "the prosecutor knows or reasonably should know tends to negate the guilt of the accused." Years later, long after he left the Department of Justice, Kline was charged by the D.C. bar and fought his censure in public.[29]

As we discussed at some length in section 2 above, the debate continues over whether *Brady* is a floor or a ceiling when it comes to revealing information. While the ethical requirements of Rule 3.8 and ABA Opinion 09-454 seem to be clearly broader than the constitutional requirements, in Kline's case the U.S. Department of Justice has taken the position that the D.C. bar had no right to require of Kline any more than was constitutionally mandated by *Brady*.[30]

This tension between the United States government and local disciplinary agencies is not new. It raged throughout the 1990s over the issue of whether DOJ lawyers should be bound by Model Rule 4.2, which states that a lawyer may not communicate with a party represented by counsel. After *United States v. Hammad*, 858 F.2d 834 (2d Cir. 1988) sanctioned a prosecutor for communicating with a represented individual who was being investigated for Medicaid fraud, then-Attorney General Richard Thornburgh, in 1989, authored what became known as the Thornburgh Memorandum.

This document claimed that because MR 4.2 might interfere with legitimate law enforcement interests, federal prosecutors were not bound to follow state ethics rules, and under the Supremacy Clause, states had no power to discipline federal

---

[29] The Kline case was widely reported, including in a thorough summary in THE NATIONAL LAW JOURNAL of June 25, 2012, *Prosecutors urge D.C. board to scrap finding that AUSA violated rule*, by Mike Scarcella. As of March 2013, the case was still pending.

[30] Adding fuel to this argument is the first paragraph of the comment to D.C.'s version of MR 3.8, which implies that the rule, despite its clear language, is not intended to "restrict" or "expand" the requirements of the Constitution and D.C. laws.

prosecutors. In 1993, new Attorney General Janet Reno issued a virtually identical memorandum. "Little Thornburgh memos" began cropping up in various states, where prosecutors couldn't resort to the Supremacy Clause, but could still argue, persuasively, their need to engage in ongoing investigations.

One of the focuses of controversy was the distinction it drew between "represented parties, the words of MR 4.2 at the time, and "represented persons," the term used by the DOJ. The ABA, angered by prosecutors saying they were not required to abide by state ethical rules largely based on the Model Rules, soon amended Rule 4.2 to state it applied to represented "persons" rather than "parties."

The fight ultimately played itself out in the congressional arena. The Citizen Protection Act (also known as the McDade-Murtha Amendment) was drafted, passed, and went into effect in 1999. This act confirmed that federal prosecutors — indeed, all government lawyers — are subject to the same professional conduct rules as all other lawyers.[31]

The extent to which prosecutors may participate directly in pre-filing prosecutorial investigations — an issue the *Hammad* court left in abeyance in its relatively narrow ruling — is still an open question. There is no consensus as to where to draw the line between proper prosecutorial investigation and violation of ethical rules. In the last generation, federal courts have, generally speaking, expanded the power of the Justice Department and other prosecutors.

8. Prosecutorial Accountability

While almost all commentators agree that prosecutors must live up to a higher ethical standard than other lawyers, most also agree that prosecutors are less likely to be subject to discipline than the average attorney. Yet the tools prosecutors have at their disposal in the last 40 years are increasingly broad. In 1974, Congress authorized federal undercover sting operations. In the mid-1980s, the strengthening of 18 U.S.C. § 1963 (commonly called the "RICO" Act), and 21 U.S.C. § 848 *et seq.* (the Continuing Criminal Enterprise Statute) gave prosecutors forfeiture tools that they did not previously have. These forfeitures enable prosecutors to seize or freeze a defendant's property, to file suit in civil courts to seize property if it can be linked to a crime, and to affirmatively question the source of a defense attorney's fees. Supreme Court rulings in the 1980s loosened the standard for search warrants; prosecutors use subpoena and search warrant powers far more aggressively against defense counsel than ever before, in an attempt to gain possession of records detailing defense counsel's clientele. Finally, in the post-9/11 era, the PATRIOT Act and other legislation and executive mandates have given even broader powers to prosecutors.

---

[31] Significantly, the sponsorship of Joseph McDade, a Pennsylvania Republican, was undoubtedly colored by his seven-week trial in 1996 in which he was acquitted of charges that he had accepted $100,000 in bribes from defense firms in exchange for supporting millions of dollars' worth of government contracts. Several jurors later described themselves as "incredulous" at the weakness of the government's case.

A generation ago, ex-prosecutor Bennett Gershman wrote an excellent law review article[32] that posits why the behavior of prosecutors is not more frequently sanctioned. First, he argued, ethical rules were designed on a private attorney-client model, in which the prosecutor increasingly does not fit; second, the prosecutor is an increasingly powerful figure, one with considerable public support, whose prosecutorial zeal is politically and practically difficult to sanction; third, prosecutorial abuse, being a more subjective matter than disciplining private attorneys for "garden variety" violations, is simply too difficult for many disciplinary agencies to tackle.

We suggest some other reasons (hardly original to us — we paraphrase here the comments of many) why prosecutors are not more often sanctioned for improper conduct. First, there is simply an absence of ordinary accountability. That is, most advocates have easily identifiable clients, to whom the lawyer must report, and whose interests the lawyer must protect. While many prosecutors feel that they indeed have a client, be it the United States government or the citizenry of a particular jurisdiction, this is not a client in the ordinary sense, the kind that makes decisions on each case. Thus, the prosecutor, not the amorphous client "the People," decides policy and what is in "the client's" best interests. Too often, this lack of accountability leads to an insular climate, where a deputy DA can sign off on his or her decisions — or, as with Colorado DA Pautler, needs only his boss' pro forma approval before acting as he chooses.

This lack of client accountability is coupled with full access to all the investigative powers that modern law enforcement can provide. Since prosecutors have these vast powers at their disposal, and are vested with enormous discretionary powers of their own, their acts take on a quasi-judicial aura. Moreover, enforcing abusive conduct is made more difficult by separation of powers problems — that is, the difficulty of officers of the judiciary branch disciplining lawyers working for the executive branch. The result is that if prosecutors decline to police themselves, they may not be policed at all.

We've noted that even where prosecutors are cited for misconduct, they are usually not named, often not disciplined, and, as significantly, their misconduct does not lead to reversal of the criminal conviction unless, under *Bagley*, the appellate court determines the result was reasonably likely to be different. Even before *Bagley*, the Supreme Court had held that even if *Brady* error occurred, reversal was required only if the defendant was deprived of a fair trial: "[N]o purpose would be served by requiring a new trial simply because an inept prosecutor incorrectly believed he was suppressing a fact that would be vital to the defense."[33]

Moreover, *Arizona v. Youngblood*, 488 U.S. 51 (1988), held that when evidence that could have exonerated a defendant was destroyed (there, clothing worn by a rape victim containing semen stains), a conviction will not be reversed "unless a criminal defendant can show bad faith" on the part of the police. It is far too easy

---

[32] *Symposium: The New Prosecutors*, 53 U. Pitt. L. Rev. 393 (1992). We refer further to this article in the Supplemental Readings below.

[33] United States v. Agurs, 427 U.S. 97, 110 (1976).

to have *Brady* information fall through a *Youngblood* crack, particularly where evidence of guilt appears overwhelming.

This leaves the question of whether it possible for someone wrongfully convicted to sue a prosecutor for damages. The last decade has seen an exponential increase in the number of factual exonerations of prisoners, through the work of various "innocence projects," use of DNA evidence, discovery of other new evidence, and in some cases discovery of prosecutorial misconduct.[34] May these exonerees successfully sue the government for damages when the prosecutorial errors were intentional? The answer is rarely, and only with great difficulty.

Under *Imbler v. Pachtman*, 424 U.S. 409 (1976), government prosecutors are entitled to absolute immunity when it comes to their actions as trial advocates, regardless of the intentionality of their conduct. *Imbler* effectively limited damages cases to those involving systemic administrative violations of constitutional rights, an office's deliberate indifference to those rights, or actions that are not related to trail advocacy.

In 2011, in a 5-4 decision, the Supreme Court reversed a $14 million award for a man who spent 18 years in prison, 14 on death row, for a crime he did not commit.

CONNICK, DISTRICT ATTORNEY v. THOMPSON
131 S. Ct. 1350 (2011)

JUSTICE THOMAS delivered the opinion of the Court.

The Orleans Parish District Attorney's Office now concedes that, in prosecuting respondent John Thompson for attempted armed robbery, prosecutors failed to disclose evidence that should have been turned over to the defense under *Brady v. Maryland*, 373 U.S. 83 (1963). . . . One month before Thompson's scheduled execution, his investigator discovered the undisclosed evidence from his armed robbery trial. The reviewing court determined that the evidence was exculpatory, and both of Thompson's convictions [murder and robbery] were vacated.

After his release from prison, Thompson sued petitioner Harry Connick, in his official capacity as the Orleans Parish District Attorney, for damages under Rev. Stat. § 1979, 42 U.S.C. § 1983. Thompson alleged that Connick had failed to train his prosecutors adequately about their duty to produce exculpatory evidence and that the lack of training had caused the nondisclosure in Thompson's robbery case. The jury awarded Thompson $14 million, and the Court of Appeals for the Fifth Circuit affirmed . . . . We granted certiorari.

. . . .

[In 1985,] a crime scene technician took from one of the victims' pants a swatch

---

[34] We will not recount the statistics here. However, there are numerous compilations of innocence cases, and evaluations of the subset that involve prosecutorial misconduct. *See generally* http://www. publicintegrity.org/accountability/harmful-error?; http://www.innocenceproject.org/know/; and Fred Zacharias & Bruce Green, *The Duty to Avoid Wrongful Convictions: A Thought Experiment in the Regulation of Prosecutors*, 89 B.U. L. REV. 1 (2009), which also contains a brief but clear history of prosecutorial immunity.

of fabric stained with the robber's blood. . . . Two days before the trial, assistant district attorney Bruce Whittaker received the crime lab's report, which stated that the perpetrator had blood type B. There is no evidence that the prosecutors ever had Thompson's blood tested or that they knew what his blood type was . . . .

In late April 1999, Thompson's private investigator discovered the crime lab report from the armed robbery investigation in the files of the New Orleans Police Crime Laboratory. Thompson was tested and found to have blood type O, proving that the blood on the swatch was not his. Thompson's attorneys presented this evidence to the district attorney's office, which, in turn, moved to stay the execution and vacate Thompson's conviction[s]. . . .

Thompson then brought this action against the district attorney's office, Connick, Williams, and others, alleging that their conduct caused him to be wrongfully convicted, incarcerated for 18 years, and nearly executed. The only claim that proceeded to trial was Thompson's claim under § 1983 that the district attorney's office had violated *Brady* by failing to disclose the crime lab report in his armed robbery trial. Thompson alleged liability under two theories: (1) the *Brady* violation was caused by an unconstitutional policy of the district attorney's office; and (2) the violation was caused by Connick's deliberate indifference to an obvious need to train the prosecutors in his office in order to avoid such constitutional violations.

. . . .

The *Brady* violation conceded in this case occurred when one or more of the four prosecutors involved with Thompson's armed robbery prosecution failed to disclose the crime lab report to Thompson's counsel. Under Thompson's failure-to-train theory, he bore the burden of proving both (1) that Connick, the policymaker for the district attorney's office, was deliberately indifferent to the need to train the prosecutors about their *Brady* disclosure obligation with respect to evidence of this type and (2) that the lack of training actually caused the *Brady* violation in this case. Connick argues that he was entitled to judgment as a matter of law because Thompson did not prove that he was on actual or constructive notice of, and therefore deliberately indifferent to, a need for more or different *Brady* training. We agree.

[The opinion then emphasizes Thompson's reliance on a single occurrence of a *Brady* violation.]

. . . .

Thompson needed to show that Connick was on notice that, absent additional specified training, it was "highly predictable" that the prosecutors in his office would be confounded by those gray areas and make incorrect *Brady* decisions as a result. In fact, Thompson had to show that it was *so* predictable that failing to train the prosecutors amounted to *conscious disregard* for defendants' *Brady* rights. . . . He did not do so.

NOTES

Is there hope, then, for greater prosecutorial accountability? The works of law professors Bruce Green and the late Fred Zacharias, several of which are cited here, have long focused on fashioning reforms to increase that accountability. On the civil side, suits for damages haven't quite reached the "impossible" level. In *McGhee v. Pottawattamie County, Iowa*, 547 F.3d 922 (8th Cir. 2007), two men wrongfully sentenced to life imprisonment filed civil rights suits against police officers and prosecutors for failing to reveal *Brady* evidence about other suspects and then fabricating and then permitting perjurious testimony. The Court of Appeal allowed most of the plaintiffs' causes of actions to go forward to trial. The Supreme Court granted *certiorari* but the case was settled before it was argued.

And in New York, a man accused of serious sexual offenses who was incarcerated without bail at Rikers' Island successfully maintained a cause of action against famed sex-crimes prosecutor Linda Fairstein for the unfair pre-trial publicity he received, including statements comparing him to Jeffrey Dahmer and claiming "this was not the first time he did something like this." Because Fairstein's actions were outside the trial arena, they were not subject to absolute immunity.[35]

9. *Garcetti*

What happens when a prosecutor risks not moving forward with a prosecution in an effort to do "the right thing"? Will there be repercussions in the political arena? Can there be retaliation from within the prosecutor's own office? Consider the recent closely divided United States Supreme Court case below involving a supervising deputy district attorney in Los Angeles.[36]

GARCETTI v. CEBALLOS
547 U.S. 410 (2006)

JUSTICE KENNEDY delivered the opinion of the Court.

. . . .

In February 2000, a defense attorney contacted Ceballos about a pending criminal case. The defense attorney said there were inaccuracies in an affidavit used to obtain a critical search warrant. The attorney informed Ceballos that he had filed a motion to traverse, or challenge, the warrant, but he also wanted Ceballos to review the case. . . . After examining the affidavit and visiting the location it described, Ceballos determined the affidavit contained serious misrepresentations. . . . He relayed his findings to his supervisors, petitioners Carol Najera and Frank Sundstedt, and followed up by preparing a disposition memorandum. The memo

---

[35] *Jovanovic v. City of New York*, 2006 U.S. Dist. LEXIS 59165 (S.D.N.Y. Aug. 17, 2006). Interestingly and perhaps anomalously, the one cause of action for which "sovereign immunity" was *granted* in *McGhee* was for the prosecutor's pre-trial statements.

[36] The case was argued twice, once before and once after the appointment of Justice Alito; with eight members of the court, it appeared that the vote would be 4-4, thus upholding the circuit court.

explained Ceballos' concerns and recommended dismissal of the case. On March 2, 2000, Ceballos submitted the memo to Sundstedt for his review. . . .

Despite Ceballos' concerns, Sundstedt decided to proceed with the prosecution, pending disposition of the defense motion to traverse. The trial court held a hearing on the motion. Ceballos was called by the defense and recounted his observations about the affidavit, but the trial court rejected the challenge to the warrant.

Ceballos claims that in the aftermath of these events he was subjected to a series of retaliatory employment actions. . . . Ceballos sued in the United States District Court for the Central District of California, asserting, as relevant here, a claim under Rev. Stat. § 1979, 42 U. S. C. § 1983. He alleged petitioners violated the First and Fourteenth Amendments by retaliating against him based on his memo of March 2.

Petitioners responded that . . . Ceballos' memo was not protected speech under the First Amendment. Petitioners moved for summary judgment, and the District Court granted their motion. Noting that Ceballos wrote his memo pursuant to his employment duties, the court concluded he was not entitled to First Amendment protection for the memo's contents. . . .

The Court of Appeals for the Ninth Circuit reversed, holding that "Ceballos's allegations of wrongdoing in the memorandum constitute protected speech under the First Amendment." . . .

We granted certiorari, 543 U. S. 1186 (2005), and we now reverse.

. . . .

The question becomes whether the relevant government entity had an adequate justification for treating the employee differently from any other member of the general public. This consideration reflects the importance of the relationship between the speaker's expressions and employment. A government entity has broader discretion to restrict speech when it acts in its role as employer, but the restrictions it imposes must be directed at speech that has some potential to affect the entity's operations.

. . . .

The controlling factor in Ceballos' case is that his expressions were made pursuant to his duties as a calendar deputy. . . . . That consideration — the fact that Ceballos spoke as a prosecutor fulfilling a responsibility to advise his supervisor about how best to proceed with a pending case — distinguishes Ceballos' case from those in which the First Amendment provides protection against discipline. We hold that when public employees make statements pursuant to their official duties, the employees are not speaking as citizens for First Amendment purposes, and the Constitution does not insulate their communications from employer discipline.

. . . .

Ceballos did not act as a citizen when he went about conducting his daily professional activities, such as supervising attorneys, investigating charges, and preparing filings. In the same way he did not speak as a citizen by writing a memo that addressed the proper disposition of a pending criminal case. . . .

. . . Supervisors must ensure that their employees' official communications are accurate, demonstrate sound judgment, and promote the employer's mission. Ceballos' memo is illustrative. It demanded the attention of his supervisors and led to a heated meeting with employees from the sheriff's department. If Ceballos' superiors thought his memo was inflammatory or misguided, they had the authority to take proper corrective action.

JUSTICE BREYER, dissenting.

Like the majority, I understand the need to "affor[d] government employers sufficient discretion to manage their operations." And I agree that the Constitution does not seek to "displac[e] . . . managerial discretion by judicial supervision." Nonetheless, there may well be circumstances with special demand for constitutional protection of the speech at issue, where governmental justifications may be limited, and where administrable standards seem readily available — to the point where the majority's fears of department management by lawsuit are misplaced. . . .

This is such a case. The respondent, a government lawyer, complained of retaliation, in part, on the basis of speech contained in his disposition memorandum that he says fell within the scope of his obligations under *Brady* v. *Maryland*, 373 U. S. 83 (1963). The facts present two special circumstances that together justify First Amendment review.

First, the speech at issue is professional speech - the speech of a lawyer. Such speech is subject to independent regulation by canons of the profession. Those canons provide an obligation to speak in certain instances. And where that is so, the government's own interest in forbidding that speech is diminished. . . .

Second, the Constitution itself here imposes speech obligations upon the government's professional employee. A prosecutor has a constitutional obligation to learn of, to preserve, and to communicate with the defense about exculpatory and impeachment evidence in the government's possession. *Kyles* v. *Whitley*, 514 U. S. 419, 437 (1995); *Brady, supra*. . . .

Where professional and special constitutional obligations are both present, the need to protect the employee's speech is augmented, the need for broad government authority to control that speech is likely diminished, and administrable standards are quite likely available. Hence, I would find that the Constitution mandates special protection of employee speech in such circumstances.

NOTES

Does it make sense to treat a government lawyer — indeed, a prosecutor — the same as any government employee for free speech purposes? Or does Justice Breyer's reliance on not only the position of "lawyer" but of "prosecutor," and his multiple references to the *Brady* case, make more sense? If a prosecutor is not afforded the free speech Breyer suggests, would s/he be able to fulfill all the duties articulated in Section 1 above? See particularly Standard 3-3.9. Would it affect the actions of the DAs in the problem?

Was it surprising to you that only Justice Breyer saw fit to mention Ceballos' role as prosecutor? Is it possible that eight other Supreme Court justices simply missed the issue? One critic, calling *Garcetti* the "worst" modern Supreme Court case, said that the "majority relegated Deputy DA Ceballos to the role of a mere functionary on an assembly line. . . ."[37]

D. SUPPLEMENTAL READINGS

1. Ellen S. Podgor, *The Role of the Prosecution and Defense Function Standards: Stagnant or Progressive?*, 62 HASTINGS L.J. 1159 (2011). Professor Podgor examines the ABA standards in their current and unpublished 4th draft form and evaluates whether these purely aspirational standards have sufficient value. She observes that by their own terms the Standards are "not intended to be used as criteria for the judicial evaluation of alleged misconduct of the prosecutor to determine the validity of a conviction," and discuses their efficacy in that light.

2. *Donnelly v. DeChristoforo*, 416 U.S. 637 (1974), is perhaps typical of cases in which the United States Supreme Court, then and in the years since, found the prosecutor's behavior in error, but refused to reverse the conviction. During summation, the prosecutor stated, "I quite frankly think that they [defendant and his attorney] hope you find him guilty of something a little less than First Degree murder." The jury convicted the defendant of first degree. Such comments, held the Court, did not meet the previously outlined standard required for reversal: "consistent and repeated misrepresentation." It was in this case, in dissent, that Justice Douglas made the remarks quoted decades later by Judge Kozinski in *Kojayan*, above.

3. *United States v. Ofshe*, 817 F.2d 1508 (11th Cir. 1987). This case represents perhaps the most extreme example of a prosecutor communicating with a defendant: using an informant who is also the defendant's lawyer. Ofshe, facing drug charges, hired attorney Glass. When Glass himself became the target of an investigation, Assistant United States Attorney Scott Turow (yes, the famous author) wired Glass for a meeting with Ofshe. When Ofshe discovered this, his other attorney moved to set aside the indictment, a motion which was denied. The court held this remedy was not necessary because Glass was instructed not to violate the attorney-client privilege (though how this could be avoided is not made clear), and because no useful information was developed.

4. *People v. Eubanks*, 927 P.2d 310 (Cal. 1996). Silicon Valley trade secrets prosecutions, while sometimes criminal, can be very expensive to investigate. In *Eubanks*, when a local DA accepted money from the aggrieved party to hire an expert to help investigate a trade secrets prosecution, the California Supreme Court held that even though the money was for investigation and not otherwise improper, the independence of prosecutorial discretion was compromised by the

---

[37] Jeffrey W. Stempel, *Tending to Potted Plants: The Professional Identity Vacuum in* Garcetti v. Ceballos, 12 NEV. L.J. 703 (2012). This article is further summarized in the Supplemental Readings.

private party assisting in the investigation.

5. Two N.Y. TIMES articles by Jonathan D. Glater exploring issues of "celebrity justice" are *Stewart's Celebrity Created Magnet for Scrutiny*, N.Y. TIMES, Mar. 7, 2004, and Glater and Nick Madigan, *Weighing Celebrity Justice: Blind or Biased*, N.Y. TIMES, Jun. 15, 2005. The articles address the role celebrity plays in criminal justice system, and refer to other "celebrity" prosecutions, among them Mike Tyson's and the child molesting charges against Michael Jackson.

6. Are prosecutors abusing their power in their prosecution of corporations and their higher-ups? In *Convictions Drive Home the Point Again*, WASHINGTON POST, May 26, 2006, Steven Pearlstein contends that the convictions of former Enron executives Ken Lay and Jeff Skilling were selective prosecutions, and that lawyers have escaped responsibility and may have profited from the prosecution of others by hiding behind the attorney-client privilege. In *Over Before It Started*, N.Y. TIMES, Jan. 14, 2005, Joseph A. Grundfest claims that Arthur Andersen was destroyed not at trial, but when it was indicted. He argues that prosecutors have the power to destroy corporations simply by indicting them on serious charges and that this prosecutorial power should be subject to review to ensure that is not abused.

7. After September 11, 2001, the U.S. implemented a federal registration and fingerprinting system in order to track people with temporary visas. Several articles have been critical of that program as resulting in the arrests or detentions of hundreds of innocent Middle Eastern men and teenagers who voluntarily complied with the program. *See, e.g.*, these two early pieces: Karen Brandon, *INS Detentions Spark Protests; Debate Grows Over Targeting of Middle Easterners in the U.S.*, CHICAGO TRIBUNE, Dec. 20, 2002, and Peter Skerry, *Muslims Never Had to Unite — Until Now*, WASHINGTON POST, Jan. 5, 2003.

8. Jeffrey L. Kirchmeier, Stephen R. Greenwald, Harold Reynolds, Jonathan Sussman, *Vigilante Justice: Prosecutor Misconduct in Capital Cases*, 55 WAYNE L. REV. 1327 (2009), describes the kinds of prosecutor misconduct that may occur in capital cases, and discusses suggestions to help prevent and remedy such misconduct. The prosecutor's role is especially important in death penalty cases because the prosecutor is a determining force in the decision of whether the death penalty will be sought.

9. In *Banks v. Dretke*, 540 U.S. 668 (2004), the Supreme Court gave some hope to defendants seeking post-conviction redress for *Brady* error. In *Banks*, the prosecutor failed to disclose that the key witness was a paid informant and allowed the witness to testify falsely that he had never spoken to the police, then relied on the false evidence in closing argument. The Supreme Court held that Banks was entitled to seek post-conviction remedy because his failure to investigate the informant and develop impeachment information was the direct result of the prosecutor's ongoing misrepresentations concerning the informant.

10. In *The Professional Discipline of Prosecutors*, 79 N.C. L. REV. 721 (2001), Fred Zacharias evaluates the prospect of future discipline against prosecutors in the post-McDade Act era. Zacharias notes the long-standing Supreme Court rule under *Imbler v. Pachtman*, 424 U.S. 409 (1976), that prosecutors are immune from civil suit because other adequate remedies exist to discipline their misconduct. Recognizing the checkered history of discipline by state agencies, Zacharias evaluates whether, where, and how the new authority of the states over prosecutorial behavior is likely to result in discipline, and the extent to which it is likely to make a real difference. More recently, the late Professor Zacharias teamed with former prosecutor Bruce Green of Fordham on several pieces addressing similar issues about how to improve on the poor record of disciplining prosecutors, including Fred Zacharias & Bruce Green, *The Duty to Avoid Wrongful Convictions: A Thought Experiment in the Regulation of Prosecutors*, 89 B.U. L. REV. 1 (2009)

11. Jeffrey W. Stempel, *Tending to Potted Plants: The Professional Identity Vaccum in* Garcetti v. Ceballos, 12 NEV. L.J. 703 (2012). In an unusually blunt and pointed article, Professor Stempel strongly criticizes the *Garcetti* case, not on the constitutional free speech grounds that were the focus of most of the discussion, but on the failure of the court to treat Ceballos as not only a lawyer but a prosecutor, and the need for such prosecutors to have sufficient independence, when seeing a case they feel should not be prosecuted, to have the discretion to dismiss that case without being sanctioned by their superiors. Professor Stempel also addresses the inconsistent reasoning found in *Garcetti* on the one hand and *Connick v. Thompson* on the other.

12. Not all prosecutors are out there doing bad things. Many are among the most honorable and ethical of attorneys. Mark Godsey's, *False Justice and the 'True' Prosecutor: A Memoir, Tribute, and Commentary*, OHIO STATE J. OF CRIM. LAW, Vol. 9 (Jan. 12, 2012), *available at* http://ssrn.com/abstract=1983944, tells that story.

PROBLEM 24: WHAT'S A CITY ATTORNEY TO DO?

A. INTRODUCTION

One of the least understood ethical conundrums facing lawyers concerns the role of the civil government attorney. This is an area that has received far too little attention from ethicists and ethics opinions, though it causes great concern for practicing government lawyers. There are several important questions about their roles. First, whom does the government attorney represent, the larger governmental entity (*e.g.*, the state or municipality), or the particular governmental agency to whom the lawyer directly answers? Second, who speaks for the client and from whom must the governmental attorney take direction? Third, does attorney-client confidentiality and the attorney-client privilege exist in the ordinary sense, and if so, with whom? Finally, how does the government attorney reconcile representing a governmental entity and also the individuals employed by that entity?

As we shall see, there are often no clear answers to these questions. Moreover the answers to these difficult questions will be different depending on the size and complexity of the governmental organization at issue. We have already discussed some of the difficulty a counsel for a corporation or partnership has in resolving these issues. Their problems are compounded when the lawyer is counsel to a government or a governmental agency. Examine the situation faced by Joe Hannah.

B. PROBLEM

I

Joe Hannah is a deputy city attorney for the City of Big Boondock. The city attorney's office is responsible for representing the city as well as its agencies and its employees while acting within the scope of their employment.

Joe is currently assigned the city's real property assessment division. This division assesses the value of all properties within the city limits for tax purposes. The higher the assessed value of the property, the more taxes collected by the city.

Part of Joe's job is to represent the Office of Assessor in appeals before the assessment appeals board. The appeals board is an administrative board set up by the city to resolve disputes between the assessor's office and property owners regarding the assessed value of their land. In addition to representing the assessor's office in those appeals, Joe is also responsible for advising the appeals board on evidentiary questions that arise.

Roger Sturges is a property owner whose land was recently assessed at $350,000. Sturges felt that this assessment was far too high and appealed to the assessment appeals board. Before the appeals hearing, Joe reviews papers that Sturges' counsel has filed urging a lower assessment based on comparable property in the area. Joe realizes that Sturges' argument is strong, but may turn on the admissibility of the information forming the basis of the "comp" analysis. When Joe shares this information with Chief Assessor Martine Ferrara, Ferrara tells Joe: "Let's stand by our assessment. There's no reason for the city to lose all of that tax revenue unless it's absolutely necessary. And who knows whether Sturges has information that's admissible."

QUESTIONS

1.   May Joe represent the Assessor's Office in Sturges' appeal to the Board while at the same time advising the Board regarding evidentiary questions that arise during that appeal?

2.   What if the evidentiary issues *do not* have a direct impact on the ultimate assessment determination?

3.   Should Joe be able to advise the Board on whether Sturges' evidence is admissible or supports a lower assessment even though doing so would hurt the city's position? What if he does and the Board chooses to ignore that information?

4.   Should or must Joe inform a "higher" authority within city government? If so, whom?

5.   What if the Board were advised by another attorney in Joe's office? Does that solve these problems?

II

Joe has been hearing rumors that individual assessors have been extorting money from property owners in exchange for lower assessment valuations. When Joe confronts Arnold Shostrand, one of the assessors, about these rumors, Shostrand acknowledges that it is not uncommon for other assessors to suggest to property owners that they are willing to "deal." Shostrand insists, however, that he found this practice "disgusting," and only participated in the scam on two isolated occasions.

QUESTIONS

Should Joe report the assessors' practice? If so, to whom? Would doing so violate a duty of confidentiality to Shostrand?

III

The Boondock *Daily Grind* gets wind of the assessors' practice of extorting money in exchange for lower property valuations and publishes an exposé. Citizens throughout Big Boondock are outraged. Within two weeks, three lawsuits are filed by property owners against the city. Joe is assigned to represent the city.

Later in that week, Joe receives a call from the mayor, who says that the suits are an embarrassment to the current administration. The mayor urges Joe to settle the suits quickly so that it is all old news by the time of the next election.

QUESTIONS

1.   Can Joe represent both the city and the individual assessors? What if Joe believes that the city could argue that the assessors were acting outside the course and scope of their employment? What if there are punitive damages claims against the assessors individually that are not available against the city as an entity? If he represents the city and the assessors, how does he deal with maintaining confidential communications?

2.   May Joe take into account the mayor's request in reaching a decision on whether to settle or go to trial? *Must* he consider the mayor's views? What if, instead of the mayor, it is the City Council applying the pressure to settle?

C. READINGS

1. Conflicting Advice in Los Angeles

To give a flavor of the kinds of conflicts of interest that can confront a city attorney, we turn to the aftermath of the Rodney King case. The issue at hand: whether the suspended Los Angeles Police Chief Darryl Gates should be discharged because of the LAPD's poor performance during the King beating and subsequent rioting, or whether he should be reinstated. Los Angeles has more people and a larger economy than many states. Intra-administrative conflicts are bound to exist in such a complex jurisdiction; the Gates matter can hardly have been the first. But in the Gates case the whole country was watching. How should a city attorney deal with answering to more than one "client"?

Rich Connell, *City Atty. Role Raises Conflict of Interest Issue*
Los Angeles Times, April 9, 1991[1]

A potential conflict of interest by the Los Angeles city attorney's office — which has given legal advice to opposing factions in the Darryl F. Gates controversy — was raised as a central legal issue Monday in the court battle over the police chief's reinstatement.

City Atty. James K. Hahn's office told the Police Commission that it had the legal authority to place Gates on leave and, within days, advised the City Council on a legal maneuver to reverse the action, documents and interviews show.

"There appears to exist ample legal authority, in both law and practice, to support the imposition of an involuntary administrative leave on the chief of police," Hahn's office advised the Police Commission in a confidential March 27 legal opinion, a copy of which was obtained by The Times.

Commissioners said they relied on the city attorney's advice last Thursday when they ordered Gates to take a 60-day paid leave, pending completion of an investigation of the Rodney G. King beating.

In a closed session the next day, the council asked Hahn and several of his office's

---

[1] Copyright © 1991 by Los Angeles Times. Reprinted by permission.

lawyers for advice on legal steps it was considering taking to reinstate Gates. One of the council's tactics — settling a lawsuit that Gates was expected to file — was approved by the council Friday. . . .

As part of their argument against the settlement, attorneys for the commissioners and civil rights groups alleged that Hahn had a conflict of interest that should invalidate the settlement.

Hahn has a "gross, unlawful three-cornered conflict of interest, which precludes his serving either the legitimate interests of the city or the public interests," said Pete L. Haviland, an attorney for several civil rights groups trying to block the settlement. The judge postponed a ruling on the issue.

Hahn's office denied there was a conflict in its advice to the Police Commission and City Council because both panels are part of the same legal entity - the city of Los Angeles. . . .

Erwin Chemerinsky, USC law professor and an expert on legal ethics, said Hahn's office appeared to have a conflict of interest.

"A lawyer can't represent adverse interests in a single matter," he said, adding that "the question of how to deal with Daryl Gates at this time is a single question."

"Once (Hahn) advised the commission, he was the lawyer for the commission," Chemerinsky said. "He shouldn't be then helping the council undo what the commission did on the basis of his legal advice."

. . . Chemerinsky said it would have been preferable for Hahn to disqualify his office from giving advice to both the commission and council.

. . . .

Mike Qualls, Hahn's spokesman, said the city attorney has only one client — the city of Los Angeles — and the power to settle lawsuits rests with the City Council. . . .

Council President John Ferraro said the city attorney's staff answered questions and assured council members that what they were doing was legal. "They helped draw up the motion," he said.

Qualls said the city attorney has remained neutral in the dispute between the commission and the council and there was nothing contradictory in the legal advice provided to the two panels. He said the only potential conflict of interest would have been representing the city in an adversarial case against Gates, whose department it also represents in numerous lawsuits.

NOTES

Should the city attorney have advised just the police commission, or just the city council? Should the council have paid for independent outside counsel, a method used in several states? What about the council members' rights to have their chief lawyer, City Attorney Hahn, advise them? The answers to these questions turn at least in part on the question of who is the client.

2.   Who Is the Client?

Three weeks after the above article appeared, former Los Angeles City Attorney Burt Pines wrote an editorial page opinion for the *Los Angeles Times* that defended Hahn's advising both the police commission and the city council. He cited a memorandum he himself had written, saying that the city attorney had only one client — the city itself.

"This precept is fundamental to understanding why the city attorney does not have a conflict of interest in advising various city departments that may sharply disagree with one another at any particular time," opined Pines. "These departments are not separate legal entities but simply administrative arms of the city, a municipal corporation. Only that corporation is the city attorney's client. Only that municipal corporation is a legal entity, able to sue or be sued."[2]

Pines cited numerous instances where both he and his successor, Ira Reiner, resolved conflicts among the city's thirty-some departments and commissions. He argued that the very reason a city attorney can resolve such "squabbles" is that the client remains the municipality. Moreover, to give separate counsel to all 30 departments and 18 elected city officials would involve astronomical cost and potential advocacy of one department's interests as against another, instead of finding the best objective solution for the city as a whole.

Who is right, Pines or Professor Chemerinsky? Pines' prose sounds persuasive, but does it hold up in the face of what appears to be clearly contradictory advice given by Hahn's office in the Gates case? After all, if the city attorney is one big law firm, how can it justify giving conflicting opinions in the same matter? In the Gates affair, the advice given seemed to be more than antithetical; it appeared that the advice given the council was *adverse* to that given the Police Commission. Must we change the meaning of conflicts of interest in the government context to conform to the reality of what governments today actually do and can afford?

Before we analyze the loyalties and duties owed by the government attorney, let us explore identifying the client a little further. Neither the ABA nor most states have specific rules defining the roles and responsibilities of the government attorney. Model Rules 1.7 and 1.13 both make reference to the government lawyer, but provide virtually no black-letter guidance. When MR 1.13 was created in 1983, Comment 6 to the rule said this:

> [D]efining precisely the identity of the client and prescribing the resulting obligations of such lawyers may be more difficult in the government context. Although in some circumstances the client may be a specific agency, it is generally the government as a whole.

After the 2002–2003 changes, the same Comment, renumbered 9, said the following:

> Defining precisely the identity of the client and prescribing the resulting obligations of such lawyers may be more difficult in the government context and is a matter beyond the scope of these Rules . . . . Although in some

---

[2] Los Angeles Times, April 30, 1991.

circumstances the client may be a specific agency, it may also be a branch of government, such as the executive branch, or the government as a whole.

This is not encouraging. The 1983 rule was vague enough, but the more modern version retreats significantly from that earlier version. In 1983, the rule suggested two alternatives and a default position. Today there is no default position and the issue of who is the client is expressly "beyond" the rules. Not much guidance has become no guidance. The ABA rules will be of little aid and comfort to either James Hahn or Joe Hannah.

There is an understandable reason for this retrenchment. Government lawyers represent a wide variety of governmental entities. Small entities such as towns or school districts are likely only to have outside counsel, and then only as needed. Cities vary greatly in size, from a few thousand people to millions. It is typical of city attorneys, even in large cities like LA, to consider the entire city the client rather than the agency within the city. Whether that is so is open to question, but in considering state governments, the argument that the particular government attorney represents the agency rather than the entire state seems to make more sense. Finally, as far as the federal government is concerned, it seems simply too big to be the client of *all* federal government lawyers. We look again at the issue of who the client is, especially in the federal context, in Section 10.

One final point here: To what extent does the government lawyer need to know who the client is? Some years back, commentator, R.P. Lawry wrote two interesting law review articles that disputed the need to specifically identify the client in the government context.[3] Identifying the client is not really possible in the traditional sense, Lawry argued. It is more important for the government attorney to determine *from whom to take direction* on matters for which the lawyer is responsible. We saw an important and similar issue in the representation dilemma facing Esperanza Dejos in Problem 8.

3. How Limited Is the Governmental Attorney-Client Privilege?

Whatever else it was, the "Whitewater" scandal during the Clinton administration gave legal scholars a veritable bouquet of issues concerning the proper behavior of lawyers. We already examined, in Problem 5, whether deputy White House counsel Vincent Foster's attorney-client privilege survived his death. In the last problem, we examined issues relating to whether Independent Counsel Kenneth Starr had abused his power as special prosecutor. Here, we focus on attorney-client privilege and confidentiality in the government context.

Three cases stemming from the Whitewater investigation illuminate the status of the government attorney-client privilege. First in time was *In re Grand Jury Subpoena Duces Tecum*, 112 F.3d 910 (8th Cir. 1997), *cert. denied*, 117 S. Ct. 2482 (1997), in which Starr sought notes taken by White House lawyers about conversations with then-first lady Hillary Rodham Clinton concerning Mrs.

---

[3] *Who Is the Client of the Federal Government Lawyer? An Analysis of the Wrong Question*, 37 Fed. B.J. 61 (1978); *Confidences and the Government Lawyer*, 57 N.C.L. Rev. 625 (1979).

Clinton's testimony before a federal grand jury and her activities following the death of Foster. In a 2-1 decision that the Eighth Circuit termed a case of first impression, Mrs. Clinton's lawyers were compelled to turn their notes over to the Independent Counsel. The court wrote that even assuming the existence of an attorney-client privilege, there is a "strong public interest in honest government and in exposing wrongdoing by public officials" that is inconsistent with asserting an attorney-client privilege in the face of a criminal investigation. The majority relied on *United States v. Nixon*, 418 U.S. 683 (1974), in which then-president Nixon was forced to turn over audiotapes relating to the Watergate affair. Though Nixon's claim was one of "executive privilege," the Supreme Court's *Nixon* holding affirmed, in the Eighth Circuit's view, "the general principle that the government's need for confidentiality may be subordinated to the needs of the government's own criminal justice processes."

A year later, it was President Clinton and his lawyers on the spot, and time for the D.C. Circuit's own case of first impression. As you read this case, keep your eye on the question of who this court says is Bruce Lindsey's client.

IN RE LINDSEY
148 F.3d 1100 (D.C. Cir. 1998), reported with previously-sealed portions at
158 F.3d 1263 (D.C. Cir. 1998)

PER CURIAM.

In these expedited appeals, the principal question is whether an attorney in the Office of the President, having been called before a federal grand jury, may refuse, on the basis of a government attorney-client privilege, to answer questions about possible criminal conduct by government officials and others. To state the question is to suggest the answer, for the Office of the President is a part of the federal government, consisting of government employees doing government business, and neither legal authority nor policy nor experience suggests that a federal government entity can maintain the ordinary common law attorney-client privilege to withhold information relating to a federal criminal offense. . . . *See United States v. Nixon*, 418 U.S. 683, 707–12 (1974); *In re Sealed Case (Espy)*, 121 F.3d 729, 736–38 (D.C. Cir. 1997). In the context of federal criminal investigations and trials, there is no basis for treating legal advice differently from any other advice the Office of the President receives in performing its constitutional functions. The public interest in honest government and in exposing wrongdoing by government officials, as well as the tradition and practice, acknowledged by the Office of the President and by former White House Counsel, of government lawyers reporting evidence of federal criminal offenses whenever such evidence comes to them, lead to the conclusion that a government attorney may not invoke the attorney-client privilege in response to grand jury questions seeking information relating to the possible commission of a federal crime.

. . . .

On January 30, 1998, the grand jury issued a subpoena to Bruce R. Lindsey, Deputy White House Counsel and Assistant to the President. On February 18,

February 19, and March 12, 1998, Lindsey appeared before the grand jury and declined to answer certain questions . . . . On March 6, 1998, the Independent Counsel moved to compel Lindsey's testimony. The district court granted that motion on May 4, 1998.

. . . .

The attorney-client privilege protects confidential communications made between clients and their attorneys when the communications are for the purpose of securing legal advice or services. It "is one of the oldest recognized privileges for confidential communications." *Swidler & Berlin v. United States*, 118 S. Ct. 2081 (1998).

The Office of the President contends that Lindsey's communications with the President and others in the White House should fall within this privilege both because the President, like any private person, needs to communicate fully and frankly with his legal advisors, and because the current grand jury investigation may lead to impeachment proceedings, which would require a defense of the President's official position as head of the executive branch of government, presumably with the assistance of White House Counsel. The Independent Counsel contends that an absolute government attorney-client privilege would be inconsistent with the proper role of the government lawyer and that the President should rely only on his private lawyers for fully confidential counsel.

. . . .

Courts, commentators, and government lawyers have long recognized a government attorney-client privilege in several contexts. . . . "In the governmental context, the 'client' may be the agency and the attorney may be an agency lawyer." In Lindsey's case, his client - to the extent he provided legal services - would be the Office of the President.

. . . .

Recognizing that a government attorney-client privilege exists is one thing. Finding that the Office of the President is entitled to assert it here is quite another.

. . . .

The grand jury, a constitutional body established in the Bill of Rights, "belongs to no branch of the institutional Government, serving as a kind of buffer or referee between the Government and the people," while the Independent Counsel is by statute an officer of the executive branch representing the United States. For matters within his jurisdiction, the Independent Counsel acts in the role of the Attorney General as the country's chief law enforcement officer. Thus, although the traditional privilege between attorneys and clients shields private relationships from inquiry in either civil litigation or criminal prosecution, competing values arise when the Office of the President resists demands for information from a federal grand jury and the nation's chief law enforcement officer. . . .

The question whether a government attorney-client privilege applies in the federal grand jury context is one of first impression in this circuit. . . . In *Swidler & Berlin*, the Supreme Court, [a]fter finding that the Independent Counsel was asking the Court "not simply to 'construe' the privilege, but to narrow it, contrary to the weight of the existing body of caselaw," . . . concluded that the Independent Counsel had not made a sufficient showing . . . .

In the instant case, by contrast, there is no such existing body of caselaw upon which to rely and no clear principle that the government attorney-client privilege has as broad a scope as its personal counterpart. Because the "attorney-client privilege must be 'strictly confined within the narrowest possible limits consistent with the logic of its principle,'" and because the government attorney-client privilege is not recognized in the same way as the personal attorney-client privilege addressed in *Swidler & Berlin*, . . . pursuant to our authority and duty under Rule 501 of the Federal Rules of Evidence to interpret privileges "in light of reason and experience," we view our exercise as one in defining the particular contours of the government attorney-client privilege.

When an executive branch attorney is called before a federal grand jury to give evidence about alleged crimes within the executive branch, reason and experience, duty, and tradition dictate that the attorney shall provide that evidence. With respect to investigations of federal criminal offenses, and especially offenses committed by those in government, government attorneys stand in a far different position from members of the private bar. Their duty is not to defend clients against criminal charges and it is not to protect wrongdoers from public exposure. The constitutional responsibility of the President, and all members of the Executive Branch, is to "take Care that the Laws be faithfully executed." U.S. Const. art. II, § 3. Investigation and prosecution of federal crimes is one of the most important and essential functions within that constitutional responsibility. . . . Unlike a private practitioner, the loyalties of a government lawyer therefore cannot and must not lie solely with his or her client agency.

. . . As Judge [Jack B.] Weinstein put it, "if there is wrongdoing in government, it must be exposed . . . . A [government lawyer's] duty to the people, the law, and his own conscience requires disclosure . . . ."

Lloyd Cutler, who served as White House Counsel in the Carter and Clinton Administrations, discussed the "rule of making it your duty, if you're a Government official as we as lawyers are, a statutory duty to report to the Attorney General any evidence you run into of a possible violation of a criminal statute." . . . Similarly, during the Nixon administration, Solicitor General Robert H. Bork [according to an interview Bork gave in 1997] told an administration official who invited him to join the President's legal defense team: "A government attorney is sworn to uphold the Constitution. If I come across evidence that is bad for the President, I'll have to turn it over. I won't be able to sit on it like a private defense attorney."

. . . .

In sum, it would be contrary to tradition, common understanding, and our governmental system for the attorney-client privilege to attach to White House Counsel in the same manner as private counsel. When government attorneys learn, through communications with their clients, of information related to criminal misconduct, they may not rely on the government attorney-client privilege to shield such information from disclosure to a grand jury.

TATEL, CIRCUIT JUDGE, dissenting from Part II and concurring in part and dissenting in part from Part III.

The attorney-client privilege protects confidential communication between clients and their lawyers, whether those lawyers work for the private sector or for government. Although I have no doubt that government lawyers working in executive departments and agencies enjoy a reduced privilege in the face of grand jury subpoenas, I remain unconvinced that either "reason" or "experience" (the tools of Rule 501) justifies this court's abrogation of the attorney-client privilege for lawyers serving the Presidency. . . .

My colleagues and I have no disagreement . . . about political advice given to the President by advisers who happen to be lawyers. Such advice is protected, if at all, by the executive privilege alone. Our disagreement centers solely on whether a grand jury can pierce the attorney-client privilege with respect to official legal advice that the Office of White House Counsel gives a sitting President.

. . . .

This court now holds that for all government attorneys, including those advising a President, the attorney-client privilege dissolves in the face of a grand jury subpoena. . . . Clients, in this case Presidents of the United States, will avoid confiding in their lawyers because they can never know whether the information they share, no matter how innocent, might some day become "pertinent to possible criminal violations." . . . As a result, Presidents may well shift their trust on all but the most routine legal matters from White House counsel, who undertake to serve the Presidency, to private counsel who represent its occupant.

. . . .

I think the court seriously underestimates the independent role and value of the attorney-client privilege. Unlike the executive privilege — a broad, constitutionally derived privilege that protects frank debate between President and advisers — the narrower attorney-client privilege flows not from the Constitution, but from the common law. . . . In other words, the unique protection the law affords a President's communications with White House counsel rests not, as my colleagues put it, on some "conceit" that "lawyers are more important to the operations of government than all other officials," but rather on the special nature of legal advice, and its special need for confidentiality, as recognized by centuries of common law.

. . . .

Accordingly, before abrogating the official attorney-client privilege for all future Presidents, this court should have remanded to the district court to allow the Independent Counsel to recall Lindsey to the grand jury to determine whether, with respect to each question that he declines to answer, he can demonstrate the elements of the attorney-client privilege, namely that each communication was made between privileged persons in confidence "for the purpose of obtaining or providing legal assistance for the client." If Lindsey failed to meet this burden, that would end the matter. . . . On the other hand, if Lindsey demonstrated that his communications involved official legal advice, the district court could use the remand to enrich the record. . . . This would create an infinitely more useful record for us, or eventually the Supreme Court . . . .

NOTES

Lindsey expanded considerably on the Hillary Clinton case by, among other things, clearly reaffirming the existence of a governmental attorney-client privilege. (Interestingly and importantly, without stopping to analyze the issue anew, the opinion adheres to — and almost assumes — the proposition that the "client" of a government lawyer is the agency, in Lindsey's case the Office of the President.)

But how narrow is the *Lindsey* holding? On its facts, it deals only with a situation in which two parts of the federal executive branch are at odds with each other, and there is an active federal criminal grand jury investigation.[4] But it is also reasonable to interpret the *Lindsey* opinion far more broadly. Judge Tatel, early in his dissent, concludes that the majority's opinion applies to "all government attorneys," wherever they may be. Moreover, *Lindsey* uses broad language supporting "public interest in honest government and in exposing [governmental] wrongdoing," and relies on a "tradition and practice" of federal lawyers reporting evidence of a crime "whenever such evidence comes to them." This language, and *Lindsey*'s reference to the statements of three well-known commentators from across the political spectrum, Jack B. Weinstein, Lloyd Cutler, and Robert Bork, while not necessary to the court's holding, seem to imply an *affirmative* duty to reveal criminal conduct whenever it occurs in a government context — or at least a federal government context — even without subpoena.

However, the *Lindsey* view is by no means unanimously adopted. Circuits have split when attorneys for state officers assert attorney-client privilege in the course of criminal investigations. In 2002, the Seventh Circuit followed a 1997 Eighth Circuit decision, and held that chief legal counsel for a state's Secretary of State could not assert the privilege before a federal grand jury.[5] But in 2005, the Second Circuit held that that the chief legal counsel for the Governor could assert attorney-client privilege before a federal grand jury that was investigating state corruption.[6]

Do you think both privilege positions can be supported by the current version of Comment 9 to Rule 1.13? Or could these differing results be part of the fallout from an overly vague rule? Reconsider the policy rationales for having the attorney-client privilege in a government setting. Should it matter if the government lawyer worked for the Chief Executive (the President or Governor) or reported to a head of a governmental agency?

---

[4] Narrowing the facts still further, the case deals only with the Office of President itself, although in *Espy*, the third Whitewater privilege case and cited in *Lindsey*, the court similarly limited the attorney-client privilege of a cabinet member, then-Secretary of Agriculture Mike Espy.

[5] In re A Witness Before the Special Grand Jury 2000-2 (Witness), 288 F.3d 289 (7th Cir. 2002).

[6] In re Grand Jury Investigation (John Doe), 399 F.3d 527 (2d Cir. 2005).

4. Limits on Confidentiality? Cindy Ossias Blows the Whistle

Lindsey leaves many questions unanswered, including these: If the attorney-client privilege is abrogated by an active investigation into criminal activity, what about *confidentiality*, a concept that we have seen is far broader than the evidentiary privilege? Is a governmental attorney permitted affirmatively to blow the whistle in the face of wrongdoing when there is no ongoing investigation? Might whistleblowing even be *required*, as some of those quoted in *Lindsey* suggest?

The dicta in *Lindsey* does not stand alone in raising these issues. Indeed, Comment 9 to MR 1.13 states, in part, "Thus, when the client is a governmental organization, a different balance may be appropriate between maintaining confidentiality and assuring that the wrongful act is prevented or rectified, for public business is involved." In order to protect the abilities of government employees to disclose government wrongdoing to public scrutiny, the federal government passed two reform acts to protect such conduct, in 1978 and 1989. Several states have also passed such "whistleblowing" statutes.

These employees may include lawyers, with the ordinary rules of confidentiality suspended. However, how far a lawyer may go in abrogating confidences is only beginning to be tested. In California, the first test came from the actions of California Department of Insurance lawyer Cindy Ossias.

Ossias was a staff attorney for the California Department of Insurance (DOI) when she began reviewing insurance companies' good-faith compliance with claims resulting from the 1994 Northridge earthquake. Eventually, she and a team of DOI staffers reported that four insurance companies had violated their duties to settle earthquake claims in good faith. Her group recommended substantial financial penalties, restitution, and remedial action. But after giving the recommendations to Insurance Commissioner Chuck Quackenbush, Ossias and her colleagues were suddenly excluded from the process of negotiating with the insurers.

Ossias soon learned that Quackenbush had cut deals with the insurers to pay nominal sums totaling $12 million — a small fraction of the nine-figure totals she had recommended — as contributions to foundations established by Quackenbush. She was shocked to learn that certain of the DOI/insurer settlement agreements found the insurer had not acted in bad faith, or were used as platforms for self-serving statements by the insurers themselves. Her team's original unfavorable reports had been buried.

Early in 2000, suspicion began to focus on Quackenbush's actions, both in the state legislature, and in the Los Angeles *Times*, where a reporter was investigating whether Quackenbush was using the newly-created foundations as a resource for his own personal public relations benefit. When Ossias was asked by an acquaintance from the state Assembly's insurance committee what was going on, she provided the Assembly committee copies of the four original recommendations and supporting documentation. The story — both the insurers' sweetheart deal and Quackenbush's foundation boondoggle — hit the front pages across California, and remained there for months. In June 2000, Ossias, now subpoenaed by the Assembly to testify, described what she believed to be Quackenbush's malfeasance. Within a week, Quackenbush had resigned in disgrace.

As for Ossias, after her disclosure the Office of Trial Counsel of the State Bar of California opened an investigation into her conduct. One conclusion trial counsel could have reached is that the state, rather than the office of insurance commissioner, was her true client, especially when the chief of her agency acted as he did. But trial counsel did not take this arguably easier way out. Instead, the bar prosecutors bit the bullet and exonerated Ossias on whistleblowing *and* public policy grounds. The text of the letter from trial counsel to Ossias' counsel Richard Zitrin appears below in its entirety save for citations.

CALIFORNIA STATE BAR TRIAL COUNSEL, LETTER TO COUNSEL FOR CINDY OSSIAS
State Bar Case No. 00-O-12989 (October 11, 2000)[7]

The State Bar of California

Office of the Trial Counsel-Enforcement

October 11, 2000

Dear Mr. Zitrin:

We are sending this letter to you based on our understanding that you represent Ms. Ossias in this matter. Please let us know immediately if this understanding is incorrect.

We are writing to advise you that we have decided to close our investigation relating to whether Ms. Ossias violated the Rules of Professional Conduct or the State Bar Act when she disclosed materials from the Department of Insurance to legislative staff members. We have concluded that Ms. Ossias did not engage in conduct which warrants disciplinary prosecution.

In reviewing this matter, we found that the facts were not in serious dispute. Ms. Ossias, while employed as an attorney with the Department of Insurance, provided legislative committees with materials pertaining to the department's settlement of claims against insurance companies arising out of the Northridge Earthquake. We have carefully reviewed the question of whether Ms. Ossias violated client confidences, whether Ms. Ossias complied with the obligations of attorneys representing an organization, and whether Ms. Ossias' conduct was permissible under the California Whistleblower Protection Act.

We have not found it necessary to decide whether the Department of Insurance could have asserted that the documents in question were confidential as to legislative committees. Rather, we have determined that Ms. Ossias' conduct should not result in discipline because: (1) it was consistent with the spirit of the Whistleblower Protection Act; (2) it advanced important public policy consider-

---

[7] This letter is reprinted here, as it has been elsewhere, with the consent of Cindy Ossias. As the subject attorney, Ossias has the right to keep such a letter confidential. She has chosen, however, to allow its widespread publication.

ations bearing on the responsibilities of the office of insurance commissioner; and (3) it is not otherwise subject to prosecution under the guidelines set forth in this office's Statement of Disciplinary Priorities.

We note that the acting insurance commissioner, based on reports from the California Highway Patrol and the California attorney general's office, commended Ms. Ossias for her actions and reinstated her to active employment with the department.

We appreciate the cooperation that we have received from you and your client in this matter. Please feel free to contact us if you have any questions or concerns.

Sincerely,

Donald Steedman

Deputy Trial Counsel

NOTES

What does this letter mean? Los Angeles *Times* reporter Virginia Ellis, who first broke the Quackenbush story, wrote that the statements in the State Bar's letter could represent "an important breakthrough," possibly "the first decision of its kind in the nation." It is only a letter, without clear precedential value. Nevertheless, the letter appears to have obvious public policy significance, although the State Bar's general counsel claimed, after the fact, that no policy position should be inferred from the document, merely an exercise of "prosecutorial discretion." The letter, written by senior staff counsel who had been told it would be made public, seems to accept Ossias' affirmative actions in a manner consistent with the *dicta* in *Lindsey*.[8]

Moreover, both new Comment 9 and old Comment 6 to ABA MR 1.13 contain this sentence: "[I]f the action or failure to act involves the head of a bureau, either the department of which the bureau is a part or the government as a whole may be the client for purpose of this Rule."

Ultimately, the Ossias letter, like the *Lindsey* opinion, speaks for itself. Read it again and make up your own mind. The letter opens the door to many questions: Why did trial counsel avoid the easy way out by stating that "we have not found it necessary" to determine whether the Department of Insurance (as opposed to the state or a legislative committee) had a confidential relationship with Ms. Ossias? Did the bar prosecutors want to address the case's public importance head on? Was their reference to the state's Whistleblower Protection Act an effort to create a safe harbor for public lawyers? Since the whistleblower statute cited applied specifically to state employees, was the reference to Ossias' conduct having "advanced important public policy considerations" an indication that these considerations might apply to lawyers other than government attorneys, such as in-house counsel? Finally, was any precedent established, or was this simply a case of "prosecutorial discretion," as the Bar claimed?

---

[8] Note, however, that the *Lindsey dicta* implies not merely that a lawyer in Ossias' position may blow the whistle, but that she *must*.

5. Representing Different Governmental Agencies

Have courts and ethics opinions supported governmental lawyers who represent different agencies at the same time? The answer is "it depends." And sometimes even within states there are clearly contradictory holdings. For example, in *In re Opinion 415*, 407 A.2d 1197 (N.J. 1979), the New Jersey Supreme Court used a strict "appearance of impropriety" standard to disallow joint representation of two different governments, a municipality and the surrounding county. But in another case, the court held that a single government lawyer may represent several different boards that are part of the same township, when there is little likelihood of a conflict arising. *DeLuca v. Kahr Bros.*, 407 A.2d 1285 (N.J. Super. Ct. 1979), required the boards to consent to being defended by the same counsel, but permitted the joint representation as being in the public interest. Nevertheless, the state ethics advisory committee, in New Jersey Opinion 560 (1985), applied the narrow "appearance of impropriety" standard to a lawyer's representation of different agencies within the same governmental entity, warning against this even where there is no apparent conflict.

What guidance exists in California for Messrs. Hahn and Pines? Perhaps not surprisingly, there are somewhat conflicting messages in the case law. *Civil Service Comm'n of San Diego Cty. v. Superior Court*, 163 Cal. App. 3d 70 (1984) concerned an underlying labor dispute. County counsel had advised both the county department of social services and the civil service commission, which eventually found against the department. But county counsel, concluding the commission was in error in deciding for the employees against the county, then filed an action on the county's behalf to overturn the commission's decision. The court disqualified county counsel, holding that in light of the necessary independence of a civil service commission, it was too simplistic to conclude that "the county" was the only client, given that they were adverse in a lawsuit. Yet the court provides a balanced holding.

CIVIL SERVICE COMM'N OF SAN DIEGO COUNTY v. SUPERIOR COURT
163 Cal. App. 3d 70 (1984)

While we have determined that county counsel must be disqualified from representing the County in this case, we wish to indicate the limits of our holding. First, it should again be emphasized that a conflict of this nature only arises in the case of and to the extent that a county agency is independent of the County such that litigation between them may ensue. Second, disqualification of county counsel is not necessarily mandated in future cases involving quasi-independent agencies. We have noted that a fundamental conflict arises whenever county counsel is asked to represent both the Commission and the County. Moreover, it is clear from the course of this case that county counsel, with good reason, views his primary responsibility as being to the board of supervisors. If the Commission is afforded access to independent legal advice, however, there is no reason county counsel may not continue to vigorously represent the County even when such representation results in litigation against the Commission. We need not and do not decide whether the Commission, appropriately informed and advised in a given case, could validly waive the conflict at the advisory stage. At most, we deal here with a manifestation of the system's general insensitivity to conflict of interest questions as they affect the government attorney. By our comments we do not mean to suggest that government attorneys must necessarily be treated identically with attorneys in private practice. But neither are they immune from conflict problems similar to those that confront the private bar. Our decision is but one small step in what should be a continuing process to develop standards of conduct, which accurately reflect the realities of practice in the private and public sectors.

NOTES

Both Messrs. Hahn and Pines and the ethics experts who dispute them can take some comfort from this case. On the one hand, the court prevented representation in litigation after counsel gave advice to two different government agencies. The Commission and the County here were both, as Pines put it, "a legal entity, able to sue or be sued." On the other, the giving of advice leading up to the suit was not, in and of itself, criticized by the court. State Bar of California Formal Opinion 2001-156 (2001) — an opinion that had been at least 10 years in the making — ultimately wound up in close accord with *Civil Service Comm'n*: The City Attorney has one client except that "Constituent sub-entities may become separate clients only if they have lawful authority to act independently of the public entity and if they take a position contrary to the overall public entity's position on a matter within the ambit of the constituent sub-entities' independent authority."

In 1992, another California appeals court affirmed that advising two agencies of the same municipality may be permissible. In *Howitt v. Superior Court*, 3 Cal. App. 4th 1575 (1992), county counsel was allowed to represent one government agency (here, a sheriff's department) in an employee hearing before an appeals board, while also giving advice to that appeals board. The court permitted the dual representation so long as appropriate screening procedures protected the independence of the separate deputy county counsel.

6. Representing the Government and Its Individual Employees

The most frequent forum for employer/employee conflicts is the lawsuit against a municipality and its police officers. Consider *Dunton v. County of Suffolk*, 729 F.2d 903 (2d Cir. 1984). There, plaintiff sued Suffolk County (N.Y.) and two of its police officers for malicious prosecution and battery. On appeal, the court found that the defendant police officers had been deprived of a fair trial, as the county and the cops had all been represented by the same counsel. The lawyer argued, successfully, that the county was not liable because the officers were acting outside the scope of employment. The court held that where there was a "likely conflict of interest," the trial court should carefully scrutinize the arrangement before the county attorney may represent all parties.

In response to this case, Suffolk County proposed to set up a panel of three lawyers, and have the officers choose their attorneys from among the three. In *Suffolk Cty. Patrolmen's Benevolent Ass'n v. County of Suffolk*, 751 F.2d 550 (2d

Cir. 1985), the union representing the two officers sued the county to seek the appointment of independent counsel chosen by the defendants themselves. The court refused to extend *Dunton*. While the defendants were entitled to independent counsel, it was up to the county to select the attorneys; otherwise the county would have no way of controlling costs.

Connecticut has a statutory requirement of indemnification for its police officers. General Statute 7-101-a requires a municipality to "protect and save harmless any municipal officer from financial loss or expense . . . arising out of any claim . . . ." This is certainly a pure solution, albeit not economical, and thus not likely to achieve widespread adoption. Even with indemnification, however, the U.S. District Court in Connecticut has required the fully informed consent of individual employees to the joint representation. *Manganella v. Keyes*, 613 F. Supp. 795 (D. Conn. 1985).

Cases in other jurisdictions have both extended and limited *Dunton*. In a Texas police brutality case, *Shadid v. Jackson*, 521 F. Supp. 87 (E.D. Tex. 1981), the court held that when a city and its police officer employees were to be represented by the same counsel, in "circumstances present[ing] . . . an obvious potential for conflict," the conflict is unwaivable, and separate representation is required. But in *Rodick v. City of Schenectady*, 1 F.3d 1341 (2d Cir. 1993), the court found that, because a trial had already occurred, and the police officers accused of undue force and misconduct had not shown any actual prejudice to their case because of joint representation by Schenectady's counsel, no *Dunton* review was needed. Would the outcome have been different had the appellants moved for disqualification of the city's attorney before trial?

The *Barkley* case below contains a thorough ethical analysis of conflicts in the governmental attorney sphere. Compare it with the cases cited above.

BARKLEY v. CITY OF DETROIT
514 N.W.2d 242 (Mich. Ct. App. 1994)

This is an action for declaratory judgment concerning the duty of defendant, the City of Detroit, to provide legal counsel to police officers being sued for injuries allegedly inflicted by the officers during the performance of their official duties. Plaintiffs, who are all police officers and members of the Detroit Police Officers Association (DPOA), and the City of Detroit, were named as defendants in nine separate civil suits that alleged various acts of police misconduct. At issue is whether ethical considerations prevent attorneys from the city's law department from fulfilling the city's obligation to provide counsel for plaintiffs in those civil actions. . . .

The Detroit Charter, § 6-403 provides that, "upon request, the corporation counsel may represent any officer or employee of the city in any act or proceeding involving official duties." [Also, the] Detroit Code states that, "where there is willful misconduct or lack of good faith in the doing of such acts, the same shall not constitute the performance of the official duties . . . ."

Detroit Code, art. XI, § 13-11-5 provides that the corporation counsel shall represent an employee in an underlying suit until the city council determines otherwise. . . . However, the collective bargaining agreement . . . provid[es] that the city council's determination is subject to final and binding arbitration and that representation will be provided in the underlying suit until the conclusion of arbitral proceedings.

. . . .

The trial court held that there is indeed a conflict of interest that arises when the city council refuses to provide representation and an employee seeks to overturn that decision through arbitration. That conflict arises because the corporation counsel would be representing the employee in the underlying suit while at the same time representing the city in the arbitration proceeding, in effect, arguing for the employee in one forum and against the employee in another. The parties do not challenge this determination, which we agree is a correct holding.

The trial court also held that, once a conflict arises, the city should pay for the employee to be represented in the underlying suit by independent counsel. . . . The court further found that no conflict of interest existed before an adverse determination by the city council. . . . Plaintiffs argue that a conflict arises when the corporation counsel represents both the city and an employee in an underlying suit while at the same time arguing to the city counsel that no representation should be provided. We agree.

. . . .

The [Michigan State Bar] Ethics Committee has [stated]:

> Where a City Attorney rendered advice on a matter to members of City Council who later sued the City over the same matter, the City Attorney may defend the City in the case only if he did not gain and did not appear to gain confidential information from the council members involved and his contact with them would not affect or appear to affect his independent professional judgment on behalf of the City. [Informal Opinion CI-335 (January 16, 1978).]

. . . .

The ethical issue presented is whether the representation of these individual plaintiffs by an attorney from the city's law department "may be materially limited by the lawyer's responsibilities" to the city, given that these plaintiffs obviously do not wish to consent to such dual representation. In such a situation, the parties seem to agree that an actual conflict is unlikely because access to the party perceived to have the deeper pockets would be obtained by showing that the employee acted within the scope of employment, thereby imposing liability on the city. However, there is a danger that the evidence will show otherwise and liability will rest solely on the individual plaintiff. . . . Therefore, such dual representation should not be undertaken.

We now return to the issue whether the city's law department should be treated in the same manner as a private law firm, so that the disqualification of one attorney should be imputed to others. *See* MRPC 1.10. We find that it should. . . .

It might be argued that a so-called "Chinese wall" might be erected such that a disqualified attorney would have neither any role in the case nor any contact with the attorneys actually involved. . . . The present case, however, does not involve a particular attorney with a particular disqualification. Rather, because all attorneys in the department represent the city and owe it the duties discussed above, none of them are free to also represent an individual employee once a conflict arises. For this purpose, we find that the department should be considered a law firm.

We, therefore, hold that assuming that the city law department is representing the city in the underlying suit, no attorney from the city law department may also represent plaintiffs in the same suit.[9]

This, however, does not mean that plaintiffs should be allowed to choose who will represent them at city expense. . . . [T]he city may select plaintiffs' counsel in the underlying cases as long as it selects an independent and unbiased counsel with none of the ethical problems discussed above. . . .

NOTES

Note that in *Barkley*, two issues were involved, and only the second concerned representing both the city and the officers in the litigation. When two different but related parties are sued, one party's theory of the case can create problems for the other. Thus, where a police director who sought advice of counsel when acting in his official capacity was later sued in his individual capacity, he raised advice of counsel as the basis of his qualified immunity defense. The city was also sued, and claimed attorney-client privilege to protect the communications between the police director and the city attorney. The Sixth Circuit had to resolve whether the *director* invoking advice of counsel impliedly waived the *city's* attorney-client privilege held by the city. The Court said no: "Having concluded that a municipality can assert the attorney-client privilege in civil proceedings, we now hold that a municipal official's assertion of the advice of counsel defense does not require the City to relinquish the privilege it holds." *Ross v. City of Memphis*, 423 F.3d 596, 603 (6th Cir. 2005).

7. Screening Revisited

Note the reference in the *Howitt* case (*see* Section 5 *above*) to screening as a justification for allowing two different departments of the county counsel to represent two different agencies of the same government. *Screening*, you may recall from Problem 10, is the evolving and increasingly permitted tactic resorted to by law firms in an effort to prevent their total disqualification. In *Barkley*, the court correctly points out that in that particular case, the systemic nature of the conflict — with the party being the municipality itself, not merely different agencies within the city government — means that screening of separate attorneys would not solve the conflict of interest. But the language of the court's opinion

---

[9] [7] We do not decide whether different departments of, for example, the Attorney General's office, may represent parties on both sides of a dispute. Although some references were made in this regard, that is not an issue before us.

certainly allows for the possibility that setting up a screen would be permitted in an appropriate case.

Indeed, it appears that, whether stated or not, principles of screening are frequently behind those court decisions that permit representation of two or more different governmental agencies by the same government "law firm," a circumstance that simply would not be allowed for a private firm in most states, at least if the agency is considered the client. Anyone who is considered a "client" is going to have significant expectations about confidentiality of communications. Several cases make reference to the fact that one office of government lawyers has little or no interaction with another office, thus allowing confidences to be preserved and justifying dual representation. This is particularly true in the case of the federal government.

Sometimes, the courts have acknowledged de facto screening. *In re Lee G.*, 1 Cal. App. 4th 17 (1991), concerned the dependency of a minor. Two separate and distinct offices of county counsel were permitted to represent both the department of social services, seeking to place the child away from the mother, and the conservator for the mother. The court pointed to the lack of connection between the two offices in denying the mother's motion for independent counsel.

City of Santa Barbara v. Superior Court 122 Cal. App. 4th 17, (2004) presents a different fact scenario that permitted screening. There, an attorney representing homeowners in litigation against the City of Santa Barbara left her private law firm and joined the city attorney's office. Rather than disqualifying the entire city attorney's office because of the new attorney's conflict, the court found satisfactory "screening measures established by the city attorney" that were "both timely and effective in protecting the [homeowners'] confidences."

As we discussed in Problem 10, screening of government lawyers has special status after the fact as well. That is, screening is far more liberally allowed when the lawyer in question is a former government attorney. Model Rule 1.11 directs itself specifically and extensively to this question.

But what if *the boss* has the conflict? The California Supreme Court decided that vicarious disqualification of an entire government law firm was required when the elected San Francisco City Attorney had, in private practice, represented a client that was being sued by the city in a matter substantially related to the chief attorney's prior representation.[10] The Court found that as the chief attorney of his office, the City Attorney could neither successfully delegate the representation nor create a valid ethical screen.

8. The Part-Time Government Lawyer

What happens when a lawyer works part-time as a government attorney and part-time in a private practice? Several states have used a broad "appearance of impropriety" standard, which excludes any conflicting employment. And when the constitutional rights of the criminally accused are at stake, the restrictions are even more pronounced. In *Utah v. Brown*, 853 P.2d 851 (Utah 1992), the court

---

[10] City & County of San Francisco v. Cobra Solutions, Inc., 135 P.3d 20 (Cal. 2006).

appointed a part-time municipal prosecutor as a criminal defendant's trial counsel. The court held that "as a matter of public policy and pursuant to our inherent supervisory power over the courts, as well as our express power to govern the practice of law, counsel with concurrent prosecutorial obligations may not be appointed to defend indigent persons." The defendant's conviction was reversed and a new trial ordered.

Compare Brown to a more recent 1997 Utah Supreme Court case. In *V-1 Oil Company, aka V-1 Propane v. Dept of Environmental Quality*, 939 P.2d 1192 (Utah 1997), the court held that an administrative governmental agency, the Solid and Hazardous Waste Control Board, could appoint one of its own employees to preside at a formal hearing on a respondent's alleged hazardous waste violation. The agency employee was a part-time staff attorney in the same division charged with investigating and prosecuting violations. The lawyer's duties did not involve investigating the kind of violation at hand (underground storage leaks). Still, the state court of appeals disqualified the appointee. The Supreme Court reversed, denying the assumption that the lawyer-appointee would automatically act in the interest of his employer, the Board: "His duty of loyalty toward his employer required him to function as an impartial adjudicator. [F]ailure to do so would constitute a serious breach of loyalty. We do not accept the proposition that the employing agency is a client or that the appointee owes the same duty of loyalty to that agency that he would owe a client." Do you agree?

Is *V-1* easily reconciled with *Brown*? Is there a legitimate distinction because *Brown* involved a criminal case while *V-1* only involved civil administrative penalties? What about when the penalties have a quasi-criminal effect?

9. The Government Lawyer as Employee

It is significant that government attorneys are not only the legal advisors to their entities, but also the employees of those entities. One emerging issue, which can affect corporate house counsel as well as government lawyers, is what happens when an attorney is terminated or otherwise leaves employment unwillingly. Can the lawyer sue for discrimination, wrongful discharge, and so on? Would such a suit involve revealing attorney-client confidences and secrets? For example, what if the lawyer is privy to information demonstrating the agency's lack of good faith in its open hiring policy? May the lawyer use this information later in an employment suit? If a lawyer may do this, it may have a chilling effect on how much confidential information is disclosed to such attorneys in the first place.

May government attorneys be disciplined for their attempts to bring matters to the attention of their superiors where they feel the government's interests would be best served? Recall *Garcetti v. Ceballos*, 547 U.S. 410 (2006), in the last problem. A sharply divided United States Supreme Court has now answered this question "yes," at least as to First Amendment grounds.

Another issue, more likely to affect governmental attorneys than their brothers and sisters in the private sector, is organized labor efforts. Issues of confidentiality and its breach arise when all deputy city counsel, for instance, unionize or threaten a strike unless they receive an acceptable collective bargaining agreement. These issues have not yet thoroughly been addressed by the courts of most states, a situation we expect will change in the near future.

At least one state, California, has permitted public attorneys to unionize and even to sue their own employers through their employee associations. In *Santa Clara County Counsel Attorneys Assn. v. Woodside*, 869 P.2d 1142 (Cal. 1994), the court upheld a California statute that permitted government lawyers to form collective bargaining units and sue if they believed, as what happened in this case, that the employer had failed to negotiate in good faith. The court stopped short of "approv[ing] the general proposition that an attorney suit against a present client is ethically permissible." "[W]e are not unmindful," wrote the court, "of the fact that attorneys suing their clients, in any circumstance, put a strain on the attorney-client relationship, and may tend to diminish the client's confidence in their attorneys' loyalty." But, emphasizing that the legislature had specifically given public attorneys a limited statutory employment right, the court allowed the lawsuit to proceed.

10. Who Is the Client, Revisited

The following article demonstrates how difficult it can be to define who a government attorney's client really is. Especially in the context of the federal government lawyer, can it ever be defined with precision?

L.J. Pendlebury, Bar, *Agencies Haggle Over Defining "Client": For Whom Does the Government Lawyer Toil?*
LEGAL TIMES, November 14, 1988[11]

Who is a lawyer's client? For private attorneys, that question is usually a simple one. But take a Customs Service lawyer: Is this lawyer's client the Customs Service, the Treasury Department, or the whole U.S. government?

This may sound like only a matter of semantics, but it is much more. A debate being waged in government circles and at the D.C. Bar is bringing to the surface strong differences over the definition of *client* for government lawyers, and the issue's ultimate resolution could significantly affect how these lawyers function. . . .

. . . .

At the monthly meeting of the bar's board of governors last Tuesday, President-elect Charles Ruff of Covington & Burling, a former U.S. attorney for the District, focused the issue sharply.

Ruff objected vigorously to a special bar committee's proposal to ask the appeals court to define the government lawyer's *client* as the agency, department, or individual whose interests the attorney is directly representing.

Under this definition, the hypothetical Customs Service attorney would represent only the service or any individual he or she is assigned to represent. The lawyer's duty would run only to those clients.

Moreover, if this lawyer shared confidential information with any other office, including another agency within the Treasury Department like the Internal Revenue Service, he could face a bar disciplinary proceeding for violating the confidentiality of his client, the Customs Service.

The court's version doesn't distinguish between private and government lawyers for the purpose of the ethics rules.

Ruff strenuously contended that in view of the complexities of the issue, the bar ought to define the client in every possible instance or, if that is impossible, just stay away from the issue and leave it up to the agencies themselves.

"I wonder whether we're serving any real purpose here by serving up an all-purpose definition of who the client is," said Ruff. "It is not our role to solve the problems of the world regarding the inner workings of government lawyers."

Just a "Rule of Thumb"

Joe Sims, partner in the D.C. office of Cleveland's Jones, Day, Reavis & Pogue, who chaired the special bar committee, pointed out that the report calls its conclusion merely a "rule of thumb, a benchmark from which deviations can be made as appropriate."

Sims later conceded, however, that "it is optimistic in the extreme to think you can serve up an ethics rule that can spell out exactly who the government client is in all cases."

Despite Sims' concession, the measure passed overwhelmingly, with Ruff the only dissenter. The bar committee will now submit to the court suggested revisions of the ethics rules that attempt to define the client in a narrow manner.

. . . .

[The D.C. bar received a series of comments on its proposals from high-ranking government lawyers.]

Russell Bruemmer, general counsel of the Central Intelligence Agency, for example, described interagency meetings at which "lawyers from within the executive branch communicate with each other and discuss legal issues in a manner that goes beyond the interests of a particular agency."

Bruemmer suggested that, in such a meeting, the client of the lawyers present might be the United States or, at least, the executive branch.

William Parler, general counsel of the Nuclear Regulatory Commission, asked whether a federal attorney might run afoul of confidentiality rules if he responds to a White House or congressional oversight committee request for information.

Parler also wondered how a government attorney should respond if the Office of Government Ethics requests a meeting regarding the activities of officials in the attorney's agency. Would a breach of attorney-client privilege occur?

The Federal Bar Association proposed going even farther than the Sims committee in limiting the definition of the client. In a letter submitted by association president Bonnie Gay, a Justice Department lawyer, the voluntary bar group urged that the client agency be clearly described as "the lowest common denominator, . . . a bureau or office and not the entire department or other bureaus or offices with which the attorney does not have a close working relationship."

D. SUPPLEMENTAL READINGS

1. *Ward v. Superior Court*, 70 Cal. App. 3d 23 (1977), is an older case similar to the facts in our problem. It involved a volatile dispute between the Los Angeles County assessor and the county board of supervisors that ended in litigation. The assessor, one Philip Watson, ultimately sued the board in his individual capacity "and as a taxpayer and resident of the County" for violations of the Civil Rights Act (42 U.S.C. § 1983). When county counsel represented the board, Watson moved to disqualify that office, since it represented him as well, as assessor. The trial court granted the motion, but the appeals court reversed. It held that the assessor's office is "merely an arm of county government" supervised by the board, and that communications between county counsel and the assessor, "an agent of the county," could not "be considered secret confidential communication so as to bar the county, acting through the board of supervisors, from obtaining that information." This harsh language on confidentiality may have been motivated by the personal nature of Watson's lawsuit against the county.

2. Michael Stokes Paulsen, *Who "Owns" the Government's Attorney-Client Privilege?*, 83 MINN. L. REV. 473 (1998). This is a good overview evaluating the attorney-client privilege in the context of an Independent Counsel investigating executive branch officials.

3. Two significant articles addressing whistleblowing by governmental attorneys are Roger C. Cramton, *The Lawyer as Whistleblower: Confidentiality and the Government Lawyer*, 5 GEO. J. LEG. ETHICS 291 (1991), and Richard C. Solomon, *Wearing Many Hats: Confidentiality and Conflicts of Interest Issues for the California Public Lawyer*, 25 SW. U. L. REV. 265 (1996). Cramton's piece is a valuable study charting the interrelationship between the ethical rules on whistleblowing and confidentiality and the recent development of whistleblowing statutes.

4. Jesselyn Radack, a federal whistleblower in the case of "American Taliban" John Walker Lindh, has written two articles worthy of note. In *The Government Attorney-Whistleblower and the Rule of Confidentiality: Compatible at Last*, 17 GEO. J. LEGAL ETHICS 125 (2003), she discusses the new, broader MR 1.6 exceptions and whistleblower protection laws, as they combine to provide the beginnings of a solution for government attorney-whistleblowers. In *Tortured Legal Ethics: The Role of the Government Advisor in the War on Terrorism*, 77 U. COLO. L. REV. 1 (2006), she explores both an agency and public interest approach to the ethical duties of government lawyers. She argues for the primacy of a public interest approach when government lawyers give advice "on morally perilous questions."

5. The New Jersey Supreme Court has written several opinions dealing with the ethical requirements of the governmental attorney. In *In re Opinion 552*, 507 A.2d 233 (N.J. 1986), the court overturned its own advisory committee on professional

ethics, ruling that a municipal attorney may represent the city and its employees in a federal discrimination action where the defendants have potential diverging interests, provided there is a substantial identity of interests between them. In *In re Opinion 452*, 432 A.2d 829 (N.J. 1981), the court affirmed the opinion of its ethics panel that it was a conflict of interest for two partners in the same law firm to work for the same city as municipal prosecutors and attorneys for the planning board. In *In re Opinion 653*, 623 A.2d 241 (N.J. 1993), the court ruled no inherent conflict existed when two partners in the same law firm served in positions for the same county, one as county counsel and the other as counsel to the county vocational school board.

6. Heather E. Kimmel, *Note: Solutions to the City Attorney's Charter-Imposed Conflict of Interest Problem*, 66 OHIO ST. L.J. 1075 (2005), is a law review note discussing conflict of interest problems that may arise when city attorneys are required by charter to represent both the mayor and the city council, and other difficulties dealing with who is the client dilemma.

7. *United States v. Reynoso*, 6 F. Supp. 2d 269 (S.D.N.Y. 1998), involves a liberalized screening standard for quasi-governmental lawyers, such as those contracted to do defense work through New York's Legal Aid Society. In *Reynoso*, the prosecution requested to disqualify a federal Legal Aid Society lawyer because another legal aid lawyer had represented a witness in the current case four years before on another matter. The defendant wanted to keep his lawyer. The court denied the motion, which had been joined by the former client/witness.

8. In an interesting juxtaposition of two matters also relating to public defender conflicts, on April 15, 2013, the Georgia Supreme Court approved Formal Advisory Opinion 10-1, answering the question "May different lawyers employed in the circuit public defender office in the same judicial circuit represent co-defendants when a single lawyer would have an impermissible conflict of interest in doing so?" in the negative. A month earlier, a Georgia appellate court rejected a defendant's effort to overturn his conviction because another public defender in the same office had previously represented the two victims in his case on other matters. *Johnson v. State*, 739 S.E.2d 469 (Ga. Ct. App. 2013). Said the *Johnson* court in a footnote: "Our Supreme Court is currently considering whether 'the rules for imputing conflicts operate within a single circuit public defender's office in the same manner as those within a law firm.' We need not reach this question because we find no evidence of any actual conflict or adverse effect arising from Johnson's representation by two members of the same public defender's office at different times."

9. James R. Harvey III, *Note: Loyalty in Government Litigation: Department of Justice Representation of Agency Clients*, 37 WM. & MARY L. REV. 1569 (1996), examines the issue of whom the Department of Justice represents, and what happens in situations in which an agency such as DOJ is asked to litigate a matter it does not consider to be in the government's best interest. Harvey examines the ethical standards that define the duty of both the individual lawyer and the agency itself. We have seen this issue play out recently in the Obama administration and Attorney General Holder's refusal to defend the Defense of Marriage Act in court.

10. Federal government lawyers must comply with more than one set of ethics rules — the same rules as their private practitioner counterparts, as well as the ethics rules and requirements applicable to those in government service. These rules are not always the same, and some even carry criminal penalties. Peggy Love's article, *Ethics and Professional Conduct for Federal Government Attorneys*, 25 ABA NAT. RESOURCES & ENV'T 40 (2011), examines some of the important ethical obligations under the Standards of Ethical Conduct for Employees of the Executive Branch, 5 C.F.R. Part 2635, and compares them to the ABA Model Rules, focusing particularly on outside activities and side-switching when leaving government service.

11. Pam Smith, *Court Bangs Head on "Ethical Wall,"* THE RECORDER (San Francisco), March 9, 2006, has a good discussion of the ethical issues raised by *City & County of San Francisco v. Cobra Solutions, Inc.*, cited in section 7 of the Readings.

12. Steven K. Berenson, *The Duty Defined: Specific Obligations that Follow from Civil Government Lawyers' General Duty to Serve the Public Interest*, 42 BRANDEIS L.J. 13 (2003), discusses the differences between a civil government lawyer's ethical duties in serving the public interest and those of a private practitioner.

Chapter 9

THE LAWYER ACTING AS ADVISER

PROBLEM 25: ADVISING THE CORPORATE CLIENT THAT'S MADE A MISTAKE

A. INTRODUCTION

What should in-house counsel do when confronted with a corporation's mistakes? Is there an obligation to tell the company to "do the right thing"? Is there ever an obligation to "blow the whistle" and reveal the error? When? When the corporation has clearly made a mistake that poses a serious physical threat to the public? What about mistakes, or frauds, that don't involve physical harm? And what is the effect of new rules — both from the ABA and the federal government — that address a corporate client's fraudulent conduct? Moreover, what consequences are likely for the whistleblowing in-house counsel?

B. PROBLEM

Ernesto Valencia is chief assistant general counsel to Giant Automobile, Inc., one of the nation's "Big Four" automotive companies.

I

Giant's electronics division produces its own smart-phone interfaces for all Giant cars. Giant's electronics laboratory tests have disclosed that the standard smart-phone interface uses a defective Bluetooth "pairing" mechanism that will require re-pairing phones with the car speakers approximately every 50–60 "use instances," or anytime the phone is removed from the car. Eventually, the Bluetooth interface will stop working completely, after approximately 700 pairings, which for most customers will likely be shortly after the one-year warranty expires. The Bluetooth problem has now been changed for newer vehicles, but 1,200,000 Giants with phone-paring problems are on the road.

The complete Bluetooth package, including new software and the labor to reinstall it, costs Giant about $82 a car. Despite the fact that almost all the pairing failures occur outside the warranty period, Giant has received a large number of calls and emails from people complaining that their phone can no longer be paired with the speakers in their car.

QUESTIONS

1. May Valencia advise Giant to replace the Bluetooth units for those who have complained? Should he? May he inform his client that if it does nothing, the probability of legal action against Giant is slight, since even in a class action, monetary damages would be difficult to show?

2. What about customers who bought these models but who have not complained? Since there is an admitted defect, should Ernie advise that *all* the pairing systems be recalled and replaced?

3. Assume the new Bluetooth "fix" is far more expensive than the old defective one. May Ernie advise Giant that it may continue to sell cars with the old system and just deal with complaints as they arise?

4. May Ernie say anything about the defect to anyone outside Giant? What if he discovers evidence of a fraudulent financial arrangement between Giant and the subcontractors producing the defective system?

II

Giant has discovered in controlled proving grounds tests that its most popular model, the Venezia Sedan, has defective brake fluid distribution that under certain changes in climatic conditions can cause complete brake failure. There are two million Venezias on the road.

Company climate experts and statisticians have written a report noting that the likelihood of complete brake failure is slight, and estimating that complete brake failure is likely to cause no more than one accident per every 100,000 vehicles per year. It is not known precisely how many of these accidents would result in a fatality, but based on reports "in the field," the company's internal auditors have been able to identify a small number of "serious accidents" — between 15 and 20 per year — as being caused by the brake failure.

Finally, repair of the Venezias is complicated. The cost to repair these vehicles is estimated at $135 per car. That would cost the company $270,000,000 for a complete recall of all 2,000,000 Venezias.

QUESTIONS

1. May Valencia advise the company to litigate all claims as they occur, on grounds of proximate cause, contributory negligence, etc.?

2. When these facts are presented to him, must or should Ernie advise Giant to recall all affected cars? What should he do if Giant refuses? What *may* he do? Would the analysis be different if Valencia were outside counsel?

3. Does it matter that the estimated number of accidents each year is 15 or 20? What if it were 50? Or 200? Or 3?

4. Does it matter that the cost of a recall is $270,000,000? What if it were only $27,000,000? What if it were $2,700,000,000, and would put Giant in bankruptcy? May Ernie consider the potentially ruinous consequences both financially and emotionally of the car company going broke on Giant workers and their families?

5. Does it matter what version of the ABA Model Rules applies in Ernie's state? Or if Ernie is in California, where the state versions of Model Rules 1.6 and 1.13 are different? Which rule, 1.6 or 1.13, trumps the other?

6. Regardless of the rules, Ernie will have to make a decision balancing ethics rules, personal morality, and the economic reality of facing the possible loss of his job. We might call it in-house counsel's "trilemma." How should he balance these considerations?

C. READINGS

1. Should Counsel Ever "Blow the Whistle"?

At what point should general counsel "blow the whistle" on his or her own client — the company that employs the lawyer? "Bean counters," or actuarial analysts, can determine the risk of harm to the public of all kinds of products that have an inherent level of danger stemming from their use. Are these merely actuarial statistics relating to the "cost" of a human life, or is there a point at which such danger, including death, must be prevented by the company? Or by the lawyer acting if the company refuses to act? Professor David Luban uses one of corporate America's most famous and dramatic examples of death caused by a product — the Ford Pinto — to posit an ethical requirement of whistleblowing. As you read about the Pinto case, consider whether the revised ABA Model Rules would result in a different course of action or change the responsibilities for lawyers in the 21st century.

DAVID LUBAN, LAWYERS AND JUSTICE:
AN ETHICAL STUDY
ch. 10 (1988)[1]

The Pinto Case

The shockers came on three successive days, October 13, 14 and 15, 1979, in three successive front-page *Chicago Tribune* headlines:

> October 13 FORD IGNORED PINTO FIRE PERIL, SECRET MEMOS SHOW

> October 14 HOW FORD PUT A PRICE TAG ON AUTOS' SAFETY

> October 15 U.S. OFFICIAL SEES COVER-UP IN FORD SAFETY TEST POLICY

Of course, everyone knew about the celebrated exploding Pinto long before that time. In February 1978, a California jury had awarded $125 million — later reduced to $6.6 million by a judge — to a teenager who had suffered horrendous burns in a Pinto accident. . . . [T]he *Tribune*'s research was initiated because a grand jury in

---

Indiana had indicted Ford for reckless homicide in the burning deaths of three teenage women whose 1973 Pinto had exploded after being struck from behind by a van on August 10, 1978.

The secret internal Ford memos revealed in the first two *Tribune* articles made it all the worse. They seemed to show a level of foreknowledge and coldblooded calculatedness on Ford's part that appalled many readers.

The first day's memos showed that Ford engineers knew that Pinto gastanks would be pierced by bolts when struck from behind at speeds as low as 21 m.p.h. This would allow gasoline to leak out, so that any spark, caused, for example, by metal scraping over pavement, would explode the fuel supply. Other memos discussed several modifications in the Pinto design that would make it safer. These were rejected on the grounds that they cost too much money (various figures were cited, ranging from $5.08 to $11 per car), and because some would decrease trunk space.

According to the first *Tribune* article, a Ford memo of November 10, 1970 commented that government-proposed fuel tank safety standards "are too strict and come too soon. Ford executives list lesser standards that the Department of Transportation 'can be expected to buy' as alternatives." A "confidential" memo dated April 22, 1971 recommended that one of the safety devices not be installed until 1976, to save Ford $20.9 million. Another "confidential" memo of October 26, 1971 stated that no additional "fuel system integrity" changes would be made until "required by law." As a result of lobbying by the auto industry, the more stringent legal requirements did not go into effect until 1977; the 1977 Pinto was designed to meet the new requirements.

These memos, in short, indicated that Ford engineers and executives were aware of Pinto's design problem, and that instead of repairing it, they acted deliberately to avoid regulatory and financial consequences to the company. The next day's revelations were summarized by Lee Strobel of the *Tribune* as follows:

> Saving 180 people from burning to death and another 180 from suffering serious burns in car fires each year would not be worth the cost of adding $11 per car for safety improvements, Ford Motor Co. officials concluded in a financial study obtained by the *Tribune* from court files.

> After preparing a cost analysis that amounted to putting a price tag on human lives and suffering, the automaker concluded that the $11 increased cost on 12.5 million cars and light trucks would be almost three times greater than the estimated costs stemming from persons killed and injured in vehicles lacking the safety measures, according to the document.

> The document does not state whether or not Ford viewed the costs as being related to potential legal liability payments.

. . . .

Ford was acquitted of reckless homicide in the Indiana trial. . . . [T]he key to the defense lay in the facts of the Indiana case. The young women's car was struck by a van moving fifty m.p.h., enough to rupture the fuel tank on any comparable car. . . . According to the *Tribune*, Ford engineers had known since 1968 that fuel tanks in the position of the Pinto's were liable to rupture "at very low speed," and discussions of how to deal with the problem in Pintos had been going on since at least 1970. Yet until the lawsuits began, the public had no inkling of the matter. . . . During 1976 and 1977 alone "thirteen Pintos — more than double the number that might be expected in proportion to their numbers — were involved in fiery rear-end crashes, resulting in deaths" while the VW Rabbit and Toyota Corolla suffered none. Some might say that it is a mistake to dwell on the particulars; it makes our reactions too emotional. On the contrary, I think that in problems such as this we cannot afford to forget the three teenagers who perished in a one-thousand-degree fire. And, if the *Tribune* stories are accurate, Ford knew precisely what it was doing. Shouldn't someone at Ford have made the information public in an act of preventive whistleblowing?

The obvious people to do so would have been Ford engineers or executives. I wish to consider a different problem, however, and that is whether attorneys in Ford's legal department (its "general counsel") who reviewed the cost-benefit and crash-test documents should have disclosed the terrible menace posed by the Pinto fuel tank. According to former Ford executive Harley Copp, the lawyers "definitely knew" what was in those documents.

It is perhaps obvious that, before calling [famed columnist] Jack Anderson or the Department of Transportation, a Ford attorney should have gone through internal company procedures to get the Pinto recalled or to reverse the decision to build unsafe Pintos. Reminding the client of the common good (in the fashion of Brandeis) is after all the fundamental requirement of morally activist legal practice. Let us suppose, as would perhaps have been the case, that this proved fruitless. Then, unless some special argument to the contrary can be found, the attorney should have alerted the public to the menace of the Pinto. . . . Ask not with whom the buck stops, it stops with thee. Life is unfair. . . .

What's Wrong With Trading Lives for Cash?

. . . [A]ssuming that the facts of the case are as the newspapers stated them, did Ford do anything immoral?

This question sounds absurd. If allowing innocent people to be immolated for no other reason than cold, cold cash isn't immoral, what is? . . .

Despite this understandable reaction, there is another way to look at the matter. What was it that Ford did? It traded off cost for safety. But that is what car manufacturers must also do. Safety costs money, and people may not be willing to pay the price. Hence, the cheaper, in both senses, car. . . . Government regulations set minimum safety standards, but after these are met, the marketplace sets the level of safety.

. . . .

To a sophisticated reader, Ford's cost-benefit study is nothing to get excited about. First of all, that number of deaths is simply an actuarial statistic and does not by any means show a callous attitude toward human life, any more than does a similar study by your insurance company or by the manufacturer of the safest car money can buy. . . . One hundred and eighty deaths out of 12.5 million vehicles translates into the statistic that the gastank Ford was using increased your chance of death by one in seventy thousand over the safer alternative. . . . (Many people would bet their lives against eleven dollars at seventy thousand to one odds; you take a worse bet by far every time you ride without a seatbelt.)

. . . .

So, at any rate, goes the argument.

We should reject this argument for several reasons. The most important and obvious one is that the Pinto did not represent a safety-versus-price trade-off. It represented a blunder. Ford could have built Pintos with safer over-the-axle rather than puncturable behind-the-axle gastank mountings, but it did not, because it had tooled up too quickly. Its cost-benefit analyses did not, as a consequence, address the question of safety-versus-price; rather, they addressed the question of recall-versus-price, given the prior mistake.

. . . .

What the Rules Say

To begin our analysis of the corporate lawyer's problem, let us review the requirements of the ethical codes. First of all, it is important to realize that in their official formulations the rules of confidentiality may not cover the Pinto case. That is because the Pinto problem concerns preventive whistleblowing, and even in its most stringent formulations, confidentiality is absolute only regarding past events. Thus, the ABA . . . Model Rules allow a lawyer to reveal information relating to the representation of a client "to prevent the client from committing a criminal act that the lawyer believes is likely to result in imminent death or substantial bodily harm . . . ."

One might wonder whether the purely statistical risk to Ford owners would allow preventive whistleblowing under these last rules. The answer, I believe, is "yes."

None of these rules, I believe, is perfect.

NOTES

Since Professor Luban wrote his book, the rules have changed more than once. As we shall shortly see, they have moved closer to Luban's morality-based position, though they are not yet there. Note Luban's reference to Ford's efforts to postpone new car safety regulations. In Problem 2, we saw references to Lloyd Cutler's efforts to postpone other car safety regulations. Clearly, putting off safety requirements had a material beneficial economic effect for automakers.

Luban clearly believes that lawyers should be held morally accountable. That is particularly relevant here, as Ernesto Valencia struggles to determine his appropriate course of conduct. Is the moral imperative sufficient to cause Valencia to act? Do you agree with Luban that there is also an *ethical* imperative, at least in the case of the Pinto's flaming gas tanks? Or is his claim that whistleblowing is *ethically* required colored by his belief that it is *morally* required?

Professor Luban himself acknowledges that evaluating the "price range" for life is not an evil thing so much as it is routine, something that governmental agencies do on an almost daily basis. How do "price of life" evaluations affect a lawyer's decision on whether to blow the whistle? Luban says that it is not the price of lives lost in the Pinto case that created the ethical mandate to disclose, but the fact that the lives were being lost because of Ford's "blunder."[2] Do you agree that this trumps the value-of-life analysis?

If you agree there is an ethical imperative, when does that imperative operate? Is it enough to be reasonably certain about ensuing death or great bodily injury? Or must there be no doubt? And how imminent must the harm be? Where does the Venezia fit under both moral standards and under the old and new (post-2003) ABA rules?

2.   Roger Tuttle's *Mea Culpa*

In his 1985 book about A. H. Robins and their lawyers,[3] Morton Mintz describes the trials of Roger Tuttle. In the 1970s Tuttle served as a Robins in-house lawyer; by 1984 he was a law professor in Oklahoma when he testified in deposition about the role of Robins' general counsel's office a decade earlier. In his testimony, Tuttle admitted that early in 1975, as lawsuits over Robins' defective Dalkon Shield mounted and government scrutiny increased, he was told by his boss, General Counsel and corporate vice president William A. Forrest, to oversee the destruction of "troublesome" Shield documents — those that pointed to the dangers of the Dalkon Shield and to Robins' early knowledge of those dangers.

At the time, Tuttle not only said nothing, but had the destruction carried out. As a "sop to my conscience," he ordered his subordinates to do the job, using the same forced-air furnace Robins used to burn contaminated drugs to destroy hundreds of documents.[4] Had these documents become public, tens of thousands of women with Shields still implanted would have learned of their danger and been able to remove them before further damage was done. And, of course, sue Robins. A decade later at his deposition, Tuttle was asked by the plaintiffs' lawyers about these women, and what if anything was done to warn them. Nothing, he admitted, nor was anything disclosed to the FDA.

Tuttle clearly recognized the gravity of his failure to speak out. He testified that he was well aware of the implications of the documents as evidence, and acknowledged that destroying them was both legally and morally wrong. Tuttle also admitted that he "personally lacked the courage to throw down the gauntlet," knowing that his job was at stake. "[W]ith a wife and two young children, I'll have to confess to you that I lacked the courage to do then what I know today was the right thing."

---

[2] The Pinto defect is not all that unusual. Some of the more recent examples of products that were "blunders" appear in Problem 22.

[3] AT ANY COST: CORPORATE GREED, WOMEN AND THE DALKON SHIELD (Pantheon 1985).

[4] Forrest and those acting under Tuttle's direction all denied Tuttle's charges.

Tuttle didn't forsake his morals entirely. Instead of destroying everything he was asked to, he selected the "most damaging of the documents" and saved copies, hiding them in the basement of his home. He turned these over at the time of his deposition. A few months later, all of the Minnesota Dalkon Shield cases were settled, in no small measure due to the information he provided.

3.   Sea Change, Part One — Sarbanes-Oxley and the SEC

The rules affecting Ernesto Valencia and his fellow in-house counsel — and, in many respects, outside counsel as well — changed substantially in the new millennium. First came the Sarbanes-Oxley Act, then the passage of SEC ethics rules, then the completion of the two-step modification to ABA Model Rules 1.6 and 1.13. We will look at each in turn, starting with an article about another financial implosion — Global Crossing — and the passage of Sarbanes-Oxley, followed by our Notes describing the SEC rules.

Michelle Cottle, *Why No One Blames The Lawyers*
NEW REPUBLIC, October 14, 2002[5]

By late last summer Roy Olofson, then the vice president of finance for Global Crossing, was convinced something was rotten with the company's books. Hit hard by the deflating telecom bubble, Global Crossing, Olofson suspected, had begun using a range of accounting tricks to artificially inflate its revenue statements. So on August 6, 2001, he sent a five-page letter to the corporation's general counsel, James Gorton, outlining his concern that company shareholders and bankers, as well as the Securities and Exchange Commission (SEC), had been intentionally misled about the organization's financial health.

Faced with Olofson's accusations, Gorton asked Global Crossing's outside counsel, the New York law firm of Simpson Thacher & Bartlett, to launch an independent inquiry. After conducting a round of interviews and reviewing company documents, the firm reported its findings back to Gorton. On February 4, 2002, Global Crossing issued an official statement asserting that after "consultation with outside counsel," management was confident that the company's accounting methods had been appropriate and that it had made adequate disclosure both to the public and to the SEC. The "allegations made by Mr. Olofson were without merit."

Today, of course, it seems clear that the folks at Simpson Thacher missed a few details. Global Crossing is under investigation by both the SEC and the U.S. Attorney's office in Los Angeles for possible accounting and disclosure improprieties. The New York attorney general is scrutinizing the company's relationships . . . while the Labor Department examines its employee stock policies. Some four dozen class-action suits alleging violations of securities law have been filed . . . . This week both Gorton, who left the firm early this year, and Chairman Gary Winnick appeared before a House Energy and Commerce subcommittee to discuss — among other things — the contents of Olofson's letter. Meanwhile [Global] filed for the fourth-largest bankruptcy in history. . . .

What about all that "consultation with outside counsel"? Apparently, Simpson Thacher's review followed the see-no-evil model that Vinson & Elkins made famous in its review of Enron . . . . The Simpson Thacher team not only failed to contact Global Crossing's board of directors and its outside auditor, the now-defunct Arthur Andersen, it didn't even interview Olofson. Rather, attorneys relied largely on information provided by a handful of company executives, many of whom may have been involved in — or knowingly benefited from — the schemes in question. . . .

But as subpoenas are issued, briefs filed, and Global Crossing self-destructs in spectacular Enron style, it's business as usual at Simpson Thacher. The firm faces no threat of legal action from the government or the public. . . . This, despite the fact that . . . the cozy relationship between Global Crossing and Simpson Thacher may well have inclined the law firm to conduct a less-than-strenuous inquiry. In addition to the millions in legal fees . . . , a number of Simpson Thacher attorneys owned stock in the telecom company. . . .

Simpson Thacher shouldn't get off that easily — nor should the legal profession as a whole. When accused of professional misconduct, lawyers often argue that their code of ethics — with its emphasis on protecting the client — actually requires them to dispense cutting-edge (read: questionable) legal advice and to overlook a client's suspicious behavior . . . . Many legal ethicists, however, say such arguments intentionally misinterpret certain aspects of the rules governing lawyers . . . . Members of the bar have periodically tried to increase lawyers' public accountability by loosening these attorney-client privilege rules. But a vocal opposition has successfully countered with ominous scenarios about what would result: Clients will no longer be honest with their attorneys, attorneys will be afraid to launch zealous defenses of their clients, and our entire legal system will come tumbling down . . . .

Reform-minded lawyers, however, point to a number of flaws in these apocalyptic claims. For starters, says Jonathan Macey, a professor at Cornell University Law School, one of the most pervasive problems in corporate law is that lawyers forget who "the client" is. "The lawyer's true ethical responsibility is to the corporation, not the individual officer who hires him," says Macey . . . .

The new wave of corporate scandals has again spotlighted the need for change. In March, [Illinois law Professor Richard] Painter drafted a letter to SEC Commissioner Harvey Pitt — signed by 40 reform-minded law professors — recommending that the commission enforce tougher ethics standards for lawyers. Three weeks later Painter received a polite rebuff from SEC general counsel David Becker, suggesting that the professor take the matter up with Congress. So Painter did just that, sending his recommendations to Senator John Edwards, who used them as the basis for an amendment to the Sarbanes-Oxley corporate-accountability act, which President Bush signed on July 30. The amendment directs the SEC to establish rules of conduct for all lawyers doing business with the commission. These rules must, among other things, require lawyers to report "evidence of material violation of securities law or breach of fiduciary duty" to a client company's general counsel or CEO. If the CEO or counsel fails to respond adequately, the lawyer must proceed up the chain of command to the audit committee or even the full board of directors.

Reformers say Sarbanes-Oxley should be uncontroversial since it allows lawyers to keep even the dirtiest of client secrets in the family. "It's really rather tame," says Stephen Gillers, vice dean and professor of legal ethics at New York University. "It does not mandate reporting outside, and so in no way compromises confidentiality or privilege." Nonetheless, the American Bar Association (ABA), which has repeatedly beaten back efforts at external oversight, lobbied hard against the amendment.

. . . .

Sarbanes-Oxley may not be enough. An even hotter topic under debate is a lawyer's right (and responsibility) to report a client's misdeeds to outside parties such as the SEC. Currently, the ABA's Model Rules . . . allow lawyers to breach confidentiality only when failure to do so is likely to result in imminent death or substantial bodily harm. Not long ago the ABA's Ethics 2000 committee recommended expanding this exemption to include preventing a client from "using the lawyer's services to commit a crime or fraud." The change was rejected . . . .

Stunned by the passage of Sarbanes-Oxley and desperate to head off further government meddling, the ABA has pledged to revisit the confidentiality issue at its February [2003] meeting.

. . . .

Some observers believe that by refusing to seriously address ethics reform until this latest series of scandals . . . , the legal profession has outsmarted itself. For years lawyers, like accountants, have done as they please, assuming they would always remain totally self-regulating, says [Columbia law Professor John] Coffee. "Both professions have behaved much like French aristocrats one year before the revolution. . . . And now it's gonna cost both of them."

NOTES

Section 307 of the Sarbanes-Oxley Act, passed in July 2002, mandated that the Securities & Exchange Commission promulgate "minimum standards of professional conduct for attorneys appearing and practicing before the Commission in . . . the representation of public companies."

On January 29, 2003, the SEC complied, adopting much of § 307's language. The SEC required that an attorney representing a client (or "issuer") must report up the ladder to the chief legal officer or chief executive officer of the company when the lawyer "becomes aware" of "evidence of a material violation of securities law or breach of fiduciary duty or similar violation" by the company or any of its agents. If the general counsel or CEO does not respond "appropriately" to the evidence, the attorney must report it to an independent audit committee or to the company's full board of directors.

The SEC rules also require the general counsel or chief legal officer to conduct a reasonable inquiry once the matter has been reported to that individual. The general counsel must then notify the reporting attorney of the results of the inquiry, and, unless s/he believes that no material violation is involved, take reasonable steps to ensure that the client takes appropriate remedial measures and makes appropriate disclosures. (The SEC rules also clarified — as if there were any doubt — that lawyers represent the entity rather than the officers or other corporate constituents, and that attorneys must therefore act in the best interests of the entity.)

Disclosures under this rule, of course, would involve the company "going public," but the SEC rules currently do not independently require that either the reporting lawyer or the GC do more than perform their duties to make and take all reasonable reporting steps *within* the company. But when the SEC promulgated its rules in early 2003, it also drafted a proposed rule that would require that if internal reporting was insufficient, the lawyers would have to withdraw and notify the SEC. It is here that the next battle may be fought.

What about Global Crossing? The company went bankrupt, but went more quietly than its Houston neighbor, Enron, without indictments or much fanfare.[6]

4. Sea Change, Part Two — The ABA Model Rules

As the last article mentions, the ABA House of Delegates had a pitched battle over the exceptions to confidentiality relating to financial fraud. In 2002, although those changes failed, the ABA did modify and simplify the "death or substantial bodily harm" exception to Model Rule 1.6 with relatively little controversy. As we discussed in Problems 4 and 5, these changes focused the issue on *harm* rather than behavior. Thus, if "slow-harm" dangers like toxic pollutants in the groundwater table are as dangerous as deadly car defects or even ex-spouses armed for revenge, they are also disclosable. And the new rule no longer requires that the client be the actor at all, only that the harm be "reasonably certain." The American Law Institute approved similar changes in its Restatement of the Law Governing Lawyers.

As for the financial fraud changes, the battle was renewed in the summer of 2003, as this article describes.

Patricia Manson, *Lawyer-Ethics Code Undergoes Sea Change*
CHICAGO DAILY LAW BULLETIN, August 12, 2003[7]

Reversing course, American Bar Association delegates have approved an ethics rule allowing lawyers to blow the whistle on a client who has made the lawyer an unwitting pawn in a financial scheme.

The policy-making House of Delegates had rejected an identical proposal to amend Rule 1.6 at the ABA's 2001 annual meeting.

But citing the accounting scandals and corporate meltdowns that have occurred since then, proponents pushed the measure at the current annual meeting — and on Monday they won.

And on Tuesday, proponents also successfully urged delegates to amend Rule 1.13 to allow attorneys — either in-house counsel or outside lawyers — to reveal

---

[6] For those wanting to read about Global's demise and an argument about why Global didn't suffer the same fate as Enron, read Timothy L. O'Brien, *A New Legal Chapter for a 90s Flameout*, N.Y. TIMES, August 15, 2004.

[7] Copyright © 2013 by Law Bulletin Publishing Company. Reprinted by permission.

confidential information in some circumstances if a corporate client refuses to address a violation of law . . . .

Peter F. Langrock of Middlebury, Vt., said a lawyer should not be forced to stand by and do nothing when an erring client manipulates the lawyer to inflict harm on others. "I didn't go to law school, I didn't spend 43 years practicing law, to have a client make use of my services to perpetrate a fraud on a widow who's trying to save money toward her daughter's education," Langrock said.

But opponents took a different view of the proposed changes to Rule 1.6. Former ABA president William G. Paul of Oklahoma City argued that the rule "asks us to barter away a piece of our professional soul" by breaching the obligation to maintain the confidentiality of communications with clients.

. . . .

In a 218-201 vote, delegates amended Rule 1.6 to allow lawyers to reveal confidences in order to block a client from using the lawyer's services in a financial fraud or crime.

Delegates also amended Rule 1.6 to permit lawyers to disclose confidences in a bid to repair any substantial harm that the client's wrongful acts have inflicted . . . . Tuesday, delegates came back to amend Rule 1.13 to require attorneys who represent corporations or other organizations to report to authorities within the client the unlawful conduct of an officer or employee.

Delegates also modified Rule 1.13 to allow an attorney to go outside the organization with confidential information if the organization's authorities fail to act in the face of a violation of the law.

Attorneys may reveal such information only if they reasonably believe that the move is necessary to prevent substantial harm to the client.

NOTES

Of course, only individual states will determine what the disciplinary rules will be. How many of the ABA reforms to either Rule 1.6 or Rule 1.13 are adopted by the states is an evolving process, though several states had acted before the ABA, and many others have since. States continue to have wide differences about permissive vs. mandatory disclosure. Thus, the broad exceptions to confidentiality in New Jersey, for example, have only passing resemblance to the narrow exceptions in California.[8]

The "up-the-ladder" requirements of Sarbanes-Oxley and the SEC, the possibility — discussed by many "SOX" commentators — that the application of those requirements may be broadened to include a much wider range of entities than publicly-traded corporations, and the possibility of going outside the

---

[8] The ABA and the Bureau of National Affairs publish the ABA/BNA Lawyers' Manual On Professional Conduct, which presents an annual survey "keeping score" on various rules changes, including this one. It can be accessed through WestLaw or Lexis with the title "*MOPC 1 — Model Standards — State Ethics Rules — Variations*."

corporation raised by both federal law and the 2003 version of Model Rule 1.13, are areas in-house counsel must research carefully before deciding what to do. Note that MR 1.13 refers to protecting the *client*, not the public. Regardless of the results of research, of course, lawyers will always be confronted by the moral issues Professor Luban raises.

5. Can Corporate Criminal Guidelines Foster Ethical Conduct?

Before the SOX-SEC transformation and the new Ethics 2000 ABA Rules, there were the corporate criminal sentencing guidelines. These guidelines, which date from the early 1990s, offer a series of challenges to in-house and outside counsel, and continue to be important today, as we will see in section 8 below. The following article relates to the corporate sentencing guidelines as they were created, and the impact that they had on corporate behavior. After this piece, we'll examine how the guidelines were most recently changed, effective November 1, 2010.

Joseph J. Fleischman, William J. Heller & Mitchell A. Schley, *The Organizational Sentencing Guidelines and the Employment At-Will Rule as Applied to In-House Counsel* 48 Bus. Law. 611 (1993)[9]

The Organizational Sentencing Guidelines (Guidelines) place new and serious professional obligations on in-house counsel. Both in-house and outside counsel may face professional disciplinary proceedings, and, in extreme circumstances, civil and criminal liability, if they do not withdraw from the lawyer-client relationship and report continuing corporate wrong-doing to prosecuting authorities, even if the report may involve information protected by the attorney-client privilege. These external pressures often conflict with the lawyer's paramount duties of loyalty and confidentiality to the client.

. . . .

The Guidelines determine an organization's penalty for violating federal-criminal law. Under the Guidelines, the sentencing judge performs an eight-step analysis to determine the amount of the mandatory fine. Each organization begins with a "base" fine which can range from $5,000 to $72.5 million, and a culpability score of five points, which can be increased or decreased depending on several factors. This culpability score is applied as a multiplier against the base fine, and it can have a significant impact upon the amount of the ultimate penalty levied against the corporation. The culpability score is a function of aggravating factors, which increase the score, and mitigating factors, which decrease the score.

Points are added — and penalties are increased under the Guidelines — for:

1. willful ignorance or condoning behavior by "high level" personnel or pervasive intolerance by "substantial authority" personnel;

---

[9] Copyright © 1993. Reprinted by permission of the authors.

2. prior criminal or civil adjudications based on similar conduct;

3. violations of an injunction or judicial order; and

4. willful obstruction or knowing failure to prevent the crime.

Points are subtracted — and penalties are mitigated under the Guidelines — for:

1. the existence of an "effective" compliance program to prevent and detect violations of law;

2. self-reporting promptly after becoming aware of the violation and prior to government investigation;

3. organizational cooperation; and

4. acceptance of responsibility. . . .

The Guidelines offer significant reductions in fines when the organization implements an effective compliance program . . . .

Frequently, and understandably, the burden of implementing a compliance program falls to counsel, especially in-house counsel. They also have responsibilities under the rules of professional conduct, such as the duty to maintain a client's confidences. Indeed, they may jeopardize their licenses to practice law for failure to comply with these ethical rules, which may conflict with the Guidelines' disclosure and other requirements.

. . . .

With the advent of the Guidelines, in-house counsel, to whom most corporations turn for legal compliance, now have a reinforced duty to detect wrongdoing and to disclose it to the entity, and possibly to prosecuting authorities. Yet, the very act of enforcing compliance or disclosing wrongdoing may lead to a sharp conflict between in-house lawyers and their supervisors.

NOTES

After a number of years of debate, in April 2010, the United States Sentencing Commission finalized revisions to the corporate sentencing guidelines, which became effective that November. By then, most larger corporations had set up compliance protocols in reaction to the sentencing guidelines. The 2010 guideline revisions allowed more flexibility in sentencing, permitting as many as three "downward departure" levels in sentencing if the compliance program maintained by the corporation was sufficiently effective. However, the amendments also spelled out in clear terms what the requirements for such "sentencing breaks" entailed, among other things: the chief compliance officer must report directly to the board of directors with "express authority to communicate personally" with the board; the corporation must detect its own malfeasance *and* report it before it is detected externally; and after the malfeasance is discovered, the corporation must provide restitution to those harmed, report to and cooperate with the federal government, and assess and if necessary change its current compliance program, preferably with independent outside assistance.

6. Roger Balla's Stand

As the title of the last article indicates, the authors include a rather lengthy discussion of the availability of employment law remedies to in-house counsel who feel compelled to blow the whistle on their employers. Corporations have defended against retaliatory discharge and similar allegations brought by whistleblowing lawyers by arguing that such claims, necessarily based on communications between counsel and client, are barred by the attorney-client privilege and the confidential relationship. Read what happened to one in-house counsel who, under the affirmative reporting language of Illinois' version of MR 1.6 had a duty, rather than a mere option, to report his client's wrongdoing.

BALLA v. GAMBRO, INC.
584 N.E.2d 104 (Ill. 1991)

The issue in this case is whether in-house counsel should be allowed the remedy of an action for retaliatory discharge. . . .

Gambro is a distributor of kidney dialysis equipment manufactured by Gambro Germany. Among the products distributed by Gambro are dialyzers which filter excess fluid and toxic substances from the blood of patients with no or impaired kidney function. The manufacture and sale of dialyzers is regulated by the United States Food and Drug Administration (FDA). . . .

Appellee, Roger J. Balla, is and was at all times throughout this controversy an attorney licensed to practice law in the State of Illinois. On March 17, 1980, appellee executed an employment agreement with Gambro which contained the terms of the appellee's employment. . . . [A]ppellee's specific responsibilities included, inter alia . . . compliance with applicable laws and regulations. . . .

In July 1985, Gambro Germany informed Gambro in a letter that certain dialyzers it had manufactured, the clearances of which varied from the package insert, were about to be shipped to Gambro. . . . Appellee told the president of Gambro to reject the shipment because the dialyzers did not comply with FDC regulations. The president notified Gambro Germany of its decision to reject the shipment on July 12, 1985.

However, one week later the president informed Gambro Germany that Gambro would accept the dialyzers and "sell [them] to a unit that is not currently our customer but who buys only on price." Appellee contends that he was not informed by the president of the decision to accept the dialyzers but became aware of it through other Gambro employees. Appellee maintains that he spoke with the president in August regarding the company's decision to accept the dialyzers and told the president that he would do whatever was necessary to stop the sale of the dialyzers.

On September 4, 1985, appellee was discharged from Gambro's employment by its president. The following day, appellee reported the shipment of the dialyzers to the FDA. The FDA seized the shipment and determined the product to be "adulterated . . . ."

On March 19, 1986, appellee filed a four-count complaint in tort for retaliatory discharge seeking $22 million in damages.

. . . .

We agree with the trial court that appellee does not have a cause of action against Gambro for retaliatory discharge. . . . In this case it appears that Gambro discharged appellee, an employee of Gambro, in retaliation for his activities, and this discharge was in contravention of a clearly mandated public policy . . . . In appellee's eyes, the use of these dialyzers could cause death or serious bodily harm to patients. As we have stated before, "[t]here is no public policy more important or more fundamental than the one favoring the effective protection of the lives and property of citizens." However, in this case, appellee was not just an employee of Gambro, but also general counsel for Gambro.

In his brief to this court, appellee argues that not extending the tort of retaliatory discharge to in-house counsel would present attorneys with a "Hobson's choice." According to appellee, in-house counsel would face two alternatives: either comply with the client/employer's wishes and risk both the loss of a professional license and exposure to criminal sanctions, or decline to comply with the client/ employer's wishes and risk the loss of a full-time job and the attendant benefits. We disagree. . . . In-house counsel do not have a choice of whether to follow their ethical obligations as attorneys licensed to practice law, or follow the illegal and unethical demands of their clients. In-house counsel must abide by the Rules of Professional Conduct. Appellee had no choice but to report to the FDA.

. . . .

If extending the tort of retaliatory discharge might have a chilling effect on the communications between the employer/client and the in-house counsel, we believe that it is more wise to refrain from doing so.

Our decision not to extend the tort of retaliatory discharge to in-house counsel also is based on other ethical considerations. Under the Rules of Professional Conduct, appellee was required to withdraw from representing Gambro if continued representation would result in the violation of the Rules of Professional Conduct. . . . [A]ccording to appellee's claims herein, his continued representation of Gambro would have resulted in a violation of the Rules of Professional Conduct. Appellee argues that such a choice of withdrawal is "simplistic and uncompassion- ate, and is completely at odds with contemporary realities facing in-house attor- neys." These contemporary realities apparently are the economic ramifications of losing his position as in-house counsel. However difficult, economically and perhaps emotionally, it is for in-house counsel to discontinue representing an employer/ client, we refuse to allow in-house counsel to sue their employer/client for damages because they obeyed their ethical obligations.

JUSTICE FREEMAN, dissenting:

I respectfully dissent from the decision of my colleagues. In concluding that the plaintiff attorney, serving as corporate in-house counsel, should not be allowed a claim for retaliatory discharge, the majority first reasons that the public policy implicated in this case, i.e., protecting the lives and property of Illinois citizens, is adequately safeguarded by the lawyer's ethical obligation to reveal information about a client as necessary to prevent acts that would result in death or serious bodily harm. I find this reasoning fatally flawed.

The majority so reasons because, as a matter of law, an attorney cannot even contemplate ignoring his ethical obligations in favor of continuing in his employment. I agree with this conclusion "as a matter of law." However, to say that the categorical nature of ethical obligations is sufficient to ensure that the ethical obligations will be satisfied simply ignores reality. Specifically, it ignores that, as unfortunate for society as it may be, attorneys are no less human than nonattorneys and, thus, no less given to the temptation to either ignore or rationalize away their ethical obligations when complying therewith may render them unable to feed and support their families.

I would like to believe, as my colleagues apparently conclude, that attorneys will always "do the right thing" because the law says that they must. However, my knowledge of human nature, [is] more than sufficient to dispel such a belief.

. . . .

. . . [T]his court must take whatever steps it can, within the bounds of the law, to give lawyers incentives to abide by their ethical obligations, beyond the satisfaction inherent in their doing so. We cannot continue to delude ourselves and the people of the State of Illinois that attorneys' ethical duties, alone, are always sufficient to guarantee that lawyers will "do the right thing." In the context of this case, where doing "the right thing" will often result in termination by an employer bent on doing the "wrong thing," I believe that the incentive needed is recognition of a cause of action for retaliatory discharge.

NOTES

Who do you think is right in *Balla* about the "contemporary realities" of how general counsel will behave, the majority or the dissent? Recall that even "good" lawyers like Roger Tuttle don't always act ethically with their jobs on the line.

Note that Illinois' affirmative duty to report, rather than working in Roger Balla's favor, seemed to hurt his case. Do you think the court would have upheld his ability to sue if Illinois only had a permissive disclosure rule? It is interesting that *Balla* does not bar Balla's claim because it would necessarily violate the attorney-client privilege. To the contrary, it seems to *require* the lawyer to disclose.

7.   Whither Protection for In-House Whistleblowers?

The case law regarding in-house counsel suing an employer for retaliatory discharge is now rather extensive, though the effect of Sarbanes-Oxley and the SEC rules has not yet significantly impacted these cases. We review that case law here.

Balla was one of the first reported cases, although, not the first Illinois case. *Herbster v. North Am. Co. For Life & Health Insurance*, 501 N.E.2d 343 (Ill. App. Ct. 1986), cited with approval in *Balla*, barred a suit by in-house counsel who refused to do what Roger Tuttle did — destroy documents that showed his company's fraud. *Balla'* s approval of *Herbster* is odd in light of *Herbster*'s different approach towards a lawyer's duties. Citing *Upjohn*, *Herbster* emphasized that "confidential communications related by a client remain inviolate by the attorney both during the attorney-client relationship and after it has been terminated." *Herbster*'s somewhat oblique holding criticized both sides for "focus[ing] on the privilege aspect of the relationship only. We find that all aspects are so necessary to our system of jurisprudence that extending this tort to the attorney-client relationship here is not justified." And what are these aspects? "The mutual trust, exchanges of confidence, reliance on judgment, and personal nature of the attorney-client relationship [that] demonstrate the unique position attorneys occupy in our society."

In another 1991 case the court in *Mourad v. Automobile Club Insurance Ass'n*, 465 N.W.2d 395 (Mich. Ct. App. 1991), concluded that in-house counsel who had refused to let his non-attorney employees supervise lawyers had a *contract* cause of action for wrongful discharge, based on an implied understanding that the lawyer was bound by ethical rules, and could not be terminated without just cause if expected to act outside those rules.

While *Mourad* was limited to contract claims, in the years since courts have begun to recognize causes of action for retaliatory discharge. In 1994, the California Supreme Court in *General Dynamics Corp. v. Superior Court*, 876 P.2d 487 (Cal. 1994), agreed that a "just cause" contract action applied and upheld a retaliatory discharge *tort* claim based on in-house counsel Andrew Rose's assertion that he was discharged because of the advice he had given to his corporate employer about the company's required course of conduct. Soon after, a Massachusetts court, in *GTE Products Corp. v. Stewart*, 653 N.E.2d 161 (Mass. 1995), cited *General Dynamics*, and also recognized a retaliatory discharge tort.

But these two cases give only modest comfort to in-house counsel who feels an ethical compulsion to speak out. While *General Dynamics* allowed counsel's remedies against a former employer, it permitted a tort cause of action only where "it can be established without breaching the attorney-client privilege or unduly endangering the values lying at the heart of the professional relationship." Where did this leave matters? California then had a strict confidentiality rule, ostensibly with no exceptions, so establishing a case without violating confidences would be a daunting task. But the court's opinion completely dodged this question, focusing instead on the narrower privilege: "[M]any of the cases in which house counsel is faced with an ethical dilemma will lie outside the scope of the statutory privilege," such as the crime fraud exception, or where "disclosure is necessary to prevent the commission of a criminal act likely to result in death or substantial bodily harm . . . ."

In *Stewart*, plaintiff house counsel fared less well. First, the *Stewart* court required that "the claim can be proved without any violation of the attorney's obligation to respect client confidences and secrets," a far broader prohibition than abrogating only the privilege. Indeed, *Stewart* noted that exceptions to confidentiality "are extremely limited." Then, stating that Stewart did not show "that remaining in his position would have required him to violate his ethical obligations as an attorney," or that, despite a poor performance review soon after he urged the company to comply with federal hazardous waste requirements, he had made a *prima facie* showing, the court granted summary judgment against him. Similarly, in *Willy v. Coastal States Management Co.*, 939 S.W.2d 193 (Tex. App. 1996), a case that had bounced around the Texas courts for so long that a 1986 version had been cited in *Balla*, the court allowed a retaliatory discharge tort at least in theory, then created the same Catch-22 for former in-house counsel Willy, saying he could not prove his claim without resorting to forbidden client confidences.

A more permissive interpretation of wrongful discharge suits (and in this particular case a sex discrimination claim) is *Kachmar v. Sungard Data Systems, Inc.*, 109 F.3d 173 (3d Cir. 1997), in which a Sungard subsidiary's allegedly discriminatory policies towards women were challenged by in-house counsel Lillian Kachmar, who was eventually fired. Not only did the court allow her causes of action to go forward, but the court wrote: "We do not suggest that concerns about the disclosure of client confidences in suits by in-house counsel are unfounded, but these concerns alone would not warrant dismissing a plaintiff's case, especially where there are other means to prevent unwarranted disclosure of confidential information." The court then cited *General Dynamics*' suggestions of protective orders, limited admissibility of evidence, and *in camera* hearings. *Kachmar* is particularly interesting because the nature of the company's violation did *not* involve potential harm to the public at all, nor did Kachmar have to refuse to act in an unethical manner.

But the Fifth Circuit came to a very different conclusion in *Douglas v. DynMcDermott Petroleum Operations Co.*, 144 F.3d 364 (5th Cir. 1998), where corporate in-house counsel complained first in-house and then to the EEOC about job discrimination, was fired, and won a substantial trial court judgment for sex and race discrimination. The opinion overturned that award and called Douglas' revelation of attorney-client confidences a violation of her ethical obligations.

Thus far, two cases, one from Montana's Supreme Court and a second from Tennessee's, stand as notable exceptions to both the *Balla* and *General Dynamics* rules. *Burkhart v. Semitool, Inc.*, 5 P.3d 1031 (Mont. 2000), held that "in-house counsel may maintain an action for employment related claims against an employer-client, and that such claims are within the contemplation of Rule 1.6 of the Montana Rules of Professional Conduct, which permits an attorney to reveal confidential attorney-client information to establish a claim in a controversy between the lawyer and the client."

Two years later came *Crews v. Buckman Laboratories International, Inc*, which evaluated *Balla*, *General Dynamics*, and *Burkhart*, and came to its own inventive conclusion. We provide this brief excerpt of this case, which concerned a deputy in-house counsel who blew the whistle on her boss, the general counsel, because the GC did not have a license to practice law in Tennessee.

CREWS v. BUCKMAN LABORATORIES
INTERNATIONAL, INC.
78 S.W.3d 852 (Tenn. 2002)

[T]his case does not present the typical retaliatory discharge claim. Consequently, while the special relationship between a lawyer and a client does not categorically prohibit in-house counsel from bringing a retaliatory discharge action, other courts have held that it necessarily shapes the contours of the action when the plaintiff was employed as in-house counsel [*citing General Dynamics* and *Stewart.*] Indeed, the California Supreme Court went so far as to forewarn lawyers that those who revealed confidential information in a retaliatory discharge suit, without a basis for doing so under the ethics rules, would be subject to disciplinary proceedings.

. . . .

If we perceive any shortcomings in the holdings of *General Dynamics* and *Stewart,* it is that they largely take away with one hand what they appear to give with the other. Although the courts in these cases gave in-house counsel an important right of action, their respective admonitions about preserving client confidentiality appear to stop just short of halting most of these actions at the courthouse door. With little imagination, one could envision cases involving important issues of public concern being denied relief merely because the wrongdoer is protected by the lawyer's duty of confidentiality . . . .

Model Rule 1.6(b)(2) permits a lawyer to reveal "information relating to the representation of a client" when the lawyer reasonably believes such information is necessary "to establish *a claim or defense* on behalf of the lawyer in a controversy between the lawyer and the client. . . ." (emphasis added). Although some commentators have asserted that this provision merely permits lawyers to use confidential information in fee-collection disputes as under the Model Code, the plain language of the Model Rule is clearly more broad than these authorities would presume.

We agree with the approach taken by the Model Rules, and pursuant to our inherent authority to regulate and govern the practice of law in this state, we hereby expressly adopt a new provision in Disciplinary Rule 4–101(C) to permit in-house counsel to reveal the confidences and secrets of a client when the lawyer reasonably believes that such information is necessary to establish a claim or defense on behalf of the lawyer in a controversy between the lawyer and the client. This exception parallels the language of Model Rule of Professional Conduct 1.6(b)(2), and we perceive the adoption of a similar standard to be essential in protecting the ability of in-house counsel to effectively assert an action for discharge in violation of public policy.

In summary, we hold that in-house counsel may bring a common-law action of retaliatory discharge . . . . Furthermore, in accordance with an Order [changing the ethics rule] filed simultaneously with the judgment and opinion in this case, we hold that a lawyer may ethically disclose the employer's confidences or secrets when the lawyer reasonably believes that such information is necessary to establish a claim against the employer. However, the lawyer must make every effort practicable to avoid unnecessary disclosure of the employer's confidences and secrets; to limit disclosure to those having the need to know the information; and to obtain protective orders or make other arrangements minimizing the risk of unnecessary disclosure.

NOTES

What about recourse for in-house counsel under the whistleblower protection statutes that exist in most states? So far, these have generally not been applied to lawyers, at least those in private employment.[10] One notable exception is New Jersey, which has long had a narrower view of attorney-client confidentiality than most venues. In *Parker v. M & T Chemicals, Inc.*, 566 A.2d 215 (N.J. Super. Ct. 1989), in-house attorney Sheldon Parker was demoted when he refused to participate in receiving deposition transcripts from a competitor's case that were subject to a protective order.

Pointing out that "the commission of a crime or fraud is excepted from the attorney-client privilege," the court had little difficulty in holding the whistleblower statute applicable to lawyers: "[I]t reinforces the Court's constitutional mission to encourage and insure the ethical practice of law. We see no constitutional incompatibility and will not read in-house attorneys out of the Act's protection." As for confidentiality (as opposed to the privilege), the court said: "The employer-client is still free to file an ethics complaint against the former employee-attorney . . . . The attorney is still subject to the same discipline as before the adoption of the [Whistleblower] Act."

Despite the fact that *Parker* was decided in 1989, few courts have since evaluated the question of whether state whistleblower act protection should be afforded in-house lawyers.[11] The whistleblower provisions of Sarbanes-Oxley may turn out to be a more fruitful area for redress, if lawyers can argue that their retaliatory discharge was due to the lawyers abiding by their SOX reporting mandates.[12]

It is of more than passing interest that of all these cases, only *Balla* and *Douglas* actually involved an in-house lawyer who went *outside* the company to blow the whistle. And in *Balla*, that occurred only *after* Balla had been fired. Thus, in almost every reported case, termination came about not as a result of public disclosure of the company's practice, but rather, *private, internal* pressure on the part of in-house counsel to get the company to do the right thing.

One lawyer who did go outside the company was Dimitrios Biller, in-house counsel for Toyota USA, who showed that whistleblowers have to be extremely careful when reporting outside the corporation. Biller left Toyota in 2007, claiming

---

[10] Recall our discussion of public attorneys' whistleblowing in Problem 24.

[11] One court that did was the Minnesota Supreme Court in *Kidwell v. Sybaritic, Inc.*, 784 N.W.2d 220 (Minn. 2010) *With a rather complicated set of facts and a plurality opinion, the court* held that while the Minnesota whistleblower statute *might* apply to in-house counsel, it did not apply to Kidwell. A three-justice minority argued that the statute *should* apply because the law whistleblower statute did not exclude attorneys, and public policy weighed heavily in Kidwell's favor.

[12] *See, e.g., Van Asdale v. Intern'l Game Technology*, 577 F.3d 989 (9th Cir. 2009).

he was forced to resign after he confronted company higher-ups with what he said was Toyota's "conspiracy to conceal, withhold and destroy evidence." When he left, he took 6,000 pages of documents with him, and sued Toyota. Toyota eventually settled with Biller for a $3.7 million severance package, but themselves sued Biller for violations of attorney-client confidentiality and privilege. In 2012, Toyota's $2.6 million arbitration award against Biller was affirmed by the Ninth Circuit.[13] The lesson? If you decide to "walk the righteous road," walk very carefully.

8. Whither (Wither?) the Corporate Attorney-Client Privilege? Part One — Prosecutorial Pressure

Note the "modern" use of the corporate sentencing guidelines to extract privilege waivers, as discussed in this next article.

David B. Fein & Robert S. Huie, *Attacks on Client Privilege Increasing: Government Insistence on Waiver Jeopardizes Values of Corporate Privilege*
CONNECTICUT LAW TRIBUNE, June 23, 2003[14]

Federal prosecutors increasingly demand waiver of attorney-client privilege and work product protection at the inception of investigations. As described by Deputy Attorney General Larry Thompson in his January 2003 memorandum, entitled "Principles of Federal Prosecution of Business Organizations," waiver is not "an absolute requirement," but prosecutors should consider willingness to waive "as one factor in evaluating the corporation's cooperation." . . . Pursuant to the 2003 revisions, prosecutors use willingness to cooperate as one of eight factors to determine whether to bring charges against a business organization.

Although prosecutors demand waiver more frequently, corporate privilege continues to serve an essential purpose. Attorney-client privilege and work product privilege protect communications between attorneys and their corporate clients. As the U.S. Supreme Court recognized 20 years ago in *Upjohn Co. v. United States*, corporate privilege is essential because it facilitates "communication of relevant information" between attorneys and clients. Such uninhibited dialogue enables companies to comply with applicable laws, because compliance with "the vast and complicated array of regulatory legislation confronting the modern corporation" is "hardly an instinctive matter." Without legal advice unfettered by the risk of disclosure, corporations may be less able to make informed decisions in accordance with the law. . . . Without assurances that communications will remain confidential, organizations may not only be hindered in their efforts to determine what laws apply and how to follow them, but may turn a blind eye to existing wrongdoing.

Federal prosecutors who aggressively pursue waiver show little regard for the importance of privilege. Prosecutors . . . not only decide whether to seek criminal

---

[13] Biller et al. v. Toyota Motor Sales USA et al., 668 F.3d 655 (9th Cir. 2012). For several articles about this case from the legal press, see the references in the Supplemental Readings.

[14] Copyright © 2013 by ALM Properties, LLC. Reprinted with permission from the June 23, 2003 Connecticut Law Tribune. All rights reserved. Further duplication without permission is prohibited.

charges, but they also determine what charges and sentences to seek. Since principles of corporate criminal liability are extremely broad, almost all acts of all employees may be imputed to the organization. . . . Given that authority, [p]rosecutors requesting waiver present corporations a difficult choice between seeking leniency and safeguarding privilege.

Tough Choices

. . . Government requests for corporate waiver often arise at the outset of an investigation, and almost certainly prior to any resolution of possible enforcement actions. On occasion, companies must decide whether to waive without even knowing what information they are ceding. In all these events, it is unlikely the company will know what benefits, if any, it will receive by virtue of its waiver.

In some situations, waiver may result in prosecution rather than leniency. Perhaps the most chilling example of this first problem is the 2002 indictment of Arthur Andersen. According to public reports, Andersen agreed to waive attorney-client privilege during the government investigation in an effort to cooperate and was rewarded with an indictment . . . . At Andersen's criminal trial, . . . once-privileged communications between Andersen employees and Andersen in-house counsel . . . formed the basis for the jury's conviction. . . .

Although the government's decision to charge Andersen led many experienced white-collar practitioners to question the value of a company waiving privilege, the pressure to waive still exists. Credit Suisse First Boston ("CSFB") recently decided to waive its attorney-client privilege, possibly out of fear of corporate prosecution . . . after [prosecutors] learn[ed] of a December 2000 e-mail message by CSFB star banker Frank Quattrone, regarding "time to clean up those files." . . . At the prosecutors' request, CSFB waived its attorney-client privilege with respect to some e-mail communications between Quattrone and CSFB's attorneys. A chain of e-mail messages between Quattrone and CSFB's then-general counsel surfaced, showing that, at the time Quattrone urged others to destroy documents, he had already been told of the government investigations of CSFB. Quattrone was subsequently indicted on obstruction of justice and witness tampering charges.

. . . .

Waiver essentially turns a corporation's lawyers into an investigative arm of the government. Some commentators have pointed out that this arrangement allows prosecutors to evade the Fifth Amendment: whereas employees might invoke their right against self-incrimination when questioned by the government, they are unable to assert it against their employer without the very real possibility of losing their jobs. As a result, employees who know that privilege has been or will be waived are understandably skittish about talking with the corporation's lawyers. . . .

Better Solutions?

. . . Ultimately, a policy change is called for to resolve the present dilemma. One solution is for the DOJ to reconsider, on a department-wide basis, the appropriateness of its requests for waiver of attorney-client privilege by organizations . . . .

A recent report by the SEC suggests a more feasible, albeit partial, solution. The Sarbanes-Oxley Act . . . directed the SEC to report findings to Congress [that] recommend amending the Securities Exchange Act of 1934 "to allow parties who choose to produce privileged or protected material to do so without fear that their production to the Commission will be deemed to waive privilege or protection as to anyone else." . . . Whether Congress will act on this recommendation remains to be seen.

NOTES

We note that with respect to the Fifth Amendment, unlike individuals, corporations have no such privilege.

It is of more than passing interest that both Arthur Andersen, the entity and Frank Quattrone, the individual had their convictions set aside by appeals courts. These events, especially the Andersen reversal, in light of the reality of Andersen's demise, have made prosecutors a bit more guarded about pressing too hard for privilege waivers lest they force other entities out of business without ultimately getting a conviction.

Criticism of federal prosecutors demanding waivers has been fairly constant, including since the 2010 sentencing guidelines amendments. In 2011, a Wall Street Journal blog complained that "the federal government isn't giving companies adequate credit for compliance programs. That's because companies and prosecutors are steering them out of the traditional criminal justice process, in deferred prosecution agreements and non-prosecution agreements." Thus, "there is little hard evidence that companies are receiving the promised consideration for their compliance programs, since judges are largely absent from the process."[15]

Meanwhile, the Department of Justice in both the Bush and Obama administrations has repeatedly denied that it is forcing corporations to waive attorney-client confidentiality and privilege. In their own internal regulation No. 9-28.710, entitled "Attorney-client and Work Product Protections," DOJ regulators, citing *Upjohn*, claim that they well appreciate the "extremely important function" that these protections give corporations. "For these reasons," they state, "waiving the attorney-client and work product protections has never been a prerequisite under the Department's prosecution guidelines for a corporation to be viewed as cooperative."

"Nonetheless," notes the DOJ, "[e]veryone agrees that a corporation may freely waive its own privileges if it chooses to do so; indeed, such waivers occur routinely when corporations are victimized by their employees or others, conduct an internal investigation, and then disclose the details of the investigation to law enforcement officials in an effort to seek prosecution of the offenders. However, . . . [w]hat the government seeks and needs to advance its legitimate (indeed, essential) law enforcement mission is not waiver of those protections, but rather the facts known

---

[15] *See* Joe Palazzolo, *Corporate Sentencing Guidelines: 20 Years Later*, WALL STREET JOURNAL on-line, October 31, 2011, commenting on a report by the Ethics Resource Center evaluating the first twenty years of the corporate sentencing guidelines.

to the corporation about the putative criminal misconduct under review . . . ."

The tension over corporate compliance and privilege waiver thus continues.

One other note: the last article begins with the traditional apologia for why the corporate attorney-client privilege is essential. Do you agree? Before deciding, first read the following section.

9. Whither (Wither?) the Corporate Attorney-Client Privilege? Part Two — Corporate Self-Destructive Behavior

Only 30 years after the Supreme Court in *Upjohn* formally affirmed the corporate attorney-client privilege, many commentators, some of them in-house counsel, see serious signs that this privilege may be eroding. The use by prosecutors of pressured waivers, as in the Salomon Brothers case, is one reason for this concern, as is the increasing prevalence — and the possible trend — of decisions that allow causes of action for in-house counsel who refuse to act unethically. On another front, Loyola (Los Angeles) law Professor Robert Benson has moved to revoke the corporate charter of Union Oil of California (Unocal), charging that it is a "repeat offender" in environmental and labor matters. If such petitions gain any currency, they would also undermine the corporate privilege.

The most significant challenge, however, comes from courts' increasing use of the crime-fraud exception to the privilege. In that arena, no one has caused corporate officers and boards more concern than the tobacco companies, for it has been in tobacco cases that the crime-fraud exception has been most widely applied.[16]

By the 1950s, tobacco companies had set up a system of reporting unfavorable information directly to lawyers in an effort to protect as much as possible under the umbrella of the attorney-client privilege. One memo from in-house counsel advised that "direct lawyer involvement is needed in all [company] activities pertaining to smoking and health, from conception through every step of the activity," while another, from outside counsel, advised that a survey on the dangers of smoking be directly commissioned by lawyers, so that "[s]hould the results prove unfavorable, there will be nothing in the [survey takers'] records to subpoena. . . ."[17]

The Council on Tobacco Research (CTR), created in the 1950s by a consortium of tobacco companies, had a "special projects" unit that we discussed in Section 6 of Problem 18. After Judge H. Lee Sarokin released the CTR information in *Haines v. Liggett Group, Inc.*, 140 F.R.D. 681 (D.N.J. 1992) it mattered little that he was

---

[16] The following paragraphs are adopted from Zitrin & Langford, THE MORAL COMPASS OF THE AMERICAN LAWYER, 1999, Copyright © 1999 by Ballantine Books, a division of Random House. Used with permission of the authors and publisher.

[17] *See* Christine Hatfield, *The Privilege Doctrines — Are They Just Another Discovery Tool Utilized by the Tobacco Industry to Conceal Damaging Information?*, 16 PACE L. REV. 525 (1996), quoting a 1984 memo from Brown & Williamson in-house counsel J. Kendrick Wells, and Mike France, *Inside Big Tobacco's Secret War Room*, BUSINESS WEEK, June 15, 1998, quoting a 1968 Arnold & Porter memo.

reversed by the Third Circuit in *Haines v. Liggett Group, Inc.*, 975 F.2d 81 (3d Cir. 1992), and disqualified from the case. His opinion, already published, served as a road map for those trying to crack open "Big Tobacco's" shield of secrecy by exposing the industry's abuse of the attorney-client privilege. In 1997, a Florida court voided the tobacco companies' privilege on crime-fraud grounds, ultimately resulting in a $144 billion verdict in favor of the state to reimburse health care costs.[19]

Finally, the floodgates opened when, in March 1998, Minnesota Judge Kenneth J. Fitzpatrick ordered the public release of 865 tobacco company documents. Fitzpatrick accused the industry of claiming privilege for many documents "clearly and inarguably not entitled to protections." This "intentional and repeated misuse" of the privilege "is intolerable in a court of law . . . ."[20] By the end of April 1998, when the Supreme Court denied the tobacco companies' requests for a stay, a congressional committee ordered the public release of 39,000 tobacco documents. It was the beginning of the end of the tobacco companies' longstanding "hardball" defense of cigarettes.

The tobacco companies are not alone, however, when it comes to lawyers' involvement in possible fraud and the use of the crime-fraud exception. We saw in Problem 18 how in 1999, one Georgia court found General Motors and its lawyers complicit in concealing information about a key witness, voiding the attorney-client and work product privileges, and forcing GM into an expensive settlement. It appears that courts are more willing to investigate the propriety of questionable corporate attorney-client privilege claims than ever before.

Finally, in New York, a federal district court voided a company's attorney-client privilege after finding that its in-house lawyer's act of negotiating the environmental details of a contract was a business matter, not the practice of law.[21] The case, never appealed, raised eyebrows because the judge did not consider *any* of the lawyer's work to be privileged. "It is my view that courts have steadily been narrowing [corporate] attorney-client privilege," Nikko general counsel, C. Evan Stewart, a frequent commentator on corporate privilege issues, wrote soon afterwards.

D. SUPPLEMENTAL READINGS

1. Marianne Lavelle, *Placing a Price on Human Life*, THE NATIONAL LAW JOURNAL, October 10, 1988, is a valuable review of how various entities, including governments, put a value on human life. This unpleasant but nevertheless real issue will almost inevitably be considered in evaluating facts such as those posited in this Problem. The range Lavelle found was from $70,000 to $132 million, with the

---

[19] *American Tobacco Company v. Florida*, 697 So. 2d 1249 (Fla. Dist. Ct. App. 1997). For the verdict, see newspapers of July 15, 2000, *e.g.*, Rick Bragg, *Jurors in Florida Give Record Award in Tobacco Case*, N.Y. TIMES at 1.

[20] *State by Humphrey v. Philip Morris, Inc.*, 1998 Minn. App. LEXIS 431 (Mar. 17, 1998). This case produced several published opinions in the Northwest Reporter, but not this particular one.

[21] Georgia-Pacific Corp. v. GAF Roofing Mfg. Corp., 1996 U.S. Dist. Lexis 671 (S.D.N.Y. Jan. 24, 1996).

average jury verdict for a male in his 30's right in the middle at $950,000.

2. Frank Partnoy, *The Cost of a Human Life, Statistically Speaking*, THE GLOBALIST (The Global Society, July 21, 2012), *available at* http://www.theglobalist. com/storyid.aspx?storyid=9692 is a more recent evaluation of the "value of life" from a San Diego law professor and expert on modern world financial markets. This interesting piece discusses how human life is evaluated in various milieus: the economy, the value of labor, the effect of raising the nation's speed limit, the value of the elderly versus young lives, and so on. Partnoy then discusses how various entities, including governmental agencies in the U.S., put a dollar figure on the value of life.

3. Elizabeth Chambliss, *Empirical Studies of the Legal Profession: What Do We Know about Lawyers' Lives? The Professionalization of Law Firm In-House Counsel*, 84 N.C. L. REV. 1515 (2006), is an article by a law professor who also holds a Ph.D. in sociology. She used focus groups, interviews, and participant observation to gather information on the evolution of the professionalization of in-house counsel.

4. It seems that innumerable Sarbanes-Oxley articles exist. Jeffrey I. Snyder, *Regulation of Lawyer Conduct Under Sarbanes-Oxley: Minimizing Law-Firm Liability by Encouraging Adoption of Qualified Legal Compliance Committees*, 24 REV. LITIG. 223 (2005), discusses the period prior to passage of the Sarbanes-Oxley Act and "what, if anything, the legal profession might have done differently to prevent the sweeping nature of the regulation under the Act." Then Snyder discusses the ramifications of the SEC rules, the possibility of compulsory "noisy withdrawal," and the reason why corporations should adopt the compliance committee structure created by the SEC.

5. Two more good SOX articles are: Andrew Longstreth, *In the New Era of Internal Investigations, Defense Lawyers have Become Deputy Prosecutors*, 27 AM. LAW. 68 (February 2005) (in which he explains how lawyers must now help in investigations of corporate wrongdoing lest they themselves be subjected to sanctions) and Meredith M. Brown, *Reporting By Lawyers of Evidence of Material Violations*, 1462 PLI/CORP 535 (2005) (in which she provides a thorough and cogent explanation of the reporting requirements of Sarbanes-Oxley).

6. Thomas Morgan, *The Client(s) of a Corporate Lawyer*, 33 CAPITAL U. L. REV. 17 (2004), is an article by one of the nation's respected senior ethics theorists, a professor at George Washington, with a different point of view. Morgan argues that "a lawyer's role is clean and simple . . . . [T]he lawyer exists to implement that which the client wants to do and could do itself if the client had the lawyer's training and experience. The lawyer's duty is not to think; it is to accept the directions given by those people who are authorized to direct . . . ." Morgan acknowledges recent modifications to the ethics rules, but encourages lawyers not to act like "Lone Rangers."

7. H. Lowell Brown, *The Crime-Fraud Exception to the Attorney-Client Privilege in the Context of Corporate Counseling*, 87 KY. L.J. 1191 (1999), is an article that reviews the status of this longstanding but somewhat elusive privilege exception and how corporate counsel should behave in order to maximize privilege protection for their clients.

8. The saga of Dimitrios Biller, National Managing Counsel of Toyota's National Rollover Program, and his legal battles with Toyota, was discussed briefly in section 7. Some good summaries with differing perspectives on Biller and his situation are: Gael O'Brien's blog, *Columns on Ethics, Leadership and Life,* (January 7, 2011, http://theweekinethics.wordpress.com/2011/01/); Holland, Hart LLP, *Ninth Circuit Upholds Arbitration Award Against Former Employee,* NATIONAL EMPLOYMENT LAW LETTER, May 2012 (various cites in various states, *see, e.g.,* 17 No. 8 NEV. EMP. L.); and several articles in the Westlaw Automotive Journal that follow both Toyota's and Biller's cases as they climbed through the court system.

10. We usually think of reporting as the responsibility of in-house counsel, but what are the responsibilities of the plaintiff's bar? According to the NEW YORK TIMES' *S.U.V. Tire Defects Were Known In '96 But Not Reported,* by Keith Bradsher, (June 24, 2001), in 1996 personal injury lawyers and traffic safety consultants identified a pattern of tire failures from the Firestone ATX tires, but they did not report those defects to government regulators because they did not want to jeopardize their own cases on behalf of plaintiffs.

11. The Ethics Resource Center, *The Federal Sentencing Guidelines For Organizations at Twenty Years: A Call to Action for More Effective Promotion and Recognition of Effective Compliance and Ethics Programs Report of the Ethics Resource Center's Independent Advisory Group on the 20th Anniversary of FSGO,* 2012. The 21 independent members of the ERC Advisory Group (former law enforcement officials, judges, prosecutors, academics, and compliance/ethics practitioners) conclude "[t]he FSGO have successfully encouraged most companies to make ethical conduct a priority," but there are still "some key adjustments in government policies and private sector practices," according to the group's president. The complete report is available at http://fsgo.ethics.org.

12. Christine Hatfield, *The Privilege Doctrines — Are They Just Another Discovery Tool Utilized by the Tobacco Industry to Conceal Damaging Information?,* 16 PACE L. REV. 525 (1996), is a thorough account of the tobacco companies' use and abuse of corporate attorney-client privilege.

13. ARTHUR MILLER, ALL MY SONS (1949). This play, by the Pulitzer Prize-winning playwright, revolves around the consequences of one man's interpretation of his corporate responsibility. Although it does not deal with the legal profession, the story is a compelling and clear tale centered on business ethics.

PROBLEM 26: WHAT'S MOST IMPORTANT — WHAT YOU SAY, HOW YOU SAY IT . . . OR WHETHER YOU SHOULD SAY IT AT ALL?

A. INTRODUCTION

This problem raises a series of escalating issues for the lawyer who is asked for advice. First, how should an attorney approach the task of giving the advice? That is, how much may the attorney point a client in a particular direction, or tell the client the likelihood of "getting caught"? Second, when does a lawyer know a client is using the advice for a fraudulent purpose? The approach to the issue of knowledge is similar to what we have encountered before (for example, *see* Problems 15 and 16).

Third, what duty does the lawyer have to investigate the veracity of the client's story, or at least not turn a blind eye to what's going on? Fourth, what should the lawyer do when the client wants more than advice — perhaps active assistance in what may be fraudulent conduct, say in the form of a statement to a regulator or an opinion letter to a client (an issue we'll carry over into the next problem)? We will look at several scandals involving lawyers, while examining the lines between appropriate and inappropriate advice, advice and active assistance, and advice vs. advocacy.

B. PROBLEM

I

Laura Pomeranian is a lawyer specializing in immigration matters. One day she is visited by an old client, Solomon Tovarich, whose family Pomeranian has helped over the years. The following conversation takes place:

> "Laura," says Solomon, "my best friend Mischa's family is visiting from Ukraine. His brother and sister-in-law and their beautiful daughter Elena. And they say things are no better there. Sure, it's better for some than the old days, but for Jews it's even worse. Mischa's brother says it's too late for them, but Elena is twenty and wants to emigrate. But with the quotas filled, it's impossible. I was thinking, I'm a widower, my kids are grown, I got a good job, maybe I could marry Elena. She's a beautiful young lady, intelligent. She could stay here, go to college."

> "You know, Sol, marrying a foreigner to avoid immigration quotas is a serious crime."

> "I'm aware of that," replies Tovarich. "Why do you think I came to you?"

Consider the following alternative responses that Pomeranian could make to Tovarich. For purposes of this problem, assume the legal accuracy of the advice given.

Scenario #1: "If this is what you really want, my advice to you is to court Elena every minute while she's here on her visitor's visa. Spend holidays with her, your birthday, and hers. Look for a new apartment together, and furnish it. Even write her love letters. And she should do the same. She'll have to be convincing about why a young woman like her is falling in love with an old goat like you."

"Is all that necessary?"

"Only if you want immigration to believe that this is a marriage made of love, not quotas."

Scenario #2: "Well, Sol, I'll go through it piece by piece. The key issue is whether your marriage to Elena is one of convenience. That is, are you marrying her for real, or to get her a legal 'status adjustment' that would let her stay in the States? Marrying her so she can live here would be defrauding the Immigration Service."

"So what will Immigration do?" asks Tovarich.

"Well," says Pomeranian, "immigration applications are now investigated by the USCIS, which is part of Homeland Security. They can't investigate every marriage, and you're not in the ethnic groups they scrutinize most closely, but they do check out a sizable random sample. They do investigate a much higher sample of people who fit their sham marriage 'profile.' I guarantee that with your age difference and the full immigration quota, you fit right into that profile."

"Of course, whether your marriage is real or a sham is a question of fact. The USCIS can only look at how the two of you act and what you say to determine the legitimacy of your marriage. For example, if you can prove you spent months in each other's company before you got married, or exchanged long letters of devotion and affection, or were always together on important occasions, that would all tend to show that your marriage is for real."

"I'll guarantee you something else: If they do investigate, you'll each be interviewed separately, and they'll ask you where you were on various dates you might be expected to remember — July 4, Thanksgiving, your birthday, hers. They'll ask you where you've been in the week just before the interview. They'll ask what kind of toothpaste and soap she uses. If your answers don't match, they'll use it against you and probably see it as fraud. But if it's clear by your answers that you've really spent the time together, it will be very strong evidentiary support for a marriage made in heaven."

"Laura, that's very helpful. Every day I'm more in love."

QUESTIONS

1. Is the first scenario unethical? Ethically, does it differ from the second?

2. Recall Professor Freedman's penknife and *Anatomy of a Murder* scenarios discussed in Problem 16. How do those scenarios compare to these?

3. Suppose Tovarich decides to go forward with his plan to marry Elena, and asks Pomeranian for her help in filling out the necessary documents for Elena's legal status. May Laura help him? What else, if anything, should Pomeranian consider before giving herself to this effort?

4. Suppose the USCIS challenges Tovarich's marriage and the issue turns on his state of mind as to the reason for the marriage. Could Laura represent Solomon before the USCIS? Does it matter whether she prepared the papers originally? Finally, which do you find easier, preparing the documents or defending the couple afterwards? Why?

II

Consider Professor Newman's article and the discussion of the "torture memo" in section 2 below in addressing these questions.

1. How similar is the advice in Newman's tax scenario to the advice government lawyers gave in the torture memo?

2. Do lawyers have an obligation to advise clients about the moral implications of their actions?

3. Do government lawyers have a higher duty than private counsel to give disinterested advice?

C. READINGS

1. How Should Lawyers Advise Their Clients?

To what extent does the lawyer owe a duty of full disclosure? What about where the lawyer believes the client may put the advice to improper use? Or where the lawyer thinks the advice may encourage the client to "get away with" something because of the small likelihood of getting caught? Should these issues affect how the lawyer gives advice? Here is a view from a professor who teaches both ethics and tax about one of the most complex of all areas of legal counseling — tax advice.

Joel S. Newman, *The Audit Lottery: Don't Ask, Don't Tell?*
Tax Notes 1438, March 6, 2000[1]

In Book II of Plato's *Republic*, Socrates tells of the shepherd Gyges, who discovered a ring that would make him invisible whenever he wished. With a twist of the ring, he could do anything he pleased, and never get caught. For centuries, philosophers have argued over whether Gyges should have lived a moral life anyway.

The tax version of Gyges's ring is the audit rate, which has rarely exceeded 2 percent of all returns filed. Of course, 98 percent invisibility does not quite reach the 100 percent invisibility that Gyges achieved, but it is close enough for tax work. Many taxpayers have twisted the ring, and played the audit lottery. They have taken questionable or worse positions on tax returns, betting that they would not be audited. . . .

Whether Gyges the taxpayer should twist the ring and play the audit lottery is one thing. Whether his lawyer should tell an unknowing Gyges what the ring can do is quite another. I propose to discuss the latter question. May a lawyer discuss the audit lottery with her client? Must she?

. . . .

[T]he national audit rate for the average, individual taxpayer is very low. If we know that our client is indeed average, with none of the peculiarities that might raise an IRS eyebrow, then the audit probability is indeed 1 percent. Why can't we tell them that?

The problem arises if we know that our client intends to take a questionable or worse position on a tax return. Arguably, advising such a client that, with a low audit rate, he is unlikely to get caught is tantamount to helping the client break the law. However, if we don't tell the client, then we are failing in an essential lawyering function. Some people already know about the low audit rate. Shouldn't everyone know? Shouldn't all taxpayers start with the same information in their dealings with their government?

Model Rules of Professional Conduct

The Model Rules of Professional Conduct do not provide many helpful answers, but they do ask the right questions. That is more than the specific tax authorities do. The relevant portion of Model Rule 1.2(d) is set forth below. Its two clauses have been separated, so that its possible contradictions will be more apparent:

> A lawyer shall not counsel a client to engage, or assist a client, in conduct that the lawyer knows is criminal or fraudulent, but a lawyer may discuss the legal consequences of any proposed course of conduct with a client. . . .

For the remainder of this discussion, then, consider a client who wishes to take a position on a tax return that in your view is neither criminal, fraudulent, nor even frivolous. However, you do not believe that the position satisfies the realistic possibility standard of [the tax code] . . . . May you tell that client about the low audit rate?

. . . Model Rule 1.2(d)['s] uses of "counsel," "assist," and "legal consequences" are especially intriguing.

"Counsel" and "Assist"

Here is the argument for a broad interpretation of "counsel" and "assist." Advising a client on a proposed course of action usually means helping her to weigh its costs and benefits. Anything that lowers the costs in the client's eyes will make the course of action more probable. Telling her that she probably won't get caught is one way of lowering those projected costs. Therefore, discussing the low audit rate is counseling and assisting the client to engage in the conduct.

The interpretation sketched out above is too broad. Assume that the client proposes criminal or fraudulent conduct. Pursuant to the broad interpretation, any time a lawyer discusses a legal consequence of that conduct that is even remotely positive, the lawyer is counseling or assisting that conduct. Therefore, the first clause of Rule 1.2(d) ["counsel" or "assist"] would contradict the second ["discuss legal consequences"]. Surely, such contradictions were not intended.

Mere advice, without more, should never be construed as a violation of Model Rule 1.2(d). If it were, then it would be very difficult for lawyers to give any advice at all. Advice is, after all, the most worthwhile thing we have to give.

"Legal Consequences"

The notion of what constitutes law, and hence, what constitutes "legal consequences" has been greatly expanded, thanks to the Legal Realism movement. No longer a sterile discussion of statutes and cases, an analysis of "legal consequences" now must include consideration of the way in which government actually works. Surely, such an analysis properly includes a consideration of governmental enforcement patterns. However, one must be careful not to take this notion too far. Without proper limits, encouraging lawyers to discuss enforcement patterns leads to the notion that what is lawful is whatever one can get away with . . . .

Yet, within limits, it is not only appropriate, but necessary to consider patterns of government enforcement when advising clients about legal consequences. Two relevant parameters concern the difference between "never enforced" and "rarely enforced," and the difference between intentional and unintentional underenforcement.

Never Enforced and Rarely Enforced

Imagine that there is a statute on the books in your state that criminalizes the playing of bingo, even if no money changes hands, even if the game is played among friends in their private homes. Imagine further that this statute has not been enforced for 50 years, and that the local prosecutors have no intention of ever enforcing it again. Your client proposes to play bingo, at home with his friends, for no money.

If you tell your client that playing bingo is a crime, and say no more, then you are doing your client a major disservice. Your statement would not be an accurate description of the legal consequences of playing bingo. There is general agreement that if a law is never enforced, it is appropriate, and necessary, to say so.

When one goes from "never enforced" to "rarely enforced," certainty and consensus break down. However, [w]ho among us has not had the experience of driving at 62 in a 55-mile-per-hour zone, only to be passed by almost everyone else on the road, including a few state troopers? Clearly, the enforcers know that the law is being broken. Yet, they rarely choose to enforce it. . . . As to the question of what the law is, the speed limit is not really 55. As to the question of consequences, the legal consequences of driving 62 in a 55-miles-per-hour zone are usually zero. . . .

Intentional vs. Unintentional Underenforcement

Tax law enforcement, however, is not the same as traffic enforcement. There is no tax law counterpart to going just a little bit over the speed limit. If your tax return is incorrect, even just a little bit, and the IRS finds out about it, you will be required to correct it, and to pay whatever taxes, interest, and penalties that might result.

It is the IRS problem with detection, however, that is the rub. In a sense, our traffic laws are not fully enforced because the government won't enforce them; our tax laws are not fully enforced because the government can't enforce them. Arguably, instances of "the government won't" can properly be discussed with clients; instances of "the government can't" cannot. . . .

However, even if the underlying distinction between "can't" and "won't" is accepted, it is not clear which side tax law enforcement is on. Note that it would not be impossible for the IRS to audit every return. The . . . IRS has never had the personnel to audit more than a tiny fraction of submitted returns. Hasn't this been going on long enough so that we can call it a policy? . . . [S]urely the taxpaying public at least has a right to know of the conscious underfunding of IRS, and of its consequences in policy and practical terms.

The Moral Dimension: Crime and Fraud Redux

[Denver ethics Professor] Stephen Pepper argues that the propriety of discussing legal consequences and enforcement policy with respect to a proposed course of conduct should depend on how bad the proposed course of conduct would be. He distinguishes *malum prohibitum* — something that is prohibited only because the law says so - from *malum in se* — something that is wrong by its very nature. A lawyer should feel perfectly free to discuss any and all legal consequences of a breach of a contract, but a lawyer should be much more circumspect in discussing the legal consequences of murder. On his continuum, Pepper locates taking an aggressive position on a tax return as somewhere in the middle.

. . . .

Bear in mind that the lawyer is merely communicating information. It is up to the client whether or not to use that information, and how. We should be loath to assume either that our morals are better than our clients', or that we should be making decisions that are properly theirs to make. . . .

Lawyers should give their clients all relevant information. They may then, if they wish, give their clients their opinion on the moral dimensions of the client's decision. They may even enter into a moral dialogue with the client, and try to persuade the client to do the right thing, in their view. Having done all of those things, however, the lawyer must then let the client decide.

Conclusion

Had he asked me, I would have told Gyges exactly what the ring could do. Of course, I would have insisted on being paid in cash for my advice up front, before he disappeared on me.

NOTES

Professor Newman raises many issues in his lucid statement of the problem. Are you fully persuaded by his arguments? Do you accept Newman's reasoning for negating the distinction between an IRS that "can't" rather than "won't" enforce? Or is it too facile, like his statement that "the speed limit is not really 55" because it's rarely enforced at that level? Do you accept the argument that lawyers who advise their clients in ways that could be put to fraudulent use are "merely communicating information"? Is there, as MR 1.2, comment 9 states, really a "critical distinction" between analyzing legal issues and recommending fraud? What about when your client's fraudulent intent is clear? Finally, does Professor Pepper's distinction between *malum prohibitum* and *malum in se* make sense?

2. Advising on Torture[2]

In the days after September 11, 2001, Americans captured a severely wounded Abu Zubaydah, an important Osama bin Laden lieutenant. By the Spring of 2002, Zubaydah, still gravely wounded, was taken to a safe house in Thailand by a CIA security team. There, after he was sufficiently recovered, Zubaydah was at first interrogated by FBI agents using standard interviewing techniques. The FBI tried to convince him they knew the details of his participation in terror by showing him a box of blank audiotapes that they said, falsely, contained recordings of his phone calls.

While Zubaydah soon began providing information, the CIA agents present believed that he was withholding far more than he told, and took over the interrogation. With the CIA in charge, Zubaydah, still weak, was subjected to coercive interrogation techniques including being stripped, held in an icy-cold room without bed or blankets, sometimes until he turned blue, and blasted with the earsplitting sounds of loud heavy-metal rockers. The FBI objected to both the legality and the utility and of these techniques, but its voice was drowned out.

The NEW YORK TIMES reported that three former CIA officials said that their "techniques had been drawn up on the basis of legal guidance from the Justice Department, but were not yet supported by a formal legal opinion." Accordingly, then CIA Director George Tenet requested a legal memo to protect the interrogators and their superiors from any future prosecution under the 1994 anti-torture act and to ensure — or at least claim — compliance with the United Nations' Convention Against Torture.

The Justice Department's Office of Legal Counsel (OLC) was assigned the task of writing the memo. The head of OLC, Jay Bybee, now a federal appeals judge, eventually signed the August 1, 2002 "torture memo," but the memo was a group effort. OLC staff, particularly John Yoo, now returned to his University of

---

[2] These facts are taken from various news reports, including David Johnston, *At a Secret Interrogation, Dispute Flared over Tactics*, N.Y. TIMES, Sept. 10, 2006, Adam Liptak, *How Far Can A Government Lawyer Go?*, N.Y. TIMES, June 27, 2004, and other information variously reported by David Johnston, Neil A. Lewis and others for THE NEW YORK TIMES, Mike Allen, Dana Priest, Professor Kathleen Clark (whose piece on the torture memo appears in Problem 27), for THE WASHINGTON POST, and Stuart Taylor for the NATIONAL REVIEW and the NATIONAL LAW JOURNAL.

California law professorship, drafted the memo, while then White House Counsel Alberto Gonzales, his staff, then Attorney General John Ashcroft's staff, and even Vice President Dick Cheney's legal counsel gave input on drafts. Among other things, the memo stated that treatment of prisoners such as Zubaydah was not torture unless it was "equivalent in intensity to the pain accompanying serious physical injury, such as organ failure, impairment of bodily function, or even death."

Although the Bush administration disavowed the Bybee memo in mid-2004, as late as September 9, 2006, President Bush maintained that the Zubaydah interrogation was legal: "These procedures were designed to be safe, to comply with our laws, our Constitution and our treaty obligations," Mr. Bush said. Moreover, he said, "the Department of Justice reviewed the authorized methods extensively and determined them to be lawful."

Was the Bybee torture memo a matter of lawyers giving the clients — here, the CIA and, indeed, the President — the advice they wanted to hear, to the denigration of reasonable interpretations of law? Did the memo involve "willful blindness" to the facts, or to the law governing torture? Or were the memos honest advice within the bounds of colorable claims of law?

In 2004, NEW YORK TIMES legal affairs reporter Adam Liptak interviewed several former high-ranking government lawyers about the "torture memo" to test "the ethical and moral limits of what lawyers can and should do in advising their clients."

"When a government is . . . faced with options," Harvard Professor Charles Fried, a former solicitor general under Reagan, told Liptak, "surely one of the questions it asks — but only one of them — is, what does the law require? Another question is, is it effective? Another is, is it moral? Those are not the same questions." The lawyer, said Fried, should be answering the first question.

Walter Dellinger, who was in charge of the OLC under Clinton, told Liptak that the OLC's job traditionally had been to provide *disinterested* advice. And Philip Lacovara, who served in the Nixon administration and was also a Watergate prosecutor, told Liptak that "If you set loose very smart and very energetic lawyers and tell them their task is to justify the unjustifiable, they will do it," he said.

Obviously, the torture memos raise a host of important questions. One, of course, is whether the authors may slant their opinion to what the recipient wants to hear, or whether they must they provide the "disinterested" advice that Walter Dellinger advocated. Another is whether *government* lawyers should take into account that on some level they represent the public. The Liptak article quoting Dellinger references FDR's Attorney General, Francis Biddle, who opposed the internment of American citizens of Japanese ancestry during World War II, though Biddle was overruled. And in late 1973, with the Watergate investigation exploding around President Nixon, both Attorney General Elliot Richardson and Deputy AG William D. Ruckelshaus refused Nixon's order to fire special prosecutor Archibald Cox, and were as a result themselves summarily fired. But in this situation, may the OLC take into account — as Alberto Gonzales and John Yoo have argued —

issues of national security and the war on terrorism?

3.   Knowledge and the Story of O.P.M.'s Lawyers

Lawyers who compromise their ethics by the way they advise their clients are hardly a new story. Each recent decade seems to have had its own top-rated scandal. In the early 2000's, it was Enron. In the 1990s, it was the Lincoln Savings & Loan debacle, about which more later. In the 1980s, it was the extraordinary story of O.P.M. Leasing. There is much to be learned from each of these stories. We begin with O.P.M. (the acronym stood for "other people's money") and its attorneys, the New York firm of Singer, Hutner, Levine & Seeman.[3]

Starting in the early 1970s, Singer Hutner began representing O.P.M. Leasing, Inc. O.P.M. was founded in 1970, the brainchild of two partners, childhood friends, and brothers-in-law, Myron Goodman and Mordecai Weissman. O.P.M.'s business involved purchasing computers — the old-fashioned main-frame kind — from IBM, and then leasing them to companies like Rockwell International, AT&T, and Polaroid. The more O.P.M. leased, the more banks were willing to lend money for more computers, using the leases with the megacompanies as collateral. By the late '70s, O.P.M. was one of the country's five largest computer-leasing companies, all of it done with O.P.M., "other people's money."

This apparent success masked the reality that the entire business was a fraud, a pyramid scheme. Not only were most of the leases fake, most of the computers never existed. The same computer would be used again and again for different leases and different loans. O.P.M.'s biggest "client," Rockwell, was less an actual client than a name used on forged leases, created by Goodman crouching under a glass-top table to shine a flashlight through signature pages that Weissman traced onto fake documents. In all, according to investigative reporter Stewart Taylor, Jr., between 1978 and 1981 alone, O.P.M. obtained almost $200 million in loans from 19 lenders secured by forged Rockwell leases.

Not long after it opened its doors, O.P.M. became Singer Hutner's largest client. The lawyers had no indication of anything amiss until June 1980 when Goodman, knowing his accountant had discovered the Rockwell fraud and was threatening to tell all, first swore his attorneys to secrecy, and then told them he had done something wrong, something he couldn't fix because it would take millions of dollars he didn't have. According to Taylor, Goodman refused to be specific about his wrongdoing, in light of senior partner Joseph L. Hutner's statement that he couldn't promise to keep the details confidential, because O.P.M. itself was the firm's client.

While Goodman kept his story vague, the accountant hired his own lawyer, William J. Davis, to meet with O.P.M.'s counsel. Davis later described his meetings

---

[3] In developing this narrative, we are indebted to Stuart Taylor, Jr., whose fascinating and comprehensive article, *Ethics and the Law: A Case History*, N.Y. Times, Jan. 9, 1983 (Magazine), describes the case in detail, and to Heidi Li Feldman, *Can Good Lawyers Be Good Ethical Deliberators?*, 69 S. Cal. L. Rev. 885 (1996). The narrative itself is adapted from our treatment in Zitrin & Langford, The Moral Compass of the American Lawyer (1999), for which we owe thanks to Ballantine Books and Random House.

with Joseph Hutner as "a macabre dance." He says he offered Hutner a letter from the accountant outlining the fraud, but Hutner "didn't want it [and] didn't want to know what was in it." Hutner behaved, said Davis, as if he were about to "clamp his hands over his ears and run out of the office." Meanwhile, Goodman, while admitting to past mistakes, swore to his lawyers that his days of dishonesty were behind him.

But the lawyers knew it wasn't that simple. The accountant's message had gotten through: A Singer Hutner memorandum drafted during this period referred to evidence of multimillion-dollar frauds. To get that money, O.P.M. had used the law firm's own opinion letters about the worthiness of the loans, which in turn were based on fake documents. Even worse, the firm knew that in the accountant's opinion, O.P.M., "in order to survive, would probably have to continue the same type of wrongful activity," and thus continue to use the firm's opinion letters.

Given all this, Singer Hutner considered stopping all its work for O.P.M. But no firm wants to lose its largest client; if Goodman's assurances could be taken at face value, all his "mistakes" were in the past. The lawyers decided to seek the advice of an outside expert in legal ethics. They chose Henry Putzel 3d, who had taught ethics at Fordham University and came recommended by the law school's dean. Putzel gave Singer Hutner the answers the firm wanted to hear.

First, Putzel concluded that despite the accountant's opinion, Singer Hutner knew of "no fact which in any way indicated the commission of an ongoing fraud." Therefore, said Putzel, the firm had no duty to say anything about what had happened in the past, including telling the banks that existing, *ongoing* loans were based on false information. Second, relying on Goodman's new assurances, the firm could even continue to close new loans for O.P.M. Third, it was not necessary for Singer Hutner to check to be sure each new O.P.M. deal was legitimate so long as Goodman swore in writing that it was, which of course he was only too happy to do by simply adding to his litany of lies.

So during the summer of 1980, Singer Hutner continued to assist O.P.M. in obtaining new loans. They claimed later that they didn't "know" Goodman was continuing his fraudulent ways, though Davis, the accountant's lawyer, had written a memorandum after his June meeting with Hutner that remarked on his firm's "apparent willingness to stick his head in the sand and ignore these problems." But the lawyers couldn't keep their heads in the sand forever. In September 1980, Goodman admitted more details about his past frauds and acknowledged that they totaled over $80 million. At that point, with the evidence overwhelming and, according to Stewart Taylor, some partners concerned about their fees and O.P.M.'s possible bankruptcy, the law firm finally decided to resign as counsel.

But with Putzel's approval, Singer Hutner did not resign at once. Rather, they set up a staged withdrawal between September and December to ensure that the client was not abandoned without a lawyer, which the firm feared would immediately put the company under. The lawyers justified staying on despite Goodman's admissions because yet again, he swore that all fraud had finally stopped.

O.P.M. found new lawyers to represent them: Peter Fishbein and his firm of Kaye, Scholer, Fierman, Hays & Handler. In October, Fishbein called his old friend Hutner to ask whether there were any problems with O.P.M. that caused Singer Hutner to give up its largest client. But Putzel instructed Hutner he couldn't tell Fishbein anything about fraud without violating O.P.M.'s confidentiality. The end result was that Kaye, Scholer, knowing nothing of O.P.M.'s past history, assisted O.P.M. in obtaining another $15 million in bogus loans before the fraud was exposed. Putzel even advised Singer Hutner that it could not tell O.P.M.'s own in-house lawyer about the frauds.

When O.P.M.'s house of cards collapsed and the tangled web of litigation began, everyone got a lawyer, including the lawyers, Singer Hutner, and the lawyers' lawyer, Putzel. O.P.M. went into bankruptcy and Goodman and Weissman were sent to prison. Lawsuits flew, and Singer Hutner wound up paying $10 million. The firm collapsed, but the principals went on practicing law, none sanctioned by the bar, and all claiming they did the right thing.

Perhaps the most sanctimonious was Putzel, whose legal brief defended his seemingly indefensible advice: Under the adversary system, "a lawyer's primary obligation . . . must be to his client, rich or poor, likeable or despicable, honest or crooked." There are times, Putzel's lawyers argued, when lawyers are "duty-bound to stand up for and protect liars and thieves." But here, by advising Singer Hutner essentially to turn a blind eye toward the truth, had Putzel encouraged the lawyers to stand up and *assist* liars and thieves?

The O.P.M. case raised many questions back in the 1980s about the extent to which lawyers could suspend disbelief and ignore obvious reality. Here is what Stuart Taylor wrote in the conclusion of his *New York Times Magazine* article:

"Whether or not Singer Hutner violated the ethical code, a basic question remains: Is there not something wrong with a code that can plausibly be used to justify the extreme lengths to which Singer Hutner went to protect its criminal client? Indeed, there is growing concern both inside and outside the legal profession that the current rules make it too easy for lawyers to condone or even actively assist their clients' ongoing crimes, frauds and cover-up conspiracies."

First, is what Singer Hutner did so clearly the active assistance that Taylor claims it is? Or is it more a matter of "willful blindness," a term we'll see again. Do you think such disingenuous behavior could happen again in today's more sophisticated legal environment? Some argue that it has already, in the Enron case and elsewhere, and that little has changed.

4. Knowledge and the Duty to Investigate

What should a law firm like Singer Hutner be required to do to verify the legitimacy of the client's statements and position? Should some investigation be required, such as one might do before filing a complaint to avoid Rule 11 attack, before advice is given? Or at least before an opinion is rendered? If the lawyer takes what the client says at face value, at what point is that no longer enough? Look at ABA Model Rule 1.1 and the Comments to 1.2 and see if they provide any insight. What is the difference between the standard of "knowing" and one of "should have known"?

The ABA has addressed this issue on numerous occasions over the years. In 1974, ABA Formal Opinion 335 discussed an attorney's duty of inquiry when giving an opinion about whether the sales of securities have to be registered under the Securities Act of 1933: "It is, of course, important that the lawyer competently and carefully consider what facts are relevant to the giving of the requested opinion and make a reasonable inquiry to obtain such of those facts as are not within his personal knowledge." Where the lawyer does not have "sufficient confidence as to all the relevant facts," or fails to make further inquiries, the attorney should not provide the client with an opinion.

In ABA Revised Formal Opinion 346 (1982), the ABA analyzed the role of a lawyer in rendering an opinion on the propriety of a tax shelter, an issue we'll directly examine in section 8. Opinion 346 reiterated the requirements of Opinion 335 to investigate and inquire, and stated:

> The lawyer who accepts as true the facts which the promoter tells him, when the lawyer should know that a future inquiry would disclose that these facts are untrue, also gives a false opinion. It has been said that lawyers cannot "escape criminal liability on a plea of ignorance when they have shut their eyes to what was plainly to be seen."

After Enron and other scandals (see the next section), the ABA set up a Task Force on Corporate Responsibility, which issued a report in 2002 that among other things argued that lawyers were too ready to "accept management's instructions and limit their advice and/or services to a narrowly defined scope, ignoring the context or implications of the advice they [gave]."[4]

The report noted that "[t]here has also been criticism of corporate lawyers for turning a blind eye to the natural consequences of what they observe and claiming that they did not 'know' that the corporate officers they were advising were engaged in misconduct." While the task force recommended that the definition of "knowledge" be expanded to include what some have termed "willful blindness,"[5] these recommendations were largely ignored.

Thus, the most important cases focusing on a lawyer's duty to investigate questionable corporate activity remain these from the early '90s, such as these three federal circuit court cases:

In *FDIC v. O'Melveny & Myers*, 969 F.2d 744 (9th Cir. 1992), a savings and loan association that hired O'Melveny to perform due diligence to confirm the accuracy of its private placement statements. When the FDIC took over as receiver, it sued O'Melveny for its willful blindness in failing to investigate the institution's fraud. The Ninth Circuit held that while a law firm had no obligation to "ferret out fraud,"

---

[4] *See* 58 Bus. Law. 189 (2002)

[5] *See, e.g.,* Roger C. Cramton, George M. Cohen & Susan P. Koniak, *Legal and Ethical Duties of Lawyers After Sarbanes-Oxley*, 49 Vill. L. Rev. 725 (2004).

it did have to undertake a "reasonable independent investigation" into whether the fraud existed.[6]

In *FDIC v. Clark*, 978 F.2d 1541 (10th Cir. 1992) the Tenth Circuit followed the *O'Melveny* reasoning in allowing the FDIC to sue an outside law firm for failing to investigate despite clear signs that the management of its client, a bank, had committed fraud by securing a series of unauthorized loans through the bank. When a lawsuit was filed against the bank alleging that the bank president had conspired to defraud the bank, the law firm accepted the president's explanation, did not report the allegations to the board of directors, and did nothing to investigate the claims.

Kline v. First Western Government Securities, Inc., 24 F.3d 480 (3d Cir. 1994), is the third such case. Here, though, the law firm wrote an opinion letter relied on by third-party investors. The Third Circuit concluded that the law firm's failure to conduct any investigation meant it could be held liable for acting with "reckless disregard" of the opinion's veracity. We'll discuss this case in the next Problem, when we look more directly at opinion letters.

5.   Enron: Legal Advice as Cover-Up, or Just Client Protection?

We are all familiar with the story of Enron — the rise, the fall, the scams, and the criminal convictions of CFO Andrew Fastow and CEO Ken Lay. The roles of Enron's many lawyers, especially Vinson & Elkins, have also been closely examined. Did the lawyers advise and then appropriately act as advocates, defending Enron as they are sworn to do? Or did their advice and assent to frauds make them co-conspirators in Enron executives' crimes? Read the following.

Robert W. Gordon, *A New Role for Lawyers?: The Corporate Counselor After Enron*
35 Conn. L. Rev. 1185 (2003)[7]

Lawyers seem to have played a relatively minor part in the theater of deception and self-dealing that has led to the collapse of Enron and other corporate titans of the 1990s. The spotlight has been on the grasping managers at the heart of the drama, debased accounting standards and practices, . . . opportunistic investment bankers, conflicted stock analysts, and a credulous business press. But lawyers — both in-house lawyers and outside law firms — were participants in many of the central transactions that ultimately brought about the companies' ruin.

---

[6] This case was reversed by the United States Supreme Court on the grounds that the FDIC had no standing to bring tort claims against O'Melveny. *See* 512 U.S. 79, 114 S. Ct. 2048.

[7] Copyright © 2003 by Connecticut Law Review. Reprinted by permission.

I. *Some Problems with What Lawyers Did*

Non-Disclosure by (Technical) Disclosure

Securities laws require accurate and transparent financial statements, so that investors can know the financial condition of the company. Enron arranged to borrow money from banks through transactions disguised as sales of real assets. No real assets ever changed hands, nor were they going to; Enron was going to repay the money with interest and cancel the sales. . . . Lawyers wrote opinions certifying the disguised loans as "true sales." Enron moved other debt off of its own books by creating sham transactions with limited-partner-entities. By law, these must be "independent" — i.e., conform to the (incredibly lax) requirement that a minimum of investors (three percent) must be from "outside" the parent firm. In some cases, even the outside investors were creatures of Andrew Fastow, Enron's CFO. Lawyers — both inside the company and outside counsel — approved all of these transactions. More generally, lawyers repeatedly facilitated Enron's strategy of structuring dubious transactions so that nobody could understand them, by using language to describe them in proxy and financial statements that, although literally and technically correct, was in practice completely opaque . . . .

Facilitating Self-Dealing

Special Purpose Entities ("SPEs") paid enormous sums to managers (again, Enron officers — Fastow's subordinates and designates) for managing them. Fastow personally received over $30 million in management fees from one set of SPEs. . . . Fastow had a "strong desire" to avoid disclosure of his compensation, and apparently was accustomed to treating the lawyers as his own personal vassals. The lawyers — in this case, Vinson & Elkins ("V&E")— obliged, by reasoning that since it was uncertain how much Fastow would eventually earn from all the transactions, Enron did not have to disclose even what he had already earned. In their SEC filings, the lawyers also asserted, as required by law, that these "related-party" transactions were negotiated at "arm's-length" and on "comparable terms" to deals with non-related parties, but apparently did not look for any factual support for these assertions, although the deals seemed questionable on their face.

The Investigation that Wasn't

Sherron Watkins, a vice president for corporate development at Enron, warned company chairman Kenneth Lay that the company was about to "implode in a wave of accounting scandals" because of dubious accounting by Enron's auditors, Arthur Andersen, for the many limited-partnership investment deals it had used to keep debt off the parent company's books and inflate Enron's earnings. Watkins . . . advised the chairman to ask an independent outside law firm to investigate, noting that Enron's regular law firm of V&E should be disqualified because it had signed off (given "true sale" opinions) on some of the deals and had a conflict of interest. Contrary to her advice, Lay did ask V&E to review the transactions . . . . V&E, overlooking its own conflict and the patent contradiction in Lay's instructions to avoid looking at the very source the whistleblower had identified as the cause of the problem, duly reported back that the transactions seemed fine — because Andersen had, after all, approved them.

Was there anything illegal or unethical about what these lawyers did? Scholars who have studied these transactions in detail have argued that there was, that the lawyers' conduct subjects them to potential liability for criminal fraud, civil fraud, and violation of the securities laws. In addition, they could face discipline under state ethical codes for facilitating fraud, or malpractice liability for failing to competently represent their actual clients, the corporate entities. . . .

II. *Some Excuses for What the Lawyers Did*

It is clear that the advice both in-house lawyers and outside law firms gave to the managers of Enron and other companies like it was instrumental in enabling those managers to cream off huge profits for themselves while bringing economic ruin to investors, employees, and the taxpaying public. Although the lawyers were not principally responsible for these acts, [s]uch fraud could not have been carried out without the lawyers' active approval, passive acquiescence, or failure to inquire and investigate. Nonetheless, not only the lawyers involved but large numbers of practitioners and bar committees . . . vigorously justify the conduct as consistent with the highest conceptions of legal, ethical, and professional propriety . . . . Observers from outside the profession, and even some from within the profession, are tempted to say that the lawyers were simply weak and corrupt, or, for those who prefer to talk this way, that the lawyers were rational economic actors. They want the client's business, in an intensely competitive market, and so they will wish to approve anything senior management of the client firm asks, averting their eyes from signs of trouble and their noses from the smell of fish. Asking too many questions and (horrors) refusing to bless a transaction risks losing the client to another firm across town. Demonstrating ingenuity in giving the managers the results they want despite apparent legal obstacles wins praise and repeat business. Sailing close to or even over the line of illegal conduct is not unduly risky, because lawyers who advise on complex transactions for corporate clients almost never face sanctions.

. . . .

Law as Neutral Constraint: The Lawyer as Risk-Manager

In this view, law is simply a source of "risk" to the business firm; it is the lawyers' task to assess and, to the extent possible, reduce it. These lawyers do not feel a moral imperative, as libertarians do, to defy or undercut the law; but neither do they feel one to comply . . . .

. . . The lawyer objectively assesses the risks, then games the rules to work around the constraints . . . . If some constraints are unavoidable he "not only may but should" advise breaking the rules and paying the penalty if the client can still make a profit.

[This defense was] not available in the case of Enron, for the obvious reasons that managers were looting the companies for their own benefit while concealing debts and losses from workers and investors. When the lawyers and accountants outwitted the pesky regulators — who, had they known what was happening, might have put a stop to it — they were not helping heroic outlaws add value to the economy and society by defying timid convention, but enabling, if not abetting, frauds and thieves. Nor were the professionals objectively, if amorally, assessing risks and weighing benefits against costs of efficient breach. It seems not to have occurred to them that outsiders might find out that the many-sided transactions with special entities were not actually earning any real returns, but merely concealing debts and losses, and that when that happened, Enron's stock price would tumble, and with it, all the houses of cards secured by that stock. The company they advised is now facing at least seventy-seven lawsuits as a result of its conduct. At best, the lawyers were closing their eyes to the risk of disaster; at worst, they were helping to bring it on.

"We Din' Know Nothin' ": The Lawyer as Myopic or Limited-Function Bureaucrat

These are claims that the lawyers were not at fault because their role was limited: We didn't know, we weren't informed; the accountants said the numbers were okay; management made the decisions; our representation was restricted to problems on the face of the documents or to information submitted to us.

Many of these claims of innocent ignorance now look pretty dubious. Some of the outside law firms, such as V&E and Andrews & Kurth, in fact worked closely with Andersen accountants in structuring many of the transactions. Sometimes they expressed doubts about the deals. An in-house lawyer, Jordan Mintz, once even hired an outside law firm to look more closely into some of Fastow's deals. Ronald Astin of V&E repeatedly objected to some of Fastow's deals, saying they posed conflicts or weren't in Enron's best interests; but . . . in V&E's report on the whistleblower Watkins' allegations, Astin minimized suspected problems. In the end, the doubting lawyers never pressed the issues.

Some of their claims of limited knowledge are plausible, however, because Enron never trusted any one set of lawyers with extensive information about its operations — it spread legal work out to over 100 law firms. If one firm balked at approving a deal, as V&E occasionally did, Enron managers would go across town to another, more compliant firm such as Andrews & Kurth. Even Enron's General Counsel, James Derrick, had no means of controlling or supervising all of the legal advice the company was receiving, because the different divisions all had their own lawyers and outside firms. . . .

The Lawyer as Advocate

The classic defense of the corporate lawyer's role, both most often advanced and held in reserve if other defenses fail, is of course that we are advocates, whose duty is zealous representation of clients. We are not like auditors, who have duties to the public; our duties are only to our clients. Our job is to help them pursue their interests and put the best construction on their conduct that the law and facts will support without intolerable strain, so as to enable them to pursue any arguably-legal ends by any arguably-legal means . . . .

For the advocate . . . [t]he lawyer does not look for truth or justice, although of course to play his role he needs to know what courts are likely to say, and how far he can get them to see the facts and bend the rules his client's way . . . .

What is less clear and more debated about the corporate lawyer-as-advocate is whether he has any obligation to try to induce his clients to comply with the law. It is clear that the lawyer may not actively help clients engage in what he knows to be a crime or a fraud. . . .

In the post-Enron debates — as in the wake of past corporate scandals — the view of the lawyer-as-advocate has most often been invoked to resist rule-changes that would give corporate lawyers positive obligations as monitors or gatekeepers of the legality of corporate conduct, especially by requiring them to report, if all else fails, managers' violations of law to authorities. Law firms and bar associations almost always take the position that such reporting requirements would . . . pervert their function as confidential advisors and advocates. If clients do not trust their lawyers, they will not be candid and forthcoming with the information that the lawyers need to do their job.

But what is their job? One view . . . is that the lawyer needs his client's trust so that he can learn about possibly illegal plans and take steps to stop them. The argument for confidentiality here recognizes that one of the lawyer's functions is to monitor compliance and head off wrongdoing — not just to put the best face on things if the client goes ahead and breaks the law.

NOTES

Does Gordon's comment that lawyers will "wish to approve anything senior management of the client firm asks" sound familiar in the context of the torture memo? While the motive Gordon ascribes is "losing the client to another firm across town," the end results may not be that dissimilar. And what about the lawyer as "risk-manager"? Does that have some similarity to Professor Newman's perspective?

6. Lincoln Savings, Its Lawyers, *Their* Lawyer, and "Litigation Counsel"

During the 1980s, several hundred savings and loan associations failed, many of which were engaged in improprieties on a grand scale.[8] The savings and loan scandals rocked the financial world and the country. The most highly publicized was that involving Lincoln Savings & Loan and its chief, Charles Keating, Jr. This scandal reached into the United States Senate, where in 1987, five senators, the so-called "Keating Five," were accused of improperly trying to persuade the Federal Home Loan Bank Board to back off of its investigation of Lincoln. Keating and Lincoln engaged in massive frauds that would cost taxpayers billions after it finally collapsed in 1989. The federal Office of Thrift Supervision (OTS), was charged with

---

[8] The *O'Melveny* case in section 4 arose out of one such failure.

cleaning up the S&L mess, and was not satisfied with going after just Keating and Lincoln.

On March 2, 1992, the OTS set out after Lincoln's attorneys, the New York firm of Kaye Scholer, Fierman, Hays & Handler and its managing partner Peter Fishbein — the same lawyer and law firm that took over OPM a decade before. The OTS, accusing Kaye, Scholer of conspiring with Lincoln to provide false information to the Bank Board and assisting Lincoln's fraudulent conduct, froze the law firm's assets. Within a matter of days, Kaye Scholer — its assets frozen, its lines of credit being called in by its banks — settled its dispute with OTS for $41 million. Two partners, including Fishbein, the firm's driving force, agreed to never again represent federally insured deposit institutions.

Kaye Scholer and Fishbein maintained their innocence throughout, and placed the blame for the settlement on the high-handed tactics of the OTS, including freezing the law firm's assets. Indeed, many felt that the OTS's tactics *were* extreme and overreaching, and may have unfairly invaded the attorney-client relationship — a claim not unlike those made by corporate lawyers objecting to prosecutors' pressures to waive the attorney-client privilege, as we saw in the last problem. The validity of these claims of overreaching notwithstanding, many believed that Kaye Scholer's focus on the "big brother" tactics of OTS was used to deflect scrutiny from the law firm's own conduct.

That conduct, according to the OTS accusations, involved Kaye Scholer interposing itself between regulators and Lincoln during two federal examinations, and then providing banking regulators with incomplete and incorrect statements, while withholding material facts about questionable transactions, Lincoln's net worth, and the compromising circumstances under which the accounting firm of Arthur Andersen — the same Arthur Andersen that later imploded after the Enron affair — resigned.

Some felt Kaye Scholer's conduct was far worse than the bare-bones OTS accusations. *American Lawyer* reporters Susan Beck and Michael Orey wrote a lengthy article in May 1992 entitled *They Got What They Deserved*, which chronicled Kaye Scholer's behavior, including this language, taken from the law firm's public 1987 submission to the Bank Board on behalf of Lincoln, as evidence of Kaye Scholer's complicity:

- "Lincoln unquestionably is not in unsafe and unsound condition. To the contrary, as set forth below, Lincoln's new management has created an extraordinarily successful, financially healthy institution."

- "Lincoln prudently manages and thus minimizes the risks associated with real estate lending."

- "In making real estate loans, Lincoln has always undertaken very careful and thorough procedures to analyze the collateral of the borrower. What is unusual about Lincoln's underwriting is its particular emphasis on, and the thoroughness of its understanding of, the collateral."

- "The ultimate proof of the pudding of Lincoln's comparative advantage, its sound investment selection, and its prudent underwriting is the unqualified success of Lincoln's program."

The *American Lawyer* exposé also documented that the law firm knew of backdated documents that were authored after a key deadline but dated the month before to grandfather in the investments in question. It described Kaye Scholer as "intimately familiar" with Lincoln employees' efforts to take files that were "empty or inadequate" and create documents after-the-fact that were "intended to look like they were part of the file at the time the investment or loan was made." The exposé also accused Kaye Scholer of knowing that files were "sanitized" by removing negative information about borrowers or risky investments, and numerous other instances of complicity with Lincoln. Indeed, a reading of Kaye Scholer's publicly-submitted documents raises many of these same issues.

Like Singer, Hutner before it, Kaye Scholer hired outside ethics counsel — in this case, one of the deans of the profession, Professor Geoffrey Hazard, then at Yale.

Kaye Scholer, with Hazard's support, claimed that its conduct was appropriate because it was acting as Lincoln's "litigation counsel" — much as Enron's lawyers later claimed their behavior was justified in their roles as "advocates." Although no litigation was then pending between federal regulators and Lincoln, Kaye Scholer claimed that it undertook Lincoln's representation only after an adversary relationship had already developed between Lincoln and the Bank Board. This, claimed the law firm, meant that its submissions to the bank regulators, including a lengthy June 1987 submission that responded to the 1986 examination, were the responses of litigation counsel "advancing arguments on its client's behalf which it believed were supported by the facts and law, without going further and disclosing weaknesses in its client's position." For his part, Professor Hazard, according to the law firm's press release, gave the opinion that had the firm complied with the Bank Board, it "would have violated the standards of ethical conduct . . . applicable to Kaye Scholer in its role as litigation counsel."

Could Kaye Scholer, by declaring the situation to be adversarial, change from advisor to "litigation counsel" by fiat? Years later, could Enron's lawyers justify their conduct in signing off on phantom deals as "advocates" under the same theory? One month after the short but sharp Kaye Scholer affair, Professor Hazard set forth his view of litigation counsel's responsibilities, in his next *National Law Journal* column on ethics, just seven weeks after the Kaye Scholer "affair" had begun.[9]

Because Kaye Scholer settled the case so quickly, Hazard noted, "the major issue in the case has not been resolved[:] a lawyer's duty concerning disclosure of facts adverse to a client, and to what third parties that duty runs." Hazard noted that lawyers often have to make adverse disclosures in discovery, including providing "smoking gun" documents. But, most significantly, he argued that "the litigation lawyer's disclosure duty remains tightly circumscribed. Clearly it does not require an inquisitorial search of the client's mind." More fundamentally, "a lawyer for a client in litigation is not a grand inquisitor against the client. . . ."

---

[9] Geoffrey C. Hazard, *Ethics*, THE NATIONAL LAW JOURNAL, April 27, 1992.

Some questioned how strongly Professor Hazard had really supported Kaye Scholer's position. *American Lawyer*'s Beck and Orey reported that Kaye Scholer actually prepared the text of Hazard's opinion statement, that it was prepared before the full OTS charges and documentation had been filed, and that it contained assumptions of fact that took up 14 of the opinion's 22 pages.

Nevertheless, Hazard's central point on the issue was that in the Lincoln Savings matter, Kaye Scholer was acting not as advisory counsel but as "litigation counsel" with respect to the Bank Board. That is, in his view the firm's duty to disclose "remain[ed] tightly circumscribed." Most observers did not accept this justification, as most today have not accepted Vinson and Elkins' claim of acting as advocates. Those who deconstructed Hazard's opinion after-the-fact (and with, of course, the easy clarity of hindsight) were widely critical of the "litigation counsel" claim, pointing out that a required report to the Bank Board did not come close to reaching an adversarial level that could justify the law firm being in litigation mode. Similarly, there intuitively seems little reason to excuse Enron's lawyers' behavior as "advocacy" when their work product was used to create and approve sham transactions.

7. Kaye Scholer, "Factual Assertions," and Three Bar Opinions

William H. Simon, Columbia law professor and prolific writer on issues of lawyers' morality and personal responsibility, wrote an extensive review of the Kaye Scholer case in 1998 that applies with equal force to Enron.[10] The problem, said Simon, was not so much the use of the term "litigation counsel" but "the distinction between factual assertion and argument." Kaye Scholer, he claimed, violated its ethical duties by claiming to make factual assertions while actually engaging in argument. Vinson & Elkins and other Enron lawyers, one might argue, did the same.

Three interesting ethics opinions emerged from the Kaye Scholer affair. First, in New York, a disciplinary investigation was opened but eventually closed with no action taken. Second, the ABA issued Formal Opinion 93-375 (August 6, 1993), which concluded that "in representing a client in a bank examination, a lawyer may not under any circumstances lie to or mislead agency officials, either by affirmative misstatement or by omitting a material fact . . . ." "However," continued the opinion, mirroring the words of Kaye Scholer's defense, "she is under no duty to disclose weaknesses in her client's case or otherwise to reveal confidential information that would be protected under Rule 1.6."

Third, however, in California, Formal Opinion 1996-146, also seemingly written with an eye on Kaye Scholer, and perhaps anticipating Enron, asked the following question: May a lawyer for a subdivision developer, knowing that substandard plumbing material has been used by a sub-contractor, write a letter to homeowners saying "The warranty in your contract means that [developer] has promised that all materials, including plumbing lines, meet plans, and specifications, including all

---

[10] *The Kaye Scholer Affair: The Lawyer's Duty of Candor and the Bar's Temptations of Evasion and Apology*, 23 LAW & SOC. INQUIRY 243 (1998).

code requirements. The warranty speaks for itself." While strictly true, and while the lawyer does not represent the original malfeasant, the letter clearly seems to mislead. The opinion concludes that the lawyer *may not* write such a letter: "A lawyer acts unethically where she assists in the commission of a fraud by implying facts and circumstances that are not true in a context likely to be misleading."

8.   Putting the Advice into Action

Beyond lawyers who advise on the law or on arguably improper courses of action are those who provide opinions of questionable accuracy. And beyond those lawyers are those who appear to be involved in actually helping to implement strategies of questionable legality.[11] One recent example is the Texas firm of Locke Liddell's[12] assistance to Ernst & Young in helping E&Y implement a massive tax fraud — a fraud that saw four E&Y executives convicted of felonies, at least two lawyers go to jail, and Ernst & Young finally avoiding criminal liability only by paying a $123 million fine in early 2013.

In 1999, Ernst & Young created several tax shelters for "extremely high wealth" individuals. The most well-known "product" was a "contingent deferred swap," or CDS. But CDS and the other "products" were never legitimate. CDS was simply an illegal tax dodge that was set up to "defer" huge one-time profits, such as those dot-comers received when they exercised stock options, long enough to give those "ordinary income" profits better tax treatment as long-term capital gains. Later, the IRS estimated that the tax dodges amounted to hundreds of millions in tax savings.

To implement its plan successfully, E&Y needed a formal tax opinion letter.[13] It went forward even though its own most respected tax lawyer, when asked about such an opinion letter, stated his complete opposition to what he saw as a transparent, highly questionable transaction.

E&Y needed a reputable tax lawyer at a reputable firm to write the letter. It chose R. Brent Clifford of Locke Liddell. Clifford and other Locke Liddell lawyers worked on the opinion letter while exchanging ideas about its text with Ernst & Young personnel along the way. The letter, known in tax circles as a "should" letter, was an assertion that CDS had a "70 to 80 per cent likelihood of success," in Clifford's words. Only when the opinion letter was completed did E&Y sell its product, to approximately 200 high wealth people in all. When it sold the tax shelter package, it told its clients to obtain the Clifford opinion letter for a $50,000 fee to Locke Liddell.

When the IRS refused to consider the tax dodge, the Department of Justice went after Ernst & Young, which at first tried to cover up its wrongdoing, making things worse. But the CDS purchasers went after both the accounting firm and Locke, Liddell, claiming that since they had purchased the opinion letter directly

---

[11] Recall the two ABA opinions addressing such issues that we discussed in section 5.

[12] During the period of the fraud, the aftermath, and the accusations, the firm had several names, which we abbreviate here with the name by which the firm was known when the problems began.

[13] There were actually two related opinion letters, required by tax laws. We simplify here.

from the law firm, they were the law firm's clients, and were entitled to competent, unconflicted representation.

The lawsuits against Locke Liddell were eventually settled in 2009. By then, Ernst & Young personnel had been criminally changed, and it was widely rumored that Clifton would be indicted. He was not, nor was he disciplined by the bar.[14]

In November 2012, the Dallas firm of Winstead Attorneys trumpeted Clifton's arrival as a new shareholder: "With nearly 30 years of experience, Clifton is a recognized and highly reputable attorney . . . [r]ecognized as a Texas Super Lawyer and listed in *Chambers USA* (Tax), *The Best Lawyers in America* . . . ."[15]

Recall the "critical distinction" made in comment 9 to Model Rule 1.2. On what side of the line between "presenting an analysis of legal aspects of questionable conduct" and "recommending the means by which a crime or fraud might be committed with impunity" did Brent Clifton's opinion letter fall? By writing a "should" letter, Clifton seems to have gone well beyond analyzing questionable conduct, the kind of advice Professor Newman claimed he could and should give in his article in section 1, towards actively assisting in illegality.

D. SUPPLEMENTAL READINGS

1. Stewart Taylor, Jr.'s excellent classic article about O.P.M., *Ethics and the Law: A Case History*, from THE NEW YORK TIMES MAGAZINE of January 9, 1983, gives the complete story of O.P.M. in the words of one of our most astute observers of the legal profession. The article is worth reading for anyone wanting to know more about the whole case, with "gory" details. One example: Myron Goodman, told at last by his lawyers that they will no longer assist in his frauds, standing "at the head of the law firm's staircase, shaking with anger," and shouting, "If you . . . bring down the company, I will bring down this firm."

2. Stephen Gillers & Roy D. Simon, Jr., *The Kaye Scholer File, in* REGULATION OF LAWYERS: STATUTES AND STANDARDS (1993 ed.), provides an interesting and thorough treatment of the Kaye Scholer case, largely because of the inclusion of a comprehensive excerpt of the OTS charging document.

---

[14] This story has been widely reported, including: Michael Cohn, *Ernst & Young to Pay $123 Million to Settle Tax Shelter Fraud Charges*, ACCOUNTING TODAY, March 4, 2013; Patricia Hurtado, *Ex-Jenkens & Gilchrist Lawyer Gets 8 Years in Tax Case*, TEXAS LAWYER, March 2, 2013; Michael Rapoport, *Ernst & Young Pays $123 Million to Settle With U.S. Over Tax Shelters*, THE WALL STREET JOURNAL, March 1, 2013; Robert W. Wood, *Ernst & Young's $123M Non-Prosecution Agreement Over Tax Shelters: Priceless*, FORBES.com, March 1, 2013; Joel Rosenblatt, *Locke, Lord Settles Lawsuit Over Tax-Shelter Letters* (Update2) BLOOMBERG NEWS SERVICE, July 2, 2009; Zach Lowe, *Will More Lawyers Be Over Alleged Ernst & Young Tax Shelter Fraud?*, THE AMERICAN LAWYER, September 16, 2008; Lindsay Riddell, *Five sue Ernst and Young over failed tax dodge*, SILICON VALLEY BUSINESS JOURNAL, February 16, 2007; and *Miers's Firm Backed Sham Shelter*, Senate Report Says, BLOOMBERG NEWS, October 10, 2005.

[15] Perhaps the biggest effect on any individual at Locke Liddell was probably that during the early 2000s, Harriet Miers, nominated by President Bush for the United States Supreme Court, was serving as co-manager of the firm. Though this was undoubtedly not the principal reason Miers withdrew her candidacy, it certainly didn't help matters.

3. Susan P. Koniak, *When Courts Refuse to Frame the Law and Others Frame It to Their Will*, 66 S. CAL. L. REV. 1075 (1993). Professor Koniak reviews the Kaye Scholer case in the context of powerful law firms and powerful governmental regulatory agencies acting with little oversight from the judicial system. Koniak has long written on the duty to investigate or, here, not bury one's head in the sand.

4. Two Georgetown articles on willful ignorance come to similar conclusions a dozen years apart. David Luban, *Contrived Ignorance*, 87 GEO. L.J. 957, 976–80 (1999), argues that lawyers should not be able to play ostrich to contrive to remain ignorant. In *The Ethics of Willful Ignorance*, 24 GEO. J. LEGAL ETHICS 187 (2011), Rebecca Roiphe citing Luban, argues that the ABA rules about "actual knowledge" are too narrow, give lawyers "greater leniency" than anyone else, don't ultimately help the client, and allow the kind of "turning a blind eye" behavior that some of our examples reflect.

5. In *Legal and Ethical Duties of Lawyers after Sarbanes-Oxley*, 49 VILL. L. REV. 725 (2004), ethicists Roger C. Cramton, George M. Cohen, and Susan P. Koniak, claim that lawyers have affirmative duties under Sarbanes-Oxley that most states already require without SOX. While SOX is a good start, these professors argue that it is just a beginning. They urge firmer "reporting up" requirements, and the implementation of "reporting out" requirements, i.e., those that require going outside the corporation's highest authority.

6. William H. Simon, *Wrongs of Ignorance and Ambiguity: Lawyer Responsibility for Collective Misconduct*, 22 YALE J. ON REG. 1 (2005). Professor Simon focuses on "deliberate ignorance and calculated ambiguity" as "key recurring themes in modern scandals from Watergate to Enron." Simon discusses lawyers' efforts to avoid responsibility, the "trend in recent legal doctrine, exemplified by the Sarbanes-Oxley Act, to strengthen duties of inquiry," and the established legal bar's resistance to the regulation.

7. *Federal Deposit Ins. Corp. v. O'Melveny & Meyers*, 969 F.2d 744 (9th Cir. 1992), is a difficult case to negotiate, but an important one. It holds that a law firm could have a duty to a corporation's investors to reveal fraud on the part of insiders. The case was overruled on other grounds dealing with choice of law, at 512 U.S. 79 (1994).

8. *Brouwer v. Raffensperger, Hughes & Co.*, 199 F.3d 961 (7th Cir. 2000), expanded the interpretation of the civil RICO statute by reinstating causes of action against a defendant law firm. The Seventh Circuit held that personal participation in the operation or management of an enterprise is not necessary in order to violate the racketeering statute. It is enough to allege that a law firm knowingly agreed to facilitate the operation of an enterprise.

9. Debra Baker, *Island Castaway*, 84 A.B.A. J. 54 (1998). Baker's article describes how lawyers' active involvement in designing offshore "asset-protection trusts" for use by clients with fraudulent intentions began to come under close scrutiny in the late 1990s. This active involvement has some similarities with the Locke Liddell efforts described above.

10. There were several federal appeals court cases addressing the propriety of "offshore asset protection trusts" shortly after Baker's article was published. A

Second Circuit case, *S.E.C. v. Brennan*, 230 F.3d 65 (2d Cir. 2000), refused to exempt the SEC from the stay provisions of the Bankruptcy Code in its effort to repatriate assets even though the SEC had already won a judgment against defendants, who created the offshore asset protection trust *during* trial and then declared bankruptcy *right after* trial. The Ninth Circuit, though, in *FTC v. Affordable Media, LLC*, 179 F.3d 1228 (9th Cir. 1999), upheld a trial court's order demanding the defendants repatriate monies held offshore, despite defendants' claim of "inability to comply with a judicial decree." "It is readily apparent," said the court, "that [trustors] the Andersons' inability to comply . . . is the intended result of their own conduct — their inability to comply and the foreign trustee's refusal to comply appears to be the precise goal of the Andersons' trust."

PART FOUR

THE PRESSURES, ECONOMICS, AND DIVERSITY
OF MODERN PRACTICE

"My fantasy of getting up from my desk, walking out my office, going to the head of my department and quitting to be a bartender is sounding extremely appealing. HELP!"

—a young lawyer posting on a *Greedy Associates* on-line "chat-room" board

Chapter 10

THE LAWYER AS PART OF THE LAW FIRM STRUCTURE

PROBLEM 27: THE SENIOR ASSOCIATE'S SERIOUS DILEMMA

A. INTRODUCTION

Clients ask lawyers for their opinions all the time. Sometimes, they want these opinions in the formal setting of an opinion letter, a document the client can rely on in determining how to act. How far may a lawyer stretch his or her own beliefs in drafting an opinion letter? Is it acceptable to draft a letter that does not comport with one's own objective opinion but may be justifiable under the facts or the law as it could be interpreted? If the opinion "stretches" the law, must the lawyer tell *that* to the client?

The problem of writing an opinion letter is a difficult enough issue. But it is even more difficult where a law firm associate is being asked, or perhaps *told*, to write an opinion letter in which he or she does not believe. Should a law firm have rules that permit associates to refuse to perform an assignment if they consider it improper? What if the associate is not sure whether performing the work is unethical? What about the duty of the law firm to the client, the duty of the associate to the partner *and* the client, and the duty to report? Consider the difficult dilemma of Stephen Green.

B. PROBLEM

I

Stephen Green is a senior associate at Swenson & DeLuca, a mid-sized firm that specializes in litigation and real estate law. Stephen has been at Swenson for only 18 months, but he first spent almost six years in the regional counsel's office of the Environmental Protection Agency. He has become his firm's resident expert on hazardous substances and toxic torts. Sheila Dern, one of the firm's real estate partners, asks Stephen to meet with one of her best clients, George Reynolds. Reynolds owns a building that had been leased for the last 10 years to a company whose business used extensive quantities of a chemical called Thorzac. The company recently went bankrupt, and now Reynolds is looking to sell the building.

At the meeting, Reynolds tells Stephen and Sheila that he has been approached by Doggy-Days, a company that boards and trains dogs, about purchasing

Reynolds' building. But Reynolds knows that the prior lessee intentionally placed some Thorzac in a man-made cement pond because it seemed to help the growth of the pond's lily pads. Stephen and Sheila tell Reynolds that not disclosing to the buyer the presence of hazardous waste could make him liable for civil and even criminal penalties.

"I know that," says Reynolds, "but what about this Thorzac? Is it hazardous or not? Look, I don't know anything about disposing of hazardous waste. If this stuff is considered hazardous, my once-valuable piece of property may not be worth spit. And I need to move quick; this dog guy is ready to buy."

Sheila asks Stephen to research Thorzac and get back to her within three days.

Stephen reviews the federal law and his state's laws. He knows that a waste is deemed hazardous if it either is specifically identified as such by the EPA, or if it is: toxic; corrosive; an irritant; a "strong sensitizer"; flammable; or generates pressure through decomposition. Stephen finds that Thorzac has not been specifically identified by the EPA as hazardous. So Stephen knows he must determine whether it has any of the proscribed characteristics.

Thorzac has only come into common usage in the last several years. After some initial investigation, Stephen doesn't think Thorzac fits the last four definitions for hazardous waste, but he is concerned about what appear to him to be its corrosive and toxic properties.

Stephen uncovers four studies that examine Thorzac. The earliest, conducted under a grant from Thorzac's manufacturer, concluded that its toxicity could not be established. Two other studies, one at a Midwestern university, the other the most recent study by a public interest research group called SafeChem, show preliminary results that indicate toxicity, and showed that prolonged exposure to Thorzac causes birth defects in rats. Neither study proved that the chemical had an effect on humans. Moreover, the SafeChem study also concluded that Thorzac has corrosive properties, and that it is capable of penetrating building materials so that the fumes may be present long after the chemical itself has been removed.

Stephen meets with Sheila. Privately, he is convinced that a regulatory agency using the common definition of "toxic," would conclude that Thorzac fit the definition: "having the capacity to produce personal injury or illness to humans through ingestion, inhalation, or absorption through the body surface." Stephen suggests they hire an expert, but Sheila reminds him that time is too short, and that Reynolds wants to move on the sale right away. "Besides," she says, "*you're* the expert." They then discuss Stephen's research.

"What does all that mean, Stephen?" says Sheila when Stephen is finished. "Look, I just talked to George this morning, and he made it real clear that what he needs is an opinion letter from us saying Thorzac is not a hazardous substance, as that term is now defined. He's sitting on a 4.5 million dollar property that he may not be able to sell to anyone."

"I understand that, Sheila," says Stephen, "but I think Thorzac fits the definition of a hazardous substance. I don't see how I can write an opinion letter saying it's not."

"Nonsense," Sheila replies. "We can't base our opinion on a study by SafeChem. They're not close to being neutral. Besides, their results are just preliminary, and other studies disagree. If that's all you've been able to find, I don't have any problem with an opinion letter that says that Thorzac is 'not a hazardous substance as that term is now defined.' What's wrong with that? And by the way, I want *you* to write this, not me. You're the guy who worked for the EPA. George is going to need *your* opinion, not mine."

QUESTIONS

1. Should Stephen write the opinion letter? *May* he? Can he refuse the assignment before he gets started? How?

2. If Stephen is considering refusing to write the letter, how sure would he have to be that he is right? What if although he *believes* Thorzac is hazardous, he cannot be certain that the EPA would reach the same conclusion, at least based on current evidence? Is this enough to warrant his refusal to write the letter?

3. In the end, what alternatives, if any, does Stephen have to writing the letter?

4. Would Stephen be in a different position if Swenson & DeLuca had been hired to defend Reynolds in a lawsuit filed by Doggy-Days for Reynolds' failure to disclose the Thorzac?

5. Suppose that, on Sheila's advice, Reynolds does not disclose the presence of Thorzac to Doggy-Days. Should Stephen tell Doggy-Days about the Thorzac and the dangers he believes it presents? Should he tell Doggy-Days to keep the dogs out of the pond?

II

In reviewing his bills for submission at the end of the month, Stephen asked Sheila's secretary for her "pre-bills" to make sure Stephen had the correct dates for client meetings and his conferences with Sheila. In reviewing her pre-bills, however, Stephen discovers that Sheila had billed for over 20 hours of meetings with him while he was out of the country on vacation. What should Stephen do with this information? And what is the likely cost to him if he takes action?

C.   READINGS

1.   Peter Kelly Takes a Stand

The following article describes the trials and tribulations of a young lawyer who felt he had to take a stand in reporting the unethical behavior of one of his firm's partners. One of the questions any associate in Peter Kelly's — or Stephen Green's — position will have to answer is whether it is "worth it" to make the ethical but sometimes very difficult choice. Kelly, if asked, maintains that it was, although his decision cost him dearly, as the article describes. Ask yourself how you would go about making this choice if you were in his position.

James M. Altman, *Associate Whistle Blowing*
NEW YORK LAW JOURNAL, September 10, 1999[1]

Discovering that a partner at your law firm has engaged in a significant violation of New York's Code of Professional Responsibility is not merely disillusioning. The Code's imperative to report the ethical misconduct of your fellow lawyers also places you in a potential conflict with your firm and puts you at personal risk. Just how complicated and serious such a situation can become is illustrated by the case of Peter Kelly, the former Hunton & Williams associate who allegedly was discharged for blowing the whistle on the fraudulent billing of partner Scott Wolas, now a fugitive from justice.[2] Ultimately, Mr. Kelly sued Hunton and won a settlement on the eve of trial, but not before joblessness and presumably a lot of angst along the way. Mr. Kelly's case is a cautionary tale that raises many questions about how to act ethically without jeopardizing your employment when you suspect that one of your "superiors" has engaged in unethical conduct.

The factual recitation of Judge John Gleeson's decision in *Kelly v. Hunton & Williams*[3] denying the firm's summary judgment motion reads like a John Grisham novel. Mr. Kelly joins Hunton's New York office in 1990 as a first-year litigation associate. The office's tightly knit litigation department has fewer than 10 partners and associates. Mr. Kelly works primarily for Mr. Wolas and Franklin Stone, another partner, and with Christopher Mason, then an associate. His first-year reviews are highly complimentary and he earns the maximum pay raise for his class. But during that first year, apparently because he was involved in preparing attorneys' fee applications, Mr. Kelly begins to suspect Mr. Wolas of billing for time not worked. He shares his suspicions with Joseph Saltarelli, another litigation associate, whose own experiences confirm Mr. Kelly's concern.

During his second year, Mr. Kelly tells Mr. Mason, now a partner, that he believes Mr. Wolas is engaged in billing fraud. Unbeknownst to Mr. Kelly, Mr. Mason, along with partner Mr. Stone, has been investing heavily with Mr. Wolas in what, it later turns out, is a multi-million dollar Ponzi scheme. "Mason respond[s] curtly, telling [Kelly] that things are not always what they seem, and that Mr. Wolas's billing is not [his] concern." Shortly thereafter, Mr. Kelly starts to get negative feedback about his work.

Mr. Saltarelli expresses his concerns about Mr. Wolas's billing to the managing partner of the New York office. The managing partner refuses to approach Mr. Wolas . . . , suggesting instead that Mr. Saltarelli raise it with Mr. Wolas "in a non-accusatory manner, under the guise of asking his help in explaining billing records. . . ."

---

[1] Copyright © 2013 ALM Media Properties, LLC. Reprinted with permission from the "September 10, 1999 edition of the New York Law Journal. All rights reserved. Further duplication without permission is prohibited.

[2] [Editors' Note: Wolas to date has never been apprehended. After he fled New York, he reappeared in Orlando in the mid-1990s as securities broker "Allen Hengst," then disappeared in December 2000 after defrauding several dozen people out of about $20 million. *See, e.g., Broker vanishes, so does cash,* ORLANDO MORNING CALL, Feb 12, 2001, and Lynn Cowan, *American Express broker used stolen identity,* DOW JONES NEWSWIRES, August 13, 2003.]

[3] 1999 U.S. Dist. Lexis 9139 . . . .

Having been advised that they might have an ethical obligation to disclose Mr. Wolas's billing irregularities to disciplinary authorities, Messrs. Kelly and Saltarelli and another litigation associate meet a few months later with James Jones, the former managing partner of the New York office, about Mr. Wolas's billing. Eventually, he informs them that the former managing partner of Hunton's flagship office in Richmond will investigate.

Mr. Mason and another partner, aware of the investigation, meet with Mr. Kelly the day before he is to be interviewed about Mr. Wolas's billing. They give Mr. Kelly a Hobson's choice: either be fired immediately, without severance pay and a favorable job reference, or announce his resignation, stay with the firm for several months, and get a favorable reference. Mr. Kelly chooses the coerced resignation.

Hunton then concludes billing fraud was not clearly established and informs Mr. Kelly he has no duty to file a disciplinary complaint with authorities.

Four years later, Mr. Kelly sues Hunton for breach of contract under *Wieder v. Skala*, the 1992 New York Court of Appeals decision holding that a law firm cannot discharge an associate for insisting that the firm report to disciplinary authorities the professional misconduct of one of its lawyers. By that time, Mr. Wolas has vanished, leaving Hunton as a co-defendant in multi-million dollar lawsuits brought by investors in Mr. Wolas's Ponzi scheme. Mr. Kelly seeks more than $250,000 in compensatory damages, plus punitive damages of more than $2.5 million. A month after Judge Gleeson denies Hunton summary judgment, the parties settle for an undisclosed sum.

Professional Duty

Hunton's alleged conduct shows just how a law firm should *not* respond when one or more associates questions whether a firm lawyer is acting unethically. Law firms have a professional duty to create an atmosphere supportive of ethical practice. That certainly includes refraining from taking action against an associate who raises an ethical issue. But for some firms, that duty is sometimes trumped by economics or firm politics. . . . .

Even if the firm was the loser, Mr. Kelly surely did not achieve anything close to a complete triumph. He was plagued by his discharge and an unfavorable reference from his only legal employer. Unable to secure suitable legal employment in New York, the lawyer moved to Texas, but the circumstances of his discharge traveled with him. After a year's unemployment, he obtained a lawyering job, but his legal career had been derailed . . . .

Yet Mr. Kelly did the right thing. Indeed, he did the only thing an ethical associate could do. . . . [O]nce Mr. Kelly's suspicions ripened to "knowledge," [New York] DR 1-103(A) required him to report Mr. Wolas's fraudulent billing, lest he himself commit an ethical violation . . . .

Mr. Kelly's career was derailed because he had not lined up another job by the time Hunton clearly showed it was unreceptive to his ethical concerns. . . . [M]ore than a year and a half after he joined the firm, Mr. Kelly was still well regarded. He probably could have left for employment with another firm without any problem.

. . . If by then he felt he had "knowledge" of Mr. Wolas's fraud, Mr. Kelly could have satisfied his ethical obligation by filing a disciplinary charge shortly after securing a new job.

. . . .

It is often difficult for an associate to assess the likely reaction of law firm partners to concerns about possible ethical improprieties. There are numerous factors to consider: How committed is the firm to professional standards? Has the firm established a mechanism — such as an ethics committee or an outside ethical adviser — for dealing with such situations? Does the alleged impropriety reflect carelessness or intentional misconduct? What is the magnitude of the transgression? Can the impropriety be rectified and, if so, how easily? How powerful within the firm, both economically and politically, is the offending lawyer? Can the offending lawyer save face vis-a-vis the firm?

[If] your firm is unlikely to shoulder its own responsibility to create an ethical environment. . . . then it is probably prudent to start evaluating your job prospects before raising the issue with the firm. If you miscalculate and raise the issue to an unreceptive firm, then it becomes more urgent to think seriously about leaving before the situation deteriorates.

As the *Kelly* case demonstrates . . . [t]he stakes can be enormous.

NOTES

At least Peter Kelly had Howard Wieder's precedent on his side. In 1987 Wieder insisted that the partners at his 12-lawyer firm report for discipline a fellow associate who was engaged in a pattern of lying to and deceiving clients. The law firm did so three months later — begrudgingly, says Wieder — and shortly thereafter fired Wieder.

Wieder maintained he was fired for insisting on reporting his colleague. "All I did was what I am ethically bound to do," Wieder told *Manhattan Lawyer*. He sued for retaliatory discharge, but saw his case thrown out by both the trial court and intermediate appeals court, both holding Wieder had no cause of action under New York's at-will employment law. The Court of Appeals finally gave Wieder satisfaction, reversing the lower courts and reinstating his dismissed causes of action against the firm. Here is a brief excerpt from the high court's opinion:

> We agree with plaintiff that in any hiring of an attorney as an associate to practice law with a firm there is implied an understanding so fundamental to the relationship and essential to its purpose as to require no expression: that both the associate and the firm in conducting the practice will do so in accordance with the ethical standards of the profession.[4]

Note that unlike the retaliatory discharge cases we examined in Problem 25, the law firm is only an employer, not a *client*. This avoids one of the principal obstacles to maintaining a cause of action for retaliatory discharge: client confidentiality.

---

[4] Wieder v. Skala, 609 N.E.2d 105 (N.Y. 1992).

Despite this and despite the fact that most states, like New York, *require* lawyers to report ethical violations, neither the law nor the courts have always been sympathetic to the Peter Kellys of the legal world. Before leaving this subject, we should report the good news: Kelly, who went to law school in Texas, has become a successful trial and appellate lawyer in Houston, highly-regarded in the legal community.

We will return to the issue of the ethical obligations of law firm associates, and partners, but first a word or two from one of the deans of legal ethics, Professor Geoffrey Hazard.

2.   Advice from Professor Hazard

How should a young lawyer deal with being asked to do something that he or she is convinced is unethical? Read Professor Hazard's advice.

Geoffrey C. Hazard, *Ethics*
THE NATIONAL LAW JOURNAL, January 17, 1994[5]

On several occasions, I have had telephone calls from former students asking how they should respond to demands by supervising lawyers that they do something seriously unethical. Should they go along, thus violating the rules of ethics and perhaps other laws as well; or should they risk losing their jobs? . . .

The problem arises when both a junior and senior are working on a legal task involving a judgment call that has significant ethical consequences.

One example is . . . whether a corporate matter involving possible illegal activity — for example, illegal payments — should be referred upward in the corporate chain of command. In litigation, the problem may be whether certain files containing potentially damaging information are within the scope of the opposing party's discovery demand . . . .

When clear-cut illegality is involved, the ethical question is not difficult to answer — or should not be. A junior lawyer who assists in illegal conduct is equally as responsible as a senior lawyer, whether in the context of disciplinary charges, civil liability or criminal responsibility . . . . If the ethical question is plausibly arguable, however, then the junior lawyer may look to the senior lawyer to determine the question and, at least in the disciplinary context, may invoke that determination by way of exculpation. Rule 5.2 of the Model Rules of Professional Conduct provides:

> A subordinate lawyer does not violate the Rules of Professional Conduct
> if that lawyer acts in accordance with a supervisory lawyer's resolution of
> an arguable question of professional duty.

As a practical matter, however, the situation confronting the junior may be very perilous. Put bluntly, the senior may engineer the assignment so the junior is directly responsible while the senior leaves no fingerprints. For example, the junior

---

may be invited or instructed to sign the disclosure opinion or the pleading to which Rule 11 applies. Or the senior may absent himself conveniently when the crucial decision has to be made. Afterward, it can be foretold, the senior and the junior may have very different recollections of their roles in the transaction.

When a junior lawyer calls me for advice in such a situation, my initial inquiry - after getting the facts — is this: Is there a lawyer in your shop who has real clout in the organization, and whom you really trust? Having "real clout" means being able to carry the day with the senior partners or a management committee. . . .

Unfortunately, there may not be anyone trustworthy in the firm who has clout. In that event, the question to the junior will be to the effect of: How many children do you have and how big is your mortgage? That is, can you afford to quit your job? If quitting is a realistic possibility, then the junior's career plan should be redirected along that line. A shop that demands juniors be the fall guys in ethics matters is no place to work, if one can help it.

The possibility of legal redress is only a last resort, notwithstanding decisions such as *Wieder v. Skala*. The chances of winning or getting a good settlement may be less than even.

The firm will have drawn the wagons around, for its professional reputation is also at stake. If redress is realized, it will come later, after wracking controversy, great expense and damage to the junior's professional reputation and employability . . . .

No one can say how often these situations arise, and doing a survey of the subject would be ludicrous. I believe the problem is pervasive with respect to relatively minor infractions, however, and more than occasional in terms of serious ones. The incidence certainly is far greater than would appear from grievance proceedings and malpractice litigation.

NOTES

Clearly, Hazard's suggestion to find a trustworthy superior with clout in the law firm is good advice. But as he himself recognizes, this may be almost impossible for many if not most associates.

Professor Hazard's question — "How many children do you have and how big is your mortgage?" — can hardly be comforting to Stephen Green. And how comforting is recourse to MR 5.2? How sure must Stephen be in order to refuse the orders of his superior, Sheila? Or does this rule beg the question, since Stephen, not Sheila, is the expert?

Hazard focuses on partners who set up the associate so that the partner "leaves no fingerprints." Just as common may be the law firm whose day-to-day operations involve questionable ethics that are ingrained in that firm's "culture." These questionable practices may relate to several of the issues raised in this volume, such as discovery practices, trial tactics, or billing irregularities. They may include an attitude that fosters, say, writing opinion letters of questionable propriety. When the firm's culture is involved, it means that "just saying no" becomes even more difficult, and the likelihood of finding a sympathetic partner with clout even more remote, since the partners with clout are the ones who set the tone for the firm.

3. To Report or Not to Report?

We now look more closely at two questions that face associates like Stephen Green: the "shield" offered by MR 5.2 and the duty to report unethical conduct under MR 8.3. Professor Hazard states that MR 5.2 may provide a shield, but notes the "practical" problems. Given the requirement under MR 8.3 to report misconduct when there is a "substantial question about that lawyer's . . . fitness,"[6] how much of a "safe harbor" does Rule 5.2 provide associates? Not much in the view of many observers. First, MR 5.2 only applies to "reasonable resolution" of "an arguable question of professional duty." Clear breaches of duty simply can't be ducked. Second, some commentators believe that it's a mistake to assume that the supervising lawyer knows the situation better than the subordinate. Stephen Green is an excellent example of that. Third, Sarbanes-Oxley and other newer regulations are not always consistent with MR 5.2.[7]

The strongest statement of the duty to report violations comes from *In re Himmel*, 533 N.E.2d 790 (Ill. 1988), which held that lawyers have an "absolute duty" to report unethical behavior. Apparently, *Himmel* has had an effect. The number of lawyer-reported ethical violations dramatically increased in Illinois since *Himmel*. Michael Oths, then president of the National Organization of Bar Counsels, told the *National Law Journal* in 1999 that the Illinois reporting rate was much higher than in any other state.[8]

Needless to say, as Messrs. Kelly and Wieder learned, it's just not as simple as reporting ethics violations when they occur and then going about one's business. Kelly, as the article notes, would have been far better off strategically to have left the firm for another job, and then, from a safe distance, report the unethical conduct directly to the disciplinary authorities.

But most people don't operate that way; they want to work things out "within the family," if possible, as both Kelly and Wieder tried to do. Indeed, *Himmel* itself is conspicuously silent on the degree of evidence a lawyer must have before the duty to report to a disciplinary agency is triggered.

In a case that garnered widespread publicity, when partner Colette Bohatch tried to report what she believed were billing improprieties to her managing partner at a Texas law firm, the managing partner exonerated the accused partner and "encouraged" Bohatch herself to leave. Bohatch sued for constructive discharge and for the firm's retaliatory conduct, including denying her access to clients, reducing her partnership compensation, and breaching the fiduciary duties owed by partners to one another. On appeal, the court allowed Bohatch's claim for

---

[6] Our review shows that as of early 2013, only three jurisdictions do not have mandatory reporting: California, Georgia, and Washington.

[7] *See, e.g.*, Lisa H. Nicholson, *Sarbox 307's Impact on Subordinate In-House Counsel: Between a Rock and a Hard Place*, 2004 MICH. ST. L. REV. 559 (2004).

[8] *See* Darryl Van Duch, *Partner Accused, Career Damaged*, NATIONAL L.J. March 8, 1999.

breach of the partnership compensation agreement, but reversed the remainder of her award, including $4 million in punitive damages.[9] A dissent argued that the failure to allow a breach of fiduciary duty claim allowed the law firm to punish a partner for trying to get the firm to comply with its ethical duties.

But other courts have been similarly unsympathetic. A District of Columbia court denied an attorney a retaliatory discharge remedy after she was dismissed for reporting ethical violations to her superiors, though they allowed her to pursue a defamation claim for falsehoods in her work evaluations.[10]

And in Florida, a court refused to apply the state whistleblower statute to a lawyer who was discharged after informing the bar of a partner who had diverted funds from his former firm. The court held that the statute only protects an individual who reports a violation of a "law, rule, or regulation" to a government agency, not someone who reports a *disciplinary* violation to the Bar.[11] Finally, in Illinois, home of *Himmel*, a 1998 case refused to allow an associate to sue a law firm after he was fired for objecting to superiors on three occasions about a partner's repeated violations of the Fair Debt Collection Agency Act.[12] The court pointed out that after all, the associate should have gone directly to the disciplinary board, as required in *Himmel*. A vigorous dissent emphasized the effect of the majority's opinion: harsh economic and practical disincentives for speaking out.[13]

Despite some recent cases of lawyer/whistleblower heroism (*see* Supplemental Reading No. 3), there are few state courts beyond New York's that allow retaliatory discharge claims. And even these are after-the-fact claims. There continues to be *no* ethics rules that "explicitly prohibit a lawyer or law firm from retaliating against an attorney who makes an external report of misconduct to disciplinary authorities."[14]

4. The Torture Memorandum — May a Lawyer Give Less Than an "Honest" Opinion? — A Case Study

Stephen Green has been asked to write an "opinion letter" in which he does not personally believe — the one that the client wants. May he do this? To help examine this question, we take a look at perhaps the most explosive opinion letter in recent years — the Justice Department's "torture memorandum." While there are obvious differences between the torture memorandum and Stephen's pending Thorzac memorandum, the analysis of the ethics of writing the torture

---

[9] Bohatch v. Butler & Binion, 977 S.W.2d 543 (Tex. 1998).

[10] Wallace v. Skadden, Arps, Slate, Meagher & Flom, 715 A.2d 873 (D.C. 1998).

[11] Snow v. Ruden, McClosky, Smith, Schuster & Russell, P.A. 896 So. 2d 787, 791–792 (Fla. Dist. Ct. App. 2005).

[12] Jacobson v. Knepper & Moga, P.C., 706 N.E.2d 491 (Ill. 1998).

[13] Recall that Illinois was also the state that denied the claims of Roger Balla, discussed in Problem 25.

[14] Alex Long, *Whistleblowing Attorneys and Ethical Infrastructures*, 68 MD. L. REV. 786 (2009). Long calls it "an embarrassment that the legal profession does not do more to encourage firm lawyers to raise concerns within their firms about suspected misconduct and protect those who comply with their ethical obligations to report serious misconduct . . . ."

memorandum, here by Washington (St. Louis) law professor Kathleen Clark, who has developed a sub-specialty in "security law," is both interesting and illuminating.

Kathleen Clark, *Ethical Issues Raised by the OLC Torture Memorandum*
1 NAT'L SECURITY L. & POL'Y 455 (2005)[15]

In the fall of 2001, the Bush Administration was looking for a place to imprison and interrogate alleged al Qaeda members away from the prying eyes of other countries and away from the supervision of US courts. The Defense Department believed that the Naval Base at Guantanamo, Cuba might work, and so commissioned the Justice Department's Office of Legal Counsel (OLC) for legal advice on whether federal courts would consider habeas petitions filed by prisoners at Guantanamo, or whether they would dismiss such petitions as beyond their jurisdiction. On December 28, 2001, OLC responded with a thorough and balanced analysis of whether federal courts would assert habeas jurisdiction. It explained the arguments against such jurisdiction, but also explored weaknesses in that argument and possible strengths in the opposing position. The memo opined that federal courts would not exercise jurisdiction, but explained the risk of a contrary ruling. Acting in reliance on this memo, the government started imprisoning and interrogating alleged al Qaeda members at Guantanamo the following month cognizant of the risk that a federal court might find habeas jurisdiction.

In 2004, the Supreme Court considered habeas corpus claims by prisoners at Guantanamo, and reached a result contrary to that predicted by the Justice Department memorandum, ruling that the district court did have jurisdiction. The fact that the Court came to a different conclusion than that advanced by OLC does not, however, mean that the OLC attorneys failed to fulfill their professional obligations to their client. The authors appropriately explained the risk of an adverse decision, and they provided enough information for the client to understand that risk and make decisions accordingly.

Whenever a lawyer offers a legal opinion, there is a possibility that other legal actors will take a contrary view. If the lawyer apprises the client of that risk and explains the magnitude of that risk, the lawyer has adequately advised and informed the client. The authors of the habeas jurisdiction memo certainly met this standard.

During the summer of 2002, CIA officials grew frustrated with the interrogation of al Qaeda member Abu Zubaydah, who had stopped cooperating with his interrogators. The CIA wanted to use harsher interrogation techniques against Zubaydah, but sought the imprimatur of the Justice Department for those techniques. In particular, they were concerned that certain harsh techniques might violate the international Convention Against Torture and implementing federal legislation, which makes it a crime to engage in torture under color of law outside the United States. White House Counsel Alberto Gonzales commissioned OLC for legal advice about the scope of the torture statute . . . . Deputy Assistant Attorney

---

[15] First published in the Journal of National Security Law & Policy. Copyright © 2005 by Kathleen Clark. Reprinted by permission of the author.

General John Yoo drafted a memorandum that was signed in August 2002 by Assistant Attorney General Jay Bybee . . . . The government apparently acted in reliance on this memorandum in setting interrogation policies for alleged al Qaeda members.

The Bybee Memorandum purported to provide objective legal advice to government decision makers. Nevertheless, its assertions about the state of the law are so inaccurate that they seem to be arguments about what the authors (or the intended recipients) wanted the law to be rather than assessments of what the law actually is . . . .

I. *The Substantive Inaccuracies in the Bybee Memorandum*

The Bybee Memorandum consists of 50 pages of text supporting three assertions: (1) the federal criminal statute prohibiting torture is very narrow in scope, applying only where an interrogator specifically intends to cause the kind of extreme pain that would be associated with organ failure or death; (2) an interrogator who is prosecuted for violating the torture statute may be able to use an affirmative defense to gain an acquittal; and (3) the torture statute would be unconstitutional if it interfered with the President's war-making powers, including the power to detain and interrogate enemy combatants as he sees fit. The memorandum's claims about the state of the law in each of these areas are grossly inaccurate.

The first major inaccuracy is in the memorandum's assertion that the federal criminal statute prohibiting torture applies only where a government official specifically intends to and actually causes pain so severe that it "rise[s] to . . . the level that would ordinarily be associated with . . . death, organ failure, or serious impairment of body functions." This claimed standard is bizarre for a number of reasons. . . . [T]his legal standard is lifted from a statute wholly unrelated to torture. It comes from a Medicare statute setting out the conditions under which hospitals must provide emergency medical care. That statute . . . define[s] "emergency medical condition" as one in which failure to provide medical care could result in "serious jeopardy" to an individual's health, "serious impairment to bodily functions," or "serious dysfunction of any bodily organ or part." The Bybee Memorandum twists this legal standard, and . . . purports to give interrogators wide latitude to cause any kind of pain short of that associated with "death, organ failure, or serious impairment of body functions."

A second major inaccuracy is the memorandum's discussion of [the] defenses available . . . — necessity and self-defense. . . . The memorandum's analysis of the self-defense option is somewhat measured. It . . . does not assert that such an affirmative defense would necessarily succeed. The memorandum also asserts that an interrogator charged with torture might well be able to gain an acquittal using the necessity defense. Yet as David Luban has noted, the memorandum never mentions the fact that the Convention Against Torture itself seems to proscribe such a defense when it declares that " '[n]o exceptional circumstances whatsoever, whether a state of war or . . . any other public emergency, may be invoked as a justification of torture.' " . . .

A third major inaccuracy is found in the memorandum's discussion of presidential authority. The Bybee Memorandum asserts that the President can, at least under some circumstances, authorize torture despite the federal statute prohibiting it. This position is based on a expansive view of inherent executive power, but the memorandum does not even mention — let alone address — *Youngstown Sheet & Tube Co. v. Sawyer*, the leading Supreme Court case on this aspect of separation of powers. *Youngstown* . . . invalidated President Truman's seizure of the nation's steel mills during the Korean War, seriously undermin[ing] any claim of unilateral executive power. The Bybee Memorandum does not even acknowledge that the constitution explicitly grants to *Congress* the power to define "Offences against the Law Of Nations . . ." which suggest[s] that Congress was well within its constitutional authority in banning torture.

On each of these three points . . . the Bybee Memorandum presents highly questionable legal claims as settled law. It does not present either the counter arguments to these claims or an assessment of the risk that other legal actors — including courts — would reject them. Despite these obvious weaknesses, the memorandum apparently became the basis for the CIA's use of extreme interrogation methods. . . . In fact, much of the memorandum was used verbatim in . . . the [written] basis for Defense Department policy.

The legal analysis in the Bybee Memorandum was so indefensible that it could not — and did not — withstand public scrutiny. Press reports about and excerpts from the memorandum began to surface in early June, 2004, and there was a wave of criticism. The Justice Department resisted congressional pressure to turn over the memorandum, insisting that the president had a right to confidential legal advice. When *The Washington Post* posted the complete text of the memorandum on its Web site, the wave of criticism turned into a flood. Eight days later, the Bush administration disavowed the memorandum. Six months later, in December 2004, OLC issued a new torture memorandum that offered legal analysis that was more accurate, repudiating the Bybee Memorandum's analysis . . . .

II. *Ethical Analysis of the Bybee Memorandum*

The substantive inaccuracies in the Bybee Memorandum are so serious that they implicate the legal ethics obligations of its authors. In analyzing the legal ethics implications, it is important to make three preliminary observations. First, lawyers who work for the federal government are subject to state ethics rules . . . . Both Jay Bybee and John Yoo were subject to the D.C. Rules of Professional Conduct . . . .

Second, these OLC lawyers had as their client an organization — the executive branch of the United States government — rather than any individual officeholder. Although White House Counsel Alberto Gonzales requested the Bybee Memorandum, he was not the client. Instead, he was simply a constituent of the organizational client. Ordinarily, lawyers must accept the decisions made by such constituents when those constituents are authorized to act on behalf of the organization. But where a lawyer knows that a constituent is acting illegally and that conduct could be imputed to the organization, the lawyer must take action to prevent or mitigate that harm . . . .

Third, in analyzing the performance of the lawyers who wrote the Bybee Memorandum, it is important to analyze whether they were acting as legal advisors or as legal advocates.

When a lawyer gives legal advice, she has a professional obligation of candor toward her client. In advising a client, the lawyer's role is not simply to spin out creative legal arguments. It is to offer her assessment of the law as objectively as possible. The lawyer must not simply tell the client what the client wants to hear, but instead must tell the client her best assessment of what the law requires or allows.[16]

David Luban has described this obligation of candor in the following way: [Where] there is not absolute agreement among lawyers about the state of the law . . . , knowledgeable lawyers' opinions usually fall somewhere in a range similar to the familiar bell curve. If a lawyer advised a client that the law is at an extreme end of that bell curve (rather than . . . where most knowledgeable lawyers would view it), then the obligation to give candid legal advice requires the lawyer to inform the client that the lawyer's interpretation is at the extreme end . . . .

In giving legal advice, a lawyer may provide advice that is contrary to the weight of authority, spinning out imaginative, even "forward-leaning" legal theories for the client to use. When doing so, however, the candor obligation requires the lawyer to inform the client that the weight of authority is contrary to that advice.

. . . .

The harm to the client from failing to advise about the illegal character of proposed conduct may be even greater when the client is an entity rather than an individual. Indeed, a lawyer working for an entity client has an enhanced obligation to guard the interests of the entity against wrongdoing by the entity's constituents.

The Bybee Memorandum purports to offer legal advice. Its authors, Jay Bybee and John Yoo, had an obligation to be candid with their client, the executive branch. The constituent who requested the Bybee Memorandum, Gonzales, may have wanted a particular answer to his questions about the torture statute. But the OLC lawyers had a professional obligation to give accurate legal advice to their client, whether or not the client's constituents wanted to hear it. Based on the available facts, it appears that Bybee and Yoo failed to give candid legal advice, violating D.C. Rule 2.1, and that they failed to inform their client about the state of the law of torture, violating D.C. Rule 1.4 . . . .

If bar disciplinary authorities investigate Yoo and Bybee, these two attorneys . . . might assert that the ethical obligations of candor and adequately informing their client did not apply because the Bybee Memorandum was never intended as legal advice in the traditional sense. In fact, David Luban and other scholars have speculated that this Bybee Memorandum was not intended as legal advice at all, but instead as an immunizing document, to ensure that CIA officials who engage in torture would not be prosecuted for that conduct . . . .

---

[16] [51] Comment 1 to D.C. Rule 2.1 states that "a lawyer should not be deterred from giving candid advice by the prospect that the advice will be unpalatable to the client." . . . Model Rule 2.1 is identical . . . .

But if the authors of the Bybee Memorandum intended to immunize torturers in this way, they might have violated a different ethical rule which prohibits an attorney from assisting a client's criminal conduct . . . .

Bybee and Yoo are not the only government lawyers for whom the Bybee Memorandum may raise ethical concerns. News reports indicate that several White House lawyers reviewed drafts of the Bybee Memorandum. Did the White House lawyers object to the flawed analysis in the memorandum, or did they instead actually insist that the memorandum include such analysis? . . .

Not all government lawyers accepted the patently inaccurate claims of the Bybee Memorandum. Career military lawyers who were involved in developing Defense Department interrogation policy objected to the Bybee Memorandum, and they went up the chain of command to register their objections. The contrast between the career military lawyers . . . and most of the politically appointed lawyers, who championed it, is quite striking.

NOTES

Obviously, torture memoranda have become politically charged. But it would be unfortunate if scholars avoided evaluating these documents on that basis. Harold Koh, then Yale Law School Dean, offered this evaluation:

> To me, the saddest part of this entire episode is not how the President's lawyers failed, but how they failed to understand how they had failed. . . . [W]e see hard cases all the time, where lawyers are forced to choose between law and morality . . . . But here, sadly, morality and law pointed in the same direction. Nor was this just government lawyers doing their job . . . . You are under no obligation as a government lawyer to tell your boss how to violate the law, particularly since a government lawyer's prime obligation is not to his or her boss, but rather, to uphold and protect the Constitution and laws of the United States of America.[17]

Recall that in Problem 24, we asked "Do government lawyers have a higher duty than private counsel give disinterested advice?" Here we ask a related question: "Does a *private* lawyer, who is not 'litigation counsel,' have the duty to write a disinterested letter?" Or, turning things around, "Does a lawyer have a duty to write only an opinion letter that states what he truly believes?"

The ABA rules are not clear on these questions. The Restatement does shed some light on related questions. In § 95, Comment (c), the Restatement discusses the lawyer's: "duty" to "provide a fair and objective opinion"; ability to rely on facts provided by others; and writing of an opinion based on factual assumptions known or suspected to be untrue ("not without express disclosure"). The ABA's Business Law Section has a subcommittee that specifically addresses opinion letters, but their "principles," codified in 1998, don't provide entirely clear answers either.

---

[17] Harold Hongju Koh, *Can the President Be Torturer In Chief?*, 81 IND. L.J. 1145, 1165, 1166 (2005).

5.   Duties to Third Parties? Liability

Opinion letters, of course, are not used just by clients, but by third parties with whom the client is attempting to do business. Clearly, Mr. Reynolds intends to use Stephen Green's letter in his efforts to sell his property. Clients often give their lawyers' opinion letters to others to further their goals. In the 1990s, a rather extensive series of court cases developed discussing lawyers' liability to third parties where their opinion letters have been passed on by the client and the lawyer knows the opinion is not accurate.

Petrillo v. Bachenberg, 623 A.2d 272 (N.J. Super. Ct. 1993), *aff'd,* 655 A.2d 1354 (N.J. 1995), is an early and oft-cited case. A seller of land had performed soil testing that revealed the land was unsuitable for a septic system. The seller's lawyer, knowing the problem, nevertheless provided the buyer with a misleading single report that gave a false sense of security about the transaction. When the buyer sued, the court found that when the lawyer handed over the test results, he assumed a duty to the buyer to render reliable information, even though the document was not created by the lawyer.[18]

In *Rubin & Cohen v. Schottenstein, Zox & Dunn,* 143 F.3d 263 (6th Cir. 1998), the court *en banc* reversed a three-judge panel and held the lawyers for a company liable where the attorneys, knowing that the company had advised potential investors to contact them, confirmed, inaccurately, the financial soundness of the company. The court emphasized that the lawyers knew exactly why their input was being sought, and that the investors had a right to rely on the lawyers' candor. Similarly, in *Vega v. Jones, Day, Reavis & Pogue,* 121 Cal. App. 4th 282 (2004), the court allowed a fraud claim where the law firm for a company that was purchasing another had written a disclosure schedule that was not candid about how the client was financing the purchase. This "half-truth" was tantamount to "active concealment."

A 1995 Colorado case[19] held that where a lawyer's opinion letter to *the client* about the merits of a lawsuit was used by the client to entice third-party purchasers, and the lawyers *knew* that the letter was being used, the lawyers could be liable to the third parties for misrepresentation (though not ordinary professional negligence).[20] If Stephen Green "knows" how Reynolds will use his letter, he could be in the same boat.

Ackerman v. Schwartz, 947 F. 2d 841 (7th Cir. 1991), goes half a step further. There, investors in a fraudulent tax shelter brought an action for securities fraud against an attorney who wrote the client an opinion letter that incorrectly stated that investors would be entitled to tax credits. The court decided that the lawyer had no affirmative duty to blow the whistle on his clients or to correct the letter. The lawyer did not agree to have his letter circulated to investors. But when the

---

[18] Note the similarities between this case and the facts in California Formal Opinion 1996-146, discussed in Problem 26.

[19] Mehaffy, Rider, Windholz & Wilson v. Central Bank Denver N.A., 892 P.2d 230 (Colo. 1995).

[20] *See also* McCamish, Martin, Brown & Loeffler v. F. E. Appling Interests, 991 S.W.2d 787 (Tex. 1999).

lawyer did not object when his clients included his letter in an offering, the court concluded that this was enough to hold the attorney liable as a principal in the fraud.[21]

Kline v. First Western Government Securities, Inc., 24 F.3d 480 (3d Cir. 1994), which we referenced in the last problem, held that a law firm that wrote an opinion letter relied on by third-party investors could be liable to third-party investors even when it did not know that the opinion letter was false. The firm's failure to conduct any investigation meant it could be held liable for acting with "reckless disregard" of the opinion's veracity.

In *Kline*, the law firm wrote an opinion about the tax consequences of an investment. The opinion letter contained a disclaimer that the lawyers based its opinion solely on its client representations and had done no due diligence regarding these representations. When the IRS refused favorable tax treatment, the investors sued the law firm. The Third Circuit court held that the disclaimer did not protect the law firm. Thus:

> When the opinion or forecast is based on underlying materials which on their face or under the circumstances suggest that they cannot be relied on without further inquiry, then the failure to investigate further may support an inference that when the defendant expressed the opinion it had no genuine belief that it had the information on which it could predicate that opinion.

Several courts since the Enron scandal have picked up on this same "reckless disregard" standard to find 10b-5 securities violations.[22]

More recently, of course, we have the scandals we've discussed in Problem 26. In the Enron matter, the court, discussing Vinson & Elkins, said this:

> This Court concludes that professionals, including lawyers and accountants, when they take the affirmative step of speaking out, whether individually or as essentially an author or co-author in a statement or report, whether identified or not, about their client's financial condition, do have a duty to third parties not in privity not to knowingly or with severe recklessness issue materially misleading statements on which they intend or have reason to expect that those third parties will rely.[23]

---

[21] This factual scenario is not unlike the Locke Liddell situation in Problem 26, except that there, the end-users argued with some success that *they too* were the clients of Ernst & Young's law firm, making their claims direct ones.

[22] *See* Rebecca Roiphe, *The Ethics of Willful Ignorance*, 24 GEO. J. LEGAL ETHICS 187 (2011), especially at fn 140: "Lawyers may also be held liable for participating in their clients' fraud under section 10b-5(a) and (c) if they know (or are reckless in not knowing) that their clients' trades are manipulative. Despite the disagreement over the extent of lawyer liability, courts do hold individuals liable for material misrepresentation under the securities laws if they are reckless in their disregard of the underlying facts."

[23] In re Enron Corp. Sec., Derivative & ERISA Litig., 235 F. Supp. 2d 549, 610–11 (S.D. Tex. 2002). The district court cited both *Rubin & Cohen* and *Ackerman*. It was estimated that V&E eventually settled with various plaintiffs for $25 to $30 million.

Should identifying the law firm be the test of lawyer liability? Should lawyers be immune so long as the third parties don't know the lawyers are involved? The answers are "no" according to trial judge in the Enron litigation, who was less concerned with who signed documents than with the fact that the law firm was a *de facto* "co-author" that participated in issuing the statements, knowing third parties would rely on them.

Then, in 2008, the United States Supreme Court held that aiders and abettors, or so-called "secondary" or "accessory" actors, could not be held liable for 10-b5 damages.[24] This decision may limit the liability of law firms when their names are not directly linked to the false statement or opinion in question. Thus, a case arising out of the Refco brokerage scandal, *Pacific Inv. Mgmt. Co. v. Mayer Brown LLP*, 603 F.3d 144 (2d Cir. 2010) followed *Stoneridge* in holding that the false statement had to be "attributed" to the lawyer or law firm, even if the firm had created the statement for the client.[25]

In two companion state cases, one brought by Refco's receiver against accountants and others, and the other brought as a shareholders' derivative suit by the victims of one of the participants in the fraud, American International Group, Inc., the New York State Court of Appeals, in a 4-3 vote, allowed those accused to use the affirmative defense of *in pari delicto*, a principle of agency law that means that courts will not intercede to resolve a dispute between two wrongdoers, and thus avoid liability.[26] The *Kirschner* majority disagreed with contemporaneous decisions in both New Jersey and Pennsylvania, both cited in the Supplemental Readings. How courts in the future may treat these situations could depend on how this trio of cases is evaluated.

6.   Duties to Third Parties? Disclosure

What about the ability of a law firm to disclose its client's financial fraud and wrongdoing? Until 1992, there was nothing that a lawyer could do; the rules of confidentiality were simply too stringent. That year, the ABA issued one of its most controversial opinions, complete with a rare dissent, Formal Opn. 1992-366, which

---

[24] *Stoneridge Investment Partners v. Scientific-Atlanta, Inc.*, 552 U.S. 148 (2008).

[25] Refco was a brokerage that went public in 2004. A year later, the fraud of Phillip Bennett, Refco's CEO and 50% owner, became public. Beginning in 1998, Bennett and others had orchestrated a succession of fraudulent loans that hid hundreds of millions of dollars of uncollectible debt from the public, falsely inflating Refco's value. Refco filed for bankruptcy protection, investors and lenders lost as much as $2.4 billion, and Bennett pled guilty and was sentenced to 16 years in prison. Joseph Collins of Mayer Brown was convicted of conspiracy and fraud charges in July 2009. His conviction was overturned and he was again convicted in 2012. See the factual summaries in this and the following case; and Chad Bray, sentenced to seven years was overturned and he was again convicted in 2012. See the factual summaries in this and the following case; and Chad Bray, *Refco Lawyer Convicted of Criminal Charges – Again*, WALL STREET JOURNAL law blog, November 16, 2012; and *U.S. Attorney for the Southern District of New York* press release, *available at* http://www.justice.gov/usao/nys/pressreleases/November12/CollinsVerdictPR.php?print=1.

[26] *Kirschner v. KPMG LLP*, 938 N.E.2d 941 (N.Y. 2010). The court split between traditional agency law and public policy, with the dissent arguing that immunity should not be granted to "the outside actor, hired to perform essential gatekeeping and monitoring functions, [who] actively colludes with corrupt corporate insiders."

became known as the "noisy withdrawal" opinion. That opinion found that:

- "A lawyer *must* withdraw from any representation of the client that, directly or indirectly, would have the effect of assisting the client's continuing or intended future fraud"; and

- A lawyer may withdraw while *disavowing* the lawyer's work product to prevent its use in the client's continuing or intended future fraud, "even though this may have the collateral effect of disclosing inferentially client confidences" — the so-called "noisy withdrawal."

In 2002, the ABA House of Delegates changed the Model Rule itself, MR 1.6(b), to add two subsections, (b)(2) and (b)(3), that liberalized the exceptions to confidentiality to allow for these circumstances by rule. A decade later, many states have adopted this permissive whistleblowing. This only applies, as did the opinion, when the client's fraud uses the lawyer's work product inappropriately.

7. Discipline for Law Firms?

Would a system that disciplines law firms as well as lawyers help associates like Stephen Green? Would it tend to improve a law firm's "culture"? University of Arizona law Professor Ted Schneyer wrote this next article 20 years ago as a cutting-edge statement of the case in favor of law firm discipline. Schneyer's thesis continues to be the subject of significant debate, but since this wide-ranging and commonsense article, exactly *two* states (and only two) have developed rules disciplining law firms.

Ted Schneyer, *Professional Discipline for Law Firms?*
77 Cornell L. Rev. 1 (1992)[27]

1. In 1989 a partner at Baker & McKenzie made improper racist and sexist remarks while interviewing a University of Chicago Law School student for a job with the firm. Shortly after the incident was reported to the firm, the interviewer opted for early retirement. But matters did not end there. Instead of treating the incident as the isolated wrongdoing of a "bad apple," the school insisted that the firm submit a written description of the measures it was taking to prevent similar incidents before the school would allow the firm to recruit on campus again. The firm complied with this demand. . . .

2. A company represented by Fried, Frank, Harris, Shriver & Jacobson sued the federal government to obtain documents under the Freedom of Information Act. The company's name was to be kept confidential under a protective order. In 1989, Fried, Frank inadvertently filed in court an unredacted document that divulged the client's name.

. . . .

4. A federal judge determined that Lord, Bissell & Brook aided in a violation of the antifraud provisions of the securities laws by failing to notify the shareholders

---

[27] Copyright © 1992 by Cornell University and the Cornell Law Review. Reprinted by permission.

of its client company when the firm learned that the earnings of an intended merger target had been grossly inflated in merger documents. A partner working on the case held stock in the target company and was interested in the deal's success. The judge, however, refused to grant the SEC an injunction that would have required Lord, Bissell & Brook to change its internal procedures to discourage such incidents in the future. The court noted the professional duty of the firm's lawyers to "conform their conduct to the dictates of the law" and expressed confidence that the firm would voluntarily take "appropriate steps." But the firm failed to take those steps and was later sued for securities violations in a similar matter, which resulted in a 24 million dollar settlement.

. . . .

Disciplinary agencies have always taken individual lawyers as their targets. They have never proceeded against law firms either directly, for breaching ethics rules addressed to them, or vicariously, for the wrongdoing of firm lawyers in the course of their work. The traditional focus on individuals has probably resulted from the system's jurisdictional tie to licensing, which the state requires only for individuals, and from the system's development at a time when solo practice was the norm.

Legal practice, however, has changed . . . . While only thirty-eight American law firms had more than fifty lawyers in the late 1950s, by 1986 over 500 firms did so and over 250 had more than 100 lawyers. [Having branch offices] has made intrafirm coordination both more difficult and more important. Firms have also become highly leveraged - that is, the ratio of relatively inexperienced associates to partners has risen as high as four-to-one. The proportionally larger number of inexperienced lawyers within firms has heightened the need for supervision. . . .

As law firms grow, the potential harm they can inflict on clients, third parties, and the legal process grows as well. At the same time, the law firm, at least the larger firm, is ripening into an institution that presents new opportunities for bureaucratically controlling the technical and ethical quality of law practice. . . .

So far, however, those who make disciplinary policy have taken little notice of these developments. True, the . . . Model Rules of Professional Conduct, note that "the ethical atmosphere of a firm can influence the conduct of its members." The Model Rules also make clear for the first time that supervisory lawyers are responsible for monitoring their subordinates, an obligation with particular significance in the hierarchical setting of a large firm. But the ABA, the state supreme courts that adopt the ABA codes, and the agencies that assist the courts in disciplinary enforcement have yet to confront the infrequency of disciplinary proceedings against lawyers in firms.

Proceedings against lawyers in large or even medium-sized firms are very rare. In 1981–82, for example, more than eighty percent of the lawyers disciplined in California, Illinois, and the District of Columbia were sole practitioners, and none practiced in a firm with over seven lawyers. Yet, judging from the frequency with which larger firms and their lawyers are the targets of civil suits, motions to disqualify, and sanctions under the rules of civil procedure disciplinable offenses occur with some regularity in those firms. . . . .

These factors may help to explain the infrequency of disciplinary proceedings against large-firm lawyers, but additional explanations, so far neglected, have important implications for disciplinary policy. These explanations stem from the nature of group practice. First, even when a firm has clearly committed wrongdoing, courts may have difficulty, as an evidentiary matter, in assigning blame to particular lawyers, each of whom has an incentive to shift responsibility for an ethical breach onto others in the firm. Many, perhaps most, of the tasks performed in large firms are assigned to teams. Teaming not only encourages lawyers to take ethical risks they would not take individually, but also obscures responsibility. . . .

Second, even when courts and disciplinary agencies can link professional misconduct to one or more lawyers in a firm as an evidentiary matter, they may be reluctant to sanction those lawyers for fear of making them scapegoats for others.
. . .

Third and most important, a law firm's organization, policies, and operating procedures constitute an "ethical infrastructure" that cuts across particular lawyers and tasks. . . . Even a firm with a well-defined management structure does not delegate the duty to make firm policy and maintain an appropriate infrastructure solely to management. To varying degrees this remains every partner's business — and sometimes, as a result, no one's . . . .

[A] disciplinary regime that targets only individual lawyers in an era of large law firms is no longer sufficient. Sanctions against firms are needed as well.

. . . .

A disciplinary system for law firms may not be immediately attractive to the lawyers who practice in firms. It could, after all, encourage their firms to monitor their work and limit their individual discretion more sharply — phenomena to which many lawyers are hostile. Yet a system of law firm discipline may actually benefit these lawyers. It could promote firm practices that reduce the risk not only of discipline but also of civil liability, disqualification, and other nondisciplinary sanctions.

The Emerging Status of Law Firms as Appropriate Disciplinary Targets

[This] idea is not as radical as it may seem. Close administrative analogies exist. The stock exchanges and the Securities and Exchange Commission maintain disciplinary systems for brokerage houses, and not just for the individuals who work in those firms. . . . And of course law firms as such are already subject to civil liability, fee denials, and disqualification; these sanctions complement lawyer discipline as a regulatory technique. Moreover, four developments in modern ethics rules and disciplinary techniques suggest that the legal profession is already edging toward the use of law firm discipline.

A. Prophylactic Ethics Rules

Modern ethics rules already require lawyers to take certain prophylactic measures to prevent misconduct . . . . [Thus,] when one lawyer in a firm is barred from handling a case on conflict grounds, other lawyers in the firm are generally barred as well. This rule seeks to avoid the risk that a lawyer who possesses confidential information about a client will be tempted or pressed to communicate that information to others in the firm.

When one views ethics rules in this modern light, as a tool to minimize lawyers' opportunities to commit fundamental wrongs, disciplining law firms for failing to take preventive, institutional measures hardly seems a radical step.

B. *Firm-Directed Ethical Norms*

A second and more curious point about modern ethics rules is that occasionally they directly address law firms. . . . Moreover, bar association ethics opinions sometimes construe ethics rules that do not explicitly address law firms as if they did. For example, one ABA opinion holds that when a lawyer who is handling a client's matter leaves her firm, the withdrawal [rules], though addressed only to individual lawyers, require the firm to continue representation. . . .

Since only licensed individuals are now subject to professional discipline, these rules and interpretations seem odd. . . . Yet the rules may not be mere slips of the professional tongue. They have a common theme: each rule deals with matters that in law firms require collective action. . . .

C. *Ethics Rules on Matters of Law Firm Governance*

. . . [E]thics rules have also begun to regulate matters of law firm governance that bear on ethical compliance. These rules, themselves prophylactic in nature, so far are addressed only to individual lawyers. . . .

Of special interest here is MR 5.1(a), which recognizes that the duty to prevent ethical breaches within a law firm is a matter of indirect as well as direct supervision. The rule requires lawyers who have "supervisory authority over the professional work of a firm" to "make reasonable efforts to ensure that the firm has in effect measures giving reasonable assurance that all lawyers in the firm conform to the rules of professional conduct." . . . Clearly, MR 5.1(a) is concerned with matters of ethical infrastructure.

. . . .

So long as the rule's up-to-date recognition of the importance of firm infrastructure is tied to the horse-and-buggy of individual discipline, the rule seems likely to remain so. . . . Accordingly, . . . we may have to give disciplinary authorities the options of fining or censuring the firm or putting it on probation.

D. *The Growing Use of Firm-Appropriate Disciplinary Sanctions*

Before 1970, many states used disbarment or suspension from practice as their chief disciplinary sanction. A system of law firm discipline could never rely heavily on analogous sanctions.

. . . .

The post-1970 development of probation as a sanction illustrates the shift toward a disciplinary philosophy compatible with firmwide discipline. . . . Probation is used "to help lawyers who have violated the disciplinary rules, but whose conduct likely can be corrected so that they can continue to serve the public." . . . When probationers work in a firm, their partners are used as supervisors and are required to ensure that the probationers use proper office practices.

CONCLUSION

A number of questions remain concerning the implementation of a system of law firm discipline which this Article has not fully addressed — how to fund the system, how disciplinary bodies will gain jurisdiction over law firms, whether they should also take jurisdiction over other entities in which lawyers practice, and who should have jurisdiction over a firm with branches in several states. These matters are secondary. For now, debate should focus on the merits of the general proposal.

NOTES

Note Professor Schneyer's discussion of the development of "ethical infrastructures" for law firms. Since this article was written, many more firms have developed such infrastructures, perhaps out of necessity given Sarbanes-Oxley and the other regulatory pressures. In addition, of course, the growth of big firms has exploded exponentially.

Recall the Bowen McCoy article in Chapter 1 about the inability of several mountain trekkers to develop a group ethic that could have helped a holy man to safety while individuals acting alone could not. Do you see a parallel between McCoy's lesson on corporate ethics and Schneyer's arguments about ethical infrastructures? Interestingly, Schneyer uses corporate models for his proposals on developing law firm ethical cultures and firm-wide discipline. Schneyer's most recent article suggests using the regulatory program used in New South Wales, Australia as a model.[28] He is still fighting the fight.

In the years since Schneyer's ambitious article, only two states, New York and New Jersey, have formally instituted law firm discipline. In New York, the basic rule of general application, DR 1-102 (no one may violate disciplinary rules, interfere with the administration of justice, etc.), was amended to apply to law firms. Other rules were amended to require that law firms "ensure that all lawyers in the firm conform" to the ethics rules, and that firms must "supervise, as appropriate," the work of associates, partners, and nonlawyers alike. New York now also requires that law firms keep records sufficient to run adequate firm-wide conflicts checks.[29] Given the history of discipline as an individual lawyer-by-lawyer matter, these changes are substantial, though they have not — at least not yet — produced a pattern of firm-wide discipline. There have been several, but relatively few, cases of law firm discipline in these two states, mostly in New Jersey, the country's most client-protective state.[30] Meanwhile, several other states, including

---

[28] Ted Schneyer, *On Further Reflection: How "Professional Self-Regulation" Should Promote Compliance with Broad Ethical Duties of Law Firm Management*, 53 ARIZ. L. REV. 577 (2011).

[29] DR 5-105(E).

[30] *See, e.g.*, In re Sills Cummis Zuckerman, Radin Tischman Epstein & Gross, 927 A.2d 1249 (N.J.

California, have intimated that law firm discipline may be in their futures.[31]

8.   Modern Law Firm Culture and "Greedy Associates."[32]

With the continued consolidation and mergers of big firms and the increasing view that law is a business first and a profession second, mentoring for young associates has become more problematic.

Any law firm's culture is a combination of its personality, its traditions, and its core values. These core values include many issues we have discussed in this volume, such as policies about the kinds of clients the firm takes, or how the firm acts towards its opponents. These values also include how much the firm focuses on making more money as opposed to "quality of life" issues — everything from part-time partnerships to parental leave policies.

Firms also define their cultures by the way they treat their associates. Some firms see their younger lawyers as profitable engines to be run at full tilt, and make little effort to convince them to stay the course to partner, while others are far more nurturing.

But firms with strong mentoring programs are increasingly rare. Many law firms give little or no feedback to their new attorneys. Annual reviews often last a mere 30 minutes. Associates come to know that they will get little insight into the quality of their work, and a lot of talk about billing.

Law firms do make efforts of varying kinds to inculcate their young lawyers with the firm's core values. To the extent economic realities permit, activities for "summer associates" — the law student interns who form the recruitment pool for permanent jobs — are often opportunities to wine and dine while the firm puts on its best face. In good economic times, law firms promote retreats and annual meetings as a chance for all employees to "bond." Instead, at many firms these events are expensive weekends where drinking or playing golf form the social schedule, and the business meeting focuses on the firm's financial health and billable hour quotas. Many firms offer little opportunity at these retreats to consider or create new directions or philosophies.

Some firms provide training for young associates from more senior lawyers or outside consultants, while others have senior partners who serve as real role models and mentors. These firms, seemingly fewer and farther between as BigLaw gets bigger and mergers continue, and frequently "smaller" firms of from 25 to 75

2007); In re Rovner, Allen, Seiken, and Rovner, 754 A.2d 554 (N.J. 2000); In re Ravich, Koster, Tobin, Oleckna, Reitman & Greenstein, 715 A.2d 216 (N.J. 1998); In re Jacoby & Meyers, 687 A.2d 1007 (N.J. 1997), and in New York, In re Wilens & Baker, 9 A.D.3d 213 (N.Y. App. Div. 2004).

[31] The California effort also comes from case law. Thus, in *People Ex Rel. Herrera, v. Stender*, 212 Cal. App. 4th 614 (2012), the City and County of San Francisco, through its elected City Attorney, accused a lawyer *and his law firm* of unfair business practices. The court found that the law *firm* should be . required to abide by the California ethics rules. While this firm was but one lawyer, admitted in another state, the reasoning may become expanded in the future.

[32] We are again indebted to the Ballantine Books division of Random House for "borrowing" in this section from pages 87–91 of RICHARD ZITRIN & CAROL M. LANGFORD, THE MORAL COMPASS OF THE AMERICAN LAWYER (1999).

lawyers, are those that insightful associates might want to look for. But increasingly, it is a world of lawyer mobility, lateral transfers — experienced lawyers from other firms who arrive with "books of business" — megafirms, and diminishing firm loyalty.

When law firms become revolving doors and values and traditions give way to free market economics and the question "What have you done for me lately?" the associate, at the bottom of the food chain, usually feels the pressure the most. Increasingly, these young associates have turned to their peers for what we might term "self-mentoring." Among the most popular outlets for peer talk therapy and general venting have been chat rooms both on- and off-line (the local sports bar) and, unfortunately for the short-sighted, social media sites like Facebook. A decade ago, "Greedy Associates" boards, or chat groups, had sprung up on the Internet. These "boards," more like clubs, are still around, offering a measure of privacy (and anonymity) while permitting candid speech. The following excerpted article is our own take on this phenomenon.

RICHARD ZITRIN & CAROL M. LANGFORD, THE MORAL COMPASS: ASSOCIATED STRESS
American Law Media and Law News Network (1999)[33]

Greedy associates care. They care about pay, perks, and prestige, and whether their firm is as hot as the competition. On line, they post the latest in salaries, bonuses, mergers, and layoffs, with Internet links to news stories announcing major law firm changes.

Greedy associates kvetch. They complain when they have to spend Labor Day in the office while their partners enjoy the weekend. And they complain when the partners *are* in the office: "Which is worse: knowing the partner for whom you are working is enjoying his Labor Day with his family, or having him hovering to make sure you are working diligently on his project?"

Greedy associates are comedians. "Newbies" who don't know the lingo had better be quick studies. And sometimes, "GAs" will even joke about themselves, their lives — even their sex lives, or the lack thereof . . . .

And they do it all publicly, on line, in a series of "Greedy Associates" clubs, or "boards". . . . Originally the boards served to exchange information about the perks offered by "BIGLAW." They still do, but they've expanded well beyond this limited scope. There are regional GA boards, specialized boards, boards for summer associates. . . . The most popular and interesting is "RealGAs," [which] has posts about salaries, bonuses, and raises. But there are also wide-ranging discussions about almost everything, from the pros and cons of punitive damages, to moral philosophy, to where to vacation in Greece. . . .

It's impossible to profile the average Greedy Associate with accuracy, since people don't identify themselves by their real names. To do so would make it impossible for a candid discussion of what's troubling them. . . . Still, it's possible

---

to make some generalizations, particularly about those who post rather than just lurk.

Greedy associates are egotistical, sharp-tongued, prideful, competitive, and bright. Mostly bright. And young — young enough to be egotistical, sharp-tongued, prideful, and competitive about how bright they are — and to constantly compare their intelligence to others. Typical is their intentional misspelling of the word "REdiculous," their creation of "sock puppet" alter egos who are free to express themselves sarcastically, even scatalogically, in ways their usual identities would not, and their on-line identities themselves: Lady Greediva, postassociatestressdisorder and the like.

Greedy associates are also disillusioned. They grouse about doing work paralegals could easily handle, far from the action and even farther from the courtroom, on cases they don't choose for clients they don't know or, even worse, don't like. The irony is that these highly intelligent young lawyers — many, if one can believe their claims, from the top of their class at the best law schools — feel they're being wasted on tasks better suited for "lesser" beings. But though many would deny it on line, beneath the hard shell of cynicism and sarcasm — the side they tend to show on the GA boards — lurk some sensitive souls.

Greedy associates worry. They worry about the meaning of their lives, why they've chosen a profession that forces them to give up so much for, well, so *much*, at least economically. But their unhappiness is palpable.

They are expected to perform quickly, at a high level of competence, and with a billable hours quota that makes the forty-hour work week look like chump change. . . . One RealGAs associate put it this way: It's like the high school competition she used to hate — swim under water for as long as possible, and see who can hold her breath and stay under water the longest. . . .

The Greedy Associates boards do more than provide an outlet for the frustrations of the law business. They also allow participants to create their own group culture. Even though people's true identities remain anonymous, many on-line comments and most of the messages we've received "off-list" show that GAs are fiercely loyal to and protective of each other. To many, the culture of the Board, and their loyalty to its participants, is more real than what they find in their own firms.

But for some, it's not enough. Wrote one Greedy Associate in a moment of despair:

> "Does anyone else on this board feel like being a lawyer in BIGLAW is slowly but surely deadening them inside? It is such mind-numbing work that I feel like I'm losing my sense of humor and find it very difficult to appreciate anything, either inside or outside work. Pure ambivalence. I've gotta get out before I go completely postal. FYI — I'm stuck here working with a partner to turn a document that does not need to be turned. It's in an area of law for which I have no experience that I got roped into because I'm a new lateral and haven't learned the politics yet. When does this end? I'm sick of being an adult and having most of my waking life dictated by people I don't like or respect, doing work for which there is no passion. My fantasy of getting up from my desk, walking out my office, going to the head

of my department and quitting to be a bartender is sounding extremely appealing.

HELP!"

We must find a way to give those who swim under water a chance to come up for air.

D. SUPPLEMENTAL READINGS

1. The incredible story of law student/whistleblower Richard G. Poff, Jr. sounds like a tale from a Grisham novel. Michael D. Goldhaber has written an excellent *National Law Journal* article, *Crazy in Alabama*, December 20, 1999, describing how Poff blew the whistle on well-known Alabama lawyer Robert "Coach" Hayes and his partners, only to find himself sued by Hayes for slander (despite Hayes's criminal conviction and bar suspension), thrown in jail by one judge, and ordered to undergo a psychiatric evaluation by another. Also worth reading is the Alabama Supreme Court opinion in *Poff v. Hayes*, 763 So. 2d 234 (Ala. 2000), reversing the seven-figure default judgment entered in favor of Hayes after a judge improperly denied both Poff's pre-trial motions and his right to jury trial.

2. Two articles from the GEORGETOWN JOURNAL OF LEGAL ETHICS on the duty to report misconduct that so damaged Peter Kelly are Arthur F. Greenbaum, *The Attorney's Duty to Report Professional Misconduct: A Roadmap for Reform*, 16 GEO. J. LEGAL ETHICS 259 (2003), and Nikki A. Ott and Heather F. Newton, *A Current Look at Model Rule 8.3: How Is it Used and What Are Courts Doing About It?*, 16 GEO. J. LEGAL ETHICS 747 (2003).

3. The saga of Louis C. Schneider's upstanding conduct is told through several articles available on line. First, Debra Cassens Weiss' *A Letter Left on a Copier Spurs an Associate's Ethical Response*, ABA JOURNAL, June 17, 2008, tells how Schneider, then a recently-admitted associate, discovered evidence that his boss' client trustee account was overdrawn when he read a letter left on the copier glass. After checking with the Bar, Schneider reported his boss for discipline. He left that firm and went out on his own. In January 2012, however, Schneider was again reporting someone to the bar, this time a deputy DA whom he had been dating, and who lied about their relationship and another relationship with a judge. Schneider also reported *himself* for being less than forthcoming about his part in the matter. Only the DA was charged with a disciplinary offense. *See* Jeff German, *Second romance cover-up alleged*, LAS VEGAS REVIEW-JOURNAL, January 4, 2012.

4. Lisa H. Nicholson, *Sarbox 307's Impact on Subordinate In-House Counsel: Between a Rock and a Hard Place*, 2004 MICH. ST. L. REV. 559 (2004), addresses the superior/subordinate duties post-Sarbanes-Oxley, and cites to Carol M. Rice, *The Superior Orders Defense in Legal Ethics: Sending the Wrong Message to Young Lawyers*, 32 WAKE FOREST L. REV. 887 (1997), an oft-cited piece with an excellent discussion of this difficult relationship.

5. Alex Long, *Whistleblowing Attorneys and Ethical Infrastructures*, 68 MD. L. REV. 786 (2009), quoted in section 3 above. Long, who has written several articles on similar subjects, offers a review of the state of the law, and some ideas for legislative and common law solutions, and ethics rule modifications.

6. ABA Section on Business Law, Committee on Legal Opinions, *Legal Opinion Principles*, 53 Bus. Law. 831 (1998), contains a complete and useful set of principles for writing opinion letters. The site http://apps.americanbar.org/buslaw/tribar/ is the home of the "Legal Opinion Resource Center," and contains a wealth of information including a number of links to other helpful documents relating to lawyers and formal opinions.

7. *R.T.C. v. Latham & Watkins*, 909 F. Supp. 923 (S.D.N.Y. 1995), is one of the relatively rare 1990s-vintage cases to find no liability owed by a law firm. Here, however, the firm issued an opinion letter valid under one state's laws but reviewed by buyers in other states. The court attributed a certain level of sophistication to the buyers of the securities involved.

8. Two other northeastern courts came out differently than the New York high court in *Kirschner*: *NCP Litig. Trust v KPMG LLP*, 901 A.2d 871 (N.J. 2006) and *Official Comm. of Unsecured Creditors of Allegheny Health Educ. & Research Found. v PricewaterhouseCoopers, LLP*, 989 A.2d 313 (Pa. 2010). The comparison among these three cases, which both the majority and dissenting opinions undertook in *Kirschner*, is worth examining, and may foretell something of the future.

9. The debate continued between the two Schneyer articles cited in the Readings with several valuable point-counterpoint articles, including these two: Julie R. O'Sullivan, *Professional Discipline for Law Firms? A Response to Professor Schneyer's Proposal* 16 Geo. J. Legal Ethics 1 (2002), and Ted Schneyer, *A Tale of Four Systems: Reflections on How Law Influences the "Ethical Infrastructure" of Law Firms*, 39 S. Tex. L. Rev. 245 (1998).

10. Joshua E. Perry, *The Ethical Costs of Commercializing the Professions: First-Person Narratives from the Legal and Medical Trenches*, 13 U. Pa. J.L. & Soc. Change 169 (2010), discusses the tension between being both a professional and a businessperson in the practice of law or medicine, callings that traditionally were marked by "a commitment to provide service to the public that goes beyond the economic welfare of the practitioner." Professor Perry describes a "moral tension between serving self-interests and meeting the needs of patients/clients as an important, under-identified, and ultimately corrosive component of contemporary professional life."

PROBLEM 28: BILLING PRACTICES AT PRAGER & DAHMS

A. INTRODUCTION

As clients become more concerned about the cost of legal services, and the legal marketplace, saturated with lawyers, becomes more competitive, billing practices of lawyers have come under close scrutiny. The traditional practice of sending an unannotated bill and expecting it to be paid is as anachronistic as black-and-white TV. It was replaced long ago by the billable hour, which remains by far the most commonly used billing standard. Questionable billing practices continued under hourly billing systems, in large firms and small law offices alike, as we'll discuss. And everyone in law school is familiar with the pressures on young lawyers to meet their billable hour requirements.

Many believe that the billable hour regime is on the wane, to be replaced by a number of other mechanisms, such as yearly retainers, flat fees, and "value billing." But for the moment we are still in the hourly-billing era, with all the issues it brings. And solutions other than this billing method are likely to cause their own set of problems.

B. PROBLEM

I

Carrie Waters was excited to accept an offer at Prager & Dahms, a large Southland City law firm. Carrie was told that as a new associate, she would receive a basic salary of $125,000 per year, plus a year-end $10,000 bonus if she billed over the requisite 1,850 hours, and another $10,000 if she could get her billings up to 2,100 hours.

Seven months have passed. Carrie is frustrated because she barely makes her billing quota and thinks she will never reach the year-end bonus goal. Moreover, she is concerned that if she doesn't reach bonus status, Prager & Dahms might give her a bad year-end review for not pulling her weight. She tells her concerns to her friend Billy Shears, a fifth-year Prager & Dahms associate. Shears tells Carrie that billing is an art and that there are certain "tricks of the trade" that will help her make her billing goals.

QUESTIONS

1. First, Shears advises Carrie that he bills for any and all time that he spends on a case. He tells her that he bills even when he thinks about a case while showering in the morning. He calls it "strategizing client's case" or "evaluating tactics for trial."

2. Second, Shears informs Carrie that since she often flies to Capital City to sit in at routine depositions, she should bill one client for traveling to and from the

deposition and simultaneously bill another client for reviewing documents for that client on the same flight. "I do it each time I travel," he says.

3. Shears suggests billing clients in minimum quarter-hour increments instead of tenths of an hour (six minutes). "That way," Shears tells Carrie, "if I call opposing counsel and he or she is not in, I leave a voice mail message and bill a quarter-hour. When I call again that afternoon and get voice mail again, it's another quarter-hour. Two one-minute phone calls, a half-hour billed!"

4. Shears tells Carrie that he recently worked on a complex antitrust research issue. He devoted over 30 hours to the project: 20 hours researching and 10 drafting a winning brief. One month later, Shears was assigned another case with the same issues. Shears simply modified the brief he had already prepared and changed the parties' names. He spent two hours revising the brief, but charged the client 20 hours for the same research and writing he had billed on the previous project. "I had the special expertise," he said. "The second client got a 10 hour discount and has nothing to complain about."

Evaluate Shears' tactics and advice.

II

Thurston Prager, founding partner of Prager & Dahms, has been a practicing trial lawyer for over 35 years. He is a very experienced and well-respected attorney who charges $700 per hour for his time, and still runs the firm through its management committee.

QUESTIONS

1. When new clients are brought to the firm, Prager prefers to negotiate fixed or partially fixed billing arrangements with his clients. His fee agreements for litigation typically involve a flat fee through filing a complaint or responsive pleading and then an hourly fee for work beyond that point. He notes both he and the firm make more money that way. Is that ethical?

2. Prager requires a minimum charge of two hours for any court appearance, no matter how brief it is. Last week, Prager scheduled three consecutive court appearances starting at 9:00 a.m. He was finished by 10:15. He billed six hours of work and then went out to the golf course. Is this proper?

3. Prager has suggested to the firm's compensation committee that the bonus system for associates should change. Instead of paying flat bonuses, he presents the idea of basing the bonus on the total *income* brought in by that associate. This, he reasons, will reduce the amount of time of first and second year associates that their reviewing partners "write down" as being wasted or part of the associates' learning curve and thus unbillable to the client. Prager also believes that this bonus system will encourage associates to work harder on cases that are billed out at the highest rates, which in turn will generate more profit for the firm. Is this proper?

C. READINGS

1. The Development of "Billable Hours"

It hasn't been that long since hourly billing was considered the wave of the future. Fifty or sixty years ago, the amount of the typical lawyer's bill was determined by what the attorney considered appropriate. This method of billing involved a largely subjective assessment of the value of legal services, and resulted in a fee that was somewhere in between today's "flat fee" and what we today would call "value billing," a term we will look at later in these readings.

One major difference between the "good old days" and modern practice is that in years past, the bill was rarely based on a formal fee agreement or even an engagement letter. Many lawyers of an earlier era felt it was unprofessional or at least undignified to have written fee agreements with clients. As recently as a generation ago, a written fee agreement was unusual except in contingency cases, where the lawyer's fee was based on a percentage of the recovery. The American Bar Association rules have only required a client's informed consent to a written *contingency* fee contract since the Ethics 2000 changes were implemented in 2002, and still do not require written fee contracts in non-contingency cases, though many individual states, including California, do have such a requirement.

Many localities had standard rates for certain kinds of services, such as real estate closings, simple wills, and probates. In many states, some of these rates, such as probate fee schedules, became codified. Other rates were institutionalized in the rules of local practice and in ethics rules. Thus, both the Model Code and the Model Rules still use as one of the factors to be considered in determining the propriety of a fee "the fee customarily charged in the locality for similar legal services." Formalized fee schedules, including schedules setting minimum fees, were widely used 40 years ago, until the United States Supreme Court held, in *Goldfarb v. Virginia State Bar*, 421 U.S. 773 (1975), that these fee schedules violated antitrust laws.

The modernization of law practices and centralization of lawyers in larger firms are circumstances that called for more uniform billing practices. And the consumers of legal fees began to think that they should be paying on the same time-for-money basis that much of America used to earn its wages. Indeed, the 1950s saw an enormous increase in hourly billing not only for lawyers, but for other service people, from auto mechanics and plumbers to accountants. Only physicians and dentists seemed to escape this trend.

Hourly billing had numerous advantages over the traditional discretionary billing methods it replaced. The "time sheet" became a way to quantify a lawyer's work, allowing the consumer to be sure that "you get what you pay for." But hourly billing presented its own host of problems. The currency of the new law firm became hours, and the measurement of the worth of law firm associates — and of many partners as well — became "billable hours."

As the starting salaries in large law firms escalated dramatically in the 1980s and again in the late 1990s, so too did the billing requirements, which climbed beyond 1,800 billable hours a year to 2,000, 2,200 and more for associates in some firms. Below, we will examine at length the effect of these billable hours requirements on the associates who must meet them. For the moment, though, put aside the issue of whether lawyers can render ethical, competent representation at that exhausting level. There is little question among commentators and ample empirical evidence that we practice law today in an environment ripe for billing abuses.

Many factors are at work in addition to the escalation of billable hours requirements themselves: the profession's increasing bottom-line obsession during the last generation; the cyclical recessions in the law "industry" in 1987, 2000, and 2008 and onward, resulting in what has come to be called an "eat-what-you-kill" mentality, or every-lawyer-for-oneself; the roller-coaster resurgences of law firm profitability, at unprecedented levels: at the end of the 1990s, with the steep, sudden, and dramatic rise in salaries, even for first-year associates; and in the recovery period after the 2000 dot.com and stock market busts as the law profession (perhaps now more accurately called the "law business") reached and then passed the first few years of the new millennium.

2. Clients Start Fighting Back About Overbilling

Unfortunately for the consumer of legal services, then, the development of hourly billing was hardly a panacea, creating its own new problems. After a period of acceptance, clients, especially large "institutional" clients, who used to pay their lawyers' periodic invoices automatically, began not only to question their bills, but to fight back. They now routinely question bills, demand discounts as frequent clients, and look proactively at billing alternatives, as we'll discuss in sections 6 and 7.

In the 1990s, a number of big corporate clients began bringing in outside auditors to examine their lawyers' bills. In the area of insurance defense, these audits quickly ran into trouble as violative of the third party insured's attorney-client privilege, an issue we discussed in Problem 12. But for other corporations, hiring companies such as Legalgard of Philadelphia became a way to check to see whether cases were being overbilled or even worse — that law firms were virtually stealing from their clients.

Back in 1992, John J. Marquess, who ran Legalgard and now runs a similar company, Legal Loss Control, told the *New York Times'* David Margolick that one client had told him " 'If you can't trust your lawyer, it's like not being able to trust your wife,' I told him, 'Based on what your legal costs have looked like for the last five years, maybe you should go home and check what your wife is doing.' "[1]

Marquess described to Margolick discovering a Century City lawyer who thrice had billed a client for a 50-hour workday; a Los Angeles lawyer who recycled the same legal research in 135 cases, charging the same hourly fee each time; and a Chicago law firm that put 79 of its 82 lawyers to work defending a single products

---

[1] David Margolick, *At the Bar: Keeping Tabs on Legal Fees Means Going After the People Who Are Hired to Go After People*, N.Y. TIMES, March 20, 1992.

liability case, resulting in a $6 million fee for what Marquess said was worth, at most, $200,000.

In other horror stories, we have discovered these examples worth noting here:

• Gary and Maureen Fairchild, husband and wife, worked individually at their separate Chicago law firms creating not just fraudulent bills but fraudulent clients, and padded those bills with personal expenses, extra hours, and more. Both were caught, disbarred, and charged with felonies. Professor Lisa Lerman of Catholic University, perhaps the most prolific writer on the subject of inappropriate billing practices, profiled this particular couple in *The Slippery Slope from Ambition to Greed to Dishonesty*, 30 HOFSTRA L. REV. 879 (2002).

• Bobby Glenn Adkins Jr. of Marietta, Georgia billed his clients in three matters for "legal services" that was actually time spent prosecuting lawsuits and perfecting liens against these same clients, and defending himself on disciplinary charges. He was disbarred in 2004.

• Raleigh, North Carolina bankruptcy Attorney Mark Kirby was indicted on 16 counts of billing fraud. Among his offenses were: "double billing" clients enough to manage 90 hours in one day; and billing a total of *13,000 hours* in a 13-month period, even though that period, calculated at 24 hours a day seven days a week, was only 9,500 hours long. Kirby somehow managed to get a hung jury in federal court before a plea negotiation resolved his case.

• Kansas lawyer Larry L. Myers billed 43.5 hours on a routine estate matter in *one hour* increments, even for matters that took only one-quarter of an hour. In 2006, however, citing his "remorse," the Kansas Supreme Court did not suspend him but disciplined him only by censure, which a minority of the court would have given only a private censure.[2]

Of course, it is not the extreme and outrageous story that is our main focus here, nor the occasional surprisingly minimal sanctions, but the issue of day-to-day overbilling or at the least, pressures to overbill. We will examine this a bit further in the next article and the notes that follow.

3. Overbilling at the Top

According to John Marquess, the worst billing offenders seemed to be prestigious law firms charging "Wall Street" rates. Can this be? And if it is so, then why? Is it simply the "bureaucracy and arrogance" that Marquess cites? The Fairchilds were both successful lawyers at large Chicago firms. Or are there other explanations for the "blue chip" overbillers described in the following article?

---

[2] In re Myers, 127 P.3d 325 (Kan. 2006).

Michael D. Goldhaber, *Overbilling is a Big-Firm Problem Too*
THE NATIONAL LAW JOURNAL, October 1999[3]

Every few months, an elite firm partner is caught in a billing or expense fraud. Predictably, the rogue's partners dismiss him as "just one rotten apple." Then the issue of overbilling is ignored until the next scoundrel comes along.

A new study in the *Georgetown Journal of Legal Ethics*, "Blue-Chip Billing," takes a longer view and tallies the rotten apples. Lisa Lerman of Catholic University . . . counts exactly 16 elite firm partners during the past 10 years who allegedly stole at least $100,000 in a billing or expense scam. Seven were managing partners. "I wanted to make a point about rot at the top," Professor Lerman says.

She sees her 16 cases as "the tip of an iceberg."

Professor Lerman would bring the iceberg into view, if only she could. She uses her study as an occasion both to look back on the outrageous cases we know about and to speculate about the outrageous cases we don't know about. She partly blames the bar for failing to catch overbillers.

"There's a complete disconnect between the occurrence of misconduct and the rate of discipline," she says in an interview. In her article, she writes, "The lawyer regulatory system has focused most of its attention on lawyers whose practices are far more modest than the sixteen lawyers on this list."

"Blue-Chip Billing" trots out a host of silk-stocking rascals, among them: Scott Wolas, the fugitive who allegedly padded bills to mask the time he spent on a Ponzi scheme to resell Scotch whiskey in Asia; Webster Hubbell, the former associate U.S. attorney general and chair of the Arkansas bar ethics committee who used Rose Law Firm funds to pay off 10 personal credit cards; and Harvey Myerson, who spent his $2.5 million in fraudulent billings on dog food, toupees and helicopter rides.

How Common?

"They are terrible cases, no question," says Robert O'Malley, of the American Legal Assurance Society, which insures firms against legal malpractice claims, "but she's got 16 cases out of millions of client representations. I don't think what she describes is widespread."

Cornell Law School ethics professor Roger Cramton counters, "These big cases are clearly outliers, but systematic bill padding is pretty widespread."

Most attorneys draw a sharp line between padding and fraud. "Inefficient or excessive billing is not remotely in the same category as falsifying bills," says Steven Krane, of Proskauer Rose L.L.P.

Yet Professor Lerman believes that there's plenty of outright fraud, and the

---

more subtle cases of overbilling are often blameworthy. "It's a significant deception when you put down four hours and you've only worked one," she says. Other academics agree.

William G. Ross, author of the book "The Honest Hour: The Ethics of Time-Based Billing by Attorneys" (1996) conducted surveys in the early '90s. About half the lawyers surveyed confessed to at least some double-billing . . . . "This is a problem that most definitely goes beyond 16 people," Professor Ross said in an interview.

. . . .

Professor Lerman suggests that big firms get away with more because they "send huge bills to large institutional clients every month." She also argues that abuses flow from arrogance, and that "law firms are magnets for people with convention-center-size egos."

Finally, Professor Lerman attributes the crisis to the billable hour. "By setting annual billable targets for lawyers," she writes, "law firms may invite — perhaps almost require — dishonest recordation of time."

Professor Ross found that even in the early 90s, half of all associates recorded billing more than 2,000 hours. Taking into account routine slack time, 2,000 honestly recorded billables translates into 3,000 hours worked — more than eight hours, seven days a week — by Professor Ross's reckoning. . . .

But if big-firm lawyers are routinely padding, they're not getting caught. A 1981-82 study cited by Professor Lerman showed that 80% of those disciplined that year in California, Illinois and Washington, D.C., were sole practitioners — and none practiced in firms of more than seven lawyers. An updat[ed] survey by *The National Law Journal* shows that . . . solos and small firms dominate the time of bar discipline offices.

. . . .

Auditor John Toothman, of the Arlington, Va., firm The Devil's Advocate, . . . tells firms not to rent expensive space or depend on a few clients because high overhead and sudden drops in business ratchet up the pressure to overbill. He also tells lawyers to lower their expectations: If they want to get rich, they should switch fields. . . .

. . . James J. Grogan, chief counsel to the Illinois disciplinary commission, reports that indeed, "Illinois' big billing cases have come to us by virtue of *Himmel* reporting."[4] Illinois, out of proportion to its size, accounted for three of the 16 cases on Professor Lerman's all-time baddie list, and all three were brought to the bar by their partners, through *Himmel* reports.

None of the 16 cases came from Texas, where last year the high court held that Houston's Butler & Binion was permitted to expel a partner after she had reported suspected overbilling by another partner. . . .

Professor Lerman herself offers no prescriptions, but her avowed ambition, in

---

[4] See our discussion in Problem 27.

calling attention to what she perceives as the crisis of big-firm overbilling, is characteristically sweeping. "My aspiration," she says, "is to make it unsafe."

NOTES

Professor Lerman and Professor Ross have focused much of their work on billing issues, from slightly different perspectives, as this article indicates. Lerman, often using real-life examples to illustrate her points, has also closely examined the issue of lawyers as liars. Ross has used surveys and statistics both to crunch billing numbers and to demonstrate lawyer dissatisfaction. Some of their work product is further described in the Supplemental Readings.

American Lawyer, the flagship magazine of the ALM legal periodical network, conducts an annual survey of big-firm associates. Among other issues, they ask associates whether their law firms train them in how to keep track of their time. Over a third said "no." Does cheating go on?

"I know people who sit down at the end of the day and say, 'What's a defensible amount of time . . .?' " one New York associate told the New Jersey Law Journal. "They think of what number they can rationally allocate to each task. The way that you write your time can be an art, and people can get quite creative."[5]

What role in overbilling does the firm play? Is it the dominant one: the creation of a firm culture where this behavior is expected? Or is pointing the finger at their law firm just an excuse for unethical associates?

4.   The ABA Speaks Out on Billing Practices

Some agree with ALAS's Robert O'Malley that Professor Lerman's examples and Professor Ross' statistics are not indicative of widespread billing fraud. But what about relatively common practices that law firms have traditionally used? Where should the line be drawn? In 1993, the ABA's ethics committee spoke out strongly on the propriety of a wide range of billing practices, a view that remains the ABA's — and many states' — current thinking. We excerpt that important opinion here. Note that our problem closely tracks several issues raised in the opinion.

---

[5] Helen Coster, *The Inflation Temptation: What Have You Done for your Client in the Past Six Minutes?*, NJLJ, October 1, 2004.

AMERICAN BAR ASSOCIATION FORMAL OPINION 93-379,
Billing For Professional Fees, Disbursements, and Other Expenses
(December 6, 1993)[6]

The legal profession has dedicated a substantial amount of time and energy to developing elaborate sets of ethical guidelines for the benefit of its clients. Similarly, the profession has spent extraordinary resources on interpreting, teaching and enforcing these ethics rules. Yet, ironically, lawyers are not generally regarded by the public as particularly ethical. One major contributing factor to the discouraging public opinion of the legal profession appears to be the billing practices of some of its members.

It is a common perception that pressure on lawyers to bill a minimum number of hours and on law firms to maintain or improve profits may have led some lawyers to engage in problematic billing practices. These include charges to more than one client for the same work or the same hours, surcharges on services contracted with outside vendors, and charges beyond reasonable costs for in-house services like photocopying and computer searches. Moreover, the bases on which these charges are to be assessed often are not disclosed in advance or are disguised in cryptic invoices so that the client does not fully understand exactly what costs are being charged to him.

The Model Rules of Professional Conduct provide important principles applicable to the billing of clients, principles which, if followed, would ameliorate many of the problems noted above. The Committee has decided to address several practices that are the subject of frequent inquiry . . . .

The first set of practices involves billing more than one client for the same hours spent. In one illustrative situation, a lawyer finds it possible to schedule court appearances for three clients on the same day. He spends a total of four hours at the courthouse, the amount of time he would have spent on behalf of each client had it not been for the fortuitous circumstance that all three cases were scheduled on the same day. May he bill each of the three clients, who otherwise understand that they will be billed on the basis of time spent, for the four hours he spent on them collectively? In another scenario, a lawyer is flying cross-country to attend a deposition on behalf of one client, expending travel time she would ordinarily bill to that client. If she decides not to watch the movie or read her novel, but to work instead on drafting a motion for another client, may she charge both clients, each of whom agreed to hourly billing, for the time during which she was traveling on behalf of one and drafting a document on behalf of the other? A third situation involves research on a particular topic for one client that later turns out to be relevant to an inquiry from a second client. May the firm bill the second client, who agreed to be charged on the basis of time spent on his case, the same amount for the recycled work product that it charged the first client?

The second set of practices involve billing for expenses and disbursements. . . .

Disclosure of the Bases of the Amounts to be Charged

At the outset of the representation the lawyer should make disclosure of the basis for the fee and any other charges to the client. This is a two-fold duty, including not only . . . the basis on which fees and other charges will be billed, but also a sufficient explanation in the statement so that the client may reasonably be expected to understand.

. . . .

A corollary of the obligation to disclose the basis for future billing is a duty to render statements to the client that adequately apprise the client as to how that basis for billing has been applied. [For hourly fees,] a billing setting out no more than a total dollar figure for unidentified professional services will often be insufficient. . . . [B]illing other charges without breaking the charges down by type would not provide the client with the information the client needs to understand the basis for the charges.

Professional Obligations Regarding the Reasonableness of Fees

Implicit in the Model Rules and their antecedents is the notion that the attorney-client relationship is not necessarily one of equals, that it is built on trust, and that the client is encouraged to be dependent on the lawyer, who is dealing with matters of great moment to the client.

. . . .

[T]he lawyer who has agreed to bill on the basis of hours expended does not fulfill her ethical duty if she bills the client for more time than she actually spent on the client's behalf. In addressing the hypotheticals regarding (a) simultaneous appearance on behalf of three clients, (b) the airplane flight on behalf of one client while working on another client's matters and (c) recycled work product, it is helpful to consider these questions, not from the perspective of what the client could be forced to pay, but rather from the perspective of what the lawyer actually earned. A lawyer who spends four hours of time on behalf of three clients has not earned twelve billable hours. A lawyer who flies for six hours for one client, while working for five hours on behalf of another, has not earned eleven billable hours. A lawyer who is able to reuse old work product has not re-earned the hours previously billed and compensated when the work product was first generated. Rather than looking to profit . . . the lawyer who has agreed to bill solely on the basis of time spent is obliged to pass the benefits of these economies on to the client. The practice of billing several clients for the same time or work product . . . is contrary to the mandate of . . . Model Rule 1.5.

Moreover, continuous toil on or over-staffing a project for the purpose of churning out hours is also not properly considered "earning" one's fees. One job of a lawyer is to expedite the legal process . . . .

If . . . the lawyer is particularly efficient in accomplishing a given result, it nonetheless will not be permissible to charge the client for more hours. . . . [T]he economies associated with the result must inure to the benefit of the client, not give rise to an opportunity to bill a client phantom hours . . . .

Charges Other Than Professional Fees

. . . The Rules provide no specific guidance on the issue of how much a lawyer may charge a client for costs incurred over and above her own fee. However, we believe that the reasonableness standard explicitly applicable to fees under Rule 1.5(a) should be applicable to these charges as well.

. . . In the absence of disclosure to the client in advance of the engagement to the contrary, the client should reasonably expect that the lawyer's cost in maintaining a library, securing malpractice insurance, renting of office space, purchasing utilities and the like would be subsumed within the charges the lawyer is making for professional services.

At the beginning of the engagement lawyers typically tell their clients that they will be charged for disbursements. When that term is used clients justifiably should expect that the lawyer will be passing on to the client those actual payments of funds made by the lawyer on the client's behalf. . . .

[I]n the absence of disclosure to the contrary, it would be improper if the lawyer assessed a surcharge on these disbursements over and above the amount actually incurred. . . .

Perhaps the most difficult issue is the handling of charges to clients for the provision of in-house services. In this connection the Committee has in view charges for photocopying, computer research, on-site meals, deliveries and other similar items. Like professional fees, it seems clear that lawyers may pass on reasonable charges for these services. Thus, in the view of the Committee, the lawyer and the client may agree in advance that, for example, photocopying will be charged at $.15 per page, or messenger services will be provided at $5.00 per mile. However, the question arises what may be charged to the client, in the absence of a specific agreement to the contrary. . . . [U]nder those circumstances the lawyer is obliged to charge the client no more than the direct cost associated with the service (i.e., the actual cost of making a copy on the photocopy machine) plus a reasonable allocation of overhead expenses directly associated with the provision of the service (e.g., the salary of a photocopy machine operator).

NOTES

The billing practices described in this opinion are hardly the most outrageous we have seen in these readings. No one is billing 135 clients for the same opinion, or 785 hours in one month. Indeed, many law firms have engaged in some of these practices for years, and many lawyers consider them perfectly appropriate. Take the cross-country plane ride. Do you agree that a lawyer, already committed to a paid trip on behalf of Client A, cannot work on Client B's file and bill it? The lawyer would still be paid for the plane ride while reading John Grisham's latest novel instead. And why shouldn't a law firm be able to "value bill" by charging for work done for another client? What if this work is the product of the firm's expertise, rather than just the lucky coincidence the ABA opinion implies? Perhaps the ABA committee's point relates more to notice and consent than to per se unreasonableness. Its analysis, after all, begins with a discussion on disclosure about billing practices, rather than unfairness. Would such notice and consent have resolved the examples posited by the ABA?

Note the ABA's concern over the public image of lawyers. Will abiding by Opinion 93-379 improve the image of lawyers? How easy will it be to comply, given the pressure to produce billable hours? Might the answer lie in law firms being more modest in their billable hours requirements, or in restructuring salaries? What other alternatives might work?

5. Happy, Healthy, and Ethical — and Still Billing?

We now return to Professor Patrick Schiltz, who has written eloquently and straightforwardly (and, admittedly, with both a perspective and an attitude) about the dangers to associates inherent in the cultures of large firms. In our earlier excerpt,[7] Schiltz discussed generally how a young lawyer could remain ethical. In this excerpt, Schiltz's position is blunt, unlikely to achieve uniform agreement from his readers. But he is clear-eyed and direct. Here he focuses on money: law firms' bottom-line mentality, playing the money "game," and what he sees as the associate's inevitable path toward billing abuse.

Patrick J. Schiltz, *On Being a Happy, Healthy, and Ethical Member of an Unhappy, Unhealthy, and Unethical Profession*
52 VAND. L. REV. 871 (1999)[8]

Thirty years ago, most partners billed between 1200 and 1400 hours per year and most associates between 1400 and 1600 hours. As late as the mid-1980s, even associates in large New York firms were often not expected to bill more than 1800 hours annually. Today, many firms would consider these ranges acceptable only for partners or associates who had died midway through the year.

[Schiltz cites studies by Professor William Ross, the ABA, Michigan Law School, and Altman Weil Pensa, a legal consulting firm, all showing that a high percentage of associates bill over 2000 hours a year, many as much as 2150 to 2400 hours per year.] Workloads, like the job dissatisfaction to which they so closely relate, are not distributed equally throughout the profession. Generally speaking, lawyers in private practice work longer hours than those who work for corporations or for the government. . . . Within private practice, the general rule of thumb is the bigger the firm, the longer the hours. . . .

The long hours that big firm lawyers must work is a particular source of dissatisfaction for them. While roughly half of all attorneys in private practice complain about not having enough time for themselves and their families, in big firms, the proportion of similarly disaffected lawyers is about three quarters. . . .

---

[7] *See* Problem 2.

[8] Copyright © 1999 by Patrick J. Schiltz. Reprinted by permission of the author.

[Y]oung attorneys in large firms who are interested in finding a new job are more likely than similarly situated associates in small firms to be motivated by "a desire for more personal time."

The unhappiness of lawyers may puzzle you. At first blush, these billable hour requirements may not seem particularly daunting. You may think, "Geez, to bill 2000 hours, I need to bill only forty hours per week for fifty weeks. If I take an hour for lunch, that's 8:00 a.m. to 5:00 p.m., five days per week. No sweat." Your reaction is common among law students — particularly among law students who are in the process of talking themselves into accepting jobs at big firms. Your reaction is also naive.

There is a big difference — a painfully big difference — between the hours that you will *bill* and the hours that you will *spend at work*. If you're honest, you will be able to bill only the time that you spend working directly on matters for clients. Obviously, you will not be able to bill the time that you spend on vacation, or in bed with the flu, or at home waiting for the plumber. But you will also not be able to bill for much of what you will do at the office or during the workday — going to lunch, . . . visiting your favorite websites, going down the hall to get a cup of coffee, reading your mail, . . . attending the weekly meeting of your practice group, filling out your time sheet, . . . sending e-mail to friends, preparing a "pitch" for a prospective client, . . . interviewing a recruit, doing pro bono work, reading advance sheets, . . . attending CLE seminars, writing a letter about a mistake in your credit card bill, going to the dentist, . . . and so on.

Because none of this is billable — and because the average lawyer does a lot of this every day — you will end up billing only about two hours for every three hours that you spend at "work." And thus, to bill 2000 hours per year, you will have to spend about sixty hours per week at the office, and take no more than two weeks of vacation/sick time/personal leave. If it takes you, say forty-five minutes to get to work, and another forty-five minutes to get home, billing 2000 hours per year will mean leaving home at 7:45 a.m., working at the office from 8:30 a.m. until 6:30 p.m., and then arriving home at 7:10 p.m.— and doing this *six days per week*, every week. That makes for long days, and for long weeks. And you will have to work these hours not just for a month or two, but year after year after year . . . .

The Money

. . . The vast majority of law students — at least the vast majority of those attending the more prestigious schools (or getting good grades at the less prestigious schools) — want to work in big firms. And the reason they want to work in big firms is that big firms pay the most.

Of course, students deny this. . . . Or they reluctantly admit that, yes, they really are after the money, but they have no choice: Because of student loan debt, they *must* take a job that pays $80,000 per year. $60,000 per year just won't cut it.

Most of this is hogwash. As I will explain below, almost all of the purported non-monetary advantages of big firms either do not exist or are vastly overstated. Moreover, there are few lawyers who could not live comfortably on what most corporations or government agencies pay, whatever their student loan debt.

. . . .

Clients insist on getting good work at low hourly rates. . . . If clients do not get what they want, they will move their business to one of the thousands of other lawyers who are chomping at the bit to get it. Raising billing rates to pay for spiraling salaries is simply not much of an option for most firms. As a result, firms get the extra money to pay for the spiraling salaries in the only way they can: They bill more hours. . . .

I am leaving out one wrinkle — an important wrinkle that you should know about [that] big firm partners euphemistically refer to as "leverage." I like to call it "the skim." Richard Abel calls it "exploitation." The person being exploited is you.

It is common for the top partners in the biggest firms to earn upwards of $2 million per year. . . . Not one of these highly paid partners could personally generate the billings necessary to produce such an income. . . .

Basically, what happens is that big firms "buy associates' time 'wholesale and sell it retail.' " Here is how it works: As a new associate in a large firm, you will be paid about one-third of what you bring into the firm. . . . Another third will go toward paying the expenses of the firm. And the final third will go into the pockets of the firm's partners. Firms make money off associates. That is why it's in the interests of big firms to hire lots of associates and to make very few of them partners.

. . . .

This, then, is life in the big firm: It is in the interests of clients that senior partners work inhuman hours, year after year, and constantly be anxious about retaining their business. And it is in the interests of senior partners that junior partners work inhuman hours, year after year, and constantly be anxious about retaining old clients and attracting new clients. And it is in the interests of junior partners that senior associates work inhuman hours, year after year . . . . And most of all, it is in everyone's interests that the newest members of the profession — the junior associates — be willing to work inhuman hours, year after year, and constantly be anxious about *everything* — [including] their billable hours. The result? Long hours, large salaries, and one of the unhealthiest and unhappiest professions on earth.

The "Game"

. . . Almost every one of these problems would be eliminated or at least substantially reduced if lawyers were simply willing to make less money. . . . The notion that lawyers could get by with less money is not exactly absurd. In 1994, the median income for American men employed full-time during the entire year was $31,612; for women, the comparable figure was $23,265. In 1995, the median income for partners in firms of all sizes was $168,751. . . . Even in the smallest firms (firms of eight or fewer lawyers), the median income for partners was $134,294. . . . It's not as if lawyers are just scraping by.

. . . Lawyers could enjoy a lot more life outside of work if they were willing to accept relatively modest reductions in their incomes. Take, for example, a partner who is billing 2000 hours and being paid $200,000. If we assume that a 20%

reduction in billable hours will translate into a 20% reduction in pay . . . , this lawyer could trade $40,000 in income for 600 more hours of life outside work (assuming that three hours at work translates into two hours billed).

Our hypothetical partner has a choice, then: He can make $200,000 per year and work many nights and most weekends — routinely getting up early, before his children are awake, driving to the office, eating lunch at his desk, leaving the office late, picking up dinner at the Taco Bell drive-through window, and then arriving home to kiss the cheeks of his sleeping children. Or he can make $160,000 per year and work few nights and weekends. He can spend time with his spouse, be a parent to his children, enjoy the company of his friends, pursue a hobby, do volunteer work, exercise regularly, and generally lead a well balanced life — *while still making $160,000 per year*. If all such lawyers making $160,000 per year sat down and asked themselves, "What will make me a happier and healthier person: another $40,000 in income (which, after taxes, will mean another $25,000 or so in the bank) or 600 hours to do whatever I enjoy most?," it is hard to believe that many of them would take the money.

But many of them do take the money. Thousands of lawyers choose to give up a healthy, happy, well-balanced life for a less healthy, less happy life dominated by work. And they do so merely to be able to make seven or eight times the national median income instead of five or six times the national median income. Why? Are lawyers just greedy?

Well, some are, but it is more complicated than that. For one thing, lawyers . . . don't sit down and think logically about why they are leading the lives they are leading any more than buffalo sit down and think logically about why they are stampeding. That is the primary reason I am writing this Article: I hope that you *will* sit down and think about the life that you want to lead before you get caught up in the stampede.

More importantly, though, the flaw in my analysis is that it assumes that the reason lawyers push themselves to make so much money is the money itself. . . . What you need to understand, though, is that [t]hey are doing it for a different reason.

Big firm lawyers are, on the whole, a remarkably insecure and competitive group of people. Many of them have spent almost their entire lives competing to win games that other people have set up for them. First they competed to get into a prestigious college. Then they competed for college grades. [Eventually] they competed to get hired by a big law firm.

Now that they're in a big law firm, what's going to happen? Are they going to stop competing? Are they going to stop comparing themselves to others? Of course not. . . . They're playing a game. And money is how the score is kept in that game.

Why do you suppose sixty year old lawyers with millions of dollars in the bank still bill 2200 hours per year? Why do you suppose lawyers whose children have everything money can buy but who need the time and attention of their parents continue to spend most nights and weekends at the office — while continuing to write out checks to the best child psychologists in town? . . .

What's driving these lawyers is the desire to *win the game.* . . . If a lawyer's life is dominated by the game — and if his success in the game is measured by money — then his *life* is dominated by money. For many, many lawyers, it's that simple.

. . . .

Becoming Unethical

Unethical lawyers do not start out being unethical; they start out just like you — as perfectly decent young men or women who have every intention of practicing law ethically. They do not become unethical overnight; they become unethical just as you will (if you become unethical)— a little bit at a time. And they do not become unethical by shredding incriminating documents or bribing jurors; they become unethical just as you are likely to — by cutting a corner here, by stretching the truth a bit there.

Let me tell you how you will start acting unethically: It will start with your time sheets. One day, not too long after you start practicing law, you will sit down at the end of a long, tiring day, and you just won't have much to show for your efforts in terms of billable hours. It will be near the end of the month. You will know that all of the partners will be looking at your monthly time report in a few days, so what you'll do is pad your time sheet just a bit. Maybe you will bill a client for ninety minutes for a task that really took you only sixty minutes to perform. However, you will promise yourself that you will repay the client at the first opportunity by doing thirty minutes of work for the client for "free." In this way, you will be "borrowing," not "stealing."

And then what will happen is that it will become easier and easier to take these little loans against future work. And then, after a while, you will stop paying back these little loans. You will convince yourself that, although you billed for ninety minutes and spent only sixty minutes on the project, you did such good work that your client should pay a bit more for it. After all, your billing rate is awfully low, and your client is awfully rich.

And then you will pad more and more — every two minute telephone conversation will go down on the sheet as ten minutes, every three hour research project will go down with an extra quarter hour or so. You will continue to rationalize your dishonesty to yourself in various ways until one day you stop doing even that. And, before long — it won't take you much more than three or four years — you will be stealing from your clients almost every day, and you won't even notice it.

You know what? You will also likely become a liar. A deadline will come up one day, and, for reasons that are entirely your fault, you will not be able to meet it. So you will call your senior partner or your client and make up a white lie for why you missed the deadline. . . . And then, in preparing a client for a deposition, you will help the client to formulate an answer to a difficult question that will likely be asked — an answer that will be "legally accurate" but that will mislead your opponent. And then you will be reading through a big box of your client's documents — a box that has not been opened in twenty years — and you will find a document that would hurt your client's case, but that no one except you knows exists, and you will simply "forget" to produce it in response to your opponent's discovery requests.

Do you see what will happen? After a couple years of this, you won't even notice that you are lying and cheating and stealing every day that you practice law. None of these things will seem like a big deal in itself . . . . But, after a while, your entire frame of reference will change. You will still be making dozens of quick, instinctive decisions every day, but those decisions, instead of reflecting the notions of right and wrong by which you conduct your personal life, will instead reflect the set of values by which you will conduct your professional life — a set of values that embodies not what is right or wrong, but what is profitable, and what you can get away with. The system will have succeeded in replacing your values with the system's values, and the system will be profiting as a result.

Does this happen to every big firm lawyer? Of course not. It's all a matter of degree. The culture in some big firms is better than in others. . . . The big firm at which I practiced [for six years as an associate and two as a partner] was as decent and humane as a big firm can be. Similarly, some big firm lawyers have better values than others. I owe a lot to a partner who sacrificed hundreds of hours of his time and tens of thousands of dollars of income to act as a mentor to me and to many other young lawyers like me.

. . . .

"Big Picture" Advice

My "big picture" advice is simple: Don't get sucked into the game. Don't let money become the most important thing in your life. Don't fall into the trap of measuring your worth as an attorney — or as a human being — by how much money you make.

If you let your law firm or clients define success for you, they will define it in a way that is in their interest, not yours. It is important for them that your primary motivation be making money. . . . If you end up as an unhappy or unethical attorney, money will most likely be at the root of your problem.

You cannot win the game. If you fall into the trap of measuring your worth by money, you will always feel inadequate. There will always be a firm paying more to its associates than yours. . . . There will always be a lawyer at your firm making more money than you. . . . You will run faster and faster and faster, but there will always be a runner ahead of you, and the finish line will never quite come into view . . . .

Most likely, when you were a child, your parents or grandparents told you money does not buy happiness. They were right.

NOTES

We recognize this excerpt does not paint a rosy picture. Adding her strong voice is noted ethicist and prolific writer Deborah Rhode, who in an article focused mostly on women, wrote this about the life of the modern-day associate, male or female:

> Lawyers remain perpetually on call — tethered to the workplace through cell phones, emails, faxes, and beepers . . . . Particularly in large firms, unmarried associates report finding it "difficult to have a cat, much less a family." As one lawyer responded to a bar survey on quality of life: "This is not a life."[9]

Remember that Judge Schiltz comes to a much more upbeat conclusion in the segment we excerpted in Problem 2. Please feel free to return to that excerpt to reread his advice about how to be happy, healthy, *and* ethical.

6. "BigLaw" Rides the Rollercoaster

A few days before the turn of the millennium and less than a year after Schiltz's article was published, a relatively modest-sized Silicon Valley firm, Gunderson, Dettmer, Stough, Villeneuve, Franklin & Hachigian, jumped first-year associates' salaries to $150,000 a year — $125,000 plus guaranteed bonuses of $25,000. This was not the small, incremental leap-frogging increase that marked the salary wars of the '80s and '90s, and made Schiltz's then-recent salary estimates ($60,000 versus $80,000) seem ridiculously puny. It was a "statement" by the new kids on the block, clearly fueled by the boomtown-like dot.com economy. It was, founding partner Scott Dettmer told *California Lawyer*, a "benchmark . . . to attract high-powered laterals from out of town . . . and to hold on to associates who were otherwise tempted to move to start-ups."[10]

In the first months of 2000, the salary war focus quickly shifted from Wall Street to Silicon Valley. By mid-January, Silicon Valley giants Cooley Godward, Wilson Sonsini, and Gray Cary had matched Gunderson, Dettmer. Other San Francisco giants soon followed suit, including Morrison Forester, Heller Ehrman, and Brobeck, Phleger, and Harrison, which had become the richest and largest Northern California-based firm. Those that were slow to act found themselves attacked by the habitues of on-line "greedy associates" boards, who monitored and reported every move in detail.

Was this only about lawyers making more money? Not exactly. There were increased expectations as well. Brobeck, for example, claimed to raise its salaries above the Gunderson benchmark. But in order to earn the extra money, the 1,950 annual billable hours previously required of Brobeck associates would no longer be enough. To earn incremental bonuses to get them to Gunderson levels, associates would need to raise their "billables" to 2,100, 2,250, and — for the big payoff — 2,400 hours a year. Brobeck chairman Tower Snow, Jr. announced, somewhat anomalously, "We don't want our people working these excessive hours, but if they do, we want to acknowledge them." More than a few found this statement disingenuous.

The Silicon Valley salary escalation seemed to affirm then-Professor Schiltz's analysis: that young lawyers would play "the game" and work many more hours for

---

[9] Deborah L. Rhode, *Gender and the Profession: The No-Problem Problem*, 30 HOFSTRA L. REV. 1001 (2002).

[10] CALIFORNIA LAWYER, July 2000. *See* Supplemental Reading 4.

just a few more dollars than the competitor paid, and that many law firms saw associates as commodities to be bought wholesale and sold retail.

With lawyers leaving — or threatening to leave — for in-house dot.com jobs, complete with stock options, dozens of firms raised their salaries by extraordinary percentages between December 1999, when Gunderson moved, and the beginning of the NASDAQ's downturn in March 2000. A year later, with the NASDAQ at less than half its previous level and "start-up" closings already an old story, most associates' salary structures remained the same. But the business environment that surrounded the law firms had changed materially for the worse. Many a newly-minted dot.com house counsel was not just out of stock options but out of work. A few law firms had found it necessary to lay off associates — the fungible commodities Schiltz described. Gunderson, which started it all, cancelled its guaranteed bonuses, effectively dropping its salaries by $20,000.[11]

By 2003, Brobeck had collapsed into bankruptcy. In 2009, Heller Ehrman followed suit; some sources reported that one of Heller's big problems was a series of huge cases that settled early, leaving the firm without sufficient billings to sustain its overhead.[12]

Since then, law firm salaries have ridden on the same roller-coaster as the American economy: recovery in mid-decade, followed by a crushing recession in 2008. By the time 2009 rolled in, big changes were in store for "BigLaw," the nation's 200 or 250 largest firms. These changes have affected new graduates and junior associates the most, as the following article, by a long-time partner at the nation's biggest BigLaw firm, DLA Piper, explains. Not only that: Many knowledgeable observers, including Neil Dilloff, doubt that the billable hour, the focus of much of Judge Schiltz's attention, will continue for long as the gold standard billing.

Neil J. Dilloff, *The Changing Cultures and Economics of Large Law Firm Practice and their Impact on Legal Education*
70 Md. L. Rev. 341 (2011)[13]

The practice of law, especially in large law firms, has been affected significantly by recent economic conditions. The recession of 2008–2009 brought about a new way of doing business for BigLaw. The year 2009 was the worst ever for law firm layoffs: more law firms laid off more employees than in all past years combined. Major law firms laid off more than 12,100 people — over one-third of whom were lawyers. (It is likely that the number of layoffs was dramatically underreported.) Moreover, some major law firms simply disappeared [into bankruptcy, including Heller Ehrman] . . . .

For the most part, the economic impact on BigLaw within the past couple of years has been all bad. The Wall Street Journal characterized the job market for

---

[11] *See* series in The Recorder (San Francisco) by Renee Deger, including *Gunderson's Guaranteed Bonus a Goner*, June 13, 2001.

[12] *See, e.g.*, Jonathan Glater, *Billable Hours Giving Ground at Law Firm*, N.Y. Times, Jan. 30, 2009.

[13] Copyright © 2011 by The Maryland Law Review. Reprinted by permission.

lawyers as "one of the worst . . . in decades." Law firms have hired fewer associates, drastically curtailed or eliminated summer associate programs, eliminated expenditures for outside training programs, reduced fringe benefits, deferred start dates or rescinded offers, frozen or scaled back salaries, and promoted fewer associates to partner. While necessary, these actions have negatively impacted morale, resulted in less institutional loyalty, and led to increased lawyer mobility.

Corporate America is the target of large law firms. As a direct result of the recent economic stress felt by large corporations, the annual escalation of legal fees has subsided greatly. Large corporate clients now demand and receive discounts. Some corporations are also reducing the number of law firms they use. Others are assigning outside counsel less work to decrease legal expenses, which has resulted in "beauty contests" among law firms in which price and quality are significant considerations. In the past, this "marketing-to-market" has been anathema to big firms, but this is no longer true.

In response, most large law firms now have little choice but to offer large hourly discounts, fixed fees, and alternate fee arrangements to their largest clients. According to a recent report, seventy-eight percent of associates, partners, and staff at corporate law firms charge certain clients a discounted rate. In addition, firms are using contingency fees, a mainstay of plaintiffs' firms, or hybrid arrangements, in which firms charge a lower hourly rate or fixed fee plus a contingency . . . . At least one major law firm intends to become "the leader in providing high-end legal services on a fixed fee basis." It remains to be seen whether discounts and these other fee changes will stick . . . .

Another significant billing trend is the much-discussed, but long-awaited, erosion of the billable hour. Several large corporations, including Pfizer, Microsoft, UPS, Cisco, Tyco, and United Technologies, have entered into annual flat fee arrangements with certain select law firms. These portfolio or fixed-fee arrangements allow clients to pay a predetermined sum of money for all work performed within a fiscal year, irrespective of the number of hours it takes the firm to perform the work. Such arrangements provide certainty to the client, who can better control its legal fee budget, and the law firm, which can count on a specified revenue stream for the year. This paradigm forces the law firm to be more efficient and prevents the client from being billed unnecessary hours.

Changes to billing practices may significantly impact the way BigLaw promotes from within. Until recently, many associates were able to move up the law firm ladder through hard work alone because billable hours were the primary criterion for success. As the billable hour becomes subordinate to alternate fee structures, however, these other attributes will become more important. Primarily, efficiency will separate mere worker bees from future partners. As fixed fee arrangements take hold, the star associate will no longer be the one who took thirty billable hours to research an issue and write a detailed memorandum. Instead, firms will covet the associate who can come up with the correct answer in a timely and cost-effective manner.

Perhaps the most refreshing and cleansing impact on the eventual, albeit slow, demise of the billable hour will be a return to the correct incentives for associates (and partners, for that matter). When an associate is paid handsomely for working many hours and sees his ascension in the firm as dependent on the quantity of these hours and how much money they bring into the firm, the temptation to round upward, perform nonessential tasks, and spend more time than necessary on a task increases. This ethical issue, prevalent in all law firms — big, midsize, and small — is the bane of honest lawyers and clients.

. . . .

[Meanwhile, c]lients have devalued junior associates. At least one large corporation now refuses to pay for work produced by junior associates and has openly stated that it views these newer attorneys as "worthless." This is certainly a gross overstatement, but the message is clear: clients want work-ready lawyers and have little to no patience for learning curves. As such, learning at the clients' expense is history . . . .

NOTES

Dilloff's review of the way things will be is a prequel to the principal focus of his article: that law schools will have to provide "real world experiences" for their students, a necessity if junior associates are to remain valuable: "Lawyers deal with real people with real problems; law students should as well. [L]aw schools have a golden opportunity to increase their relevance to the real world practice of law by implementing changes in their curricula that meet the challenges of tomorrow's large law firm practice."

Interestingly, Dilloff and Schiltz, from very different perspectives, both see the ethical problems associates face with the billable hour. One wonders, though, whether the yearly flat fee arrangements some large corporations are now looking for might result in another ethical dilemma for the "worker bees": whether to put in the requisite effort to do the best possible job given that the premium for these associates will be "efficiency." Only time will tell, as the change from billable hours is still in its nascent stages.

7.   Modern Alternatives to Hourly Billing

In light of the problems that hourly billing has caused, BigLaw is not the only place looking to change their billing methods. Dilloff and others have noticed a significant uptick in the number of BigLaw partners leaving to start their own firms, often "boutiques" that have particular specialties, in areas like patent litigation, taxation, mass tort litigation, or class actions. These more cost-effective shops are just as, if not more, likely to look for new billing regimes. And, as we've noted many times in this volume, over half our nation's lawyers remain small-firm and solo practitioners who also need — and already use — a variety of ways to charge for legal services. Here are a few of them:

Flat or fixed fees have long been used by criminal defense lawyers, estate planners, and others to set the value of their services. As Dilloff notes, larger firms and their clients are looking at flat annual retainers. Also on the table are flat fees where the task involved is familiar and relatively quantifiable. Often, this is called "value billing" or "task-based" billing. A modification of the flat fee arrangement is one where the attorney charges hourly up to a maximum cap for a particular case. The advantage to the client of such arrangements is clear: knowing from the outset what the highest possible fee will be. The advantage to the lawyer is that, so long as the services are well performed, the client will be happy if the lawyer finds ways to save time and costs. The disadvantage to the lawyer, however, is that very careful time estimates are required, and they don't always prove accurate. A law firm may find itself committed to a case that is taking far more time than the flat or maximum fee covers. This can be a disadvantage to the client as well, since a law firm in such circumstances might be disinclined to spend all the time necessary to do the best possible job on the client's case.

One more caveat about flat or fixed fee arrangements: Some courts have criticized, even invalidated, flat fees deemed "non-refundable."[14] But many other courts have found that flat-fee or non-refundable fee contracts are not necessarily improper, for instance where the law firm does the work,[15] makes itself available on an as-needed basis,[16] or is fired for refusing to engage in requested action that it believes might be unethical.[17]

Hybrid hourly and contingency fees, also referenced by Dilloff, allow lawyers from small shops who are not sufficiently confident about a matter to take it entirely on contingency to represent clients who can't or don't want to pay the full hourly freight. These situations might include business, real estate, or insurance litigation, where monetary damages are at stake but where the liability issues are more complicated than those of the typical personal injury contingency case. Hybrid fees mean the lawyer gets a substantially discounted hourly fee, and then a discounted contingency fee in the event the case is successful.

Incentive bonuses are similar to these hybrid fees. Here, the attorney might receive a reduced hourly rate plus a percentage bonus for any recovery over a specified sum of $X, or any savings to the client of more than $Y. Both hybrid fees and incentive bonuses have the advantages to the lawyer of rewarding both the time spent and results obtained, while helping the client by reducing the expenditures substantially if the case is not successful.

Discounts and "blended" rates, where the law firm charges a single median rate for the work of both partner and associate, are becoming more common, particularly where the law firm and client have known each other for a long time. Discounts to the firm's best clients may be a way of keeping those clients happy in smaller firms as in large ones. But by creating a compensation "hierarchy," firms of any size may also be encouraging lawyers to spend their available time on matters compensated at higher rates. Moreover, many observers believe that the most frequent abuses for "churning files" (overworking them) and "writing up" (or inflating) hours occur in the field of insurance defense, a highly competitive area in which substantial hourly discounts are often given.

---

[14] *See, e.g.*, Matter of Cooperman, 633 N.E.2d 1069 (N.Y. 1994); In re Hirschfeld, 960 P.2d 640 (Ariz. 1998).

[15] In re Gastineau, 857 P.2d 136 (Or. 1993).

[16] Kelly v. MD Buyline, Inc., 2 F. Supp. 2d 420 (S.D.N.Y. 1998) (limiting the scope of *Cooperman*).

[17] Ryan v. Butera, Beausang, Cohen & Brennan, 193 F.3d 210 (3d Cir. 1999).

No fee arrangement is perfect. But as clients become more sensitized to the need for control over fees, they and their lawyers will work more closely to come up with acceptable solutions.

D. SUPPLEMENTAL READINGS

1. Volume 50, No. 4 of the RUTGERS LAW REVIEW contained four valuable articles about unethical billing practices, all based on Lisa Lerman's narrative of the true story of a lawyer named, for purposes of publication, "Nicholas Farber." Her *Scenes From a Law Firm*, 50 RUTGERS L. REV. 2153 (1998), is accompanied by articles by William Ross, billing auditor James P. Schratz, and Lawrence J. Fox, formerly both an ABA ethics committee chair and a big-firm managing partner.

2. In addition to the article cited in the Readings, Lisa Lerman's contributions to this subject include *Blue-Chip Bilking: Regulation of Billing and Expense Fraud by Lawyers*, 12 GEO. J. LEGAL ETHICS 205 (1999), a preliminary version of that piece that appeared in the 1998 Symposium Issue of THE PROFESSIONAL LAWYER entitled *Regulation of Unethical Billing Practices: Progress and Prospects*, and *Teaching Moral Perception and Moral Judgment in Legal Ethics Courses: A Dialogue About Goals*, 39 WM. & MARY L. REV. 457 (1998), in addition to the piece on the Fairchilds cited in the body of the Readings.

3. William G. Ross' article, *The Ethics of Hourly Billing*, 44 RUTGERS L. REV. 1 (1991), is perhaps the first significant article dealing with a modern analysis of lawyers' billing practices. It includes the lawyers survey mentioned in Goldhaber's article, in which Ross found, among other matters, that the vast majority of lawyers believed that their colleagues padded their bills, and 50% acknowledged that they had billed two clients for the same period. Ross authored the book THE HONEST HOUR: THE ETHICS OF TIME-BASED BILLING BY ATTORNEYS (1997), and summarized it in the 1998 PROFESSIONAL LAWYER symposium issue. He has also written on the insurance auditing controversy, *An Ironic and Unnecessary Controversy: Ethical Restrictions on Billing Guidelines and Submission of Insurance Defense Bills to Outside Auditors*, 14 ND. J. L. ETHICS & PUB. POL'Y 527 (2000).

4. In two relatively recent articles, Douglas R. Richmond, who is a risk manager for malpractice insurers, has defended the much maligned billable hour. In *For a Few Dollars More: The Perplexing Problems of Unethical Billing Practices by Lawyers*, 60 S.C. L. REV. 63 (2008), he submits that there is a "continuum of customary billing practices," from thievery to somewhat marginal, through honest. He believes that "cases of outright billing fraud have a disproportionately negative effect on the legal profession," but argues that "hourly billing is, as a matter of practice and principle, fair and fine." He then outlines where things go wrong with the worst offenders, and submits that the solution is that "principled firms cannot tolerate the presence of lawyers who fraudulently bill." If they crack down, he sees the billable hour as continuing to be the primary billing method. He has also written a more condensed analysis, *An Inconvenient Truth: There is Nothing Wrong with the Billable Hour*, 19 ABA PROF. LAW. 3 (2009).

5. Two others who have written extensively on billing issues: Professor Carl T. Bogus, whose article *The Death of an Honorable Profession*, 71 IND. L.J. 911 (1996), is an excellent contribution to the discussion about the effect of money on the practice of law; and in a more colloquial vein, Darlene Ricker, a lawyer and LOS ANGELES TIMES editor, has written several interesting articles on billing abuses, including *Greed, Ignorance and Overbilling*, ABA JOURNAL (August 1994).

6. Patrick Schiltz's article, reprinted above, was part of a symposium issue of the VANDERBILT LAW REVIEW, Volume 52, number 4, with the title *Attorney Well-Being in Large Firms: Choices Facing Young Lawyers*. Other articles provided perspectives on Schiltz's "feature" piece, and Schiltz closed with a response to those other commentators. These other articles provide varied and valuable viewpoints on Schiltz's theme.

7. In a slightly different vein, the July 2000 issue of CALIFORNIA LAWYER contains an excellent series of articles on life, salary escalation, and the expectations of both law firms and associates. The enlightening profiles and interviews with associates and partners include one with the woman who is believed to have been Gunderson's first beneficiary of Silicon Valley generosity.

8. Susan Saab Fortney's *An Empirical Study of Associate Satisfaction, Law Firm Culture and the Effects of Billable Hour Requirements*, 64 TEX. B. J. 1060 (2001), is an effective summary of associate unhappiness.

9. More recently, Martha Neil has written a series of articles on the effect of the last recession on the law firm "industry," at least two of which were cited in Dilloff's Maryland Law piece excerpted above: *Pay Cuts Accelerate at Law Firms Across the Country*, A.B.A. J., June 30, 2009, *available at* http://www.abajournal.com/news/article/pay_cuts_accelerate_at_law_firms_across_the_country/ and *Some BigLaw Leaders Still Ponder: How Low Can Associate Salaries Go?*, A.B.A. J., October 6, 2009, *available at* http://www.abajournal.com/news/article/some_biglaw_leaders_still_ponder_how_low_can_associate_salaries_go/.

10. Dennis Curtis & Judith Resnik, in *Teaching Billing: Metrics of Value in Law Firms and Law Schools*, 54 STAN. L. REV. 1409 (2002), review Deborah Rhode's book, IN THE INTERESTS OF JUSTICE: REFORMING THE LEGAL PROFESSION and argue that "law schools ought to join in the conversation about the role of hourly billing in shaping concepts of professionalization."

11. Christine Parker and David Ruschena, Australian lawyers, offer *The Pressures of Billable Hours: Lessons from a Survey of Billing Practices Inside Law Firms*, 9 U. ST. THOMAS L.J. 619 (2011). They review a Queensland Billing Practices Survey in which "[l]awyers from twenty-five private law firms answered questions about the billing systems, office culture, and ethics policies of their firms." They found a frequent "cultural disconnect" between partners and "employee-lawyers" because "junior lawyers feel that their firms are only interested in revenue production while senior lawyers feel that they value ethics and quality first." It sounds quite familiar . . . .

PROBLEM 29: IS THERE A GLASS CEILING AS LAWYERS CLIMB THE LAW FIRM LADDER?

A. INTRODUCTION

Racial, cultural, gender, sexual preference, and other biases are facts of life in our society. In Problem 14, we looked as how some of these biases can affect us as advocates and counselors. Now we look at these same issues from the inside of the profession. Some biases are overt; most in today's world come in more subtle forms. They affect the practice of law every bit as much as they do other walks of life. Some might argue that countering such biases in the form of ethical requirements is using ethics in an effort to be "politically correct." Others contend that the fundamental inequalities of our society, some of which are described in the readings below, warrant the conclusion that the ethical lawyer is the lawyer who does what is possible to understand, deal with, and affirmatively counteract such biases.

Of course, all decisions to *not* hire, or promote, women or minority attorneys don't automatically signal bias, either overt or subtle. But vigilance is required to ensure that such biases do not determine the outcome. Take the case of Sharon Chau.

B. PROBLEM

Sharon Chau is an attractive, ambitious, Asian attorney at Donovan, Kemper, Newcomb & Yates, an Ocean City law firm with 20 partners and 35 associates. She has been working there for eight years. During this time, she has had a few opportunities to try her own cases, and has developed a reputation as a skillful and aggressive trial lawyer. She has even attracted a few small and modest-sized new clients to DKNY.

Chau, however, makes an effort to leave the office by 5 p.m. and is not frequently seen by the partners "grinding out the hours" at work. In the last three years, she has averaged about 150 fewer billable hours per year than the average senior associate.

At DKNY, the third Friday of the month has traditionally been reserved by the litigation unit for after-work socializing over drinks at the Olympian Club. Chau, however, rarely joins the group. Except for one or two close friends, she does not often see her colleagues outside the office. Moreover, she is not often available to socialize with clients during evening hours. Rather, Chau goes home to take care of her two children, Jessica, 5, and Matthew, 9. After Jessica was born, Chau took one year of maternity leave from DKNY. She is now a single parent. She often prepares briefs or for trial at home, after the kids are in bed.

Next month Chau will be reviewed by the DKNY partners to determine whether she should be offered partnership. If it is offered, she would be the first female minority partner of the firm. The DKNY partners currently include two white females, both married without children, one Spanish-surnamed male whose family has resided in suburban La Vista for three generations, and one older Japanese-American male who heads the international trade department and also maintains an office in Japan. The remainder of the partners are Caucasian men.

Two weeks before the partnership meeting, Chau is approached by partner James Taylor. They have been cordial in the past, but she only knows him professionally. Taylor tells Chau that he would like to take her to dinner to discuss her future at DKNY, and if things go as he anticipates, he can almost guarantee her partnership at the firm.

QUESTIONS

1. You are a voting member of the partnership committee. Discuss *all* the pros and cons of inviting Chau to become a partner at DKNY, whether "appropriate" or not. Which factors do you feel are appropriate to consider?

2. Suppose the partnership committee votes no partnership, telling Chau that their decision is based on her time constraints and billable hours. Are these valid reasons?

3. Just prior to the partnership meeting, one male and one female partner ask Chau numerous questions regarding her family life and responsibilities. Chau asks the other female partner whether she was subjected to the same questions, and she replies "no." Is there a legitimate basis for such questioning?

4. Before the partnership meeting, while completing an assignment for Newcomb, Chau overhears him saying to Yates, "I can't believe that Chinese company stole that trademark right from under us. You've got to watch them, you know, they're always sneaky and quiet until they want something, and then they'll do anything . . . ."

Chau is extremely upset when she hears this, but she is also concerned about her job. What actions, if any, should Chau take? Should she discuss the matter with other members of the firm?

5. Is Taylor's dinner invitation proper? Should she accept? What if she believes that Taylor's vote could determine the outcome? Would it matter if Taylor is one of the two partners who supervises Chau's work?

C. READINGS

1. Women in the Legal Workplace

For the past 30 years, almost half of law school populations have been women. Thus, law firms should have no problem finding academically qualified women candidates to employ. Once inside the firm, however, problems can arise for the woman associate. The National Association of Women Lawyers began doing annual surveys charting the progress of women in "BigLaw" in 2005. In 2011, NAWL gave this dismal report: Six percent of managing partners at the 200 largest American law firms were women, only fifteen percent of these firms had at least one woman on their management committee, and only fifteen percent of firm equity partners were women. "This sixth year of the survey presents a sobering picture of the prospects for women in 'BigLaw.' Not only do women represent a decreasing percentage of lawyers in big firms, they have a far greater chance of occupying positions like staff attorneys, counsel, and fixed-income equity partners with diminished opportunity for advancement or participating in firm leadership," said the report.[1]

What is causing this ongoing disparity? Two long-standing causes are still around: the "me-not-me" dilemma (to be a good lawyer you must "be like a man"), and the "mommy track" problem (when, if ever, and at what price can women lawyers have children). The "me-not-me" syndrome occurs most clearly in the courtroom; the image of the good advocate is one who is aggressive and forceful, and "plays the game" by rules that have traditionally been masculine. "Being like a man" in the courtroom may give rise to accusations of being overly "aggressive" or "insensitive," while acting more feminine may bring accusations about ineffectiveness. It is a fine line to have to walk.

Or, as Deborah Rhode, one of the nation's leading ethicists and an expert on gender equality, wrote about gender stereotypes:

> [C]haracteristics traditionally associated with women are at odds with those traditionally associated with professional success, such as assertiveness, competitiveness, and business judgment. Some lawyers and clients still assume that women lack the aptitude for complex financial transactions or the combativeness for high-stakes litigation. Yet professional women also tend to be rated lower when they adopt "masculine," authoritative styles, particularly when the evaluators are men. Female lawyers routinely face some variation of this double standard and double bind. They risk appearing too "soft" or too "strident," too "aggressive" or not "aggressive" enough. And what is assertive in a man often seems abrasive in a woman.[2]

Rhode is far from alone. In 2010 two University of Hawai'i professors — one a law professor, the other a psychologist — tried to prove their hypothesis about systemic stereotyping of women through an empirical study of law students. The study "confirmed that implicit gender bias is in fact widely present among a law student sample." Significantly, the stereotyping was prevalent in both male *and female* students.[3]

These and other problems faced by women lawyers in the law firm setting are addressed by the following article, which describes the thin tightrope to success women lawyers must walk. Although written in 1990, it could have been written last week.

---

[1] WOMEN LAWYERS' JOURNAL, Vol. 96, Nos. 2 and 3 (2011), and *available at* http://nawl. timberlakepublishing.com/files/WLJ_vol96nos2_3_loresSpreads.pdf.

[2] Deborah L. Rhode, *Gender and the Profession: The No-Problem Problem*, 30 HOFSTRA L. REV. 1001 (2002).

[3] Justin D. Levinson & Danielle Young, *Implicit Gender Bias in the Legal Profession: An Empirical Study*, 18 DUKE J. GENDER L. & POL'Y 1 (2010).

Mona D. Miller, *Breaking Through the Glass Ceiling*
CALIFORNIA LAWYER (August 1990)[4]

In 1977, when I graduated from law school, I thought if I worked very hard and did my best, I could eventually become a partner at the medium-sized Los Angeles law firm I was about to join. And I did, although by that time the firm had grown and I was less naive about the ways in which women associates are expected to conform to a predominantly male culture. A hopeful, headlong plunge into the law and the determination to do an enormous amount of work are helpful, but they simply aren't enough. . . .

While probably no more sexist than the world at large, law firms, caught in a mire of cut-throat competition, rising overhead and the shifting loyalties of clients and partners, are hardly oases of egalitarianism. Women associates must deal with latent and open sexism, a dearth of role models and minority status. Though women now make up 50 percent of many law school classes, the ratio of women partners is increasing by only 1 percent a year.

. . . .

To become a partner, a woman must . . . present herself in a way that conforms to the firm's perception of its requirements. Different firms value different qualities, and they may not in fact value what they say they value.

. . . .

Whether sexist or just used to the comfort of the familiar, men often have difficulty acknowledging competence in a woman. Some can hardly believe they've encountered it. I'll never forget a juror telling me after a long trial that a young male partner and I had won, "You weren't as bad as I thought you'd be."

Thus a female associate must not only have ability, her "style" — her personality and way of communicating, her attitudes and expression — must instill confidence in her superiors. She needs to be able to present herself as a highly competent lawyer and inevitable future partner without seeming threatening, overpowering, abrasive, abusive, self-righteous, or (at the other end of the spectrum) defensive, overanxious, insecure, hysterical, rigid, or, God forbid, humorless. (A sense of humor is essential for survival in this profession.) Women need to select and maintain a professional demeanor that does not offend yet does not leave room for warmth or friendliness to be mistaken for a sexual overture.

A woman in a big firm cannot afford to be so different that the men feel uncomfortable with her. And the range of behaviors male partners tolerate from women associates is, in my experience, both narrower and different from what they tolerate in a man. . . .

Even a woman's physical appearance is more closely examined. I have heard male partners complain about female associates' excessive weight, makeup or lack of makeup, strong perfume or wrinkled suits while overlooking the creases or badly

---

[4] Copyright © 1990 by the California Lawyer. Reprinted by permission.

fitting suits, untucked shirt tails, scuffed shoes or bloodstained shirts on some of their male colleagues.

Motherhood is another area where the gap between a firm's self-image and what really goes on within its walls is apparent. Maternity-leave policies are driven by economic realities. Some partners view a firm's maternity-leave policy as a generous gift, not something to which the associate is entitled. A senior associate I knew who might otherwise have received a handsome discretionary bonus for long hours found her bonus reduced pro rata for the time she took off for maternity leave. I question whether the same thing would have happened to a male associate temporarily disabled by a back or leg injury for the same period of time.

Though a firm may claim to be pro-family, women who defer partnership to have children make some partners very uneasy. The women's commitment is questioned because they may not be available for work at night or on weekends, or because they are not treating partnership as the be-all-and-end-all of existence. Some partners are simply uncomfortable hearing about infants. One attorney mother I know says she avoids the "B" word with certain partners.

Too much talk about one's child may seem unprofessional, but focusing exclusively on work may bring a woman criticism to which a man would not be subject. Older partners may be offended by a new mother's "premature" return to work. On the other hand, a woman who works fewer hours with reduced compensation may cause amazing resentment. . . .

At some point you have to ask yourself how much compromise is too much. Where do you draw the line in conforming to male-dominated institutional values? You'll know when something inside you rebels. I didn't have to draw that line; it started drawing itself.

. . . .

I drew the line . . . early in my career, when I was the "grunt" worker on a huge antitrust team and had the opportunity to meet a manager of the corporate client and review some records in Fresno. I had worked very hard on the case and looked forward to getting out of the library to see our client's plant, but there was no reason the trip had to take place immediately. I was anticipating with great pleasure a visit from a sister I saw only once or twice a year. When the senior partner announced he was sending me to Fresno for a week, I said something like "Oh, no, that's the week my sister's coming to L.A."

The more senior (and male) associate advised me privately that I'd made a big mistake. I should have expressed how thrilled and happy I — a nobody who'd been slaving away on this case 10 hours a day for months — was at being sent on a wonderful and exciting business trip. A sister's visit was a totally unacceptable reason not to want to go, calling my entire level of commitment into question. Apparently months of well-executed work could be erased by a spontaneous remark.

I later apologized to the partner in charge [but] the trip was rescheduled to a better time for me. Undoubtedly, I had foolishly communicated my feeling that making the trip just then was not essential; no superior ever wants his decisions criticized, especially by a woman . . . .

Since that time I have supervised many associates and I now have more sympathy for the senior partner than I did . . . . People who are inflexible about their personal schedules make life harder for the rest of us. But the prevalent myth among some lawyers that no life outside the firm should ever intrude into office discussions strikes me as sick and inherently sexist in a world where working mothers usually bear more child-rearing responsibilities than their husbands, and wives deal more than husbands with the physical and emotional maintenance of the home. . . . I don't think emphasis on a more balanced approach to work, leaving time for family and community, should be treated as a sign of inexcusable weakness.

. . . .

I did have help from many male colleagues. These men assumed I would be able to deal with whatever came my way, which forced me to learn a great deal and to develop a thicker skin. At the same time, some of them recognized the power they had to control the tone of various encounters. Their willingness to step in and deflect sexist comments eliminated the need for me to respond and face being branded as "defensive" or "humorless."

Nevertheless, while useful mentors and allies may be found along the way, the person who engineers a woman's arrival into the partnership is the woman.

NOTES

Some have argued that the issues raised by the Miller piece are "quality of life" rather than gender issues. Is Miller correct that these issues affect women much more strongly than men? Should these issues be treated as sex-neutral, or is it legitimate to understand that they affect women more?

2.   The "Mommy Track" and Caretakers

Mona Miller eventually resigned her partnership after the birth of her daughter and returned to practice with another firm on a part-time basis. Should the "mommy track" force women to resign their partnerships? Can there be a part-time partner at a firm? On one hand, many feel the bias against women with kids has continued unabated. When Southwestern law Professor Judy Sloan role-plays with her students divided into law firms deciding on female candidates, the "pregnant woman" rarely gets the job. On the other, in the years since Miller's article, more firms are looking at these possibilities, in an effort to keep lawyers, mostly but not exclusively women, who have other personal priorities but who want to continue with the "serious" practice of law. But that doesn't necessarily make it easier.

In June 1998, Florida Attorney Alice Hector, a partner and senior trial lawyer at a large Miami law firm, lost a custody battle with her ex-husband because, with an iffy employment record, he was adjudged more available as a parent to their children. The ruling, *Young v. Hector*, 740 So. 2d 1153 (Fla. Dist. Ct. App. 1999), shocked the legal world. In an unusual proceeding, the Florida appeals court agreed to rehear the case *en banc* and a year later changed its decision, using the same original citation to wipe the previous opinion off the books. Many women found the original *Hector* opinion outrageous, but many also reported having succeeded in merging partnership careers with lives as parents. Almost all those who succeeded cited unusually supportive spouses, nannies who were "like a member of the family," and the reality of working two full-time jobs.

One surprising "mommy track" stumbling block, according to some younger woman attorneys, is that older women who have "made it," while they may be mentors and role models, are sometimes of little help in encouraging changes such as part-time partnership tracks. Indeed, some claim that some older women lawyers are often among those most resistant. "I'm not going to make exceptions for anybody in my court," a woman judge said at a recent bias seminar. "I dealt with my child care problems; attorneys appearing in my court will simply have to deal with theirs." This is an understandable point of view, but is it reasonable?

We invite anyone with doubts about whether women routinely face subtle forms of "mommy track" bias to try this test. Lawyer X attends an afternoon judicial conference, such as a pretrial settlement conference. After waiting their turn on the calendar, the lawyers go into chambers, where X tells the judge the following: "Your Honor, I really need to be out of here by 4:30. You know, I'm a single parent, and I have to pick up my little girl at day care by 5:15." If X is a man, the likely response from the bench — be the judge man or woman — is sympathy and understanding, even a positive reaction ("Gee, what a caring Dad.") But if X is a woman, the likely response is anger at her request for "special favors," and a negative reaction ("Having kids is fine, but she's not taking her law practice seriously enough.") Try this test empirically; unfortunately, the results have been borne out by the similar experiences of many lawyers.

The following article describes one poignant real-life experience.

Stuart Hanlon, *Getting It*
CALIFORNIA LAWYER (April 2000)[5]

I recently was forced to withdraw from the case of *People v. Sara Jane Olson aka Kathleen Soliah*, for personal but very simple reasons: I am a single father of two young boys, ages eight and twelve, and my wife, attorney Kathleen Ryan, died more than two years ago of leukemia. When I agreed to be one of Sara's lawyers I thought it would be a six-to-eight-week trial involving the charges that she and others supposedly connected to the Symbionese Liberation Army (SLA) planted bombs under two Los Angeles police cars in 1975. My commitment to live in Los Angeles four or five nights a week for the period of time seemed workable during the school year because I had family lined up to help take care of my sons. The prosecution . . . decided to expand the scope of the trial to include other evidence [of SLA activity including] the kidnapping of Patricia Hearst. The court agreed . . . and a likely two-month trial suddenly became a six-to-eight-month trial.

Within hours, I came to the conclusion that I could not leave my kids for that long a period, and shortly thereafter I asked to withdraw as counsel. This was an extremely difficult decision to make because I was committed to represent Sara. I strongly believe in her innocence. . . . I knew that leaving the case would put both Sara and [my co-counsel] Susan Jordan in a difficult situation. Whenever a lawyer leaves a case, especially a massive one like this, there is a void. . . . However, the decision was clear: My children's needs were more important than any professional considerations.

I was surprised by the positive publicity surrounding my withdrawal. I was portrayed as sacrificing a high-profile case for the sake of my children and taking the moral high road. It was not only embarrassing but strange. After all, I was just a lawyer quitting a case. Then I realized that I was receiving all this attention because it was so unusual for a man to give up anything in his professional life for the sake of his family. If I had been a female attorney in the same situation, there would have been nothing heroic about quitting to care for my children. It would have been expected. . . . [I]n fact, if I had been a woman and had *not* left the case, I probably would have been criticized for being cold and uncaring. . . .

I have had to think a lot about sexual stereotypes since the death of my wife. . . . Sexism is nothing new in our society or in the law. Most female attorneys reading this will probably think, *Duh! Didn't you get this before?* And the answer would be, no I didn't. If Kathy were still alive, I would have gone off to Los Angeles for six months without much of a thought and left her to not only care for our two children but also her very demanding domestic law practice. . . .

I hope the publicity surrounding my withdrawal and my personal situation helps some of us men in the legal profession understand the difficult and painful choices that are faced every day by lawyers, prosecutors, and judges who also happen to be women and mothers. No articles are written about how terrific they are or how difficult their professional choices are.

There is one very big difference between those women and myself: I was forced into this situation by the death of a wonderful person, lawyer, and mother, yet I receive credit for my choices because I am awkward in my new role, and it is uncommon for men to have to make such decisions. Kathleen and many other professional women embrace their roles as mothers and manage the balance between their professional and family lives with grace and ease. I, for one, have learned how difficult their choices are.

3.   Women as "Rainmakers," and "Networking"

"Rainmaking," or creating business, is what many of the most successful lawyers are all about. But rainmaking means being able to "network," the traditional way lawyers obtain clients. And there remain serious *de facto* gender and racial barriers to effective networking, such as the woman lawyer who has difficulty inviting the male client out to dinner. As Jean MacLean Snyder, a successful rainmaking woman lawyer put it some years ago, "Men take clients out. They take their wives, and the clients — almost always men — take their wives. Women have to renegotiate all of that, right from picking up the phone to say, 'Would you like to go out to dinner?' Or maybe, 'Could I take you out to dinner?' . . . Is the woman going to bring her husband with her? Does the client bring his wife?"[6]

Even those women who successfully "learn the rules of the man's world" may find it still does not completely level the playing field. Inequality is shown in recent statistics. According to a NAWL survey in late 2009, 72% of the 200 largest law firms surveyed had no women among their top five rainmakers, about half had no women among their top ten, and one-third had only one.[7]

Women lawyers fight back, of course. In October 2012, the Law Practice Management Section of the ABA put on a "Women Rainmakers Mid-Career Workshop," in which women "rainmakers" provided marketing, mentoring, and networking opportunities to other women lawyers. Perhaps most importantly, the workshop was hands-on, with one-on-one "coaching sessions," mock "pitch sessions" to mock boards of directors, and the like. Of course, the need for such specialized programs underscores the problem that women face when it comes to access to business.

4. Minorities and Race: The San Francisco Experience

If the road is tougher for women than men, it may be even more difficult for members of minorities, especially, according to the statistical and anecdotal evidence, African-Americans. In the post-President Obama era, the chance of an African-American to succeed at the highest level cannot be questioned. But almost unanimously, scholars who have studied race in America agree on one thing: The election of a black president hardly means we are living in a post-racial era. Just look at our law firms.

In the late 1980s and throughout the 1990s, bar associations and many law firms, including BigLaw firms, made substantial efforts to increase the hiring and promotion of minority lawyers. For some big firms, their reasons were both altruistic and bottom-line related. For others, it may have been the pressure of closer media scrutiny, especially from the American Lawyer Media group, which owns legal newspapers around the country, and which kept detailed tallies of minority hirings and promotions.

In 1989, the Bar Association of San Francisco began a concerted effort to increase the percentages of minority associates and partners in its member law firms. Specific goals were targeted: 15% minority associates or junior counsel and 5% minority partners or senior counsel by the end of 1995; and 25% and 10%, respectively, by the end of the year 2000. San Francisco, a West Coast legal center with a progressive reputation and a widely diverse population that includes large numbers of African-Americans, Latinos, and Asian-Americans, was perhaps the ideal locus for such a plan.

---

[6] Jean MacLean Snyder, Oral remarks at 1990 ABA litigation symposium, reprinted in *Woman As Rainmakers*, LITIGATION (1991).

[7] *See* Lorelei Laird, *Lessons from Female Rainmakers*, 2011, National Association of Female Executives, reported at http://www.workingmother.com/best-companies/lessons-female-rainmakers; and notes from ABA Law Practice Management Section Law Firm Marketing Strategies Conference, 2010.

When it issued its interim report in December 1993, the bar association noted a substantial increase in the numbers of minority attorneys, an increase that applied across-the-board to large, mid-sized, and small firms, and corporate law departments. During this period, the Association itself had its first minority presidents, a Chinese-American and an African-American. The positive result was clearly due in significant part to a system-wide approach, led by the bar, which made law firm diversity the right road to take, and used this form of "peer pressure" to counter and begin to change deep-seated cultural attitudes. Nevertheless, many firms fell well short of the targeted goals.

Perhaps a more significant problem, however, was that to some observers, while minority hiring had increased, the corporate world's willingness to spread business to minority attorneys lagged far behind. At the annual dinner of the California Minority Counsel Program, then-bar President Ray Marshall threw down the gauntlet, stating that the program "had not helped increase professional opportunities" for "partners of color."[8]

By 1998, while the program's progress had continued for associates, it had slowed substantially for minority partners, especially those who were not Asian. A San Francisco *Daily Journal* survey found that in California's 20 largest firms, most of them based in the Bay Area, only 38 of the over 3,000 partners were African-American, and 11 of the 20 firms had either one or *no* black partners. Periodic reports in 1999 and 2004 showed that firms remained close to on track for minority associates, but had continued to fall well short of their partnership goal. The bar's own report showed that in the largest firms that were the focus of the study, only 6% of partners were minorities. Worse, in San Francisco's "large mid-sized firms" minority partners comprised 2.6%, a rate the 1999 report described as "dismal." Significantly, the report also found that law firms with affirmative programs to encourage diversity did far better than those that adopted a "color blind" approach.

The disappointing numbers reported in 2004 caused the Bar's leadership to redouble its efforts, by including members of the minority bar counsel program on its board of directors, increasing the number of minority law student scholarships, and, perhaps most significantly, raising the visibility of the issue once again. However, the goals have not nearly been met.

5. Are Minority Attorneys Losing Ground?

If increasing minority hiring was so difficult in San Francisco, with strong bar support and many firms buying into the program, what is it like in other areas of the country? The record in the last decade is not good, and if anything shows that minority representation, especially in big firms, has not grown, and has actually decreased for African Americans. *American Lawyer*'s 2010 "diversity scorecard" showed that in late 2008 and 2009, when the recession hit law firms hard, the percentage of minority lawyers at "BigLaw" firms went down for the first time in a decade. Minority lawyers were one and one-half times more likely to be laid off than white attorneys. African American attorneys suffered the greatest percentage

---

[8] Michael J. Hall, *BASF Leader Calls Minority Plan Weak*, L.A. & S.F. Daily J., October 24, 1994.

decrease.[9] By the end of 2012, the situation had gotten worse for black lawyers, according to a report by Vault.com in cooperation with the Minority Corporate Counsel Association.

Vera Djordjevich, *Are African-American Attorneys Losing Ground?*
vault.com, *available at* http://blogs.vault.com/blog/workplace-issues/are-african-american-attorneys-losing-ground/, February 28, 2013[10]

Despite a recessionary blip, for the most part we have seen steady — albeit slow — progress for minority lawyers over the years.

That said, not all minority groups are faring equally well. While the number of Asian Americans and Hispanics among summer associates, for example, is increasing, the percentage of African-American law students hired has declined — even as the number of black students enrolled in law school has grown . . . .

Why are young African-American lawyers leaving firms at a disproportionate rate? Perhaps one reason is that, while the chances of making partner at a BigLaw firm are slim for everyone these days, the possibilities seem even more remote for African-Americans. In 2011, law firms reported that less than 3% of attorneys promoted to partnership were African-American.

According to Vault's annual Associate Survey, in which thousands of law firm associates assess their employers on various workplace issues, African-Americans consistently report the lowest levels of overall job satisfaction among racial/ethnic groups. Feedback from African-American associates reveals certain common threads:

While some firms do well at the ground level, the lack of color among the upper echelons is discouraging:

- "There are not many minorities, especially African-Americans and Latinos, in the partnership."

- "It is discouraging for ethnically diverse young associates to not see or have an impressionable number of ethnically diverse partners at the firm."

The firm brings in diverse attorneys, but then does little to engage or help them develop:

- "They are having a difficult time keeping minorities — specifically people of color. We don't feel like there is anyone here that is really trying to retain us and to help us grow as attorneys, which means it's time to go."

- "With a couple of exceptions, minority associates seem to get ignored a bit when it comes to work. Minorities do not seem to have the same opportunity to bill as many hours as white attorneys do."

- "In my experience, few lawyers of color have mentors or sponsors in their

---

[9] Emily Barker, *Minority Lawyers Losing Ground at Big Law Firms, New Report Shows*, THE AMERICAN LAWYER, March 2, 2010.

[10] Copyright © vault.com. Reprinted by permission.

corner or really meaningful opportunities to connect with influential lawyers at the firm." . . .

Retention is stronger when mentoring is not simply a pro-forma activity but an organic aspect of the culture:

- "The firm's Chief Diversity Officer and lead hiring partner have worked very hard to ensure that we have a diverse group of associates; having and being a mentor is a natural part of working here (not something that feels artificial or contrived). As a diverse associate, I can say that the mentorship I have received here has been a significant factor in my development as an attorney and in my choice to stay at the firm; the culture here is open and I have no hesitation about knocking on a variety of partners' doors to ask questions about workflow or other issues."

- "The chair of our diversity committee is really committed to these issues. Minorities and women really mentor each other and make an effort to retain those individuals in the firm. I can say that from personal experience, falling into both categories."

Affinity groups and other gatherings for attorneys of similar backgrounds can provide valuable opportunities to share experiences and build relationships . . .:

- "As a minority associate, I was initially hesitant about working in [a geographic area that] lacks a great deal of diversity. However, I've found [the firm] and the community to be extremely welcoming and engaging. [The firm] works with minority professional networking groups to help young associates ease their way into the community."

NOTES

In THE GOOD BLACK: A TRUE STORY OF RACE IN AMERICA (1999), author Paul M. Barrett describes, at page 55, one white partner's view of affirmative action: "There are lots of minorities, African-Americans in particular, who are running around with Harvard and Yale degrees and who are not qualified in any sense" to practice law with his firm.

Read the following article, which seems, unfortunately, to affirm the prevalence of this attitude, and recounts, among other things, the story of Lawrence Munchin, the title character of THE GOOD BLACK.

Leonard M. Baynes, *Falling Through the Cracks: Race and Corporate Law Firms*
77 ST. JOHN'S LAW REVIEW 785 (2002)[11]

[S]ome lawyers of color who work in corporate law firms still have remarkably different experiences than their white counterparts. For instance, in the 1990s, Cleary, Gottlieb, Steen & Hamilton established a "critical mass" of minority associates: thirty African Americans, fourteen Latinos, and twenty-four Asian

---

[11] Copyright © 2002 by St. John's Law Review Association. Reprinted by permission.

Americans. Most of the African American associates hired during this period, however, left the firm. Unfortunately, this problem is not confined to Cleary. By the third year, most associates of color leave corporate law firms; whereas, forty percent of associates in general leave during the same time frame. . . .

Evan Davis, a Cleary partner, blamed the departure of many of the African American associates on "the prejudice of low expectations," the type of "subconscious prejudice [that] affects people of color." Former Cleary attorney Roslyn Powell described the problem this way: "Senior associates felt that their views were ignored. You get lousy work assignments, then they say that everything you do is wrong [or they say that] you can't write." . . . Another former black Cleary associate stated that "[Cleary] assume[s] blacks are interested in pro bono, but not corporate transactions. There's this view that we're not really interested in corporate work."

Others focused on Cleary's management structure as the problem. It had "no formal departments" but instead was "organized around informal groups of partners and associates who focus on specific areas of practice such as mergers and acquisitions, tax, intellectual property, or litigation." . . . Some reported that the informality resulted in the formation of racial cliques that kept African American associates from receiving good work assignments. For most of the African American associates, the coup de grace was Cleary's failure to invite senior African American associate Lynn Dummett into the partnership ranks. After the partnership meeting deciding Ms. Dummett's fate, rumors spread that racist comments were made at the meeting. [Many saw this] as a signal that the firm was uninterested in diversifying its partnership ranks.

. . . .

Two very important discrimination cases [have] caused corporate heads to spin. In the first case, Andargachew Zelleke, a cum laude graduate of Harvard Law School, who was of Ethiopian ancestry, alleged that while working at White & Case, senior associate Donald Ries made racially derogatory comments against him. At the time of the suit, White & Case had three Latino partners but no African American partners, [and] only eight African American associates but sixteen Latino ones. [Reis's alleged] comments were . . . (1) Mr. Zelleke was only admitted to Harvard because of affirmative action; (2) Mr. Zelleke was a "black prince"; and (3) Mr. Zelleke "is so stupid because he is half-black." Mr. Ries denied making the derogatory statements; however, other associates allegedly confirmed the charges . . . .

Given Mr. Zelleke's biracial background, White & Case attorneys allegedly were confused over his racial identity. The executive partner of the Los Angeles office wrote: "In the first place, Andy Zelleke's skin is not black . . . . We hire Mexican lawyers. Are they black? I don't know whether they're black or not. Some of them have very dark skin. Do I care? I don't care." This confusion over Mr. Zelleke's racial identity seems disingenuous and misses the point. First, Mr. Zelleke requested that the law firm list him as black in its EEO records. Second, . . . despite how he described himself or appeared, he apparently faced discrimination because of his black identity. Ultimately, White & Case and Mr. Zelleke agreed to a $505,000 negotiated judgment to resolve the lawsuit. It was reputedly "the first race-discrimination lawsuit by an attorney to result in a formal judgment against a major firm."

. . . .

In the second case, Lawrence Mungin, an African American, Harvard-educated bankruptcy associate, sued his former law firm, Katten Muchin & Zavis, alleging that they racially discriminated against him. The jury awarded Mr. Mungin $2.5 million in damages, including punitive damages of $1.5 million. The Washington Post reported that the award was the largest discrimination judgment against a law firm.

At the time of Mr. Mungin's employment, the firm had only four African American attorneys out of 350 attorneys nationwide, and Mr. Mungin was the only African American attorney in the Washington, D.C. office. Mr. Mungin alleged that the law firm discriminated against him by paying him less than other lawyers in his entering class, by failing to provide him with quality assignments, and by failing to consider him for partner. As several of the department's partners left the firm, Mr. Mungin's status became more precarious. The law firm told him that "he had to handle first-year associate work," even though he was a seventh-year associate. Additionally, the firm lowered his billing rate from $185 to $125 per hour. In his seventh year, the firm failed to officially review his performance. One partner, however, did evaluate him, stating:

> Much of Larry's time is consumed by routine tasks, such as drafting status letters to our client. Occasionally we receive a challenging assignment from AIG [a large client], which Larry accomplishes with great skill. AIG is a very difficult client and Larry's ongoing efforts to coordinate with me have made a potentially troublesome situation, relatively easy. I do not believe that, for the most part, AIG offers challenging work to Larry. Larry nonetheless accomplishes the tasks for AIG with a helpful attitude and a willingness to tackle the unique problems this client presents.

Katten's head partner found this evaluation lauded Mr. Mungin's "affability," not his technical expertise and discounted the evaluation because he did not respect the partner who wrote it. Mr. Mungin was humiliated by the evaluation, and when asked to read it from the witness stand, he cried . . . .

In a highly unusual decision, the D.C. Circuit reversed and remanded the jury verdict. At the hearing, although Mr. Mungin's qualifications were not challenged by defense counsel at the lower court or on appeal, Judge Randolph, *sua sponte*, asked about Mr. Mungin's grades at Harvard and whether he had been fired from his previous law firms. It seems that Judge Randolph engaged in the same stereotypes about African American attorneys that some of the partners in Katten Muchin had. So it should come as no surprise that the D.C. Circuit, by a 2-1 vote, found that no reasonable jury could find for Mr. Mungin and reversed the jury verdict. . . .

6. Minority Partners and Systemic Issues

Harvard Professor David Wilkins has long examined and written about the experience of African American lawyers in large corporate law firms. Centering his research on Chicago, Wilkins continues to write on these issues, including the experiences of principals of black-owned firms, the future for black lawyers in the post-Obama era, and, in this earlier article, the high attrition rate of African-American lawyers who had already become partners in large firms. In this piece, Wilkins conducted interviews with over 150 law firm partners or former partners, developing a clear-eyed view at some of the systemic roadblocks to the success of black lawyers, even those who had supposedly "made it" as "BigLaw" partners.

David B. Wilkins, *Partners Without Power? A Preliminary Look at Black Partners in Corporate Law Firms*
2 [Hofstra] J. Inst. Stud. Leg. Eth 15 (1999)[12]

Discussions about law firm diversity tend to treat increasing the number of minority partners as both the ultimate goal and the end of the analysis. The emphasis that diversity advocates place on partnership statistics is understandable.

Nevertheless . . . just because a minority lawyer becomes a partner does not mean that he or she will stay a partner. In today's competitive environment, partnership is no longer the equivalent of tenure. . . . [A]lthough the term "partner" invokes reassuring connotations of equality, it is now painfully clear that some law firm partners are substantially more equal than others. . . . Partners who make the biggest contribution to the bottom line also tend to have significant influence over firm management. . . .

[M]inority partners are located at the bottom end of the partnership pecking order. . . . Because they have less seniority and clout than their white peers, minority partners are more likely to look for other employment opportunities. . . . At the same time, minority partners live in constant fear of the kind of demotion or even outright expulsion that happens to partners who have neither the financial nor the political resources to protect their interests inside the firm.

[Wilkins then discusses "the vanishing black partner," described his anecdotal evidence, gathered by scores of interviews of African-American partners in Chicago's large firms, and what statistics are available, all which show great attrition among black partners.]

The Markets of Power

Partners . . . compete in three distinct markets: the *external* market for clients, the *internal* market for referrals, and the market for *labor*. Each of these markets utilizes a different form of currency.

As many have noted, the currency that brings success in the external market is *connections*. . . . The internal market operates on a different currency . . . *reciprocity*. Partners are more likely to refer business from their existing clients to those who can both do the work well . . . and who can return the favor by sending work back. . . .

Finally, the currency in the labor market is *clout* . . . . In a world in which all partners are not created equal, savvy senior associates understand that their best strategy for maximizing their chances of winning the [partnership] tournament lie in developing working relationships with powerful partners whose views will carry weight at partnership time. . . .

Partners with power are, therefore, those partners with significant reservoirs of connections, reciprocity, and clout. Black partners, unfortunately, face significant barriers to obtaining each of these three forms of capital.

Why the Last Typically Remain Last

. . . Racism . . . cannot provide the full explanation for why black lawyers remain partners without power in many firms. [But a]cknowledging that black professionals are subject to the same forces that affect their white coworkers does not mean, as some conservative commentators have suggested, that black professionals have "transcended" race. . . . When placed in the context of the natural predisposition of human beings to favor those who are most like themselves, it is clear that the simple credo of "class not race" fails accurately to account for the role that race plays in the lives of middle class blacks ".

[B]lack lawyers who become partners have had to overcome obstacles that, although not different in kind from those encountered by their white peers, are nevertheless rendered more difficult because of race. Chief among these obstacles is the problem of finding mentors. . . . Black lawyers consistently report that they have difficulty finding partners who are willing to enter into these crucial relationships.

The blacks who make partner have found a way to surmount this challenge. Some have done so by having superior academic credentials, for example, graduating from an elite law school. . . . Thus, seventy-seven percent of all of the black partners listed in the Minority Partners Handbook in 1995 graduated from one of the eleven elite schools from which corporate firms typically recruit, with fully 47% attending either Harvard or Yale law school. . . . Contrary to the skeptic's assertion, therefore, with respect to educational credentials, the average black partner is *better* qualified than his or her white peers.

. . . .

If neither racism nor their own lack of ability dooms the careers of black partners, then why are these lawyers, nevertheless, disproportionately represented among the partners without power? The answer to this question lies in the complex intersection among the institutional dynamics of elite firms, race, and the strategies for becoming a partner with power; strategies that are quite different from those that lead to success as an associate . . . . Moreover, unlike their peers, black partners must also negotiate these pressures in an environment in which they still face negative stereotypes and preconceptions because of their race.

. . . .

A. *The Politics of Rain*

Connections are the currency of the external market for new clients. Given this reality, it should come as no surprise that black partners are at a disadvantage in this market. As one prominent black partner ruefully notes:

> We don't sit in the corporate boardrooms, and our mothers and fathers don't sit in the corporate boardrooms. We're not members of the $40,000-a-head country club and neither are our mothers and our fathers. We're just not naturally networked — because of the history of our country, quite frankly — into the kinds of business opportunities or avenues that our white counterparts are networked into.[13]

To be sure, there are many white partners whose mothers and fathers don't sit on corporate boards either. Unlike the so-called "golden age," elite firm lawyers are no longer chosen primarily on the basis of their social pedigree. Nevertheless, it remains true that blacks are less likely than whites to have the kind of contacts from which important business relationships are developed.

. . . .

There is, however, one area where many black partners have the kind of contacts that produce lucrative business. One of the salient developments in the post civil rights era has been the rise in black political power . . . . Predictably, many black partners have made cultivating black political contacts a major part of their rainmaking strategy.

This political strategy, however, is a double edge sword. The example of the city of Chicago is illustrative. On the positive side, many black lawyers in Chicago's large firms saw their fortunes rise considerably when Harold Washington was elected Mayor in 1983. . . . Washington made it clear that any firm wishing to do business with the city of Chicago would have to demonstrate its commitment to diversity. . . . Several of the black lawyers I interviewed benefitted directly . . . . This reality became bitterly apparent to many black partners in Chicago when Harold Washington died unexpectedly shortly after his reelection in 1987 [and was replaced] by Richard M. Daly (who is white). . . . The repercussions of this new state of affairs for the careers of several black partners in Chicago were both swift and severe. In one particularly graphic example, the day after Washington died, the managing partner of a large Chicago firm called in the firm's only two black partners, both of whom had brought in significant city work, and asked them how they intended to support themselves now that Washington was dead.

B. *Getting the Franchise — and Keeping It*

. . . Law firms distribute partner work for existing clients in three ways: inheritance, referrals, and cross marketing. Black partners appear to face significant obstacles in each of these arenas.

1. Inheritance — Although few like to admit it, many of today's senior partners

---

[13] Chicago partner Frederick H. Bates, quoted in Steven Keeva, *Unequal Partners*, ABA J., February 1993. *See* the Supplemental Readings for a further description of this article.

acquired their most important clients the old fashioned way: they inherited them. The process is as familiar as it is rarely discussed. Senior partners with important client relationships bequeath them to favored junior colleagues. As the term implies, this process is traditionally done when the senior partner is about to retire. . . .

The black partners in my study have had little success in the inheritance market. In one of my first interviews, a black partner in a major firm in Chicago, challenged me to find one example of a black partner who had either assumed a leading role for one of the firm's important institutional clients or was being groomed to do so in the future. After more than sixty interviews with black lawyers who are either senior associates or partners in Chicago, I have yet to find a single example. . . .

2. One of the primary benefits of working in a law firm, as opposed to being a solo practitioner, is the potential for internal referrals. Clients frequently call a lawyer with whom they have a close relationship about a problem outside of that lawyer's areas of expertise. . . . The question remains, however, which of his partners the lawyer will call. . . .

Once again, black lawyers are less likely than their peers to get all or part of the franchise in a given area. . . . To the extent that black lawyers have had fewer mentors as associates, and tend to be more isolated as partners, they are less likely to have the kind of cross-cutting relationships throughout the firm that generate significant referral business. . . .

Finally, to the extent that referring partners seek return business, the barriers black partners face in the external and inheritance markets are likely to impede their chances for referrals as well. . . .

3. *Cross Marketing* — The final mechanism for generating and allocating business from existing clients is cross marketing. . . . The essence of cross marketing is simply taking a proactive stance towards referrals. Rather than waiting for the client to call with a new kind of problem, law firms are increasingly approaching existing clients about the possibility of doing work for them in other areas. . . .

Several black partners . . . felt that they were excluded from these marketing initiatives for the same reasons that they were largely left out of the inheritance and referral markets. Rarely are black partners considered by their peers to be the "best" lawyers to convince a client to send additional business to the firm. . . .

When they are invited, black partners frequently complain that they are only there for show, perhaps because the client is concerned about diversity, and are rarely given credit for any work that subsequently comes in.

. . . .

And so the circle continues. Black partners have a harder time getting clients from the outside, which in turn undermines their participation in the internal referral market, which in turn stymies their efforts to secure the services of senior associates, which in turn places added burdens on their efforts to recruit clients and solicit referrals. Given this reality, it is no wonder that many black partners have decided to seek their fortunes in arenas other than the large law firm.

NOTES

Suzanne Baer, a New York bar association diversity consultant, reinforces Wilkins' view. Baer was quoted in Steven Keeva's *ABA Journal* article about a fundamental difference between the way white and black Americans see the world: "When you grow up never having to deal with racism, always seeing positive portrayals of people like yourself in the mass media, it creates an adult who has the ability to access wealth and do client development with some confidence, because that person knows that the door he or she is knocking on is going to have a white person behind it. This compensates for the fact that he or she doesn't have family connections. It's very hard for people to understand this automatic benefit . . . even if you're wealthier than the white boy who sat next to you in school."

The election of President Obama has changed this in a fundamental way, as Professor Wilkins notes, but big questions remain:

> It is one thing to say that every little boy or girl might grow up to be President of the United States. It is quite a different thing to see a black President acting on the world stage every day of the week . . . . Whether the nation's first black President produces coattails that go beyond inspiring the young, however, remains to be seen.
>
> . . . .
>
> What is certain, however, is that there are likely to be many new black corporate lawyers precisely because there has been an Age of Obama. Just as corporate jobs have always been a stepping stone to high level positions in government, the reverse is also true . . . . Given the number of high-level black lawyers in the Obama administration, this trend will undoubtedly accelerate in the years when these now highly desirable lawyers leave office . . . . Whether these new black corporate lawyers will ever manage to do anything that causes as dramatic a shift in the racial landscape as the election of Barack Obama, of course, remains to be seen. But the very fact of their presence in ever greater numbers in corporate America allows us at least to dream . . . .[14]

7. Facing Dual Discrimination

African-American as well as other minority women lawyers often face dual discrimination. One more word from Professor Wilkins' 2010 article: "[B]lack women, notwithstanding their growing numbers in the black professional class, continue to lag behind both their black male and white female peers in terms of professional opportunities and success." This is especially true of the road to large firm partnership. In 1988, one black woman judge from Atlanta estimated the number of black women lawyers in partnership track positions as *one*. Things have improved since then, but not by that much.

---

[14] David B. Wilkins, *The New Social Engineers in the Age of Obama: Black Corporate Lawyers and the Making of the First Black President*, 53 How. L.J. 557 (2010).

Government and public service work remains much more a part of the minority woman's legal world. A 1998 survey showed 2% of white lawyers — and 2% of male minority attorneys — took public interest jobs after law school. The percentage for minority women was three times higher. For women, this may be one of the indirect effects of the "mommy track." But this may also be due in part to self-selection — a personal commitment to be in a more public service-oriented part of the profession.

The next article, from the *ABA Journal*, tells a more recent version of the story of — why women of color are vanishing from large law firms.

Jill Schachner Chanen, *Early Exits*
A.B.A. Journal (August 2006)[15]

From her office in a curved-glass building in downtown Chicago, Tina Tchen has all the trappings of success: a view, positions in national bar associations and a partnership at one of the country's most prestigious law firms — Skadden, Arps, Slate, Meagher & Flom. To those who know her, Tchen's success is no surprise. A graduate of a top law school, she's worked hard to earn her reputation as a bet-the-company trial lawyer.

What is surprising, though, is that Tchen decided to stick it out at a law firm at all. According to a new study by the ABA's Commission on Women in the Profession, few women of color ever get the kinds of equal opportunities that Tchen received to put them on the road to partnership. As a result, most choose to leave their firms rather than stay and fight for equality.

The study, *Visible Invisibility: Women of Color in Law Firms*, explores the experiences of these women. And what it shows is not pretty.

According to the study, women of color are leaving large law firm practices in droves because they are the victims of an uninterrupted cycle of institutional discrimination.

. . . .

Women of color say race and gender still carry a lot of baggage in the workplace. And nowhere is that baggage more of a burden for them than in large law firms where the good-old-boy network of white male leadership still predominates.

The issue has taken on heightened importance for law firms of late as corporate clients are starting to demand diversity — not just in the composition of their legal teams, but also in entire firms. But many women of color report that law firms in general continue to be unresponsive. Though most law firms are making efforts to diversify through recruiting, it seems few pay attention to what happens once women of color actually start working full time at the firm.

Behind the Findings

The commission's study is not the first to spotlight this situation. Study after study show that minority female lawyers have exceptional attrition rates in large law firms, defined as 25 attorneys or more. By some measures, nearly 100 percent of these women leave law firms within eight years. Other studies put the number closer to 66 percent within five years . . . .

"There are very few women of color in law firms. We are basically invisible," says Paulette Brown, a lawyer . . . in Short Hills, N.J., who co-chaired the study for the women's commission.

Brown, who notes that she is one of just three African American women partners in large law firms in the entire state of New Jersey, says that law firm leaders have been ignoring this problem for far too long . . . .

Using data obtained from self-administered questionnaires and from focus groups, the study has produced one-of-a-kind qualitative and quantitative data highlighting the differences in the hiring, development and advancement of women of color when compared to their male and nonminority counterparts in law firms, says Arin Reeves, a Chicago lawyer and diversity consultant who served as a co-chair of the study for the commission.

. . . .

Reeves says she sees women of color slipping through the cracks of law firms. Others, she says, are pushed out, while still more read the tea leaves and jump. "We are losing incredible talent from our profession because we have not been able to value, integrate and respect women of color," she says.

"The attrition has different points of origination, but, I think for a lot of law firms, . . . even if you decide to jump; you are not making the decision to jump in an ideal world where you have the same opportunities," Reeves adds.

Skirting the Periphery

While many law firms have diversity initiatives that focus on either gender or race, few — if any — pay attention to the overlap of these factors known as "intersectionality," says Reeves. And that's where many of the problems lie. "Women of color often are twice removed," she explains. As a result, she says, they tend to feel isolated and operate on the periphery in law firms.

[M]any of these women of' color working in large law firms are recruited from top law schools and often are at the top of their class, [but] 43.5 percent of the women surveyed reported missing out on desirable assignments because of race or gender . . . compared to 25 percent of men of color, 38.6 percent of white women and 1.9 percent of white men . . . .

Like others, Tehen suspects that minority women are inadvertently overlooked when work assignments are made. It likely happens because of individuals' comfort zones. "The people handing out the work are more comfortable with others like themselves, and since the majority of the people handing out the work are white men it is just perpetuating itself."

. . . .

Seattle lawyer Jacqueline Parker, now first vice president and counsel of Washington Mutual Bank, came to work at a large law firm with several years of experience in banking and finance and still found herself being denied opportunities. "I wanted to do financial services work, and if the partners and senior associates were not willing to give it to me, that is when I knew that it was time to find another opportunity," she says.

It was not until Parker approached a black partner at her firm and asked why she was not being given the opportunities she wanted that she was introduced to a senior white lawyer with substantial business in her preferred practice area.

Parker says the relationship she developed with these two lawyers helped her not only at the firm, but also in her law career. "I got absolutely invaluable feedback about what I did right and wrong," she says. But she wonders what would have happened without the support of these lawyers who took her under their wings.

Indeed, Parker's experience points to another issue raised by the surveyed women of color: the lack of mentoring . . . .

Finding a mentor is difficult enough, but it's tougher for minority women lawyers because there are so few senior women of color in law firms to whom they can relate.

. . . .

Reports of Overt Racism

Perhaps the most noteworthy finding of the women's commission study, however, was that nearly half of minority women lawyers reported that they are experiencing frequent and blatantly racist behavior in the workplace. According to the study, some 49 percent of the women of color surveyed reported experiencing demeaning comments or other types of harassment.

. . . .

The [anonymous] Am Law 100 associate says many women she knows have found that, no matter how well-educated they are, they cannot endure the treatment they suffered at these law firms because of racism. "It breaks my heart because their spirits were broken here," she says. This lawyer says she does not know why she has put up with the discrimination she personally has experienced, but she now is enjoying seeing senior lawyers be solicitous to her after she developed a substantial book of business. "I've learned that black does not matter; green does."

NOTES

As we have noted before, in many respects, overt racism is relatively easy to deal with — the enemy you know. The more insidious indirect issues — heavy recruiting but little mentoring, or not understanding the true circumstances facing women of color after they're hired — are more difficult to address. The solution, as the last lawyer quoted notes, is developing one's own book of business. But developing that business is where latent racial issues provide among the biggest hurdles.

8.   Is Bias an Ethical Issue?

The answer to this question is, increasingly, "yes." In the past 20 years, many states have passed disciplinary rules prohibiting discrimination by lawyers. Unlike most rules, whose development begins on a national level through the ABA, individual states, often motivated by local lobbying, have taken the lead in developing bias rules. As a result, and because these rules have little in the way of precedent to guide their direction, the substance of the rules varies widely from state to state.

By 1995, over half the states had anti-bias rules. In about 10 states, bias misconduct must be connected to the practice of law, and does not cover such issues as discrimination in employment. Other jurisdictions — including three of the nation's largest, New York, California, and the District of Columbia — have barred employment discrimination as well.

Nevertheless, the enforcement impact of rules prohibiting employment discrimination is likely to be slight. D.C.'s rule has generated very few complaints. And in New York and California, prohibited conduct may not result in discipline unless there is first a civil adjudication that the lawyer's conduct was wrong, a precondition that severely limits the rules' impact.

Since 1995, some of the focus has shifted from discrimination against women and minorities to bias encountered by gays and lesbians and those with disabilities. The National Association for Law Placement (NALP) began tracking lawyers by sexual preference in 1996. Everyone involved with the process admits this is harder than to track the progress of minorities and women, as sexual preference is not physically apparent, and because — at least in some parts of the country — sexual preference is not a characteristic lawyers always openly acknowledge. Whether it is because of increased hiring or increased self-reporting, the numbers of gay and lesbian attorneys hired at law firms seem to have risen significantly.

Disabled lawyers face a far more difficult hurdle. A 1996 NALP survey showed that only 54% of disabled lawyers found full-time law jobs, and less than half of those jobs were in private practice. Often the profession itself makes it harder even to become a lawyer. Dee Jones, a 2012 graduate of Vermont Law School, had to sue the National Association of Bar Examiners just to be allowed to take the Multistate Professional Responsibility Exam with the accommodations she needs. Jones, who is legally blind and has an auditory learning disability, won a preliminary injunction requiring the bar examiners to allow her to use a computer during the MPRE. The computer allows Jones, who hopes to practice disability law, to use two types of software that enlarge text, highlight words in different colors and read text aloud, so that she can fully comprehend the material.[16]

---

[16] *See*   http://www.vermontlaw.edu/Experience_VLS/Student_Highlights/Student_News_and_ Achievements/Federal_Judges_Rules_in_Favor_of_Blind_VT_Law_School_Student.htm.

Are anti-discrimination rules effective? These rules, Washington, D.C. lawyer David Isbell told the *National Law Journal*, are "likely to serve mainly a hortatory purpose" rather than be a "major disciplinary tool." But if Isbell, who served as chair of the ABA ethics committee that considered such a rule, is correct, are anti-bias rules justified? Yes, says Isbell, because they "set a useful standard" that lawyers should try to meet. Still, one must wonder how deep the commitment to anti-bias rules runs among state regulatory agencies if regulations are drafted without enough teeth to make them truly enforceable. Should a civil adjudication of discrimination be necessary when, for example, a criminal adjudication of theft is not required to discipline lawyers who steal money from their client trustee accounts?

9. Bias in the Courts

Bias in the legal profession is not limited to the words and actions of lawyers. Indeed, if anything our courts are slower to change than the rest of the profession. One problem that has gotten widespread publicity in recent years is the lack of minority clerks working at the United States Supreme Court. In the late 1990s, *USA Today* and *Legal Times*, the Washington D.C. Law Daily, reported that only seven of the 394 clerks hired by the nine sitting justices were African-American, and only four were Latino. Tony Mauro, longtime Supreme Court reporter for *American Lawyer* and its affiliates, reported that civil rights and minority bar groups attempted to sit down with then-Chief Justice Rehnquist in 1998 to discuss the situation, but he refused to meet with them.[17]

The nation's highest court hasn't fared much better when it comes to women clerks. Indeed, for the Fall 2006 Supreme Court term, only seven of the 37 law clerkships went to women, half the number for previous year, according to Pulitzer-prize-winning Supreme Court reporter Linda Greenhouse in the *New York Times*.[18] The *Times* reports that from 2000 to 2006 only 7% of Justice Scalia's clerks were women, and only 11% of Justice Kennedy's. With the two newest justices being women, this trend may now change.

And the high court is not alone. A September 1998 report found that of 66 research attorneys at the California Supreme Court (these are permanent staff positions, not law clerks who cycle through the courts), there were two Asian-Americans, one African-American, and no Latinos. The only minority member of the First District Court of Appeals' 52-lawyer research staff was a single Latino lawyer.[19] The statistics today are better, but not where they should be.

Lack of minority research attorneys is just the tip of the iceberg. Judges' power means that their behavior often is not subject to the same checks found in most law firms. In 1990, a California commission found widespread sex discrimination among the state's judges. The commission's report cited "openly hostile" attitudes, demeaning remarks, inappropriate sexual advances, even telling dirty jokes on the

---

[17] Tony Mauro, *Supreme Court Doors Opening Slightly*, LEGAL TIMES & AM. LAW. MEDIA, March 6, 2000. This article discusses a conference at Howard University that focused on this issue.

[18] Linda Greenhouse, *Women Suddenly Scarce Among Justices' Clerks*, N.Y. TIMES, August 30, 2006.

[19] *See* Greg Mitchell, *No Place at the Table*, THE RECORDER (San Francisco), Sept. 18, 1999.

bench. "Across the board," said the report, "we see one common thread — and that is the lack of credibility that women receive, whether they are lawyers or other participants in the process."

In the years since, sex discrimination on the bench has materially abated, but it has not ceased. We invite anyone with doubts about whether women routinely face subtle forms of bias from the bench to try the test we discuss in section 2 above about the disparate reactions to the male and female lawyers needing to care for their children.

Occasionally, overt incidents of sexism or racism continue to occur. In two 1999 cases, one Arizona judge, among numerous other offenses, e-mailed raunchy sexual material to his staff, while a Syracuse, New York judge — among other charges — commiserated with a prosecutor by describing an elderly murder victim as "just some old nigger bitch." The Arizona judge resigned and the New York judge was removed.

As these readings have consistently pointed out, bias is usually not a matter of prejudice this overt, but rather subtle and almost unstated forms of unequal treatment. This unequal treatment is often due to people's expectations of the situation, expectations that have developed over many years by a society dominated by white males — the traditionally predominant group from which judges are selected. The more this changes over time, the more these issues will fade. Where courts no longer only have one or two seated women or minority judges but many, it is natural that the attitude of their white male colleagues will evolve and affect those appearing before the bar.

10. Making Diversity Work in the Law Firm

The writer of this last piece is not a lawyer, but someone who works often with law firms. As a management consultant dedicated to "creative cultural changes," Jacob Herring knows firsthand the problems of dealing with diversity issues. In this hard-hitting article, as valuable today as it was in our first edition, he suggests that the negative messages minority members get from law firms originate from cultural assumptions about people of color. His many thoughtful and provocative ideas about bias in the workplace, its causes and its remedies, make this an excellent close to our discussion.

Jacob H. Herring, *Diversity in the Workplace*
San Francisco Attorney (October/November 1992)[20]

If you're looking for resistant hold-outs regarding workforce diversity, look no farther than most U.S. law firms.

For over 15 years I have worked with Fortune 100 companies and government agencies in . . . managing and valuing racial and gender diversity, and my experience tells me that diversity, at its best, thrives in an environment where it receives the support of the organization. Corporations that made the transition to

---

[20] Copyright © 1992 by Jacob N. Herring. Reprinted by permission.

the diverse workplace in the early-to-mid '70s are now working on issues of true corporate culture change: they know that minority men and white women have different experiences, and they are striving to reduce barriers to allow *all* their employees to achieve in their organizations.

This is rarely the case with law firms, which by nature represent the conservative tendencies to maintain the status quo. . . . Combining a lack of awareness with a determination to reinforce comfortable "norms," law firms have barriers to achieving, much less encouraging, workforce diversity. The partners, by-and-large, are not trained in management skills and concepts, and many approach human issues as legal problems to be litigated rather than issues directly related to how people respond to each other.

The vast majority of American companies and law firms were built for, by, and about able, married, apparently straight white men. . . . Thus, women, people of color, gays and lesbians, and people of varied physical and learning abilities get left out of the overall culture of their respective [organizations].

Almost all of the firms with which I work perceive themselves to be liberal on issues of race and gender; in their own perception, they are more liberal than the next individual or firm, and their deep, genuine *feelings* about diversity sometimes remain unrecognized and unexamined.

I assume that when individuals in an outwardly sincere attempt to embrace and foster diversity send messages that convey racist or sexist attitudes, they are genuinely not conscious of the impact of such messages. . . .

[A]ll of us, to varying degrees, have been programmed to see each other not as we in fact are — as unique individuals — but as the culture would have us see each other. Our culture programs us to think about and see each "other" in particular ways.

For example, cultural assumptions about white men are that they are generally insensitive, racist, sexist, power-hungry, ruthless . . . .

Blacks are considered lazy, irresponsible, violent and dumb.

Hispanics are considered possessors of many of the same dubious "characteristics" as blacks, with "hot-blooded" and "hot headed" thrown in for good measure.

Asians are assumed to be hard workers, not very assertive, and usually submissive.

And women — assumed to be someone else's possessions, sex objects, and nurturers — are further limited through some religious groups' influence that dictate "woman's place."

This cultural assumptions programming is provided by parents, schools, churches, the media — via messages that are reinforced until one believes them. Once the cultural assumptions are believed or accepted without examination, they become institutionalized. After awhile, one accepts them as valid because the cultural assumptions are most of what one has heard about the "other" group.

Cultural assumptions are so powerful that they can alter the way we see individuals with whom we interact daily and in intimate relationships, such as marriage. But cultural assumptions are absolutely devastating and most limiting when applied to groups with which we have very little interaction, leaving no opportunity to dispel myths.

Thus, the black male partner who is seen on-site after hours is assumed to be "up to something"; the physically attractive female associate "invites" flirting; the hispanic associate lives for a "good time."

Another reason that women, minorities, and "others" (read: not straight while males) get negative messages in and from law firms is due to certain innate characteristics of communication.

Communication is composed of two major elements: digital communication and analog communication. Digital communication consists of words put together in a grammatical and syntactical fashion. It has the advantage of being precise and elegant, but can also mislead and, in fact, lie. Analog communication is everything else beyond digital communication, such as the context in which something is said. Voice volume, pitch, and rhythm, body language, gestures, etc. . . .

In face-to-face interactions, 65% or more of what is communicated is analog communication. It is the ambiguity of analog communication that presents the problem. While people may use digital communication to say things that are socially acceptable, their analog communication sends negative messages — leaving individuals or full departments off memo rotations, not informing people about meetings, etc. . . .

Sometimes people send negative messages that do not represent their true intent, like the male partner who lauds a female associate for "finally learning to think like a man," or the sincere associate who mentions to his new-found colleague over drinks that "I don't even think of you as being black anymore!"

Minorities and white women are predisposed to make or give negative interpretations of dominant group behavior (read: white in general or white men in particular), because their cultures and their experience in and out of work over a lifetime tell them that negative interpretations are more often valid than not, and are the least risky approach to workplace survival. While white men are ignorant of the cultural assumptions made about them, they unknowingly play those cultural assumptions out, not realizing that they are being scrutinized. . . .

White men are unique in that they are the only group in our society that truly perceives themselves as individuals, with little or no *group* identity. So, one white male observing another behaving in a way that reinforces the negative cultural assumptions about white men does not usually speak up to check the offensive behavior of his colleague. And, in fact, does not usually *feel the need* to do so.

Minorities, white women, and disabled people at least *feel* that they want to check the offending behavior of others in their groups, and a lot of their behavior is governed by how it reflects not only on them as individuals, but also on them as a group. They do this because they know that negative behavior on their part or on the part of their same-group peers will result in each member of the group receiving negative image reinforcement.

. . . .

Those who are not white males, then, get small, ambiguous, subtle messages — "micro-gressions" — that make them feel bad. A significant number of people of color and white women are predisposed to interpret such messages negatively, resulting in feelings of alienation, anger, and rage. Such feelings get in the way of bonding with the firm's partners and other associates. . . .

In order to change this, the partners must examine their own organizations' cultures and . . . be willing to change those elements that interfere with diversity, because the behavior of employees is more determined by the corporate or organizational culture and structure than by anything else. . . .

Profit motives aside, partners who are dead serious about encouraging diversity in their law firms and client bases see it from a moral and creative perspective, and they see how it's going to help them and achieve their higher goals. They already know *why* they want to embrace diversity; they just want to know *how* to make it happen. . . . Some law firms attempt to embrace diversity because they have to — clients, partners, the Bar, and other influences are pressuring them. They often are not resistant so much as indifferent, and indifference still creates roadblocks to bringing about effective change and true diversity. Those who adamantly resist, choosing to act at their own pace or not at all, find in time that their inaction may be quite detrimental when valuable associates "vote with their feet" by leaving. . . .

While preparing for the global marketplace of the future, *all* American corporate environments, in order to maintain their positions, to stimulate growth from within, and to "do the right thing," need to address issues of workplace diversity, and law firms should become the pioneers in managing it. After all, it is the interpretation of law that not only governs, but defines what we as a society should be and do.

NOTES

Note that while Herring begins by saying law firms are behind other businesses in dealing with diversity issues, he ends by holding out hope that they can lead the way in the future. Is he being overly optimistic? Or are law firms, schooled in the law and focused on what society should be and should do, the best place to look for progressive change?

Does Herring's article still resonate today? Here is what the two University of Hawai'i professors had to say about stereotypes in 2010:

One of the most telling facts about stereotypes is that they emerge early in life, often influencing children as young as three years old. These impressionable children, who are constantly engaged in interpreting the world around them, quickly learn to ascribe certain characteristics to members of distinct ethnic and social groups. Such associations derive from cultural and social beliefs, and are learned directly from multiple sources, including the children's parents, peers, and the media. As the children grow older, their stereotypes harden, . . . remain largely unchanged and become implicit (or automatic). In the context of gender stereotypes, children are likely to learn at an early age that men are "competent, rational, assertive, independent, objective, and self confident," and women are "emotional, submissive, dependent, tactful, and gentle."

Does that sound familiar? We lawyers have made progress since the first edition of this book was published. And we still have a long way to go.

D. SUPPLEMENTAL READINGS

1. RAND JACK & DANA CROWLEY JACK, MORAL VISION AND PROFESSIONAL DECISIONS: THE CHANGING VALUES OF WOMEN AND MEN LAWYERS (1989). Chapter 5 of this book is excerpted in 57 FORDHAM L. REV. 933 (1989). This study, by an attorney and a developmental psychologist, while done some time ago, is a thorough and interesting look at the different roles played by men and women in the law firm setting, and the ways in which women must "pattern" themselves to adapt to this setting.

2. Cynthia Grant Bowman, *Women and the Legal Profession,* 7 AM. U. J. GENDER SOC. POL'Y & L. (1998), is an interesting article that reaffirms the slower progress of women up the law firm ladder but also argues that the subtle forms of discrimination against women in litigation have become more overt in recent years.

3. Stanford ethics Professor Deborah L. Rhode has written several important and cogent academic pieces on women and the law, including: *The Subtle Side of Sexism,* 16 COLUM. J. GENDER & L. 613 (2007); *Gender and the Profession: The No-Problem Problem,* 30 HOFSTRA L. REV. 1001 (2002) (both discussing the self-reinforcing cycle of stereotypic expectations and calling for gender bias education); *Perspectives on Professional Women,* 40 STAN. L. REV. 1163 (1988), *Myths of Meritocracy,* 65 FORDHAM L. REV. 585 (1996) and *Lesbians in the Law: Sex-Based Discrimination: Common Legacies and Common Challenges,* 5 S. CAL. REV. L. & WOMEN'S STUD. 11 (1995).

4. Several valuable articles on women in the law are: Anna M. Archer, *From Legally Blonde to Miss Congeniality: The Femininity Conundrum,* 13 CARDOZO J.L. & GENDER 1 (2006) (focusing on the role of films in perpetuating gender stereotypes in the legal profession); Christine Alice Corcos, *We Don't Want Advantages: The Woman Lawyer Hero and Her Quest for Power in Popular Culture,* 53 SYRACUSE L. REV. 1225 (2003), which explains popular culture's impact on images of women attorneys — and the disadvantage they face because of the lack of woman iconic heroes; Patricia Hatamyar & Kevin M. Simmons, *Are Women More Ethical Lawyers? An Empirical Study,* 31 FLA. ST. U. L. REV. 785 (2004), an interesting project showing that woman are significantly less likely to be disciplined by the bar than men; and Judith L. Maute, *Writings Concerning Women in the Legal Profession, 1982–2002,* 38 TULSA L. REV. 167 (2002), a thorough review of the literature on this subject.

5. *Hishon v. King & Spalding,* 467 U.S. 69 (1984), held that a woman lawyer who was denied an invitation to become a partner could state a cognizable claim of sex discrimination under Title VII of the 1964 Civil Rights Act.

6. Steven Keeva, *Unequal Partners,* ABA JOURNAL (February 1993), which we excerpted in our first edition, is an important and thorough article about the dissatisfaction and high attrition rates of black partners, that particularly in Chicago. Keeva has long been a staff writer and editor for the *ABA Journal*. Like Professor Wilkins, he interviewed many African-American partners, and gained substantial insight into the difficult road black partners face even after partnership.

7. Berkeley law Professor Marjorie M. Shultz has written frequently and cogently on racial issues, including the volume WHITEWASHING RACE: THE MYTH OF A COLOR-BLIND SOCIETY (2003), whose title speaks for itself. She and Sheldon Zadeck are the authors of an extensive and important study funded by the Law School Admissions Counsel on racial and other biases in law school- and bar-related examinations. They focus on what "predictors" make for good lawyers, and found that examination scores were both culturally biased and poor predictors of performance as a lawyer. *Final Report, Identification, Development, and Validation of Predictors for Successful Lawyering*, 2008.

8. Eli Wald, *A Primer on Diversity, Discrimination, and Equality in the Legal Profession or Who is Responsible for Pursuing Diversity and Why*, 24 GEO. J. LEGAL ETHICS 1079 (2011), is a lengthy and thorough review of the status of diversity and the difficult hurdles to be faced, by a frequent writer on this subject.

9. In addition to the more recent effort excerpted above, the ABA JOURNAL has produced two important articles about black women in the law: Nina Burleigh, *Black Women Lawyers — Coping With Dual Discrimination*, (June 1, 1988), and Arthur S. Hayes, *Color-Coded Hurdle* (February 1999). The latter article came from a particularly valuable February 1999 issue of the ABA JOURNAL magazine featuring 16 different articles on race and the law.

Chapter 11

MENTAL HEALTH, SUBSTANCE ABUSE, AND THE REALITIES OF MODERN PRACTICE

PROBLEM 30: A LAWYER IN TROUBLE AND HIS FRIENDS ON THE SPOT

A. INTRODUCTION

Lawyers work high stress jobs in a high stress world. The rewards of the profession can be great, but so are the pressures. Lawyers' work can be impaired by mental illness, especially depression, and all sorts of addictions — to drugs, painkillers, alcohol, gambling, even sex, especially given the instant availability of the Internet. The incidence of lawyer drug abuse — all drugs, but most particularly alcohol — is high: higher than for other professions. And when a lawyer loses control to addiction, be it to alcohol, drugs, or something else, the lawyer's colleagues — and clients — often suffer as well. Here, our problem focuses on alcoholism, but the same issues would apply in similar ways to many other circumstances.

B. PROBLEM

Bill "Rabbit" Worthington is partner at the firm of Dill, Strait & Smith, one of the oldest and most prestigious law firms in town. Worthington has been with the firm for over 30 years. His colleagues call him "Rabbit" because of his creativity in facing and solving new legal problems. They used to say at Dill, Strait that he could take an impossible case and pull a rabbit out of his hat to win it, hence his nickname.

I

Recently, things have changed for Worthington. At first he seemed simply less efficient and energetic. Everyone thought he was just going through a "lazy spell." But there began to be other telltale signs. He seemed to get little done after lunch, and those who ate with him noted that his lunchtime "glass" of wine had become three or four. "Rabbit" had long had an "open door" policy, encouraging late afternoon "schmoozing" with young associates who wanted the benefit of his counsel; his office had been dubbed "the Rabbit warren" because of all the traffic and activity centered there. In the past several months, though, Rabbit's door has stayed closed most afternoons, and he often doesn't emerge at all until he heads for home.

Chuck Chenier is the firm's managing partner, and a friend of Rabbit's since law school. He has begun noticing a strong smell of alcohol on Rabbit's breath in the afternoons. He has also observed that Worthington just doesn't seem like "the old Rabbit." What, if anything, should he do about this?

II

Another year has gone by. Chuck Chenier talked to Rabbit, who promised to "get myself under control," but otherwise Chuck has taken no action. In the past several months, the associates who work with Rabbit have noticed problems with his work. He lost one client's original documents, only to find them months later in another client's file. One late afternoon, as the deadline for filing neared, his draft memo of a key motion was nowhere to be found, and as usual he never had placed it on the office's file server. Worse, no one knew where Rabbit was. His secretary searched through his newest files on his computer and finally found it buried under "miscellaneous." He now loses paperwork so often that his secretary has begun to open his mail and keep a copy of everything in a cabinet known as "Rabbit's file."

Jane Diaz is a second year associate at the firm. She was originally thrilled that one of the partners she was assigned to work with was Worthington. Jane had heard of him, and at first found him to be just like she imagined, but she increasingly became aware of Rabbit's work sloppiness and found herself having to "cover" for him more and more. Last week, she and Worthington were with a major client who was being deposed by opposing counsel. It was Jane's first "big" case, and she was excited. Rabbit "defended" the deposition, but to Jane just didn't seem to be paying attention. He failed to object several times to questions that Jane thought were obviously irrelevant and prejudicial. His breath smelled like alcohol, though Jane wasn't sure anyone else could detect it.

QUESTIONS

1.   What should Jane do? Should she discuss the matter with Chuck Chenier? Should she talk directly to Worthington? Or is the matter simply not something she should tackle herself?

2.   What, if anything, should Chenier do?

3.   What, if anything, should be done about Rabbit's clients? Should they be told anything, and if so, what should they be told?

III.

Think about what you would do if you discovered that a good friend and colleague, your fellow law student or associate, had developed a mental health, substance abuse, or gambling problem. Is there anything that you would feel you would do or *must* do?

C. READINGS

1. Recent Statistics on Lawyers and Depression

As this first article explains, lawyers have the dubious distinction of having the highest rate of depression of any profession. And studies show a clear correlation between depression and drug and alcohol abuse as people attempt to self-medicate. We do not include this article to scare you, or give you the feeling that you're next. Rather, we want you to know the reality so that you know what we lawyers are facing, and so you can better prepare yourself to avoid becoming a statistic.

Joan E. Mounteer, *Depression Among Lawyers*
33 COLORADO LAWYER 35 (2004)[1]

Everyone experiences the occasional "blue day" or a period of feeling "down." It also is normal to feel sadness or grief after a loss. Sadness is a part of life. But chronic feelings of sadness are not a normal part of life. Depression, a serious medical disorder, differs vastly from the transitory state of feeling "down in the dumps."

Depression produces a profound low mood and influences a person's thoughts, feelings, health, and behavior. It is an illness, just like heart disease and cancer are illnesses. At one time or another, depression will afflict more than 25 percent of the population. It strikes all ages, all races, all economic groups, and both sexes. . . . Fortunately, depression can be successfully treated in approximately 80 percent of cases.

Depression is not something to be ashamed of. It is not a character flaw or a sign of personality weakness. Moreover, it is not a "mood" that a person can "snap out of," any more than a person can "snap out of" diabetes. Depression strikes the legal profession more often than any other profession . . . .

Symptoms of Depression and Contributing Factors

According to Dr. Amiram Elwork, a clinical psychologist and director of the Law & Psychology Training Program at Widener University in Minnesota, the symptoms of depression come in clusters and include the following:

- Persistent sad, anxious, "empty" mood
- Feelings of hopelessness, pessimism
- Feelings of guilt, worthlessness, helplessness
- Loss of interest or pleasure in ordinary activities, including sex
- Withdrawal from family and friends
- Sleep disturbances (insomnia, early morning waking, or oversleeping)
- Eating disturbances (either loss or gain of appetite and weight)

---

[1] The excerpted material is reproduced by permission. Copyright © 2004 Colorado Bar Association. All rights reserved.

- Decreased energy, fatigue, being "slowed down"
- Thoughts of death or suicide, suicide attempts
- Restlessness or irritability
- Increased alcohol consumption (self-medication)
- Difficulty concentrating, remembering, making decisions
- Physical symptoms (such as headaches, digestive disorders, and chronic pain) that do not respond to treatment.

Depression in the Legal Profession

In a study of more than 100 occupations, lawyers had the highest rate of depression. In fact, lawyers are almost four times more likely to experience depression than the general population. Aside from depression, one in four lawyers also experience feelings of inadequacy and inferiority in personal relationships, as well as anxiety or social alienation, at much higher rates than the population at large.

Especially among lawyers, depression can be life-threatening. . . . A disproportionate number of lawyers commit suicide, unfortunately during middle age, when they would be most productive. Some attribute this to the depressed lawyer's typical retreat into isolation, which greatly enhances the risk of acting on suicidal thoughts. . . . Why is depression such a problem in the profession? First, the increase in the number of lawyers likely has led to increased competition and diminishing personal relationships with other lawyers. Second, new technology creates an unrelenting and faster work pace. Also, the law is overwhelmingly complex today. Changing legal standards make it difficult to know how to advise clients, and courts render so many decisions that it is not easy to understand what the law actually is. The only certainty is that whatever the causes, lawyers suffer increased rates of burnout, disillusionment, and dissatisfaction, which can lead to attorney neglect of files, anxiety, depression, substance abuse, or suicide.

Because depression impacts productivity in the workplace, lawyers toiling under its burdens can cause irreparable damage to clients, law firms or offices, and the legal profession, as well as to their own health. A major hurdle for depressed lawyers is to realize they are, in fact, depressed. Depression is insidious. Often, those who suffer from depression do not recognize it as such. This may be because those who have lived with suffering for so long are used to feeling depressed or are out of touch with their feelings — being depressed can have a numbing effect.

Empirical research suggests that lawyers have personality characteristics that distinguish them from the general population. . . . Lawyers are trained to be rational and objective. This training, combined with the devaluation of emotional concerns and feelings, can become obstacles to seeking help. Due to their unique personality traits, lawyers may not recognize their own problem until the disciplinary committee comes knocking on the door.

NOTES

Not every lawyer suffers from depression, any more than all lawyers are alcoholics. But since many lawyers have personalities that make it *difficult to recognize symptoms*, being aware of this fact should help increase our awareness and watchfulness — in our friends and in ourselves. A special warning to women: Empirical studies show both that physiologically, some addictions, such as to alcohol, progress much more rapidly in women than in men, and that women are far more likely to keep a problem hidden.

2. A Case History of a Lawyer in Trouble

What happens when a lawyer uses drugs or alcohol to excess? When no one intervenes to prevent such behavior, the consequences can be a swift slide down a slope towards legal oblivion. At first, the consequences may be personal to the attorney, but over time, the clients of that lawyer and the lawyer's firm will likely begin to feel the effects. Read what happened to one fallen lawyer and how his misfortune affected his life, both negatively and positively.

Barbara Mahan, *Disbarred*
CALIFORNIA LAWYER (July 1992)[2]

Most lawyers expect a lot from their careers. They endure three rough years of law school, a grueling bar exam and the long hours necessary to establish a practice. In return they hope for such benefits as a high salary, respected status and the satisfaction of helping clients.

Sometimes it works out that way; sometimes it doesn't. . . . Lawyers become disenchanted with what they do, or how they do it, or what it brings them. They make mistakes — little ones at first, then bigger and bigger ones. The system they swore to uphold doesn't seem worth the effort anymore. They violate the standards of the profession or the law itself. Stories about these lawyers we hear only in whispers, or read in the stilted prose of a State Bar disciplinary report.

The accounts below come from five former lawyers who were either disbarred or resigned because they were certain they would be disbarred. Banished from the profession, they testify here from the legal underground. They agreed to be interviewed . . . [because] they believed either that telling their stories would help others or that it would help them face and accept their pasts. . . .

Two of the former lawyers who speak here . . . abused alcohol or drugs. That is not a coincidence. The State Bar estimates that 30 to 50 percent of discipline cases are related to substance abuse.

From their vantage outside the profession, these men touch on several common themes. One is the economic and social cost of being forced from their work. Disbarred lawyers not only lose their ticket to practice law; they lose their financial security. Many go bankrupt. Their marriages or relationships fail, their friends drift away, their colleagues don't call, their health begins to falter.

---

[2] Copyright © 1992 by Barbara Mahan. Reprinted by permission.

Another theme is the depth of their personal loss. Cast from legal society, they question their identities and self-worth. They agonize at failing their fathers and their own children. Some wonder if there is any point in going on; they contemplate escape or suicide.

A third is the difficulty of starting over. Educated for the law, former practitioners can't or don't want to find a new career. Many become paralegals, doing much of the same work they performed as lawyers at substantially less pay. Those who attempt new kinds of work usually struggle for a period after making the switch.

A final, unexpected theme is a growing sense of social responsibility. Two lawyers who once were consumed by addictions now help others stop abusing drugs and alcohol. . . .

After they resigned or were disbarred, some of these men became better fathers, sons, husbands and friends. They saw clearly some things that had been clouded or hidden. Their failures, in varying degrees, appear to have led to redemption. Deprived of their profession, they gave more of themselves to other people than they ever had before.

In reviewing their stories, one cannot help wondering whether these former lawyers would have achieved the same advances in self-awareness and social commitment had they not suffered the loss of their profession. . . .

David K. Demergian

By his second year out of law school, David Demergian had reached a level of success that many young lawyers dream of. He had established his own practice in San Diego, landed some top real estate clients and was making well into six figures a year. He had an expensive home, a pretty wife, a Mercedes and a baby daughter. But for Demergian, it wasn't enough.

In 1983 he started pulling this dream life apart. He fell in love with his secretary and left his wife and child. Single for the first time in years, he threw himself into a fast lane of parties and women. He began representing topless and bottomless clubs, dancers and drug defendants. It made him feel good to walk into exotic bars and be treated like a big shot.

In late 1984 his secretary introduced him to freebase cocaine, and within a short time he was hooked. His addiction, which lasted only seven months, cost him his profession, his financial solvency and his self-respect. He believes it also cost him his father's life.

Demergian, 39, has turned his life around since his disbarment. Once concerned chiefly with the power, prestige and trappings of the law, he now works as a law clerk, drafting documents to which he cannot sign his name. He has married again, has another daughter and spends a lot of time with his girls. . . .

In his spare time Demergian works with lawyers and judges who are alcoholics and addicts. A consultant for The Other Bar [a rehabilitation program sponsored by the California State Bar], Demergian gets up to 40 calls a month for help, from people in trouble and from their families, colleagues and friends. He tells them his story of catastrophe and hope, and attempts to offer others what he wishes he could have found: a way off the path toward self-destruction before everything was lost.

Until I got hooked on freebase cocaine around December 1984, my law practice had been exemplary. But by January or February 1985, I no longer went into the office. I stayed home every day, calling in for trials, saying I was sick. All day long I smoked cocaine. The high ends quickly, and the crash is lower than anything you can imagine. So every 10 or 15 minutes I would take another hit. Then I would clean my place. I had all this energy. I arranged my shirts in my closet alphabetically by color. I recorded oldies from the radio, 20 cassettes of them, and cross-indexed the songs. I only went to the office late at night to use the computer for my oldies index and to pick up any money that came in.

In seven months I went through $80,000. Unfortunately, only $60,000 of it was mine. In April or May 1985 I took $20,000 from a client trust fund, the proceeds of the sale of a client's house in a divorce settlement. I had run out of money. . . . I told myself I would pay it back. The denial involved in my addiction was frightening and extreme. . . .

On Father's Day 1985 around 3 a.m. my doorbell rang. I had been up all night having a party, and there were half-naked girls and drugs all around. I opened the door and there on the doorstep was my father, who was a doctor. He had flown out from Wisconsin because Stephanie, the woman who is now my wife, called him and said, "Your son is killing himself with drugs." My father and I had always been close. But I wouldn't let him in. The tears were streaming down his face when I slammed the door.

My father and Stephanie began conspiring to get me into treatment. I went into a drug treatment center, but I was not committed to it and I left. Over the next three days I went through a lot of cocaine. At the end I was as pitiful and incomprehensibly demoralized as a human being can be. . . . An old friend showed up at my place and stayed with me until he found a hospital that would take me. I went back into treatment June 28, 1985, and I have been clean ever since.

In the program I learned rigorous honesty. After I was in the hospital three days, I borrowed the money from my parents and paid back my client. When I got out, I called all my clients and told them everything. They all stayed with me except the drug dealers.

Ironically, after I got well . . . I got a notice of my interim suspension from the State Bar effective January 1987.

The stress of helping me get into treatment killed my father. He had a stoke a year and half after I recovered and passed away about the time I was sending out the . . . notices to close out my practice. He was only 57. He got me through as much as he could and then he died.

After my suspension, I got a job as a law clerk for a small firm, starting out at $800 a month. Then the State Bar hearings began. No one except me thought it would result in disbarment, because I had no prior discipline [record] and I had more than 70 letters of support from lawyers and judges. But deep in my heart I knew I should be disbarred.

About a year after my sobriety I got involved with The Other Bar. At first I thought it would look good for my discipline case. Then it became something I really believed in. As it started to get inside me, I thought maybe I could help other people avoid what happened to me. In the last three years I have helped maybe 100 people. It's one of the things that lets me sleep at night. I lie there and see dozens of faces of lawyers who are still practicing and alive because of me.

I make $4,600 a month as a law clerk doing general civil litigation research and writing. . . . I was eligible to apply for reinstatement in January 1992, but I was not sure I would do it right away. It's real important to me to get my license back because they took it away. But being a lawyer isn't so important anymore. I used to care about the power, the prestige, the money. Now I want to preserve the happiness I have. . . .

NOTES

The effect on the clients of a lawyer who abuses drugs or alcohol is not always as graphic as in the case history described above. But the abilities of lawyers to perform their fiduciary duties to their clients — to put the causes and needs of their clients first — often become seriously impaired when lawyers are more concerned with their substance addictions. Deadlines are missed, responses are not filed, and more subtle lapses — some of which the client may not be able to discover — occur with increasing regularity.

Psychologists, management consultants, and other experts in the field offer a great deal of advice about how friends and colleagues might deal with the problem attorney. But most experts would tell us that the most important advice they can give is the following: Don't ignore the problem, or even worse, participate in the cover-up. Take action, because inaction will be viewed as tacit acceptance of the situation. The more difficult it is to take action, because of friendship or close long-term business relationships with your colleague, the more important taking action becomes.

And as for David Demergian? Almost four years to the day after he was disbarred, he was readmitted to active practice. He has had an unblemished record in the 20 years since.

3. Lawyers' Problems? Let Us Count the Ways

In the spring of 2011, the Texas Advocate published an excellent article by two members of the state's Lawyer's Assistance Program.[3] This program, like many other similarly-titled programs in state bars across the country, helps lawyers by identifying typical problems lawyers face, suggesting preventive measures for them to take, and providing solutions through various available means. We will discuss some of this article's suggested preventive steps in section 9 below. For now, though, we focus on the daunting list of problems that, according to this

---

[3] Sara E. Dysart & Ann D. Foster, *Practicing Law and Wellness: Modern Strategies for the Lawyer Dealing with Anxiety, Addiction and Depression*, 54 THE ADVOCATE (Texas) 4 (2011) (The "Best of" Litigation Update).

article, lawyers can too commonly face, and that may interfere with both their professional and private lives.

• *Anxiety disorders*, including panic attacks, often with symptoms of worry, fatigue, sleeplessness, difficulty in concentration, irritability, and muscle tension. "Overzealous representation," the authors write, "often creates or masks anxiety."

• *Addiction by Substance Use and Substance Abuse or Dependence*: This includes "alcohol, amphetamines — including methamphetamine, caffeine, club drugs, cocaine, crack cocaine, hallucinogens, heroin, marijuana, myriad prescription drugs, nicotine, sedatives, steroids, and an intoxicating mix of all the above (polysubstance abuse/dependency)." When things reach the abuse stage, symptoms become more serious: legal problems, increased tolerance to the drug, increasingly risky behavior, time and effort focused largely on finding and taking the drug, and so on.

• *"Process Addictions"*: The primary two addictions in this category are gambling and sexual activity and/or pornography online. But other addictions may include such ordinarily positive things as exercise, working, eating, even shopping, when done obsessively or compulsively.

• *Depression and "Mood Disorders"*: Mood disorders include bipolarity, and burnout and Post Traumatic Stress Disorder, including "compassion fatigue," in which the pressures of repeatedly performing to "save" clients create a PTSD-type series of symptoms.

4. How Forgiving Is Our Disciplinary System About Alcohol and Other Illnesses?

Until 30 years ago, disciplinary systems had little sympathy for lawyers committing errors that were attributable to alcoholism or other impairment if clients were harmed in the process. That began to change in 1987 when, in the leading case of *In re Kersey*, 520 A.2d 321 (D.C. 1987), the District of Columbia Court of Appeals set a standard for mitigation due to alcohol abuse that has been widely adopted by other states. Lawyer Kersey, an alcoholic since high school, committed 24 ethics violations, three of which involved misappropriating client funds. But Kersey then completed an alcohol detoxification program and on appeal found support from a special D.C. disciplinary committee that requested mitigating his punishment from disbarment to something less severe. The court created a "but for" standard that in Kersey's case meant that but for his alcoholism, his misconduct would not have occurred.

The appeals court engaged in a sophisticated discussion of the nature of alcoholism, including that it involves both voluntary and involuntary behavior, and that abuse of alcohol does not necessarily result in actions taken against clients. Ultimately the court agreed to stay Kersey's disbarment, and placed him on five years of probation that required close supervision by three monitors, who observed his sobriety, his law practice, and his finances.

Mitigation of discipline due to alcoholism or other illness is by no means a universally held view, however. In New Jersey, Kersey surely would have been disbarred under the so-called "Wilson rule." In *In re Wilson*, 409 A.2d 1153, 1154 (N.J. 1979), the New Jersey Supreme Court held it "almost invariable" that mitigation cannot be considered in disciplining a lawyer who misappropriates client funds. Disbarment is permanent in New Jersey, with no possibility of later reinstatement, like the second chance David Demergian received. So the effect of the *Wilson* rule is huge. This rule was specifically applied to include mitigation due to alcoholism in *In re Hein*, 516 A.2d 1105 (N.J. 1986):

> [T]he evidence showed that [Hein's] misappropriation had been the result of the extensive pressure of coping with his alcohol dependency and its ravaging effects upon his life and practice . . . . We have no doubt that the alcoholism contributed to the loss of critical control of judgment, but cannot conclude that the evidence warrants a departure from the principle that we set forth in In re Wilson.[4]

Even when misappropriation of client funds is not the issue, the New Jersey Supreme Court has been quite tough on lawyers even if they are completely rehabilitated. In *In re Willis*, 552 A.2d 979 (N.J. 1989), the court reviewed the decision of a split disciplinary board: four votes for a one-year suspension from practice, and three votes favoring only a public reprimand in light of the extraordinary rehabilitation Willis had undergone. Willis' violations were a one-year failure to file a tax return and "six acts of unethical conduct that demonstrated a pattern of neglect." The high court emphasized at some length Willis' exemplary behavior and complete rehabilitation and mused about what it should do: He had become "an inspiration to many and a credit to the bar. Should we concentrate solely on his past ethical infractions and ignore his remarkable recovery?" And this: "Outside the courtroom, he has taken his message into public schools, to meetings of Alcoholics Anonymous, and to lawyers wrestling with substance abuse. Should we ignore his good works? What message would that send to similarly afflicted lawyers? How would that protect the public interest?" Ultimately, though, the court supported the Board majority, though it lowered the suspension from a year to six months.

And in D.C. itself, the more lenient *Kersey* view adopted by many other states did not hold sway when it came to illegal drug use. D.C. had extended the *Kersey* theorem to broadly allow mitigation in such cases as depression, bipolar disorder, or addiction to prescription drugs. But the court refused to allow mitigation in a case of a lawyer's *illegal* use of cocaine, holding that a principal tenet of the *Kersey* rule was a lack of criminal conduct.[5]

Obviously, justice will not be equally dispensed, but will depend on one's jurisdiction *and* one's perspective about the primacy of client protection versus clear lawyer rehabilitation. The landscape is ever-changing. Now that several states have legalized marijuana, how would a court following the *Kersey* opinion deal with malfeasance due to marijuana in a state where its personal use is legal?

---

[4] 516 A.2d at 1107. Prior to *Hein*, in *In re Jacob*, 469 A.2d 498, 501 (N.J. 1984), the court had held that mitigation due to mental illness would require "a loss of competency, comprehension or will of a magnitude that could excuse egregious misconduct," a standard attorney Jacob could not meet. New Jersey has long been seen as the one of the toughest states on disciplining lawyers or, put the other way, one of the most client-protective states in the country.

[5] In re Marshall, 762 A.2d 530, 536–37 (D.C. 2000).

5. Defining the Ethical Requirements, and Two ABA Opinions on Impairment

Before returning to the most important issue — how to prevent or overcome the various pitfalls that can befall a lawyer — we take one more side road to examine to what extent the Model Rules require that incompetence due to "impaired work" be reported.[6]

Rules describing the responsibilities of supervising and subordinate lawyers are largely silent on the issue of what to do about an impaired colleague. Even in Illinois, where *Himmel*[7] gives lawyers an "absolute duty" to report, rates of reporting lawyer impairment have hardly skyrocketed.

This reality raises many questions. What actions should be taken? Should an impaired lawyer be removed from a case? Reported to a firm committee? Reported to a board of professional discipline? Fired? Should the lawyer's career be considered, and if so, to what extent?

As it relates to clients, what should they be told? Where the client is being hurt, don't other law firm members have an obligation to protect that client's interests? If the lawyer's individual fiduciary duty is imputed to each member of the law firm, isn't "whistleblowing" to the client necessary? Even if an ethics complaint doesn't follow for the impaired lawyer, could a law firm be liable for malpractice and breach of fiduciary duty if a client later learns that the firm failed to advise about a partner's impairment? Finally, how else other than "whistleblowing" might the goal of client protection be accomplished?

In 2003, the American Bar Association published two separate ethics opinions dealing with the impaired lawyer. Formal Opinion 03-429 (2003) addresses impaired attorneys within their law firms while Formal Opinion 03-431 (2003) focuses on the responsibility of other attorneys who observe impairment in a lawyer from another firm. On the one hand, it is laudable that the ABA has directly addressed this important issue, not once but twice. On the other, some see the opinions as begging more questions than they answer. The focus of the opinions is where it should be — on the client. But the opinions are relatively narrow and do little to directly help the impaired lawyer or the lawyer's firm, nor do they fully solve client protection issues.

Opinion 429's focus is on whether the lawyer is so impaired that his or her ability to represent clients with the "legal knowledge, skill thoroughness and preparation reasonably necessary for the representation" has been materially affected. In other words, does the lawyer remain "competent, diligent, and effective"? The opinion notes that it is important to distinguish "erratic" behavior that doesn't impair competence[8]

---

[6] *See* MR 8.3, and ABA Model Code, DR 1-103(A).

[7] 533 N.E.2d 790 (Ill. 1988). See the discussion in Problem 27.

[8] The opinion uses the example of Tourette's Syndrome, which need not impair a lawyer, although if not carefully treated could lead to arguable impairment due to the involuntary tics and verbalizations it involves.

Opinion 429 requires the law firm to create "measures giving reasonable assurance that all lawyers in the firm conform to the Rules of Professional Conduct." To that end, firms should develop policies specifically for impaired lawyers. The opinion does not explain how small firms and sole practitioners — still a majority of the American bar — can develop such policies, particularly in light of the difficulties lawyers — indeed, anyone — have in recognizing their *own* impairment.

The opinion is even less definitive on the question of disclosure. While there "may" be an obligation to disclose the situation to the client so that the client can "make informed decisions regarding the representation," the trigger for disclosure is unclear, and the disclosure should be made in a way that "to the extent possible, should be conscious of the privacy rights of the impaired lawyer." When it comes to reporting the lawyer for disciplinary purposes, the opinion again warns about jumping to conclusions, and indicates that no reporting is necessary if no client was harmed.

On disclosure, Formal Opinion 429 and Formal Opinion 431 both pay careful attention to client confidentiality. Whether reporting one's own colleague or a lawyer from another firm, the reporting lawyer must be careful not to violate client confidentiality, which, as we have learned, is quite broad and includes more than a client's communications. Opinion 431 strongly urges lawyers to get the client's informed consent before reporting and also admonishes that the reporting lawyer must be confident that the condition of the other lawyer rises to the level of "material impairment." But as we have seen, triggering the reporting standards of "honesty, trustworthiness or fitness as a lawyer" differs substantially from state to state. This limits the opinions' utility.

6. Intervention

One way to be proactive with members of one's own firm — and one's friends and families — was pioneered by, among others, the Chicago's Lawyer Assistance Program, which established an "intervention" protocol many years ago. Interventions can be high risk affairs, but trainings such as Chicago's LAP program's have had considerable success. Such interventions often have the same message conveyed by psychologists — the need to be tough, especially with those with whom we are close. Some discipline counsel continue to feel that treating alcoholism as a disease may be letting lawyers off the disciplinary hook. How would you balance these considerations in the case of "Rabbit" Worthington?

Tripp Baltz, *Presenting The Hard Facts of a Liquid Habit to Impaired Lawyers*
CHICAGO LAWYER (December 1991)[9]

She glares across the circle of people at her sister, the alcoholic lawyer, and begins.

"For as long as I remember, you've been tearing up every family gathering and

---

ruining every holiday," she says, her voice quaking.

"At my house you get drunk and pass out," she continues. "We could go to your house; you get drunk and pass out. At a restaurant, you get drunk and embarrass everybody. You throw up in the bathroom, and you fall down . . . ."

Cook County Circuit Judge Warren D. Wolfson breaks in. "Lemme stop it at this point," he says. "This would not happen."

Lawyer's Assistance Program interventions are no place for emotional outbursts, Wolfson explains. Participants must stick to retelling specific events of what they have seen and heard and how they felt about it. Things like always tearing up family gatherings "are throw-aways. You can't have it," he says.

Wolfson and other LAP intervention veterans were conducting a training session for about 40 lawyers and judges who volunteered to be intervenors — people who confront attorneys with substance abuse problems in hopes of creating change.

. . . .

Through LAP, intervenors confront lawyers or judges addicted to alcohol or other drugs with their problem to try to breach the impaired attorney's denial and encourage him or her to seek treatment. Intervenors work in teams of three, including a judge and at least one recovering alcoholic.

Intervenors surround alcoholics with reality, [Former LAP President Michael J.] Howlett explained prior to the training session. They encourage family, friends and co-workers — the witnesses and victims of the chaos of alcoholism — to present hard facts of drinking to the impaired attorney.

LAP intervenors . . . come from all parts of the legal community[:] three sitting judges, one retired judge and a smattering of solo practitioners, corporate counsel and government agency attorneys.

The group is a mix of women and men, jackets and suits, tight-knotted ties and open collars, thin gray hairs and long curly locks.

. . . .

Based on intervention services, LAP is not a disciplinary organization, a temperance society or a recovery program.

"We don't shake tambourines and beat drums," Wolfson says. "We treat alcoholism as a treatable disease. We share the common conviction that we care about chemical abuse victims and their families, friends, co-workers, partners and associates. We try to get all parts of the person's life."

The relationship between trained intervenors and the judges and attorneys who receive assistance through LAP is privileged under Rule 1.6 of the Illinois Supreme Court's Code of Professional Conduct, Howlett says.

"What is said at an intervention never goes out," he says. To retain the LAP privilege and the right to participate in an intervention, one has to stay for the entire training program, he says. During the next four hours, no one will leave

. . . .

Wolfson describes how a team prepares for an intervention. The team interviews the addicted lawyer's family, friends and co-workers who are willing to participate as if they were preparing witnesses. Some of those interviewed will accompany the LAP team when it confronts the addicted person.

Intervenors plumb for solid evidence and specific events.

"We're lawyers," Wolfson says. "We know how to ask the question; we know how to get the information. We need information that will stand up. It can't be hearsay. It can't be gossip or rumor.

"It has to be specific, and you will need to lay the same kind of foundation you would need to get a conversation into evidence: who was there, when was it, what happened."

Intervenors advise participants to write down on yellow legal pads the facts and incidents that will be useful later, Wolfson says.

. . . .

"If the alcoholic senses a weak point, he'll go after it like a dog after a rabbit," he says.

So if a participant falters or loses heart, Howlett says, the intervention team is there to gently nudge him or her back to the purpose by reminding them of something they wrote down.

"If a partner talks in terms of, 'Well, I'm not so sure that George has a problem,' then an associate can remind him, 'Well, we did find him walking down the center of the L tracks twice. And we know that he's talked his way out of the last three DUI tickets.' "

"Or the last time we entertained a client, he put his face in the salad," Howlett says. "We engage in what I call the duck school of diagnosis. Walks like a duck, talks like a duck, hangs around with ducks, acts like a duck — it's a drunk . . . ."

"It's an equal opportunity disease: men and women, all races, makes no difference. We take the position that this is a disease that doesn't recognize any barriers," he says.

Throughout the session, the trainers used the term "alcoholic" to refer to any person impaired by substance abuse or addiction.

. . . .

Wolfson . . . explains the importance of setting limits: Having a person deliver the message that the lawyer's job is in peril if they fail to seek treatment.

"There is no more powerful motivator" than the prospect of losing your job, Wolfson says. "The limit-setter will often be the last person to speak at an intervention, designated as the clean-up hitter," he says.

Murphy adds, "You gotta make sure they mean it, and you make sure they're gonna say it." Partners sometimes back down. "It's like impeachment," he groans

. . . .

"We had a head of public office say they were going to fire this person if they didn't get help," he continues. When we got to the point where the hammer was supposed to fall, and we turned to the supervisor and said, 'Is there anything you want to say to him now?' he said, 'Get help, or I'm going to be disappointed.'

"You have nothing further to say? 'Get help or I'm really going to be disappointed.' Wasn't there something you wanted to say about his job? 'Yeah, if he doesn't get help, he's not going to be very good at his job.'"

Howlett, like an entertainer on stage, relates the ironic humor of the story. But he follows through with its seriousness: "It was sad because it takes a lot of courage to do what we ask these people to do. You have to prepare them well enough and give them the support that will carry them through it."

The alcoholic cannot argue with the participants' feelings, Murphy says.

"We're going to hit them with facts, but we're going to tell them how that made you feel," he says. "And we want them to know that the feeling hurts that person."

"The alcoholic can do all kinds of bad things, and he thinks he's only hurting himself. We want to now let him know he's hurting these people. We want to get all these people to give them that message."

. . . .

When everyone is prepared, the judge on the team calls the subject and invites him to a meeting in the judge's chambers, saying there are a number of people concerned about him, Howlett says. The alcoholic usually knows the reason for the call, he says.

. . . .

Howlett instructs Wolfson to start the mock intervention. Trainees playing the concerned people in the alcoholic lawyer's life sit in a circle in Wolfson's chambers. The judge greets Sue, who takes her seat at the center of the circle. After Sue's sister has spoken, an associate tells her story.

"First of all, I'm glad I can work for you," she says. "You were the prime reason I joined this firm. You have an excellent reputation, and I have learned a lot. Over the last couple of years, though, things have gone downhill . . . ."

Howlett interrupts. "Get to the drink," he says.

Wolfson backs him up: "Here again, it's much too general. . . . You can't just say her work's getting worse."

"You have to say, 'Last Tuesday, there was a client waiting in the office, a Mr. Jones; and when you didn't come back from work, I had to meet with him. When you came back later that day, you smelled of alcohol and I had to lie to a partner about where you were.'"

. . . .

A recovering alcoholic rises to describe the role he plays at an intervention. "You won't find this on my resume," he begins. . . .

"One of the big things I always say to them is that the other people in this room talk about how hard it is and how difficult it is for them to be here and for you to be here."

"They don't know how difficult it is. There are only two people in the room who know how difficult it is for you to be here." Now only his voice and the low rattle of the air conditioning can be heard in the room.

"I've been there," he continues. "I sat in that chair; I walked down the same road as you. I sat in the same bars. I ruined my life. I, too, had a drinking problem."

. . . .

The intervention should last less than an hour, Wolfson says.

. . . .

[B]efore the intervention, a member of the team will have arranged for a bed for the subject at a treatment facility . . . . Treatment usually starts with the alcoholic entering an in-patient program that lasts 28 days and exposes him to the medical and academic side of the disease, Howlett says. But it also begins his relationship with Alcoholics Anonymous, Howlett says, one he will most likely continue for the rest of his life as long as he stays in recovery.

"I welcome you to all this," Howlett says as the session comes to an end. "I have found that it is, next to what I do as a husband and a father, the most significant thing I do with my time."

. . . .

Wolfson: "When a 6- or 7-year-old child turns to her father and says, 'I want my daddy back, please get help,' there isn't a dry eye in the room."

NOTES

Note the idea of setting clear limits and sticking with them. The emphasis on "not changing the finish line" by giving second chances again and again is central to the intervention's success. So is the emphasis on alcoholism as a disease. But while alcoholism and other drug addictions are now well recognized as diseases, emphasizing the "disease" aspect over "tough love" can lessen personal responsibility. Interventions have to walk this tightrope. It's important to remember that these diseases are *chronic*, and relapse may be only a drink or a pill away.

7. Stress, Dissatisfaction, and Wellness

If there were better ways to avoid stress in the first place, perhaps fewer people would get to the point of needing intervention. From time to time, various surveys have attempted to measure lawyers' stress. What have you done to prepare yourself to meet and deal with this stress? The best time to put a workable plan in place is now, in law school, before the reality of the daily practice of law has begun to take its toll.

In 1999, a group of forward-thinking law professors led by Larry Krieger of Florida State University began an on-line discussion group on "humanizing" legal education. By 2001, the group had put on workshops and a conference that, as Capital University Professor Susan Daicoff, one of the group's coordinators, put it, focused on "ways of practicing law and resolving legal disputes that are positive, healing, and humanistic." In addition to more traditional views, the group looked well beyond the legal profession itself, examined holistic solutions, and made a conscious effort to begin searching for better ways of protecting the health of the minds and bodies of lawyers and law students alike. In the last few years, the group has coalesced more formally around the concept of "humanizing legal education." An increasing number of professors have written on wellness and personal satisfaction and how to get it. They include Professor Krieger, whose several articles have helped lead the way. We excerpt here his 2005 piece, a prescription for wellness actually written to assist law professors in teaching humanizing values.

Lawrence S. Krieger, *The Inseparability of Professionalism and Personal Satisfaction: Perspectives on Values, Integrity and Happiness*
11 CLINICAL LAW REV. 425 (2005)[10]

There is a lot of talk about "professionalism" in law schools and the legal profession today, with little evidence of positive impact . . . . One crucial reason that our rhetoric fails is that it is contradicted by the competitive, outcome-oriented institutional values one typically finds dominating law schools and the highly visible and commercialized segments of the profession. It is reasonable that law students and young lawyers "tune out" the noble but dissonant messages about professionalism, but the regrettable result is that many of them fail to really comprehend the foundations of their future working life.

Professionalism training typically amounts to telling law students and lawyers that they should act in certain ways, for generally noble reasons including the high calling of our profession; and that they'd better do so, for more coercive reasons including the potential for bar discipline. Neither of these motives — guilt or fear — is likely to be effective in producing the desired result. Rarely, if ever, is one's actual life experience — including one's happiness and career satisfaction — raised as part of the professionalism discussion. This fact further enables students to distance themselves from a discussion they perceive as theoretical rather than personal.

I will argue (1) that satisfaction and professional behavior are inseparable manifestations of a well-integrated and well-motivated person; and (2) that depression and unprofessional behavior among law students and lawyers typically proceed from a loss of integrity - a disconnection from intrinsic values and motivations, personal and cultural beliefs, conscience, or other defining parts of their personality and humanity. . . .

Values and Personal Satisfaction as a Perspective for Teaching Professionalism

I begin with a strong dose of the truth for my students. This is something too rarely done at our schools . . . . I tell students the truth about the dismal results of surveys on attorney mental health and career satisfaction, and I tell them the truth about the egregiously low standard of behavior often encountered among attorneys and judges in the real world they are preparing to enter . . . . Not surprisingly, students are often taken aback when they see data summaries showing lawyers to have the highest incidence of depression of any occupation in the United States, or to suffer other forms of emotional distress up to 15 times more frequently than the general population.

I transition to the positive side of our topics by focusing on the values and motivations common to most people . . . . First, it is no coincidence that there is a perception among the public, scholars, and bar leaders alike that values like money, power, and an uncompromising drive to win are displacing values like integrity, decency, and mutuality among many lawyers. The second reason for this focus makes the discussion most relevant to students and lawyers: Those values and motivations that promote or attend professionalism have been empirically shown to correlate with well being and life satisfaction, while those that undermine or discourage professionalism empirically correlate with distress and dissatisfaction. These conclusions are supported by both recent empirical studies and classical humanistic theory describing psychological health and maturity.

Professionalism and Satisfaction as Dual Expressions of Psychological Maturity

I present professionalism to law students as a combination of developed legal skills and various personal virtues that we typically seek in lawyers: broad vision/wisdom, integrity and honesty, compassion, respect for others and for differences, unselfishness, the desire to serve others and one's community, self-confidence, individualism, and a real commitment to justice . . . .

Modern psychology classifies both values and motivation as either intrinsic or extrinsic. A person is intrinsically motivated when he chooses a self-directed action which he genuinely enjoys or which furthers a fundamental life purpose, while extrinsically motivated choices are directed towards external rewards (i.e. money, grades, honors), avoidance of guilt or fear, or pleasing/impressing others . . . .

Attorneys who are deeply committed to their own values are less likely to pursue the values or desires of their clients with unethical or abusive tactics. And a lawyer who chose her career path for the most fundamental intrinsic reason — because she genuinely enjoys the work — will generate a better work product and be consistently happy at work, thereby creating a positive effect on her clients, adverse counsel, court personnel. The converse is also true — an attorney who does the work primarily for the money or to bolster his image will be more frustrated with the process, less effective, and much less pleasant to work with (or against).

Understanding Integrity As Physical And Psychological Health

One more principle that illuminates the relationship between personal satisfaction and professionalism is integrity. Integrity is clearly a foundation of professionalism, but its effect on personal well-being is perhaps even more direct. In fact, integrity is conceptually synonymous with health. Although we may commonly think of "health" in terms of the body and "integrity" in terms of the personality or character, the essence of each is the same — a condition of wholeness or integrated functioning within one's self. Furthermore, the functioning of the personality and of the physiology are closely interrelated: a person's level of personal integrity affects his physical health and well-being directly. For example . . . lying or deceptive behavior, which clearly manifests a loss of character integrity, is often attended by the experience of psychological anxiety and physical stress . . . .

We may certainly discourage lying, deception, manipulation of fact or law, or abuse of people or process because such behavior is "unprofessional." But the impact will be multiplied if we also explain that such behavior erodes integrity by separating the lawyer from key parts of her self — her conscience, sense of decency and/or intrinsic values.

NOTES

Does this correlation between integrity and health make sense to you? Or is Professor Krieger just trying to "sell" law students on putting morality ahead of winning, money, and the other traditional trappings of success? His article is supported by ample empirical evidence. For example, noted Stanford ethicist Deborah Rhode has written that lawyers who choose public interest work are 68% happier than their peers.

But is this empirical evidence determinative? Might this "humanizing" group be naïve, or have they understood a basic truth? Finally, and most importantly, is the path Professor Krieger suggests one worth taking? Recall David Dermagian's words: "I used to care about the power, the prestige, the money. Now I want to preserve the happiness I have."

8.   Stress, Drugs, and the Rock 'n' Roll of Law Practice

Even if you adopt Professor Krieger's wellness standards, it would be simplistic to ignore the reality of a law firm practice, and both the peer pressure and professional pressure it creates. The peer pressure to go out drinking, for example, can be substantial at certain firms, where it can become a way of life for most of the lawyers who practice there. Young associates who do not carefully consider these issues can get swept up into a lifestyle they did not affirmatively choose. It is always difficult to resist the expectations of one's own law firm. It can be hard to "just say no" without standing out among your friends and colleagues, or, perhaps worse, your superiors. Many associates report that partners expect them to go out drinking with clients, reminding them that "wining and dining" is what the client wants and expects. Thus, doing this becomes a matter of economic survival rather than strictly a matter of choice.

It would also be simplistic to say that merely working out at the local athletic club, jogging or mountain biking on weekends, or reading a good book every night at bedtime — all worthwhile activities — will enure all of us from using — and sometimes abusing — drugs or alcohol, or protect against all mental health issues. First, many lawyers, particularly young associates faced with seemingly insurmountable billable hours requirements, may be too tired, too overworked, or too burned out to always keep their stress-reduction programs in place. Second, many lawyers *like* to have a drink or two when they socialize, and feel, correctly, that it never negatively affects their performance.

Where should the line be drawn? Should it be only when the clients of the lawyer are actually adversely affected? What about when it appears that those clients' rights may be seriously endangered? Should any lawyer who uses illegal drugs or gets obviously drunk be subject to discipline, or at least brought to a bar intervention program? Or would this be legislating morality? Indeed, *should* lawyers be imposing such moral values on others? Neither these nor other questions are completely clear. What is clear is the need to give serious consideration to these issues that affect so many of today's practicing lawyers. And, of course, for each of us to consider our own behavior in terms of our own well-being.

9.   Further Thoughts on the Best Cure: Prevention

Texas' Dysart and Foster have come up with a dozen suggestions for how to prevent problems by maintaining personal well-being. They are worth summarizing here.

Sara E. Dysart and Ann D. Foster, *Practicing Law and Wellness: Modern Strategies for the Lawyer Dealing with Anxiety, Addiction and Depression*
54 THE ADVOCATE (Texas) 4 (2011)[11]

Prevention is directly related to the concept of self-care. Quite simply: Take care of yourself. It's your responsibility. It is not anyone else's responsibility. If you don't take care of the physical, mental, emotional and spiritual aspects of your life, you will spin out of balance, becoming strong in one area and weak in another. The result is that you become more vulnerable to the "dis-ease" that fuels anxiety, addiction and depression . . . . So what's a lawyer to do?

1. *Take inventory.* We all know that any business that fails to take inventory is bound to fail. People are no different. Taking an inventory or snapshot of your daily life can give you an idea of where you are and — of equal importance — where you want to go . . . . Here's an exercise to help with this type of inventory: Draw a circle and divide the circle into wedges representing the time spent on your daily activities. Are you happy with the allocation of time and energy? Are there areas where you spend the majority of your time and you wish you'd spend less? Are there areas where you devote minimal or no time but wish you did? There is no right or

---

[11] Copyright © 2011 by The Advocate (Texas). Reprinted by permission.

wrong allocation [but if] your inventory highlights areas of concern, what can you do to change them?

2. *Schedule time for what's important to you.* Wishing and wanting to change are important ingredients for change but action is important too . . . . First things really do come first. Try it! We learn from both good and bad results. . . . Be kind to yourself if you slip back into old patterns. Be aware and try again. It will happen if you try.

3. *Practice saying "no" and "yes" and really mean it.* Boundaries are important to self-care . . . . In essence, they help define relationships between you and everyone else. . . . Know that you have a right to personal and professional boundaries. Set clear and decisive limits and let people know what you expect and when they have crossed the line, acted inappropriately or disrespected you. Likewise, don't be afraid to ask for what you want, what you need and what actions to take if your wishes aren't respected. Recognize that others' needs and feelings and demands are not more important than your own . . . . Practice saying no and yes when appropriate and remain true to your personal and professional limits. Don't always accommodate everyone. Self-care is necessary; you don't always want to try to please others at your own expense. Above all, trust and believe in yourself. You know what you need, what you want and value. Don't let others make the decisions for you . . . .

4. *Take a stress inventory and employ effective stress management methods to help you cope.* Don't put this off. Stress takes its toll on everyone . . . . Find out what your stressors are, how you react to stress, what works to help dissipate its physical and mental effects and schedule healthy solutions into your daily life[:] Aerobic activity . . . ; deep breathing techniques like the "Relaxation Response"; mindfulness-based stress reduction (MBSR); camaraderie with friends and colleagues; daily meditation; regular participation in hobbies outside the law such as fishing, gardening, painting, dancing, golf and swimming; biofeedback; volunteer service to others; yoga; tai chi; qigong; massage; acupuncture, etc. Look for activities that activate the parasympathetic nervous system to relax your mind and body, rest and rejuvenate.

5. *Eat right, get enough sleep and exercise.*

6. *Get organized.* Organization is day-by-day chaos relief.

7. *Quit smoking.*

8. *Put your financial house in order.* Living beyond your personal or professional means is a ticket to hell. Take a look at your finances, get out of debt and plan for retirement. This is easy to say but sometimes hard to accomplish. Law students graduate with a staggering amount of debt (average debt is about $100,000) but there is some help available: Law student loan forgiveness programs; loan repayment options (standard, extended, graduated, income contingent); set up a pay off through "snowballing" efforts (pay off the smallest debt first with a payment equal to regular scheduled payment plus 10 percent of your adjusted income) [etc.]

9. *Develop interests outside the law.* Try to develop or maintain interests completely unrelated to the practice of law. This will provide you with opportunities

to take a well deserved break from your work, and, quite frankly, helps to make you a far more emotionally well-developed and interesting person . . . .

10. *Give a little back.* Try to do something kind for someone at least once a week. The more anonymous you can be about it, the better. Try something small. If you have the time, volunteer your time to help another. Don't make the activity about you — it should be about giving to others. Whatever measure you take, large or small, remember that it will not only help others, but it will also serve to build your self-esteem, help put your life in perspective, and help to develop and maintain a vital connection with the community in which you live.

11. *Develop or maintain a sense of spirituality.* Spirituality doesn't necessarily mean religion. [I]nquire within, find what works for you, and then pay attention to it. If a particular religion or spiritual practice works for you, put it into action in your life. If getting out in nature is a spiritual experience for you, go regularly. Whatever you choose, let it give you some perspective on your life, helping to reduce anxiety, worry and guilt.

12. *A sense of humor is critical.* Don't take yourself so seriously. It doesn't matter how big and important you are, or would like to be, what your salary is, or for which firm you work. If you can't laugh at yourself, you're a heart attack waiting to happen. And seriously, life is a lot less fun. Try this as an experiment: At least once a week, do something fun that involves no competition . . . . Nothing relieves stress and tension better than a good laugh.

NOTES

We add a few supplemental thoughts of our own:

• *Be yourself.* You are the only person you can be, and the only one you need to please. Try to improve yourself, sure, but first accept and love who you are. When you do, it will be easier for others to accept and love you too. And if you don't meet every personal or professional goal, forgive yourself as you would anyone else.

• *Do something for yourself every day.* When you draw that "circle with little wedges" that the Texas lawyers suggest, is there something in the circle *today* that you want to do? There should be.

• *Make sure there's room for family and friends in your daily life.* Our spouses and partners, children, and friends give us the "supplies" to keep us positive in the roughest of times. After a day isolated writing a brief or stressing over the key "deal-breaker" language of a contract, even a few minutes of undivided attention between you and your loved ones can make all the difference.

• *Remain positive and optimistic.* Lawyers are professional pessimists. We are paid to look past what is likely to happen and worry about what might *possibly* go wrong — the "worst case scenario." We are taught not to try our cases from strength, but to examine the case's weaknesses to figure out a way around them. But this pessimistic thinking is far less successful in life. It's a mind-set best left behind at the end of the day.

• *Give and you shall receive.* You have read here repeatedly, from Professors Krieger and Rhode to the Texas LAP attorneys, how acting with integrity, working in the public interest, doing good works, doing something kind for another, all help our own wellness. We add our voices to theirs. Lawyers are by their nature care-givers. These acts make us happier.

• *Remember: You can't take care of others unless you take care of yourself first.* This is an old maxim that is almost axiomatic. But it is true of all care-givers, and important not to forget.

D.   SUPPLEMENTAL READINGS

1. Rachel Tarko Hudson, *Pick your Poison: Abuse of Legal Versus Illegal Substances as Mitigation in Attorney Disciplinary Cases*, 22 GEO. J. LEGAL ETHICS 911 (2009). This article reaffirms the extent of substance abuse among lawyers and engages in a lengthy and intelligent review comparing New Jersey's strict no-mitigation rule with Pennsylvania's far more lenient rule, and then evaluating the District of Columbia's stance, which Hudson describes as "unequal treatment."

2. *Office of Disciplinary Counsel v. Braun*, 553 A.2d 894 (Pa. 1989) is the Pennsylvania Supreme Court case that first allowed mitigation for mental illness. *Office of Disciplinary Counsel v. Peck*, No. 200 DB 2003 (Pa. Aug. 28, 2006), discussed by Hudson, available through the Administrative Office of the Pennsylvania Courts but not otherwise publicly reported, allowed mitigation under the *Braun* standard even though the lawyer misappropriated client funds — automatic disbarment in New Jersey — and abused illegal cocaine as well as alcohol (not mitigating in D.C.). Peck also, while under the influence, lied during his first administrative hearing, but later rehabilitated and was still allowed to use mitigation.

3. *Willner v. Thornburgh*, 738 F. Supp. 1 (D.D.C. 1990). Willner, an attorney who had been offered a job in the Antitrust Division of the Justice Department, objected to the department policy of requiring a drug test for each new employee. The federal district court agreed, and barred the testing.

4. George Edward Bailey, *Impairment, the Profession and Your Law Partner*, 11 [ABA] PROFESSIONAL LAWYER, 2 (1999), presents an excellent overview of how to cope with the impaired lawyer in the law firm setting. The article discusses impairment, discipline, mitigation, and the *Kersey* case and the New Jersey no-mitigation rule.

5. A good article by Maureen Hynd, *A Friend in Need May be a Malpractice Claim Waiting to Happen*, in the January 2004 issue of W. VA. LAWYER (2004), focuses on the malpractice consequences of the conduct of impaired lawyers.

6. Carol M. Langford, *Depression, Substance Abuse, and Intellectual Property Lawyers*, 53 KANS. L. REV. 875 (2005). This co-author's article is adopted from a report done for the ABA Intellectual Property Section Ethics Committee that surveyed intellectual property lawyers nationwide on these issues. It includes empirical information on the prevalence of alcoholism and drug addiction in lawyers in general as well as a review of state disciplinary case law on these subjects.

7. Professor Larry Krieger manages this excellent site on humanizing legal education: http://www.law.fsu.edu/academic_programs/humanizing_lawschool/humanizing_lawschool.html.

8. Len Klingen, *The Mentally Ill Attorney*, 27 NOVA L. REV. 157 (2002). This straightforward article examines what lawyers should do to prevent and mitigate the harm to their clients caused by their mental illness, what clients can do to mitigate their own damages, and what the lawyer's partners and the Bar should do to limit damages when a lawyer is mentally ill. He notes that lawyers are not subject to discipline for being mentally ill, but rather for the behaviors that follow if their illness goes undetected and untreated. He gives examples of the types of mental illnesses lawyers may suffer from and specific protections a client, lawyer, and law firm can provide.

9. The UNIVERSITY OF PITTSBURGH LAW REVIEW had an excellent symposium issue in the spring of 2008 on lawyers with disabilities. These two first-rate pieces from that symposium issue stand out: Laura Rothstein, *Law Students and Lawyers with Mental Health and Substance Abuse Problems: Protecting the Public and the Individual*, 69 U. PITT. L. REV. 531 (2008) and Michael L. Perlin, *"Baby, Look Inside Your Mirror": The Legal Profession's Willful and Sanist Blindness to Lawyers with Mental Disabilities*, 69 U. PITT. L. REV. 589 (2008).

10. David Margolick, *At The Bar: 15 Years Later, Disbarred Lawyer Can't Erase Horror's Stigma*, N.Y TIMES, May 15, 1993, tells the sad though compelling story of former attorney Robert T. Rowe. In 1978, in a moment of insanity brought on in part by PTSD from the Korean War, the strain of caring for a deaf and blind son, and his loss of a job and reliance on his wife's working two jobs, Rowe killed his entire family — his son, a daughter, and his wife — with a baseball bat. Found not guilty by reason of insanity and released from a mental institution after eight years, Rowe started a new family, did volunteer work, and then applied to lift his indefinite suspension from the bar. Though healthy and "fully able to practice his profession" according to psychiatrists, the New York court said no, describing him, somewhat oddly, as "guilty of serious *professional* misconduct" (our emphasis).

Chapter 12

THE ECONOMICS OF LAWYERING

PROBLEM 31: COUNSELORS IN ACTION GO FOR THE GOLD

A. INTRODUCTION

Among the images of lawyers most readily available to the public on a daily basis are those left by their advertisements and other efforts to solicit business. Before the United States Supreme Court stepped in during the late 1970s, there was simply *no* advertising; ethics rules required that even law firm letterheads and business cards meet strict standards of dignity and decorum. The majority of America's lawyers may long to return to those times, but between 1977 and 1995, the Supreme Court decided nine cases that broadly evaluated the commercial-free-speech rights of lawyers to both advertise their services and solicit prospective clients. By the time the Court was through, it had rather clearly defined the constitutional boundaries of lawyers' commercial free speech. In the years since 1995, many states have increased prohibitions against certain advertisements and solicitations. Some of these regulations may be constitutionally overbroad, but for the most part their constitutionality has not been further tested.

By "advertising," we mean just that: the general promotion of one's services and availability. "Solicitation" is a somewhat more complicated concept. "Capping and "running," the traditional term for lawyers sending "agents" out to directly solicit business from the public, is still clearly banned in every American jurisdiction. The degree to which an attorney may approach or "target" specific persons, either individually or as a group, to offer legal services — what we describe as "solicitation" — has been defined by the Supreme Court's series of cases. As a result, the First Amendment as interpreted by the Court has ensured that substantial lawyer advertising and a degree of lawyer solicitation is here to stay. Exactly where the lines are or should be drawn remains an ongoing tug-of-war, with a few courts having recently re-entered the fray.

B. PROBLEM

The law firm of Garcia, Weir, and Lesh decides to open a chain of "legal clinics" called "Counselors In Action" (C.I.A.), in the five largest regional markets in the state. They plan to charge lower fees for most routine services. Garcia, Weir, & Lesh believe that if they can capture market volume, they will be able to make more profit than if they operated as a more conventional law firm. Moreover, they think that by bringing clients in for these simple services, they may be able to develop a more lucrative personal injury practice. While most of C.I.A.'s staff attorneys are from local law schools, Garcia and Weir attended Harvard, while Lesh attended Stanford. Garcia, Weir. and Lesh all have had considerable success as trial lawyers over the years. The C.I.A. staff attorneys, however, are largely inexperienced.

I

C.I.A. decides to advertise. It hires an advertising and public relations firm to help promote business. The agency proposes the following print ad copy that will also appear on the firm's website:

a. "Counselors In Action employs among the most qualified lawyers in town. Many of our lawyers attended the most prestigious law schools and have won many large trials and settlements. You can count on Counselors In Action to win."

b. "Here's what Counselors In Action's senior trial lawyers have accomplished: *Garcia* has won his last twelve trials; *Weir* is a past recipient of the Trial Lawyer Network's 'Advocate of the Year' award; and each of *Lesh's* last six jury successes has been in the high six figures."

c. "In personal injury cases, you pay *nothing* except a portion of the award *you* recover. No recovery means no fee. And you will get the personal, professional, top-flight service you should expect."

Are these advertisements appropriate? Do they meet ethical requirements? Can the firm use this trade name and call itself a "legal clinic"?

II

The ad agency suggests the firm hire television actors Patrick Robinson and singer Kris Ting-Stewart to portray the typical C.I.A. attorney in a series of TV spots. Ethical? Appropriate?

III

The partners realize that C.I.A.'s chances of success will be maximized if they emphasize personal injury claims. The agency suggests a direct mail approach to anyone in the metropolitan areas where their offices are located whenever an injury accident report is filed with the public repository. They suggest that the mailing be a personalized letter introducing the firm and a brochure emphasizing C.I.A.'s personal injury experience. They also suggest that one of the partners follow up the letter with a phone call. Ethical? Appropriate?

IV

In a further effort to spur business, the web site designer prepares a website that provides "tips" to potential plaintiffs looking for attorneys to take their cases. These tips do little more than regurgitate applicable professional rules regulating contingent fee contracts and suggested questions for clients to ask lawyers they are contemplating hiring. The site also encourages clients to contact the firm by e-mail with any questions. Is this ethical? Are there special problems with advertising on the Internet that do not exist for other media?

C. READINGS

1. *Bates v. State Bar*

The way it used to be, lawyers simply didn't advertise. Outside of "dignified" business cards and letterheads and a listing in a directory for attorneys such as Martindale-Hubbell, lawyers were not supposed to promote their services. Solicitation of business — at least in the usual commercial sense — was simply forbidden. Canon 27 of the ABA's 1908 Canons put it this way: "The most worthy and effective advertisement possible . . . is the establishment of a well-merited reputation for professional capacity and fidelity to trust. This cannot be forced, but must be the outcome of character and conduct . . . ." Much of this sentiment remained expressed in Canon 2 of the Model Code, especially in DRs 2-101 through 2-104, even though these rules were anachronisms largely unenforceable after the Supreme Court's constitutional cases.

Of course, it was not entirely true that lawyers never solicited business, but rather that they did so outside of public scrutiny: in boardrooms, at business luncheons, and at country clubs. As the practice of law became more diverse in the 1970s, younger lawyers searched for new avenues of attracting business. As Justice Blackmun implied in the seminal *Bates* case excerpted below, it was no longer possible for lawyers to hold themselves above other trades with the idea that the law must be an especially "dignified" profession. The traditional ban on lawyer advertising, said Blackmun, was more a rule of etiquette than ethics.

In *Bates*, two Arizona lawyers opened a legal clinic and advertised their services with the newspaper ad, included in the appendix to the court's opinion, that we reproduce below. Justice Blackmun evaluated each of the Arizona Bar's reasons for banning advertising, rejected each in turn, and reversed the lawyers' discipline.

BATES v. STATE BAR OF ARIZONA
433 U.S. 350 (1977)

The issue presently before us is a narrow one. First, we need not address the peculiar problems associated with advertising claims relating to the *quality* of legal services. Such claims probably are not susceptible of precise measurement or verification and, under some circumstances, might well be deceptive or misleading to the public, or even false. Appellee does not suggest, nor do we perceive, that appellants' advertisement contained claims, extravagant or otherwise, as to the quality of services. Accordingly, we leave that issue for another day. . . .

The heart of the dispute before us today is whether lawyers . . . may constitutionally advertise the *prices* at which certain routine services will be performed. Numerous justifications are proffered for the restriction of such price advertising. We consider each in turn:

1. *The Adverse Effect on Professionalism.* . . . It is claimed that price advertising will bring about commercialization, which will undermine the attorney's sense of

dignity and self-worth. . . . Advertising is also said to erode the client's trust in his attorney: Once the client perceives that the lawyer is motivated by profit, his confidence that the attorney is acting out of a commitment to the client's welfare is jeopardized. . . .

[W]e find the postulated connection between advertising and the erosion of true professionalism to be severely strained. At its core, the argument presumes that attorneys must conceal from themselves and from their clients the real-life fact that lawyers earn their livelihood at the bar. . . .

The absence of advertising may be seen to reflect the profession's failure to reach out and serve the community: Studies reveal that many persons do not obtain counsel even when they perceive a need because of the feared price of services or because of an inability to locate a competent attorney . . . .

It appears that the ban on advertising originated as a rule of etiquette and not as a rule of ethics. . . . Since the belief that lawyers are somehow "above" trade has become an anachronism, the historical foundation for the advertising restraint has crumbled.

2. *The Inherently Misleading Nature of Attorney Advertising.* It is argued that advertising of legal services inevitably will be misleading (a) because such services are so individualized with regard to content and quality as to prevent informed comparison on the basis of an advertisement, (b) because the consumer of legal services is unable to determine in advance just what services he needs, and (c) because advertising by attorneys will highlight irrelevant factors and fail to show the relevant factor of skill.

We are not persuaded that restrained professional advertising by lawyers inevitably will be misleading . . . . The only services that lend themselves to advertising are the routine ones: the uncontested divorce, the simple adoption, the uncontested personal bankruptcy, the change of name, and the like — the very services advertised by appellants.

. . . .

The third component is not without merit: Advertising does not provide a complete foundation on which to select an attorney. But it seems peculiar to deny the consumer, on the ground that the information is incomplete, at least some of the relevant information needed to reach an informed decision. The alternative — the prohibition of advertising — serves only to restrict the information that flows to consumers. Moreover, the argument assumes that the public is not sophisticated enough to realize the limitations of advertising, and that the public is better kept in ignorance than trusted with correct but incomplete information. We suspect the argument rests on an underestimation of the public. . . .

3. *The Adverse Effect on the Administration of Justice.* Advertising is said to have the undesirable effect of stirring up litigation. . . . Advertising, it is argued, serves to encourage the assertion of legal rights in the courts, thereby undesirably unsettling societal repose. There is even a suggestion of barratry.

But advertising by attorneys is not an unmitigated source of harm to the administration of justice. It may offer great benefits. Although advertising might increase the use of the judicial machinery, we cannot accept the notion that it is always better for a person to suffer a wrong silently than to redress it by legal action. As the bar acknowledges, "the middle 70% of our population is not being reached or served adequately by the legal profession." . . .

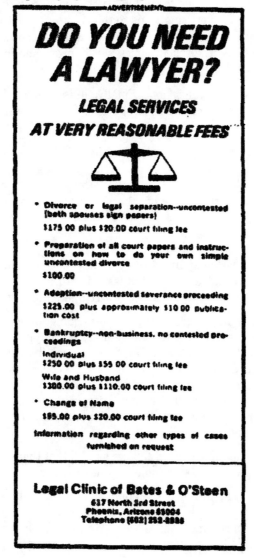

4. *The Undesirable Economic Effects of Advertising.* It is claimed that advertising will increase the overhead costs of the profession, and that these costs then will be passed along to consumers in the form of increased fees . . . .

These two arguments seem dubious at best. Neither . . . appears relevant to the First Amendment. . . .

5. *The Adverse Effect of Advertising on the Quality of Service.* It is argued that the attorney may advertise a given "package" of service at a set price, and will be

inclined to provide, by indiscriminate use, the standard package regardless of whether it fits the client's needs.

Restraints on advertising, however, are an ineffective way of deterring shoddy work. An attorney who is inclined to cut quality will do so regardless of the rule on advertising. . . . Even if advertising leads to the creation of "legal clinics" like that of appellants' — clinics that emphasize standardized procedures for routine problems — it is possible that such clinics will improve service by reducing the likelihood of error.

6. *The Difficulties of Enforcement.* Finally, it is argued that the wholesale restriction is justified by the problems of enforcement if any other course is taken. . . .

We suspect that, with advertising, most lawyers will behave as they always have: They will abide by their solemn oaths to uphold the integrity and honor of their profession and of the legal system. For every attorney who overreaches through advertising, there will be thousands of others who will be candid and honest and straightforward. . . .

    . . . .

In holding that advertising by attorneys may not be subjected to blanket suppression, and that the advertisement at issue is protected, we, of course, do not hold that advertising by attorneys may not be regulated in any way . . . .

Advertising that is false, deceptive, or misleading of course is subject to restraint. . . . For example, advertising claims as to the quality of services — a matter we do not address today — are not susceptible of measurement or verification; accordingly, such claims may be so likely to be misleading as to warrant restriction. Similar objections might justify restraints on in-person solicitation. We do not foreclose the possibility that some . . . warning or disclaimer or the like, might be required of even an advertisement of the kind ruled upon today so as to assure that the consumer is not misled . . . .

As with other varieties of speech, it follows as well that there may be reasonable restrictions on the time, place, and manner of advertising. . . .

The constitutional issue in this case is only whether the State may prevent the publication in a newspaper of appellants' truthful advertising concerning the availability and terms of routine legal services. We rule simply that . . . the present application of the disciplinary rule against appellants to be violative of the First Amendment.

NOTES

Was *Bates* a decision whose time had come, a case that simply reflected the changing needs of society? It is interesting to read Justice Blackmun's analysis of the Arizona Bar's arguments from the perspective of time passed and new cases decided. Which of the Bar's arguments seem anachronistic and exclusionary by today's standards? Which of Justice Blackmun's points seem strong and which weak? How do you feel about Blackmun's argument that enforcement will not be a problem because only a very few in the profession will overreach and distort? Has this prediction proved correct? Blackmun states that the *Bates* opinion is limited to its facts. His conclusion specifically notes that many other forms of advertising and solicitation are not deemed acceptable by virtue of the *Bates* decision. Has it worked out this way? Or did *Bates* open Pandora's box, letting all manner and means of undignified and unpleasant legal advertising escape?

2. *Bates'* Supreme Court Progeny: Advertising

Before we examine some specific examples and recent advertising cases, we summarize below the other Supreme Court cases since *Bates* that primarily addressed *advertising*. Later we will do the same for the cases emphasizing *solicitation*. This is a substantial revision to our organization of this material. There is no bright line between advertising and solicitation; indeed, "targeted advertising" is a form of solicitation, as we will soon see. Nevertheless, we believe that the dual issues of advertising and solicitation are better understood if we deal with each separately.

• *In re R.M.J.*, 455 U.S. 191 (1982). Missouri had limited advertising to very specific categories of information. Attorney R.M.J. circulated a professional announcement that said that he was admitted in both Missouri and Illinois, that he practiced "personal injury" and "real estate" law (rather than the approved terms "tort law" and "property law"), and that he was admitted to practice before the United States Supreme Court. Justice Powell spoke for the Court. In agreeing with *R.M.J.*, Powell drew a distinction between truthful and misleading advertising:

> Truthful advertising related to lawful activities is entitled to the protections of the First Amendment. But when the particular content or method of the advertising suggests that it is inherently misleading or when experience has proved that in fact such advertising is subject to abuse, the States may impose appropriate restrictions. Misleading advertising may be prohibited entirely. But the States may not place an absolute prohibition on certain types of potentially misleading information, e.g., a listing of areas of practice, if the information also may be presented in a way that is not deceptive. . . .

> Although the potential for deception and confusion is particularly strong in the context of advertising professional services, restrictions upon such advertising may be no broader than reasonably necessary to prevent the deception.

• *Zauderer v. Office of Disciplinary Counsel*, 471 U.S. 626 (1985) is a case of advertising "targeted" at a particular audience, here women who had used the Dalkon Shield. This case could be considered either an advertising or solicitation case, or both. We include it here because it involved attorney Zauderer's print advertisement, placed in 36 newspapers throughout Ohio. While the ad specifically asked women, "Did you use this IUD?," provided information about the dangers of the Dalkon Shield in particular, and according to the court garnered Zauderer 106 clients, it lacked any element of direct solicitation, as Justice White noted in reversing the reprimand imposed in Ohio:

> Because appellant's statements regarding the Dalkon Shield were not false or deceptive, our decisions impose on the State the burden of establishing that prohibiting the use of such statements to solicit or obtain legal business directly advances a substantial governmental interest.

> . . . Although some sensitive souls may have found appellant's advertisement in poor taste, it can hardly be said to have invaded the privacy of those who read it. More significantly, appellant's advertisement — and print advertising generally — poses much less risk of overreaching or undue influence [than more direct solicitation]. Print advertising may convey information and ideas more or less effectively, but in most cases, it will lack the coercive force of the personal presence of a trained advocate [and] is not likely to involve pressure on the potential client for an immediate yes-or-no answer to the offer of representation. . . . Accordingly, the substantial interests that justified the ban on in-person solicitation upheld in *Ohralik*[1] cannot justify the discipline imposed on appellant for the content of his advertisement.

White also directly addressed the issue of "dignity," which for so long had operated to govern attorney conduct:

> [A]lthough the State undoubtedly has a substantial interest in ensuring that its attorneys behave with dignity and decorum in the courtroom, we are unsure that [this] is an interest substantial enough to justify the abridgment of their First Amendment rights. . . . [T]he mere possibility that some members of the population might find advertising embarrassing or offensive cannot justify suppressing it.

However, because Zauderer's ad said that clients would pay no fee unless they received money (that is, he charged a contingency fee), but *failed to say* that they might have to pay *costs*, this failure to disclose was misleading and thus subject to discipline.

• *Peel v. Attorney Registration & Disciplinary Comm'n*, 496 U.S. 91 (1990). Attorney Peel put on his letterhead that he was certified by the National Board of Trial Advocacy. The Court supported Peel, holding the letterhead was neither actually nor inherently misleading.

• *Ibanez v. Florida Board of Accountancy*, 512 U.S. 136 (1994). Ibanez was an attorney who also was a CPA and a certified financial planner (CFP). Her plans to use these designations on her letterhead and business cards, as well as in her yellow pages advertising, ran afoul of the Florida Board of Accountancy (but not the State Bar). The Accountancy Board reprimanded her for "false, deceptive and misleading advertising." The Supreme Court reversed, finding Florida's position "entirely insubstantial." In dissent, Chief Justice Rehnquist and Justice O'Connor complained that the designated initials, particularly the little-known "CFP," might be inherently misleading.

---

[1] We will summarize this case below.

• *Milavetz, Gallop & Milavetz, P.A. v. United States*, 559 U.S. 229 (2010) was a case primarily about the constitutionality of provisions of the Bankruptcy Abuse Prevention and Consumer Protection Act of 2005 that arose in a declaratory relief action filed by a bankruptcy law firm that wanted to find out, in advance, what it could and could not do. However, in her majority opinion, Justice Sotomayor analyzed the *Zauderer* disclosure requirements in determining that the law firm had to make certain disclosures — that it was a "debt relief agency" under the act, and that their debt relief assistance could result in bankruptcy at a significant monetary cost to their clients — in order to avoid being misleading.

In most instances, these and other cases have referenced the detailed test for determining the regulation of commercial free speech defined in another Supreme Court case, *Central Hudson Gas & Elec. Corp. v. Public Serv. Comm'n*, 447 U.S. 557, 566 (1980).

3. How Much Has Changed? It Mostly Comes Down to "Misleading"

In *Bates*, Justice Blackmon envisioned "restrained professional advertising" that would avoid being "inevitably misleading." "The only services that lend themselves to advertising are the routine ones," he wrote: "the uncontested divorce, the simple adoption, the uncontested personal bankruptcy . . . ." Though most lawyers now accept Blackmon's interpretation of the First Amendment, his prognostication about what services would be advertised was considerably less accurate. But the primary issue, clearly articulated by Blackmon in *Bates*, remains whether an advertisement is "false, deceptive, or misleading."

How far have lawyers gone in promoting their services in the years since *Bates*? Anyone familiar with the legal marketplace knows some of the ways. Telephone yellow pages became saturated with print ads containing assurances, approvals and certifications, and pictures of the stars of the show — the lawyers who make those assurances. Ads continue to proliferate on radio and late night television. "Targeted" mailings are sent to people with particularized legal problems. Here are a few other advertising "innovations":

The 800 Number Hotline. Law firms, and consortiums of law firms, have set up 800 number "hotlines" to answer simple questions, and to generate cases in the event the simple question can't be answered on the phone. Some lawyers for a time tried 900 numbers, where the customer who called paid a per-minute fee.

Free Seminars are offered in areas of law that are either lucrative or of particular concern to specific groups, such as seminars on estate planning for the elderly. Those that attend the seminars may be encouraged to engage the services of the lawyers conducting the program.

Private Referral Services. Many bar associations run nonprofit referral services that qualify lawyers by experience and refer potential clients to those lawyers. Some states like California formally regulate such services, and the ABA has similar standards, compliance with which gives the service the right to say it is "ABA approved."

Private referral services operate outside this scheme, many emphasizing personal injury referrals, advertising and operating through their on-line presence. Some "referral services" simply turn out to be law firms or groups of firms. Other "referral services" that are not law firms don't qualify lawyers based on knowledge and experience; they simply carve out geographical territory and "sell" that territory one or more lawyers. These programs proliferate for two reasons. First, consumers have long sought out referral services on the assumption they provide trustworthy information about lawyers from an objective source. Second, lawyers and non-lawyers alike see them as potential profit centers, especially since referral services and those who run them (who need not be lawyers) are still not subject to regulation in most states. As described, however, these entities are inherently misleading because they are not "lawyer referral services" as the term is generally defined.

Endorsements and Testimonials are used in television ads to encourage prospective clients to call "their" lawyer. In one series of frequently shown California TV spots, famous baseball personalities were used to encourage callers in both English and Spanish to hire a particular group of lawyers. Past clients of lawyers are used for testimonials, and in some cases, actors are hired to do the testimonials.

Thus, we have this case in point: the New York law firm of Worby Groner Edelman & Napoli Bern. The Worby firm has been principal liaison counsel for the victims of the 9-11 tragedy in the consolidated litigation formally known as *In re World Trade Center Disaster Site Litigation*. In Problem 11 we quoted from one opinion in this case that examined Worby's conflicts of interest. In March 2011, the compelling advertisement reproduced below appeared at a fundraiser for 9/11 police and firefighters. But the ad was a fake.

Robert Keiley, the firefighter whose photo appears beside the quote "I was there" *wasn't* there at the World Trade Center in 2001, and didn't join the fire department until 2004. When the photo was taken, for a departmental fire prevention ad, Keiley was holding his fire helmet, not a picture of the 9-11 devastation, which was PhotoShopped in by Worby's ad agency.

Keiley, who didn't know his photo was being used by Worby, was furious: "It's an insult to the Fire Department. It's an insult to all the families who lost people that day," he told the New York *Post*. "It makes me look like I'm cashing in on 9/11." Keiley's best friend lost his brother on 9/11. "I had friends who died on 9/11," Keiley said. "How can I look their families in the eye if they see this picture?" Keiley told a reporter.

When the Worby firm directed all calls to its ad agency, the agency spokesperson said that Keiley's image could be used for "really anything you want." The ad, however, was quickly pulled by Worby.

4. Advertising in a Modern and High-Tech World

With use of the Internet, the ads lawyers use have changed from Yellow Pages spreads to pop-ups and banners purchased on search engines and desirable websites. More recently, lawyers have become bloggers. Tweeters, Facebook friends, and Instagram senders. What has this meant for advertising?

For a recent Inns of Court program, California attorney John Steele, an ethics consultant and adjunct professor at UC Berkeley, came up with a list of websites that each have their own different protocols, and a list of questions to be asked of each site. Steele examined (in alphabetical order) Avvo, Facebook, Groupon, LinkedIn, and Twitter, as well as lawyer blogs, or "blawgs."

Two questions were omnipresent: "Is it advertising?" and "Is client confidentiality protected?" For Avvo, an endorsement site, Steele also asked, "Is the advertising authored by you, the lawyer?; Are you responsible for the accuracy of what is said on the page describing you?; Do you have a duty to correct inaccurate statements posted by others?; and May you ask your own clients to rate you highly?" LinkedIn also raised questions about client endorsements and factual accuracy. Groupon caused Steele to express concern about fee-splitting. And blogs raised a host of issues for Steele, from whether a blog is an ad at all to whether outcomes and testimonials need disclaimers about obtaining favorable results in future cases.

On a listserv on which Steele posted his list, ABA staff counsel Will Hornsby, a recognized expert on attorney advertising, reminded that while new tech-based media are important to understand and recognize, it's most important to "move the discussion from the forms of tech-based media to concentrate on the content and context of the message." His observation makes sense. As new forms of advertising come along, the same rules apply: Is it advertising, and thus subject to commercial free speech regulation? Is it false or misleading? And are there other issues, such as adequate disclosures or disclaimers that are legitimate constitutional restraints?

As for blogs, in February 2013, the Virginia Supreme Court decided the case of Horace F. Hunter, Richmond criminal defense lawyer and author of the blog "This Week in Richmond Criminal Defense." Read this analysis of whether Hunter's blog could result in a disciplinary offense.

HUNTER v. VIRGINIA STATE BAR ex rel THIRD DIST. COMM.
2013 Va. LEXIS 28 (Feb. 28, 2013)

I. FACTS AND PROCEEDINGS

Horace Frazier Hunter, an attorney with the law firm of Hunter & Lipton, PC, authors a trademarked blog titled "This Week in Richmond Criminal Defense," which is accessible from his law firm's website, www.hunterlipton.com. This blog, which is not interactive, contains posts discussing a myriad of legal issues and cases, although the overwhelming majority are posts about cases in which Hunter obtained favorable results for his clients. Nowhere in these posts or on his website did Hunter include disclaimers.

As a result of Hunter's blog posts on his website, the [Virginia State Bar (VSB)] launched an investigation. During discussions with the VSB about whether his blog constituted legal advertising, Hunter wrote a letter to the VSB offering to post a disclaimer on one page of his website:

> "This Week in Richmond Criminal Defense is not an advertisement[;] it is a blog. The views and opinions expressed on this blog are solely those of attorney Horace F. Hunter. The purpose of these articles is to inform the public regarding various issues involving the criminal justice system and should not be construed to suggest a similar outcome in any other case."

However, the negotiations stalled and no disclaimers were posted . . . .

On March 24, 2011, the VSB charged Hunter . . . . Specifically, the VSB argued that he violated rules 7.1 and 7.2 because his blog posts discussing his criminal cases were inherently misleading as they lacked disclaimers. The VSB also asserted that Hunter violated Rule 1.6 by revealing information that could embarrass or likely be detrimental to his former clients by discussing their cases on his blog without their consent.

In a hearing on October 18, 2011, the VSB . . . presented a former client who testified that he did not consent to information about his cases being posted on Hunter's blog and believed that the information posted was embarrassing or detrimental to him, despite the fact that all such information had previously been revealed in court. . . . The VSB also entered all of the blog posts Hunter had posted on his blog to date. At that time, none of the posts entered contained disclaimers. Of these thirty unique posts, only five discussed legal, policy issues. The remaining twenty-five discussed cases. Hunter represented the defendant in twenty-two of these cases . . . . In every criminal case described, Hunter's clients were either found not guilty, plea bargained to an agreed upon disposition, or had their charges reduced or dismissed.

At the hearing, Hunter testified that he has many reasons for writing his blog — including marketing, creation of a community presence for his firm, combating any public perception that defendants charged with crimes are guilty until proven innocent, and showing commitment to criminal law . . . . Hunter admitted that he only blogged about his cases that he won. . . . Following the hearing, the VSB held that Hunter violated Rule 1.6 by "disseminating client confidences" obtained in the course of representation [that] "would be embarrassing or be likely to be detrimental" to clients and he did not receive consent from his clients to post such information. The VSB further held that . . . Hunter's website contained legal advertising based on its factual finding that "[t]he postings of [Hunter's] case wins on his webpage advertise[d] cumulative case results." Moreover, the VSB found that at least one purpose of the website was commercial. The VSB further held that he violated Rule 7.2 by "disseminating case results in advertising without the required disclaimer" because the one that he proposed to the VSB was insufficient.

. . . .

II. ANALYSIS

Rule 7.1(a)(4), which is the specific portion of the Rule that the VSB argued that Hunter violated, states:

> (a) A lawyer shall not . . . use or participate in the use of any form of public communication if such communication contains a false, fraudulent, misleading, or deceptive statement or claim. For example, a communication violates this Rule if it:
>
> > (4) is likely to create an unjustified expectation about results the lawyer can achieve . . . .

The VSB also argues that Hunter violated the following subsection of Rule 7.2(a)(3):

> (a) . . . In the determination of whether an advertisement violates this Rule, the advertisement shall be considered in its entirety, including any qualifying statements or disclaimers contained therein. Notwithstanding the requirements of Rule 7.1, an advertisement violates this Rule if it:
>
> > (3) advertises specific or cumulative case results, without a disclaimer that (i) puts the case results in a context that is not misleading; (ii) states that case results depend upon a variety of factors unique to each case; and (iii) further states that case results do not guarantee or predict a similar result in any future case undertaken by the lawyer. The disclaimer shall precede the communication of the case results. When the communication is in writing, the disclaimer shall be in bold type face and uppercase letters in a font size that is at least as large as the largest text used to advertise the specific or cumulative case results and in the same color and against the same colored background as the text used to advertise the specific or cumulative case results.

In response to these allegations, Hunter contends that speech concerning the judicial system is "quintessentially 'political speech'. . ." [and not] transformed into commercial speech simply because one of multiple motives is commercial. The VSB responds that Hunter's blog posts are inherently misleading commercial speech.

Turning to Hunter's argument that his blog posts are political, rather than commercial, speech, we note that "[t]he existence of 'commercial activity, in itself, is no justification for narrowing the protection of expression secured by the First Amendment.'" However, when speech that is both commercial and political is combined, the resulting speech is not automatically entitled to the level of protections afforded political speech.

. . . .

Here, Hunter's blog posts, while containing some political commentary, are commercial speech. Hunter has admitted that his motivation for the blog is at least in part economic. The posts are an advertisement in that they predominately describe cases where he has received a favorable result for his client . . . .

Moreover, the blog is on his law firm's commercial website rather than an independent site dedicated to the blog. . . . The website uses the same frame for the pages openly soliciting clients as it does for the blog, including the firm name, a photograph of Hunter and his law partner, and a "contact us" form.

This non-interactive blog does not allow for discourse about the cases, as non-commercial commentary often would by allowing readers to post comments. [Cites to recent articles on blogging as largely interactive.] Instead, in furtherance of his commercial pursuit, Hunter invites the reader to "contact us" the same way one seeking legal representation would contact the firm through the website.

Thus, the inclusion of five generalized, legal posts and three discussions about cases that he did not handle on his non-interactive blog, no more transform Hunter's otherwise self-promotional blog posts into political speech, "than opening sales presentations with a prayer or a Pledge of Allegiance would convert them into religious or political speech."

Having determined that Hunter's blog posts discussing his cases are commercial speech, we must determine whether the expression is protected by the First Amendment. . . . Next, we ask whether the [test is met under] *Central Hudson Gas & Elec. Corp. v. Public Serv. Comm'n*, 447 U.S. 557, 566, 100 S.Ct. 2343 (1980) . . . .

The VSB . . . argues that the posts are inherently misleading. While we do not hold that the blog posts are inherently misleading, we do conclude that they have the potential to be misleading "because the public lacks sophistication concerning legal services . . . ." *Bates*, 433 U.S. at 383. . . . While the States may place an absolute prohibition on inherently misleading advertising, "the States may not place an absolute prohibition on certain types of potentially misleading information if the information also may be presented in a way that is not deceptive." *In re R.M.J.* Here, the VSB's own remedy of requiring Hunter to post disclaimers on his blog posts demonstrates that the information could be presented in a way that is not misleading or deceptive.

Thus, we must examine whether the VSB has a substantial governmental interest in regulating these blog posts . . . . [*Bates*] expressed concern that the public may lack the sophistication to discern misstatements as to the quality of a lawyer's services. Therefore, the VSB has a substantial governmental interest in protecting the public from an attorney's self-promoting representations that could lead the public to mistakenly believe that they are guaranteed to obtain the same positive results if they were to hire Hunter.

The VSB's regulations permit blog posts that discuss specific or cumulative case results but require a disclaimer to explain to the public that no results are guaranteed. This requirement directly advances the VSB's governmental interest . . . . [Further] we hold that the disclaimers required by the VSB are "not more extensive than is necessary to serve that interest." *Central Hudson*, 447 U.S. at 566.

We thus conclude that the VSB's Rules 7.1 and 7.2 do not violate the First Amendment. As applied to Hunter's blog posts, they are constitutional and the panel did not err.

[The court then discusses the First Amendment as it relates to Virginia's Rule 1.6 on confidentiality, which the Court quotes.]

The VSB argues that it can prohibit an attorney from repeating truthful information made in a public judicial proceeding even though others can disseminate this information because an attorney repeating it could inhibit clients from freely communicating with their attorneys or because it would undermine public confidence in the legal profession. Such concerns, however, are unsupported by the evidence . . . .

. . . .

JUSTICE LEMONS, dissenting:

I agree with the majority's resolution of the Rule 1.6 issue. However, I dissent from the majority's determination that Hunter is guilty of violating Rules 7.1(a)(4) and 7.2(a)(3) and that Hunter must post a disclaimer that complies with Rule 7.2(a)(3).

. . . .

Hunter's blog contains articles about legal and policy issues in the news, as well as detailed descriptions of criminal trials, the majority of which are cases where Hunter was the defense attorney. The articles also contain Hunter's commentary and critique of the criminal justice system. He uses the case descriptions to illustrate his views.

Speech concerning the criminal justice system has always been viewed as political speech. As political speech, Hunter uses his blog to give detailed descriptions of how criminal trials in Virginia are conducted. He notes how the acquittal of some of his clients has exposed flaws in the criminal justice system.

The majority asserts that because Hunter only discusses his victories, his blog is commercial. The majority does not give sufficient credit to the fact that Hunter uses the outcome of his cases to illustrate his views of the system. Hunter testified that one of the reasons he maintained the blog was to combat "the public perception that is clearly on the side that people are guilty until they're proven innocent." For example, when discussing one of the cases where his client was found not guilty, he concludes the post by explaining that this case is an "example of how innocent people are often accused of committing some of the most serious crimes. That is why it is important not to judge the guilt of an individual until all the evidence has been presented both for and against him."

. . . .

The majority also focuses on the location of Hunter's blog, and asserts that because the blog is accessed through the law firm's website and is not interactive, that demonstrates the blog is commercial in nature. While going through the law firm's website is one way to access the blog, it is also possible to go directly to the blog without navigating through the firm's website. Further, the fact that the blog is not interactive in no way commercializes the speech . . . .

Hunter conceded that one of the purposes of the blog was marketing. Although the United States Supreme Court has never clearly decided whether political speech is transformed into commercial speech because one of the multiple motivations of the speaker is marketing and self-promotion, its jurisprudence leads to the conclusion that Hunter's speech is not commercial . . . .

Even if there is some commercial content to Hunter's speech, any commercial content is intertwined with political speech. When commercial and political elements are intertwined in speech, the heightened scrutiny test must apply to all of the speech . . . .

NOTES

Hunter was publicly reprimanded. He publicized his own State Bar case openly on his website, further adding to his visibility. He even appeared on an ABA continuing education DVD discussing the first-level appellate case.

The importance of this case should not be underestimated. As the advertisement for the ABA video noted, "If your law firm has a blog and you have not paid attention to the matter of *Horace Hunter v. Virginia State Bar,* you want to participate in this ethics CLE that addresses what amounts to a case of first impression . . . ."

Case of first impression indeed. First, as both the majority and the dissent recognized, *Hunter* had to decide an issue that the Supreme Court had never addressed: whether *hybrid* political and commercial speech should be governed by the highest or the lower *Central Hudson* First Amendment scrutiny. Second, the court was on new ground in addressing the free-speech rights of what some call "blawgers," or lawyer-bloggers. Finally, *Hunter* also addressed client confidentiality issues, though the court gave this rather minimal attention.

The effect on "blawgers" could be substantial. "Hunter's case has some lawyers — for whom blogging has become commonplace . . . questioning whether the bar is overreaching in its regulation of online speech," wrote a Washington *Post* reporter after the intermediate appellate court opinion in 2011. Washington, D.C. lawyer Carolyn Elefant, who blogs at *My Shingle,* wrote then that even though her blog, unlike Hunter's, steers clear of trumpeting winning cases, if "Hunter's news feed qua blog is an advertisement and therefore requires disclaimers, mark my words, that decision will be construed broadly to encompass even legitimate blogs that discuss substantive legal issues."

5. So What *Is* "Misleading" in Today's World?

In the absence of Supreme Court involvement after the mid-1990s, many state bars made their advertising regulations more stringent. These state regulatory agencies wield great power when the Supreme Court is not speaking. How effective are these state regulations in light of constitutional requirements? Most regulations have not been constitutionally tested. Typical of these increased regulations is the series of advertising "standards" promulgated by the State Bar of California. These standards are quite specific in nature, including, for example, detailed requirements for notices on both targeted and untargeted direct mail and disclaimers for endorsements and testimonials, including the font size and placement of the disclaimers or notices. Drafters of these provisions seem to have paid relatively modest attention to whether all of them are actually constitutional.

Some state courts, though, have taken a narrower view of commercial free speech than the Supreme Court did in the 1980s and 1990s. Indiana, with several relatively restrictive court opinions, is one such state. In *In re Keller*, 792 N.E.2d 865 (Ind. 2003), a law firm's television commercial, complete with a celebrity voice, had a script that called for the "insurance defense lawyer," upon learning that the Keller firm was opposing counsel, to say "Let's settle this one." "No, let's not," said the state Supreme Court, which issued a public reprimand.

New Jersey, another state with a history of restrictive regulation, held in 2006 that the phrase "Super Lawyer" was an impermissible and misleading marketing vehicle.[2] And the *Hunter* court itself, albeit with little analysis, let stand the Virginia rule requiring disclaimers to contain very specific details: font size and description, type face, even color of text.

While *Hunter* stands alone for the moment on blogging, other recent authorities have disagreed with the *Hunter* court as to what constitutes misleading advertising. In *Gee v. Louisiana Attorney Disciplinary Board*, 632 F.3d 212 (5th Cir. 2011), the Fifth Circuit found several of Louisiana's advertising rules unconstitutional, including the rule that forbade "a reference or testimonial to past successes or results obtained . . . ."[3] The *Gee* court also struck down the requirements as to font size, speed of speech on TV ads, and the requirement of both written and spoken disclaimers on television and electronic media.

The *Gee* court did uphold rules prohibiting "a portrayal of a client by a non-client . . . or the depiction of any events or scenes . . . that are not actually authentic without disclaimer," and prohibiting lawyers from promising results or using a trade name that "states or implies an ability to obtain results . . . ." These

---

[2] Opinion 39, N.J. Committee on Advertising (2006).

[3] Even Florida, a relatively strict lawyer-regulation state, had, as we went to press, a proposed rule that would allow lawyers to list past results if "objectively verifiable." Proposed Florida rule 4.7.3, April 2013 draft.

are two areas where courts and other authorities have almost uniformly upheld prohibitions, on the common-sense basis that both false depictions of people and events, and promising results (as opposed to listing victories) are clearly misleading.[4]

What about the issue of confidentiality under MR 1.6, which the Virginia Bar Board found Horace Hunter had breached by posting, without consent, material learned during the course of the representation that could be embarrassing or detrimental to his former clients? The Virginia Supreme Court, as we've seen, summarily discarded this issue in Hunter's favor. But isn't Virginia's Rule 1.6 a correct statement of what we discussed in Problem 5 — the broad prohibition against revealing the confidences and secrets of the client — *even if* the information might otherwise by public?

The issue of confidentiality was also addressed in District of Columbia Formal Opinion 335 (2006), which held that "a settlement agreement may not compel counsel to keep confidential and not further disclose in promotional materials or on law firm websites public information about the case . . . ." To do so would prevent counsel from informing potential clients of their experience and expertise." But on the issue of confidentiality, the DC bar disagreed with what was to become the Virginia court's view:

> If a client withholds permission for her lawyer to disclose public informa-
> tion, we agree that the lawyer must keep the information secret and that
> D.C. Rule 1.6 applies. A plaintiff settling a sexual harassment claim, for
> example, may wish to protect her privacy by not allowing her lawyer to
> publicize further any information about her case.

6. *Bates'* Supreme Court Progeny: Solicitation

As we did for advertising in section 2, we review here the Supreme Court cases on solicitation that have been decided in the years since *Bates*.

• *Ohralik v. Ohio State Bar Association*, 436 U.S. 447 (1978), and *In re Primus*, 436 U.S. 412 (1978). These two cases were the first opportunity after *Bates* for the Court to revisit the issue of commercial speech for lawyers. They were decided on the same day, and represent opposite extremes on the issue of direct, case-specific solicitation.

In *Ohralik*, Ohio Attorney Ohralik's solicitation couldn't have been much more overt or overbearing. He learned that two teenage girls had been injured in an automobile accident. He visited the parents of one, whom he knew slightly, and then went to the hospital, where he asked the girl, in traction, to sign a one-third contingency fee agreement. Two days later, he went back to the hospital and she signed.

---

[4] In *Alexander v. Cahill*, 598 F.3d 79 (2d Cir. 2010), however, the Second Circuit struck down the fictitious depiction and trade name rules at least as it applied to one law firm, which used the name "Heavy Hitters." The firm produced high-tech ads that showed the firm's lawyers surrounded by "wisps of smoke, blue electrical currents, and special effects . . . towering above local buildings. Here, the court said, it made "common sense" that no one is "likely to be misled into thinking that these advertisements depict true characteristics."

Ohralik visited the second girl at her home the day after she was released from the hospital. He carried a concealed tape recorder. He told her he represented the first girl and asked if she wanted him to represent her as well. At first, she seemed confused, but ultimately said "O.K." After she changed her mind the next day, Ohralik, who had captured their conversation on tape, insisted that the girl had entered into a binding agreement, and attempted to obtain about $2,500 in fees from her. Eventually, the first girl fired Ohralik, who sued for breach of contract. Both girls complained to the bar, and the Ohio Supreme Court handed Ohralik an indefinite suspension.

The Supreme Court easily distinguished *Bates*, and concluded that Ohralik's overt, "overreaching," in-person solicitation of clients was not commercial free speech protected under the First Amendment. Justice Powell's opinion emphasized the danger of in-person solicitation:

> Although it is argued that personal solicitation is valuable because it may apprise a victim of misfortune of his legal rights, the very plight of that person not only makes him more vulnerable to influence but also may make advice all the more intrusive. Thus, under these adverse conditions the overtures of an uninvited lawyer may distress the solicited individual simply because of their obtrusiveness and the invasion of the individual's privacy, even when no other harm materializes. . . .

> Unlike the advertising in *Bates*, in-person solicitation is not visible or otherwise open to public scrutiny. Often there is no witness other than the lawyer and the lay person whom he has solicited, rendering it difficult or impossible to obtain reliable proof of what actually took place.

Powell concluded by emphasizing the circumstances of the Ohralik solicitations: the youth of the two girls; their vulnerability, one still in the hospital, the other seen on her first day home; the lack of opportunity for either girl to think objectively about her decision; Ohralik's emphasis on "what sounded like a cost-free and therefore irresistible offer." "The facts of this case," concluded Powell, "present a striking example of the potential for overreaching that is inherent in a lawyer's in-person solicitation."

Primus concerned the actions of attorney Primus, a private lawyer who also served as a local ACLU officer and cooperating attorney, and as a consultant to the South Carolina Council on Human Relations. On behalf of the Council, Primus met with a group of women who contended they had been sterilized as a condition of receiving Medicaid, and discussed with the women their legal rights. Later, after the ACLU agreed to provide representation in a lawsuit against a particular doctor, Primus wrote a letter to a woman who had attended the meeting and who had been sterilized by that doctor. She informed the woman that the ACLU would provide free legal counsel, and that "we" would come see her to "explain what is involved." The woman showed the letter to the doctor and then called Primus to decline the offer.

Again, Justice Powell wrote for the Court, but this time he found the lawyer's actions protected, and distinguished Primus' conduct from that of Ohralik:

Unlike the situation in *Ohralik*, however, appellant's act of solicitation took the form of a letter to a woman with whom appellant had discussed the possibility of seeking redress for an allegedly unconstitutional sterilization. This was not in-person solicitation for pecuniary gain. Appellant was communicating an offer of free assistance by attorneys associated with the ACLU, not an offer predicated on entitlement to a share of any monetary recovery.

The Court relied heavily on *NAACP v. Button*, 371 U.S. 415 (1963), in determining that Primus' actions were protected by the First Amendment. Applying *Button* to the case before him, Powell concluded that "solicitation . . . for the purpose of furthering the civil-rights objectives of the organization and its members" is a protected association "for the advancement of beliefs and ideas."

Ohralik and *Primus*, though they were decided together and both deal with solicitation, are clearly distinguishable. Primus' conduct seems positively pristine in light of Ohralik's behavior, and her solicitation was by mail only, while his was in person and unusually obtrusive.

• *Shapero v. Kentucky Bar Ass'n*, 486 U.S. 466 (1988). Attorney Shapero took "targeted" advertising one giant step beyond *Zauderer*, discussed in section 2, right into the world of solicitation. He asked the state advertising commission for permission to send a letter directly to "potential clients who have had a foreclosure suit filed against them." Shapero did not know these people, only that they were facing foreclosure. The mailing, which could hardly qualify as "dignified," is worth reproducing here:

> It has come to my attention that your home is being foreclosed on. If this is true, you may be about to lose your home. Federal law may allow you to keep your home by ORDERING your creditor to STOP and give you more time to pay them.

> You may call my office anytime from 8:30 a.m. to 5:00 p.m. for FREE information on how you can keep your home. Call NOW, don't wait. It may surprise you what I may be able to do for you. Just call and tell me that you got this letter. Remember it is FREE, there is NO charge for calling.

Justice Brennan, speaking for the Court, found Shapero's proposed conduct closer to that of Zauderer than Ohralik, reasoning as follows:

> Of course, a particular potential client will feel equally "overwhelmed" by his legal troubles and will have the same "impaired capacity for good judgment" regardless of whether a lawyer mails him an untargeted letter or exposes him to a newspaper advertisement — concededly constitutionally protected activities — or instead mails a targeted letter. The relevant inquiry is not whether there exist potential clients whose "condition" makes them susceptible to undue influence, but whether the mode of communication poses a serious danger that lawyers will exploit any such susceptibility.

While the Brennan opinion upheld Shapero's right to send his letter, the Court was much more fundamentally divided in the 4-2-3 *Shapero* decision than at any time since the 5-4 decision in *Bates*. Justice O'Connor's dissent called for the reconsideration of the expansion of advertising since *Bates*, claiming the cases following *Bates* were based on "defective premises and flawed reasoning."

Florida Bar v. Went For It, Inc., 515 U.S. 618 (1995). If the above cases left the state of the law and the extent to which solicitation may be ethical in flux, nothing prepared lawyers for the Supreme Court's decision in *The Florida Bar v. Went For It, Inc.* There, Justice O'Connor, who had shown an increasing discomfort with the extent of lawyer solicitation, wrote for a 5-4 majority that upheld a Florida ban on written communications with accident victims within 30 days of the accident. Her opinion contrasted sharply with the dissent by Justice Kennedy.

O'Connor justified the Florida regulation by agreeing with the Florida Bar that "it has a substantial interest in protecting the privacy and tranquility of personal injury victims and their loved ones against intrusive, unsolicited contact by lawyers." She relied in part on a lengthy Bar summary and study containing "both statistical and anecdotal [information] supporting the Bar's contentions that the Florida public views direct-mail solicitations in the immediate wake of accidents as an intrusion on privacy that reflects poorly upon the profession." O'Connor distinguished *Shapero* by noting that the Kentucky regulation was "a broad ban on all direct-mail solicitations, whatever the time frame and whoever the recipient." She also noted that "the State in *Shapero* assembled no evidence attempting to demonstrate any actual harm."

Justice Kennedy's blistering dissent asserted that "[a]ttorneys who communicate their willingness to assist potential clients are engaged in speech protected by the First and Fourteenth Amendments," a principle "understood since *Bates*." Kennedy found it "uncontroverted that when an accident results in death or injury, it is often urgent at once to investigate the occurrence, identify witnesses, and preserve evidence. Vital interests in speech and expression are, therefore, at stake . . . ."

As for restricting speech on privacy grounds, Kennedy wrote that "we do not allow restrictions on speech to be justified on the ground that the expression might offend the listener," and thus the First Amendment must prevail. The fact that the advertising might be "offensive" or "undignified" was of no import, Kennedy noted, pointing to the opinions of the previous Supreme Court cases on commercial free speech.

Then, in unusually strong language, he wrote that "the State is doing nothing more [than engaging in] censorship pure and simple; and censorship is antithetical to the first principles of free expression." Kennedy ended his dissent by remarking: "If public respect for the profession erodes because solicitation distorts the idea of the law as most lawyers see it, it must be remembered that real progress begins with more rational speech, not less."

7. Solicitation After *Shapero* and *Went For It*

Justice Kennedy seemed to see the entire purpose of lawyer commercial-free-speech cases screeching to a halt in *Went For It*. His arguments have resonance, particularly that the majority chose to protect lawyers' public image over free speech, and that "opposing parties" (i.e., insurance companies) may step in during the 30-day ban.

But despite the dire predictions from those who agree with this view, thus far there have been relatively few judicial repercussions. Most court decisions that followed *Went For It* continued to uphold a lawyer's right to advertise and, to a lesser extent, solicit. Some distinguished *Went For It* on the basis that Florida had a substantial body of evidence to bolster that state's claim that such contacts were invasive and caused suffering, while subsequent cases have not had such evidentiary support. Rather, it has again largely been state bar regulators — and not the courts — who took the lead after *Went For It*, adopting more stringent controls on both advertising and solicitation.

In the aftermath of *Shapero*, the Louisville Courier-Journal reported that Kentucky lawyers were "plastering accident victims, accused drunken drivers and other potential customers with mail solicitations."[5] Because Kentucky's Open Records Act gave lawyers access to police accident reports, some victims were inundated by the targeted direct mail that the *Shapero* case unleashed.

Meanwhile, lawyers pushed the solicitation envelope after *Shapero* on both coasts by using free medical or scientific screening as a way to solicit clients. In New Jersey, the East Brunswick firm of Garruto, Galex & Cantor offered free chest X-rays to factory workers, in hopes of gaining clients who suffered from mesothelioma, a deadly form of cancer caused by asbestos exposure.[6]

And California attorney Gordon Stemple operated medical screening vans he called "examobiles," that traveled all over screening tire factory workers for asbestos exposure. Tire factories were known for having asbestos issues, so in addition, Stemple set up a non-profit he called the National Tire Workers Litigation Project. Stemple's solicitations never resulted in discipline, but he and his firm were eventually sued by Raymark Industries, Inc., an asbestos manufacturer, for civil RICO violations. Stempel in turn sued Raymark. Stempel's suit was dismissed, and he settled Raymark's suit for an undisclosed amount.[7]

In the years since *Went For It*, there have been fewer solicitation horror stories than those about advertising. We posit three possible reasons: First, *Went For It* and *Ohralik* had set clear solicitation boundaries. Second, lawyers have self-policed solicitation in their own back yards. Thus, in Kentucky, when targeted mail ran rampant, most complaints to the bar came from other attorneys. Third, new bar regulations focused on advertisements that bar regulators could see and even in some cases require lawyers to submit for review or archiving. Solicitation, as Justice Powell noted in *Ohralik*, is largely beyond such scrutiny.

In the years since the Supreme Court spoke, the history of advertising and solicitation regulation has been more about state regulation than Supreme Court interpretation. State disciplinary agencies fill in the gaps as best they can, subject

---

[5] Andrew Wolfson, *Lawyers Who Solicit Clients by Mail Prompt Complaints*, THE COURIER-JOURNAL (Louisville), February 24, 1991.

[6] *See* Tracy Schroth, *"Ambulance Driving"; Medical Screening for Clients Stirs Controversy*, NEW JERSEY LAW JOURNAL, March 12, 1990.

[7] *See, e.g.*, Nathan A. Schachtman and Cynthia J. Rhodes, *Medico-Legal Issues in Occupational Lung Disease Litigation*, 27 SEMINARS IN ROENTGENOLOGY 140 (1992). The Raymark settlement is reported at 14 MEALEY'S LITIGATION REPORTS-ASBESTOS 6:16 (July 19, 1991).

to eventual constitutional interpretation. But since the high court has not issued a major opinion since *Went For It*, those state regulations have filled the void, and lawyers violate them at the peril.

8. Insurance Companies, Insurance Lawyers, and Advertising

One of the most common complaints from plaintiffs' lawyers about bans on soliciting accident victims is that posited by Justice Kennedy's dissent in *Went For It*: The bans don't apply to insurance companies, allowing them to quickly contact the victims first and encourage them to settle their claims for far less than what they are worth. In effect, some insurance companies mount "anti-lawyer" campaigns designed to dissuade or distract potential claimants from hiring lawyers to pursue their claims.

Insurance companies know that the more they can avoid having claims go to court, the more money they will save. We referenced in Problem 12's Supplemental Readings the actions of Allstate Insurance Company. Allstate was sued by injured persons after they received a company pamphlet entitled, "Do I Need an Attorney?" Some criticized the pamphlet as a thinly veiled attempt to dissuade the injured parties from hiring attorneys to pursue their claims. Both a Washington trial court and the West Virginia State Bar have agreed with this.

The rules that regulate attorney advertising and solicitation do not apply to these contacts by the insurance company and its attorneys, because the contacts are not being made for the purpose of obtaining clients. For these reasons, many states using Florida-style bans have applied the bans to both sides.

There are other examples of insurance company efforts to reach early (and low) settlements with claimants. In one California case, a claims adjuster and an insurance company lawyer manipulated a couple whose baby was badly burned while in a relative's care into believing that he was acting with the couple's and their daughter's interests in mind. The lawyer involved said he had gone to court "on behalf" of insureds "dozens and dozens of times."[8]

As we learned in Problem 12, some insurance companies use their own attorney employees to represent their insureds against third party claims, though several jurisdictions still disallow this practice. Should these in-house insurance attorneys be required to indicate on their letterhead, business cards, or websites their actual relationship with the carrier? Does failure to make these disclosures mislead the insureds into thinking that their lawyers are independent of the insurers? (Some attorneys argue that placing the affiliation on stationery or business cards will mislead the insureds into thinking that the attorneys will *not* represent their best interests.)

The Nassau County (New York) Bar Association concluded that any rule, one way or the other, was too inflexible; rather, the insured should be apprised of the

---

[8] *See* Settle v. Civil Service Employees' Ins., Harper, et al., Alameda Co. (Calif.) Super. Ct. No. 754597-3. This case is reported in ZITRIN & LANGFORD, THE MORAL COMPASS OF THE AMERICAN LAWYER 132–33 (1999).

lawyer's true status and then consent to the representation.[9] California State Bar Formal Opinion 1987-91 reached a different result: Anything on the letterhead other than "Law Division" would be misleading and therefore unethical.

D. SUPPLEMENTAL READINGS

1. William Hornsby, *What You Need to Know in 2013: Lawyer Advertising and Marketing Ethics Today: An Overview*, [ABA] ATTORNEY AT WORK, DAILY DISPATCH, January 23, 2013, is a concise and well-written review from perhaps the most knowledgeable expert on lawyer advertising and solicitation, ABA staff attorney Will Hornsby. Hornsby reviews recent rules changes and what to expect in the future.

2. G.M. Filisko, who often writes for ABA periodicals, has written several good articles on advertising and solicitation. Two are noted here. *The Ethics of Online Advertising*, 41 STUDENT LAWYER (March 2013) (No. 7) is a straightforward overview of the advertising rules presented for law students and new lawyers. The second, from the ABA JOURNAL of August 2012, is *Where the Buck Stops*, and the subtitle makes Filisko's point: *Lawyers Need to Verify All the Nice Things Being Said about Them Online*. The piece quotes the Virginia Bar's chief ethics counsel James McCauley as saying "Lawyers may not know the marketing service they're subscribing to is using improper or fraudulent means to improve their search position or visibility on the Internet. But once they're made aware of that fact, they can't continue employing the vendor who's using means the lawyer couldn't use himself."

3. Geoffrey C. Hazard, Jr., Russell Pearce, & Jeffrey W. Stempel, *Why Lawyers Should Be Allowed to Advertise: A Market Analysis of Legal Services*, 58 N.Y.U. L. REV. 1084 (1983), is a fascinating article describing in great depth the need for advertising certain types of legal services as a way to generate demand and economies of scale. But the authors feel advertising is not useful in the delivery of certain types of legal services. Looked at in the rearview mirror, this earlier take on where advertising would lead and where it would be useful is an interesting window on the time right after *Bates*.

4. North Carolina State Bar Ethics Comm., Formal Op. 2012-1 (July 20, 2012) held that client testimonials in attorney advertisements need not be accompanied by a disclaimer unless the endorsements "go to the outcome of a case or matter." Thus, the typical disclaimer that prior successes are not indicative of future results is necessary only for "hard" endorsements that "indicate a particular favorable result," and are not needed for "soft" client testimonials, *i.e.*, general praise for an attorney's abilities. One might speculate that "endorsements" on LinkedIn would similarly require no disclaimer if re-published on a firm's website.

5. Steven A. Delchin & Sean P. Costello, *Show Me Your Wares: The Use of Sexually Provocative Ads to Attract Clients*, 30 SETON HALL L. REV. 64 (1999). This article details and explains the ramifications of Rosalie Osias' ad campaign for mortgage clients that used sexy pictorial content to attract clients. It uses Osias'

---

[9] *See* Nassau Bar Ethics Opinion 95-5 (1995).

ads as a basis for analyzing the law-as-profession/law-as-business debate. What seems to astound everyone is the success of Ms. Osias' campaign.

6. Michael Conroy, *Clash of Titans: Groupon v. The Model Rules of Professional Conduct*, IOWA L. REV., (Forthcoming March 2013), *available at* http://ssrn.com/abstract=2232143 or http://dx.doi.org/10.2139/ssrn.2232143 is a law student note that tackles an interesting subject: whether lawyers may advertise through "daily deals" such as through Groupon. Conroy argues that lawyers may ethically sell their services this way as a reasonable cost of advertising authorized by Rule 7.2, and that the money retained by the daily deal company is not an impermissible fee split.

7. Nina Keilin, *Client Outreach 101: Solicitation of Elderly Clients by Seminar Under the Model Rules of Professional Conduct*, 62 FORDHAM L. REV. 1547 (1994). The issue raised in this article remains extremely important, particularly as the practice continues almost unabated. Lawyers and, often, non-lawyers with lawyer "adjuncts' set up "educational seminars" on wills, trusts, and senior entitlements to attract elderly potential clients. The article describes the vulnerability of the elderly to the pressures that can be exerted by lawyer "salespeople."

8. *Ficker v. Curran*, 119 F.3d 1150 (4th Cir. 1997). Despite the Supreme Court's holding in *Florida Bar v. Went For It*, the Fourth Circuit held that an attorney is permitted to send written solicitations to criminal defendants within 30 days of their arrest. The court distinguished between civil cases, where the potential clients would be the ones to bring the lawsuits and had ample time beyond the 30 days to decide what to do, and criminal cases, where the client is charged against his will, cases come to trial quickly, and an attorney is needed from the outset.

9. *In re Anis*, 599 A.2d 1265 (N.J. 1992). A well-written opinion by the New Jersey Supreme Court discussing the uncharted waters of ethical decency, after a law firm contacted the parents of one of the victims of the air disaster over Lockerbie, Scotland, the day after the body of their son had been identified.

10. Amy Busa & Carl G. Sussman, *Expanding the Market for Justice: Arguments for Extending In-Person Client Solicitation*, 34 HARV. C.R.-C.L. L. REV. 487 (1999). The authors argue that legal services attorneys and others who provide services to low income persons should be able to solicit them in person. They argue that the state's interest in seeing that such persons have access to the courts outweighs any countervailing dangers of solicitation.

11. There are surprisingly few recent academic articles that survey issues of Internet solicitation. One of the more useful is Cyrus D. Mehta & Elizabeth T. Reichard, *The Ethics of Practicing Law on the Internet: Advertising, Client Confidentiality and Avoiding the Unauthorized Practice of Law*, 145 PLI/NY 351 (2004), which provides a brief set of guidelines for advertising on the Internet, including a discussion of the risks of engaging in the unauthorized practice of law, and a section on how Internet technologies such as e-mail affect formation and confidentiality issues relating to the attorney-client relationship.

12. Thomas J. Watson, a risk manager for a legal malpractice insurance carrier published *Lawyers and Social Media: What Could Possibly Go Wrong?* in 2012

WISCONSIN LAWYER (May 2012). His answer, of course, was "everything." A valuable practical piece.

PROBLEM 32: THE ECONOMICS OF LEGAL SERVICES FOR INDIGENT CLIENTS

A. INTRODUCTION

Early in the history of common-law countries, lawyers — or their precursors — worked without compensation,[1] Today, of course, things are much different. Lawyers expect their clients to pay for the services they render. Every lawyer is exhorted by aspirational ethical guidelines to help represent the poor and disadvantaged, the people who can't otherwise afford the services of an attorney. But in most places these guidelines are mere exhortation, while the legitimate legal needs of millions go unmet. What should be the responsibility of *all* lawyers to assist in providing legal services to those in need?

B. PROBLEM

I

You have just been hired to head the Gold County Legal Services Office. This is the only office in the entire county serving indigent and fixed income clients in civil matters on a no fee basis. The local bar association has a *pro bono* panel, but it doesn't come close to meeting all the needs of the poor. The only other services offered for free are those of the public defender in criminal cases.

Your resources are severely limited. Your staff is working as hard as can be expected but is not nearly able to handle all the problems that come in. After some time to assess the situation, you realize you face a number of important decisions.

1. A number of clients come to you complaining that Len Lord, one of the big rental property owners in the county, has raised rents each year by 10% or more despite a county ordinance limiting rent raises to the rate of inflation or 3.0%, whichever is less. You and your staff have handled a few individual cases, but you realize that the best approach would be a multi-party "private attorney-general" or public interest lawsuit designed to force Lord to stop his practice as to all tenants, many (but not all) of whom would qualify for legal aid services. On the other hand, you know that such litigation will be costly and very time consuming for your staff.

Should the legal aid office undertake the suit? May you refuse it when you know that many renters will get no relief otherwise?

2. After six months, the time/cost studies you have instituted show that child custody and visitation cases take up a disproportionately large amount of staff time. In addition, your clients have been able to prevail in just 18% of the cases. Many have come to you with requests for custody where you believe they stand little or no chance of success. You also find that bankruptcy cases take too much staff time, especially since the bankruptcy court is located 80 miles away.

---

[1] Theodore Frank Thomas Plucknett, CONCISE HISTORY OF THE COMMON LAW, ch. 12 (1956) (Indianapolis: Liberty Fund, 2010).

(a) May you decide to refuse to handle all child custody and visitation proceedings? May you screen these cases and take only the ones you or your staff believe are truly meritorious? Or that you think you will actually win?

(b) May the legal aid office refuse all bankruptcy matters if you arrange instead to have a volunteer lawyer give a do-it-yourself seminar once a month to explain how people can handle their own bankruptcy filings? May you refuse these cases even if you don't give this seminar?

3. You recently circulated a survey in which your clientele had an opportunity to voice their opinions about the issues most important to them. The three issues at the top of the list were housing and homelessness, family law issues, and basic and emergency health care. May you make these three areas your highest priority? What if you discover that the fourth most important issue in your survey was social security, but that a very high percentage of seniors/disabled who responded listed this concern number one? May you ignore this, and thus ignore the seniors' greatest need on the theory of "the greatest good for the greatest number"? Or must you take social security cases?

II

Now put yourself in the position of a first- or second-year associate in a large downtown firm. You want to do *pro bono* public work, but the firm has a requirement of 2,150 billable hours, which of course takes a tremendous commitment of your time. Besides, your firm does not have a substantial *pro bono* commitment. You haven't been able to find a partner who will serve as a *pro bono* mentor or support your desire to do this work. And the firm has told you that any *pro bono* work you do will not be credited towards your billable hours.

What can you do? What should you do? Finally, what are your thoughts about *law students* being required to perform *pro bono*? What does *pro bono* really mean anyway?

C. READINGS

1. Life as a Legal Aid Lawyer

What is life like in the legal aid fast lane? Read this article about dedicated young attorney Robert Doggett.

Richard Zitrin, *Five Who Got It Right*
13 WIDENER L.J. 209 (2003)[2]

THE TRUE BELIEVER — Robert Doggett, Texas Rural Legal Aid, Austin, Texas.

In the 1970s, many legal aid offices had federal funding, and young, idealistic law graduates could get fellowships that gave them the opportunity to spend a few years representing poor people. Some stayed on as staff lawyers. But the days when the needs of the poor were a high funding priority are long gone. Many legal services agencies have closed, and financial woes are a constant strain for those that remain.

Today's legal aid lawyers must accept personal costs if they want to represent the poor. They will be grossly underpaid. They will be overwhelmed with work. Far more people will need their services than even the best of them can possibly handle. Yet, some still seek this work. Those few who, like Robert Doggett, decide to make a career of representing poor people make a long-term commitment to personal sacrifice. [Here in his own words is Robert Doggett's story.]

My clients are poor people. They have problems they don't deserve and didn't cause. Most aren't well educated and have little power. They're the least likely to complain or have the resources to change their situation. But they're the ones who need help the most. My job is to help as best as I can.

When I got out of law school, I went to work for the Dallas Tenants Association. Part of my job was to try and keep people from being homeless, and we were very effective at that. In court I'd see people representing themselves and getting evicted in about ten seconds. So I'd jump in and say "Excuse me, judge; just a moment." I'd walk up to the person and say, "It seems like you need some help; I'm free and I'd be happy to help you." The judges just hated that! It would slow down their docket and the eviction process. But when I got involved, they would actually have to hear evidence on the issues. I still did some of those cases long after my job changed because I just couldn't stop — I hear such horrible stories.

Now, a lot of people tell me they're against what I'm doing. But if you tell people the facts of a particular case, then they say, "Of course, that's different." Once I worked on a tenant's action where the people in a housing complex lost their utilities and air conditioning for two months. It was a hot Texas summer, and the landlord was doing nothing. He even threatened to call the cops on us. It was so bad we got some good TV coverage.

Anyway, it's getting extremely ugly when I get a call at home at 8:00 on a Saturday morning from the landlord's lawyer. He says "It's fixed, I promise, it's all fixed. So I want you to call off Monday's hearing." We call to check with the tenants and it's true: after 63 days, the problems are fixed! So my co-counsel and I get back on the phone with the landlord's lawyer, and he says "I want to put somebody on the line named Dorothy and I want you to do me a favor. Just confirm the truth." Then he says "Now, Dorothy, can you hear? I have the tenants' lawyers on the line."

It turns out Dorothy is the owner's mother-in-law. It seems she saw the stories on TV, realized it was one of her son-in-law's complexes, and felt shamed. The attorney told me that at Shabbas dinner — they're Jewish — she blew a gasket and said to fix the problems, no matter what the cost. So the lawyer wanted me to confirm that everything was fixed. It's funny, we like to think that we're the saviors, that it's our great legal work that fixes things, when this time it was the defendant's mother-in-law.

I worked four years at the Tenants Association. I was their only attorney. My first year, I worked for $25,000 and then they raised me to $30,000. My student loans? I never really liked to add them up back then, but they were in the $50,000 zone. It wasn't real good; I just couldn't afford to pay them. But I was lucky. My rent was low and my wife's law school had a loan forgiveness program for public service. Last year I paid the loans off. It only took twelve years!

When I started law school, I was on the standard career track. If somebody had said "You're going to be doing Legal Aid work," I'd have said "No way." But I quickly realized that there were things happening out in the real world that I had never been exposed to before. A friend invited me to help him interview applicants for a free legal clinic.

Maybe it was meeting these people and understanding what they had been through. They'd tell me their whole life story hoping I'd help. We had to tell a lot of people that we couldn't help them, and that was very disturbing to me. They poured their guts out and nothing was going to come of it just because there weren't enough volunteer attorneys.

So I got involved with the law student *pro bono* committee at Southern Methodist. I pulled just about every trick in the book to get students to do volunteer work. One time I wrote an article for the school newspaper called "This Has Nothing to Do with Sex." It didn't! It was about *pro bono* work. I know, it's a cheap trick.

I interviewed with the big firms. I ate at all the fancy places in town my last year. I had one offer from a good firm. But I knew fighting for an insurance company or a big bank wouldn't really get me going, and if I don't get excited about what I'm doing, I'm not going to do as good a job. Besides, living from vacation to vacation was not my idea of life . . . .

So when I turned down the offer from the firm, I had no job. That was the most difficult part. My father wasn't thrilled when I told him.

My parents were both puzzled. They knew I had a lot of student loans. I got a birthday card a few years ago saying something like, "We are proud of what you are doing. We are still not really sure why." For years, my mom wondered why I do what I do. She would like to feel she doesn't have to worry about me anymore. When I worked in Dallas, every once in a while when she wanted to do me a favor my Mom would have my dry cleaning done. She'd pick up my suits and shirts, have them cleaned, and bring them back, just to save me a little money.

I finally did get to work for Legal Services of North Texas. In one of my first cases there, I represented some low income folks on a hazardous waste problem, something legal services traditionally hasn't done. But the environment is an issue that affects poor people more than most. They have a hazardous waste blender in West Dallas that is an extreme danger to the community right across the street, and the State agency had the audacity to say that we didn't have the right to be heard in the permit process. All we were after was the same level of protection as anyone else.

The homes across from the plant are owned by the residents. They're all Hispanic. Most of them speak broken English at best and they generally don't get involved in lawsuits, but the stench coming from the plant was so bad they couldn't go outside. They were afraid for their kids. We had testimony about the stench, but the agency still said "Sorry, it doesn't prove the odors come from the plant." We finally got a court opinion saying it's absurd for a state agency to deny us the right to be heard.

Poverty work comes down to benefits, family issues and housing and consumer issues. At this point, I am not scared of any issue. Just get me up to speed on it, let's find the problem and go after it.

Usually, though, Rule No. 1 is "Don't file a lawsuit." You have to break Rule No. 1 once in a while, but it's a rule you start with. Lawyers are trained to be technicians, to look to the law to solve problems. But I was trained to think of more creative ways. If we sue and lose, the other side will claim that everything they were doing was fine, even if that's not what the judge said. I walk into a room full of people and say "How many of you think a judge is going to solve your problems today? I am dying to file a lawsuit." Nobody raises their hand . . . .

Bill Bridge, my evidence professor and a very good listener, taught me something. I said "Hey, I'll just get one of these regular jobs and do *pro bono* work on the side, and I can pay off my student loans in a couple of years." He looked at me and said "You know what's going to happen if you do that? You'll work your butt off, come home at 9:00 at night and there is no way you're going to have time to do *pro bono* work. Don't fool yourself."

I went from a small country town to Plano, a nice suburb, but hardly a cultural melting pot, graduated from Texas A&M, then to SMU law school, and I turned out like this! After ten years of practice in two legal aid jobs, I was 33 and living in the same apartment I had when I was in law school. I lived there for 13 years. The price was right!

My parents were both conservative Republicans, but we were always taught "do unto others." Until my dad died a few years ago, he worked for a refrigeration company. I remember going with him to people's houses at 3:00 a.m. holding a flashlight while he repaired a busted refrigerator. He was always willing to help people no matter when, day or night.

Personal life? Frankly it's hard to have time for one. But I finally found someone who lived in Austin. Raman moved to Dallas to start at the Public Defender's office. She and I got married a few years ago. We're compatible because we're both very intolerant of intolerance.

Raman never much liked Dallas, so we eventually went to Austin. She works part-time for the Texas Innocence Project and part-time for Texas Appleseed. We both love what we do. A family? Let's say we don't have kids yet but we're in intense negotiations.

[And] regardless of where I live or exactly what I'm doing, I don't have any intention of stopping this work, ever.

NOTES

Robert Doggett is a long way from the novice attorney straight out of law school who began his career with only training his student *pro bono* experience. He became a recognized expert in housing and environmental issues involving poor people to the point at which he was hired by the Dallas City Attorney to help deal with the issue from the government side. His job was to teach staff attorneys the techniques he had developed to successfully sue slumlords. After that stint, he returned to legal aid in Austin. He is a senior staff lawyer for Texas Rural Legal Aid, where he still works cases while mentoring younger attorneys. His wife Raman continues to do similar work on the criminal side. Robert considers himself a "lifer." As for the results of his and Raman's "intense negotiations," they have two beautiful young girls.

2. Making Choices About Which Cases to Take

How do lawyers like Robert Doggett confront problems similar to those faced in Gold County: underfunding, understaffing, and far too many cases to choose from?

Ralph Jimenez, *Veto Will Affect Legal Assistance for State's*
THE BOSTON GLOBE, June 12, 1994[3]

Every week, the Manchester office of New Hampshire Legal Assistance receives several hundred pleas for help from people who are losing their homes, facing utility shutoffs or being denied pension, health care or welfare benefits.

On Thursdays, the office staff rides a trembling shower stall of an elevator up to the dingy Elm Street rooms where they meet to decide whose case they can afford to take and who will get a pamphlet explaining their rights and an apology. Next year, because of a gubernatorial veto, more people will get an apology instead of their day in court, the nonprofit organization's lawyers said.

"It's an agonizing, triage decision," Elliott Berry, a legal assistance lawyer since 1976, said of the Thursday meetings. "We decide who is likely to make it without our help and who is likely to lose no matter what we do. Then we try to concentrate on who we can do the most for. But it really is like playing God and it's by far the worst part of the job. I can't remember our resources ever being thinner than they are now."

. . . On Wednesday, Gov. Stephen E. Merrill vetoed a bill that would have raised $240,000 for Legal Assistance by adding a $5 surcharge to the court fees paid by those who file civil lawsuits. [T]he governor faulted Legal Assistance for suing the state in the past and said he does not intend to provide money to an organization that intends to haul the state into court in the future. . . .

"I am not trying to do away with Legal Assistance. I think as they were originally intended to be, which is an organization to help the poor and needy, they did a good job and continue to do a good job," Merrill said. "But I don't want to encourage them to become a cause-oriented organization that continues to spend too much of its

---

[3] Copyright © 1994 by The Boston Globe. Reprinted with permission courtesy of The Boston Globe.

time lobbying and too much of its time bringing litigation against the state in matters that, in my opinion, are not related to poverty."

. . . .

[Both Legal Assistance Director Robert] Gross and Berry, however, say class action suits by Legal Assistance were a major force behind reforms that have made New Hampshire's mental health and penal systems a model for the nation. And such suits are filed only when other means have failed to solve a problem shared by many people, Gross said. . . .

Legal Assistance gets the bulk of its $1.7 million budget from two sources, the federal Legal Services Corp.[4] and a program that captures the interest earned on temporary bank accounts held in trust briefly by lawyers for clients. Federal funds are off because New Hampshire's poor were last officially counted in 1989 — before recession swelled their numbers, Gross said. And low bank interest rates have cost the agency $200,000 a year. With 18 lawyers to cover the state and more than 24,000 calls for help — 10,000 to the Manchester office alone — a low-income resident's odds of securing a lawyer are less than one in seven.

NOTES

This article was written in 1994. Has the situation changed? In the years immediately after this article, legal assistance took even more hits, including a 25% decrease in federal funding between 1996 and 2000, and a 1996 Congressional act prohibiting federally-funded legal services organizations from engaging in class actions.[5] Was Governor Merrill right that New Hampshire Legal Assistance did not sufficiently steer clear of politics? And how about class actions? Are they a necessary part of the work of representing the poor? Most of Robert Doggett's work in the past 10 years has been in class actions.

Today, triage "case conferences" happen all over the country. And in most places, no longer does the Legal Services Corporation or the state provide much funding. To the extent that organizations want public funds, they often have to choose between accepting that funding and not taking on class actions or declaratory relief cases, and other similar conditions. Some organizations have simply turned down public funds if accompanied by conditions they consider too onerous. But private funding for legal aid has never been easy and is certainly not getting easier. Does all this affect your thoughts about how to use case selection as a strategy to avoid the ethical dilemma of not being able to represent all people who are worthy?

---

[4] The "LSC" is a private nonprofit corporation funded by Congress to provide grants to civil legal aid programs.

[5] However, in *Legal Services Corp. v. Velazquez*, 531 U.S. 533 (2001), the Supreme Court, *citing* First Amendment grounds, prohibited Congress' ability to limit funds to Legal Services Corporation organizations that challenged existing welfare laws.

3. Tough Lawyers Making Tough Choices

Here are just a few current statistics about the legal needs of the poor and middle class:

- *1-to-6,415*: The ratio of free legal services attorneys available to the number of low-income Americans who need one.

- *63 million*: The number of low-income Americans qualifying for free legal help in 2010. One-third of them are children.

- *71%*: The percentage of legal needs of low-income households that are not met by the court system. The figure is also high for moderate-income households at 61%.

- *Less than 20 percent*: The number of low-income Americans' legal needs that are being met according to a 2009 study conducted by the LSC.

- *90%*: The number of civil litigants in high-volume city courts who don't have access to a lawyer.

- *$15.8 million*: The amount of money cut from the Legal Services Corporation's fiscal year 2011 budget, further reducing funds for civil legal aid to low-income Americans. This comes after years and years of other deep cuts.[6]

This means a lot of tough decisions for legal services lawyers everywhere.

Sometimes, the tough choices made by well-meaning but understaffed and financially strapped public service attorneys arouse the ire of the very communities they are trying to serve. In early 1994, the Legal Assistance Foundation of Chicago realized it too was only serving a small percentage of those in need. But when the foundation chose to close an office in a largely Latino area, the closing resulted in distress and outrage in both the Spanish-speaking community and the leadership of the Spanish-speaking bar.

Compounding the problem is the fact that even if funding isn't *legally* tied to various limitations, such as not suing the state, practicalities often limit a program's available scope. Robert Doggett ran into such a problem when the associates he recruited from Dallas' Akin, Gump found themselves in court opposing a landlord who was a good friend of several of the firm's partners. More overt conflicts of interest, of course, can knock potential *pro bono* volunteers right off a case.

4. IOLTA, and How It's Not Nearly Enough

When Ronald Reagan was president, he made a concerted effort to end legal services programs. Even though he was unsuccessful in killing the national civil legal services program entirely, he was successful in significantly reducing funding

---

[6] These figures and many others can be found in David Liu, *Civil Legal Aid by the Numbers*, CENTER FOR AMERICAN PROGRESS (August 9, 2011) (americanprogress.org/issues/open-government/news/2011/08/09/10080/civil-legal-aid-by-the-numbers).

for these programs.[7] By 1983, 61 LSC-funded programs lost 30% or more of their staff attorneys, and LSC reported a 25% decline in the number of legal services offices operating nationwide. IOLTA (Interest On Lawyer Trust Accounts), created during the Reagan era attacks, did move modest amounts of interest from client trust accounts to legal aid organizations.

Today virtually every lawyer in private practice maintains an IOLTA account. These funds were, however, never sufficient to meet need, and diminish markedly when interest rates are low. In addition, parties unhappy with some of the work legal services has done have claimed IOLTA programs caused them financial loss, and have taken some of their challenges to the United States Supreme Court. After you read *Brown v. Legal Foundation*, below, consider whether you think IOLTA accounts are an appropriate source of funding for legal services to the poor. Who or what should bear the financial burden of providing legal services to those who cannot afford them? Most states have declined to pick up much of a share of the funding burden.

BROWN v. LEGAL FOUNDATION OF WASHINGTON
538 U.S. 216 (2003)

JUSTICE STEVENS delivered the opinion of the Court.

The State of Washington, like every other State in the Union, uses interest on lawyers' trust accounts (IOLTA) to pay for legal services provided to the needy. Some IOLTA programs were created by statute, but in Washington, as in most other States, the IOLTA program was established by the State Supreme Court pursuant to its authority to regulate the practice of law. In *Phillips v. Washington Legal Foundation*, 524 U.S. 156, 118 S.Ct. 1925, 141 L.Ed.2d 174 (1998), a case involving the Texas IOLTA program, we held "that the interest income generated by funds held in IOLTA accounts is the 'private property' of the owner of the principal." We did not, however, express any opinion on the question whether the income had been "taken" by the State or "as to the amount of 'just compensation,' if any, due respondents." We now confront those questions.

As we explained in *Phillips*, in the course of their legal practice, attorneys are frequently required to hold clients' funds for various lengths of time . . . . Before 1980 client funds were typically held in non-interest-bearing federally insured checking accounts. Because federal banking regulations in effect since the Great Depression prohibited banks from paying interest on checking accounts, the value of the use of the clients' money in such accounts inured to the banking institutions.

In 1980, Congress authorized federally insured banks to pay interest on a limited category of demand deposits referred to as "NOW accounts." In response to the change in federal law, Florida adopted the first IOLTA program in 1981 authorizing the use of NOW accounts for the deposit of client funds, and providing that all of the interest on such accounts be used for charitable purposes. Every State in the

---

[7] Cynthia F. Adcock writes extensively about *pro bono* programs in law schools, including its history in the 1970s and 1980s. See further reference in the Supplemental Readings.

Nation and the District of Columbia have followed Florida's lead and adopted an IOLTA program, either through their legislatures or their highest courts. The result is that . . . today, because of the adoption of IOLTA programs, [t]he aggregate value of those contributions in 2001 apparently exceeded $200 million.

. . . .

A state law that requires client funds that could not otherwise generate net earnings for the client to be deposited in an IOLTA account is not a "regulatory taking." A law that requires that the interest on those funds be transferred to a different owner for a legitimate public use, however, could be a *per se* taking requiring the payment of "just compensation" to the client. Because that compensation is measured by the owner's pecuniary loss — which is zero whenever the Washington law is obeyed — there has been no violation of the Just Compensation Clause of the Fifth Amendment in this case.

NOTES

There are, happily, a few rays of sunshine on this otherwise bleak landscape: the efforts on the part of a number of law schools to offer full or substantial payment of student loans for any graduate working in low-paying public interest law jobs, federal loan forgiveness programs for law graduates who go into public service work, and efforts by state bars to require law students to provide legal services to the underserved as a prerequisite to admission.

When it comes to loan forgiveness, New York University School of Law, long committed to extensive programs in the public interest, led the way creating a program that repays one-tenth of that lawyer's student loans, up to a 100%, for every year a graduate remains in a public service job. The purpose of programs like these is clear: to encourage new lawyers to go into public interest fields by substantially reducing their concern about repaying loans. "If [students] want a career in public service," the executive director of N.Y.U.'s Public Interest Law Center told the *New York Times*, "we can tell them . . . nothing will stand in your way. The choice is yours."[8]

And since the College Cost Reduction and Access Act of 2007, federal loan forgiveness programs and repayment structures have both improved, through the Act's "Public Service Loan Forgiveness Program," which provides for loan forgiveness after 10 years of public service employment and its "Income-Based Repayment" component, which helps reduce monthly payments to help make educational debt manageable. These have helped immeasurably in allowing law graduates to take lower paying jobs, often ones where lower income clients can receive legal services. We will further examine *pro bono* service requirements, including a movement to require law students to complete "*pro bono*" service, below.

Of course, even if a graduate wishes to get a public interest job to take advantage of this legislation, public service jobs are very limited, and getting one is

---

[8] *See* N.Y. TIMES, November 9, 1994.

becoming as competitive as getting a job with the biggest of BigLaw firms. The limits relate directly to the funding problems such programs face. Do you think loan forgiveness is an acceptable way of encouraging people to do public service work? How should we define "public service work"?

5.   The (Unfulfilled?) Promise of *Gideon*

What about indigent people facing criminal charges?

Every law student knows that *Gideon v. Wainwright*[9] provides a constitutional obligation under the Sixth and Fourteenth Amendments to provide counsel to indigent defendants in felony cases, and that the right to counsel has been extended over time to any potential loss of liberty. However, what is less known is that this requirement is all too often not met, as public defenders regularly face crushing caseloads to the point where in some parts of the country the promise of *Gideon* is a hollow one.

Washington (St. Louis) Vice-Dean Peter Joy, in part summarizing the work of others, recently evaluated the major factors contributing to poor quality of defense services:[10] excessive caseloads, lack of funds for expert witnesses and investigators, and extremely low pay rates for court-appointed lawyers and contracted defense services. Civil legal services programs must limit their caseloads to levels at which they can perform competently and leave many others unrepresented. Unlike those programs, public defenders and others under court appointment or government contract have a very different problem. Their ethical duty is to represent *all* those facing loss of liberty, and provide them all with competent and diligent representation. But how can they remain competent under the Constitution and *Gideon* in the face of caseloads that *can't* be cut down?

The ABA provides no exception to the competence requirements for lawyers representing the indigent, saying "Once representation has been undertaken, the functions and duties of defense counsel are the same whether defense counsel is assigned, privately retained, or serving in a legal aid or defender program." *The American Bar Association Standards for Criminal Justice, Defense Function*, 4-1.2(h).

In addition, ABA Formal Opinion 06-441 (2006) opines that if workload excesses prevent a lawyer from providing competent and diligent representation to existing clients, competence dictates that attorney must not accept new clients. These two somewhat inconsistent positions highlight the serious questions our nation faces as we consider whether all those accused of a crime are able to receive competent representation given the limited resources available.

---

[9] 372 U.S. 335 (1963)

[10] Peter A. Joy, *Ensuring the Ethical Representation of Clients in the Face of Excessive Caseloads*, 75 Mo. L. Rev. 771 (2010), *citing, inter alia*, Norman Lefstein & Georgia Vagenas, Restraining Excessive Defender Caseloads: The ABA Ethics Committee Requires Action, Champion, December 2006.

6.   Walking the Walk: Accomplishing *Pro Bono* Work

At least as currently funded, it's clear that the legal needs of all Americans cannot be met by legal services organizations alone. Much has been said and much more written about the need for *pro bono* work to bridge the gap.

What is a *pro bono* obligation anyway? While it is possible to debate the definition, such as whether *pro bono* legal work must be performed for free (*e.g.* could there be a low cost alternative, sometimes called "low-bono"), whether a student can earn academic credit and still call the work *pro bono*, or whether the work can relate to non-legal matters, we'll start first with the more inclusive definition used by West's Encyclopedia.

> *Pro bono* adj. short for *pro bono publico*, Latin "for the public good," legal work performed by lawyers without pay to help people with legal problems and limited or no funds, or provide legal assistance to organizations involved in social causes such as the environment, consumers, minorities, youth, battered women and education organizations and charities.[11]

Many of the nation's largest and most prestigious firms have come to consider *pro bono* an important part of their practice. Some, like New York's Cravath, Swaine & Moore, have taken on impact litigation to preserve important rights for people who could not otherwise afford representation. Others send their attorneys to legal aid clinics, or to assist lawyers like Robert Doggett in handling their overwhelming caseloads. A few, like Morgan, Lewis & Bockius, not only count all *pro bono* hours towards the billable hour requirement, but don't limit those hours once a case is accepted. Washington, D.C.'s Hogan & Lovell created a separate community services department within the firm with the specific task of handling *pro bono* cases. Schulte, Roth & Zabel, based in New York and D.C., employs a Special Counsel for *pro bono* Initiatives. D.C.'s Crowell & Moring hired a full-time lawyer to coordinate *pro bono* work. She does everything from deciding what kinds of cases to take, to exhorting her colleagues to do the work and matching them with the most appropriate cases, to overseeing the work and providing training, backup, guidance, and quality control. Many firms have similar in-house programs (though many more do not).

In many localities, state, local, and specialty bar associations have taken the lead by making *pro bono* work by its member firms a high priority item. Partly because it gives its *pro bono* participants a high profile, complete with awards and an annual party attended by the Supreme Court's Chief Justice and the local state and federal presiding judges, the Bar Association of San Francisco has helped persuade literally thousands of attorneys from scores of firms both to take on cases in the bar's own extensive *pro bono* projects and to undertake *pro bono* matters on their own. And the ABA frequently uses its influence, and sometimes its monthly magazine, to encourage practicing lawyers to make a *pro bono* commitment. For instance, the cover story of the February 2013 *ABA Journal* describes six lawyers

---

[11] WEST'S ENCYCLOPEDIA OF AMERICAN LAW (2d ed. 2008).

and their inspiring *pro bono* work.[12]

Though they have traditionally lagged behind lawyers in private practice, many corporate law departments now also provide significant *pro bono* services. The ABA's Standing Committee on Pro Bono and Public Service, Corporate Counsel, reports[13] "Corporations are coming to the forefront of the world of *pro bono*. Many corporate legal departments have long-standing *pro bono* programs and policies through which these corporations and their in-house lawyers have given back to their respective communities through the free legal representation of low-income individuals and community-based or non profit organizations," and provides a wide range of resources to help lawyers who want to do *pro bono* work. The Association of Corporate Counsel (ACC) also has an active program to help member corporations support *pro bono*. Overall, private practice attorneys provide significantly more *pro bono* hours than do corporate or government attorneys. *Supporting Justice III: A Report on the Pro Bono Work of America's Lawyers*, americanbar.org. Chicago, IL, USA: American Bar Association (March 22, 2013).

What can a young associate bring to the *pro bono* table? Plenty. Robert Doggett recalls having to cover two courts and searching for a body — any body with a bar card — to stand in front of one judge alongside a client in need. Does that actually help? Many *pro bono* coordinators have remarked that the "mere" presence of a lawyer can change the situation for *pro se* clients; perfect examples are landlord-tenant and family law matters.

Whether a young lawyer has the opportunity to do this work depends in large part on the individual and in large part on the law firm. We include here an example of a story about *pro bono* work, written when the author was a young tax attorney at a large New York firm.

Victor E. Fleischer, *Needlework and Soap Operas on Death Row* law.com, May 7, 2001[14]

This is how you find out you are next: an execution order that you — the condemned — must sign. No reassuring words like habeas corpus or executive clemency. No phone call from your lawyer, because you do not have one. "I, Larry L. Jenkins Jr., shall be executed by the Department of Corrections at such penal institution and on such a date and time within the aforementioned time period as may be designated by said Department . . . ."

You sign the order. You do what you are told. Certainly you don't know the law. What do you know? Georgia still has the electric chair. You've heard about Old Sparky, the chair used in Florida. You've seen the pictures. You wonder if next month it will be a picture of you . . . .

What you need is a lawyer. You need a lawyer to explain that the execution order

---

[12] *Working for free: Lawyers incorporating pro bono into their lives talk about its rewards, challenges*, ABA JOURNAL, February 2013, *available at* http://www.abajournal.com/magazine/article/working_for_free/.

[13] http://apps.americanbar.org/legalservices/probono/corporate_counsel.html.

[14] Copyright © 2001 by Victor E. Fleischer. Reprinted by permission of the author.

is just a legal chess move — the attorney general's procedural gambit to force a habeas petition to be filed quickly. You need a lawyer to take a second look at the trial that landed you on death row.

I am writing this article to encourage other big-firm associates to get involved with death penalty work. . . .

Larry Jenkins became a client of Davis Polk & Wardwell shortly before his execution order went into effect. In hopes of taking a death penalty case, our firm had been in contact with Terri Piazza, a member of the tireless staff of the nonprofit Georgia Resource Center in Atlanta . . . . [I]n March 1999, I signed my very first court paper as a lawyer: Motion for Stay of Execution. An unusual court paper for anyone to file, let alone a junior associate in the tax department at a large firm in New York City.

A few weeks later I visited our new client on death row at the Diagnostic and Classification Center in Jackson, Ga. Many things I learned that day were trivial, yet I will never forget them. I learned that mentally retarded persons, like Larry Jenkins, usually look "normal." I learned that Larry spends 23 hours a day in his cell, mostly watching television. I learned that crocheting is the new hobby on death row. (Who knew? Apparently the prison gives the inmates plastic needles and yarn, and the inmates can send away for patterns.)

Larry had crocheted a picture of Jesus to give to Terri. . . . Larry and I talked about his favorite soap operas, "General Hospital" and "All My Children." Larry explained that he does his needlework during the commercials, because he has to pay full attention during the soaps. I learned that Larry was in ninth grade when he was arrested for murder. Finally we talked about basketball, which at least is something I know a little about. Larry confirmed that every hoops fan outside New York, including those on Georgia's death row, hates the Knicks.

I also learned on that day that I had a client who needed me. I have spent much of my three years in the practice of law feeling a bit daunted by the often surreal nature of my work — facing abstruse questions like whether the tax-straddle rules apply to prepaid forward contracts. Not exactly the cliffhanger material of "Law and Order" . . . . On Larry's case we argue about whether the jury would have sentenced this young man to death if he had received a fair trial. That's a prime-time question.

And the human connection to my client is more real than anything I've personally felt on a conference call. My billable work has been stimulating, challenging and rewarding . . . . But the one time in my short legal career I have not harbored any doubts about what I was doing was that afternoon when I walked out of that prison, thinking about needlework, soap operas, and Larry Jenkins. If I am ever asked what I accomplished before I turned 30, I will speak with pride about my work for Larry Jenkins. It is the one thing I have done so far with my J.D. that I will someday tell my grandchildren about.

. . . .

Many of the best and brightest law school graduates each year come to New York to work for big firms. We all have been fortunate enough to receive outstanding legal educations. Some of us have spent a year or two clerking for the federal courts and working on death penalty cases. We have a responsibility to put that training to use.

I urge you to speak up. Write a quick e-mail to the *pro bono* coordinator, or the recruiting coordinator, or a partner, at your firm. . . . Visit www.probono.net to get an idea of the resources that are available. Talk to the dedicated lawyers at local organizations . . . who stand ready to guide volunteer lawyers through the process. Talk to lawyers at other firms who have been involved with a case. The clients are waiting, and they need you.

NOTES

Victor Fleischer continues his work as a valued member of the New York City bar's capital punishment committee. There are several obvious points to be learned from this article. We mention two: First, while Fleischer calls for representation of those on death row without counsel, the call could be for many other indigent clients in many other situations — people on the verge of homelessness facing eviction without counsel, others in need of disability insurance such as SSDI who are too disabled to handle the paperwork themselves. Only the names — and the legal issues — are different. The stories, though, are no less compelling.

Second, Fleischer got as much out of the experience as the client, an experience that is very common. Clearly, many lawyers dedicate themselves devotedly to *pro bono* work. Significantly, however, despite the participation of these attorneys in both big firms and small — many of the attorneys who give the most time are small-firm and solo practitioners who simply integrate *pro bono* into their regular case load — and the joy they get from their experience, not only are there are far more in need of legal services than those receiving help, but the evidence is that the gulf is growing wider, as the statistics in section 3 above demonstrate.

While many private law firms do extensive *pro bono* work, some averaging as much as 100 hours or more per lawyer per year, others do little or none and others have individual lawyers who do *pro bono* but feel unsupported by their firms. "I do *pro bono* work myself and started a firm *pro bono* committee, but frankly, the committee consists mostly of me," complains one lawyer of our acquaintance, a partner in a 200-lawyer firm. "I get no support from my partners. Most of them think I'm wasting time — time I could turn into billable hours. So the associates I try to encourage are instead discouraged from helping me." Even in firms that extol the virtues of *pro bono* and emphasize their commitment, *pro bono* may not be accorded an equal status. Tellingly, while Crowell & Moring's hiring of a full-time *pro bono* coordinating lawyer is laudable, that lawyer occupies a non-partnership track position.

In other words, with the defunding of legal services programs, the recessions in the legal profession after 2000 and again from 2008 onward, and the pressures young lawyers feel to make a living and perform according to their superiors' expectations, a pervasive and increasing need for assistance exists.

7. A Call for Mandatory *Pro Bono*

Should every lawyer, as an ethical duty, be *required* to perform *pro bono* service? The issue has been debated for decades among legal services lawyers, bar association officials, and other representatives of both the profession and public interest groups. But little consensus has been reached.

One of the most compelling and widely discussed and reproduced statements favoring mandatory *pro bono* was the testimony of Orville H. Schell, then President of the Association of the Bar of the City of New York, before a U.S. Senate Judiciary subcommittee almost 40 years ago. Schell concluded not only that *pro bono* was "one of profession's principal obligations," but that there was "a longstanding general lack of commitment by lawyers" to do this work. Most controversial was his view that *pro bono* service should be mandatory: "Not to have it enforceable will leave the providing of these services right where it is now, on the shoulders of a few lawyers of good will while the great majority go merrily on their way." Moreover, Schell took the position that lawyers could neither buy themselves out of doing *pro bono*, nor fulfill it by doing good works — such as for churches or schools — that were not legal services.

Schell's reasoning did not rest on the frequently advanced theory that lawyers hold a monopoly on legal work through their licensing; he pointed out that "plumbers and TV repairmen" were also licensed. Instead he cited lawyers' role in the administration of justice:

> "I am now convinced, as a philosophical matter that lawyers, unlike groups such as plumbers, manufacturers of can openers, oil barons (unhappily), undertake an obligation to the public when they enter the bar. That obligation is to devote some portion of their professional life to the delivery of legal services at non-compensatory rates, or no fees at all."

> "Believing, then, that the profession does have such an obligation, I submit that, one way or the other, it must be made an enforceable obligation."[15]

Schell's remarks, given much play at the time, were immediately controversial. Some argued that "mandatory *pro bono*" was indentured servitude, others that it was an oxymoron — after all, how could anything done *pro bono* be "mandatory"? Nothing much came of his pronouncement other than to set the stage for future debate. Moreover, in addition to raising the fundamental question of whether *pro bono* work should be required at all, Schell's statement contained many of the elements of what has become a long-running continuing debate on mandatory *pro bono*. Among them are these:

> • Should lawyers be entitled to buy themselves out of participation in *pro bono* by paying a fee, or by allowing more junior lawyers in their firm to do the work for them, or must everyone participate, as Schell believes?

> • Should doing non-legal community service suffice, or is the very nature of *pro bono* work legal?

---

[15] Testimony from the U.S. Subcommittee on Judiciary subcommittee, February 3, 1974.

• Should the *pro bono* work necessarily be on behalf of poor people, or should work "on behalf of the legal system or legal profession" also be allowed?

• Should those in public interest work or in the public sector also be required to do *pro bono*?

• What about sole practitioners who claim they struggle to make it as it is, and who see many potential clients whom they consider "*pro bono*" because they provide these people uncompensated advice without it resulting in a case? And, as always,

• How will *pro bono* projects be funded?

Let us add one other question: Should "*pro bono*" include work that, if successful, might result in a substantial attorneys' fee award to the law firm? We know of several firms that have appeared to base their selection of *pro bono* "impact" cases on the likelihood of being awarded fees down the road. We question whether that is truly "*pro bono*" or more in the nature of a contingency fee case.

8.   Should — and Can — Mandatory *Pro Bono* Be Legislated?

The legal system faces ever increasing demands for access to the courts. In a separate arena, alternate law-school educational model proposals, such as two-year law school degrees followed by "apprenticeships" that provide limited representation to the underserved, are being seriously circulated. The timing may be right to revisit the discussion on mandatory *pro bono*, despite historical opposition.

Interestingly, some of those most strongly in favor of mandatory *pro bono* have been attorneys from larger, well-established firms who, like Orville Schell, who see a clear professional obligation. These lawyers also understand that associates who wish to do *pro bono* in a law firm with little *pro bono* history are likely to encounter enormous resistance unless they are fulfilling a requirement of the profession.

Just as interesting is the fact that some of the strongest opponents of mandatory *pro bono* are legal services attorneys themselves, who feel that forcing a lawyer to do *pro bono* may provide their programs with "volunteer" attorneys who are neither ready nor willing to do the job, nor motivated to learn. Many public service lawyers would rather see the money that would be spent for mandatory *pro bono* systems going to enhance their own programs' limited budgets.

The debate over defining what constitutes *pro bono* continues to cause controversy. In the late 1990s, that controversy exploded after a Colorado advisory committee recommended a minimal mandatory *pro bono* scheme. This recommendation was well thought through — the product of an 18-month effort by a committee of the state's Judicial Advisory Council. "It is the best way to increase the level of services," Ed Kahn, co-chair of the council's legal services committee, told the *ABA Journal*. "It won't solve the problem, but if we increase the level of services, it will be a substantial step in the right direction."[16]

The step the committee recommended was modest: lawyers would have to give 25 hours of *pro bono* service a year, at least half which would be free legal work to the needy. A "buyout" clause would have allowed those who preferred to pay $1000 in lieu of doing the work, with the money designated for legal service.

But lawyers deeply resented the idea. According to the ABA Journal, there was "intense opposition from almost every bar organization around the state." A survey by the Denver Bar Association showed 90% of its members opposed the plan. By June 1999, not only was this proposal disapproved by the Colorado Supreme Court, but the court also refused to implement a reporting requirement similar to that instituted in Florida in 1993 (discussed below).

Does that mean the issue died completely in Colorado? No, but change is slow and usually incremental. In 2005, Colorado Rule of Civil Procedure 260.8 went into effect. This rule, like similar rules in a growing number of states, among them Delaware, New York, Tennessee, Washington, and Wyoming, permits lawyers who provide *pro bono* representation — or who mentor law students or other lawyers — to receive one hour of continuing legal education credit for every five otherwise-billable hours of *pro bono*, to a maximum of nine credits for each 3-year compliance period. Work for a bar association or "access to justice" organization may count towards CLE.

This plan met with little resistance, and had the co-sponsorship of many of Colorado's major bars. But at nine credit hours every three years, lawyers will "max out" at 45 billable hours, or only 15 hours a year. Thus, this new rule is hardly ambitious, especially compared to the previous proposal.

When the Florida Supreme Court approved a plan that would require every lawyer in the state to report each year the amount of free services that lawyer provided to the poor, it was the first of its kind in the country. This does not amount to mandatory *pro bono*. It is only a reporting requirement; actually doing the work is *not* required. Those who report that they have not done *pro bono* work can expect to have their names publicized by the bar. But this was enough to have one lawyer who heads a group emphasizing "lawyers' rights" to compare the reporting and disclosure tactics to McCarthyism. Indeed, the plan was challenged on due process and equal protection grounds, but upheld by the Eleventh Circuit in *Schwarz v. Kogan*, 132 F.3d 1387 (11th Cir. 1998).

The Florida plan makes several concessions. One exempts judges and many government attorneys, while another allows law firms to "collectively discharge" their obligation by having a few in the firm do *pro bono* work not only for themselves but on behalf of their colleagues as well. The rule also contains a provision allowing lawyers to buy out of the requirement for a $350 per year donation to legal aid, an idea that troubled Chief Justice Rosemary Barkett enough to cause her to voice her objections in a concurring opinion.

Finally, the Florida plan reached an interesting balancing test on the significant issue of defining *pro bono*. The court held that the work must involve "legal services

---

[16] Debra Baker, *Mandating Good Works*, ABA JOURNAL (March 1999).

to the poor" and the "working poor." But the court also said that working with charitable, civic, religious, or educational organizations might qualify if the work is done "in matters predominantly designed to address the needs of poor persons."

The Florida plan did require work for "the poor." Should "freebies for friends of friends," also count toward *pro bono* work?

The Florida plan remains a work in progress that has not been widely adopted elsewhere. As Colorado Supreme Court Chief Justice Mary Mallarkey put it, "we view the mandatory reporting as a step toward the imposition of mandatory *pro bono* requirements. Since we are unwilling to arrive at that destination, we are also unwilling to take the first step."[17] Nevertheless, the Florida Bar has reported that the plan had materially increased *pro bono* participation among the state's attorneys. But many lawyers who have long *pro bono* histories boycotted the reporting requirements, at least in the rule's early years, on the grounds that it was both offensive and too little.

9. *Pro Bono* from All Lawyers, Starting at the Top

Northwestern University Law Professor Steven Lubet argues that representing the poor is not a political issue, but one of professionalism, with service as the professional ideal, to be undertaken by all. We excerpt the portion of his law review article that focuses on the "real world" practice of law — here, on the 11th floor of a courthouse in Chicago, and the arrival on that scene of a famous lawyer.

Steven Lubet, *Professionalism Revisited*
42 Emory L.J. 197 (1993)[18]

[P]ro bono obligations [are] personal . . . . I call [it] the Eleventh Floor Principle, and it is best explained through a vignette from my own early days in practice.

For two years after I graduated from law school, I worked in a legal services office on Chicago's west side. From my first day on the job I became our office's "consumer law expert,"which required me to spend considerable time in the courtrooms on the eleventh floor of the civic center. . . .

In the early 1970s the eleventh floor was a no-man's land for poor people. It housed the landlord-tenant and collection courts, and therefore saw an endless stream of hapless individuals come before the bench to be processed. The all but inevitable outcome of every case was either an eviction or a wage garnishment . . . . The defendants were almost always unrepresented. If they had defenses, they had no way of recognizing or raising them. The best result that a defendant could hope for, whether liable or not, was usually a few extra days in his or her apartment or a few extra months to pay a debt.

---

[17] *See, e.g.,* Sue Lindsay, *Lawyers Won't Be Forced Into Free Work,* Rocky Mountain News, June 3, 1999.

[18] Copyright © 1993 by Emory Law Journal and Steven Lubet. Reprinted by permission of the author.

The worst feature of the eleventh floor, however, was not the judgments that were entered [but] the way that the defendants were treated. The judges were nasty and peremptory. They rushed through the cases without allowing the defendants to talk, and they ridiculed defendants who attempted to say a few words in their own behalves. The clerks and bailiffs were worse, refusing to answer questions or to give explanations. The only advice they would give was "sit down and wait until your case is called." . . .

Every courtroom on the eleventh floor seemed to operate in continual bedlam. The plaintiffs' attorneys were always huddled and talking to each other. The clerks were always shouting orders to the ill-fated defendants. The judges were also barking out their judgments — seven days to move, thirty days to pay, add on the attorney's fees, and do not ask any questions. To me, the noise represented the character of the entire place; I thought of it as the din of injustice.

Legal services lawyers were seen as interlopers, people who wanted to ruin everyone else's easy time. We were tolerated, but just barely. I think that the judges considered us to occupy a position about half a step higher than the indigent defendants. These were courtrooms badly in need of reform.[19]

Then one day, when I was sitting in one of the worst courtrooms waiting for my daily portion of judicial abuse, it happened. A pinstriped, downtown lawyer walked up to the bench and said, "Your Honor, I would like to present Mr. Albert Jenner." In 1975, the late Albert Jenner was probably the most well known and widely respected lawyer in Chicago. A named partner in Jenner & Block, he was most famous as the Republican counsel to the Senate Watergate Committee. Many believed that Mr. Jenner was the man most responsible for the eventual committee vote to impeach President Nixon. His visage — stern countenance, ramrod posture, piercing eyes, and signature bow tie — was well known to every Chicagoan who owned a television set. Albert Jenner was a man of unrivaled prominence, integrity, and power, and he had apparently come to the eleventh floor as a favor to a friend or employee.

Once Mr. Jenner's presence was announced, the entire courtroom suddenly metamorphosed. The muttering plaintiffs' bar fell silent. Clerks began answering inquiries from unrepresented defendants. The judge actually asked questions about the facts and the law. It was as though we were now in a real courtroom where justice, and people, mattered . . . .

More than anything else imaginable, the unexpected presence of an important lawyer recast procedures on the eleventh floor. The judges and court personnel began to worry about how they appeared. Instead of facing only disinterested regulars and perceived no-accounts, they now had to be concerned about the well-to-do and powerful. For the rest of that day it was possible to practice law on the eleventh floor as though we were in a real courtroom. By the next week, unfortunately, the residual effects of Mr. Jenner's visit had worn off . . . . There is a lesson in this digression. The presence of a prominent lawyer can have a

---

[19] [28] I am not suggesting that defaulting tenants should not be evicted or that deadbeats should not be compelled to pay their debts. I am not arguing for "politically biased" outcomes. Rather, my point is that the process was bad. . . . Respect for the law was diminished and neutral justice suffered. . . .

transformative effect on a courtroom. And there are many courtrooms that are in serious need of transformation. While the eleventh floor of the 1970s might have been unique in its combination of clerical squall and juridic torpor, there are numerous others today that differ only as a matter of degree.

. . . .

Again, it is not "politically biased" to say that justice is best done in the sunlight . . . . Eleventh floor type courts are essentially lawless in that they operate without reference to the norms, rules, and procedures that are intended to govern our judicial system. The required presence of important lawyers at all levels of the judicial system would provide a robust corrective against this hazard.

NOTES

What is Professor Lubet's point? Is it that when *every* lawyer, no matter how great or "important," participates, not only the poor but the entire system benefits? Is it that Jenner dignified both the courts and the poor people who appeared there?

Finally, what if the potential *pro bono* attorney we're talking about is *you*, not Albert Jenner? Do you agree that it will be *your* responsibility as a lawyer to do *pro bono* work? If so, should we legislate such an obligation to make it part of the privilege of practicing law? Is Orville Schell correct to distinguish lawyers from plumbers, the manufacturers of can openers, and oil barons? If he is, does that make lawyers' obligations to the needs of society different as well?

10.   How About Our Law Schools?

If lawyers are encouraged to contribute *pro bono* work, what about law students? Or law professors? Increasingly, law schools are providing opportunities to do *pro bono* work, both through clinical programs that represent people too poor to otherwise afford a lawyer, and stand-alone *pro bono* programs, often largely student-run. Left on their own, however, with only the spirit of volunteerism to guide them, it can be hard for law students to step forward to participate in *pro bono* service. When Robert Doggett did, he found it was a hard sell when he tried to enlist others.

Now it may be getting a bit easier. First, many law schools have, if not jumped, at least stepped onto the *pro bono* wagon. There are two law school models. The first is a pure *pro bono* model, in which students earn no academic credit for their work with the underserved. By 2010, 18% of law schools responding to the ABA now *require* an average of 35 hours of such service in order to graduate. The second is to consider at least some in-house live-client clinical opportunities as *pro bono*. According to an ABA Survey, by 2010 over 85% of responding law schools offered in-house live-client clinical opportunities.[20] One can argue that clinical programs, while extremely valuable, are not pure *pro bono* programs, since students receive credit toward their law school degrees, and also because some

---

[20] *A Survey of Law School Curricula: 2002–2010*, ABA, Catherine L. Carpenter, (Ed. P4 of Executive Summary).

clinics do not serve the traditionally underserved.[21]

No matter the definition of *pro bono* one uses, however, we have heard from countless lawyers, many of them former students, that their *pro bono* experience was the most gratifying work they've done. While preliminary data available thus far do *not* necessarily support the conclusion that encouraging *pro bono* in law school leads to doing more *pro bono* work in practice,[22] whether this is borne out can only be answered with more data.

There will soon be more opportunities to gather that information, because, starting in 2015, law school graduates from any law school will be *required* to complete 50 hours of *pro bono* work before being admitted to practice in New York. Under this program, participation in a live-client clinical program may be counted towards those hours.

Why institute this requirement? According to the September 2012 Court of Appeals press release, it is that there is "more needed to be done to bridge the continuing access to justice gap, which, exacerbated by the tenuous economy, has resulted in thousands of litigants who cannot afford legal representation to pursue their basic rights involving housing, family and other essential matters." In the words of Chief Judge Jonathan Lippman, the force behind the program:

> "There should be no higher aspiration for a lawyer than to work in the public interest, with this new rule going a long way to foster the values of *pro bono* legal assistance and public service that are so fundamentally rooted in our profession, providing prospective attorneys with valuable experience in areas of the law that serve the greater good and promoting such engagement as a regular part of their professional lives."[23]

Although no state has turned its immediate attention from mandatory *pro bono* for students to mandatory *pro bono* for practicing attorneys, so far reaction to the law student plan has been surprisingly positive. No state has yet followed suit on the *pro bono* pre-admission plan either, although little time had passed as we went to press. California, Massachusetts, and New Jersey were all exploring such a rule. The March 2013 ABA Journal called the New York rule a "Change Heard Round the World," and quoted Pro Bono Institute President Esther Lardent, as saying that "[w]hile it's a New York rule, it really has implications beyond New York."[24] And the addition of California could have "a ripple effect throughout the country."[25]

---

[21] Leigh Jones, *Want to Graduate? Brush Up on Your Pro Bono*, 79 MIAMI DAILY BUS. REV., May 13, 2005.

[22] *See* Robert Granfield, *Institutionalizing Public Service in Law School: Results on the Impact of Mandatory Pro Bono Programs*, 54 BUFF. L. REV. 1355 (2007), and Scott L. Cummings, Rebecca L. Sandefur, *Beyond the Numbers: What We Know — and Should Know — About American Pro Bono*, 7 HARV. L. & POL'Y REV. 83 (2013).

[23] Both quotes are from the press release of the Chief Administrative Judge of New York, www.nycourts.gov/press, September 19, 2012.

[24] James Podgers, *New York's new rule requires bar applicants to perform 50 hours of pro bono*, ABA JOURNAL, March 2013.

[25] Karen Sloan, *Pro Bono Mandate Gains Steam*, THE NATIONAL LAW JOURNAL, April 22, 2013, *available*

What do you see as an appropriate *pro bono* requirement for law students? Should it be mandatory at all? Or *for* all? Should clinics not be counted as *pro bono* because students are "getting" something, including credits towards their degree? Or could it be simply a requirement students just have to fulfill? If mandatory, is 50 hours before gaining bar admission enough? What about requiring faculty members' participation? Would this encourage you as a student?

D.   SUPPLEMENTAL READINGS

1. Glenn Cohen's article *Rationing Legal Services*, 5 J. OF LEGAL ANALYSIS 221 (2013), provides an extensive discussion of issues to be considered when allocating resources to needed services, analogizes to rationing in the international medical field, and concludes by suggesting eight tangible recommendations he believes could be adopted without overwhelming administrative burden or cost.

2. Scott L. Cummings & Rebecca L. Sandefur, *Beyond the Numbers: What We Know — and Should Know — About American Pro Bono*, 7 HARVARD L. & POL'Y REV. 83 (2013), provides an excellent overview of *pro bono* as an introduction to a report on the "New Measurement" movement that is beginning to gather information to answer the question of whether *pro bono* is an effective or efficient way to provide access to justice.

3. Deborah L. Rhode, professor of law and director of Stanford's ethics center, has written extensively about the need for lawyers' *pro bono* commitment. *Cultures of Commitment: Pro Bono for Lawyers and Law Students*, 67 FORDHAM L. REV. 2415 (1999), discusses the meaning of *pro bono* and the various ways it can be implemented in a law school setting, and reviews what has been done to date. *Pro Bono in Principle and in Practice: Public Service and the Professions*, STANFORD LAW AND POLITICS (2006), includes an extensive empirical study that demonstrates how little *pro bono* work the average lawyer does and how much is thus left undone.

4. Abner J. Mikva, *Casualties of the Salary War*, law.com, AMERICAN LAW MEDIA and THE RECORDER [San Francisco], May 3, 2000, gives us the perspective of this former chief judge of the D.C. circuit, member of Congress, and chief White House counsel about the dearth of *pro bono* in light of today's salaries and hourly demands.

5. More recent work by Deborah Rhode (here with Scott Cummings) provides a systematic look at the professionalization of *pro bono* programs in large firms and the challenges they face in the current economic climate. Scott L. Cummings & Deborah L. Rhode, *Managing Pro Bono: Doing Well By Doing Better*, 78 FORDHAM L. REV. 2357 (2010). They find that *pro bono* programs are profoundly shaped by the interests of law firm lawyers, evident in the emphasis placed on the satisfaction of lawyers rather than clients. They conclude with a series of recommendations on how firms might enhance the quality of *pro bono* work and at the same time better assist clients in need.

---

at   http://www.law.com/jsp/nlj/PubArticleNLJ.jsp?id=1202596770850&Pro_Bono_Mandate_Gains_ Steam&slreturn=20130420011104.

6. Reed Elizabeth Loder, *Tending the Generous Heart: Mandatory Pro Bono and Moral Development*, 14 GEO. J. LEG. ETHICS 459 (2001), looks at *pro bono* from the perspective of moral theory. Professor Loder argues that while one can't teach morality by insisting on *pro bono*, doing this work often enhances lawyers' moral development.

7. Lawrence J. Fox, *Should We Mandate Doing Well By Doing Good?*, 33 FORDHAM URB. L.J. 249 (2005), is an article by a noted ethics guru *and* recipient of the ABA's *Pro Bono* Publico Award. Fox announces his recent conversion to the belief that *pro bono* work should be mandatory and explains his reasoning in thoughtful and clear terms, including the monopoly lawyers continue to have on legal services.

8. Michael Millemann, *Mandatory Pro Bono in Civil Cases: A Partial Answer to the Right Question*, 49 MD. L. REV. 18 (1990). An excellent comprehensive survey of the history of *pro bono* in the Anglo-American tradition of jurisprudence, and his suggestion, as the title implies, of requiring such *pro bono*.

9. The ABA's THE PROFESSIONAL LAWYER has two 2012 point-counterpoint articles on recent the New York mandatory *pro bono* requirements. In support is Benjamin P. Cooper, who has written *Mandatory Pro Bono for New York Bar Applicants: Why Not?* Douglas R. Richmond, in *A New York State of Mind*, is not convinced. (THE PROFESSIONAL LAWYER, Vol. 21, No. 3, at pages 3–5 and 6–8 (2012).)

10. For student perspectives on the value of *pro bono* programs in law schools, see Vance Salter and Jan Jacobowitz's anecdotal report *As The Twig Is Bent: Law Student Insights Regarding Pro Bono and Public Interest Law*, 86 FLORIDA BAR JOURNAL (May 1, 2012), *available at* http://ssrn.com/abstract=2227409, and learn what these students have found out about *pro bono* and themselves.

11. In *Beyond Externships and Clinics: Integrating Access to Justice Education into the Curriculum* (October 15, 2011), Cynthia F. Adcock provides a succinct summary of clinical and *pro bono* programs today. *Available at* http://papers.ssrn.com/sol3/papers.cfm?abstract_id=2060323.

12. One proposed solution to providing at least some access to the court system for people of limited means has been the development of limited performance agreements, and new rules in many states that allow for limited-scope representation (or "unbundled services"). Stephanie Kimbro, *Using Technology to Unbundle in the Legal Services Community*, HARVARD J. OF LAW & TECHN. Occasional Paper Series, February 2013 is an article on how best to unbundle legal services. Whether her operating premise — an assumption that legal services clients are not "deserving valuable full-service resources for legal cases that truly require the continuous, full attention of a licensed lawyer" — is correct or not, her article is valuable in helping to facilitate limited-scope representation.

PART FIVE

OTHER ATTORNEY CONDUCT ISSUES

Chapter 13

ADMISSIONS, DISCIPLINE, AND SOME OTHER RULES OF LAWYERING

Is there a difference between a business and a profession? What does it mean to be admitted to practice law? To retain a license to practice? What should members of the public be able to assume when they seek a lawyer? In this chapter, we look at professional conduct issues — admission and discipline — and also address a few issues not discussed elsewhere.

Is there a difference between a lawyer who is a licensed member of a profession and a businessperson who has learned about law and says "I am equipped to give legal advice"? We believe there is a significant difference. A great deal of business involves knowledge of the law but a being a "businessperson" does not equate to being a legal professional. What is the difference? As one modern dictionary states: A profession arises when any trade or occupation transforms itself through "the development of formal qualifications based upon education, apprenticeship, and examinations, the emergence of regulatory bodies with powers to admit and discipline members, and some degree of monopoly rights."[1]

The members of a profession often create and enforce their own performance standards. This is certainly true of law, where both the rules of ethics and decisions about bar admissions and discipline are determined almost entirely by professional organizations, subject only to court review. This works, argue professionals, both for their own mutual benefit and for the benefit of their clients, patients, or congregants. They say that the difference is not, as some claim, some sort of elitist belief that professionals are "better" than businesspeople, or lawyers "better" than plumbers. Neither is the difference one based on training and expertise, as there are many experts in many trades, business and plumbing among them. The difference may be partly explained by the formal nature of a lawyer's licensure. But many, even most, fields require, or at least prefer, some sort of license — from securities trader to contractor to plumber.

We believe that what most distinguishes a professional relates to the expectations a member of the public has about what the professional knows and does, what is expected from that professional in terms of quality of the work, and what happens if that person fails. Someone who seeks help from a professional can and should assume not only that the professional has a sufficient base of knowledge and has made a commitment to follow the rules of the profession, but also that the individual has made a commitment to put the client's or patient's needs before his or her own

---

[1] ALAN BULLOCK & STEPHEN TROMBLEY, THE NEW FONTANA DICTIONARY OF MODERN THOUGHT 689 (London: Harper-Collins, 1999).

desire for gain. Unlike in business, with a professional, such as a lawyer, one should never need to say *caveat emptor.*

The discipline of legal ethics is largely about the standards American lawyers have created for themselves: standards created because of the understanding that the services lawyers provide to clients are an essential component to the existence of a civil society. Lawyers' professional discipline is rarely regulated by an independent state agency; rather regulation is done by legal entities — usually a state bar or the courts. Most lawyers believe that without regulation internal to the profession, attorneys run the risk of losing their professional independence, and independence of judgment and action on behalf of their clients helps protect a functioning civil society. In this chapter, we discuss how lawyers create and enforce these standards and some of the tensions that come when there are pressures to relax or eliminate those standards.

A.   ADMISSION TO THE BAR

There are three principal requirements for admission to the bar: extensive education, passing a bar examination, and being found to be of good moral character. These requirements are supposed to help guarantee that those who hire attorneys, whether mega-corporations or individuals of modest means, can assume their lawyers are competent, diligent, and willing to put their own interests aside in favor of their clients' interests. The first two, extensive education and passing a comprehensive bar examination, address general competence. The third, a determination of good moral character, addresses whether an otherwise well-trained person will perform honorably and within the bounds of ethical propriety.

Though the image of lawyers has become tarnished in the past few decades, and despite a significant decline in the number of law school applicants since 2010, becoming a lawyer remains a popular career choice. This is still the case although students in the United States face more rigorous requirements before being admitted to the bar than do students in any other Western country, with the exception of Canada. In this chapter, we first look briefly at educational and examination requirements for admission, then evaluate what is meant by "good moral character," and finally take a look at how the modern practice of law is affected by our federal system, in which each jurisdiction has its own set of standards of admission.[2]

The American Bar Association keeps data on various indicators including the number of lawyers nationwide. In 2012, the ABA reports that the legal profession looked like this:[3]

---

[2] Requirements for obtaining a license to practice law are available online from the American Bar Association Section of Legal Education and Admissions to the Bar and the National Conference of Bar Examiners (NCBE) at www.abanet.org/legaled/bar.html.

[3] http://www.americanbar.org/content/dam/aba/migrated/marketresearch/PublicDocuments/lawyer_demographics_2012_revised.authcheckdam.pdf.

NUMBER OF LICENSED LAWYERS - 2011
1,245,205*

*Source: ABA Market Research Department, 4/2012

GENDER	1980**	1991**	2000**	2005**
Male	92%	80%	73%	70%
Female	8%	20%	27%	30%

**Sources: *The Lawyer Statistical Report*, American Bar Foundation, 1985, 1994, 2004, 2012 editions.

AGE	1980*	1991*	2000*	2005*
29 yrs. or less	15%	10%	7%	4%
30-34	21%	16%	12%	9%
35-39	15%	18%	14%	13%
40-44	9%	18%	15%	13%
45-54	16%	18%	28%	28%
55-64	12%	10%	13%	21%
65+	13%	10%	12%	13%
Median	39	41	45	49

*Sources: *The Lawyer Statistical Report*, American Bar Foundation, 1985, 1994, 2004, 2012 editions.

RACE / ETHNICITY	1990**	2000**	2010**
White, not Hispanic	92.6%	88.8%	88.1%
Black, not Hispanic	3.3%	4.2%	4.8%
Hispanic	2.5%	3.4%	3.7%
Asian Pacific American, not Hispanic	1.4%	2.2%	3.4%
American Indian, not Hispanic	0.2%	0.2%	—
Native Hawaiian or Pacific Islander, not Hispanic	.04%	.04%	—

**Source: 1990, 2000 U.S. Census, Bureau of the Census.

NOTE: U.S. Census considers Hispanic an ethnicity, not a race. Persons of Hispanic origin can be of any race.

These numbers provide a few different insights. First, while the percentages of women and racial minorities have grown, they have done so substantially more slowly in recent years than in earlier surveys, with the notable exception of Asian Pacific lawyers. Second, the profession is graying, growing older as post-World War II "baby boomers" age, as with American populace as a whole.

1. Educational Requirements and the Bar Exam

Completing a law school education requires adequate grades throughout a full curriculum, including many challenging doctrinal courses, extra requirements such as moot court, and in a growing number of schools clinical or experiential courses. Once an aspiring lawyer completes law school, however, America's federal system, and the fact that both procedural and substantive law vary widely from state to state, means students must be admitted to practice state by individual state. Each state and other venues, including the District of Columbia and Puerto Rico, has established its own requirements for admission. While some jurisdictions cooperate with others on their bar exams, for the most part passing a bar exam is required for each and every state where one wants to practice. Though there still are three states, California, Washington, and Vermont, that allow a would-be lawyer to "read the law" (i.e., to sit for the bar examination without having to attend law school), such individuals are increasingly rare. Almost all would-be lawyers in America have first completed seven years of higher education: four years in an accredited college plus an additional three years of law school.

Historically each state approved each law school whose graduates wanted to take that state's bar exam. Some, like New York, even approved each program of undergraduate education. With the development of American Bar Association accreditation standards, however, today's norm is for students who have completed a degree at an ABA accredited law school to be allowed to sit for the bar in the state(s) of their choice.[4]

Whether a law school graduate eventually becomes a lawyer may have a lot to do with where that student takes the bar exam because of the disparity in exam difficulty and bar-passage rates. For example, in California and New York, two states in which a large percentage of new lawyers want to practice, between 40% and 55% of those taking the exams fail, while some other states have pass rates above 80%.[5]

Some argue that the bar exam is a superficial hurdle and passage has little to do with a person's ability to practice law, while others argue it is an important measure of minimal competence that protects the public. Whether the bar helps protect prospective clients or helps protect those already in practice from competition, not only must every prospective lawyer take an exam (except in Wisconsin, where "diploma privileges" give graduates of Wisconsin law schools bar admission without an exam), the exams are ordinarily quite difficult. Most states also require that students pass the Multistate Professional Responsibility Examination, though the number of correct answers required to pass does vary from state to state. Generally, local federal rules allow admission automatically to the federal district courts within a state once that lawyer has been admitted to practice in that state's courts.

Attacks on bar examinations by those claiming they violate constitutional or antitrust protections have consistently failed. So have attacks based on concerns about the widely disparate standards from one state to another. The right of states to limit the number of times someone may take an exam has also been consistently upheld.[6]

---

[4] There are also a few states such as California with state-accredited law schools that are unaccredited by the ABA. Students who attend these schools may sit for the bar only in that particular state.

[5] http://focusbarreview.com/bar-exam-pass-rates-by-state.html.

[6] *See, e.g.*, Younger v. Colorado State Bd. of Law Exm'rs, 625 F.2d 372 (10th Cir. 1980); Poats v. Givan, 651 F.2d 495 (7th Cir. 1981).

More recently, challenges have been raised based on data that support the argument that the bar exam creates an unnecessary barrier to admission to practice and may be culturally biased. For example, an ABA report evaluating California's bar exam found that for the July 2004 exam, 74.6% of white takers passed, while only 48.2% of African-Americans, 53.4% of Hispanics, and 65.5% of Asians (grouped together here) succeeded.[7] There are no reported successful challenges to bar exams based on race or ethnicity,[8] but some of the experiments with the bar exam, and especially performance based testing (see the Multistate Performance Test (MPT)) have been introduced in the hope that the outcomes for test takers using the MPT will be racially neutral.

Under the Americans With Disabilities Act, 42 U.S.C. § 12101–12213, persons with learning disabilities are entitled to reasonable accommodations when taking the bar exam. The disability must be one that substantially affects a major life activity. Thus, the court in *Bartlett v. New York State Board of Law Examiners*, 2 F. Supp. 2d 388 (S.D.N.Y. 1997), allowed a woman with reading speed and comprehension problems several accommodations including: "double time" to take the exam; the use of a computer to answer essay questions; permission to circle multiple choice answers in the examination booklet as opposed to being required to draw in circles on an answer sheet; and a large-print version of the exam. On the other hand, Deanna Jones, a student at Vermont Law School, had to sue the National Conference of Bar Examiners (NCBE) in 2011 to get permission to use software she needed. She won, and although the NCBE tried to withhold her results, she passed the MPRE and the Vermont bar exam and has been admitted to practice.[9]

2.   What Should Race and Gender Have to Do with Law School Admission?

We address issues of diversity within in the profession in Problem 29 and briefly in section 1 above. What about getting into law school in the first place? The number of women at law schools continues to rise and some minority groups show substantial increases in law student population. But when it comes to African-American law students, enrollment may actually be decreasing.[10] At the University of California's Boalt Hall law school, the focal point of the Supreme Court's famed *Bakke* decision on affirmative action over 35 years ago,[11] there was a year after the

---

[7] ABA, *available at* http://www.abanet.org/minorities/publications/g9/v11n1/mountains.html. There is also interesting empirical data, developed primarily by Marjorie Schultz, a law professor at Berkeley, and her colleague Sheldon Zedeck, a psychology professor, that demonstrate a racial bias in the LSAT exam.

[8] *See* Pettit v. Ginerich, 582 F.2d 869 (4th Cir. 1978) and Delgado v. McTighe, 522 F. Supp. 886 (E.D. Pa. 1981) for two examples of where such challenges failed.

[9] Jones v. National Conference of Bar Examiners, 801 F. Supp. 2d 270 (D. Vt. 2011). *See* http://www.huffingtonpost.com/2011/08/08/deanna-jones-legally-blin_n_920843.html.

[10] John Nussbaumer, *Misuse of the Law School Admissions Test, Racial Discrimination, and the De Facto Quota System for Restricting African-American Access to the Legal Profession*, 80 St. John's L. Rev. 167 (2006).

[11] Regents of Univ. of Cal. v. Bakke, 438 U.S. 265 (1978), which held that race and ethnicity may be

passage of the anti-affirmative-action Proposition 209 in which only one African-American joined the entering class.

Douglas Laycock, Professor of Law at the University of Texas, has worked on affirmative action issues for legal teams representing both the University of Texas[12] and the American Law Deans Association as *amicus curiae* in *Grutter v. Bollinger*, defending affirmative action at the University of Michigan law school. In this excerpt from his article about affirmative action cases, he explains the underlying rationale for affirmative action in *Bakke* and *Grutter* and the current state of the law on "diversity" in the admissions process.

Douglas Laycock, *The Broader Case for Affirmative Action, Desegregation, Academic Excellence, and Future Leadership*
78 Tul. L. Rev. 1767 (2004)[13]

"Diversity" is the Supreme Court's chosen ground for upholding race-based affirmative action in admissions to higher education.[14] "Diversity" has multiple meanings, and the United States Supreme Court's opinion in *Grutter v. Bollinger* substantially expanded those meanings and shifted their base. But however defined, diversity is not the only reason for affirmative action, and perhaps not the best label for what diversity has grown to include.

. . . .

Affirmative action has been the most effective method, and generally the only effective method, of desegregating schools with highly selective admission standards. Perhaps least understood of all the reasons for affirmative action, directly considering race preserves selective admission standards and thus protects academic excellence. Affirmative action is needed to create a leadership class for a diverse American future, including the rapidly approaching time when some states will be led by their minority populations. Affirmative action is a partial remedy for the effects of past and present discrimination in public elementary and secondary education. And no race-neutral means work nearly as well . . . .

In his controlling opinion in *Regents of the University of California v. Bakke*, Justice Powell chose diversity as the ground for upholding race-based affirmative action in university admissions. In a system based on precedent, his solo choice created powerful incentives a quarter-century later for the lawyers representing the University of Michigan in *Grutter v. Bollinger* and *Gratz v. Bollinger*, and a prominent path of least resistance for justices inclined to uphold affirmative action in those cases . . . . And so the law is that affirmative action in university admissions is permissible because diversity in higher education is a compelling governmental interest.

For Justice Powell, diversity meant diversity of background and experience

---

taken into account in admissions, but only if done flexibly, and where race is not the sole factor considered for admission.

[12] Hopwood v. Texas, 78 F.3d 932 (5th Cir. 1996).

[13] Copyright © 2004 by the Tulane Law Review. Reprinted by permission.

[14] [1] *Grutter v. Bollinger*, 539 U.S. 306, 328 (2003).

within the classroom, for the purpose of improving the educational experience in that classroom. This was explicitly a First Amendment interest in the "robust exchange of ideas." His brief discussion contained just a passing hint about improved race relations; combining thoughts from the first and last sentences of a paragraph suggests that studying with racially diverse medical students might help future doctors "serve a heterogeneous population . . . with understanding."

For the majority in *Grutter*, diversity starts with Justice Powell's opinion and includes Justice Powell's meaning. But diversity in *Grutter* is a much broader concept, anchored more in racial justice and the values of the Equal Protection Clause than in the First Amendment. In the longer and more elaborated discussion in *Grutter*, diversity is about promoting racial tolerance and understanding; developing workers, citizens, and leaders for a racially diverse society; and preserving the legitimacy of American government. Diversity in Justice Powell's sense is a plausible reason for affirmative action in admissions; diversity in *Grutter*'s sense is a much better reason.

. . . Diversity is emphatically not confined to racial and ethnic diversity. If a university's admissions process considers race, it must also "meaningfully" consider "all factors that may contribute to student body diversity." But the Court twice pointed out that the university need not give equal weight to all diversity factors, and it upheld a Michigan program that gave special weight to "one particular type of diversity, that is, racial and ethnic diversity with special reference to the inclusion of students from groups which have been historically discriminated against, like African-Americans, Hispanics and Native Americans, who without this commitment might not be represented in our student body in meaningful numbers."

3.   Comparing Educational Processes: The Making of a Lawyer in America, Europe, and Asia

In most of the world, graduate education, whether in engineering, medicine, or law, is part of a student's undergraduate university education. Even though high school programs in many other countries are longer and often more rigorous than in the US, this still means that a newly qualified lawyer in Spain, for example, might be 21 years old and have taken only theoretical courses in law, while her sister in the States is at least 24 or 25 and has completed seven years of education after high school. The EU is working towards increasing consistency in legal education, through the "Bologna Process," which is designed to help harmonize education across all member nations and allow for lawyers from one country to represent clients in another. As with much of the harmonization of laws across the EU, the Bologna Process is still very much in development, but will be important for American lawyers to watch.

Looking beyond years in school as a measure of competence, some American law professors are more interested in emulating the period of apprenticeship found in commonwealth-based countries. Barristers in the United Kingdom, for example, must complete a "pupilage" in order to qualify for the kind of trial work that falls under that tier of the licensing system. And in Canada, *more* preparation is required than in the States: rigorous law school admission standards (24,000 applications for fewer than 2700 law school seats); three years of classroom study;

and a months-long "articling" — or apprenticeship requirement.[15]

In Asia legal education in the last century often was based on European models, mixed with traditional practice. Today, legal systems in Taiwan, Korea, and even China pay close attention to American systems and teaching modalities. One of the most interesting, to American eyes at least, is the experience of Japan, which in the late 1990s had only about 26,000 lawyers to serve the needs of over 100,000,000 people. For the new millennium, Japan adopted a series of significant reforms to its legal system largely based on American jurisprudence. Among these reforms was the creation in 2005 of over 60 graduate-level law schools, and a change to the bar exam designed to substantially increase the bar passage rates for law school grads and thus increase the number of lawyers. Before this change, only 2–3% of prospective lawyers passed the rigorous bar entry examinations. Under the new system, exam passage has increased to about 30%, but as in the United States, Japan has found the number of law school applicants dropping sharply since 2010, despite the still-small number of current practicing attorneys. Moreover, some — both within the bar and particularly more traditional academicians — have resisted the new changes. The jury is still out on whether law schools, at least at their current numbers, will thrive in Japan.[16]

4. In Search of a Uniform Definition of Good Moral Character

The third leg in gaining bar admission is a determination of good moral character, now a prerequisite for membership in every state. Definitions of "good moral character" are anything but uniform. Courts and state bars have done better establishing what good moral character is *not* than what it is; there are well over 100 cases in which courts have examined applicants' moral fitness to practice law. This negative definition, evolving over time, includes a connection between "good moral character" and contemporary politics. Today, for instance, the issue of sexual orientation would be unlikely to defeat one's effort to gain bar membership, but as recently as 20 years ago, acknowledged homosexuality, or even "cohabitation," could well have resulted in a negative "character" finding in some states.

The history of the "good moral character" requirement is permeated with politics and subjective judgments. In colonial times, Massachusetts required the approval of one's moral qualifications by three sitting judges. Given the strict Puritanical politics of the time, it is likely that the requirement also served as

---

[15] *See* Christopher Guly's three-part series on modern Canadian law schools in *The Lawyers Weekly*, September 24, October 1, and October 8, 2010, especially part 2, *Demand for Law Spots High*. The length of the apprenticeship varies somewhat from province to province.

[16] *See generally Symposium: Successes, Failures, and Remaining Issues of the Justice System Reform in Japan*, U.C. HASTINGS COLLEGE OF THE LAW, including Session 3 on legal education, September 7, 2012, for which co-author Richard Zitrin was a speaker, video *available at* http://hastingsmedia.org/Downloads/japan/JapanJusticeSys_session1_03.mp4; and the following: Miki Tanikawa, *A Japanese Legal Exam That Sets the Bar High*, N.Y. TIMES, July 10, 2011; Colin P.A. Jones, *Japan's New Law Schools: The Story So Far*, 27 ZEITSCHRIFT FSR JAPANISCHES RECHT 248 (2009). Setsuo Miyazawa, Kay-Wah Chan, and Ilhyung Lee, *The Reform of Legal Education in East Asia*, 4 ANNU. REV. LAW AND SOC. SCI. 333 (2008); and KAHEI ROKUMOTO, LEGAL EDUCATION, IN LAW IN JAPAN: A TURNING POINT, ch. 8 (Daniel H. Foote ed., 2007).

something of a political and religious loyalty test. Until the early part of this century, moral character was almost always determined colloquially through one's reputation and acquaintances. Those seeking to become lawyers usually belonged to families with ties to the legal profession. Few women, blacks, or Jews were admitted. In the South, until Reconstruction, membership was limited to those who could gain entrance to the state's Inns of Court, literally an "old boys" club open to very few.

Beginning in the 1890s and continuing into the 1930s, states began to adopt more systematic forms of background screening. Undoubtedly, the growing complexity and diversity of society had much to do with this. So did the growing immigrant populations. Also of importance was the emergence of large workers', populist, and radical movements that focused attention on the efforts to exclude political "undesirables" from the bar.[17]

Still, quite a few made it in. For instance, the National Lawyers Guild was formed by mostly Jewish radical lawyers employed by the federal Works Products Administration in New York City. One of the Guild's first campaigns was to send a brigade of volunteer lawyers to fight with the "Abraham Lincoln brigade" on the loyalist side in the Spanish Civil War.

In the years after World War II, the fitness issue, not surprisingly, was Communism. In 1957, the Supreme Court addressed the issue in two cases decided on the same day. In *Schware v. Board of Bar Examiners of New Mexico*,[18] the Court held that the New Mexico Bar could not exclude applicant Schware, a former Communist party member who had used aliases and had been arrested at numerous demonstrations, since those activities were 15 years old or more and Schware had no current negative comments about his character. The Court found that qualifications for bar admission "must have a rational connection with the applicant's fitness or capacity to practice law." In the second case, *Konigsberg v. State Bar of California*, the Court used the same "rational connection" standard in evaluating the propriety of asking an applicant about past Communist party participation.[19]

Because a lawyer's duty is ultimately to the public, any significant doubts about a Bar applicant's character have traditionally been resolved in favor of protecting the public by denying admission to the applicant.[20] But circumstances certainly vary. Bars are more likely to examine high profile cases closely, while other admissions matters not attracting public attention are more likely to slide through.[21]

---

[17] *See* JEROLD S. AUERBACH, UNEQUAL JUSTICE: LAWYERS AND SOCIAL CHANGE IN MODERN AMERICA (1976).

[18] 353 U.S. 232 (1957).

[19] 353 U.S. 252 (1957). Other cases have qualified this rule in various ways. See particularly, two cases decided together, In re Anastaplo, 366 U.S. 82 (1961), and Konigsberg v. State Bar of Cal., 366 U.S. 36 (1961), known colloquially as Konigsberg II; *see also* Baird v. State of Arizona, 401 U.S. 1 (1971), and Law Students Civ. Rights Research Council, Inc. v. Wadmond, 401 U.S. 154 (1971).

[20] Deborah L. Rhode, *Professionalism in Perspective: Alternative Approaches to Nonlawyer Practice*, 1 J. INST. STUD. LEG. ETH. 197, 199 (1996).

[21] Richard Zitrin, *The Moral Compass: Why the Bar Sometimes Overreaches on Discipline*, THE [SF]

To help clarify what is meant by "good moral character," the American Bar Association has issued a comprehensive list of relevant conduct that might warrant further inquiry before examiners decide whether the applicant is fit to practice law. The list includes:

- unlawful conduct
- academic misconduct
- making of false statements, including omissions
- misconduct in employment
- acts involving dishonesty, fraud, deceit, or misrepresentation
- abuse of legal process
- neglect of financial responsibilities
- violation of an order of a court
- evidence of mental or emotional instability
- evidence of drug or alcohol dependency
- denial of admission to the Bar in another jurisdiction on character and fitness grounds
- disciplinary action by a lawyer disciplinary agency or other professional disciplinary agency of any jurisdiction.[22]

The requirement of good moral character is ostensibly used as a forecast of how one might act as a lawyer. But there are no significant studies showing that character determinations are accurate. All disbarred or disciplined attorneys were once deemed of good moral character. Whether the estimated 0.2% denied admission nationwide based on character issues turn out any better — or any worse — than non-lawyers is not known. Some argue that the fact most lawyers don't "get into trouble" proves the value of the requirement. Prior bad acts are often seen as indicative of future bad acts. But clearly, there will continue to be constitutional limits on the use of "character" as a litmus test.

Yet bar associations may inquire into conduct that is arguably protected by the First Amendment. As one example, Paul Converse was denied admission by the Nebraska State Bar Commission for being what his own lawyer described as a "pain in the neck." He had demonstrated hostile, abusive, and disruptive behavior throughout his law school career, including threatening frivolous litigation, contacting the press when he felt slighted by his law school, and creating and marketing shirts featuring the law school dean in a compromising position. He argued that he could not be denied admission based solely on his inappropriate behavior. The Supreme Court of Nebraska, however, affirmed the denial.[23]

RECORDER and law.com on line, October 2, 2011 and Richard Zitrin, *The Moral Compass*, Column no. 5, unpublished, April 2012.

[22] A.B.A. Section on Legal Education & Admissions, Comprehensive Guide to Bar Admission Requirements, *2013 The Code of Recommended Standards for Bar Examiners.*

[23] In Re Converse, 602 N.W.2d 500 (Neb. 1999).

Another example is Matthew Hale, who was the head of a church that had as three of its major tenets the hatred of minorities, admiration of Adolph Hitler, and a belief in "RAHOWA," or racial holy war. Nevertheless, Hale declared that he would have no trouble taking the lawyers' oath to support the United States and Illinois constitutions. What do you think about whether being an avowed racist, standing alone, is sufficient grounds for rejecting bar membership? The Illinois hearing panel found that Mr. Hale's beliefs were in absolute contradiction to the letter and spirit of Rule 8.4(a), which in subsection (5) requires that a lawyer shall not engage in conduct that is prejudicial to the administration of justice. Specific examples cited by the hearing panel were to "not engage in adverse discriminatory treatment of litigants, jurors, witnesses, lawyers, and others, based on race, sex, religion, or national origin." While Hale was "absolutely entitled to hold these beliefs," said the panel, in its opinion those beliefs meant he did not possess the requisite character and fitness for admission to the practice of law. His application was denied, and the denial upheld.[24]

5.   Other "Character" Grounds for Denying Admission

We now look briefly at some of the other grounds that courts and bars have cited in making findings that an applicant is not of good moral character.

Lack of Candor. One of the most frequently cited reasons for denying admission is the failure to answer truthfully while applying for membership. False, misleading, or evasive answers on bar applications may, in and of themselves, be sufficient grounds for finding a lack of fitness to practice. For example, in the case of *In re Greenberg*, 614 P.2d 832 (Ariz. 1980), the Arizona Supreme Court held that falsely testifying before the bar's committee was enough of a breach of the duty of candor to deny admission based on lack of good moral character. The rules on this issue vary materially from state to state, but candor is generally a big-ticket item.

Conviction of a Crime. Felony convictions usually stack the cards against the applicant, although the passage of time after the completion of a sentence, coupled with clear rehabilitation, may result in leniency about admission in some states. This lenient attitude is by no means guaranteed and is applied unevenly. Admission is more likely after commission of a misdemeanor, but criteria are applied unevenly as are admissions with past felonies. In one California matter, a lawyer was admitted to practice less than 10 years after his Florida felony conviction for "grand larceny by check." Within a decade, he had been charged with several counts of disciplinable misconduct.[25]

Non-criminal Behavior. Sometimes applicants have not broken laws but have behaved in the past in such a way as to call into question their fitness to practice. This behavior could be anything from cheating on a high school physics test to underage drinking. Since most state bars put a premium on candor, it makes sense for applicants to candidly admit past transgressions such as prior illegal drug use

[24] In re Matthew F. Hale, M.R. 16075, Order of November 12, 1999; Hale v. The Committee on Character and Fitness of the Illinois Bar, 530 U.S. 1261 (2000).

[25] Matter of Drexel A. Bradshaw, State Bar of California case No. 06-0-14611.

even if it didn't result in criminal charges. But such admissions may then raise character and fitness questions.

One of the better-known recent examples of such an applicant is Steven Glass, the "star" of the movie *Shattered Glass*, the story of how a young journalist deceitfully invented dozens of stories that never happened and when discovered engaged in an elaborate cover-up. Some years after he was exposed, Glass went to Georgetown Law School and eventually moved to California. He passed the California bar exam in 2007, but the Bar's Committee of Bar Examiners, in charge of the admissions process, found that he had not shown he was of "good moral character." Glass appealed to the State Bar Court and convinced both a trial judge and the court's Review Department that he should be admitted. At trial, Glass acknowledged the gravity of his mistakes, but argued that he had shown by clear and convincing evidence that he had been rehabilitated. During the course of the trial, he presented 22 witnesses, including a federal judge who flew out to California to testify in person, two psychiatrists who were largely unrebutted by the Bar's Office of Trial Counsel (OTC) and a named-partner boss, for whom Glass worked as a paralegal, who testified to Glass's exceptional efforts during six years of a close working relationship.

Despite all that evidence and two court decisions in Glass' favor, the Bar's trial counsel decided to appeal the admissions decision to the California Supreme Court, where the matter stands as this book goes to press. What standard must an applicant in this situation meet? Is clear and convincing evidence enough? And how hard and long should bar examiners fight such decisions? Some people speculated that Glass' high visibility may have been part of why the California bar examiners were so adamant in fighting his admission. Is "setting an example" in a high visibility case a justifiable reason to refuse to accept the courts' decisions?

Drug Use. Drug use and drug dependency or abuse seem to be viewed differently than 20 years ago, perhaps as the result of all the students of the 1960s and since who are now active participants in the admissions and disciplinary process, not to mention holders of high office. Illegal drug use has often been excused when accompanied by strong evidence of rehabilitation and a substantial passage of time. Conviction for possession of a small quantity of marijuana has been held insufficient in several states to disqualify an applicant. The New Jersey Supreme Court has recognized that drug addiction is a treatable disease.[26] A prior criminal record, where all of the offenses were related to drug addiction begun as a teenager, and where 12 years had passed since such offenses and 13 since the last drug use, was held not to be grounds for denying admission in Maryland.[27]

Mental Health. Should law students have to worry about past mental health issues like this bar applicant?

> "So, I didn't realize that the character and fitness part of the Bar can ask for in-depth disclosure of all your mental health medical records until recently, and now I'm worried.

---

[26] In re Strait, 577 A.2d 149 (N.J. 1990).

[27] Application of A.T., 408 A.2d 1023 (Md. 1979).

"Background: I was diagnosed as depressed and then re-diagnosed as bipolar, in college, and have been on medication for about 5 years. Personally, I think I was just having severe anxiety (due to an abusive relationship at the time), but the medicine seemed to help, so I stayed on it. I haven't had any mental health counseling for about 3 years or any mental health problems or crises for at least 4 years, and the only thing I still do is take the medication. I am now in law school and have to see a psychiatrist for a re-evaluation as to whether to continue my prescription or go off the medication. I am worried because it seems like all the character and fitness questionnaires put bipolar in the same category as serious stuff like schizophrenia, so I am wondering whether: 1. I should see about getting rediagnosed *(sic)* as something other than bipolar (i.e. just anxiety), and 2. Whether going off the medication would be an important/essential thing to do in order to avoid any problems on the character and fitness section of the bar. Also, do I have to send them my mental health records from all of college, or just from law school? Do the records just need to include the conclusions of psychiatrists, or also all the notes of counseling sessions I had with regular counselors on campus? It seems totally invasive, stigmatizing and unfair that they ask for mental health records, and I wish I could have the freedom to get general counseling for the stress of law school without worrying about it, but I guess that's how things are."[28]

The mental health of applicants is something that has long been of concern to state bar boards. "The purpose is not to thin the herd of people admitted to practice, but to ascertain whether they're able to function," Erica Moeser, then President of the National Conference of Bar Examiners, told the *ABA Journal* in 2000. But how much attention should be focused on diagnoses and how much on the actual, observable behavior of the applicant? Partly in response to changes in perception about what mental health means, and partly in response to the Americans With Disabilities Act, state bars are changing what sorts of questions they ask about mental health. Because there have been so many changes on this issue — some bars, like Connecticut, eliminated all mental health questions to applicants and then added some back in — the most we can say is that how each state deals with the connection between mental health and the ability to effectively represent clients, is a moving target.

Financial Problems. The Supremacy Clause prevents a state from denying admission to the bar solely because of an applicant's filing for bankruptcy. Florida addressed the issue of debt decades ago, and held that the mere fact that debts are incurred beyond a debtor's present ability to repay is not sufficient to warrant denial of admission,[29] though where a precipitous bankruptcy was filed before even the first installment of a debt was due, that constituted grounds for denial of admission based on financial irresponsibility.[30]

---

[28] As found on www.top-law-schools.com/forums/viewtopic.php?f=3&t=89016.

[29] In re Groot, 365 So. 2d 164 (Fla. 1978).

[30] In re G.W.L., 364 So. 2d 454 (Fla. 1978).

Thus, money problems separate from bankruptcy have been held relevant in determining admission to the practice of law. In New York, *In re Anonymous*, 549 N.E.2d 472 (N.Y. 1989) denied admission to an applicant who had displayed an inability to handle finances and suffered a bankruptcy, but the court specifically found the bankruptcy not to be the sole reason for denial. More recently New York made waves when, in 2009, Robert Bowman, a graduate of UC Hastings College of Law, after finally passing the NY Bar on the fourth try, was denied admission because by then he had accrued more than $400,000 in student debt.

In light of the challenges faced by many law graduates to repay loans, especially loans not covered by Income-Based Repayment (IBR) and/or public service loan forgiveness (PSLF) programs, a Ninth Circuit decision in the spring of 2013 may provide some guidance to state bars considering student debt as a condition of admission. In *Hedlund v. Education Resources Inst.*, 718 F.3d 848 (9th Cir. 2013), the court applied the so-called *Brunner* Test[31] in holding that law graduate Hedlund's debt could not be discharged unless he proved three things: he could not maintain, based on current income and expenses, a minimal standard of living if required to repay the loans; his current financial situation was likely to persist for a significant part of the repayment period; and he had made a good-faith effort to repay the loans. The court then found that Hedlund, having met this test, could discharge the great bulk of his law school student debt in bankruptcy.

Personal Lifestyles. Recent decades have seen a material liberalization of how the courts look at applicants' private lives. Even in relatively conservative states courts have held that an applicant who is living with someone of the opposite sex outside of marriage would not today be denied admission,[32] and that it is not appropriate to ask an applicant about the commission of homosexual acts, since to do so would violate the *Schware/Konigsberg* "rational connection" standard.[33]

That is not to say that all personal behavior is acceptable. In In re Application of Wylie, 733 N.E.2d 588 (Ohio 2000), for example, the court held that an applicant seeking bar admission failed to establish that he possessed the requisite character, fitness, and moral qualifications for admission to the practice of law, where, *inter alia*, he had been charged with sexual harassment at the workplace.

Miscellaneous other issues: A law graduate violated bar-examination rules by continuing to write after time was called. She was allowed to reapply after one year.[34] A law graduate who is an undocumented alien has had bar admission put on hold while the Florida Supreme Court rules on a request from the Florida Board of Examiners as to whether undocumented aliens are eligible for admission to the bar. The case was still pending at our press deadline.[35]

---

[31] Brunner v. New York State Higher Education Services Corp., 831 F.2d 395 (2d Cir. 1987).

[32] Cord v. Gibb, 254 S.E.2d 71 (Va. 1979).

[33] In re N.R.S., 403 So. 2d 1315 (Fla. 1981).

[34] In re Application of Parker, 985 N.E.2d 476 (Ohio 2013).

[35] Case No. SC11 — 2568, Florida Board of Bar Examiners RE: Question as to whether Undocumented vs. Immigrants are eligible for admission to the Florida Bar, http://www.floridasupremecourt.org/pub_info/summaries/briefs/11/11-2568/Filed_03-07-2012_Respondent_Brief.

6. Some Problems of Multiple Jurisdictions

It is thought that New Jersey tries to be tough on bar admissions to discourage lawyers from New York and Pennsylvania, both bigger neighbors with large legal centers, from invading their courts *en masse*. Most states participate to some extent in a system of "reciprocity," which gives experienced counsel the opportunity to gain admission in another state based on that experience, a series of personal references, and sometimes a foreshortened (and much easier) bar examination. New Jersey does not, making it as difficult for experienced lawyers from a neighboring state to gain admission as it is for new law school graduates (maybe more difficult, since the experienced lawyer may be much less prepared or less willing to take a bar exam). Of course, anyone from Pennsylvania or New York who is ready and able to take the full New Jersey bar exam and pass it will still be admitted to practice in that state. But what about the federal courts, which after all are arms of the United States government? May the federal courts in New Jersey still restrict membership to New Jersey bar members? Yes, according to *In re Roberts*, 682 F.2d 105 (3d Cir. 1982), which noted that cases in federal court often rely on state law.

Although not itself an admissions case, the California Supreme Court's ruling in *Birbrower, Montalbano, Condon & Frank v. Superior Court*, 949 P.2d 1 (Cal. 1998) raised important issues about the practice of law in a "foreign" jurisdiction. *Birbrower* prohibited a New York law firm from collecting fees from a dissatisfied California client because the firm, in advising the client about settling a pending arbitration matter, had practiced law in California without a license. The *Birbrower* court broadly defined both "the practice of law" and "in California," implying that the latter term might include a "virtual" electronic presence without physically being in the state.

Despite some states' restrictiveness, the modern day practice of law is full of lawyers with national venues, especially those who work for companies that do business throughout the country. Within a few weeks of the *Birbrower* decision, the Hawai'i Supreme Court, which frequently adopts California judicial reasoning, decided *Fought & Co. v. Steel Engineering & Erection*, 951 P.2d 487 (Haw. 1998). The *Fought* court evaluated *Birbrower* both from the perspective of what constitutes the practice of law, with which it largely agreed, and what constituted a lawyer's presence in the state, where it diverged from the California case.

Before the Hawai'i court was the application of the phrase "within the jurisdiction." Fought, an Oregon company, used its longtime Oregon lawyer to advise it on issues relating to Hawai'i litigation over construction of Maui's airport. Fought also had local counsel. The court recognized that it was dealing with a case of first impression, then allowed Fought's lawyer to collect fees owed to Fought in the litigation as the prevailing party. The court noted that the fact that the dispute was litigated in Hawai'i should not in itself cost Fought the use of its trusted longtime counsel, particularly since counsel's advice was general, and was transmitted back in Oregon. Thus, the phrase "within the jurisdiction" was more

---

pdf. A similar case in California was mooted by 2013 legislation permitting such admission under specified circumstances.

narrowly construed than the *Birbrower* court's interpretation of "in California."

If private counsel represent their clients on an *ad hoc* basis, they can seek admission in the new jurisdiction *pro hac vice*, or for the purposes of the particular litigation. But what if they are in-house counsel? May a lawyer admitted in New York working as deputy general counsel in California advise a Delaware corporation about how to defend a lawsuit in federal court in Arizona? If some accommodation for this kind of situation is not made, the practical consequences for thousands of businesses and perhaps tens of thousands of lawyers are enormous.

By 1999, 14 states and the District of Columbia had decided to allow non-admitted house counsel to practice.[36] Several other states have tried to solve this problem by setting up two classes of practitioners, including one that would allow in-house counsel to do most of the transactional work required of them without having to pass the bar examination. Some years ago, in some of these states, in-house counsel themselves objected, railing against what they perceive as second-class status.[37] Over time, however, this legitimizing status proved too important in most venues, and many such two-tiered programs have developed in recent years.

A principal problem remains individual states' protectionism. For some small states, like New Hampshire, Nevada, and even New Jersey, though it has a much larger bar, protectionism may be perceived as necessary for survival of their bar. For others, like California or New York, the protectionism seems more like purely a desire for control. There has also been a concern raised that reciprocity agreements may allow individuals who take "easier-to-pass" bar exams in one state to then get "credit" when they come to California or New York, where passing the bar is much more difficult.

Nevertheless, almost all in the profession recognize that the practice of law no longer stops at the borders of each state. Large corporations and many individuals find themselves involved in legal matters that are increasingly national — and often international — in scope. Our nation and world continue to get smaller through better technology, quicker communication, and the use of the Internet. Many in the organized bar have not only begun to grapple head-on with the issue of how to deal with multijurisdictional practice, but have called for substantial change.

In 2000, the American Bar Association formed a commission to study multijurisdictional practice. That commission's work did not ultimately change the ABA rules, but the Ethics 20/20 Commission, which we've discussed earlier in this volume, addressed and reformed some of these same issues. In California, a Supreme Court advisory task force on multijurisdictional practice published preliminary recommendations in mid-2001 that broke materially from the court's reasoning in *Birbrower*. The task force recommended a "registration" procedure for in-house counsel, and, more significantly, a narrowing of the definition of "the practice of law" to allow out-of-state attorneys to perform more functions traditionally reserved for California-admitted lawyers, including in arbitrations

---

[36] Carol A. Needham, *Permitting Lawyers to Participate in Multidisciplinary Practices: Business as Usual or the End of the Profession as We Know It?*, 84 Minn. L. Rev. 1315 (2000).

[37] *See* Richard A. Zitrin, *In-House Outlaws?*, Cal. Law., December 1990.

such as in *Birbrower*. This thinking is hardly unique to California. Increasingly, bar groups have begun to recognize the need for a "national" bar, at least in general federal court practice and certain kinds of legal matters, such as the transactional advice given to Fought & Co. by its Oregon counsel on its Hawai'ian case, and for certain kinds of lawyers, such as in-house and public interest attorneys.

We addressed multijurisdictional issues in Problem 11, but for purposes of admission and discipline we note that many see the outcome as inevitable: the walls between the states crumbling, slowly at first for litigation and other matters unique to each state, but crumbling all the same. And discipline of interstate attorneys for "practicing law without a license" remains a controversial issue, rarely exercised, with the most common suggestion being the submission of out-of-state lawyers to the jurisdiction of the state in which they engage in work for their clients.

B. DISCIPLINE OF LAWYERS

1. An Overview of Lawyer Discipline

The highest court of each state, acting under its inherent judicial powers, has the ultimate decision whether to discipline an attorney admitted to practice before it.[38] In addition, all federal courts have similar authority that can be imposed independently of the states.

Where did these courts get these inherent powers? They generally declared them for themselves, reasoning that their state constitutions would not have provided for courts without some inherent ability to regulate those who appear before them. Without exception, courts' inherent powers to review and determine the suitability of lawyers to practice before them have been upheld. So, too, has been the power of courts to order the creation of an "integrated bar," meaning, one that requires all the state's lawyers to be members. These mandatory bars are sometimes set up by statute.[39] The emergence of an integrated bar in most states has given the courts a more effective way to enforce discipline, by using the bar as its investigative arm. While the way this is accomplished varies significantly from state to state, in most states, integrated bars serve to investigate instances of discipline, issue complaints, and conduct administrative hearings. In some states, this work still rests on the shoulders of volunteer lawyers.

There are many "Top Ten" lists of the reasons lawyers run into discipline difficulty. One representative and concise lists sets forth the top ten reasons clients file ethics complaints against attorneys as: failure by the lawyer to communicate

---

[38] It is difficult to provide definitive data comparing how states handle disciplinary complaints because of distinctions in terminology. The ABA Center for Professional Discipline does an annual report. Surveys from 1998–2011 appear on the Center's website: http://www.americanbar.org/content/dam/aba/administrative/professional_responsibility/2011_sold_final_report.authcheckdam.pdf.

[39] The formation and purposes of mandatory bars have been approved twice by the United States Supreme Court. *See* Keller v. State Bar of Cal., 496 U.S. 1 (1990) and Lathrop v. Donohue, 367 U.S. 820 (1961). In *Keller*, however, the Court circumscribed the ability of an integrated bar to take positions on political issues not directly related to the legal profession, since dues-paying members have no choice about their mandatory membership.

with the client; lack of diligence in working on the case; failure to keep client funds in trust; disagreements over fees; improper advocacy; personal behavior outside of law practice; incompetence; misleading advertising and solicitation; conflicts of interest; and revelation of confidential information.[40]

If, for one of these ten reasons or a multitude of others, the administrative hearing that follows filing and investigating a complaint results in a finding that the complaint against a lawyer is valid, a wide variety of sanctions may be imposed, from private or public reprimands to probation, often with conditions such as restitution, participation in counseling, or periodic audits of the practice by a monitor, to suspension and disbarment. Just as with criminal cases, plea bargaining is common in almost every state, with the respondent attorney often agreeing to a probationary period with certain conditions, possibly including an interim suspension, in order to avoid a more serious penalty. An attorney who fights the case through a hearing generally has the right to an adjudication before the state's supreme court. Since the proceedings are "quasi-criminal,"[41] due process safeguards are available to the respondents, albeit often with somewhat lax rules of evidence and with fewer of the constitutional exclusionary defenses available to criminal defendants.

For example, in *In Re Pressman*, 658 N.E.2d 156 (Mass. 1995), the court held that a lawyer who had testified before a federal grand jury pursuant to an order that his testimony could not be used against him in a criminal case was not immunized from use of that testimony in disbarment proceedings. The court held that state judges did not have to follow a federal trial judge's grant of immunity in a later bar proceeding involving Pressman's accepting bribes.

While it is not easy to discover the reasons people are denied admission to practice, every state has some system for publishing information about disciplined lawyers. Many states make it relatively easy to see what lawyers who got in trouble did and what the consequences were. California, for example, publishes monthly reports both in the Bar's own journal[42] and *California Lawyer*, a monthly magazine available to all California practitioners. And the Bar's own website publishes information under the name of each lawyer who has been disciplined beyond a so-called "private reproval."

Other states, like Illinois, make the information available but it takes quite a bit of time to sort through if one wants to know what the lawyers did and how they were punished.[43]

A few lawyers have also become legal journalists or columnists who write about discipline and other legal ethics issues. With a primary audience of lawyers, these lawyer-columnists can help readers understand how the disciplinary system works and what trends in discipline they foresee. In California, for example, Diane Karpman, who has a regular column, "Ethics Byte" in the California Bar Journal,

---

[40] Loren Singer, *Preventing Problems in Legal Ethics*, LEGAL INTELLIGENCER, April 26, 1996.

[41] In Re Ruffalo, 390 U.S. 544 (1968).

[42] *Available at* http://www.calbarjournal.com/June2013/AttorneyDiscipline/Disbarments.aspx.

[43] *See* http://www.iardc.org/co_recentdiscdec.html.

wrote recently about her perception that the California disciplinary pendulum, which she believes shifts every decade or two, is about to radically switch once again.[44] As evidence, she cites action taken by the Supreme Court of California, in referring 24 cases back to the State Bar Court for possible further discipline.

On the other hand, Richard Zitrin, this volume's co-author, writes a column called "The Moral Compass" for the San Francisco *Recorder,* a legal newspaper, and www.law.com, American Law Media's on-line presence. His three-article series sees the California bar's discipline system as ineffective and not changing for the better despite the 24-case "recall."[45]

In addition to legal journalists, the popular press often comments when it sees a trend. The Minnesota Star Tribune published an article titled, "Lawyer sanctions in Minnesota could set record; is economy a factor?" This story, which got wide coverage when the ABA Journal picked it up,[46] covered the facts that a record number of lawyers in Minnesota had been disciplined; suspensions have become increasingly harsh (30 days for telling an opposing lawyer he hoped she would "sleep with the fishes"; at least 15 months for having an affair with a divorce client and billing her for time spent having sex); and disbarments more frequent (a scheme to obtain tax credits on behalf of education software companies).

Can lawyers be subject to discipline for making false statements or misrepresentations in a private business transaction totally unrelated to his law practice? Yes, they can. *See, State Sav. & Loan Ass'n v. Cor* ey, 488 P.2d 703, 711 (Haw. 1971) 406 U.S. 920 (1972), *rehearing denied,* 407 U.S. 934 (1972) and *People v. Rishel,* 50 P.3d 938 (Colo. 2002), finding violations of Rules 8.4(b) (prohibiting a "criminal act that reflects adversely on the lawyer's honesty, trustworthiness or fitness as a lawyer in other respects") and (c) (prohibiting conduct involving dishonesty, fraud, deceit or misrepresentation), and 1.15(b) (requiring lawyers to deliver and account for funds and property). *Rishel* arose in connection with a lawyer's dishonest handling of pool of funds used for Rockies season tickets, unrelated to the provision of legal services).

Can lawyers pass responsibility for bad actions on by outsourcing work? No, they may not. Both the Bar Association of the City of New York and the ABA[47] allow outsourcing. The New York opinion offers an extensive six-step list for the outsourcing, including that the admitted lawyer (1) assumes responsibility for the work and assures its quality, (2) supervises the "off-shore" lawyers in "vigilant and creative" ways such as interviewing them and conducting reference checks, (3) sees that confidential information of the client is protected, (4) checks for conflicts that

---

[44] Diane Karpman, *Focus returns to tighter discipline with Supreme Court's return of 24 cases,* THE CALIFORNIA BAR JOURNAL, (State Bar of California) (July 2012).

[45] *The Moral Compass: Bar Discipline, Part 3: Solutions Difficult in Bar Discipline Problems,* THE [S.F.] RECORDER and law.com on-line, November 21, 2011; *The Moral Compass: Bar Discipline, Part 2: Sometimes Too Aggressive,* THE [S.F.] RECORDER and law.com on-line, October 3, 2011; *The Moral Compass: Bar Discipline, Part 1: How Bad? Really Bad,* THE [S.F.] RECORDER and law.com on-line, September 19, 2011.

[46] ABAJournal.com, posted May 14, 2013, 5:55 AM CDT by Debra Cassens Weiss.

[47] Ass'n of the Bar of the City of New York Formal Opinion 2006-3; ABA Formal Opinion 09-451 (August 5, 2008).

an off-shore (such as Indian) firm might have, (5) bills only the direct cost to the client, and (6) obtains advance consent from the client to outsource, particularly if the role of the off-shore firm is likely to be substantial. The ABA's opinion is less specific and less clear on the requirement of client consent. But clearly, as the New York opinion notes, passing the buck on competence to someone not in the country much less admitted in the jurisdiction is a non-starter.

Perhaps the most famous lawyer to be pursued by a state bar is President Clinton. On June 7, 2000, Little Rock lawyer Marie-Bernarde Miller was appointed by the Arkansas Supreme Court's Committee on Professional Conduct to pursue its recommendation for Clinton's disbarment. The complaint was based on a finding of contempt in which a judge concluded that the president had misled the court and opposing counsel in deposition testimony about the nature of his relationship with Monica Lewinsky. Previous Arkansas cases involving lying under oath had not resulted in disbarment. Ethics experts argued the propriety of setting an example or creating a higher level of responsibility for lawyers who hold public office, vs. the equal application of the law.

President Clinton agreed to give up his Arkansas law license for five years as part of a deal struck with the Arkansas Committee on Professional Conduct. Clinton acknowledged that some answers he gave about Lewinsky during a 1998 deposition were false and that he "knowingly gave misleading and evasive answers." However, he maintained that he did not intend to lie. Today the Arkansas Judiciary website lists William Jefferson Clinton as an attorney admitted since 1973 with no obvious mention of his suspension.

What about behavior that may not relate to conduct as a lawyer but is, let us say, downright offensive? The Legal Profession blog [http://lawprofessors.typepad.com/legal_profession/] often reports on behavior of this kind. For example, in 2011 a lawyer in Arizona was suspended for one year after yelling at two medical records clerks over the phone. He told one that she was "nothing but a slut who worked for a copy service." (He claimed that he had called her a "slug," but her testimony that she could tell the difference between "g" and "t" was apparently persuasive). When the attorney was told by a second records clerk that she would get back to him, he stated that he was so excited that he "just came all over himself." His defense that he was physically incapable of that profanity undoubtedly did not help his cause. In this context, one year may seem to some like light punishment.[48]

And finally, what about practicing lawyers who don't pay their student loans? The Illinois Bar reports that Olufemi F. Nicol, "who was licensed in 1994, was suspended for six months and until further order of the Court. At a time when he was earning a $190,000 annual salary from a Chicago law firm, he avoided in bad faith the repayment of approximately $78,000 in education loans guaranteed by the Illinois Student Assistance Commission."[49]

---

[48] In the Matter of a member of the State Bar of Arizona, Meyer L. Ziman, Bar No. 002624 PDJ 2011-9067.

[49] *See* http://iln.isba.org/blog/2011/09/26/illinois-supreme-court-disbars-12-suspends-43-censures-10.

2. Law Firm Discipline

Discipline usually comes down to an individual matter, even where the attorney claims the questioned conduct was motivated by intrafirm culture or solidarity, following a boss' orders, fear of getting fired, or defending one's client at any cost. Conversely, there is generally no imputed misconduct for the actions of others in the firm. But this may be changing. Thus, while individual attorneys are subject to criminal prosecution for their unlawful acts of misconduct, such as stealing their clients' funds, this criminal liability has only recently begun to be applied to law firms. In 1994, a New York trial court held that a law partnership could be indicted for the crime of fraud even though only one partner was actually involved.[50] New Jersey was the first state to impose law firm discipline when it reprimanded Jacoby & Meyers in 1997 for depositing trust account funds out-of-state, rather than in New Jersey banks. The New Jersey court relied heavily on a 1993 report of the New York Committee on Professional Responsibility, which, as we discussed in Problem 27 eventually led to New York becoming the first state to formalize law firm discipline. The New Jersey court, however, stopped short of fining the offending firm, deciding instead to study the issue of whether a fine would be proper. It remains to be seen how widespread law firm discipline will become, and what level of punishment will be permitted.

As we saw in Problem 30, most state bars now have drug and alcohol intervention programs that protect confidentiality for any disclosures made by attorneys seeking help. Some of these confidentiality "cones of silence" are stronger than the confidentiality required by the attorney-client privilege. While few question the value of these programs, many recognize that they create an inherent conflict with the disciplinary enforcement goals of the bar. To the extent addictions are considered diseases, the bar's programs must serve to treat and protect lawyers seeking help. But often, as we have seen, addictions are accompanied by professional incompetence, even client abandonment. To solve this dilemma, some jurisdictions have set up systems where lawyers seeking help can voluntarily retreat from practice for a period of time to participate in treatment, an idea we endorse.

3. Should Lawyers Discipline Lawyers?

Although discipline is subject to review by a state's highest court, in almost every state the day-to-day workings of the disciplinary system are conducted in-house by state bars or staffs of lawyers hired by courts for that specific function. Some argue that a system in which lawyers police lawyers is like having the fox guarding the henhouse. They see that in contrast, physicians, psychologists, and other mental health professionals are usually disciplined by an independent state agency or an arm of the state's attorney general. On the other hand, disciplining one's own profession has long been regarded as a component of professionalism.

In 1992, the ABA Commission on Professionalism reported that while discipline in most states was conducted in a much more professional manner than it had been

---

[50] People v. Lessoff & Berger, 1994 N.Y. Misc. LEXIS 33 (Feb. 4, 1994).

20 years before, the mechanisms of lawyer discipline still left many problems unsolved. First among these problems was the continued failure to have a truly independent enforcement scheme. Among the other problems noted by the ABA commission and other observers are these: Too many complaints in too many states still take too long to adjudicate, and those who complain often find the system unresponsive, self-protective, and too willing to give wrist-slaps for all but the most egregious conduct. Too much of the disciplinary system continues to operate in secret; understandable efforts to protect falsely accused lawyers can have the effect of shielding for too long dishonorable members of the profession whose guilt has been proved. Certain kinds of matters simply don't get prosecuted. Many state bars expressly refuse to prosecute non-lawyers for engaging in the unauthorized practice of law. And some of the most common complaints, such as fee disputes and negligence, are ignored by some enforcement agencies, even where these complaints also allege fraud or gross incompetence, on the theory that such clients have adequate civil remedies.

Standardizing a penalty for ethical rule violations has proven difficult in many states. But are inconsistent outcomes evidence that the discipline system doesn't work, or evidence that punishments are being tailored to the offender? Most judges don't see minimum sentencing guidelines (imposed by legislators) as a useful tool to the administration of justice. With bar discipline, judges still have flexibility to look at each case. Thus, in insisting that the dismissal of disciplinary cases for driving under the influence of alcohol be reviewed, the Michigan Supreme Court concluded that "attorney misconduct cases are fact-sensitive inquiries that turn on the unique circumstances of each case."[51]

In an attempt to minimize exposure to risk, many law firms have committees or designated in-house counsel charged with responsibility to avoid ethics violations, evaluate conflicts of interest, and prevent malpractice. One author has suggested that these internal processes will eventually generate information that law firms can provide to sophisticated prospective clients. Such committees and procedures could serve as selling points; market forces, rather than disciplinary systems, would thus control a law firm's conduct.[52] It remains to be seen, of course, whether market forces can control large law firms, much less attorney ethics.

4.　Civil and Other Remedies

In most states, talk of reform continues mostly to be little more than just talk. Clients who want results have increasingly taken their disputes to the civil courts. Most states' courts make it clear that a lawyer's violation of the disciplinary rules does not create a civil cause of action or provide conclusive evidence of a civil wrong. But most of these courts also agree that where the violation of such rules is relevant to the issues alleged in the civil case, that violation may serve as evidence in support of the civil claim.[53] Some states have also held that, as a matter of public

---

[51] Grievance Administrator v. Deutch and Howell, 565 N.W.2d 369, 377 (Mich. 1997).

[52] *See* Elizabeth H. Gorman, *Explaining the Spread of Law Firm In-House Counsel Positions: A Response to Professor Chambliss*, 84 N.C.L. Rev. 1577, 1578 (2006).

[53] *See, e.g.*, Fishman v. Brooks, 487 N.E.2d 1377 (Mass. 1986); Mirabito v. Liccardo, 4 Cal. App. 4th

policy or to deter lawyers' violations of their fiduciary duties to their clients, unethical conduct may also result in a denial of attorneys' fees.[54]

As we have seen, other remedies for the unethical behavior of lawyers come in the form of sanctions imposed by courts for such matters as the frivolous filing of lawsuits or breaches of discovery requirements. In addition, certain agencies, especially within the federal government, reserve the right to exclude a lawyer from practice before those agencies. Other agencies, such as the Securities and Exchange Commission, the Internal Revenue Service, and the Customs and Immigration Service, also monitor the behavior of lawyers appearing before them. Of course, the SEC's lawyer reporting regulations have garnered by far the most attention, but how actual admission to practice and lawyer discipline will be affected remains to be seen. And courts, particularly federal courts, including specialized courts such as bankruptcy courts, continue to reserve the right to exclude from practice before them lawyers they find to be unfit. The federal government, through the Department of Justice's Executive Office for Immigration Review (EOIR), for example, has issued rules for immigration practitioners (who, like Social Security advocates, may be lawyers, but who may also be non-lawyer representatives).

C. THE UNAUTHORIZED PRACTICE OF LAW AND MULTIDISCIPLINARY PRACTICE

1. A Brief Overview of Unauthorized Practice

The answer to the question of what constitutes the unauthorized practice of law is both deceptively simple in some respects and quite complicated in others. Clearly, someone who represents himself or herself to be a lawyer but who actually has not gained admission to practice is engaged in the unauthorized practice of law. So, too, is a suspended or disbarred lawyer who continues to represent clients. But what about a lawyer who is a member of one state bar but appears on pleadings in federal district court in another state? Or an attorney admitted in one state who works in another state as in-house counsel, advising the corporate client on transactional matters that relate primarily to federal law?

On the other end of the spectrum are non-lawyers who seek to perform legal or quasi-legal tasks without a lawyer's supervision. Whether they call themselves paralegals or legal assistants, they in effect have challenged the essence of the profession itself, by questioning its ability to maintain a monopoly. Is their involvement in drafting simple documents or giving advice about how to fill in the blanks on legal forms enough to constitute the unauthorized practice of law? Are those who do this work defrauding the public or serving a public need? Does their work provide consumers with a needed choice? We take a brief look below at these issues.

---

41 (1992); Lipton v. Boesky, 313 N.W.2d 163 (Mich. Ct. App. 1981).

[54] *See, e.g.*, Goldstein v. Lees, 46 Cal. App. 3d 614 (1975); In re Estate of Halas, 512 N.E.2d 1276 (Ill. App. Ct. 1987).

First, however, a word about enforcement. Many states still have statutes making the unauthorized practice of law a misdemeanor, while others regard it as contempt of court. Many state bars, such as those in Texas and Massachusetts, continue to maintain active unauthorized practice of law departments to specifically deal with the issue, while other bars have completely abandoned their "UPL" units. Still others, like California, have re-instituted UPL units because of the massive amount of non-lawyer fraud taking place, particularly in immigrant and first-generation communities. But whether enforcement is left to the state bar, the courts, or on those rare occasions when traditional law enforcement agencies sit up and take notice, prosecution for the unauthorized practice of law is uneven at best, and has diminished or all but disappeared in several states.

There are several reasons for this. First, the last decade has seen a significant increase in the willingness of courts and agencies to allow nonlawyer representatives to participate in the legal system, especially in conjunction with "unbundled" services for the poor. Second, many states are dissuaded from prosecuting such cases both by the costs of prosecuting and the relatively low priority that the cases are given. If prosecution is done by a state bar, unauthorized practice problems often take a back seat to the substantive violations of practicing lawyers; if prosecution is turned over to law enforcement, unauthorized practice is considered less important a crime than ordinary criminal offenses. Third, many lawyers now recognize that on certain routine matters, their fees effectively eliminate them from being hired. The practical reality is that many people find themselves in need of legal help without the means of affording a lawyer. This is true both for individuals of modest means and for companies that operate nationally but may still need economies of scale.

Because lawyers understand that the clients they are too expensive to serve still need legal help, some are less inclined to crack down when these people get help from other non-lawyers. The problem, of course, is that some non-lawyers, particularly in immigrant communities, severely exacerbate the plight of the unrepresented, through ignorance or, far too often, outright fraudulent conduct.

2. What Is Meant by "The Practice of Law"?

It stands to reason that before one can evaluate the *unauthorized* practice of law, it is necessary to define what constitutes the practice of law. Efforts to create a uniform definition have not met with much success. An overly simplistic definition comes from a 90-year-old California Supreme Court case, *People v. Merchants Protective Corp.*, 209 P. 363 (Cal. 1922), which provided this tautological definition that the practice of law is any "legal advice and counsel and the preparation of legal instruments and contracts by which legal rights are secured." This language was quoted and reaffirmed in the *Birbrower* case cited above in section (A)(7), and remains the essence of California's definition.

A more complicated definition? Here is one court's attempt. In *Norvell v. Credit Bureau of Albuquerque*, 514 P.2d 40 (N.M. 1973), the New Mexico Supreme Court listed six factors demonstrating the practice of law: 1) representation of parties before judicial or administrative bodies; 2) preparation of pleadings and other papers incidental to actions and special proceedings; 3) management of such actions and proceedings; 4) giving legal advice and counsel; 5) rendering services that require using legal knowledge and skill; and 6) preparing instruments such as contracts by which rights are secured. This definition may not be perfect — among other things, it gives rise to the need for other definitions, such as what is meant by "legal advice" or "legal knowledge." But it is similar to and probably as good as most efforts in most other states.

3. Defining What Non-lawyers May Do

Many states have examined the kinds of services that non-lawyers will and will not be permitted to perform. In some states, courts have become less concerned about the quality of legal assistance and more with providing people at least *some* form of assistance. In several states, some use of nonlawyer legal assistants has been sanctioned by statute.

Below is a brief look at some areas of law, or at least what many still consider "the practice of law," that are now considered by some states permissible territory for nonlawyer assistance. The kinds of relatively routine services described here are typical of those areas in which non-lawyers are being afforded more and more opportunities for work. How much leeway exists continues to vary greatly from state to state.

Real Estate Transactions. Increased mobility in the last 40 years has resulted in many states relaxing the rules on what real estate brokers and salespersons may do to complete the necessary legal steps required in a real estate transaction, including, in some states, the escrow closing itself. Other states allow title insurance companies wide latitude in drafting documents, and at least one state, Indiana, allows some bank officials to fill out real estate papers. A few states still prohibit — or at least attempt to prohibit — non-lawyers from doing anything at all. Very generally, northeastern states tend to require more lawyer involvement in home sales than in the west, where greater mobility literally came with the territory. Thus, while lawyers' involvement in property closings remains common in New York or New Jersey, such involvement is almost non-existent in sales of California residences, where real estate brokers and title companies perform all the services.

Landlord-Tenant Matters. Some states, such as Maryland and California, allow registered legal assistants to provide services in eviction cases. Florida allows a variety of non-lawyers to file many of the documents necessary for evictions, default judgments, and uncontested writs of possession.

Administrative Law. The Social Security Administration permits non-lawyers to provide representation in both adversarial and nonadversarial proceedings, as does the United States government on citizenship and immigration issues, by regulating (and thus accepting) non-lawyers. Several states allow non-lawyers to appear in administrative hearings and appeals. Other states allow non-lawyers at unemployment hearings. New Jersey courts provide a wide spectrum of avenues available to non-lawyers who want to represent others, explicitly set forth in that state's administrative code.

Tax Law. Accountants, for-profit tax preparation companies, and even unions and, in some parts of the country, notary publics[55] commonly assist people with tax forms, and in effect give tax advice. CPAs, some former Internal Revenue Service agents and specially enrolled non-lawyers who have passed an IRS examination may appear with clients in certain tax forums.

Family Law. While most states hold to a traditional lawyers-only line, a few states like Florida allow non-lawyers to help parties complete domestic relations forms. In Washington, parties to divorces who are not represented by counsel may be assisted by a court-sponsored Family Law Facilitator Program. Similar programs exist in other states.

Wills and Trusts. Many bookstores offer will kits (*see* below). But helping someone write a will has been found in one state to be the unauthorized practice of law where those providing the help also received a bequest.[56]

Other Areas of Law. An increasing number of states, including California and West Virginia, now allow non-lawyers to represent people before worker's compensation appeals boards. Several states allow non-lawyers to represent individuals before public utilities commissions, planning boards, and appeals boards. Most states allow non-lawyers in labor hearings and arbitrations; indeed, many arbitrators are themselves non-lawyers.

Computer Software and Books. In the late 1990s, the state of Texas launched an attack on both computer software and books, claiming that Nolo Press' popular self-help literature and programs like Quicken Family Lawyer constituted the unauthorized practice of law. The disciplinary authorities eventually backed down in the case of Nolo Press. But the Texas Supreme Court's Unauthorized Practice of Law Committee successfully won a summary judgment motion enjoining the sale in Texas of Quicken Family Lawyer (QFL) because the software package constituted the unlawful practice of law.[57] "QFL" involves more than "merely instructing someone how to fill in a blank form," said the court. "QFL" conducts an "interview" with the user, customizes documents, and selects certain documents over others. This, the court concluded, all met the definition of practicing law.

The attack on software and books provoked controversy in all quarters and distress in many. After all, neither computer software programs nor books require human interaction of any kind, and self-help, often thought to have constitutional protections, has been part of the legal landscape for a very long time. In the aftermath of the QFL case, Texas amended its unauthorized practice statute to exclude software that conspicuously states it is "not a substitute for the advice of an attorney," after which the injunction against QFL was lifted.[58]

---

[55] In some segments of society, such as much of the Spanish-speaking community, notary publics are regarded as important functionaries, as they are in much of Latin America and the Mediterranean countries of Europe.

[56] *See* Marks v. Estate of Marks, 957 P.2d 235 (Wash. Ct. App. 1998).

[57] Unauthorized Practice of Law Committee v. Parsons Technology, Inc., 1999 U.S. Dist. Lexis 813 (N.D. Tex. Jan. 22, 1999).

[58] For more discussion of changes to UPL wrought by software, legal forms on websites, and so forth, see Problem 6.

4. Multidisciplinary Practice (MDP): Non-lawyer Practice on a Large Scale

MDP ordinarily refers to the increasingly frequent practice of lawyers working in concert with others, such as accountants, financial advisers, and insurance and real estate brokers, in one organizational entity, sometimes itself called an MDP. Ordinarily these MDPs either involve "unbundled" services for the poor[59] or involve many clients and lots of money. In late 1999, accounting giant Ernst and Young financed the opening of a new, and short-lived, Washington, D.C. law firm, called McKee, Nelson, Ernst & Young. McKee and Nelson, the lawyer components in the firm's name, felt they were able to risk such an open undertaking with Ernst & Young because the District of Columbia features the most liberal interpretation of Rule 5.4, prohibiting law firms from sharing fees with a non-lawyer — the heart of MDP — in the country. The D.C. rule allows lawyers both to share fees and form partnerships with non-lawyers such as accountants.

But while sharing fees and partnerships may have become accepted in some places, especially in Europe, many lawyers in the States have expressed serious concerns over their desire to maintain independent professional judgment, avoid conflicts of interest, and keep confidences.

Among the groups most interested in multidisciplinary work are accounting firms such as Ernst & Young. Many lawyers worry that partnership and financial pressures from non-lawyer accountants would potentially interfere with their independent judgment. Moreover, they note that accountants operate under different conflict of interest rules — screening, for example, is a commonly used strategy when conflicts arise — and instead of requiring relatively strict confidentiality, accountants are often in the position of being *required* to disclose information to various regulatory and oversight agencies.

It is not just the wealthy who are interested in the possibilities of multidisciplinary practice. There are many who believe that more must be done to support lawyers working with psychologists, land use planners, nurses, social workers, and a myriad of other professions. Louise Trubek and Jennifer Farnham write that as access to the court system has grown more difficult for low and moderate income clients, a number of inventive strategies have arisen to help address the shortages of legal assistance to these communities.

> Some involve providing limited legal services and relying on the client as his or her own advocate. Examples of this are unbundling, do-it-yourself systems, advice hotlines, and community legal education. A contrasting strategy is to increase impact and individual litigation using lawyers in a conventional law office where the lawyer is the dominant authority, perhaps assisted by nonlawyer support personnel. . . . At the other end of the economic spectrum from high-powered MDPs are so-called social justice collaboratives. This type of practice emphasizes working closely with other

---

[59] See our discussions in Problem 5 and Problem 32

professions, lay advocates and community agencies to meet a variety of needs and overcome barriers.[60]

Trubek and Farnham are just two of those who believe that more must be done to support lawyers working with psychologists, land use planners, nurses, social workers, and a myriad of other professions. While these partnering efforts are less dependent on the bottom line than are partnerships with large accountancy and financial firms, they raise as many issues of multidisciplinary practice as do partnerships with large accountancy and financial firms.

5.   The Swing of the Pendulum

In the beginning of this chapter we discussed what it means to be a professional, and why self-regulation is seen by so many lawyers as being a key to an independent legal system that works for all — individuals, organizations, and the government of which the judiciary is such an important part. Professional independence, and the accountability so essential to maintaining that independence, has not always been the norm. After the Civil War, the United States had what amounted to an "open bar." Because some believed (or said they believed) that bar associations were actually "secret trade unions of a privileged class, not equally open to all citizens . . . undemocratic and un-American," states began to regulate lawyers in a manner that at once democratized and also lowered, or eliminated, certain previously required qualifications.[61] One hundred and fifty years later, after slow and steady progress to create an (admittedly imperfect) professional system of admission and discipline that is more ecumenical, diverse, and egalitarian, where are we now?

Reading Model Rule 5.4, one might conclude that not much has changed in the legal profession's insistence on keeping itself separate from other professionals. But while Rule 5.4 may reflect today's reality, the world is continuing to change. The importance of lawyer independence is being challenged from many quarters. Some, including the outspoken Professor William Simon, whom we have noted elsewhere in this volume, question, for example, the rationale for confidentiality, claiming that the isolation of lawyers undermines their accountability to their clients and thus their usefulness. He relies upon this belief in the relative unimportance of confidentiality, at least in the business context, to support his conclusion that those who call themselves "business lawyers" should regulate their behavior differently, and see themselves more as partners to their business clients.[62]

Simon is not alone. Professor Thomas Morgan, one of the senior lions among legal ethicists, predicts a world that makes distinctively legal questions less common. He sees a world in which legally-trained non-lawyers will be more fully

---

[60] Louise G. Trubek and Jennifer J. Farnham, 7 CLINICAL L. REV. 227 (2000–2001).

[61] Louise L. Hall, *A Lawyer's Pecuniary Gain: The Enigma of Impermissible Solicitation*, 5 GEO. J. LEGAL ETHICS 393 (1991).

[62] *See* William H. Simon, *Introduction: The Post-Enron Identity Crisis of the Business Lawyer*, 74 FORDHAM L. REV. 947, 952 (2005). If this topic interests you, you should look at the other articles in this colloquium.

integrated into the process of helping clients address the substantive challenges they face, while what is seen as a distinctively legal question will become more narrowly defined.[63] Meanwhile, Richard Suskind, in a number of books and articles, including the well-known "The End of Lawyers," describes the changes he anticipates in the future practice of law, in particular what he describes as the increasing "commoditization" of legal services: "There is nothing terribly scientific about commoditizing legal services. It simply means that you define the typical tasks you typically complete for typical type of project, document the process by which those tasks are completed, and put a flat fee price on the deliverables for the client."[64] For the moment, at least, commentators with these perspectives remain a modest minority. But a day when these visions of lawyering are broadly accepted may be neither so far off nor so far-fetched.

D. SUPPLEMENTAL READINGS

1. On the topic of the definition and role of a profession, Susan Saab Fortney quotes Julius Henry Cohen as saying "Ours is a profession . . . . The sins of one of us are the sins of all of us." to set the stage for her examination of accountability as a fundamental aspect of professionalism. Susan Saab Fortney, *Law as a Profession: Examining the Role of Accountability*, 40 FORDHAM URB. L.J. 177 (2012). Fortney considers a lawyer's resistance to mandatory legal malpractice insurance, and even insurance disclosure requirements, as signs of lack of that accountability

2. Is there any value in looking at bar admissions information given the correlation, or lack thereof, with subsequent lawyer discipline? According to Leslie C. Levin, Christine Zozula, and Peter Siegelman, in their *A Study of the Relationship between Bar Admissions Data and Subsequent Lawyer Discipline*, while many of the responses on the admissions application are statistically associated with an elevated risk of future discipline, these variables make very poor predictors of subsequent misconduct. *Available at* http://ssrn.com/abstract=2258164 or http://dx.doi.org/10.2139/ssrn.2258164, (March 15, 2013).

3. Timothy T. Clydesdale, *A Forked River Runs Through Law School: Toward Understanding Race, Gender, Age, and Related Gaps in Law School Performance and Bar Passage*, 29 LAW & SOC. INQUIRY 711 (2004). This well-documented article contains extensive data on admissions and admissions tests, performance in law school, and bar passage rates across different groups. It argues for reducing reliance on the LSAT admissions test, supporting first year students with mentoring and tutorial programs, and increasing the diversity of law school faculty as ways of helping to improve diversity in the profession.

4. M.A. Cunningham, *The Professional Image Standard: An Untold Standard of Admission to the Bar*, 66 TUL. L. REV. 1015 (1992). This article discusses the political aspects of the term "fitness" to practice law, and its use as it relates to

[63] Thomas D. Morgan, *Calling Law a "Profession" Only Confuses Thinking About the Challenges Lawyers Face*, 9 U. ST. THOMAS L.J. 542 (2011). *See also* Thomas D. Morgan, *The Last Days of the American Lawyer* (January 27, 2010), *available at* http://ssrn.com/abstract=1543301 or http://dx.doi.org/10.2139/ssrn.1543301.

[64] RICHARD SUSKIND, THE END OF LAWYERS?: RETHINKING THE NATURE OF LEGAL SERVICES (2008).

applicants of various racial, economic, gender, and sexual preference backgrounds.

5. Jane Gross, *A Killer in Law School: Admirable or Abominable?*, NEW YORK TIMES, September 13, 1993, tells the story of James Hamm, convicted of murder in 1974 and attending an Arizona law school 20 years later, and evaluates the question of whether this fully-rehabilitated ex-convict should be admitted to the practice of law. In 2000, Eben Gossage, an admitted former drug addict once convicted of manslaughter for killing his sister, who later became a law student and passed the bar exam in 1993, failed to gain admission to the California bar. The bar examiners cited more recent traffic infractions as heavily as they did the past manslaughter. *See, e.g.*, Kevin Livingston, *Convicted Killer Denied Bar Card*, THE RECORDER (San Francisco), August 15, 2000.

6. Other articles addressing the "character and fitness" portion of the bar admissions process are these: Tricia S. Heil, *From Gatekeeping to Disbarment and Back Again: Chemical Dependency and Mental Health Issues in Licensing and Discipline*, 64 TEX. B. J. 158 (2001), explains how the character and fitness process works; Stephanie Denzel, *Second-Class Licensure: The Use of Conditional Admission Programs for Bar Applicants with Mental Health and Substance Abuse Histories*, 43 CONN. L. REV. 889 (2011) examines similar issues. Both Jon Bauer's *The Character of the Questions and the Fitness of the Process: Mental Health, Bar Admissions and the Americans With Disabilities Act*, 49 UCLA L. REV. 93 (2001), and Laura Rothstein's *Law Students and Lawyers with Mental Health and Substance Abuse Problems: Protecting the Public and the Individual*, 69 U. PITT. L. REV. 531, (2008) (also mentioned in Problem 30) are more pointed. They critically examine the legality of bar admissions agencies' increased focus on mental health, especially under the Americans With Disabilities Act.

7. Emelie E. East, *Note: The Case of Matthew F. Hale: Implications for First Amendment Rights, Social Mores and the Direction of Bar Examiners in an Era of Intolerance of Hatred*, 13 GEO. J. LEGAL ETHICS 741 (2000). This is a relatively balanced and well-documented review of the Hale case, its pleadings, and its constitutional issues, leaning towards Hale's admission.

8. Carla D. Pratt, *Should Klansmen Be Lawyers? Racism as an Ethical Barrier to the Legal Profession*, 30 FLA. ST. U. L. REV. 857 (2003), takes off from the Hale matter and argues that "in order to possess the requisite moral character to be an . . . attorney, an individual must subscribe to the core value of equal justice that serves as a cornerstone of our entire system of justice."

9. Carol A. Needham, *Splitting Bar Admission into Federal and State Components: National Admission for Advice on Federal Law*, 45 KAN. L. REV. 453 (1997). This thoughtful article advocates national admission for practice in federal courts. Her more recent piece, *Permitting Lawyers to Participate in Multidisciplinary Practices: Business as Usual or the End of the Profession as We Know It?*, 84 MINN. L. REV. 1315 (2000), provides a reality-check discussion about issues regarding multijurisdictional and multidisciplinary practice.

10. The vast majority of states now require Mandatory Continuing Legal Education, or MCLE. The website, http://www.abanet.org/cle/mcleview.html, is an excellent web resource that warehouses information on each state's MCLE requirements.

11. For another view of unauthorized practice of law issues, see Sheryl B. Shapiro, *American Bar Association's Response to Unauthorized Practice Problems Following Hurricane Katrina: Optimal or Merely Adequate?*, 20 Geo. J. Legal Ethics 905 (2007).

12. Some feel strongly that lawyers do a poor job of regulating themselves. See James E. Moliterno, *The Trouble with Lawyer Regulation*, 62 Emory L.J. 885 (2013); Washington & Lee Legal Studies Paper, *available at* http://ssrn.com/abstract=2264351.

13. Lawrence Fox, *Accountants, the Hawks of the Professional World: They Foul Our Nest and Theirs Too, Plus Other Ruminations on the Issue of MDPs*, 84 Minn. L. Rev. 1097 (2000). With this and a number of other articles, the ever-outspoken Mr. Fox rails eloquently against the attack on lawyers' professional independence that he sees coming from the "Big 5" (now Big 4) accounting firms and other proponents of MDPs.

TABLE OF CASES

[References are to pages]

[References are to pages]

[References are to pages]

Q

R

S

[References are to pages]

Y

Z

TABLE OF RULES AND OPINIONS

[References are to page and note numbers.]

[References are to page and note numbers.]

[References are to page and note numbers.]

[References are to page and note numbers.]

INDEX

[References are to pages.]

I-1

[References are to pages.]

[References are to pages.]

[References are to pages.]

[References are to pages.]

[References are to pages.]

[References are to pages.]

[References are to pages.]

[References are to pages.]

ISBN 978-0-7698-5303-1

9 780769 853031

90000 >